Elgar Encyclopedia of Post-Keynesian Economics

Elgar Encyclopedia of Post-Keynesian Economics

Edited by

Louis-Philippe Rochon

Full Professor, Laurentian University, Canada, Editor-in-Chief of Review of Political Economy *and Founding Editor Emeritus of* Review of Keynesian Economics

Sergio Rossi

Full Professor of Economics, University of Fribourg, Switzerland

Edward Elgar PUBLISHING

Cheltenham, UK • Northampton, MA, USA

© Louis-Philippe Rochon and Sergio Rossi 2023

All rights reserved. No part of this publication may be reproduced, stored in a retrieval system or transmitted in any form or by any means, electronic, mechanical or photocopying, recording, or otherwise without the prior permission of the publisher.

Published by
Edward Elgar Publishing Limited
The Lypiatts
15 Lansdown Road
Cheltenham
Glos GL50 2JA
UK

Edward Elgar Publishing, Inc.
William Pratt House
9 Dewey Court
Northampton
Massachusetts 01060
USA

A catalogue record for this book
is available from the British Library

Library of Congress Control Number: 2022948745

This book is available electronically in the **Elgar**online
Economics subject collection
http://dx.doi.org/10.4337/9781788973939

Printed on elemental chlorine free (ECF)
recycled paper containing 30% Post-Consumer Waste

ISBN 978 1 78897 392 2 (cased)
ISBN 978 1 78897 393 9 (eBook)

Typeset by Cheshire Typesetting Ltd, Cuddington, Cheshire
Printed and bound in the USA

Contents

List of contributors	xiii
Introduction to the *Elgar Encyclopedia of Post-Keynesian Economics*	xvii
A Tract on Monetary Reform Aldo Barba	1
Accelerator effects Fabio Freitas	2
AD–AS model Anil Aba	3
Agent-based modelling Corrado Di Guilmi	4
Aggregate demand Geoff Harcourt and Peter Kriesler	6
Animal spirits Sheila Dow	7
Asset backed securities Clara Capelli and Eugenio Caverzasi	8
Asymmetric information Lino Sau	9
Austerity Aldo Barba	11
Balance of payments Gilberto Libanio and João P. Romero	12
Balance of payments constrained growth Anthony Thirlwall	13
Balance of trade João P. Romero and Gilberto Libanio	15
Balanced budget Arne Heise	17
Bank lending and creditworthiness Fábio Terra	18
Bank lending and expectations Fábio Terra	19
Banking and finance Noemi Levy-Orlik and Jorge Bustamante-Torres	20
Banking regulation Peter Docherty	22
Banking School Eugenio Caverzasi	24
Banks Marcelo Milan	25
Basel Agreements Yannis Panagopoulos	27
Behavioural economics Mathieu Dufour	29
Bretton Woods Mario Cedrini	30
Bubbles – credit Lino Sau	31
Bubbles – financial Steve Keen	33
Business cycles Ekaterini Tsouma	34
Business cycles and prey–predator models Geoff Harcourt and Peter Kriesler	35
Cambridge Circus Maria Cristina Marcuzzo	37
Cambridge equation Luigi L. Pasinetti and Ariel L. Wirkierman	38
Capacity utilization Attilio Trezzini and Daria Pignalosa	40
Capital controls Luis Reyes	41
Capital flows Pablo Bortz	43
Capital requirements Ted P. Schmidt	44
Capital theory controversies Geoff Harcourt and Peter Kriesler	45
Capitalism Marco Veronese Passarella	47
Capitalism – stages of John E. King	48
Capitalism – varieties of Guillaume Vallet	49
Carbon tax Étienne Espagne and Antoine Godin	51
Central bank independence Sergio Rossi	52

Central bank–treasury relations 54
Flavia Dantas

Central banking 56
Peter Docherty

Central banking – developing economies 58
Esteban Pérez Caldentey

Chicago School 59
Luigi Ventimiglia

Clearing balances 61
Edoardo Beretta

Common currency area 62
Arslan Razmi

Compensation thesis 64
Simona Bozhinovska

Complex systems 65
Corrado Di Guilmi

Consumer behaviour 67
Robert H. Scott

Consumer choice 68
Anil Aba

Consumption theory 69
Ted P. Schmidt

Contagion effects 70
Luigi Ventimiglia

Corn model 72
Marco Missaglia

Corporate debt 73
Melanie G. Long

Credit 74
Robert H. Scott

Credit constraints 75
Nicolas Piluso and Louis-Philippe Rochon

Credit default swaps 77
Daniele Tori

Credit divisor 78
Jonathan Massonnet

Credit easing 79
Olivia Bullio Mattos

Credit money 81
David M. Fields

Credit multiplier 82
Plamen Ivanov

Credit-led boom 84
Fernando Toledo and Jorge Carrera

Critical realism 85
Ariane Agunsoye

Crowding-in and crowding-out 87
Najib Khan

Cumulative causation 88
David M. Fields

Currency board 90
Shirley Gedeon

Currency hierarchy 91
Fernando Ferrari Filho

Currency School 93
Robert W. Dimand

Current accounts 94
Christos Pierros

Debt deflation 96
Steve Keen

Debt – external 98
Luis Reyes

Debt – household 99
Aldo Barba

Debt – non-financial corporate sector 100
Fernanda Ultremare

Debt – public 101
Alain Parguez and Slim Thabet

Debt-led boom 102
Fernando Toledo and Jorge Carrera

Deindustrialization and economic growth 104
José Gabriel Palma

Deindustrialization, 'premature' deindustrialization and the Dutch disease 106
José Gabriel Palma

Demand-led growth 109
Marco Missaglia

Dependency theory 111
David M. Fields

Deregulation 112
Ivan Velasquez

Development 114
Amitava Dutt

Development banking 115
Konstantinos Loizos

Dollar dominance *Adrien Faudot*	117	Euthanasia of the rentier *Ana Laura Viveros*	146
Dollarization *Wesley C. Marshall*	118	Exchange rates *Aleksandr V. Gevorkyan*	148
Double-entry bookkeeping *Matheus Grasselli*	119	Exchange rates – fixed vs flexible *Luigi Ventimiglia*	149
Dual economy *Marco Missaglia*	120	Exchange rates – managed *Aleksandr V. Gevorkyan*	150
Dutch disease *Adrien Faudot*	122	Exogenous money *Yannis Panagopolous*	152
Ecological macroeconomics *Étienne Espagne, Antoine Godin and Romain Svartzman*	123	Expectations *Ekaterini Tsouma*	153
		Fallacy of composition *Jonathan Massonnet*	154
Ecological microeconomics *Richard P.F. Holt*	125	Feminist economics *Melanie G. Long*	156
Econometrics – role of *Florent McIsaac*	127	Finance – initial vs final *Andrea Carrera*	157
Economic Dynamics *Heinrich Bortis*	128	Finance and development *Wesley C. Marshall*	159
Economic geography *Jordan Ayala*	130	Finance in developing countries *Noemi Levy-Orlik*	160
Economic Growth and the Balance-of-Payments Constraint *Paulo Robilloti*	132	Finance motive *Claude Gnos*	161
Economic integration *Mehdi Ben Guirat*	133	Financial crises *Mathieu Dufour*	163
Effective demand *Claude Gnos*	135	Financial deepening *Diego Guevara*	164
Employer of last resort *Antoine Godin*	136	Financial fragility *Steve Keen*	165
Endogenous money *Louis-Philippe Rochon*	138	Financial innovations *Marcelo Milan*	166
Entrepreneurial State *Esteban Cruz Hidalgo, José Francisco Rangel Preciado and Francisco M. Parejo Moruno*	139	Financial instability hypothesis *Mathieu Dufour*	168
		Financial liberalization *Konstantinos Loizos*	169
Essays in the Theory of Economic Growth *Heinrich Bortis*	140	Financial macroeconomics *Vincent Duwicquet*	171
Euro *Sergio Rossi*	142	Financial regulations *Domenica Tropeano*	172
European Monetary Union *Guillaume Vallet and Hamed Karamoko*	144	Financial risk *Melanie G. Long*	174
Eurozone imbalances *Luis Reyes*	145	Financial sectoral balances *Christos Pierros*	175

Financialization *Plamen Ivanov*	176	Heterodox economics *Paolo Ramazzotti*	209
Fiscal consolidation *Shakuntala Das*	177	Historical time *Charles M.A. Clark*	211
Fiscal deficits *Malcolm Sawyer*	179	Horizontalism *Matteo Deleidi*	212
Fiscal multiplier *Aldo Barba*	180	Hysteresis *Mark Setterfield*	213
Fiscal policy *Arne Heise*	181	Imperfect competition *Maria Cristina Marcuzzo*	215
Foreign-exchange reserves *Aleksandr V. Gevorkyan*	183	Income distribution *Eckhard Hein*	216
Free trade *Mohamed Aslam*	185	Income multiplier *Jo Michell*	218
Full employment *Paolo Paesani and Antonella Palumbo*	186	Induction and deduction *Edward Teather-Posadas*	220
Functional finance *John E. King*	187	Inequality *James K. Galbraith*	221
General Theory – interpretations of *Robert W. Dimand*	189	Inflation *Sergio Rossi*	223
Gibson paradox *Enrico Sergio Levrero*	192	Inflation – conflict theory of *Malcolm Sawyer*	224
Globalization *Wesley C. Marshall*	194	Inflation – cost-push *Carlo Cristiano*	225
Goodwin cycles *Robert A. Blecker*	195	Inflation targeting *Ulaş Şener*	226
Government deficits and inflation *Hassan Bougrine*	197	Innovation *Nicola De Liso*	228
Government deficits and money creation *Hassan Bougrine*	198	Institutional economics – core ideas *Slim Thabet*	230
Growth *Amitava Dutt*	199	Institutional economics – origins *William E. McColloch*	231
Growth – unequal *Ricardo Araujo*	201	Interest rate – long term *Salvatore Perri*	233
Growth – wage-led vs profit-led *David M. Fields*	202	Interest rate, natural *Basil Oberholzer*	234
Harrod's dynamics *Esteban Pérez Caldentey*	203	Interest rate and income distribution *Enrico Sergio Levrero*	235
Harrod's foreign trade multiplier *Germán D. Feldman*	204	Interest rate rules *Achilleas Mantes*	237
Harrod's trade cycle *Cédric Rogé*	206	Interest rate targeting *Hassan Bougrine*	239
Harrodian instability *David M. Fields*	208	Interest rates and investment *Matteo Deleidi*	240

International clearing union *Hassan Bougrine*	241	Liquidity preference *Suranjana Nabar-Bhaduri*	268
International financial architecture *John T. Harvey*	243	Mark-up pricing *Jordan Melmiès and Florian Botte*	270
International monetary system *Pablo Bortz*	245	*Maturity and Stagnation in American Capitalism* *Fernando Rugitsky*	271
Investment – theories of *William E. McColloch*	246	Methodology *Sheila Dow*	272
Investment theory – ecological *Basil Oberholzer*	248	Microfoundations *John E. King*	274
Investment theory – Kaleckian *Malcolm Sawyer*	249	Military Keynesianism *John E. King*	275
Investment theory – Keynesian *Robert H. Scott*	250	Modern money theory *Shakuntala Das*	276
Involuntary unemployment – explanations of *Ítalo Pedrosa*	251	Monetary circuit *Edouard Cottin-Euziol and Louis-Philippe Rochon*	278
Involuntary unemployment – origins of *Esteban Cruz Hidalgo, Francisco M. Parejo Moruno and José Francisco Rangel Preciado*	253	Monetary circuit – French School *Alain Parguez*	279
IS–LM model *Fernando Toledo and Demian T. Panigo*	254	Monetary circuit – Italian School *Marco Veronese Passarella*	280
Job guarantee *Esteban Cruz Hidalgo, Francisco M. Parejo Moruno and José Francisco Rangel Preciado*	255	Monetary integration *Guillaume Vallet and Hamed Karamoko*	282
		Monetary policy *Peter Docherty*	283
Kaleckian economics *John E. King*	256	Monetary policy dominance *Fábio Terra*	285
Keynes effect *Peter Docherty*	258	Monetary policy transmission mechanism *Devrim Yilmaz*	286
Keynes Plan *Sergio Rossi*	259	Monetary theory of production *Alain Parguez and Slim Thabet*	287
Keynesian cross diagram *Maurizio Solari*	261	Money and banking *Jo Michell*	288
Kuznets curve *Daniela Tavasci*	263	Money as a means of payment *Sergio Rossi*	290
Land rents *Dirk Löhr and Oliver Richters*	264	Money creation – history of *Wesley C. Marshall*	292
Lender of last resort *Ted P. Schmidt*	265	Money creation – nature of *Maurizio Solari*	293
Lexicographic preferences *Anil Aba*	266	Money illusion *Robert W. Dimand*	295
Limits to substitution revisited: energy *Oliver Richters*	267	*Money in Motion* *Enrique Delamónica*	296

Monopoly Capital *Peter Kriesler*	298	Pasinetti's index *Sylvio Antonio Kappes*	326
Monopoly power *Ilhan Dögüs*	299	Pasinetti's paradox *Alex Pelham*	327
NAIRU *Corrado Di Guilmi*	301	Phillips curve *Florent McIsaac and Luis Reyes*	328
Negative interest rate policy *Guillaume Vallet and Louis-Philippe Rochon*	302	Ponzi finance *Ted P. Schmidt*	330
		Post-Keynesian economics – a big tent? *John E. King*	331
Neoclassical economics *Hassan Bougrine*	303	Post-Keynesian economics and Marxian economics *Jelle Versieren*	333
Neo-liberalism *Anil Aba*	305		
New Consensus in Macroeconomics *Alvaro Martín Moreno Rivas*	306	Post-Keynesian social policy *Enrique Delamónica*	334
New fiscalism *Wesley C. Marshall*	308	Power *Camilo Andrés Guevara*	336
New Keynesianism *Esteban Pérez Caldentey*	309	Pricing *Jordan Melmiès and Florian Botte*	338
Non-ergodicity *Matheus Grasselli*	310	Principle of increasing risk *Aleksandr V. Gevorkyan*	339
Okun's law *Antonella Palumbo, Claudia Fontanari and Chiara Salvatori*	312	Production of Commodities by Means of Commodities *Enrico Sergio Levrero*	341
Oligopoly and Technical Progress *Joseph Halevi*	313	Profit *Laurent Cordonnier*	342
Open economy macro models *Robert A. Blecker*	314	Property premium *Frank Decker*	343
Orthodox dissenters *Diego Guevara*	316	Property theory of money *Frank Decker*	344
Overdraft economies *Severin Reissl*	317	Public finance *Camilo Andrés Guevara*	346
Paradox – Kalecki's *Peter Kriesler*	319	Quantitative easing *Vijayaraghavan Ramanan*	347
Paradox of costs *YK Kim*	321	Quantum macroeconomics *Sergio Rossi*	349
Paradox of debt *YK Kim*	321	Rationality *Roderick O'Donnell*	350
Paradox of liquidity *Lídia Brochier*	322	Reflux mechanism *Vijayaraghavan Ramanan and Louis-Philippe Rochon*	352
Paradox of thrift *Robert H. Scott*	324		
Paradox of tranquillity *Eugenio Caverzasi*	325	Regional economic integration and free trade agreements *Mohamed Aslam*	353

Regulation School *Matthieu Montalban*	355	Stock–flow consistent models *Antoine Godin*	386
Remittances *Salewa Olawoye-Mann*	357	Structural economic dynamics *Luigi L. Pasinetti and Nadia Garbellini*	388
Rentier income *Hanna Szymborska*	358	Structuralism *Amitava Dutt*	389
Reserves – role of *Domenica Tropeano*	359	Structuralism and post-Keynesianism *Esteban Pérez Caldentey*	390
Satisficing *J. Barkley Rosser, Jr.*	361	Structuralism – Latin American *Fernando Rugitsky*	392
Savings *Orsola Costantini*	362	Subprime financial crisis *Eugenio Caverzasi*	393
Secular stagnation *William E. McColloch*	363	Supermultiplier *Ricardo Summa*	395
Securitization *Carryl Oberson*	365	Sustainable development *Jerry Courvisanos*	396
Selected Essays on the Dynamics of Capitalist Economy 1933–1970 *Malcolm Sawyer*	367	Target-return pricing *Jordan Melmiès and Florian Botte*	398
Settlement balances *Edoardo Beretta*	368	TARGET2 system *Sergio Rossi*	399
Settlement system *Edoardo Beretta*	369	Technological change *Nicola De Liso*	400
Shadow banking – extent of *Rudy Bouguelli*	371	Terms of trade *Fernando Rugitsky*	401
Shadow banking – origins *Alicia Girón*	373	*The Accumulation of Capital* *William E. McColloch*	403
Social classes *John E. King*	374	*The Great Transformation* *Gareth Dale*	404
Socialization of investment *Roderick O'Donnell*	376	*The Path of Economic Growth* *Joseph Halevi*	406
Sraffian economics *Attilio Trezzini*	377	*The Scourge of Monetarism* *Peter Docherty*	407
Stabilizing an Unstable Economy *Aleksandr V. Gevorkyan*	379	*The Structure of Post-Keynesian Economics* *Joseph Halevi and Peter Kriesler*	409
Stagflation *Nathaniel Cline*	380	*The Theory of the Leisure Class* *Christos Pierros*	410
Stagnation policy *Eckhard Hein*	382	Thirlwall's law *Esteban Pérez Caldentey*	412
State – entrepreneurial *Slim Thabet*	384	Tobin tax *Gonzalo Combita Mora*	413
State – role of *David M. Fields*	385	Too-big-to-fail financial institutions *Carryl Oberson*	414

Trade and development 416
Amitava Dutt and Najib Khan

Trade cycles 417
Esteban Cruz Hidalgo, Francisco M. Parejo Moruno and José Francisco Rangel Preciado

Transformational growth 418
Enrique Delamónica

Transmission mechanism of monetary policy – income distribution 420
Sylvio Antonio Kappes

Traverse, path dependency, and economic dynamics 421
Ettore Gallo

Traverse, path dependency, and economic equilibrium 423
Peter Kriesler

Twin deficits 424
Vincent Duwicquet

Uncertainty 426
Amitava Dutt

Uncertainty – ontological and epistemological accounts 427
Roderick O'Donnell

Unemployment 428
Flavia Dantas

Universal basic income 431
Marshall Steinbaum

Veblen effect 433
Guglielmo Forges Davanzati

Verdoorn's law 434
Alvaro Martín Moreno Rivas

Wages 436
Enrico Sergio Levrero

Washington Consensus 437
Mario Cedrini

Wealth distribution 439
Fernando Rugitsky

Wealth effect 440
Vera Dianova

Zero interest rate policy 441
Paolo Paesani

Contributors

Anil Aba, Yaşar University, İzmir, Turkey

Ariane Agunsoye, Goldsmiths, University of London, UK

Ricardo Araujo, University of Brasilia, Brazil

Mohamed Aslam, University of Malaya, Kuala Lumpur, Malaysia

Jordan Ayala, University of Missouri, Kansas City, USA

Aldo Barba, University of Naples 'Federico II', Italy

Mehdi Ben Guirat, Laurentian University, Sudbury, Canada

Edoardo Beretta, University of Lugano, Switzerland

Robert A. Blecker, American University, Washington, DC, USA

Heinrich Bortis, University of Fribourg, Switzerland

Pablo Bortz, National University of San Martín and National University of the West, Argentina

Florian Botte, University of Lille and Université du Littoral Côte d'Opale, France

Hassan Bougrine, Laurentian University, Sudbury, Canada

Rudy Bouguelli, Université Paris Cité, France

Simona Bozhinovska, University of Sorbonne Paris Nord, France

Lídia Brochier, Federal University of Rio de Janeiro, Brazil

Olivia Bullio Mattos, St. Francis College, New York, USA

Jorge Bustamante-Torres, Universidad Nacional Autónoma de México, Mexico

Clara Capelli, Bethlehem University, Palestine

Andrea Carrera, Complutense University of Madrid, Spain

Jorge Carrera, National Scientific and Technical Research Council, National University of La Plata, and Central Bank of Argentina

Eugenio Caverzasi, University of Insubria, Italy

Mario Cedrini, University of Turin, Italy

Charles M.A. Clark, St. John's University, New York, USA

Nathaniel Cline, University of Redlands, USA

Gonzalo Combita Mora, Universidad Nacional and Universidad de la Salle, Colombia

Laurent Cordonnier, University of Lille, France

Orsola Costantini, United Nations Conference on Trade and Development, Geneva, Switzerland

Edouard Cottin-Euziol, University of the Antilles, Martinique, France

Jerry Courvisanos, Federation University Australia, Ballarat, Australia

Carlo Cristiano, University of Pisa, Italy

Esteban Cruz Hidalgo, University of Extremadura, Spain

Gareth Dale, Brunel University, London, UK

Flavia Dantas, SUNY Cortland, USA

Shakuntala Das, Global Institute for Sustainable Prosperity, USA

Nicola De Liso, University of Salento, Lecce, Italy

Frank Decker, University of Sydney Law School, Australia

Enrique Delamónica, UNICEF, New York, USA

Matteo Deleidi, University of Bari, Italy, and University College London, UK

Corrado Di Guilmi, University of Technology Sydney, Australia

Vera Dianova, Franklin University Switzerland, Lugano, Switzerland

Robert W. Dimand, Brock University, St. Catharines, Canada

Peter Docherty, University of Technology Sydney, Australia

Ilhan Döğüs, independent economist

Sheila Dow, University of Stirling, UK

Mathieu Dufour, Department of Social Sciences, Université du Québec en Outaouais, Canada

Amitava Dutt, University of Notre Dame, USA, and FLACSO, Ecuador

Vincent Duwicquet, University of Lille, France

Étienne Espagne, Agence Française de Développement and Centre de Recherche sur le Développement International, France

Adrien Faudot, Grenoble Alpes University, Grenoble, France

Germán D. Feldman, National University of General San Martín, Buenos Aires, Argentina

Fernando Ferrari Filho, Federal University of Rio Grande do Sul, Brazil

David M. Fields, University of Utah and Salt Lake Community College, Salt Lake City, USA

Claudia Fontanari, University of Roma Tre, Italy

Guglielmo Forges Davanzati, University of Salento, Lecce, Italy

Fabio Freitas, Federal University of Rio de Janeiro, Brazil

James K. Galbraith, University of Texas at Austin, USA

Ettore Gallo, New School for Social Research, New York, USA

Nadia Garbellini, Università degli Studi di Modena e Reggio Emilia, Italy

Shirley Gedeon, University of Vermont, USA

Aleksandr V. Gevorkyan, St. John's University, New York, USA

Alicia Girón, Universidad Nacional Autónoma de México, Mexico

Claude Gnos, University of Burgundy, Dijon, France

Antoine Godin, University Sorbonne Paris Nord, France

Matheus Grasselli, McMaster University, Hamilton, Canada

Camilo Andrés Guevara, Universidad de La Salle, Colombia

Diego Guevara, Universidad Nacional de Colombia, Colombia

Joseph Halevi, Macquarie University, Sydney, and International University College of Turin, Italy

Geoff Harcourt†, University of New South Wales, Sydney, Australia

John T. Harvey, Texas Christian University, Fort Worth, USA

Eckhard Hein, Berlin School of Economics and Law, Germany

Arne Heise, University of Hamburg, Germany

Richard P.F. Holt, Southern Oregon University, USA

Plamen Ivanov, University of Winchester Business School, UK

Sylvio Antonio Kappes, Federal University of Ceará, Brazil

Hamed Karamoko, Grenoble Alpes University, Grenoble, France

Steve Keen, University College London, UK

Najib Khan, Prince Sultan University, Riyadh, Saudi Arabia

YK Kim, University of Massachusetts, Boston, USA

John E. King, La Trobe University, Melbourne, Australia

Peter Kriesler, University of New South Wales, Canberra, Australia

Enrico Sergio Levrero, University of Roma Tre, Italy

Noemi Levy-Orlik, Universidad Nacional Autónoma de México, Mexico

Gilberto Libanio, Universidade Federal de Minas Gerais, Belo Horizonte, Brazil

Dirk Löhr, Trier University of Applied Sciences, Environmental Campus Birkenfeld, Germany

Konstantinos Loizos, Centre of Planning and Economic Research, and National and Kapodistrian University of Athens, Greece

Melanie G. Long, College of Wooster, USA

Achilleas Mantes, Agence Française de Développement, Paris, France, and School of Oriental and African Studies, University of London, UK

Maria Cristina Marcuzzo, La Sapienza University, Rome, Italy

Wesley C. Marshall, Universidad Autónoma Metropolitana, Mexico City, Mexico

Jonathan Massonnet, University of Applied Sciences and Arts Western Switzerland, Switzerland

William E. McColloch, Keene State College, USA

Florent McIsaac, French Development Bank, France

Jordan Melmiès, University of Lille, France

Jo Michell, University of the West of England, Bristol, UK

Marcelo Milan, Federal University of Rio Grande do Sul, Porto Alegre, Brazil

Marco Missaglia, University of Pavia, Italy

Matthieu Montalban, University of Bordeaux, France

Alvaro Martín Moreno Rivas, National University of Colombia, Bogotá, Colombia

Suranjana Nabar-Bhaduri, Bucknell University, Lewisburg, USA

Roderick O'Donnell, University of Sydney, Sydney, Australia

Basil Oberholzer, Centre for Development and Environment, University of Bern, Switzerland

Carryl Oberson, University of Fribourg, Switzerland

Salewa Olawoye-Mann, York University, Toronto, Canada

Paolo Paesani, University of Rome Tor Vergata, Italy

José Gabriel Palma, University of Cambridge, UK and University of Santiago, Chile

Antonella Palumbo, University of Roma Tre, Italy

Yannis Panagopoulos, Centre of Planning and Economic Research, Athens, Greece

Demian T. Panigo, National Scientific and Technical Research Council, Buenos Aires, Argentina

Alain Parguez[†], University of Franche-Comté, Besançon, France

Francisco M. Parejo Moruno, University of Extremadura, Spain

Luigi L. Pasinetti, Università Cattolica del Sacro Cuore, Milan, Italy

Marco Veronese Passarella, Link Campus University of Rome, Italy, and University of Leeds, UK

Ítalo Pedrosa, Federal University of Rio de Janeiro, Brazil

Alex Pelham, Spokane Falls Community College, Washington, USA

Esteban Pérez Caldentey, Economic Commission for Latin America and the Caribbean, Santiago, Chile

Salvatore Perri[†], University of Catanzaro, Italy

Mathieu Dufour, University of Québec in Outaouais, Gatineau, Canada

Christos Pierros, National and Kapodistrian University of Athens and Labour Institute INE-GSEE, Greece

Daria Pignalosa, University of Roma Tre, Italy

Nicolas Piluso, University of Toulouse, France

Vijayaraghavan Ramanan, independent researcher, India

Paolo Ramazzotti, University of Macerata, Italy

José Francisco Rangel Preciado, University of Extremadura, Spain

Arslan Razmi, University of Massachusetts at Amherst, USA

Severin Reissl, University School for Advanced Studies, Pavia, Italy, and European Institute on Economics and the Environment, Italy

Luis Reyes, Kedge Business School, France

Oliver Richters, Carl von Ossietzky University Oldenburg, Germany

Paulo Robilloti, Escola Superior de Propaganda e Marketing, Brazil

Louis-Philippe Rochon, Laurentian University, Sudbury, Canada

Cédric Rogé, University of Lille, France

João P. Romero, Universidade Federal de Minas Gerais, Belo Horizonte, Brazil

J. Barkley Rosser, Jr., James Madison University, Harrisonburg, USA

Sergio Rossi, University of Fribourg, Switzerland

Fernando Rugitsky, UWE Bristol, UK

Chiara Salvatori, University of Roma Tre, Italy

Lino Sau, University of Torino, Italy

Malcolm Sawyer, University of Leeds, UK

Ted P. Schmidt, SUNY Buffalo State College, New York, USA

Robert H. Scott, Monmouth University, West Long Branch, USA

Ulaş Şener, Berlin School of Economics and Law, Germany

Mark Setterfield, New School for Social Research, New York, USA

Maurizio Solari, University of Fribourg, Switzerland

Marshall Steinbaum, University of Utah, Salt Lake City, USA

Ricardo Summa, Federal University of Rio de Janeiro, Brazil

Romain Svartzman, University College London, UK

Hanna Szymborska, Birmingham City University, UK

Daniela Tavasci, Queen Mary University of London, UK

Edward Teather-Posadas, Colorado State University, USA

Fábio Terra, Federal University of ABC, Brazil

Slim Thabet, University of Picardie Jules Verne, Amiens, France

Anthony Thirlwall, University of Kent at Canterbury, UK

Fernando Toledo, National University of La Plata and Central Bank of Argentina

Daniele Tori, Open University Business School, Milton Keynes, UK

Attilio Trezzini, University of Roma Tre, Italy

Domenica Tropeano, University of Macerata, Italy

Ekaterini Tsouma, Centre of Planning and Economic Research, Athens, Greece

Fernanda Ultremare, Federal University of Rio Grande do Norte, Brazil

Guillaume Vallet, Grenoble Alpes University, Grenoble, France

Ivan D. Velasquez, Bucknell University, USA

Luigi Ventimiglia, Queen Mary University of London, UK

Jelle Versieren, University of Antwerp, Belgium

Ana Laura Viveros, Universidad Nacional Autónoma de México, Mexico

Ariel L. Wirkierman, Goldsmiths, University of London, UK

Devrim Yilmaz, Agence Française de Développement, Paris, France

Introduction to the *Elgar Encyclopedia of Post-Keynesian Economics*

More than 45 years ago, in the *Journal of Economic Literature*, Eichner and Kregel (1975, p. 1294) proclaimed the rise of a 'new paradigm in economics' and predicted that 'post-Keynesian theory has the potential for becoming a comprehensive, positive alternative to the prevailing neoclassical paradigm'. This, we argue, it has achieved. Indeed, as Kerr (2005, p. 475) argues, 'Post Keynesian economics has evolved from a loosely associated grouping of dissenting ideas to a body of theories addressing a particular vision of interrelated aspects of the capitalist process.'

Nowhere has this been made more evident than in the aftermath of the global financial crisis that burst in 2008, and again during the COVID-19 crisis of 2020–21, which have both shown the degree to which post-Keynesian economics is not only relevant to the real world, but is also, *de facto*, the only body of thought able to offer any relevant policy recommendations. This should not be surprising, since post-Keynesian economics is about understanding the real world and how it operates, and as such it is able to propose relevant policies to address problems of unemployment, and other problems arising from a lack of aggregate demand. In light of the COVID-19 pandemic, in many countries, governments adopted post-Keynesian-inspired policies, and increased public spending some 10-fold, if not more, by supporting wages, workers and incomes through a panoply of programmes. Talks of 'building back better', which includes in some corners greener and fairer, are taking deep root in many countries.

Of course, COVID-19 presented some theoretical and policy challenges, which post-Keynesians were all too happy to take into account. Specifically, issues regarding supply problems, such as supply-chain constraints, would pose a serious challenge. Both the *International Journal of Political Economy* and the *Review of Political Economy* published full issues dedicated to the economic and policy challenges posed by COVID-19.

By contrast, mainstream economic theory is unable to offer anything relevant. Still based largely on substitution effects, and the representative agent who is looking to maximize his/her utility, mainstream theory still focuses its economics on only two polar opposite scenarios: equilibrium (and convergence to equilibrium) or 'black swans', which are events that are very rare and (therefore) unpredictable. This is why mainstream models are considered 'fair weather' models (Goodhart, 2009, p. 352), meaning they can only explain economies that do not deviate too widely from their long-run (equilibrium) position.

Mainstream-inspired economic policies are designed in this sense to remove any obstacles or imperfections that impede a prompt return to equilibrium. Any event that deviates from this established scenario must be treated as an exogenous shock in order to make sense. As such, financial crises lie outside the established parameters of 'fair weather' and, as we all witnessed, mainstream economists had nothing to offer except perhaps more austerity policies (fiscal largesse being an imperfection), or at least dire warnings of impending inflation.

But post-Keynesians reject models of gravitation, stability or convergence as the norm, since the economy is governed by uncertainty and endogenous processes, the outcome of which is difficult to predict (although many do incorporate discussions of equilibrium, though the notion of equilibrium is very different, and certainly not a centre of gravitation).

Moreover, uncertainty is treated very differently by post-Keynesians. It is not simply the possibility of unpredictable shocks or 'black swans'. Rather, it is part and parcel of the production and growth process. Whereas in mainstream models uncertainty explains the possibility of events like 'black swans', for post-Keynesians uncertainty is embedded in the behaviour of individuals and firms (as well as governments and central banks), and leads to possible expectations being frustrated with consequences. Terzi (2010) is correct when he claims in the title of his paper, in the *Journal of Post Keynesian Economics*, that 'Keynes's uncertainty is not about black or white swans'. For Keynes, and presumably post-Keynesians, uncertainty affects our decisions and motives: 'the future outcomes of today's economic decisions are largely influenced by agents' current behavior and beliefs' (Terzi, 2010, p. 564).

LOUIS-PHILIPPE ROCHON AND SERGIO ROSSI

As a result, post-Keynesians do not often discuss 'exogenous' shocks, relying rather on a view that considers events and crises as endogenous to the development of capitalism, as proposed by Minsky (1986). In this sense, it is difficult to see what post-Keynesians would consider a true 'black swan'. For instance, the 2008 global financial crisis was certainly the inevitable result of a hyper-financialized economy, bound to collapse. As for COVID-19, Bellofiore (2021, p. 394) has made the argument that it should be considered an endogenous crisis as well: 'the [COVID-19] health crisis is not an exogenous shock: it is inherent in the capitalist social form of production and consumption.'

These very different views of the world are important if economic theory is expected to lead to the development of economic policies, which it should. As Galbraith (2021, p. 67) explains, 'economics is a policy discipline.' As stated above, mainstream theory has had very little to offer in terms of policy to deal with either the financial crisis or COVID-19, since this theory is focused on stability and convergence to equilibrium. Clearly, if these events are treated as 'black swans', being by definition exogenous to the body of thought, what possible policies can emanate from this? Nothing at all.

By contrast, the post-Keynesian view treats these events as endogenous, enabling heterodox economists to formulate relevant policies. As such, post-Keynesians have always embraced an activist fiscal State, for economic but also for moral reasons. And if the 2008 global financial crisis marked 'the return of the Master' (that is, Keynes), the health crisis saw him moving in and settling in quite well. Governments addressed the collapse of aggregate demand with *aplomb* (see Seccareccia and Rochon, 2020; and Rochon and Seccareccia, 2021). Whether this newly found Keynesianism is here to stay is a different question altogether. In the end, post-Keynesian theory may be relegated to the foxhole, again, to be revived in the next crisis. Time will tell.

Finally, these two very different approaches are grounded as well in very different definitions of economics, or as Shapiro (1977, p. 552) argues, 'differences in their treatment of economic life'. For instance, neoclassical economics is concerned about internal consistency and the mechanisms by which the system gravitates back to its position of equilibrium, and the problems or welfare of the individual. This inward-looking classic definition of economics, being the study of the efficient allocation of scarce resources, does not seem to offer anything about today's growing ills such as secular stagnation, income inequality, and much more.

By contrast, heterodox economics is outward-looking, and focuses precisely on the problems that ill this society; it is about power, social conflict, income distribution, and economic growth, and the overall society or community. Arestis (1992, p. 90) defines post-Keynesian economics as 'the study of how actual economic systems are able to expand their outputs over time by producing and distributing the resulting social surplus'. This definition has nothing to do with internal consistencies: the world is too messy to be preoccupied with neat, convergence mechanisms.

As Eichner (1979, p. 168) concludes, 'the advantage of the post-Keynesian approach is that it enables one to confront the problems directly and openly rather than to conceal them under simplifying assumptions.'

A short history of post-Keynesian economics

While post-Keynesian[1] economics is well established today as a credible and whole alternative to mainstream views, what about its origins?

It is somewhat difficult to clearly identify, let alone pinpoint, when precisely post-Keynesian theory began as a positive contribution to economic theory, in part because many of the ideas that form the core of post-Keynesian economics date back a few centuries, and in part because it is difficult to agree on a date or period when many of these ideas came together to form a school of thought properly speaking.

However, to help us identify when post-Keynesian economics began, we are guided by two observations: first, we know it must have begun sometime after Keynes. In his magistral *History of Post-Keynesian Economics*, King (2002) argues post-Keynesian economics began in 1936. But it is difficult to argue that anything 'post' began during Keynes's reign. Moreover, it is unclear how 'post-Keynesian' Keynes was. For instance, Kaldor (1983, p. 47) has argued that 'the real author of the so-called "neoclassical synthesis" was not Paul Samuelson, it was Keynes himself'.

Second, the usual Cambridge protagonists and friends in Keynes's inner circle, like Michał Kalecki, Nicolas Kaldor, or Joan Robinson – whom Harcourt and Kerr (2009, p. 1) called 'the greatest woman economist' – are certainly involved. Indeed, Asimakopulos (1988–89, p. 261) identifies 'Michal Kalecki and Joan Robinson [as] two of the major contributors to what is called today post-Keynesian economics', whereas King (2013, p. 493) argues that '[t]he most important of the British Post Keynesians[2] were Joan Robinson (1903–1983) and Nicholas Kaldor (1908–1986)'. King (2002, p. 5) even calls Robinson the 'founding mother'. Arestis and Skouras (1985) dedicate their book to 'the memory of the first post-Keynesians', of which Robinson is one.

These arguments are used below to try to identify, as best as we can, the roots of post-Keynesian economics. Yet, in tracing the roots of post-Keynesian economics, it is important to differentiate between the theoretical roots (a body of theoretical arguments), or what we can argue to be the emergence of post-Keynesian theory, on the one hand, and the institutional roots, on the other, or the emergence of a post-Keynesian school – that is, the creation of an identifiable group of economists around specific social networks (conferences, journals, organizations).

Tracing the institutional roots of post-Keynesian economics

Regarding the institutional roots, indeed, today there are a number of journals that focus on the publication of heterodox and post-Keynesian ideas, like the *Review of Political Economy*, the *Review of Keynesian Economics*, the *Journal of Post Keynesian Economics*, the *International Journal of Political Economy*, the *European Journal of Economics and Economic Policy*, the *Cambridge Journal of Economics*, among many others. There are also a number of organizations, like the Post-Keynesian Network, the Post-Keynesian Economics Society, the Association des Etudes Keynésiennes in France, not to mention a proliferating number of Rethinking Economics movements. Universities offering heterodox courses and doctoral programmes are also numerous today, including the New School for Social Research, the University of Massachusetts Amherst, Bucknell University, University of Utah, Colorado State University, the University of Missouri-Kansas City, in the United States alone. These institutions cement and promulgate the theory, which in turn must necessarily precede the creation of these social networks and institutions: after all, you need a theory around which to congregate.

In discussing the history of post-Keynesian economics, these two are at time conflated. Yet we believe we gain in separating them, as this brings much clarity to the discussion.

But these institutional roots emerged, there is no doubt, only in the early 1970s in the United States, where Alfred Eichner was an instrumental part of the movement to create a network of meetings – no less because of his close relationship with Joan Robinson. Of course, in the United Kingdom, at Cambridge, you had the usual Circus protagonists and friends of Keynes. Yet, there was no conscious effort at that time to organize or crystalize the work of the Cambridge economists into an official 'school'. Pasinetti (2005, p. 839) has argued that 'the Cambridge group certainly misbehaved in the process of organizing a proper School. In many scientific disputes, they often displayed individualistic attitudes, and sometimes even egoistic behaviour, rather than adopting a spirit of cooperation, which would have kept and fostered the unity of the Keynesian School. Their voices were sometimes discordant. Though they always agreed on fighting the Neoclassical School, they often quarrelled among themselves, usually over trivial issues.' This individualistic behaviour certainly contributed to the failure to create a post-Keynesian school in the United Kingdom. This would only develop later, with the new generation of economists, like Victoria Chick and Philip Arestis, who created in 1988 the Post-Keynesian Economics Study Group.

Lee (2000, p. 9) has argued that it is in the United States that a post-Keynesian school of economics began to emerge in 1969, when Alfred Eichner contacted Joan Robinson about his research, and '[b]y April 1971 Eichner began wondering whether the time was not ripe for a Post Keynesian revolution in the United States' (Lee, 2000, p. 23).

Their correspondence is discussed by Turner (1989) and Lee (2000), and the influence of Robinson on the burgeoning American movement is clear. In fact, in discussing Eichner's work during this period, it was Robinson who first referred to this kind of work as 'post-Keynesian' (Turner, 1989, p. 191), and by 6 April 1971, Eichner was now calling this new paradigm 'post-Keynesian' (Turner, 1989, p. 191), although Lee (2000d, p. 145) claims that Eichner used the term as early as April 1969, in a letter to Robinson: 'In a letter to Robinson in April 1969, Eichner mentioned that he was making his students familiar with 'the post-Keynesian Robinson–Kaldor type of growth model".

Shortly after that, in December 1971, Robinson was invited by John Kenneth Galbraith, incoming president of the American Economic Association (AEA), to give the Richard T. Ely Presidential Address – the first woman to do so – giving her famous talk, 'The Second Crisis of Economic Theory' (Robinson, 1972). That year, these meetings were held in New Orleans, 26–29 December 1971.

> 8:00 p.m. **Richard T. Ely Lecture**
> Presidential
> Salon *Chairman:* JOHN KENNETH GALBRAITH,
> Jung Hotel Harvard University
> **AEA** *Speaker:*
> "The Second Crisis of Economic Theory,"
> JOAN ROBINSON, University of Cambridge and University of Waterloo

Eichner had previously seen an opportunity of capitalizing on Robinson's presence at the 1971 meeting of the AEA, and suggested they organize a meeting of their own on 28 December, to gather heterodox and like-minded economists in an effort to begin what would become, in the United States, the post-Keynesian school. Such a gathering was meant to be the first of many, under the umbrella name of the Political Economy Club, and Eichner's vision was to have chapters of this club established throughout the United States.

The first meeting, however, was by invitation only, and the invitation, signed by Robinson, was sent initially to thirty scholars, in which Robinson indicated her concerns over 'the vulgar version of neo-classical theory' taught in American universities, and urged her guests to attend a dinner to discuss 'what can be done to remedy the situation' (Lee, 2000b, p. 116).

Seventeen scholars in total attended the meeting, notably Tom Asimakopulos, Kenneth Boulding, Victoria Chick, Paul Davidson, Alfred Eichner, John Gurley, Donald Harris, Jan Kregel, Robert Lekachman, Hyman Minsky, and Edward Nell.

However, the first meeting was not exactly a success, with different viewpoints and interests being expressed. At this meeting Robinson officially suggested to the group that the emerging school be called 'post-Keynesian' (Lee, 2000, p. 146). Although the name was initially rejected, Eichner would continue using it over the following few years.

In the years leading up to the New Orleans meeting, according to Lee (2000), heterodox economists were coming together under other heterodox associations, such as the Union for Radical Political Economy, the Association for Evolutionary Economics, and the Association for Social Economics. These associations had their respective journals as well. These were natural allies for post-Keynesians, as all were in essence 'pluralist, left-leaning heterodox networks' (Hodgson, 2019, p. 44). But it was at the 1971 meeting that discussions took place specifically to create a post-Keynesian group or association.

The 1971 New Orleans meeting therefore marks the beginning of a so-called post-Keynesian school: a conscious act to build institutions to support, defend, develop, and propagate the economics of Keynes (and Kalecki). As Lee (2000. p. 26) argues, '[t]hese initial activities by Eichner constituted, in the United States, the beginning of Post Keynesian economics as an identifiable body of ideas supported by a network of economists and institutions.' The meeting created a new sense of urgency: post-Keynesians were being excluded from academic positions and journals, and from participating in an official capacity in the annual meetings, such as those of the AEA. This observation led to an exchange of letters between Eichner and various members of the AEA, but to no avail. Nevertheless, post-Keynesians felt they were living in 'revolutionary times' (King, 2002, p. 122) on the heels of the Cambridge controversies, which many thought sounded the death knell of neoclassical economics.

The Political Economy Club gathered again the following year, at the December 1972 AEA meeting in Toronto, where Eichner organized a meeting entitled 'The Possibility of an Alternative to the Neo-Classical Paradigm: A Dialogue Between Marxists, Keynesians and Institutionalists'. This meeting, however, was not part of the official AEA programme and was held clandestinely. Eichner presented his paper, 'Outline for a New Paradigm in Economics', alongside Minsky's presentation, 'An Alternative to the Neo-Classical Paradigm: One View', both of which are printed in full in Lee (2000, pp. 147–59). In this presentation, Eichner now openly refers to 'post-Keynesians', and quite regularly so.[3]

After the meeting, Eichner concluded that 'the session reinforced my belief that it is possible to develop an alternative to the neo-classical paradigm, that the differences between Marxists, neo-Marxists, Keynesians, post-Keynesians, institutionalists and grants economists are not necessarily incompatible' (quoted in Lee, 2000, p. 27). Yet, he warns that '[a]t the same time, however, the development of an alternative paradigm will not be easily accomplished, especially since the member of the various schools insist on emphasizing entirely different types of problems' (quoted in Lee, 2000b, p. 145).

The following year, under the guise of a Union for Radical Political Economy session, feeling discouraged, Eichner, with the help of Edward Nell, organized a session at the 1973 Allied Social Sciences Associations in New York City, entitled 'Post-Keynesian Theory as a Teachable Alternative Macroeconomics', featuring presentations by both Eichner and Kregel. This constitutes the first time an entire session on post-Keynesian economics was put together in an official capacity, in the United States.

8:30 a.m. **Post-Keynesian Theory as a Teachable**
Hilton   **Alternative Macroeconomics**
Sutton South
URPE   The Implications of the Sraffa Model, E.J. NELL, The New School

Cambridge Theory, JAN KREGEL or DON HARRIS, Stanford University

Investment and Pricing in the Mega-Corp, ALFRED EICHNER

The following year, at the AEA meeting in San Francisco in 1974, Eichner organized another similar session, entitled 'Alternative Approaches to Economic Theory', in which he and Kregel presented their now-famous 1975 *Journal of Economic Literature* paper.

The session was well attended and, according to Lee (2000, p. 28), 'Eichner felt that the larger audience which attended the session went away with the impression that Post Keynesian theory was beginning to emerge.'

8:30 am
St. Francis, Georgian Room
URPE

Alternative Approaches to Economic Theory

Chairperson: HOWARD J. SHERMAN, University of California, Riverside

Institutionalism and Marxism, LAURENCE SHUTE, University of Massachusetts, Boston

Post-Keynesian Theory: The New Paradigm in Economics, ALFRED S. EICHNER, State University of New York, Purchase, and J. A. KREGEL, Southampton University

The Grand Tradition: Theories of Surplus from Quesnay to Sraffa and Notes on the Neo-classical Interlude, JESSE G. SCHWARTZ and VIVIAN C. WALSH, University of Waterloo, Ontario

Discussion: DOUGLAS F. DOWD, California State University, San Jose

Despite these initial activities, however, programmes for the 1974–78 period show no additional sessions being organized on topics related to post-Keynesian economics at the AEA. However, the 1975 publication of Eichner and Kregel's paper in the *Journal of Economic Literature* marked a definite moment in the establishment of a post-Keynesian school. This was followed a few years later by Shapiro's (1977) article in the *Journal of Economic Issues*, marking the emergence of a distinct post-Keynesian school. Indeed, Shapiro's article (which is grossly underappreciated today) echoes many of the same arguments made by Eichner and Kregel (1975), but was clearly more accessible and addressed to like-minded readers. With hindsight, Eichner (1979, p. vii) admitted his 1975 article may have been 'pitched at too high a technical level'.

Moreover, it was during this time that Weintraub became interested in Eichner's and Robinson's activities, and the idea of a post-Keynesian journal was born. Following an event held at Rutgers University in April 1977 (see below), Weintraub is quoted as saying, 'We've got to form a journal. I'm going to ask Ken Galbraith for some money' (Turner, 1989, p. 197). Although the idea of creating a journal supportive of Keynes's ideas was always part of Weintraub's plans going back to the 1960s, 'nothing happened until 1977' (Lee, 2000, pp. 30–31).

The efforts of the last six years or so culminated in the creation of the *Cambridge Journal of Economics*, in the United Kingdom, in the spring of 1977, by the Cambridge Political Economy Society,[4] and the *Journal of Post Keynesian Economics*, in the United States, in the fall of 1978.[5] This is quite an accomplishment given that post-Keynesian economics only six years earlier was still in its very beginning. In a matter of a few years really, post-Keynesian economics had arrived.

The *Journal of Post Keynesian Economics* was first announced publicly in the programme of the 1978 AEA conference.

ECONOMICS

from M.E. Sharpe, Inc.

Journal of Post Keynesian Economics

Editors: Paul Davidson, Rutgers University, and Sidney Weintraub, University of Pennsylvania

JPKE will publish articles by economists whose views differ in many details, but who are united on one overriding conviction: the job of economics is to describe the real world, then to provide a reliable guide to public policy. This cannot be done by standing pat on outmoded theory or by treating modern economic institutions as an inconvenient afterthought. Fresh ideas are already plentiful. JPKE is dedicated to the systematic discussion now urgently needed.

Contributors to early issues
Bruno S. Frey, John Kenneth Galbraith, Edward M. Graham, Aron Katsenelinboigen, Lawrence R. Klein, Abba Lerner, Joan Robinson, Warren J. Samuels, Francis Seton, James Tobin

A special feature of the first issue:
A Symposium on Carter's Economic Program

First issue: Fall 1978

A quarterly publication. Subscription:
Institution $25; Individual $17; Student $12.

Other institutional support followed, with Eichner establishing a friendship with Mike Sharpe, thereby giving post-Keynesians a publishing outlet for books. Eichner's *Guide* was published there in 1979, although the idea to publish a book that offered an alternative to neoclassical economics had been floated around since 1972, initiated by Nell's anti-neoclassical book. The articles in the book, which appeared in *Challenge* magazine the year before, are written purposely for 'the neophyte in economics' in contrast to Eichner's more technical 1975 *Journal of Economic Literature* paper.[6]

In addition, post-Keynesians were beginning to congregate around Rutgers University, starting in the later 1970s and early 1980s.

It was while at Rutgers University that Paul Davidson, who was department chair, along with Eichner thought of the idea of a one-day event dedicated to post-Keynesian views. This meeting – on post-Keynesian theory and inflation (inflation being an important topic at that time) – was another key moment in the history of post-Keynesian economics. The aim was clear: to serve 'as a forum for the exchange of ideas and scholarship by those economists whose work falls within the tradition established by Keynes, Kalecki, Robinson, Kaldor, and Sraffa' (cited in Lee, 2000, p. 31). It was for the first time an entire event, as opposed to a session, bringing together the leading post-Keynesian scholars and held specifically to discuss post-Keynesian theory. In this sense, it was a very important step forward.

By every account, the meeting was well attended: Eileen Appelbaum, John Burbidge, Paul Davidson, Alfred Eichner, Geoff Harcourt, Jan Kregel, Fred Lee, Robin Marris, Will Milberg, Hyman Minsky, Basil Moore, Edward Nell, Stephen Rousseas, Lawrence Seidman, Nina Shapiro, Lorie Tarshis, and Sidney Weintraub, among others, including a young Mario Seccareccia, who was still a graduate student at McGill University at the time and, upon hearing about the event, decided to drive down and attend it.[7]

As mentioned above, the meeting was eventful in another important way: the large gathering of like-minded scholars convinced Sydney Weintraub that the time was right for a journal dedicated to the work of Keynes and his followers. From there, as mentioned above, the idea of the *Journal of Post Keynesian Economics* was born, and its first number appeared the following year.

There is no denying that the event had a considerable impact on many attendees, and created important social and academic relationships among the participants. It energized a nascent movement and contributed to a number of other post-Keynesian activities over the next few years, including a second meeting at Rutgers University in 1981, one at the University of Ottawa in 1981, and another one in 1984 (where Rochon remembers attending some sessions as an undergraduate), as well as the (in)famous Trieste gatherings from 1981 to 1985.

Post-Keynesians and the 1970s

From the discussion above we can argue that post-Keynesian economics, as we understand it today, emerged in the United States as a school of thought in the 1970s, including the use of the name 'post-Keynesian' as early as 1972. In conclusion, the 1970s proved to be a very productive decade, where much was accomplished, although 'much of the detailed argument remains to be worked out' (Eichner, 1979, p. 167). Before that, it is difficult to see any movement towards the creation of a social network or association, either in the United States or in the United Kingdom.

So, while the institution of post-Keynesian economics and the use of the word was established in the early 1970s (originally with a hyphen, by the way), what about the intellectual or theoretical roots? Did it emerge only then, or perhaps its structure was well in place by then, as it had emerged before? Vernengo (2019, Internet) argues that 'before the 1970s it was difficult to talk about Post Keynesianism as clearly separated from the mainstream, since the very idea of heterodoxy was not yet fully developed'. Here, Vernengo clearly refers to the post-Keynesian institution. In what follows, we offer a different interpretation as to the post-Keynesian vision.

Tracing the intellectual roots of post-Keynesian economics

Overall, starting in the mid-to-late 1960s, American and British post-Keynesians were very active in getting published, and it was clear that there was a burgeoning school of thought emerging and some loose, still embryonic institutions.

It is impossible in this space to mention the numerous papers and books published during this period, although we should mention Paul Davidson, who had been working on a version of the post-Keynesian theory of money, early in the 1960s, culminating in Davidson (1965; see Rochon, 1997, for an alternative discussion of Keynes's finance motive, however), and by 1970 he was at the University of Cambridge, UK, on sabbatical, while working on his book, *Money and the Real World* (Davidson, 1972), with Joan Robinson figuring prominently in discussions surrounding his book. Indeed, Robinson had been instrumental, having read every chapter of Davidson's book and giving extensive comments on the content.[8]

LOUIS-PHILIPPE ROCHON AND SERGIO ROSSI

That year, Kaldor (1970) published his paper on endogenous money and 'the new monetarism' in the *Lloyd Banks Review*. Jan Kregel, another prominent post-Keynesian, spent 1968–69 at Cambridge, UK, taking courses with Joan Robinson; he co-wrote, with Alfred Eichner, their famous paper on post-Keynesian economics in the *Journal of Economic Literature* (Eichner and Kregel, 1975), and authored an introductory textbook, *The Reconstruction of Political Economy: An Introduction to Post-Keynesian Economics*, in 1973 (Kregel, 1973; with a foreword by Joan Robinson) – the same year Robinson authored an introductory book with John Eatwell, titled *An Introduction to Modern Economics* (Robinson and Eatwell, 1973). We must also mention early books by Weintraub (1958, 1959), both of which focused heavily on inflation.

All of these writings would certainly qualify as claiming the mantle of establishing post-Keynesian theoretical or intellectual roots. And in many ways, they did. But we would submit that there is a more obvious choice: the intellectual roots of post-Keynesian theory date back to the mid-1950s. Logic would suggest that the intellectual roots of post-Keynesian economics began at Cambridge, UK, and since Joan Robinson – one of the 'pioneering Keynesian' (Harcourt, 1995) – was at the heart of virtually every early development of an emerging school, especially in the United States, it may have in fact begun with her.

Yet, to claim that Robinson – 'the most influential figure within Cambridge heterodox economics' (Hodgson, 2019, p. 32) – was instrumental in building post-Keynesian economics is uncontroversial. King (2002, p. 50) argues that 'Robinson was well on the way to becoming the most influential representative of the so-called "Left Keynesians"'. Rima (1991, p. 4) discusses 'the magnitude of her post-Keynesian legacy', and how instrumental she was in 'laying the foundation for the post-Keynesian paradigm'. Marcuzzo (2018, p. 130) argues that Joan Robinson is what may just unite the various strands of heterodox or post-Keynesian economics: 'Post-Keynesian economics ... is a very composite group of people often at odds with each other, but I think united in the belief that Joan Robinson is the leading and iconic figure with whom most of them could identify.'

Joan Robinson's influence was undoubtedly great, and she was aware of the need, on the one hand, of countering the Keynesians and the monetarists and, on the other, of the need to weave together the economics of Keynes, Kalecki, and Sraffa and to present an overall post-Keynesian vision – two of the building blocks to tearing down one approach in order to replace it with another. Hence, her approach was both negative (critical) and positive (contribution). This is the work of someone who is keenly aware of the need to establish not simply elements of a theory, but an entire, credible alternative to the mainstream.

However, it is not until the publication of Robinson's *Accumulation of Capital* in 1956 – which Robinson considered her magnum opus – that an attempt is made, in the very same way as *The General Theory* (Keynes, 1936) itself (both books published when the authors were of the same age; see Harcourt and Kerr, 2013, p. ix), to establish an all-encompassing approach to Cambridge economics after Keynes – an attempt at a synthesis or a vision. The book, which is certainly 'a long and difficult work' (King, 2016, p. 318), should be considered as central to post-Keynesian economics.

In that sense, Robinson's (1956) book is the first by a follower of Keynes not focusing on a narrow topic, but presenting an overall vision, which included weaving together the views of Keynes, Kalecki, and Sraffa. Indeed, the intellectual roots of post-Keynesian theory are to be found in *The Accumulation of Capital*. Vernengo (2019, Internet), however, argues that '[p]erhaps the three books that mark the modern birth of PK economics are Paul Davidson's *Money and the Real World* and Hyman Minsky's *John Maynard Keynes*, and Alfred Eichner's *A Guide to Post Keynesian Economics*. All these books emphasize the fundamental instability of capitalism, associated to the fundamental uncertainty related to the investment process, and the increasingly fragile financial structures that are built in the process of investment.' Yet, these elements are also to be found in *The Accumulation of Capital*.

As a matter of fact, Robinson's (1956) book contains virtually all the elements of post-Keynesian economics as it stands today. Klein (1989, p. 258) describes the book, and more specifically Part 1, as 'truly a masterful statement of economic principles, especially principles of macroeconomics, that could serve better than almost any other "Principles" textbook in laying bare the fundamental aspects of our subject to the beginner'.

This is not the first time *The Accumulation of Capital* was thought of as a textbook. In his review of the book, Barna (1957, p. 493) refers to the book precisely as a textbook: 'The achievement of Mrs. Robinson is that she has written a full-scale textbook on what is probably the most important post-war subject.' The comparison of *The Accumulation of Capital* to possibly the first post-Keynesian 'textbook' certainly is in the spirit of the argument presented here.

For instance, Robinson's (1956) book contains considerable attention to uncertainty and historical time, a discussion of the importance of social class analysis, conflict and power, a specific discussion of Keynes's economics into the long run, the principle of aggregate demand, income distribution, the process of production, credit, money, and banking, in addition to economic growth and accumulation, the short run and the long run, as well as the dynamics of transitioning between these two periods – in short, all the elements that are key to a positive contribution to a body of work forming the early seeds of what will become known as 'post-Keynesian economics'. In fact, in using the name 'post-Keynesian' in a 14 March 1986 letter to Marjorie Turner, Eichner specifically links the name to *The Accumulation of Capital* (cited in Lee, 2000a, p. 5):

> As for why I always hyphenate post-Keynesian, it is because that is the way we initially started doing it. Later it became to distinguish those who followed the line of inquiry by Joan in *The Accumulation of Capital* from among the broader group of post-Keynesians who, while opposed to the dominant neoclassical theory or at least important parts of that theoretical perspective, nonetheless did not accept Joan's arguments, particularly with respect to what is known as long-period, or steady-state growth, analysis.

Also, Robinson (1956) discusses in great details the functioning of a truly modern economic system and displays a sense of realisticness: reliance on a realistic portrayal of the economic system. In her 1956 book there is a clear discussion of the theory of the monetary circuit. Her aim was to reconstruct economics: 'Joan Robinson saw a formidable task ahead, consisting in nothing less than a reconstruction of economic theory. This led, after a decade of intense work, to the publication of her second major contribution to economic theory – *The Accumulation of Capital* (1956)' (Pasinetti, 1987, p. 216).

Eichner (1980, p. 40) has argued this point: 'It was Joan Robinson in *The Accumulation of Capital* (1956) who first synthesized these three disparate visions in a single work of originality which marks the beginning of a distinctly separate post-Keynesian theory.' And though not referencing her book, Kregel (1973, p. 3) argues that post-Keynesian economics is 'most closely associated with the writings of Professor Joan Robinson'.

Marcuzzo (2018, p. 127) claims that '[n]otwithstanding her criticisms, Robinson argued for an integration of Sraffa's results into a Marshallian and Keynesian framework, so as to give birth to a true alternative to neoclassical economics, which she labelled Post-Keynesian', and quotes a passage from Robinson (1973). Yet, this desire to 'give birth' to an alternative to neoclassical economics, to offer a theory certainly on par with it, was well present in *The Accumulation of Capital* – a book that, as stated above, contains all the elements of modern post-Keynesian economics, a book that is rooted in Keynes's analysis and a desire to extend it to the long run, a book that brings together various strands of post-Keynesian economics: the post-Keynesian vision.

This said, and to be generous, Robinson's book is not the only candidate for having sparked the beginning of post-Keynesian economics. We can argue there was a 'trilogy of sparks' at Cambridge, UK, at that time.[9] Along with Robinson's *Accumulation of Capital*, we can include Michał Kalecki, discussed above, who published his *Theory of Economic Dynamics* in 1954, and Nicholas Kaldor's (1955–56) *Alternative Theories of Income Distribution*, in which the author includes a 'Keynesian' approach to distribution, thus marking a positive contribution to theories of economic growth. While these last two contributions were narrower in scope, *The Accumulation of Capital* can be viewed as a grand approach, touching a number of bold ideas.

This would correspond to Lavoie's (2014, p. 31) statement that '[i]t could also be tempting to say that post-Keynesianism started in 1956, when Kaldor and Robinson put forth what was then called the Cambridge, Anglo-Italian or Neo-Keynesian theory of distribution as an alternative to the neoclassical theory based on the marginal productivity'.

But not everyone would agree. Lerner (1957, p. 693) had described the book as an 'irritation'. More recently, in reviewing the book on the

50th anniversary of its publication, at Rochon's request, King (2016, p. 328) argued, 'It seems to me that they represent an admission of defeat. *AC* was a noble failure, and Robinson knew it before she had finished writing.'

Whether the book was a 'noble failure' or not, the fact remains that it was a remarkable attempt at putting forth a complete synthesis that later became post-Keynesian economics.

Finally, as stated above, Robinson (1960, p. xiii) uses the expression 'post-Keynesian economics', which King (2002, p. 9) claims was used in a chronological way, to refer to the work of 'a remarkable group of economists [who] started a stream of economic thought' (Pasinetti, 1987, p. 217), in Cambridge, UK. Among the body of exceptional work of the time, the 'trilogy of sparks' discussed above stands out, and contains what we believe are the intellectual seeds of the post-Keynesian school that will begin to emerge in the next fifteen years. In this way, certainly unknowingly, the use of the expression 'post-Keynesian' by Robinson is best understood as precisely that body of work that was developing at Cambridge, UK, at that time and which formed the beginning of an emerging school of thought of that name. Chronologically or not, the expression is absolutely *à propos*. This view is supported by Lee (2000d, p. 145; italics ours): 'In 1959 Robinson used the term in a chronological sense, *but also to refer to her own theoretical work and that of her Cambridge colleagues, such as Nicholas Kaldor.*'

Moving forward

Becoming a 'positive alternative to the prevailing neoclassical paradigm' is only half the battle, of course. While post-Keynesian economics stands today as a whole and coherent alternative to neoclassical or mainstream economics, the next crucial step is the same as in the last seven decades: to win over the profession, which is currently in a state of despair (Rochon and Rossi, 2021, Ch. 2), and policy makers. In many ways, this has begun: Mariana Mazzucato advises governments, Heathey Boushey works in the Biden administration, and Stephanie Kelton has close ties to Bernie Sanders and parts of the Democratic Party in the United States.

But it remains overall a difficult task. The exercise is even more frustrating when you realize the number of critical and post-Keynesian ideas that have crept up and been adopted by mainstream authors. Indeed, Lavoie (2014) discusses the growing list of what he calls 'mainstream dissenters' (Stiglitz, Krugman, Sen, North, Rodrick, among others) – scholars who are not shy about teetering on the 'edge of [mainstream] economics' (Colander et al., 2004, p. 486). Areas in which the mainstream has borrowed some post-Keynesian or heterodox ideas include (among other things) monetary policy, complexity, and environmental issues.

In a letter to Alfred Eichner, on 11 July 1973, Joan Robinson writes '[t]here will soon be lots of books coming out on our side of the question and this will provide ammunition for people who are fed up with having to teach what they don't believe in. There is no hope of shifting the old guard but I think the students will be on our side and we have to work it through them' (quoted in Lee, 2000, p. 163).

In 2022, there is an abundance of articles, books, journals and, in the last few years at least, textbooks on post-Keynesian and heterodox economics: for instance, Lavoie (2014), Blecker and Setterfield (2019), and Rochon and Rossi (2021), among others. This is a welcome development, but the economics profession seems as tone deaf as ever to the (ir)relevance of their views.

In line with this, the number of students graduating with theses on heterodox and post-Keynesian themes is truly impressive. Armed increasingly with technical skills, some are now being hired in neoclassical 'citadels'.

This encyclopaedia

We have decided to embark on another encyclopaedic adventure, following our *Encyclopedia of Central Banking* (Rochon and Rossi, 2015), since we really feel there is a growing need of an encyclopaedia of post-Keynesian economics for a variety of stakeholders, notably for the younger generations of economists who have not had the occasion to know that an alternative to the ideas of the mainstream exists and can provide viable solutions to the current major economic problems around the world. We hope this volume finds itself in their hands.

This is the reason why we collected over 300 entries from about 170 authors, who have been so kind to write in an accessible way one or more articles gathered in this volume. The task, indeed, has been monumental and has taken much of our time and energy during more than five years. It was not an easy task but we believe it was worth carrying out, especially so now that the pandemic crisis has further aggravated the economic situation of several categories of economic agents and particularly those that already suffered much from the negative consequences of the 2008 global financial crisis. It is also with a view to improve the living conditions of these people that we made such a collective effort. Let us hope that it will deliver before long several positive results for the common good.

Louis-Philippe Rochon and
Sergio Rossi[10]

Notes

1. We will not deal here with the spelling of post-Keynesian economics, but the debate, often ridiculed by the younger generation, is an important one and goes to the very heart of how we define ourselves – as a large tent or as a narrow community. According to Lavoie (2014, p. 44), '[t]he relevant taxonomy today seems to be that "Post Keynesian" is a narrow-tent designation, while "post-Keynesian" covers a broader tent.'
2. The term 'British Post Keynesians' used in the above quote is meant to differentiate between the British and the American approaches. While there are certainly some important differences between these approaches, there are considerable similarities as well.
3. Note that the expression 'post-Keynesian' itself was used both by Kaldor (1955–56) and Robinson (1960). For Robinson (1960, p. xiii), '[my research] belongs to the field of what is sometimes called post-Keynesian economics.' According to King (2002, p. 9), however, it was used in a chronological sense: 'When Robinson wrote of "post-Keynesian economics" (Robinson, 1960a, p. xiii) [see Robinson, 1960], she was referring to her own theoretical work and that of Cambridge colleagues like Kahn and Kaldor.' Yet, an argument can be made that this chronological use of the work oddly enough corresponds to the work of the founding members of the school itself. Only a decade later, as argued above, was Robinson using the expression to refer specifically to a school of thought.
4. The *Cambridge Journal of Economics* was created in 1977, largely as a result of the move of the *Economic Journal* away from Cambridge the year before (Hodgson, 2019, p. 44).
5. It is worth mentioning that Joan Robinson published a paper in both inaugural journals. In the 1978 AEA programme, an advertisement announcing the creation of the *Journal of Post Keynesian Economics* appears.
6. While Robinson did write the 11-page Foreword to the book, she was not that enthusiastic. In a letter to Paul Davidson, she admits, 'I am rather bothered by the way Al Eichner sets up as spokesman for what all Post Keynesians think and then slips in fancy ideas of his own. I hope you are keeping an eye on him' (quoted in Lee, 2000, p. 39, fn 42).
7. Lee (2000, p. 39, fn 44) says that Luigi Pasinetti was also in attendance, although his name does not appear in Lee's (2000d, p. 150) list. In an email dated 18 August 2021, Mario Seccareccia confirms Pasinetti was not there.
8. In a private email, Davidson explained how every morning he would arrive at the office where notes from Robinson would await him.
9. We are grateful to Pablo Bortz for such a wonderful expression.
10. We would like to thank Marc Lavoie and Mario Seccareccia for their comments. All errors remain ours.

References

Arestis, P. (1992), *The Post-Keynesian Approach to Economics: An Alternative Analysis of Economic Theory and Policy*, Aldershot, UK and Brookfield, MA, USA: Edward Elgar.

Arestis, P. (1996), 'Post-Keynesian economics: towards coherence', *Cambridge Journal of Economics*, **20** (1), 111–35.

Arestis, P. and T. Skouras (1985), *Post-Keynesian Economic Theory: A Challenge to Neo-Classical Economics*, Sussex, UK: Wheatsheaf; and Armonk, NY, USA: M.E. Sharpe.

Asimakopulos, A. (1988–89), 'Kalecki and Joan Robinson: an "outsider's" influence', *Journal of Post Keynesian Economics*, **11** (2), 261–78.

Barna, T. (1957), 'Review of *The Accumulation of Capital*', *Economic Journal*, **67** (267), 490–93.

Bellofiore, R. (2021), 'The winters of our discontent and the social production economy', *Review of Political Economy*, **33** (3), 394–413.

Blecker, R. and M. Setterfield (2019), *Heterodox Macroeconomics Models of Demand, Distribution and Growth*, Cheltenham, UK, and Northampton, MA, USA: Edward Elgar.

Colander, D., R. Holt and B. Rosser Jr. (2004), 'The changing face of mainstream economics', *Review of Political Economy*, **6** (4), 485–99.

Davidson, P. (1965), 'Keynes's finance motive', *Oxford Economic Papers*, **17** (1), 47–65.

Davidson, P. (1972), *Money and the Real World*, London: Palgrave.

Eichner, A. (1979), *A Guide to Post-Keynesian Economics*, Armonk, NY: M.E. Sharpe.

Eichner, A. (1980), *Toward a New Economics: Essays in Post-Keynesian and Institutionalist Theory*, Armonk, NY: M.E. Sharpe.

Eichner, A.S. and J.A. Kregel (1975), 'An essay on Post-Keynesian theory: a new paradigm in economics', *Journal of Economic Literature*, **13** (4), 1293–311.

Galbraith, J. (2021), 'What is economics? A policy discipline for the real world', *Real World Economic Review*, 96, 67–81.

Goodhart, C. (2009), 'The continuing muddles of monetary theory: a steadfast refusal to face the facts', in E. Hein, T. Niechoj and E. Stockhammer (eds), *Macroeconomic Policies on Shaky Foundations: Whither Mainstream Economics?*, Marburg: Metropolis, pp. 351–69.

Harcourt, G. (1995), 'The structure of Post-Keynesian economics: the core contributions of the pioneers', *History of Economics Review*, 45, 95–105.

Harcourt, G. and P. Kerr (2009), *Joan Robinson*, London: Palgrave Macmillan.

Harcourt, G. and P. Kerr (2013), 'Introduction', in J. Robinson, *The Accumulation of Capital*, Basingstoke: Palgrave, third edition, pp. vii–xxx.

Hodgson, G. (2019), *Is There a Future for Heterodox Economics? Institutions, Ideology and a Scientific Community*, Cheltenham, UK, and Northampton, MA, USA: Edward Elgar.

Kaldor, N. (1955–56), 'Alternative theories of distribution', *Review of Economic Studies*, **23** (2), 83–100.

Kaldor, N. (1970), 'The new monetarism', *Lloyds Bank Review*, July, pp. 1–17.

Kaldor, N. (1983), 'Keynesian economics after fifty years', in D. Worswick and J. Trevithick (eds), *Keynes and the Modern World*, Cambridge, UK: Cambridge University Press, pp. 1–48.

Kalecki, M. (1954), *The Theory of Economic Dynamics*, London: Routledge.

Kerr, P. (2005), 'A history of Post-Keynesian economics', *Cambridge Journal of Economics*, **29** (3), 475–96.

Keynes, J.M. (1936), *The General Theory of Employment, Interest and Money*, London: Macmillan.

King, J.E. (2002), *A History of Post Keynesian Economics Since 1936*, Cheltenham, UK, and Northampton, MA, USA: Edward Elgar.

King, J.E. (2013), 'A brief introduction to Post Keynesian macroeconomics', *Wirtschaft und Gesellschaft*, **39** (4), 485–508.

King, J.E. (2016), 'Joan Robinson's *Accumulation of Capital* after 60 years', *Review of Keynesian Economics*, **4** (3), 316–30.

Klein, L. (1989), 'The economic principles of Joan Robinson', in G. Feiwel (ed.), *Joan Robinson and Modern Economic Theory*, London: Palgrave Macmillan.

Kregel, J. (1973), *The Reconstruction of Political Economy: An Introduction to Post-Keynesian Economics*, London: Palgrave Macmillan.

Lavoie, M. (2014), *Post-Keynesian Economics: New Foundations*, Cheltenham, UK, and Northampton, MA, USA: Edward Elgar.

Lavoie, M. (2021), 'Wynne Godley's monetary circuit', *Journal of Post-Keynesian Economics*, **44** (1), 6–23.

Lee, F.S. (2000), 'Alfred S. Eichner, Joan Robinson and the founding of Post Keynesian economics', *Research in the History of Economic Thought and Methodology*, 18C, pp. 9–40.

Lee, F.S. (2000a), 'Preface', *Research in the History of Economic Thought and Methodology*, 18C, pp. 3–7.

Lee, F.S. (2000b), 'Organizing the U.S. Post Keynesians and macrodynamics, 1971–1972', *Research in the History of Economic Thought and Methodology*, 18C, pp. 115–59.

Lee, F.S. (2000c), 'On the genesis of Post Keynesian economics', *Research in the History of Economic Thought and Methodology*, 18C, pp. 1–258.

Lee, F.S. (2000d), 'The organizational history of Post Keynesian economics in America, 1971–1995', *Journal of Post Keynesian Economics*, **23** (1), 141–62.

Lerner, A. (1957), 'Review of Joan Robinson's *The Accumulation of Capital*', *American Economic Review*, **47** (2), 693–99.

Marcuzzo, M.C. (2018), 'Joan Robinson's challenges on how to construct a Post-Keynesian economic theory', *Annals of the Fondazione Luigi Einaudi*, 52, 119–34.

Minsky, H.P. (1986), *Stabilizing an Unstable Economy*, New York: McGraw-Hill.

Pasinetti, L.L. (1987), 'Joan Violet Robinson', in J. Eatwell, M. Milgate and P. Newman (eds), *The New Palgrave: A Dictionary of Economics*, London: Macmillan, pp. 212–17.

Pasinetti, L.L. (2005), 'The Cambridge School of Keynesian economics', *Cambridge Journal of Economics*, **29** (6), 837–48.

Rima, I. (1991), *The Joan Robinson Legacy*, London: Routledge.

Robinson, J. (1952), 'Generalising the *General Theory*', in *The Rate of Interest and Other Essays*, London: Macmillan, pp. 67–142.

Robinson, J. (1956), *The Accumulation of Capital*, London: Macmillan.

Robinson, J. (1960), *Exercises in Economic Analysis*, London: Macmillan.

Robinson, J. (1972), 'The second crisis in economic theory', *American Economic Review*, **62** (1), 1–10.

Robinson, J. (1973), *Collected Economic Papers, Volume IV*, Oxford: Blackwell.

Robinson, J. and J. Eatwell (1973), *An Introduction to Modern Economics*, London: McGraw-Hill.

Rochon, L.-P. (1997), 'The finance motive: a reassessment. Credit, liquidity preference and the rate of interest', *Review of Political Economy*, **9** (3), 277–93.

Rochon, L.-P. and S. Rossi (eds) (2015), *The Encyclopedia of Central Banking*, Cheltenham, UK, and Northampton, MA, USA: Edward Elgar.

Rochon, L.-P. and S. Rossi (eds) (2021), *An Introduction to Macroeconomics: A Heterodox Approach to Economic Analysis, Second Edition*, Cheltenham, UK, and Northampton, MA, USA: Edward Elgar.

Rochon, L.-P. and M. Seccareccia (2021), 'What have we yet to learn from the COVID-19 crisis', *Review of Political Economy*, **33** (3), 373–6.

Seccareccia, M. and L.-P. Rochon (2020), 'What have we learned from the COVID-19 crisis: domestic and international dimensions and policy options for a post-coronavirus world: introduction', *International Journal of Political Economy*, **49** (4), 261–4.

Shapiro, N. (1977), 'The revolutionary character of Post-Keynesian economics', *Journal of Economic Issues*, **11** (3), 541–60.

Terzi, A. (2010), 'Keynes's uncertainty is not about black or white swans', *Journal of Post Keynesian Economics*, **32** (4), 559–65.

Turner, M. (1989), *Joan Robinson and the Americans*, London: Routledge.

Vernengo, M. (2019), 'The state of Post-Keynesian economics and its connections with other heterodox perspectives', *American Review of Political Economy*, **14** (1).

Weintraub, S. (1958), *An Approach to the Theory of Income Distribution*, Philadelphia: Clifton.

Weintraub, S. (1959), *A General Theory of the Price Level, Output, Income Distribution, and Economic Growth*, Philadelphia: Chilton Company.

Louis-Philippe Rochon and Sergio Rossi

A Tract on Monetary Reform

A Tract on Monetary Reform – first published in December 1923 – is a collection of five essays, which largely reproduces material published by Keynes in 1922 in the 'Reconstruction Supplements' of the *Manchester Guardian Commercial*.

Keynes's analysis of the functioning of the capitalist system always feeds on economic events of the time. Those of the *Tract* revolved around the inflationary tendency that started in 1914, followed by a deflationary trend since 1920. The first two chapters deal with the evils proceeding from instability in the purchasing power of money, also in connection with the part played by the exigencies of war finance. The third chapter develops the theoretical foundations of the analysis, that is, Keynes's constructive work on the Quantity Theory of Money (QTM). The last two chapters are about remedies. A work of a fine literary quality blending the language of the theorist and the practitioner with that of the polemicist and the persuader, the *Tract* aroused enormous interest and numerous controversies.

The first chapter, 'The consequences to society of changes in the value of money', later reprinted in *Essays in Persuasion*, is the most important of the entire collection. Dangers – and advantages – deriving from inflation and deflation can only be understood in light of their distributive effects. Keynes does this by dividing the social body into the investing class, the business class, and the earning class. His idea is that inflation redistributes wealth in a manner very injurious to the investor, very beneficial to the businessperson, and probably beneficial to the wage earner as well. After a start where a given level of production is assumed, the discussion then opens to the ways in which changes in the value of money affect that level. The conclusion is that 'inflation is unjust and deflation is inexpedient. Of the two perhaps deflation is, if we rule out exaggerated inflations such as that of Germany, the worse; because it is worse, in an impoverished world, to provoke unemployment than to disappoint the *rentier*' (Keynes, 1923/1971, p. 36). These themes are developed further in the second chapter, 'Public finance and changes in the value of money', through an articulated analysis of devaluation and capital levy as alternative means of containing excessively high claims of State's creditors. The capital levy is considered as the rational method, although scarcely feasible politically.

Chapter 3, 'On the theory of money and exchange' could be seen, with the benefit of hindsight, as the first act of the long battle undertaken by Keynes against the QTM. As a matter of fact, from a theoretical point of view, it is only an important example of the Cambridge approach to the QTM and to the credit cycle. The QTM is considered, in any case, as 'fundamental. Its correspondence with fact is not open to question' (p. 61), a certain unease towards it emerging only in the denial that it could be used mechanistically, so that a given variation in the quantity of money generates an analogous variation in prices, without influencing the other elements of the equation (it is in this framework that Keynes coined the famous expression 'In the long run we are all dead'). The QTM is also the basis of Keynes's purchasing power parity theory of the exchange rate.

The last two chapters lead again to the monetary policy issues topical at the time: (i) devaluation versus deflation; (ii) stability of prices versus stability of exchange; (iii) restoration of a gold standard. As regards the first issue, Keynes argues that deflation is not desirable and, in many countries, it is not even possible, because 'the burden which it would throw on the taxpayer would be insupportable' (p. 119). As regards the second issue, 'when stability of the internal price level and stability of external exchanges are incompatible, the former is generally preferable' (p. 132). With regard to the latter issue, Keynes's idea is that the gold standard – both an old-fashioned gold standard and a gold standard managed jointly with the United States – is harmful. A regulated non-metallic standard, according to Keynes, was already a fact, having, whilst economists dozed, 'crept into the real world by means of bad fairies – always so much more potent than the good – the wicked ministers of finance' (p. 138). Monetary stability had to be achieved through money management, and money management meant the regulation of credit, to be implemented without any constraints imposed by a metallic standard.

ALDO BARBA

See also

Cambridge Circus; Inflation; Inflation – conflict theory of; Money illusion; Rentier income

ALDO BARBA

Reference

Keynes, J.M. (1923/1971), *A Tract on Monetary Reform*, in *The Collected Writings of John Maynard Keynes, Vol. IV*, London: Macmillan.

Accelerator effects

Accelerator effects refer to the feedback process relating economic activity and business investment in circulating and fixed capital goods. This kind of effect is an important element in post-Keynesian analyses of both business cycles and economic growth. In fact, the interaction between accelerator and multiplier effects (or the supermultiplier effect) is an important ingredient of some post-Keynesian models of business cycles and economic growth.

The acceleration principle, understood here in its more general form known as the capital stock adjustment principle or 'flexible accelerator' (see Goodwin, 1948 and Chenery, 1952), is the main theoretical hypothesis advanced to explain these effects. Underlying this principle (in all its variants) is the idea that the process of capitalist competition leads to the existence of a normal capital–output ratio (hereafter, NCOR) that governs business investment decisions (Matthews, 1959). The NCOR depends on the technical capital–output ratio and the normal degree of capacity utilization. For given technical conditions of production and income distribution, the chosen technical capital–output ratio is the one that tends to prevail as a result of the cost-minimizing process induced by capitalist competition. Thus, changes in technology and in income distribution may modify the technical capital–output ratio. In particular, modifications in relative prices engendered by changes in income distribution may lead to changes in the cost-minimizing ratio. However, according to the Cambridge controversies on capital theory, it cannot be presumed *a priori* that, in general, there is an inverse relationship between NCOR and the rate of profit (or interest) as supposed by simple models based on neoclassical theory (for instance, the Solow model). On the other hand, the normal degree of capacity utilization is determined, among other things, by the historically established convention of what are the 'normal' ratios of the peak to average demand (see Ciccone, 1986; 1987). These ratios would explain the amount of planned spare capacity maintained in various sectors of the economy to prevent firms from losing market shares to their competitors when demand is relatively high on the market for produced goods and services.

Hence, given technical conditions, income distribution, and the long-run patterns of output fluctuations, the NCOR is also given. The latter establishes a direct relationship between the levels of output expected to prevail in the future and the required capital stock (capacity) that can normally support these projected levels of output (including its peak levels) while covering production expenses and allowing, at least, the obtainment of a minimum required (normal) rate of profit. It follows that if the profit rate in a production activity happens to be lower than this minimum, such a production activity is not a viable one in the long run, and investment in this activity would tend to be interrupted. Conversely, when the profit rate is not below the minimum one, net investment tends to promote the adjustment of the available capital stock to the corresponding level defined by the NCOR and the projected output levels. Moreover, in a situation where there is no binding supply constraint, the relationship just mentioned turns into a causal relation in which demand changes projected into the future provoke changes in the capital stock to adjust capacity to demand in line with the NCOR. Thus, investment is the means by which capitalist competition leads to the adjustment of capacity to demand. And the accelerator or capital stock adjustment principle becomes the foundation of a post-Keynesian theory of investment demand in which the latter is conceived as a derived or induced demand.

More specifically, according to the capital stock adjustment principle, when the actual capital–output ratio (ACOR) is above (below) its normal level, capitalist competition would prevent the maintenance of costly unused capacity (the risk of firms losing market share) by affecting investment in a way that gradually makes the rate of capital accumulation smaller (bigger) than the projected rate of output growth. For a sufficiently gradual reaction of business investment to the gap between actual and normal ratios, there would be, *ceteris paribus*, an adjustment of the ACOR towards the NCOR and, concomitantly, the convergence of the rate of capital accumulation towards the expected trend rate of output growth. Therefore, over a sequence of business cycles and provided the projected growth rate of output is positively related to the observed trend rate of growth of demand, there would be a tendency for the trend rates of growth of investment and capital accumulation to be explained by the trend rate of growth of demand. In these circumstances, for a given trend rate of output growth, accelerator effects are characterized by the fact that demand fluctuations projected into the future tend to cause more than proportional oscillations in business investments in such a way that the investment–output ratio features a pro-cyclical pattern. On the other hand, in what regards the analysis of longer-run output trends, accelerator effects are captured by the fact that changes in the trend rate of demand growth provoke changes in the same direction of the trend level of the share of business investment in output.

FABIO FREITAS

See also

Capacity utilization; Capital controversies; Fiscal multiplier; Income multiplier; Supermultiplier

References

Chenery, H.B. (1952), 'Overcapacity and the acceleration principle', *Econometrica*, **20** (1), 1–28.
Ciccone, R. (1986), 'Accumulation and capacity utilization: some critical considerations on Joan Robinson's theory of distribution', *Political Economy: Studies in the Surplus Approach*, **2** (1), 17–36.
Ciccone, R. (1987), 'Accumulation, capacity utilization and distribution: a reply', *Political Economy: Studies in the Surplus Approach*, **3** (1), 97–111.
Goodwin, R.M. (1948), 'Secular and cyclical aspects of the multiplier and the accelerator', in L.A. Metzler, H.S. Perloff and E.D. Domar (eds), *Income, Employment, and Public Policy: Essays in Honor of Alvin H. Hansen*, New York: W.W. Norton, pp. 108–32.
Matthews, R.C.O. (1959), *The Trade Cycle*, Cambridge, UK: James Nisbet.

AD–AS model

The aggregate demand–aggregate supply (AD–AS) model is among the elementary theoretical models to represent and analyse price and output fluctuations at the macroeconomic level. As opposed to the classical view, which claims production is supply constrained in the long run, the AD–AS model assumes the aggregate supply curve, in the short run, could be upward sloping.

The model consists of three curves: aggregate demand, short-run aggregate supply, and long-run aggregate supply. In the output/price space, the aggregate demand curve is downward sloping owing to the wealth effect, the interest-rate effect, and the exchange-rate effect. As the price level rises, for given wages, individuals' real wealth falls. As a result, their consumption is reduced. Hence, a reduction in the total amount of consumption implies a lower aggregate output ($Y = C + I + G + NX$): the wealth effect yields a negative relationship between the price level and output.

Also, as the price level rises, people need more cash to buy goods and services; hence, they tend to liquidate their asset holdings. This reduction of the supply of savings in the market for loanable funds increases interest rates, which in turn reduces the equilibrium level of investment. A fall in investment immediately implies a fall in output. For that reason, the interest-rate effect entails a negative relationship between the price level and output.

Third, as an increasing price level drives up domestic interest rates, foreign savers will demand more stocks and bonds. This will lead to an appreciation of the domestic currency. As the domestic currency becomes more valuable, produced goods will become more expensive for foreigners. Consequently, net exports will fall, leading to a fall in output.

Wealth, interest-rate, and exchange-rate effects contribute to the downward-sloping aggregate demand curve. Anything changing consumption, investment, government expenditures, or net exports leads to a shift in the aggregate demand curve.

Long-run aggregate supply, on the other hand, is a vertical curve reflecting the full employment of resources. Output, in the long run, is considered to be constrained by available resources and production technology. As a result, any policy increasing aggregate demand does not increase output but leads to higher prices. This is the classical notion of money neutrality: changes in nominal variables do not affect real variables.

In the short run, though, the aggregate supply curve could be upward sloping owing to a variety of market imperfections (Mankiw, 2014). For instance, according to the sticky-wage theory (which states that nominal wages are sticky in the short run owing to job contracts and social norms), when actual prices exceed the expected prices and labour costs stay the same, production becomes more profitable than planned. Hence, firms increase production (Y). This implies a positive relationship between prices and output.

Another imperfection is sticky prices. Many, if not all, prices are not perfectly flexible in the short run. As such, when there is a monetary injection, firms with flexible prices increase their prices. However, firms with menu costs do not respond as quickly, so that their prices remain lower than others. As a result, customers increase their demand for these relatively cheaper products. This stimulates firms with menu costs to increase production.

Lastly, there is the misperceptions theory, according to which firms cannot tell whether their prices increase because their products are more in demand or there is an overall increase in the prices of all goods. Some firms, failing to recognize it is an increase in the prices of all goods (inflation), may increase their output and hire more workers. The result, again, is a positive relationship between prices and output.

Although the AD–AS model has been a widely used pedagogical tool in mainstream macroeconomics, it is a very disputed area of research. It was meant to be a representation of Keynesian economics, but as argued by Colander (1995) it is in fact a seriously flawed model. The standard mainstream version of the model withholds many logical inconsistencies and there is not much empirical evidence supporting it (Moseley, 2010). A fundamental criticism from a post-Keynesian perspective is that the standard Marshallian model always equates aggregate demand and aggregate supply but, in contrast to Say's Law, actually 'there is no insurance that all the goods produced will be sold' (Lavoie, 2014, p. 278). In that case, the level of effective demand would be the main binding factor in determining employment of resources. Based on this, the post-Keynesian AS curve is flat for all levels of output below full capacity utilization and would bend to be vertical near full capacity, where the supply constraint begins to be binding. Last but not least, the behavioural dynamics of the AD–AS model are too mechanical in the sense that it underplays the role of expectations, uncertainty, and historical time (Dutt and Skott, 2006).

ANIL ABA

See also

Fiscal policy; Monetary policy; Money illusion; Neoclassical economics; Wealth effect

References

Colander, D. (1995), 'The stories we tell: a reconsideration of AS/AD analysis', *Journal of Economic Perspectives*, **9** (3), 169–88.
Dutt, A.K. and P. Skott (2006), 'Keynesian theory and the AD–AS framework: a reconsideration', *Contributions to Economic Analysis*, **277**, 149–72.
Lavoie, M. (2014), *Post-Keynesian Economics: New Foundations*, Cheltenham, UK, and Northampton, MA, USA: Edward Elgar.
Mankiw, N.G. (2014), *Principles of Macroeconomics*, Stamford, CT: Cengage Learning.
Moseley, F. (2010), 'Criticisms of aggregate demand and aggregate supply and Mankiw's presentation', *Review of Radical Political Economics*, **42** (3), 308–14.

Agent-based modelling

Agent-based modelling (ABM) is a computational methodology for building, solving, and analysing models populated by a large number of fully heterogeneous agents, connected through an incomplete network, who follow simple behavioural rules and interact with each other. The resulting aggregate dynamics and empirical regularities are not known a priori and cannot be inferred from individual behaviour, determining an open-ended state of spaces (Tesfatsion, 2017).

Agent-based models are computationally solved by means of computer simulations and can be used to represent complex systems, in which nonlinear, chaotic, or out-of-equilibrium forms of behaviour are possible.

The three main characteristics of ABM are: heterogeneity of agents, their interaction, and evolutionary dynamics. Populations in agent-based models display (full) heterogeneity at the agent level. This feature is in contrast with heterogeneity as normally treated in dynamic stochastic general equilibrium models where agents are classified in categories and heterogeneity is not defined at micro-level but at some meso-level of aggregation. In ABM, agents cannot be fully rational and have a limited (local) knowledge of their ecosystem. As a result, they adopt simple behavioural rules (heuristics) and adaptive expectations.

Owing to their limited vision of the system and information sets, agents interact with each another at local level. They receive constant feedback from the system. Three main consequences of interaction and feedback can be identified. First, the map of interactions at local level defines a network topology, whose characteristics determine the time evolution of the system. Second, the feedback effects at systemic level generate endogenous and persistent novelty with infinite possible outcomes. As a consequence, an open-ended state of spaces must be considered, since it is not possible to pre-identify a finite range of feasible outcomes. Third, the aggregate structure emerges from agents' interactions: the system is characterized by emergent properties that are not implied nor can be inferred by agents' behaviour.

The chain of feedback effects through time defines an evolutionary dynamic. The system and the single parts or sub-parts change over time and these changes are mutually interdependent. The evolution of agents takes place through the retention of those characteristics that are necessary for survival and the innovation of those features that are less compatible with the changes in the environment.

A corollary of these three characteristics is that agent-based models are typically non-ergodic, owing to strong path dependency: no final equilibrium state can be identified.

The implementation of agent-based models is articulated in four phases. First, a virtual economy populated by various types of agents (for instance, households, firms, banks, government) is constructed, in which each agent is endowed with internal states and behavioural routines. Second, the initial conditions and parameters' values are quantified (calibration). This phase involves the definition of the parameters' range that allows the model to reproduce relevant empirical evidence (validation). The validation is performed through direct estimation from the data, or by minimizing the distance between the model's results and the data to reproduce, or by means of meta-modelling (representation of the model as an explicit approximate relationship between input and output variables). The third phase concerns the numerical simulations. No further intervention by the modeller occurs at this stage and the dynamics are only driven by agents' interactions. Simulations run in discrete time and, at each time step, a set of agents is activated through the pre-defined behavioural rules and idiosyncratic stochastic processes. Their heuristic decisions mutually affect each other according to the network topology. At the end of each time step, aggregate variables are computed by summing individual quantities and the system state is updated, determining a change in the agents' set of information. At the end of the simulation the fourth phase of implementation takes place: the emergent properties of the system are recorded, statistically analysed, and tested through repetitions of the simulations (Monte Carlo replications). The analysis involves the sensitivity study: quantifying the change in the simulations' results associated to variations in the parameter set.

ABM was introduced in macroeconomics during the 1990s and has proved to be able to replicate a number of stylized facts at both the microeconomic and macroeconomic levels. Its modelling approach can explain evidence such as the persistence of heterogeneity, the emergence of fat-tail distributions, and extreme events (see Gallegati et al., 2017). The adoption and implementation of ABM in economics has been criticized, besides reasons related to its non-standard modelling approach, for the difficulties in identifying the causal chains within the model, owing to the use of numerical simulations (Di Guilmi et al., 2017), and for the degree of freedom of the modeller, who is not constrained by the need of an equilibrium analytical solution (Foley, 2017). Recent developments are addressing these issues by introducing global sensitivity analysis, which allows for the multidimensional exploration of the parameter space, and meta-modelling, which can identify the main variables affecting the results and can shed light on the causal relationships among the different parameters and variables (Saltelli et al., 2008).

CORRADO DI GUILMI

See also

Behavioural economics; Methodology; Microfoundations; Stock–flow consistent models; Traverse, path dependency, and economic dynamics

References

Di Guilmi, C., M. Gallegati and S. Landini (2017), *Interactive Macroeconomics*, Cambridge, UK: Cambridge University Press.

Foley, D.K. (2017), 'Crisis and theoretical methods: equilibrium and disequilibrium once again', *New School for Social Research Department of Economics Working Paper*, No. 1703.

Gallegati, M., A. Palestrini and A. Russo (2017), *Introduction to Agent-Based Economics*, Amsterdam: Academic Press.

Saltelli, A., M. Ratto, T. Andres, F. Campolongo, J. Cariboni, D. Gatelli, M. Saisana and S. Tarantola (2008), *Global Sensitivity Analysis: The Primer*, Cornwall: Wiley.

Tesfatsion, L. (2017), 'Modeling economic systems as locally-constructive sequential games', *Journal of Economic Methodology*, **24** (4), 384–409.

Aggregate demand

In a letter to Roy Harrod (August 30, 1936), Maynard Keynes wrote: 'To me the most extraordinary thing, regarded historically, is the complete disappearance of the theory of demand and supply for output on a whole, *i.e.* the theory of employment, *after* it had been for a quarter of a century the most discussed thing in economics' (Keynes, 1978, p. xv, italics in the original). So it was that the core of the system in his magnum opus, *The General Theory of Employment, Interest and Money* (1936), is his aggregate demand and supply functions. Their intersection gives the point of effective demand at which the short-period equilibrium or rest state of the economy is established.

There are two different concepts of aggregate demand in *The General Theory*. The first and most fundamental is the total of employment offered, and consequent output produced, based on the expectation of each entrepreneur/firm of what their immediate prices (if they are price-takers) or sales (if they are price-makers) are to be. Those producing consumption goods have in mind either the prices they expect to receive, so that they offer employment up to the point that their marginal costs equal these prices; or they have in mind what their sales are to be, so that they offer employment that makes possible output equal to their expected sales.

Those producing capital goods mostly respond to orders for fixed capital goods and to desired investment in stocks/inventories (similar procedures are followed by producers of intermediate goods). The totals of all the outcomes of responding to these expectations fall on a 45° line relating them to either total employment offered or output to be produced. The aggregate supply function also falls on the 45° line, as it shows the expected proceeds needed to offer levels of employment.

Keynes set out these ideas in *The General Theory*: 'in a given situation of technique, resources and factor cost per unit of employment, the amount of employment, both in each individual firm and industry and the aggregate, depends on the amount of the proceeds which the entrepreneurs expect to receive from the corresponding output' (Keynes, 1936, pp. 24–25).

The second concept of aggregate demand is what the all-seeing economist in principle may observe: the totals of the levels of overall consumption expenditure arising at different levels of personal disposable income of Keynes's aggregate consumption or prosperity to consume function plus the aggregate levels of planned investment expenditure at any point in time. (For simplicity we are assuming a closed economy without a government.)

The values of the two concepts of aggregate demand only match up at the point of effective demand. Here, the employment, output, income and spending arising from the firms reacting to their expected prices or sales creates the income levels that lead to spending that fulfils these expectations. Moreover, if the economy is not initially at the point of effective demand, the corresponding unexpected prices or sales are signals that lead firms to change their employment and output levels so as to move the economy towards the point of effective demand, provided that there is no feedback into expected planned expenditures.

This may be contrasted with the mainstream aggregate supply and demand analysis, where both are functions of the aggregate price level, with given expectations. Although the short-run situation is consistent with involuntary unemployment, in the long run it is assumed that the aggregate supply curve is vertical at full employment, or the natural rate level of unemployment. It is this assumption, said to originate in some mystical powers of markets as long as prices and money wages are 'flexible', that explains why there is no unemployment in the long run. However, these functions, especially the long-run aggregate supply curve, are very different from those discussed by Keynes and post-Keynesians.

Had the bulk of post-war students been taught the economics of Keynes through the

CORRADO DI GUILMI / GEOFF HARCOURT AND PETER KRIESLER

structure he analysed, they would have had no trouble in explaining the stagflation episode of the 1970s. An imported cost inflation or an autonomous rise in money wages would have raised the aggregate supply function, resulting in a lower level of employment and a higher overall price level. The latter in turn could have induced an inflationary spiral, signalling the need for radically different policies than were in fact implemented. The rise of monetarism and then Lucasianism and the neo-liberal era may well have been averted.

GEOFF HARCOURT AND
PETER KRIESLER

See also

Effective demand; Keynesian cross diagram; Stagflation; *The General Theory of Employment, Interest and Money*; Unemployment – involuntary

References

Keynes, J.M. (1936), *The General Theory of Employment, Interest and Money*, London: Macmillan.

Keynes, J.M. (1978), *The Collected Writings of John Maynard Keynes, Volume VII: The General Theory of Employment, Interest and Money*, London: Macmillan.

Animal spirits

Animal spirits first arose in modern macroeconomics in Keynes's *General Theory* (Keynes, 1936), playing a key role in investment decisions, and thus central to his theory of aggregate demand.

> Most, probably, of our decisions to do something positive … can only be taken as a result of animal spirits – of a spontaneous urge to action rather than inaction, and not as the outcome of a weighted average of quantitative benefits multiplied by quantitative probabilities. (Keynes, 1936, p. 161)

In spite of the importance Keynes placed on animal spirits, they did not accord with the rationality calculus of the microfoundations programme, and the concept fell into disuse (Dow and Dow, 1985). For example, Coddington (1982) argued that any element of irrationality meant that all decision-making was irrational.

This dichotomisation between rationality and irrationality persists in renewed mainstream attention to animal spirits in the wake of the financial crisis: in the form of a random shock to beliefs, or more generally as 'noneconomic motives and irrational behaviours' (Akerlof and Shiller, 2009, p. x). In public discourse the term is used more narrowly to refer to irrational optimism, which is seen as a major factor in the build-up to the financial crisis and thus to be discouraged.

However, post-Keynesian economists have consistently analysed animal spirits as integral to Keynes's view that, given fundamental uncertainty, rationality alone is insufficient to justify action; animal spirits, along with conventional judgement, are required. Post-Keynesian thinking on uncertainty, and particularly the degrees of uncertainty, has evolved in such a way as to challenge the mainstream dichotomisation of certainty and uncertainty, rationality and irrationality (see, for instance, Runde and Mizuhara, 2003). By emphasising the conventional content of expectations, and the capacity for degrees of uncertainty, the modern post-Keynesian literature has taken analysis of animal spirits forward. Contrary to the mainstream approach, animal spirits are understood less as a matter of individual psychology and more as the outcome of social conventions and social structures.

Thus Marchionatti (1999) takes forward Keynes's analysis of the investment decision by considering how the structure and environment of the firm influence animal spirits. For Schumpeter (1934), the structure of industrial organisation (firm size, firm age, corporate governance and so on) is important for the scope and character of animal spirits. Further, for Marshall (1919), the success of any organisation is due in large part to the political, social and economic atmosphere. Marchionatti (1999, p. 431) identifies this atmosphere with the 'rules of the social game', based on a shared ideology or 'mental model'.

This is taken further by Dow and Dow (2011), who apply this understanding of animal spirits to organisation, innovation and behaviour in the financial sector and to reactions to austerity policies in the wake of the financial crisis. On the one hand, they consider the interplay between animal spirits and evidence; while on the other hand they argue that the factors contributing to animal spirits are open to policy intervention. This latter point is developed by Dow (2014), where animal spirits are considered in terms of unsubstantiated optimism, low uncertainty perception and low uncertainty aversion. A distinction is drawn between animal spirits with respect to expanding capacity on the one hand and animal spirits with respect to innovation on the other. The first case is analysed primarily in terms of fluctuations in spontaneous optimism and uncertainty perception, while the emphasis for the second is more on the enduring dispositions of organisations and individuals. Animal spirits in both contexts are shown to be influenced by structural factors, which are open to policy management.

SHEILA DOW

See also

Aggregate demand; Financial crises; Microfoundations; Rationality; *The General Theory of Employment, Interest and Money*

References

Akerlof, G.A. and R.J. Shiller (2009), *Animal Spirits: How Human Psychology Drives the Economy, and Why It Matters for Global Capitalism*, Princeton, NJ: Princeton University Press.

Coddington, A. (1982), 'Deficient foresight: a troublesome theme in Keynesian economics', *American Economic Review*, **72** (3), 480–87.

Dow, A. and S. Dow (1985), 'Animal spirits and rationality', in T. Lawson and H. Pesaran (eds), *Keynes' Economics: Methodological Issues*, Armonk, NY: M.E. Sharpe, pp. 46–65. Reprinted in S. Dow, *Foundations for New Economic Thinking: A Collection of Essays*, London: Palgrave Macmillan, 2012, pp. 33–51.

Dow, A. and S. Dow (2011), 'Animal spirits revisited', *Capitalism and Society*, 6 (2), article 1, available online at https://www.degruyter.com/view/j/cas.2011.6.issue-2/1932-0213.1087/1932-0213.1087.xml; last accessed 4 April 2019.

Dow, S. (2014), 'Animal spirits and organization', *Journal of Post Keynesian Economics*, **37** (2), 211–32.

Keynes, J.M. (1936), *The General Theory of Employment, Interest and Money*, London: Macmillan.

Marchionatti, R. (1999), 'On Keynes's animal spirits', *Kyklos*, **52**, 415–39.

Marshall, A. (1919), *Industry and Trade*, London: Macmillan.

Runde, J. and S. Mizuhara (eds) (2003), *The Philosophy of Keynes's Economics: Probability, Uncertainty and Convention*, London and New York: Routledge.

Schumpeter, J.A. (1934), *Capitalism, Socialism and Democracy*, London: Allen and Unwin.

SHEILA DOW / CLARA CAPELLI AND EUGENIO CAVERZASI

Asset backed securities

Asset backed securities (ABSs) are bonds resulting from the transformation of financial assets. The value of ABSs – and of the cash flow they generate – is based on a pool of underlying assets, usually securitized loans but also, although much less frequently, royalties and stocks. In some cases, it is possible to distinguish ABSs based on the kind of loans backing the security; for instance, Mortgage Backed Securities (MBSs) can be Residential, Commercial, or Student Loans Asset Backed Securities.

Closely related to ABS are the Collateralized Debt Obligations (CDOs), a structured form of ABSs sliced into tranches with different seniorities. Senior tranches are the first receiving payments and the less exposed to default risk of the underlying assets. The process of their creation and sale involves different financial actors, and can be exemplified as follows. A financial institution that has issued a loan and holds it as an asset in its balance sheet can sell it to a Special Purpose Vehicle (SPV), namely a specialized subsidiary company. The SPV packages the loan with other loans into a new asset (an ABS), which is then sold on the financial markets and can be further transformed into a CDO. The institution that issued the loans collects the payments on the original loans and passes them to the holder of the security.

Although MBSs and CDOs can be considered as two subsets or specific types of ABSs, very often the term ABS is used to refer to securities backed by assets other than mortgages, with MBS referring to a distinct financial product.

Even though very similar financial instruments based on collateralized loans were used as early as the eighteenth century (Frehen et al., 2014), the introduction of ABSs in the modern financial system dates back to the 1970s in the United States, when Government-Sponsored Enterprises issued their first MBS: the Government National Mortgage Association (or 'Ginnie Mae') in 1970; the Federal Home Loan Mortgage Corporation (or 'Fannie Mac') in 1971; and the Federal National Mortgage Association (or 'Fannie Mae') in 1983 (see Segoviano et al., 2013). The private sector started issuing ABSs in 1985 (Sperry Univac Corporation). In the same year, this financial innovation was also adopted in Europe, first in the United Kingdom (1985) and later in the rest of the continent.

Conversely, CDOs were introduced by the private sector; the first one was issued by the Imperial Savings Association, which failed in 1990. The deregulation of the financial sector of the 1980s and 1990s gave a great impulse to the growth of ABSs: on the eve of the subprime mortgage crisis of 2007–2008, they were among the most traded products in the financial markets and one of the causes that led to the outbreak of the crisis itself.

On the one hand, ABSs allowed the loan originators (both banks and non-banking financial institutions) to exchange an illiquid asset (that is, the loan) for a liquid one (such as bank deposits), thus giving them the possibility to expand their portfolios while meeting Basel-type capital requirements. On the other hand, ABSs transferred the risk from the originators to the final investor (that is, the holder of the security), which in turn profoundly undermined the stability of the financial system, as the loan originators no longer had the incentive to carefully assess their borrowers' creditworthiness (Kregel, 2008).

The spectacular success of ABS radically changed the financial systems. Banks shifted from a traditional 'originate to hold' business model, in which loans were issued and kept in the balance sheets, to an 'originate to distribute' model. According to Caverzasi et al. (2019), such shift led to a metamorphosis of the credit system, as loans became in the first place the input for the process of production of complex financial assets. This is part of the broader transformation of the US economic system – and, more generally, of the advanced capitalist economies – that goes under the name of financialization.

CLARA CAPELLI AND EUGENIO CAVERZASI

See also

Deregulation; Financial innovations; Financialization; Securitization; Subprime financial crisis

References

Caverzasi, E., A. Botta and C. Capelli (2019), 'Shadow banking and the financial side of financialisation,' *Cambridge Journal of Economics*, **43** (4), 1029–51.
Frehen, R., W.N. Goetzmann and K.G. Rouwenhorst (2014) 'Dutch securities for American land speculation in the late eighteenth century,' in E.N. White, K. Snowden and P. Fishback (eds), *Housing and Mortgage Markets in Historical Perspective*, Chicago, University of Chicago Press, pp. 287–304.
Kregel, J. (2008) 'Minsky's cushions of safety – systemic risk and the crisis in the U.S. subprime mortgage market,' *Levy Economics Institute of Bard College Public Policy Brief*, No. 93.
Segoviano, M., B. Jones, P. Lindner and J. Blankenheim (2013), 'Securitization: lessons learned and the road ahead,' *International Monetary Fund Working Paper*, No. WP/13/255.

Asymmetric information

The analysis of asymmetric information and its implications for macroeconomics in terms of market failures (that is, involuntary unemployment, credit and/or equity rationing, banking and financial crisis, and so on) have been under scrutiny since the end of the 1980s (Stiglitz, 2004).

Post-Keynesian economists have stressed particularly the relevance of asymmetric information in financial markets, since the latter play a central role in determining the path of an economy. The aims of their analyses were twofold: on one hand, to show the relevance of the financial structure for investment decisions and, on the other, to investigate how a monetary economy may evolve towards financial instability and crisis.

Post-Keynesian economists have considered how differences in the information available to firms and providers of external finance may give rise to finance constraints (see Fazzari and Athey, 1987; Dymski, 1992; Fazzari and Variato, 1994; Sau, 1999).

In contrast with the well-known Modigliani–Miller theorem (1958), post-Keynesians have shown indeed that the financial structure matters for investment decision and that limits to real activity come from the financial system rather than from technology or preferences. This means that investment projects that would increase the value of firms and would be undertaken according to neoclassical theory might be constrained by financial markets.

These approaches are in compliance with one of Keynes's main contributions: to develop conditions under which 'money', broadly conceived, mattered for the real performance of the macroeconomy. In this regard, asymmetric information has provided useful insights into the 'foundations' of the traditional Keynesian concepts of borrowers' and lenders' risk. These 'principles' are rooted in the relationship between entrepreneurs and lenders. Entrepreneurs seek funds in excess of those generated internally to finance their projects, while lenders evaluate whether it is worthwhile to meet these requests.

As regards lenders' risk, since information is asymmetric, the probability distributions over uncertain project outcomes differ between borrowers and lenders. If the same general equilibrium interest rate that cleared the market for external finance in the full information case were to prevail with asymmetric information, borrowers with poor quality projects could behave opportunistically. Lenders recognize this incentive, and therefore they charge a higher rate of interest to borrowers of all qualities when information is asymmetric.

Keynes (1936, p. 284) claimed that as investment spending rises, lenders become more reluctant to finance marginal projects. Minsky (1975) characterizes this risk as an increase of the marginal supply price of investment to firms as investment expands (Fazzari and Mott, 1986–87).

As to borrowers' risk, Minsky (1975, p. 35) described this risk as 'doubts in the mind of the entrepreneur', and argued that this is the only relevant financial factor if 'a man ventures his own money' (ibid.). Nevertheless, if borrowers' risk arises from entrepreneurs' risk aversion, then diversification seems to provide the obvious solution.

Nevertheless, under asymmetric information, to undertake a profitable investment project, a firm's insiders may have to commit more of their own capital either as a direct means to finance the project or as collateral to obtain outside funds. This requirement forces entrepreneurs to forego diversification opportunities if they want to invest.

The topic of asymmetric information opened, during the 1990s, a debate and has sparked controversy (see Van Ees and Garretsen, 1993; Crotty, 1996). Some post-Keynesian authors have indeed disputed that what is relevant in Keynesian approaches is radical/fundamental uncertainty, rather than asymmetric information. Van Ees and Garretsen (1993), for instance, have argued that the hypothesis of complementarity between these two methodological approaches cannot be supported.

By contrast, Dymski (1993) has proposed a relationship and a complementary between the two approaches: in good/tranquil times (bank) behaviour in financial markets can be characterized as decision making under asymmetric information. However, in turbulent periods the analysis of decision making under fundamental uncertainty is more appropriate to analyse behaviour in financial markets.

This controversy has remained open (see Piégay, 2000) and is beyond the scope of the present overview. Problems of asymmetric information do exist and deserve the attention of economists. However, such an analysis will necessarily be partial in nature, as it can only take place on the *ceteris paribus* assumptions of a given state of the world and a given amount of information.

LINO SAU

See also

Credit constraints; Financial crises; Financial instability hypothesis; Uncertainty; Unemployment – involuntary

References

Crotty, J.R. (1996), 'Is New Keynesian investment theory really "Keynesian"? Reflections on Fazzari and Variato', *Journal of Post Keynesian Economics*, **18** (3), 333–357.
Dymski, G. (1988), 'A Keynesian theory of bank behavior', *Journal of Post Keynesian Economics*, **10** (4), 499–526.
Dymski, G. (1992), 'A "new view" of the role of banking firms in Keynesian monetary theory', *Journal of Post Keynesian Economics*, **14** (3), 311–320.
Dymski, G. (1993), 'Keynesian uncertainty and asymmetric information: complementary or contradictory?', *Journal of Post Keynesian Economics*, **16** (1), 49–54.
Fazzari, S.M. and M.J. Athey (1987), 'Asymmetric information, financing constraints, and investment', *Review of Economics and Statistics*, **69** (3), 481–487.
Fazzari, S.M. and T.L. Mott (1986–87), 'The investment theories of Kalecki and Keynes: a study of firm data 1970–82', *Journal of Post Keynesian Economics*, **9** (2), 171–187.
Fazzari, S.M. and A.M. Variato (1994), 'Asymmetric information and Keynesian theories of investment', *Journal of Post Keynesian Economics*, **16** (3), 351–369.
Keynes, J.M. (1936), *The General Theory of Employment, Interest and Money*, London: Macmillan.
Minsky, H.P. (1975), *John Maynard Keynes*, New York: Columbia University Press.

Piégay, P. (1999–2000), 'The New and Post Keynesian analyses of bank behavior: consensus and disagreement', *Journal of Post Keynesian Economics*, **22** (2), 265–283.

Sau, L. (1999), 'Financial structure, asymmetric information and H.P. Minsky's investment theory revised', *Economia politica*, **14** (2), 211–242.

Stiglitz, J.E. (2004), 'Information and the change in the paradigm in economics', *The American Economist*, **48** (1), 17–49.

Van Ees, H. and H. Garretsen (1993), 'Financial markets and the complementarity of asymmetric information and fundamental uncertainty', *Journal of Post Keynesian Economics*, **16** (1), 37–48.

Austerity

There is little doubt as to what austerity is: a restrictive stance of fiscal policy, made of public spending retrenchments, tax increases (particularly on lower incomes), or a combination of both. Austerity means to use budget manoeuvres to reduce public and/or private expenditure. From a Keynesian point of view, the effects of austerity measures on income and employment levels are clear: an increase in the economy's propensity to save does not increase investment, but tends to reduce income levels, leaving investment and saving unchanged. This occurs notably in the most favourable case, where the contraction of income does not encroach upon investment, thereby contributing to an even sharper contraction of income eventually.

Given all this, the most problematic aspect with respect to austerity policies concerns the objectives policymakers pursue in the name of austerity. As a mean of reducing aggregate demand, and therefore the use of plants and labour, austerity tends in the first instance to contract revenues and profits. Capitalists should join the popular classes most affected by these manoeuvres in opposing them. Yet, they do not. What must therefore be explained is why capitalists favour a fiscal policy stance that apparently moves against their own interests. Put another way, from a Keynesian point of view, the problem posed by austerity policies is why they are so insistently invoked by the ruling classes and so stubbornly implemented by the governments at their service.

There are two main reasons in this regard. First, there are 'non-self-inflicted austerity policies', which concern foreign debt. A country that has a deficit in its trade balance must borrow from abroad. In this case, austerity represents the *redde rationem* of the foreign creditor who, no longer willing to exchange goods and services against rights on the future production of the deficit country, would impose a halt on its growth rate and through it the restoration of the equilibrium in its balance of trade. To this end, austerity acts in two ways. On the one hand, as we pointed out, it stops the accumulation of debt. On the other hand, it favours settlement. Consider for example that privatisation policies, which are often an important aspect of austerity packages, provide foreign creditors with an asset that can conveniently satisfy their rights in 'real' terms.

Second, there are 'self-inflicted austerity policies', implemented by the domestic ruling classes without any pressure from the outside. The rationale behind austerity in this case is more elusive. It must be understood by tracing it back to the distributional effects that inevitably follow from expansionary policies aimed at achieving permanently high levels of production and employment. To the extent that the economic system operates permanently close to full employment, the disciplinary action exercised by the unemployed on the claims of the employees tends to weaken, thus generating a shift in the balance of power in favour of the workers in the incessant dispute between them and the capitalists on the division of the social product. High employment tends to favour high wages, which, if persistent, become standard for workers. This increases their ability to oppose a contraction of wages, and to obtain a wage growth at least in line with that of productivity. If this happens, the rate of profit will not increase, and may even shrink if wage growth is greater than productivity growth. The higher real wages will further increase aggregate demand and therefore economic growth and wages, in a virtuous circle. Although virtuous for society as a whole, this circle reduces the rate of profit. Austerity is the policy through which the capitalists break it. The self-inflicted austerity policies are therefore an expression of the fact that capitalists prefer low rates of economic growth coupled with full control over the accumulation pace and the determinants of income distribution, to a high growth regime with an ensuing loss of control on both (Kalecki, 1943). It must also be considered that austerity, especially if prolonged, necessarily implies lower taxes and thus lower government spending. The erosion of the economic role of the State in the economy allows capitalists to conquer non-market services industries (such as health, education, transport and utilities), whose weight has become very relevant in deindustrialised advanced economies.

Until the radical turn of the early 1980s towards free-market policies, austerity policies were meant to cause momentary slowdowns that, though aimed at re-establishing the 'disciplinary mechanism', were followed by expansionary policies, to be once again discontinued in the event of another economic and social overheating. With the change in the balance of power that has emerged from that turning point, these disciplinary episodes have evolved into a regime where economic growth is permanently held back by restrictive policies (or at least by policies that are never expansive over a prolonged period of time). This development has reached a paroxysm in Europe where, thanks to the political alibi provided by the smokescreen of 'supranational' institutions, austerity has taken root to the point of being implemented even in the strongly recessive context determined by the financial crisis that started in 2008.

ALDO BARBA

See also

Aggregate demand; Financial crises; Fiscal multiplier; Fiscal policy; Income distribution

Reference

Kalecki, M. (1943), 'The political aspects of full employment', *Political Quarterly*, **14** (4), 322–30.

Balance of payments

The balance of payments is a statistical statement that summarizes transactions between residents and non-residents in a given country over a period of time. Transactions resulting in a payment to non-residents are entered as a debit in the balance of payments, while transactions resulting in an inflow of resources from foreigners are entered as a credit.

The balance of payments divides international transactions into three accounts, according to the definition provided by the International Monetary Fund (2009), which is also used by the United Nations' System of National Accounts. The first one is the current account, which refers to exports and imports of goods and services. These, in turn, are divided into three finer categories within the current account: goods trade (exports or imports of merchandise), services trade (payments for legal assistance, tourists' expenditures, transport services, engineering services, among others), and income transfers (international interests, rents and dividends, as well as personal transfers and international aid). The second account within the balance of payments is the capital account, which records transactions of non-produced non-financial assets, such as land, as well as capital transfers between countries. Thirdly, there is the financial account, which records purchases and sales of financial assets, such as stocks, corporate bonds and government debt.

The sum of the balances on the current and capital accounts represents the net lending or borrowing by a given country with regard to the rest of the world. This result is equal to the net balance of the financial account, which means that the financial account measures how the foreign surplus or deficit is being financed.

It should be noticed that, in the double-entry accounting system that underlies the balance of payments, international transactions give rise to two offsetting entries. Hence, the current account balance, the financial account balance and the capital account balance automatically add up to zero.

In an open economy, keeping the balance of payments' current account in equilibrium is critical in order to sustain long-run economic growth. When domestic output and income increase, so does the demand for imports of goods and services. Starting from a trade equilibrium, if exports do not increase at the same rate as imports, then the country will run a trade-balance deficit. If a country runs successive trade deficits, then it will constantly increase its foreign debt, which will eventually worsen its income account balance owing to increasing interest payments.

There are typically two rebalancing mechanisms to correct current account deficits: exchange rate depreciation and domestic adjustment via deflation and/or recession. In both cases, exports become more competitive and imports tend to decline, leading to an improvement in the trade balance that eventually corrects the disequilibrium in the current account.

When rebalancing mechanisms are absent, foreign debt keeps rising. At a certain point, the increasing foreign debt will make creditors suspect the debtor country will not be able to honour its obligations, or that the trade deficit might lead to an exchange rate devaluation, which would generate a capital loss to the creditors. Hence, this leads to a halt in international finance and, consequently, to an unsustainable loss of reserves – expressed as a deficit in the balance of payments' financial account. This situation is known as currency crisis or 'sudden stop', because suddenly the country running the current account deficit does not have the foreign currency required to finance its imports (see McCombie and Thirlwall, 1994).

Sudden stops normally lead to drastic currency depreciations, as well as to sharp decreases in domestic output and national income. Both movements are rebalancing mechanisms, as mentioned before, and contribute to reduce the demand for imports and to bring the current account balance back to its equilibrium. Between 1991 and 2015 a total of 46 balance-of-payments crises have been identified in 34 emerging countries (Eichengreen and Gupta, 2016).

Two indicators are widely used to measure a country's degree of foreign indebtedness: the ratio of the current account deficit to GDP, and the net stock of foreign liabilities (NFL) to GDP. Empirical evidence suggests that the probability of a currency crisis increases considerably once the country's NFL exceeds 50 percent of GDP or becomes about 20 percentage points above its historic average. Further, the speed at which these indicators are increasing is also a warning indicator (Catão and Milesi-Ferretti, 2014).

To avoid currency crises, governments might also take measures that seek to bring the current account balance back to equilibrium. Such measures are often focused on reducing imports, by imposing import restrictions (tariffs, quotas, and so on). Policies aiming to increase exports, such as subsidies or other types of incentives, are also an alternative. Promoting exchange rate depreciations is also an option that impacts both exports and imports. Yet, these actions take some time to affect the trade balance, and often generate disturbances that impact negatively on GDP growth.

A balance-of-payments equilibrium, therefore, constitutes a constraint on output growth in the long run. Although trade deficits can be temporarily financed by capital inflows, if the structural problems that lead to these recurrent deficits are not resolved in due time, economic growth must be reduced in order to reduce import growth and bring the trade balance back to equilibrium. As structural changes take considerable time, the balance of payments represents an effective constraint on growth for most economies, especially underdeveloped ones (Thirlwall, 1979; Moreno-Brid, 2003).

GILBERTO LIBANIO AND JOÃO P. ROMERO

See also

Balance-of-payments constrained growth; Balance of trade; Exchange rates; Foreign-exchange reserves; Trade and development

References

Catão, L.A.V. and G.M. Milesi-Ferretti (2014), 'External liabilities and crises', *Journal of International Economics*, **94** (7), 18–32.

Eichengreen, B. and P. Gupta (2016), 'Managing sudden stops', *Work Bank Policy Research Working Paper*, No. 7639.

International Monetary Fund (2009), *Balance of Payments and International Investment Position Manual*, sixth edition, Washington, DC: International Monetary Fund.

McCombie, J.S.L. and A.P. Thirlwall (1994), *Economic Growth and the Balance-of-Payments Constraint*, Basingstoke: Macmillan.

Moreno-Brid, J. (2003), 'Capital flows, interest payments and the balance-of-payments constrained growth model: a theoretical and empirical analysis', *Metroeconomica*, **54** (2–3), 346–65.

Thirlwall, A.P. (1979), 'The balance of payments constraint as an explanation of international growth rate differences', *Banca Nazionale del Lavoro Quarterly Review*, **128**, 45–53.

Balance of payments constrained growth

The balance of payments constrained growth model (BPCGM) in its 'modern' form was first developed by Thirlwall (1979). The central proposition of the model is that no country can grow faster in the long run than the rate consistent with balance-of-payments equilibrium on current account unless it can finance ever-growing deficits, which in general it cannot. There is a limit to the deficit-to-GDP ratio, and a limit to the external-debt-to-GDP ratio, above which financial markets get nervous. If the real exchange rate is not an efficient balance-of-payments adjustment mechanism because, for some reason, the real exchange rate is not flexible, or because the Marshall–Lerner condition is not satisfied,[1] economic growth will have to slow down to keep the growth of imports in line with the growth of exports.

The idea that a shortage of foreign-exchange reserves may constrain the economic growth of countries, and that plentiful foreign-exchange reserves will benefit such a growth, is not new. Mercantilism (Mun, 1664), dual gap analysis (see for instance Chenery and Bruno, 1962), Prebisch's (1950) centre–periphery model and Harrod's (1933) foreign trade multiplier all focus on exports and foreign-exchange reserves as conducive in various ways to faster economic growth (see Thirlwall, 1992).

The central result of Thirlwall's BPCGM is that if current account equilibrium is a long-run requirement, and the real exchange rate (or real terms of trade) does not adjust, a country's economic growth rate (g) will equal x/π, where x is the growth of real exports and π is the income elasticity of demand for imports. It can be shown that this result is the dynamic analogue of Harrod's static foreign trade multiplier result that $Y = X/m$ where Y is the level of GDP, X is the level of exports and m is the marginal propensity to import, which is derived from the same assumptions as the dynamic result (Thirlwall, 1982). McCombie (1985) has also shown that this dynamic Harrod's trade multiplier result can be thought of as the workings of Hicks's supermultiplier, where export growth allows all other components of demand to grow faster than otherwise would be the case, because export growth can pay for the import content of consumption, investment and exports themselves.

Parametric tests of the model include testing whether it is relative price changes or economic growth that adjusts to balance-of-payments disequilibrium (Alonso and Garcimartin, 1998–99), and whether the estimated income elasticity of demand for imports from an import demand function (π^*) does not differ significantly from the π that makes the balance-of-payments equilibrium growth rate equal to the actual rate (this is the McCombie test, see McCombie, 1989).

There is now a mass of empirical evidence supporting the view that economic growth in many countries, particularly developing countries, is constrained by the balance of payments (McCombie and Thirlwall, 2004; Thirlwall, 2011; Soukiazis and Cerqueira, 2012), and that economic growth adjusts to balance-of-payments disequilibrium, not to the real exchange rate. Of course, not all countries in the world can be balance-of-payments constrained, but it only requires a few countries not to be constrained (by running huge balance-of-payments surpluses) for all the rest to be so.

A balance-of-payments deficit can have serious negative real effects on an economy, contrary to the prevailing orthodoxy that deficits are merely a form of consumption smoothing (Obstfeld and Rogoff, 1995), or they are even a sign of success because deficits on current account are merely the mirror image of a surplus on the capital account. Two points can be made in reply. First, countries are not indifferent to their exchange rate, and if it starts to depreciate, interest rates are likely to rise to attract foreign capital and this will impact negatively on domestic investment. Second, it is necessary to distinguish autonomous capital inflows from accommodating flows. Foreign direct investment flows may be a sign of success, but accommodating debt-creating flows at high interest rates are certainly not.

ANTHONY THIRLWALL

See also

Exchange rates – fixed versus flexible; External debt; Foreign-exchange reserves; Harrod's foreign trade multiplier; Supermultiplier

Note

1. The Marshall–Lerner condition states that for a fall in the exchange rate to improve the balance of payments, the sum of the (negative) price elasticities of demand for exports and imports must sum to greater than unity in absolute value.

References

Alonso, J.A. and C. Garcimartin (1998–99), 'A new approach to balance of payments constraint: some empirical evidence', *Journal of Post Keynesian Economics*, **21** (3), 259–82.

Chenery, H. and M. Bruno (1962), 'Development alternatives in an open economy: the case of Israel', *Economic Journal*, **72** (285), 79–103.

Harrod, R. (1933), *International Economics*, London: Macmillan.

McCombie, J.S.L. (1985), 'Economic growth, the Harrod trade multiplier and the Hicks super-multiplier', *Applied Economics*, **17** (1), 55–72.

McCombie, J.S.L. (1989), 'Thirlwall's law and balance of payments constrained growth – a comment on the debate', *Applied Economics*, **21** (5), 611–29.

McCombie, J.S.L. and A.P. Thirlwall (2004), *Essays on Balance of Payments Constrained Growth: Theory and Evidence*, London and New York: Routledge.

Mun, T. ([1664] 1923), *England's Treasure by Foreign Trade*, Oxford: Basil Blackwell, reprinted edition.

Obstfeld, M. and K. Rogoff (1995), 'The international approach to the current account', in G.M. Grossman and K. Rogoff (eds), *Handbook of International Economics*, New York: North Holland, Vol. 3, pp. 1737–99.

Prebisch, R. (1950), *The Economic Development of Latin America and its Principal Problems*, New York: ECLA, UN Department of Economic Affairs.

Soukiazis, E. and P. Cerqueira (eds) (2012), Models of Balance of Payments Constrained Growth: History, Theory and Empirical Evidence, London and New York: Palgrave Macmillan.

Thirlwall, A.P. (1979), 'The balance of payments constraint as an explanation of international growth rate differences', *Banca Nazionale del Lavoro Quarterly Review*, **36** (128), 45–53.

Thirlwall, A.P. (1982), 'The Harrod trade multiplier and the importance of economic growth', *Pakistan Journal of Applied Economics*, **1** (1), 1–21.

Thirlwall, A.P. (1992), 'The balance of payments as the wealth of nations', in J. Ball (ed.), *The Economics of Wealth Creation*, Aldershot, UK, and Brookfield, USA: Edward Elgar, pp. 134–70.

Thirlwall, A.P. (2011), 'Balance of payments constrained growth models: history and overview', *PSL Quarterly Review*, **64** (259), 307–51.

Balance of trade

The balance of trade is the difference between exports and imports of goods and services of a given country over a period of time. These transactions are recorded in the goods and services account of the balance of payments, which registers transactions of items 'that are outcomes of production activities' (International Monetary Fund, 2009, p. 149) and represents the largest component of the current account. As a matter of fact, trade in goods is usually responsible for the highest share of the balance of trade, despite the increasing importance of trade in services in the global economy.

When the monetary value of a country's imports exceeds that of its exports, the country has a trade deficit. A country has a trade surplus when the value of its exports exceeds that of its imports.

The trade balance indicates the size and direction of international borrowing. When a country has a trade deficit, it is buying more from abroad than it is selling to the rest of the world. Yet, a country can only import more than it exports if it can finance the difference. A country with a trade deficit, therefore, must increase its net foreign debts by the exact amount of that deficit. Analogously, a country with a trade surplus is receiving more from what it exports than what it is paying for its imports. Hence, this country is financing the trade deficits of its trading partners by lending to them. These results can also be interpreted as intertemporal trade. In this interpretation, a country with a trade deficit is importing present consumption goods and exporting future consumption goods, while a country with a trade surplus is exporting present consumption goods and importing future consumption goods.

If a country faces a series of trade deficits, which are not compensated by a surplus in the incomes account, then its foreign debt will keep increasing. This situation is not sustainable and will eventually lead to a halt in international finance (McCombie and Tharnpanich, 2021). When this happens, we say the country is facing a currency crisis or a sudden stop.

In an open economy, therefore, since trade deficits cannot be financed indefinitely, keeping the balance of trade in equilibrium is crucial for current account equilibrium, to avoid currency crises and to sustain economic growth. Since the demand for imports increases along with domestic output, in the long run, starting from a trade equilibrium, exports must increase at the same rate as imports to prevent trade imbalances. The United States, however, is not subject to this constraint in the same manner as other countries are. Since the US dollar functions as the international currency, it can finance its trade deficit indefinitely, as long as the trading partners continue to accept payments in US dollars issued by the country. Yet, this 'exorbitant privilege' has its limits as well (Eichengreen, 2008).

The pace of growth of exports and imports is determined by the competitiveness of the domestic production in relation to its foreign contenders. In particular, the demand for exports and for imports is determined by both price and non-price competitiveness.

ANTHONY THIRLWALL / JOÃO P. ROMERO AND GILBERTO LIBANIO

Price competitiveness has limited impact in the long run. On the one hand, if the sum of the price elasticities of demand for exports and imports is not smaller than −1, then the Marshall–Lerner condition is not fulfilled and changes in relative prices do not affect the balance of trade or exert only negligible impacts on it (Bahmani et al., 2013). On the other hand, if relative purchasing power parity is valid, then relative prices tend to remain stable in the long run, not affecting the balance of trade (Taylor and Taylor, 2004). This means that short-term improvements in terms of trade, such as the 2000s commodities boom, tend to reverse after some time, providing only a temporary impact on the balance of trade (Caldentey and Vernengo, 2010).

Non-price competitiveness is associated with factors such as product quality, marketing, and distribution networks. In the traditional export and import demand functions, these factors are captured in the income elasticities of demand. Hence, if the domestic and foreign incomes are growing at the same rate, then income elasticities are the main determinants of the growth rates of exports and imports, as well as of the balance of trade (Thirlwall, 1979).

Finally, it is also crucial to note that price and income elasticities change markedly between sectors. Consequently, the sectoral composition of exports and imports is a central underlying determinant of the balance of trade (Araújo and Lima, 2007). More specifically, while high-tech goods present high income-elasticity of demand, low-tech and primary goods present low income-elasticity of demand and high price-elasticity (Gouvea and Lima, 2010; Romero and McCombie, 2016).

Considering the problems associated with recurrent trade imbalances, governments often take measures that seek to keep the balance of trade in equilibrium. Such measures may consist in imposing import restrictions such as tariffs or quotas, in order to reduce imports, or may focus on increasing exports, by adopting policies such as subsidies or other types of incentives. Exchange-rate depreciations are also an option that impacts both exports and imports in the short run.

Nonetheless, in order to structurally resolve the tendency of recurrent deficits in the balance of trade, it is critical to implement public policies that aim to shift production and exports towards high-tech industries and to improve product quality, to increase the income elasticity of the demand for exports (Romero, 2019). These measures may involve industrial, technological and exchange-rate policies (Missio et al., 2015).

João P. Romero and Gilberto Libanio

See also

Balance of payments; Balance of payments constrained growth; Exchange rates; Foreign-exchange reserves; Trade and development

References

Araújo, R.A. and G.T. Lima (2007), 'A structural economic dynamic approach to balance-of-payments-constrained growth', *Cambridge Journal of Economics*, **31** (5), 755–74.

Bahmani, M., H. Harvey and S.W. Hegerty (2013), 'Empirical tests of the Marshall–Lerner condition: a literature review', *Journal of Economic Studies*, **40** (3), 411–43.

Caldentey, E.P. and M. Vernengo (2010), 'Back to the future: Latin America's current development strategy', *Journal of Post Keynesian Economics*, **32** (4), 623–44.

Eichengreen, B. (2008), *Globalizing Capital: A History of the International Monetary System*, Princeton, NJ: Princeton University Press.

Gouvea, R.R. and G.T. Lima (2010), 'Structural change, balance-of-payments constraint, and economic growth: evidence from the multisectoral Thirlwall's law', *Journal of Post Keynesian Economics*, **33** (1), 169–204.

International Monetary Fund (2009), *Balance of Payments and International Investment Position Manual*, sixth edition, Washington, DC: International Monetary Fund.

McCombie, J.S.L. and N. Tharnpanich (2021), 'Balance-of-payments constrained growth', in L.-P. Rochon and S. Rossi (eds), *An Introduction to Macroeconomics: A Heterodox Approach to Economic Analysis, Second Edition*, Cheltenham, UK, and Northampton, MA, USA: Edward Elgar, pp. 469–93.

Missio, F., F. Jayme Jr., G. Britto and J.L. Oreiro (2015) 'Real exchange rate and economic growth: new empirical evidence', *Metroeconomica*, **66** (4), 686–714.

Romero, J.P. (2019), 'A Kaldor–Schumpeter model of cumulative growth', *Cambridge Journal of Economics*, **43** (6), 1597–621.

Romero, J.P. and J.S.L. McCombie (2016), 'The multi-sectoral Thirlwall's law: evidence from 14 developed European countries using product-level data', *International Review of Applied Economics*, **30** (3), 301–25.

Taylor, A. and M. Taylor (2004), 'The purchasing power parity debate', *Journal of Economic Perspectives*, **18** (4), 135–58.

Thirlwall, A.P. (1979), 'The balance of payments constraint as an explanation of international growth rate differences', *Banca Nazionale del Lavoro Quarterly Review*, **32** (128), 45–53.

Balanced budget

Fiscal rules are regarded as a means of making fiscal policy more transparent and less arbitrary. Their value, however, depends on the extent to which they are credibly followed by political actors and their effectiveness in reaching their intended goals.

Although several fiscal policy rules have been discussed in the literature – including debt rules, and expenditure and revenue rules – the balanced budget rule has recently become the main focus of both academic discussion and policy action (see for instance Alesina and Perotti, 1995; Alesina and Giavazzi, 2014). While academic debate has focused on the effectiveness of the balanced budget rule in binding the hands of political actors, policy action has forged ahead by imposing balanced budget rules in ever more countries (see Lledó et al., 2017). In 1985, the United States passed its first federal Balanced Budget Act in order to cope with a rapidly increasing fiscal deficit at the federal level. In 1997, meanwhile, the European Union (EU) implemented the Stability and Growth Pact, which introduced a balanced budget rule for EU member States intending to join the European Monetary Union, and in 2012 even obliged Eurozone members to constitutionally safeguard this balanced budget rule via the 'Fiscal Compact' (officially termed the Treaty on Stability, Coordination and Governance in the Economic and Monetary Union). Many other developed, emerging and developing countries followed suit.

The feasibility of any balanced budget rule clearly depends on its intended aims. From a mainstream perspective, the 'debt bias' of governments subject to the pressure of political rationality (maximizing votes) rather than economic rationality (maximizing welfare) serves to focus attention on the sustainability of public finances. A rigorously enforced, balanced budget rule may prove effective at constraining structural deficit spending. Nevertheless, if the objective of a balanced budget rule is not simply to constrain public deficits but also to secure fiscal sustainability at minimum cost, mainstream economics can no longer provide a coherent rationale for such a rule. Hyperstable, hyper-rational New Classical macroeconomics may repudiate deficit spending as a tool of stabilization policy due to its adherence to 'Ricardian equivalence', yet aspects of intergenerational burden-sharing and the complementarity of public and private investment as a basis for economic development would refute the idea of zero public debt as an 'optimal' debt rule toward which any economy following a balanced budget rule will necessarily converge in the long run, should positive nominal GDP growth rates be assumed to be the ordinary outcome of economic development. In contrast to balanced budgets, structural deficits are therefore viable even in the face of sustainability requirements, as long as a constant, 'targeted' public debt ratio is maintained over the business cycle.

From a post-Keynesian perspective, on the other hand, deficit spending is a crucial means of reducing the gap between aggregate demand and potential output. A balanced budget rule that addresses structural deficits rather than total, unadjusted deficits may be feasible in times of small business cycle fluctuations, which can be regulated by 'automatic stabilizers' (for instance short-term deficits accruing from revenue losses and spending increases in cyclical downturns). In times of greater recession and, more importantly, long-lasting output gaps, unemployment, and zero-interest rates, fiscal policy needs to be able to assume the function of the 'spender of last resort'. Balanced budgets, especially when they are recklessly enforced under the auspices of austerity programmes, are not only bound to dampen economic recovery and prolong a recessive development (see for instance Botta and Tori, 2018); they are also certain to curtail public investment spending in the long run, since investment expenditure is easier to cut than public consumption spending, which has a more direct effect on voters.

If the 'spender of last resort' function cannot consistently be fulfilled by a balanced budget rule (as a symbol of 'sound finance'), and if game theory nonetheless suggests that a fiscal rule is required to overcome free-rider behaviour (particularly among governments of small, open economies), such a rule must contribute to maintaining full employment and ensuring price stability and fiscal sustainability. Abba Lerner's concept of functional finance (as opposed to the mainstream notion of sound finance), which focuses public deficit spending on maintaining aggregate demand (see Lerner, 1943), along with Keynes's concept of capital budgeting, which aims to close the gap between actual private investment and potential full-employment saving (see Keynes, 1943, 1945), and the classical 'golden rule' (public investment financed by public deficits) would all be good candidates for a fiscal rule capable of challenging the balanced budget rule.

ARNE HEISE

See also

Aggregate demand; Fiscal consolidation; Fiscal deficit; Fiscal policy; Functional finance

References

Alesina, A. and F. Giavazzi (2014) (eds), *Fiscal Policy after the Financial Crisis*, Chicago, IL: University of Chicago Press.
Alesina, A. and R. Perotti (1995), 'The political economy of budget deficits', *International Monetary Fund Staff Papers*, **42** (1), 1–31.
Botta, A. and D. Tori (2018), 'The theoretical and empirical fragilities of the expansionary austerity theory', *Journal of Post Keynesian Economics*, **41** (3), 364–98.
Keynes, J.M. (1943), 'The long-term problem of full employment', in D.E. Moggridge (ed.), *The Collected Writings of John Maynard Keynes*, Vol. XXVII, London: Macmillan, pp. 320–25.
Keynes, J.M. (1945), 'National debt inquiry: the concept of a capital budget', in D.E. Moggridge (ed.), *The Collected Writings of John Maynard Keynes*, Vol. XXVII, London: Macmillan, pp. 405–13.
Lerner, A. (1943), 'Functional finance and federal debt', *Social Research*, **10** (1), 38–53.
Lledó, V., S. Yoon, X. Fang, S. Mbaye and Y. Kim (2017), 'Fiscal rules at a glance', March, available online at https://www.imf.org/external/datamapper/fiscalrules/Fiscal%20Rules%20at%20a%20Glance%20-%20Background%20Paper.pdf; last accessed 4 April 2019.

Bank lending and creditworthiness

Uncertainty is an unavoidable characteristic for all economic agents, including banks. The latter deal with what Rochon (2006) calls 'micro-uncertainty' – that is, the uncertainty they face when lending to a specific client (it is important to note that with the advance of big data, the decision of lending has increasingly focused on the client itself and not on classes of clients). Uncertainty is the impossibility of knowing the whole set of information about clients, meaning that there is always some information that is either unknown or does not exist when banks decide whether to lend. As a matter of fact, when clients demand credit, banks do not know if they are presenting all relevant information about their income, their wealth, the risk of their project and so forth. Thus, banks need to assess the creditworthiness of their clients to decide granting or denying credit to a borrower.

Several factors are considered in the evaluation of credit risk, such as the moral, liquidity, solvency, and the disappointment-of-expectations risks. This assessment is not independent of what Rochon (2006) calls 'macro-uncertainty', defined as how banks consider and predict key macroeconomic variables, such as aggregate demand. In this sense, banks must deal with both micro-uncertainty (the uncertainty in lending to a specific borrower) and macro-uncertainty (the uncertainty in lending to all borrowers).

Cleary, uncertainty complicates the evaluation of creditworthiness; so how do banks deal with that? Wolfson (1996) explains that banks set both price and non-price measures to manage their limited assessment of how much a client is creditworthy. Price measures refer to the interest rate banks charge on a client (according to what Rochon (2006) calls 'the robustness of creditworthiness'; in other words, more creditworthy borrowers will generally have a lower premium). Non-price requirements are qualitative and quantitative aspects that banks gather about a borrower, such as collaterals, the size of credit lines, loan covenants, client's history with the bank, and some ratios as debt/equity, debt/income and debt/cash flow (Moore, 1988). It is important to mention that nowadays banks also exchange information between themselves to better evaluate clients' creditworthiness, and central banks help them as well. In Brazil, for instance, the central bank monitors each national identification number that borrows above a certain amount. This is a monetary policy macroprudential measure that helps banks to classify creditworthy clients.

Banks combine both price and non-price measures to assess each borrower, in their attempt to minimize credit risk. Older or prime clients tend to be given more flexible credit

Bank lending and expectations

In neoclassical economics, banks are mere financial intermediaries where households deposit savings and investors borrow these to fund their investment plans. Hence, banks are passive firms that exist to facilitate the encounter of savers and borrowers. Moreover, banks cannot lend without prior savings, and so investment cannot occur without savings. Consequently, not only do savings precede investment, but they also are a precondition to the existence of the latter.

In post-Keynesian economics, by contrast, banks are not mere intermediaries but issue money and provide credit lines. They market a broad range of financial services, although the key service they offer is credit. Like any other firm, banks actively set up competitive strategies to gain market shares.

For post-Keynesian economists, banks do not need to collect savings to lend. They actually operate in an overdraft system like those of advanced economies and provide loans through a simple balance-sheet operation: they inscribe a loan on the assets side and an equivalent deposit on the liabilities side. Hence, credit is granted in this operation, which in turn creates money endogenously. Banks collect savings from depositors not as a requirement to lend, but to enlarge their businesses.

In post-Keynesian theory, money creation is the usual bank response to credit demand. As Keynes (1930/2013, p. 197) wrote in *A Treatise on Money*, 'Credit is the pavement along which production travels; and the bankers, if they knew their duty, would provide the transport facilities to just the extent it is required in order that the productive powers of the community can be employed at full capacity.'

All economic agents, including banks, face uncertainty – an unavoidable feature of the economy. If future outcomes cannot be known for certain, agents can only have expectations about them. In this sense, when deciding whether to extend credit to borrowers or not, banks facing uncertainty cannot be sure of how right their expectations of both the customers' creditworthiness in particular and economic activity in general are. Rochon (2006) calls the former 'micro-uncertainty' and the latter 'macro-uncertainty'. Nevertheless, customers also back their economic decisions, such as conditions, while high-risk borrowers as well as new clients have tight (or tighter) credit conditions. These conditions change in accordance with the business cycle. At the end of a boom or during a bust, even clients ranked at intermediary and good tiers of creditworthiness can become credit restricted as banks' liquidity preference soars; in this case, bank lending only reaches the safest, that is, the greatest creditworthy borrowers.

Finally, in post-Keynesian economics banks are not credit constrained as in New Keynesian economics, where banks are constrained consistent with the money multiplier model. In the latter, credit constraints emerge from banks unwilling to lend owing to a credit demand higher than the available supply of credit. For post-Keynesians, however, there is no such thing as a lack of resources to supply credit, because banks endogenously grant loans to attend the credit demand of any non-bank agents. Thus, banks are not subject to insufficient resources to lend, since they create these resources. However, banks can be at different stages of uncertainty (or, as Wolfson (1996) recalls from Keynes (1936), at different states of confidence), which are accompanied by diverse assessments of creditworthiness and, consequently, by a looser or tighter lending behaviour. In other words, as Rochon (2006) argues, banks may choose not to lend.

FÁBIO TERRA

See also

Credit constraints; Credit divisor; Credit money; Endogenous money; Uncertainty

References

Keynes, J.M. (1936), *The General Theory of Employment, Interest and Money*, London: Macmillan.

Moore, B.J. (1988), *Horizontalists and Verticalists: The Macroeconomics of Credit Money*, Cambridge, UK: Cambridge University Press.

Rochon, L.-P. (2006), 'Endogenous money, central banks and the banking system: Basil Moore and the supply of credit', in M. Setterfield (ed.), *Complexity, Endogenous Money and Macroeconomic Theory: Essays in Honour of Basil J. Moore*, Cheltenham, UK, and Northampton, MA, USA: Edward Elgar, pp. 220–43.

Wolfson, M. (1996), 'A Post Keynesian theory of credit rationing', *Journal of Post Keynesian Economics*, **18** (3), 443–70.

borrowing, on their expectations. Therefore, the relationship between expectations and bank lending influences the supply of, and demand for, credit.

Regarding the supply of credit, banks form two main expectations. The first assesses clients' creditworthiness; the other outlooks on the whole economy. Wolfson (1996) listed several sources of uncertainty that banks face when evaluating customers' creditworthiness, such as those related to assessing how trustful is the information that clients deliver, how good their collaterals and business plans are and how stable is their income. If customers do not pass banks' requirements to lend, they become credit restricted.

Expectations of banks about the economic future also affect the supply of credit. If their 'macro-uncertainty' hurls distrust on their business outlooks, they will not lend, ensuring a reduction in the rhythm of economic activity. Even borrowers that were previously creditworthy can become credit restricted when banks hold mistrustful expectations.

'Macro-uncertainty' also regards expectations of non-bank agents, and it has the power to impact credit demand, bank lending and economic activity. If households and entrepreneurs have pessimistic perspectives of the future, they do not borrow, even when banks do not restrict credit. When both banks and non-bank agents have positive expectations, credit demand increases and pushes economic activity. In this sense, as Cottin-Euziol and Rochon (2022) argue, banks' expectations relative to those of borrowers must be considered.

Expectations and bank lending have a strong relationship. At the 'micro-uncertainty' level, banks assess the creditworthiness of clients in a microeconomic stance, whereas within 'macro-uncertainty' banks consider the future of the whole economy. Nevertheless, both levels affect bank lending and, consequently, economic activity. 'Macro-uncertainty' also affects the expectations borne by banks' customers, either households or entrepreneurs, impacting credit demand and, consequently, bank lending. Finally, expectations vary over time and contribute to set both the boom and bust phases of business cycles. As Minsky (1986) argued, the relationship between expectations and bank lending is not neutral to economic activity.

FÁBIO TERRA

See also

Animal spirits; Endogenous money; Money and banking; Neoclassical economics; Uncertainty

References

Cottin-Euziol, E. and L.-P. Rochon (2022), 'The monetary circuit', in M. Vernengo, E. Perez-Caldentey and B.J. Rosser Jr (eds), *The New Palgrave Dictionary of Economics*, London: Palgrave, forthcoming.

Keynes, J.M. (1930/2013), *A Treatise on Money. Volume II: The Applied Theory of Money*, in *The Collected Writings of John Maynard Keynes, Volume VI*, Cambridge, UK: Cambridge University Press.

Minsky, H.P. (1986), *Stabilizing and Unstable Economy*, New Haven: Yale University Press.

Rochon, L.-P. (2006), 'Endogenous money, central banks and the banking system: Basil Moore and the supply of credit', in M. Setterfield (ed.), *Complexity, Endogenous Money and Macroeconomic Theory: Essays in Honour of Basil J. Moore*, Cheltenham, UK, and Northampton, MA, USA: Edward Elgar, pp. 220–43.

Wolfson, M. (1996), 'A Post Keynesian theory of credit rationing', *Journal of Post Keynesian Economics*, **18** (3), 443–70.

Banking and finance

The financial system, in which banks and non-bank financial institutions operate, provides liquidity to the economy (households, non-financial sector and financial sector). While both categories of institutions operate in the same system, the main difference between banks and non-bank financial institutions is that the former grant credit on demand *ex nihilo* (from scratch), while the latter perform the function of financial intermediation, circulating the rentier capital among all capitalists.

This raises questions about the role of savings and the rate of interest. Economic theories have different explanations about both the role of savings in the financial circuit and the definition and determinants of the rate of interest.

Neoclassical theory assumes three fundamental arguments: (1) savings determine investment and income; (2) the rate of interest is a real variable, which is in turn determined by the equilibrium between investment and savings; and (3) the maximum level of production and employment is reached when savings and investment are equal. Combined, these arguments imply that savings are associated with finance; therefore, finance is derived from financial intermediation, overlooking money creation by banks' credit.

The heterodox approach, however, offers different arguments altogether, which is well summarized by the notion of non-neutral and endogenous money: banks provide credit out of thin air that finances production (including investment), which in turn creates income. More importantly, savings are the result of investment; prices are not flexible, and the rate of interest is a monetary variable set by the central bank, which influences a panoply of other rates, including the long-term interest rate. In this framework, banks create money, regardless of any real asset, with a causality that goes from assets to liabilities. In other words, bank credits create debts (deposits). The limit to the provision of bank credit depends only on the borrowers' ability to pay back their debt, which is subject to different explanations.

Keynes (1936, 1937) and Minsky (1986) situate banks at the beginning of the monetary circuit: they issue money as a result of a demand for credit. Although the interest rate is inversely related to the money supply (Keynes, 1936), both authors also argue that banks can modify their volumes of credit regardless of the amount of their assets. Hence, bank credit also depends on banks' liquidity preference (Keynes, 1937).

According to this view, the cancellation of bank credits depends on the liquidity preference of individuals, that is, the recirculation of non-spent (hoarded or financial) savings across financial markets (Keynes's liquidity preference theory) or firms' financial structure, (Minsky's hypothesis of financial instability). In these frameworks, financial markets are responsible for not providing savings to close the economic circuit or issuing excess credit in relation to firms' income in the first period of production. Keynes (1937) named this process as 'funding', where it is assumed that long-term securities collect unspent income (savings) and enable entrepreneurs to pay off their debts to banks. Thereby, long-term securities are tied to investment returns (dividends) and capital market liquidity creates financial cycles (Minsky, 1986).

A central argument for both Keynes (1936, 1937) and Minsky (1986) is that the funding process is highly unstable, owing to speculative activities that take place in the financial market, summed up in the liquidity preference theory, where professional investors operate along with agents that determine the future interest rate through the present perception of future rates of interest (dominated by psychological factors).

Minsky (1986) replaces liquidity preference theory with the financial instability hypothesis. He argues that investment finance comes from bank advances that, at the beginning of the cycle, offer a large amount of liquidity, at low interest rates. This increased liquidity raises firms' leverage rate, which increases faster than income (owing to the asymmetry between debt and income) that, in turn, reduces bank credit volumes and raises their interest rate, creating a business cycle. Minsky's analysis is different from Keynes's in so far as financial institutions instead of financial investors induce speculation by increasing debts faster than income, through financial innovation that unfolds business cycles. This view does not acknowledge that credits granted for production purposes generate profits that cancel debts (see Lavoie and Seccareccia, 2001).

The monetary circuit school offers an alternative vision: banks provide credit on demand and its volume is determined by the solvency of their borrowers. Liquidity is channelled to production, which expands income (influx phase) and its counterpart is the cancellation of debts (reflux phase) (see Parguez and Seccareccia, 2000). In this framework, money is structurally endogenous and non-neutral (Rochon, 1999), which means that loans create deposits (liquidity) and expand income, which annuls debts once workers and capitalists spend their wages and profits. There is a dissensus about whether banks finance only the circulating capital of production (wages and production inputs) (Seccareccia, 2003) or also the purchase of finished investment goods (Rochon, 1999).

For 'circuitists', the relevant rate of interest is determined by the central bank. The banks' lending rate, whose movement is not affected by the volume of credits (Rochon, 2006), is higher than the central bank's rate of interest, owing to the fact that banks add a margin to it. This means that the rate of interest is an 'administered price' determined by the central bank, which guarantees commercial banks' liquidity (lender of first resort) and affects the redistribution of income.

NOEMI LEVY-ORLIK AND JORGE BUSTAMANTE-TORRES

See also

Endogenous money; Financial instability hypothesis; Liquidity preference; Monetary circuit; Money creation – nature of

References

Keynes, J.M. (1936), *The General Theory of Employment, Interest and Money*, London: Macmillan.
Keynes, J.M. (1937), 'Alternative theories of the rate of interest'. Reprinted in *The Collected Writings of John Maynard Keynes, Vol. XIV*, London: Macmillan, 1973, pp. 201–14.
Lavoie, M. and M. Seccareccia (2001), 'Minsky's financial fragility hypothesis: a missing macroeconomic link?', in R. Bellofiore and P. Ferri (eds), *Financial Fragility and Investment in the Capitalist Economy: The Economic Legacy of Hyman Minsky, Volume II*, Cheltenham, UK, and Northampton, MA, USA: Edward Elgar, pp. 76–96.
Minsky, H.P. (1986), *Stabilizing an Unstable Economy*, New Haven and London: Yale University Press.
Parguez, A. and M. Seccareccia (2000), 'The credit theory of money: the monetary circuit approach', in J. Smithin (ed.), *What is Money?*, London and New York: Routledge, pp. 101–23.
Rochon, L.-P. (1999), *Credit, Money and Production: An Alternative Post-Keynesian Approach*, Cheltenham, UK, and Northampton, MA, USA: Edward Elgar.
Rochon, L.-P. (2006), 'Endogenous money, central banks, and the banking system: Basil Moore and the supply of credits', in M. Setterfield (ed.), *Complexity, Endogenous Money and Macroeconomic Theory: Essays in Honour of Basil J. Moore*, Cheltenham, UK, and Northampton, MA, USA: Edward Elgar, pp. 170–86.

Banking regulation

The mainstream approach to banking regulation imposes restrictions on the behaviour of individual banks designed to ensure their safety, and, through this effect on individual institutions, the safety of the entire banking system. The need for such measures arises from the traditional function banks play in accepting deposits at relatively short maturities and making loans at longer maturities. This maturity mismatch makes banks susceptible to confidence problems when loan defaults increase. In the absence of central bank support, increased loan defaults can create depositor concern about a bank's ability to repay their funds, and this can trigger a bank run with the potential for depositors at other banks to question the safety of deposits at their own institutions. Bank runs can thus be contagious, with the possibility that problems at a single institution can spread to the entire banking system (Bhattacharya et al., 1998, pp. 751–5).

Governments thus tend to provide a range of measures aimed at protecting the viability of banks when they experience sudden increases in deposit redemptions. Most common among these measures are lender-of-last-resort facilities and deposit insurance schemes. The first ensures that banks have access to liquidity at times of increased deposit redemptions without the need for asset fire sales. The second is designed to strengthen depositor confidence that their funds will be returned even if the bank collapses. The problem with these safety measures, however, is that they create moral hazard for bank managers. A manager is, for example, more likely to make a risky loan that is hoped will generate high profits if the bank is protected in the case where the borrower defaults. Containing this moral hazard is the traditional function of prudential bank regulation in mainstream theory. Regulation places limits on the risk-taking behaviour of bank managers, so that governments can provide safety nets without increasing the probability that borrowers will default and banks will fail (Mishkin, 2001, p. 8).

Post-Keynesian economists have not traditionally devoted a great deal of attention to prudential regulation but much of the above analysis is consistent with post-Keynesian theory. Post-Keynesians place considerable emphasis on the importance of banks in rendering the money supply endogenous and making corporate investment independent from saving (Moore, 1988). This enables aggregate demand to play a decisive role in determining output and employment. Post-Keynesians have also carefully analysed the role of banks in generating financial crises, and how these crises can feed back negatively on the banking system to disrupt its ongoing operations, reducing investment, income and employment (Minsky, 1982). In addition, Dow (1996) stresses the key role of liquidity as a means of dealing with economic uncertainty and highlights the liquidity-generating function of banks. Together, these post-Keynesian perspectives highlight the important role banks play in the economy, justifying both the provision of the government

NOEMI LEVY-ORLIK AND JORGE BUSTAMANTE-TORRES / PETER DOCHERTY safety net and the need for regulation to reduce moral hazard.

Bhattacharya et al. (1998, pp. 756–60) and Mishkin (2001, pp. 8–15) identify various historical approaches to bank regulation. The two most common approaches have been liquidity requirements, which mandate the holding of a minimum proportion of deposit funds in the form of liquid assets, and risk-based capital regulation that requires loans to be financed with a minimum proportion of capital (as opposed to deposits) and for this proportion to rise as the riskiness of loans increases. The objective of liquidity requirements is to ensure that banks have funds on hand to repay deposits if they are redeemed. The objective of capital regulation is to ensure that bank shareholder funds are sufficient to absorb losses from loan defaults so that deposits are not jeopardized. Post-Keynesians have endorsed both types of these requirements (Dow, 1996; Palley, 2004; Docherty, 2008; Crotty and Epstein, 2009). The trend in Western economies from the 1980s until the financial crisis of 2007–2008 was away from liquidity regulation and towards risk-based capital regulation. But since the crisis, that trend has been reversed with a renewed emphasis on liquidity regulation.

Each of these regulatory approaches perceives the risk of increased loan defaults as exogenous to the banking system. An alternative approach, however, suggested by Minsky (1964, 1982), is that increased default risk can be generated endogenously, within the banking system itself (see Ramskogler, 2011; Tymoigne, 2014). This can happen when banks lend to finance expansions in investment spending and purchases in asset markets that subsequently experience price inflation. Increased debt-to-income ratios and reduced holdings of liquidity across the economy tend to characterize such boom conditions (Minsky 1964, pp. 325–6; 1982, pp. 62–8). Loan defaults can increase under these conditions if interest rates rise, if incomes fall, or if asset price expectations are suddenly revised downwards. In such cases, the negative effects on banks described earlier can be generated (Minsky, 1964, p. 331). Post-Keynesians have, therefore, been among those who advocate the variation of prudential bank regulations in a counter-cyclical manner to moderate the build-up of risk that can occur during booms (Palley, 2004; Docherty, 2008; Crotty and Epstein, 2009; and Dow, 2017; see also Borio, 2005). Higher capital requirements in periods of faster-than-usual asset price inflation, for example, force banks to fund a greater proportion of lending with expensive capital. This either reduces the supply of credit as banks scale back that supply to match available bank capital, or it increases the cost of loans to borrowers as banks pass on the increased cost of funding loans with more capital. The latter reduces the difference between the expected return borrowers receive on asset holdings, and the cost of borrowing. As this difference falls, so does the profitability of holding assets, and this, in turn, reduces both the demand for assets and the demand for bank credit. Such an active approach to prudential bank regulation has come to be called macroprudential regulation in contrast to the microprudential approach of mainstream banking theory outlined above (Galati and Moessner, 2013). A question mark over this macroprudential approach, however, is whether alternative, non-bank financing channels will be substituted for bank funding when policy is tightened during the boom, so that the policy ultimately fails to prevent asset price increases. Docherty (2020) argues that even if this substitution occurs, ring-fencing banks from continued exposure to the markets in which asset prices are rising enhances banking system stability, and this is a key aim of macroprudential regulation.

In the end, the importance of banks in post-Keynesian theory for investment financing, liquidity provision and the generation of financial instability underscores the need for bank regulation, which incorporates both microprudential and macroprudential components.

PETER DOCHERTY

See also

Endogenous money; Financial crises; Financial instability hypothesis; Lender of last resort; Money creation – nature of

References

Bhattacharya, S., A.W.A. Boot and A.V. Thakor (1998), 'The economics of bank regulation', *Journal of Money, Credit and Banking*, **30** (4), 745–70.

Borio, C. (2005), 'Monetary and financial stability: so close and yet so far', *National Institute Economic Review*, **192**, 84–101.

Crotty, J. and G. Epstein (2009), 'Crisis and regulation: avoiding another meltdown', *Challenge*, January–February, 5–26.

PETER DOCHERTY

Docherty, P. (2008), 'Basel II and the political economy of banking regulation–monetary policy interaction', *International Journal of Political Economy*, **37** (2), 82–106.
Docherty, P. (2020), 'Prudential bank regulation: a post-Keynesian perspective', *European Journal of Economics and Economic Policies: Intervention*, **17** (3), 399–412.
Dow, S.C. (1996), 'Why the banking system should be regulated', *Economic Journal*, **106** (436), 698–707.
Dow, S.C. (2017), 'Central banking in the twenty-first century', *Cambridge Journal of Economics*, **41** (6), 1539–57.
Galati, G. and R. Moessner (2013), 'Macroprudential policy: a literature review', *Journal of Economic Surveys*, **27** (5), 846–78.
Minsky, H.P. (1964), 'Longer waves in financial markets: financial factors in the more severe depressions', *American Economic Review*, **54** (3), 324–35.
Minsky, H.P. (1982), *Can 'It' Happen Again?*, New York: M.E. Sharpe.
Mishkin, F.S. (2001), 'Prudential supervision: why is it important and what are the issues?', in F.S. Mishkin (ed.), *Prudential Supervision: What Works and What Doesn't*, Chicago: Chicago University Press, pp. 1–29.
Moore, B.J. (1988), *Horizontalists and Verticalists: The Macroeconomics of Credit Money*, Cambridge, UK: Cambridge University Press.
Palley, T.I. (2004), 'Asset-based reserve requirements: reasserting domestic monetary control in an era of financial innovation and instability', *Review of Political Economy*, **16** (1), 43–58.
Ramskogler, P. (2011), 'Credit money, collateral and the solvency of banks: a post Keynesian analysis of credit market failures', *Review of Political Economy*, **23** (1), 69–79.
Tymoigne, E. (2014), 'Measuring macroprudential risk through financial fragility: a Minskian approach', *Journal of Post Keynesian Economics*, **36** (4), 719–44.

Banking School

The Banking School originated as one of the two sides, together with the so-called Currency School, involved in a two-decade debate that took place in England after the 1825 crisis until the end of 1840s on the organization of the English monetary and banking system, and on the rules to be followed by the Bank of England.

The debate was later interpreted beyond the contingency of the regulation of the English monetary system of the nineteenth century and was regarded as part of the broader and ongoing theoretical debate on monetary theory (Goodhart and Jensen, 2015). Within this framework, the Banking School is considered as a precursor of the endogenous money theory, particularly of post-Keynesian monetary theory (Lavoie, 2014), whereas the Currency School backed an exogenous view of money supply and is associated with what later became the monetarist tradition (Humphrey, 1988).

Nonetheless, at that time the debate focused mainly on regulation and practical aspects (Schumpeter, 1954/2006). While the Currency School developed its regulatory advices moving from specific axioms, the approach of the Banking School was non-theoretical and its opposition to its counterpart was based on a technical analysis of the functioning of the banking system (Goodhart and Jensen, 2015). This is why, according to Fetter (1965), the Banking School happened to lack theoretical rigor.

The main exponents of the former were Thomas Tooke, John Fullarton, and James William Gilbart; while Thomas Joplin, Samuel Jones Lloyd, and Robert Torrens were the main members of the Currency School. John Stuart Mill also took part in the debate on the side of the Banking School; however, his affiliation to this group is controversial, because later on Stuart Mill changed his view to more orthodox positions (see Arnon, 2011). This debate built on a previous controversy between Bullionists and anti-Bullionists, with the Banking School descending from the latter. While accepting the position of the Bullionists on the desirability of the convertibility regime, the members of the Banking School rebutted all the major theoretical elements of the Bullionists' analysis, which were conversely accepted and developed into policy advices by the Currency School.

The main points of disagreement were: (i) the definition of money, (ii) the nature of money supply, and (iii) the determination of the price level. Each of these points marked a neat contraposition with the tenets of the Currency School.

Tooke (1844, pp. 17–22) maintained that the idea, supported by the Currency School, that only coins and bank notes ought to be considered as money was based on a misconception, since other means of payments, such as deposits, cheques (with the latter allowing for the transfer of the former), and bills of exchange fulfilled the same functions.

The Banking School considered the supply of money to be demand-driven. Neither commercial banks nor the central bank held the power to increase the amount of credit instruments in circulation above the level desired by the public. This was valid also for bank notes, as illustrated by Fullarton's law of reflux: while banks held the power to issue notes, their circulation depended on the will of the public. (The law of reflux has been equated with the real-bills doctrine; on the difference between the two, see Skaggs, 1991.) The quantity of money in circulation was therefore seen as an endogenous variable determined by the level of demand.

This strictly relates to the third point, that is, the determination of the price level. The Banking School opposed the quantity theory of money embraced by the Currency School, which ascribes changes in the price level to changes in the amount of money in circulation. The causality was reversed in Tooke's perspective: it is the price level that determines the quantity of money (to wit, credit instruments used for transactions) in circulation. A rise (or fall) in the price level was rather due to a rise (or fall) in the level of demand, given the contingent level of supply in the market for produced goods and services. This reasoning did not apply to inconvertible papers issued by the government, as this represented an additional source of demand and hence had an impact on prices.

These views were at odds with the perfect-circulation principle advocated by members of the Currency School, on which they grounded their reform proposal, then implemented in the 1844 Bank Charter Act.

According to this view, the ideal system would be the one in which gold was the only means of transaction. Since this was unattainable and undesirable for practical reasons, the solution was to structure the monetary system in order to ensure that circulation would change along with the amount of gold in the economy. This, known as the currency principle, motivated the creation of two separate departments in the Bank of England, namely, the Issue Department and the Banking Department. The former had the monopoly on the issuance of notes, whose quantity had to be maintained in a stable proportion with the gold held by the Bank of England. The latter could deal in deposits and credits as a regular bank.

However, the Bank of England was unable to meet the rules established by the 1844 Act in both the 1847 and 1857–58 crises. This came as no surprise to Tooke, who had foreseen the impossibility of respecting these rules in case of major shocks (Arnon, 2011, p. 222). The Banking School reform proposals were limited to the quantity of reserves, which in its view should have been large enough to be able to face fluctuations in gold movements.

Albeit not succeeding in imposing their view during the debate, the Banking School's ideas have not been abandoned and made a comeback with the post-Keynesian school of thought. 'The Banking School thus supported endogenous money, reversed causality and the need to focus attention on credit instead of money aggregates, just as modern post-Keynesians do' (Lavoie, 2014, p. 184).

EUGENIO CAVERZASI

See also

Currency School; Endogenous money; Financial regulations; Money creation – nature of; Reserves – role of

References

Arnon, A. (2011), Monetary Theory and Policy from Hume and Smith to Wicksell: Money, Credit and the Economy, Cambridge, UK: Cambridge University Press.

Fetter, F.W. (1965), *Development of British Monetary Orthodoxy, 1797–1875*, Cambridge, MA: Harvard University Press.

Goodhart, C. and M. Jensen (2015), 'Currency School versus Banking School: an ongoing confrontation', *Economic Thought*, **4** (2), 20–31.

Humphrey, T. (1988), 'Rival notions of money', *Federal Reserve Bank of Richmond Economic Review*, **74** (5), 3–9.

Lavoie, M. (2014), *Post-Keynesian Economics: New Foundations*, Cheltenham, UK, and Northampton, MA, USA: Edward Elgar.

Schumpeter, J.A. (1954/2006), *History of Economic Analysis*, London and New York: Routledge.

Skaggs, N.T. (1991), 'John Fullarton's law of reflux and central bank policy', *History of Political Economy*, **23** (3), 457–80.

Tooke, T. (1844), An Inquiry into the Currency Principle: The Connection of the Currency with Prices and the Expediency of a Separation of Issue from Banking, London: Longman, Brown, Green and Longmans.

Banks

Banks have a central importance in post-Keynesian macroeconomics. Through their

EUGENIO CAVERZASI / MARCELO MILAN

lending activities, they are the endogenous suppliers of money in capitalist economies, thus shaping macroeconomic trends. Keynes was well aware of their importance, having stated that '[c]redit is the pavement along which production travels and the bankers if they knew their duty, would provide the transport facilities to just the extent it is required in order that the productive powers of the community can be employed at full employment' (Keynes, 1931, p. 197). As such, 'in general, banks hold the key position in the transition from a lower to a higher scale of activity' (Keynes, 1937, p. 668).

In light of this, banks have the power or rather 'hold the key' to start a finance–investment–saving–funding process consistent with what proponents of the monetary circuit approach argue. In doing so they allow – or not – the taking of positions in capital assets.

Most definitions of banks are functional, in the sense that they are characterized by their role in the economy. For instance, Minsky (1986, p. 249) argues that '[f]inancing other than through retained earnings involves contracts denominated in money and banks are organizations that arrange for and engage in the financing of business'. Others highlight their dual nature: 'banks are firms that carry out banking [provision of liquidity and the creation of credit] functions' (Dymski, 1988, p. 500). Commercial banks, despite their growing integration with investment banking and other services that point to a universal type of institution, have received more emphasis (see Minsky, 1986; Wray, 2013).

Post-Keynesians propose a theory of a monetary production economy, which is in sharp contrast to a barter or money-less one (Dillard, 1988). Banking for post-Keynesians should be discussed within a sequence of events that involve first the relationship between banks and bank borrowers; and second between banks and the central bank. In both cases, the money supply is endogenous, as discussed by Lavoie as early as 1984. Borrowers demand credit, which banks supply endogenously, provided borrowers are creditworthy, and, similarly, central banks supply endogenously the settlement balances demanded by banks, if needed. In both cases, therefore, the endogenous nature of money and central bank money is emphasized, which stands in direct contradiction to the monetarist argument of an exogenous supply of money imposed by central banks. Indeed, as Moore (1978, p. 125) puts it: 'Money does not enter the system like manna from heaven – or from the sky via Milton Friedman's helicopter.' For monetarists like Friedman, banks are passive in the transmission mechanism of monetary policy, in which the supply of money, as a multiple of bank reserves obtained from the central bank, is fixed in a discretionary manner. (For a criticism of the monetarist approach, see Kaldor (1978).) There are some differences between post-Keynesian scholars in this regard, and they hinge on whether or not central banks accommodate the demand for reserves at a fixed interest rate, or if they adjust their loans to banks to the perceived risks of excessive credit-funded expenditures by changing the policy rate of interest.

There are several features that make banks special in post-Keynesian economics. There is an interdependence between supply of short-term liquidity on the liabilities side of banks' balance sheets and longer-term credit granting on their assets side. Given the intrinsic mismatch between asset and liability maturities, banks are leveraged and need to refinance frequently. This means that they are financially fragile institutions by design (Dymski, 1988). Since they occupy a key position in the economy, they are intrinsically destabilizing.

One source of refinancing short-term banks' liabilities that minimizes this consequence is a lender of last resort (a central bank). The banks' financial fragility can also be addressed by means of deposit insurance, avoiding problems of runs to discount the liability issued at par with central bank money. Banks earn a profit mainly by the difference between interest paid on liabilities and interest received on assets (spread or mark-up), plus service fees and an asset portfolio for trading and earning interest or capital gains on securities.

Banks are not constrained by central bank reserves in their decisions to make loans to potential customers, if they are likely to be returned along with acceptable marked-up interest payments. Banks' refusal implies that some of the agents demanding credit do not receive it, not owing to asymmetric information as in the orthodox view of credit rationing, but because of uncertainty (Rochon, 2006). Just like other agents, banks also face fundamental uncertainty and have a liquidity preference to cope with both illiquidity and insolvency risks (Monvoisin and Pastoret, 2003).

Keynes (1931) had already shown how banks face the challenge of balancing profitability (extending loans) and safety (keeping excess liquid assets over short-term liabilities). On the other hand, financial innovations in other parts of the financial system have been causing disintermediation, with banks losing business to other institutions. Thus, corporations could issue commercial papers instead of borrowing working capital from banks. This means that in the near future banks, as we have come to know them, may disappear, diluted in a more complex type of institution. But money and liquidity will remain central to understand capitalist economies.

MARCELO MILAN

See also

Chicago School; Endogenous money; Monetary circuit; Monetary policy transmission mechanism; Money creation – nature of

References

Dillard, D. (1988), 'The barter illusion in Classical and Neoclassical models', *Eastern Economic Journal*, **14** (4), 299–318.
Dymski, G.A. (1988), 'A Keynesian theory of bank behavior', *Journal of Post Keynesian Economics*, **10** (4), 499–526.
Kaldor, N. (1978), *Further Essays in Applied Economics*, London: Duckworth.
Keynes, J.M. (1931), *A Treatise on Money. Volume II: The Applied Theory of Money*, London: Macmillan.
Keynes, J.M. (1937), 'The "ex-ante" theory of the rate of interest', *Economic Journal*, **47** (188), 663–9.
Lavoie, M. (1984), 'The endogenous flow of credit and the Post-Keynesian theory of money', *Journal of Economic Issues*, **18** (3), 771–97.
Minsky, H.P. (1986), *Stabilizing an Unstable Economy*, New York: McGraw Hill.
Monvoisin, V. and C. Pastoret (2003), 'Endogenous money, banks and the revival of liquidity preference', in L.-P. Rochon and S. Rossi (eds), *Modern Theories of Money: The Nature and Role of Money in Capitalist Economies*, Cheltenham, UK, and Northampton, MA, USA: Edward Elgar, pp. 18–40.
Moore, B.J. (1978), 'Monetary factors', in A.S. Eichner (ed.), *A Guide to Post-Keynesian Economics*, White Plains, NY: M.E. Sharpe, pp. 120–38.
Rochon, L.-P. (2006), 'Endogenous money, central banks and the banking system: Basil Moore and the supply of credit', in M. Setterfield (ed.), *Complexity, Endogenous Money and Macroeconomic Theory: Essays in Honour of Basil Moore*, Cheltenham, UK, and Northampton, MA, USA: Edward Elgar, pp. 170–86.
Wray, L.R. (2013), 'What do banks do? What should banks do? A Minskian perspective', *Accounting, Economics and Law: A Convivium*, **3** (3), 277–311.

Basel Agreements

All Basel Agreements were basically inspired by and discussed in the framework of the so-called 'bank capital channel' of the monetary transmission mechanism, which suggests that monetary authorities, through the bank's capital required ratio(s), control the amount of loans – and the composition of a bank's trading book – which constitute the risky assets held by a bank. This mechanism is therefore in accordance with (or part of) the mainstream monetary policy, which argues bank liabilities (deposits) create bank assets (loans) (see Rochon, 1999 for a critical discussion).

The liberalization of the banking industry, especially in advanced economies, contributed to a lending boom–bust cycle that had to be restricted for reasons of economic and financial stability (Goodhart et al., 2004). Commercial banks' 'loop' economic performance as well as their low equity capital (relative to other sectors of the economy) were an issue that worried the Basel Committee on Banking Supervision (BCBS) given banks' insolvency risks. In light of this, the BCBS issued in the late 1980s some directives for the G-10 banks. Initially, the Basel I Agreement (see Basel Committee on Banking Supervision, 1988) established the basic architecture for setting minimum-risk-based capital requirements for banking organizations in order to stabilize the international financial system. At the time, Basel I recognized only credit risk exposure as the important element of the risk equation for banks.

The capital adequacy agreement of Basel I (1988) imposes internationally approved weights for different types of risk, including off-balance-sheet risks, and required banks, subscribing to the agreement, should maintain a ratio of 8 per cent of equity capital (consisting of Tier 1 and Tier 2 equity elements) to Risk-Weighted Assets (RWA) as a cushion to the credit and market risk exposures. More analytically, Risk Weights (RW) that vary from

0 to 100 per cent are applied to both banking and trading book categories of assets to derive RWA. Thus, in order to derive RWA, the exposure of each credit and trading categories with the corresponding RW were multiplied and in this way the required equity capital was calculated for every bank. At a later stage, due to trading book expansion, the BCBS recognized also the importance of the market risk exposure for banks.

This capital ratio was meant to limit the loans banks were making. For instance, if banks' actual ratios were below 8 per cent, banks had either to increase their capital base or, because of the cost implied in issuing new equity, to reduce lending and liquidate tradable securities, in order to restore the predetermined 8 per cent ratio level.

Through the Basel II Agreement (see Basel Committee on Banking Supervision, 2006), the BCBS was compelled to issue some further clarifying 'directives' on three main issues. More analytically, it introduced:

- New formulas (the standardized and the Internal Rate Based methods) for a more accurate estimation of the actual banking book (credit risk) exposure, considering not only the collateral but also the haircuts attached to it.
- Some increased number of banking book categories with an analogous increase in the financial collateral, for a more accurate calculation of the credit risk exposure.
- A re-estimation of the bank's equity capital, taking into account the bank's exposure to the operational risk as well.

Later on, the Basel III Agreement (see Basel Committee on Banking Supervision, 2011, 2017) new 'directives' extended the Basel I and II mandates. As Ennis and Price (2011) underlined, Basel III retains the RW scheme of Basel II. Although it initially retained the 8 per cent minimum equity capital, it progressively required a gradual increase, which led to an equity requirement of 8.5 per cent and 10.55 per cent, for Tier 1 capital and total capital respectively, no later than 2019. Additionally, the BCBS introduced two more 'directives' related to banks' liquidity risk measures (Basel Committee on Banking Supervision, 2010): the Liquidity Coverage Ratio, which establishes a minimum level of high-quality liquid assets to withstand an acute stress scenario lasting one month, and the Net Stable Funding Ratio, which ensures that the longer-term assets or activities are funded by more stable medium- or longer-term liability and equity financing.

From the point of view of heterodox and post-Keynesian economics, reservations exist concerning the ability of monetary authorities to constrain, through the monetary transmission mechanism, the commercial banks' ability for new lending expansion. These reservations are expressed in light of the theory of endogenous money, concerning the credit creation process, which is not limited to the loans versus deposits causality relationship but is further extended to the loans versus capital relationship.

YANNIS PANAGOPOULOS

See also

Capital requirements; Credit money; Endogenous money; Financial crises; Financial instability hypothesis

References

Basel Committee on Banking Supervision (1988), 'International convergence of capital measurement and capital standards', Basel: Bank for International Settlements, April.
Basel Committee on Banking Supervision (2006), 'International convergence of capital measurement and capital standards: a revised framework (the comprehensive version)', Basel: Bank for International Settlements, June.
Basel Committee on Banking Supervision (2010), 'Basel III: international framework for liquidity risk measurement, standards and monitoring'. Basel: Bank for International Settlements.
Basel Committee on Banking Supervision (2011), 'Basel III: a global regulatory framework for more resilient banks and banking systems', Basel: Bank for International Settlements, June.
Basel Committee on Banking Supervision (2017), 'Basel III: finalizing post-crisis reforms', Basel: Bank for International Settlements, December.
Ennis, H. and D. Price (2011), 'Basel III and the continuing evolution of bank capital regulation', *Economic Brief*, 6, 1–6.
Goodhart, C.A.E., B. Hofmann and M. Segoviano (2004), 'Bank regulation and macroeconomic fluctuations', *Oxford Review of Economic Policy*, **20** (4), 591–615.
Rochon, L.-P. (1999), *Credit, Money, and Production: An Alternative Post-Keynesian Approach*, Cheltenham, UK, and Northampton, MA: Edward Elgar.

Behavioural economics

Behavioural economics is a research programme lying at the intersection of psychology and economics. Taking as a starting point the deficiencies of the rational-agent paradigm as a way to depict human beings in economic models, it aims to better delineate actual human behaviour by studying how humans perceive and process information, and the way they form beliefs and expectations. In doing so, it typically adopts a methodological individualist standpoint, focusing on the agent and its cognitive processes, often using the neoclassical rational agent (NCRA) as a benchmark to identify divergent behaviour.

The NCRA is characterized by an optimizing behaviour over all known alternatives, in an effort to maximize individual utility. Seeking to provide an alternative to this depiction of human agents, Simon (1955, 1956, 1972) made an early foray into the study of individual cognitive processes and devised the concept of bounded rationality. Because gathering information is itself costly and human beings have limited computing abilities, they will tend to aim for certain levels of satisfaction rather than an overall maximization of their utility, a behaviour Simon calls 'satisficing'. In so doing, they will use rules of thumb or heuristics to sift through available information and make a decision regarding the issue at hand. This implies a vision of rationality different from that of the NCRA, wherein humans adapt their objectives and the methods to reach them in accordance with their limitations.

Researchers in what gradually came to be known as behavioural economics identified several heuristics used by human beings in their decision-making processes (see Kahneman et al., 1982, and Kahneman and Tversky, 2000, for the results generated in that literature). Prominent examples include availability and representativeness. Information that is more easily brought to mind ('available') will have more weight in the decision-making process, which could influence subjective probability distributions. Similarly, since they can only process a limited amount of information, people will tend to focus on a subset of cases that are deemed representative of the general situation.

Finance is one of the main fields of study in which these heuristics have been marshalled, as they provided a way to explain how observed behaviour differed from what would have been expected if markets had been populated by NCRA (Shiller, 1998; Barberis and Thaler, 2002). Many economists, using the NCRA as the reference point for rationality, see those heuristics as generating biases that can lead to 'irrational' behaviour and possibly generate market fluctuations or crises. Such an analysis is typically conducted from a methodological individualist standpoint, with overall dynamics in models being the result of aggregated individual actions (Dow, 2011).

This differs from the usual approach in post-Keynesian economics, exemplified by Minsky's emphasis on social conventions and market sentiment. However, these heuristics can also be seen as a way for individuals to operate in a world of fundamental uncertainty (Perron-Dufour, 2012). For example, availability and representativeness could combine to decrease the subjective probability of a financial crisis as time passes after such an event. Memories of the crash will wane and become less salient over time, while firms that are able to grow will come to be seen as representative of the new state of affairs. Such an analysis could be associated with a Minskian framework to generate a theory of financial cycles and crises.

MATHIEU DUFOUR

See also

Financial instability hypothesis; Methodology; Microfoundations; Rationality; Uncertainty

References

Barberis, N. and R. Thaler (2002), 'A survey of behavioral finance', *National Bureau of Economic Research Working Paper*, No. 9222.
Dow, S. (2011), 'Cognition, market sentiment, and financial instability', *Cambridge Journal of Economics*, **35** (2), 233–45.
Kahneman, D. and A. Tversky (2000), *Choices, Values and Frames*, Cambridge, UK: Cambridge University Press.
Kahneman, D., P. Slovic and A. Tversky (eds) (1982), *Judgement under Uncertainty*, Cambridge, UK: Cambridge University Press.
Perron-Dufour, M. (2012), *A Minskian Approach to Financial Crises with a Behavioural Twist: A Reappraisal of the 2000–2001 Financial Crisis in Turkey*, Doctoral dissertation, University of Massachusetts, Amherst.
Shiller, R.J. (1998), 'Human behavior and the efficiency of the financial system', *National Bureau of Economic Research Working Paper*, No. 6375.

MATHIEU DUFOUR

Simon, H.A. (1955), 'A behavioral model of rational choice', *Quarterly Journal of Economics*, **69** (1), 99–118.

Simon, H.A. (1956), 'Rational choice and the structure of the environment', *Psychological Review*, **63** (2), 129–38.

Simon, H.A. (1972), 'Theories of bounded rationality', in C.B. McGuire and R. Radner (eds), *Decision and Organization: A Volume in Honor of Jacob Marschak*, Amsterdam: North-Holland Publishing Company, pp. 161–76.

Bretton Woods

Bretton Woods is the name of the town, in New Hampshire, where 44 nations gave life, in July 1944, to the first and only fully negotiated international monetary system. Drawing lessons from the impossibility of re-establishing a properly working gold standard in the inter-war period and the troublesome implications this failure had (the Great Recession, generalized mercantilism, protectionism, trade and exchange controls), negotiators forged a new international architecture aimed at reviving multilateral free trade for the post-war period. The outcome of the Bretton Woods conference resulted mainly from a confrontation between the two reform proposals elaborated by world-famous economist John Maynard Keynes for Britain and Harry Dexter White for the United States.

The climate of intellectual convergence that characterized the negotiations helped to reach consensus on a system of fixed but adjustable pegs linking national currencies to the US dollar, which was convertible to gold at the fixed exchange rate of 35 US dollars an ounce. A newly born institution, the International Monetary Fund (IMF) should act as guardian of monetary stability: it should provide liquidity to countries recording chronic or severe balance-of-payments deficits, allowing them to borrow in reserve currencies up to the total amount of a quota initially subscribed by countries themselves according to their economic importance (only 25 per cent of which in gold or strong currencies). In case of fundamental disequilibrium – but the notion was left undefined – countries could recur to devaluation. The multilateral payments system established at Bretton Woods required the removal of all forms of exchange controls, but permitted member countries to regulate capital-account transactions, to avoid the potentially harmful effects of hot money flows. The World Bank (*de facto* a fund, while the IMF is actually a bank) was also established in order to finance reconstruction and development projects, as well as to provide low-income countries with loans they could not obtain on a commercial basis.

In exchange for the benefits of hegemony, the United States acted as a world growth locomotive during the Bretton Woods regime, granting other powers (Japan and European countries in particular) the possibility of implementing export-led growth strategies. Europe's return to convertibility in 1958 (the Treaty of Rome establishing the European Economic Community was signed a year earlier) meant that the world should not fear dollar shortage any longer, and rather be concerned with a possible dollar glut. As early as 1960, Belgian economist Robert Triffin formulated his famous 'dilemma' (Triffin, 1960): when a national currency is used as an international reserve asset, its issuing country is compelled to run current account deficits to provide reserves to the rest of the world, but an excess dollar circulation ends up undermining confidence in this currency's value. The system indeed broke down in 1971. Decades of Keynesian fine-tuning policies, the Great Society programme in the United States and the Vietnam war led President Nixon of the US, in 1971, to suspend dollar convertibility, while inflationary pressures nurtured by oil crises in the 1970s impeded the reconstruction of a global fixed-exchange-rate regime.

Retrospectively, the Bretton Woods thirty 'glorious' years of unprecedented global economic growth appear correlated with the 'embedded liberalism' of the order: as Ruggie (1982) famously remarked in a Polanyian perspective, multilateral free trade was predicated upon State interventionism. The 'hyperglobalization' model of the Washington Consensus will sanction 'deviations' from the rules of the globalization game by means of the disciplinary power of conditionalities imposed by the IMF in exchange for financial assistance. During the Bretton Woods epoch, conversely, globalization was a means, not an end. It was the by-product of the (Keynesian) pursuit of full employment and growth in domestic economies by means of both monetary and fiscal policies, accompanied by gradual liberalization of trade (ensured by the 'loose' General Agreement on Tariffs and Trade).

MATHIEU DUFOUR / MARIO CEDRINI

The Bretton Woods agreement finally rejected many revolutionary aspects of Keynes's plan. Specifically, his ideas of using a truly supranational unit of account, the bancor (instead of a national reserve currency), for settling imbalances (by means of a 'technical' institution like the Clearing Union), and of ensuring creditors' involvement in international adjustment by sanctioning positive bancor balances continue to be most important references for global reform. Keynes played a decisive role in creating the system's condition for success, by endowing it with an expansionary bias, and making it defend, and promote, policy space and a variety of policies and capitalisms.

MARIO CEDRINI

See also

Exchange rates; International Clearing Union; International financial architecture; International monetary system; Keynes Plan

References

Cesarano, F. (2006), *Monetary Theory and Bretton Woods: The Construction of an International Monetary Order*, Cambridge: Cambridge University Press.
Helleiner, E. (2014), *Forgotten Foundations of Bretton Woods: International Development and the Making of the Postwar Order*, Ithaca: Cornell University Press.
Rodrik, D. (2011), *The Globalization Paradox: Democracy and the Future of the World Economy*, New York: Norton.
Ruggie, J.G. (1982), 'International regimes, transactions, and change: embedded liberalism in the postwar economic order', *International Organization*, **36** (2), 379–415.
Skidelsky, R. (2002), *John Maynard Keynes, Vol. III, Fighting for Britain, 1937–1946*, London: Macmillan.
Triffin, R. (1960), *Gold and the Dollar Crisis: The Future of Convertibility*, New Haven: Yale University Press.

Bubbles – credit

Post-Keynesian economists have produced a substantial body of literature that investigates the liaison dangereuse of financial stability between the process of credit creation and that of asset bubbles. This line of reasoning is concerned particularly with the tradition of Hyman Minsky (1972) (see Rochon, 1999a, 1999b; Toporowski, 2000; Papadimitriou and Wray, 2001; Rochon and Rossi, 2003; Sebastien, 2008; Keen, 2013) and it is in contrast with the so-called 'irrelevance view' adopted by the theorists of the efficient-market hypothesis.

More recent approaches (Stockhammer and Ramskogler, 2009; Ramskogler, 2011) have tried to enrich post-Keynesian macroeconomic models with the analysis of endogenous money as a potential source of instability. Indeed, lending enables demand to increase in the aggregate, thereby financing a growth in economic activity and rising prices on asset markets. These post-Keynesian approaches are very different from the conventional 'financial accelerator' models, because the latter relied on agency costs, owing to asymmetric information, and acted through the interest rate rather than through the volume of credit.

A credit bubble is a sustained and accelerating growth of bank loans (overlending) relative to GDP. This promotes a boom in both the economic activity and in asset prices. The role of credit in macroeconomic cycles can be summarized as follows: there is first an upswing in economic activity as the economy expands, and banks and financial markets provide an expanding volume of credit to finance the growth of both consumption and investment, particularly where regulation is lax and competition among banks and non-bank financial institutions is intense. If there is excess capacity, upward pressure on wholesale and retail prices is subdued. Hence, the central bank has no obvious reason to tighten and stem the growth of money and credit, leading to a further expansion of output and further increase in credit.

In turn, higher property and securities prices encourage overlending and investment activity. However, as lending expands, increasingly risky investments are underwritten. The demand for risky investments rises with the supply, since, in the prevailing environment of stable prices, nominal interest rates and therefore yields on safe assets are low. In search of yield, investors dabble increasingly in risky investments (Minsky, 1972). Their appetite for risk is stronger still to the extent that these trends coincide with the development of new technologies, in particular network technologies of promising but uncertain commercial potential, and because of the process of financial innovations by banks and non-bank financial institutions.

MARIO CEDRINI / LINO SAU

Eventually, all these investment activities, together with the wealth effect on consumption, produce signs of inflationary pressures, causing the central bank to tighten. Eventually, the financial bubble is pricked and, as asset prices decline, the economy is left with an overhang of ill-designed, non-viable investment projects, distressed banks, and heavily indebted households and firms, aggravating the subsequent downturn and opening the door to a debt–deflation spiral. The longer the asset-price inflation is allowed to run, the greater are the depletion of the stock of sound investment projects and the accumulated financial excesses. Further, the more severe becomes the subsequent downturn. The credit boom thus contains the seeds of the subsequent crisis. This implies that economic booms and rising asset prices in part rely upon accelerating debt, but since this positive and infinitive expansion is not feasible, a credit bubble will be defined by the transitions from positive to negative debt acceleration.

Post-Keynesian economists attribute financial crises to a prick in the bubble in stock and securities markets, fuelled by a combination of financial innovations and ample credit in an unregulated financial environment (Dejuán and Dejuán-Bitriá, 2018). Crises may be conceived as a 'credit boom gone wrong'. Nevertheless, post-Keynesian authors have also stressed that the consequences of credit expansion and the extent of the subsequent boom may depend on the structure and regulation of the financial sector.

Financial innovations magnified the impact of these accommodating credit conditions, and central banks did little to pre-empt their effects. The consequences included property booms, increasing consumer debt, surging investment and rising securities prices, particularly those of high-tech firms. They included growing worries about the stability of financial institutions and markets.

One possible post-Keynesian policy implication is that policy-makers should act pre-emptively to prevent the development of unsustainable credit booms that might have seriously negative macroeconomic and financial consequences when they turn to bust. Central banks should concern themselves not just with commodity-price inflation but also with asset-price inflation, especially in periods of technological dynamism when asset-market inflation has a particular tendency to overshoot. They should tighten their interest rate policy when they see credit expanding rapidly and asset-market conditions responding enthusiastically, and do so even if commodity-price inflation remains subdued.

LINO SAU

See also

Credit; Credit money; Endogenous money; Financial innovations; Financial instability hypothesis

References

Dejuán, Ó. and D. Dejuán-Bitriá (2018), 'A predator–prey model to explain cycles in credit-led economies', *Review of Keynesian Economics*, **6** (2), 159–79.
Keen, S. (2013). 'Predicting the "global financial crisis": post-Keynesian macroeconomics', *Economic Record*, **89** (295), 228–54.
Minsky, H.P. (1972), 'Financial instability revisited: the economics of disaster', in Board of Governors of the Federal Reserve System (ed.), *Reappraisal of the Federal Reserve Discount Mechanism*, Washington, DC: Board of Governors of the Federal Reserve System, vol. 3, pp. 95–136.
Papadimitriou, D. and L.R. Wray (2001), 'Minsky's analysis of financial capitalism', in R. Bellofiore and P. Ferri (eds), *The Economic Legacy of Hyman Minsky, Volume 1: Financial Keynesianism and Market Instability*, Cheltenham, UK, and Northampton, MA, USA: Edward Elgar, pp. 123–46.
Ramskogler, P. (2011). 'Credit money, collateral and the solvency of banks: a Post Keynesian analysis of credit market failures', *Review of Political Economy*, **23** (1), 69–79.
Rochon, L.-P. (1999a), *Credit, Money and Production: An Alternative Post-Keynesian Approach*, Cheltenham, UK, and Northampton, MA, USA: Edward Elgar.
Rochon, L.-P. (1999b), 'The creation and circulation of endogenous money', *Journal of Economic Issues*, **33** (1), 1–21.
Rochon, L.-P. and S. Rossi (eds) (2003), *Modern Theories of Money: The Nature and Role of Money in Capitalist Economies*, Cheltenham, UK, and Northampton, MA, USA: Edward Elgar.
Sebastien, C. (2008), 'A Post-Keynesian model of accumulation with a Minskyan financial structure', *Review of Political Economy*, **20** (3), 319–31.
Stockhammer, E. and P. Ramskogler (2009), 'Post Keynesian economics: how to move forward', *European Journal of Economics and Economic Policies: Intervention*, **6** (2), 227–46.
Toporowski, J. (2000), *The End of Finance: The Theory of Capital Market Inflation, Financial Derivatives and Pension Fund Capitalism*, London and New York: Routledge.

Bubbles – financial

As frequently occurs in economics, the still-dominant theoretical definition of financial bubbles uses factors that are themselves poorly defined. Financial bubbles are defined as 'transient upward accelerations of the observed price above a fundamental value. The paradox is that the determination of a bubble requires, in this definition, a precise determination of what is the fundamental value' (Filimonov and Sornette, 2013, p. 3699).

The definition of the 'fundamental value' of a financial asset was dominated by the Efficient Markets Hypothesis/Capital Assets Pricing Model (EMH/CAPM) assertions that (a) it is the sum of discounted future cash flows and (b) asset markets rationally anticipate this value, making deviations from it no more than random walks (see Sharpe, 1964; Fama, 1970). This definition, therefore, denies the possibility of financial bubbles, and much early research work considered conditions under which these bubbles could nonetheless occur while constrained by the assumption of rationality, as defined by neoclassical economics, which includes accurate expectations of the future (Fama and French, 2004, p. 26). Archetypal here was the work of Allen and Gorton (1993), who used an overlapping generations model to assert that bubbles could arise from agency relationships, even though 'the fundamental [value] … is [by assumption] known to all traders … [and it is assumed that] [a]ll agents know the structure of the model and the distributions of the random variables, but do not observe the particular realizations of random variables' (Allen and Gorton, 1993, pp. 816–17).

The 'rational bubble' literature subsided somewhat after the leading advocates of the EMH/CAPM admitted its empirical failure in 2004 (Fama and French, 2004), the broad stock market underwent undeniable booms and crashes in the periods 1995–2003 (when the S&P 500 index more than trebled in five years, then almost halved in three years) and 2003–09 (when it almost doubled in six years, then more than halved in one and a half years), and the Great Recession of 2007–10 coincided with the stock and housing market collapses. After these events, neoclassical literature turned to evaluating its earlier consensus 'that asset bubbles could be effectively ignored with little real adverse economic impact' (Evanoff et al., 2012, p. 3). Evanoff et al.'s (2012) volume provides a good overview of this process, with five pivotal pre-Great Recession papers, and responses to them by neoclassical authors after the crisis.

Kindleberger and Aliber's (2015, p. 21) more pragmatic definition takes financial cycles for granted, defines a bubble as 'a generic term for the increases in the prices of securities or currencies in the mania phase of the cycle that cannot be explained by the changes in the economic fundamentals', and notes that '[b]ubbles always implode; by definition a bubble involves a non-sustainable pattern of price changes or cash flows' (Kindleberger and Aliber, 2015, p. 1). Since Kindleberger and Aliber's (2015) analysis is based on Minsky's financial instability hypothesis, 'pro-cyclical increases in the supply of credit in good times and the decline in the supply of credit in less buoyant economic times' (Kindleberger and Aliber, 2015, p. 25) play a large role in their explanation of financial bubbles.

Jordà et al.'s (2016) empirical work confirms the significance of the expansion and collapse of credit for the formation and collapse of financial bubbles – 'the more credit grows in the expansion, the more dangerous the situation gets' – and the deleterious impact of bubbles on economic performance: 'About two-thirds of all postwar recessions, 41 out of 65, are associated with bubble episodes.' But they note the difficulty of distinguishing 'booms driven by speculation from those driven by fundamental economic forces' (Jordà et al., 2016, pp. 3–4).

Sornette's (2017) econophysics-inspired approach argues that 'stock market crashes are caused by the slow build-up of long-range correlations leading to a global cooperative behavior of the market and eventually ending in a collapse in a short, critical time interval', where 'critical' has the physics meaning of 'the explosion to infinity of a normally well-behaved quantity' (Sornette, 2017, p. 23). His market model is founded on simple heuristics, based on the existence of uncertainty about future returns, imitative behaviour by traders, and the existence of hierarchies of traders. This leads to both reinforcing feedbacks and waves in pricing financial assets, which manifest themselves in 'log-periodic' fluctuations overlaid on a power-law acceleration of prices in the rising phase of a bubble. The singularity aspect of the log-periodic fluctuations also enables the prediction of when a bubble will burst. He established the Financial Crisis Observatory to test

STEVE KEEN

the predictive success of his 'log-periodic power law singularity' model, and claims considerable success in out-of-sample predictions of the timing of stock market bubble bursts (Sornette, 2017, p. xvii).

Phillips et al. (2011) undertake a similar study using more conventional, though very sophisticated, recursive econometric techniques, built on the concept of 'financial exuberance' (Phillips et al., 2011, p. 202), to help identify periods of explosive price growth.

Though economics rarely reaches a consensus, the empirical facts of the first two decades of the twenty-first century seem to be leading the discipline towards a consensus that bubble formation and collapse is a normal, if potentially pathological, aspect of asset markets. Fundamental value, however, remains elusive.

STEVE KEEN

See also

Bubbles – credit; Financial crises; Financial fragility; Financial instability hypothesis; Neoclassical economics

References

Allen, F. and G. Gorton (1993), 'Churning bubbles', *Review of Economic Studies*, **60** (4), 813–36.
Evanoff, D.D., G.G. Kaufman and A.G. Malliaris (2012), *New Perspectives on Asset Price Bubbles*, New York: Oxford University Press.
Fama, E.F. (1970), 'Efficient capital markets: a review of theory and empirical work', *Journal of Finance*, **25** (2), 383–417.
Fama, E.F. and K.R. French (2004), 'The capital asset pricing model: theory and evidence', *Journal of Economic Perspectives*, **18** (3), 25–46.
Filimonov, V. and D. Sornette (2013), 'A stable and robust calibration scheme of the log-periodic power law model', *Physica A*, **392** (17), 3698–707.
Jordà, O., M. Schularick and A.M. Taylor (2016), 'Bubbles, credit, and their consequences', *Federal Reserve Bank of San Francisco Economic Letter*, 2016-27, available online at https://www.frbsf.org/economic-research/publications/economic-letter/2016/september/equity-and-housing-bubbles-and-consequences/ (last accessed 23 April 2021).
Kindleberger, C.P. and R.Z. Aliber (2015), *Manias, Panics, and Crashes: A History of Financial Crises*, New York: John Wiley & Sons.
Phillips, P.C.B., Y. Wu and J. Yu (2011), 'Explosive behavior in the 1990s NASDAQ: when did exuberance escalate asset values?', *International Economic Review*, **52** (1), 201–26.

Sharpe, W.F. (1964) 'Capital asset prices: a theory of market equilibrium under conditions of risk', *Journal of Finance*, **19** (3), 425–42.
Sornette, D. (2017), *Why Stock Markets Crash: Critical Events in Complex Financial Systems*, Princeton, NJ: Princeton University Press.

Business cycles

Business cycles (BCs) are widely accepted as the sequences of upward and downward movement in overall economic activity. According to Kalecki (1937), a BC is formed by the dynamic process consisting of a series of upward and downward cumulative processes. The justification of the 'cycle' concept is related to the idea of regularity. This is stressed, for example, in the reference to trade cycles by Keynes (1936, p. 314), who identifies a 'recognisable degree of regularity in the time-sequence and duration of the upward and downward movements.' Still, the precise expression 'business cycle' is sometimes regarded as misconceived, since there is actually no 'periodicity' involved. This fact is inherent in the early Burns and Mitchell (1947) working definition referring to a sequence of recurrent but not periodic changes. In that sense, BCs constitute *ex ante* not directly observable and hardly predictable economic fluctuations. Even though unsystematic, they are persistent and diffused across different economic sectors and countries, often exhibiting synchronization patterns. Depending on whether the focus is on the sequences of upward and downward fluctuations in the level of or in trend-adjusted economic aggregates, the concepts of the 'classical cycle' or the 'growth cycle' are employed.

The occupation with BCs basically concentrates on BC analysis and BC theorizing. BC analysis generally refers to the study of BC characteristics and stylized facts, by means of BC measurement and dating of successive reference dates. The latter mark the turning points, called peaks and troughs, which specify the course of the BC or the BC 'chronology,' consisting of BC phases – expansions and contractions for BCs and accelerations and slowdowns for growth cycles. BC dating and measurement are conducted on the basis of diverse techniques, from simple and ad hoc to more sophisticated formal statistical and econometric procedures. Evidently, growth cycle analysis additionally involves trend-cycle separation and trend adjustment. Overall, BC analysis is conducted at both the individual level by economists and at the level of research by planning agencies, including specialized institutes. Such are the National Bureau of Economic Research, the Centre for Economic Policy Research and the Economic Cycle Research Institute, which provide BC chronologies widely accepted and applied as benchmarks for comparisons and evaluations.

The advance of BC theories centers on the exploration of the causes for the occurrence of such economic fluctuations, accepting that these do not constitute temporary crises interrupting normality. The pursuit of related considerations results in a wide variety of existing theoretical and empirical research, evolving over time against the background of: different schools of thought about the functioning of the economic system and more advanced presumptions about perceptions and expectations by the agents; changing economic, sociological and political conditions; more sophisticated mathematical and econometric modeling techniques, alongside significant improvements in data production and acquisition. The often conflicting and contradicting reasoning behind the re-appearance of BCs starts with disagreement as to whether they constitute a problem of economic instability or just reflect a mechanism for the interaction of the economy with the underlying environment. In trying to explain their emergence and replicate their recorded features, the fundamental dichotomies expand over endogenous and exogenous forces, impulse and propagation mechanisms, demand and supply factors, real and nominal impacts, the degree of stability or instability of private demand, the maintenance and departure from equilibrium, but also the necessity and effectiveness or ineffectiveness of interventionary monetary and fiscal policy.

According to post-Keynesian theorizing, and along the lines of Keynesian thought and early trade cycle models, such as the one by Kaldor (1940), BCs arise endogenously. They constitute phenomena related to the normal functioning of the economy, reflecting the cyclicality and instability inherent in capitalist economic systems. Effective demand is most central to post-Keynesian BC theories, with investment fluctuations, in particular, lying at the heart of the shift between BC phases. Exogenous shocks and policy actions are supplementary, as capitalist economies do 'not rely upon exogenous shocks to generate business cycles,' which are compounded out of both internal dynamics and 'the system of interventions and regulations designed to keep the economy operating within reasonable bounds' (Minsky, 1992, p. 8).

Despite the presumed importance of BC research, its prosperity historically displays cyclicality itself, booming in periods of severe and protracted economic fluctuations and slumping in their absence. Overall, it remains a particularly demanding and difficult task, since BCs constitute the result of unique dynamic configurations of events, they are not always alike and may underlie changing features and stylized facts and, finally, they cannot be explained mono-causally, as they arise from the interaction of various impulses and a synthesis of elements. Still, BC analysis and theorizing offer helpful tools for various other levels of economic research, such as forecasting of business conditions and the investigation of the link and interaction between economic growth and fluctuations.

EKATERINI TSOUMA

See also

Aggregate demand; Effective demand; Fiscal policy; Monetary policy; Trade cycles

References

Burns, A.F. and W.C. Mitchell (1947), *Measuring Business Cycles*, New York: National Bureau of Economic Research.
Kaldor, N. (1940), 'A model of the trade cycle,' *Economic Journal*, **50** (197), 78–92.
Kalecki, M. (1937), 'A theory of the business cycle,' *Review of Economic Studies*, **4** (2), 77–97.
Keynes, J.M. (1936), *The General Theory of Employment, Interest and Money*, London: Macmillan.
Minsky, H.P. (1992), 'The financial instability hypothesis,' *Jerome Levy Economics Institute of Bard College Working Paper*, No. 74.

Business cycles and prey–predator models

Richard Goodwin (1913–96) wrote the seminal papers linking the causes of business cycles to prey–predator models as he developed his theory of cyclical growth. Goodwin was a pupil of Joseph Schumpeter at Harvard in the 1930s. Schumpeter argued that the trend and cycle were indissolubly mixed, inseparable, so that the statistical procedure of detrending time series to reveal the cycle had no justification in theory. From early on in his career Goodwin developed this fundamental insight (see Goodwin, 1948, 1949, 1950, 1953, 1955; Harcourt, 2015), culminating in his now classic paper, 'A growth cycle', a chapter in Charles Feinstein's *Festschrift* for Maurice Dobb (see Goodwin, 1967).

Goodwin's paper linked his core insight to Vito Volterra's prey–predator model (see Volterra, 1931). His model is an application of the analogy of the 'symbiosis of two populations – partly complementary, partly hostile', which results in over-shooting and under-shooting in each to produce wave-like growth processes over time. In the original model, predators consume the prey, reducing their numbers substantially. As a result, predators starve, reducing, in turn, their numbers. This reduction in the number of predators allows the prey to reproduce to large numbers, which subsequently leads to increased numbers of predators; and so the growth cycle is repeated. Goodwin (1982, p. 167) writes that this 'is helpful in understanding ... the dynamical contradictions of capitalism ... especially when stated in a Marxian form'. He analysed the fight over wages and profits and the resulting feedback on real variables, which brought about a growth cycle, that is to say, alternative periods of fast and slow, even negative, economic growth over time. So high wages are associated with low profits, which lead to low levels of investment and, therefore, lower output and economic growth and higher unemployment. This, in turn leads to lower wages and increasing profits, which induces more investment, raising the level of output and of economic growth while reducing unemployment – which induce higher wages, reproducing the growth cycle.

Joan Robinson pointed out to Goodwin that he was assuming Say's Law, to wit, that capital and labour were always fully employed in his 1967 model. So, in subsequent developments, involuntary unemployment at the points of effective demand could occur.

Goodwin's final version of the model is in his 1987 magnum opus, *The Dynamics of a Capitalist Economy*, co-authored with Lionella Punzo (see Goodwin and Punzo, 1987). In it he entwined the aggregate cyclical fluctuations papers with their impact on production interdependence associated with Wassily Leontief's input–output models and, though for different purposes and insights, Piero Sraffa's classic, *Production of Commodities by Means of Commodities* (see Sraffa, 1960).

The elements of Goodwin's theory include inventory cycles in which under-shooting and over-shooting of production in contrast to sales and attainment of desired levels of inventories are key features. When output levels reach new heights, induced investment in fixed capital comes into play. Alfred Marshall's distinction between fixed and variable costs is invoked with the implication that capital and outlays associated with its finance are 'fixed' for a very much longer period of time in the downward then in the upward direction – 'a simple application of Marshall's famous principle that the short period is very much shorter for expansions than for contractions' (Goodwin, 1982, p. 177).

His theory is summed up in a succinct paragraph: 'when ... the economy has finally accumulated enough capital, investment is reduced, sales fall, investment is further reduced and sales fall further .... Whereas investment will be reduced to the same level as in the last depression, sales will not because of the great additions during the boom to the body of "fixed outlays" ... a high level of sales will not be entirely lost .... In each swing the economy goes higher than ... previously, but it does not swing back lower ... because of the nature of the cost structure' (Goodwin, 1982, p. 117).

Then because the cycle could exist without the trend but not vice versa, Goodwin considers a Harrod-type process of economic growth to show that 'the trend will generate a cycle just as easily as the cycle will create the trend' (Goodwin, 1982, p. 118).

In Kalecki's last article in the *Economic Journal* in 1968, 'Trend and business cycles reconsidered', he independently comes to a similar understanding as Goodwin: 'In fact, the long-run trend is but a slowly changing component of a chain of short-period situations: *it has no independent entity*' (Kalecki, 1968, p. 165, emphasis added).

Paul Samuelson independently wrote at least two articles on similar themes (see Samuelson, 1967, 1971) but, most uncharacteristically, did not cite Goodwin's papers. In his 1967 paper, 'A universal cycle?', he writes that he '[takes his] clue from biology. A.J. Lotka and V. Volterra some forty years ago wrote down simple equations for "the struggle for existence". They postulate two species, an exploiting or hunting species ... and an exploited or hunted species .... Call them tigers and rabbits; bacteria and men; or capitalists and proletariat' (Samuelson, 1967, p. 473).

GEOFF HARCOURT AND PETER KRIESLER

See also

Business cycles; *Economic Dynamics*; Effective demand; *Essays in the Theory of Economic Growth*; Harrod's dynamics

References

Goodwin, R.M. (1948), 'Secular and cyclical aspects of the multiplier and accelerator', in L.A. Metzler (ed.), *Income, Employment and Public Policy: Essays in Honor of Alvin H. Hanson*, New York: Norton, pp. 108–32.
Goodwin, R.M. (1949), 'The multiplier as matrix', *Economic Journal*, 59 (236), 537–55. Reprinted in R.M. Goodwin (1983), *Essays in Linear Economic Structures*, London: Macmillan, pp. 1–21.
Goodwin, R.M. (1950), 'Does the matrix multiplier oscillate', *Economic Journal*, 60 (240), 764–70. Reprinted in R.M. Goodwin (1983), *Essays in Linear Economic Structures*, London: Macmillan, pp. 22–9.
Goodwin, R.M. (1953), 'The problem of trend and cycle', *Yorkshire Bulletin of Economic and Social Research*, 5 (2), 81–98. Reprinted in R.M. Goodwin (1982), *Essays in Economic Dynamics*, London: Macmillan, pp. 112–21.
Goodwin, R.M. (1955), 'A model of cyclical growth', in E. Lundberg (ed.), *The Business Cycle in the Post-War World*, London: Macmillan, pp. 203–21. Reprinted in R.M. Goodwin (1982), *Essays in Economic Dynamics*, London: Macmillan, pp. 122–40.
Goodwin, R.M. (1967), 'A growth cycle', in C.H. Feinstein (ed.), *Socialism, Capitalism and Steady Growth: Essays Presented to Maurice Dobb*, Cambridge: Cambridge University Press, pp. 54–8.
Goodwin, R.M. (1982), *Essays in Economic Dynamics*, London: Macmillan.
Goodwin, R.M. (1983), *Essays in Linear Economic Structures*, London: Macmillan.
Goodwin, R.M. and L.F. Punzo (1987), *The Dynamics of a Capitalist Economy: A Multi-Sectoral Approach*, Oxford: Polity Press in association with Basil Blackwell.
Harcourt, G.C. (2015), 'Fusing indissolubly the cycle and the trend: Richard Goodwin's profound insight', *Cambridge Journal of Economics*, 39 (6), 1569–78.

Kalecki, M. (1968), 'Trend and business cycles reconsidered', *Economic Journal*, 78 (310), 263–76.
Lotka, A.J. (1925), *Elements of Physical Biology*, Baltimore: Williams and Wilkins Company (second edition 1957, New York: Dover Publications).
Samuelson, P.A. (1967), 'A universal cycle?', *Operations Research – Verfahren*, 3, 307–20.
Samuelson, P.A. (1971), 'Predator–prey oscillations in ecological and economic equilibrium', *Proceedings of the National Academy of Sciences of the United States of America*, 68, 980–3.
Sraffa, P. (1960), *Production of Commodities by Means of Commodities*, Cambridge, UK: Cambridge University Press.
Volterra, V. (1931), *Leçons sur la théorie mathématique de la lutte pour la vie*, Paris: Editions Jacques Gabay.

Cambridge Circus

The 'Circus' was the informal group that met between late 1930 and the spring of 1931 to discuss Keynes's *Treatise on Money*, including not only Richard Kahn, James Meade, Piero Sraffa, and Joan and Austin Robinson, but also some of the most brilliant economics students of the next generation. According to Joan Robinson, it was first proposed by Sraffa and organized as an official venture (Robinson, 1978, p. xii).

The discussions within the Circus went in parallel with the drafting of the 'multiplier' article by Kahn (1931), which was written between the summer of 1930 – during a holiday in the Tyrol (Kahn, 1984, p. 91) – and the early months of 1931 and published in June of that year (Marcuzzo, 2011).

In the literature there is disagreement as to the influence of the 'Circus' (and Kahn's in particular) on Keynes's transition from the *Treatise* to the new ideas, which formed the core of *The General Theory* (Marcuzzo, 2002). Moggridge (1994, p. 111) remarks that 'Kahn's accounts of the "Circus" ... taken together with those of other participants, provide valuable grist for the mills of historians of economics'. An instance of such a skepticism can be found in Patinkin (1976) to whom Kahn (1984, p. 105) retorted: 'Don Patinkin disputes the importance commonly attributed to us [the Circus] in assisting Keynes to write the *General Theory*. In so far as he relies on documents, he is fully entitled to make his case. Others can judge. For my own part I feel myself unable to arouse any feeling of passion over events which took place so long ago.' Skidelsky (1992, p. 448) also had some doubts: 'Much more important than the Circus's collective contribution to Keynes's progress was Kahn's personal contribution.'

Some evidence of the discussions within the Circus (of which there is no written documents, but only later recollections) comes mainly from Joan Robinson. One of the topics being discussed was the relation between demand and output. In the *Treatise*, equilibrium is postulated when saving is equal to investment and profits are normal. An increase in investment causes an increase in prices and profits. The peculiarity of the argument in the *Treatise* is that, if part of the profit is spent, prices arise all the more. If profits are saved, prices and profit will continue to fall. The Circus pointed out (seemingly by Austin Robinson) that '[i]f businessmen increase consumption when profits rise, there will be an increase in the output of goods and services, with not necessarily any rise in prices at all' (Robinson, 1978, p. xiii).

Thus, one of the main contributions of the Circus, with the help of Kahn's multiplier, was to urge Keynes to consider the changes in output, rather than in prices and profits, following an increase in investment.

A second topic was the distinction between the *ex post* identity between saving and investment, and the *ex ante* condition according to which investment is the causal element in the relationship. Again, in Joan Robinson's recollections: '[a]t the Circus, we had got used to the idea that investment determines saving both in a static and in an incremental sense .... An *increase* in the rate of expenditure on investment, beginning at a particular moment, quickly brings about an equal increase in the flow of saving, through the mechanism of the multiplier' (Robinson, 1980, p. 391).

In conclusion, we may agree with the assessment of the role the Circus provided by one of its protagonists, Austin Robinson: 'there came to be a two-way traffic, with Keynes sometimes accepting our criticisms, sometime letting us know through Kahn his own developing ideas. Kahn as the messenger had some ideas how Keynes's thinking was developing. The rest of us never quite knew which of our ideas and suggestions had reached Keynes. We knew later, when *The General Theory* appeared, that many of the ideas were ideas with which we had been playing in the period November 1930 to March 1931' (Robinson, 1994, pp. 9–10).

MARIA CRISTINA MARCUZZO

See also

A Treatise on Money; Income multiplier; Savings; The Accumulation of Capital; The General Theory of Employment, Interest and Money

References

Kahn, R. (1931), 'The relation of home investment to unemployment', *Economic Journal*, **41** (162), 173–98.
Kahn, R. (1984), *The Making of Keynes's General Theory*, Cambridge, UK: Cambridge University Press.
Marcuzzo, M.C. (2002), 'The collaboration between J.M. Keynes and R.F. Kahn from the *Treatise* to the *General Theory*', *History of Political Economy*, **34** (2), 421–48.
Marcuzzo, M.C. (2011), 'The "elusive figure who hides in the preface of Cambridge books". An appraisal of Richard Kahn's contributions', in C. Gehrke, N. Salvadori, I. Steedman and R. Sturn (eds), *Classical Economics versus Modern Theories: Essays in Honour of Heinz D. Kurz*, Abingdon: Routledge, Vol. II, pp. 185–206.
Moggridge, D.E. (1994), 'Richard Kahn as an historian of economics', *Cambridge Journal of Economics*, **18** (1), 107–16.
Patinkin, D. (1976), 'From the *Treatise* to the *General Theory:* the development of the theory of effective demand', *History of Political Economy*, **8** (1), 64–82.
Robinson, A. (1994), 'Richard Kahn in the 1930s', *Cambridge Journal of Economics*, **18** (1), 7–10.
Robinson, J. (1978), 'Reminiscences', in *Contributions to Modern Economics*, Oxford: Blackwell, pp. ix–xxii.
Robinson, J. (1980), 'Review of The Collected Writings of John Maynard Keynes. Volume XXIX: The General Theory and After – A Supplement. Edited by Donald Moggridge', *Economic Journal*, **90** (358), 391–3.
Skidelsky, R. (1992), *John Maynard Keynes: Volume II: The Economist as Savior, 1920–1937*, London: Macmillan.

Cambridge equation

The Cambridge equation is a relation of logical consistency between the rate of profits

(P/K), the natural rate of growth (g_n) and the propensity to save out of total profits (s_p), which states that:

$$\frac{P}{K} = \frac{1}{s_p} g_n \qquad (1)$$

if a dynamic equilibrium with full employment is to be maintained through time.

When Domar's (1946) dynamic equilibrium solution – that is, exponential growth of investment at a steady rate such that total effective demand would grow hand in hand with productive capacity – was coupled with Harrod's (1948) natural growth rate $g_n = n + \lambda$, to wit, the maximum expansion rate supported by technical conditions (the growth of labour force n and of labour productivity λ), growth theory came to an impasse. For a given aggregate savings-to-income ratio (s) and technique in use (synthesized by capital-output ratio κ), the equilibrium relation

$$\frac{s}{\kappa} = g_n \qquad (2)$$

could only be satisfied by a fluke, as all three magnitudes were considered constant. The Cambridge equation (1) was proposed to give a Keynesian answer to the Harrod–Domar dilemma: it specifies the long-run functional distribution of income between wages and profits, which produces precisely the saving ratio (s) required by equilibrium growth in equation (2).

Equation (1) is a fundamental relation of Keynesian income distribution theory (Kaldor, 1955) that links profits to savings through the ownership of the capital stock. Its logic runs as follows (Pasinetti, 1962): in any production system, wages are distributed amongst members of society in proportion to the amount of labour they contribute, whereas profits are distributed in proportion to the amount of capital they own. Thus, if ownership of capital derives from accumulated savings, in the long run, profits (P) will turn out to be distributed in proportion to contributed savings (S), for each social category.

But as long as there is a social category that derives all its income, and therefore savings, exclusively from profits, then the saving behaviour of just this group will determine the actual value of the ratio of profits to savings for the whole system. And the rate of profits (P/K) implied by this ratio of profits to savings (P/S) will be the one given by equation (1). At such a basic level of investigation, the Cambridge equation is independent of the institutional set-up of the advanced industrial society under study.

To see this, consider first a capitalist system. Capitalists may control the stock of fixed assets but not the entire financing of its creation, as workers – by saving (S_w) – own part of the capital stock through loans to the capitalists, receiving part of the profits (P_w). But as long as capitalists, differently from workers, save exclusively out of profits $S_c = s_c P_c$, then (see Pasinetti, 1974, pp. 127–8):

$$\frac{P}{S} = \frac{P_c + P_w}{S_c + S_w} = \frac{P_w}{S_w} = \frac{P_c}{S_c} = \frac{P_c}{s_c P_c} = \frac{1}{s_c} \qquad (3)$$

so that, in a dynamic equilibrium ($S = I$) with full employment, equation (3) collapses to equation (1) with $s_p = s_c$, namely, the propensity to save out of total profits coincides with (though is not identical to) the capitalists' propensity to save (s_c). Crucially, workers' propensity to save, though influencing the distribution of income between capitalists and workers (P_c/Y), does not influence the long-run rate of profits (P/K) nor the functional income distribution between profits and wages (P/Y).

On the other hand, in a socialist system, where only the State accumulates, that is, $s_p = 1$, the Cambridge equation (1) establishes an equality between the natural rate of growth and a natural rate of profits:

$$\frac{P}{K} = g_n \qquad (4)$$

implying that aggregate investments coincide with aggregate profits, and aggregate consumption coincides with aggregate wages, although individual wages and interest payments on individual savings are partly consumed and partly saved. In such a system, the technique in use yields the highest per-capita consumption, so that the natural rate of profits is efficient (Pasinetti, 1974).

The logic behind equation (1) renders apparent the pre-institutional character of functional income categories (wages and profits): they underlie, but do not directly correspond to, visible social categories (such as workers and capitalists) specific to an institutional set-up, exemplifying the separation between pre-institutional and institutional layers of analysis (Pasinetti, 2007).

To sum up, through the Cambridge equation, the Keynesian theory of income distribution establishes a continuity with the concept of residual income featuring in the Classical economists, but it reverses its causal direction by inverting the contrasting roles of wages and profits: if a dynamic equilibrium with full employment is to be maintained, investment requirements induced by the natural growth rate (g_n) and the propensity to save out of profits (s_p) set the share of total profits, so that it is the wages that, so to speak, become the surplus of the system. Even more importantly, when the relations are stripped down to their essentials, that is, in the purest case in which $s_p = 1$, and therefore (1) becomes $(P/K) = g_n = \hat{n} + \lambda$, the natural rate of profits is determined, fundamentally, not by the 'quantity of capital' (as long asserted by mainstream economics), but by the sum of the rates of growth of labour and of the productivity of labour.

LUIGI L. PASINETTI AND ARIEL
L. WIRKIERMAN

See also

Effective demand; *Essays in the Theory of Economic Growth*; Income distribution; Pasinetti's paradox; Wages

References

Domar, E. (1946), 'Capital expansion, rate of growth, and employment', *Econometrica*, **14** (2), 137–47.
Harrod, R.F. (1948), *Towards a Dynamic Economics*, London: Macmillan.
Kaldor, N. (1955), 'Alternative theories of distribution', *Review of Economic Studies*, **23** (2), 83–100.
Pasinetti, L.L. (1962), 'Rate of profit and income distribution in relation to the rate of economic growth', *Review of Economic Studies*, **29** (4), 267–79.
Pasinetti, L.L. (1974), *Growth and Income Distribution: Essays in Economic Theory*, Cambridge: Cambridge University Press.
Pasinetti, L.L. (2007), *Keynes and the Cambridge Keynesians: A 'Revolution in Economics' to be Accomplished*, Cambridge: Cambridge University Press.

Capacity utilization

The size of productive capacity is usually measured through the technically maximum output obtainable through a set of durable means of production and the non-durable means of production and labour necessary to run them at the highest intensity. Accordingly, the degree to which the firm plans to use newly installed capacity, that is, the normal degree of utilization, should be understood as the ratio between the level of output that the firm expects to produce on average over the life of the plants and the maximum level of output defining productive capacity. It is an *ex ante* measure and implies a margin of spare capacity as an intended result. Actual utilization is instead an *ex post* magnitude, determined by the levels of output actually produced. It is certainly lower or at most equal to full utilization and may be higher, lower or equal to normal utilization.

The variability of the degree of utilization of productive capacity can take two distinct forms, as the firm can modify either the duration of operations (resorting to overtime labour or adopting a multiple-shift system) or their speed.

The definition of a technique of production necessarily implies the specification of the optimal intensity of use of the means of production. The notion of normal utilization of productive capacity is therefore relevant in the theoretical fields in which techniques of production are involved: the theory of prices, where normal utilization determines the methods of production implicit either in the production function or in the price equations, and the theory of economic growth, where it determines the desired capital–output ratio and the decisions to invest. In fact, the determination of the normal degree of utilization has been addressed in the analysis of radically different problems and with different theoretical approaches (see Trezzini and Pignalosa, 2021).

The general terms in which the problem of determining the degree of utilization is usually set, together with the elaboration of the basic principles for the treatment of the issue, can be traced back to Marx's analysis. Subsequently, the issue appears, albeit implicitly, in the debate of the 1920s and 1930s on the cost functions in which, for a given productive plant, the output level corresponding to the minimum unit cost is determined (Viner, 1931). The contribution of Steindl (1952) reveals the relevance of the notion for the theory of demand-led accumulation, inspiring a later approach to the issue (beginning with Ciccone, 1986) that emphasizes the role of the expected fluctuations of output in the determination of the size and the normal degree of capacity utilization. Kurz (1986) claims the necessity of addressing the issue in the framework of the choice of technique, which he develops along the lines of the Classical theory. His approach is taken up by subsequent contributions (see for instance Nikiforos, 2013). A further strand of analysis, stemming from the seminal work of Marris (1964), extends the neoclassical theory of the firm by explicitly considering the variability of the speed or the duration of capital utilization.

In the heterogeneity of the literature, a principle that meets with general consensus is the one according to which normal utilization is that which the firm plans upon installing the productive capacity and is determined in such a way as to maximize profits. This requires assessing the effect that different degrees of utilization have on the average cost of fixed and circulating capital and on the cost of labour, taking into account the technical conditions of production, the distributive variables – including the level of the wage differential for non-standard working hours – and the level of output to be produced. In this regard, a divergence of views emerges on how to deal with the fact that the lifetime of plants extends over several production cycles, each of which is associated with an expected (possibly different) level of output. While in most analyses the variability of output levels is not given an analytical role (see for instance Marris, 1964 and Kurz, 1986), in some contributions it is seen as a crucial determinant of normal utilization (see for example Steindl, 1952 and Ciccone, 1986).

Within demand-led growth analyses, the need to combine an autonomous role for aggregate demand in the growth process with an exogenous determination of distribution requires clarifying whether actual utilization should be assumed to equal normal utilization in the long run and whether normal utilization should be conceived as endogenous to demand (Hein et al., 2012; Trezzini and Palumbo, 2016). Consequently, the concept of normal capacity utilization has assumed a crucial role in the ongoing debate over the theory of demand-led growth, becoming the focus of a growing body of literature.

ATTILIO TREZZINI AND DARIA PIGNALOSA

See also

Aggregate demand; Effective demand; Growth – wage-led vs profit-led; Income distribution; Harrodian instability

References

Ciccone, R. (1986), 'Accumulation and capacity utilization: some critical considerations on Joan Robinson's theory of distribution', *Political Economy: Studies in the Surplus Approach*, **2** (1), 17–36.

Hein, E., M. Lavoie and T. van Treeck (2012), 'Harrodian instability and the "normal rate" of capacity utilization in Kaleckian models of distribution and growth: a survey', *Metroeconomica*, **63** (1), 139–69.

Kurz, H. (1986), 'Normal positions and capital utilization', *Political Economy: Studies in the Surplus Approach*, **2** (1), 37–54.

Marris, R. (1964), *The Economics of Capital Utilization: A Report on Multiple Shift Work*, Cambridge, UK: Cambridge University Press.

Nikiforos, M. (2013), 'The (normal) rate of capacity utilization at the firm level', *Metroeconomica*, **64** (3), 513–38.

Steindl, J. (1952), *Maturity and Stagnation in American Capitalism*, Oxford: Oxford University Press.

Trezzini, A. and A. Palumbo (2016), 'The theory of output in the modern classical approach: main principles and controversial issues', *Review of Keynesian Economics*, **4** (4), 503–22.

Trezzini, A. and D. Pignalosa (2021), 'The normal degree of capacity utilization: the history of a controversial concept', *Centro Sraffa Working Paper*, No. 49.

Viner, J. (1931), 'Cost curves and supply curves', *Zeitschrift für Nationalökonomie*, **3** (1), 23–46.

Capital controls

Capital controls are 'measures that restrict capital transactions (or transfers and payments necessary to effect them) by virtue of the residency of the parties to the transaction. Controls may be economy-wide, sector-specific (usually the financial sector), or industry specific (for example, "strategic" industries in the case of controls on FDI)' (Ostry et al., 2011, pp. 3–4).

There are differences between controls on inflows or liability flows (for instance, foreign acquisition of domestic assets) and controls on outflows or asset flows (resident acquisition of foreign assets) (see Ghosh et al., 2014). Both types of control are part of the macroprudential toolkit, along with exchange-rate-related measures (which target specific currencies) and other measures (which target volumes of transactions, usually denominated in a given currency, such as the US dollar).

ATTILIO TREZZINI AND DARIA PIGNALOSA / LUIS REYES

Controls on outflows of capital can be useful to avoid or minimize the negative impact of capital flights. Epstein (2005) defines the latter as a combination of capital and unrecorded outflows. His 2005 book focuses on the link between the two and on what can be done to make capital to flow in the right direction (that is, from north to south).

Controls on inflows of capital have been met with visceral opposition, despite the fact they have gained greater recognition in recent years as useful tools to manage exchange rate risks (International Monetary Fund, 2012). Opponents to capital controls often get confused between controls on outflows – which were widespread during the interwar period plagued with capital flight – and hot money flows, competitive devaluations, exchange restrictions, protectionism and imploding global trade (Ghosh and Qureshi, 2016). The sour experience of that period and similar episodes afterwards left an important mark in the discussions that led to a reduced intensity in the use of this policy instrument, and ultimate full neglect (see Ghosh and Qureshi, 2016).

In the Bretton Woods regime, controls on outflows in advanced G-7 economies were much higher than those on inflows, and the latter remained relatively constant. Over the same period, emerging markets were more protectionist on both fronts, especially with respect to inflows (Ostry et al., 2011). This, together with a broader set of measures (with its pros and cons) helped several Latin American economies develop an often-criticised though successful import-substitution strategy, very close in spirit to what is described by Prebisch (1950).

In contrast to the trends observed during the Bretton Woods era, advanced economies' use of capital controls has been gradually falling, and they are currently less used in Europe and Latin America as compared to other regions. Asia, in contrast, still makes active use of this tool (Ostry et al., 2011).

In their defence of capital controls, Crotty and Epstein (1999) cite three ways in which controls can be useful to rebalance political and economic power. These controls (1) restrict the ability of rentiers and multinationals to 'run away', which in turn may contribute to (2) strengthening labour's bargaining power and recognise that, in order to be effective, (3) they must be coupled with economic intervention by the State. The authors further argue that the long-run unprofitability of not implementing capital controls can serve as an argument against the short-run unprofitability of implementing them, as perceived by investors in financial markets.

Rey (2018) studies the global financial cycle and finds it is inversely related to the VIX (a measure of implied stock-market volatility), so that when financial investors perceive low volatility, financial bubbles build up. Conversely, when stock-market volatility is high, episodes of capital flight occur (with the exception of foreign direct investment). Naturally, the less the economy is financially repressed, the more vulnerable it is to financial crises.

In order to tame the cycle, Ocampo (2012) argues the enforcement of capital controls on inflows is desirable during boom periods in order to avoid exchange rate appreciation, the risks associated with rising current account deficits and/or useless foreign exchange reserve accumulation. In contrast, in times of crisis authorities must avoid capital flight. This implies that they must implement controls on outflows. This is compatible with Rey's (2018) analysis.

An important question related to financial liberalisation is the loss of national sovereignty, which is at stake when domestic firms are controlled (partially or fully) by foreign individuals with interests that may be contradictory to national development goals. Part of that sovereignty lost could be regained by imposing controls on foreign direct investment inflows, as the Chinese case has shown (Herr, 2008), despite constant bashing against this and other successful economies (McKinnon and Schnabl, 2014).

LUIS REYES

See also

Bretton Woods; Capital flows; Exchange rates – fixed vs flexible; Exchange rates – managed

References

Crotty, J. and G. Epstein (1999), 'A defense of capital controls in light of the Asian financial crisis', *Journal of Economic Issues*, **33** (2), 427–33.

Epstein, G.A. (ed.) (2005), *Financialization and the World Economy*, Cheltenham, UK, and Northampton, MA, USA: Edward Elgar.

Ghosh, A. and M. Qureshi (2016), 'What's in a name? That which we call capital controls', *International Monetary Fund Working Paper*, No. 16/25.

Ghosh, A., M. Qureshi, J. Il Kim and J. Zalduendo (2014), 'Surges', *Journal of International Economics*, **92** (2) 266–85.

Herr, H. (2008), 'Capital controls and economic development in China', in P. Arestis and L.F. de Paula (eds), *Financial Liberalization and Economic Performance in Emerging Countries*, London: Palgrave Macmillan, pp. 142–72.

International Monetary Fund (2012), 'The liberalization and management of capital flows: an institutional view', *International Monetary Fund Policy Paper*, available online at https://www.imf.org/external/np/pp/eng/2012/111412.pdf.

McKinnon, R. and G. Schnabl (2014), 'China's exchange rate and financial repression: the conflicted emergence of the renminbi as an international currency', *China & World Economy*, **22** (3), 1–35.

Ocampo, J.A. (2012), 'The case for and experience with capital account regulations', in A. Bhattacharya (ed.), *Regulating Global Capital Flows for Long-Run Development*, Boston: Boston University, pp. 13–21.

Ostry, J., A. Ghosh, M. Chamon and M. Qureshi (2011), 'Capital controls: when and why?', *International Monetary Fund Economic Review*, **59** (3), 562–80.

Prebisch, R. (1950), 'Bases for the discussion of an anti-cyclical policy in Latin America', in Economic Commission for Latin America (ed.), *The Economic Development of Latin America and Its Principal Problems*, New York: United Nations Department of Social Affairs, pp. 49–59.

Rey, H. (2018), 'Dilemma not trilemma: the global financial cycle and monetary policy independence', *National Bureau of Economic Research Working Paper*, No. 21162.

Capital flows

Capital flows reflect the acquisition of assets and incurrence of liabilities of one economic unit, resident in a specific country, with non-residents of that country. As such, they capture debt and equity claims between residents of different countries, and are registered in the financial account of the balance of payments. Though equity flows, particularly foreign direct investment, are the predominant type of capital flows, debt flows in the form of portfolio investment and bank loans have been the most dynamic and volatile component of capital flows.

Since the obverse of net capital flows is the current account balance, mainstream literature interprets capital flows as 'foreign savings' (when in deficit) available to fund domestic investment (McKinnon, 1973) or, equivalently, as the outcome of domestic consumption and saving intertemporal decisions of forward-looking domestic agents (Obstfeld and Rogoff, 1995). This argument, however, does not stand close scrutiny in the specific field of international finance, beyond the diverse critiques to the optimizing framework of neoclassical economics.

The first thing worth mentioning in this regard is that capital flows are concentrated between advanced economies, which contradicts the corollary of marginal productivity theory: instead of flowing to economies with a lower degree of development and capital stock (and therefore higher real profitability), capital movements are directed towards mature capitalist economies.

Second, from a post-Keynesian perspective it is important to distinguish between savings and finance. The former are determined by investment decisions, public deficits and the trade balance, while finance (in the form of credit) is an important determinant of investment.

Third, and because of the previous argument, gross capital flows have an importance of their own beyond net measures, because they imply debt relations with counterparty risk, among other risks. As an example, though the current account balance between the United States and Europe was roughly in balance, gross capital flows between these regions were a major determinant of the dissemination and severity of the 2008 crisis (Avdjiev et al., 2016).

Fourth, the determinants of capital flows (particularly portfolio and other investment flows) are not merely the reflection of the conditions in the recipient economy. They are rather influenced by expected capital gains and risk perceptions in global financial centres, with the US dollar playing a major role because it is a funding currency (Kaltenbrunner, 2015; Harvey, 2019). In this sense, capital flows display a Minskyan dynamic of ebb and flow according to risk perceptions and the build-up of external vulnerabilities, described by Kindleberger as cycles of 'manias, panics and crash' (Kindleberger and Aliber, 2005).

Fifth, there is a growing importance of institutional investors such as hedge funds, pension funds, cash pools and asset managers investing in short-term assets with higher yield–risk relations, instead of 'productive investment' (Bonizzi and Kaltenbrunner, 2019).

The increasing role of these type of investors and the variety of views and risk-aversion attitudes help to explain one of the conundrums of international finance: the positive comovement between capital inflows and outflows (Avdjiev et al., 2018).

Sixth, even equity flows are substantially influenced by financial conditions, because they include merger and acquisition expenditures and intra-company debt instrumented via tax havens.

Lastly, since capital flows do not necessarily obey the conditions prevalent in recipient countries (particularly developing economies), they cause abrupt and volatile changes in exchange rates, asset prices (such as stock exchanges, real estate and financial systems) and income distribution (Bortz, 2016). Therefore, there is a strong rationale for implementing capital controls for governments to regain certain autonomy for the conduct of economic policy according to domestic considerations (see Keynes, 1973, pp. 148–9; Grabel, 2012).

PABLO BORTZ

See also

Current accounts; Development; Finance and development; Income distribution; Neoclassical economics

References

Avdjiev, S., B. Hardy, S. Kalemli-Özcan and L. Servén (2018), 'Gross capital flows by banks, corporates and sovereigns', *Bank for International Settlements Working Paper*, No. 760.
Avdjiev, S., R. McCauley and H.S. Shin (2016), 'Breaking free of the triple coincidence in international finance', *Economic Policy*, 31 (87), 409–51.
Bonizzi, B. and A. Kaltenbrunner (2019), 'Liability-driven investment and pension fund exposure to emerging markets: a Minskyan analysis', *Environment and Planning A: Economy and Space*, 51 (2), 420–39.
Bortz, P.G. (2016), *Inequality, Growth and 'Hot Money'*, Cheltenham, UK, and Northampton, MA, USA: Edward Elgar.
Grabel, I. (2012), 'Dynamic capital regulations, IMF irrelevance and the crisis', in K.P. Gallagher, S. Griffith-Jones and J.A. Ocampo (eds), *Regulating Capital Flows for Long-Run Development*, Boston: Frederick S. Pardee Center for the Study of Longer Range Development at Boston University, pp. 59–69.
Harvey, J. (2019), 'Exchange rates and the balance of payments: reconciling an inconsistency in Post Keynesian theory', *Journal of Post Keynesian Economics*, forthcoming.
Kaltenbrunner, A. (2015), 'A Post Keynesian framework of exchange rate determination: a Minskyan approach', *Journal of Post Keynesian Economics*, 38 (3), 426–48.
Keynes, J.M. (1973), *The Collected Writings of John Maynard Keynes, Vol. XXV: Activities 1940–1944. Shaping the Post-War World: The Clearing Union*, London: Macmillan.
Kindleberger, C. and R. Aliber (2005), *Manias, Panics and Crashes: A History of Financial Crises*, Hoboken, NJ: John Wiley & Sons, fifth edition.
McKinnon, R. (1973), *Money and Capital in Economic Development*, Washington, DC: Brookings Institution.
Obstfeld, M. and K. Rogoff (1995), 'The intertemporal approach to the current account', in G. Grossman and K. Rogoff (eds), *Handbook of International Economics, Vol. III*, Amsterdam: North Holland, pp. 1731–99.

Capital requirements

Capital requirements are regulatory controls used to limit the leverage of financial institutions. Under current Basel rules, for example, bank assets are weighted by risk, and the growth of assets is constrained by a minimum ratio of equity-to-assets.

Minsky (1986) was one of the earliest proponents of using capital requirements to restrain the destabilizing effect of banking and as a formal tool of monetary policy. Since banks are profit-seeking entities that generate profit through the granting of credit lines, and they have exhibited an extraordinary proclivity to circumvent regulations through innovations, the most effective way to restrain bank credit is regulating the growth of assets (loans) via capital-asset ratios.

> As things stand now, the adequacy of bank capital is a concern of bank examination and supervision, not of monetary policy. In order to constrain the disequilibrating potential, to protect against debt deflation, and to remove the bias due to the higher asset-equity ratios allowed to giant banks, the Federal Reserve should be authorized to set an asset-equity ratio for all banks – that is, all institutions with deposits subject to transfer by check or withdrawal on demand. A 5 per cent asset–equity ratio seems reasonable, especially if capital absorption by covert bank liabilities is taken into account. The Federal Reserve should have a right to vary the ratio if aggregate bank

capital is compromised. A capital-adequacy condition should not be administered as a straightjacket, and a penalty constraint upon dividends should be assessed for significant shortfalls of capital. (Minsky, 1986, p. 356)

In addition to his call for capital requirements to restrict bank leverage, there are two other important points Minsky raises in the above quotation: the inclusion of off-balance sheet assets (what he called 'covert liabilities'), and the use of dividend policy to restrain bank (and therefore credit) growth. In relation to the second point, Minsky stated that if large profitable banks retained earnings in excess of what is consistent with non-inflationary credit growth, then it would also be necessary to control payout ratios. That is, banks would be required to raise dividend payouts, reducing retained earnings (equity) to a level consistent with non-inflationary credit growth.

Bank capital requirements were formally proposed through the 1988 Basel Accords, originally established by the Basel Committee on Banking Supervision, made up of the Group of Ten central bank governors. The first set of standards (known as Basel I) was implemented in 1992 and subsequent iterations were adopted in 2004 (Basel II). Given the existing standards proved inadequate to prevent the 2008 global financial crisis, Basel III was announced in 2010 to further strengthen the capital requirement rules. In addition to raising the minimum standards, a minimum liquidity requirement and operational risk standard were adopted.

Basel III utilizes several capital ratio measures that banks are required to meet. The narrowest ratio is Common Equity Tier 1 (CET1) capital relative to risk-weighted assets (RWA). CET1 is comprised of common equity and retained earnings, while asset types are categorized into different risk classes ranging from cash and government securities that carry a weight of zero, to corporate bonds carrying a weight of one, and certain real estate assets with weights greater than one. Currently, banks with assets in excess of 50 billion US dollars are required to maintain a ratio of CET1 to RWA of 4.5 per cent plus a capital conservation buffer of 2.5 per cent, creating a minimum ratio of 7 per cent. Banks failing to meet this minimum may be subject to constraints on dividend distributions, buybacks and compensation.

The second measure, Tier 1 capital, includes CET1 plus capital assets like preferred stock, and carries a minimum value of 8 per cent. Tier 2 capital incorporates Tier 1 plus unsecured subordinated debt and requires a minimum ratio of 10.5 per cent. Last, the leverage ratio uses CET1 capital relative to average total assets, including off-balance sheet values (as Minsky suggested). Basel III also added a counter-cyclical buffer, ranging from 0 to 2.5 per cent, to be used by central banks at their discretion. The counter-cyclical buffer would typically be raised during an expansion and lowered in a recession. With the exception of Minsky's suggestion to control dividend policy as a way to restrain inflationary credit growth, the current Basel rules essentially adhere to those he prescribed over 30 years ago.

TED P. SCHMIDT

See also

Basel Agreements; Bubbles – credit; Credit; Debt deflation; Financial instability hypothesis

References

Bank for International Settlements, 'Basel III: international regulatory framework for banks', Basel: Bank for International Settlements, available online at https://www.bis.org/bcbs/basel3.htm (last accessed 6 November 2020).

Minsky, H.P. (1986), *Stabilizing an Unstable Economy*, New York: McGraw-Hill.

Capital theory controversies

The capital theory controversies were a series of debates on high theory between economists mainly based in Cambridge, United Kingdom (for instance Joan Robinson, Piero Sraffa, Luigi Pasinetti) and Cambridge, Massachusetts (like Paul Samuelson and Robert Solow) in the 1950s–1970s. Although the debates were ostensibly about the problem of measuring capital, they were actually about the nature and meaning of capital and the question of what is the appropriate way to analyse a contemporary capitalist economy.

The controversies arose when Joan Robinson (1953–54) asked how capital was measured in the aggregate production functions – in what units? 'The first puzzle is to find a unit in which capital may be measured as a *number* (i.e. an index) which is independent of relative prices and distribution, so that it may be inserted in a production function where along with labour ... it may explain the level of output ... [and] analyse distribution' (Harcourt, 1969/1986, pp. 146–7, emphasis in original). Joan Robinson argued that it was impossible to develop the concept of a quantity of capital independently of the rates of interest (profits) and wages. As this was extremely destructive of mainstream theory, it fuelled a long and technical debate – culminating in Samuelson's summing up of a symposium in the *Quarterly Journal of Economics* in 1966, where he admitted it was not possible to derive any such model outside of what is effectively a one-commodity model. (In 1962, Samuelson unsuccessfully attempted to show that the four 'parables' reflecting that price is always and everywhere an index of scarcity and which were true of one-commodity models remained robust when extended to n-commodity models.) As a result, the marginal productivity theory of distribution and the inverse relationship between the value of capital (and therefore investment) and the rate of interest (profits) were shown to have no theoretical foundation.

The problem is that within conventional economics there are two pricing rules. For given quantities of the factors of production, price must equate supply and demand for given resources, while for produced output, price must cover costs with a uniform rate of profits. Because capital is both a factor of production and a produced good, it is required to satisfy both price conditions simultaneously, which is not feasible.

Joan Robinson (1953–54) argued that the problem with the analysis was much deeper than the question of the measurement of capital, and stressed the use of inappropriate methods of analysis. She was critical of the use of comparisons of long-period equilibrium (differences) to analyse actual changes (processes) without any analysis of movements between long-period equilibria and of how the economy was able to get into long-period equilibrium.

As to the meaning of capital, Joan Robinson (1953–54) argued that meaning depended on the 'vision' of the social system the analyst had in mind. There are two principal 'visions': first, the mainstream Fisherian where the consumer queen trying to maximize her life-time utility through saving and consumption decisions calls the tune and all other players and institutions dance to her tune; secondly, there is the classical, Marxian, Veblenesque, Keynesian, Kaleckian, Kaldorian and Robinsonian 'vision' whereby the ruthless and swashbuckling capitalist class (all three, industrial, commercial and financial) calls the tune and all other classes and institutions respond.

All supply and demand theories fall under the first 'vision', and in the 1970s and 1980s their highest form or reference point was the Arrow–Debreu general equilibrium model. This led to attempts to show that the Cambridge, United Kingdom, critique could be extended to all variants of supply and demand models and especially to the general equilibrium model (see for instance Lazzarini, 2015). However, with the rise in importance of endogenous growth models, Piketty's (2014) best seller concerning the distribution of income and wealth, and the return of the mainstream to using small models (except for dynamic stochastic general equilibrium models), the original critique of the meaning and measurement of capital in the aggregate production function has returned to the agenda (see Harcourt, 2015). Alongside all these developments there have been discussions of the indissoluble link between analysis and ideology (see Cohen and Harcourt, 2003).

GEOFF HARCOURT AND
PETER KRIESLER

See also

Aggregate demand; Capitalism; Growth – wage-led vs profit-led; Paradox of costs; Profit

References

Cohen, A.J. and G.C. Harcourt (2003), 'Whatever happened to the Cambridge capital theory controversies?', *Journal of Economic Perspectives*, **17** (1), 199–214.

Harcourt, G.C. (1969), 'Some Cambridge controversies in the theory of capital', *Journal of Economic Literature*, **7** (2), 369–405. Reprinted in O.F. Hamouda (ed.), *Controversies in Political Economy: Selected Essays of G.C. Harcourt*, Brighton, Sussex: Wheatsheaf Books, 1986, pp. 145–206.

Harcourt, G.C. (2015), 'Review article of Thomas Piketty, *Capital in the Twenty-First Century*', *Economic and Labour Relation Review*, **26** (2), 314–21.

Lazzarini, A. (2015), 'Some unsettled issues in a second phase of the Cambridge–Cambridge controversy', *Review of Radical Political Economics*, **47** (2), 256–73.

Piketty, T. (2014), *Capital in the Twenty-First Century* (translated by Arthur Goldhammer), Cambridge, MA, and London: The Belknap Press of Harvard University Press.

Robinson, J. (1953–54), 'The production function and the theory of capital', *Review of Economic Studies*, **21** (2), 81–106.

Samuelson, P.A. (1962), 'Parable and realism in capital theory: the surrogate production function', *Review of Economic Studies*, **29** (3), 193–206.

Samuelson, P.A. (1966), 'A summing up', *Quarterly Journal of Economics*, **80** (4), 568–83.

Capitalism

Capitalism is a mode of economic, social and political organization, based on the private ownership of the means of production and a 'free'-wage labour market (see Marx, 1857–8, 1867). Its origin traces back to the developments of banking and merchant activities during the so-called Italian Renaissance (that begun in Tuscany in the fourteenth century and peaked in the two following centuries). However, it was the rise of British industrial manufacture in the mid-eighteenth century (that is, the first industrial revolution) that marked the inception of modern capitalist era (see, for instance, Foley and Duménil, 2008). Although different types of capitalism can be identified, all capitalist economies display some distinctive characteristics compared to other economic systems. Capitalist economies are monetary economies of production, where commodities are produced by means of equipped labour.

The process of production gets started when a money capital is exchanged by the owner/manager of the means of production (that is, the representative of capital) against labour force and other inputs. The use of equipped labour force in the production sphere allows producing an output, which is then brought to the market for sale. The process comes to an end when the capitalist recovers the initial sum plus a money profit. Karl Marx (1885) described this sequence through the well-known formula for the cycle of money capital, M–C–M' (transformation of money capital into commodities, and transformation of commodities into more money), as opposed to the simple circulation form, C–M–C (transformation of commodities into money, and transformation of the money back into commodities of different kind). The monetary surplus value, $M' = M + \Delta M$, arises from the fact that the time spent by workers in the production process exceeds the time necessary to produce their subsistence (as the acquisition of labour force is the only external purchase for the capitalist class). The point is that capitalism is not a system where economic agents cooperate to produce specific use values. Rather, it is an impersonal and conflictual system aiming at maximizing the exchange value of products, hence capitalists' surplus value (or gross profit), through the exploitation of workers.

According to Marx, capitalism is marked by some laws of motion, notably, the tendency for the profit rate to fall, the concentration and centralization of capital, the fall in relative wages, and cyclical crises. While the idea of a falling profit rate is quite contentious, most dissenting economists and social scientists recognize the other tendencies.

At a lower level of aggregation and abstraction, three different forms of capitalism can be identified: *laissez-faire* or liberal market capitalism, coordinated or mixed capitalism, and State capitalism. Ideally, a liberal market economy is a system where prices and quantities of products are utterly determined by the ebb and flow of unregulated (or lightly regulated) markets. The State does not interfere with private business: it just sets the rules of the game. Capital accumulation is a private affair. Arguably, a pure *laissez-faire* capitalist system has never existed. However, Anglo-Saxon countries are usually regarded as (mostly) liberal market capitalist economies. In contrast, northern European countries are frequently mentioned as examples of coordinated capitalism, meaning a society characterized by a strong welfare system, regulated markets and a mix of private and government enterprise (see, for instance, Soskice and Hall, 2001).

The Rhine or German model, the Japanese model and, to some extent, the Mediterranean model can be thought as subsets of coordinated capitalism. The second wave of capitalist globalization, which has been taking place since the early 1990s, has thinned the distinction between the two types of capitalism though. As a matter of fact, coordinated capitalist countries have recorded an expansion of the sphere of influence of the market, while Anglo-Saxon countries have sometimes rediscovered the role of the State in supporting domestic productions. Finally, the label 'State capitalism' is sometimes used to refer to the Soviet Union model (see, for example, Cliff, 1974). This is quite controversial though, as it entails that there can be capitalism without private accumulation. In principle, the economy is fully planned under State capitalism (either in a centralized or decentralized way), while the State owns the means of production. Capital accumulation is not banned. It is managed by the State in the interest of the population. China's economic model is sometimes associated with State capitalism because of the use of economic planning. However, market forces and private enterprise are key drivers of the Chinese economy. This is the reason China should be rather referred to as a market socialist system, where Chinese authorities see a mixed economy as a preliminary stage in the process of developing a socialist economy.

MARCO VERONESE PASSARELLA

See also

Capitalism – stages of; Capitalism – varieties of; Chicago School; Globalization; Monetary theory of production

References

Cliff, T. (1974), *State Capitalism in Russia*, London: Pluto Press.
Foley, D. and G. Duménil (2008), 'Marx's analysis of capitalist production', in S.N. Durlauf and L.E. Blume (eds), *The New Palgrave Dictionary of Economics*, London and Basingstoke: Palgrave Macmillan, second edition, available online at https://link.springer.com/content/pdf/10.1057%2F978-1-349-95121-5_2164-1.pdf (last accessed on 12 August 2019).
Marx, K. (1857–8), *Grundrisse: Foundations of the Critique of Political Economy*, London: Penguin Books/New Left Review, 1993.
Marx, K. (1867), *Capital: A Critique of Political Economy, Volume 1*, London, Penguin Books/New Left Review, 1976.
Marx, K. (1885), *Capital: A Critique of Political Economy, Volume 2*, London, Penguin Books/New Left Review, 1978.
Soskice, P.A. and D.W. Hall (2001), *Varieties of Capitalism: The Institutional Foundations of Comparative Advantage*, Oxford: Oxford University Press.

Capitalism – stages of

Many mainstream economists believe that fundamental economic theory is timeless and eternally true, since it is derived from the essential properties of 'human nature'. In contrast, most post-Keynesian economists maintain economics must be to some extent historically specific, changing as the economic system changes, along with the social, political and institutional framework within which it is embedded. This has practical as well as purely intellectual significance, since the most important economic problems, and the policy measures that are required to address them, will also change over time. Hence post-Keynesian economists take a strong interest in identifying the various stages of capitalism, often drawing on the institutionalist and radical-Marxian literature in their work.

Hyman Minsky distinguished four stages of capitalism in the United States, each with a distinct relationship between the financial and non-financial sectors of the economy (Nersisyan, 2010). In the first, 'commercial' stage, self-finance through retained earnings was the general rule. This was followed by the 'finance' stage, in which businesses became heavily dependent on banks to finance their activities, and the (largely unregulated) financial sector assumed much greater importance. The deep problems that arose as a result led to its replacement by the third, 'managerial' stage, with a much greater degree of financial regulation by the federal government and the emergence of a welfare State. Towards the end of his life Minsky identified a newly emerging fourth stage of 'money manager capitalism', in which managers of money replace managers of industry as the leading players in the economy and encourage them to concentrate exclusively on the maximization of shareholders' value. This generates a new 'downsize and distribute' model in which there are fewer jobs and less favourable terms and conditions of employment, and also gives rise to increased financial fragility and macroeconomic instability. Minsky did not live to see the global financial crisis of 2007–08, but it would not have surprised him.

Many post-Keynesian economists have adopted this analysis of the new stage of capitalism, usually describing it, however, as an era of 'financialization' rather than 'money manager capitalism'. Others would object that Minsky's stages place too much stress on finance and not enough on other dimensions of the problem, including the nature of production, the degree of competition, international economic relations, and the broader socio-political underpinnings of the capitalist economic system. In terms of

MARCO VERONESE PASSARELLA / JOHN E. KING

production, we might follow the French regulation school and distinguish a pre-industrial stage, classical factory production, 'Fordism' and 'post-Fordism', perhaps with a most recent 'post-industrial stage' in which finance and intangible capital play a much greater role. In classical nineteenth-century factory production, economies of scale are quite small, a high degree of competition prevails, and the role of the State in the economy is minimal. The mass-production, assembly-line techniques that in the first three-quarters of the twentieth century characterized the Fordist stage generated massive economies of scale, a very high degree of industrial concentration, and general acceptance of the need for a much greater economic role for the government, not least in maintaining effective demand. In the post-Fordist stage, beginning around 1975, 'flexible specialization' replaced the assembly line, with small-batch production of highly differentiated products to supply niche markets under conditions of continuous innovation and quality enhancement. This was widely regarded as the technological foundation of neoliberal capitalism (Howard and King, 2008).

If less emphasis were to be placed on technology, and more on the degree of competition, at least three stages might be distinguished: pre-1870 classical or competitive capitalism, monopoly capital (Baran and Sweezy, 1966), and the highly but imperfectly competitive post-1980 globalized capitalist system. This overlaps to some extent with the three stages of international economic relations: national rivalry before 1939, United States' hegemony from 1945 to the 1980s, and the new stage of national rivalry initiated by the rise of China and the (relative) decline of the United States after 1990 (Macdonald, 2015). Finally, and probably most important, is the classification by socio-political characteristics, in which mercantilism gives way to classical or *laissez-faire* capitalism, followed by 'organized' capitalism, with much greater State intervention, and finally to the neoliberal stage, in which the overriding power of the market is stressed and the need for tight regulation is denied.

There is, of course, a vast literature on all these questions, involving social philosophers, political scientists and sociologists as well as economists. Three final questions might be posed. First, how do all these distinct but overlapping sets of stages relate to each other? Can we simply choose one or more of them to meet the problem at hand, or can they be synthesized into a single, more or less coherent typology? Second, how are they related to the patterns of long waves in global economic activity that continue to fascinate economic historians, and in particular to the apparent (but disputed) return of relative stagnation early in the twenty-first century? Does this point to the emergence of a new stage of disorganized capitalism (Streeck, 2016)? Third, what of the future? Are we at the beginning of a new, post-neoliberal stage of capitalism, in which the growth of information technology, robotics, intangible capital, and intellectual property will pose very different policy problems from those of the neoliberal stage? Perhaps we stand on the threshold of a new kind of society, beyond work, scarcity, and capitalism itself: fully automated luxury communism (Bastani, 2018).

JOHN E. KING

See also

Capitalism; Capitalism – varieties of; Financial fragility; Financialization; Regulation School

References

Baran, P.A. and P.M. Sweezy (1966), *Monopoly Capital: An Essay on the American Economic and Social Order*, New York: Monthly Review Press.

Bastani, A. (2018), *Fully Automated Luxury Communism: A Manifesto*, London: Verso.

Howard, M.C. and J.E. King (2008), *The Rise of Neoliberalism in Advanced Capitalism: A Materialist Analysis*, Basingstoke: Palgrave Macmillan.

Macdonald, J. (2015), *When Globalization Fails: The Rise and Fall of Pax Americana*, New York: Farrar, Strauss & Giroux.

Nersisyan, Y. (2010), 'Money manager capitalism', in J.E. King (ed.), *The Elgar Companion to Post Keynesian Economics*, Cheltenham, UK, and Northampton, MA, USA, second edition, pp. 409–14.

Streeck, W. (2016), *How Will Capitalism End?*, London: Verso.

Capitalism – varieties of

Weber's (1905/1989) seminal book on *The Protestant Ethic and the Spirit of Capitalism* nailed the probabilist relationship between the Protestant culture and the emergence of such an economic system in Western countries.

JOHN E. KING / GUILLAUME VALLET

The originality of Weber's work is to insist on the increasing relevance of instrumental rationality as a key feature of capitalism. In addition to private property and profit-seeking forms of behaviour, the application of instrumental rationality in all domains of life has been a significant facet of Western societies since the eighteenth century.

Moreover, Schumpeter (1917) added to this framework the importance of money as the central institution of evolving capitalism. Through his 'claim theory of money', Schumpeter stressed that money finances future production in capitalism. Specifically, bank credits finance entrepreneurship, in the sense that economic agents become entrepreneurs when they become debtors (Schumpeter, 1917, p. 206).

However, there cannot be a single model of capitalism. On the contrary, we should deal with the concept of varieties of capitalism (VoC) (see Hall and Soskice, 2001; Amable, 2003). Understanding capitalism through its different varieties is key to comprehending its dynamics through the existence of several spheres of capital accumulation evolving over time and over geographical locations (Boyer, 2003).

According to the different institutional frameworks specific to each country, or groups of countries, it is possible to identify several features that distinguish the models of capitalism. Each of these features captures paramount ways in which the institutions affect economic structures and the behaviour of economic agents (firms in particular). Specifically, the VoC approach insists on the importance of industrial relations, vocational training and education, corporate governance, inter-firm relations, cooperation between workers, and organization.

At the macroeconomic level, the ties between these five features are built through institutions and culture, as Weber (1905/1989) pointed out, inducing the identification of macroeconomic models of capitalism. Among others, two great models can be put forward:

- The liberal market-economy model: firms coordinate their activities primarily through hierarchical and competitive market arrangements. Market institutions provide a high degree of coordination of economic agents' forms of behaviour (on the labour market for instance). In this model, State intervention is not the norm.
- The coordinated market economy: in this model, firms are more dependent on non-market relations such as the State to coordinate market actors. Economic relations are characterized more by cooperation, and the model of competition between companies is not the most relevant aspect. Companies are likely to coordinate with other actors.

On the whole, the VoC approach facilitates an understanding of the functioning and reproduction of capitalism. Through its varieties, capitalism as an economic system rests on peculiar combinations of State interventionism and market forces, with such a combination allowing the production of public goods, which are crucial to triggering growth and development. As a result, the VoC approach criticizes the 'one best way' logic of the economic development process, in terms of uniqueness. Moreover, the VoC approach is relevant to understanding the resilience of capitalism beyond the built-in contradictions that Marxist scholars have emphasized (see Boyer, 2018). According to the VoC approach, institutions matter in capitalism, in the sense that they demonstrate that economic action is always embedded in economic and social structures.

GUILLAUME VALLET

See also

Capitalism; Capitalism – stages of; Credit money; Development; Money and banking

References

Amable, B. (2003), *The Diversity of Modern Capitalism*, Oxford: Oxford University Press.
Boyer, R. (2003), 'L'anthropologie économique de Pierre Bourdieu', *Actes de la recherche en sciences sociales*, **150**, 65–78.
Boyer, R. (2018), 'Marx's legacy, Régulation theory and contemporary capitalism', *Review of Political Economy*, **30** (3), 284–316.
Dore, R., W. Lazonick and M. O'Sullivan (1999), 'Varieties of capitalism in the twentieth century', *Oxford Review of Economic Policy*, **15** (4), 102–120.
Hall, P.A. and D. Soskice (eds) (2001), *Varieties of Capitalism: The Institutional Foundations of Comparative Advantage*, Oxford: Oxford University Press.
Schumpeter, J.A. (1917), 'Money and the social product', *International Economic Papers*, **6**, 148–211.
Weber, M. (1989), *L'éthique protestante et l'esprit du capitalisme*, Paris: Pocket Agora, first published in English in 1905.

Carbon tax

The carbon tax is a fiscal policy aimed at incentivizing economic agents' behaviour towards low-carbon actions.

The concept comes from Pigou (1920) and is related to the neoclassical theory of externalities. In this approach, the good or bad involuntary outputs of the production or consumption processes should be internalized through a pricing mechanism in order to restore the social-welfare optimum. A neoclassical alternative to carbon pricing is the carbon market mechanism, stemming from Coase (1960), where economic agents exchange a limited amount of emission permits on a market. Although a price mechanism to orient agents' behaviour can have some virtues in a broader climate-policy framework, this original concept of the carbon tax runs into at least two fundamental categories of critiques in a post-Keynesian framework.

The first category of critiques deals with the way the carbon price is calculated. The value of a carbon tax should be equal to the value of the externalities generated by carbon emissions, or what Nordhaus (2017) calls 'the social value of carbon'. In a cost–benefit approach, the social value of carbon amounts to the value of the damages generated by an additional ton of carbon. In a cost-effectiveness approach, it equals the cost of mitigating the required amount of emissions. These latter two approaches have generated a wide array of social values of carbon: Stiglitz et al. (2017) suggest an amount between 40 and 80 US dollars in 2020 (and 50–100 dollars in 2030); Nordhaus (2017) suggests 31 US dollars in 2015 with a 3 per cent annual increase; Ricke et al. (2018) suggest much higher ranges of social values of carbon when looking at country-level values (from 177 to 805 US dollars per ton of CO_2 in actualized values).

Hence, these values vary substantially from one modelling exercise to the other. Nevertheless, the modelling framework used to generate them is very similar at some level of abstraction and can be challenged on different aspects. First, climate damages, because they are conceived as a loss of potential GDP, can easily be compensated by capital accumulation in a supply-driven model. More economic growth can then become the solution to lower the relative impacts of damages and justify the idea that we should postpone action.

Second, most climate-economy models fail to account for the critical role played by uncertainty in the entire decision process. This fact is recognized by some modellers for climate-related values and their economic impacts (Weitzman, 2009; Pindyck, 2013). The entire optimization process based on an uncertain climate evolution and on uncertain (and currently undervalued) climate damages is thus at best dubious. But economic uncertainty also involves a specific understanding of the behaviour of economic agents.

This is the third point. The coordination of agents around a specific price takes place in a context of radical uncertainty. Institutions influence individual behaviour to lower the level of uncertainty and make expectations (and financial decisions) possible. If those institutions, among which the monetary and the financial systems are key, do not factor in future climate changes, then the coordination of economic agents' expectations will be strongly biased (Aglietta and Espagne, 2016) and no carbon price alone will replace that necessary institutional transformation. Pricing mechanisms are thus just one tool among others to develop an institutional framework coherent with a low-carbon pathway. In this framework, there is no such thing as an optimal carbon price, and no reason why the allocation of property rights and pricing mechanisms in general can restore the current path of the economy (Gowdy and Erickson, 2005), which has no reason to be at equilibrium.

The second category of critiques develops the idea that pricing (or market-based) mechanisms as sole (or even main) tools for climate-policy designs are flawed for political-economy reasons. In concrete terms, the choice of a carbon-tax trajectory is the product of a more or less institutionalized bargaining process. The use of models can only help explain an argument, not tell any absolute truth about the right trajectory (Espagne et al., 2018). In this respect, even if models give some insights on theoretical social values of carbon, the actual carbon price chosen is often far away from the value that a society (or the world) actually attributes to mitigating climate change and reflects more the prevailing power structure. Political acceptability and efficiency depend on the position of social groups regarding the carbon tax. The efficiency of mitigation action cannot be considered separately from fairness.

It is usually said that the macroeconomic effect of a carbon tax strongly depends on how its receipts are used. These funds can reduce other distorting taxes, be invested into low-carbon investments, or redistributed lump sum. But a fundamental question remains: is the carbon tax and the ensuing transition contractionary or expansionary? The post-Keynesian approach usually considers that the transition can be expansionary because of an increase in physical capital investment, innovation, and research and development spending leading to demand increase and income generation. In practice, the research work carried out by ecological macroeconomists has, however, only slightly touched the carbon-tax issue, considering it as a mere marginal tool for climate policy (Bovari et al., 2018), and preferring to focus on directly incentivizing green investment (Dafermos et al., 2017), regulating the financial system (Campiglio et al., 2017) so that it aligns with a low-carbon path, or developing a degrowth narrative (Jackson and Victor, 2016).

ÉTIENNE ESPAGNE AND ANTOINE GODIN

See also

Financial regulations; Fiscal policy; Neoclassical economics; Pricing; Uncertainty

References

Aglietta, M. and É. Espagne (2016), 'Climate and finance systemic risks, more than an analogy? The climate fragility hypothesis', *Centre d'études prospectives et d'informations internationales Working Paper*, No. 2016-10.
Bovari, E., O. Lecuyer and F. Mc Isaac (2018), 'Debt and damages: what are the chances of staying under the 2°C warming threshold?', *International Economics*, **155**, 92–108.
Campiglio, E., Y. Dafermos, P. Monnin, J. Ryan-Collins, G. Schotten and M. Tanaka (2018), 'Climate change challenges for central banks and financial regulators', *Nature Climate Change*, **8** (6), 462–8.
Coase, R.H. (1960), 'The problem of social cost', in *Classic Papers in Natural Resource Economics*, London: Palgrave Macmillan, pp. 87–137.
Dafermos, Y., M. Nikolaidi and G. Galanis (2017), 'A stock-flow-fund ecological macroeconomic model', *Ecological Economics*, **131**, 191–207.
Espagne, É., A. Pottier, B.P. Fabert, F. Nadaud and P. Dumas (2018), 'SCCs and the use of IAMs: let's separate the wheat from the chaff', *International Economics*, **155**, 29–47.
Gowdy, J. and J.D. Erickson (2005), 'The approach of ecological economics', *Cambridge Journal of Economics*, **29** (2), 207–22.
Jackson, T. and P.A. Victor (2016), 'Does slow growth lead to rising inequality? Some theoretical reflections and numerical simulations', *Ecological Economics*, **121**, 206–19.
Matikainen, S., E. Campiglio and D. Zenghelis (2017), 'The climate impact of quantitative easing', *Grantham Research Institute on Climate Change and the Environment Policy Paper*, available online at http://www.lse.ac.uk/GranthamInstitute/wp-content/uploads/2017/05/ClimateImpactQuantEasing_Matikainen-et-al-1.pdf (last accessed on 18 June 2019).
Nordhaus, W.D. (2017), 'Revisiting the social cost of carbon', *Proceedings of the National Academy of Sciences*, **114** (7), 1518–23.
Pigou, A.C. (1920), *The Economics of Welfare*, London: Macmillan.
Pindyck, R.S. (2013), 'Climate change policy: what do the models tell us?', *Journal of Economic Literature*, **51** (3), 860–72.
Ricke, K., L. Drouet, K. Caldeira and M. Tavoni (2018), 'Country-level social cost of carbon', *Nature Climate Change*, **8** (10), 895–900.
Stiglitz, J.E., N. Stern, M. Duan, O. Edenhofer, G. Giraud, G. Heal, E. Lèbre la Rovere, A. Morris, E. Moyer, M. Pangestu, P.R. Shukla, Y. Sokona and H. Winkler (2017), *Report of the High-Level Commission on Carbon Prices*, available online at https://static1.squarespace.com/static/54ff9c5ce4b0a53decccfb4c/t/59244eed17bffc0ac256cf16/1495551740633/CarbonPricing_Final_May29.pdf (last accessed on 18 June 2019).
Weitzman, M.L. (2009), 'On modeling and interpreting the economics of catastrophic climate change', *Review of Economics and Statistics*, **91** (1), 1–19.

Central bank independence

Central bank independence is meant to be the cornerstone of contemporary monetary policy: the central bank should be independent of the general government sector, that is, it must not be obliged to finance the public sector's deficit through a purchase of government bonds on the primary market. This is supposed to avoid inflationary pressures generated by monetary authorities whose mandate is to guarantee price stability on the market for produced goods and services.

The independence of central banks became an issue in the 1970s, when Keynesian policies to support aggregate demand on the product market (hence wage and employment levels) were increasingly criticized as being unable to address the issues of stagflation – a mix of stagnation and inflation – observed in a number of Western economies at that time. In this period, many central banks were not independent of the relevant government, which means that they were buying an increasing volume of government bonds on the primary market, as a result of which monetary aggregates and prices on the goods market increased beyond the rate of growth of real GDP.

The neoliberal counter-revolution that occurred near the end of the 1970s across the world gave rise to an institutional transformation as regards central banks, whose independence in respect of the general government sector was justified with the alleged neutrality of money as well as monetary policy on 'real' magnitudes such as employment and real GDP growth over both the short and long run (see Friedman, 1968).

Since then, the independence of central banks has taken different forms. Goal independence occurs when the central bank is free to decide the goals of its monetary policy with regard to both their nature and their magnitude. In a number of cases, for instance for the European Central Bank, the goal of price stability is given by constitution (or statutes), but the central bank is in a position to decide the price index to be used to measure inflation as well as the rate of inflation that corresponds to price stability on the market for produced goods and services. It is well known, for example, that the European Central Bank has defined price stability as a year-to-year increase in the harmonized index of consumer prices 'below, but close to, 2 per cent over the medium term' (European Central Bank, 2018, Internet). Instrument or operational independence means that the central bank decides what monetary policy tool best allows it to achieve a given objective and the extent of its utilization over a self-defined period of time. Negative interest rates, for instance, have been introduced since the bursting of the global financial crisis in 2008 by some central banks that are allowed to choose the best instrument(s) to guarantee price stability or any other monetary policy goal. Financial and personal independence makes sure that a central bank has its own budget and their officials are appointed without any explicit political influence.

In the 1990s, a growing literature provided different indices to measure a central bank's independence (see Grilli et al., 1991; Cukierman, 1992; Alesina and Summers, 1993), in an attempt to support the idea that this independence provides better economic policy results than the lack of it. Post-Keynesian economists criticized this independence on several grounds, notably, as regards its causal link with economic performance, and the fact that it does not consider all stakeholders' interests in an economic system (see Wray, 2007).

More recently, namely since the bursting of the global financial crisis in 2008, central bank independence from the banking sector has been questioned. It appears in fact that central bank decisions are influenced by the health of the banking sector: when the latter shows a systemic fragility, or there is a looming banking crisis, the central bank does 'whatever it takes' (Draghi, 2012, Internet) to support banks in trouble. This central bank dependence is further reinforced by the fact that a number of central bank governors have worked in their career for a major financial institution, so that they are familiar with a number of their managers. These issues should be investigated deeply and could provide a much different perspective on the alleged merits of central bank independence pointed out in the literature.

SERGIO ROSSI

See also

Aggregate demand; Inflation; Monetary policy; Monetary policy transmission mechanism; Money illusion

References

Alesina, A. and L. Summers (1993), 'Central bank independence and macroeconomic performance: some comparative evidence', *Journal of Money, Credit and Banking*, **25** (2), 151–62.

Cukierman, A. (1992), *Central Bank Strategy, Credibility and Independence*, Cambridge: MIT Press.

Draghi, M. (2012), 'Speech at the Global Investment Conference in London', 26 July, available online at http://www.ecb.int/press/key/date/2012/html/sp1 20726.en.html; last accessed 4 April 2019.

European Central Bank (2018), 'The definition of price stability', available online at https://www.ecb.europa.eu/mopo/strategy/pricestab/html/index.en.html; last accessed 4 April 2019.

Friedman, M. (1968), 'The role of monetary policy', *American Economic Review*, **58** (1), 1–17.

Grilli, V., D. Masciandaro and G. Tabellini (1991), 'Political and monetary institutions, and public financial policies in the industrial countries', *Economic Policy*, **6** (13), 341–76.

SERGIO ROSSI

Wray, L.R. (2007), 'A post Keynesian view of central bank independence, policy targets, and the rule versus discretion debate', *Journal of Post Keynesian Economics*, **30** (1), 119–41.

Central bank–treasury relations

In most countries, central banks act as fiscal agents of their federal governments, intermediating the flow of payments between the treasury (and other government agencies) and the non-government sector. Central banks operate as the government's bank: they accept deposits, make electronic payments, and clear checks drawn on the treasury account. They also provide securities services to the treasury organizing auctions and redemptions of treasury securities. There is little controversy that this relationship requires the obvious coordination between the central bank and the treasury so that fiscal operations proceed smoothly. However, the mainstream view stops short: it assumes that beyond this coordination, the central bank and the treasury are (and should be) mostly independent.

Post-Keynesian economists, especially Modern Money Theorists (MMTs), reject this view. They emphasize the defensive nature of the relationship between the central bank and the treasury. First, most central banks around the world conduct monetary policy by setting overnight interest rate targets, which they can meet with precision by (endogenously) accommodating the demand for reserve balances via open-market operations or paying interest on the excess reserve balances held by private banks on their accounts with central banks (see Moore 1988, 1991; Wray 1998, 2012). Note that in modern monetary systems central banks do not have control over monetary aggregates, or the money supply, as is commonly presented in textbook expositions. In fact, money is created endogenously by the domestic financial system, and central banks have no choice but to horizontally accommodate the demand for reserves for clearing, settlement, and other purposes at the interest rate target.

Central banks must react by adding or draining reserves from the banking sector to offset the impact that daily treasury operations (government spending and taxation) have on these reserves. In the absence of the central bank's daily defensive actions, the overnight interest rates would deviate (sometimes widely) from the target (or corridor). Modern central banks must coordinate daily with the treasury to ensure that the adequate reserves for the banking sector after fiscal operations (see Wray, 1998; 2012; Bell and Wray, 2003). The actual institutional process through which this coordination happens varies from country to country, but this fundamental relationship remains valid for most countries regardless of regulatory or specific sets of operational procedures adopted by their central banks.[1]

The typical simplified exposition of a central bank's balance sheet has the treasury's deposit account, as well as private banks' reserve accounts, on the liabilities side. Reserve balances and central bank notes (cash) are liabilities of central banks. On the assets side are securities (credit market instruments), loans to domestic banks, gold, and foreign exchange reserves. When the government spends, the central bank initiates an electronic transfer of funds from the treasury's account to the payee's bank account held as a liability to a commercial bank. The treasury's reserve account is debited by the amount of the transaction. The commercial bank's liability (payee's demand deposit) increases by the amount of the treasury payment, while its assets (reserve balances at the central bank) also increase by the same amount. The treasury's reserve account is debited, and the commercial bank's reserve account is credited.

Let us assume that the amount of reserves balances held by the banking system prior to this transaction was consistent with the overnight rate target (and that the central bank does not pay interest on excess reserves). Hence, the treasury spending operation has increased the amount of reserves available to the banking sector beyond what banks desired. This puts downward pressure on the overnight rate of interest, as banks try to eliminate their excess reserves. The central bank would have to intervene by draining the excess reserves (for example, with repurchase agreements or outright sales of securities in the open market) to meet its overnight target rate of interest, since banks cannot eliminate excess reserves via inter-bank lending. The central bank's holding of government securities is debited while the bank's asset shift forms (from central bank reserves to government securities).

When the government taxes, the opposite happens. The treasury's account is credited, and the banking sector loses reserves. Assuming everything else is constant, this puts upward pressure on the overnight rates of interest, as banks bid each other for additional reserves. Again, banks cannot increase the amount of aggregate reserves via inter-bank borrowing. The central bank would have to add reserves to the banking sector (for instance, buying securities in the open market) to prevent the overnight rate of interest from rising above the target.

Some central banks (as in the United States or Canada) pay interest on excess reserves held by banks and charge them an interest on overdrafts, which effectively establishes a corridor within which the overnight rate of interest fluctuates. Note that minimum reserve requirements, which some countries legally require, do not change the logic above (see Wray, 1998). Banks need reserves for clearing, settlement, and other liquidity purposes, and central banks must meet that demand to ensure the smooth functioning of the domestic payments system and their interest rate targets; the explanation above remains valid even if banks were not legally required to hold reserves.

In summary, when the government (treasury) spends, it injects reserves into the economy; when it taxes, it drains reserves. In the absence of the central bank's daily defensive actions, the overnight interest rates would deviate (sometimes widely) from the target (or corridor). In theory, if the treasury received payment flows of the same amount as payment outflows each day, the net reserve effect would be zero; and no defensive action from the central bank would be required. The daily flow of payments between the government and the private sector changes the composition and size of the central bank's balance sheet, the quantity of reserves available to the banking sector, and ultimately the form in which banks hold their assets.

Post-Keynesian economists, especially MMTs, reject the mainstream thesis of central bank independence and conclude that the close cooperation between the central bank, depository institutions, and the treasury in sovereign countries makes the traditional distinction between monetary and fiscal policy irrelevant (see Bell, 2000; Bell and Wray, 2003; Wray, 2012). MMT tends to consolidate the treasury's and the central bank's balance sheets, which admittedly abstracts from operational constraints,[2] to drive home the larger points that (i) monetary policy actions are mainly defensive, and (ii) sovereign nations that issue their own currency in a floating exchange rate regime are not financially constrained in their ability to deficit spend.[3] The logical conclusion is that, in sovereign countries, taxes and government bonds do not finance government spending (see Bell, 2000): government deficits are financed via the creation of reserves first ('high-powered money'), which must be drained from the banking sector via government bonds if the monetary authority is to hit its positive interest rate target and maintain the integrity of the domestic payments system. On this point, it is important to note that chronic public deficits require the primary sales of treasury securities in the primary markets to drain the chronic positive net reserve effect. The purpose of the sale of governments bonds is not government financing but to allow the central bank to hit its overnight target rate of interest. The operations of the treasury and the central bank are deeply intertwined by the design of modern monetary systems. Fiscal policy is on the driver's seat, as fiscal deficits vertically inject 'high-powered money' into private balance sheets.

In conclusion, the analysis presented above contrasts with the mainstream view of central bank–treasury relations. First, government deficits tend to put a downward pressure on the overnight inter-bank rate of interest. To meet its interest rate target, the central bank must horizontally accommodate banks' demand for reserves. This reverses the causality presented in the loanable-funds argument. Further, it negates the mainstream view that monetary policy and fiscal policy are (or should be) independent. Most of the central bank's daily operations are defensive to offset the net reserve impact of daily fiscal operations. Finally, fiscal deficits inject reserves (high-powered money) into the balance sheet of the non-government sector, which then requires the sale of government bonds to drain the excess reserves and allow central banks to meet their interest rate targets.

FLAVIA DANTAS

See also

Endogenous money; Fiscal deficits; Fiscal policy; Modern money theory; Money and banking

Notes

1. What follows is a simplified exposition of the reserve effect from treasury operations. It

abstracts from institutional complexities and procedural intricacies to make the larger point general and easier to comprehend. Post-Keynesians have produced a vast literature focusing on a detailed institutional examination of the clearing and settlement process between the central bank and banks, the treasury and the central bank, and the treasury and the non-government sector. For example, the treasury keeps tax-and-loans accounts with private banks to facilitate this coordination between the Federal Reserve and the US Treasury (see Bell, 2000). Fullwiler (2011, 2013, 2017) has explored the intricate and complex set of procedures between the Federal Reserve and the US Treasury. Other post-Keynesian authors have explored this in countries such as Canada (Lavoie, 2019), Australia (Mitchell and Mosler, 2002) and Brazil (Rezende, 2009).

2. The two operational constraints imposed on the treasury and the central bank in most countries are as follows: (i) the treasury needs positive balances on its account at the central bank before it can spend, that is, it is legally prohibited from 'overdrafting' their accounts at the central bank; (ii) central banks cannot credit reserves directly to the treasury's account, or directly purchase newly issued government bonds. Instead, the treasury sells bonds directly to private banks (and other non-government entities), and central banks purchase and sell government bonds in secondary markets, usually as they conduct open-market operations.

3. This proposition is not accepted by all post-Keynesian authors (see Gnos and Rochon, 2002; Rochon and Vernengo, 2003; Lavoie, 2013). For a response to some of the criticisms raised by post-Keynesians to MMTs, see Tymoigne and Wray (2013).

References

Bell, S.A. (2000), 'Do taxes and bonds finance government spending?' *Journal of Economic Issues*, **34** (3), 603–20.

Bell, S.A. and L.R. Wray (2002), 'Fiscal effects on reserves and the independence of the Fed,' *Journal of Post Keynesian Economics*, **25** (2), 263–71.

Fullwiler, S. (2011), 'Treasury debt operations: an analysis integrating social fabric matrix and social accounting matrix methodologies', *Social Science Research Network Working Paper*, available at https://ssrn.com/abstract=1825303 or http://dx.doi.org/10.2139/ssrn.1825303

Fullwiler, S. (2013), 'An endogenous money perspective on the post-crisis monetary policy debate', *Review of Keynesian Economics*, **1** (2), 171–94.

Fullwiler, S. (2017), 'Modern central bank operations: the general principles,' in L.-P. Rochon and S. Rossi (eds), *Advances in Endogenous Money Analysis*, Cheltenham, UK, and Northampton, MA, USA: Edward Elgar, pp. 50–87.

Gnos, C. and L.-P. Rochon (2002), 'Money creation and the State: a critical assessment of chartalism,' *International Journal of Political Economy*, **32** (3), 41–57.

Lavoie, M. (2013), 'The monetary and fiscal nexus of neo-chartalism: a friendly critique,' *Journal of Economic Issues*, **47** (1), 1–31.

Lavoie, M. (2019), 'Advances in the Post-Keynesian analysis of money and finance,' in P. Arestis and M. Sawyer (eds), *Frontiers of Heterodox Economics*, Basingstoke, UK, and New York: Palgrave Macmillan, pp. 89–192.

Mitchell, W.F. and W. Mosler (2002), 'Public debt management and Australia's macroeconomic priorities,' Center for Full Employment and Equity Working Paper, No. 02–13.

Moore, B.J. (1988), *Horizontalists and Verticalists: The Macroeconomics of Credit Money*, Cambridge, UK: Cambridge University Press.

Moore, B.J. (1991), 'Money supply endogeneity: "reserve price setting" or "reserve quantity setting"?' *Journal of Post Keynesian Economics*, **13** (3), 404–13.

Rezende, F. (2009), 'The nature of government finance in Brazil,' *International Journal of Political Economy*, **38** (1), 81–104.

Rochon, L.-P. and M. Vernengo (2003), 'State money and the real world: or chartalism and its discontents,' *Journal of Post Keynesian Economics*, **26** (1), 57–68.

Tymoigne, E. and L.R. Wray (2013), 'Modern money theory 101: a reply to critics,' *Levy Economics Institute of Bard College Working Paper*, No. 778.

Wray, L.R. (1998), *Understanding Modern Money: The Key to Full Employment and Price Stability*, Cheltenham, UK, and Northampton, MA, USA: Edward Elgar.

Wray, L.R. (2012), *Modern Money Theory: A Primer for Macroeconomics for Sovereign Monetary Systems*, Basingstoke, UK, and New York: Palgrave Macmillan.

Central banking

Two aspects of central banking have been of particular interest to economists. The first is historical and concerns the circumstances under which central banks were established, their legislative foundations, and their accumulation of additional roles through time. The second is analytical and is often approached by comparing the operation of monetary systems with central banks to those without them (so called free-banking systems). A number of valuable treatments of central banking combine both aspects (see, for instance, Goodhart, 1988).

FLAVIA DANTAS / PETER DOCHERTY

Whichever aspect is on view, a common set of questions tends to be asked. What is it that central banks do? How did central banks come to perform these functions? Which of them should central banks continue to perform, and which could be performed by other institutions? Should central banks be independent of executive government? Post-Keynesian economists have distinctive answers to these questions.

Central banks have historically performed a range of functions including: banker to the government; issuing and managing national currencies including their exchange with foreign currencies; acting as the bankers' bank; maintaining financial stability; operating national payments systems; conducting monetary policy; and regulating commercial banks (see Mishkin, 2019, pp. 370–71). Post-Keynesian economists stress the stability-enhancing function of central banks, but also have distinctive views about the objectives for monetary policy and how these objectives are achieved.

The central bank's role in promoting financial stability follows from post-Keynesian beliefs about the inherent instability of unregulated banking. This view is associated most closely with Minsky's financial instability hypothesis (Minsky, 1982, pp. 59–70, 90–116; see Goodhart, 1988, pp. 47–55). The problem with unregulated banking is that competitive pressures can periodically lead banks to overextend credit. This generates higher borrower debt-to-income ratios, increased speculative activity, more optimistic expectations for the future course of asset prices, and asset price inflation. If asset price expectations are suddenly revised downwards or interest rates rise, loan defaults can increase and banks can be placed under financial stress, and this can lead to bank failures with negative effects on both output and employment.

During such periods of crisis, there is a difference between the interests of individual banks and those of the banking system as a whole. It is in the interest of individual banks to hoard liquidity, since depositors may withdraw funds from banks in which they have lost confidence, and banks may need liquid resources to repay these deposits. It is, however, in the interest of the system as a whole that solvent banks experiencing deposit withdrawals are able to borrow liquidity to allay depositor fears. Central banks should, therefore, lend freely to such institutions according to post-Keynesian economists, to prevent widespread bank failure (Dow, 2017). While private banks in a free-banking system may recognize the value of lending to competitors in such circumstances, this will cause conflicts of interest as lenders impose restrictions on borrowers to reduce the moral hazard of future over-lending (Goodhart, 1988, pp. 57–75). Lender-of-last-resort lending should thus be provided by a public institution that is above such competitive concerns (Goodhart, 1988, p. 53; Dow and Smithin, 1999, pp. 80–84).

Once the importance of this stability-enhancing function of central banks has been understood, the possibility of its monetary policy function follows. If banks are required to hold liquid reserves at the central bank as part of the regulatory framework that follows from stability-enhancement, a demand for liquidity during normal times is created. The central bank is then able to affect the price and availability of such liquidity, and these are the traditional tools of monetary policy.

Post-Keynesian economists have distinctive views about the objectives of monetary policy and its transmission to the rest of the economy, stressing the importance of full employment and the role of income distribution in the way monetary policy affects the macroeconomy (Rochon and Setterfield, 2007). The stability-enhancing function also suggests that central banks are the appropriate body to regulate commercial banks (Docherty, 2008, pp. 101–3). This follows from the need to manage the moral hazard created by the provision of emergency liquidity support to commercial banks during crises (Dow, 2017, p. 1548).

The orthodox case for making central banks independent from executive government rests on the assertions that inflation is caused by excess money supply, that managing this problem should be the primary goal of monetary policy, and that elected governments will be tempted to ignore this goal in favour of generating economic growth and reduced unemployment at convenient points in the electoral cycle. Post-Keynesian economists reject the principle of money neutrality upon which this case is built, and this leaves open the possibility of alternative monetary policy objectives. Post-Keynesian economists assert that these should include full employment but this is legitimately a matter for social and political determination, suggesting that central banks need not be independent of executive government.

PETER DOCHERTY

Aspromourgos (2011, p. 644), however, observes that central bank independence is not necessarily anti-democratic, provided that the central bank remains under the ultimate authority of the legislature.

Recognizing the role of a publically operated central bank for the promotion of financial stability and full employment is thus an important dimension of post-Keynesian economics.

PETER DOCHERTY

See also

Central bank independence; Financial instability hypothesis; Lender of last resort; Monetary policy; Monetary policy transmission mechanism

References

Aspromourgos, A. (2011), 'Can (and should) monetary policy pursue a zero real interest rate, permanently?', *Metroeconomica*, **62** (4), 635–55.

Docherty, P. (2008), 'Basel II and the political economy of banking regulation-monetary policy interaction', *International Journal of Political Economy*, **37** (2), 82–106.

Dow, S.C. (2017), 'Central banking in the twenty-first century', *Cambridge Journal of Economics*, **41** (6), 1539–57.

Dow, S.C. and J. Smithin (1999), 'The structure of financial markets and the 'first principles' of monetary economics', *Scottish Journal of Political Economy*, **46** (1), 72–90.

Goodhart, C.A.E. (1988), *The Evolution of Central Banks*, Cambridge, MA: MIT Press.

Minsky, H.P. (1982), *Can 'It' Happen Again? Essays on Instability and Finance*, Armonk, NY: M.E. Sharpe.

Mishkin, F.S. (2019), *The Economics of Money, Banking and Financial Markets*, twelfth edition, New York and London: Pearson.

Rochon, L.-P. and M. Setterfield (2007), 'Interest rates, income distribution, and monetary policy dominance: Post Keynesians and the "fair rate" of interest', *Journal of Post Keynesian Economics*, **30** (1), 13–42.

Central banking – developing economies

The greater majority of central banks in developing countries are molded on the norms and legislation of those of developed countries. Their monetary policy strategies are limited to maintaining price stability and ensuring the adequate functioning of the payments system. The political and instrument independence of central banks provides the required credibility to achieve their stated objectives.

However, there are glaring differences between developed and developing economies, which severely undermine the adequate transplantation and application of the monetary policies strategies followed by developed countries. A key difference is that developing countries do not issue an internationally acceptable means of payment (an international reserve currency). This limits to a great extent the countercyclical role of monetary policy.

An expansionary monetary policy, through a decline in interest rates or an increase in the money supply, seeking to bring output in line with its potential level, can be short-cut due to an ensuing disequilibrium in the balance of payments. Owing to their narrow productive and export base, most developing countries are highly dependent on imports of goods and services. As a result, the behaviour of imports is highly sensitive to any increase in income, even below full-employment conditions.

Any expected depreciation of the nominal exchange rate may not lead to increased exports to help correct the current account deficit or lead to increased economic growth. Even if the nominal exchange rate translates into a depreciation of the real exchange rate, its short-term effects on exports of goods and services may be negligible, as these are in general invoiced in a foreign currency. Thus, the adjustment tends to fall on the imports side. Also, given the high imports content of investment, a depreciation of the nominal exchange rate increases imports costs and thus discourages the purchase of foreign machinery and equipment with detrimental effects for medium- and long-term economic growth.

At the same time, a depreciating exchange rate can have significant detrimental financial effects. To the extent that local assets issued in domestic currency are held by foreign investors, a depreciation of the exchange rate will translate into a capital loss and prompt greater risk perceptions and, in the absence of a reversal in monetary policy, induce capital outflows.

Besides having inflationary consequences (in developing economies inflation is driven to a great extent by costs), a depreciation of the exchange rate can also affect the balance sheet of the economic agents and in particular of the general government and the non-financial corporate sector.

Total external debt represents roughly 62 percent of the gross domestic product of developing economies and emerging markets (Institute for International Finance, 2020). Depreciation not only raises debt service costs, and outgoings, but also swells liabilities by increasing the local-currency value of outstanding debt. If the collateral for the debt is denominated in local currency, a depreciation will also cause this asset to lose value. In the case of the non-financial corporate sector this can aggravate the existing currency mismatch that has increased since 2007 for most developing regions (Chui et al., 2016). In order to protect themselves, firms must purchase foreign currencies to balance their accounts. Depending on their size and importance in the market and the number of firms behaving in this way, currency purchases can create further pressure for devaluation of the nominal exchange rate, ultimately increasing the external debt of the firms operating in the non-tradable goods sector.

At the same time, the subordinate role of developing economies in the international currency hierarchy can aggravate the intensity of contractionary monetary policies. Developing economies must provide a risk premium to foreign investors to hold assets in the local currencies of developing economies. In the face of capital outflows and currency depreciation, the required increase in the domestic rate of interest must be higher than that warranted by interest parity theorems (the difference between the domestic and international rate of interest must equal the exchange rate depreciation plus the risk premium).

The role of currency subordination is manifest in developing countries' increased accumulation of international reserves and central banks' recurrent interventions in the spot, forward and derivative markets as part of their monetary policy frameworks (Borio, 2019).

ESTEBAN PÉREZ CALDENTEY

See also

Central bank independence; Exchange rates; Foreign-exchange reserves; Inflation – cost-push; Monetary policy

References

Borio, C. (2019), 'Monetary policy frameworks in EMEs: inflation targeting, the exchange rate and financial stability,' *Bank for International Settlements Annual Economic Report 2019*, Basel: Bank for International Settlements, pp. 31–53.

Chui, M., E. Kuruc and P. Turner (2016), 'A new dimension to currency mismatches in the emerging markets: non-financial companies', *Bank for International Settlements Working Paper*, No. 550.

Institute for International Finance (2020), *Global Debt Monitor: Attack of the Debt Tsunami*, Washington, DC: Institute for International Finance.

Chicago School

When economists mention the 'Chicago School' of economics, they refer to both geography and intellectual or ideological ideas. Indeed, the heart of this school is the Department of Economics at the University of Chicago, and it is therefore known as the 'Chicago School'.

However, the evolution of the Chicago School generally had three phases. The 'old school' was developed in the 1930s and 1940s, with Frank Knight, Jacob Viner and Henry Simons. Nevertheless, it was with the 'new/second school' of the 1950s and 1960s, whose main proponents were Milton Friedman (1976 Nobel Prize) and George Stigler (1982 Nobel Prize), that the theoretical apparatus of monetarism, underpinning many economic policies implemented in Chile, the United States and the United Kingdom in the 1980s, took shape. Finally, the 'third school' extended into microeconomics, macroeconomics and finance with Gary Becker (1992 Nobel Prize), Robert Lucas (1995 Nobel Prize) and Eugene Fama (2013 Nobel Prize), respectively.

Throughout its history, the expansion of the Chicago School and its growing intellectual hegemony have been supported by private funds, sponsoring either conservative pro-free-market research (Volker Fund) or research linked to the financial industry: in 1960, thanks to a grant from Merrill Lynch, the Center for Research in Security Prices (CRSP) was established as an integral part of the University of Chicago. The CRSP played a pivotal role in the development of financial economics as a sub-discipline. Fischer Black and Myron Scholes (1997 Nobel Prize) were directors of the CRSP. Its success provided the theoretical apparatus underpinning the increasing dominance of finance in the economy, development of the derivatives market and financial deregulation.

Throughout its evolution, the Chicago School has maintained its hostility towards alternative paradigms, including the imperfect competition approach and, infamously, the Keynesian Revolution. However, while the first school aimed to accommodate them within the theoretical scaffolding of neoclassical theory, the second one, in its opposition to the possibility of market failures, evolved along two clearly distinct and interrelated paths that underpinned the intellectual hegemonic character of the Chicago School and paved the way to neoliberalism: one was Friedman's theoretical system aimed at the condemnation of aggregate demand stabilizing fiscal and monetary intervention; the other one extended the neoclassical paradigm – examples are the theories of human capital (Gary Becker and Theodore W. Schultz), property rights and transaction costs (Ronald H. Coase) (see Fonseca, 2021). Its research agenda was then dubbed as imperialist, as a result of its venturing into other fields of social sciences and based on the idea that the economic approach is the only one 'in social sciences which explains a wide range of human behaviour' (Brenner, 1980, p. 180). This second school then represented the last stronghold against the Keynesian Revolution.

The new (or second) Chicago School emerged as an alternative to the neoclassical synthesis and developed with both a complete adhesion to the assumptions of the marginalist tradition and from the monetarist critique to Keynes. First, methodologically, economics is seen as the study of (rational) behaviour in a relationship between ends and scarce means, subject to alternative uses. Second, the stability of various functions is a pivotal assumption that allows for explanation and predictability, even within the School, at the expense of realism (Friedman, 1953); more specifically, Friedman (1956), known as the 'modern quantity theorist', maintained that the velocity of circulation of money is a stable function of the rate of return of various assets (Chick, 1973). Third, money supply is assumed to be exogenous and non-neutral only in the short run. In the long run, it affects only the general price level (vertical Phillips curve). Therefore, monetary and fiscal policies aiming to support aggregate demand might even be destabilizing in the short run.

However, within the third school, Lucas (1972), in unifying rational expectations and the notion of markets in continued equilibrium, maintained that agents anticipate the effects of policy interventions. As a result, the Phillips curve becomes vertical also in the short run. Only those economic policies that surprise agents are effective.

There was a debate on whether Lucas and Sargent and the 'new classical' school could be called 'monetarists' or should they be distinguished from Friedman's monetarism. A central difference between the two is that Friedman was a (self-declared) Marshallian while the 'new classical' economists were Walrasians. This difference is, according to Friedman himself (see Hoover, 1984), much relevant in terms of methodology as it is in terms of a different approach to the very identity of economics as a discipline and of the economic problem: the Marshallian partial equilibrium is 'an engine for the discovery of concrete thrusts' (Friedman, 1949, p. 490). The Walrasian general equilibrium is, for Friedman, a comprehensive structure characterized by mathematical elegance. However, despite Friedman's critiques to new classical economics, the third school is seen as an extension of Friedman.

Post-Keynesian economists of the Cambridge School responded, first, methodologically, by rejecting the marginalist consumer sovereignty and stressing the importance of entrepreneurs' expectations and the central role of monetary and financial variables. This overturned the relationship between microeconomics and macroeconomics, and established macroeconomic foundations for microeconomics (see Roncaglia, 2019). Second, they re-emphasized the volatility of entrepreneurs' expectations in terms of both returns on investment projects and in determining the effective demand and future interest rates, pivotal for the speculative demand for money, which is the largest and most unstable component of the demand for money. Third, money supply is endogenously credit-driven, and financial institutions have a predominant role (Kaldor, 1982). Fourth, for post-Keynesian economists, money is non-neutral, and the notion of self-equilibrating markets is rejected: expectations and liquidity preference affect the rate of interest and the investment level, which, via the multiplier, determine income and employment. As a consequence, monetary policy should target the interest rate and not the money supply, unlike in the quantity theory of money. Money is non-neutral in both the short and long run. Post-Keynesian economists reject long-run economic analysis in that sense: the long run is a series of short-run periods (Robinson, 1956).

In terms of policy prescriptions, then, not only should interventions provide liquidity during crises, but financial institutions and operators should also be continuously monitored and regulated, to reduce the transmission mechanisms of crises (Minsky, 1986).

LUIGI VENTIMIGLIA

See also

Endogenous money; Liquidity preference; Monetary policy; Money illusion; Phillips curve

References

Brenner, R. (1980), 'Economics – An imperialist science?', *Journal of Legal Studies*, **9** (1), 179–88.
Chick, V. (1973), *The Theory of Monetary Policy*, London: Gray-Mills.
Fonseca, G. (2021), *The Chicago School*, available online at https://www.hetwebsite.net/het/schools/chicago.htm (last accessed 17 March 2021).
Friedman, M. (1949), 'The Marshallian demand curve', *Journal of Political Economy*, **57** (4), 463–95.
Friedman, M. (1953), *Essays in Positive Economics*, Chicago: University of Chicago Press.
Friedman, M. (1956), 'The quantity theory of money: a restatement', in M. Friedman (ed.), *Studies in the Quantity Theory of Money*, Chicago: University of Chicago Press, pp. 3–21.
Hoover, K.D. (1984), 'Two types of monetarism', *Journal of Economic Literature*, **22** (1), 58–76.
Kaldor, N. (1982), *The Scourge of Monetarism*, Oxford: Oxford University Press.
Lucas, R.E. (1972), 'Expectations and the neutrality of money', *Journal of Economic Theory*, **4** (2), 103–24.
Minsky, H.P. (1986), *Stabilizing an Unstable Economy*, Yale: Yale University Press.
Robinson, J. (1956), *The Accumulation of Capital*, London and New York: Palgrave Macmillan.
Roncaglia, A. (2019), *L'età della disgregazione: storia del pensiero economico contemporaneo*, Rome: Laterza.

Clearing balances

'The deposits of the bank of the dealer at the central bank are what mainstream authors call reserves; central bankers now refer instead to clearing balances or settlement balances' (Lavoie and Seccareccia, 2016, p. 110). As defined in Part 204.3 (v) of the US Code of Federal Regulations, 'clearing balance means the average balance held in an account at the Federal Reserve Bank by an institution over a reserve maintenance period to satisfy its contractual clearing balance with a Reserve Bank' (Office of the Federal Register, National Archives and Records Administration, 2011, p. 108). More generally, banking institutions ranging from small retail depositories to big money centre banks maintain clearing balances in their account at the local central bank. However, interestingly enough, 'in addition to complying with a Federal Reserve System regulation for holding a required reserve balance, many banks simultaneously meet an additional requirement to hold a clearing balance in their account at a Federal Reserve Bank' (Stevens, 1993, p. 2).

Hence, depository institutions could voluntarily decide prior to 12 July 2012 to hold such types of balances in their account at the Federal Reserve in addition to obligatory reserve requirements. According to Naber et al. (2017, Internet), there were at least four reasons explaining the phenomenon of complying with additional contractual and self-determined reserve requirements:

1. a preference by some banks to pay for Federal Reserve service charges with earning credits, which has in fact been possible since 1981. Therefore, 'these credits [are used] to defray the cost of the Federal Reserve services it uses, such as check clearing and wire transfers of funds and securities' (Board of Governors of the Federal Reserve System, 2005, p. 31);
2. contribution of clearing balances to maintain reserve balances at a desired level;
3. rates offered on clearing balances sometimes seen as particularly interesting;
4. additional motives like decisional inertia.

As these four points indicate, clearing balances are attractive for economic, policy-related and behavioural reasons. At the same time, the demand for Federal Reserve balances is made of required reserve balances, contractual clearing balances and excess reserve balances. According to Bennett et al. (1997, p. 108), the rising amount of clearing balances – mainly, in order to earn implicit interests – has not been accompanied by a comparable trend in total account balances, which have in some cases even declined over the past years. Hence, required clearing balances contribute to the accumulation of 'earning credits', which can be used to pay for services without affecting reserve balances. 'The clearing balances held by an institution generate earnings credits, which may be used to offset the cost of eligible Federal Reserve services. Earning credits are applied to an institution's monthly billing service charges' (Federal Reserve Bank of Philadelphia, 2008, Internet). If such payments for services were on the contrary to be directly charged to the bank's reserve account, then reserve balances would shrink as explained by the Federal Reserve Bank of Chicago (1994, p. 22). Until January 2004 the interest rate accruing to contractual clearing balances was the Federal Funds rate, although at that point it was changed to '90% of the yield on the 3-month Treasury bill, a change that reduced the earnings credit rate slightly. The rate was changed again in January 2005 to 80% of the yield on the 3-month Treasury bill' (Carpenter and Demiralp, 2008, p. 6). The fact that institutions have decided to progressively redirect funds toward contractual clearing balances is, therefore, mainly because – unlike excess reserves (namely funds exceeding banks' reserve requirements) – the earning credits deriving from contractual clearing balances can be used to offset eligible Federal Reserve service charges. More generally, according to Croushore (2007, p. 242), banks keep clearing balances to allow for a simplified reconciliation of accounts across banks.

EDOARDO BERETTA

See also

Central banking; Monetary policy; Money and banking; Settlement balances; Settlement system

References

Bennett, P., S. Hilton and B. Madigan (1997), 'Implementing US monetary policy with low reserve requirements', *Bank for International Settlements Conference Paper*, No. 3, pp. 107–20.
Board of Governors of the Federal Reserve System (2005), *The Federal Reserve System: Purposes & Functions (Ninth Edition)*, Washington, DC: Board of Governors of the Federal Reserve System.
Carpenter, S. and S. Demiralp (2008), 'The liquidity effect in the Federal Funds market: evidence at the monthly frequency', *Journal of Money, Credit and Banking*, **40** (1), 1–24.
Croushore, D. (2007), *Money and Banking. A Policy-Oriented Approach*, Boston and New York: Houghton Mifflin Company.
Federal Reserve Bank of Chicago (1994), *Modern Money Mechanics: A Workbook on Bank Reserves and Deposit Expansion*, Chicago: Federal Reserve Bank of Chicago.
Federal Reserve Bank of Philadelphia (2008), *Contractual Clearing Balances – Fact Sheet*, Philadelphia: Federal Reserve Bank of Philadelphia, available online at https://www.philadelphiafed.org/-/media/bank-resources/forms/clearing_balance_fact_sheet.pdf.
Lavoie, M. and M. Seccareccia (2016), 'Money and banking', in L.-P. Rochon and S. Rossi (2016), *An Introduction to Macroeconomics: A Heterodox Approach to Economic Analysis*, Cheltenham, UK, and Northampton, MA, USA: Edward Elgar, pp. 97–116.
Naber, J.M., R. Sambasivam and M.-F. Styczynski (2017), 'Demand for voluntary balance requirements: the U.S. experience with contractual clearing balances from 2000 to 2007', *FEDS Notes*, Washington, DC: Board of Governors of the Federal Reserve System, January 4.
Office of the Federal Register, National Archives and Records Administration (2011), *Code of Federal Regulations – Title 12 (Banks and Banking) – Parts 200 to 2019, Revised as of January 1, 2011*, Washington, DC: US Government Printing Office.
Stevens, E.J. (1993), 'Required clearing balances', *Federal Reserve Bank of Cleveland, Economic Review*, **29** (4), 2–14.

Common currency area

Analysing official dollarization, Edwards (2001, p. 250) notes, 'this rather drastic piece of advice – giving up the national currency – is being dispensed on the basis of very limited empirical and historical evidence.' Looking at the evolution of Common Currency Areas (CCAs) leaves one thinking similar thoughts. On the one hand, many countries are now CCA members, while, on the other hand, evidence about performance is scant, especially for the pre-euro decades, and one often has to fall back on theory to make sense of the limited experience. The severity and duration of the euro-area crisis have reinvigorated interest in CCA issues.

CCAs are defined as regions that (1) share a currency but not a fiscal authority or national government, and (2) have a formal voice in the setting of CCA monetary policy. Given these criteria, CCA member countries, according to Hagan and Bredenkamp (2018), now constitute over 15 per cent of the global economy. The four major CCAs are the Central African Economic and Monetary Community, the West African Economic and Monetary Union, the Eastern Caribbean Currency Union, and the European Monetary Union (EMU).

A substantial body of theoretical literature explores the pros and cons of CCAs, much of which, starting with Mundell (1961), involves the theory of Optimum Currency Areas (OCAs). Arguments in favour of such arrangements include increased microeconomic efficiency, lower transaction costs, elimination of risk of speculative attacks on national currencies, enhanced inflation-fighting credibility, development of the banking system, reduced risk premia on bonds, lower real interest rates, and denser trade linkages between members. Arguments against include the loss of monetary sovereignty and seigniorage, absence of exchange-rate-based stabilization, limited space for a domestic lender of last resort, and the inability to use the inflation tax in exceptional circumstances.

The loss of the stabilizing functions of national monetary policy and exchange rates becomes costlier in the presence of nominal rigidities and asymmetric shocks. Coping mechanisms could take the form of intermember factor mobility, wage and price flexibility, and within-union fiscal transfers (Mundell, 1961), high levels of trade integration (McKinnon, 1963), or a diversified economic structure (Kenen, 1969). Whether or not these criteria are endogenous is itself controversial. For example, some have argued that monetary integration may foster intra-industry trade, make inter-member relative price changes more effective, promote business-cycle synchronization, and reduce exposure to asymmetric real shocks. Meeting the preconditions for an OCA may, therefore, be a less pressing concern. Krugman (1993), by contrast, argues that reduced transaction costs will lead countries to become more specialized in their comparative advantage sectors. An implication is that integration will raise the likelihood of members experiencing sector-specific asymmetric shocks.

The costs of union membership may be higher from a post-Keynesian perspective, however, and indeed Arestis and Sawyer (2001) have argued that currency unions induce a deflationary bias. For one, contrary to assumptions underlying much mainstream analysis, hysteresis may make the effects of demand shocks more persistent. This, in turn, makes the unavailability of counter-cyclical stabilization costlier. Exchange rate movements may be effective if the extreme Keynesian assumption of producer currency pricing is to be believed, although one would have to counterbalance this with the reluctance of developing economies to let their currencies freely adjust due to the 'fear of floating'. Finally, the lack of exchange rate adjustment and national-level monetary coordination implies that the favourable view of fiscal policy traditionally taken by post-Keynesian economists needs to be qualified.

Consider EMU circumstances in 2011: countries with high unemployment (say Spain) may have found it desirable to fiscally expand relative to low unemployment countries (say Germany). However, Germany had experienced current account surpluses and Spain was a deficit country. In the absence of exchange rate adjustment, this national fiscal mix will then magnify external imbalances and instability. In this sense, fiscal efficacy may increase the costs of exchange rate inflexibility. One must note, however, that cost-push inflation, not significantly influenced by monetary aggregates, makes the loss of monetary sovereignty and the implied benefits from discipline less significant.

Recent EMU experience has re-energized old debates. While initially bond markets integrated rapidly, inflation differentials persisted and greater capital-market integration appears not to have led to the expected benefits from risk diffusion. Moreover, country-based risk premia made a dramatic comeback following global financial problems in 2008–09. While inter-member countries' labour mobility increased, evidence suggests that the initial frictions relative to US regions appear to have survived. Moreover, the lack of fiscal union and a lender of last resort has taken its toll, while member countries have not proven immune to current account issues. CCAs remain vulnerable to the problems experienced by fixed exchange rate regimes since the gold standard, and post-Keynesian emphasis on the use of policy instruments for stabilization remains as relevant as ever.

ARSLAN RAZMI

ARSLAN RAZMI

See also

Dollarization; European Monetary Union; Hysteresis; Inflation – cost-push; Lender of last resort

References

Arestis, P. and M. Sawyer (2001), 'Will the euro bring economic crisis to Europe?', in P. Arestis, M. Baddeley and J. McCombie (eds), *What Global Economic Crisis?*, London: Palgrave Macmillan, pp. 78–103.
Edwards, S. (2001). 'Dollarization: myths and realities', *Journal of Policy Modeling*, 23 (3), 249–65.
Hagan, S. and H. Bredenkamp (2018), 'A framework for currency unions and IMF lending', *International Monetary Fund Blog*, 16 March, available online at https://blogs.imf.org/2018/03/16/a-framework-for-currency-unions-and-imf-lending/; last accessed 4 April 2019.
Kenen, P.B. (1969), 'The optimum currency area: an eclectic view', in R.A. Mundell and A.K. Swoboda (eds), *Monetary Problems of the International Economy*, Chicago, IL: University of Chicago Press, pp. 41–60.
Krugman, P. (1993), 'Lessons of Massachusetts for EMU', in F. Torres and F. Giavazzi (eds), *Adjustment and Growth in the European Monetary Union*, Cambridge, UK: Cambridge University Press, pp. 241–69.
McKinnon, R.I. (1963), 'Optimum currency areas', *American Economic Review*, 53 (4), 717–25.
Mundell, R.A. (1961), 'A theory of optimum currency areas', *American Economic Review*, 51 (4), 657–65.

Compensation thesis

The compensation thesis is a theoretical approach with respect to money creation, central bank intervention and exchange rate policy, which is presented by its proponents as an alternative to the standard adjustment mechanism in an open economy with fixed or managed exchange rates (Lavoie, 2001, 2014, Ch. 7; Serrano and Summa, 2015; Angrick, 2017). It revolves around two main claims: (1) the interest rate is exogenous and its level is determined by the central bank, regardless of the exchange rate regime; and (2) in the specific case of a fixed exchange rate regime, the central bank can have control over its domestic interest rate only if it has already acquired a large enough stock of foreign reserves or if it can easily obtain them. Those expected outcomes depend on the particular views about interest rate and exchange rate determination upon which this approach is based.

Concerning the first claim, interest rate targeting happens for the same reasons it does in a closed economy. As soon as any inflow of foreign currency gets transferred into domestic currency, the operations of the central bank are directed toward day-to-day liquidity management with the purpose of setting the level of the base rate of interest. The operations of the central bank are treated along the lines of the monetary policy implementation literature (Bindseil, 2004; Fullwiler, 2017). Various components on the central bank balance sheet are expected to compensate for an increased domestic liquidity in the system, whether it comes from an increase in foreign reserves (which reflects open-economy and exchange-rate considerations) or from any other autonomous factor. The exact components at play depend on the monetary policy implementation framework set in place in a specific country. An increase in foreign reserves may be compensated by a reduction in credits to the domestic economy (government securities or advances to banks), or by an increase in government deposits at the central bank or in the issuance of central bank bills.

Concerning the second claim, as long as the central bank can supply the demanded foreign currency for a given exchange rate level, it can defend the parity of its choice. The central bank can supply this quantity if it has enough foreign reserves available or if it can easily obtain a swap or a public loan in foreign currency. Therefore, while the stock of foreign reserves available could not influence the exchange rate or the interest rate at a given moment, it could rather impose a policy constraint on the level those two variables can take for a given period of time. That being said, a country that accumulates foreign reserves as a result of strong exports would be expected to be less constrained by the policy choice of these two levels than a country that depends on foreign indebtedness to provide for this stock of foreign reserves. This buffer would allow for a range of possible combinations of those two levels, without any direct link between them and possibly driven by different policy objectives that the central bank could have.

The basis of the approach is the question of money creation, and the absence of the automatic adjustment comes as a result of money being considered demand-led and endogenous. Its conclusions apply only to the cases where the reflux mechanism is at play. The interest rate in question is the base rate of the central bank, a very short-term rate on its liabilities. The possibility of other rates being affected by capital flows, such as the long-term rate or any other rate out of direct control of the central bank, could still exist (Taylor, 2004, 2008; Lavoie, 2021).

There are a few studies that attempted to empirically test the compensation thesis (Lavoie and Wang, 2012; Angrick, 2017). This strand of literature tests for long-term relationships between foreign reserves and the separate components of the balance sheet that can have a compensating role, as recalled above, and between foreign reserves and the monetary base. What is important to point out is that, following the theoretical interpretation, only the components in domestic currency could have a compensating role and those are the only operations this interpretation could be applied to. The foreign inflows that do not get transferred into domestic currency would not increase central bank reserves, thus there would be no need for a compensating measure for the purpose of interest rate targeting. The interpretation of the relationship between foreign reserves and the monetary base could be more ambiguous; as both variables have different determinants, there is a possibility that they could move in the same or opposite directions without it having any influence on the process of money creation.

SIMONA BOZHINOVSKA

See also

Central banking; Endogenous money; Exchange rates – fixed vs flexible; Money creation – nature of; Reflux mechanism

References

Angrick, S. (2018), 'Global liquidity and monetary policy autonomy: an examination of open-economy policy constraints', *Cambridge Journal of Economics*, **42** (1), 117–35.
Bindseil, U. (2004), *Monetary Policy Implementation: Theory, Past, and Present*, Oxford: Oxford University Press.
Fullwiler, S. (2017), 'Modern central-bank operations: the general principles', in L.-P. Rochon and S. Rossi (eds), *Advances in Endogenous Money Analysis*, Cheltenham, UK, and Northampton, MA, USA: Edward Elgar, pp. 50–87.
Lavoie, M. (2001), 'The reflux mechanism in the open economy', in L.-P. Rochon and M. Vernengo (eds), *Credit, Growth and the Open Economy*, Cheltenham, UK and Northampton, MA, USA: Edward Elgar, pp. 215–42.
Lavoie, M. (2014), *Post-Keynesian Economics: New Foundations*, Cheltenham, UK, and Northampton, MA, USA: Edward Elgar.
Lavoie, M. (2021), 'Two post-Keynesian approaches to international finance: the compensation thesis and the cambist view', in B. Bonizzi, A. Kaltenbrunner and R. Ramos (eds), *Emerging Economies and the Global Financial System*, London and New York: Routledge, pp. 14–27.
Lavoie, M. and P. Wang (2012), 'The "compensation" thesis, as exemplified by the case of the Chinese central bank', *International Review of Applied Economics*, **26** (3), 287–301.
Serrano, F. and R. Summa (2015), 'Mundell–Fleming without the LM curve: the exogenous interest rate in an open economy', *Review of Keynesian Economics*, **3** (2), 248–68.
Taylor, L. (2004), 'Exchange rate indeterminacy in portfolio balance, Mundell–Fleming and uncovered interest rate parity models', *Cambridge Journal of Economics*, **28** (2), 205–27.
Taylor, L. (2008), 'A foxy hedgehog: Wynne Godley and macroeconomic modelling', *Cambridge Journal of Economics*, **32** (4), 639–63.

Complex systems

A complex system can be defined as a system composed of different parts or sub-parts whose interaction among themselves and with the environment gives rise to emergent forms of behaviour.

Complex systems are normally characterized by strong heterogeneity, feedback effects, nonlinearities, and path dependency (time is non-reversible). The analysis of complex systems focuses on how agents with limited information in a context of uncertainty coordinate to generate a particular set of emergent properties.

The components and sub-components of complex systems display structural and behavioural heterogeneity. They interact among each other, usually at local level, according to a (possibly time-variant) network topology. As a result of their interaction they may spontaneously organize in clusters or in hierarchal structures. A further consequence of the interaction is that agents dynamically evolve through learning and adaptation. Agents retain the characteristics that are necessary for survival and innovate in order to survive in a dynamically evolving environment. The interaction determines feedback effects that in turn can originate nonlinearities. The resulting uncertainty about the possible evolution of the system and the fact that each agent has only a partial view of the system and a limited information set imply a level of rationality that is typically different from full rationality as defined in economics.

A further consequence of interaction and the resulting nonlinearities is the absence of a predefined or predictable macro-dynamics. Aggregate outcomes emerge from micro-level interactions and are therefore defined as emergent properties: they cannot be inferred from the behaviour of the system's individual components. Moreover, there can be no (spontaneous) tendency toward a Nash equilibrium, given the different possible evolution paths, and a multiplicity of possible final states or attractors is possible.

Emergent properties in complex systems display a fractal structure: every subset of results replicates the statistical properties of the whole, at a suitable single level of magnification in case of self-similarity or at dual level of magnification in case of self-affinity. The fractal structure implies the possibility of extreme events, defined as sudden transitions of larger magnitude than previous transformations ('punctuated dynamics' as defined by Sornette, 2006). These transitions are the result of self-organized criticality (Bak, 1996): the spontaneous organization of a system in a critical state that is modified by external factors, originating phase-transition events that display a fractal structure.

The behaviour of systems revealing self-organized criticality has been studied in the so-called sand-pile experiments, in which a series of regular and homogenous exogenous shocks hitting a system generates transitions that are different in size and occur at irregular time intervals. These events are defined as avalanches and their distribution is power law. The power law probability distribution function for a quantity x can be expressed as:

$$p(x) = \left(\tfrac{x}{x_0}\right)^{-\alpha} \qquad (1)$$

where x_0 is the minimum value for which a power law tail emerges (threshold or scale parameter) and α is the slope parameter.

The power law distribution is scale-invariant: independently from the size of any event $x_1 > x_0$, the proportion of events larger than x_1 follows an invariant scaling law according to the slope coefficient of the power law distribution α. The emergence of a power law distribution is therefore a consequence of the fractal structure of the system's emergent properties. This type of distribution can account for extreme (rare) events. Its emergence is due to a range of different possible stochastic processes and in general signals the presence of self-organizing criticality.

Power law distributions are ubiquitous in economics and finance: they have been detected for example for firms' size, individual income, firms' bankruptcies, countries' GDP, and stock returns. Other economic phenomena can be interpreted as a consequence of self-organizing criticality; for example, the fact that firms' heterogeneity persists through time in terms of technology, productivity, profits, and growth rates (Dosi et al., 2010) and there is no evidence of reversal to the mean. Also, innovations do not emerge following a continuous homogeneous process but can rather be characterized as avalanches: they are clustered in time and space, and their size is drawn from a very skewed distribution (Silverberg and Verspagen, 2007).

CORRADO DI GUILMI

See also

Lexicographic preferences; Microfoundations; Neoclassical economics; Power; Uncertainty

References

Bak, P. (1996), *How Nature Works: The Science of Self-Organized Criticality*, New York: Copernicus.

Dosi, G., S. Lechevalier and A. Secchi (2010), 'Introduction: interfirm heterogeneity – nature, sources and consequences for industrial dynamics', *Industrial and Corporate Change*, **19** (6), 1867–90.

Silverberg, G. and B. Verspagen (2007), 'The size distribution of innovations revisited: an application of extreme value statistics to citation and value measures of patent significance', *Journal of Econometrics*, **139** (2), 318–39.

Sornette, D. (2006), *Critical Phenomena in Natural Sciences. Chaos, Fractals, Selforganization and Disorder: Concepts and Tools*, Berlin: Springer.

Consumer behaviour

One area of research where post-Keynesian economics has not made a substantial contribution is consumer behaviour, although few post-Keynesian economists have broached the topic – such as Joan Robinson (1956, 1962), Alfred Eichner (1987), and Marc Lavoie (1994). There are others whose contributions challenge the neoclassical economics view of consumer behaviour, such as James Duesenberry (1949) and Thorstein Veblen (1899/2017). One reason for this neglect is that many post-Keynesian economists are more interested in macroeconomics. Building upon Keynes's *General Theory*, post-Keynesian authors often focus on macroeconomic issues, such as finance, government, and central banking. Consumer theory is also nebulous and getting inside the minds of consumers is outside the area of expertise of most post-Keynesian economists. The overarching assumptions and generalizations made by neoclassical economics about consumer behaviour were never accepted by post-Keynesian authors, but an accepted alternative has not materialized. Behavioural economics is developing a far better alternative to consumer behaviour that many post-Keynesian economists are beginning to accept.

Neoclassical (orthodox) economics has a simplistic model of rational economic human, who makes consumption decisions that account for all known factors, such as substitutes, prices, available income, future income, and so on. This theory of consumer behaviour is known as consumer choice theory, which is composed of three assumptions. First, consumers make purchases to maximize their happiness (that is, utility maximization). Second, consumers have insatiable wants that are never satisfied. Last, people consume up to the point where the marginal benefit of consuming one more good/service equals the marginal cost of that good/service. According to post-Keynesian economists, consumer choice theory is at best a ridiculous oversimplification of consumer decision making and at worst completely wrong.

Lavoie (1994) assimilated earlier post-Keynesian counter-arguments to consumer choice theory. Post-Keynesian economics is pluralist; hence Lavoie (1994) gathered together concepts developed across economic schools of thought and other social sciences. Lavoie (1994) asserts that people in the real world do not have full information about prices, substitutes, and utility maximization. In fact, people often have limited information and limited income that constrains their options to a much narrower field than that supposed by neoclassical economics. Rather than a maximization principle, people's choices are lexicographically ordered according to desirability but also practicality: needs weighed at the bottom progressing to wants up the scale. People must pay for needs (bottom of the scale), then allocate any remainder to wants (next higher level of the scale). Real income affects how far up the consumption scale someone can go. Thus, income is a more important factor in consumption decisions than substitutions.

Duesenberry (1949) found that consumption is more complex than most people realized. He developed the relative income hypothesis (RIH), which has two parts. First, people are quick to increase their consumption when income rises, but are slow to decrease consumption when income falls. One reason for this is that consumer spending involves long-term financial contracts that are hard to break, such as mortgages and car loans. But also, spending becomes a habit that is hard to break, which helps explain the second part of RIH. Duesenberry found that people did not consume according to income only, but rather relative to others in their social circle. Veblen made this observation in his book *The Theory of the Leisure Class*, published in 1899. He found that people want to live one strata above their current income/wealth. Thus, people consume based on their neighbours and also the rich, who set consumer trends with their conspicuous consumption. People do not make consumer decisions in a vacuum; they are always influenced by many other agents.

People's preferences are constantly changing and being manipulated. Thus, no consumer can make a long-term purchase (like a car, coat, or house) knowing how it will maximize their happiness in the future. Post-Keynesian economists assert that the world is non-ergodic, thus the past is not a perfect (or even good) predictor of the future. What you feel about a car today will likely change over the course of ownership. Likewise, even short-term decisions are influenced by many exogenous factors such as advertising (overt or subliminal) and social environments. People are influenced by norms, habits, marketing, and peers.

ROBERT H. SCOTT

An important development to challenge consumer choice theory is behavioural economics. No strong linkage exists between behavioural economics and post-Keynesian economics, but many of the findings of behavioural economics challenge neoclassical foundations. Some important findings are that people are biased and heavily influenced by factors that are irrational and exogenously determined. People often make sub-optimal decisions because of fear, ignorance, social influence, and/or other myriad influences. These robust findings are not new to post-Keynesian economists, but they are putting an end to neoclassical thinking on consumer behaviour.

ROBERT H. SCOTT

See also

Behavioural economics; Lexicographic preferences; Microfoundations; Neoclassical economics; Post-Keynesian economics – a big tent?

References

Duesenberry, J. (1949), *Income, Saving and the Theory of Consumer Behaviour*, Cambridge, MA: Harvard University Press.
Eichner, A. (1987), *The Macrodynamics of Advanced Market Economies*, Armonk, NY: M.E. Sharpe.
Lavoie, M. (1994), 'A Post-Keynesian approach to consumer choice', *Journal of Post Keynesian Economics*, **16** (4), 539–62.
Robinson, J. (1956), *The Accumulation of Capital*, London: Macmillan.
Robinson, J. (1962), *Economic Philosophy*, London: C.A. Watts & Co.
Veblen, T. (1899/2017), *The Theory of the Leisure Class*, London and New York: Routledge.

Consumer choice

Consumer choice theory attempts to explain how individuals make consumption decisions. It was developed during the Marginalist Revolution of the late nineteenth century, and further scrutinized in the mid-twentieth century. It is the entry point and one of the essential features of neoclassical microeconomics; in fact, the entire mainstream macroeconomics is built upon the consumer choice foundations.

According to this view, the consumer is considered to be the most fundamental decision maker in a free-market economy. Placing the consumer choice into the core of microeconomic theory also coincides with the liberal doctrine of consumer sovereignty. Consumers can exercise their power to demand, or not to demand, any goods and services in the market. Hence, their preferences are immediately reflected in the markets and in the allocation of resources.

At theoretical level, the representative individual is assumed to be a rational decision maker whose objective is to maximize her or his utility, subject to a budget constraint. The rationality assumption implies the individual's preference ordering satisfies three key microeconomic axioms: completeness, transitivity, and non-satiation. Only then will there exist a utility function that represents the individual's preferences. Ideally, this needs to be a Cobb–Douglas function, which is twice continuously differentiable, so that the applied calculus does not fail.

The individual then solves a constraint optimization problem that yields her or his optimal consumption bundle. The Walrasian demand function is also derived from this constrained optimization. Virtually, the individual demand curve's downward slope reflects diminishing marginal utility, which is at the heart of all mainstream microeconomic theory. The market demand curve, then, is simply the horizontal summation or aggregation of all individual demand curves. Lastly, in conjunction with the supply function derived out of the profit maximizing behaviour of the competitive curve, equilibrium prices are determined. On that account, consumer choice is one of the essential elements of the mainstream price theory.

For all that rigour and elegance, the neoclassical consumer choice framework fails to be a satisfactory theory. Hyper-rationality is far from explaining how individuals actually behave. Kirman (1992) argues its mathematical convenience and yielding analytically tractable results provide support for the mainstream consumer choice theory. Empirical evidence clearly shows the basic assumptions of rationality are simply false. Friedman (1953), on the other hand, states that the hyper-rationality assumption is plausible, because it explains the data. According to Friedman's epistemology, criticizing the neoclassical model for its unrealistic assumptions is digressive: as long as it explains the data, the model is useful. But then, it is very much possible to build numerous different models that can fit the data. Deciding on which theory to follow boils down to the relevance of their assumptions. Even though neoclassical choice theory yields downward sloping demand curves that roughly fit the data, from a methodological perspective, unrealistic assumptions undermine the validity of theoretical models (Blaug, 1992).

Although the unit of analysis is 'class' in heterodox economics, the post-Keynesian approach gives some illuminating insights into consumer choice. As opposed to the axiomatic approach of neoclassical economics, heterodox economists assert the data at the microeconomic level could, and should, be theorized without unrealistic hyper-rationality assumptions (Shaikh, 2012). Social conventions, habits, heuristics, and rules-of-thumb have more power in explaining consumer choice than optimizing behaviour. Roy (1943), who first advocated the post-Keynesian theory of consumer choice, argued there is a hierarchy of needs that could be represented by lexicographic preferences. Lavoie (1994) has identified six principles of post-Keynesian consumer choice theory: procedural rationality, satiable wants, separability of needs, subordination of needs, growth of needs, and non-independence. Lexicographic preference ordering with satiation thresholds, as suggested by Georgescu-Roegen (1954), serves as a more relevant alternative to the Cobb–Douglas preferences.

ANIL ABA

See also

Behavioural economics; Methodology; Microfoundations; Neoclassical economics; Pricing

References

Blaug, M. (1992), *The Methodology of Economics: Or, How Economists Explain*, Cambridge, UK: Cambridge University Press.
Friedman, M. (1953), 'The methodology of positive economics', in *Essays in Positive Economics*, Chicago, IL: University of Chicago Press, pp. 3–43.
Georgescu-Roegen, N. (1954), 'Choice, expectations and measurability', *Quarterly Journal of Economics*, **68** (4), 503–534.
Kirman, A.P. (1992), 'Whom or what does the representative individual represent?', *Journal of Economic Perspectives*, **6** (2), 117–136.
Lavoie, M. (1994), 'A Post Keynesian approach to consumer choice', *Journal of Post Keynesian Economics*, **16** (4), 539–562.
Roy, R. (1943), 'La hiérarchie des besoins et la notion de groupes dans l'économie de choix', *Econometrica*, **11** (1), 13–24.
Shaikh, A. (2012), 'Rethinking microeconomics: a proposed reconstruction', *Department of Economics Working Paper*, New School for Social Research, No. 6.

Consumption theory

Modern consumption theory emerged to explain the empirical observation that the long-run average propensity to consume (APC) was relatively stable, a fact inconsistent with the simple short-run Keynesian consumption function. Post-Keynesian consumption theory can be identified with two strands of thought: Duesenberry's (1949) relative income hypothesis (RIH), and the class-based models of economic growth and income distribution found in Kaldor (1956) and Pasinetti (1962).

Duesenberry's (1949) RIH was the first attempt to provide a theory explaining the stability of the APC. It relies on the assumption that households are influenced by social and institutional factors like habit and class position – Veblen's (1899/2017) notion of emulation. In this view, the level of consumption is a function of both the level of income and income relative to other households, which suggests households are slow to adjust consumption as their income changes. For example, if income falls, households tend to maintain current consumption patterns by either reducing current savings, consuming out of past savings, increasing the use of debt, or increasing household income by increased labour force participation (for example, a spouse entering the labour force).

The Kaldor and Pasinetti models, derived from Kalecki's profit equation, were developed to explain the factors that determine the profit rate and profit share in the long run. Kaldor (1956) and Pasinetti (1962) start with the assumption of two separate classes of households, namely, capitalists and workers, who consume out of profits and wage income respectively. However, as Pasinetti (1962) showed, the labouring class can be divided further into any number of sub-classes (with their own saving propensities) without affecting the result of the model (the profit share is determined by the spending decisions of the capitalist class).

ANIL ABA / TED P. SCHMIDT

Mainstream consumption theory, based on the assumption of a representative rational household that maximizes consumption relative to expected lifetime income, has been dominated by the well-known theories of Friedman's (1957) permanent income hypothesis, and Modigliani and Brumberg's (1954) life-cycle hypothesis. However, their inability to explain the secular decline in the US personal savings rate from the mid-1970s until the 2008 financial crisis has brought about renewed interest in heterodox views.

Wolff (1981), using wealth distribution data, provided support for the class-based model, concluding that an appropriate model describing savings (or wealth accumulation) behaviour should categorize households into three classes: a capitalist class that owns most of the privately held capital wealth, a primary working class that consists of relatively skilled workers who display life-cycle behaviour, and a secondary working class that consists of less-skilled workers who typically have low or no savings.

More recently, researchers have used post-Keynesian consumption theory to explain both the secular decline in savings and the connection between the rise in inequality and household debt. For example, van Treeck (2014), after summarizing recent behavioural evidence on household consumption that supports the RIH, suggests that a major cause of the global financial crisis was a consequence of households using debt to maintain relative consumption standards as income inequality increased. Mason (2018), however, provides a critique of this view, arguing that the 'debt as a means to maintain living standards' is inconsistent with the fact that much of the debt is associated with the purchase of assets (mainly housing). Schmidt (2018) suggests that the secular decline in the US personal savings rate can be explained using Wolff's class-based model of households, where the secular decline is explained as three distinct periods, each influenced by a different class.

TED P. SCHMIDT

See also

Consumer behaviour; Consumer choice; Financial crises; Income distribution; Kaleckian economics

References

Duesenberry, J. (1949), *Income, Saving and the Theory of Consumption Behavior*, Oxford: Oxford University Press.
Friedman, M. (1957), *A Theory of the Consumption Function*, Princeton: National Bureau of Economic Research.
Kaldor, N. (1956), 'Alternative theories of distribution', *Review of Economic Studies*, **23** (2), 83–100.
Mason, J.W. (2018), 'Income distribution, household debt, and aggregate demand: a critical assessment', *Jerome Levy Economics Institute at Bard College Working Paper*, No. 901.
Modigliani, F. and R. Brumberg (1954), 'Utility analysis and the consumption function: an interpretation of cross-sectional data', in K.K. Kurihara (ed.), *Post-Keynesian Economics*, New Brunswick, NJ: Rutgers University Press, pp. 388–438.
Pasinetti, L. (1962), 'Rate of profit and income distribution in relation to the rate of economic growth', *Review of Economic Studies*, **29** (4), 267–79.
Schmidt, T.P. (2018), 'Does rising inequality explain the secular decline in the US personal savings rate?', paper presented at the URPE 50th Anniversary Conference, University of Massachusetts, Amherst, 28 September.
van Treeck, T. (2014), 'Did inequality cause the U.S. financial crisis?', *Journal of Economic Surveys*, **28** (3), 421–48.
Veblen, T. (1899/2017), *The Theory of the Leisure Class*, London and New York: Routledge.
Wolff, E.N. (1981), 'The accumulation of household wealth over the life-cycle: a microdata analysis', *Review of Income and Wealth*, **27** (1), 75–96.

Contagion effects

Contagion is an empirical phenomenon that describes the transmission of a shock across countries, particularly during crises. Contagion was experienced during the Great Depression (1930s) and the debt crisis in the 1980s. However, it received most academic interest after a series of currency collapses in the 1990s, when the intensity and extent of the transmission of these shocks surprised both practitioners and academics: unlike during past crises, relatively small economies had a large global effect, even when there were no strong trading relationships between the affected countries; for example, between Mexico and Argentina in 1994, East and Southeast Asian countries in 1997, and Russia and Brazil in 1998. Similarly, in 2007, the small subprime securitized assets market in the United States (size 860 billion US dollars) had a huge impact on the global financial market (size 25 trillion US dollars) (Rigobon, 2016).

The definition of contagion is, however, contentious. A 'broad' definition is concerned with wide-ranging types of linkages between two countries, including trade and financial linkages. According to a stricter definition, contagion is associated with an unanticipated shock and/or the change in beliefs or expectations of a crisis in country B, once country A has been hit by a crisis, beyond similarities in economic fundamentals and linkages. A further strict definition concentrates on crisis times.

Theoretically, the risk that a country is affected by contagion is usually considered to depend on the linkages, real and financial, with another country that act as channels through which transmission occurs. A typical example of real linkage is trade. The trade balance of country B might deteriorate as a result of an export decrease to country A, undermining economic growth and external finances as investors reassess country B's risk, and currency devaluation might follow (Glick and Rose, 1999). Competitive devaluations might also contribute to the propagation of shocks from one country to another (Corsetti et al., 2000).

Alternatively, contagion can be transmitted by financial linkages, often responsible for the propagation of shocks even in the absence of real linkages. First, a lender might stop lending to an economy just because its capital position in another economy has worsened. Second, the balance sheet of financial investors may be affected in a similar way by severe market-to-market price adjustments. Third, investors who need to rebalance their portfolios create contagion. For example, given a shock investment, funds may anticipate liquidity issues due to future losses or redemptions or decreased value of leveraged investors' collateral and start selling other assets to raise cash (Kaminsky and Reinhart, 2000).

In terms of applied research, models can be classified into four categories. First, there are asymmetric information and expectation-formation models (herding behaviour among investors). Second, macroeconomics feedback models aim to explain how an adverse expectation of one event makes this event more probable. Third, models of liquidity and bank runs describe when a large number of customers withdraw their bank deposits, fearing the bank's insolvency. Fourth, 'wake-up call' models look at whether a crisis in one country provides new information about the seriousness of a problem somewhere else (Masson, 1999).

However, post-Keynesian economists have looked both at crises and at contagion from the starting point that markets in general, and financial markets in particular, are prone to crises that are endogenously created even when exogenously triggered (Arestis and Glickman, 2002). The trigger exposes an endogenous fragility that is often the result of the lowering of the margins of safety and the taking on of an increasing level of risk (Kregel, 1998). The intensity and duration of the effects of a shock and of its propagation depend on the pre-existing fragility, which can be mitigated by financial regulation and capital controls (Jomo, 1998; David, 2008).

LUIGI VENTIMIGLIA

See also

Capital controls; Capital requirements; Financial crises; Financial instability hypothesis; Financial regulations

References

Arestis, P. and M. Glickman (2002), 'Financial crisis in South-East Asia: dispelling illusion the Minskyan way', *Cambridge Journal of Economics*, **26** (2), 237–60.
Corsetti, G., P. Pesenti, N. Roubini and C. Tille (2000), 'Competitive devaluations: toward a welfare-based approach', *Journal of International Economics*, **51** (1), 217–41.
David, A. (2008), 'Controls on capital inflows and the transmission of external shocks', *Cambridge Journal of Economics*, **32** (6), 887–906.
Glick, R. and A.K. Rose (1999), 'Contagion and trade: why are currency crises regional?', *Journal of International Money and Finance*, **18** (4), 603–17.
Jomo, K.S. (1998), 'Malaysian débâcle: whose fault?', *Cambridge Journal of Economics*, **22** (6), 707–22.
Kaminsky, G.L. and C.M. Reinhart (2000), 'On crises, contagion, and confusion', *Journal of International Economics*, **51** (1), 145–68.
Kregel, J. (1998), 'Yes, "it" did happen again: a Minsky crisis happened in Asia', *Levy Economics Institute Working Paper*, No. 234.
Masson, P. (1999), 'Multiple equilibria, contagion, and the emerging market crises', *International Monetary Fund Working Paper*, No. 99/164.
Rigobon, R. (2016), 'Contagion, spillover and interdependence', *European Central Bank Working Paper*, No. 1975.

LUIGI VENTIMIGLIA

Corn model

According to Ricardo (1817), the so-called 'corn model' served as an analytical introduction to the problem in which he was really interested: the determination of the level (and above all, the trend) of the rate of profit, the central category of a capitalistic economic system.

In itself, the corn model is extremely simple. Think of an economy subdivided into two sectors, the agricultural sector and the iron sector (which we call the rest of the economy). Assume that in the agricultural sector a single commodity is produced, corn, which is also used as the unique mean of production. In other words, corn is used to pay workers in advance (this is their real wage); corn seeds constitute the unique intermediate input. As output and capital are different quantities of the same thing (corn), the rate of profit in the agricultural sector may be computed as a material ratio, namely the ratio between the surplus of corn (total production minus seeds minus wages) and the quantity of corn advanced as capital (seeds plus wages). As such, the prices of corn and iron are just not needed to calculate the rate of profit prevailing in the agricultural sector. As to the rate of profit prevailing in the iron sector, it must be the same as that in agriculture.

Indeed, assume this is not the case and, for instance, the rate of profit earned in the iron sector is higher than the agricultural rate of profit. Capitalists would move their capital from the agricultural to the iron sector, the relative price of iron would fall because of increased relative supply and then the profit rate in the iron sector would move back to the same level realized in the agricultural sector. In short: the agricultural rate of profit, which is determined as a material ratio and independently from relative prices, coincides with the rate of profit for the economy as a whole. This is not just an 'average' profit rate; this is the profit rate earned in each single sector of the economy, and it only depends on what happens in agriculture. If, due to population pressure, fewer and fewer fertile lands are to be cultivated, the agricultural surplus will reduce relative to the amount of capital (corn) needed in the production process, thereby lowering the profit rate in agriculture and therefore in any other sector of the economy. A 'differential' rent will emerge: capitalists will compete against each other to get the right to cultivate the most fertile plots, and land owners will take advantage of such competition and extract a rent. As a result, the social and economic system will move toward stagnation: increasing rents, falling profits, stagnating wages. An ugly world, a return to feudalism. A 'stationary state'.

This model and its predictions were criticized from the onset, especially by Malthus. In the real world, the argument goes, there are no sectors where output and inputs are given by the same commodity. You need iron to produce corn, and you need corn to produce iron. The rate of profit cannot be calculated anymore as a material ratio, unless the labour theory of value applies in its narrowest sense (the relative price of commodities coincides with the ratio between the quantities of direct and indirect labour they incorporate). However, the labour theory of value in this narrow sense does not apply and the corn model and its bleak predictions have to be rejected.

This kind of criticism of the corn model is formally correct, of course. From the broader perspective of the history of economic thought, however, these analytical limitations are truly unimportant compared with the role this model played in the development of subsequent ideas. First, in some sense the corn model was, together with Quesnay's *Tableau économique*, the very first 'model' in the discipline. Moreover, Ricardo, more than Quesnay, was the author who first understood the importance of analytical rigour and internal coherence in the development of an economic argument. Second, the corn model, net of its limitations, is the first rigorous representation of production as a circular process, in opposition to the mainstream view where production is seen as a linear one (the idea of the production function). Needless to say, Ricardo is the intellectual father of Marx and grandfather of Sraffa and Garegnani, and *Production of Commodities by Means of Commodities* could have been renamed *Production of Corn by Means of Corn: Adjusting and Generalizing Ricardo's Corn Model*. Third, in the corn model, wages are determined by conflict, and profits are a residual. Income distribution, once again in opposition to the current mainstream view, has nothing (or very little) to do with factors' productivities.

These deep and fundamental criticisms to the current economic orthodoxy – capital is not a primary factor, distribution is not ruled

MARCO MISSAGLIA

by technology – were only proved by Sraffa (1960), but their seeds are certainly to be found in Ricardo's corn model.

MARCO MISSAGLIA

See also

Capitalism; Income distribution; Neoclassical economics; *Production of Commodities by Means of Commodities*; Profit

References

Ricardo, D. (1951 [1817]), *On the Principles of Political Economy and Taxation*, Cambridge, UK: Cambridge University Press.
Sraffa, P. (1960), *Production of Commodities by Means of Commodities. Prelude to a Critique of Economic Theory*, Cambridge, UK: Cambridge University Press.

Corporate debt

Corporations have several means of financing investment. They can issue stocks, giving stockholders claims to profits through dividends, or they can draw on retained earnings. Borrowing is a third potential source of funding. In addition to borrowing from commercial banks, corporations can offer debt products on financial markets, a practice that has grown dramatically since the 1980s (Carter, 1991). These products include corporate bonds, which have long maturities and high yields, as well as shorter-maturity notes and commercial papers.

The impact of corporate debt on investment has been neglected in mainstream economics. Modigliani and Miller's (1958) seminal work concluded that the valuation of a corporation is independent of its leverage. As a result, the cost of capital for the firm and its investment decisions do not depend on whether the firm would fund that investment by issuing stocks or by selling bonds.

Post-Keynesian economists have criticized this thesis owing to the presence of uncertainty. The Modigliani–Miller (1958) theorem assumes forward-looking agents who can assign probabilities to all future returns. By contrast, Keynes (1937) argues that most investment decisions are characterized by fundamental uncertainty, making agents unable to determine numerical probabilities with confidence.

Uncertainty will lead lenders to impose limits on firm leverage to mitigate losses in the case of an adverse event (Glickman, 1997). As Glickman notes, Kalecki (1937) also points to self-imposed constraints on corporate leverage. Firms that borrow to fund fixed investments are at greater risk of insolvency.

Hyman Minsky (1982) and Paul Davidson (1991) have stressed the interconnections between financial markets and the real macroeconomy. Credit arrangements and 'money contracts' more generally create fixed obligations (Davidson, 1991). A financialized economy is thereby dominated by 'claims, not on real assets, but on money' (Minsky, 1977, p. 21). These monetary claims facilitate economic activity in the face of uncertainty but also generate the possibility of crises when current income flows become insufficient to meet fixed obligations.

Minsky's (1982) financial instability hypothesis explores how corporate debt engenders macroeconomic volatility. Minsky claims that periods of economic stability will promote rising leverage. Firms and lenders predict continued growth in profit flows, narrow their safety margins, and increase debt-funded investment. While firms can initially repay debt ('hedge' finance), rising leverage, interest rate increases, or falling profits can render firms unable to service debt without additional borrowing ('Ponzi' finance). As the boom slows, banks cut lending to highly leveraged firms, which must liquidate assets. The result is a 'debt-deflationary process' in which investment demand and asset prices collapse.

Consistent with these predictions, corporate debt has regularly generated systemic risk. In 1970, the US transportation company Penn Central defaulted on its commercial papers after declaring bankruptcy. A loss of confidence froze the entire commercial paper market. Issuers were unable to further refinance debt, and the value of commercial papers plummeted. Corporate debt products also played a role in the 2008 global financial crisis. Commercial papers collateralized by assets including mortgage loans and automobile financing contributed to the evaporation of liquidity across financial markets when asset prices collapsed (Kacperczyk and Schnabl, 2010).

Corporate debt may again become a source of financial instability in coming years. Non-financial corporate debt in the United States has almost returned to pre-crisis levels, at about 73 per cent of gross domestic product (GDP)

as of 2018. Meanwhile, China's corporate debt level (150 per cent of GDP) remains higher than that of most other economies (Tiftik et al., 2019), raising concerns as the country's income growth continues to slow.

MELANIE G. LONG

See also

Credit money; Finance – initial vs final; Financial crises; Financial instability hypothesis; Uncertainty

References

Carter, M. (1991), 'Uncertainty, liquidity and speculation: a Keynesian perspective on financial innovation in the debt markets', *Journal of Post Keynesian Economics*, **14** (2), 169–82.
Davidson, P. (1991), 'Is probability theory relevant for uncertainty? A Post-Keynesian perspective', *Journal of Economic Perspectives*, **5** (1), 129–43.
Glickman, M. (1997), 'A Post Keynesian refutation of Modigliani–Miller on capital structure', *Journal of Post Keynesian Economics*, **20** (2), 251–74.
Kacperczyk, M. and P. Schnabl (2010), 'When safe proved risky: commercial paper during the financial crisis of 2007–2009', *Journal of Economic Perspectives*, **24** (1), 29–50.
Kalecki, M. (1937), 'The principle of increasing risk', *Economica*, **4** (16), 440–47.
Keynes, J.M. (1937), 'The general theory of employment', *Quarterly Journal of Economics*, **51** (2), 209–23.
Minsky, H.P. (1977), 'The financial instability hypothesis: an interpretation of Keynes and an alternative to "standard" theory', *Challenge*, **20** (1), 20–27.
Minsky, H.P. (1982), *Can 'It' Happen Again? Essays on Instability and Finance*, Abingdon-on-Thames, UK: Routledge.
Modigliani, F. and M.H. Miller (1958), 'The cost of capital, corporation finance and the theory of investment', *American Economic Review*, **48** (3), 261–97.
Tiftik, E., K. Mahmood and J. Zhou (2019), *Global Debt Monitor: Slowdown in 2018 – Pause or Trend?*, Washington, DC: Institute of International Finance.

Credit

Credit comes from the Latin *creditum* ('loan') or *credere* ('to believe'). Credit is a social construction whereby someone lends their surplus to someone else on the 'trust' that the counterparty will repay the loan. Credit, according to post-Keynesian economists (and anthropologists such as David Graeber), is the oldest form of spending and is the source of all money relations. Every issuance of credit automatically creates a debt (or liability). In pre-modern times credit relationships occurred among close associates or at least people in close geographic location, so due diligence and creditworthiness were easier to calculate – though default was always a possibility (owing to bad harvest, borrower's death, and so on).

As the economy became more complex, institutions emerged that began playing the role of creditor (like banks) and the legitimizer of credit (States). Credit plays a critical role in the creation of money (such as the monetary circuit) and is the impetus for economic growth. Thus, post-Keynesians call the economic system a 'monetary production economy'. The economy could also be called a 'credit production economy' with little change in effect. This perspective was first presented by Karl Marx (1867 [1992]) in Volume I of *Capital* with his M-C-M' equation, where M is money, C is commodities, and M' > M when there are profits. John Maynard Keynes advanced this thinking by stating the unique characteristics of money and the role of banks and financial markets. Keynes states in *A Treatise on Money* (1930/1950, pp. 219–220) that '[c]redit is the pavement along which production travels and the bankers if they knew their duty, would provide the transport facilities to just the extent it is required in order that the productive powers of the community can be employed at full employment'.

In Alfred Mitchell Innes's articles, 'What is money?' (1913) and 'The credit theory of money' (1914), he makes no distinction between money and credit/debt. He wrote the following regarding the purpose of credit (Innes, 1914, p. 152):

> [A] sale and purchase is the exchange of a commodity for credit. From this main theory springs the sub-theory that the value of credit or money does not depend on the value of any metal or metals, but on the right which the creditor acquires to 'payment', that is to say, to satisfaction for the credit, and on the obligation of the debtor to 'pay' his debt and conversely on the right of the debtor to release himself from his debt by the tender of an equivalent debt owed by the creditor, and the obligation of the creditor to accept this tender in satisfaction of his credit.

MELANIE G. LONG / ROBERT H. SCOTT

Neoclassical economists argue that money is neutral in the long run. Their historical viewpoint is that money did not evolve from credit, but rather emerged as a way to smooth barter transactions, and to have transactional value this early currency had valuable physical properties (like a pound of sterling). For them, money is a stock that is only adjustable exogenously by central banks or households. For example, neoclassical economists think that a bank gets deposits and can only grant credit within the limits of the fractional reserve system (that is, the money multiplier). Post-Keynesians, in contrast, assert that credit creation is demand led, that is, endogenous. As such, banks grant credit when there is demand and are not constrained by supply-side factors such as deposits or central banks, but rather are able to create credit on demand. The only constraints on the issuance of credit are the number of 'credit-worthy' borrowers.

One area where post-Keynesians have made important extensions to Keynes's analysis is with consumer credit and debt. At the time Keynes was writing there was little consumer credit available. Household consumption was constrained (largely) by their incomes, but today aggregate demand encompasses both income and debt obligations. Thus, as debt increases then aggregate demand will also increase, but can exceed income (see Brown, 2007). Minsky (1992) used a Michal Kalecki-inspired (with some added influence from Joseph Schumpeter) credit conception to develop his business-cycle model using financial instability that results from the optimism of entrepreneurs and banks in issuing credit up to a point where the system becomes unstable (credit/debt bubble) and moods turn pessimistic (becoming credit constrained). These periods and levels of pessimism and optimism follow credit issuance patterns that determine business investment that starts the monetary production cycle.

ROBERT H. SCOTT

See also

Credit money; Monetary circuit; Money and banking; Money illusion; Monetary theory of production

References

Brown, C. (2007), 'Financial engineering, consumer credit, and the stability of effective demand', *Journal of Post Keynesian Economics*, **29** (3), 427–453.

Innes, A.M. (1913), 'What is money?', *The Banking Law Journal*, **30** (5), 377–408.

Innes, A. (1914), 'The credit theory of money', available at https://www.community-exchange.org/docs/The%20Credit%20Theoriy%20of%20Money.htm (last accessed 7 November 2020).

Kalecki, M. (1971), *Selected Essays on the Dynamics of the Capitalist Economy 1933–1970*, Cambridge: Cambridge University Press.

Keynes, J.M. (1930 [1950]), *A Treatise on Money, Vol. II*, London: Macmillan.

Keynes, J.M. (1936), *The General Theory of Employment, Interest, and Money*, London: Macmillan.

Marx, K. (1867 [1992]), *Capital: A Critique of Political Economy, Volume I*, London: Penguin.

Minsky, H. (1992), 'The financial instability hypothesis', *Jerome Levy Economics Institute of Bard College Working Paper*, No. 74, available at http://www.levyinstitute.org/pubs/wp74.pdf (last accessed 7 November 2020).

Credit constraints

In the post-Keynesian theory of endogenous money (see Rochon, 1999; Lavoie, 2014), bank loans give rise to bank deposits. This position stands in contradistinction to neoclassical theory, where bank deposits determine bank loans, according to the well-known money-multiplier model. In this model, banks are restrained in their ability to lend by the amount of pre-existing bank deposits: banks can only increase their lending if their deposits increased beforehand. This view embodies the definition of rationing: faced with a demand for loans greater than the existing and pre-determined supply of loanable funds, banks must allocate efficiently savings among those who are demanding credit. Banks are nothing more than financial intermediaries.

In post-Keynesian theory, however, such ideas and terminology are rejected. Banks never face a pre-determined supply of loans and are never constrained by a lack of loanable funds. Indeed, according to the theory of endogenous money, bank assets determine bank liabilities, or rather loans determine deposits. Hence, deposits can never constrain bank lending, which is needed to finance production in both the consumption-goods sector and the investment-goods sector. Firms need access to credit to finance the process of production, and especially to pay wages.

In articles subsequent to *The General Theory*, Keynes recognized that banks play a key role in the transition to a higher level of economic activity (Keynes, 1937a/1973). He even argues that the financing constraint that can be placed on firms is a powerful method of controlling the level of investment (see Keynes, 1937b/1973). Viewed through money's endogeneity, we can conclude immediately the existence of a link between the creation of money and debt.

Given the discussion above, however, it is more appropriate to talk about credit constraints, rather than rationing. Indeed, post-Keynesian economists never see bank activities, and specifically bank lending, as being influenced by the need to 'ration' credit. Rather, banks are free to lend as much as they want. But they do face some constraints, and there will always be a 'fringe of unsatisfied borrowers', which is perfectly compatible with the horizontalist view of endogenous money (Rochon, 1999).

A true constraint on bank lending is the lack of creditworthy borrowers. If, for whatever reasons, banks judge borrowers to be non-creditworthy, they will refuse them credit. Moreover, if potential borrowers decide not to borrow, banks will be unable to lend. In this sense, banks are constrained by their willingness to lend to creditworthy borrowers, on the one hand, and by the demand arising from creditworthy borrowers, on the other hand. In neither case is lending influenced by a lack of deposits or a rationed supply.

The above discussion raises two important questions: (1) how do banks evaluate the creditworthiness of borrowers and (2) how can a decrease in the supply of bank credit have real economic consequences?

Regarding the first question, Keynes (1930, Vol. II, p. 365) suggests that the borrower's 'standing' with the bank is very important. Hence, those borrowers or firms having a good relationship or a long track record with their banks will most likely be deemed creditworthy. The bank may also consider various other variables or financial ratios such as cash flow, debt levels, and leverage ratios (see Wolfson, 1996). Ultimately, creditworthiness means only one thing: the bank's perception of the borrower's ability to repay the loan with interest in the future. It is in this way that banks 'place a bet' (Rochon, 1999) on borrowers.

Banks may therefore be led to refuse to grant loans on the basis of their assessment of their own expectations of future aggregate demand, hence their degree of confidence in the future in a framework of radical uncertainty, and the conventions in force within the banking system. In this respect, there would be a conventional leverage that banks consider acceptable, against which they compare the leverage of the firm applying for credit.

The relationship between credit and production shows the central role played by banks. As Keynes (1930) noted, banks are special – a theme picked up again by Robinson (1956).

In the end, as Keynes (1930, I, p. 212) told us, '[t]here is apt to be an unsatisfied fringe of borrowers, the size of which can be expanded or contracted, so that banks can influence the volume of investment by expanding or contracting the volume of their loans, without there being necessarily any change in the level of bank-rate, in the demand schedule of borrowers, or in the volume of lending otherwise than through the banks. This phenomenon is capable, when it exists, of having great practical importance.'

NICOLAS PILUSO AND LOUIS-PHILIPPE ROCHON

See also

Endogenous money; Monetary theory of production; Money and banking; Money creation – nature of; Uncertainty – macro vs micro

References

Keynes, J.M. (1930), *A Treatise on Money*, London: Macmillan, two volumes.
Keynes, J.M. (1937a/1973), 'Alternative theories of the rate of interest', in *The Collected Writings of John Maynard Keynes, vol XIV: The General Theory and After. Part II: Defence and Development*, London: Macmillan, pp. 201–15.
Keynes, J.M. (1937b/1973), 'The "ex ante" theory of the rate of interest', in *The Collected Writings of John Maynard Keynes, vol XIV: The General Theory and After. Part II: Defence and Development*, London: Macmillan, pp. 215–23.
Lavoie, M. (2014), *Post-Keynesian Economics: New Foundations*, Cheltenham, UK, and Northampton, MA, USA: Edward Elgar.
Robinson, J. (1956), *The Accumulation of Capital*, London: Macmillan.
Rochon, L.-P. (1999), *Credit, Money and Production: An Alternative Post-Keynesian Approach*, Cheltenham, UK, and Northampton, MA, USA: Edward Elgar.

Wolfson, M. (1996), 'A Post Keynesian theory of credit rationing', *Journal of Post Keynesian Economics*, **18** (3), 443–70.

Credit default swaps

Credit default swaps (CDS) are a form of insurance policy against fluctuations in the creditworthiness, and the potential default, of debt securities. In CDS contracts, the credit protection buyer agrees to make a series of periodic payments (premiums) to the credit protection seller until the contract reaches maturity. Should the so-called 'credit event' occur (that is, bankruptcy, failure to pay, debt restructuring, or debt repudiation), the two parties have the option (not an obligation) to settle. When this happens, the buyer will receive compensation from the seller.

CDS are the major type of credit derivatives, which can be built on a single entity or as indexes of multiple entities. Being derivate instruments, their remuneration is derived from an 'underlying' performance, which in this case is borrowers' credit quality. Credit quality, in turn, depends on the rating of the relevant debt obligation. Whenever creditworthiness deteriorates (improves), CDS prices increase (decrease), thereby generating gains for the protection buyers (sellers) that can be monetized even without the credit event occurring.

There are two important differences between typical insurance products and CDS. On the one hand, in CDS contracts the buyers are not required to have a tangible exposure to credit risk, to wit, being debtholders. Any investor willing to hedge a specific credit risk can purchase this instrument, which in this case is called 'naked CDS'. Investors buying naked CDS gamble on the worsening of the credit quality of debt securities, while an insurance company might bet on an opposite improvement. On the other hand, the amount of the payout in case of the credit event is not prearranged, and it is determined following a quite long and complex process of negotiations and auctions. Typically, this payout represents only a portion of the actual loss.

Although a wide diffusion of derivatives can be traced back to the fourteenth century, CDS represent a recent financial innovation. Developed in the early 1990s by JP Morgan Inc. to essentially transfer its credit risk exposure, CDS became a fundamental instrument within global financial markets (Augustin et al., 2014). One important problem of this market only partially addressed by the so-called 'Dodd–Frank Act' is that most derivatives transactions take place within unregulated over-the-counter markets. From the late 1990s, and especially in the run-up to the 2007–2008 global financial crisis, the volume of the CDS market expanded rapidly. At the end of 2007, the total CDS notional amount, which is the total protection being purchased on the market, reached 61.2 trillion US dollars. The credit protection sold on the market exceeded the value of the corresponding insured debt securities by approximately twelve times (Aldasoro and Ehlers, 2018). The American International Group (AIG) was the major seller of CDS, acting as the 'banking system insurer'. Owing to the lack of sufficient capital to clear debt positions once the creditworthiness of the underlying worsened, in particular in the case of Lehman Brothers, AIG became insolvent and had to be bailed out by the US government. Of course, private rating agencies with a profit structure tending to overestimate solvency played a pivotal role in this process (Kregel, 2008). The recent decade saw a sensible reduction in the outstanding amounts of CDS, coupled with a general reduction in counterparty risk (Aldasoro and Ehlers, 2018).

Conventional research focuses on the microeconomic features of CDS, evaluating them as stabilizing and beneficial tools if accurately used. Depending on specific financial actors' risk aversion, and on the extent to which regulation can reduce perverse incentives, CDS might also become dangerous (see Lando, 2020). The post-Keynesian approach considers derivatives as instruments aimed at reducing fundamental uncertainty while adding layers of financial opaqueness in credit risk transfer markets, ultimately fostering financial instability (Dow, 2015). This is the 'paradox of risk', for which the

> illusion of liquidity induces agents to take over even more risky decisions. Thus risk-reducing microeconomic financial innovations end up producing a more risky macroeconomic environment. (Lavoie, 2014, p. 21)

This echoes the Minskyian insight about the inherent instability and fragility of capitalist financial systems, fostered by profit-oriented financial innovation introduced during 'tranquil times' (Minsky, 1977).

The invention of CDS provided insurance from risk to the benefit of growing assets securitization. Before the summer of 2007, the overconfidence in mortgage-backed securities as liquid and safe assets was fuelled by the opportunities of risk-spreading provided by CDS. While the largest banks kept on securitizing most of their mortgage loans, big insurance companies supported credit provision via CDS. Being freed from their position of 'risk absorber', banks found in subprime mortgage lending a profitable opportunity (Botta et al., 2015; 2020). The endogenous creation of risk through CDS production becomes even clearer when considering that while they were envisioned as a risk hedging innovation, their 'naked' version often embodied an opportunity for speculation (Crotty, 2009).

DANIELE TORI

See also

Basel agreements; Financial crises; Financial innovations; Financial instability hypothesis; Paradox of tranquillity

References

Aldasoro, I. and T. Ehlers (2018), 'The credit default swap market: what a difference a decade makes', *BIS Quarterly Review*, June, 1–14.

Augustin, P., M.G. Subrahmanyam, D.Y. Tang and S.Q. Wang (2014), 'Credit default swaps: a survey', *Foundations and Trends in Finance*, 9 (1–2), 1–196.

Botta, A., E. Caverzasi and D. Tori (2015). 'Financial–real-side interactions in an extended monetary circuit with shadow banking: loving or dangerous hugs?', *International Journal of Political Economy*, 44 (3), 196–227.

Botta, A., Caverzasi, E. and Tori, D. (2020). 'The macroeconomics of shadow banking', *Macroeconomic Dynamics*, 24(1), 161–190.

Crotty, J. (2009), 'Structural causes of the global financial crisis: a critical assessment of the "new financial architecture"', *Cambridge Journal of Economics*, 33 (4), 563–580.

Dow, S.C. (2015), 'Addressing uncertainty in economics and the economy', *Cambridge Journal of Economics*, 39 (1), 33–47.

Kregel, J. (2008), 'Using Minsky's cushions of safety to analyze the crisis in the US subprime mortgage market', *International Journal of Political Economy*, 37 (1), 3–23.

Lando, D. (2020), 'Credit default swaps: a primer and some recent trends', *Annual Review of Financial Economics*, 12, 177–92.

Lavoie, M. (2014), *Post-Keynesian Economics: New Foundations*, Cheltenham, UK, and Northampton, MA, USA: Edward Elgar Publishing.

Minsky, H.P. (1977), 'The financial instability hypothesis: an interpretation of Keynes and an alternative to standard theory', *Challenge*, 20 (1), 20–27.

Credit divisor

According to a number of post-Keynesian economists, the credit divisor depicts that variations in the monetary base are driven by variations in the supply of money. This mechanism was first described in the 1960s by Jacques Le Bourva (1962/1992) and reverses the causality (between the monetary base and the supply of money) stressed in the theory of the money multiplier. It is an explicit consequence of the post-Keynesian theory of endogenous money and reminds the hierarchical nature of payment systems as well.

According to the theory of the money multiplier, banks have the ability to multiply an initial balance in central bank money by collecting it (on deposit) and lending it several times. This process would be constrained by banks' (compulsory or excess) reserves in central bank money, while being predictable by the stability of the demand for money assumed by monetarists. Against this background, changes in the supply of money depend (with more or less flexibility) on changes in the monetary base, which is why the central bank would be able to control the evolution of the supply of money.

Based on an exogenous view of money, the theory of the money multiplier is flawed for several (logical and empirical) reasons:

- First, the money multiplier in fact is always equal to one, because banks are not able to multiply bank notes, in the same way that the London goldsmiths of the sixteenth century could not multiply the ingots that their customers deposited with them.
- Second, the exogenous view of money that prevails in the theory of the money multiplier runs counter to the nature of credit-money, which does not exist without being borrowed, hence without being demanded by the public (Moore, 1988).
- Finally, and from an empirical point of view, the second half of the twentieth century was marked by financial innovations that

decreased the demand for money, thus highlighting its intrinsic instability.

The endogenous nature of money requires reversing the causality between the monetary base and the supply of money: changes in the monetary base result from changes in the supply of money, the latter reflecting the variation of aggregate spending. Since money does not exist without being borrowed, its supply depends on the volume of transactions made during the relevant period, which is why Moore (1988, p. xii) suggested that the supply of money is 'credit-based and demand-driven'. This observation confirms that 'loans make deposits', particularly when firms go into debt with banks to pay wages, that is, to monetize current output. To be precise, bank deposits are created as soon as the payer draws on a credit line granted by a bank. The endogeneity of money is also verified for the monetary base, which proceeds from the need (by banks) for balances in central bank money for interbank settlements, but also for putting bank notes into circulation.

Accordingly, both the supply of money and the monetary base are not determined by the central bank, which has to adjust its monetary interventions to the level of economic activity; otherwise it would be detrimental to the functioning of the payments system and would threaten financial stability. Against this background, and contrary to what the theory of the money multiplier implies, the supply of money is not conditioned by prior reserves in central bank money. After having verified the creditworthiness of borrowers, banks issue money at the request of the public and then turn to the central bank in order to obtain funds. Since changes in the supply of money precede (and cause) changes in the monetary base, it follows that the supply of money is not a multiple of the monetary base. The monetary base is a quotient of the supply of money, hence the existence of the credit divisor as stated by post-Keynesian economists.

Therefore, the credit divisor reflects the hierarchical nature of the payments system: the public uses bank money for its everyday transactions (as a matter of fact, a note issued by the central bank is put into circulation on the basis of money issued by commercial banks), while banks use central bank money as a means of final payment for interbank settlements. Since no one can pay with one's own acknowledgement of debt, every payment involves three actors, namely, the payee, the payer and the issuer of the means of payment, which is why money is never issued independently of transactions. As a result, the central bank is not able to directly influence the supply of money but uses in this respect some policy rates of interest, which are supposed to influence the cost of borrowing for the public, and thus the demand for money. In light of this operational framework for monetary policy, which is now recognized by many central banks around the world (Bindseil, 2014), reserve requirements play a negligible role, thereby nullifying the theory of the money multiplier definitively.

JONATHAN MASSONNET

See also

Credit money; Endogenous money; Financial innovations; Money as a means of payment; Money creation – nature of

References

Bindseil, U. (2014), *Monetary Policy Operations and the Financial System*, Oxford: Oxford University Press.

Le Bourva, J. (1962 [1992]), 'Money creation and credit multipliers', *Review of Political Economy*, 4 (4), 447–76.

Moore, B.J. (1988), *Horizontalists and Verticalists: The Macroeconomics of Credit Money*, Cambridge, UK: Cambridge University Press.

Credit easing

The expression 'credit easing' was first mentioned by Ben Bernanke, the then US Federal Reserve's (Fed) Chairman of the Board of Governors, in January 2009. In a speech given at the London School of Economics, Bernanke highlighted the Fed's response to the global financial crisis of 2007–08 and distinguished it from what the Bank of Japan (BoJ) had done from 2001 to 2006. In the latter case, monetary policy was focused on the liability side of the BoJ's balance sheet, targeting the quantity of bank reserves and hoping to increase credit and broader measures of money, like M1 and M2. According to Bernanke, such a programme (called 'quantitative easing') did not work, as reserves were kept idle at the BoJ. The Fed, however, focused on the asset side of its balance sheet, with the quantity of bank reserves being a consequence of its policy of providing

JONATHAN MASSONNET / OLIVIA BULLIO MATTOS

loans to banks and buying securities – defined as credit easing by Bernanke (2009).

This unconventional monetary policy began in 2008 after traditional instruments were shown to be insufficient to deal with the crisis, especially after hitting the so-called zero-lower bound for interest rates in December. Bernanke (2009) divided these unconventional policies into three groups: (i) provision of short-term liquidity to solvent financial institutions; (ii) provision of liquidity to borrowers in credit markets; and (iii) purchasing mortgage-backed securities, agency debt, and long-term Treasuries through Large Scale Asset Purchases programmes. The policy aims included: restoring financial markets and improving the balance sheet of financial institutions, reducing interest rates for consumers and businesses, re-establishing financial intermediation, and increasing market liquidity. As a result of these policies, there was an unprecedented increase in the Fed's balance sheet from around 800 billion US dollars in 2007 to approximately 4.5 trillion US dollars in 2015.

These actions show that there was still present in the Fed a belief in traditional transmission channels of monetary policy and in the money multiplier, once it was expected that economic conditions would improve with monetary easing (Fullwiler, 2013). Nonetheless, the results in the real economy were disappointing and the recovery was extremely slow, as Papadimitriou et al. (2015) show. As is well known in post-Keynesian literature, banks do not lend reserves: they create deposits with a 'stroke of bankers' pens when they approve loans' (McLeay et al., 2014, p. 16). Thus, any policy based on reserve creation and the money multiplier was bound to fail to support aggregate demand, since this depends on banks' willingness to lend again. Policy makers were also convinced that the price level would respond to the increase in the quantity of money, which proved not to be the case.

From a post-Keynesian point of view, private agents' liquidity preference is very strong in a crisis, as they try to accumulate liquid assets for three reasons: precaution, like Keynes (1936, p. 196) puts it, 'to provide for contingencies requiring sudden expenditures and for unforeseen opportunities of advantageous purchases'; speculation, once agents keep waiting for the interest rate to increase; and because of uncertainty with regard to the level of aggregate demand in the future. In 1936, Keynes had already laid out the limitations of monetary policy when liquidity preference is high – even with money injections, economic variables do not respond as monetary authorities wish they would: 'If, however, we are tempted to assert that money is the drink which stimulates the system to activity, we must remind ourselves that there may be several slips between the cup and the lip' (Keynes, 1936, p. 173).

The Fed did what was necessary to avoid a total collapse of the national financial system. Nevertheless, there was a total misconception on the part of the Fed as to how money is actually created. For post-Keynesians, money is endogenous and for the 'real circuit' to be activated, banks must be willing to take on more risks and increase credit. This was not one of the results from the Fed's credit-easing policy. Had it created reserves to buy public debt in the primary market and to support a more active fiscal policy to increase effective demand, the results would have been much faster and greater (Farhi, 2014).

OLIVIA BULLIO MATTOS

See also

Financial crises; Liquidity preference; Monetary policy transmission mechanism; Quantitative easing; Zero interest rate policy

References

Bernanke, B.S. (2009), 'The crisis and the policy response', speech given at the Stamp Lecture at the London School of Economics, London, 13 January, available online at https://www.federalreserve.gov/newsevents/speech/bernanke20090113a.htm.
Farhi, M. (2014), 'Revelações da crise: moeda fiduciária e as relações Tesouro/Banco Central', Revista de Economia Política, 34 (3), 396–412.
Fullwiler, S.T. (2013), 'An endogenous money perspective on the post-crisis monetary policy debate', Review of Keynesian Economics, 1 (2), 171–94, Summer 2013.
Keynes, J.M. (1936), The General Theory of Employment, Interest, and Money, London: Macmillan.
McLeay, M., A. Radia and R. Thomas (2014), 'Money creation in the modern economy', Bank of England Quarterly Bulletin, 54 (1), 14–27.
Papadimitriou, D.B., G. Hannsgen, M. Nikiforos and G. Zezza (2015), 'Fiscal austerity, dollar appreciation, and maldistribution will derail the US economy', Levy Economics Institute of Bard College Strategic Analysis, May, available online at www.levyinstitute.org/publications/fiscal-austerity-dollar-appreciation-and-maldistribution-will-derail-the-us-economy.

Credit money

The fundamental starting point in understanding credit money is recognition of the fact that a capitalist economy is perforce a monetarized production system, that is, real economic activity is presupposed by the degree to which banks make loans to firms to spur capitalist investment (see Arestis and Eichner, 1988). In this sense, the laws of motion of capital accumulation, as determined by the need to expand output, are christened by the means of banking. The capacity for firms to purchase the amounts of labour and material inputs necessary for satisfying expectations of profit extraction and, hence, for workers to receive wages, is assigned by the scope of debt commitments.

In order for capitalism to 'go ahead with assurance' (Keynes, 1937, p. 247), it depends on a struggle for economic existence shaped and fashioned by the deontic power of credit granting (Ingham, 2004, p. 204). Strictly speaking, without a rise in debt, economic growth essentially comes to a halt; investment expenditures stem from the need to borrow in excess of any pre-existing amount of financial resources (Seccareccia, 2011). Thus, credit is a social technology of deferred payment and settlement that delineates a relatively secure contractual claim for entrepreneurs to cope with uncertainty, manage sales, and, thus, facilitate long-run operational expansion as determined by the level of effective demand (Moore, 1989; Dunn, 2000; Ramskogler, 2011). If there is a restriction on credit, as a matter of course, any attempts for increased production are rendered nugatory (Kahn, 1931, pp. 174–5).

Credit is the pavement along which production travels and the bankers if they knew their duty, would provide the transport facilities to just the extent it is required in order that the productive powers of the community can be employed at full employment. (Keynes, 1973, p. 197)

[H]ow can capitalists invest more than what remains from their current profits after spending part of them for personal consumption? This is made possible by the banking system in various forms of credit inflation. ... [W]ithout credit inflation there would be no fluctuations in investment activity. Business fluctuations are strictly connected with credit inflation. (Kalecki, 1990, pp. 148–9)

The role of banks is to grant entrepreneurs absolute command over property (Marx, 1894, p. 570), allowing firms to pay out money for capital goods and the wage bill, to keep production and distribution going in advance of receiving profits from expected sales of consumer goods. The implication is that an appropriate portion of profits eventually accumulated by firms will be alienated by the financier; namely, firms will have to deduct interest payments from their collateralized deposit schedules of future revenue – this is the reflux mechanism (see Lavoie, 1999). This social process constitutes a monetary circuit (Graziani, 1997), which can be elucidated using Marx's reproductive schema (Lucarelli, 2010):

$$M^* - M - C' - M' - M^{*'}$$

where M^* represents bank loans to firms to facilitate the production process ($M - C' - M'$),

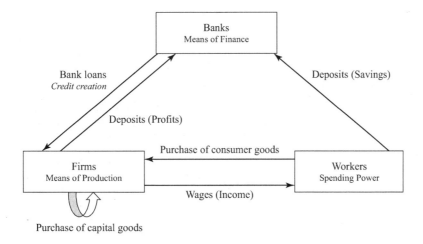

DAVID M. FIELDS

which eventually is converted into $M^{*'}$, that is, the payment of interest to the financier out of realized profits M'. As such, not only is there exploitation of labour concerning the extraction of profits, but there is also a conflict within the capitalist class itself, as firms, working on credit must contend with proceeds relegated to the banking sector (Panico, 1980).

Rates of interest regulate the rate of profit (Sraffa, 1960, p. 3). The presence of finance makes it so that the actual centre of distributive conflict in capitalism does not necessarily lie at the point of production, but is governed by an exogenous variable that reflects the leverage of credit. High rates of interest, for instance, would induce firms to prefer short-termism instead of long-term productive investment, since access to credit is expensive. The social cost of this speculative strategy is, invariably, the process of nominal wage suppression.

The means by which financial institutions supply loans allow entrepreneurs to have access to debt irrespective of streams of potential earnings. This 'elasticity' of capitalist production is a monetary social space that concretizes the abstract social expression of capitalist social relations (Ingham, 1996). Hence, capitalism is a credit-driven social structure, whereby money is endogenously created in response to real forces in the economy.

DAVID M. FIELDS

See also

Effective demand; Endogenous money; Monetary circuit; Monetary theory of production; Money creation – nature of

References

Arestis, P. and A. Eichner (1988), 'The post-Keynesian and institutionalist theory of money and credit', *Journal of Economic Issues*, **22** (4), 1003–21.
Dunn, S. (2000), 'Fundamental uncertainty and the firm in the long run', *Review of Political Economy*, **12** (4), 419–33.
Graziani, A. (1997), 'A Marxist theory of money', *International Journal of Political Economy*, **27** (2), 26–50.
Ingham, G. (1996), 'Money is a social relation', *Review of Social Economy*, **54** (4), 507–29.
Ingham, G. (2004), *The Nature of Money*, Cambridge, UK: Polity Press.
Kahn, R.F. (1931), 'The relation of home investment to unemployment', *Economic Journal*, **41** (162), 173–98.
Kalecki, M. (1990), *Capitalism: Business Cycles and Full Employment. Collected Works of Michal Kalecki, Volume I*, Oxford, UK: Clarendon Press.
Keynes, J.M. (1937), 'Alternative theories of the rate of interest', *Economic Journal*, **47** (186), 241–52.
Keynes, J.M. (1973), *The Collected Writings of John Maynard Keynes, Vol. XIII: The General Theory and After. Part 1: Preparation*, London: Macmillan.
Lavoie, M. (1999), 'The credit-led supply of deposits and the demand for money: Kaldor's reflux mechanism as previously endorsed by Joan Robinson', *Cambridge Journal of Economics*, **23** (1), 103–13.
Lucarelli, B. (2010), 'Marxian theories of money, credit, and crisis', *Capital and Class*, **34** (2), 199–214.
Marx, K. (1894), *Capital, Vol. III*, New York: International Publishers.
Moore, B.J. (1989), 'The endogeneity of credit money', *Review of Political Economy*, **1** (1), 65–93.
Panico, C. (1980), 'Marx's analysis of the relationship between the rate of interest and the rate of profits', *Cambridge Journal of Economics*, **4** (4), 363–78.
Ramskogler, P. (2011), 'Credit money, collateral and the solvency of banks: a post-Keynesian analysis of credit market failures', *Review of Political Economy*, **23** (1), 69–79.
Seccareccia, M. (2011), 'The role of public investment as principal macroeconomic tool to promote long-term growth', *International Journal of Political Economy*, **40** (4), 62–82.
Sraffa, P. (1960), *Production of Commodities by Means of Commodities*, Cambridge, UK: Cambridge University Press.

Credit multiplier

The better part of mainstream economists still models the money supply as exogenous and banks as passive institutions transferring deposits from savers to borrowers (Allen et al., 2020). The financial intermediation view, treating money as manna fallen from heaven, is reflected in the Basel framework through the capital adequacy ratio (CAR), which is simply a revised version of the 'old' credit multiplier (that is, the minimum reserve requirements) as Panagopoulis and Spiliotis (2015) underline.

The past version was ingrained in Monetarist-affiliated central banks by Friedman and Schwartz's (1963, pp. 790–91) definitions of central bank money, the money stock and their relationship through a credit multiplier. For the latter to be an effective monetary policy tool, 'the main source of the fluctuations of the money stock [had to be] … supply-side' with 'central banks [having] no problem in controlling the monetary base' (Lavoie, 1984, p. 777). This flawed Monetarist idea, in post-Keynesian eyes, is derived from the following well-known equation:

$$M = B / [(R/D) + (C/M) - (RC/DM)] \quad (1)$$

where the monetary base (B) equals the sum of the reserves of commercial banks (R) plus the currency in the hands of the public (C), whereas the money stock (M) is equal to this same currency (C) plus public deposits held by commercial banks (D). In the Monetarist world, the R/D ratio is fixed by the legal minimum reserve requirements, whilst the public's liquidity preference (C/M) is fairly stable: '[Monetarists] generally admit that the ratios C/M and even R/D are not constant, but ... sufficiently stable ... [allowing] the central bank [to impose] the money stock of its choice, through open-market operations' (Lavoie, 1984, p. 777). Thus, the central bank can set R, the reserve requirement, and thereby control B, the amount of 'high-powered money'. In simplest terms, the mainstream view can be reduced to equation (2):

$$M = mB \quad (2)$$

where causality is read from right to left with the dependant variable, the money stock (M), a function of the relationship of the monetary multiplier (m) and the independent variable, the monetary base (B).

In contradistinction to mainstream (Monetarist) economists, post-Keynesians model the stock of money as endogenous and demand-driven by creditworthy entrepreneurs. In this framework of economic thought, with roots in the writings of Le Bourva (see Lavoie, 1992), monetary aggregates are a residue of credit aggregates. Consequently, post-Keynesians developed the credit divisor ($1/m$) to counterbalance the mainstream multiplier view, whereby the dependent variable, the monetary base (B), is a residue of the independent variable, the money stock (M), as shown in equation (3).

$$B = (1/m) \, M \quad (3)$$

To wit, post-Keynesians contend that 'causality runs from higher credit needs, to higher bank deposits, to higher required reserve' (Lavoie, 1984, pp. 776–7) with central banks accommodating the needs of commercial banks' reserve requirements, in harmony with horizontalism (see Rochon, 2020).

In more recent times, the debate shifted. With the development of the bank regulatory framework (that is, Basel II and III), a 'new' credit multiplier and equity emerged at its epicentre (Panagopoulis and Spiliotis, 2015, pp. 23–4). The mainstream, now, maintains that CAR is employed by central banks to control the supply of bank loans through two channels: either through changing assets' risk weights to control the 'net' exposure; or changing the equity definitions (that is, Tier I and Tier II).

Post-Keynesians, again, call for a reversed relationship, although two internal positions exist. For horizontalists, if bank assets perform and profits will be generated, these will 'cause' (retained) earnings and thus satisfy equity requirements. For structuralists, the causality is bi-directional: if their hypothesis holds, then equity leads to monetary expansion and equally monetary expansion leads to equity creation.

The validity of all views on the credit multiplier are directly related to the question on the money supply's causality. With post-Keynesians, chiefly of horizontalist leanings, prevailing over the mainstream in the first round of the battle, it is rather possible that this school of thought will triumph again.

PLAMEN IVANOV

See also

Credit divisor; Credit money; Endogenous money; Money and banking; Money creation – nature of

References

Allen, F., G. Covi, X. Gu, O. Kowalewski and M. Montagna (2020), 'The interbank market puzzle', *Bank of England Staff Working Paper*, No. 862.

Friedman, M. and A. Schwartz (1963), *A Monetary History of the United States, 1867–1960*, Princeton: Princeton University Press.

Lavoie, M. (1984), 'The endogenous flow of credit and the Post Keynesian theory of money', *Journal of Economic Issues*, **18** (3), 771–97.

Lavoie, M. (1992), 'Jacques Le Bourva's theory of endogenous credit-money', *Review of Political Economy*, **4** (4), 436–46.

Panagopoulis, Y. and A. Spiliotis (2015), 'Bank capital and the new credit multiplier', in L.-P. Rochon and S. Rossi (eds), *The Encyclopaedia of Central*

Banking, Cheltenham, UK and Northampton, MA, USA: Edward Elgar, pp. 23–24.

Rochon, L.-P. (2020), 'The economics of Basil Moore: slow progress toward horizontalism', *European Journal of Economics and Economic Policies: Intervention*, **17** (3), 313–24.

Credit-led boom

Credit-led booms are positive and exceptional deviations from the relationship between credit and economic activity (Dell'Ariccia et al., 2012). These events can be analysed from either a cross-country perspective – based on local or idiosyncratic qualities – or a global approach – focused on significant interactions between financial centres and peripheral economies. In any case, credit-led booms are intrinsically associated with the depth and functioning of the financial system (commercial banks, non-bank financial institutions, and capital markets) and depend on the interaction of credit supply and demand.

The early signs of increasing leverage trends are connected to the initial feeling of relaxation of risk perceptions, which Minsky originally identified as the first stage of credit-led booms (Cencini and Rossi, 2015). The arrival of a 'Minsky moment' – when economic agents' desire to sell is greater than their desire to buy (Aliber and Kindleberger, 2015) – implies a reversion of overoptimism and tightened subjective risk perception during the final stage of credit-led booms. Economic agents' expectations deteriorate, and credit availability vanishes owing to negative spillovers from this procyclical credit pattern (Minsky, 1986).

A key aspect of credit-led booms is the role of changes in subjective expectations, according to Keynes's (1936/2018) famous 'beauty contest' idea. New inventions or discoveries, changes in regulations, tastes or even rumours are significant variables for understanding credit-led booms from the very beginning, as well as reversals associated with the 'Minsky moment'. Tranquil times characterized by 'hedge' financial positions pave the way for boom-and-bust episodes full of 'speculative' and 'Ponzi' financial schemes. Balance sheets of banks and non-bank financial institutions usually deteriorate when they move on from boom to bust stages (Kregel, 2015).

From a cross-country perspective, the failure to coordinate agents getting different kinds of lending – in a framework of widespread credit availability – could explain the undesirable effects that credit-led booms may trigger. Central banks' regulations are critical to prevent, at the macroeconomic level, the negative consequences arising from agents' credit decisions. Traditional drivers of credit-led booms involve lax regulations of financial systems, misjudgement of risk exposures by commercial banks, and fragile expectation formation processes by economic agents. The expansion of credit supply relates to financial deregulation practices, financial innovation, and changes in banks' risk assessment strategies. Increased credit availability channels funds to investment and opens up greater opportunities for economic growth. Nevertheless, speedy credit expansion can lead to more financial vulnerability, excessive leverage, and the formation of bubbles in the prices of real and financial assets.

From a global approach, Emerging Markets and Developing Economies (EMDEs) are substantially exposed to international financial flows, thus transmitting, generating and amplifying credit-led booms, particularly in the face of deficient regulation and supervision of the financial system. Global financial cycle literature captures the way interaction between financial centres and peripheral economies lies at the foundation of credit-led booms in EMDEs. Early credit inflows are good predictors of credit bust coming to an end. Indeed, a Minskyan 'displacement' occurs when the risk appetite of global investors decreases. In such a case, it is frequent to find herd behaviour and capital flight from EMDEs to global financial centres.

At an early stage, credit-led booms in EMDEs usually boost consumption and investment opportunities, cause their GDP to expand, and increase real and financial asset prices as well as collateral values. However, at the end of credit-led booms, nominal exchange rate pressures and financial capital outflows are commonplace – worsening the quality of banks' balance sheets, and, in some circumstances, bringing about runs on bank deposits. External agents that operate in EMDEs (such as transnational enterprises or global investment funds) typically get credit in international capital markets and channel it to EMDEs' financial systems, generating 'cascade finance'. In particular, commercial banks in EMDEs are the traditional recipients of external inflows. They further increase both local credit availability – by relaxing credit rationing – and the chances of experiencing credit-led booms (Borio and Zhu, 2007; Adrian and Shin, 2008).

Credit-led booms pose significant challenges to economic policy. Deregulations and liberalization of financial systems proved to be detrimental to macro-financial stability, as exemplified by credit-led booms and their negative spillovers. Hence, it is essential to develop macro and micro prudential policies that may cushion a procyclical credit behaviour. The Basel I regulatory framework encourages domestic and external financial deregulation. In turn, the transition to Basel III norms and, particularly, the partial re-regulation supported by the G20 and the Financial Stability Board call for a rigorous monitoring of the banking sector, asset markets, global financial investors, shadow banking, and non-bank financial institutions loan facilities as provided by dynamic provisioning rules (Bank for International Settlements, 2010). Central banks are then called to face the challenge of avoiding a vicious interaction between leverage increases and financial institutions' behaviour, which could magnify credit procyclicality.

FERNANDO TOLEDO AND JORGE CARRERA

See also

Basel agreements; Credit money; Financial crises; Financial instability hypothesis; Financial regulations

References

Adrian T. and H. Shin (2008), 'Financial intermediaries, financial stability and monetary policy', *Federal Reserve Bank of New York Staff Report*, No. 346.
Aliber, R. and C. Kindleberger (2015), *Manias, Panics, and Crashes: A History of Financial Crises*, seventh edition, Basingstoke: Palgrave Macmillan.
Bank for International Settlements (2010), 'Basel III: a global regulatory framework for more resilient banks and banking systems', Basel Committee on Banking Supervision, Basel: Bank for International Settlements.
Borio, C. and H. Zhu (2007), 'Capital regulation, risk-taking and monetary policy: a missing link in the transmission mechanism?', *Bank for International Settlements Working Paper*, No. 268.
Cencini, A. and S. Rossi (2015), *Economic and Financial Crisis: A New Macroeconomic Analysis*, Basingstoke and New York: Palgrave Macmillan.
Dell'Ariccia, G., D. Igan, L. Laeven and H. Tong (2012), 'Policies for macrofinancial stability: how to deal with credit booms', *International Monetary Fund Staff Discussion Note*, No. 12/06.
Keynes, J.M. (1936/2018), *The General Theory of Employment, Interest, and Money*, Basingstoke and New York: Palgrave Macmillan.
Kregel, J. (2015), 'Keynes, Minsky and international financial fragility', paper presented at the 11th International Keynes Conference on Globalized Capitalism, Hitotsubashi University, 20–22 March.
Minsky, H.P. (1986), *Stabilizing an Unstable Economy*, New Haven, CT: Yale University Press.

Critical realism

Critical realism evolved out of a direct critique of positivism and a general challenge to mainstream economic approaches. In particular, in the aftermath of the global financial crisis, calls for critical realist approaches have increased (see Mäki, 2011; Lee, 2012).

Contrary to mainstream economics, critical realists advocate a non-formalistic methodological framework, which is related to different assumptions about the social ontology of capitalism. Social reality does not consist of 'isolated atoms', that is to say, variables leading to the same results independent of the framework, but of meanings, values and relations that are fundamentally interrelated (Lawson, 2009, p. 763). Since knowledge of the world is constantly changing, shaped by historical and social environments, only a partial view of the world is possible and development of theory never ends in a final product (Sum and Jessop, 2013).

In contrast to positivistic approaches that consider the world to be based on empirically observed events, critical realists argue that reality consists of three different domains. In addition to the empirical domain comprised of observed events, the actual and real domains exist independently of the researcher's experience. While the actual domain represents observable events, the real domain consists of latent, underlying mechanisms that generate events, but cannot be observed (Danermark et al., 2002). Reality thus does not only include experienced events but also not experienced events produced by underlying structures and mechanisms existing independently of individual beliefs. Owing to the fact of not being able to access all layers of reality such as the real domain, hypotheses are developed to depict the underlying mechanisms of a phenomenon (Elder-Vass, 2010).

A main aspect of critical realist research is the concept of demi-regularities, to wit, semi-predictable events that are contingent on the interaction of multiple causal mechanisms. Instead of seeing one factor always causing an actual event, events are evolving, based on the interaction of diverse causal mechanisms. Even if causal mechanisms are repeated in diverse situations producing the same underlying real effects, they might not necessarily lead to the same empirical or actual events. This is due to the fact that other causal facts might interact with them (Lee, 2012). The concept of causality is therefore not treated in a positivistic way, in which a causal relation is assumed to be empirically regular, but causal mechanisms are contingent and seen as tendencies (Elder-Vass, 2010).

As economic researchers aim to explain underlying causal mechanisms for an empirical phenomenon and finding answers to 'why' and 'how' questions through developing hypothetical models, retroduction is prevalent in critical realist research (Downward and Mearman, 2007). The major task of retroduction is explaining an observed event based on logical inference (Blaikie, 2009). A recurring methodology used in critical realist studies is case study research employing a mixed methods design. This often includes qualitative data in the form of primary data such as interviews and quantitative data in the form of economic statistics. The aim is to capture the impact of social relations on economic phenomena without ignoring the reverse effect; that is, the interactions between structure and agency (Marsh, 2009; Elder-Vass, 2010). By employing mixed methods, middle-range theories rather than grand theories are developed, presenting the interconnection between micro-level and macro-level analyses (Danermark et al., 2002).

Critical realist approaches have made an important contribution to economics, in particular in the field of financialization. Critical realist research concerning financialization can be divided into three main themes: the changing nature of the economy in light of a growing role of finance (Jessop, 2015; Bracking, 2016), financialized housing (Lawson, 2006; Soaita and Dewilde, 2019) and the impact of finance on everyday life (Jefferson, 2007; Ruwanpura, 2007). Studies in the first theme argue that critical realist approaches are necessary because of being able to incorporate sociological and political aspects and conduct an integrated analysis since financial markets cannot be studied in isolation (Munoz, 2016; Monaghan and O'Flynn, 2017). Secondly, critical realist studies discuss changes in housing networks on the basis of path-dependency and multi-causality, stressing the importance of social relations. This is illustrated by Wood (2018), who incorporates both macro-structural changes (policies promoting homeownership) and micro-interactional aspects (construction of social norms) to show how new social norms have supported the mortgage-led accumulation regime in the United Kingdom. Finally, research focusing on the impact of financialization on everyday life depicts, amongst others, how the increasing role of finance in wider aspects of society leads to rising inequalities. Morgan and Olsen (2011), for instance, reveal that micro-finance leads to rising debt levels and reinforces existing power inequalities based on class, caste and poverty.

ARIANE AGUNSOYE

See also

Financial crises; Financialization; Income distribution; Methodology; Neoclassical economics

References

Blaikie, N. (2009), *Designing Social Research*, second edition, Cambridge, UK: Polity Press.
Bracking, S. (2016), *The Financialisation of Power: How Financiers Rule Africa*, London and New York: Routledge.
Danermark, B., M. Ekström, L. Jakobsen and J.C. Karlsson (2002), *Explaining Society: Critical Realism in the Social Sciences*, London and New York: Routledge.
Downward, P. and A. Mearman (2007), 'Retroduction as mixed-methods triangulation in economic research: reorienting economics into social science', *Cambridge Journal of Economics*, 31 (1), 77–99.
Elder-Vass, D. (2010), *The Causal Power of Social Structures – Emergence, Structure and Agency*, Cambridge, UK: Cambridge University Press.
Jefferson, T. (2007), 'Two studies of women's retirement incomes in Australia: assessing some outcomes of pluralism in economic research', *Cambridge Journal of Economics*, 31 (3), 363–78.
Jessop, B. (2015), 'The symptomatology of crises, reading crises and learning from them: some critical realist reflections', *Journal of Critical Realism*, 14 (3), 238–71.
Lawson, J.M. (2006), *Critical Realism and Housing Research*, London and New York: Routledge.

Lawson, T. (2009), 'The current economic crisis: its nature and the course of academic economics', *Cambridge Journal of Economics*, **33** (4), 759–77.

Lee, F. (2012), 'Critical realism, grounded theory, and theory construction in heterodox economics', *Munich Personal RePEc Archive Paper*, No. 40341, available online at https://mpra.ub.uni-muenchen.de/40341/1/MPRA_paper_40341.pdf.

Mäki, U. (2011), 'Scientific realism as a challenge to economics (and vice versa)', *Journal of Economic Methodology*, **18** (1), 1–12.

Marsh, D. (2009), 'Keeping ideas in their place: in place of thin constructivism', *Austrian Journal of Political Science*, **44** (4), 679–96.

Monaghan, L.F. and M. O'Flynn (2017), 'The Madoffization of Irish society: from Ponzi to sociological critique', *Finance and Banking*, **68** (4), 670–92.

Morgan, J. and W. Olsen (2011), 'Aspiration problems for the Indian rural poor: research on self-help groups and micro-finance', *Capital and Class*, **35** (2), 189–212.

Munoz, J. (2016), 'A qualitative case study of the Mexican stock market (BMV) from the perspective of critical realism and grounded theory', in F.S. Lee and B. Cronin (eds), *Handbook of Research Methods and Applications in Heterodox Economics*, Cheltenham, UK, and Northampton, MA, USA: Edward Elgar, pp. 388–99.

Ruwanpura, K.N. (2007), 'Shifting theories: partial perspectives on the household', *Cambridge Journal of Economics*, **31** (4), 525–38.

Soaita, A.M. and C. Dewilde (2019), 'A critical-realist view of housing quality within post-communist EU States: progressing towards a middle-range explanation', *Housing, Theory and Society*, **36** (1), 44–75.

Sum, N.L. and B. Jessop (2013), *Towards a Cultural Political Economy*, Cheltenham, UK, and Northampton, MA, USA: Edward Elgar.

Wood, J.D.G. (2018), 'The integrating role of private homeownership and mortgage credit in British neoliberalism', *Housing Studies*, **33** (7), 993–1013.

Crowding-in and crowding-out

Fiscal policy defines a government's spending behaviour. A contractionary fiscal policy can be defined as the government's decision to cut its spending and/or to increase the existing tax rate. An expansionary fiscal policy, on the other hand, may require a government's direct intervention in the economy through an increase in its own expenditures (Buiter, 1977).

Assuming a balanced budget, an expansionary fiscal policy is expected to lead to a budget deficit, unless the government's excess expenditures are compensated with an increase in fiscal revenues. However, during unexpected shocks to the economy, the government is forced to boost its spending and lower the tax rate at the same time, so that firms and households can contribute to aggregate demand by augmenting their own expenditures (Andrade and Duarte, 2016). This dual action of increased spending and reduced tax revenues often exacerbates budget deficits. The expected influence of this increased public spending on the overall economic activity, whether conducive or adverse, generally depends on two possible propagating mechanisms, namely crowding-in and crowding-out.

Crowding-in is a macroeconomic phenomenon that occurs when an expansionary fiscal policy stimulates the level of the private sector's spending. If the economy is under-utilizing its capacity, and there are unemployed resources, the government's fiscal expansion can persuade the private sector to use part of the available resources, thereby increasing the level of capacity utilization via private spending. During unexpected shocks to the economy, governments resort to expansionary fiscal measures that share a common objective of supplementing aggregate demand to reroute the economy to its steady-state growth trajectory (Balcerzak and Rogalska, 2014). The expansionary measures can be designed as a stimulus package to spur government spending, in addition to a tax reduction for firms and/or households. This stimulus package, directed towards building or improving public infrastructure, is expected to result in a higher income for firms and households, thereby increasing aggregate demand and supply. As a consequence, investment activity returns to normalcy. The economy is also expected to return to its steady-state growth trajectory. This positive impact of the government's expansionary fiscal policy on attracting private spending is called the 'crowding-in effect'.

Crowding-out is a macroeconomic phenomenon that occurs when an expansionary fiscal policy fails to stimulate the level of the private sector's spending. Instead, savings are diverted from the private sector towards the public sector (Friedman, 1978).

If an expansionary fiscal policy is directed towards an activity (such as national defence) that may fail to spur aggregate demand or supply, the undesirable outcome could be a reduction in spending by firms and households.

The logic behind this crowding-out effect is that households are the only source of the supply for loanable funds, whereas the demand for these loanable funds mainly comes from firms. With an expansionary fiscal policy, the government becomes a competitor with the firms for the limited amount of loanable funds (Buiter, 1977). When the economy faces a recession, the creditworthiness of firms and households is negatively impacted, whereas the government still enjoys its own creditworthiness. Hence, households prefer to lend their loanable funds to the government by purchasing government bonds, and firms end up postponing their investment decisions owing to the higher cost of borrowing as a result of higher interest rates.

In addition, assuming that the economy is running at its full capacity with a fixed aggregate supply, the government could also dissuade resources away from the private sector and towards 'forced savings', thus leading to an upward pressure on the price level (Friedman, 1978, p. 597). This crowding-out effect can have a twofold impact. On one side, public spending in the real sector, particularly on infrastructure, can crowd out investment from the private sector, thereby leading to the 'real crowding-out' effect. On the other side, the government's deficit financing through interest-bearing debt instruments can dissuade providing savings to the private sector in order to lend to the public sector, leading to the 'financial crowding-out' effect (Friedman, 1978, p. 597).

The two effects are often dubbed 'fiscal multiplier', owing to the fact that public spending is expected to multiply GDP either positively or negatively, resulting in an upward or a downward multiple of the GDP (Maric, 2015).

The literature seems to provide a consensus over the short-run effectiveness of a government's expansionary fiscal policy. An expansionary fiscal policy leading to a crowding-in effect is plausible in the short run. However, its long-run effects are debatable. The literature also seems to suggest a cautious approach to expansionary fiscal policy, particularly in the long run, to avoid a debt-trap due to the crowding-out effect.

NAJIB KHAN

See also

Aggregate demand; Capacity utilization; Fiscal deficits; Fiscal multiplier; Fiscal policy

References

Andrade, J.S. and A.P. Duarte (2016), 'Crowding-in and crowding-out effects of public investments in the Portuguese economy', *International Review of Applied Economics*, 30 (4), 488–506.

Balcerzak, A.P. and E. Rogalska (2014), 'Crowding out and crowding in within Keynesian framework. Do we need any new empirical research concerning them?', *Economics and Sociology*, 7 (2), 80–93.

Buiter, W.H. (1977), 'Crowding out and the effectiveness of fiscal policy', *Journal of Public Economics*, 7 (3), 309–28.

Friedman, B.J. (1978), 'Crowding out or crowding in? Economic consequences of financing government deficits', *Brookings Papers on Economic Activity*, 3, 593–641.

Maric, Z. (2015), 'Crowding out vs. crowding in effects in transitional countries', *Perspectives of Innovations, Economics and Business*, 15 (4), 126–36.

Cumulative causation

A central tenet of mainstream economic analysis is the assumption that there is a stationary state towards which an economic system is headed, if all the correct production function variables are sufficiently 'plugged in'. The concept of cumulative causation rejects this static approach and takes a dynamic and evolutionary approach to manifest the extent to which an economic system actually moves through historical time.

Cumulative causation is the notion that social reality is an evolving processual novelty; in other words, the operation of causality concerning social phenomena continually feeds upon and in turn transforms the conditions on which the causality operates. This suggests that cause-and-effect sequences in the future derive from cause-and-effect sequences in earlier times (Veblen, 1898; Hodgson, 2001; Lawson, 2015). The capacity for an economic system to expand depends on its past successes.

In this regard, cumulative causation elucidates institutional configurations and interdependencies that set in motion particular path dependencies. Capital accumulation, for instance, is historically contingent upon dynamics that give rise to self-perpetuating cycles of rapid or slow (or even negative) economic growth, respectively. As Kaldor (1977) poignantly noted, while inventions were significant in the process of industrialization in

NAJIB KHAN / DAVID M. FIELDS

the eighteenth century, none of these would have had the same long-run effect had it not been for the evolution of labour productivity, as evidenced by the development of the factory system from cottage industry. Economic growth is due primarily to increasing returns (Young, 1928); augmentations of the size of the market, that is, the level of effective demand, begets an extension and, thus, specialization of the social division of labour.

> [Increasing returns constitute] the development of skill and know-how; the opportunities for easy communication of ideas and experience; the opportunity of ever increasing differentiation of processes and of specialization in human activities. (Kaldor, 1970, p. 484)

Accordingly, it can be argued that Marx's conception of the development of the forces of production, as interrelated with the development of the social division of labour, is an antecedent to the determinant of productivity as outlined by the principle of cumulative causation (Ricoy, 2003). A 'widening sphere of circulation' (Marx, 1973, p. 407), and, thus, increasing demands for the means of production induce

> specialisation of the instruments of labour, by the formation of detail labourers, and by grouping and combining the latter into a single mechanism, division of labour in manufacture creates a qualitative gradation, and a quantitative proportion in the social process of production; it consequently creates a definite organisation of the labour of society, and thereby develops at the same time new productive forces in the society. (Marx, 1867, p. 364)

A path dependency of long-run economic progress, hence, is an income effect, in which the rate of growth of induced investment and the rate of growth of consumption are attuned to the rate of growth of autonomous expenditures (Kaldor, 1970). If the rate of autonomous expenditures is significantly low over historical time, an economic system will undergo an evolutionary trajectory towards economic stagnation, that is, a social condition of underdevelopment (Myrdal, 1957). To abstractly demonstrate it, let I (total investment) $= f(Y)$, where Y equals total output, which is total income from the effects of autonomous expenditures. Since the level of effective demand determines the level of economic activity, we can derive that $Y = \varphi Z$, where φ is the multiplier, and Z is the level of autonomous expenditures in the economy.

A decisive effect of a permanent increase in the demand for a good is an increase of the productive capacity through investment in fixed capital, which in turn fosters an increase in more employment owing to demand for said assets.

Let us propose the stylized fact that workers consume their wage bill and capitalists save profits. We can write $Y = W + \Pi$, where Y is total income (output), W is gross wages and Π is gross profits; total income Y (output) is the sum of gross wages and gross profits in the economy. Savings, as a residual, are equal to the excess of income over consumption, which is equal to gross profits. Increases in effective demand not only lead to increases in employment, but, with increases in consumption due to increased employment, allowing for wages to rise with productivity, gross profits aggrandize. If expected future earnings are met by demand, profits are directed towards more investment, and hence more employment. This, in turn, fosters more investment, and hence more profit. If shocks are avoided, a long-run full employment position of stability is ultimately reached.

On the basis of cumulative causation, we can determine the extent to which an economic system is a social process of scale. It illuminates the particular mechanisms of how production is 'continually transformed and revolutionized' (Marx, 1891, pp. 39–40), given historically specific social conditions, and how, thus, productivity is a calibration of increasing returns.

DAVID M. FIELDS

See also

Business cycles; Effective demand; Growth; Power; Traverse, path dependency, and economic dynamics

References

Hodgson, G. (2001), 'Darwin, Veblen and the problem of causality in economics', *History and Philosophy of the Life Sciences*, **23** (3–4), 385–423.

Kaldor, N. (1970), 'The case for regional policies', *Scottish Journal of Political Economy*, **60** (5), 481–91.

Kaldor, N. (1977), 'Capitalism and industrial development: some lessons from Britain's experience', *Cambridge Journal of Economics*, **1** (2), 193–204.

Lawson, T. (2015), 'Process, order and stability in Veblen', *Cambridge Journal of Economics*, **39** (4), 993–1030.

Marx, K. (1867), *Capital, Vol. I*, New York: International Publishers.

DAVID M. FIELDS

Marx, K. (1891), *Wage Labour and Capital*, Moscow: Progress Publishers.
Marx, K. (1973), *Grundrisse*, Harmondsworth: Penguin.
Myrdal, G. (1957), *Economic Theory and Underdeveloped Regions*, London: Gerald Duckworth.
Ricoy, C. (2003), 'Marx on division of labour, mechanization and technical progress', *European Journal of the History of Economic Thought*, **10** (1), 47–79.
Veblen, T. (1898), 'Why is economics not an evolutionary science?', *Quarterly Journal of Economics*, **12** (4), 373–97.
Young, A. (1928), 'Increasing returns and economic progress', *Economic Journal*, **38** (152), 527–42.

Currency board

A currency board is a fixed-exchange-rate regime in which the monetary authority (central bank) commits to pegging the domestic currency to a foreign anchor currency. It issues domestic currency that is fully backed by the reserves of foreign assets and stands ready to exchange its currency on demand for the anchor foreign currency at a fixed exchange rate. New emission of domestic currency must be backed 100 per cent with foreign exchange, and so the total amount of its domestic base money corresponds to the value of the currency board's holdings of foreign reserve assets. In this sense the supply of reserves is passive. Only when domestic banks or residents present foreign currency to the currency board for conversion into domestic currency will the domestic monetary base be changed. Unlike traditional central banks that may hold (monetize) government debt, currency boards may only hold foreign exchange reserves as assets; to wit, there is no fiduciary issue in a currency board system.

The prohibition against holding domestic assets (sovereign debt, mortgages, discount loans to banks) has implications concerning the ability of a currency board to carry out monetary policy. Although a traditional central bank may pursue discretionary monetary policy by altering its portfolio of domestic assets to change the monetary base or to support the exchange rate, the monetary authority under a currency board regime is unable to do this. Under this monetary arrangement neither monetary aggregates nor the domestic interest rate can be considered as pure monetary domestic instruments and used accordingly. With domestic currency convertible to the reserve currency at a fixed price, the currency board has no control over the quantity of domestic currency in circulation; this is determined by the demand to hold it. The currency board's role in determining the supply of reserves is entirely passive, 'acting like a warehouse, storing reserves in the form of foreign currency securities and issuing notes and coin in their pace' (Lewis, 2002, p. 129). It may neither purchase assets from commercial banks via the discount window nor engage in open-market operations. Hence the monetary base is beyond its control. Under the rule-based currency-board regime, market forces determine the monetary base; it is increased when the private sector sells foreign currency to the central bank at the fixed exchange rate and is decreased when the private sector purchases foreign currency from it to finance a balance-of-payments deficit (Williamson, 1995).

While currency boards back 100 per cent of their base money with the anchor currency, it is important to note that reserves are only a fraction of the value of the marketable domestic financial assets that are denominated in their currencies. In countries under existing currency boards, reserves back less than half of the domestic M2 money supply (currency, demand deposits, time and savings deposits), the remainder being backed by domestic assets such as sovereign debt and loans. The expansion of the domestic M2 money supply is theoretically limited by the reserve requirement, which is set by the currency board and designed to prevent erratic changes in the money multiplier (Kopcke, 1999).

The metaphor most often cited to explain the simplicity and rule-bound nature of the currency board regime borrows from the price-specie flow mechanism of Hume's gold standard (see Hanke and Schuler, 1991, 1994; Williamson, 1995; Kopcke, 1999). In these accounts, a current-account deficit will lead to a reduction in the monetary base, as the public trades domestic currency for foreign currency. This will cause a rise in domestic interest rates, a fall in aggregate demand, and a depreciation of the real exchange rate that set into motion a restoration of equilibrium. The contraction in the money supply also reduces demand for labour and other factors of production, reducing the country's prices relative to other countries. A variant of this analysis uses the insight of the fixed-exchange-rate version of the Mundell–Fleming model, where

DAVID M. FIELDS / SHIRLEY GEDEON

under a fixed-exchange-rate regime it is impossible to simultaneously have independent monetary policy, open capital markets, and a fixed exchange rate (the so-called 'impossibility of the Holy Trinity'). Money supply endogeneity is traced as follows: Δ international reserves →Δ monetary base →Δ broad money (Dornbusch and Giavazzi, 1999; Wolf et al., 2008).

The claim that the currency board provides an automatic adjustment to the domestic money supply that mirrors the surplus on the balance of payments holds only if the sole source of new foreign reserves derives from positive net exports. While the currency board's reserve holdings are directly related to the acquisition of foreign reserves, the existence of open capital markets means that foreign reserves can also be acquired independently of foreign trade, namely through net private capital inflow and workers' remittances. In the formerly socialist countries of Bulgaria, Bosnia-Herzegovina, Estonia and Lithuania, where currency boards were established in the mid 1990s, this occurred through financial sector foreign direct investment, namely, the establishment of branches and subsidiaries of banks from Western Europe. Through their subsidiaries, parent banks transferred funds earmarked as foreign liabilities on the domestic banks' balance sheets that were largely absorbed by the non-tradables sectors such as consumer durables, real estate, financial assets and construction. The direct inflow of foreign reserves caused the monetary base to increase, and, via the multiplier, the broad money supply. Despite current-account deficits in all four countries, domestic money supply growth reached as high as 25 per cent annually, counter to the classical argument summarized above. During the global financial crisis of 2007–08, international banking groups withdrew liquidity from the local subsidiaries, creating great strain on the currency board as the monetary base contracted, necessitating international intervention to stabilize the banking systems (Gedeon, 2009; Ostry et al., 2010).

The singular advantage of the currency board regime is that it depoliticizes the monetary system and closes the door for central bank financing of government deficits. This can provide credibility to the fixed exchange rate and encourage the private domestic sector to hold domestic currency and deposits, thereby supporting economic development and financial sector deepening. However, the fact that a currency board regime permits a completely open door to foreign funds means that neither a dearth of deposits by domestic residents nor a shortage of reserves need lead to a slowdown in bank lending (and hence money supply growth) so long as foreign reserves can be borrowed from international financial markets.

SHIRLEY GEDEON

See also

Aggregate demand; Endogenous money; Exchange rates – fixed vs flexible; Exchange rates – managed; Financial crises

References

Dornbusch, R. and F. Giavazzi (1999), 'Hard currency and sound credit: a financial agenda for Central Europe', *European Investment Bank Papers*, **4** (2), 24–32.
Gedeon, S. (2009), 'Money supply endogeneity under a currency board regime: the case of Bosnia and Herzegovina', *Journal of Post Keynesian Economics*, **32** (1), 97–114.
Hanke, S.H. and K. Schuler (1991), *Currency Boards for Eastern Europe*, Washington, DC: Heritage Foundation.
Hanke, S.H. and K. Schuler (1994), *Currency Boards for Developing Countries: A Handbook*. San Francisco: ICS Press.
Kopcke, R.W. (1999), 'Currency boards: once and future monetary regimes?', *New England Economic Review*, May, 21–37.
Lewis, M.K. (2002), 'Currency boards and currency arrangements in transition economies', in Z. Sevic (ed.), *Banking Reforms in South East Europe*, Cheltenham, UK, and Northampton, MA, USA: Edward Elgar, pp. 125–46.
Ostry, J.D., A.R. Ghosh, K. Habermeier, M. Chamon, M.S. Qureshi and D.B.S. Reinhardt (2010), 'Capital inflows: the role of controls', *International Monetary Fund Staff Position Note*, No. 10/04.
Williamson, J. (1995), *What Role for Currency Boards?*, Washington, DC: Institute for International Economics.
Wolf, H.C., A.R. Ghosh, H. Berger and A. Gulde (2008), *Currency Boards in Retrospect and Prospect*, Cambridge, MA: MIT Press.

Currency hierarchy

John Maynard Keynes, in many of his writings, proposed the reform of the international monetary system (IMS). For instance, in *A Treatise on Money* (1930/1976, vol. 2) he outlined a

SHIRLEY GEDEON / FERNANDO FERRARI FILHO

proposal for the operation of a supernational central bank to ensure the stability of commodity prices and the liquidity of the world economy, while in his *Proposals for an International Clearing Union* (1944/1980) he suggested the bancor as a supranational currency to be used in the IMS.

Considering that the configurations of all IMS – from the gold standard to the Bretton Woods regime and, mainly, after the collapse of the latter regime, that is, the years of the flexible US dollar standard – have been asymmetric and centred on a national currency, Keynes's proposal aimed at eliminating the inherent hierarchical characteristic of an IMS anchored in a national currency. In other words, knowing that in a national economy money is imposed by the State and its sovereignty is determined by the medium of exchange, unit of account and store of value functions, while in the world economy the use of a national currency as an international currency is determined by the economic and political power of a specific country (as a result, in the IMS national currencies are not equivalent in terms of degree of convertibility and liquidity), according to Keynes it was necessary to abolish the privileges of national currencies that were used as international currencies. This idea is, clearly, observed in Keynes's revolutionary *Proposals for an International Clearing Union*: 'We need an instrument of international currency having general acceptability between nations. ... We need a quantum of international currency, which is neither determined in an unpredictable and irrelevant manner ... nor subject to large variations depending on ... reserve policies of individual countries' (Keynes, 1944/1980, p. 168). By the way, the degree of convertibility and liquidity of some currencies at the international level is mainly determined by the economic and political power of their issuing country in the world. This is the reason why the US dollar has been the main currency and has influenced all economies in the world since the end of the Second World War.

Keynes's attention regarding the creation of an autonomous international currency is, in the field of international political economy, called currency hierarchy, that is, the degree of convertibility and liquidity that some national currencies have in the world economy.

Going into this direction, Cohen (1998, 2015) created the concept of hegemonic currency that is related to the fact that some countries, owing to their geopolitical power in the world, have the capacity to issue debts, in their own currencies, both domestically and internationally. Given that, Cohen (1998) defines monetary sovereignty and argues that a national currency becomes an international currency because economic agents 'choose' the currency that brings more confidence to them. In other words, the acceptance of a national currency as an international currency is given by demand. Moreover, based on the ideas of liquidity premium and policy space, he elaborates a 'monetary pyramid' to show why some currencies are demanded and others are not; thus, the 'monetary pyramid' explains why there is a currency hierarchy in the world.

Similarly, Prates (2017) argued that, since the collapse of the Bretton Woods regime in the early 1970s, the IMS, in a framework of financial globalization, has been more asymmetric, and, as a result, the idea of currency hierarchy has dominated the international relationships between countries, mainly between central and peripheral currencies. Thus, given that the asymmetries of the IMS have created different degrees for hegemonic currencies, she adapted the Cohen's 'monetary pyramid' to central and peripheral currencies. To sum up, according to Prates (2017), at the top of the 'monetary pyramid' are the highest currencies, that is, those currencies that have more liquidity premium and those economies that have high monetary sovereignty (policy space in the world). These are the case of the US dollar, the first at the top, and the euro, the second one. Sterling pounds, yens, Swiss francs and Canadian dollars are located in the middle of the pyramid, while emerging currencies, such as those of China and of some Latin American countries, which have a low liquidity premium and monetary sovereignty, are at the floor of the pyramid.

In a post-Keynesian perspective, Davidson (1994) presents a proposal for reforming the IMS that goes in the same direction as Keynes's international clearing union. After defining a specific taxonomy to explain the economic dynamism of an open unionized monetary system (UMS) and an open non-unionized monetary system, he describes the rules required to operate an IMS according to a UMS. Like Keynes (1944/1980), Davidson's proposal is to create an IMS able to regulate the international liquidity and to stabilize the exchange rate regime from speculation activity, among others.

To conclude, it is important to mention that the internationalization of a national currency, in an international political economy perspective, is based on the economic (trade and financial) integration and geopolitical power of the issuing country in the world economy (De Conti, 2011). Further, the international financial crisis of 2007–08, and the 'great recession' in 2009–10, have brought the idea of restructuring the IMS as a necessary condition for the world to bring back economic stability. Thus, as Keynes (1944/1980, p. 176) noted, the world economy needs 'the substitution of an expansionist, in place of a contractionist' regime. Without eliminating the global currency asymmetries and reforming the IMS, the world economy will continue to be 'a by-product of the activities of a casino' (Keynes, 1936/2007, p. 159).

FERNANDO FERRARI FILHO

See also

A Treatise on Money; Bretton Woods; International financial architecture; International monetary system; Keynes Plan

References

Cohen, B.J. (1998), *The Geography of Money*, London and Ithaca: Cornell University Press.
Cohen, B.J. (2015), *Currency Power: Understanding Monetary Rivalry*, Princeton: Princeton University Press.
Davidson, P. (1994), *Post Keynesian Macroeconomic Theory*, Aldershot and Brookfield: Edward Elgar.
De Conti, B.M. (2011), *Les politiques de change et monétaire: les dillemnes affrontés par les pays à monnaies périphériques*, Paris: Université Paris 13, PhD dissertation.
Keynes, J.M. (1930/1976), *A Treatise on Money, Volume II*, New York: AMS Press.
Keynes, J.M. (1944/1980), *Activities 1940–1944: Shaping the Post-War World – The Clearing Union (The Collected Writings of John Maynard Keynes, Volume XXV)*, London: Macmillan.
Keynes, J.M. (1936/2007), *The General Theory of Employment, Interest and Money*, London: Palgrave Macmillan.
Prates, D.M. (2017), 'Monetary sovereignty, currency hierarchy and policy space: a post-Keynesian approach', *Texto para Discussão*, Instituto de Economia/Unicamp, No. 315, available at https://www.eco.unicamp.br/images/arquivos/artigos/3554/TD315.pdf (last accessed 7 November 2020).

Currency School

The Currency School emerged in Great Britain in the 1830s and developed principles, intended to make a mixed metallic and paper currency behave like a metallic currency, that were embodied in Sir Robert Peel's Bank Charter Act of 1844. The monetary economists George Warde Norman (1833), Robert Torrens (1840), Mountifort Longfield, Samuel Jones Loyd (later Lord Overstone) (later collected in Overstone, 1857), and J.R. McCulloch (1831) spoke for the Currency School in debates with the Banking School (for instance, Thomas Tooke, John Fullarton, and John Stuart Mill) and Free Banking School (such as James William Gilbart and Poulett Scrope) over the decennial rechartering of the Bank of England. The Currency School drew inspiration from David Ricardo's contributions to the bullionist controversy two decades before (collected in Ricardo, 1951–73, Vol. III), especially his 1810–11 *The High Price of Gold Bullion: A Proof of the Depreciation of Bank Notes*, and followed Ricardo's exposition of the quantity theory of money and the price-specie flow mechanism of trade adjustment. The ideas of the Banking School stemmed from Henry Thornton's writings and speeches in that controversy when Britain was on an inconvertible paper standard during the Napoleonic Wars.

Just as Ricardo had criticized the Bank of England for excessive issue of bank notes during the period of inconvertibility, the Currency School blamed the Bank of England for amplifying the credit cycle instead of varying the money supply in the interest of stability (even though one of them, George Warde Norman, was a director of the Bank of England for most of the time from 1821 to 1872). Loyd and others of the Currency School argued that, with a pure metallic currency, gold inflows or outflows would immediately change the currency in circulation, adjusting the price level and bringing the gold flows to an end. Such gold flows would only have the same effect with a mixed currency if the paper money in circulation was varied in proportion to the precious metals. The Currency School attributed price increases and gold outflows to excessive issue of bank notes, with the gold outflow threatening the convertibility of the notes. The currency principle held that a mixed metallic and paper currency (coin plus notes of the Bank of England

and of Scottish and country banks) should be managed to behave like a metallic currency and to avoid gold drains (see Daugherty (1942–43), Skaggs (1999) and Arnon (2011) on the doctrines of the Currency and Banking Schools).

The Currency School did not accept that interbank clearing would limit overissue of bank notes, especially in view of the size and privileges of the Bank of England compared to the country banks and Scottish banks. While recognizing that credit instruments such as deposits and bills of exchange could affect prices, the Currency School did not include them in the money supply and held that the quantity of credit instruments varied with the quantity of coins and notes in circulation. In contrast, the Banking School considered bank notes just one among many forms of credit and viewed the quantity of notes in circulation as demand-determined, so that overissue of notes was impossible. This divergence between the views of the Currency and Banking Schools on the role of credit and the exogeneity or endogeneity of the money supply continued and continues to resonate in later monetary debates.

Embodying the currency principle, the Bank Charter Act of 1844 limited the maximum quantity of country-bank notes and placed a 100 per cent marginal reserve requirement in gold coins or bullion on Bank of England notes issued beyond a fixed fiduciary issue of 14 million British pounds. The Bank of England was divided into a new Issue Department, which issued bank notes in return for gold, and a Banking Department, which made loans and took deposits, holding its reserves against those deposits in bank notes. Thus, when bank notes were presented to the Issue Department for redemption in gold, the Bank of England could not reissue those notes, so a gold drain would automatically contract the note issue. The division of the Bank of England into two departments reflected the Currency School's wish to regulate the note issue, which could be either excessive or deficient without appropriate management, but not to regulate other banking activities. The suspensions of the Bank Act of 1844 during the crises of 1847, 1857, and 1866 were greeted by the Banking School as vindication of their rejection of the currency principle but were dismissed by Loyd and others of the Currency School as transient episodes of little significance.

ROBERT W. DIMAND

See also

Banking School; Credit money; Endogenous money; Exogenous money; Reserves – role of

References

Arnon, A. (2011), *Monetary Theory and Policy from Hume and Smith to Wicksell*, Cambridge, UK: Cambridge University Press.
Daugherty, M.R. (1942–43), 'The Currency–Banking controversy', *Southern Economic Journal*, **9** (2), 140–55 and **9** (3), 241–51.
McCulloch, J.R. (1831), *Historical Sketch of the Bank of England*, London: Longmans.
Norman, G.W. (1833), *Remarks upon Some Prevalent Errors with Respect to Currency and Banking and Suggestions to the Legislature as to the Renewal of the Bank Charter*, London: R. Hunter.
Overstone, Lord [Loyd, S.J.] (1857), *Tracts and Other Publications on Metallic and Paper Currency*, London: Harrison.
Ricardo, D. (1951–73), *The Works and Correspondence of David Ricardo*, 11 volumes, edited by P. Sraffa with M.H. Dobb, Cambridge, UK: Cambridge University Press.
Skaggs, N.T. (1999), 'Changing views: twentieth-century opinion on the Banking School–Currency School controversy', *History of Political Economy*, **31** (2), 361–90.
Torrens, R. (1840), *A Letter to Thomas Tooke, Esq., in Reply to his Objections Against the Separation of the Business of the Bank into a Department of Issue and a Department of Deposit and Discount with a Plan of Bank Reform*, London: Longman, Hurst, Orme and Brown.

Current accounts

A country's current accounts record within a given period, say, in a quarter or a year, how income is generated by production, how it is distributed to the institutional sectors, and how it is redistributed once direct taxes and current transfers are considered. In addition, they provide an overview of the institutional sectors' spending and saving decisions. The current account is comprised of three subsets, namely the production account, the primary income account, and the secondary income account. Let us consider these in turn.

The production account indicates the contribution of each of the economy's institutional sectors to the gross domestic product (GDP). Specifically, the GDP is the sum of each sector's gross value added (GVA) and the indirect taxes

Table 1 Production account of a domestic institutional sector

Produced output
− Intermediate consumption
= Gross value added
− Consumption of fixed capital
= Net value added

Table 2 Primary income account of an institutional sector

Gross value added/trade balance
+ Compensation of employees
+ Taxes on production and imports
− Subsidies
+ Property income
(Mixed income)
= Primary income, gross

received minus the subsidies paid by the public sector. Each sector's GVA is derived only once intermediate consumption is deducted from output. Output indicates the level of production within a given period, while intermediate consumption refers to the amount of goods and services completely used up in the production process (see Eurostat, 2010, pp. 68–69). Further, subtracting the consumption of fixed capital from the GVA yields the net value added.

Table 1 shows the sequence of the product account. Note that all entries are expressed in nominal values and that in the case of the external sector, production refers to exports and imports of goods and services (see International Monetary Fund, 2013, pp. 11–15).

The primary income account records the manner according to which income generated from production is allocated between institutional sectors. Primary income consists of three main categories, which are the compensation of employees, net indirect taxes, and property (or rentier) income. The compensation of employees includes wages and social contributions, actual and imputed, of both employees and employers (see European Commission et al., 2009, pp. 140–143 and Eurostat, 2014, pp. 70–76). Net indirect taxes are retrieved after subtracting subsidies on production from indirect taxes. The latter includes the value-added tax (VAT), taxes on products, taxes on export and import duties net of VAT, and other taxes on production. Finally, property income relates to the following five sources:

(a) the income generated from holding assets such as interest on deposits, securities, and loans;
(b) distributed income of corporations, for instance to the owners of equity shares;
(c) reinvested earnings on foreign direct investment, which reflect income of a resident unit from subsidiaries, associates, and branches from abroad;
(d) other investment income, attributable to insurance policy holders, pension entitlements, and collective investment fund shareholders; and
(e) rent.

Table 2 summarizes the above. Note that mixed income refers to income from self-employment and thus affects only the gross primary income of households.

Finally, the secondary income account indicates the reallocation of primary income, through current transfers. The latter are defined as transactions between institutional sectors in terms of goods, services, or assets for which there is no direct counterpart. Further, current transfers are distinguished from capital transfers as the latter involve also dispositions of assets or relinquishing of financial claims (see Eurostat, 2010, pp. 113–122). Current transfers include taxes on income, wealth, and so on, or direct taxation. They further include net social contributions, social transfers paid in cash, that is, unemployment benefits, while other current transfers concern transfers that take place between international institutions and national governments, or between resident and non-resident units and which are not capital transfers. Finally, current transfers include non-life insurance claims and premiums.

The gross disposable income is retrieved once the aforementioned transactions are taken into consideration. Particularly, in the case of households a further inclusion of social transfers in kind yields the adjusted disposable income or the social wage. In advance, when deducting consumption expenditure from disposable income the gross savings or the current account balance is retrieved. Table 3 summarizes all this.

In conclusion, current accounts allow the examination of:

(a) the growth regime and the macro-financial stability of an economy given the detailed

Table 3 Secondary income account of an institutional sector

Primary income, gross
− Taxes on income, wealth, and so on
− Net social contributions
+ Social benefits other than social transfers in kind
+ Other current transfers
= Disposable income, gross/secondary income, gross
+ Social transfers in kind
= Adjusted disposable income, gross
− Actual final consumption
Savings, gross/current account balance

exposition of the main contributions to effective demand;
(b) the manner according to which functional income is distributed;
(c) the effectiveness of fiscal policy in terms of income inequality and social protection;
(d) the process of financialization by focusing on the relative size of the rentier income, and;
(e) the presence of imbalances vis-à-vis the external sector.

CHRISTOS PIERROS

See also

Effective demand; Financialization; Fiscal policy; Growth – wage led vs profit-led; Income distribution

References

European Commission, International Monetary Fund, Organisation for Economic Co-operation and Development, United Nations, and World Bank (2009), *System of National Accounts 2008*, New York: European Commission, International Monetary Fund, Organisation for Economic Co-operation and Development, United Nations, and World Bank.
Eurostat (2010), *European System of Accounts ESA 2010*, Brussels: European Commission.
Eurostat (2014), *Manual on Government Deficit and Debt: Implementation of ESA 2010*, Brussels: European Commission.
International Monetary Fund (2013), *Balance of Payments and International Investment Position Manual (BPM6)*, Washington, DC: International Monetary Fund.

Debt deflation

Irving Fisher (1933) coined the term 'debt deflation' to describe the striking twin phenomena of excessive private debt and falling prices that characterized the Great Depression, and as a general explanation of serious economic crises in capitalism in general. Between 1929 and mid-1932, the US private debt ratio rose from 87 per cent to 143 per cent of GDP (normalizing data to coincide with post-1946 Federal Reserve data), even though debt levels fell from 91 billion to 80 billion US dollars during the same period. Though private debt was falling, the ratio of private debt to GDP rose sharply as nominal GDP fell faster still, spurred both by falls in real output of up to 15 per cent per annum between 1930 and 1932, and falls in the price level of up to 10 per cent per annum between 1931 and 1933.

Fisher (1933, p. 344, italics in the original) saw this process as the primary cause of the Great Depression:

> *the very effort of individuals to lessen their burden of debts increases it, because of the mass effect of the stampede to liquidate in swelling each dollar owed.* Then we have the great paradox which, I submit, is the chief secret of most, if not all, great depressions: *The more the debtors pay, the more they owe.*

Fisher's explanation was explicitly a non-equilibrium one. He noted that while it may be sensible to assume that economic variables tend to equilibrium,

> the exact equilibrium thus sought is seldom reached and never long maintained. New disturbances are, humanly speaking, sure to occur, so that, in actual fact, any variable is almost always above or below the ideal equilibrium .... Theoretically there ... must be over- or underproduction, over- or under-consumption, over- or underspending, over- or under-saving, over- or under-investment, and over or under everything else. It is as absurd to assume that, for any long period of time, the variables in the economic organization, or any part of them, will 'stay put,' in perfect equilibrium, as to assume that the Atlantic Ocean can ever be without a wave. (Fisher, 1933, p. 339)

Fisher asserted that non-equilibrium forces that set off the Great Depression are '*overindebtedness* to start with and *deflation* following soon after' (Fisher, 1933, p. 341, italics in the original), and mused that either on their own would be insufficient to trigger a crisis, since the other factor – inflation or low levels of debt – would counteract the forces tending to depression.

Assuming the existence of both factors, Fisher then set out a nine-stage chain-reaction process following from this initial disequilibrium. This began with distress selling by debtors to reduce their debts, which caused a contraction in the money supply, leading to falling prices, and low nominal but very high effective rates of interest that increased the burden of debt repayment even as debtors reduced their nominal debts. He saw no necessary end to this process without deliberate reflation by the government, which made him both an advocate for and fan of reflation by the Roosevelt government.

Fisher's theory was ignored by mainstream economists on the basis of the loanable funds model of banking, in which bank lending does not create money. Bernanke (2000, p. 24) wrote that while Fisher influenced Roosevelt, 'Fisher's idea was less influential in academic circles, though, because of the counterargument that debt-deflation represented no more than a redistribution from one group (debtors) to another (creditors). Absent implausibly large differences in marginal spending propensities among the groups, it was suggested, pure redistributions should have no significant macroeconomic effects.'

In contrast, debt deflation was taken up by post-Keynesian economists who understood that bank lending creates money and debt repayment destroys it (Moore, 1979), something Fisher himself was also cognizant of (see Fisher, 1932, pp. 14–16), and which is now supported by some central banks (see McLeay et al., 2014; Deutsche Bundesbank, 2017). Fisher's debt-deflation theory was the original inspiration to Hyman Minsky's financial instability hypothesis, with Minsky citing Fisher well before his first realization that the textbook IS–LM model of Keynes was erroneous (Minsky, 1969, p. 9).

Minsky's hypothesis fleshed out Fisher's by explaining how an economy could reach a position of excessive private debt via a series of credit-driven booms and busts (Minsky, 1977). Keen (1995) showed how debt deflation was a potential outcome of a complex system feedback process when the private debt to GDP ratio was added as an additional system state to Goodwin's (1967) cyclical growth model.

Keen (2016) also argues that the 2008 Great Recession was a debt-deflationary crisis, attenuated as both Minsky and Fisher asserted by high levels of government spending. Grasselli and Costa-Lima (2012) have formalized Fisher's observations on the role of government spending in destabilizing the stable bad equilibrium of the Keen model. Debt deflation remains an active area of post-Keynesian research.

STEVE KEEN

See also

Bubbles – credit; Debt-led boom; Endogenous money; Financial instability hypothesis; Paradox of debt

References

Bernanke, B.S. (2000), *Essays on the Great Depression*, Princeton, NJ: Princeton University Press.
Deutsche Bundesbank (2017), 'The role of banks, non-banks and the central bank in the money creation process', *Deutsche Bundesbank Monthly Report*, April, pp. 13–33.
Fisher, I. (1932), *Booms and Depressions: Some First Principles*, New York: Adelphi.
Fisher, I. (1933), 'The debt-deflation theory of great depressions', *Econometrica*, **1** (4), 337–57.
Goodwin, R.M. (1967), 'A growth cycle', in C.H. Feinstein (ed.), *Socialism, Capitalism and Economic Growth*, Cambridge, UK: Cambridge University Press, pp. 54–8.
Grasselli, M. and B. Costa Lima (2012), 'An analysis of the Keen model for credit expansion, asset price bubbles and financial fragility', *Mathematics and Financial Economics*, **6** (1), 191–210.
Keen, S. (1995), 'Finance and economic breakdown: modeling Minsky's "Financial Instability Hypothesis"', *Journal of Post Keynesian Economics*, **17** (4), 607–35.
Keen, S. (2016), 'Modeling financial instability', in A.G. Malliaris, L. Shaw and H. Shefrin (eds), *The Global Financial Crisis and Its Aftermath: Hidden factors in the meltdown*, Oxford and New York: Oxford University Press, pp. 67–103.
McLeay, M., A. Radia and R. Thomas (2014), 'Money creation in the modern economy', *Bank of England Quarterly Bulletin*, **54** (1), 14–27.
Minsky, H.P. (1969), 'The new uses of monetary powers', *Nebraska Journal of Economics and Business*, **8** (2), 3–15.
Minsky, H.P. (1977), 'The financial instability hypothesis: an interpretation of Keynes and an alternative to "standard" theory', *Nebraska Journal of Economics and Business*, **16** (1), 5–16.
Moore, B.J. (1979), 'The endogenous money stock', *Journal of Post Keynesian Economics*, **2** (1), 49–70.

STEVE KEEN

Debt – external

'Gross external debt is the amount, at any specific time, of disbursed and outstanding contractual liabilities of residents of a country to repay principal, with or without interest, or to pay interest, with or without principal, to non-residents' (International Monetary Fund, 1993, p. 106). 'Non-equity liabilities' may sometimes be the relevant definition of external debt, especially when dealing with a country's net position (ibid.). The latter is defined as the difference between all assets and liabilities with respect to the rest of the world, mainly made up of equity (including foreign direct investment) and non-equity (including debt).

Net lending countries have an advantage over net borrowing countries in that the former are overall holders of funds that are lent to the latter. Thus, net borrowers depend on financial resources coming from net lenders and thus on the monetary policy decisions carried out by their central banks, whose policy announcements and decisions have an impact on exchange rates and, as a consequence, on the demand and valuation of financial instruments denominated in different currencies.

When the debt requirements denominated in foreign currency are important, the risk of over-indebtedness increases sharply with the volatility of the exchange rate of the country's currency with respect to the currencies of its lenders, thus making it more vulnerable to financial crises. When most of the stock of debt is denominated in a single currency (rather than several currencies) the exposure of the economy to a sharp depreciation is naturally high. Thus, in a globalised world, exchange rate management is crucial for carrying out debt management.

The post-Volcker shock period (after 1979) is such that virtually only the United States can run capital account surpluses/current account deficits, whereas all other countries can run capital account deficits with respect to the United States, while at the same time pursuing current account surpluses. Thus, since then, all countries other than the United States must compete with each other in order to achieve export-led growth and to attract financial resources denominated in US dollars.

Virtually everywhere (with important exceptions such as Japan) a large proportion of foreign debt is currently denominated in US dollars, even when the funds are lent by non-US banks. An alternative to counter the US dollar's 'exorbitant privilege' (Eichengreen, 2010) is the creation of an alternative international monetary system strongly based on the Keynes Plan (see for instance Costabile, 2009), which would give less weight to this currency. For borrowing countries, this would be equivalent to a diversification of foreign debt, which reduces risk exposure of over-indebtedness following fluctuations in the US dollar exchange rates.

On the list of other possible solutions to counter the negative effects of this risk we can find capital controls. Ostry et al. (2011), the International Monetary Fund (2012) and Ghosh and Qureshi (2016) recognize the usefulness of these instruments. Further, Crotty and Epstein (1999) argue that they are highly likely to contribute to avoid instability generated by large capital inflows and outflows, that is, the transfer problem (Lane and Milesi-Ferretti, 2004).

The analysis of firms' capital structure may be useful in studying foreign capital dependency. The standard benchmark starts with the distinction of equity and debt liabilities. Productive firms in net lending countries decide on their structure based on domestic interest rates and stock prices. The structure of firms in net borrowing countries is defined by these too but also, and even more importantly, by foreign stock prices, interest and inflation rates. In the short run, currency appreciations are normally followed (and further enhanced) by capital inflows. Lasting expected appreciations are likely to encourage foreign direct investment (FDI), whose permanence in the net borrowing country also depends on whether regulations concerning it (or lack thereof) favour international financial profits.

The dualism between devaluations being associated with foreign debt increases, and appreciations encouraging FDI (a major outcome of the Great Moderation) explains, at least in part, the shift from foreign debt (artificially reduced in periods of appreciation) to equity financing and FDI in the past couple of decades (Lane and Milesi-Ferretti, 2007).

Currently, several international organizations (the Bank for International Settlements, the International Monetary Fund, the Organisation for Economic Co-operation and Development, and the World Bank) have joined in order to bring together the data needed to analyse external debt by country (on both asset and liability sides) consistent with the United Nations' system of national accounts (see the Joint External Debt Hub, www.jedh.org).

LUIS REYES

See also

Capital controls; Current accounts; Exchange rates; Financial crises; Keynes Plan

References

Costabile, L. (2009), 'Current global imbalances and the Keynes Plan: a Keynesian approach for reforming the international monetary system', *Structural Change and Economic Dynamics*, **20** (2), 79–89.

Crotty, J. and G. Epstein (1999), 'A defense of capital controls in light of the Asian financial crisis', *Journal of Economic Issues*, **33** (2), 427–33.

Eichengreen, B. (2010), *Exorbitant Privilege: The Rise and Fall of the Dollar and the Future of the International Monetary System*, Oxford: Oxford University Press.

Ghosh, A. and M. Qureshi (2016), 'What's in a name? That which we call capital controls', *International Monetary Fund Working Paper*, No. 16/25.

International Monetary Fund (1993), *Balance of Payments Manual*, Washington, DC: International Monetary Fund.

International Monetary Fund (2012), 'The liberalization and management of capital flows: an institutional view', *International Monetary Fund Policy Paper*, Washington, DC, USA: International Monetary Fund, available online at https://www.imf.org/external/np/pp/eng/2012/111412.pdf.

Lane, P.R. and G.M. Milesi-Ferretti (2004), 'The transfer problem revisited: net foreign assets and real exchange rates', *Review of Economics and Statistics*, **86** (4), 841–57.

Lane, P.R. and G.M. Milesi-Ferretti (2007), 'The external wealth of nations mark II: revised and extended estimates of foreign assets and liabilities, 1970–2004', *Journal of International Economics*, **73** (2), 223–50.

Ostry, J., A. Ghosh, M. Chamon and M. Qureshi (2011), 'Capital controls: when and why?', *IMF Economic Review*, **59** (3), 562–80.

Debt – household

Household debt – with particular reference to its specific component of consumer debt – is debt contracted by households to finance consumer spending, both as a consumer debt proper (credit cards, car loans, student loans and so forth), and as gross equity extraction from existing homes by borrowing in the residential mortgage market to finance consumption spending on both durable and non-durable goods.

The growth of debt-financed consumer expenditure over the decades preceding the 2008 global financial crisis went completely unnoticed by mainstream economists, who were obsessively focused instead on the growth of public debt and its alleged unsustainability. Since then, household debt has come to the centre of the economic debate, owing to the obvious role played by private debt, not public debt, in triggering the crisis. Despite this, the explanations of the phenomenon offered by the mainstream theory remain largely unsatisfactory, the analysis being carried out in light of the neoclassical theory of saving, and the problem being seen as a mistaken intertemporal choice of forward-looking agents in a full-employment economy.

The question appears in completely different terms from the point of view of post-Keynesian theory, and, more generally, of heterodox economic theory (see, for example, Cynamon and Fazzari, 2008; Barba and Pivetti, 2009; Magdoff and Foster, 2009). The premises of this alternative explanation are: (i) to refer to a theory of saving in which past income, rather than future income, determines current consumption choices; (ii) to link this theory of saving to a notion of equilibrium in which investment determines saving and not the other way around. From this standpoint, the phenomenon of rising household debt is approached in terms of the effort by low- and middle-income households to maintain, as long as possible, their relative standards of consumption in the face of persistent changes in income distribution in favour of households with higher incomes. In a framework of financial deregulation and of an easing of liquidity constraints on low- and middle-income households, which acted as permissive factors (as in the neoclassical interpretation), rising household debt is viewed as the response to falling or stagnant real wages, or to wages that – though rising – were not keeping pace with productivity growth.

This explanation solves an apparent contradiction between the trends in the distribution of income and in the saving rate recorded before the global financial crisis. It is a well-established fact that in the 1980–2008 period, income inequality in the United States increased greatly.

In the same period, the private saving rate recorded a marked decline, largely concentrated in the households sector, reaching its lowest level since the end of the Great Depression. Now, as inequality rose, the share of consumption relative to disposable income should have become smaller. This, however, has not been the case: the rise in households' saving rate that would have been brought about by the concentration of total income on the upper 10 per cent of the income distribution was more than compensated by the fall in the saving rates of the remaining 90 per cent, owing largely to increased access to household debt.

This seems to suggest that, through household debt, low wages can coexist with high levels of aggregate demand, with no need for State intervention, providing in this way a solution to the fundamental contradiction between the necessity of high and rising levels of consumption and a framework of antagonistic conditions of income distribution. Things, however, are not so simple, as the global financial crisis has made clear. In fact, the question of the long-run sustainability of substituting loans for wages must be considered. As for public debt, also for private debt the crucial factor is the difference between the rate of interest (i) and the rate of growth of income (g). If $i > g$, the debt/income ratio keeps on rising. The point here is that, while the growth of public debt, supporting g, favours the reduction of the ratio between public debt and GDP, the growth of private debt does not reverberate on the income and therefore on solvency of all indebted workers. For the latter, the share of income required over a period of time to repay their debt can very easily become unsustainable also because the interest they have to pay, especially if they have a poor credit rating, is significantly higher than that of the government.

ALDO BARBA

See also

Aggregate demand; Debt-led boom; Financial crises; Financial liberalization; Income distribution

References

Barba, A. and M. Pivetti (2009), 'Rising household debt: its causes and macroeconomic implications – a long period analysis', *Cambridge Journal of Economics*, **33** (1), 113–38.

Cynamon, B. and S. Fazzari (2008), 'Household debt in the consumer age: source of growth – risk of collapse', *Capitalism and Society*, **3** (1), 1–32.

Magdoff, H. and J.B. Foster (2009), *The Great Financial Crisis: Causes and Consequences*, New York: Monthly Review Press.

Debt – non-financial corporate sector

A distinct feature of post-Keynesian theory is its focus on interrelated balance sheets among its various member units – firms, households, governments, and even countries (see Minsky, 1975). In this perspective, non-financial corporations (NFCs) play an extremely important role connecting the credit cycle to the economic cycle. This view is built upon two arguments developed by Keynes (1936). First, investment is the driving force causing fluctuations in the level of output and employment. Second, as argued by Minsky (1975), finance holds the key to the investment process, as it sanctions NFCs' decisions to produce in a hierarchical relation that is crucial to the notion of an entrepreneurial economy. NFCs' debt is, therefore, at the heart of the financial instability hypothesis, which describes the impact of debt and its validation through the behaviour of a complex and interconnected system of assets and liabilities (Minsky, 1982; see also authors in the monetary circuit tradition, for instance, Rochon, 2006).

In investment decisions, both NFCs and the financial system speculate about firms' future cash-flow performance, which is ultimately the source of debt repayment, as well as their ability to refinance debts. Capital assets are not acquired on the basis of their physical productivity, which may be previously known, but according to the expected profitability during the production process. This speculative dimension of the acquisition of capital assets is significantly expanded by the fact that it has to be financed.

Expectations of profits determine both the flow of debt and the price of existing debt. Now, expectations of profits, which will determine future investments, depend upon realized profits, which are determined by past investments. Thus, besides providing the funds to fulfil payment commitments as they come due and helping to determine investment and financing conditions, the flow of debt to NFCs signals whether past investment decisions have succeeded. Post-Keynesian economists point out that every asset has a carrying cost and, therefore, there must be a degree of compatibility between the asset return and the cost of liabilities, as well as between cash-flow generation periods and debt payment commitments (Minsky, 1992).

For that matter, Minsky (1986) focuses his analysis on detailing and characterizing the nature of NFCs' debt, which will configure certain financial structures. The first one is 'hedge finance' and describes a portfolio whose expected cash flows offset all financial commitments, with no term and quantity mismatch between assets and liabilities. The speculative financial structure occurs when debt service is greater than expected cash flows for a determined period, even though the present value of the expected returns over the entire productive period is still greater than the present value of the payment commitments. Finally, when cash flow is insufficient to meet the debt service in all periods and the NFC has to capitalize interest on its liabilities by increasing it, there is a Ponzi financial structure. Though, agents engaged in Ponzi finance estimate that the present value of their net proceeds will be, over the long run, higher than their payment commitments.

However, the judgment of acceptable debt structures is based on subjective calculations by individuals, and a drop in the relationship between return on investment and financial commitments can lead to rapid generalized revaluations by the financial market at any time. In Minsky's (1986, p. 232) own words, '[a]lthough periods of Ponzi finance may be part of the normal cyclical experience of firms, being forced into Ponzi-financing arrangements by income shortfalls or interest costs escalation is a systemic part of the process that leads to widespread bankruptcy.'

Therefore, in a system where expectations can be frustrated and uncertainty is always present, the NFCs' debt movement follows the fluctuations in agents' liquidity preference. Changes in the perception of risk by borrowers and creditors are the fuel for the cyclical dynamics of capitalist economies.

FERNANDA ULTREMARE

See also

Debt-led boom; Financial crises; Financial instability hypothesis; Income distribution; Monetary circuit – Italian school

References

Keynes, J.M. (1936), *The General Theory of Employment, Interest and Money*, London: Macmillan.
Minsky, H.P. (1975), *John Maynard Keynes*, New York: Columbia University Press.
Minsky, H.P. (1982), 'The financial instability hypothesis: a restatement', in H.P. Minsky, *Can 'It' Happen Again? Essays on Instability and Finance*, Armonk, NY: M.E. Sharpe, pp. 90–116.
Minsky, H.P. (1986), *Stabilizing an Unstable Economy*, New Haven, CT: Yale University Press.
Minsky, H.P. (1992), 'The financial instability hypothesis', *Levy Economics Institute Working Paper*, No. 74.
Rochon, L.-P. (2006), 'Endogenous money, central banks and the banking system: Basil Moore and the supply of money', in M. Setterfield (ed.), *Complexity, Endogenous Money and Macroeconomic Theory: Essays in Honour of Basil J. Moore*, Cheltenham, UK, and Northampton, MA, USA: Edward Elgar, pp. 220–243.

Debt – public

Public debt is always conceived by policy makers as a twenty-first century wraith, often depicted as the worst deadly danger for the stability of a capitalist economy. Such a conventional vision of public debt relies on a set of specific postulates, namely:

(1) In any accounting period, the new issuance of public debt is equal to the excess of aggregate State expenditures over tax receipts. It is thereby equal to the State deficit.
(2) Since the so-called deficit is a share of State expenditures, it means that the State would only spend its already existing tax receipts.
(3) Excess spending is to be financed by selling debt titles to financial markets, thereby to private international banking institutions that determine the rate of interest to be paid by the State.
(4) The central bank must not acquire directly State liabilities as long as it is not absolutely independent from the State.
(5) Public debt is always assumed to finance excess non-productive State expenditures, thereby jeopardizing the long-run stability of a capitalist economy.
(6) A logical corollary is that long-run stability only depends on the growth of public debt and never on the growth of private debt.

FERNANDA ULTREMARE / ALAIN PARGUEZ AND SLIM THABET

It should be obvious that this set of assumptions stands in full contradiction to the ideas of the monetary circuit by forgetting specifically time and money. It is imperative therefore to give heterodox answers to the assumptions listed above. Below, we list specific answers and provide a fully consistent account of public debt.

(1) Tax income cannot finance State expenditures, because tax receipts are only generated in the reflux phase of the monetary circuit. Thereby it is absurd to postulate that State expenditures should be financed by *ex post* tax receipts.
(2) The so-called public 'deficit' is part of the State's initial expenditures. Thereby it cannot be financed by *ex post* borrowing.
(3) This means that aggregate public expenditures are undertaken out of a net creation of money operated at the State level by its banking branch, namely the central bank. When they are to be paid in the reflux phase, taxes levied across the economy destroy an equal amount of money and national income. The so-called public deficit is thereby a net creation of both money and income for society as a whole. It reflects the creation of net savings for society, including the foreign sector. Thereby, the State is not obliged to sell debt titles to banks, in order to fund its deficit. It would mean that the State is borrowing its own currency. Logically, the crucial distinction is between good deficits targeting the effort to invest for the best possible future, and bad deficits, neither planned nor wanted, being the outcome of absolute commitment to austerity.
(4) Ultimately, being the fundamental issuer of money, the State can never go bankrupt or become 'insolvent', as long as its monetary power is not jeopardized, as in the euro area. In this area, public expenditures are to be *ex ante* financed by selling debt titles to banks.
(5) Even in such an area, the accumulation of public debts to banks remains insignificant relative to pure private debts relying on nothing.

Finally, in a truly modern capitalist economy the State can never be 'insolvent' as long as it does not plan its insolvency by surrendering its sovereignty on its currency, which is the dark aspect of the euro order, as explained by Parguez (2016).

ALAIN PARGUEZ AND SLIM THABET

See also

Fiscal deficits; Fiscal policy; Interest rates and income distribution; Modern money theory; Monetary circuit – French School

References

Parguez, A. (2016), 'Economic theories of social order and the origins of the euro', *International Journal of Political Economy*, **45** (1), 2–16.
Parguez, A. and S. Thabet (2017), '¿Economía capitalista monetaria sin deflación? Enfoque circuitista-institucionalista', *Ola Financiera*, **10** (26), 1–31.

Debt-led boom

Debt-led booms are periods of sustained increments in either public or private debt-to-GDP ratios. These episodes are related to the second wave of financial globalization that emerged after the collapse of the Bretton Woods regime in the early 1970s. According to Kose et al. (2020, p. 6):

> Global debt has trended up since 1970, reaching around 230 percent of GDP in 2018. Debt has risen particularly rapidly in EMDEs [Emerging Markets and Developing Economies], reaching a peak of about 170 percent of GDP in 2018. Much of the increase since 2010 has occurred in the private sector, particularly in China. Debt in low-income countries has started to rise after a prolonged period of decline following debt-relief measures in the late 1990s and 2000s. Advanced economy debt has been broadly flat since the global financial crisis, with increased government debt more than offsetting a mild deleveraging in the private sector.

These stylized facts can be related to mounting evidence on the increasing importance of financialization (see Rochon and Monvoisin, 2019).

Post-Keynesian authors remark that debt-led booms can have various macroeconomic implications for investment and consumption, mainly through two mechanisms. First, debt-led booms could have negative consequences on different economic agents (Kalecki, 1937; Minsky, 1975). Rapid debt accumulation deteriorates the quality of balance sheets, producing considerable adverse effects on repayment capacity, shrinking available finance for future investment, and endangering the service of (outstanding) debt obligations. Second, debt-led booms could affect income transfers from debtors to creditors. Differences in marginal propensities to consume between debtors and creditors negatively affect aggregate consumption.

Moreover, debt-led booms give rise to business cycle fluctuations through two key channels (Palley, 2009): the multiplier–accelerator principle, which shows how the growth of debt can affect aggregate demand; and the increase in income levels, which leads to positive feedbacks on indebtedness and, ultimately, goes down at the end of debt cycles. At this stage, real and financial asset prices plummet, the balance sheets of commercial banks deteriorate, and the real value of collaterals falls, thus increasing their exposure to different types of risks. However, some post-Keynesian authors challenged Minskyan procyclical characterization of firms and banks' leverage (Lavoie and Seccareccia, 2001). The growth of income as debt increases can generate a countercyclical movement in leverage ratios, leading to the 'paradox of debt'.

In general, debt-led booms relate to a global scenario of low interest rates and financial innovation, causing indebtedness trends to grow. The end of debt-led booms was typically associated to systemic financial crises that went hand in hand with global recessions (in 1982, 1991, 2009). In EMDEs, these crises were triggered by negative external financial shocks: increased global investors' risk aversion, risk premia and borrowing costs, which unleashed sudden stops and deep recessions. During the 1970s, there were 519 debt-led booms (recorded) in 100 EMDEs. The median of public (private) debt-led booms was 30 (15) percentage points of GDP. The duration of public and private debt-led booms amounted to 8 years and 7 years, respectively. Interestingly, half of public debt-led booms were related to financial crises. Domestic vulnerabilities – a high short-run external indebtedness profile and a low stock of international reserves – largely amplified the negative effect of financial crises. Exchange rate, sovereign debt, and banking crises were often consequences of debt-led booms. High initial debt levels increased the duration of economic contractions and reduced that of GDP expansions. Moreover, it is worth reviewing the specific role of the public sector as the main actor responsible for fuelling these events. Actually, Taylor (1998, p. 1) reverses the frequent argument that blames the public sector for the build-up of external debt stocks: in his own words, 'external financial crises are not caused by an alert private sector pouncing upon the public sector's foolish actions such as running an unsustainable fiscal deficit or creating moral hazards. They are better described as private sectors (both domestic and foreign) acting to make high short-term profits when policy and history provide the preconditions and the public sector acquiesces.'

There are considerable challenges for designing an economic policy that may prevent debt-led booms. The allocation of lending to investment projects is vital to promote economic growth. Robust macroeconomic regimes call for fiscal, monetary and exchange rate policies coordination and are essential for avoiding negative spillovers related to debt-led booms. Macroprudential and financial regulations are necessary to accomplish these overriding tasks. After the global financial crisis that burst in 2008, there has been renewed interest in capital account management techniques by public authorities, academia and financial institutions. These facts reflect the importance of properly regulating financial capital inflows that generate the mentioned negative consequences of debt-led booms, particularly in EMDEs.

FERNANDO TOLEDO AND
JORGE CARRERA

See also

Bretton Woods; Debt deflation; Financialization; Globalization; Paradox of debt

References

Kalecki, M. (1937), 'The principle of increasing risk', *Economica*, **4** (16), 440–447.
Kose, M., P. Nagle, F. Ohnsorge and N. Sugawara (2020), *Global Waves of Debt: Causes and Consequences*, Washington, DC: World Bank Group.
Lavoie, M. and M. Seccareccia (2001), 'Minsky's financial fragility hypothesis: a missing macroeconomic link?', in R. Bellofiore and P. Ferri (eds), *Financial Fragility and Investment in the Capitalist Economy: The Economic Legacy of Hyman Minsky, Volume II*, Cheltenham, UK, and Northampton, MA, USA: Edward Elgar, pp. 76–96.

Minsky, H.P. (1975), *John Maynard Keynes*, New Heaven, CT: Yale University Press.
Palley, T. (2009), 'The simple analytics of debt-driven business cycles', *Political Economy Research Institute Working Paper*, No. 200.
Rochon, L.-P. and V. Monvoisin (eds) (2019), *Finance, Growth and Inequality: Post-Keynesian Perspectives*, Cheltenham, UK, and Northampton, MA, USA: Edward Elgar.
Taylor, L. (1998), 'Lax public sector, destabilizing private sector: origins of capital market crises', *CEPA Working Paper*, No. 6.

Deindustrialization and economic growth

Rapid deindustrialization in advanced economies reopened an age-old debate: is a unit value added in manufacturing really equal to one in primary commodities or services from the point of view of the level and especially the sustainability of long-term economic growth? This debate was also fuelled in the 1980s by rising unemployment, as economies were struggling to absorb the labour displaced from manufacturing.

From the perspective of the potential impact of deindustrialization one can classify the theories of economic growth in three camps. This requires a distinction between two concepts: 'activity' and 'sector'. Examples of the former are research and development (R&D) and education, and of the latter, manufacturing. The first camp includes Solow-type neoclassical models (both traditional and 'augmented') where economic growth is neither 'activity' nor 'sector' specific (for example, manufacturing has no special role). The second camp, while still regarding economic growth as 'sector indifferent', models it as 'activity specific' (for example, education and R&D-specific, as in Romer's, Lucas's and neo-Schumpeterian models). Finally, those in the third camp argue that economic growth is both 'sector specific' (such as in Kaldor's laws), and 'activity specific' (that is, specific to the sector playing the role of engine for economic growth).

In the first camp one finds not only the Solow-type models but also some endogenous growth ones (like early 'AK' models) in which increasing returns are somehow seen as stemming directly from within the production function – rather than being based on R&D or the production of human capital.

In the second camp increasing returns are explicitly not associated with the size, depth or strength of the manufacturing sector as such (Aghion and Howitt, 1998); with investment in manufacturing having no special feedback effect on R&D or human capital creation – other than just being 'complementary' to innovation through its effect on the profitability of research and education. 'Embodiment' *à la* Kaldor and Thirlwall cannot be accommodated in their framework.

In the third camp, the approaches to economic growth found in Kalecki, Hirschman, Kaldor, (arguably) Schumpeter, Thirlwall, Pasinetti, Prebisch, Furtado (and new Brazilian developmentalists), Taylor, Wade, Amsden, Singh, Sutcliffe, Chang, Ocampo, Ros and Palma (among others) stand out. In these 'sector-specific' theories of economic growth – which continue a long tradition that goes all the way back to Smith and Hume – the pattern of economic growth, increasing returns and the whole dynamics of the sustainability of productivity growth are crucially dependent on the structure of output and employment. Issues such as the capacity to generate and diffuse technological change, productivity growth potentials, ability to move up the 'technology ladder', externalities, synergies, balance-of-payments sustainability, gains from trade, and, in the case of developing countries, ultimately their capacity for 'catching up' with the production frontier are directly linked to the size, strength and depth of the manufacturing sector. This is also true of inequality (see Palma, 2019a).

In sum, as far as economic growth is concerned, if for the first and second camps whether one produces potato chips or micro-chips is not a fundamental issue per se (except that for the second camp it might be one, if an activity has a greater sustained impact on the profitability of R&D), for the third camp issues such as that (the structure of output and employment) relate to what long-term economic growth, and its sustainability, are all about.

Following the previous analysis, it is now possible to elucidate why for the first growth camp deindustrialization is not a particularly relevant growth issue. Only market rigidities can make it one. For Sachs and Warner (1997), for example, if neoclassical competitive conditions prevail, deindustrialization implies no hindrance to economic growth or full employment. If they do not prevail, and discovering natural gas produced some mis-adjustments in the Dutch economy, these rigidities should be dealt with at source. They are the 'disease', not deindustrialization.

Also, if 'premature' deindustrialization in developing resource-rich countries is about the transformation of output and employment structures from an artificially policy-induced-ISI-industrialization to a more deregulated-market-based-path, this can hardly be bad for economic growth.

From the point of view of the second camp, deindustrialization in 'mature' economies may or may not have an impact on economic growth per se: it would all depend on its specific form. For instance, it could actually result in a stimulus if the 'upward' deindustrialization – in the Rowthorn and Wells (1987) sense – is associated with the reallocation of resources from run-of-the-mill manufacturing activities towards more R&D-intensive specialized service activities. What follows would be an increase in the demand for R&D and human capital, making their investment more profitable – this could speed up the pace of innovation, and this the increasing returns that emerge from technical change. But as productivity growth in high-income deindustrializing countries has fallen by nearly two-thirds since 1980 (versus 1950–80), there is little evidence of these positive processes at work.

In middle-income countries, however, (as in Latin America) it is difficult to imagine how 'premature' deindustrialization could be viewed from this perspective as a stimulus for long-term economic growth, as it has diverted resources from manufacturing towards extractive activities (normally based on mature technologies) and cheap services (with minimal long-term potentials for productivity growth).

In fact, Chile (the most successful country doing this in the 1990s) did so with one of the lowest rates of investment in R&D as a share of GDP in the world (just 0.4 per cent) – or less than 2 per cent Korea's R&D expenditure. However, its failure to sustain high rates of productivity growth – which fell from 3.9 per cent (1986–98), to 2.1 per cent (in the following decade), and 0.4 per cent the following one (Palma, 2019b) – indicates that it is one thing to speed up economic growth, but another to sustain it.

Finally, although finding it difficult to accommodate the concept of 'positive' (or 'upward') deindustrialization in mature economies, the third approach to economic growth understands deindustrialization (particularly in its 'Dutch disease' form) as clearly negative for long-term economic growth – especially if 'premature'. The same is true of the current narrowing-down of the policy-space needed to fight these prospects (a phenomenon which is now found in many so-called 'trade' agreements; for the case of the 'Transpacific Treaty' see, for example, Palma, 2019b).

The collapse of productivity growth in industrialized countries since neoliberal reforms would be the likely outcome of 'wrong' policies (like radical monetarism), and 'wrong' structural change (such as financialization) excessively intensifying deindustrialization.

And one interpretation of the actual stagnation of average productivity levels in Latin America since 1980 (including Brazil, Mexico and Argentina; see Palma, 2011 and 2019b) would be that this is the likely (perhaps inevitable) consequence of 'premature' deindustrialization becoming 'uncreative destruction'.

Basically, for this third growth camp no sector can play the role of 'production frontier shifter' as well as manufacturing, since the latter is able to set in motion processes of 'cumulative causation' in terms of increasing returns, characterized by their positive feedback loops into the system, capable of generating a momentum of change that is self-perpetuating – *à la* Veblen/Myrdal or the Smith/Young/Kaldor/Taylor manner.

JOSÉ GABRIEL PALMA

See also

Balance-of-payments constrained growth; Deindustrialization, 'premature' deindustrialization and the Dutch disease; Financialization; Growth; Neoclassical economics

References

Aghion, P. and P. Howitt (1998), *Endogenous Growth Theory*, Cambridge, MA, USA: The MIT Press.

Palma, J.G. (2005), 'Four sources of "deindustrialization" and a new concept of the "Dutch disease"', in J.A. Ocampo (ed.), *Beyond Reforms: Structural Dynamics and Macroeconomic Vulnerability*, Stanford and Washington: Stanford University Press and the World Bank, pp. 71–116.

Palma, J.G. (2011), 'Why has productivity growth stagnated in most Latin American countries since the neo-liberal reforms?', in J.A. Ocampo and J. Ros (eds), *The Oxford Handbook of Latin American Economics*, Oxford: Oxford University Press, pp. 568–607.

JOSÉ GABRIEL PALMA

Palma, J.G. (2019a), 'Behind the seven veils of inequality. What if it's all about the struggle within one half of the population over just one half of the national income?', *Development and Change*, **50** (5), 1133–213.

Palma, J.G. (2019b), 'The Chilean economy since the return to democracy in 1990', *Cambridge Working Papers in Economics*, No. 1991, available at https://www.econ.cam.ac.uk/research-files/repec/cam/pdf/cwpe1991.pdf.

Rowthorn, R.E. and J.R. Wells (1987), *De-Industrialization Foreign Trade*, Cambridge, UK: Cambridge University Press.

Sachs, J.D. and A.M. Warner (1997), 'Fundamental sources of long-run growth', *American Economic Review*, **87** (2), 184–8.

Deindustrialization, 'premature' deindustrialization and the Dutch disease

A notable stylized fact of the world economy since the mid-1960s is the rapid decline in manufacturing employment in industrialized countries (a drop of more than one-third; in the United States by nearly half). Although the structure of employment has changed over the long-term course of economic development, changes of this scale and speed are unprecedented. Moreover, as some consider manufacturing a crucial driver of outward shifts of the production frontier – for instance, in post-Keynesian, structuralist and neo-Schumpeterian thought, and even in Marxian economics (see Tregenna, 2009), with Kaldor's laws being paradigmatic –, deindustrialization is likely to have a significant negative impact on long-term productivity growth.

The starting issue was the double-edged effect of discovering mineral resources; while allowing for an expansion of expenditure, they could lead to a contraction of the non-mineral traded sector – namely, the 'Dutch disease'.

Some early industrializers in East Asia also show some signs of deindustrialization in the late 1980s, and Latin American countries and South Africa also began to deindustrialize after radical economic reforms, despite their level of per capita income being far lower than those that deindustrialized earlier. This latter process was labelled by Palma (2005) as 'premature' deindustrialization. Eleven years later, Rodrik (2016) also used this concept in a similar framework.

Originally, 'Dutch disease' had a narrow meaning, that is, the appreciation of the real exchange rate in countries that have an export surge of commodities. Later on, it was also associated with the 'resource curse' hypothesis. However, Rowthorn (1994) argued that deindustrialization in advanced economies was a structural phenomenon: manufacturing employment would drop as mature economies would tend to switch employment to specialized services.

Palma (2005, 2008, 2019a) suggests that deindustrialization is a far more complex phenomenon as there are in fact four processes at work. To start, he labelled Rowthorn's 'inverted-U' relationship between manufacturing employment and per capita income as the 'the first source of deindustrialization'. Then, he indicated that there was an additional source of deindustrialization: Rowthorn's 'inverted-U' relationship has been declining over time (Figure 1).

Yet, there is a further process at work: a remarkable drop in the turning point of the 'inverted-U' relationship (Figure 2).

In fact, the per capita income associated with the turning points plummeted by half during the radical-monetarist 1980s. This led to an increase in the number of countries that had gone beyond the respective turning point (from none in 1980 to twenty in 1990).

Finally, in several countries (like the Netherlands) manufacturing employment fell more than expected. For Palma, this excess deindustrialization is not just an 'overshooting' but relates to his specific conceptualization of the Dutch disease: in countries that have an export surge of commodity (or tourism or finance), or a major shift in economic policy (such as Latin American countries in the 1980s), a unique additional degree of deindustrialization is typical – additional to the three deindustrialization forces already discussed above.

The origin of this 'disease' lies in the fact that these 'inverted-U' relationships tend to be different in natural resource-rich countries (able to generate a trade surplus in commodities) and those that are not – and therefore forced to aim for a trade surplus in manufacturing, as they have to finance inevitable trade deficits in commodities (such as Japan).

Oddly enough, taking the highest point of the curves, in this period the share of manufacturing employment in both groups of

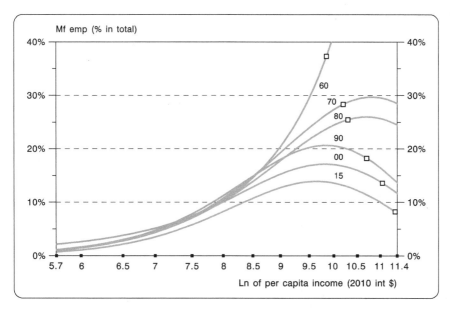

Note: squares indicate the country with the highest per capita income in each period. In this and following regressions all parameters are significant at the 1 per cent level ('t' statistics were constructed using 'White heteroscedasticity-consistent' standard errors), and the adjusted R^2 are between 66 per cent and 77 per cent. Regressions of this type simply mean to be a cross-sectional description of cross-country differences in manufacturing employment, categorized by income *per capita*. They should not be interpreted in a 'predicting' way, because there are a number of difficulties with a curve estimated from a single cross-section.

Sources: ILO and UNIDO data basis (105 countries).

Figure 1   Second source of deindustrialization: a declining relationship, 1960–2015

countries (commodity rich and poor) dropped by a similar proportion – by about half (Palma, 2019a).

In this regard, it is now possible to explain Palma's concept of the 'Dutch disease'. There is a group of (both industrialized and developing) countries that exhibit a specific additional degree of deindustrialization. The Netherlands rightly gives its name to this phenomenon (Figure 3).

What happened in the Netherlands was that a discovery of gas led to a switch from its previous 'mf'-type process of deindustrialization to a 'pc' one, moving the country along two consecutive paths of deindustrialization. The first consisted of the three processes of deindustrialization discussed above. The second corresponds to the change from having an 'mf' structure of output and employment to a 'pc' one. The Dutch disease should only be regarded as the *extra* level of deindustrialization associated with this switch. In the Netherlands it led to an extra 5 percentage points drop in manufacturing employment: the difference between this having fallen to its conditional expectation as an 'mf' country, given its income per capita (a non-Dutch-disease scenario), and to its actual post-Dutch-disease settings.

This phenomenon also occurred in countries that developed flourishing service-exporting sectors, such as tourism (Greece, Cyprus and Malta) and financial services (Switzerland, Luxembourg and Hong Kong). Surges in remittances from workers living abroad could have a similar effect.

Finally, Figure 3 also shows that this 'disease' was experienced in Latin American countries after abandoning their 'structuralist' industrialization agenda (ISI), which had aimed at achieving an 'mf' industrialization despite them being rich in natural resources. The radical change of the economic policy regime (neoliberal reforms) resulted in the Dutch disease by transforming their output and employment

JOSÉ GABRIEL PALMA

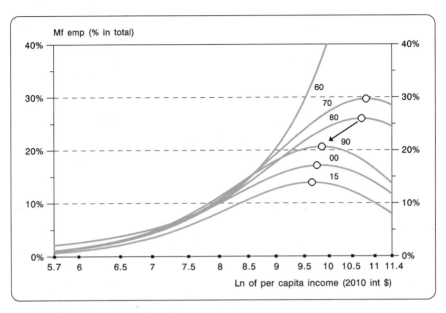

Note: circles indicate the turning point of the regressions.
Sources: ILO and UNIDO data basis (105 countries).

Figure 2   Third source of deindustrialization: a changing turning point, 1960–2015

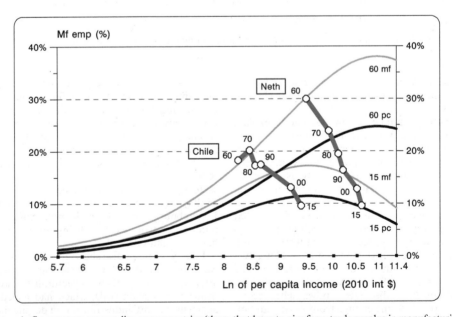

Note: 'mf' represents commodity-poor countries (those that have to aim for a trade surplus in manufacturing) and 'pc' represents primary commodity-rich countries. The difference is a dummy intercept for 'pc' countries (significant at the 1 per cent level).

Figure 3   The Netherlands and Chile: unravelling the 'Dutch disease', 1960–2015

JOSÉ GABRIEL PALMA

structure from a policy-induced 'mf' path to a resource-rich 'pc' one.

From this perspective, 'premature' deindustrialization in Latin American countries relates to these radical economic reforms obstructing their transition towards a more self-sustaining form of industrialization (à la Kaldor, 1967).

In sum, the Dutch disease should be seen as a specific type of 'excess' deindustrialization, which commodity or export-services-booming economies can easily avoid — as Finland, Malaysia, Vietnam and Latin America before 1980 did (also Chile in its nitrate boom during the 1880s, see Palma, 2019b; see also Pesaran, 1984). However, there seem to be fewer and fewer countries willing to follow such policies, leading to a process of 'uncreative destruction' in manufacturing.

JOSÉ GABRIEL PALMA

See also

Balance-of-payments constrained growth; Deindustrialization and economic growth; Dutch disease; Financialization; Neoclassical economics

References

Kaldor, N. (1967), *Strategic Factors of Economic Development*, Ithaca, NY, USA: Cornell University Press.

Palma, J.G. (2005), 'Four sources of "deindustrialization" and a new concept of the "Dutch disease"', in J.A. Ocampo (ed.), *Beyond Reforms: Structural Dynamics and Macroeconomic Vulnerability*, Stanford and Washington: Stanford University Press and the World Bank, pp. 71–116.

Palma, J.G. (2008), 'Deindustrialisation, premature deindustrialisation and the Dutch disease', in S.N. Durlauf and L.E. Blume (eds), *The New Palgrave Dictionary of Economics*, 2nd edition, London: Palgrave Macmillan, pp. 1297–306.

Palma, J.G. (2019a), 'Desindustrialización, desindustrialización "prematura" y "síndrome holandés"', *El Trimestre Económico*, **86** (344), 901–66.

Palma, J.G. (2019b), 'The Chilean economy since the return to democracy in 1990', *Cambridge Working Papers in Economics*, No. 1991, available at https://www.econ.cam.ac.uk/research-files/repec/cam/pdf/cwpe1991.pdf.

Pesaran, H. (1984), 'Macroeconomic policy in an oil-exporting economy with foreign exchange controls', *Economica*, **51** (203), 253–70.

Rodrick, D. (2016), 'Premature deindustrialization', *Journal of Economic Growth*, **21** (1), 1–33.

Rowthorn, R.E. (1994), 'Korea at the cross-roads', *Centre for Business Research Working Paper*, No. 11.

Tregenna, F. (2009), 'Characterising deindustrialisation: an analysis of changes in manufacturing employment and output internationally', *Cambridge Journal of Economics*, **33** (3), 433–66.

Demand-led growth

Economic growth, here intended as a sustained increase in average per capita incomes, essentially coincides with technical and organizational change. Then, in order to have a good theory of demand-led long-run growth, rejecting Say's law and using the principle of effective demand as the foundational stone of a macroeconomic model is not enough. Some kind of demand-induced technical change is also needed. Indeed, if the rate of growth of employment resulting from a demand-led growth model with exogenous technical change turns out to be higher (lower) than the exogenous rate of growth of labour supply, unemployment would fall (rise) indefinitely, which cannot constitute an acceptable long-run equilibrium. In any plausible description of a long-run equilibrium, the unemployment rate must be constant. How can this be guaranteed?

In the neoclassical-synthesis Keynesian models, both the 'old' AS–AD model and the New Consensus three-equation model, this is achieved through the adjustment of some components of aggregate demand, via financial markets (AS–AD) or the central bank (three-equation model). According to post-Keynesian and Kaleckian authors, there is another, crucial mechanism at work (perhaps in the longer run), usually defined as 'Marx-biased technical change' (Foley and Michl, 1999, p. 117). If labour, which constitutes such an important share of total costs, becomes more expensive, entrepreneurs will try to economize on its use, and labour-saving and productivity-enhancing machineries will be introduced. Now, post-Keynesian authors, starting from Joan Robinson (1956), noted that labour may become more costly not only, and not mainly, in response to some exogenous event (the factory acts), but also as a consequence of a buoyant economic activity that, as such, increases employment and makes labour scarcer. A positive discrepancy between

JOSÉ GABRIEL PALMA / MARCO MISSAGLIA

employment growth and labour supply growth gives rise to labour-saving (capital-using) technical change and productivity growth.

In an illuminating paper, Dutt (2006) clarifies how the introduction of this kind of Marx-biased technical change gives aggregate demand a key role in the determination of the long-run equilibrium of the economy. Think of an economy evolving on some steady-growth path, with labour productivity and per capita income growing at a constant rate. At a point, some aggregate demand shock materializes: the government or firms or households decide to spend more. The short-run consequence is to increase the growth rate of output and employment, and then create tensions in the labour market. This will put in motion two different dynamics. On the one hand, some kind of neoclassical-synthesis adjustment will reduce aggregate demand (via higher interest rates) and then push the economy back on the same steady-growth path. On the other hand, however, higher labour costs will induce entrepreneurs to adopt capital-using and productivity-enhancing techniques. This kind of adjustment, as such, makes labour relatively less scarce and, as a result, the economy moves on a new steady-growth path with a faster rate of growth of labour productivity and per capita income. This is clearly a case where aggregate demand matters in the determination of the long-run growth path of the economy, and it matters in that it modifies the path of a crucial supply factor, namely technology.

The kind of endogenous technical change we just described is based on the deliberate decision of capitalists to introduce labour-saving machineries. Such a framework may be modified in two directions.

One was the route followed by Kaldor (1957), whose very popular technical progress function (also known as 'Kaldor–Verdoorn effect') makes labour productivity growth a by-product (a somewhat unintended consequence) of capital accumulation. The idea is that the accumulation of knowledge is, as originally pointed out by Arrow (1962) and long before by Smith (1776), a by-product of mechanization. Each new machine modifies the production environment in such a way that learning is stimulated and, this way, the stock of knowledge goes up. To some extent, the knowledge accumulated within each investing firm spills over to other firms through several possible channels – workers and managers may move from one firm to the other, products incorporating the innovations circulate in the market and make some kind of 'reverse engineering' perfectly possible, and so on – and therefore the stock of knowledge for the economy as a whole becomes a function of the aggregate capital stock. It is important to realize that this kind of Kaldor–Verdoorn–Arrow–Romer technical change is not sufficient, in itself, to produce demand-led long-term growth. For the Kaldorian technical progress function to produce a fully consistent model of demand-led growth, it is of course necessary to discard Say's law and introduce some kind of investment function, for instance one with a standard accelerator term.

The other route is followed by the 'Schumpeter-meets-Keynes' literature, a very interesting stream of research initiated by some evolutionary authors (Dosi et al., 2010; see also Ricottilli, 1993, Ch. 6), where the emphasis is on studying how aggregate demand may interact with the incentive to innovate as determined by the competition struggle among capitalists, rather than the conflict between workers and capitalists. Provided that variations in aggregate demand affect, in one sense or the other, the competitive environment and therefore the incentive to innovate (the rent-seeking behaviour) of Schumpeterian entrepreneurs, once again one has a coherent theory of demand-led long-run growth.

MARCO MISSAGLIA

See also

Aggregate demand; Effective demand; Growth – wage-led vs profit-led; Interest rates and investment; Verdoorn's Law

References

Arrow, K. (1962), 'The economic implications of learning by doing', *Review of Economic Studies*, **29** (3), 155–73.
Dosi, G., G. Fagiolo and A. Roventini (2010), 'Schumpeter meeting Keynes: a policy-friendly model of endogenous growth and business cycles', *Journal of Economic Dynamics and Control*, **34** (9), 1748–67.
Dutt, A.K. (2006), 'Aggregate demand, aggregate supply and economic growth', *International Review of Applied Economics*, **20** (3), 319–36.
Foley, D. and T.R. Michl (1999), *Growth and Distribution*, Cambridge, MA: Harvard University Press.
Kaldor, N. (1957), 'A model of economic growth', *Economic Journal*, **68** (268), 591–624.

Marx, K. (1867/1977), *Capital: A Critique of Political Economy*, New York: Vintage Books, Vol. 1.

Ricottilli, M. (1993), *Teoria dello sviluppo economico*, Roma: La Nuova Italia Scientifica.

Robinson, J. (1956), *The Accumulation of Capital*, London: Macmillan.

Romer, P.M. (1986), 'Increasing returns and long-run growth', *Journal of Political Economy*, **94** (5), 1002–37.

Smith, A. (1776/1937), *An Inquiry into the Nature and Causes of the Wealth of Nations*, New York: Random House.

Dependency theory

According to Rostow (1960), all societies can be placed on a linear continuum, that is, a 'stages of economic growth' path, from undeveloped to developed. The assumption is that capitalism is a historically progressive system, which is transmitted from the privileged economically advanced countries to the rest of the world by a continual process of destruction and replacement of 'primitive' social structures (Palma, 1978). This modernization theory is a 'blame the victim' approach to problems affecting the 'Third World'. It ignores external influences, like colonialism (and neo-colonialism).

Dependency theory, on the other hand, highlights the extent to which global dialectical forces of motion and contradiction generate vast disparities of wealth and power. The world economy is reproduced as a 'world system' (Wallerstein, 1979) of 'unequal exchange' (Emmanuel, 1972; Amin, 1974, 1976). If economic growth is not reached, it is not because within the Third World there exists obstacles as a result of innate poverty arising from some form of 'backwardness' but owing to the net outflow of vital resources.

Baran and Sweezy (1960), in *Monopoly Capital*, assess the degree to which monopoly, as measured by the market concentration ratio of large capitalist firms (corporations), in economically advanced countries, ensues a fundamental division between advanced countries and impoverished ones. The result is that weaker countries suffer the retardation of the requisite forces to spawn autonomous and dynamic processes of self-governance of the conditions that engender independent social/political/economic coordination, planning and control. This constitutes a 'hierarchical [world] system with one or more leading metropolises, completely dependent colonies [even if not in name, certainly in practice] at the bottom, and many degrees of superordinate and subordination in between' (Baran and Sweezy, 1966, pp. 178–9).

Nevertheless, economic growth in the Third World, while controlling for socioeconomic income differentials, is viable (Cardoso and Faletto, 1970) if there is an 'embedded autonomy' (Evans, 1995) to engage in Keynesian aggregate demand management. This is measured by the extent to which a country does not suffer the inability to borrow in its own currency.

The essence of 'monetary sovereignty' is the cartalist (or chartalist) (Goodhart, 1998) conception that emphasizes State power to fully establish a national currency. From this perspective, 'underdevelopment', or 'dependency', is the powerlessness of a country in setting its own unit of account, which forces it to peg its currency to a reference currency of an economically advanced country. This results in a dearth of flexibility to use monetary policy and fiscal policy for domestic economic needs. Since the central bank is forced to maintain a certain level of reserves of the foreign reference currency such that the price of the domestic currency, in terms of the reference currency, does not change, this produces a negative money-multiplier that sets in motion an inherent deflationary bias, which, if not counteracted by capital inflows to spur aggregate demand, can lead to abrupt contraction of the monetary base, stunting any supposed progress towards economic supremacy (see Vernengo, 2006; Fields and Vernengo, 2012; Vernengo and Fields, 2016).

In this sense, if any form of government spending is to be engaged, an 'underdeveloped' country has to issue bonds that are not denominated in its own currency. This is a balance-of-payments constraint (Thirlwall, 2011). It amounts to the attraction of external commercial loans with the faith of the country's financial markets by foreign investors used as collateral. If confidence is lost in the strength of the country's financial markets, leading to a spread over bonds like US Treasury securities, if the foreign reference currency is the US dollar, interest rates on domestic foreign-currency-denominated bonds are likely to rise. Government spending would become very costly, removing the domestic capacity to spur public investment as an effective countercyclical policy in the face of economic stagnation.

MARCO MISSAGLIA / DAVID M. FIELDS

If development fails to occur, it is not because of 'the survival of archaic institutions', or some inability to contract some 'modern man' (Inkles, 1969) syndrome. On the contrary, it is generated by the same capitalist development that led to the domination by economically advanced countries, that is, 'the development of capitalism itself' (Frank, 1969, p. 23). It is an operation of what Myrdal (1957) referred to as international 'backwash' effect that produces falling terms of trade for economically weaker countries (Prebisch, 1950). Since the imbalance of international trade defines the mechanisms by which capital is drained from former colonized countries, there is no way for a Third World economy to 'catch up' in Rostowian fashion (Amin, 1976, p. 383).

DAVID M. FIELDS

See also

Aggregate demand; Balance-of-payments constrained growth; Capitalism; *Monopoly Capital*; Monopoly power

References

Amin, S. (1974), 'Accumulation and development: a theoretical model', *Review of African Political Economy*, **1** (1), 9–26.
Amin, S. (1976), *Unequal Development*, Brighton, UK: Harvester.
Baran, P. and P. Sweezy (1966), *Monopoly Capital: An Essay on the American Economic and Social Order*, New York: Monthly Review Press.
Cardoso, F.H. and E. Faletto (1970), *Dependência e desenvolvimento na América Latina*, Rio de Janeiro: Zahar.
Emmanuel, A. (1972), *Unequal Exchange: An Essay on the Imperialism of Trade*, New York: Monthly Review Press.
Evans, P. (1995), *Embedded Autonomy: States and Industrial Transformation*, Princeton: Princeton University Press.
Fields, D. and M. Vernengo (2012), 'Hegemonic currencies during the crisis: the dollar versus the euro in a Cartalist perspective', *Review of International Political Economy*, **20** (4), 740–59.
Frank, A.G. (1969), 'The development of underdevelopment', *Monthly Review*, **18** (4), 17–31.
Goodhart, C.A.E. (1998), 'The two concepts of money', *European Journal of Political Economy*, **14** (3), 407–32.
Inkles, A. (1969), 'Making men modern: on the causes and consequences of individual change in six developing countries', *American Journal of Sociology*, **75** (1), 208–24.
Myrdal, G. (1957), *Economic Theory and Underdeveloped Countries*, London: Duckworth.
Palma, G. (1978), 'Dependency: a formal theory of underdevelopment or a methodology for the analysis of concrete situations of underdevelopment?', *World Development*, **6** (7), 881–924.
Prebisch, R. (1950), 'El desarrollo económico de la América Latina y sus principales problemas', *Revista de Economía Argentina*, **48** (379–80), 211–66.
Rostow, W.W. (1960), *The Stages of Economic Growth: A Non-Communist Manifesto*, Cambridge, UK: Cambridge University Press.
Thirlwall, A.P. (2011), 'Balance of payments constrained growth models: history and overview', *PSL Quarterly Review*, **64** (259), 307–51.
Vernengo, M. (2006), 'Technology, finance, and dependency: Latin American radical political economy in retrospect', *Review of Radical Political Economics*, **38** (4), 551–68.
Vernengo, M. and D. Fields (2016), 'DisORIENT: money, technological development and the rise of the West', *Review of Radical Political Economics*, **48** (4), 562–8.
Wallerstein, I. (1979), *The Capitalist World-Economy, Volume 2*, Cambridge: Cambridge University Press.

Deregulation

Deregulation is a counteroffensive project against the socio-political achievements of the New Deal era. Several regulations came from institutional changes made to overcome the Great Depression of 1929 and the post-World War II era. This post-war period is characterized by stable economic growth with high market regulation. Even though these regulations and policies were successful, some mainstream authors argued against them (see Friedman, 1962). The idea that markets do not need to be regulated because they are stable and provide the best possible outcome has gained traction within the economic discussion since the 1970s. Therefore, the State's intervention should be reduced merely to a law enforcement role. Ironically, the Chicago theory of regulation and the Public Choice school provide the principal elements behind deregulation. They can be found in Buchanan and Tullock (1962), Stigler (1971), Peltzman (1976), and Becker (1983) (see also Noll, 1989; Winston, 1993; MacLean, 2017).

According to Peltzman (1989), there is a consensus among the discipline that deregulation is necessary to enhance market efficiency affected by government regulations. For these authors,

DAVID M. FIELDS / IVAN VELASQUEZ

the 'market' is a synonym for the 'economy' (see Chang, 2000). The 'consensus', however, left out heterodox economics. It presents a case against State intervention favouring a market-primacy ideology with a constant call for de-politicizing the economy. The wave of market deregulation started in the 1970s and achieved its peak in the 1980s, led by Ronald Reagan and Margaret Thatcher, and supported by the 'consensus' mentioned above. These administrations put the 'free-market' ideology into practice by reducing the State's role in the economy through tax cuts, privatizations, and a persistent attack on workers' rights and social security programmes. Deregulation facilitated the de-unionization of labour and the wage share decline (see Winston, 1993). This opened the path to the so-called neoliberal era.

The implementation of deregulation in the economies has created several economic and social issues. At the economic level, the savings and loan crisis of the 1980s and 1990s is an example of the consequences of deregulation. Deregulation created a chaotic environment for this industry through the consolidation of control frauds. That is, 'a company run by a criminal who uses it as a weapon and shield to defraud others and makes it difficult to detect and punish the fraud' (Black, 2005, p. 1). Later on, this deregulatory process created the conditions that triggered the global financial crisis of 2007–08. The financial industry's lack of regulation and supervision brought the global economy to an almost as significant crisis as the Great Depression.

Deregulation is the cornerstone of the neoliberal agenda. It is part of ten reforms that Williamson labelled the 'Washington Consensus' in 1989. Its name is due to a consensus about the reforms policymakers in Washington considered necessary for Latin America's development (see Williamson, 2004). Consequently, the 'Washington Consensus' is a synonym for deregulation and the 'free-market' doctrine imposed on developing countries. An example is the Chilean Constitution, approved in 1980 under Pinochet's dictatorship and elaborated on Buchanan's advice. This constitution implemented deregulation at all ranks. It went from privatizing health care, social security, higher education, and even water to unions' banning (see MacLean, 2017). Chile's economic success in the 1980s and 1990s is highlighted by Williamson (2004) as proof of deregulation's economic fruits. Thus, the Chilean Constitution's economic reforms became a standard of comparison for other Latin American countries. However, these reforms' social results, such as the lack of social security, higher levels of poverty, and increased income inequality, caused a wave of riots in 2019–20 in Chile, rejecting the 'free-market' ideology on which the Constitution is founded. The request for government intervention and re-regulation of the private sector was evident by approving a referendum in November 2020 for a constitutional change.

In the heterodox economics approach, markets are social institutions that appear simultaneously with the State. These institutions are only one of the elements that make up the capitalist system (see Chang, 2000). Markets continuously evolve; they are shaped, along with social goals, through regulation (legislation). Therefore, market processes are cumulative and modulated by the State's intervention through monetary and fiscal policy tools. The regulation of markets is an institutional arrangement, which is crucial and typical for a capitalist economy.

Consequently, from a heterodox economics viewpoint, regulation should evolve as markets do. Regulations cannot be static processes; they are 'legislated and the result of evolutionary processes' (Minsky, 1986, p. 7). State intervention is part of the heterodox economics theoretical approach (see Lavoie, 2006). Deregulation is inconsistent with heterodox economics. It contradicts the capitalist system's historical evolution and against its institutional framework. What is needed is an evolutionary regulation system that is fluid.

IVAN VELASQUEZ

See also

Credit-led boom; Financial crises; Financial liberalization; Neo-liberalism; Regulation School

References

Becker, G. (1983), 'A theory of competition among pressure groups for political influence', *Quarterly Journal of Economics*, **98** (3), 371–400.

Black, W. (2005), *The Best Way to Rob a Bank Is to Own One*, Austin: University of Texas Press.

Buchanan, J. and G. Tullock (1962), *The Calculus of Consent*, Ann Arbor: University of Michigan Press.

Chang, H.-J. (2000), 'An institutionalist perspective on the role of the state: towards an institutionalist political economy', in L. Burlamaqui, A.C. Castro and H.-J. Chang (eds), *Institutions and the Role of the State*, Cheltenham, UK, and Northampton, MA, USA: Edward Elgar, pp. 3–26.

Friedman, M. (1962), *Capitalism and Freedom*, Chicago: University of Chicago Press.

Lavoie, M. (2006), *Introduction to Post-Keynesian Economics*, Basingstoke, UK, and New York: Palgrave Macmillan.

MacLean, N. (2017), *Democracy in Chains*, London: Penguin Books.

Minsky, H. (1986), *Stabilizing an Unstable Economy*, New Haven and London: Yale University Press.

Noll, R. (1989), 'Comments and discussion to Sam Peltzman's article', *Brookings Papers on Economic Activity*, **20**, 48–58.

Peltzman, S. (1976), 'Toward a more general theory of regulation', *Journal of Law and Economics*, **19** (2), 211–41.

Peltzman, S. (1989), 'The economic theory of regulation after a decade of deregulation', *Brookings Papers on Economic Activity*, **20**, 1–41.

Stigler, G. (1971), 'The economic theory of regulation', *Bell Journal of Economics and Management Science*, **2** (1), 3–21.

Williamson, J. (2004), 'The strange history of the Washington consensus', *Journal of Post Keynesian Economics*, **27** (2), 195–206.

Winston, C. (1993), 'Economic deregulation: days of reckoning for microeconomists', *Journal of Economic Literature*, **31** (3), 1263–89.

Development

Although the idea and study of economic development have a very long history, it is usually accepted that the sub-discipline of development economics emerged after the Second World War. Among other factors (such as the recent independence of former colonies and Cold War rivalry), the rise of Keynesian economics with its emphasis on State activism in the economy has been associated with this emergence. However, early development economists did not believe that Keynesian and post-Keynesian ideas related to the role of aggregate demand had a role in the study of economic development. Aggregate demand was considered to be of importance for mature capitalist economies and for short-term economic problems, but not for the long-term development problems of less-developed countries (LDCs), for which development was seen as a long-term problem. The focus was more on coordinating investment decisions (discussed by Rosenstein-Rodan, 1943), low levels of saving and capital accumulation (emphasized by Lewis, 1954), agricultural bottlenecks that caused inflation (examined by Kalecki, 1976), the nature of international specialization and dependence on primary products (stressed by Prebisch, 1950, and Singer, 1950) and the balance-of-payments constraint (discussed by the structuralists and also, later in the post-Keynesian literature, by Thirlwall, 1979). Extensions of Keynes's (1936) short-period analysis with a given stock of capital to the examination of capital accumulation by Harrod (1939) and Domar (1946) led to the use of the so-called Harrod–Domar equation in development economics. However, this was only to argue that rates of economic growth had to be increased by increasing saving rates and reducing the capital/output ratio. Aggregate demand problems were neglected using erroneous arguments (see Dutt, 2013) involving high population, which created high demand (ignoring the problem of low income) and capital scarcity (neglecting the possibility of it being caused by low investment incentives).

Subsequently, especially in the 1970s and 1980s, aggregate demand made its way into the development economics literature (see Rakshit, 1982, Taylor, 1983, and Dutt, 1984). This was due to a number of factors: first, as a result of changes in the structures of many LDCs, especially semi-industrialized countries; second, owing to the perceived failures of earlier development theories to deal with the problems of LDCs, for instance in Latin America (Furtado, 1964) and South Asia (Bagchi, 1970), which seemed to be facing demand-side problems not just in the short run but also in the long run; and, third, there was the growing popularity of formal non-orthodox macroeconomic theories drawing on the work of Marx (1867) and Kalecki (1971), in addition to Keynes (1936). Some development scholars, in fact, argued that characteristics of LDCs arguably make aggregate demand issues highly relevant for them (see Dutt, 2013). These include: the fragmented nature of commodity and credit markets; the lack of stable institutions; the uncertainty generated by the instability of the economic growth process owing to the existence of a multiplicity of constraints on growth; and the importance of assets such as land, gold and precious metals, which induce potential investors to divert their assets to unproductive channels in the face of this uncertainty. What seem like supply bottlenecks may well reflect demand-side factors: for instance, low levels of aggregate demand may imply low levels of government revenue and spending on infrastructure, resulting in supply constraints in agriculture and industry, and low levels of economic growth due to the lack of aggregate demand result in slow technological change, which makes the economies externally uncompetitive, leading to foreign-exchange problems. Moreover, financial crises, often caused by destabilizing short-term international capital flows, and the resulting long-term contractionary consequences of austerity measures that reduce aggregate demand, have also been emphasized (see, for instance, Ocampo et al., 2009), leading to calls for anti-cyclical fiscal and monetary policies and the creation of a global financial order more responsive to the needs of LDCs.

AMITAVA DUTT

See also

Aggregate demand; Balance-of-payments constrained growth; Capital flows; Development banking; International financial architecture

References

Bagchi, A.K. (1970), 'Long-term constraints on India's industrial growth', in E.A.G. Robinson and M. Kidron (eds), *Economic Development in South Asia*, London: Macmillan, pp. 170–92.
Domar, E.D. (1946), 'Capital expansion, rate of growth, and employment', *Econometrica*, **14** (2), 137–47.
Dutt, A. (1984), 'Stagnation, income distribution and monopoly power', *Cambridge Journal of Economics*, **8** (1), 25–40.
Dutt, A. (2013), 'Post-Keynesianism and the role of aggregate demand in development economics', in G.C. Harcourt and P. Kreisler (eds), *Oxford Handbook of Post-Keynesian Economics*, Oxford and New York: Oxford University Press, Vol. 1, pp. 568–94.
Furtado, C. (1964), *Development and Underdevelopment*, Berkeley: University of California Press.
Harrod, R. (1939), 'An essay in dynamic theory', *Economic Journal*, **49** (193), 14–33.
Kalecki, M. (1971), *Selected Essays on the Dynamics of the Capitalist Economy, 1933–1970*, Cambridge, UK: Cambridge University Press.
Kalecki, M. (1976), *Essays on Development Economics*, Brighton: Harvester.
Keynes, J.M. (1936), *The General Theory of Employment, Interest and Money*, London: Macmillan.
Lewis, W.A. (1954), 'Economic development with unlimited supplies of labour', *Manchester School*, **22** (2), 131–91.
Marx, K. (1867), *Capital, Volume 1*, New York: International Publishers, 1967.
Ocampo, J.A., C. Rada and L. Taylor (2009), *Growth and Policy in Developing Countries: A Structuralist Approach*, New York: Columbia University Press.
Prebisch, R. (1950), *The Economic Development of Latin America and Its Principal Problems*, New York: United Nations.
Rakshit, M.K. (1982), *The Labour Surplus Economy*, Delhi: Macmillan.
Rosenstein-Rodan, P.N. (1943), 'Problems of industrialization in Eastern and South-Eastern Europe', *Economic Journal*, **53** (210–11), 202–11.
Singer, H. (1950), 'The distribution of gains between borrowing and investing countries', *American Economic Review*, **40** (2), 473–85.
Taylor, L. (1983), *Structuralist Macroeconomics*, New York: Basic Books.
Thirlwall, A.P. (1979), 'The balance of payments constraint as an explanation of the international growth rate differences', *PSL Quarterly Review*, **32** (128), 45–53.

Development banking

Development banking is a special kind of banking that is closely related to the economic and institutional development of a country. As a distinct form of banking, it originated in nineteenth-century France. Commercial banks considered it to be too risky to provide long-term financing to firms, and lacked the ability to assess such kinds of risks. In this context, the French bank Crédit Mobilier became the antecedent of development banks, because (i) it sought to achieve a combination of private financial and socio-economic returns, and (ii) it contributed to economic development both directly, through financing of investment projects, and indirectly, by diffusing technical and organizational skills and banking techniques (Cameron, 1953). On these grounds, development banks proliferated during the post-World War II period, owing to the financing needs of reconstruction and economic development and the lack of private funds for that.

The prevailing ideas among economists and policymakers for the subordination of finance to the needs of the real economy were also conducive to the idea of development banking. Development banking became outdated during the financial liberalization era of the 1980s and 1990s, but has drawn new interest recently because of its countercyclical role during the Great Recession of late 2000s (De Luna-Martínez and Vicente, 2012).

It is possible to sketch a theory of development banking by focusing on four major themes that characterize it. The first issue relates to the significance of long-term versus short-term financing. The idea is for development banks to finance grand-scale investment projects in leading sectors, in order to boost economic development (Chang and Grabel, 2005). Such projects have a long gestation period, entail high financial risk and demand a significant amount of funds, but they also promise high socio-economic returns. Commercial banks prefer projects with shorter maturities and lower risk. Hence, in theory, such projects should obtain financing on the capital markets. Yet, developing countries suffer from a double deficit, namely, economic and institutional underdevelopment. In the face of shallow capital markets and prohibitive transaction and financing costs, development banks may act as capital market substitutes (Studart, 1995, p. 75).

A second issue concerns the criteria of financing. A development bank is a financial institution with a special purpose. As a financial institution, it should take care of its own financial viability. As a special purpose entity, it should give priority to projects with high socio-economic yields, such as those that contribute to higher employment, economize on foreign-exchange reserves, or serve other goals of economic development broadly defined. Hence, development banks should strike a balance between financial and socio-economic returns, which is not a straightforward task to achieve but it rather depends on the historically specific economic conditions and government policies in each country.

A related issue is the ownership structure of development banks. The question is: in order to serve their purpose better, should they be State-owned, privately owned or a combination of these two? The answer to this question also depends on the motives of different stakeholders and the prevailing financial regime. State-owned banks are more conducive to serving government developmental goals, but at the same time are more vulnerable to political corruption. On the other hand, privately owned banks could be more successful financially even as they disregard projects with high socio-economic impact but meagre private returns. Further, State-owned banks are less likely to survive a liberalized financial system than privately owned ones.

The final issue is the bidirectional relationship between development banks and development conceived comprehensively as being both economic and institutional. Development banks boost economic and institutional development by financing industrial and public investment projects along with designing new financial products, disseminating entrepreneurial practices, management and accounting techniques or even consult the government on the institutional infrastructure of capital markets. At the same time, they themselves become the object of change by being transformed to investment banks as financial development proceeds along with economic development. In this sense, development banks' dynamic nature defines them as reflections of financial systems' development, as the latter responds to the needs of a growing real economy. Development banking survival in different economic and institutional environments such as Brazil and China but also Germany, Japan and Canada is proof of its ability to adapt successfully to changing macroeconomic and financial conditions (Loizos, 2017).

KONSTANTINOS LOIZOS

See also

Banking and finance; Development; Government deficits – and money creation; Money and banking; Trade and development

References

Cameron, R.E. (1953), 'The Crédit Mobilier and the economic development of Europe', *Journal of Political Economy*, **61** (6), 461–88.

Chang, H.-J. and I. Grabel (2005), 'Reclaiming development from the Washington Consensus', *Journal of Post Keynesian Economics*, **27** (2), 273–91.

De Luna-Martínez, J. and C.L. Vicente (2012), 'Global survey of development banks', *World Bank Policy Research Working Paper*, No. 5969.

Loizos, K. (2017), 'Alternative financial regimes and development banks in Greece 1963–2002: what have we learned?', *Economic Alternatives*, 1, 34–50, available at https://www.unwe.bg/uploads/Alternatives/Loizos_ea_en_br_1_2017-2.pdf (last accessed 8 December 2020).

Studart, R. (1995), *Investment Finance in Economic Development*, London and New York: Routledge.

Dollar dominance

Dollar dominance refers to the dominant use of the US currency in invoicing and settlement of international trade. It is also the currency in which international investments and debts are denominated. For instance, more than 60 per cent of official foreign-exchange reserves are held in US dollars. Moreover, many countries have also chosen to peg their currency to the US dollar: indeed, 60 per cent of the countries of the world do so – amounting to 70 per cent of countries once weighted by their shares in world GDP (Ilzetki et al., 2019).

This dominance has been clear since the end of the Second World War, although the dollar's global rise started during the interwar period (Eichengreen and Flandreau, 2009). The US currency is used in different proportions according to the countries and regions involved. For instance, one might say that the European Union (EU) is insulated from the dollar dominance, owing to its capacity to use the euro for its foreign trade (the US dollar invoiced 33 per cent of EU exports in 2016). In Latin America or Asia, the US dollar often invoices more than 80 per cent of exports, and this figure is even more critical in oil-exporting countries.

The literature on international currency competition has highlighted that the dollar dominance was enhanced by a combination of economic, political and institutional factors. The determinant most frequently reported in the literature is the size of the issuing countries: this makes it easier to enhance national industrial champions backed by the domestic market and secure large market shares abroad. In theory, the issuing country is assumed to issue a 'sound' currency, which is associated to both price stability and exchange rate stability. As the currency adoption is mainly a market-driven process, the government is supposed to stay away from any manipulation of the exchange rate.

Other major institutional arguments are the credibility of the central bank's monetary policy and the last-resort guarantee of monetary authorities. The issuing country's payments system should be connected to an international network easily accessible by the rest of the world. This payments system should also be linked to sophisticated financial markets providing various financial services and collecting savings. The monetary system should rest on consistent political institutions. The last-resort guarantee, which is sometimes criticized on the ground that it is inconsistent with the monetary policy's credibility, has proven to be of paramount importance in times of crisis (Fields and Vernengo, 2013). The issuing economy is usually also a military power and has an active diplomacy. Eventually, the government's strong willingness to internationalize the national currency is seen as a fundamental prerequisite.

These arguments are not independent of each other. More often than not, they overlap and reinforce each other, which is all the more necessary since the literature usually assumes the prominence of network effects, which favours currency usage. Particular attention should be paid to the fact that the literature has extrapolated the United States' and the United Kingdom's historical experiences to highlight arguments accordingly.

The US dollar dominance provides few significant economic advantages, of which the most well known is allowing the United States to issue vast quantities of government bonds. As they are considered to represent the global reserve asset, the US economy is not constrained to balance its current account and can even be encouraged to record current account deficits to fuel the global economy. Another advantage is that US exporters do not have to hedge against exchange rate fluctuations, since they are paid in their home currency. As the current international monetary regime is the source of international financial instability, post-Keynesian economists such as Davidson (1992) and Rossi (2017) have for a long time called for an international monetary reform establishing a truly multilateral and sustainable payments system.

The asymmetrical nature of the current international monetary regime also gives political advantages to the issuing economy. The use of the US dollar remains prohibited with countries – the 'rogue nations' – and organizations that are considered the United States' enemies and put on the list of the Office of Foreign Assets Control. The threat of disconnection of a bank – or an entire banking system – from the US dollar payments system is a powerful dissuasive weapon that the United States has been using increasingly.

ADRIEN FAUDOT

See also

Bretton Woods; Currency board; Currency hierarchy; International financial architecture; International monetary system

References

Davidson, P. (1992), 'Reforming the world's money', *Journal of Post Keynesian Economics*, **15** (2), 153–79.
Eichengreen, B. and M. Flandreau (2009), 'The rise and fall of the dollar (or when did the dollar replace sterling as the leading reserve currency?)', *European Review of Economic History*, **13** (3), 377–411.
Fields, D. and M. Vernengo (2013), 'Hegemonic currencies during the crisis: the dollar versus the euro in a Cartalist perspective', *Review of International Political Economy*, **20** (4), 740–59.
Ilzetzki, E., C.M. Reinhart and K.S. Rogoff (2019), 'Exchange arrangements entering the twenty-first century: which anchor will hold?', *Quarterly Journal of Economics*, **134** (2), 599–646.
Rossi, S. (2017), 'Rethinking the international monetary and financial architecture', in L.-P. Rochon and S. Rossi (eds), *A Modern Guide to Rethinking Economics*, Cheltenham, UK, and Northampton, MA, USA: Edward Elgar, pp. 302–18.

Dollarization

Dollarization is the term used when a country formally adopts the US dollar as official currency. Current examples include Ecuador (2000), El Salvador (2001), and Panama (1904). In dollarized countries, there is only one currency that serves as a means of payment within the country (Ben Guirat and Rochon, 2015). This is the narrowest example of dollarization in theory and practice, and from this starting point there are many forms of dollarization. Even amongst formally dollarized countries, there are differences in official and informal central bank mandates regarding bank regulation, macroeconomic goals, and lender of last resort functions. There are even differences in the abdication of the function of seignorage; in Panama, for example, the balboa circulates alongside the US dollar, whereas in Ecuador only the latter circulates.

While important differences exist between formally dollarized economies, even more exist in informal dollarization, which occurs when a country's economy is, to varying degrees, *de facto* – while not *de jure* – dollarized. In these cases, the official national currency operates alongside the US dollar. The more dollarized the economy, the more dominant the foreign currency in this relationship. While not the legal tender, contracts and bank deposits may to a varying degree be denominated in US dollars. The investment decisions – and debt obligations – of national governments and companies may be determined in US dollar terms to varying degrees. When participating in fully or partially dollarized countries, foreign companies will typically receive credit from abroad and then repatriate profits in US dollars.

Central bank operations can vary widely in *de facto* dollarized countries. The standard set of options is framed in the 'impossible trinity', in which authorities choose between restricting capital flows, control over the exchange rate, and the central bank's policy rate of interest. In Latin America, where many economies are *de facto* dollarized to varying degrees, the Washington Consensus approach mostly removed capital controls by the late 1980s and early 1990s, while most of the region's central banks focused on stabilizing their currencies' exchange rates. By the end of this decade, and again in general terms, countries of the region began shifting towards inflation targeting regimes.

Within the Latin American framework, the extreme example of *de facto* but not *de jure* dollarization is Argentina's Convertibility plan from 1991 to 2001. The Argentine central bank became essentially a currency board and used pesos only as a physical veil for the US dollar, which was guaranteed on a one-to-one basis. The tail end of the Convertibility plan coincided with the launch of the euro, and while neither was a case of formal dollarization in a strict sense, in both cases individual countries lost control over the national currency in all relevant senses: its quantity, distribution, and interest rate.

Both circumstances are reminiscent of the gold standard, as they share the characteristic of a State abdicating the control of its currency to financial markets. In fact, once this is done, the next political decision of paramount importance in a gold standard regime is the price to which the national currency is fixed to gold. However, once this is done, the gold standard is firmly within the realm of financial markets, and gold acts as a mechanism of automatic market adjustment: the more money flows out of the economy, the higher interest rates must

ADRIEN FAUDOT / WESLEY C. MARSHALL

be. As higher interest rates lead to lower productive investment, as well as lower production and employment, more money flows out of the economy, and fiscal crises can arise, as seen in the 1920s and 1930s in Europe, at the turn of the twenty-first century in Argentina, or in recent years in the countries of the euro's periphery. While none of these cases involved outright dollarization, the context that they offer helps to understand dollarization, at least when dealing with larger economies. Panama and El Salvador, as small economies that are highly dependent on the US economy, are indeed both the most concrete examples of dollarized economies, but are also outliers, and have avoided some of these deflationary dynamics.

Why a country would abdicate control over its currency and replace it for the US dollar or the euro, enter into a gold standard, or allow a *de facto* dollarization of its own economy are political questions. As such agreements involve ceding important functions of the State to the private sector, and have had a history of plunging nations into economic ruin, it is little surprise that such political decisions have faced harsh criticism from all sides. From critical academia, Keynes (1978) addressed the gold standard in *The Economic Consequences of Mr Churchill*. From the mainstream, the International Monetary Fund (2004), a proponent of the Convertibility plan in Argentina, issued a mea culpa shortly after the country had defaulted on loans and returned to the Argentine peso (pesofication).

WESLEY C. MARSHALL

See also

Bretton Woods; Currency board; Inflation targeting; International financial architecture; Washington Consensus

References

Ben Guirat, M. and L.-P. Rochon (2015), 'Dollarization', in L.-P. Rochon and S. Rossi (eds), *The Encyclopedia of Central Banking*, Cheltenham, UK, and Northampton, MA, USA: Edward Elgar, pp. 148–9.
International Monetary Fund (2004), 'Report on the evaluation of the role of the IMF in Argentina, 1991–2001', Washington, DC: International Monetary Fund.
Keynes, J.M. (1978), 'The economic consequences of Mr Churchill', in E. Johnson and D. Moggridge (eds), *The Collected Writings of John Maynard Keynes, Volume III: The Return to the Gold Standard*, London: Royal Economic Society, pp. 207–30.

Double-entry bookkeeping

Double-entry bookkeeping is a set of accounting conventions developed over centuries (see Lauwers and Willekens, 1994) to accurately record financial transactions. Its starting point is the basic accounting equation asserting that assets = liabilities + equity, where assets consist of resources owned, for example, by a company (such as equipment, real estate, or inventories), liabilities are obligations owed by it (such as a loan that needs to be repaid), and equity (also known as net worth) is the difference between them. Because of this balancing feature, the list of all assets and liabilities of a company is called a balance sheet and provides a snapshot of the company's financial position. As time goes by, the company incurs expenses and receives revenues, and the basic accounting equation is extended to include this so-called income statement as follows:

$$assets = liabilities + equity + (revenue - expenses)$$

Within this framework, double-entry bookkeeping stipulates that every transaction corresponds to equal and cancelling entries, called debits and credits, in at least two of the accounts described above. By convention, each account is represented by a T-shaped table, with the name of the account written across the top, debits recorded on the left-hand side, and credits recorded on the right-hand side. Notice that, unlike the normal usages of the words, a credit can either increase or decrease the value of an account, and the same is true for a debit. For example, using cash to purchase equipment should be recorded as a debit (increase) to the equipment account and a credit (decrease) to the cash account, with both being treated as assets, whereas taking up a loan to pay for the same purchase would be recorded as a credit (increase) to the loan account, treated as a liability.

Although textbooks primarily describe these conventions in the context of a company (see Wild and Shaw, 2019), they apply equally well to any other economic unit, including banks, households, central banks, or branches of the government, and underpin many important concepts in post-Keynesian economics. For example, when a bank extends a loan to a client, it follows from double-entry bookkeeping that it should record the new loan as debit (increase) in its assets while simultaneously recording a credit to at least one other account. Typically, the matching credit is an increase in the deposit account of the client, which is a liability for the bank, and the operation just described is the essence of the 'loans create deposits' assertion of endogenous money theory (see Lavoie, 2003). From the point of view of the client, the same transaction consists of a simultaneous debit to a deposit account (in this case viewed as an asset) and credit to a loan account (viewed as a liability). When generalized to entire sectors, such quadruple-entry bookkeeping for the systems of accounts on both sides of every financial transaction constitutes the basis of stock–flow consistent modelling (see Dos Santos and Zezza, 2008).

For a different example, consider quantitative easing, which consists of a central bank purchasing financial assets (say mortgage-based securities) from commercial banks. From the point of view of the central bank, this is a debit (increase) to assets matched by a credit (increase) to reserve liabilities, whereas from the point of view of the commercial bank this is a debit (increase) to one asset account (reserves) matched by a credit (decrease) to another asset account (mortgage-based securities).

As a final example, one can use double-entry bookkeeping to describe spending by a consolidated government sector plus central bank as a credit (increase) to the cash account (viewed here as a liability) and a debit (increase) to the expenses account, whereas the household or firm receiving the payment records it as a credit (increase) to the revenue account, matched by a debit (increase) to its cash account (now viewed as an asset). A detailed analysis of these types of operations and their significance for macroeconomics form the basis for modern monetary theory (see Bell, 2000).

MATHEUS GRASSELLI

See also

Endogenous money; Modern money theory; Money and banking; Quantitative easing; Stock–flow consistent models

References

Bell, S. (2000), 'Do taxes and bonds finance government spending?', *Journal of Economic Issues*, **34** (3), 603–20.
Dos Santos, C.H. and G. Zezza (2008), 'A simplified, "benchmark", stock–flow consistent Post-Keynesian growth model', *Metroeconomica*, **59** (3), 441–78.
Lauwers, L. and M. Willekens (1994), 'Five hundred years of bookkeeping: a portrait of Luca Pacioli', *Tijdschrift voor Economie en Management*, **39** (3), 289–304.
Lavoie, M. (2003), 'A primer on endogenous credit-money', in L.-P. Rochon and S. Rossi (eds), *Modern Theories of Money: The Nature and Role of Money in Capitalist Economies*, Cheltenham, UK, and Northampton, MA, USA: Edward Elgar, pp. 506–43.
Wild, J. and K. Shaw (2019), *Fundamental Accounting Principles*, New York: McGraw-Hill, 24th edition.

Dual economy

A dual economy is one where two different logics – or even two 'modes of production' (in the sense of Marx) – simultaneously operate and interact with each other. This is the case described by Sir Arthur Lewis (1954), where a fully capitalistic sector coexists and interacts with a pre-capitalistic sector, the latter being populated by petty commodity producers employing pre-modern production techniques and adopting a distributive rule based on the average rather than the marginal product of labour (see Ros, 2000).

'Development', in Lewis's (1954) analysis, coincides with the progressive absorption of the pre-capitalistic sector, whose role is to supply cheap wage goods and labour to the capitalistic sector. In this framework, an economy may be said to be developed or 'mature' when it ceases to be dual and becomes homogenously capitalistic (and only at that point one can start thinking in terms of some aggregate growth model). During the development process, people move away from the pre-capitalistic sector (often located in the countryside, but not necessarily so); independent, petty commodity producers become workers in the capitalistic sector; pre-modern production techniques are progressively abandoned; and, finally, functional income distribution worsens because capital accumulation in the modern sector proceeds at an unchanged

MATHEUS GRASSELLI / MARCO MISSAGLIA

real wage as long as an 'unlimited' supply of labour is available.

This pattern of development – for example China in the thirty years approximately from 1980 to 2010 – shares many similarities with the Marxian view according to which the destiny of petty commodity production was to be progressively and fully replaced by capitalistic production during the development process, and Lewis's (1954) unlimited supply of labour is just another name for the Marxian reserve army.

This is certainly a powerful description of the development process. The historical process, however, is always less linear than expected. Some Marxian scholars (a good example is Jaramillo, 2012) have recently developed a model where the dual character of the social fabric (especially of those economies belonging to the 'periphery' of the world capitalistic system and in those sectors where economies of scale are unimportant), far from being a transitory feature, is a permanent and structural characteristic of the economy. Petty commodity production (sometimes referred to as 'informality') coexists with capitalistic production on a permanent basis and in this respect the Marxian (and Lewisian) view is a bit too mechanical. To give just one among several possible examples, think of motorbikes. Produced capitalistically, they are becoming cheaper and cheaper, and this makes it possible for petty producers to run viable activities and resist the competition of the capitalistic sector in the transportation of people.

A different notion of dualism emerges from the post-Keynesian and structuralist traditions. Here, the conceptual basis is provided by Kalecki (1971), whose distinction between 'cost-based' and 'demand-based' prices dates back to 1943, and Hicks (1965), who referred to the same distinction between 'fixprice' and 'flexprice' sectors. *Stricto sensu*, the economy described by Kalecki and Hicks is not dual: the sectors producing fixprice and flexprice commodities do not truly follow different logics, and the distinction is only based on the possibility to accumulate and hold stocks of finished products and/or increase production rapidly in response to higher demand. When this is possible, prices are 'cost-based' ('fixprice'); otherwise, they are 'demand-based' ('flexprice') – industrial products belong to the first group, raw materials and agricultural commodities to the second. Yet, a good reason why Kalecki's and Hicks's contributions are to be included in a discourse on dualism is that they show how the presence of some structural rigidity may prevent traditional Keynesian policies from being effective. For instance, unemployment in a demand-constrained (Keynesian) manufacturing sector cannot be removed through the standard Keynesian recipe owing to the inelasticity of supply in the food sector, a kind of mechanism that is more likely to be at work in a less-developed economy where food products still constitute a significant fraction of total consumption (the purchasing power created by an expansionary demand policy ends up being spent to buy dearer food items). This is a case where a structural constraint may be such that, even if the macroeconomy is governed by the principle of effective demand, Keynesian macroeconomic policies are to be somewhat amended to be effective. Analogous structural rigidities underlie the two- and three-gap models first developed by Chenery and Strout (1966) and Bacha (1990), as well as the contributions made by some structuralist authors (Taylor, 1983; Dutt, 1991) in the discussion of development issues. In all these cases, this Kaleckian/Hicksian 'dual' scheme reveals itself to be useful in the understanding of those economies where the pure Keynesian scheme may not be applied and, yet, the application of the orthodox view cannot be accepted because of the logical fallacies of Say's law.

MARCO MISSAGLIA

See also

Capitalism; Development; Effective demand; Income distribution; *Selected Essays on the Dynamics of Capitalist Economy*

References

Bacha, E.L. (1990), 'A three-gap model of foreign transfers and the GDP growth rate in developing countries', *Journal of Development Economics*, **32** (2), 279–96.

Chenery, H.B. and A.M. Strout (1966), 'Foreign assistance and economic development', *American Economic Review*, **56** (4), 679–733.

Dutt, A.K. (1991), 'Stagnation, income distribution and the agrarian constraint', *Cambridge Journal of Economics*, **15** (3), 343–51.

Hicks, J.R. (1965), *Capital and Growth*, Oxford: Clarendon Press.

Jaramillo, E.S. (2012), 'Heterogeneidad estructural en el capitalismo. Una mirada desde el Marxismo de hoy', *CEDE Universidad de Los Andes Working Paper*, No. 2012–20.

MARCO MISSAGLIA

Kalecki, M. (1971) '"Cost-determined" and "demand determined" prices', in *Selected Essays on the Dynamics of the Capitalist Economy, 1933–1970*, Cambridge, UK: Cambridge University Press, pp. 43–61.

Lewis, W.A. (1954), 'Economic development with unlimited supplies of labor', *Manchester School of Social and Economic Studies*, **22** (2), 139–91.

Marx, K. (1977 [1867]), *Capital: A Critique of Political Economy*, New York: Vintage Books, Vol. 1.

Ros, J. (2000), *Development Theory and the Economics of Growth*, Ann Arbor: University of Michigan Press.

Taylor, L. (1983), *Structuralist Macroeconomics*, New York: Basic Books.

Dutch disease

The expression 'Dutch disease' was coined by *The Economist* in 1977 in describing the deindustrialization of the Dutch economy following the country's exploitation of the Groningen natural gas field, and the resulting appreciation of the Dutch currency's real exchange rate after the increase of its export receipts from a particular booming sector (such as the commodities sector).

Corden and Neary (1982) and Corden (1984) were at the origin of the Dutch disease core model. In their neoclassical model, they assume three sectors of activity: (i) a manufacturing sector exposed to international competition (the tradable sector), (ii) a sector sheltered from international competition (the non-tradable sector); and (iii) a booming sector (open to international trade, which can be associated with the energy sector while not limited to it). In general, the non-tradable sector includes the services sector, which is considered sheltered from international competition – although in practice some services are also easily outsourced abroad. An economic boom generates an increase in external revenues that have two significant effects on the domestic economy, leading to an increase in imports of tradable products at the expense of domestic production.

The first effect is the 'resources movement' effect. An increase in the booming sector's revenues gives rise to a higher remuneration for labour and capital in the economy as a whole. The non-tradable sector can follow the movement and increase the remuneration for labour and capital, since it is sheltered from international competition. The tradable sector is unable to increase its prices, owing to the fact that the producers of this sector are price-takers and depend on international prices. Consequently, if these businesses try to retain their workers and investors by increasing their remuneration as the two other sectors, their margins will decrease dangerously until they close down.

The second effect is the spending effect, which follows from the increase in demand by those who receive the booming sector's revenues. All other things remaining equal, the increase in demand for both the tradable and non-tradable sectors leads to higher prices in the non-tradable sector. The tradable sector, however, is unable to face the rise in demand owing to competitive external constraints. It cannot raise its prices either. Hence the additional demand will be satisfied by imports. A change in the real exchange rate is reflected in the price movements of non-tradable goods relative to tradable goods, the latter being determined by international markets. An increase in the relative prices of non-tradable goods means an appreciation of the real exchange rate.

Recently, the Dutch disease was reinterpreted by development economists. Palma (2005) used the concept to discuss economic growth and development issues in Latin America. Bresser-Pereira (2008) authored a new model of the Dutch disease, according to which the Dutch disease is equal to the difference between the 'current equilibrium', which balances intertemporally the current account of a country, and the 'industrial equilibrium', that is, the exchange rate used by companies that produce tradable (non-commodity) goods or services in order to remain competitive.

The severity of the disease varies according to the international price of the commodity. The real exchange rate of an economy hit by the Dutch disease is drifting away from the one that would allow manufacturing industries to be competitive. The stronger the price boom, or the higher the Ricardian rent drawn from the exploitation of primary resources, the more the exchange rate moves away from a level where the manufacturing industry is profitable. The Ricardian rents originate from the high productivity of domestic producers of raw materials. A common (but politically difficult) way to neutralize the Dutch disease is to establish a sovereign wealth fund that keeps abroad the proceeds of exports. Another method proposed by Bresser-Pereira (2008) is to introduce

MARCO MISSAGLIA / ADRIEN FAUDOT

a tax on exports of raw materials – that is, those goods that give rise to the disease – in order to facilitate industrial development.

It is noteworthy that the Dutch disease is related to the restructuring of productive activities and not to fossil resources' exhaustible nature. Hence, the Dutch disease model has been used to study the impact of international remittances, tourism or official development assistance, potentially resulting in real exchange rate appreciations. Although the model was initially developed to understand the difficulties of countries already industrialized, it remains useful to understand lagging development and the tendency to overvalue the real exchange rate in countries exporting mainly raw materials.

ADRIEN FAUDOT

See also

Current accounts; Development; Exchange rates; Exchange rates – fixed vs flexible; Exchange rates – managed

References

Bresser-Pereira, L.C. (2008), 'The Dutch disease and its neutralization: a Ricardian approach', *Brazilian Journal of Political Economy*, **28** (1), 47–71.
Corden, W.M. (1984), 'Booming sector and Dutch disease economics: survey and consolidation', *Oxford Economic Papers*, **36**, 359–80.
Corden, W.M. and J.P. Neary (1982), 'Booming sector and deindustrialization in a small open economy', *Economic Journal*, **92** (368), 825–48.
Palma, J.G. (2005), 'Four sources of "deindustrialization" and a new concept of the "Dutch disease"', in J.A. Ocampo (ed.), *Beyond Reforms: Structural Dynamics and Macroeconomic Vulnerability*, Stanford and Washington: Stanford University Press and the World Bank, pp. 71–116.

Ecological macroeconomics

Ecological macroeconomics is a relatively new strand of literature aiming to integrate the insights from ecological economics with those of different streams of heterodox macroeconomics. Ecological macroeconomics is an approach to macroeconomics that seeks to explicitly account for the economic system as a sub-system of the planet's biophysical systems. The field describes and analyses how systems of finance, production and distribution both depend upon, and direct the transformation of materials and energy (Althouse, 2022). Beginning in the 2000s, ecological macroeconomics took form alongside the increasing awareness of the ecological crisis at the political level, and gained momentum after the 2008 financial crisis. Examples of this growing interest include a book, *Post Keynesian and Ecological Economics* (Holt et al., 2009), the dedication of a full section of the journal *Ecological Economics* to ecological macroeconomics (Rezai and Stagl, 2016), and reviews of topics and models covered in the field (Fontana and Sawyer, 2016; Røpke, 2016; Hardt and O'Neill, 2017).

Ecological macroeconomics has offered developments in two directions: on the one hand, by integrating ecological concerns within streams of macroeconomics that had historically overlooked such concerns (Lavoie, 2014); on the other hand, by enabling ecological economists to better understand money and finance, historically a weakness in the field (Fontana and Sawyer, 2016). An example of this fruitful collaboration lies in the Stock-Flow Consistent approach, developed originally within the post-Keynesian school of thought, which has proven to be a useful tool to highlight the interactions between ecological and macroeconomic dynamics (Dafermos et al., 2017; Bovari et al., 2018; Monasterolo and Raberto, 2018).

Ecological macroeconomists have formulated proposals to regulate the financial system while facilitating long-term investments towards a low-carbon economy (Røpke, 2017; Jackson, 2017). They have suggested that several 'green' monetary policies and 'green' prudential regulations could be used to accelerate investments in the transition (Campiglio et al., 2018). For instance, establishing differential capital requirements could reward banks that are more exposed to 'green' assets and/or penalize banks with higher exposure to fossil fuels (Rozenberg et al., 2013; Campiglio, 2016). Central banks could also implement 'forward guidance' policies through which they would influence market expectations towards 'green' investments (Campiglio, 2016), or offer favourable refinancing conditions to commercial banks that have invested in low-carbon projects (Aglietta et al., 2015).

Several ecological macroeconomists also argue that public investments are critical to overcome the inability of the private sector alone to fund the low-carbon transition, due to the fundamental uncertainty related to it (Fontana and Sawyer, 2016). National and multilateral development banks can play a critical role towards this end (Aglietta and Espagne, 2016). More fundamentally, government expenditure financed through debt and/or taxes will be essential to provide the number of 'green' investments needed and to address the specific type of funding often required. For instance, installing renewable energy capacity demands important upfront costs. Going further, some authors (for example Forstater, 2003; Lawn, 2010; Godin, 2013) consider that the government could use its spending and taxation powers to finance 'green' full employment mechanisms 'including monitoring, clean up, recycling, education, and more' (Forstater, 2003, p. 21).

In short, ecological macroeconomics' proposals mostly consist in tweaking existing prudential regulations and fiscal and monetary policies towards Keynesian-oriented measures, while 'greening' them for the purpose of an ecological transition. Whereas such proposals seem to offer practical yet ambitious avenues of reform, the field's methodological toolbox remains largely embedded in a conceptual framework that approaches nature first and foremost as a type of 'capital', the depreciation of which could be avoided with so called 'green' investments. This position is informed by a pre-analytical view of a 'world of abundance' (Lavoie, 2014, p. 22), which fails to discuss critical technical (see for instance Smil, 2017), institutional (Paavola, 2007; Vatn, 2010) and ethical (Latour, 2004; Descola, 2005; Brown, 2012) dimensions that could prevent an ambitious socio-ecological transition. More particularly, the legitimate concerns of many post-Keynesian authors around the sources of economic growth (wage-led versus profit-led versus export-led) seem to be at odds with the constraints emerging from a finite world (see for instance Althouse et al., 2020). Further, the need to develop new governance schemes to protect the commons (Ostrom, 2009) does not seem to fit in the traditional conceptions of 'public versus private' ownership and management. Finally, ecological macroeconomics has not yet integrated a growing stream of research coming from environmental history, which suggests that capitalism's regimes of accumulation are deeply influenced by their reliance on abundant and easily accessible natural resources as well as relatively unpolluted ecosystems (Moore, 2015; Malm, 2016).

As of now, it is therefore unclear whether the analytical and methodological framework offered by ecological macroeconomists will be sufficient to re-embed the economic sub-system within the Earth's biophysical systems (Daly and Farley, 2011) or if a more transformative change of paradigm is needed to reconcile post-Keynesian and other streams of heterodox economics with ecological economics (Svartzman et al., 2019).

ÉTIENNE ESPAGNE, ANTOINE GODIN AND ROMAIN SVARTZMAN

See also

Capital requirements; Ecological microeconomics; Growth – wage-led vs profit-led; Heterodox economics; Stock-flow consistent model

References

Aglietta, M., E. Espagne and B. Perrissin-Fabert (2015), 'A proposal to finance low carbon investment in Europe', *Note d'analyse*, France Stratégie.

Aglietta, M. and E. Espagne (2016), 'Climate and finance systemic risks: More than an analogy? The climate fragility hypothesis', *Centre d'Etudes Prospectives et d'Informations Internationales Working Paper*, No. 2016-10, available at http://www.cepii.fr/PDF_PUB/wp/2016/wp2016-10.pdf (last accessed 7 November 2020).

Althouse, J. (2022), *Ecological Macroeconomics for a Shared Planet: Towards a Political Ecology of Money, Finance and Production*, PhD thesis, Université Sorbonne Paris Nord, Villetaneuse.

Althouse, J., G. Guarini and J.G. Porcile (2020), 'Ecological macroeconomics in the open economy: sustainability, unequal exchange and policy coordination in a center-periphery model', *Ecological Economics*, **172**, 1–29.

Bovari, E., G. Giraud and F. McIsaac (2018), 'Coping with collapse: a stock-flow consistent monetary macrodynamics of global warming', *Ecological Economics*, **147**, 383–398.

Brown, P.G. (2012), *Ethics for Economics in the Anthropocene*, New York: Teilhard Studies Number 65.

Campiglio, E. (2016), 'Beyond carbon pricing: the role of banking and monetary policy in financing the transition to a low-carbon economy', *Ecological Economics*, **121**, 220–230.

Campiglio, E., Y. Dafermos, P. Monnin, J. Ryan-Collins, G. Schotten and M. Tanaka (2018), 'Climate change challenges for central banks and financial regulators', *Nature Climate Change*, **8**, 462–468.

Dafermos, Y., M. Nikolaidi and G. Galanis (2017), 'A stock-flow-fund ecological macroeconomic model', *Ecological Economics*, **131**, 191–207.

Daly, H.E. and J. Farley (2011), *Ecological Economics, Second Edition: Principles and Applications*, Washington, DC, USA: Island Press.

Descola, P. (2005), *Par-delà nature et culture*, Paris: Editions Gallimard.

Fontana, G. and M. Sawyer (2016), 'Towards post-Keynesian ecological macroeconomics', *Ecological Economics*, **121**, 186–195.

Forstater, M. (2003), 'Public employment and environmental sustainability', *Journal of Post Keynesian Economics*, **25** (3), 385–406.

Godin, A. (2013), 'Green jobs for full employment, a stock flow consistent analysis', in M.J. Murray and M. Forstater (eds), *Employment Guarantee Schemes*, London and New York: Palgrave Macmillan, pp. 7–46.

Hardt, L. and D. O'Neill (2017), 'Ecological macroeconomics models: assessing current developments', *Ecological Economics*, **134**, 198–211.

Holt, R.P.F., S. Pressman and C.L. Spash (eds) (2009), *Post Keynesian and Ecological Economics*, Cheltenham, UK, and Northampton, MA, USA: Edward Elgar.

Jackson, T. (2017), *Prosperity Without Growth*, 2nd edition, London and New York: Routledge.

Latour, B. (2004), *Politics of Nature: How to Bring the Sciences into Democracy*, Cambridge, MA: Harvard University Press.

Lavoie, M. (2014), *Post-Keynesian Economics: New Foundations*, Cheltenham, UK, and Northampton, MA, USA: Edward Elgar.

Lawn, P. (2010), 'Facilitating the transition to a steady-state economy: some macroeconomic fundamentals', *Ecological Economics*, **69**, 931–936.

Malm, A. (2016), *Fossil Capital: The Rise of Steam Power and the Roots of Global Warming*, Brooklin and London: Verso.

Monasterolo, I. and M. Raberto (2018), 'The EIRIN flow-of-funds behavioural model of green fiscal policies and green sovereign bonds', *Ecological Economics*, **144**, 228–243.

Moore, J.W. (2015), *Capitalism in the Web of Life: Ecology and the Accumulation of Capital*, Brooklin and London: Verso.

Ostrom, E. (2010), 'Beyond markets and States: polycentric governance of complex economic systems', *American Economic Review*, **100** (3), 641–672.

Paavola, J. (2007), 'Institutions and environmental governance: a reconceptualization', *Ecological Economics*, **63** (1), 93–103.

Rezai, A. and S. Stagl (2016), 'Ecological macroeconomics: introduction and review', *Ecological Economics*, **121**, 181–185.

Røpke, I. (2017), 'Sustainability and the governance of the financial system: what role for full reserve banking?', *Environmental Policy and Governance*, **27** (3), 177–192.

Rozenberg, J., S. Hallegatte, B. Perrissin-Fabert and J.-C. Hourcade (2013), 'Funding low-carbon investments in the absence of a carbon tax', *Climate Policy*, **13**, 134–141.

Smil, V. (2017), *Energy and Civilization: A History*, Boston: MIT Press Scholarship Online.

Svartzman, R., D. Dron and E. Espagne (2019), 'From ecological macroeconomics to a theory of endogenous money for a finite planet', *Ecological Economics*, **162**, 108–120.

Vatn, A. (2010), 'An institutional analysis of payments for environmental services', *Ecological Economics*, **69**, 1245–1252.

Ecological microeconomics

Neoclassical microeconomics makes a number of assumptions regarding how individuals think and behave. It looks at economic agents as regularly knowing the choices available to them and the probabilistic outcomes of making each choice. From their choices, consumers and firms act rationally and make decisions to maximize their utility or profits based on the constraints they face and independent of the decisions of other agents.

In contrast, post-Keynesian microeconomics is guided by four facets that bring the analysis closer to the real world. First, consumers and firms confront uncertainty in their decision-making. Economic agents in general do not know all their options, the consequences of their actions or the exact utility and profits that will accrue from their choices. In this world, the future is uncertain and not known. Second, individual judgments are affected by social factors, such as human relations, conventions, habits and emulation rather than just personal choice. Post-Keynesians believe social rationality is more dominant in economic decision-making than neoclassical microeconomics allows. A third property is that economic agents' choices and constraints evolve through historical time rather than adjusting mechanically from one equilibrium point to another. The final facet is the central role institutions play in providing economic and social stability. Institutions play a vital role in post-Keynesian analysis and policy decisions.

These four facets provide a strong theoretical foundation for ecological microeconomics, which studies the relationships between agents, economic systems and nature. Following the work of Boulding (1966), economic agents extract resources such as oil, timber and fish from the environment and in the economic process of consumption and production put waste back into the environment. It is impossible for humans to make a living or satisfy their needs without interacting with nature by extracting resources and putting waste back into the ecological system. Ecological microeconomics focuses on this interaction between the environment and economic agents. It can add thereby a new dimension to post-Keynesian economic analysis. Moreover, the many insights of post-Keynesian economics can be used in ecological microeconomics.

In a post-Keynesian world of uncertainty, the role of government is to reduce uncertainty whenever possible. For instance, ecological microeconomics recognizes the need for precautionary rules to safeguard the environment. Standards to protect the quality of water and air are put into place, so individuals do not have to worry about their health and safety. Since many ecological outcomes cannot be known before they occur, principles based on critical boundaries and threshold levels are essential in our social and economic spheres to achieve sustainable development. An example is provided by the Lisbon Principles found in ecological economics (Constanza et at., 1999), which include: (1) the responsibility principle; (2) the scale-matching principle; (3) the adaptive management principle; (4) the cost-allocation principle; and (5) the full participation principle. Enforcement and implementation of these principles require institutions and policy decisions, which post-Keynesians have used and ecological microeconomics can follow.

Post-Keynesian choice theory recognizes the interdependence of most choices individuals make. This interdependence is extended in ecological microeconomics to include the environment. As well as individual and social rationality, we also need microeconomic models that bring in ecological rationality. Cases of prisoner's dilemmas found in most post-Keynesian microeconomic analysis are particularly evident with ecological problems. Besides lack of information that can lead to suboptimum outcomes, post-Keynesian and ecological economists recognize individual choices are influenced by publicity, fashion and culture, which can lead to behaviour and consumption habits that are unsustainable and environmentally harmful. Moreover, in the absence of future generations being able to register their preferences in an uncertain future, the government needs to account for the likely preferences of future generations.

The study of individual, social and ecological rationality to human nature in ecological microeconomics is compatible with the post-Keynesian view that human needs are based on a social hierarchy. Following the work of Galbraith (1958) and Earl (1983), humans form a hierarchy of needs. At the bottom of the hierarchy is the need for survival. Next comes needs for comfort and social interaction. Finally, there are the needs of self-actualization and improvement. As Lavoie (2006) points out, it is one's income that determines where one is in this hierarchy and how rapidly one can move from one level to the next. This hierarchy is important in understanding the development of consumption and production behaviour that is compatible with sustainable development.

Overall, markets fail to appropriately manage ecological problems because of uncertainty and individual inability to process information. Given the methodological approach of neoclassical economics, the latter is ill-equipped to deal with ecological rationality as compared to post-Keynesian economics.

RICHARD P.F. HOLT

See also

Behavioural economics; Ecological macroeconomics; Institutionalist economics; Neoclassical economics; Sustainable development

References

Boulding, K.E. (1966), 'The economics of the coming spaceship earth', in H. Jarrett (ed.), *Environmental Quality in a Growing Economy*, Baltimore: Resources for the Future/Johns Hopkins University Press, pp. 3–14.

Costanza, R., F. Andrade, P. Antunes, M. van den Belt, D. Boesch, D. Boersma, F. Catarino, S. Hanna, K. Limburg, B. Low, M. Molitor, J.G. Pereira, S. Rayner, R. Santos, J. Wilson and M. Young (1999), 'Ecological economics and sustainable governance of the oceans', *Ecological Economics*, **31** (2), 171–87.

Earl, P.E. (1983), *The Economic Imagination: Towards a Behavioral Analysis of Choice*, Armonk, NY: M.E. Sharpe.

Galbraith, J.K. (1958), *The Affluent Society*, London: Hamish Hamilton.

Lavoie, M. (2006), *Introduction to Post Keynesian Economics*, London: Palgrave Macmillan.

Econometrics – role of

Econometrics is the application of statistical methods to economic data. Although its role in economic research is not without criticism, as illustrated by the Keynes-versus-Tinbergen debate, the application of statistical methods to economics has contributed to the emergence of well-established empirical economic relations, such as the Pareto (1896) income distribution power laws, the Kaldor (1957) facts, or the Phillips (1958) curve. These relations occupy a central place in today's theoretical debate in economics.

Tinbergen – 1969 Nobel laureate in economics for his contribution to econometrics – published a ground-breaking macroeconometric model for the Netherlands in 1936. For the first time, the debate on economic policy was based on quantitative, empirically tested economic analysis rather than economic theory. Although some specifications of his model showed similar elements to Keynes's theory published the same year, Keynes labelled his work as 'statistical alchemy' in an article of the *Economic Journal* in 1939. Keynes (1939, p. 560) argued that Tinbergen's approach 'is a means of giving quantitative precision to what, in qualitative terms, we know already as the result of a complete theoretical analysis'. Keynes further argued that econometrics could be used only for 'curve fitting'; it could not refute economic hypotheses or evaluate economic models. Keynes stressed that econometrics – as a method – can be only applicable where the economist is able to provide a correct and indubitably complete analysis of the significant factors beforehand.

On the other hand, Tinbergen argued that economic theories could never be complete. Econometric research could be useful for scrutinizing elements of economic theories and for examining whether one theory describes reality better than another. Further, it could provide the numerical values of the coefficients in dynamic models that determine the cyclical and stability properties of the model. Finally, through a process of trial and error, it could yield suggestions for an improved specification of dynamic lags. In the aftermath of the controversy, Tinbergen's approach was increasingly used by economists, for its results in forecasting and policy recommendation, particularly with respect to monetary policy. However, Keynes's comments on the role of expectations and uncertainty in macroeconometrics, as well as specification and simultaneous equation biases, remained relevant.

Econometrics is a young discipline within which the robustness of the results depends on both the quality and the quantity of data. Over the last century, tremendous advances in the field have been developed by scholars who have significantly improved the techniques (fixing spurious regressions, convergence of estimators, nonlinearities, asymmetries, error term distributions, missing data, multi-frequency data and so on), and the data collection. The availability of new resources, both in computing power and in econometric theory, has created a race for high-dimensional and nonlinear analyses that seem to capture the complexity of the world. However, when used to infer most complex theoretical (macro)economic models, the use of econometrics alone is almost impossible, as the (key) parameters cannot be well identified (that is, similar changes in two or more parameters generate almost the same results). Moreover, when used for statistical inference, the paradigm of high-dimensional spaces gives rise to the phenomenon known as the curse of dimensionality (Bellman, 1961) (to wit, the need for numerical resources and data is superlinear with respect to dimension), generating a data scarcity problem that seems unsolvable.

FLORENT MCISAAC

See also

Aggregate demand; Microfoundations; Monetary policy; Phillips curve; Uncertainty

References

Bellman, R.E. (1961), *Adaptive Control Processes*, Princeton, USA: Princeton University Press.
Kaldor, N. (1957), 'A model of economic growth', *Economic Journal*, **67** (268), 591–624.
Keynes, J.M. (1936), *The General Theory of Employment, Interest and Money*, London: Macmillan.
Keynes, J.M. (1939), 'Professor Tinbergen's method', *Economic Journal*, **49** (195), 558–77.
Pareto, V. (1896), *Cours d'économie politique*, Paris: Droz.
Phillips, W. (1958), 'The relation between unemployment and the rate of change of money wage rates in the United Kingdom, 1861–1957', *Economica*, **25** (100), 283–99.

FLORENT MCISAAC

Tinbergen, J. (1936), 'Kan hier te lande, al dan niet na overheidsingrijpen, een verbetering van de binnenlandsche conjunctuur intreden, ook zonder verbetering van onze exportpositie? Welke leering kan ten aanzien van dit vraagstuk worden getrokken uit de ervaringen van andere lan-den?', *Preadvies van de Vereeniging voor Staathuishoudkunde en Statistiek*, 's-Gravenhage, pp. 62–108.

Economic Dynamics

The first chapter of *Economic Dynamics* (Harrod, 1973) announces the theme of the book: the need for a dynamic economics. Chapters 2 and 3 are about the theoretical framework and the instability principle. In Chapters 4 to 9, theory is put to use to consider various topics: the capital–output ratio, the rate of interest, inflation, foreign trade, international capital movements. Chapter 7 deals with some problems and conflicts, and Chapter 10 provides a general survey of the overall argument.

The book starts from the fundamental dichotomy between static and dynamic theory. Neoclassical theory since Jevons and Marshall, grounded upon the marginal principle, is essentially micro-static. Keynes is the all-important master of macro-statics. 'Macro-dynamics, with which this book deals, is concerned with the determinants of the rates of increase of the main categories of demand – those for capital goods, for exports, etc.' (Harrod, 1973, p. 11). Dynamic theory on a large scale is to be found with the old Classical economists, Adam Smith and David Ricardo particularly. As an illustration, Harrod mentions Ricardo on the dynamics of distribution: 'in different stages of society the proportion of the whole produce of the earth which will be allotted to these classes under the name of rent, profit and wages, will be essentially different' (p. 12): 'rents rise, profits fall' (p. 13).

In Chapter 2, Harrod presents the tools required for dynamic theory, that is, three growth rates already put to use in his 1939 article (p. 16).

The first equation is $G = s/C$, where 'G is a growth rate per unit of time, s is the fraction of income that is saved, and C is the accretion of capital in the same unit of time divided by the increment of goods produced in that time. This equation is a dynamized version of the fact that investment is always necessarily equal to saving' (p. 16).

The second equation is $G_w = s_d/C_r$. Here 's_d is the fraction of income that would be represented by the amount of saving that people currently want to make' (p. 17). 'C becomes C_r when the values of numerator and denominator are such that people find that the amount of capital goods on hand, fixed and circulating, is just what they find convenient' (p. 18).

Third, there is another variant of the fundamental equation, representing the natural rate of growth $G_n = s_o/C_r$ (p. 27). 'One may think of it of growth in accordance with the potential of an economy, or as the maximum possible rate of growth, subject ... to the desired balance between work and leisure' (pp. 27–8). 'The "natural" growth rate is determined by population increase and technological progress, and specifies what optimum saving ratio s_o is required in consequence of that' (p. 28).

Chapter 3 is devoted to the instability principle, which in vast parts of the economic literature has been associated with the 'Harrod knife-edge'. On this, Harrod is unequivocal: 'Nothing that I have ever written (or said) justifies this description of my view' (p. 32).

Nevertheless, it 'would be almost a miracle if the aggregate of decisions resulted in an actual growth rate equal to the "warranted" growth rate. There are likely to be some deviations all the time. But if they are of moderate dimensions, I would not suppose that they would bring the instability principle into operation. That is why I so much object to the knife-edge idea. It requires a fairly large deviation ... to bring the instability principle into play' (p. 33).

Harrod concludes: 'I am confident that the theory that the "warranted" equilibrium growth rate of *laissez-faire* capitalism, without management or interference, is unstable, stands firm; and it is the fundamental explanation of the business cycle' (p. 45).

In the subsequent chapters, Harrod goes on to apply the theoretical framework set out in Chapters 2 and 3 to various problems related to growth and employment in the main. The analysis gets very complex as it emerges from the table on page 104, which exhibits various combinations of the actual, warranted and natural growth rates, giving rise to specific types of dynamics. For example, if, in an unemployment situation, the warranted rate of growth exceeds the natural rate, the economy will head towards full employment. However, once

FLORENT MCISAAC / HEINRICH BORTIS

full employment is reached, the economy must move forward at the natural rate, which is below the warranted rate. Accordingly, recession is inevitable, unless excess saving is absorbed, for example through a fiscal deficit (p. 105).

Paradoxically, then, the foot should be put on the accelerator when unemployment is at its minimum level. To clarify the situation, this paradox requires for economic dynamics to establish its basic axioms, and to translate them into maxims of economic policy (p. 106).

Indeed, to come to grips with a complex and paradox-ridden real world, principles are required. The most plausible principles have to be distilled from an intensive study of the history of economic theories.

In the spirit of Harrod, a combination of Keynesian and Classical principles seems most appropriate (Bortis, 2021, pp. 102–3): the principle of effective demand, the labour-value principle and the surplus principle. On these principles a system of Classical–Keynesian political economy may be erected (for some elements of this system see Bortis, 2021, pp. 102–13). The Classical–Keynesian system allows us to escape from the straightjacket of static neoclassical equilibrium economics and opens the way for setting up empirical laws of economic dynamics, for example the all-important law of cumulative causation of disequilibria (Myrdal, 1957; Kaldor, 1985). An important aspect of this law is the relationship between employment and distribution (Keynes, 1936, pp. 372–4): world effective demand governs world employment, implying massive involuntary unemployment. With globalization, the free movement of labour leads to a pressure on wages everywhere. Income distribution gets more unequal. World effective demand shrinks and involuntary unemployment increases. This, in turn, exerts additional pressure on wages. A vicious circle comes thereby into being.

Methodologically, Keynes distinguishes 'between the logical theory of the multiplier [the multiplier principle], which holds good continuously, without time-lag, at all moments of time, and the consequences of an expansion in the capital-goods industries which take gradual effect, subject to time-lag and only after an interval' (Keynes, 1936, p. 122). The logical theory of the multiplier is an ever-valid principle, which is implemented through concrete expansions in the capital-goods industries (Keynes, 1936, pp. 122–5). Now, principles are necessarily of a static nature, while the realizations of principles in the real world are fundamentally dynamic. Hence Harrod's claim that Keynes is the master of macro-statics only is not appropriate.

Harrod is right to go back to the Classical economists in his search for dynamic economics. However, in this undertaking, Keynes must also be taken into account.

Indeed, Harrod's 1939 article was considered very important at that time, because it proposed an explanation of the extreme instability of capitalism exhibited in the Great Depression of the 1930s. However, in the mid 1950s a post-Keynesian countermovement set in, with Nicholas Kaldor arguing that saving adjusted to investment through changes in income distribution and that, as a rule, the realized rate of profit was above the desired profit rate. Consequently, there was an inherent tendency towards full employment at the natural rate of economic growth. This was confirmed by the unprecedented Kondratiev upswing from, broadly, 1950 to 1973, which brought about not only full employment but even over-employment, resulting in massive immigration in Germany and Switzerland for example. All this strongly reduced the importance of Harrod's 1973 *Economic Dynamics*. Subsequently, the monetarist counterrevolution of the mid 1970s literally swept away both Keynes and Harrod.

Nevertheless, Harrod should not be reduced to his 1973 book. In fact, his main work is his splendid biography of Maynard Keynes, containing Harrodian developments of Keynes's theory, for example regarding the importance of exports and the significance of the export multiplier. Given his sympathy for the old Classical economists, his profound knowledge of Keynes and his awareness of the potential of Keynes's theory, Roy F. Harrod may be considered a founding father of Classical–Keynesian political economy.

HEINRICH BORTIS

See also

Accelerator effects; Capitalism; Cumulative causation; Effective demand; Income distribution

References

Bortis, H. (2021), 'The history of economic theories', in L.-P. Rochon and S. Rossi (eds), *An Introduction*

HEINRICH BORTIS

to *Macroeconomics: A Heterodox Approach to Economic Analysis*, Second Edition, Cheltenham, UK, and Northampton, MA, USA: Edward Elgar, pp. 80–121.
Harrod, R.F. (1939), 'An essay in dynamic theory', *Economic Journal*, **49** (193), 14–33.
Harrod, R.F. (1973), *Economic Dynamics*, London: Macmillan.
Kaldor, N. (1985), *Economics Without Equilibrium*, Armonk, NY: M.E. Sharpe.
Keynes, J.M. (1936), *The General Theory of Employment, Interest and Money*, London: Macmillan.
Myrdal, G. (1957), *Economic Theory and Underdeveloped Regions*, London: Harper.

Economic geography

Economic geography is a subdiscipline of economics and human geography that seeks to explain the forces that lead to spatial variation in economic activity. It explores uneven geographic growth and development, interregional trade and the intersectoral flow of funds, transportation and communication, and the location of economic activity. Post-Keynesian economic geography emphasizes fundamental uncertainty, non-equilibrium outcomes, the non-neutrality of money, and the dependence of wealth and capital accumulation on effective demand for regional exports. Combining elements of regional multiplier theory, cumulative causation, and dependency theory, post-Keynesian economists have provided explanations for uneven regional growth and development (see Dow and Chick, 1988). Additional considerations of this approach include the persistence of regional and otherwise localized concentrations of unemployment, and the tendency for unemployment to exhibit spatial dependence (Mitchell and Juniper, 2007; Tcherneva, 2020, pp. 22–41).

Half a century of scholarship on regional growth, development, and money and finance demonstrates the intersection of economic geography and post-Keynesian economics. Kaldor, Thirlwall, Dow, and Chick were among the first authors to explicitly engage in theorizing regional development and finance from the perspective of post-Keynesian economics (Kaldor, 1966, 1970; Dow, 1987a, 1987b; Dow and Chick, 1988; Thirlwall, 1980). Their work explores regional economic growth differentials, balance-of-payments constrained regional growth, the role of financial factors and flows of funds across regions, and the importance of functional and institutional variations that arise from changes in financial regulation and banking systems. The lineage of economic thought that incorporates the spatial implications of the non-neutrality of money is traced back to August Lösch (1940) and Walter Isard (1956), two founders of regional science (see Bieri, 2017).

Localized variations in financial and institutional factors alongside the dynamics of cumulative causation, regional multipliers, and liquidity preference help explain the concentration of economic growth and development in some areas at the expense of others. There are regional disparities in the marginal efficiency of investment, and through cumulative dynamics of investment and productivity growth regional divergence is likely to persist. Regional economic growth from export demand increases productivity through internal or external increasing returns to scale. Increases in productivity provide additional competitiveness for the local export sector. As production is consumed outside of the region, these purchases lead to further output growth via a multiplier effect – according to Verdoorn's law (see Kaldor, 1966, 1970; McCombie and De Ridder, 1984). Regional or otherwise localized aggregate demand and financial flows drive cumulative processes of economic growth and decline.

Attempts to explain the uneven development of a place – systematic underdevelopment at some locations to the benefit of increased economic growth and social well-being in others – are incomplete without considering the role of money and finance, and the linkages between finance and the real allocation and distribution of resources (Dow, 1987a, 1987b; Dymski, 2011; Bieri, 2017). Building from a spatial pattern typical of many metropolitan areas in the United States, Dymski (2001) considers stock–flow imbalances across a metropolitan area with an inner core and suburban ring in a post-Keynesian spatial input–output model. This model shows how financial speculation shapes the physical development of a place, where an inflow of money in advance of any promise of a return flow of income generates changes in the built environment (Dymski, 2001). The location of firms across urban space will tend to be uneven, reinforcing patterns of structural discrimination (segregation and isolation) and poverty. Since economic activity

HEINRICH BORTIS / JORDAN AYALA

exists in space and thus operates in spaces with borders, financial and real flows across these borders alter the balance of wealth within and between neighbourhoods, regions, and nations (Dymski, 2004).

In mainstream economics, considerations of geography do not extend beyond the calculation of costs related to communication and transportation (Krugman, 1991), or topography and other physical characteristics (Gallup et al., 1999). Exogenous and non-economic place-based characteristics or stable equilibrium outcomes on a featureless geographical backdrop determine economic geography, and exogenously determined transportation costs are key (Sheppard, 2016). The treatment of space in mainstream economics, in the degree of inconsistency and omission, runs parallel to conventional theorizations of money. Mainstream economics, including urban and regional approaches, adopt the quantity theory of money, in which money can only affect prices. In addition to the spatial implications of capital accumulation and its role in shaping decisions made by the politically and economically powerful at the local to global level, it is important to understand the linkages between financial factors and the accumulation and distribution of capital (Martin, 1999; Bieri, 2017; Sheppard and Barnes, 2017). Geography and historical time are dynamic. The geography on which the social and economic world rests is not a featureless plane of x–y coordinates, but an expression of social and economic processes that shape geography.

JORDAN AYALA

See also

Balance-of-payments constrained growth; Cumulative causation; Dependency theory; Effective demand; Verdoorn's Law

References

Bieri, D. (2017), 'Back to the future: Lösch, Isard, and the role of money and credit in the space-economy', in R. Jackson and P. Schaeffer (eds), *Regional Research Frontiers, Vol. 1: Advances in Spatial Science*, Berlin: Springer, pp. 217–41.

Dow, S.C. (1987a), 'The treatment of money in regional economics', Journal of Regional Science, **27** (1), 13–24.

Dow, S.C. (1987b), 'Money and regional development', Studies in Political Economy, **23** (1), 73–94.

Dow, S.C. and V. Chick (1988), 'A Post-Keynesian perspective on the relation between banking and regional development', *Thames Papers in Political Economy*.

Dymski, G. (2001), 'Can entrepreneurial incentives revitalize the urban inner core? A spatial input–output approach', Journal of Economic Issues, **35** (2), 415–22.

Dymski, G. (2004), 'Sraffa in the city: exploring the urban multiplier', in G. Argyrous, M. Forstater and G. Mongiovi (eds), *Growth, Distribution, and Effective Demand: Alternatives to Economic Orthodoxy. Essays in Honor of Edward J. Nell*, Armonk, NY: M.E. Sharpe, pp. 220–38.

Dymski, G. (2011), 'A spatialized approach to asset bubbles and Minsky crises', in D.B. Papadimitriou and L.R. Wray (eds), *The Elgar Companion to Hyman Minsky*. Cheltenham, UK, and Northampton, MA, USA: Edward Elgar, pp. 222–45.

Gallup, J.L., J.D. Sachs and A.D. Mellinger (1999), 'Geography and economic development', International Regional Science Review, **22** (2), 179–232.

Isard, W. (1956), *Location and Space-Economy: A General Theory Relating to Industrial Location, Market Areas, Land Use, Trade, and Urban Structure*: Cambridge, MA: MIT Press.

Kaldor, N. (1966), *Causes of the Slow Rate of Growth of the United Kingdom: An Inaugural Lecture*, Cambridge, UK: Cambridge University Press.

Kaldor, N. (1970), 'The case for regional policies', Scottish Journal of Political Economy, **17** (3), 337–48.

Krugman, P. (1991), *Geography and Trade*, Cambridge, MA: MIT Press.

Lösch, A. (1940), 'Geographie des Zinses', Die Bank, **33** (2), 24–8.

Martin, R. (1999), *Money and the Space Economy*, Chichester, UK: Wiley.

McCombie, J.S. and J.R. De Ridder (1984), '"The Verdoorn law controversy": some new empirical evidence using U.S. State data', Oxford Economic Papers, **36** (2), 268–84.

Mitchell, W. and J. Juniper (2007), 'Towards a spatial Keynesian economics', in P. Arestis and G. Zezza (eds), *Advances in Monetary Policy and Macroeconomics*, Basingstoke, UK and New York: Palgrave Macmillan, pp. 192–211.

Myrdal, G. (1957), *Economic Theory and Underdeveloped Countries*, London: Duckworth.

Sheppard, E.S. (2016), *Limits to Globalization: The Disruptive Geographies of Capitalist Development*, Oxford: Oxford University Press.

Sheppard, E.S. and T.J. Barnes (2017), *The Capitalist Space Economy: Geographical Analysis after Ricardo, Marx and Sraffa*, London and New York: Routledge.

Tcherneva, P.R. (2020), *The Case for a Job Guarantee*, Cambridge, UK: Polity Press.

Thirlwall, A. (1980), 'Regional problems are "balance-of-payments" problems', Regional Studies, **14** (5), 419–25.

JORDAN AYALA

Economic Growth and the Balance-of-Payments Constraint

This book highlights the rationalization of the influence that the external sector has on economic growth of a given country. The theory of balance-of-payments-constrained growth has become a highly used approach to modelling long-run economic growth, especially by economists from the post-Keynesian tradition.

McCombie and Thirlwall (1994) built a highly simplified model that suggests an answer to the question: why do countries experience different rates of economic growth?

Like all Keynesian-inspired constructions, the authors emphasized demand. Instead of reducing economic development to just a combination of availability of labour, capital and the incorporation of technology, they drew attention to the fact that the existence of these conditions was necessary but not sufficient to provide economic growth.

Their conclusion was that the factor effectively limiting the long-term growth rate of an economy is the long-term growth rate of its exports combined with the long-term elasticity of import demand with respect to total production. This elasticity is just a number that links the percentage of growth in imports to the rate of GDP growth in the long run. For example, if it is equal to 2, a GDP growth rate of 2.5 per cent implies an increase in imports of 5 per cent. Thus, the long term is a time sufficiently large to eliminate fluctuations in GDP, imports and exports due to shocks, such as the oil crisis or changes in tariffs. The complete model that takes into account the possibility of capital movements to finance possible current account deficits is rather complex. The essence of the conclusion, however, is very simple. In the long term, the accumulation of current account deficits increases the country's liabilities and therefore increases the need for remittances of interest, royalties and dividends, which requires growing trade surpluses.

After the accumulation of sustainable liabilities, that is, in the long term, the economy has to find a balance given by the following relationship:

(increase in GDP) multiplied by (elasticity of imports) = growth rate of exports

For instance, if GDP grows at a 3 per cent long-term rate and the long-term elasticity of imports is 2, imports will grow by 6 per cent yearly. In the long run, the balance requires that the growth rate of exports should also be 6 per cent. As a result, the so-called 'Thirlwall law' says just that: an economy's higher long-term growth rate is given by the long-term growth rate of its exports divided by the long-term elasticity of import demand.

The models of open macroeconomics, such as the Mundell–Fleming model, start from a condition of equilibrium in the balance of payments as a whole; that is, the balance is given in the capital account and in the current account simultaneously. The application of this condition in the long run means that inflows in the capital account can finance imbalances in the current account, without restrictions as to the period in which this process can occur. McCombie and Thirlwall (1994), by contrast, argue that a country cannot be financed indefinitely by current account imbalances (but it can accumulate surpluses). The restriction imposed by these models, therefore, refers only to the degree of capital mobility, while the McCombie and Thirlwall model assumes that the balance, in the long run, is given by the balance in the current account.

Such an approach also provides the theoretical foundation and empirical support to justify economic growth led by foreign trade, as exports and investment based on import substitution can increase GDP growth rates and simultaneously increase the capacity of importing goods and services. Economic growth is said to be led by foreign trade as it is not just a question of suggesting export-led growth, since import substitution has similar effects on aggregate demand to that of increased exports. In other words, both the income elasticity of demand for exports and the income elasticity of demand for imports are important in determining the long-term equilibrium growth rate of the economy.

Following this theory, the most effective way to increase economic growth and reduce unemployment is the possibility of generating complementary economic growth between countries, a solution that was proposed by Keynes himself during the negotiations of the Bretton Woods agreement. Keynes proposed that the adjustment of the balance of payments between countries with different performances should be carried out by promoting economic

PAULO ROBILLOTI

growth in surplus countries in order to reduce global imbalances. However, such suggestion contained as a major obstacle the need for policy coordination between countries and international cooperation.

The implication for economic policy stemming from McCombie and Thirlwall's (1994) contribution is that the structural adjustment of the balance of payments towards higher rates of economic growth, keeping the degree of trade openness constant, must be done by changing the measure of elasticities. This necessarily implies a profound change in the competitive bases of productive sectors.

PAULO ROBILLOTI

See also

Balance of payments; Balance-of-payments constrained growth; Bretton Woods; IS–LM model; Thirwall's law

Reference

McCombie, J. and A.P. Thirlwall (1994), *Economic Growth and the Balance-of-Payments Constraint*, Basingstoke, UK, and New York: Palgrave Macmillan.

Economic integration

Economic integration refers to the harmonizing of economic policies between different countries or territories with the purpose of increasing trade, productivity and economic growth. The participating countries seek to ensure deeper economic cooperation by unifying to various degrees their monetary, fiscal and trade policies, and by decreasing or abolishing mutual trade restrictions such as tariffs, quotas or other taxes. Economic integration can occur through policies designed within regional blocs like the European Single Market and the North American Free Trade Agreement, or at the international level such as through membership in the World Trade Organization.

Classical and early neoclassical theories of economic integration (see Smith, 1776/2008; Ricardo, 1816/2015; Ohlin, 1933; Viner, 1937) are usually linked with theories of free trade, based on a general equilibrium approach, according to which countries with abundant resources develop a comparative advantage in the production of these goods. Indeed, countries that specialize in the production of such goods can gain from the least trade restrictions, and therefore achieve a higher degree of economic integration through the increase in trade (see Samuelson, 1948; Viner, 1950). Although Keynes (1946) agreed that the advantages of trade are substantial, he also 'thought that "the classical school greatly overstressed them". This was because he thought that, even in the best constructed global system, there would still be winners and losers, so that "great moderation" was necessary in pressing economic integration too far' (Skidelsky, 2005, p. 18).

Keynes's views about economic integration evolved considerably through the years after witnessing two world wars, a Great Depression and an international reconstruction effort that saw the creation of several international institutions with stated missions to help resolve economic and political problems between countries (see Eichengreen, 1984). In *The Economic Consequences of the Peace*, Keynes (1919) praised the prosperous pre-war economic relationships within the European powers and believed that greater good comes when 'the interference of frontiers and of tariffs was reduced to a minimum' (Keynes, 1919, p. 8). Consequently, he criticized the post-World War I reparation treaty against Germany and argued that, to avoid future conflicts, European economic integration should be prioritized over sanctions, precisely because 'the economic interdependence of Germany and her neighbours [is] overwhelming' (Keynes, 1919, p. 8).

However, the Great Depression seems to have tempered Keynes's position, as he advocated minimizing 'economic entanglement among nations' (Keynes, 1933, p. 181). In *The General Theory of Employment, Interest and Money*, albeit in the framework of a closed economy, Keynes (1936) elaborates further and emphasizes the critical role of effective demand as the determinant of economic output, and the importance of government expenditures as a stabilizing tool against recessions and to reach full employment (Keynes, 1936).

Contrary to neoclassical economic policy that proposes economic integration as an additional layer of economic deregulation that should allow international and regional markets to operate in a self-regulating optimal setting, Keynes was more concerned with establishing an international system that allows

PAULO ROBILLOTI / MEHDI BEN GUIRAT

States to cooperate and engage in mutually beneficial economic activities that will provide for full employment without the possibility of economic differences developing into deeper conflicts or even wars. Keynes had reservations about the post-World War II impacts of globalization, economic integration and the increase of international capital flows, and although he supported the creation of supranational institutions he feared that global economic uncertainty could be further contagious in unregulated export-driven markets and that economic domestic stabilization policies could consequently be rendered ineffective (Dimand, 2006).

Post-Keynesian economists develop Keynes's analysis against unchecked free trade and deeper economic integration for several reasons. Davidson (2015) explains that because modern technology is easily transferrable across borders, the theory of comparative advantages is hardly applicable to modern economies with expansive trade treaties, and since economic exchanges often occur between countries with unequal economic development, free capital flows and the free movement of goods and services can easily allow for the outsourcing of production to inexpensive labour markets, therefore contributing to downward flexible wages and declining labour productivity growth (Davidson, 2015). In similar fashion, Lavoie (2016) addresses the impact of trade agreements and capital mobility on wages, the bargaining power of labour and, as a result, income inequality. Kaldor (1970) and Thirlwall and Hussain (1982) also addressed issues of long-run economic growth in the framework of globalized trade and integrated economies, and although their models prescribed different policy recommendations, they both stressed the possibility of a negative impact of external competition on local markets (see Blecker, 2009). The uniting theme among post-Keynesian economists remains that economic integration policies and free trade treaties are suitable if they address issues of full employment, and that the free movement of trade and capital flows should not disrupt the implementation of domestic policies, especially the ability of national governments to pursue government spending when necessary (Kregel, 2008).

MEHDI BEN GUIRAT

See also

European Monetary Union; Fiscal policy; Free trade; Monetary policy; Regional economic integration and free trade agreements

References

Blecker, R.A. (2009), 'Long-run growth in open economies: export-led cumulative causation or a balance-of-payments constraint?', *American University Working Paper*, No. 2009-23.

Davidson, P. (2015), *Post Keynesian Theory and Policy: A Realistic Analysis of the Market Oriented Capitalist Economy*, Cheltenham, UK, and Northampton, MA, USA: Edward Elgar.

Dimand, R. (2006), 'Keynes on global economic integration', *Atlantic Economic Journal*, 34 (2), 175-82.

Eichengreen, B. (1984), 'Keynes and protection', *Journal of Economic History*, 44 (2), 363-73.

Kaldor, N. (1970), 'The case for regional policies', *Scottish Journal of Political Economy*, 17 (3), 337-48.

Keynes, J.M. (1919), *The Economic Consequences of the Peace*, London: Macmillan.

Keynes, J.M. (1933), 'National self-sufficiency', *Studies: An Irish Quarterly Review*, 22 (86), 177-93.

Keynes, J.M. (1936), *The General Theory of Employment, Interest and Money*, London: Macmillan.

Keynes, J.M. (1946), 'The balance of payments of the United States', *Economic Journal*, 56 (222), 172-87.

Kregel, J. (2008), 'What can Keynes tell us about policies to reduce unemployment and financial instability in a globalised international economy?', *METU Studies in Development*, 35 (1), 161-76.

Lavoie, M. (2016), 'Rethinking macroeconomic theory before the next crisis', Institute for New Economic Thinking, available online at https://www.ineteconomics.org/perspectives/blog/rethinking-macro-theory (last accessed on 5 August 2019).

Ohlin, B.G. (1933), *Interregional and International Trade*, Cambridge, MA, USA: Harvard University Press.

Ricardo, D. (1816/2015), *On the Principles of Political Economy and Taxation*, Cambridge, UK: Cambridge University Press.

Samuelson, P.A. (1948), 'International trade and the equalisation of factor prices', *Economic Journal*, 58 (230), 163-84.

Skidelsky, R. (2005), 'Keynes, globalisation and the Bretton Woods institutions in the light of changing ideas about markets', *World Economics*, 6 (1), 15-30.

Smith, A. (1776/2008), *An Inquiry into the Nature and Causes of the Wealth of Nations*, Oxford: Oxford University Press.

Thirlwall, A.P. and M.N. Hussain (1982), 'The balance of payments constraint, capital flows and growth rate differences between developing countries', *Oxford Economic Papers*, **34** (3), 498–510.

Viner, J. (1937), *Studies in the Theory of International Trade*, New York: Harper & Brothers.

Viner, J. (1950), *The Customs Union Issue*, New York: Carnegie Endowment for International Peace.

Effective demand

Effective demand is a key concept in Keynes's theory of employment. To introduce it, Keynes defined two functions: the aggregate supply function, $Z = \varphi(N)$, and the aggregate demand function, $D = f(N)$. Z stands for the aggregate supply price of the output resulting from a given quantity of employment *(N)*, that is, 'the expectation of proceeds which will just make it worth the while of the entrepreneurs to give that employment' (Keynes, 1936, p. 25). D stands for the proceeds that entrepreneurs expect to receive when selling the output produced by N. The effective demand that determines the volume of goods to be produced, hence employment, is '[t]he value of D at the point of the aggregate function, where it is intersected by the aggregate supply function' (p. 25). In this sense, it can explain why an economy can remain in a position of less than full employment.

The 'principle of effective demand' defined in this way was intended to counter the neoclassical view according to which the labour market adjusts itself to full employment, provided prices and wages are flexible. However, mainstream economists now consider this principle as simply a special case of neoclassical general equilibrium theory. It would simply promote a model in which quantities rather than prices are subject to adjustment. This common interpretation is all the more paradoxical since Keynes (1936, p. 27) insisted that '[t]he essential character of the argument is precisely the same whether or not money-wages, etc., are liable to change'.

The reason for this paradox is certainly to be found in the theoretical framework underlying both approaches. Mainstream economists consider the economic system as composed of markets that, ideally, allow for achieving the balance between individual preferences via the free adjustment of supplies and demands on markets for goods and labour. On this view, Keynes would have, at best, added another stone to the edifice. He would have explained that demand may play a leading role in determining employment when prices and wages are not flexible. However, Keynes clearly contrasted his vision of the economy he labelled 'money-wage' or 'entrepreneur economy' with the neoclassical representation he called 'real exchange economy' (Keynes, 1933, pp. 76–106).

In the 'real exchange economy', firms are mere intermediaries between the market for productive services and the market for produced goods. Fundamentally, productive services exchange for goods. Ultimately, exchanges even boil down to the exchange of productive services for one another, as firms and money may be disregarded (see Walras, 1954/1874, p. 225). Hence the label of 'real exchange economy'.

For Keynes, however, entrepreneurs and money play the crucial role: entrepreneurs decide on the volume of employment with reference to the money proceeds they are expecting from sales. The principle of effective demand is no doubt grounded in this view of the economy. It namely puts to the fore the entrepreneur and the successive spending and proceeds the latter is expecting to incur for a given volume of employment. As Keynes (1936/1973, pp. 24–5) argued, 'entrepreneurs will endeavour to fix the amount of employment at the level which they expect to maximize the excess of the proceeds over the factor cost.'

In this model, expected demand plays a major role. Namely, entrepreneurs would meet losses if they produced goods that would not be demanded. They consequently adapt production and hence employment to the expected demand for the goods produced. In this way, expected demand proves effective in determining output and the correlated quantity of employment. Full employment is in no way ensured.

To insist on the originality of Keynes's concept of effective demand, we may confirm that his argument is not akin to the analysis of the interplay of supply and demand on markets, embedded in the mainstream model. With reference to the usual distinction between the *ex ante* disparity of supply and demand and their *ex post* balance achieved on markets through price changes, Keynes is clear: '*Ex ante* decisions in their influence on effective demand relate solely to *entrepreneurs*' decisions. *Ex ante* saving is a very dubious concept – the decisions don't have to be made' (Keynes, 1937, pp. 182–3).

MEHDI BEN GUIRAT / CLAUDE GNOS

Accordingly, there are no distinct supply and demand forces determining employment, which would be based on the behaviour of two different categories of agents. Entrepreneurs are left to make decisions based on their own forecasts, which, as post-Keynesian economists are used to highlighting, are subject to a high degree of uncertainty. Hence the role of the current state of expectations (Keynes, 1936, pp. 46–51) and entrepreneurs' psychology.

CLAUDE GNOS

See also

Aggregate demand; Fiscal policy; Neoclassical economics; *The General Theory of Employment, Interest and Money*; Uncertainty

References

Keynes, J.M. (1933), 'The distinction between a co-operative economy and an entrepreneur economy', in *The Collected Writings of John Maynard Keynes, Volume XXIX: The General Theory and After: A Supplement*, London and Basingstoke: Macmillan, 1973, pp. 76–106.

Keynes, J.M. (1936), *The General Theory of Employment, Interest and Money*, London: Macmillan.

Keynes, J.M. (1937), '"Ex post and ex ante", "Notes from Keynes" 1937 Lectures', in *The Collected Writings of John Maynard Keynes, Volume XIV: The General Theory and After. Part II: Defence and Development*, London and Basingstoke: Macmillan, 1973, pp. 179–83.

Walras, L. (1954), *Elements of Pure Economics or the Theory of Social Wealth*, translated by W. Jaffé, London: George Allen & Unwin (first French edition 1874).

Employer of last resort

The role of employer of last resort (ELR) for the State has been pushed forward by Minsky (1965) as a response to the war on poverty that the US president J.F. Kennedy started in the 1960s. The literature offers different names for the same policy such as Job Guarantee Programme or Public Service Employment programme. Minsky strongly criticized the economic policies put in place during the war on poverty (such as tax cuts) and advocated in favour of public works in order to reach full employment, the only state of affairs that could eradicate poverty.

Since then, ELR programmes have been declined in different versions according to how to set wages and benefits, target populations, types of projects to be included in the programme, administrative ways to deal with the programme, ways to finance it, and so on. Most of these descriptions are related to the Modern Money Theory school of thought and have been widely debated with post-Keynesian literature (see Palley, 2018, or Wray et al., 2018, for recent publications on the topic).

Wray (2007, p. 9) proposes 'a universal job guarantee with a single compensation package for all participants'. He recommends providing full-time (or part-time when required by the applicant) jobs to anyone who is of legal age, able, ready and willing to work in exchange for a uniform wage and benefit package, fixed according to the living conditions in the country.

Education and training as well as job searching should be part of the activities proposed under ELR schemes. The administration of the programme should be highly decentralized in order to fit with the local realities. The federal government should provide funds for the employees and part of the capital cost of each project funded by the ELR scheme. The rest of the capital cost would be the burden of local governments. Each project would thus be implemented in cooperation between the federal and local governments and/or non-government organizations.

A rich discussion over the functions and impacts of ELR schemes has flourished, mostly within post-Keynesian literature. Their main benefits lie in the complete elimination of involuntary unemployment and its side-effects such as loss of skills or social and health costs of unemployment. This outcome has however been questioned, because it could lead to disguised underemployment (Sawyer, 2003), be structurally constrained and lead to conflict inflation, along Kalecki's line (Kalecki, 1943; Ramsay, 2002; Palley, 2018) or would lead to a low-wage full-employment equilibrium (Seccareccia, 2004). Another heavily debated aspect concerns the impact on cost-pushed inflation by an ELR scheme. While proponents of the approach claim that it would de facto create an anchor for wages, similar to a minimum-wage policy, others claim that because it would be a minimum real wage, it would exacerbate inflationary pressure owing to nominal wage increase (Kadmos and O'Hara, 2000; Moudud, 2006; Palley, 2018). It seems that the counter-cyclical aspect of policy is commonly

CLAUDE GNOS / ANTOINE GODIN

acknowledged, as well as its stabilizing aspect, as advocated by Minsky (1986). There is, however, a debate on its cost, its impact on the public deficit, and the ensuing demand-pull inflation or trade-balance worsening (Aspromourgos, 2000; Ramsay, 2002; Sawyer, 2003; see Mitchell and Wray, 2005, for a response to these critiques). Other aspects have been pushed forward, notably those praising the approach emphasizing the fight against poverty and inequality (Minsky, 1986; Wray, 2007), social justice and the right to work (Harvey, 2002) or its impact to achieving the Millennium Development Goals of the United Nations (Kregel, 2006). Critics have highlighted the opportunity cost of such a policy compared to other industrial or demand management policies, the risk of undermining the public sector or the fear of leading to compulsory work programmes (Palley, 2001, 2018; Sawyer, 2003).

The ELR's transformational aspects have been highlighted. Forstater (2004, 2006) and Godin (2013) have shown the possibility of achieving social and environmental sustainability through the use of guaranteed green job policies, while Alcott (2013) has advocated for the ELR to be a supporting tool to a degrowth policy. In a different vein, authors have stressed the potential empowerment of women and gender inclusion effects (Antonopoulos, 2007; Papadimitriou, 2008; see Abukhadrah, 2017, for a critical analysis of the design of such policy to achieve these goals). On the other hand, it seems that the structural impacts of ELR have not been thoroughly examined, as pointed out by Kadmos and O'Hara (2000) and Moudud (2006). This has been also underlined by Godin (2014), who shows that depending on the structure of the economy, an ELR could lead to inflation or not and high-wage or low-wage full employment, making the case for a careful policy design, in combination with other fiscal or industrial policies.

ANTOINE GODIN

See also

Effective demand; Fiscal multiplier; Fiscal policy; Inequality; Public finance

References

Abukhadrah S. (2017), *Can ELR Contribute to Women's Empowerment?*, PhD dissertation, Paris: Centre d'économie de l'Université Paris Nord.

Alcott, B. (2013), 'Should degrowth embrace the job guarantee?', *Journal of Cleaner Production*, 38, 56–60.

Antonopoulos, R. (2007), 'The right to a job, the right types of projects: employment guarantee policies from a gender perspective', *Levy Economics Institute Working Paper*, No. 516.

Aspromourgos, T. (2000), 'Is an employer-of-last-resort policy sustainable? A review article', *Review of Political Economy*, 12 (2), 141–55.

Forstater, M. (2004), 'Green jobs: addressing the critical issues surrounding the environment, workplace, and employment', *International Journal of Environment, Workplace and Employment*, 1 (1), 53–61.

Forstater, M. (2006), 'Green jobs: public service employment and environmental sustainability', *Challenge*, 49 (4), 58–72.

Godin, A. (2013), 'Green jobs for full employment, a stock flow consistent analysis', in M.J. Murray and M. Forstater (eds), *Employment Guarantee Schemes: Job Creation Policy in Developing Countries and Emerging Markets*, Basingstoke, UK, and New York: Palgrave Macmillan, pp. 7–46.

Godin, A. (2014), 'Job guarantee: a structuralist perspective', *Revue de la régulation*, 16, available online at https://journals.openedition.org/regulation/10988 (last accessed on 1 July 2019).

Harvey, P. (2002), 'Human rights and economic policy discourse: taking economic and social rights seriously', *Columbia Human Rights Law Review*, 33 (2), 364–471.

Kadmos, G. and P.A. O'Hara (2000), 'The taxes-drive-money and employer of last resort approach to government policy', *Journal of Economic and Social Policy*, 5 (1), article 1.

Kalecki, M. (1943), 'Political aspects of full employment', *Political Quarterly*, 14 (4), 322–30.

Kregel, J. (2006), 'ELR as an alternative development strategy', paper presented at the Levy Economics Institute conference, 'Employment Guarantee Policies – Theory and Practice', October.

Minsky, H.P. (1965), 'The role of employment policy', in M.S. Gordon (ed.), *Poverty in America*, San Francisco: Chandler Publishing Company, pp. 175–200.

Minsky, H.P. (1986), *Stabilizing an Unstable Economy*, New Haven: Yale University Press.

Mitchell, W. and L.R. Wray (2005), 'Full employment through job guarantee: a response to critics', *Center for Full Employment and Price Stability Working Paper*, No. 39.

Moudud, J. (2006), 'How State policies can raise economic growth', *Challenge*, 49 (2), 33–51.

Palley, T.I. (2001), 'Government as employer of last resort: can it work?', *Industrial Relations Research Association, 53rd Annual Proceedings*, pp. 269–74.

Palley, T.I. (2018), 'Government spending and the income-expenditure model: the multiplier, spending composition, and job guarantee programs',

ANTOINE GODIN

Forum for Macroeconomics and Macroeconomic Policies Working Paper, No. 30.
Papadimitriou, D.B. (2008), 'Promoting equality through an employment of last resort policy', Levy Economics Institute Working Paper, No. 545.
Ramsay, T. (2002), 'The jobs guarantee: a Post Keynesian analysis', Journal of Post Keynesian Economics, **25** (2), 273–91.
Sawyer, M. (2003), 'Employer of last resort: could it deliver full employment and price stability?', Journal of Economic Issues, **37** (4), 881–907.
Seccareccia, M. (2004), 'What type of full employment? A critical evaluation of government as the employer of last resort policy proposal', Investigación Económica, **63** (247), 15–43.
Wray, L.R. (2007), 'The employer of last resort programme: could it work for developing countries?', International Labour Office Economic and Labour Market Paper, No. 2007/5.
Wray, L.R., F. Dantas, S. Fullwiler, P.R. Tcherneva and S.A. Kelton (2018), 'Public service employment: a path to full employment', Levy Economics Institute of Bard College Research Project Report, April.

Endogenous money

In mainstream or neoclassical theory, the money supply is said to be under the control of the central bank and is thus considered exogenously controlled. Graphically, the money supply curve is drawn as vertical in interest rate/money space. In this view, central banks can increase or decrease the monetary base and, given a stable money multiplier, influence the total amount of money in circulation. The conclusion is that the quantity of money in circulation is independent of production, and simply is whatever the central bank chooses, consistent, however, with its inflation target. Schumpeter (1954, p. 277) has called this approach 'real analysis'. This is still predominantly what is taught in university classes.

> Real analysis proceeds from the principle that all essential phenomena of economic life are capable of being described in terms of goods and services, of decisions about them, and of relations between them. Money enters the picture only in the modest role of a technical device that has been adopted in order to facilitate transactions. (Schumpeter, 1954, p. 277)

In newer mainstream models, such as in New Consensus models, the rate of interest is an exogenous variable, and there is a version of endogenous money, although these models maintain the existence of a natural rate of interest. In this version, the decision to control rates of interest remains a policy choice of the central bank, although these short-term rates are only temporary positions on their way to their natural value. This stands in stark contrast with the post-Keynesian view (see Monvoisin and Rochon, 2006).

Indeed, post-Keynesian economists see the money creation process very differently. For them, the creation of money is linked to the productive needs of the economic system. In a simplified version of money endogeneity, commercial banks agree to lend to the private sector, whose firms must pay wages before they can collect proceeds from the sale of their goods. In this sense, money is endogenous to the needs of production, and is tied closely to the payment of wages. The so-called money supply is demand-determined through the demand for bank loans: loans create deposits and as such banks are never constrained by the lack of deposits, but only by the lack of creditworthy borrowers (see Wolfson, 1996; Rochon, 1999).

As loans are given, money appears on the liabilities side of banks' balance sheets. At that point, if banks need reserves (or settlement balances) they will seek them after, often from the central bank, which then accommodates the needs of the banking sector (Moore, 1988). Hence, both money and 'high-powered money' are considered endogenous and demand-determined.

One important conclusion is that there is an immediate link between money and debt, and we can argue that money is the physical manifestation of debt (Rochon, 1999). Schumpeter (1954, p. 278) has called this 'monetary analysis', pointing out that '[m]onetary analysis introduces the element of money on the very ground floor of our analytic structure and abandons the idea that all essential features of our economic life can be represented by a barter-economy model'. In this perspective, therefore, we cannot discuss the existence of any real variable without introducing money at the same time.

Rochon and Rossi (2013) identify two post-Keynesian versions of endogenous money, what they call the 'revolutionary' and the 'evolutionary' views. While both views accept the endogenous nature of money, they differ significantly in how money became endogenous.

In the evolutionary view, largely based on Chick's (1986) appraisal of the evolution of the banking system, money became endogenous because of the creation of certain institutions, especially the central bank. Before that, money would have been exogenous, and thus fully consistent with the neoclassical story, and perhaps consistent with the story of barter. The main conclusion of this analysis is that money is endogenous or exogenous according to the historical period considered.

According to the revolutionary theory of endogenous money, by contrast, money's 'endogeneity is not a matter of institutions but rather one of logical necessity' (Lavoie, 1996, p. 533) – a fact recognized even by Robinson (1956, p. 32). In this sense, money is endogenous irrespective of the historical period or the institutions in existence: money did not become endogenous through time.

LOUIS-PHILIPPE ROCHON

See also

Credit constraints; Interest rate – natural; Monetary theory of production; Money creation – nature of; Settlement balances

References

Chick, V. (1986), 'The evolution of the banking system and the theory of saving, investment and interest', *Économies et Sociétés*, **20** (8–9), 111–26.
Lavoie, M. (1996), 'Monetary policy in an economy with endogenous credit money', in G. Deleplace and E.J. Nell (eds), *Money in Motion: The Post-Keynesian and Circulation Approaches*, Basingstoke and New York: Macmillan and St. Martin's Press, pp. 532–45.
Monvoisin, V. and L.-P. Rochon (2006), 'The Post-Keynesian consensus, the New Consensus and endogenous money', in C. Gnos and L.-P. Rochon (eds), *Post-Keynesian Principles of Economic Policies*, Cheltenham, UK, and Northampton, MA, USA: Edward Elgar, pp. 57–77.
Moore, B.J. (1988), *Horizontalists and Verticalists: The Macroeconomics of Credit Money*, Cambridge, UK: Cambridge University Press.
Robinson, J. (1956), *The Accumulation of Capital*, London: Macmillan.
Rochon, L.-P. (1999), *Credit, Money and Production: An Alternative Post-Keynesian Approach*, Cheltenham, UK, and Northampton, MA, USA: Edward Elgar.
Rochon, L.-P. and S. Rossi (2003), 'Endogenous money: the evolutionary versus revolutionary views', *Review of Keynesian Economics*, **1** (2), 210–29.
Schumpeter, J.A. (1954), *History of Economic Analysis*, London: Allen & Unwin.
Wolfson, M. (1996), 'A Post Keynesian theory of credit rationing', *Journal of Post Keynesian Economics*, **18** (3), 443–70.

Entrepreneurial State

The entrepreneurial State is a concept popularized by Mazzucato (2013) that integrates the Keynesian and Schumpeterian traditions based on the ideas of uncertainty and innovation, respectively. However, the fundamental pillar of the investigation is ontological, that is, the destruction of the myth of the distinction between the State and the market following the work of Polanyi (1944). 'In innovation, the State not only "crowds in" business investment but also "dynamizes it in" – creating the vision, the mission and the plan' (Mazzucato, 2013, p. 35).

Referring to the 'entrepreneurial State' reflects an understanding of the role of the State that breaks with conventional wisdom. Instead of treating the State as a merely administrative, cumbersome and passive entity whose intervention is only required when some kind of market failure occurs, the State would be in charge of providing the leadership to make things happen that, left in the hands of the market and private initiative, would not occur. As a matter of fact, most of the radical innovations that have fuelled the dynamics of capitalism stem from initial investments made with capital provided by the State, from railways to the internet. The public sector is the only agent capable of dealing with radical uncertainty in those sectors where there are no expectations that such investments will materialize in goods to be sold for profitability, since it is the profit-making motive that guides private companies.

Following Keynes (1926/1978, pp. 291–2), the point is not 'to do things which individuals are doing already, and to do them a little better or a little worse; but to do those things which at present are not done at all'. The State is important not only for the traditional reasons of the need to carry out countercyclical policies when demand and investment are too low, but to create visions around important new technologies by setting the directions of change, or, in other words, to tilt the market playing field to favour certain changes over others (Mazzucato, 2016, p. 141). Therefore, we should think of the State as an important agent, not only to guarantee fiscal stimulus in times of economic crisis, but at any point in the business cycle.

Challenge-driven innovation policy (see Mazzucato et al., 2020) and mission-oriented innovation policy (see Mazzucato and Kattel, 2018) are two developments that illustrate this type of action of the entrepreneurial State. Along with the direction these changes should take to make them possible, the entrepreneurial State also addresses the issues around the type and structure of public sector organizations that are needed to provide the depth and breadth of high-risk investments; the type of evaluation criteria used to evaluate mission-oriented investments; and the distribution of risks and rewards between the State and the private sector. If the State incubates research from basic research to final product design, and companies largely prepare State-driven technology for the consumer market, the distribution of rewards cannot entirely fall into the latter. This is not one more argument to increase State revenues or close the budget deficit. As Mazzucato and Wray (2015) point out, even from the approach of endogenous money extended to the State that characterizes the so-called Modern Money Theory, sharing the benefits with the State must be done by efficiency criteria. With limits to total spending dictated by the capacity of real resources, the State's participation in the rewards of successful projects would help to compensate and politically accept the inevitable failures associated with innovation processes (Mazzucato, 2016, pp. 152–3).

In addition, as Jacobs and Mazzucato (2016, p. 21) point out, the entrepreneurial State also deals with how to configure markets to achieve co-production and the fair distribution of economic value. Here the entrepreneurial State is complemented by Keynes's (1936, p. 378) concept of socialization of investment. The State must undertake a mission that the private sector does not address itself: full employment. Following the maxim of doing those things that are currently not done at all, there are activities with important social value but that are not lucrative; for example, care work or cleaning the natural fuel of forests. Here, too, the State assumes a direct role in deciding which projects should be undertaken and for what benefits the projects should be undertaken (Mazzucato and Wray, 2015, p. 36).

ESTEBAN CRUZ HIDALGO, JOSÉ FRANCISCO RANGEL PRECIADO AND FRANCISCO M. PAREJO MORUNO

See also

Capitalism; Endogenous money; Fiscal policy; Modern money theory; *The Great Transformation*

References

Jacobs, M. and M. Mazzucato (2016), 'Rethinking capitalism: an introduction', in M. Jacobs and M. Mazzucato (eds), *Rethinking Capitalism: Economics and Policy for Sustainable and Inclusive Growth*, Chichester, UK: Wiley–Blackwell, pp. 1–27.
Keynes, J.M. (1926/1978), 'The end of laissez-faire', in *The Collected Writings of John Maynard Keynes, Vol. IX: Essays in Persuasion*, London: Macmillan, pp. 272–92.
Keynes, J.M. (1936), *The General Theory of Employment, Interest and Money*, London: Macmillan.
Mazzucato, M. (2013), *The Entrepreneurial State*, London: Anthem Press.
Mazzucato, M. (2016), 'From market fixing to market-creating: a new framework for innovation policy', *Industry and Innovation*, **23** (2), 140–56.
Mazzucato, M. and R. Kattel (2018), 'Mission-orientated innovation policy and dynamic capabilities in the public sector', *Industrial and Corporate Change*, **27** (5), 787–801.
Mazzucato, M. and L.R. Wray (2015), 'Financing the capital development of the economy: a Keynes–Schumpeter–Minsky synthesis', *Levy Economics Institute of Bard College Working Paper*, No. 837.
Mazzucato, M., R. Kattel and J. Ryan-Collins (2020), 'Challenge-driven innovation policy: towards a new policy toolkit', *Journal of Industry, Competition and Trade*, **20** (2), 421–37.
Polanyi, K. (1944), *The Great Transformation*, Boston: Beacon Press.

Essays in the Theory of Economic Growth

Essays in the Theory of Economic Growth (Domar, 1957) is made up of nine essays that have a unifying theme, that is, an application of the rate of growth as an analytical device to a specific economic problem: capital expansion and employment, capital accumulation, the effect of foreign investment on the balance of payments, depreciation and replacement, the burden of debt and national income, and a consideration of Feldman's Soviet model of growth (pp. ix and 3–4). This growth model is, in fact, not Keynesian, but is derived from a modified

Marxist scheme, the key variable being the fraction of total investment that is retained by the capital goods industry in order to produce more capital goods (p. 11).

Domar uses two distinct methods (p. 4). The first consists in taking a certain flow, for instance national income or investment, as an independent variable, and analysing the mutual interrelationships between this flow, other flows functionally related to it (a fiscal deficit or investment, for example), stocks arising from the flows (capital stock, national debt) and flows resulting from the stocks (depreciation charges, interest payments), all in growing economies. In the second method, the problem is expressed as a system of a few simple differential equations, the solution of which yields the rate of growth of some variable. It is this method that is put to use in the core Chapter 3 of the book in which the famous 1946 Domar equation is derived (pp. 70–82).

The starting point is a puzzle: according to Alvin Hansen, who was Domar's teacher and supervisor, a constant stream of investment results in a constant rather than in a rising income (p. vii). The reason is that, in Keynes's (1936) *General Theory*, investment is merely an instrument for generating income and 'does not take into account the extremely essential, elementary, and well-known fact that investment also increases productive capacity' (p. 73).

However, Keynes takes into account the capacity effect of investment, though not through a formal relation: 'New capital-investment can only take place in excess of current capital-disinvestment if *future* expenditure on consumption is expected to increase. Each time we secure to-day's equilibrium by increased investment we are aggravating the difficulty of securing equilibrium to-morrow [because of the capacity effect of investment that leads on to an increase in productive capacities]' (Keynes, 1936, p. 105, italics in the original). In fact, Keynes distinguishes 'between the logical theory of the multiplier [the multiplier principle], which holds good continuously, without time-lag, at all moments of time, and the consequences of an expansion in the capital goods industries which take gradual effect, subject to time-lag and only after an interval' (Keynes, 1936, p. 122). The logical theory of the multiplier is an ever-valid principle, which is implemented in space and time through concrete expansions in the capital goods industries, the complex consequences of which include capacity effects of investment (Keynes, 1936, pp. 122–5). From these few pages it emerges that Keynes's way of arguing is of organic complexity, because he considers the functioning of the economy as whole, a statement that holds for his entire *General Theory*. Domar, however, looks at a partial, well-specified problem, that is, to capture the capacity effect through a formal relation and to set it in relation to the income effect to discover macroeconomic equilibria between supply and demand and their relation to employment.

Employment is a function of the ratio of national income to productive capacity (p. 73). Economic equilibrium occurs when productive capacity, that is, the supply of goods, equals effective demand, given by national income. Domar postulates that productive capacity is such that full employment prevails (p. 75). Full employment is maintained if productive capacity increases at the same pace as national income (effective demand). The increase in productive capacity is given by the investment volume times the social average investment productivity (the ratio of the increase in productive capacity with respect to the investment volume). The increase in effective demand (national income) depends upon the increase of investment multiplied by the inverse of the marginal propensity to save. Equating both increments yields the equilibrium rate of economic growth, to wit, the marginal propensity to save times the social average investment productivity (p. 75). The failure of the economy to grow at this rate creates unused capacity and unemployment (p. 77).

On the whole, Domar is moderately optimistic about getting near to the equilibrium rate of economic growth, thereby avoiding diminishing profit rates, scarcity of investment opportunities, chronic unemployment and similar calamities. However, an economy may fail to get near enough to the required growth rate and the calamities will come into being. 'So economic salvation is not impossible; neither is it assured' (p. 8). The moderate optimism underlying the fundamental essay III prevails in fact in the entire volume.

However, Domar recognizes that a satisfactory theory of economic growth cannot be created from models only. It requires empirical work, that is, 'the ability to synthesize data and ideas from all social sciences, and most of all

HEINRICH BORTIS

it requires that breadth of vision and imagination and that degree of understanding which is called "wisdom". In short, it is a job for sages' (p. 12).

Now, in his *General Theory*, Keynes (1936) struggled to understand, precisely on the basis of a new vision of economic phenomena, how monetary production economies function. His conclusions regarding economic growth are revealing. First, Keynes (1936, p. 373) suggests 'that measures for the redistribution of incomes in a way likely to raise the propensity to consume may prove positively favourable to the growth of capital. ... Thus our argument leads towards the conclusion that in contemporary conditions [also valid at present] the growth of wealth, so far from being dependent on the abstinence of the rich, as is commonly supposed, is more likely to be impeded by it.' Secondly, Keynes (1936, pp. 128–31) alludes to the enormous importance for both employment and economic growth of autonomous factors: pyramids, cathedrals, old bottles filled with bank notes, buried at suitable depths, as well as exports (Keynes, 1936, Ch. 23) and, implicitly, to wars and government expenditures. These factors all have an income effect only, but no direct capacity effect. However, the new incomes created by autonomous expenditures induce the building up of new capacities in a cumulative way through a kind of supermultiplier with consumption and investment as derived magnitudes, if the balance of payments may be broadly kept in equilibrium (Keynes, 1980). Keynes was in fact the sage Domar was looking for.

HEINRICH BORTIS

See also

Balance of payments; Effective demand; Fiscal deficits; Growth; Supermultiplier

References

Domar, E.D. (1957), *Essays in the Theory of Economic Growth*, Oxford: Oxford University Press.
Keynes, J.M. (1936), *The General Theory of Employment, Interest and Money*, London: Macmillan.
Keynes, J.M. (1980), *The Collected Writings of John Maynard Keynes, Volume XXV: Activities 1940–1944. Shaping the Post-War World: The Clearing Union*, London: Macmillan.

Euro

The euro is the name of the currency adopted by countries that participate in the European Monetary Union (see Gnos, 2015). Its adoption by them was conditional on the fulfilment of a number of so-called convergence criteria enshrined in the Maastricht Treaty signed in 1992. These criteria concern inflation, interest rates, exchange rates and public finance with regard to the country's GDP (see Rossi and Dafflon, 2012). All countries joining the euro area should respect these criteria during the two years preceding their entry, and once in the euro area must comply with the so-called 'Fiscal compact', which aims in practice at yearly balanced budgets for the general government sector and a public-debt-to-GDP ratio below 60 per cent.

A number of would-be euro-area member countries managed to adopt the euro with some accounting tricks reducing in particular public debts and deficits with regard to their GDPs (see Dafflon and Rossi, 1999). Among them, Greece was in a prominent position owing to its accounting fudges, which were revealed by the newly elected government in the fall of 2009, sparking thereby the euro-area crisis. The latter made it plain that the euro area is not a single-currency area actually. The euro, in fact, is not the single currency of countries that participate in the European Monetary Union, because the European Central Bank, to date, has not been operating as a settlement institution for the national central banks of euro-area countries within the TARGET2 payments system (Rossi, 2016). This problem was revealed by the bursting of the global financial crisis in 2008, when several countries in the Southern 'periphery' of the euro area (the so-called 'PIGS', standing for Portugal, Italy, Greece and Spain) began accumulating enormous negative balances within TARGET2, as a result of the impossibility for them to sell financial assets to the 'core' countries in the euro area (to wit, Germany and some of its neighbours) in order for the former group of countries to pay for their trade deficits with regard to surplus countries like Germany (see Rossi, 2013, for analytical elaboration).

The euro, as a matter of fact, is just the name of heterogeneous national currencies that are exchanged at par, 'as if' they were part of the same monetary system. All these

HEINRICH BORTIS / SERGIO ROSSI

different currencies (all named 'euros') are not homogeneous, because they are not issued within a three-tiered banking system, on top of which there should be the European Central Bank acting as a settlement institution for national central banks within it (Rossi, 2018). The TARGET2 payments system, indeed, is a two-tiered system: on top of commercial banks one finds actually national central banks as well as the European Central Bank, which is thereby at the same institutional level of national central banks – and wrongly so (see Rossi, 2017a).

The euro-area crisis that erupted near the end of 2009 has given rise to various proposals to dispose of it. Among them, one finds the idea to reintroduce national currencies in all those countries where the euro and its associated constraints represent a dramatic straitjacket for their population (see Rossi, 2017b). There exist two possibilities in this regard. Either the country abandons the euro and comes back to its previous situation reintroducing its own national currency, or it uses the euro for international transactions only, issuing a national currency for the settlement of domestic transactions. The former solution is dangerous and short-sighted: the exchange rate of the national currency might be strongly depreciated as a result of the structural problems of the national economy (such as Greece's), and this could further aggravate the country's economic situation rather than improving it. A much better solution would be to reintroduce the national currency alongside the euro, to be used only by the national central bank in the settlement of international transactions. This would echo Keynes's proposals for an International Clearing Union issuing bancor to be used for the settlement between central banks, 'private individuals, businesses and banks other than central banks, each continuing to use their own national currency as heretofore' (Keynes, 1942/1980, p. 168).

A monetary–structural reform of the euro area in the spirit of Keynes (1942/1980) respects the endogenous nature of money (Rossi, 2018) and may elicit a large political consensus: it allows both the reintroduction of national currencies – notably in those countries that most suffer from the euro-area crisis – and keeping the euro, transforming it into a common currency in order to achieve European monetary integration and hence provide for a sound international monetary order. All this will be instrumental to move forward later on to transform the euro into a truly single currency for euro-area residents, once their countries' economic systems are really converging on structural grounds (rather than simply nominally, as encapsulated in the Maastricht Treaty).

SERGIO ROSSI

See also

European Monetary Union; Eurozone imbalances; Keynes Plan; Settlement system; TARGET2 system

References

Dafflon, B. and S. Rossi (1999), 'Public accounting fudges towards EMU: a first empirical survey and some public choice considerations', *Public Choice*, **101** (1–2), 59–84.
Gnos, C. (2015), 'European monetary union', in L.-P. Rochon and S. Rossi (eds), *The Encyclopedia of Central Banking*, Cheltenham, UK, and Northampton, MA, USA: Edward Elgar, pp. 163–5.
Keynes, J.M. (1942/1980), 'Proposals for an International Clearing Union', in *The Collected Writings of John Maynard Keynes, vol. XXV, Activities 1940–1944. Shaping the Post-War World: The Clearing Union*, London and Basingstoke: Macmillan, pp. 168–95.
Rossi, S. (2013), 'Financialisation and monetary union in Europe: the monetary–structural causes of the euro-area crisis', *Cambridge Journal of Regions, Economy and Society*, **6** (3), 381–400.
Rossi, S. (2016), 'The euro must be abandoned to achieve European monetary integration', *International Journal of Political Economy*, **45** (1), 72–84.
Rossi, S. (2017a), 'European monetary union', in J.-L. Bailly, A. Cencini and S. Rossi (eds), *Quantum Macroeconomics: The Legacy of Bernard Schmitt*, London and New York: Routledge, pp. 135–43.
Rossi, S. (2017b), 'Back to national currencies? Monetary integration in an asymmetrical currency area', in R. Mirdala and R.R. Canale (eds), *Economic Imbalances and Institutional Changes to the Euro and the European Union*, Bingley, UK, and Somerville, MA, USA: Emerald, pp. 91–111.
Rossi, S. (2018), 'Clearing houses and monetary order: domestic and international issues', paper presented at 'Clearing Houses' conference at the University of Amiens, France, 15–16 November.
Rossi, S. and B. Dafflon (2012), 'Repairing the original sin of the European Monetary Union', *International Journal of Monetary Economics and Finance*, **5** (2), 102–23.

SERGIO ROSSI

European Monetary Union

The European Monetary Union (EMU) refers to the euro area, including 19 countries belonging to the European Union (EU), and to Denmark, whose currency is pegged to the euro. It officially came into existence in 1999 with the creation of the euro and the European Central Bank (ECB). In the spirit of the European political leaders and their economic advisors, the creation of the EMU was the 'logical' outcome of the European economic integration process, which began in 1957 with the signature of the Treaty of Rome.

Indeed, following Balassa's (1961) theory, EU members have increased their degree of economic interdependence through spillover effects, making several steps forward as far as regional integration is concerned. Therefore, the idea of strengthening monetary integration between European countries is not new: during the Bretton Woods regime, at the onset of the EU, projects aimed at implementing an EMU had already emerged (for instance, the 'snake in the tunnel' mechanism in the early 1970s). After 1973, increasing instability within the international monetary system led EU members to launch the European Monetary System (EMS) in 1979, resting on nearly fixed exchange rates between the European currencies (within a band of +/− 2.25 per cent until 1993, +/−15 per cent afterwards). The scope of the EMS was to stabilize exchange rates to prepare for the introduction of the euro. Consequently, as stated by Emerson et al. (1999) in their report, the creation of the EMU was associated with the 'one market, one money' logic, resting on Optimum Currency Area theory (see Mundell, 1961). Hence, a single currency was seen as the best way to foster European market internal trade and to reduce inflation rates, to stabilize them at a low, and not volatile, level, and, more generally, to build a solid currency area.

However, the EMU was hit by the 2007–08 crisis, which morphed into a European crisis with severe economic and monetary difficulties (in Greece from 2011 and in Cyprus in 2012, for instance), which destabilized the EMU, questioning its viability. The crisis shed light on the significant imbalances between euro-area member countries (fiscal and current account imbalances, problems of competitiveness), as well as on the lack of adequate policies designed to strengthen the unity of the currency area, in the case of turmoil in particular (fiscal transfers, banking supervision, independent capacity of indebtedness at the European level). All in all, the 2007–08 crisis highlighted the weaknesses of the EMU, which were actually integral to its origins (Wyplosz, 2016).

In response to the crisis, the EMU evolved. In addition to setting up new 'unconventional' monetary policies (through 'quantitative easing' programmes, for instance), the ECB was given new enlarged missions aimed at strengthening financial and banking supervision. To that aim, the Banking Union (BU), supervised by the ECB, was launched in 2012 in order to prevent new banking crises that would weaken the EMU. Resting on three keystones ('Single Rulebook', 'Single Supervisory Mechanism' and 'Single Resolution Mechanism'), the BU is supposed to improve the functioning of the EMU. This is paramount with respect to future enlargements of the euro area including less-developed countries than its current members.

Nevertheless, the history of the EMU raises two main issues regarding its future. First, its case clearly highlights that a monetary union is not merely a zone built to foster trade. Money implies more than that, as it is related with fiscal policies, imbalances in management mechanisms, and specific monetary policy transmission mechanisms. Second, the 'one-size-fits-all' model that rests on a single currency for the EMU is called into question. If the first issue is not fully addressed, both the differences in the level of development between European countries and, above all, the different political will of European citizens associated with monetary sovereignty are likely to lead to a different functioning of the EMU in the future. Such a functioning would rest on the euro as the 'monetary hub' of the system, but in relation to other European currencies. The case of the United Kingdom, and even Switzerland (Vallet, 2012; Rossi and Vallet, 2021), whose economies are highly integrated with the euro area without having full membership, are evidence that there is a 'monetary life' outside the EMU.

GUILLAUME VALLET AND HAMED KARAMOKO

See also

Euro; Eurozone imbalances; Financial regulations; Monetary policy transmission mechanism; Quantitative easing

References

Balassa, B. (1961), *The Theory of Economic Integration*, Homewood: R.D. Irwin.
Emerson, M., D. Gros, A. Italianer, J. Pisany-Ferry and H. Reichenbach (1992), *One Market, One Money: An Evaluation of the Potential Benefits and Costs of Forming an Economic and Monetary Union*, Oxford: Oxford University Press.
Mundell, R. (1961), 'A theory of optimum currency areas', *American Economic Review*, **51** (4), 657–65.
Rossi, S. and G. Vallet (2021), 'The economic dimension', in P. Dardanelli and O. Mazzoleni (eds), *Switzerland–EU Relations: Lessons for the UK after Brexit?*, London and New York: Routledge, pp. 20–37.
Vallet, G. (2012), 'Should I stay or should I go? Switzerland and the European economic and monetary integration process', *Journal of Economic Integration*, **27** (3), 366–85.
Wyplosz, C. (2016), 'The six flaws of the Eurozone', *Economic Policy*, **31** (87), 559–606.

Eurozone imbalances

The analysis of imbalances in the Eurozone can be carried out by means of the basic accounting identity whereby the current account balance (CAB = trade balance + net income from abroad + net current transfers) equals the difference between gross domestic saving and investment, that is, the financing capacity or need of the domestic institutional sectors (see International Monetary Fund, 2020, Chs 3 and 5).

As is well known, the gradual adjustment towards a single currency with a fixed nominal exchange rate meant that overvalued currencies (namely, those of northern European countries) had to be devalued in real terms, whereas devalued currencies (that is, those of southern European countries) had to be overvalued (Duwicquet and Mazier, 2010; Comunale, 2017). This differentiated integration (see Leruth and Lord, 2015) naturally implied that, following the adjustment, countries with depreciating currencies gained competitiveness while at the same time those with appreciating currencies lost it. This meant CAB surpluses for the former and deficits for the latter, which were in turn reflected in domestic imbalances.

This also meant that the gap between saving (S) and investment (I) was persistently negative for southern European countries and positive for their northern peers, which also allowed financing of the former by the latter. This can be seen via another basic identity whereby $S - I = NKA + RT$, where NKA stands for net capital and financial account, and RT stands for reserve asset transactions. Insufficient savings to finance investment in the south meant a need for foreign capital, whereas excessive saving over investment in the north meant that these countries could conveniently fill that gap. Thus, in large part thanks to current and capital account liberalization, northern European countries hosting large private banks have financed banks (thus investment and consumption) in southern countries over a large part of the duration of the European Monetary Union project.

Attempting to fit the rules that (seemingly) work for a model country (that is, the golden rule based on Germany's 3 per cent average public deficit–GDP ratio) are unlikely to work in all countries. This can be particularly catastrophic when a country running a current account deficit faces an economic downturn that strongly reduces the financing capacity of the private sector. In this case a feasible alternative to keep the economy afloat would be that the government runs a deficit (for instance, via the automatic stabilizers) of a size necessary to fill the gap between savings and investment (reflected in the CAB deficit) that aims at minimizing the negative spillover effects to the rest of the economy. Since fiscal consolidation was sought around 2011, the result has been the infamous European debt crisis, which, as Pérez Caldentey and Vernengo (2012) argue, was the result of an imbalance between core and non-core countries inherent to the euro-area economic model.

Stockhammer et al. (2017) place the origin of the Eurozone crisis in the emergence of a debt-driven model coupled with an export-led model, which is explained by the two identities seen above. These are also the focus of Eichengreen (2010, p. 1), who mentions that 'current account imbalances, budget balances and unit labor costs are three sides of the same coin'. Lucarelli (2017) argues that this neoliberal path toward austerity and wage repression (or internal devaluation) is ultimately unsustainable and self-defeating, as the recent past has proven.

The differences in per capita GDP among member countries of the European Monetary Union have increased considerably since 2000, and are more important than those among states in the United States for the same period (Streeck and Elsässer, 2016). Monetary union may actually have fostered divergence in productivity trends (Bagnai and Mongeau, 2017). Further, it is well known that the Eurozone is not an optimum currency area, a theory influenced by Real Business Cycle theorists (De Grauwe, 2006).

It is worth asking why, in the face of the theoretical implications (which turned out to be practical) of the above-mentioned basic macroeconomic identities, and given the existing asymmetries further enhanced by the aftermath of the European debt crisis, European authorities persist in favouring northern countries' financial sector at the expense of the productive sector and southern European over-indebted public sectors.

LUIS REYES

See also

Current accounts; Euro; European Monetary Union; Exchange rates – fixed vs flexible; Fiscal consolidation

References

Bagnai, A. and C. Mongeau (2017), 'Monetary integration vs. real disintegration: single currency and productivity divergence in the euro area', *Journal of European Public Policy*, **21** (4), 353–67.
Comunale, M. (2017), 'Dutch disease, real effective exchange rate misalignments and their effect on GDP growth in EU', *Journal of International Money and Finance*, **73**, 350–70.
De Grauwe, P. (2006), 'What have we learnt about monetary integration since the Maastricht Treaty?', *Journal of Common Market Studies*, **44** (4), 711–30.
Duwicquet, V. and J. Mazier (2010), 'Financial integration and macroeconomic adjustments in a monetary union', *Journal of Post Keynesian Economics*, **33** (2), 333–69.
Eichengreen, B. (2010), 'Imbalances in the euro area', mimeo, University of California, available online at https://eml.berkeley.edu/~eichengr/Imbalances_Euro_Area_5-23-11.pdf (last accessed 30 December 2020).
International Monetary Fund (2020), *Balance of Payments Manual*, Washington, DC: International Monetary Fund, available at https://www.imf.org/external/np/sta/bop/bopman.pdf (last accessed 20 November 2020).
Leruth, B. and C. Lord (2015), 'Differentiated integration in the European Union: a concept, a process, a system or a theory?', *Journal of European Public Policy*, **22** (6), 754–63.
Lucarelli, B. (2017), 'Intra-eurozone payments: implications for the TARGET2 payments system', *Review of Radical Political Economics*, **49** (3), 343–57.
Pérez Caldentey, E. and M. Vernengo (2012), 'The euro imbalances and financial deregulation: a post-Keynesian interpretation of the European debt crisis', Levy Economics Institute of Bard College Working Paper, No. 702, available at https://ssrn.com/abstract=1980886.
Stockhammer, E., C. Constantine and S. Reissl (2017), 'Explaining the euro crisis: current account imbalances, credit booms and economic policy in different economic paradigms', Post Keynesian Economics Society Working Paper, No. 1617.
Streeck, W. and L. Elsässer (2016), 'Monetary disunion: the domestic politics of Euroland', *Journal of European Public Policy*, **23** (1), 1–24.

Euthanasia of the rentier

In *The General Theory of Employment, Interest and Money*, Keynes (1936) does not focus on the relationship between financial markets and economic activity, but in the last chapter of his book he describes the link between interest rates and capital accumulation referring to the 'euthanasia of the rentier'. In that chapter, the definition of rentiers is based on their income and involves holders of national debt, holders of fixed-interest securities of private businesses and, in general, 'big savers'; all of them are 'functionless investors' according to Keynes (1936).

This consideration of rentiers allows the development of the theory of interest. Keynes (1936) argued interest rates should be high enough to stimulate saving but, at the same time, the latter is determined by investment, which is encouraged by low interest rates (Pollin, 1997). Then, 'the demand for capital is strictly limited in the sense that it would not be difficult to increase the stock of capital up to a point where its marginal efficiency had fallen to a very low figure' (Keynes, 1936, p. 375). Therefore, the euthanasia of the rentier means a painless death of functionless investors, due to low interest rates that stimulate capital investment, thereby reducing the profitability rate of these rentiers, because they cannot exploit the scarcity-value of capital.

The concept of 'rentier' is related to both liquidity preference and uncertainty. Investors could choose between money and other capital assets according to their liquidity premium and carrying costs. According to Keynes, the State should create the circumstances to induce investors to hold long-term capital assets more than short-term assets. In that sense, 'socialisation of investment will prove the only means of securing an approximation to full employment' (Keynes, 1936, p. 379), and if there is a 'necessity of central controls to bring about an adjustment between the propensity to consume and the inducement to invest, there is no more reason to socialise economic life than there was before' (p. 380).

Minsky (1975) revisits the debtor–creditor relationship, how this precipitates economic crises, and the euthanasia of the rentier. He explains that investment could be financed by retained earnings or issuing stocks. If a firm decides to use retained earnings to finance investment, it is not exposed to fluctuations occasioned by short-term interest rates. However, the financial fragility of the firm occurs when interest payments increase owing to an increase in short-term interest rates. When firms are generally unable to compensate the interest payment and must sell assets to get money, the economy will enter into a debt-deflation that can give rise to a depression.

According to Minsky (1975), in the framework of an extreme degree of uncertainty, the liquidity premium of money could be higher than the return from assets. In that case, a reduction of nominal interest rates to increase the capitalization rate may not be enough to induce investment. This result can be explained by rentiers' consumption preferences[1] or because the return to capital is decreasing (Minsky, 1975; Watkins, 2010). However, Minsky (1975, p. 152) considers that 'in order to achieve the euthanasia of the rentier, it may be necessary to first achieve the income distribution that Keynes argued would exist after euthanasia was achieved'.

The redistribution of income away from rentiers and long-term economic growth would only occur if the policy of low interest rates is accompanied by fiscal stimulus. However, a policy of high interest rates in favour of rentiers does not create the conditions for recovery in case of recession. Seccareccia and Lavoie (2016) explain three reasons for this fact. The first reason is related to the paradox of frugality, since high interest rates would negatively affect investment, and consequently reduce production and employment. The second refers to the low marginal propensity to consume of high-income groups such as rentiers. The third is that a high interest rate policy against inflation has a negative effect on wages and benefits.

ANA LAURA VIVEROS

See also

Debt deflation; Financial fragility; Liquidity preference; *The General Theory of Employment, Interest and Money*; Uncertainty

Note

1. According to Minsky (1975, p. 152), '[o]ne reason may be that the rich turned to consuming capital-intensive bundles of goods rather than philosophy and culture and that their example filtered down to the not so rich. Thus a variety of conspicuous consumption became generalized, and this conspicuous consumption has led to a continuing capital shortage.'

References

Davis, J.B. (2010), 'Uncertainty and identity: a post Keynesian approach', *Erasmus Journal for Philosophy and Economics*, **3** (1), 33–49.

Keynes, J.M. (1936), *The General Theory of Employment, Interest and Money*, London: Macmillan.

Mattos, O.B., F. Da Roz, F.O. Ultremare and G.S. Mello (2019), 'Unconventional monetary policy and negative interest rates: a Post-Keynesian perspective on the liquidity trap and euthanasia of the rentier', *Review of Keynesian Economics*, **7** (2), 185–200.

Minsky, H.P. (1975), *John Maynard Keynes*, New York: McGraw Hill.

Pollin, R. (1997), '"Socialization of investment" and "euthanasia of the rentier": the relevance of Keynesian policy ideas for the contemporary US economy', in P. Arestis and M. Sawyer (eds), *The Relevance of Keynesian Economic Policies Today*, London and Basingstoke: Palgrave Macmillan, pp. 57–77.

Seccareccia, M. and M. Lavoie (2016), 'Income distribution, rentiers, and their role in a capitalist economy: a Keynes–Pasinetti perspective', *International Journal of Political Economy*, **45** (3), 200–23.

Watkins, J. (2010), 'Rescuing the rentier – Neoliberalism, social imbalance, and the current economic crisis: a synthesis of Keynes, Galbraith, and Minsky', *Journal of Economic Issues*, **44** (2), 471–8.

Exchange rates

The exchange rate expresses the value of a national currency in units of another currency. Despite being a staple element of international macroeconomics, there is no general theory of exchange rate determination or why exchange rates fluctuate. The most common explanation refers to the purchasing power parity (PPP) (see for instance Cassel, 1918) and efficient market clearing.

The absolute PPP implies one price for the same good ('law of one price'), where exchange rates are expressed as a ratio of two countries' price levels on baskets of identical goods and services. Under relative PPP, the exchange rate adjusts to compensate for two countries' inflation differentials. For instance, the Big Mac index (*The Economist*, 2019) tracks the price of the Big Mac around the world. The theory suggests that after exchanging your currency into another currency, the price of the Big Mac should be the same. Yet, the absolute PPP approach finds limited empirical support, while the relative PPP has limited accuracy for exchange rate forecasts. One possible reason is that over time and countries, market structures change, measures of prices for comparable baskets vary, and prices across countries do not adjust consistently owing to global value chains' competitive pressures and other factors.

In the uncovered interest parity model, exchange rates reflect the price of a financial asset driven by perceived capital gains (or losses) in forward markets. A higher domestic interest rate sends a signal of a possible currency devaluation. As monetary policy drives the domestic and foreign interest rate differentials, the exchange rate is said to overshoot (Dornbusch, 1976), or disproportionately adjust, initially impacting the financial markets. This is then followed by a gradual change in the goods prices (sticky prices) and eventual long-term exchange rate adjustment. Under the covered interest parity, the difference between the spot and forward exchange rates is set in perfect foresight with no arbitrage. In the portfolio-balance model, the exchange rate is derived from an optimal balance of demand for domestic cash balances and holdings of domestic or foreign-currency denominated bonds.

The post-Keynesian literature adds certain extensions to the above, though rather dispersedly (Ramos and Prates, 2018). Here, while institutional factors emphasize the dominant positions of some currencies, fundamental uncertainty explicitly refers to the persistent volatility in foreign-exchange markets (see for instance Gevorkyan and Gevorkyan, 2012; Lavoie, 2014). In developing economies, currency hierarchy translates in the country's monetary policy dependence on the larger trading partner's business cycle (see for example Andrade and Prates, 2013). For instance, institutional dependence on the fluctuations of the value of the US dollar is visible in the small economies of the Caribbean (Downs and Khemraj, 2019). Similarly, currency values of the smallest economies of Eastern Europe and the former Soviet Union move in the directions of the largest regional trading partners, namely the European Union or Russia (see Gevorkyan, 2017).

Finally, currency values evolve out of international capital markets (Harvey, 2019). Traders speculate based on interest rate differentials, carry trade, directly influencing currency values as 'animal spirits' fuel capital markets volatility (Ramos and Prates, 2018). This differs from the portfolio-balance model in that the speculative activities create persistent instability in foreign-exchange markets rather than leaning towards a stable equilibrium.

National central banks operate with a range of exchange rate policies, such as a hard peg (where the value of an exchange rate is fixed to a reserve currency, for instance the US dollar, and is mainly sustained with reliance on foreign-exchange reserves), a floating arrangement with flexible currency value adjustments, and a soft peg, which allows for some currency value flexibility within acceptable boundaries.

An estimated 12.5 per cent of countries follow a hard peg and 34.4 per cent the floating regime, and a majority (46.4 per cent) have varying degrees of the soft peg. The soft peg is common to emerging markets (with commodity exporters opting for a more fixed regime) and a free-floating regime is mainly characteristic of the larger industrialized economies such as the United States, the United Kingdom, and the euro area (International Monetary Fund, 2020).

Exchange rates are one of the most difficult, yet integral, concepts in contemporary macroeconomics. Institutional aspects of the currency periphery, fundamental uncertainty, and speculative trends across global capital markets, on top of competitive macroeconomic

ALEKSANDR V. GEVORKYAN

fundamentals, form the contemporary framework of exchange rate determination. Owing to the dynamic nonlinear nature of the global markets, the pressures on theoretical explanatory models of exchange rates remain urgent and persistent.

ALEKSANDR V. GEVORKYAN

See also

Currency hierarchy; Exchange rates – fixed vs flexible; Exchange rates – managed; Monetary policy; Uncertainty

References

Andrade, R.P. and D.M. Prates (2013), 'Exchange rate dynamics in a peripheral monetary economy', *Journal of Post Keynesian Economics*, 35 (3), 399–416.
Cassel, G. (1918), 'Abnormal deviations in international exchanges', *Economic Journal*, 28 (112), 413–15.
Dornbusch, R. (1976), 'Expectations and exchange rate dynamics', *Journal of Political Economy*, 84 (6), 1161–76.
Downs, D. and T. Khemraj (2019), 'Foreign exchange pressure in Barbados: monetary approach or monetary dependence?', *Review of Political Economy*, 31 (2), 159–77.
Gevorkyan, A.V. (2017), 'The foreign exchange regime in a small open economy: Armenia and beyond', *Journal of Economic Studies*, 44 (5), 781–800.
Gevorkyan, A.V. and Ar.V. Gevorkyan (2012), 'Redefined fundamental uncertainty, fiscal rules, fiscal net, fiscal sustainability and emerging markets scenarios', *Aestimatio, the IEB International Journal of Finance*, 5, 126–61.
Harvey, J.T. (2019), 'Exchange rates and the balance of payments: reconciling an inconsistency in Post Keynesian theory', *Journal of Post Keynesian Economics*, 42 (3), 390–415.
International Monetary Fund (2020), *Annual Report on Exchange Arrangements and Exchange Restrictions: 2019*, Washington, DC: International Monetary Fund.
Lavoie, M. (2014), *Post-Keynesian Economics: New Foundations*, Cheltenham, UK, and Northampton, MA, USA: Edward Elgar.
Ramos, R.A. and D.M. Prates (2018), 'The Post-Keynesian view on exchange rates: towards the consolidation of the different contributions in the ABM and SFC frameworks', *Texto para discussão* #352, Unicamp. Instituto de Economia, Campinas.
The Economist (2019), 'The Big Mac index', available online at www.economist.com/news/2019/07/10/the-big-mac-index (last accessed on 27 August 2019).

Exchange rates – fixed vs flexible

The 1997 East Asian crisis prompted a reclassification of exchange-rate regimes by the International Monetary Fund in a spectrum of ten official regimes: from one corner solution of the pure fixed regime (dollarization), which implies a complete loss of control over domestic monetary policy, to various intermediate managed regimes (for example, crawling peg, managed floating), to the opposite-corner solution of the free-floating regime (Fisher, 2001), in which the central bank can maintain its independence, and intervention occurs only exceptionally, to address disorderly market conditions (Reinhart and Rogoff, 2004).

The classification of various exchange-rate regimes is essential, because each regime provides an indication of the underlying monetary policy and the ability of an economy to react to imbalances. It is also complex for at least three reasons: first, countries may have multiple official rates; second, the gap between the official, *de jure*, regime, and the actual, *de facto*, regime may be substantial (for example, countries may experience a parallel unofficial market); third, each country has its own way of implementing an exchange-rate regime.

Theoretically, the mainstream view is aligned to the two corner solutions. On the one end, hard pegs are, first, considered to be useful against inflation, since they act as a price anchor. Second, this regime provides discipline for macroeconomic policies, preventing governments' expansionary policies. Third, allegedly, fixed exchange rates discourage speculating activity, which may push the exchange rate far away from its optimum level (in terms of resource allocation). On the other end, pure floating regimes are preferred (Friedman, 1953), because they allow the exchange rate to bear the weight of the adjustment in response to a shock, eluding or reducing the impact on other economic variables. In a free-market view, the role of private speculation improves stability, as financial losses are a deterrent to irrational behaviour. This has become the preferred solution at the behest of international financial institutions (Epstein and Yeldan, 2008).

In practice, however, not many countries adopt a pure free-floating regime. Particularly for developing countries, there are two causes of 'fear of floating'. First, these countries are significantly open and tend to have a high pass-through from exchange rates to import prices, which is an issue when the central bank's mandate is primarily inflation targeting and inflation stabilization (Calvo and Reinhart, 2002). Second, these countries experience excessive dollarized liabilities, which might be due to the impossibility of issuing debt in local currency, the so-called 'original sin' (Eichengreen et al., 2007).

Post-Keynesian economists maintain that Keynes viewed stability in a different way: concerned about the different nature of trade and financial flows, he envisaged a mechanism that should limit the size of the current-account balance and use that limit to implement short-term measures of capital-flow control. Therefore, he recommended an exchange rate with some flexibility and active intervention in the market (Kregel, 2015). The monetary authority should use interest rates to affect exchange rates and, consequently, exports and effective demand. Accordingly, following Keynes's resistance to peg solutions, post-Keynesian economists have opposed the creation of currency areas. For example, the countries of the euro area gave up their monetary and exchange-rate policies for the Stability and Growth Pact, which does not contain any countercyclical mechanism, given the requirements and the size of a balanced budget (Arestis et al., 2001).

LUIGI VENTIMIGLIA

See also

Bretton Woods; Central bank independence; Effective demand; Exchange rates; Monetary policy

References

Arestis, P., C. McCauley and M. Sawyer (2001), 'An alternative stability pact for the European Union', *Cambridge Journal of Economics*, **25** (2), 113–30.
Calvo, G. and C. Reinhart (2002), 'Fear of floating', *Quarterly Journal of Economics*, **117** (2), 379–408.
Eichengreen, B., R. Hausmann and U. Panizza (2007), 'Currency mismatches, debt intolerance and original sin: why they are not the same and why it matters', in S. Edwards (ed.), *Capital Controls and Capital Flows in Emerging Economies: Policies, Practices, and Consequences*, Chicago: University of Chicago Press, pp. 121–70.
Epstein, G.A. and E. Yeldan (2008), 'Inflation targeting, employment creation and economic development: assessing the impacts and policy alternatives', *International Review of Applied Economics*, **22** (2), 131–44.
Fisher, S. (2001), 'Exchange rate regimes: is the bipolar view correct?', *Journal of Economic Perspectives*, **15** (2), 3–24.
Friedman, M. (1953), 'The case for flexible exchange rates', in *Essays in Positive Economics*, Chicago: University of Chicago Press, pp. 157–203.
Kregel, J. (2015), 'Keynes, Minsky and international financial fragility', available online at http://www.ier.hit-u.ac.jp/extra/doc/WS2015/E-Kregel.pdf (last accessed on 23 March 2019).
Reinhart, C.M. and K.S. Rogoff (2004), 'The modern history of exchange rate arrangements: a reinterpretation', *Quarterly Journal of Economics*, **119** (1), 1–48.

Exchange rates – managed

Central banks, especially in developing economies, often rely on a mix of monetary policy measures and foreign-exchange market interventions to maintain a managed floating exchange rate regime. In this arrangement, a pro-active central bank intervenes to change the direction of the domestic currency's exchange rate depending on a diverse set of policy priorities. These interventions may be made on a regular basis or only occasionally, based on pre-announced or unannounced currency value targets, thereby giving the regime a more common 'dirty float' name. The managed float arrangement stands in contrast to more narrowly defined fixed or free-floating exchange rate regimes.

The International Monetary Fund's (2020) *Annual Report on Exchange Arrangements and Exchange Restrictions* catalogues a broad range of specific exchange rate policies that fit the contours of a managed regime with a majority of countries maintaining de facto 'dirty float' arrangements. The *Report* mentions heightened uncertainty and external shocks that can influence some countries' decisions, as their central banks attempt to defend the national currency.

A soft currency peg, broadly capturing the managed exchange rate regime (outside of the hard peg, or fixed exchange rate), includes (1) pegs with horizontal bands (currency value maintained within a predefined corridor); (2) crawling pegs (adjustments to currency value are made periodically); (3) a combination of both as crawling pegs; and (4) managed float without a predetermined exchange rate path. In addition to other currency value (exchange rate) targets, central banks rely on monetary anchors or a combination of both in their exchange rate management policies.

In a peripheral monetary economy (that is, a developing country), central banks intervene to tame foreign-exchange markets' volatility or defend domestic currency from short-term instability of international capital flows (see Andrade and Prates, 2013; Ramos and Prates, 2018). Central banks rely on a range of policy instruments varying with the economy's financial markets' development. Most common polices include active purchases and sales of foreign-exchange reserves (especially in the large commodity-exporting emerging markets) and are often paralleled by more innovative use of derivatives, repurchase agreements or other policy measures in structurally weaker economies aimed at balancing the domestic currencies under sporadic changes in foreign-exchange flows, remittances and manufactured imports dependencies (Gevorkyan, 2017). In addition, while international reserves are generally comprised of a mixed basket of reserve currencies, recent research and empirical evidence point to a rising relevance of gold in the foreign-exchange reserve balance composition across emerging markets (Gevorkyan and Khemraj, 2019).

The reality of exchange rate management mechanics in developing countries also varies with the economy's structural system. For instance, Lavoie and Wang (2012) explore an automatic compensation for the case of China, whereby the People's Bank of China accumulates foreign reserves and simultaneously has the funds deposited into the government's deposit account at the central bank. In this automatically compensating offset, there is no change to the monetary base consistent with the Mundell–Fleming sterilization. This works in a situation of large State-owned exporters earning foreign exchange and selling it to the central bank.

In contrast to such exception, Khemraj (2014) proposes that central banks target the foreign-exchange spread in their local market by one-sided sales of Treasury bills to investors. The interest on government securities then compensates investors for switching from a foreign-currency asset to a domestic security. This compensation mechanism looks at a world after financial liberalization and one with little or no capital controls. In this model, exchange rate management replaces non-remunerated excess reserves – possibly engendered by expenses from central bank deposits – with domestic interest-bearing securities (Khemraj, 2018). It is not an automatic process, but one that is policy based, as argued by Andrade and Prates (2013) and Gevorkyan (2017).

It is likely that some form of managed float exchange-rate arrangements will continue to dominate across emerging markets. The maturity of domestic financial markets seems to matter in the country's shift to a free float. Yet, as uncertainty about capital flows persists in the currency periphery framework and as external shocks become more severe, as the Covid-19 pandemic has illustrated, it would be reasonable to expect developing countries to continue to rely on mixed strategies of managed float exchange-rate regimes. At the same time, while possibly addressing countries' financial and macroeconomic vulnerabilities, the proliferation of the diverse domestic currency regime arrangements will continue to complicate efforts to develop a unified theory of exchange rate dynamics.

ALEKSANDR V. GEVORKYAN

See also

Bretton Woods; Central bank independence; Exchange rates; Exchange rates – fixed vs flexible; Monetary policy

References

Andrade, R. and D.M. Prates (2013), 'Exchange rate dynamics in a peripheral monetary economy', *Journal of Post Keynesian Economics*, **35** (3), 399–416.
Gevorkyan, A.V. (2017), 'The foreign exchange regime in a small open economy: Armenia and beyond', *Journal of Economic Studies*, **44** (5), 781–800.
Gevorkyan, A.V. and T. Khemraj (2019), 'Exchange rate targeting and gold demand by central banks: modeling international reserves composition', *Emerging Markets Finance and Trade*, **55** (1), 168–80.
International Monetary Fund (2020), *Annual Report on Exchange Arrangements and Exchange Restrictions: 2019*, Washington, DC: International Monetary Fund.
Khemraj, T. (2014), *Money, Banking and Foreign Exchange Market in Emerging Economies*, Cheltenham, UK, and Northampton, MA, USA: Edward Elgar.
Khemraj, T. (2018), 'Monetary policy and excess liquid assets in small open developing economies', in L. Briguglio (ed.), *Handbook of Small States:*

ALEKSANDR V. GEVORKYAN

Economic, Social and Environmental Issues, London and New York: Routledge, pp. 205–17.

Lavoie, M. and P. Wang. (2012), 'The "compensation" thesis, as exemplified by the case of the Chinese central bank', *International Review of Applied Economics*, **26** (3), 287–301.

Ramos, R.A. and D.M. Prates (2018), 'The Post-Keynesian view on exchange rates: towards the consolidation of the different contributions in the ABM and SFC frameworks', *Texto para discussão*, No. 352, Instituto de Economia, Campinas.

Exogenous money

One of the traditional debates in economic literature concerns the question about the endogenous or exogenous nature of money. From the point of view of the mainstream (orthodox theory), money is an exogenous magnitude, and the central bank is basically in a position to control the money supply process. This principal institutional role of the monetary authorities was represented in different time periods by three mainstream sub-schools like Monetarism, New Keynesianism and the New Consensus. Let us present these schools of thought briefly.

According to Monetarists, any exogenous money supply increase can give rise to an output effect only in the short run. Further, the central bank is the dominant player in the financial system and operates to 'fine tune' the economy. Paraphrasing Friedman's views, any money supply expansion could be considered as endogenous to the monetary base and rather exogenous to the economy's aggregate demand. In causality terms, any kind of money exogeneity will imply that 'each of the different money stocks is the product of the monetary base and a money multiplier' (Meltzer, 1995, p. 63). Consequently, credit demand 'satisfaction' should be under the 'approval' of money supply growth. Thus, credit is an endogenous reaction to an exogenous shift of money growth, as this is initiated by the monetary base.

Overall, the Monetarist approach basically seems to strengthen the central bank's role and if not to neglect, at least to diminish the role and importance of financial institutions (banks) in the evolution of economic activity through the 'credit channel'. This 'credit channel' atrophy, inside the orthodox framework, was basically brought forward by the New Keynesians.

New Keynesian monetary theory supplements the 'money channel' pinpointed by the Monetarists with the 'credit channel', primarily focusing on commercial banks' asset management (as loan supply). For New Keynesians, the 'credit channel' is a supply-driven story (Panagopoulos and Spiliotis, 2008). This new (supply) channel is discussed by New Keynesians to explain fluctuations in the real economy. It is decomposed in two parts: the lending channel (see Bernanke and Blinder, 1988), from the point of view of banks, and the balance-sheet channel, from the point of view of firms (see Bernanke and Gertler, 1995).

With regard to the money channel, New Keynesians recognize that this (auxiliary) channel is a kind of central banks' reaction function (to some unexpected shocks). Actually, most prominent economists of this school are split between two views. One view is that there is a long-run relationship between money and output, initiated by the monetary aggregates, while the other view claims that this relationship weakens or even breaks down and a relation emerges between interest rates or spreads with real output.

By contrast, the New Consensus view appears to be developed around Taylor's (1993) insights and particularly through his interest rate policy rule, as an attempt for restoring the prime role of the central bank and, thus, the 'protagonist' role of the 'money channel'. The general philosophy behind this view is that the economy, in the short run, deviates from its Wicksellian equilibrium. However, owing to the central bank's administrative intervention – through the Taylor's policy rule – the economy will eventually gravitate towards its long-run equilibrium values. More specifically, if aggregate demand factors (like the loan demand) are able, in the short run, to lead the level of output away from its equilibrium level, it is the Taylor rule that is in charge of restoring the long-run Wicksellian equilibrium between the policy rate of interest and output. Therefore, according to the New Consensus framework, in the 'tug of war' between monetary authorities and the real economy, the former is in a position, as a dominant player, to restore any predetermined equilibrium target.

YANNIS PANAGOPOLOUS

See also

Aggregate demand; Endogenous money; Financial crises; Monetary policy transmission mechanism; Money and banking

References

Bernanke, B. and A. Blinder (1988), 'Credit, money, and aggregate demand', *American Economic Review*, **78** (2), 435–39.

Bernanke, B. and M. Gertler (1995), 'Inside the black box: the credit channel of monetary policy transmission', *Journal of Economic Perspectives*, **9** (4), 27–48.

Clarida, R., J. Gali and M. Gertler (1999), 'The science of monetary policy: a New Keynesian perspective', *Journal of Economic Literature*, **37** (4), 1661–707.

Meltzer, A. (1995), 'Monetary, credit and (other) transmission processes: a monetarist perspective', *Journal of Economic Perspectives*, **9** (4), 49–72.

Panagopoulos, Y. and A. Spiliotis (2008), 'Alternative money theories: a G7 testing', *Journal of Post Keynesian Economics*, **30** (4), 607–29.

Taylor, J.B. (1993), 'Discretion versus policy rules in practice', *Carnegie–Rochester Conference Series on Public Policy*, **39**, 195–214.

Expectations

Expectations in economics can be defined as informed guesses about non-observable future economic events, variables and measures, which are central to forward-looking present choices and decision-making. They are commonly formed by individual agents, economic entities and institutions, such as consumers, investors, households, firms and public authorities, when active in any kind of economic activity. Consumers and households, for instance, base their decisions on expectations about future income streams and expected prices, investors and firms about expected costs and profits, and public authorities about expected public revenues and expenditures.

The enormous importance of expectations in economics lies in the fact that shaping expectations and incorporating these in any kind of decision and action impact on general economic activity. Keynes (1936) views the concept of expectations as a determining factor of output and employment. He argues that business supply decisions of entrepreneurs depend on the expectations they form as to consumers' willingness to pay for the produced commodities. These expectations on prospective investment yields (whether short-term or long-term) determine in turn the amount of offered employment by firms. Friedman (1968) stresses the concept of expectations about price developments in his seminal work on the natural rate of unemployment, in relation to the celebrated Phillips curve. General acknowledgment of the outmost significance of shaping and accounting for expectations in economic decision-making motivates research on adequate and sophisticated ways to formally incorporate this notion in economic theory and analysis. Insofar as dynamics and the differentiation between short-run and long-run analysis are introduced, different concepts of expectations attract historically the scientific interest of economists and are applied via different theories and models. Among the most prominent ones are static, adaptive and rational expectations.

The concept of static or naïve expectations postulates that agents do not anticipate any changes. In the early cobweb theory of price determination (Ezekiel, 1938), for example, producers expect future prices to equal present prices. Along the same lines, agents may expect the future inflation rate to remain the same, ignoring potentially crucial information on inflation policy available at the time of shaping expectations.

Adaptive expectations are introduced to formalize the more dynamic concept that expectations are formed on the basis of (weighted) past realizations. Farmers, for example, take into account past prices when forming their expectations on future prices (Nerlove, 1958), while 'the expected rate of change in prices seems to depend in some way on what the actual rates of change were in the past' (Cagan, 1956, p. 37). Inherent in the concept of adaptive expectations is a 'backward-looking' feature, allowing for systematic errors, alongside the lack of any consideration of current conditions and potentially anticipated shocks.

Agents that form expectations on the basis of all available information, including any anticipation of potential future policy changes, are said to be rational. The roots of the rational-expectations hypothesis lie in the early work of Muth (1961, p. 330), who views rationality as being 'a principle applicable to all dynamic problems'. He defines as 'rational' the expectations (that is, the informed predictions of future events) that 'are essentially the same as the predictions of the relevant economic theory' (p. 316). Expectations formed by rational agents are central to the influential critique by Lucas (1976) on policy evaluation and, overall, constitute a major element of a great number of sophisticated macroeconometric models. Still, the assumption of the formation of rational expectations is also subject to significant criticism, on the basis of several arguments such as the strongly dynamic features of the economic system, the underlying uncertainty, imperfect knowledge, the partial or limited non-identical and asymmetric access to information by agents, alongside the cost for its acquisition and procession.

The key role of expectations in post-Keynesian theorizing relates to the impact on agents' decision-making of the underlying uncertainty, due to which expectations are influenced by social conventions and rules of thumb. The fundamental role of uncertainty and its repercussions for the formation of expectations imply the non-acceptance of the rational-expectations hypothesis, as well as the rejection of the argument of policy ineffectiveness by post-Keynesian economists. In conjunction with uncertainty, unstable expectations feed investment instability, which in turn drives overall economic instability.

Any realistic formation of expectations, even if following a process of gradual learning, remains a complex issue, owing also to psychological factors guiding the decision-making process. Heuristics, conflict, human nature and emotions might also be involved. As Keynes (1936, p. 162) argues, 'individual initiative will only be adequate when reasonable calculation is supplemented and supported by animal spirits', while 'if the animal spirits are dimmed and the spontaneous optimism falters, leaving us to depend on nothing but a mathematical expectation, enterprise will fade and die' (p. 162).

EKATERINI TSOUMA

See also

Behavioural economics; Effective demand; Money illusion; *The General Theory of Employment, Interest and Money*; Uncertainty

References

Cagan, P. (1956), 'The monetary dynamics of hyperinflation', in M. Friedman (ed.), *Studies in the Quantity Theory of Money*, Chicago and London: University of Chicago Press, pp. 25–117.
Ezekiel, M. (1938), 'The cobweb theorem', *Quarterly Journal of Economics*, **52** (2), 255–80.
Friedman, M. (1968), 'The role of monetary policy', *American Economic Review*, **58** (1), 1–17.
Keynes, J.M. (1936), *The General Theory of Employment, Interest and Money*, London: Macmillan.
Lucas, R.E. (1976), 'Econometric policy evaluation: a critique', *Carnegie-Rochester Conference Series on Public Policy*, **1** (1), 19–46.
Muth, J.F. (1961), 'Rational expectations and the theory of price movements', *Econometrica*, **29** (3), 315–35.
Nerlove, M. (1958), 'Adaptive expectations and cobweb phenomena', *Quarterly Journal of Economics*, **72** (2), 227–40.

Fallacy of composition

Formally speaking, a fallacy of composition occurs when the 'premise that the parts of a whole are of a certain nature is improperly used to infer that the whole itself must also be of this nature' (Britannica, 2009). Popularized in economics by Samuelson's (1948) textbook, *Economics: An Introductory Analysis*, this form of sophism is often cited as a wrong way to infer conclusions at the macroeconomic (the whole) level from microeconomic reasoning (the parts). The most famous (already at that time) fallacy of composition is probably the 'paradox of thrift' described by Keynes (1936/2007) in *The General Theory of Employment, Interest and Money* and taught in introductory courses of macroeconomics. This is called a 'paradox' because the effects that can be reasonably expected from an increase in the saving rate of an individual household, to wit, a decrease in the level of consumption (of this household), do not occur when an increase in the saving rate for the totality of households is considered. For the set of households taken as a whole, higher saving rates lead respectively to lower aggregate consumption, lower firms' sales, lower output and, therefore, to lower aggregate saving.

By focusing primarily on global magnitudes, post-Keynesian economists have highlighted the *a priori* existence of several fallacies of composition that threaten the logical consistency of reasoning in macroeconomics. Besides the paradox of thrift there are, for instance, the paradox of costs, the paradox of public deficits, the paradox of profit-led demand and the adding-up constraint (see Lavoie, 2014, pp. 16–22 for further details on this subject matter). All these paradoxes stem from the peculiar nature of transactions on the labour market, as well as from the logical implications of the formation and the expenditure of national income, to wit, the creation and the final destruction of purchasing power. In this respect, national income acts as a bridge between microeconomics and macroeconomics, since it proceeds from transactions among economic agents (in particular through the payment of wages) but refers to a purchasing power over the whole community.

Drawing from methodological individualism, which pretends to explain any social phenomenon referring to individual motives, neoclassical theory cannot grasp the distinctiveness of macroeconomics, but also cannot articulate in a coherent manner microeconomics and macroeconomics. The reductionist nature of neoclassical theory was already highlighted by Keynes (1936/2007, p. 23, italics in the original) as follows:

> I have called my theory a *general* theory. I mean by this that I am chiefly concerned with the behavior of the economic system as a whole, with aggregate incomes, aggregate profits, aggregate output, aggregate employment, aggregate investment, aggregate saving rather than with the incomes, profits, output, employment, investment and saving of particulier industries, firms or individuals. And I argue that important mistakes have been made through extending to the system as a whole conclusions which have been correctly arrived at in respect of a part of it taken in isolation.

In the aftermath of the Lucas (1976) critique of postwar Keynesian structural macroeconometric models, the search (carried out by New-Classical theorists) for microeconomic foundations of macroeconomics logically led to the use of the representative agent assumption in neoclassical macroeconomic modelling. Since this assumption implicitly reduces the determination of national income to the calculation of the real cost of production of a unique firm, it remains undermined by the existence of a fallacy of composition owing to the neglect of what Keynes (1936/2007, p. 23) called 'effective demand'. Supposing a competitive environment comprised of a single firm, the representative agent assumption legitimizes wage devaluation policies, which would result in an increase of profits without reducing the level of employment eventually. In reality, the determination of the level of employment depends on the profits that firms expect to draw from sales on the product market, the origin of which lies in the income (to wit, the purchasing power) that wage earners gained from their productive activities on the labour market.

The above recalls the interdependence between the labour market and the product market for the determination of national income, the latter being simultaneously a cost of production globally and an economic claim (to wit, a purchasing power) over the whole national product. These two complementary sides of the concept of national income are brought together under the principle of effective demand, which represents both a global supply, namely, the formation of national income, and a global demand, namely, the expenditure of national income in the form of consumption or investment.

> [T]he volume of employment is given by the point of intersection between the aggregate demand function and the aggregate supply function; for it is at this point that the entrepreneurs' expectation of profits will be maximised. The value of D at the point of the aggregate demand function, where it is intersected by the aggregate supply function, will be called *the effective demand*. (Keynes, 1936/2007, p. 25, italics in the original)

The principle of effective demand bridges the gap between microeconomics and macroeconomics, since it brings together the expectations of entrepreneurs in terms of proceeds and the determination of the 'product as a whole' (Keynes, 1936/2007, p. xvi). Keynes (1936/2007) already highlighted that, more than methodological problems in their own right, fallacies of composition in macroeconomics (the paradox of thrift especially) are illusions initiated by neoclassical theory, which is based on a set of postulates about the behaviour of *homo œconomicus*.

The monetary circuit approach of Keynes (1930/2011, p. 134; 1936/2007) deconstructs analytically and economically the relationships existing between microeconomics and macroeconomics in a monetary production economy. It ranges economic transactions in a (non-dichotomous) coherent framework according to their macroeconomic (payment of wages, consumption expenditures) or microeconomic (financial market transactions) scope (see also the theory of money emissions initiated by Schmitt, 1966). Against this background, *The General Theory of Employment, Interest and Money* and the *Treatise on Money* are still crucial for grasping contemporary problems like financialization and recall that economics is a science of human action enacting global, macrological, laws.

JONATHAN MASSONNET

Human effort and human consumption are the ultimate matters from which alone economic transactions are capable of deriving any significance; and all other forms of expenditure only acquire importance from their having some relationship, sooner or later, to the effort of producers or to the expenditure of consumers. (Keynes, 1930/2011, p. 134)

JONATHAN MASSONNET

See also

Effective demand; Monetary circuit; Paradox of costs; Paradox of debt; Paradox of thrift

References

Britannica (2009), 'Fallacy of composition', in *Encyclopaedia Britannica*, available at http://www.britannica.com.
Keynes, J.M. (1930/2011), *A Treatise on Money. Two Volumes Complete in One, Volume 1. The Pure Theory of Money*, Mansfield Centre, CT: Martino.
Keynes, J.M. (1936/2007), *The General Theory of Employment, Interest and Money*, Basingstoke and New York: Palgrave Macmillan.
Lavoie, M. (2014), *Post-Keynesians Economics: New Foundations*, Cheltenham, UK, and Northampton, MA, USA: Edward Elgar.
Lucas, R.J. (1976), 'Econometric policy evaluations: a critique', *Carnegie-Rochester Conference Series on Public Policy*, 1 (1), 19–46.
Samuelson, P.A. (1948), *Economics: An Introductory Analysis*, New York: McGraw-Hill.
Schmitt, B. (1966), *Monnaie, salaires et profits*, Paris: Presses universitaires de France.

Feminist economics

Feminist economics emerged as a unique school of economic thought in the 1980s and 1990s, although feminism already influenced political economy much earlier (Agenjo-Calderón and Gálvez-Muños, 2019). It has been defined broadly as a 'lens' that centres gender inequality as an area of research (Van Staveren, 2010) with a normative goal of reducing such inequality (Strober, 1994). Feminist economists have called for an expansion of economic inquiry to include care provisioning and unpaid work in the household (Austen and Jefferson, 2010).

Lavoie (2002) has argued that feminist and post-Keynesian economists share criticisms of neoclassical economics, creating a starting point for collaboration. Like post-Keynesians, feminist economists have questioned the assumptions of rationality and atomism (see Bergmann, 1990; Strober, 1994). At the same time, the feminist paradigm is often seen as encompassing a particularly wide range of approaches, with some researchers applying mainstream methods (see Blank and Reimers, 2003; Van Staveren, 2010).

Several new areas of research have emerged combining insights from the two schools of thought. Feminist macroeconomists have adapted structural models to incorporate gender wage gaps and occupational segregation (Seguino, 2020). Unlike neoclassical models that focus on gender equality's positive long-term impacts on economic growth, these Kaleckian models allow shifts in women's outcomes to generate short-run impacts that vary based on the economy's structural characteristics.

The results point to a more complicated relationship between income distribution and economic growth. In profit-led economies, an increase in women's wages can initially reduce economic growth (Seguino, 2020). Related empirical work on employment and income distribution has found that conflict over scarce 'good jobs' can lead women's job quality to fall as their labour force participation rate rises (Seguino and Braunstein, 2019).

Recent extensions to these models assess how care provisioning affects macroeconomic outcomes. Braunstein et al. (2020) propose a conceptual model in which societies differ in the level of care provided, the distribution of caring labour, and care's relationship to investment demand. Based on these characteristics, both 'high road' and 'low road' regimes are possible. In the high-road regime, economic growth is compatible with greater gender equality and greater care provisioning, while the opposite is true for the low-road regime.

An additional strand of research work assesses the distributional implications of financialization and monetary policy. Elson and Cagatay (2000) argue that central banks have promoted low inflation to benefit white male creditors ('deflationary bias'). Seguino and Heintz (2012) confirm that white women and black men and women experience greater employment costs from contractionary monetary policy. Other research work explores how structural inequality perpetuates gaps in wealth accumulation and leaves women and people of colour more vulnerable during financial crises (see for instance Dymski et al., 2013).

JONATHAN MASSONNET / MELANIE G. LONG

The Covid-19 pandemic has had disproportionate impacts on women, both reducing employment and intensifying care responsibilities (see Craig and Churchill, 2020). The distributional characteristics of the crisis and its relationship to social reproduction open the door to additional work at the intersection of post-Keynesian and feminist economics.

MELANIE G. LONG

See also

Growth; Growth – wage-led vs profit-led; Income distribution; Inequality; Neoclassical economics

References

Agenjo-Calderón, A. and L. Gálvez-Muñoz (2019), 'Feminist economics: theoretical and political dimensions', *American Journal of Economics and Sociology*, **78** (1), 137–66.
Austen, S. and T. Jefferson (2010), 'Feminist and post-Keynesian economics: challenges and opportunities', *Cambridge Journal of Economics*, **34** (6), 1109–22.
Bergmann, B.R. (1990), 'Feminism and economics', *Women's Studies Quarterly*, **18** (3–4), 68–74.
Blank, R.M. and C. Reimers (2003), 'Economics, policy analysis, and feminism', in M.A. Ferber and A.J. Nelson (eds), *Feminist Economics Today: Beyond Economic Man*, Chicago: University of Chicago Press, pp. 157–74.
Braunstein, E., R. Bouhia and S. Seguino (2020), 'Social reproduction, gender equality and economic growth', *Cambridge Journal of Economics*, **44** (1), 129–56.
Craig, L. and B. Churchill (2020), 'Working and caring at home: gender differences in the effects of Covid-19 on paid and unpaid labor in Australia', *Feminist Economics*, **26** (1), 1–17.
Dymski, G., J. Hernandez and L. Mohanty (2013), 'Race, gender, power, and the US subprime mortgage and foreclosure crisis: a meso analysis', *Feminist Economics*, **19** (3), 124–51.
Elson, D. and N. Cagatay (2000), 'The social content of macroeconomic policies', *World Development*, **28** (7), 1347–64.
Lavoie, M. (2002), 'The tight links between post-Keynesian and feminist economics', *Post-Autistic Economics Review*, **11**, 189–92.
Seguino, S. (2020), 'Engendering macroeconomic theory and policy', *Feminist Economics*, **26** (2), 27–61.
Seguino, S. and E. Braunstein (2019), 'The costs of exclusion: gender job segregation, structural change and the labour share of income', *Development and Change*, **50** (4), 976–1008.
Seguino, S. and J. Heintz (2012), 'Monetary tightening and the dynamics of US race and gender stratification', *American Journal of Economics and Sociology*, **71** (3), 603–38.
Strober, M.H. (1994), 'Rethinking economics through a feminist lens', *American Economic Review*, **84** (2), 143–7.
Van Staveren, I. (2010), 'Post-Keynesianism meets feminist economics', *Cambridge Journal of Economics*, **34** (6), 1123–44.

Finance – initial vs final

Financing the production process is Keynes's (1937a, 1937b) object of inquiry in two well-known articles published in the *Economic Journal*, where he defined finance as a new creation of money, issued by banks with the aim of funding firms' productive activities.

Indeed, in a closed economy with no government, bank loans are granted to firms to pay wages and produce new inventories of goods (Lavoie, 2014). This short-term phenomenon is known as 'initial finance'. In such a vertically integrated economy without a public sector, bank loans are then used by firms to carry out investment activities over time. In particular, capital goods are financed by corporate shares, new bank loans, and retained profits (Lavoie, 2014). This phenomenon is called 'final finance'.

On one side, the phenomenon of 'initial finance' has been a major object of inquiry of monetary-circuit traditions, particularly in Canada, France, Switzerland, and Italy (see Schmitt, 1966; Parguez, 1975; Barrère, 1990; Graziani, 2003; and Lavoie, 2014). In this theoretical framework, firms' production planning is thought to be the spur of bank credit, according to the saying 'loans make deposits' (see Lavoie, 2003). Therefore, supply decisions are thought to precede demand on the product market, and 'initial finance' is needed to allow for the initial payment of firms' production costs (wages). It is only when production costs are finally covered that companies' debt to the banking system is extinguished and, if profits are made through the process, a stock of goods is appropriated by firms.

On the other side, focusing on the role of effective demand, post-Keynesian economists at large have set out to explain the 'final finance' concerning the autonomous determinants of demand in an open economy with government; namely, autonomous consumption, investment, public spending, and exports (see, for instance,

MELANIE G. LONG / ANDREA CARRERA

Davidson, 1982, 1986). Autonomous demand is thought to be financed through the banking system, with the exception of exports, which are generated by autonomous foreign demand. Bank credit, together with the multiplier effect explained by Keynes (1936), induces spending and generates new output. Accordingly, demand generates supply on the market for produced goods and services (see Cesaratto, 2017, for analytical elaboration).

As Cesaratto (2017) argues, initial-finance research fails to explain, *inter alia*, investment funding. Investment, namely the production of investment goods, is thought to be financed either through individual savings, especially according to the Italian monetary-circuit tradition (see Graziani, 2003; Fontana and Realfonzo, 2005), or via profits, along the lines of the Dijon–Fribourg School (Schmitt, 1966; Cencini, 2005; Rossi, 2007). Indeed, savings from wages and savings from profits have often been thought to be the source of investment activities (see Carrera, 2019, for a detailed explanation). This viewpoint harks back mainly to Classical economists, to Keynes, and to seminal post-Keynesian contributions (see, for instance, Robinson, 1937; Kaldor, 1956; Pasinetti, 1962). Accordingly, initial credit to production does not include the funds required to carry out investment activities.

It is worth noting that some investigations have been started aiming to integrate the financing of initial production and final payments, looking for a reconciliation between Keynes's post-1936 research on finance and monetary-circuit theories (see Rochon, 1997). Recently, Cesaratto (2017) sought to buttress the attempts made in particular by Davidson (1986) and Dalziel (1996), among others, to reconcile initial and final finance. The post-Keynesian reconciliation is based on the following, simple steps: (1) the initial credit to production is made according to companies' orders or expectations; (2) final payments are made thanks to the revenues generated by the income (super)multiplier; (3) further autonomous spending and investment may be financed through a new credit granted by banks.

ANDREA CARRERA

See also

Effective demand; Income multiplier; Monetary circuit; Money and banking; Money creation – nature of

References

Barrère, A. (1990), 'Signification générale du circuit: une interprétation', *Économies et Sociétés* ('Série Monnaie et Production', 6), **24** (2), 9–34.
Carrera, A. (2019), *A Macroeconomic Analysis of Profit*, London and New York: Routledge.
Cencini, A. (2005), *Macroeconomic Foundations of Macroeconomics*, London and New York: Routledge.
Cesaratto, S. (2017), 'Initial and final finance in the monetary circuit and the theory of effective demand', *Metroeconomica*, **68** (2), 228–58.
Dalziel, P.C. (1996), 'The Keynesian multiplier, liquidity preference, and endogenous money', *Journal of Post Keynesian Economics*, **18** (3), 311–31.
Davidson, P. (1982), *International Money and the Real World*, London: Macmillan.
Davidson, P. (1986), 'Finance, funding, saving, and investment', *Journal of Post Keynesian Economics*, **9** (1), 101–10.
Fontana, G. and R. Realfonzo (eds) (2005), *The Monetary Theory of Production: Tradition and Perspectives*, Basingstoke and New York: Palgrave Macmillan.
Graziani, A. (2003), *The Monetary Theory of Production*, Cambridge, UK: Cambridge University Press.
Kaldor, N. (1956), 'Alternative theories of distribution', *Review of Economic Studies*, **23** (2), 83–100.
Keynes, J.M. (1936), *The General Theory of Employment, Interest and Money*, London: Macmillan.
Keynes, J.M. (1937a), 'Alternative theories of the rate of interest', *Economic Journal*, **47** (186), 241–52.
Keynes, J.M. (1937b), 'The "ex ante" theory of the rate of interest', *Economic Journal*, **47** (188), 663–9.
Lavoie, M. (2003), 'A primer on endogenous credit-money', in L.-P. Rochon and S. Rossi (eds), *Modern Theories of Money: The Nature and Role of Money in Capitalist Economies*, Cheltenham, UK, and Northampton, MA: Edward Elgar, pp. 506–43.
Lavoie, M. (2014), *Post-Keynesian Economics: New Foundations*, Cheltenham, UK, and Northampton, MA: Edward Elgar.
Parguez, A. (1975), *Monnaie et macroéconomie*, Paris: Economica.
Pasinetti, L.L. (1962), 'Rate of profit and income distribution in relation to the rate of economic growth', *Review of Economic Studies*, **29** (4), 267–79.
Robinson, J.V. (1937), *Introduction to the Theory of Employment*, London: Macmillan.
Robinson, J.V. (1956), *The Accumulation of Capital*, London: Palgrave Macmillan.
Rochon, L.-P. (1997), 'Keynes's finance motive: a re-assessment. Credit, liquidity preference and the rate of interest', *Review of Political Economy*, **9** (3), 277–93.

Rossi, S. (2007), *Money and Payments in Theory and Practice*, London and New York: Routledge.
Schmitt, B. (1966), *Monnaie, salaires et profits*, Albeuve, CH: Castella.

Finance and development

Economic development is one of the longest and most intensely debated issues in economics. As universally applied, there are two competing views. One was developed by Smith (1776/2010) and argues that there is a natural order. Much like individuals who possess vices and virtues (some preordained and some acquired) that may or may not be conducive to personal wealth, the wealth of nations is also dependent on such factors. The opposing view, most convincingly presented by Polanyi (1944), is that of social order.

As applied to countries that have not developed, there are likewise two opposing views. One view is well captured by Rostow (1960), who proposes development as linear and positive. All countries are on the path to development, only some are further along than others. It is assumed that developed countries will automatically remain that way, and that economic growth is synonymous with economic development. The opposing view is given by Furtado (1978), who argues that economic development is neither linear nor positive: countries can underdevelop for centuries (that is, the equilibrium of underdevelopment). Furthermore, Furtado (1978) places the ultimate emphasis on culture, rather than economic growth, as a determinant for economic development, arguing that the latter is impossible without the former.

Differing views on financing for development follow from the viewpoint taken on development. From the natural-order viewpoint, peripheral countries suffer from the 'original sin' of not being able to issue bonds in their own currency, and therefore find themselves confronted with the 'impossible trinity'; that is, they can control interest rates or the exchange rate, but not both under conditions of financial opening. The need for external financing is also attributed to natural factors. In the more recent versions of this viewpoint, authors such as McKinnon (1973) argue that developing economies are capital deficient. As these countries have ample opportunities for investment but lack capital, the economic policy recommendation is financial opening.

From the viewpoint of social order, developing countries are equipped with central banks and treasuries, and therefore do not have to suffer from the original sin. The country is not naturally scarce of capital, but rather is an exporter of capital. The impossible trinity need not exist, as capital controls can be utilized. From a social-order perspective, the international order dictates a hierarchy of access to financing, and the access to foreign capital becomes an external constraint. In Latin America, those favouring the natural-order conception often suggest that such constraints can be resolved through economic reform and foreign investment, while those embracing the social-order viewpoint argue that social and political change is prerequisite.

The natural international order does not stand up to scrutiny, as the last half century has seen two important changes in the international monetary order that cannot be convincingly argued as natural. The first occurred with the Bretton Woods agreement, which established a socially regulated monetary order led by national governments and international monetary institutions. The second change has occurred with the unwinding of this order and a return to a market order led by global banks.

In the first period, national economies maintained capital controls to regulate international capital flows, while domestically development banks financed development projects. There were no systemic financial or banking crises. In the second period, development banks were closed or relegated, capital controls were lifted, and national and even regional financial crises became common. This experience is common to both developed and developing countries, albeit with important exceptions and differences.

In his lecture on national self-sufficiency, Keynes (1933, p. 758) argued to 'let goods be homespun whenever it is reasonably and conveniently possible, and, above all, let finance be primarily national'. During the Keynes's inspired Bretton Woods international financial system, national State financing reached a historic high in the North Atlantic. As the historical process of globalized financialization has returned national financing to international credit markets, a predatory double monetary circuit (Parguez, 2010) has emerged in which dollar flows originate in the dollar money centres, spread around the globe, and return with gains.

ANDREA CARRERA / WESLEY C. MARSHALL

Financialization (the return to a market-led global monetary order) has at least up to present validated the arguments of the critical school of development within Latin America (Furtado, 1978), and also the social-global order Polanyian viewpoint (Polanyi, 1944; Polanyi-Levitt, 2013).

WESLEY C. MARSHALL

See also

Bretton Woods; Capital controls; Development; International financial architecture; International monetary system

References

Furtado, C. (1978), *El Desarrollo Económico: Un Mito*, Mexico: Siglo XXI editores.
Keynes, J.M. (1933), 'National self-sufficiency', *The Yale Review*, **22** (4), 755–69.
McKinnon, R.I. (1973), *Money and Capital in International Development*, Washington, DC: Brookings Institution.
Parguez, A. (2010), 'Doble circuito monetario depredador: los costos de la plena integración al sistema financiero y productivo multinacional', *Ola Financiera*, **3** (6), 1–33.
Polanyi, K. (1944), *The Great Transformation*, Boston: Beacon Press.
Polanyi-Levitt, K. (2013), *From the Great Transformation to the Great Financialization*, London: Zed Books.
Rostow, W.W. (1960), *The Stages of Economic Growth: a non-Communist Manifesto*, Cambridge, UK: Cambridge University Press.
Smith, A. (1776/2010), *The Wealth of Nations*, London: Simon and Brown.

Finance in developing countries

Finance is composed of bank advances and is used to produce goods and services, including capital goods (Rochon, 1999). Bank credits cover the circulating capital of the production processes of both consumption goods and capital goods. This needs to be differentiated from capital market liquidity that stems from profits that provide the means to acquire finished capital goods (Graziani, 2003). In developing countries, the domestic production of capital goods is weak and capital markets are shallow and small, thereby big amounts of credits are required to import finished capital goods.

The discussion of finance availability for the production process is straightforward. Following the monetary circuit theory, the first phase (named influx) takes place with bank advances based on firms' demand, which are used to hire workers and buy inputs, thereby expanding the wage bill and profits. In this framework, banks only accommodate the credit demand from solvent borrowers (Rochon, 1999), which is unrelated to cyclical movements but can be modified by banks' liquidity preference, a concept developed by Keynes (1971). The last phase (named reflux) takes place when workers and capitalists acquire goods and services, increasing firms' income, which cancels their debts and thereby closes the monetary circuit.

In this process, three issues should be emphasized. First, as the theory of the monetary circuit suggests, the creation and destruction of debt takes place in a single period, although it can be extended to include overlapping periods (Rochon, 2006), in order for banks to continue their operation. Second, profits create firms' internal funds or circulate as financial capital, which provides the means to acquire finished capital goods. Third, central banks set interest rates that need to remain constant, because higher interest rates can increase firms' costs above their income receipts, and thus create payments defaults.

In an integrated economy, with strong capital accumulation, investment creates its own finance, through profits (usually from past periods) that convert into internal funds (entrepreneurs' savings), which are used to buy capital goods or to provide liquidity to firms' illiquid balance sheets. Therefore, non-bank financial institutions (and capital markets) are key to understand the whole production process. This argument is based on Kalecki (1971), who claimed that firms' own savings along with rentier finance is one of the investment determinants. This is also acknowledged by Graziani (2003), who argued that banks finance circulating capital, while profits are related to finished capital goods' purchase. This argument is subject to controversy, since some post-Keynesian economists (Rochon, 1999) believe that the purchase of capital goods can also be financed by bank credit, arguing that relying too much on internal funds is akin to reinstating the saving–investment causality of neoclassical theory.

Profits have a central role in closing the production process, which becomes the curse of

WESLEY C. MARSHALL / NOEMI LEVY-ORLIK

developing countries since these economies do not produce capital goods. Investment goods are imported, and thereby profits are not produced in the domestic markets and big volumes of credit are needed to acquire finished capital goods. The lack of (or the weak) capital good sector requires special schemes of finance, or external capital inflows (and credits), which depend on international market conditions.

In the era of industrialization, developing economies set up either social devices or public institutions (funded with government credit lines) to finance the acquisition of imported finished capital goods, while in the neoliberal era investment finance depended on external private capital inflows (foreign direct and portfolio investment) that took advantage of developing economies.

In this framework, government direct intervention in mobilizing financial resources to acquire investment is crucial, especially during industrialization processes of developing economies. These arrangements were functional during the different industrialization periods, where public investment headed the process of capital accumulation, along with 'cheap money' policies, and monetary devices that channelled credit to key economic activities. This process developed smoothly in the first two tiers of the industrialization processes (Cameron, 1972) as well as in the East Asian industrialization (Amsden, 1989) that took place within closed economies and with simple technological sectors, or had strong government foreign multinationals' regulation, imposing technological transfers, with strong government leadership in terms of finance and industrialization policies.

Latin American countries underwent a unique industrialization process. Finished capital goods were imported, for which governments provided credits at low rates of interest, and multinationals were not obliged to transfer technology. The industrialization process based on the so-called 'import substitution industrialization model' had high investment coefficients, although machines and equipment were mainly imported, and strong capital markets were not built. Once governments ceased to intervene directly in economic activity, a de-industrialization process unfolded, and 'primarization' or 'maquila' processes re-emerged in the region.

NOEMI LEVY-ORLIK

See also

Development; Finance – initial vs final; Monetary circuit; Money and banking; Profit

References

Amsden, A. (1989), *Asia's Next Giant, South Korea, and Late Industrialization*, Oxford and New York: Oxford University Press.

Cameron, R.M. (1972), *Banking and Economic Development*, Oxford and New York: Oxford University Press.

Graziani, A. (2003), *The Monetary Theory of Production*, Cambridge, UK: Cambridge University Press.

Kalecki, M. (1971), *Selected Essays on the Dynamics of the Capitalist Economy, 1933–1970*, Cambridge, UK: Cambridge University Press.

Keynes, J.M. (1973), 'Alternative theories of the rate of interest', in *The Collected Writings of John Maynard Keynes, Volume XIV*, London: Macmillan, pp. 201–14.

Rochon, L.-P. (1999), *Credit, Money and Production: An Alternative Post-Keynesian Approach*, Cheltenham, UK, and Northampton, MA, USA: Edward Elgar.

Rochon, L.-P. (2006), 'Endogenous money, central banks, and the banking system: Basil Moore and the supply of credits', in M. Setterfield (ed.), *Complexity, Endogenous Money and Macroeconomic Theory: Essays in Honour of Basil J. Moore*, Cheltenham, UK, and Northampton, MA, USA: Edward Elgar, pp. 170–86.

Finance motive

Keynes introduced this motive for holding money in his 1937 post-*General Theory* articles on the interest rate (Keynes, 1937a, 1937b). To start production, he argued, firms have to secure a 'provision of cash' or 'financial provision' provided by banks or the market.

This argument is part of Keynes's revolutionary approach to macroeconomics. It is namely in line with the theory of a 'monetary economy of production' Keynes sketched in the early 1930s in opposition to the neoclassical model, which he labelled a 'real exchange economy' (Keynes, 1933). Contrary to neoclassical economists, who see money as a neutral instrument in an exchange economy, Keynes laid focus on the crucial functions of money and the role of entrepreneurs in a production economy.

As subsequently depicted by the Keynes principle of effective demand introduced in *The*

NOEMI LEVY-ORLIK / CLAUDE GNOS

General Theory (Keynes, 1936), entrepreneurs are deemed to decide on production and hence on the volume of employment with a view 'to maximise the excess of the proceeds over the factor cost' (Keynes, 1936, p. 25). The interplay of supply and demand on markets, praised by neoclassical writers, is not primary in the economic process; it is contingent upon entrepreneurs' quest for monetary profits and the volume of production they consequently decide upon. The introduction of the finance motive completes this story. Considering investing in production, entrepreneurs have to secure a financial provision they will use to pay for production costs. This provision is thus designed to bridge the gap 'between the time when the decision to invest is taken and the time when the correlative investment and saving actually occur' (Keynes, 1937b, p. 208).

The definition of the finance motive actually gave Keynes an opportunity to further specify his vision of the monetary economy of production. As he put it:

> 'finance' has nothing to do with saving. ... 'Finance' and 'commitment to finance' are mere credit and debit book entries, which allow entrepreneurs to go ahead with assurance. ... Credit, in the sense of 'finance', looks after a flow of investment. It is a revolving fund which can be used over and over again. It does not absorb or exhaust any resources .... Each new net investment has new net saving attached to it. The saving can be used once only. It relates to the net addition to the stock of actual assets. (Keynes, 1937b, p. 209)

The distinction between finance and saving is in accordance with the distinction between the successive formation and spending of income that is key in Keynes's theory of unemployment. The formation of the community's income results from the employment given by the entrepreneurs (see Keynes, 1936, p. 23). Saving is the excess of income over consumption (pp. 62–3). Finance precedes entrepreneurs' investment in production, and thus the formation of the community's income. Consequently, it is not to be confused with saving, which is an allocation of the formed income.

Keynes indicated that finance and the commitment to finance offered by banks 'are mere credit and book entries' (Keynes, 1937b, p. 209). This indication relates to another aspect of the Keynesian revolution: Keynes's constant endeavour to renew monetary theory. In the case under consideration, he emphasized that banks' monetary commitments and the ensuing payments consist in book entries that do not 'absorb or exhaust any resources' (ibid.). They contrarily result in the formation of resources, to wit, income that will be partly spent on consumption and partly saved. Being not dependent on pre-existing (and presumably limited) resources, the banks' commitment may be repeated 'and used over and over again' (ibid.). This will repeatedly allow the formation of income. Interestingly, Keynes mentioned that the financial market can also provide a financial provision to entrepreneurs. This simply implies that investors will translate income deposits they hold with banks into debts issued by firms. Does it mean that firms will borrow and spend investors' savings? It will be so, if firms spend the money on investment goods, just as consumers spend their own incomes or incomes they borrow, when buying consumption goods. If firms spend it to pay factor cost, that is, for the payment of wages, they will form new incomes corresponding to the newly produced goods. The spending of a sum of money may amount to the spending or to the formation of incomes, according to whether it results in the purchase or the production of goods.

CLAUDE GNOS

See also

Effective demand; Finance – initial vs final; Monetary circuit; Money illusion; Savings

References

Keynes, J.M. (1933), 'The distinction between a co-operative economy and an entrepreneur economy', in *The Collected Writings of John Maynard Keynes, Volume XXIX: The General Theory and After: A Supplement*, London and Basingstoke: Macmillan, 1973, pp. 76–106.

Keynes, J.M. (1936), *The General Theory of Employment, Interest and Money*, London: Macmillan.

Keynes, J.M. (1937a), '"Ex post and ex ante", "Notes from Keynes" 1937 lectures', in *The Collected Writings of John Maynard Keynes, Volume XIV: The General Theory and After. Part II: Defence and Development*, London and Basingstoke: Macmillan, 1973, pp. 179–83.

Keynes, J.M. (1937b), 'The "ex ante" theory of the rate of interest', *Economic Journal*, **47** (188), 663–9. Reprinted in *The Collected Writings of John Maynard Keynes, Volume XIV: The General Theory and After. Part II: Defence and Development*, London and Basingstoke: Macmillan, 1973, pp. 215–23.

Financial crises

Financial crises are moments of disruption in the regular functioning of financial markets. They have been happening for many centuries, can be national or international in scope, and can have a multiplicity of possible causes and consequences (Kindleberger, 2000). Post-Keynesian theory lays particular stress on endogenous factors that are conducive to financial crises and the ramifications that these crises can have in the rest of the economy.

While financial crises can be triggered by external causes, post-Keynesian theory shows that the dynamics inherent to a modern capitalist economy are liable to create situations conducive to crises. The financial instability hypothesis formulated by Minsky (1982, 1986) outlines one such mechanism in which real and financial sectors are interlinked. In a state of fundamental uncertainty, expectations about future states of the economy will largely be based on a host of market conventions and psychological determinants. As an economic expansion proceeds, these expectations are likely to become increasingly positive, gradually leading to less cautious investment and financing practices. This will in turn bring more fragility in the economy, in particular in the financial sector. The situation may eventually become untenable, creating the conditions for a crisis. (For analyses of financial crises from a Minskyian perspective, see Kregel (2008) and Wray (2009) for the 2007–2008 subprime crisis, and Schroeder (2002) for a discussion of crises in developing countries.)

Financial crises often have widespread impacts on the economy. Typically, they entail a decrease in the availability of financial capital and an increase in financing costs, and they are likely to have an influence on different sectors of the economy. If credit dries up, for example, some non-financial firms may find it difficult to roll-over their debts and to have enough liquidity to service their financial commitments, especially if they have undertaken long-term investments. In the case of a currency crisis, as happened in South-East Asia in the late 1990s, there might also be an important negative impact on the exchange rate, compounding the problem for firms or governments indebted in foreign currency. That said, the burden of adjustment is seldom shared equally. Workers are often hit especially hard by financial crises and some groups with better access to liquidity may even gain by recuperating assets from troubled firms or simply benefit from the difficulties of their competitors (see Lee and Jayadev, 2005; Dufour and Orhangazi, 2009).

Given the deleterious effects of financial crises and the fact that they can arise endogenously through the normal functioning of a capitalist economy, post-Keynesian economists often recommend a set of macroprudential regulations to help avert their occurrence or mitigate their impact (see Minsky, 1986; Dow, 2011; Lavoie, 2014). Proper regulations will depend on the situation, but the broad idea is to foster sufficient safety margins, limit speculative activities, and increase vigilance over the system. Various indicators of fragility should be monitored, along with the possible development of financial innovations that could have destabilizing effects. Monetary authorities could also aim to steer market sentiment and conventions. Finally, the scope of regulations can extend to lenders and borrowers and include, for example, relatively high levels of down payments necessary to be eligible for a mortgage loan, margin requirements to restrain financial speculation, or credit controls.

MATHIEU DUFOUR

See also

Basel agreements; Financial innovations; Financial instability hypothesis; Financial regulations; Uncertainty

References

Dow, S. (2011), 'Cognition, market sentiment and financial instability', *Cambridge Journal of Economics*, **35** (2), 233–49.

Dufour, M. and O. Orhangazi (2009), 'The 2000–2001 financial crisis in Turkey: a crisis for whom?', *Review of Political Economy*, **21** (1), 101–22.

Kindleberger, C.P. (1978/2000), *Manias, Panics and Crashes: A History of Financial Crises*, New York: John Wiley and Sons.

Kregel, J. (2008), 'Minsky's cushions of safety', *Jerome Levy Economics Institute Public Policy Brief*, No. 93.

Lavoie, M. (2014), *Post-Keynesian Economics: New Foundations*, Cheltenham, UK, and Northampton, MA, USA: Edward Elgar.

Lee, K.-K. and A. Jayadev (2005), 'Capital account liberalization, growth and the labor share of income: reviewing and extending the cross-country evidence', in G.A. Epstein (ed.), *Capital Flight and Capital Controls in Developing Countries*,

Cheltenham, UK, and Northampton, MA, USA, pp. 15–57.
Minsky, H.P. (1982), *Can 'It' Happen Again? Essays on Instability and Finance*, Armonk, New York: M.E. Sharpe.
Minsky, H.P. (1986), *Stabilizing an Unstable Economy*, New Haven, CT, USA: Yale University Press.
Schroeder, S.K. (2002), 'A Minskian analysis of financial crisis in developing countries', *Center for Economic Policy Analysis Working Paper*, No. 2002–09.
Wray, L.R. (2009), 'The rise and fall of money manager capitalism: a Minskian approach', *Cambridge Journal of Economics*, **33** (4), 807–28.

Financial deepening

Financial deepening is traditionally an orthodox concept that can be understood as the growing offer and provision of financial products. It is accompanied by a significant degree of financial openness and deregulation in financial markets. Financial deepening is perceived as a critical factor for economic growth, poverty reduction, and even minor inequality levels by the conventional approach. Thus, this concept is interpreted in standard economics as a positive element for the economy. Eschenbach (2004) argues that financial deepening grounds on the empirical works of Gerschenkron (1962), Cameron et al. (1967), and Goldsmith (1969). They used econometric methods to research the connection between finance and economic growth.

During the 1970s, McKinnon (1973) and Shaw (1973) raised concerns favouring financial deepening and against financial repression. They highlighted the financial sector's role in increasing savings through the proper incentives based on the neoclassical idea of saving channelling investment. One of their main recommendations was to eliminate interest rate ceilings, advocating free market 'best allocation' logics for the financial system to achieve this objective. These policy recommendations were a crystal response against the Keynesian paradigm based on Keynes's (1936) and Tobin's (1965) works that supported government intervention in the credit market.

In the 1980s, critics of the financial deregulation paradigm emerged from a neostructuralist approach based on Taylor (1983), who argues that unorganized capital markets have an essential responsibility in developing countries by determining whether financial deepening and liberalization are associated with economic growth. Stiglitz (1989) criticizes financial liberalization based on the idea of market failures in financial markets. Despite these critics, new arguments emerged during the 1990s and 2000s favouring financial deepening and its relationship with better economic growth and better income distribution. King and Levine (1993) emphasize the role of financial deepening to promote innovation. They argue that savings are channelled to the most productive investments through deep financial systems, increasing the likelihood of innovation and technological progress. Demirgüç and Levine (2009) share the optimism about financial deepening, arguing that it helps improve income distribution and reduce inequality through the positive impact of finance on individuals. They argue that easy access to the credit market would increase parents' investment in education for their children. Thus, this will reduce the number of young people who leave their studies to work in case of an adverse shock that may reduce family income.

Therefore, financial deepening proponents justify that the deepening and growth of the financial sector at all levels (intermediated and non-intermediated) is positive for society. However, in heterodox economics, financial deepening and financial liberalization are widely criticized. The term used in the last three decades is financialization. It refers to the problematic dimension of the rise and complexity of the financial sector and its interaction with the so-called 'real' sector of the economy.

The housing bubble that inflated in the United States during the first decade of the twenty-first century, known as the subprime bubble, is a clear example of how problematic and complex financial markets are. This has been already pointed out by Minsky (1977), who stated that fragility increases as financial deepening elements rise. For example, as debt grows and liquidity declines, economic units go from hedge positions toward speculative and Ponzi positions (see Minsky, 1977).

After the 2008 great recession, the problematic dimension of financial deepening arose in the literature. For instance, some authors (see Arcand et al., 2015) have recognized the 'too much finance hypothesis' trying to identify a threshold above which financial development no longer has a positive effect on economic growth. They found that finance can hurt GDP

MATHIEU DUFOUR / DIEGO GUEVARA

growth if credit to the private sector is more than 100 per cent of GDP. In spite of this, deepening finance is still one of the main approaches for economic development. The most dramatic face of financial deepening is having the economy working for finance instead of the finance working for the economy.

DIEGO GUEVARA

See also

Development; Finance and development; Financial instability hypothesis; Financial liberalization; Financialization

References

Arcand, J., E. Berkes and U. Panizza (2015), 'Too much finance?', *Journal of Economic Growth*, **20** (2), 105–48.
Cameron, R., O. Crisp, H. Patrick and T. Richard (1967), *Banking in the Early Stages of Industrialisation: A Study in Comparative Economic History*, New York: Oxford University Press.
Demirgüç-Kunt, A. and R. Levine (2009), 'Finance and inequality: theory and evidence', *World Bank Policy Research Working Paper*, No. 4967.
Eschenbach, F. (2004), 'Finance and growth: a survey of the theoretical and empirical literature', *Tinbergen Institute Discussion Paper*, No. 2004–039/2.
Gerschenkron, A. (1962), *Economic Backwardness in Historical Perspective: A Book of Essays*, Cambridge, MA: Harvard University Press.
Goldsmith, R. (1969), *Financial Structure and Development*, New Haven, CT: Yale University Press.
Keynes, J.M. (1936), *The General Theory of Employment, Interest and Money*, London: Macmillan.
King, R. and R. Levine (1993), 'Finance and growth: Schumpeter might be right', *Quarterly Journal of Economics*, **108** (3), 717–38.
McKinnon, R. (1973), *Money and Capital in Economic Development*, Washington, DC: Brookings Institution.
Minsky, H.P. (1977), 'Banking and a fragile financial environment', *Journal of Portfolio Management*, **3** (4), 16–22.
Shaw, E.S. (1973), *Financial Deepening in Economic Development*, New York: Oxford University Press.
Stiglitz, J.E. (1989), 'Markets, market failures, and development', *American Economic Review*, **79** (2), 197–203.
Taylor, L. (1983), *Structuralist Macroeconomics: Applicable Models for the Third World*, New York: Basic Books.
Tobin, J. (1965), 'Money and economic growth', *Econometrica*, **33** (4), 671–84.

Financial fragility

Financial fragility is the capacity of the financial system to break down, causing payments for assets, goods and services to fail, thus leading to disruptions to the entire economy. The term is widely used in both neoclassical (Bernanke and Gertler, 1990; Douglas and Raghuram, 2001; Gennaioli et al., 2012; Agarwal et al., 2018) and post-Keynesian literature (Minsky, 1995; Chick, 1997; Bezemer and Grydaki, 2014; Mittnik and Semmler, 2018; Nishi, 2019), but these two schools of thought differ greatly over how to define and measure it, as well as over what its causal mechanisms are.

The provision of borrowed money is essential to the phenomenon, but neoclassical analysis presumes the false loanable funds model of banking (McLeay et al., 2014) in which non-banks lend to other non-banks through financial intermediaries, and money is neither created nor destroyed by credit transactions, while post-Keynesians use the correct endogenous-money model of banking in which banks originate money and debt, with lending creating money and repayment destroying it.

Bernanke and Gertler (1990) is representative of the neoclassical treatment. They define a 'financially fragile situation' as one where 'potential borrowers ... have low wealth relative to the sizes of their projects' (Bernanke and Gertler, 1990, p. 88). They construct a two-period (a 'savings' period and a 'consumption' period) general equilibrium model, in which all citizens receive an equal endowment in the savings period. Entrepreneurs decide between a certain return on their endowment, or a higher randomly distributed return from an investment, for which they must borrow from non-entrepreneurs. Non-entrepreneurs decide whether to accept the certain return, or lend to entrepreneurs at a higher rate of interest, with the risk that some entrepreneurs will achieve a lower return than the certain rate of interest and therefore be unable to pay. This raises issues of asymmetric information and agency costs, and '[i]f borrower net worth is low enough, agency costs become overwhelming, and there is no contract for which evaluation of investment projects is profitable' (Bernanke and Gertler, 1990, p. 99). The authors provided no mechanism by which financial fragility might rise over time, and were ambivalent about the impact of higher leverage on financial fragility.

DIEGO GUEVARA / STEVE KEEN

Post-Keynesian analysis is grounded in Minsky's analysis of factors endogenous to a capitalist economy that lead to rising financial fragility over time. These include changes in investor and speculator expectations over a business cycle under conditions of fundamental uncertainty, changes in the balance sheets of private banks – which are the primary creators of money and debt – and a tendency for private debt to rise relative to GDP over a number of economic cycles, since '[i]n a heavily indebted economy: 1. even minor declines in profits and wages can lead to increases in nonperforming assets in the portfolios of financial institutions; 2. even minor increases in interest rates can lead to increases in nonperforming assets in the portfolio of financial institutions; 3. even minor increases in wages can lead to pressure on profit flows and therefore to an increase in nonperforming assets' (Minsky, 1995, p. 198).

Minsky (1995) placed all economic units on a spectrum between robustness and fragility, with the most robust being 'hedge' units whose cash flows exceed their financial commitments at all times. 'Speculative' units could cover interest commitments, but not all principal repayment, and thus needed to be able to roll over debt to survive. 'Ponzi' units could cover neither interest nor principal payments needed to borrow to meet interest commitments, and were reliant upon asset sales in a rising market to remain solvent. Changes in expectations over one business cycle lead to a shift in the fragility spectrum from 'hedge' in the aftermath to a preceding debt-induced crisis to 'speculative' in the recovery phase and 'Ponzi' in the boom, when 'euphoric expectations' (Minsky, 1969, p. 224) become widespread. On top of this within-cycle tendency towards increased financial fragility, there is a multi-cycle tendency for the level of private debt to grow faster than GDP (Keen, 1995, 2017), which increases the financial fragility of the entire economy over time, and which can culminate in a financial crisis like the Great Depression. Governments can attenuate this process by large deficits (Minsky, 1995, p. 205) that increase the net equity position of the entire private sector and reduce financial fragility.

STEVE KEEN

See also

Endogenous money; Financial instability hypothesis; Financial regulations; Money and banking; Neoclassical economics

STEVE KEEN / MARCELO MILAN

References

Agarwal, V., G.O. Aragon and Z. Shi (2018), 'Liquidity transformation and financial fragility: evidence from funds of hedge funds', *Journal of Financial and Quantitative Analysis*, **54** (6), 2355–81.
Bernanke, B. and M. Gertler (1990), 'Financial fragility and economic performance', *Quarterly Journal of Economics*, **105** (1), 87–114.
Bezemer, D. and M. Grydaki (2014), 'Financial fragility in the Great Moderation', *Journal of Banking and Finance*, **49** (C), 169–77.
Chick, V. (1997), 'Some reflections on financial fragility in banking and finance', *Journal of Economic Issues*, **31** (2), 535–41.
Douglas, W.D. and G.R. Raghuram (2001), 'Liquidity risk, liquidity creation, and financial fragility: a theory of banking', *Journal of Political Economy*, **109** (2), 287–327.
Gennaioli, N., A. Shleifer and R. Vishny (2012), 'Neglected risks, financial innovation, and financial fragility', *Journal of Financial Economics*, **104** (3), 452–68.
Keen, S. (1995), 'Finance and economic breakdown: modeling Minsky's 'financial instability hypothesis'', *Journal of Post Keynesian Economics*, **17** (4), 607–35.
Keen, S. (2017), *Can We Avoid Another Financial Crisis? (The Future of Capitalism)*, London: Polity Press.
McLeay, M., A. Radia and R. Thomas (2014), 'Money creation in the modern economy', *Bank of England Quarterly Bulletin*, **54** (1), 14–27.
Minsky, H.P. (1969), 'Private sector asset management and the effectiveness of monetary policy: theory and practice', *Journal of Finance*, **24** (2), 223–38.
Minsky, H.P. (1995), 'Financial factors in the economics of capitalism', in H.A. Benink (ed.), *Coping with Financial Fragility and Systemic Risk*, Boston: Kluwer Academic, pp. 3–14.
Mittnik, S. and W. Semmler (2018), 'Overleveraging, financial fragility, and the banking–macro link: theory and empirical evidence', *Macroeconomic Dynamics*, **22** (1), 4–32.
Nishi, H. (2019), 'An empirical contribution to Minsky's financial fragility: evidence from non-financial sectors in Japan', *Cambridge Journal of Economics*, **43** (3), 585–622.

Financial innovations

Financial innovations, understood as the introduction of new financial products or business practices by existing or new financial institutions, have been a remarkable feature of advanced capitalist economies. In post-Keynesian economics, these innovations have been dealt with mainly in terms of their macroeconomic impacts. The most important issues discussed are the consequences for monetary policy, followed by the effects on financial instability and capital accumulation.

Regarding the consequences for monetary policy, early post-Keynesian economists discussed financial innovations relative to the ability of monetary authorities to target a given stock of money (Minsky, 1957; Rousseas, 1960, 1984). According to them, the 1950s and 1960s saw the introduction of one innovation in the US money market, namely the federal funds, which, it is argued, affected the implementation of monetary policy: according to Minsky (1957), the federal funds provided banks with the ability to expand deposits above banks' reserves supplied by the Federal Reserve (Fed). Further, repurchase agreements, that is, the ability to revert the initial deal with the Fed, enabled banks to loan out more funds for a given amount of deposits. Thus, banks could inject more liquidity into the economy regardless of the willingness of the central bank. Later, the introduction of time deposits and certificates of deposits as a form of liability management by US banks represented a major burden on the Fed, since the deposits were no longer the only relevant option for raising funds.

In the real world, monetary policy operates by targeting a short-term policy rate of interest, not monetary aggregates. Hence, if central banks target a higher interest rate when demand for credit goes up, it first causes idle balances to become active (dis-hoarding), and, therefore, it affects the velocity of circulation of any given money stock, making it impossible for the Fed to control monetary aggregates and the corresponding expenditures. Also, once the process of dis-hoarding is complete, additional restrictive policies will incentivize innovations, that is, the creation of new liquid assets, altering the financial structure, this time shifting the velocity of money, not just moving along the same velocity function, and thus affecting the capacity of monetary policy to influence portfolio decisions (wealth composition) regarding liquid assets, and also the ability to control lending by making it more expensive.

Post-Keynesian structuralists have mostly dealt with financial innovations. Their focus on velocity is relevant, since it is related to liquidity conditions and, therefore, the relationship between the flow of effective demand and the stock of old and new liquid assets. Horizontalists' approach has received less attention. For instance, Rochon (1999) claims that the process of financial innovation emphasized by structuralists like Minsky is considered from a very long-run perspective. This is an important point. If liquidity changes induced by the endogenous supply of credit happen continuously, discrete financial innovations are insufficient to highlight a central feature of modern monetary economies.

Besides central bank interest-rate setting, financial regulation in general, like constraints on the size and composition of assets and liabilities, has been identified as a major incentive for the introduction of financial innovations (Skott, 1995). For example, if regulations require financial institutions to keep a given leverage ratio, the latter may start developing off-balance sheet transactions to circumvent the norm.

Regarding the second impact, by tapping pools of idle funds, that is, wealth kept in the form of illiquid assets, to make credit available to firms by turning them into liquid or tradable ones, in addition to the ability of banks to create credit *ex nihilo*, financial innovations allow more debt to be held, leading to a movement from 'hedge' to 'speculative' or 'Ponzi' positions, increasing the fragility of the whole economy (Carter, 1989). It could also inflate asset price bubbles. More recently, innovations in consumer credit allowed easier access to debt-financed spending by households, contributing to the financial crash of 2007–08 (Lavoie, 2015).

Financial innovations are also related to the paradox of liquidity: they apparently increase the liquidity of existing assets, but actually reduce it. Indeed, as the tradability of assets goes up, quasi-monies are created, enhancing the substitutability of liquid assets, causing previously less-liquid assets to become more liquid. This is the velocity effect stressed by Rousseas (1960, 1984). This boosted liquidity increases the likelihood of asset price bubbles. When the frenzy fuelled by credit disappears, these new liquid assets are quickly sold, causing their prices to plummet. Markets freeze, and what seemed to be liquid over the boom becomes illiquid during the bust. The paradox of risk shows how financial innovations intended to manage risks at the microeconomic level cause an increased systemic risk, since they create a false feeling of safety, given that the risk is not

MARCELO MILAN

reduced but only redistributed across many portfolios (Lavoie, 2015).

The consequences of financial innovations for capital accumulation have been considered neutral regarding the supply of finance (initial supply of liquidity for investment plans) and funding (matching the maturity of financial obligations and the real assets purchased). Yet, they have an impact on the types of financial institutions and instruments, such as the shrinking difference between short- and long-term securities, or the disappearing segmentation of the banking sector as it evolves into a universal form. In this regard, globalization has caused financial markets to become more homogeneous in terms of institutions and practices. Securitization has provided another source of finance and funding, causing traditional banks to lose room as providers of short-term liquidity. Finally, the appearance of institutional investors has provided long-term funding opportunities (Skott, 1995; Carvalho, 1997).

Summing up, financial innovations change the liquidity of existing assets or introduce new liquid assets, with major consequences for the structure of the financial system and therefore for monetary policy, given the creation of new financial institutions, or with existing institutions introducing them by changing the scope of their business and enhancing competition for profits. Since the transaction velocity of different assets is modified in the process, the overall liquidity and its distribution are also transformed. As an outcome, monetary policy is furthered challenged in its already asymmetric ineffectiveness to stabilize the trajectory of the economy, and the latter tends to become more unstable owing to the very financial innovations introduced to avoid the consequences of interest rate changes and/or existing financial regulations.

MARCELO MILAN

See also

Effective demand; Financial crises; Financial liberalization; Financial regulations; Monetary policy

References

Carter, M. (1989), 'Financial innovation and financial fragility', *Journal of Economic Issues*, **23** (3), 779–93.

Carvalho, F.J.C. (1997), 'Financial innovation and the post Keynesian approach to the "Process of capital formation"', *Journal of Post Keynesian Economics*, **19** (3), 461–87.

Lavoie, M. (2015), *Post-Keynesian Economics: New Foundations*, Cheltenham, UK, and Northampton, MA, USA: Edward Elgar.

Minsky, H.P. (1957), 'Central banking and money market changes', *Quarterly Journal of Economics*, **71** (2), 171–87.

Rochon, L.-P. (1999), *Credit, Money and Production: An Alternative Post-Keynesian Approach*, Cheltenham, UK, and Northampton, MA, USA: Edward Elgar.

Rousseas, S. (1960), 'Velocity changes and the effectiveness of monetary policy, 1951–57', *Review of Economics and Statistics*, **42** (1), 27–36.

Rousseas, S. (1984), 'Financial innovation and control of the money supply: the Radcliffe Report revisited', in M. Jarsulic (ed.), *Money and Macro Policy*, Dordrecht: Kluwer-Nijhoff Publishing, pp. 47–61.

Skott, P. (1995), 'Financial innovation, deregulation and Minsky cycles', in G. Epstein and H. Gintis (eds), *Macroeconomic Policy after the Conservative Era: Studies in Investment, Saving and Finance*, Cambridge, UK: Cambridge University Press, pp. 255–73.

Financial instability hypothesis

Developed by Minsky (1982, 1986), the financial instability hypothesis seeks to explain the recurrence of financial crises in modern capitalist systems, in which crises can arise endogenously. It contrasts with more conventional explanations that rely on exogenous shocks. For Minsky (1982), stability is 'destabilizing', as periods of economic expansion will tend to encourage economic agents to engage in behaviour that will increase the fragility of the economy and possibly result in a financial crisis. The financial instability hypothesis thus states that modern capitalist systems are inherently unstable.

Minsky's (1982, 1986) framework is steeped in the post-Keynesian tradition. From the perspective of financial markets, Minsky argues, the economy can essentially be seen as a world of money claims distributed over time, supported by the cash flow generated by households, government, and businesses. Of these, business debt holds a central importance and Minsky (1982, 1986) makes it the centrepiece of his analysis. In the process, he takes full account of the fundamentally uncertain nature of the future, the fact that modern capitalist economies are denominated in money, and the unidirectional flow of time, which implies that investments may be irreversible and assets hard to liquidate in case of financial strain.

Debts are incurred and credit bestowed on the expectation that businesses will earn enough receipts over costs to be able to service them. For the economy as a whole, these expectations are validated if price and output levels are such that enough firms are in a position to fulfil gross payments and refinance their debts. However, the level of funds available in the economy depends on investment, so that firms' ability to support their current liability structure depends on expectations about the future, notably about future investment. In Minsky's (1982, p. 65) words, 'the ability to debt-finance new investment depends upon expectations that future investment will be high enough so that future cash flows will be large enough for the debts that are issued today to be repaid or refinanced.' Under fundamental uncertainty, expectations about future investment or the evaluation of different debt structures will necessarily be subjective, which creates systemic instability.

Minsky (1982) argues that expectations are pro-cyclical, with a certain inertia in the upswing. This amounts to saying that, from being relatively or even overly prudent after a crash, agents will become increasingly optimistic as an economic expansion proceeds. Business will also start to pick up, allowing some of the bolder firms to prosper. The safety margins put in place after the crash will gradually be seen as being overly cautious, leading to an increase in investment as well as in leverage ratios. Increases in investment demand will then further feed the expansion and possibly generate a boom economy. Minsky also argues that this could be reinforced by a propensity to make financial innovations during a boom. Shortly put, tranquillity on financial markets will induce increasing amounts of risk-taking, which will make the system more fragile and undermine its stability. In this regard, Minsky (1982) differentiates three broad types of financing positions: 'hedge finance' (receipts are higher than debt commitments and financing costs), 'speculative finance' (receipts are higher than financing costs, but not enough to cover principal), and 'Ponzi finance' (receipts are not enough to cover financing costs). He then argues that there is a tendency for the proportion of firms in speculative or Ponzi positions to increase as the expansion proceeds, increasing thereby systemic fragility.

While increased risk-taking on the part of investors can fuel an economic expansion for a while, it can also trigger dynamics leading to its own demise. As an example, Minsky (1982) outlines a possible endogenous process whereby the boom could end. Increases in investment and the concomitant demand for financing may lead to increase in interest rates, either because the financing curve is not perfectly elastic or because inflationary pressures resulting from the boom trigger interest rate increases by the central bank. Some firms may then start experiencing trouble in making payments, putting some strain on creditors and leading the latter to put pressure on other firms if they start recalling some loans. At the same time, expectations may start shifting and some creditors could become reluctant to refinance debts that were typically rolled over. Building pressure may eventually lead to a crisis, especially if there is a sudden reversal of expectations by a large subset of individuals.

MATHIEU DUFOUR

See also

Financial crises; Financial fragility; Financial innovations; *Stabilizing an Unstable Economy*; Uncertainty

References

Minsky, H.P. (1982), *Can 'It' Happen Again? Essays on Instability and Finance*, Armonk, NY: M.E. Sharpe.

Minsky, H.P. (1986), *Stabilizing an Unstable Economy*, New Haven, CT: Yale University Press.

Financial liberalization

Financial liberalization emerged as a policy recommendation during the 1980s and 1990s against the regulated financial regime that prevailed during the 1950s and 1960s. In the post-World War II era of reconstruction and development, interest rates were set by the government at administered low levels and credit was allocated to priority sectors to boost economic development. However, stagflation during the 1970s gave rise to a critique against these policies that took the form of the McKinnon–Shaw model of financial repression and liberalization.

According to this model, in a 'savings causing investment' framework, the problem becomes how households allocate their savings between bank deposits and 'unproductive assets' such as cash, gold, or land. When the government imposes ceilings on deposit rates of interest keeping them below their equilibrium levels, savings are diverted from bank deposits to 'unproductive assets', thereby decreasing investment financing. Further, ceilings on loan rates of interest threaten banks' financial viability, whilst government subsidies on these rates perpetuate a vicious circle of failed firms and increased subsidies without any significant effect on economic development. Therefore, the main policy recommendation is to increase real interest rates in order to reach their higher equilibrium levels. Then, the 'savings causing investment' argument predicts reallocation of portfolios in favour of deposits, a rise in bank loans and a concomitant rise in investment expenditure (Fry, 1995, pp. 24–6).

New structuralists (Van Wijnbergen, 1982, 1983; Taylor, 1983) challenged the McKinnon–Shaw argument because the latter disregards the existence of curb money markets in developing economies. These markets are both an alternative to deposits and 'unproductive assets' as outlets for savings, and an alternative source of financing for firms that are unable to obtain a bank loan. Hence, the curb market rate clears the credit market and enters the supply function as a cost of financing working capital. Hence, the combined demand and supply effects of restrictive monetary policy during financial liberalization might lead to stagflation rather than economic growth.

Financial liberalization programmes in developing economies during the 1980s and 1990s raised issues of financial instability and banking crises along with concerns about the necessary institutional development and regulation of the financial system. Besides, starting from 1989, financial liberalization policies constitute an indispensable part of the 'Washington Consensus' promoted by the International Monetary Fund (IMF) and the World Bank as a policy prescription for developing countries.

The above developments gave rise to a more comprehensive critique of the financial repression and liberalization thesis emerging from a post-Keynesian institutional perspective (Arestis, 2005; Arestis and Stein, 2005; Marangos and Whalen, 2011). This critique is articulated in four major points. First, as interest rates rise, the effects of adverse selection or moral hazard due to banks' excessive risk-taking call for financial regulation. This is more so within a fundamentally uncertain environment wherein financial innovation invites financial instability. The East-Asian crisis of the 1990s was an example of how financial liberalization increased Minskian financial fragility. A second point is that the McKinnon–Shaw model is deeply rooted in a distorted saving–investment causality. However, if the causality runs from investment to saving, and within banks' balance sheets from loans to deposits, higher real interest rates can only discourage investment, reduce income and hence decrease savings. In addition, the McKinnon–Shaw model disregards the significance of stock markets despite their role in destabilizing international short-run capital flows and the fact that their development is considered to be a condition for financial liberalization programmes sponsored by the IMF and the World Bank. Finally, the institutions-augmented Washington Consensus cannot provide a remedy to the defects of the original model so long as one-size-fits-all recipes for institutional reforms cannot account for different institutional and cultural backgrounds that condition the way economic agents behave and respond to reforms within a fundamentally uncertain environment (Loizos, 2018).

KONSTANTINOS LOIZOS

See also

Financial crises; Financial fragility; Financial instability hypothesis; Financial regulations; Uncertainty

References

Arestis, P. (2005), 'Washington Consensus and financial liberalization', *Journal of Post Keynesian Economics*, **27** (2), 251–71.

Arestis, P. and H. Stein (2005), 'An institutional perspective to finance and development as an alternative to financial liberalisation', *International Review of Applied Economics*, **19** (4), 381–98.

Fry, M.J. (1995), *Money, Interest and Banking in Economic Development*, second edition, Baltimore: Johns Hopkins University Press.

Loizos, K. (2018), 'The financial repression–liberalization debate: taking stock, looking for a

synthesis', *Journal of Economic Surveys*, **32** (2), 440–68.
Marangos, J. and C.J. Whalen (2011), 'Evolution without fundamental change: the Washington Consensus on economic development and its significance for post-Keynesian institutionalism', in C.J. Whalen (ed.), *Financial Instability and Economic Security after the Great Recession*, Cheltenham, UK, and Northampton, MA, USA: Edward Elgar, pp. 153–78.
Taylor, L. (1983), *Structuralist Macroeconomics: Applicable Models for the Third World*, New York: Basic Books.
Van Wijnbergen, S. (1982), 'Stagflationary effects of monetary stabilization policies: a quantitative analysis of South Korea', *Journal of Development Economics*, **10** (2), 133–69.
Van Wijnbergen, S. (1983), 'Interest rate management in LDC's', *Journal of Monetary Economics*, **12** (3), 433–52.

Financial macroeconomics

Financial macroeconomics is the study of the national and international financial system. It is particularly interested in the interactions between real variables (production, employment, investment, consumption and so on) and financial variables (such as interest rates, credits, securities, exchange rates). To understand financial macroeconomics, it is first helpful to consider the mechanisms underlying the financial growth regime. In a second step, one should focus on the macroeconomic effects of financial integration. Finally, the influence of monetary variables must be taken into account.

Since the Fordist crisis, finance has taken an increasingly important place in the economy. As Boyer (2000) points out, a finance-led accumulation regime is possible but may prove unstable in the event of a reversal of confidence in financial markets. As a matter of fact, the development of financial markets has significantly altered macroeconomic dynamics. In a regime of financialized economic growth, consumption and investment can be stimulated despite stagnant wages. The provision of credit to households by stimulating consumption, demand for real estate and demand for equities can drive up house prices and equities, leading to wealth and capital-gains effects on consumption. The credit supply can also be favoured for households and companies with an increasing value of financial and real-estate assets that can be used as collateral for the credit granted. In the most favourable cases, the higher demand for goods and services will lead to an increase in the rate of production capacity utilization and in the profit rate, which will stimulate business investment. In a financialized system, however, corporate profits will not only be used to finance productive investment. Companies will tend to distribute dividends and favour financial accumulation (notably, share buy-backs, mergers and acquisitions, increased cash flow). Unlike the Fordist regime, the financialized regime is characterized by a disconnection between profit and investment (Cordonnier and Van de Velde, 2015). The excessive supply of credit as well as the increase in risk-taking in line with the increase in asset returns will encourage financial instability and the recurrence of financial crises. A rise in interest rates will create tensions on both real-estate and equity markets that could lead to a systemic financial crisis as experienced in the United States in 2007.

Financial macroeconomics also focuses on international financial trade and gross financial positions. The 2008 global financial crisis showed that capital flows were much larger between the United States and Europe than between the United States and Asia (Borio and Disyatat, 2011). The analysis of the international financial assets and liabilities of economic agents makes it possible to measure the diffusion effects of a crisis at the international level. Given the close link between European banks and the US financial system, the financial crisis will then spread to European banks with a magnitude proportional to the gross positions vis-à-vis the United States. Banks that have accumulated assets whose value has fallen sharply will be in difficulty, particularly if their external debt is high, especially for banks indebted in foreign currencies and whose domestic currency has depreciated. Banks' solvency problems are transferred to the State if the latter recapitalizes them. The private-debt crisis gives rise thereby to a public-debt crisis if the State pursues a counter-cyclical policy to emerge from the recession.

While greater financial integration can be a vehicle for spreading crises, it can also, in theory, allow risks to be shared. The international diversification of portfolios could absorb an asymmetric shock through the holding of financial securities and international credit. A country affected by a decline in domestic income may benefit from external income (dividends and interest) received from other countries as well as foreign loans that will smooth domestic income and stabilize consumption and GDP. In the case of the United States this mechanism appears insufficient to smooth personal income distribution, especially during the 2009 recession when capital income proved pro-cyclical (Duwicquet and Farvaque, 2018).

Monetary policy plays an important role in terms of financial stability. The level of central banks' interest rates and their diffusion to other interest rates, asset prices and exchange rates have important effects on the financial system. Lower interest rates will also boost the supply of credit and the prices of both financial and real-estate assets. In a situation of low interest rates and insufficient demand on the market for produced goods and services, companies will seek to reduce their equity supply and go into debt to invest in both real-estate and financial markets, inducing higher asset prices. Monetary policy can cause bubbles or financial instability in a framework of internationalization of financial exchanges. The US financial cycle can have an impact on gross international capital flows and lead to capital outflows to emerging countries that can lead to a currency crisis. The exchange rate is also the subject of numerous studies in financial macroeconomics. An exchange rate that is not adapted to the fundamentals of the economy can lead to significant misalignments (undervalued currency for some countries and overvalued for others). An overvalued currency will penalize exports and encourage imports, which will worsen the trade balance, reduce industry's share of value added and increase unemployment. As Davidson (1999, p. 65) points out, '[t]o reduce entrepreneurial uncertainties and the possibility of massive currency misalignments in any fixed exchange rate system, Keynes recommended the adoption of a fixed, but adjustable, exchange rate system.'

The euro appears to be overvalued for the southern countries of the euro area (including France) and undervalued for the northern countries (particularly Germany). These exchange rate misalignments are partly responsible for the differences in the level of public debt and employment between euro-area countries. The 'quantitative easing' policy carried out by the European Central Bank from 2015 onwards has made it possible to reduce interest rates on government securities and on loans to businesses and households, thereby reducing the debt burden. Similarly, the depreciation of the euro in real terms allows the euro area as a whole to generate trade surpluses. Despite these favourable financial factors, the euro area still suffers from insufficient aggregate demand at the time of writing (March 2021). The implementation of a fiscal stimulus oriented towards ecological transition could be supported by the issuance of Eurobonds.

VINCENT DUWICQUET

See also

Financial crises; Financial fragility; Financial instability hypothesis; Financialization; Profit

References

Borio, C. and P. Disyatat (2011), 'Global imbalances and the financial crisis: link or no link?', *Bank for International Settlements Working Paper*, No. 346.
Boyer, R. (2000), 'Is a finance-led growth regime a viable alternative to Fordism? A preliminary analysis', *Economy and Society*, **29** (1), 111–45.
Cordonnier, L. and F. Van de Velde (2015), 'The demands of finance and the glass ceiling of profit without investment', *Cambridge Journal of Economics*, **39** (3), 871–85.
Davidson, L. (ed.) (1999), *The Collected Writings of Paul Davidson, Volume 3: Uncertainty, International Money, Employment and Theory*, London and Basingstoke: Macmillan.
Duwicquet, V. and E. Farvaque (2018), 'US interstate risk sharing: a post-crisis examination', *Pacific Economic Review*, **23** (2), 296–308.

Financial regulations

Financial regulations have always been designed according to the institutional features of financial systems. Historically, the first form of financial regulation aimed at controlling the excessive expansion of means of payments. In a system based on a precious metal, the excessive expansion of means of payments could threaten the convertibility of paper money into gold or other metals. Restrictions in the issue of banknotes were therefore imposed in many countries. Yet, financial innovation was successfully used to circumvent regulation. In monetary systems without gold and with a central bank, financial regulations tried to limit the expansion of loans and deposits to a multiple of reserves. Reserves, however, were not binding, as in periods of economic growth the expansion of loans and deposits of all banks taken jointly would occur without any lack of reserves for the banking system as a whole. In the downward phase of the business cycle, the central bank accommodated the demand for reserves by banks to avoid a depression.

In the period after World War II up to the 1970s, financial regulations became a tool not so much to reduce the expansion of means of payments but rather to steer the industrial development of countries. Since the 1929 financial crisis very important regulations had been introduced, such as the bank deposit insurance and limits to free competition in the United States, the separation between commercial and investment banks, and a series of institutions (banks as well as corporations) financed by the State through injection of central bank reserves or capital, whose task was to pursue a public purpose – be it the economic development of an otherwise lagging-behind country or the expansion of a particular industrial sector. For example, public-owned banks and corporations were an important economic policy tool for reconstruction after the disasters of war for many European and Asian countries. Banks were therefore constrained in the setting of their interest rates on loans as well as in the volumes lent through direct credit controls. The State controlled thereby both the credit supply and the cost of credit.

From the 1980s onwards, this type of regulation was dismantled. Financial liberalization was either autonomously pursued or imposed as a condition for receiving foreign loans. The consequences were higher interest rates and credit bubbles, which often morphed into financial crises. Then an international regulation of banks was attempted through a transnational organization, namely the Basel Committee for Banking Supervision (BCBS). The rules designed by it were based on new fashionable techniques for the calculation of risk. Their main goal was to constrain the banks' assumption of risk and to avoid thereby financial crises. Capital rules were in the first version quite roughly designed with a simple classification of assets into risk grades. In the successive versions of Basel (II and III) regulation, the proportion of capital to assets was prescribed in a more modular way to improve the correctness of the weights attached to assets. The weights were calculated according to the standard deviation of the assets' price from an historical average. The risk was seen as a characteristic of assets rather than depending on the institutional design of markets and on the behaviour of agents operating in them. The result was an enormous expansion of the banking and financial sector with respect to any measure of real economic activity and a huge financial crisis. In fact, risk weights could be easily gamed by banks and the regulation itself provided avenues for elusion. For example, the risk of assets could be stripped by entering into derivatives contracts. This gave extraordinary impulse to the derivatives markets. The global financial crisis of 2007–08 revealed how mistaken was the idea of calculating risks with statistical metrics and cancelling them through derivatives. Yet, after the crisis, in the overhaul of regulation designed by the BCBS, the same basic principles were maintained while some new measures, such as the liquidity coverage ratio and the leverage ratio, were added with the aim to constrain the composition of assets and liabilities and to reduce the size of banks' balance sheets (Basel Committee for Banking Supervision, 2013; Tropeano, 2018, pp. 55–78). This contributed to a reduction of leverage in the banking sector. At the same time, non-bank financial institutions (NBFIs) continued to expand and to increase their ties to banks; some NBFIs, the cash-rich ones, increasingly contributed to the funding of banks, while other NBFIs, the leveraged ones, borrowed from them (Aldasoro et al., 2020). This occurred both at the domestic level and across countries' borders. Most of these transactions were denominated in US dollars. The Covid-19 pandemic crisis is again causing liquidity problems and will probably cause solvency problems in the future in a framework in which leverage is still high and debt is higher than in 2007.

DOMENICA TROPEANO

See also

Basel Agreements; Financial crises; Financial fragility; Financial instability hypothesis; Financial liberalization

References

Aldasoro I., W. Huang and E. Kemp (2020), 'Cross-border links between banks and non-bank financial institutions', *Bank for International Settlements Quarterly Review*, September 2020, pp. 61–74, available at https://www.bis.org/publ/qtrpdf/r_qt2009e.pdf (last accessed 8 February 2021).

Basel Committee on Banking Supervision (2013), *Basel III: The Liquidity Coverage Ratio and Liquidity Risk Monitoring Tools*, Basel: Bank for International Settlements, available at https://www.bis.org/publ/bcbs238.pdf (last accessed 8 February 2021).

Tropeano, D. (2018), *Financial Regulation in the European Union After the Crisis: A Minskian Approach*, London and New York: Routledge.

Financial risk

Mainstream microeconomic theory posits that agents are able to assign numerical probabilities to a complete set of potential future economic outcomes. Financial risk, therefore, is defined as the variance of these distributions. Such a conception of risk is key to the neoclassical claim that markets will price risk accurately, and financial risk management tools such as Value-at-Risk are embodiments of this theory (Lockwood, 2015).

Post-Keynesian economists have argued that this definition of financial risk overstates the certainty with which agents can predict future outcomes. These critiques are based in the distinction between risk and uncertainty introduced by Keynes (1937) and Knight (1921). Keynes (1937) disputes the idea that all outcomes can be assigned a numerical probability. For events such as 'the prospect of a European war ... or the price of copper and the rate of interest twenty years hence', he argues 'there is no scientific basis on which to form any calculable probability whatever' (Keynes, 1937, p. 214).

Based on this critique, the financial risk associated with many long-term investments cannot be described probabilistically (Davidson, 1991). Moreover, the mainstream treatment of risk combined with the assumption of rational expectations eliminates most sources of actual financial risk. Glickman (1997) criticizes the Modigliani–Miller theorem for suggesting that bankruptcy can only result from a chance series of poor outcomes for an 'otherwise sound' firm. By assumption, incorrect expectations cannot be a source of insolvency.

Scepticism about agents' ability to calculate the risk of future economic events has led post-Keynesian economists to a series of alternative propositions about financial risk. First, both risk and uncertainty about those risks influence investment. To the extent that a firm can form expectations about future outcomes, its likelihood of investing will depend on its confidence that its expectations are accurate (Keynes, 1936).

Second, tolerance for risk is linked to banks' and firms' liquidity preference (Mott, 1985). This is made clear in Kalecki's (1937) principle of increasing risk as well as in more recent work (for instance Glickman, 1997). Given uncertainty, lenders and firms may be unable to calculate the risk of an investment, but they can assess their risk of incurring irreversible losses in the case of an adverse outcome. One result of this perspective on risk will be upper limits on firm leverage. Firms are aware that rising leverage makes them vulnerable to insolvency, and creditors fear that they will be unable to mitigate losses through the liquidation of assets in the case of a highly leveraged firm.

A major post-Keynesian innovation has been to link financial risk to macroeconomic stability, most notably in Hyman Minsky's (1982) financial instability hypothesis. Minsky argues that agents' tolerance for leverage and therefore risk will rise when economic prospects are good. In line with Keynes's (1937) description of decision-making under uncertainty, firms that experience protracted prosperity and undertake many successful investments are likely to predict that this current success will continue. Such optimism encourages firms to reduce their margin of safety by increasing leverage and prompts the deregulation of financial activities.

As the most highly leveraged firms begin to show signs of financial vulnerability, the supply of credit to these firms will diminish, and a rise in interest rates or reduction in income flows will result in their insolvency. Because firms and lenders are interconnected by their financial obligations, the result will be a widespread financial crisis. Debt holders will seek to liquidate assets to repay their debt, prompting a 'debt-deflationary process' of falling asset prices and reduced investment spending.

The 2008 global financial crisis can be seen as an illustration of post-Keynesian notions of financial risk. Firms and lenders took on more financial risk by increasing leverage, emboldened by widespread economic optimism and financial innovations. Meanwhile, in line with post-Keynesian critiques regarding uncertainty, probabilistic financial risk measures failed to predict the crisis (Lockwood, 2015).

MELANIE G. LONG

See also

Debt deflation; Financial crises; Financial instability hypothesis; Liquidity preference; Principle of increasing risk

References

Davidson, P. (1991), 'Is probability theory relevant for uncertainty? A Post-Keynesian perspective', *Journal of Economic Perspectives*, **5** (1), 129–43.
Glickman, M. (1997), 'A Post Keynesian refutation of Modigliani–Miller on capital structure', *Journal of Post Keynesian Economics*, **20** (2), 251–74.
Kalecki, M. (1937), 'The principle of increasing risk', *Economica*, **4** (16), 440–7.
Keynes, J.M. (1936), *The General Theory of Employment, Interest, and Money*. London: Macmillan.
Keynes, J.M. (1937), 'The general theory of employment', *Quarterly Journal of Economics*, **51** (2), 209–23.
Knight, F.H. (1921), *Risk, Uncertainty and Profit*, New York: Hart, Schafner, and Marx.
Lockwood, E. (2015), 'Predicting the unpredictable: Value-at-Risk, performativity, and the politics of financial uncertainty', *Review of International Political Economy*, **22** (4), 719–56.
Minsky, H.P. (1982), *Can 'It' Happen Again? Essays on Instability and Finance*, Abingdon-on-Thames, UK: Routledge.
Mott, T. (1985), 'Towards a Post-Keynesian formulation of liquidity preference', *Journal of Post Keynesian Economics*, **8** (2), 222–32.

Financial sectoral balances

Financial sectoral balances refer to a national account identity indicating that the net lending or net borrowing positions of all institutional sectors of an economy always sum up to zero. The net lending or net borrowing position for each institutional sector is retrieved once gross capital formation and capital transfers, including capital taxes, are added on the current account balance. In the case of the general government sector, its net lending or net borrowing position reflects the fiscal surplus or deficit, while in the case of the external sector the net lending or net borrowing position is the reverse of the balance of payments. In this respect, the identity could be expressed as follows:

$$NL_h + NL_{nf} + NL_b + FB - BoP = 0 \quad (1)$$

in which NL is the net lending or net borrowing position, FB is the fiscal budget (either a deficit or a surplus), and BoP is the balance of payments, while the subscripts h, nf, and b represent households, non-financial corporations, and financial corporations respectively. Identity (1) states that in order for one sector to record a surplus, or to hold a net lending position, the other sectors ought to jointly list a deficit, or a net borrowing position.

In post-Keynesian literature, the implications of this relation are critically correlated with the demand and growth regime of the economy. If the private sector and in particular households record a deficit and the external sector a surplus, the economy is characterized as debt-led. Internal demand is driven by private debt, with international trade having a negative contribution to economic growth (Dodig et al., 2016). On the contrary, a persistent surplus in the balance of payments, as well as in the balance of all domestic sectors, indicates that economic growth relies heavily on the export performance of the economy, thus the latter is considered as export-led. Finally, a surplus for the household sector, a balance-of-payments deficit, and negative values in the balance of corporations and the general government sector imply that demand is driven mostly by public spending and investment activity. Thereby, the growth regime of the economy is domestically demand-led.

Nonetheless, financial sectoral balances have equally important fiscal and trade policy implications. Aggregating the private sector into one institutional unit yields:

$$NAFA = BoP - FB \quad (2)$$

where $NAFA$ is the net acquisition of financial assets by the private sector. Equation (2) shows that the accumulation of financial wealth by the private sector critically depends on the balance of payments and the fiscal budget. In the presence of either a surplus vis-à-vis the external sector or a fiscal deficit, the private sector becomes wealthier and vice versa.

The causality between these three variables is controversial. In mainstream economic thinking, the assumption of the loanable funds theory indicates that a fiscal deficit would likely absorb funds from the private sector in order to finance the deficit generating an external deficit. On the contrary, in the post-Keynesian domain, and in particular in the Stock–Flow Consistent (SFC) methodology and the Modern Money Theory (MMT), the causality is utterly different.

In the SFC approach, pioneered by the work of Godley (1999), financial sectoral balances serve as the ultimate tool in detecting macro-financial instability. A prolonged period of dissipation of private sector wealth, for instance when the NAFA is negative, implies that the economy is unstable and a recession is looming. This is precisely the mechanism that allowed SFC practitioners to detect *ex- ante* the Great Recession (Bezemer, 2010). In this framework, fiscal deficit has a stabilizing role for the economy. Its impact is constrained by the structural competitiveness of the economy and the willingness of the private sector to hold public sector liabilities (Godley, 1999).

With regards to the first constraint, in an import-oriented economy the fiscal deficit ought to exceed the deficit in the balance of payments in order to ensure the wealth accumulation of the private sector. Thereby, the causality runs from the balance of payments towards fiscal policy (Godley and Lavoie, 2007, Ch. 6). With respect to the second constraint, if the fiscal deficit exceeds the level of public liabilities the private sector is willing to hold, then the balance of payments deteriorates since interest on debt paid abroad increases substantially. In both cases, the stability of the macro-financial system becomes subject to the ability of the public sector to service its debt. In the MMT framework, the constraints are either resource related or depend on the currency in which the public sector liabilities have been issued (Wray, 2015).

CHRISTOS PIERROS

See also

Current accounts; Fiscal policy; Growth; Growth – wage-led vs profit-led; Twin deficits

References

Bezemer, D.J. (2010), 'Understanding financial crisis through accounting models', *Accounting, Organizations and Society*, **35** (7), 676–88.
Dodig, N., E. Hein and D. Detzer (2016), 'Financialisation and the financial and economic crises: theoretical framework and empirical analysis for 15 countries', in E. Hein, D. Detzer and N. Dodig (eds), *Financialisation and the Financial and Economic Crises*, Cheltenham, UK, and Northampton, MA, USA: Edward Elgar, pp. 1–41.
Godley, W. (1999), 'Seven unsustainable processes', *Jerome Levy Economics Institute of Bard College Special Report*, available at http://www.lev yinstitute.org/pubs/sr/sevenproc.pdf (last accessed 9 November 2020).
Godley, W. and M. Lavoie (2007), *Monetary Economics: An Integrated Approach to Credit, Money, Income, Production and Wealth*, Basingstoke and New York: Palgrave Macmillan.
Wray, L.R. (2015), *Modern Money Theory: A Primer on Macroeconomics for Sovereign Monetary Systems*, second edition, Basingstoke and New York: Palgrave Macmillan.

Financialization

Epstein (2005, p. 3) famously defined financialization as 'the increasing importance of financial markets, financial motives and financial institutions, and financial elites in the operation of the economy and its governing institutions'. Even if the definition of this expression lacks focus, post-Keynesian economists, almost universally, believe that 'financialization involves the replacement of industrial or production capitalism by a more predatory form of financial capitalism, or casino capitalism' (Rochon, 2012, p. 167). In this quote, Rochon obliquely draws on the post-Keynesian distinction between productive (that is, industrial) versus unproductive (that is, household) credit creation by the banking sector.

The structural break towards unproductive liquidity creation can be traced back to the early 1980s. A growing number of studies indicate that the stock of unproductive credit, such as household debt, exploded around that time. Bezemer (2012) notes a drastic increase in the household debt over GDP ratio: from a ratio of 2 in the 1950s and 1960s to more than 4 in the early 2000s. Bezemer and Hudson (2016), analysing a balanced sample of 14 OECD countries covering the period from 1990 to 2012, also point to the growing share of household mortgage in credit markets, rising from 20 per cent of total credits to over 50 per cent. The seeds of the Finance, Insurance and Real Estate (FIRE) sector were thus sown.

Within this period of financialization, Hudson (2010) estimates interest payments on mortgage loans accounted for 70 per cent of all interest payments in the United States, demonstrating the transformation of real estate to the financial sector's new favourite client. Yet, Bezemer et al. (2016) empirically prove that this gigantic mortgage credit wave has contributed negatively to the income growth of households. For post-Keynesian economists, the explanation of this economic phenomenon, and its implications, is straightforward.

The creation of unproductive liquidity in mortgage markets fails to induce growth in household income; rather, it contributes to increases in household debt stock. As a result, an ever-increasing component of disposable income goes to serve the increased interest payments towards the FIRE sector. This income transfer process gives rise to highly unequal societies, busying economic highbrows over the last decade. The result is a two-tiered rentier economy (Bezemer and Hudson, 2016).

Post-Keynesian economists have firmly established that expansion of unproductive credit, such as household mortgages, is positively correlated to the probability of crises. With the high household debt levels (serviced out of wages), even a marginal income reduction may escalate and lead to defaults. As a result, Stockhammer (2012, p. 62) notes that 'the fragility of the system has increased as the resilience of households against temporary shocks has decreased'. Thus, another by-product of financialization is the heightened fragility of the financial system.

Since the onset of financialization in the 1980s, the number of US banks has halved to about seven thousand in 2010, leading to increased bank asset concentration. In turn, this has made the sector more fragile by making a few too-big-to-fail banks. This development highlights the shift of importance of shadow banks (such as hedge funds) in the economy. Through their active collaboration and participation (along with originating banks) in financial engineering (that is, credit default swaps and securitization), theoretically 'de-risking' the latter by selling low-quality subprime mortgages to the former has also led to the increased fragility of the system, as Minsky (1977) hypothesized.

The enlargement of the FIRE sector 'burns' the real economy, and the Keynesian entrepreneurial economy wanes, whilst the fragility of the financial system increases, as does economic inequality. These are some of the current consequences of the financial sector's malformation and overdevelopment over the last four decades. Is it now time to reign in credit creators upon the sound principles of monetary production economy (Keynes, 1930)?

PLAMEN IVANOV

See also

Financial instability hypothesis; Liquidity preference; Monetary theory of production economy; Money and banking; Shadow banking – origins

References

Bezemer, D. (2012), *Creating a Socially Useful Financial System*, Address to the Institute for New Economic Thinking, Berlin, Germany, April 14.

Bezemer, D. and M. Hudson (2016), 'Finance is not the economy: reviving the conceptual distinction', *Journal of Economic Issues*, **50** (3), 745–68.

Bezemer, D., M. Grydaki and L. Zhang (2016), 'More mortgages, lower growth', *Economic Inquiry*, **54** (1), 652–74.

Epstein, G. (ed.) (2005), *Financialization and the World Economy*, Cheltenham, UK, and Northampton, MA, USA: Edward Elgar.

Hudson, M. (2010), 'The transition from industrial capitalism to a financialized bubble economy', *The Levy Institute of Economics Working Paper*, No. 627.

Keynes, J.M. (1930), *A Treatise on Money, Volume 2*, London: Macmillan.

Lavoie, M. (2012), 'Financialization, neo-liberalism, and securitization', *Journal of Post Keynesian Economics*, **35** (2), 215–33.

Minsky, H.P. (1977), 'The financial instability hypothesis: an interpretation of Keynes and an alternative to "standard" theory', *Nebraska Journal of Economics and Business*, **16** (1), 5–16.

Nersisyan, Y. and L.R. Wray (2010), 'The global financial crisis and the shift to shadow banking', *The Levy Economics Institute Working Paper*, No. 587.

Rochon, L.-P. (2012), 'Financialization and the theory of the monetary circuit: fiscal and monetary policies reconsidered', *Journal of Post Keynesian Economics*, **35** (2), 167–9.

Stockhammer, E. (2012), 'Financialization, income distribution and the crisis', *Investigación Económica*, **71** (279), 39–70.

Fiscal consolidation

Fiscal consolidation refers to policy measures adopted by governments intended to reduce fiscal deficits and accumulation of public debt. A government's fiscal deficit occurs when its spending exceeds its revenue from taxes, while fiscal surplus happens when government spending is less than its revenue from taxes. Key indicators identified for fiscal prudence include fiscal deficit and public debt as percentages of gross domestic product (GDP).

The purpose of a fiscal-consolidation strategy is to bring the cyclically adjusted primary budget to balance by gradually reducing the debt-to-GDP ratio over a given period of time. The primary budget is the government fiscal balance excluding its interest payments. The consolidation process is a period of fiscal adjustment whose duration is usually measured in terms of number of years, while the content of the process is determined by the proportions of the public deficit reduced by spending cuts or by revenue increases.

The fiscal reform pursued as part of a consolidation strategy consists of a combination of tax reforms, expenditure control, reforms in the management of public debt, and reduction in discretionary spending through reducing capital expenditure on public investment.

Fiscal consolidation spans several decades and countries around the world have adopted different forms of consolidation based on their fiscal position. The effects of consolidation depend on their design, composition (expenditure-based or tax-based – tax hikes versus spending cuts), the length of the consolidation, their consistency over time (that is, whether spending cuts are permanent or transitory), and the state of the economy.

Conventionally, fiscal-consolidation efforts are considered successful when expenditure cuts average more than 1.2 percent of GDP while successful revenue-based consolidations average around 1.1 percent of GDP. However, attempts to reduce public deficits with fiscal consolidation can have a long-lasting negative impact on the state of the economy, as it has been observed post-recession in 2008.

Most policymakers favour spending cuts in the consolidation strategy, as they believe that rising fiscal deficit is caused by government spending. However, data from the Bureau of Economic Analysis over a span of five decades show that government spending relative to GDP has been rather flat, and therefore rising government spending in the form of stimulus packages or transfer payments cannot be held responsible for increasing federal debt and deficit in the United States (Wray, 2019).

Further, the empirical evidence for the United States indicates that the collapse of tax revenues during recessions mainly contributed to the growth of public deficit and debt-to-GDP ratios in the post-war period (Wray, 2019). Tax revenues tend to be strongly pro-cyclical, meaning that they tend to increase during an economic expansion but fall sharply in a recession, while government spending is weakly counter-cyclical, implying that even though spending falls during an economic boom it does not rise much in bust. Thus, tendencies of strong pro-cyclicality of tax revenues and weak counter-cyclicality of government spending have caused fiscal deficits to rise sharply during recessions but not fall as sharply during expansions.

Empirical evidence (Fata and Summers, 2008; Russek and Kowalewski, 2015) also suggests that there is no determinate relationship between economic growth and public deficits. The size of these deficits increases when economic growth is below potential GDP while public deficit decreases when GDP growth is above potential. In the aftermath of the 2008 global financial crisis, countries around the world implemented fiscal-consolidation strategies primarily based on spending restraints aiming to reduce fiscal deficits and boost economic growth. Such consolidation paths as recommended by the International Monetary Fund for both advanced and emerging economies required: substantial reduction in government spending; deep cuts in wages, pensions, and social benefits; sharp increases in taxes or reduced tax concessions; increased property taxes, increased rates of value-added tax, increased worker social insurance contributions, phasing out subsidies, targeting social safety nets, labour market liberalizations; extensive privatization of public resources and State-owned assets; public sector layoffs and winding down of stimulus measures. These structural reforms during deep recessions proved to be detrimental for the recovery. Most advanced countries including the United States experienced a negative impact of this fiscal consolidation on their GDP growth rates and have not been able to return to the pre-crisis level of GDP growth with such a strategy. This trend is far more accentuated in European economies and, in particular, in Greece, which had a drastic cutback in government expenditures, especially health-care expenditures, thereby giving rise to significant increases in income inequality and unemployment.

Severe austerity measures embraced in the name of fiscal consolidation have not served well either developed or developing nations. Attempts to reduce public debt through fiscal consolidation have been self-defeating and led to higher public-debt-to-GDP ratio through their long-term negative impact on output. The purpose of fiscal consolidation, therefore, should not be targeted towards reducing public debt and deficit as percentages of GDP to an arbitrary chosen figure. Rather, it must be undertaken with an eye on its impact on the economy in terms of unemployment, inequality, and growth.

SHAKUNTALA DAS

See also

Financial crises; Fiscal deficits; Fiscal policy; Income distribution; Income multiplier

References

de Rugy, V. and J. Salmon (2020), 'Flattening the debt curve: empirical lessons for fiscal consolidation', *Mercatus Center George Mason University Research Paper*, available at https://www.mercatus.org/publications/government-spending/flattening-debt-curve-empirical-lessons-fiscal-consolidation (last accessed 1 February 2021).

Fata, A. and L.H. Summers (2008), 'The permanent effects of fiscal consolidations', *Journal of International Economics*, **112**, 238–50.

Russek, F. and K. Kowalewski (2015), 'How CBO estimates automatic stabilizers', *Congressional Budget Office Working Paper*, No. 2015-07.

Wray, L.R. (1998), *Understanding Modern Money: The Key to Full Employment and Price Stability*, Cheltenham, UK, and Northampton, MA, USA: Edward Elgar.

Wray, L.R. (2019), 'Congressional testimony: reexamining the economic costs of debt', hearing before the House Budget Committee, 20 November, Washington, available at http://www.levyinstitute.org/pubs/tst_11-20-19.pdf (last accessed 2 February 2021).

Fiscal deficits

The fiscal (budget) deficits of governments refer to the difference between government revenues (largely taxation) and expenditures (see Sawyer, 2021). Here we focus on deficits, but there can also be a budget surplus; as such many of the points made below would act in reverse in the case of the budget being in surplus rather than deficit.

Reference to government means the consolidated accounts of all tiers of government, recognizing that the central government often places limits on the spending and revenues of the lower tiers of government, and provides fiscal transfers to lower tiers. A central government has a particular relationship with the central bank acting as its bank and issuer of the currency, which lower tiers of government may not have.

Different measures of the budget deficit are used. A 'current deficit' is the difference between government current expenditure and revenues, whereas a 'primary deficit' is the difference between government current expenditures other than interest payments on debt and capital expenditure and tax revenue. There is also a 'total deficit' based on all government expenditures. Some have advocated a 'golden rule' for fiscal policy under which governments would borrow to fund capital expenditures but with current budgets on average in balance. A 'structural budget position' is one calculated from prevailing government expenditure plans and tax rates on the basis that the economy is operating at 'potential output'.

The essence of the post-Keynesian perspective comes from the sectoral balance equation, and the degree to which private demand is sufficient to ensure full employment (Arestis and Sawyer, 2004). The sectoral balance equation can be written as follows:

$$G - T \text{ (budget deficit)} = S - I \text{ (net private savings)} + M - X \text{ (current account deficit} = \text{capital account surplus)}$$

When the equation above is viewed as an accounting identity, it indicates that private agents' behaviour has an impact on the amount of the budget deficit. Let us undertake two thought experiments that differ in terms of the proposed level of government expenditure and tax rates: in a case where savings turn out to be relatively high, investment relatively low and capital inflow relatively large, then the budget deficit will turn out to be relatively larger. When there is perceived to be low private demand (which would be reflected in high savings, low investment, low net exports), then government should boost demand via its fiscal position through a combination of higher expenditures and lower tax rates. Indeed, the general post-Keynesian perspective would be that the purpose of fiscal policy and the intentions for budget deficit should be to balance the economy (that is, to strive for full employment; see Lerner, 1943, and Kalecki, 1944) rather than to balance the budget (sound finance). A budget deficit is required when there is the potential for private saving to exceed private investment, which means that funds for the budget deficit will become available, and indeed a budget deficit enables potential saving to be realized.

A balanced budget would involve the right-hand side in the sectoral balance equation above to be zero. Thus, if a balanced budget is to be realized, that condition would need to be satisfied. The post-Keynesian perspective is that in general that condition would not be satisfied. Indeed, it is found that, in general, governments run deficits, and public debt is cumulated deficits.

The sustainability of a fiscal deficit can be judged along the following lines. A total budget deficit of b relative to GDP maintained over time would lead to a public debt to GDP ratio of $d = b/g$, where g is the nominal GDP growth rate. A primary deficit relatively to GDP of b^* would lead to a debt ratio of $b^*/(g - r)$, where r is the rate of interest on government debt. Its sustainability would then require that $g > r$. There has been much discussion as to whether that condition typically holds. In any event, a small difference between the rate of economic growth and the interest rate would lead to a large debt ratio. A total budget deficit is the one relevant for aggregate demand purposes, though it should be noted that stabilization of the debt ratio would involve the primary budget position moving into surplus.

MALCOLM SAWYER

See also

Aggregate demand; Fiscal consolidation; Fiscal multiplier; Fiscal policy; Income multiplier

References

Arestis, P. and M. Sawyer (2004), 'Fiscal policy matters', *Public Finance*, **54** (3–4), 133–53.
Kalecki, M. (1944), 'Three ways to full employment', in Oxford University Institute of Statistics, *The Economics of Full Employment*, Oxford: Blackwell, pp. 39–58.
Lerner, A. (1943), 'Functional finance and the Federal debt', *Social Research*, **10** (1), 38–51.
Sawyer, M. (2021), 'The role of fiscal policy', in L.-P. Rochon and S. Rossi (eds), *An Introduction to Macroeconomics: A Heterodox Approach to Economic Analysis*, Cheltenham, UK, and Northampton, MA, USA: Edward Elgar, pp. 355–75.

Fiscal multiplier

The multiplier is the relationship that the Keynesian theory establishes between the aggregate demand components that are autonomous with respect to the income level and the equilibrium level of income. It is the reciprocal of the marginal propensity to save.

In a situation of less than full employment, the injection of new autonomous demand through an expansionary fiscal policy raises production to meet the higher demand. This leads to an equivalent increase in national income. The recipients of this additional income will increase consumer spending but to a lesser extent, due to saving. This will further increase production, income, consumption, and so on. Adding all these smaller and smaller increases, the cumulative change in the level of national income is such as to ensure that the dissaving of the public sector will be fully offset by an increase in savings from the private sector. Tax reductions generate a similar but minor effect, the ensuing increase in disposable income being partly saved in the very first round of the process. An analogous reasoning shows why the transfer payment multiplier is also smaller than the government spending multiplier. More generally, the size of tax and transfer multipliers depends on the marginal propensity to consume of those who pay taxes or benefit from transfers. Since the marginal propensity to consume decreases as income increases, the richer the transfer earner or the taxpayer, the smaller the transfer and tax multipliers.

Fiscal multipliers can be grouped into two categories, namely, 'crowding out' multipliers and 'crowding in' multipliers. In the first case, the strength of the multiplicative process is reduced, because the multiplier exerts a negative influence on investments that compensates in whole or in part the expansionary effects of public spending. Changes in interest rates are the main channel through which this replacement of private investment with public consumption could take place. In the second case, the growth of private consumption increases investment, so the expansionary action of private firms joins that of the government. The dependence of investments on the level of income and on the expectations of its future growth is the basis of this acceleration of the multiplicative process. The influence of foreign trade openness on the multiplier deserves a final consideration. To the extent that part of the income generated by fiscal expansion is spent abroad and not internally, the multiplier is reduced: in this situation, government spending dissipates some of its beneficial domestic effects, acting rather as a stimulus for the economy from which the flow of imports comes.

The size of fiscal policy multipliers is today at the centre of a bitter empirical debate. With the endless accumulation of empirical studies, however, the range of results has not narrowed, but has instead widened. Estimates of public spending multipliers vary between −3.8 and +3.8, while those of tax cut multipliers between −4.8 and +3.0 (see Van Brusselen, 2010). This vagueness stems from the fact that isolating the effect on national income of a change in government spending or taxes would involve knowing the change in income that would have occurred if the government had not changed spending or taxes. To construct the 'counterfactual' it is therefore necessary to resort to models. Three main models are used: macroeconometric forecasting models, time series models, and dynamic stochastic general equilibrium models. Each of them is based on different empirical testing strategies and different sets of hypotheses. But the key point is that the observed variety of fiscal multipliers is not just due to the different types of models. Even within the same class of models, the results are sensitive to methodological choices, data sets, behavioural assumptions, the period over which the multiplier is measured, and so on. While before 2008 it was widely believed that public spending multipliers in developed countries averaged about 0.5, starting from the global financial crisis that burst in 2008 a process of revision of this consensus has begun, which has led to values that even quadrupled that estimate (see, for example, Auerbach and Gorodnichenko, 2012). US policymakers refer to relatively high estimates, especially in periods of sharp contraction of economic activity (Reichling and Whalen, 2015). European policymakers favour much lower estimates, regardless of the economic situation, and have even gone so far as to seriously believe in the idea that public spending multipliers can be negative.

ALDO BARBA

See also

Aggregate demand; Crowding in and crowding out; Fiscal deficit; Fiscal policy; Income multiplier

References

Auerbach, A.J. and Y. Gorodnichenko (2012), 'Measuring the output responses to fiscal policy', *American Economic Journal: Economic Policy*, **4** (2), 1–27.

Reichling, F. and C.J. Whalen (2015), 'The fiscal multiplier and economic policy analysis in the United States', *Congressional Budget Office Working Paper*, 2015–02.

Van Brusselen, P. (2010), 'Fiscal stabilisation plans and the outlook for the world economy', in Banca d'Italia (ed.), *Fiscal Policy: Lessons from the Crisis*, Rome: Bank of Italy, pp. 257–76.

Fiscal policy

Fiscal policy amounts to deciding about government spending and collecting taxes. Governments may intervene in markets for allocational, distributional, or stabilization-related reasons. In order to perform the macroeconomic task of stabilizing an unstable economy in the short or long run, fiscal policy may be used in conjunction with monetary policies on the part of public authorities and wage policies on the part of private actors.

In order to dampen business cycle fluctuations in the short run and close lasting output gaps in the long run, fiscal policy needs to be able to stimulate aggregate demand in a controlled way, either by directly altering public spending or by indirectly manipulating private expenditure through tax variations. Assuming a situation of full employment, full capacity utilization, and an even balance between government spending and tax revenues, fiscal policy makes use of fiscal balances to ward off disturbances to such an equilibrium. This involves running a budgetary surplus in a business cycle upswing or in a situation where there is ongoing excess demand in relation to potential output, and running a budget deficit during a business cycle downturn or where there are lasting output gaps.

The fiscal policies adopted by governments may be adjusted to meet the requirements of the economic situation, that is, used on a discretionary basis, or they may follow a prescriptive numerical or behavioural rule. A numerical rule, such as a zero budget balance (a 'balanced budget'), is the most transparent and least flexible approach. A discretionary policy stance, meanwhile, ensures the highest level of flexibility, though at the cost of transparency and

ALDO BARBA / ARNE HEISE

credibility. A behavioural rule such as a fiscal Taylor rule (which aligns the fiscal balance with the output gap (see Taylor, 2000)) combines transparency and credibility with a certain degree of flexibility. Fiscal policy rules may be justified where we can assume a potential divergence between political rationality ('maximizing votes'), economic rationality ('maximizing welfare'), and strategic behaviour on the part of governments, particularly, but not exclusively, in small, open economies.

From a Post-Keynesian perspective, fiscal policy rules that aim to achieve full employment, price stability, and fiscal sustainability are based on the premise that a capitalist economy is not self-correcting, either in the short or long run. Such rules therefore cannot merely be designed to dampen business cycle fluctuations diverging from a full-employment, full-capacity-utilization trend, but must also address long-run problems of insufficient aggregate demand.

Perhaps the best-known Post-Keynesian behavioural fiscal policy rule is Abba Lerner's notion of 'functional finance' (as opposed to the 'sound finance' of the mainstream balanced budget rule (see Lerner, 1943)). The rule is based on three principles (see Colander, 2003): (1) that it is the government's task to maintain a certain level of aggregate demand to prevent deflationary pressures (deficient aggregate demand) and inflationary pressures (excess demand) – this is achieved by running a budget deficit or surplus of an appropriate size where necessary; (2) that it is the central bank's task to pursue a monetary policy that allows for a maximum level of private investment; (3) that if these rules conflict with mainstream principles of 'sound finance' and 'sound money', so much the worse for these principles.

The notion of 'functional finance' emphasizes the need to coordinate fiscal and monetary policy, yet neglects the role of wage policy within such macroeconomic coordination (see Heise, 2009, p. 396 ff.). Moreover, it is too broad a concept to serve as an administrative strategy. It nonetheless can be and has been developed (by John Maynard Keynes) to form the basis for 'capital budgeting' (see Keynes, 1943a, 1945), in which the public budget is split into a 'current budget' and a 'capital budget'. While the current budget consists of public consumption spending and needs to be structurally balanced, the capital budget consists of public investment expenditure and is financed through deficits. Its aim is to maintain overall investment demand on a par with full-employment savings across the business cycle: 'Thus capital budgeting is a method of maintaining equilibrium; the deficit budgeting is a means of attempting to cure disequilibrium if and when it arises' (Keynes, 1943b, pp. 352–3). Further, Keynes's conception of capital budgeting can be seen as a dynamically elaborated form of the classical golden rule of fiscal policy, which legitimizes public deficits as long as they are used for public investment spending.

Active Keynesian fiscal policy has experienced a resurgence in popularity in the wake of the global financial crisis that burst in 2008. Prior to this event, which mainstream economics did not expect to occur, most mainstream economists advocated non-Keynesian outcomes of active fiscal policy. On the basis of direct or indirect (to wit, rationally predicted) crowding-out effects (or Ricardian equivalence), such economists called into question the effectiveness of deficit spending (and rejected the harmful consequences of austerity measures). More recent empirical evidence, however, has even led the International Monetary Fund – a stronghold of mainstream economics – to acknowledge that errors had been made in this regard (see International Monetary Fund, 2012, p. 41 ff. and Blanchard and Leigh, 2013).

ARNE HEISE

See also

Aggregate demand; Fiscal deficit; Functional finance; Income multiplier; *Stabilizing an Unstable Economy*

References

Blanchard, O. and D. Leigh (2013), 'Growth forecast errors and fiscal multipliers', *International Monetary Fund Working Paper*, No. 13/1.
Colander, D. (2003), 'Functional finance, new classical economics and great-great grandsons', in E.J. Nell and M. Forstater (eds), *Reinventing Functional Finance: Transformational Growth and Full Employment*, Cheltenham, UK, and Northampton, MA, USA: Edward Elgar, pp. 35–51.
Heise, A. (2009), 'A Post Keynesian theory of economic policy – filling a void', *Journal of Post Keynesian Economics*, **31** (3), 383–401.
International Monetary Fund (2012), *World Economic Outlook October 2012: Coping with High Debt and Sluggish Growth*, Washington, DC: International Monetary Fund.

Keynes, J.M. (1943a), 'The long-term problem of full employment', in *The Collected Writings of John Maynard Keynes, Volume XXVII: Activities 1940–1946. Shaping the Post-War World: Employment and Commodities*, London: Macmillan, pp. 320–5.

Keynes, J.M. (1943b), 'Maintenance of employment: the draft note for the Chancellor of the Exchequer', in *The Collected Writings of John Maynard Keynes, Volume XXVII: Activities 1940–1946. Shaping the Post-War World: Employment and Commodities*, London: Macmillan, pp. 352–7.

Keynes, J.M. (1945), 'National debt inquiry: the concept of a capital budget (Memorandum by Lord Keynes)', in *The Collected Writings of John Maynard Keynes, Volume XXVII: Activities 1940–1946. Shaping the Post-War World: Employment and Commodities*, London: Macmillan, pp. 405–13.

Lerner, A. (1943), 'Functional finance and the Federal debt', *Social Research*, **10** (1), 38–51.

Taylor, J.B. (2000), 'Reassessing discretionary fiscal policy', *Journal of Economic Perspectives*, **14** (3), 21–36.

Foreign-exchange reserves

Foreign-exchange reserves – or international reserves (IR) – are foreign-currency denominated international liquid assets held by central banks. Typically, IR securities are denominated in what is known as reserve currencies – those most widely accepted for payment in international trade and finance transactions. Other assets may be banknotes, precious stones, gold, and so on. While the pragmatic preference might be for central banks to hold IR in currencies with no direct ties to domestic economies' trade partners (in order to minimize external shocks), historically, successive dominance of the global reserve currencies in the international financial system has limited the use of other alternatives (Eichengreen et al., 2017).

The breakdown of the Bretton Woods regime in the early 1970s spurred the early rise in IR as a policy instrument among central banks and a critical subject in academic research. It was quickly established that foreign-exchange reserves tend to rise with economic growth and strengthening current account. The IR balances would decrease with needs for larger foreign-exchange adjustment efforts, if central banks defended domestic currencies under hard pegs or managed float and become minimal under truly flexible exchange rate regimes (see Flood and Marion, 2002). This IR balance motive in support of domestic currency value would form the traditional view of the IR's role in domestic macroeconomic policy.

There was a drastic change in the IR perception following the 1997 Asian crisis and successive currency and sovereign debt crises (most notably, the defaults in Russia in 1998 and Argentina in 2001). A group of economies, aptly termed emerging markets (EMs), appeared as principal hoarders of IR. Here, while maintaining the traditional currency value focus, IR balances would rise above analytically modelled optimal levels. With the rise in prices of primary commodities through the 2000s, some of the EMs with disproportionate reliance on commodity exports saw immediate pick-up in economic growth and significant IR accumulation. The windfall in surplus foreign-exchange revenues lent an opportunity for some EMs to opt for a fixed or more stringently managed exchange rate regime, by-passing, in some cases, industrial policy. At the macroeconomic level, this confluence of events motivated domestic consumption ensuring affordability of imported consumer goods, though with evident dependency on the primary export commodity price and ability to tap international capital markets (see Gevorkyan, 2019, for an analysis of the diverse exchange rate policies).

Accumulation of IR then offers additional transactional benefits, such as mitigating either trade or sovereign debt risks (Aizenman and Turnovsky, 2002; Soesmanto et al., 2015). From a foreign financial investor perspective, a borrowing economy with significant IR balances sends a positive credibility signal to the market in hopes of attracting larger loan volumes at favourable terms. With an announced exchange rate anchor and maintaining adequate IR, the central bank is then able to thwart capital flight, minimizing a possible currency crisis scenario (Semmler and Gevorkyan, 2011; Kato et al., 2017). Such policy flexibility, even if short lived, may be viewed as a significant advantage of the post-2008 Global Financial Crisis (GFC) financial deepening across EMs, yet counterbalanced by the rising indebtedness of the structurally weaker economies.

To add to the complexity, a recent trend, following the GFC, has seen some EM central banks engaged in proactive management of the

IR composition. To some extent this follows a typical optimal portfolio management. In reality, when minimizing the volatility of an asset, or of a substantial share of IR assets denominated in a specific currency, a monetary authority is also interested in the potential returns. For example, Pina (2017) finds that assets' returns play a determinant role in the IR composition. Elsewhere, Gevorkyan and Khemraj (2019) model possibilities of substituting traditional US dollar denominated securities with increased holdings of gold in a framework of an exchange rate anchor (assuming domestic cost and import-driven inflation) under managed float regime. The authors find a range of volatility tolerance and returns maximization options consistent with central banks' foreign-exchange market priorities. It is also important to note that such a scenario of IR management allows to be partially addressed the infamous trilemma question of liberal capital markets, fixed exchange rate, and independent monetary policy.

High-income economies tend to have the largest shares of gold (as a percentage of IR), while low-income countries maintain minimal values with middle-income economies (as reported in Gevorkyan and Khemraj, 2019). Given its intrinsic value and price volatility, holding gold clearly bears some risk in the boom cycle, while offering comfort in recession (at least psychologically). Nevertheless, despite the recent rise in gold demand, including from EMs, much of the IR are still allocated in foreign-currency holdings.

As of the first quarter of 2019, close to 61.8 per cent of the world's allocated foreign-exchange reserves were denominated in US dollars (International Monetary Fund, 2019). Over the past two decades at least, this has been a relatively consistent trend, though with gradual decline in the US dollar shares and moderate gains in the euro (at 20.4 per cent), a trend explored at length by Eichengreen et al. (2017). It is somewhat premature to single out the Chinese renminbi with roughly two per cent of the globally allocated reserves.

The significance of IR for the modern open economy is in the range of opportunities that a carefully constructed foreign-exchange portfolio offers with a finely tuned monetary policy. As observed above, some of these targets include conventional exchange rate anchors, sovereign debt management, and nuanced portfolio optimization. Nevertheless, trade openness, financial deepening, and fundamental uncertainty will continue to stimulate variations in the volume and composition of IR across the world. Yet, it is foreseeable that foreign-exchange reserves will remain critical in national macroeconomic policies of EMs.

ALEKSANDR V. GEVORKYAN

See also

Bretton Woods; Exchange rates – managed; Financial crises; International financial architecture; International monetary system

References

Aizenman, J. and S.J. Turnovsky (2002), 'The high demand for international reserves in Far East: what is going on?', *Journal of the Japanese and International Economies*, **17**, 370–400.

Eichengreen, B., A. Mehl and L. Chiţu (2017), *How Global Currencies Work: Past, Present, and Future*, Princeton, NJ: Princeton University Press.

Flood, R. and P. Marion (2002), 'Holding international reserves in an era of high capital mobility', *International Monetary Fund Working Paper*, No. 02/62.

Gevorkyan, A.V. (2019), 'Exchange market pressure and primary commodity exporting emerging markets', *Applied Economics*, **51** (22), 2390–412.

Gevorkyan, A.V. and T. Khemraj (2019), 'Exchange rate targeting and gold demand by central banks: modeling international reserves composition', *Emerging Markets Finance and Trade*, **55** (1), 168–80.

International Monetary Fund (2019), 'Currency composition of official foreign exchange reserves', Washington, DC: International Monetary Fund.

Kato, M., C. Proaño and W. Semmler (2017), 'Does international reserves targeting decrease the vulnerability to capital flights?', *Research in International Business and Finance*, **44** (1), 64–75.

Pina, G. (2017), 'International reserves and global interest rates', *Journal of International Money and Finance*, **74** (C), 371–85.

Semmler, W. and A.V. Gevorkyan (2011), 'Sailing out of crisis emerging markets style: blending fiscal-monetary rules, nominal targets, and debt dynamics in some transition economies', in J.A. Batten and P.G. Szilagyi (eds), *The Impact of the Global Financial Crisis on Emerging Financial Markets*, Bingley: Emerald Group Publishing, pp. 155–95.

Soesmanto, T., E. Selvanathan and S. Selvanathan (2015), 'Analysis of the management of currency composition of foreign exchange reserves in Australia', *Economic Analysis and Policy*, **47** (1), 82–9.

Free trade

The free trade theory was developed in the eighteenth century to fulfil the expansion of capitalism in rich countries. The theory emerged to challenge the doctrine of mercantilism, which stresses that trade should be managed to enhance national economic power. Smith (1776, Ch. 3) and Ricardo (1817, Ch. 1) opposed the idea of mercantilism and offered theories for free trade to increase national wealth. Their theories claim that free trade would provide meaningful gains for all parties involved and would enhance economic growth, employment, and income through a comparative advantage (Kenen and Lubitz, 1979, p. 34). Mainstream economists agreed that free trade would work better than restricted trade in increasing the size of the trade share in the world market. Enlarging markets across national borders increases the pool of potential producers, consumers, partners, and investors, which then permits greater specialization and economies of scale, and, consequently, enhances per capita economic growth (Oxley, 1990, pp. 46–9).

The positive impact of free trade remains elusive. Implicitly, free trade works to enhance industrial expansion and enrich the rich countries rather than promoting equal welfare growth in the world as a whole. Free trade, enforced through either imperialism or colonialism or through multilateral trade agreements, has led to slower economic growth, damage to local industries, and an increase in the incidence of poverty, particularly in developing countries. Free trade is seen as a zero-sum game, where value is transferred from powerless to powerful countries, often under the use of (physical) force, that is, in the form of colonial armies, foreign-backed dictators, or economic and financial pressure.

Free trade refers to no imposition of any type of trade barriers on foreign goods and services, and allows the free flow of goods and services across countries. The removal of trade barriers, such as tariffs, or reducing tariff rates or non-tariff barriers, would lower the world price so that consumers are able to buy goods at a cheaper price. However, lowering the price by reducing trade barriers will hurt local industries, and, if local producers are unable to compete with foreign goods, then these producers will suffer a loss and the profit rate will drop or turn to negative. Subsequently, the role of profit-led growth to drive the national income would be distorted. If production of goods and services falls, this affects employment, hence workers will be fired. Consequently, the total wage bill will be lower and the role of wage-led growth in pushing effective demand collapses. In short, enhancing trade competition by removing trade barriers will hurt producers and will cause a loss of jobs for local people in the long run. The theory of free trade assumes efficient markets, but, in practice, there is immobility of labour in terms of moving from old and inefficient industries to new ones. When there is a high level of unemployment over the long run, this can give rise to an economic crisis.

Before 1930, Keynes believed in free trade; however, when the British economy fell into deep recession, Keynes abandon the belief (Bhagwati, 2002, p. 16), arguing that

> there are some important respects in which those who are not afraid to use tariffs have a broader conception of the national economic life and a truer feeling for the quality of it. Free traders, fortified into presumption by the essential truths – one might say truisms – of their cause, have greatly overvalued the social advantage of mere market cheapness, have attributed excellences which do not exist to the mere operation of methods of laissez-faire. (Keynes, 1932, p. 206)

The basis of free trade theory is wrong. It is not the absence of competition that produces underdevelopment, but rather its existence causes damage to local industries, reduces real wages, and fails to enhance effective demand. The level of competition is unequal across nations, owing to the level of technological advances, products and brands, stock of human capital, and domination in the world commodity market as regards price determination. In general, developing countries are price takers while industrial countries determine the demand for commodities (Coote, 1992, p. 45; Buckman, 2004, p. 37). Since countries are different as regards the level of economic development, to promote equal competition, trade protection should be implemented by underdeveloped or inefficient countries (Grimwade, 1996, pp. 31–4). Unrestricted international competition presents a threat to national economic development and economic plans in developing a national economy. Trade protection should be implemented to offset imperfect competition in the world and to ensure that

MOHAMED ASLAM

high-cost producers are able to compete with low-cost producers as well as to protect local businesses, jobs, and national income (Kenen and Lubitz, 1979, p. 28; Eichengreen, 1984).

Today, international trade is more complex than before the nineteenth century, even though it seems that free trade is taking place. For example, some products that are exported from developing countries face high trade barriers in rich countries, the labour force is paid less than their fair wage, and the price of commodities is determined by those demanding them (rich countries). Hence, poor countries lose foreign exchange while wealth is accumulated by rich nations. This new trade theory based on comparative (or competitive) advantages actually is not working well. Nowadays, most exports and imports are in the form of intra-firm trade. Hence, attributing the gains and losses in trading for countries is difficult to estimate. Ultimately, foreign trade occurs between multinational corporations, since they created intra-firm trade (Dicken, 2003, pp. 41 and 248).

MOHAMED ASLAM

See also

Effective demand; Growth – wage-led vs profit-led; Regional economic integration and free trade agreements; Terms of trade; Trade and development

References

Bhagwati, J. (2002), *Free Trade Today*, Princeton, NJ: Princeton University Press.
Buckman, G. (2004), *Globalization: Tame It or Scrap It?*, London: Zed Books.
Coote, B. (1992), *The Trade Trap: Poverty and Commodity Markets*, London: Oxfam.
Dicken, P. (2003), *Global Shift*, fourth edition, New York: The Guilford Press.
Eichengreen, B. (1984), 'Keynes and protection', *Journal of Economic History*, 44 (2), 363–73.
Grimwade, N. (1996), *International Trade Policy: A Contemporary Analysis*, London and New York: Routledge.
Kenen, P.B. and R. Lubitz (1979), *International Economics*, third edition, New Delhi: Prentice Hall of India.
Keynes, J.M. (1932), 'Pros and cons of tariffs', *The Listener*, 30 November. Reprinted in *The Collected Writings of John Maynard Keynes, Vol. XXI*, London: Macmillan, 1982, pp. 204–10.
Oxley, A. (1990), *The Challenge of Free Trade*, New York: St. Martin's Press.

Ricardo, D. (1817), *On the Principles of Political Economy and Taxation*, London: John Murray Publisher.
Smith, A. (1776), *An Inquiry into the Nature and Causes of the Wealth of Nations*, London: Strahan and Cadell.

Full employment

Full employment defines a situation in which the entire labour force is employed in some form or other of salaried work. Theoretical and empirical ambiguities surround this seemingly straightforward definition.

Neoclassical theories consider full employment as an equilibrium position, guaranteed by competition in the labour market and full flexibility of wages and prices. Within this theoretical framework, unemployment is the result of either rational choice (voluntary unemployment) or obstacles to market forces. These can be transitory (frictional unemployment), cyclical or structural. Structural unemployment may depend on the skill gap between unemployed workers and available jobs, technological displacement, geographical mismatch or job search costs. Considering these factors, full employment requires equality between the number of vacancies and the number of unemployed workers. The 'natural rate' models (Friedman, 1968) postulate the tendency towards this equilibrium, the only one compatible with constant inflation and identified with 'full-employment unemployment' (Hall, 1970).

Defining structural unemployment is not easy. Theoretically, one may wonder why market forces do not produce price incentives to overcome mismatch and misallocation. Empirically, to incorporate structural unemployment into full employment makes the latter indefinite.

Keynesian economists deny the notion of a self-equilibrating mechanism in the labour market and regard employment as depending on aggregate demand. When defining full employment as a socially desirable target, Keynesian economists abstain from any theoretical notion of equilibrium and rely instead on statistical measures, which pose their own problems. These stem from the effects of low unemployment on the size of the labour force (Rees, 1957), differences in 'employability' (for example young people), and possibility to lessen frictional unemployment by proper economic policies (Beveridge, 1944). These factors, and the fact that frictional unemployment is part of it, make it difficult to quantify full employment. Besides, full employment as an economic policy target must be consistent with 'acceptable' (and thus conventional) standards of labour time and wages.

Keynes (1936) regarded full employment as the 'inflation threshold' and many Keynesian economists were convinced that, as employment increased, so did prices because of either increasing costs (Keynes, 1939) or raising money wages reflecting the bargaining power of workers (Kalecki, 1943). However, neither Keynes nor Keynesian economists established any univocal relation between unemployment and inflation. It would take the Phillips curve (see Phillips, 1958; Samuelson and Solow, 1960) for that relation to emerge.

Keynesian policies for full employment had their heyday immediately after World War II, amidst preoccupation that mass unemployment would reappear with the end of the war. Beveridge (1944) conventionally set the full-employment target for Britain at 3 per cent unemployment. Official documents and legislation such as the British government's white paper (1944) and the American Employment Act (1946) contain vague formulations of the target. A United Nations report of 1949 prescribed that different nations should adopt different full-employment targets (United Nations, 1949). Rees (1957) lists various approaches to quantifying full employment (minimum unemployment, maximum employment, equality between vacancy rate and unemployment rate, and so on) finding conceptual and practical difficulties in each of them.

The 1950s saw a growing preoccupation about inflationary pressures emerging in connection with high employment levels. As policy priorities changed, full employment was interpreted as the level of structural unemployment consistent with stable nominal wages (in the traditional version of the Phillips curve) or inflation (in the subsequent expectations-augmented version). When full-employment policies revived in the early 1960s in the United States, the targeted rate of inflation was set at 4 per cent as a way to control for excessive inflationary pressures (Okun, 1962). Gradual acceptance of the Phillips curve in macroeconomic theory and policymaking made the empirical notion of full employment (including frictional and structural unemployment) dependent on the amount of inflation regarded as tolerable and therefore even more indeterminate.

With the advent of natural-rate models, the empirical assessment of equilibrium (structural) unemployment has increasingly relied on the alleged self-adjusting properties of the economy, thus often identifying in practice 'full-employment' unemployment with the moving average of the actual unemployment rate.

PAOLO PAESANI AND ANTONELLA PALUMBO

See also

Aggregate demand; Inflation; NAIRU; Neoclassical economics; Phillips curve

References

Beveridge, W. (1944), *Full Employment in a Free Society*, London: Allen & Unwin.
Friedman, M. (1968), 'The role of monetary policy', *American Economic Review*, **58** (1), 1–17.
Hall, R.H. (1970), 'Why is the unemployment rate so high at full employment?', *Brookings Papers on Economic Activity*, 3, 369–410.
Kalecki, M. (1943), 'Political aspects of full employment', *Political Quarterly*, **14** (4), 322–30.
Keynes, J.M. (1936), *The General Theory of Employment, Interest and Money*, London: Macmillan.
Keynes, J.M. (1939), 'Relative movements of real wages and output', *Economic Journal*, **49** (139), 34–51.
Okun, A. (1962), 'Potential GNP: its measurement and significance', *Cowles Foundation Paper*, No. 190.
Phillips, A.W. (1958), 'The relation between unemployment and the rate of change of money wage rates in the United Kingdom, 1861–1957', *Economica*, **25** (100), 283–99.
Rees, A. (1957), 'The meaning and measurement of full employment', in *The Measurement and Behavior of Unemployment*, Washington, DC: National Bureau of Economic Research, pp. 11–62.
Samuelson, P.A. and R.M. Solow (1960), 'Analytical aspects of anti-inflation policy', *American Economic Review*, **50** (2), 177–94.
United Nations (1949), *National and International Measures for Full Employment*, New York: Department of Economic Affairs.

Functional finance

After the collapse of Lehman Brothers in 2008 the German chancellor, Angela Merkel, drew what seemed the obvious conclusion. 'One should simply have asked the Swabian housewife,' Merkel said. 'She would have told us that you cannot live beyond your means' (*New York Times*, 2010). This 'Swabian housewife logic' was used to support the eurozone austerity package in the interests of 'sound finance'. But it is almost completely wrong (King, 2015).

The reasons were set out with great clarity by Lerner (1944, pp. 302–4). The public debt is not a burden on posterity, because if posterity repays this debt it will be paying it to the same posterity that will be alive at the time when the payment is made; it is purely a transfer from one group of citizens to another. It is not a burden on the nation, nor is it a sign of national poverty. Just as increasing the public debt does not make the nation poorer, so repaying the public debt does not make the nation richer. The interest on the public debt is not a burden on the nation, because it, too, is a transfer payment. Neither the nation nor the government can be forced into bankruptcy. The government can always meet its obligations to its citizens by borrowing from other citizens, or by issuing the money to pay them. The State cannot be thrown into a debtor's prison or debarred by a bankruptcy order from continuing its business. This is because neither the nation nor the government is an ordinary business concern (still less a Swabian housewife). The weird notion of 'a country "going bankrupt" because it has a great internal debt can only be explained as the result of private capitalists building up a conception of the state in their own image and impressing this capitalist mythology on the other members of the capitalist society' (Lerner, 1944, p. 304). Against the 'businessmen's prejudice' in favour of 'sound finance', Lerner argued for what he termed 'functional finance': macroeconomic policy should be directed towards the maintenance of full employment without demand inflation. Nothing else matters. Run a fiscal deficit when effective demand is deficient, and a fiscal surplus when it is excessive.

Simple algebraic manipulation of the national income accounting identity setting total expenditure equal to total income shows that, in a closed economy, the public sector deficit (government expenditure minus tax revenue) must equal the private sector surplus (saving minus investment). This is an identity which tells us nothing about the direction of causation. But it does tell us that, if the public sector is in surplus, the private sector must run a deficit. Conversely, if the private sector is determined to run a surplus and succeeds in doing so, then the public sector must show a deficit. This is the flow analysis.

The stock analysis is even simpler: if the government budget is in balance, the ratio of public debt to income will rise or fall, depending on whether the rate of growth of national income is greater or less than the rate of interest on the public debt. It follows that there are two ways of reducing the ratio of government debt to GDP: reduce the rate of interest or increase the rate of economic growth. Conversely, even if the budget is in balance, there are two ways in which the public-debt-to-income ratio may rise: higher interest rates or slower economic growth (Watts and Sharpe, 2013).

The opposite of functional finance is what Burger (2003) described as the shibboleth of 'fiscal sustainability', which is often used to justify austerity. It rests on the unstated, and false, proposition that the private sector is essentially stable, normally operating at full employment, with no deficiency of effective demand, so that output and employment are supply-constrained, not demand-constrained. This, Keynes would have said, is equivalent to the assumption that Say's Law operates. It follows that output and employment cannot be increased through the use of fiscal policy, in either the short period or the long period, and government spending can be reduced without any consequences for private sector balance sheets. Post-Keynesian economists strongly reject all these propositions.

The case for functional finance does become more complicated when part or all of the public debt is owned by foreigners, as Lerner noted. 'Increasing debt to other countries or to the citizens of other countries does indicate impoverishment of the borrowing country and enrichment of the lending country. Of this kind of debt the popular criticism is valid' (Lerner, 1944, p. 305). However, this did not entail that borrowing from foreigners was necessarily a bad idea. It 'may be foolish or wise according to circumstances, just as in the case of individual borrowing' (ibid.).

In fact, the open-economy implications of functional finance are profoundly subversive of Angela Merkel's 'Swabian housewife logic' and its use by the European Union to force austerity on Greece, Italy and several other vulnerable nations. In an open economy the public sector deficit is equal to the sum of the private sector surplus and the trade deficit. If there is a trade surplus, the government deficit will be less than the private sector surplus. The reverse is also true: a country with a trade deficit and a private sector surplus will have a correspondingly larger public sector deficit. But for planet Earth as a whole, imports are equal to exports, so that a serious fallacy of composition must be recognized and avoided. Any individual country can increase its trade surplus, and hence reduce its budget deficit, perhaps by screwing down wage costs, as Germany has done since the introduction of the euro, but this must come at the expense of one or more of its trading partners, whose increased trade deficits will (*ceteris paribus*) be reflected in higher budget deficits. Neomercantilist policies in one country cannot justify the imposition of austerity on others (Podkaminer, 2019).

JOHN E. KING

See also

Effective demand; Fallacy of composition; Fiscal consolidation; Fiscal deficits; Fiscal policy

References

Burger, P. (2003), *Sustainable Fiscal Policy and Economic Stability: Theory and Practice*, Cheltenham, UK, and Northampton, MA, USA: Edward Elgar.
King, J.E. (2015), 'A Post Keynesian critique of Swabian housewife logic', in A. Bitzenis, N. Karagiannis and J. Marangos (eds), *Europe in Crisis*, Basingstoke: Palgrave Macmillan, pp. 29–43.
Lerner, A.P. (1944), *The Economics of Control: Principles of Welfare Economics*, New York: Macmillan.
New York Times (2010), 'In Greek debt crisis, a window to the German psyche', *New York Times*, 4 May 2010, available online at https://www.nytimes.com/2010/05/04/business/global/04iht-euro.html?_r=0.
Podkaminer, L. (2019), 'The private saving glut and the developed countries' government financial balance', *Review of Keynesian Economics*, **7** (1), 94–107.
Watts, M. and T. Sharpe (2013), 'Immutable laws of debt dynamics', *Journal of Post Keynesian Economics*, **36** (1), 59–84.

General Theory – interpretations of

Despite a widespread sense that John Maynard Keynes's *General Theory of Employment, Interest and Money* (1936) marked a 'Keynesian revolution' in economics (an expression given traction by Klein (1947)), the message and significance of *The General Theory* was and continues to be vigorously contested. Advocacy of fiscal or monetary expansion to remedy high unemployment long pre-dated Keynes, as did recognition that public works spending would cause secondary rounds of income and spending (an idea that appears in a speech by Pericles reported by Plutarch). Keynes's breakthrough was not in policy but in the theory behind the policy. Coddington (1983) usefully classified interpretations of Keynes's *General Theory* as hydraulic, reductionist, or fundamentalist.

Hydraulic Keynesianism interpreted *The General Theory* as a small system of simultaneous equations for aggregate demand, in 1936 review articles by David Champernowne and W. Brian Reddaway and in papers by Roy Harrod, John Hicks, and James Meade presented in 1936 and published the following year (see Young, 1987), with Hicks (1937) influentially supplementing the system of equations with diagrams that later became the Hicks–Hansen IS–LM diagram (from the initials of investment = saving, liquidity preference = money supply). In Modigliani's 1944 formulation of the IS–LM interpretation of Keynes, demand shifts had real effects either in a liquidity trap (where the nominal interest rate is at the zero lower bound) or because of a rigid money wage rate, perhaps due to money illusion. This approach, which treats *The General Theory* as a special case of classical economics with nominal frictions added, captured one aspect of Keynes, namely, the policy adviser and builder of ad hoc models. Keynes had summarized his theory as a four-equation simultaneous-equations model in a December 1933 lecture at Cambridge attended by Champernowne and Reddaway (see Dimand, 1988; Rymes, 1989) but did not do so in his 1936 book, either because he was dissatisfied with the preliminary version or because he followed Marshall's advice to use mathematics as an aid to inquiry but then translate the results into English and burn the mathematics. Whereas Hicks (1937) made only passing mention of uncertainty,

JOHN E. KING / ROBERT W. DIMAND

Keynes's 1933 lecture explicitly included the 'state of the news' as an argument in each of the consumption, investment, and liquidity preference functions.

Contrary to textbook versions of the hydraulic interpretation, Keynes did not assume money illusion or an arbitrarily rigid money wage. A fixed money wage was a simplifying assumption that would be dropped in Chapter 19 of *The General Theory* and a recommendation to avoid destabilizing wage cutting. In Chapter 2, Keynes (1936) explained how, with staggered contracts, workers might rationally resist money wage cuts, which changed relative wages, but not adjustment through price level changes that affected all real wages at the same time. This would explain why money wages had been sticky in Britain, unlike in the United States, where money wages had fallen sharply in the early 1930s without reducing either unemployment or real wages. The staggered contract explanation for rational downward stickiness of money wage rates was independently rediscovered by Taylor (1979) without recollection of Keynes (1936, Ch. 2). Downward stickiness of money wage rates would imply that real wages were countercyclical, rising when output fell. Keynes (1939) accepted empirical evidence from John Dunlop and Lorie Tarshis, and theoretical arguments by Michal Kalecki about mark-up pricing, that real wages did not in general vary countercyclically, but held this finding strengthened his theory by freeing it from the first classical postulate (that the real wage varies along a downward-sloping marginal product of labour schedule).

Patinkin (1982) argued that the central message of Keynes's *General Theory* was threefold: the principle of effective demand, the proposition that the equilibrium level of national income and output Y is determined by the equation $Y = AE(Y)$, and the goods market equilibrium condition that income is equal to (planned) aggregate expenditure AE. $Y = AE(Y)$ is equivalent, when consumption is deducted from each side of the equation, to the IS equation that (for the simplest case, a closed economy with no government) investment I is equal to saving $S(Y)$. This principle of effective demand is the equivalent, for levels of equilibrium income and spending, to the finite-valued multiplier relating a change in autonomous spending to the resulting change in equilibrium income, derived between 1930 and 1933 by Giblin, Hawtrey, Kahn, Keynes, Meade, and Warming (see Dimand, 1988; Dimand and Hagemann, 2019).

In contrast to this focus on demand determining the level of equilibrium income, Swedish followers of Wicksell emphasized movements of the price level, while cyclical fluctuations were central to most of Kalecki's early essays (Kalecki, 1966). Patinkin (1982) debatably excluded from Kalecki's central message a 1933 essay about effective demand and equilibrium income, because it was an outlier among Kalecki's early writings and because it appeared in a Polish magazine comparable to Britain's *The Economist* rather than in a scholarly journal.

Reductionist interpretations of Keynes look to ground his theory in choice-theoretic microeconomic foundations, capturing another aspect of Keynes, as a Marshallian economist. Robert Clower (in papers starting in 1965, collected in Clower, 1984) and Axel Leijonhufvud (1968, 1981) urged that Keynes's rejection of what he called Say's Law,[1] that, in aggregate, supply creates its own demand, be taken seriously as a rejection of Walras's Law. Walras's Law states that, assuming local non-satiation of all agents so that budget constraints are strictly binding, summation of individual budget constraints implies that the value of aggregate excess demand is zero summed across all markets including money. Clower and Leijonhufvud argued that Walras's Law is valid for notional demands (when there are no quantity constraints) but not for effective demands: if there is an excess supply of labour, the labour that quantity-constrained workers cannot sell multiplied by the wage rate that they would have gotten if they could have sold their labour should be counted in their budget constraint for buying goods and services. An excess supply of labour need not imply excess effective demand elsewhere in the system, hence automatic restoration of full employment could not be presumed. Without mention of Clower or Leijonhufvud (or even, except on the book cover, of Keynes) Russell Cooper (1999) reformulated this interpretation of Keynes's unemployment equilibrium with the game-theoretic concept of strategic complementarity: if firms, acting together, would expand production and hire more workers, the newly hired workers would spend their wages in ways justifying that expansion of employment but there is no incentive for any single firm to hire.

ROBERT W. DIMAND

Fundamentalist interpretations of *The General Theory*, such as that by Davidson (1972 and many later publications), capture Keynes's aspect as a revolutionary thinker and emphasize Keynes (1936, Ch. 12; 1937) on fundamental uncertainty about an unforeseeable future, uncertainty that cannot be reduced to insurable risk and which makes long-period expectations about the profitability of investment highly volatile (Keynes, 1921; Knight, 1921). Keynes (1937), replying to four reviews of his 1936 book, identified fundamental uncertainty and the rejection of the classical law of markets as the crucial features distinguishing his theory from the wide range that he lumped together as 'classical economics'. Although Coddington (1983, Ch. 4) expressed forceful doubts, Keynes's view of uncertainty and long-period expectations is clearly a key part of his theory. But while uncertainty explains the volatility of the marginal efficiency of capital and of liquidity preference, other building blocks of Keynes's theory are needed to explain why the resulting fluctuations in effective demand have real and lasting effects on output and employment, not just on prices and wages.

Minsky (1975) and Tobin (1980) drew attention to Keynes's Chapter 19, 'Changes in money-wages', and to Fisher (1933), to argue that Keynes's results did not depend on money wage rigidity (see Tobin's overview chapter in Harcourt and Riach, 1997). Patinkin (1965) had claimed that the Pigou–Haberler real balance effect proved that a sufficiently lower money wage could restore full employment even in a liquidity trap through the wealth effect on consumption of more valuable money balances. Patinkin thus viewed Keynes's *General Theory* as practically relevant but theoretically trivial, as depending on a fixed money wage. But while a lower price level increases aggregate expenditure, a falling price level reduces it by increasing the value of debt (increasing the risk of bankruptcy and default) and raising the real return (lowering the opportunity cost) of holding real money balances. Faster adjustment of prices and money wages is thus destabilizing so that, for large negative demand shocks that push the economy outside what Leijonhufvud termed 'the corridor of stability', deflation moves the economy further away from, instead of back towards, potential output and full employment.

Keynes's *General Theory* continues to be, and undoubtedly will continue to be, intensively debated as differing interpretations stress Chapter 2 on the two classical postulates of the labour market, Chapter 3 on the principle of effective demand, Chapter 12 on long-period expectations, Chapter 17 on the essential properties of interest and money, or Chapter 19 on changes in money wages. These varied interpretations attest to the richness and continued theoretical interest of the great work of a brilliant multi-faceted thinker.

ROBERT W. DIMAND

See also

Aggregate demand; Effective demand; Income multiplier; Liquidity preference; *The General Theory of Employment, Interest and Money*

Note

1. Although the classical law of markets is known as Say's Law, Béraud and Numa (2018) point out that, starting with the 1826 fifth edition of his *Traité*, Jean-Baptiste Say (responding to criticism from Sismondi) formulated a monetary theory of crises that allowed for hoarding and for a role for public works to provide employment during crises – but only the 1819 fourth edition was translated into English.

References

Béraud, A. and G. Numa (2018), 'Beyond Say's Law: the significance of J.-B. Say's monetary views', *Journal of the History of Economic Thought*, **40** (2), 217–41.
Clower, R. (1984), *Money and Markets: Essays by Robert W. Clower*, Cambridge, UK: Cambridge University Press.
Coddington, A. (1983), *Keynesian Economics: The Search for First Principles*, London: George Allen & Unwin.
Cooper, R. (1999), *Coordination Games: Complementarities and Macroeconomics*, Cambridge, UK: Cambridge University Press.
Davidson, P. (1972), *Money and the Real World*, London: Macmillan.
Dimand, R.W. (1988), *The Origins of the Keynesian Revolution*, Aldershot, UK: Edward Elgar, and Stanford, CA: Stanford University Press.
Dimand, R.W. and H. Hagemann (eds) (2019), *The Elgar Companion to John Maynard Keynes*, Cheltenham, UK, and Northampton, MA, USA: Edward Elgar.
Fisher, I. (1933), 'The debt deflation theory of great depressions', *Econometrica*, **1** (4), 337–57.
Harcourt, G.C. and P.A. Riach (eds) (1997), *A 'Second Edition' of the General Theory*, London and New York: Routledge.

ROBERT W. DIMAND

Hicks, J.R. (1937), 'Mr. Keynes and the Classics: a suggested interpretation', *Econometrica*, **5** (2), 147–59.
Kalecki, M. (1966), *Studies in the Theory of Business Cycles, 1933–1939*, Oxford: Basil Blackwell.
Keynes, J.M. (1921), *A Treatise on Probability*, London: Macmillan.
Keynes, J.M. (1936), *The General Theory of Employment, Interest and Money*, London: Macmillan.
Keynes, J.M. (1937), 'The general theory of employment', *Quarterly Journal of Economics*, **51** (2), 109–23.
Keynes, J.M. (1939), 'Relative movements of real wages and output', *Economic Journal*, **49** (193), 34–51.
Klein, L.R. (1947), *The Keynesian Revolution*, New York: Macmillan.
Knight, F.H. (1921), *Risk, Uncertainty and Profit*, New York and Boston: Houghton Mifflin.
Leijonhufvud, A. (1968), *On Keynesian Economics and the Economics of Keynes*, New York: Oxford University Press.
Leijonhufvud, A. (1981), *Information and Coordination: Essays in Macroeconomic Theory*, New York: Oxford University Press.
Minsky, H.P. (1975), *John Maynard Keynes*, New York: Columbia University Press.
Patinkin, D. (1965), *Money, Interest and Prices*, second edition, New York: Harper & Row.
Patinkin, D. (1982), *Anticipations of the General Theory? And Other Essays on Keynes*, Chicago: University of Chicago Press.
Rymes, T.K. (ed.) (1989), *Keynes's Lectures, 1932–35: Notes of a Representative Student*, London and Basingstoke: Macmillan and Ann Arbor: University of Michigan Press.
Taylor, J.B. (1979), 'Staggered wage setting in a macro model', *American Economic Review: AEA Papers and Proceedings*, **69** (2), 108–13.
Tobin, J. (1980), *Asset Accumulation and Economic Activity*, Oxford: Basil Blackwell, and Chicago: University of Chicago Press.
Young, W. (1987), *Interpreting Mr. Keynes: The IS–LM Enigma*, Cambridge, UK: Polity, and Boulder, CO: Westview.

Gibson paradox

In *A Treatise on Money*, Keynes (1930, p. 198) called the co-movement between the interest rate and the price level 'the Gibson paradox', owing to a series of articles published in 1923 by A.H. Gibson in the *Banker's Magazine* in which an extraordinarily 'close correlation' between the interest rate on consols and the price level emerged for over a century. It is seen as a paradox because a monetary policy tightening is usually expected to be followed by a decrease in the price level (or a lower rate of inflation) according to the demand side channels of the monetary transmission mechanism.

Several theories have been advanced to explain this stylized fact. On the hypothesis that at equilibrium the nominal interest rate equals a given 'natural' real rate plus the expected inflation rate, Fisher (1930) argued that the Gibson paradox arises because price expectations adjust slowly after a change in inflation fuelled by a change in the growth rate of the money supply – thereby determining fluctuations in the actual real interest rate around its natural level. More precisely, following a higher price increase than before, lenders will only require with a delay repayment in monetary terms of a sum that is able to cover the drop in the value of money and, when this occurs, prices and the nominal interest rate move in the same direction and the actual real rate of interest adjusts towards its natural level.

This 'monetary' explanation of the Gibson paradox differs from the 'real' one advanced by Wicksell (1906) and shared to a great extent by Keynes (1930), according to which the market rate of interest is relatively sticky compared with the natural rate of interest (namely, the interest rate that equals savings and investment at full employment) so that, when there is a long-run tendency of the natural rate of interest to move, continuous slow movement of inflation or deflation occurs. This would be due to changes in investment driven respectively by expected extra-profits or losses when the market rate of interest is lower or higher than the natural rate. It will only stop if movement of the market interest rate in the same direction as prices brings the interest rate to the natural level again.

Friedman and Schwartz (1983) ascribed the Gibson paradox mainly to the gold standard. It also appears, however, under fiat monetary regimes, typically by using vector autoregression (VAR) models. Following Sims (1992), this has been explained by omitted information on the systematic part of monetary policy. In particular, VAR analysis would turn out to be mis-specified if it fails to include a proxy for future inflation. In this case, the result of endogenous and/or anticipatory responses to expected inflation by the central bank would emerge as a co-movement of prices and interest

ROBERT W. DIMAND / ENRICO SERGIO LEVRERO

rates: a predicted upcoming surge in inflation would be followed by an increase in the policy rate of interest, a decrease in the output gap, and – as long as the monetary policy tightening does not fully offset the inflationary shock – a rise in current inflation.

However, the practice suggested by Sims (1992) to avoid the price puzzle by including commodity prices as a proxy of expected inflation does not work for all sub-sample periods, especially in the pre-1980 period. This has been explained by Castelnuovo and Surico (2010) by the fact that the specification error in the VAR models that comes from the omission of a latent variable would manifest itself only with passive monetary regimes. In other words, only with these regimes inflation expectations become very informative on the dynamics of the economy and help to identify a monetary policy shock correctly. It has also been argued that the price puzzle would disappear when a larger information set is used, or the output gap or a new measure of monetary policy shock free from endogenous or anticipatory movements is included in the VAR model.

An alternative interpretation is that the price puzzle is not a false finding that pertains only to mis-specified VARs but, rather, it is a 'genuine' phenomenon related to a supply-cost-channel effect arising from businesspeople tending to regard interest rates as a cost. While rejected or confined only to specific conditions concerning the degree of price and wage flexibility by Castelnuovo and Surico (2010), this perspective brings to mind the original interpretation of Tooke (1838), which was initially criticized by Wicksell because – in a gold-money economy – variations in the interest rate would be accompanied by changes in relative and not absolute prices.

Recently, several studies have stressed the cost channel of monetary policy stemming from the amount of interest to be paid on working capital or on loans made to face the temporal mismatch between factor payments and sales receipts (Barth and Ramey, 2002; Christiano et al., 2005). Even before, Kalecki (1971) claimed that the degree of monopoly is likely to increase whenever overhead costs (which can be thought of as including the interest costs associated with debt servicing) rise. However, the cost-channel interpretation of the Gibson paradox does not necessarily apply only to oligopolistic conditions or to the working capital and short-term loans.

Given the money wages, the normal profits of enterprise and the methods of production, a permanent increase in interest rates – namely, in the pure cost of capital – would lead to a change in the same direction of commodity prices under the action of free competition that equals prices to the monetary costs of production (Pivetti, 1991). Workers will thus suffer a loss in their purchasing power, unless they are able to resist it by demanding higher money wages and an inflationary process is set up.

ENRICO SERGIO LEVRERO

See also

Inflation; Interest rate – natural; Interest rates and investment; Monetary policy transmission mechanism; Monopoly power

References

Barth, M.J. and V.A. Ramey (2002), 'The cost channel of monetary transmission', *NBER Macroeconomics Annual 2001*, 16, 199–256.

Castelnuovo, E. and P. Surico (2010), 'Monetary policy, inflation expectations and the price puzzle', *Economic Journal*, **120** (549), 1262–83.

Christiano, L.J., M. Eichenbaum and C.L. Evans (2005), 'Nominal rigidities and the dynamic effects of a shock to monetary policy', *Journal of Political Economy*, **113** (1), 1–45.

Fisher, I. (1930), *The Theory of Interest*, New York: Macmillan.

Friedman, M. and A.J. Schwartz (1983), *Monetary Trends in the United States and the United Kingdom*, Chicago: University of Chicago Press.

Kalecki, M. (1971), 'Costs and prices', in *Selected Essays on the Dynamics of the Capitalist Economy*, Cambridge, UK: Cambridge University Press, pp. 43–61.

Keynes, J.M. (1930), *A Treatise on Money, Volume II*, London: Macmillan.

Pivetti, M. (1991), *An Essay on Money and Distribution*, New York: St. Martin's Press.

Sims, C.A. (1992), 'Interpreting the macroeconomic time series facts: the effects of monetary policy', *European Economic Review*, **36** (5), 975–1000.

Tooke, T. (1838), *A History of Prices, and the State of the Circulation, from 1793 to 1837*, vols I and II, London: P.S. King and Son.

Wicksell, K. (1906), *Lectures on Political Economy*, vol. II, English translation by E. Classen and edited with an introduction by L. Robbins, 1935. Reprint 1978, New Jersey: Augustus M. Kelley.

Globalization

Globalization is a prime example of an expression that has been used so often that it loses meaning. In economics, it is generally accepted as meaning the opening of national borders to flows of goods and services, investment, and people. However, globalization is a word commonly used in popular culture and in many fields of study.

The fact that globalization means different things to different people is significant in itself and has even become an object of academic study (see Garrett et al., 2006). The concept of globalization is particularly tendentious, as it represents something equally tendentious: the definition of the global world order.

In the centres of global power, globalization has been largely – if not always correctly – debated in recent decades. Margaret Thatcher famously claimed 'there is no alternative' to the global capitalist market, a sentiment likewise voiced by US president Ronald Reagan around the same time.

Roughly a decade later, the free trade agreement with Mexico and the dangers of offshoring American jobs were highlighted in the presidential debates between Bill Clinton and Ross Perot. More than two decades later, the two countries again dominated the debate with Donald Trump and Theresa May supposedly representing those negatively affected by globalization.

In 2000, the International Monetary Fund (IMF) offered its vision of 'economic globalization', describing it as 'a historical process, the result of human innovation and technological progress' (International Monetary Fund, 2000, Internet). Painting the issue as a natural progression of societies and their markets, for the IMF globalization represents 'the increasing integration of economies around the world, particularly through trade and financial flows. The term sometimes also refers to the movement of people (labor) and knowledge (technology) across international borders. There are also broader cultural, political and environmental dimensions of globalization' (International Monetary Fund, 2000, Internet). The IMF weaves in the narrative of a spontaneous market order, particularly as it relates to technological change: 'there is nothing mysterious about globalization. The term has come into common usage since the 1980s, reflecting technological advances that have made it easier and quicker to complete international transactions – both trade and financial flows' (International Monetary Fund, 2000, Internet).

As a key proponent and promoter of financial globalization, it is unsurprising that the IMF adopts the position of a natural or spontaneous order, as it eliminates all relevant political considerations. It is only under the perspective of a global social order, and within the realm of political economy, that these considerations can be properly addressed. In *The Great Transformation*, Polanyi (1944) convincingly criticizes both the natural and the spontaneous market order, and proposes the hypothesis of the global social order to great effect. Polanyi-Levitt's *From the Great Transformation to the Great Financialization* (2013) maintains this viewpoint, while updating it to current globalization and financialization.

Polanyi-Levitt's (2013) viewpoint offers the most potent available remedy to the IMF's misleading definitions of globalization. Despite the IMF's statement that there is 'nothing mysterious about globalization', the IMF and other proponents of globalization have clearly contributed to the mystery surrounding globalization. Polanyi-Levitt (2013, p. 241) states that the 'introduction of "globalization" to describe the internationalization of production under control of transnational corporations is a brilliant example of the importance of language in the marketing of the neoliberal project'. Perhaps the most important consequence of the language of globalization is that when the term 'is used to replace "accelerating international trade and investment," the nation and its borders disappear from view. In language if not in reality, economics has obliterated the political jurisdiction of the nation-state' (Polanyi-Levitt, 2013, p. 241).

Polanyi-Levitt (2013, pp. 241–2) pithily states that '[g]lobalization is both a description of the increased interdependence of economies and a prescriptive agenda in the service of capital'. The macroeconomic results of globalization separate themselves from the previous period of the Keynesian inspired 'golden age' of capitalism in much higher unemployment, inflation, wealth disparities, and the return of financial crises around the globe. Rolling back successful global economic management would always be a difficult sell to the public. It is therefore only fitting that the language and theory surrounding globalization should be deceitful.

WESLEY C. MARSHALL

From the broad angle of political economy, Polanyi-Levitt (2013, pp. 241–2) provides perhaps the most complete definition of globalization: 'the elimination of national sovereignty over the allocation of national resources, including the control and regulation of capital, defines globalization as a project whose objective is the subordination of peoples and nations to capital accumulation on a global scale.'

Today, when few prominent economists dare question the spirit of free trade, Keynes's (1933, p. 758) viewpoint is more welcome than ever: 'Ideas, knowledge, art, hospitality, travel – these are the things which should of their nature be international. But let goods be homespun whenever it is reasonably and conveniently possible; and, above all, let finance be primarily national.'

WESLEY C. MARSHALL

See also

Capitalism; Financial crises; Financialization; Free trade; Power

References

Garrett, P., B. Evans and A. Williams (2006), 'What does the word "globalisation" mean to you? Comparative perceptions and evaluations in Australia, New Zealand, the USA and the UK', *Journal of Multilingual and Multicultural Development*, **27** (5), 392–412.
International Monetary Fund (2000), 'Globalization: threat or opportunity?', *Issues Brief*, No. 00/01, available at https://www.imf.org/external/np/exr/ib/2000/041200to.htm (last accessed 30 December 2020).
Keynes, J.M. (1933), 'National self-sufficiency', *The Yale Review*, **22** (4), 755–69.
Polanyi, K. (1944), *The Great Transformation*, Boston: Beacon Press.
Polanyi-Levitt, K. (2013), *From the Great Transformation to the Great Financialization*, London: Zed Books.

Goodwin cycles

Richard Goodwin (1967) developed a mathematical model to represent Karl Marx's (1867 [1976]) theory of cyclical economic crises. This 'Goodwin cycle' approach was later imported into post-Keynesian economics by Barbosa-Filho and Taylor (2006), who altered Goodwin's model by adopting a neo-Kaleckian framework in which aggregate demand depends on income distribution.

Goodwin's original model consists of a system of differential equations in two variables – the wage share and the employment rate – changes in which are related to each other in predator–prey fashion (see Grasselli and Maheshwari, 2017). When the wage share (the predator) is low and profitability is high, firms increase their investment leading to more rapid growth of the capital stock, which in turn increases employment (the prey). Higher employment then increases the bargaining strength of workers, leading to real wage increases that (for any given rate of labour productivity growth) push up the wage share. However, the higher wage share eventually 'squeezes' (reduces) the profit rate (assuming a constant capital–output ratio), causing firms to reduce their investment, at which point economic growth falls and a recession ensues. The employment rate then falls, until workers' bargaining power is reduced to the point where workers accept lower real wages, thereby restoring capitalists' profitability and sparking a recovery of investment and, ultimately, employment. As this process repeats endlessly, the economy follows (in some mathematical formulations) a 'closed orbit' that can be visualized as a continuous counterclockwise rotation on a diagram with the wage share on the vertical axis and the employment rate on the horizontal axis. Figure 1 shows a simplified version of such a Goodwin cycle (other mathematical formulations yield more complex dynamics, such as 'limit cycles').

In the neo-Goodwin model of Barbosa-Filho and Taylor (2006), the capacity utilisation rate is used instead of the employment rate as the measure of economic activity. Utilisation is determined by a neo-Kaleckian model of demand and distribution; for the model to generate neo-Goodwin cycles (counterclockwise rotations on a diagram with the wage share on the vertical axis and the utilisation rate on the horizontal axis), the case of profit-led demand must be assumed. In addition, the neo-Goodwin model incorporates a post-Keynesian specification of the labour market, in which the nominal wage rather than the real wage is determined in the labour bargaining process (see Blecker and Setterfield, 2019, Chapter 5).

Otherwise, the intuition for the counterclockwise rotations in the neo-Goodwin model is similar to that in the original version. Both

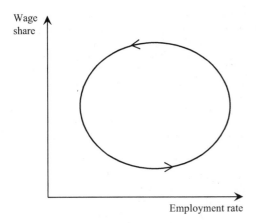

Figure 1   A simplified Goodwin cycle

the original and neo-Goodwin models require that wage increases squeeze profits and thereby reduce investment as the economy approaches the peak of the cycle, thus leading to the next downturn, and that these tendencies are reversed during the ensuring recession thereby enabling an eventual recovery. One important difference, however, is that the neo-Goodwin model does not generally yield either a closed orbit or a limit cycle. Because of additional feedback effects that are typically incorporated in neo-Goodwin models, the counterclockwise cycles can either move inward toward an equilibrium point, in which case they are stable or convergent, or spiral outward away from the equilibrium, in which case they are unstable or explosive, depending on the parameters of the model.

Goodwin cycle models (old and new) have been criticised on various grounds. The assumption of profit-led demand has been rejected by those who believe that the empirical evidence supports wage-led demand for most countries. The profit-squeeze mechanism has been questioned by those who observe that real wages are not strongly procyclical, and who believe that cyclical variations in the wage share are instead driven mainly by procyclical movements in labour productivity (see Lavoie, 2017). Skott (1989, 2017) has criticised both the original and neo-Goodwin models for oversimplifying the connections between goods markets and labour markets. New theoretical models have shown that counterclockwise rotations of the utilisation rate and wage share can be generated by economic mechanisms that do not assume either profit-led demand or a profit-squeeze.

For example, Stockhammer and Michell (2017) show that cyclical variations in Minskyan financial fragility can generate the appearance of 'pseudo-Goodwin cycles', while Setterfield and Kim (2017) show that the appearance of profit-driven cycles can be created by the dynamics of household borrowing for financing consumer expenditures. New empirical research has found that even the 'Goodwin pattern' in the data has broken down since the early 2000s (see, for example, Setterfield, 2021).

ROBERT A. BLECKER

See also

Aggregate demand; Financial fragility; Growth – wage-led vs profit-led; Income distribution; Profit

References

Barbosa-Filho, N.H. and L. Taylor (2006), 'Distributive and demand cycles in the US economy: a structuralist Goodwin model', *Metroeconomica*, **57** (3), 389–411.

Blecker, R.A. and M. Setterfield (2019), *Heterodox Macroeconomics: Models of Demand, Distribution and Growth*, Cheltenham, UK, and Northampton, MA, USA: Edward Elgar.

Goodwin, R.M. (1967), 'A growth cycle', in C. Feinstein (ed.), *Socialism, Capitalism and Economic Growth*, Cambridge, UK: Cambridge University Press, pp. 54–8.

Grasselli, M.R. and A. Maheshwari (2017), 'A comment on "Testing Goodwin: growth cycles in ten OECD countries"', *Cambridge Journal of Economics*, **41** (6), 1761–6.

Lavoie, M. (2017), 'The origins and evolution of the debate on wage-led and profit-led regimes', *European Journal of Economics and Economic Policies: Intervention*, **14** (2), 200–21.

Marx, K. (1867), *Capital: A Critique of Political Economy, vol. I*, translated by B. Fowkes, London: Penguin/Vintage, 1976.

Setterfield, M. (2021), 'Whatever happened to the "Goodwin pattern"? Profit squeeze dynamics in the modern American labour market', *Review of Political Economy*, published online, 8 June, DOI: 10.1080/09538259.2021.1921357.

Setterfield, M. and Y.K. Kim (2017), 'Household borrowing and the possibility of "consumption-driven, profit-led growth"', *Review of Keynesian Economics*, **5** (1), 43–60.

Skott, P. (1989), *Conflict and Effective Demand in Economic Growth*, Cambridge, UK: Cambridge University Press.

Skott, P. (2017), 'Weaknesses of "wage-led growth"', *Review of Keynesian Economics*, **5** (3), 336–59.

Stockhammer, E. and J. Michell (2017), 'Pseudo-Goodwin cycles in a Minsky model', *Cambridge Journal of Economics*, **41** (1), 105–25.

Government deficits and inflation

Linking inflation to government deficits stems from two ideas: (i) inflation is caused by demand forces; (ii) how deficits are financed.

To make the link between government deficits and inflation clearer, it is important to understand that government deficits lead to injection of new money into the system. In this regard, textbooks invariably repeat the same story: there are only three possible ways in which a government can pay for its spending. These are taxes, borrowing, and creation of money. Most economists tend to consider taxes as the only 'legitimate' source of revenue for the government and, therefore, argue that any expenditure above the amount of collected taxes would put the government in a deficit position. In such a case the government will have to resort to borrowing or to creation of money in order to pay for its deficit.

The last two options are immediately scorned, and the policymaker is advised to avoid using them because, supposedly, they have harmful effects for the economy. Borrowing by the government is considered bad because, supposedly, it leads to higher interest rates since the government would be competing with private investors for the limited and scarce funds. Higher interest rates would discourage private investment, attract foreign lending and cause an appreciation of the national currency – thereby leading to a loss of exports. This is the famous argument of 'crowding out'. Creation of money, on the other hand, is believed to lead to inflation.

Consequently, most governments attempt to achieve a balanced budget and are even encouraged to achieve budgetary surpluses by cutting their spending on the provision of public goods and services (infrastructure, health, education, and so on) and/or by raising taxes. Austerity and the principles of the so-called 'sound finance' are nowadays the dominant view in policymaking. In addition, central banks, at least since the 1980s, have become almost obsessed with the fight against inflation and most of them, at some point in time, have set a zero-inflation target or a target close to it. In trying to achieve their inflation target, central banks follow what they call a tight-money approach; essentially by keeping interest rates high in order to stifle credit.

However, a sober analysis of the flow of funds that follow from the creation of money to finance government spending reveals that this necessarily leads to an increase in banks' reserves and, therefore, in the amount of liquidity in the banking system. The increased liquidity can have two consequences: (1) cause the rate of interest to fall, as inter-bank lending becomes cheaper, and (2) may lead to inflation. The first effect is of more of a short-run nature and tends to manifest itself almost immediately, and clearly invalidates the 'crowding out' argument.

The second effect, which is the only one emphasized by neoclassical economists, is in fact very unlikely as long as the economy is below full employment. However, even if inflation is caused by the injection of 'too much liquidity into the system', then the government has no difficulty in withdrawing that excess amount and thereby putting a break on inflationary pressures. Indeed, if, as claimed by conservative economists, the newly created money used by the government to finance, for instance, full-employment programmes leads to the extraordinary situation where 'too much money is chasing too few goods', then, in practice, the government has at its disposal a centuries-old, tested and proven method for effectively withdrawing the extra liquidity, namely, taxation.

As Lerner (1943, 1946) argued, if the goal is to increase the total aggregate spending for the purpose of maintaining full employment and preventing deflation, the sovereign national government can create money to buy whatever it needs: paying wages to public sector employees, lending to private citizens, or giving to people as welfare payments. All these payments can be done simply by crediting the accounts of the intended recipients.

If, on the other hand, the goal is to lower total spending in the economy, perhaps in order to prevent inflation, then the government can destroy money by withdrawing it through taxing, borrowing (selling government bonds), or by selling other items in its possession. That is why Lerner (1949, p. 307) insisted that '[t]he purpose of taxation is never to raise money but to leave less in the hands of the taxpayer' – thus proving that the basic principle of 'sound finance' is fundamentally flawed. The fear of inflation from deficit spending seems unjustified, but it serves a purpose. It creates uncertainty about the efficacy of the interventionist strategy and makes policymakers reluctant to pursue an active programme that seeks to eliminate unemployment and inequality in the distribution of wealth and income.

HASSAN BOUGRINE

See also

Crowding in and crowding out; Fiscal consolidation; Fiscal deficit; Inflation targeting; Money creation – nature of

References

Lerner, A.P. (1943), 'Functional finance and the federal debt', *Social Research*, **10** (1), 38–51.
Lerner, A.P. (1946), 'An integrated full employment policy', in A.P. Lerner and F.D. Graham (eds), *Planning and Paying for Full Employment*, Princeton: Princeton University Press, pp. 163–220.
Lerner, A.P. (1949), *The Economics of Control: Principles of Welfare Economics*, New York: Macmillan (first published 1944).

Government deficits and money creation

Mainstream economists maintain that all government spending must be financed with taxes, and as such creation of money and borrowing must be avoided. In their view, taxes are the only 'earned' income for the government. This is a basic premise in the neoclassical theory of public finance and has dominated the thinking of most economists whose ideas shaped public policy.

Progressive post-Keynesian economists, on the other hand, argue that (national) government spending is routinely paid for through the creation of money by the central bank. In monetary circuit theory, for instance, since the government, represented by the Treasury (the ministry of finance), cannot create its own money, it must get advances, or a loan from the bank. In principle, it can be any bank, but for obvious reasons the preference is for the central bank.

The practice and procedures tend to vary from one country to another, but it always boils down to the same thing: the government gets a loan or a credit line from the central bank. Typically, the government puts its own securities (bonds) as a collateral. The loan to the government is recorded as an asset on the central bank's balance sheet and as a liability on the government's own balance sheet. By this process, the central bank advances money to the government simply by crediting its account. Having now secured a positive amount of money in its account – a credit to it by the central bank – the government can start making payments to its employees and other suppliers of goods and services by drawing on this credit line. All these expenditures lead to a flow of liquidity (money) from the public sector to the private sector, thus adding to the latter's liquid holdings (bank deposits). Indeed, as private agents receive their payments, they give rise to a deposit in their bank accounts – either through direct deposits or via cheques – and represent an increase in their deposits. In this regard, it is worth quoting Marriner S. Eccles (1947), chairman of the US Federal Reserve Board (1934–48), when answering questions from the members of the Committee on Banking and Currency of the House of Representatives, who wanted to know how the government pays for its expenditures. 'Question: How did you get the money to buy those $2,000,000,000 of Government securities [and advance that money to the government]? Mr. Eccles: We created it. Question: Out of what? Mr. Eccles: Out of the right to issue credit, money. Question: And there is nothing behind it, is there, except the Government's credit? Mr. Eccles: We have the Government bonds. Question: That's right, the Government's credit. Mr. Eccles: That is what your money system is.'

The process may in fact involve several successive steps, which can be summarized as follows: the cheques or deposits that increased the private agents' deposits are held by the banks as claims on the government and thus are recorded as an equal increase in their assets. Banks' claims on the government in this form are called 'reserves'. Banks can claim these reserves by presenting the cheques or deposits to the central bank, which keeps accounts for both the government and commercial banks. In a setting where the central bank is the banking arm of the government, the central bank executes the operation simply by crediting commercial banks' accounts (that is, by adding to their reserves) and debiting the government's account by an equal amount. Government spending results in a net injection of liquidity (money) into the private sector; the government is now running a deficit, but the private sector has a surplus of equal amount. We conclude that government spending increases the private sector's income and, therefore, that the accumulated deficits – the public debt – add to the private sector's financial wealth (see Bougrine, 2017).

It should be noted, however, that with the rise of monetarism and the associated ideas of 'fiscal responsibility' and 'sound finance', neoliberal policies have succeeded in imposing severe restrictions on how central banks could participate in financing government expenditures and in some cases making it illegal for central banks to advance funds to their own governments – hence, severely hampering the role of public policy in fighting poverty and other economic and social problems. Governments, such as those in the European Monetary Union, are now forced to rely on taxes and loans from private lenders, namely banks.

Note, however, that when the government remains indebted to the central bank and when the latter is publicly owned and is therefore the government's banking arm, the issue of a government's debt to its own bank becomes largely a technical issue. However, we can point out that any taxes collected by the government are deposited in its own account at the central bank as credits and would, therefore, serve to lower the amount of the debt (loan). If the government is eager to pay down its debt to the central bank, it can withdraw more money from the private sector by various ways and use the proceeds in the same way as taxes. All these withdrawals lead to a decrease in liquidity in the private sector and, from an accounting perspective, they are recorded in exactly the opposite manner of recording government spending.

HASSAN BOUGRINE

See also

European Monetary Union; Fiscal deficit; Inflation targeting; Monetary circuit; Money creation – nature of

References

Bougrine, H. (2017), *The Creation of Wealth and Poverty: Means and Ways*, London and New York: Routledge.

Eccles, M.S. (1947), *The Hearing before the Committee on Banking and Currency House of Representatives*, Eightieth Congress, Washington, DC: United States Government Printing Office, p. 52.

Growth

Post-Keynesian theory, by extending Keynes's (1936) short-run theory of unemployment to the long run, views economic growth as depending mainly on the growth of aggregate demand for goods and services, rather than on aggregate supply considerations such as saving as in the classical–Marxian theory, and on labour supply and its productivity as in the neoclassical approach, both in its old and new incarnations. A key feature of the Post-Keynesian approach is that investment behaviour is independent of saving behaviour (unlike the other approaches mentioned, which make saving and investment identically equal).

A basic Post-Keynesian growth model assumes that investment as a ratio of the capital stock (I/K) depends positively on the rate of capacity utilization ($u = Y/K$), where Y is real output, because excess capacity deters investment (Steindl, 1952). It also assumes that capitalists save a constant fraction (s) of profits and workers do not save, so that saving as a ratio of capital stock is given by $S/K = sr$, where r is the profit rate given, by definition, by $r = \pi u$, where π is the share of profits in income. Further, assuming that the profit share is fixed by the degree of monopoly, as in Kalecki's (1971) theory of mark-up pricing, goods market equilibrium, with $\dfrac{I}{K} = \dfrac{S}{K}$, is shown in the figure below at the intersection of the investment and saving curves. The growth of the capital stock (and output) is given by g. The investment line is assumed to be flatter than the saving line for macroeconomic stability: excess demand, with planned investment greater than saving, results

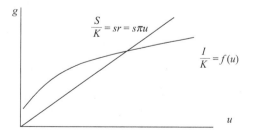

HASSAN BOUGRINE / AMITAVA DUTT

in an increase in output and capacity utilization. With investment rising less than saving, there is a stable adjustment.

An (exogenous) increase in the saving rate of capitalists reduces capacity utilization and economic growth, exhibiting the paradox of thrift. A reduction in the profit share increases capacity utilization and the rate of economic growth by distributing income from capitalists to workers who have a higher propensity to consume. This increases aggregate demand, resulting in wage-led economic growth. An increase in 'animal spirits' (which Keynes (1936) defines to be the spontaneous urge to action rather than inaction) displaces the investment curve upwards and increases economic growth as a self-fulfilling prophecy. An increase in labour productivity (for a constant profit share) leaves the rate of economic growth unaffected; if technological change increases investment (as it is embodied in capital), economic growth increases. Models such as this have been extended to incorporate endogenous technological change, financial and debt issues, inflation, endogenous income distribution, multi-sector considerations, and the environment, among others (see Dutt, 2017).

Although a model of this type (see Dutt, 1984, and Rowthorn, 1982, who assume that investment also depends on the rate of profit, because it increases profit expectations and eases financial conditions) has become popular (see Hein, 2014), it has been criticized for allowing the capacity utilization rate to be endogenous in (long-run) equilibrium rather than being equal to some exogenous 'normal' rate of capacity utilization. However, the model has been defended with the claim that there is no such thing as a 'normal' capacity utilization rate or, if it exists, it is endogenous. There are also some alternative approaches. One assumes full or normal capacity, and investment and saving adjust owing to variations in prices and hence in the profit share (see Robinson, 1962, for such a model in which investment depends on the rate of profit). Another assumes that investment adjusts in the long run to the exogenously given rate of growth of labour supply, although this implies that aggregate demand does not affect the rate of long-run economic growth (Kaldor, 1959). Another one reverts to the basic model, but assumes that investment is more responsive to capacity utilization than is saving, resulting in knife-edge instability (Harrod, 1939). Here, labour market considerations may be a stabilizer. Yet another modifies the basic model by making investment depend positively on the profit share and capacity utilization (Bhaduri and Marglin, 1990). This implies that a reduction in the profit share may reduce the rate of economic growth by reducing investment enough to outweigh the positive consumption effect, implying profit-led growth, as in neo-Marxian models (see Dutt, 1990). Finally, for an open economy, with exports and imports depending on international competitiveness, a rise in the wage share can reduce both aggregate demand and economic growth by reducing net exports. However, if the economy faces a balance-of-payments constraint, with constant (or zero) foreign debt-income ratio and international terms of trade (see Thirlwall, 1979), economic growth depends positively on external demand growth and negatively on the income elasticity of its imports.

AMITAVA DUTT

See also

Aggregate demand; Balance-of-payments constrained growth; Capacity utilization; Growth – wage-led vs profit-led; Paradox of thrift

References

Bhaduri, A. and S. Marglin (1990), 'Unemployment and the real wage: the economic basis of contesting political ideologies', *Cambridge Journal of Economics*, **14** (4), 375–93.

Dutt, A. (1984), 'Stagnation, income distribution and monopoly power', *Cambridge Journal of Economics*, **8** (1), 25–40.

Dutt, A. (1990), *Growth, Distribution and Uneven Development*, Cambridge, UK: Cambridge University Press.

Dutt, A. (2017), 'Heterodox theories of growth and distribution: a partial view', *Journal of Economic Surveys*, **31** (5), 335–51.

Harrod, R. (1939), 'An essay in dynamic theory', *Economic Journal*, **49** (193), 14–33.

Hein, E. (2014), *Distribution and Growth after Keynes*, Cheltenham, UK, and Northampton, MA, USA: Edward Elgar.

Kaldor, N. (1959), 'Economic growth and the problem of inflation', *Economica*, **26** (103), 212–26.

Kalecki, M. (1971), *Selected Essays on the Dynamics of the Capitalist Economy*, Cambridge, UK: Cambridge University Press.

Keynes, J.M. (1936), *The General Theory of Employment, Interest and Money*, London: Macmillan.

Robinson, J. (1962), *Essays in the Theory of Economic Growth*, London: Macmillan.

Rowthorn, R. (1982), 'Demand, real wages and growth', *Studi Economici*, **18** (1), 3–54.
Steindl, J. (1952), *Maturity and Stagnation in American Capitalism*, Oxford: Basil Blackwell.
Thirlwall, A.P. (1979), 'The balance of payments constraint as an explanation of the international growth rate differences', *PSL Quarterly Review*, **32** (128), 45–53.

Growth – unequal

Since the classical economists and Marx, it is widely accepted that the process of economic growth is inherently unequal. The Industrial Revolution, which is at the root of industrial society as we know it, relied heavily on a previous accumulation cycle. This allowed entrepreneurs to become owners of the capital goods extensively and hire workers to master production. In that environment, Adam Smith successfully showed that the cause of a nation's wealth is the continuous increase in labour productivity. But he also demonstrated that demand on the market for produced goods and services plays an import role in the adoption of more productive techniques. Sectors whose demand was growing were more prone to implement new production methods to foster output and meet its demand. Central to this reasoning is that learning-by-doing related to the production process is essential to explain productivity growth. Then sectors with higher demand are more prone to have faster technological progress. But the share of income spent on any particular consumption good is never constant, because personal income increases but tends to reach saturation. This phenomenon is the empirical regularity first described by Engel (1857), a German statistician of the nineteenth century.[1] Now, productivity gains translated in terms of higher per capita demand are unevenly distributed with regard to the demand for different kinds of goods. That is why the process of economic growth is inherently unequal.

Besides, Joseph A. Schumpeter added a new dimension to the process of economic growth when he considered the role of innovation. According to him, the main competition in capitalist economies is for the rents that accrue from monopolistic power. If such power is not natural, it can be searched through research and development (R&D) activities. When an entrepreneur successfully reaches an invention translated in terms of a new product, s/he immediately obtains monopoly power owing to patents and copyright. Such power guarantees that the revenues are above the costs of production, which gives rise to rents. Such rents may be reinvested in more R&D, thereby giving rise to more monopoly power. This shows that the process of innovation is also inherently uneven. An entrepreneur or firm that successfully obtains a patent for a new product can reinvest the profits that accrue from selling this product into new R&D, giving rise to more rents.

This process contrasts with the literature on economic growth that unfolded in the twentieth century. First, the models of Harrod (1939) and Domar (1946) intended to extend the Keynesian effective demand to the long run. But they cannot consider the inequalities that accrue from the process of economic growth owing to their limited framework built in terms of an aggregated economy. The neoclassical growth model proposed by Solow (1956) restricted their focus on capital accumulation and total factor productivity, which constituted the mainstream growth theory. A common element in all these models is a steady-state path of economic growth that precludes any possibility of uneven growth. With their emphasis on the supply side, these models built initially regarding aggregated frameworks are unfitted to consider the possible links between economic growth and changes in the demand composition that lead to unbalanced growth.

Amongst the scholars who paid attention to unbalanced economic growth, Baumol (1967) features prominently. He assigns to the industrial sector the role of being the progressive industry, while the service sector is stagnant as regards productivity growth. Assuming that the real outputs (or volume shares) of both stagnant and advanced sectors grow at the same rate, there is an unbalanced labour allocation. The backward sector tends to absorb all economy's labour. Moreover, as a consequence, the productivity of the whole economy tends to stagnate. This outcome became known in the literature as the 'Baumol cost disease'. Although dealing with unbalanced growth, Baumol has a neoclassical pedigree, which manifests in his model owing to its strong focus on the supply side, with demand playing next to no role. Although he had provided essential insights on how technological factors can lead to unbalanced growth, this fact is very unsettling insofar as there are more subtle and compelling reasons for demand-side sources of structural changes. To further consider the role of demand, Pasinetti (1993) highlighted that the dynamic patterns of human needs and preferences give rise to entirely different consumer demand compositions and, therefore, particular production structures and employment in each economy. Accordingly, the Pasinettian theory of consumption based on an income-driven rule of non-proportional expansion of demand delivers unbalanced economic growth as the outcome of income and relative-price effects simultaneously considered.

RICARDO ARAUJO

See also

Capitalism; Effective demand; Growth – wage-led vs profit-led; Neoclassical economics; Monopoly power

Note

1. Note that although Engel's formulation concerned mainly food, his law holds for other products.

References

Baumol, W.J. (1967), 'Macroeconomics of unbalanced growth: the anatomy of urban crisis', *American Economic Review*, **57** (3), 415–26.
Domar, E. (1946), 'Capital expansion, rate of growth, and employment', *Econometrica*, **14** (2), 137–47.
Engel, E. (1857), 'Die Produktions- und Konsumtionsverhältnisse des Königreichs Sachsen', *Zeitschrift des Statistischen Bureaus des Königlich Sachsischen Ministeriums des Innern*, **3** (8–9), 1–54.
Harrod, R. (1939), 'An essay in dynamic theory', *Economic Journal*, **49** (193), 14–33.
Pasinetti, L.L. (1993), *Structural Economic Dynamics: A Theory of Economic Consequences of Human Learning*, Cambridge, UK: Cambridge University Press.
Solow, R.M. (1956), 'A contribution to the theory of economic growth', *Quarterly Journal of Economics*, **70** (1), 65–94.

Growth – wage-led vs profit-led

A central concern of post-Keynesian macroeconomics is the interaction between economic activity and the resulting distribution of income. This issue is crucial in understanding whether rising wage shares bolsters demand and increases the rate of capacity utilization, which, in turn, induces capitalists to invest, or whether rises in the profit share serve as the primary stimulus.

If the propensity to consume out of wages is higher than that to consume out of profits, redistributing income away from wage earners would depress total consumption. However, it could also stimulate investment expenditures because of a higher profit share, which would in essence counteract the depressing effect of lower consumption expenditures on effective demand. Depending on which of these effects dominates, there are two possibilities that can emerge: (i) greater consumption expenditure owing to higher real wages and lower profit share (wage-led growth), or (ii) greater investment expenditure owing to higher profit share and lower real wages (profit-led growth) (see Bhaduri, 2007).

A large body of work has investigated these issues empirically (see Barbosa-Filho et al., 2006; Hein and Vogel, 2008; Stockhammer and Onaran, 2013; Oyvat et al., 2020). Yet, the primary theoretical difference lies in the treatment of capitalist investment (Caldentey and Vernengo, 2013).

On the one hand, wage-led growth models, inspired by the contributions of Nicholas Kaldor, estimate the degree to which capitalist investment is derived from demand attuned to the growth of autonomous spending, that is, the accelerator.

In contrast, profit-led models, influenced by the work of Joan Robinson, see capitalist investment as an independent function subordinate to the rate of profit. Changes in income distribution have ambiguous effects on capital accumulation, which ultimately rests on the exact specification of the investment function in relation to an approximate remunerated risk, that is, a normal rate of profit, of adequately employing capital.

Steindl (1952/1976) advanced the argument that increases in the profit rate would lead to higher profit shares, which would inevitably be contractionary owing to increases in the degree of monopoly power, resulting in chronic economic stagnation and over-accumulation, unless offset by sources of surplus capital absorption, like foreign trade and financialization. The profit rate, therefore, should be treated as an endogenous variable,

RICARDO ARAUJO / DAVID M. FIELDS

assuming an open economy (Blecker, 1989). Nominal currency depreciations, for instance, would make domestic goods more internationally competitive, and the resulting boost to net exports could outweigh decreases in domestic consumption brought about by the lower wage share. With the distributive share of total income between labour and capital moving towards property wealth owing to financialization (see Van Arnum and Naples, 2013), particularly in the case of the United States, domestic consumption expenditure can be buoyed by the substitution of rising real wages with rising household debt (Barba and Pivetti, 2009).

Generally speaking, countries should not be uniquely classified as either wage or profit led. Time horizons should be considered. The relative magnitudes of the effects of income distribution on the components of aggregate demand are likely to vary depending on the course of the business cycle. As Blecker (2016) explains, the positive effects of higher profit shares on investment are mainly short-run phenomena, while the sensitivity of workers' consumption to their income is likely to be stronger in the long run.

DAVID M. FIELDS

See also

Accelerator effects; Effective demand; Financialization; Income distribution; Monopoly power

References

Barba, A. and M. Pivetti (2009), 'Rising household debt: its causes and macroeconomic implications – a long-period analysis', *Cambridge Journal of Economics*, 33 (1), 113–37.

Barbosa-Filho, N.H. and L. Taylor (2006), 'Distributive and demand cycles in the US economy – a structuralist Goodwin model', *Metroeconomica*, 57 (3), 389–411.

Bhaduri, A. (2007), 'On the dynamics of profit-led and wage-led growth', *Cambridge Journal of Economics*, 32 (1), 147–60.

Blecker, R.A. (1989), 'International competition, income distribution and economic growth', *Cambridge Journal of Economics*, 13 (3), 395–412.

Blecker, R.A. (2016), 'Wage-led versus profit-led demand regimes: the long and the short of it', *Review of Keynesian Economics*, 4 (5), 373–90.

Caldentey, E.P. and M. Vernengo (2013), 'Wage and profit-led growth: the limits to Neo-Kaleckian models and a Kaldorian proposal', *Levy Economics Institute of Bard College Working Paper*, No. 775.

Hein, E. and L. Vogel (2008), 'Distribution and growth reconsidered: empirical results for six OECD countries', *Cambridge Journal of Economics*, 32 (3), 479–511.

Oyvat, C., O. Öztunali and C. Elgin (2020), 'Wage-led versus profit-led demand: a comprehensive empirical analysis', *Metroeconomica*, 71 (3), 458–86.

Steindl, J. (1952/1976), *Maturity and Stagnation in American Capitalism*, New York: Monthly Review Press.

Stockhammer, E. and O. Onaran (2013), 'Wage-led growth: theory, evidence, and policy', *Review of Keynesian Economics*, 1 (1), 61–78.

Van Arnum, B.M. and M.I. Naples (2013), 'Financialization and income inequality in the United States, 1967–2010', *American Journal of Economics and Sociology*, 72 (5), 1158–85.

Harrod's dynamics

Roy F. Harrod (1900–78) is mostly known for his contributions to economic dynamics. Following the logic of physical mechanics, Harrod divided economics into a static and a dynamic branch. The former dealt with states of rest, and the latter with the study of the causes of the rate at which an object moves at a point in time. He identified three situations in economics that could qualify as static in its mechanical sense: a stationary equilibrium, comparative statics and a situation of constant change over time.

Harrod thought that, with the exceptions of the 'old classical school' (Adam Smith, David Ricardo, John Stuart Mill), economists including Keynes had focused on perfecting static equilibrium analysis and had excluded the dynamic elements from the corpus of economic theory. Harrod sought to fill this gap by providing a framework of concepts relevant to dynamics and analogous to that found in statics. Harrod started from the premise that statics and dynamics formed part of a single and indivisible theory, and that the analysis of the determinants of the level of activity (statics) preceded that of dynamics.

Harrod provided the first articulated view of dynamics in *The Trade Cycle* (1936). In strict analogy with the analysis of statics, he coined the notion of 'a steady rate of advance' (a situation in which the ratio of the increment of output to the previous level is constant), which provided the reference point for the explanation of the trade cycle. In Harrod's theory, the

DAVID M. FIELDS / ESTEBAN PÉREZ CALDENTEY

upwards/downwards cumulative movements of the trade cycle are driven by the endogenous interaction between the multiplier and the accelerator.

An increase (decline) in the rate of investment pushes up (reduces) the rate of increase of consumption via the multiplier effect. This in turn requires, by the workings of the accelerator, a rise (fall) in the level of investment. By the logic of the multiplier, this entails a rise (fall) in the level of income and consumption; and the consequent increase (fall) in consumption leads via the accelerator to an increase (reduction) in the level of investment.

In *An Essay on Dynamic Theory* (Harrod, 1938; 1939), its key innovation – that is, the fundamental equation – provided a further and definitive development of Harrod's dynamics and its central core, namely the instability principle. He defined the fundamental equation in terms of the warranted rate of economic growth (that rate of economic growth that validates the capital accumulation decisions of entrepreneurs). Along with the warranted rate of economic growth, Harrod introduced the natural (the maximum rate of growth allowed by population, technology and preferences, assuming full employment) and the actual rate of economic growth. In *An Essay on Dynamic Theory*, instability results from the independency of the three components of the fundamental equation (the rate of economic growth, the propensity to save, and the incremental capital–output ratio), and Harrod describes the trade cycle in terms of the cumulative deviations of the actual from the warranted rate of economic growth and the endogeneity of the warranted rate over the course of the cycle.

Harrod's approach to dynamics permeated his writings on a variety of subjects including imperfect competition, international competition, economic development and macroeconomic policy (Harrod, 1957; 1961; 1973). His initial optimism about the development of dynamics gave place to disappointment and frustration over the misunderstanding, misinterpretation and misrepresentation of his view on dynamics, which became increasingly identified with a balanced-growth model. Far from being a *fait accompli*, Harrod's dynamic economics simply became an agenda for future research and there is much work to be done in laying out the foundations of a truly Harrodian dynamic economics.

ESTEBAN PÉREZ CALDENTEY

See also

Accelerator effects; Development; Harrod's foreign trade multiplier; Harrod's trade cycle; Income multiplier

References

Harrod, R.F. (1936), *The Trade Cycle*, Oxford: Clarendon Press.
Harrod, R.F. (1938), 'An essay in dynamic theory', in D. Besomi (ed.), *The Collected Interwar Papers and Correspondence of Roy Harrod, Vol. III*, Cheltenham, UK, and Northampton, MA, USA, 2003, pp. 1188–212.
Harrod, R.F. (1939), 'An essay in dynamic theory', *Economic Journal*, **49** (193), 14–33.
Harrod, R.F. (1957), *International Economics*, Chicago: University of Chicago Press.
Harrod, R.F. (1961), *Topical Comment*, New York: St. Martin's Press.
Harrod, R.F. (1973), *Economic Dynamics*, New York: Macmillan.
Pérez Caldentey, E. (2019), *Roy Harrod*, London: Palgrave Macmillan.

Harrod's foreign trade multiplier

Roy F. Harrod introduced the notion of the 'foreign trade multiplier' in Chapter VI of his 1933 book, *International Economics*. Extending Kahn's (1931) employment multiplier to international trade and published three years before Keynes's *General Theory*, Harrod (1933) puts forward the idea that the level of industrial output is explained by the principle of the foreign trade multiplier, which, at the same time, provides the mechanism for keeping the balance of payments in equilibrium (Kaldor, 1981, p. 601).

This twofold condition is derived from the validity of the principle of effective demand within an open economy and from the implied necessary balance between exports and imports. If exports fall short of imports, and the balance-of-payments deficits cannot be persistently financed, income and employment will fall. The adjustment mechanism is well known in peripheral economies: the balance-of-payments crisis will lead to a currency depreciation, which, by deteriorating income distribution, will exert its contractionary effects on aggregate output (see Braun and Joy, 1968).

Following Harrod (1948, pp. 119–22), the foreign trade multiplier can be formalized as follows. Assume an open economy where there are no autonomous components of aggregate demand other than exports (X), and in which all domestic income (Y) is consumed either to purchase domestic goods (cY) or imports (mY). Terms of trade are assumed to be constant and the exchange rate is fixed. There is no saving and investment, and no government activity. Therefore:

$$Y = C^d + X \quad (1)$$

$$E = (c + m)Y \quad (2)$$

where C^d is the income received from the sale of goods at home, E is the level of expenditure, and c and m are, respectively, the proportion of income spent on domestic and foreign goods.

The internal equilibrium is obtained from imposing both the equality between total income and total expenditure ($Y = E$) and the condition that income received from the sale of goods at home is equal to the expenditure on home-made goods ($C^d = cY$) (Harrod, 1936/1965). Thus, from equations (1) and (2) one derives the expression for the foreign trade multiplier:

$$Y = \frac{x}{m} \quad (3)$$

In other words, this is 'the product of the reciprocal of the proportion of income devoted to goods made abroad and the value of exports' (Harrod, 1933/1942, p. 123).

The validity of equation (3) also implies external equilibrium, which means that trade is balanced:

$$X = mY = M \quad (4)$$

Note that there is no need for any kind of adjustment to make the level of domestic activity compatible with the external sector.

As Pérez Caldentey (2019, pp. 280–1) points out, condition (3) is expressed in its instantaneous formulation, but it can also be derived as a chain of successive spending. Let income in period 1 be equal to exports earnings for the same period ($Y = X$). In period 2, exports earnings are spent at home in the proportion $(1 - m)X$. In the next period, the proportion of the income spent by exporters at home is equal to $(1 - m)^2$. The chain of spending continues until the entire exports earnings of the initial period are spent in the economy. For the nth period, the total income is equal to the income earned by exporters plus the income earned by those producing domestic goods. The multiplier is derived by subtracting the initial level of income from the expression for period n. This yields:

$$\Delta Y = \Delta X[1 + (1 - m) + (1 - m)^2 + \ldots + (1 - m)^n]$$

The expression in square brackets is a geometric series, whose limit as $n \to \infty$ is:

$$\lim_{n \to \infty} \frac{1 - (1 - m)^n}{1 - m} = \frac{1}{1 - (1 - m)} = \frac{1}{m} \quad (5)$$

Some decades later, Kaldor (1970) rediscovered Harrod's idea in his lecture on the case for regional policies, given to the Scottish Economic Society, where he established its dynamic analogue, by means of which he explained differences in output growth rates. This influential notion was later developed formally by Thirlwall (1979) in his characterization of the balance-of-payments constrained growth rate:

$$y = \frac{x}{\pi} \quad (6)$$

where y is the rate of growth of real income, x is the rate of growth of export volumes, and π is the income elasticity of demand for imports. Price-elasticities of both exports and imports are assumed to be small, relative to income elasticities.

To obtain condition (6) from expression (3), let us start by expressing the latter in its difference form, and divide both sides by Y. Then, multiply and divide the right-hand side by X. Finally, recalling that $X = M$, we obtain:

$$y = \frac{\Delta Y}{Y} = \frac{\Delta X}{X} \frac{M}{Y} \frac{1}{m} = \frac{x}{\pi}$$

It is then clear that, being the dynamic version of the foreign trade multiplier, Thirlwall's Law describes an export-led growth model.

Notice that the moment we relax one of the key assumptions of the foreign trade multiplier and allow for autonomous components of effective demand other than exports, the equilibrium level of output and its growth rate are no longer necessarily determined by exports. In this case, the balance-of-payments equilibrium acts as an upper bound for output, as many

Latin American structuralist scholars used to stress (see, for instance, Prebisch, 1949/1986), while its normal level may well stand below it.

GERMÁN D. FELDMAN

See also

Balance-of-payments constrained growth; Effective demand; Income multiplier; Structuralism and post-Keynesianism; Thirlwall's Law

References

Braun, O. and L. Joy (1968), 'A model of economic stagnation: a case study of the Argentine economy', *Economic Journal*, **78** (312), 868–87.
Harrod, R.F. (1933/1942), *International Economics*, second edition, Cambridge, UK: Cambridge University Press.
Harrod, R.F. (1936/1965), *The Trade Cycle*, New York: Augustus M. Kelley.
Harrod, R.F. (1948), *Towards a Dynamic Economics*, London: Macmillan.
Kahn, R.F. (1931), 'The relation of home investment to unemployment', *Economic Journal*, **41** (162), 173–98.
Kaldor, N. (1970), 'The case for regional policies', *Scottish Journal of Political Economy*, **17** (3), 337–48.
Kaldor, N. (1981), 'The role of increasing returns, technical progress and cumulative causation in the theory of international trade and economic growth', *Economie Appliquée*, **34** (4), 593–617.
Pérez Caldentey, E. (2019), *Roy Harrod*, London and New York: Palgrave Macmillan.
Prebisch, R. (1949/1986), 'El desarrollo económico de la América Latina y algunos de sus principales problemas', *Desarrollo Económico*, **26** (103), 479–502.
Thirlwall, A.P. (1979), 'The balance of payments constraint as an explanation of international growth rates differences', *Banca Nazionale del Lavoro Quarterly Review*, **32** (128), 45–53.

Harrod's trade cycle

Harrod's (1936, 1939) analysis of the business cycle is based on two main determinants, namely, the principle of instability and imperfect competition.

The principle of instability emerges from Harrod's (1936, 1939) work on the dynamics of capitalism, which is an extension of Keynes's (1936) ideas in the medium run. In this task, Harrod (1939) mobilizes the concepts of the actual growth rate g, the warranted growth rate g_w and the natural growth rate g_n. The latter refers to the rate of economic growth required to maintain full employment. The warranted growth rate is 'the rate of growth which, if it occurs, will leave all parties satisfied that they have produced neither more nor less than the right amount. Or, to state the matter otherwise, it will put them into a frame of mind which will cause them to give such additional orders as will maintain the same rate of growth' (Harrod, 1939, p. 16).

The dynamics of the actual growth rate is the result of the dialectic that is tied around the multiplier and the accelerator. The multiplier links the evolution of income to the growth rate of investment – a link that depends on the share s of income that is saved. The accelerator determines the quantity of units of capital required to produce an additional unit of good, taking into account the technology and the interest rate. When, for example, actual demand turns out to be higher than anticipated by entrepreneurs ($g > g_w$), the quantity of installed capital is likely to be deemed insufficient and thus induce an acceleration of investment. This implies, via the multiplier effect, an increase in demand. Outside the warranted growth path, the growth rate of investment does not generate an increase in demand in proportion to the increase in productive capacity. The gap between g and g_w widens.

The dynamic equilibrium of full employment can only occur when $g = g_n = g_w$. The problem with Harrod's principle of instability is that the forces that could lead to a reconciliation of g and g_w are also those that cause g_w and g_n to divorce. Suppose, for example, that $g < g_w = g_n$. A depreciating loop is then triggered by the fact that $g < g_w$ and nothing hinders it, if there is no change in the parameters that define g_w (the social savings rate s, the interest rate, the level of public spending, the capital coefficient and so on). To stop the process of cumulative depression, it is thus necessary to change the value of g_w, which then moves away from g_n.

As Hicks (1949) pointed out, the instability of the dynamic equilibrium of full employment is not sufficient to explain economic fluctuations. It remains to be explained why the economy has a tendency to oscillate.

It is at this point that imperfect competition comes into play in Harrod's analysis through the relative movements of prices and production costs along the business cycle. On this

GERMÁN D. FELDMAN / CÉDRIC ROGÉ

point, Harrod (1936) differs from Keynes (1936) by not assuming a decline in marginal labour productivity. Harrod's argument is based on what he calls 'the law of diminishing elasticity of demand' (1936, p. 21), which implies that the degree of monopoly increases in the upswing and falls in the downswing.

Thus, the decline in the mark-up that accompanies the phase of economic recession is likely to lower the social savings rate s (and thus g_w) via the resulting distributional effects.

Let us assume that the present situation is characterized by an effective growth rate g lower than the warranted growth rate g_w. This leads to a drop in production owing to the slowdown in investment. As explained, this reaction only amplifies the initial imbalance. Now, if the fall in household and corporate savings rates accompanies the slowdown in capital accumulation, g_w falls as well. If this decline is large enough, it is possible that, at some point in time, g_w will fall below g (point A in the figure), propelling the economy onto an accelerated growth path. Indeed, this time firms see their inventories shrink and try to cope by accelerating their investments, which again amplifies the imbalances (but in the other direction) and sustains the cumulative process. However, this expansion cannot be sustained over the long run, because the agents' savings rate rises as the economic outlook improves, which pushes the warranted growth rate upwards. On the other hand, if the labour supply does not grow fast enough, which happens as the economic system approaches full employment, the growth of g will slow down and even stop (point C in the figure). Of course, investment also results in a substitution of capital for labour, that is, an increase in the coefficient of capital, which makes it possible to slow down the growth rate initiated by the increase in the social savings rate. But Harrod (1936, 1939) believes that this should necessarily lead to the moment when the effective growth rate falls below the required growth rate and then begins a new phase of recession.

Thus, the non-linear behaviour of the investment and savings functions that results from Harrod's principle of instability and his 'law of diminishing elasticity of demand' are likely to explain both economic cycles and growth. It must be noted that this fundamental point is almost systematically ignored in standard presentations of Harrod's growth model (see for instance Barro and Sala-i-Martin, 1995, p. 17; Acemoglu, 2008, p. 26).

Shaded areas in the figure correspond to recessions. At point C, there is a return in the cycle owing to difficulties in finding available labour as full employment approaches. Unemployment is reduced during the BD phase and increases each time g is below g_n. It is noticeable that the turnaround of the cycle takes place before reaching full employment and it is not at all evident that full employment is reached during the cycle. In particular, if

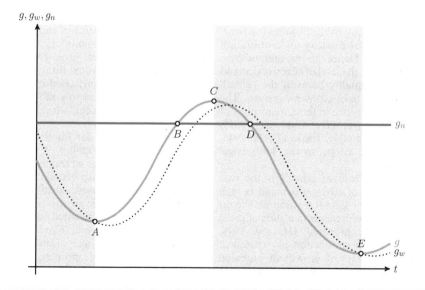

Cédric Rogé

point D is the point at which the unemployment rate is lowest, there is no evidence that it is zero.

CÉDRIC ROGÉ

See also

Accelerator effects; Capitalism – stages of; Free trade; Growth – wage-led vs profit-led; Income multiplier

References

Acemoglu, D. (2008), *Introduction to Modern Economic Growth*, Princeton: Princeton University Press.
Barro, R.J. and X. Sala-i-Martin (1995), *Economic Growth*, New York: McGraw-Hill.
Harrod, R.F. (1936), *The Trade Cycle: An Essay*, Oxford: Clarendon Press.
Harrod, R.F. (1939), 'An essay in dynamic theory', *Economic Journal*, **49** (193), 14–33.
Hicks, J.R. (1949), 'Mr. Harrod's dynamic theory', *Economica*, **16** (62), 106–21.
Keynes, J.M. (1936), *The General Theory of Employment, Interest and Money*, London: Macmillan.

Harrodian instability

The fundamental essence of Harrodian instability is that without the presence of requisite stabilizing mechanisms to ensure a steady-state rate of economic growth, where actual output is kept in pace with potential output, there is a tendency towards a long-run unstable condition of either capacity overutilization (an overheating economy) or capacity underutilization (excess capacity). Hence, to prevent adverse path dependencies, the level of effective demand must guarantee equality between the 'actual' and 'warranted' rate of economic growth. The possibility of divergence in these trend rates of economic growth (see Pérez Caldentey, 2019, pp. 173–257), assumed by Harrod (1939, 1948, 1973), has become known as the 'knife edge' (Kregel, 1980).

The warranted rate of growth is the rate at which the level of effective demand is high enough such that the long-run economic expansion will 'leave entrepreneurs in a state of mind in which they are prepared' (Harrod, 1948, p. 82) to carry on production as scheduled. It represents the rate of growth of potential output that would only occur if investment over the long run is such that demand stably adjusts itself to the level and growth rate of planned productive capacity (Trezzini and Pignalosa, 2021), which may not necessarily constitute full employment (Serrano et al., 2019). As such, the so-called 'natural', or neo-Wicksellian, rate of (un)employment is thoroughly rejected. Given the extent to which uncertainty is prevalent, due to the coercive laws of capitalist competition (Marx, 1977, p. 433), it is unreasonable to assume that economic growth at the warranted rate should be fully expected, as the growth of 'actual' output can deviate from desired degrees of capacity utilization, resulting in static fluctuation (Hicks, 1965).

The potential for Harrodian instability can be abstractly manifested by a multiplier accelerator model (Allain, 2021), namely $I = f(Y)$, where I is total productive investment, and Y equals total output, which is total income from the effects of autonomous expenditures, that is, capitalist expenditure on improving production based on positive lagged changes in disposable income – this is the Keynesian multiplier of induced demand leading to positive expectations of future economic growth. We can derive a steady-state equilibrium level of employment with the following equation: $Y = \varphi Z$, where φ is the multiplier and Z is the level of autonomous expenditures in the economy. The unambiguous outcome of a permanent increase in the level of effective demand is an increase in capacity utilization via investment in fixed capital.

Hence, we can write $Y = W + \Pi$, where Y is total income (output), W is gross wages and Π is gross profits. Increases in demand not only lead to increases in employment, but with increases in consumption resulting from increasing employment, gross profits increase as well. Hence, if expected future earnings are met by demand and surpassed by production, profits are directed towards more investment and increase employment, which, in turn, fosters more investment.

In this sense, in order for the economy to avoid Harrodian instability, Y must be the condition at which the warranted rate of economic growth equals the actual rate of output. A cumulative and unstable position arises if the actual rate of economic growth is either greater than or less than the warranted rate. The former case will induce capitalists to over-accumulate; the latter will encourage disinvestment. The overall macroeconomic property can be represented by the following figure displaying the

CÉDRIC ROGÉ / DAVID M. FIELDS

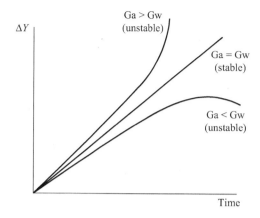

'knife edge' growth path, in which *Ga* is the actual growth rate, and *Gw* is the warranted growth rate; ΔY is the change in total output, and, by implication, productive investment.

The central question is what stabilizing mechanism is necessary to prevent Harrodian instability due to capitalist investment being insufficient? In order to ensure that the wage share and the level of economic activity do not fall, the answer is capacity-enhancing public investment, so that autonomous expenditures adjust the warranted rate of economic growth, and by definition the actual rate of economic growth, to a long-run equilibrium position of full employment (Moudud, 2009). 'To lift employment to any desired degree of fullness... requires a very ambitious, dynamically variable fiscal policy' (Goodwin, 1997, pp. 162–3).

DAVID M. FIELDS

See also

Capacity utilization; Dependency theory; Effective demand; Growth; Unemployment

References

Allain, O. (2021), 'A supermultiplier model of the natural rate of growth', *Metroeconomica*, **72** (3), 612–34.
Goodwin, R. (1997), 'Keynes and dynamics', in G.C. Harcourt and P.A. Riach (eds), *A Second Edition of the General Theory*, London and New York: Routledge, pp. 162–3.
Harrod, R. (1939), 'An essay in dynamic theory', *Economic Journal*, **49** (193), 14–33.
Harrod, R. (1948), *Towards a Dynamic Economics*, London: Macmillan.
Harrod, R. (1973), *Economic Dynamics*, London: Macmillan.

Hicks, J. (1965), *Capital and Growth*, Oxford: Oxford University Press.
Kregel, J. (1980), 'Economic dynamics and the theory of steady growth: an historical essay on Harrod's "knife-edge"', *History of Political Economy*, **12** (1), 97–123.
Marx, K. (1977), *Capital, Vol. I*, New York: Vintage.
Moudud, J.K. (2009), 'The role of the State and Harrod's *Economic Dynamics*: toward a new policy agenda?', *International Journal of Political Economy*, **38** (1), 35–57.
Pérez Caldentey, E. (2019), *Roy Harrod*, Basingstoke, UK: Palgrave Macmillan.
Serrano, F., F. Freitas and G. Bhering (2019), 'The trouble with Harrod: the fundamental instability of the warranted rate in the light of the Sraffian supermultiplier', *Metroeconomica*, **70** (2), 263–87.
Trezzini, A. and D. Pignalosa (2021), 'The normal degree of capacity utilization: the history of a controversial concept', *Centro Sraffa Working Paper*, No. 49.

Heterodox economics

Heterodox economics (HE) is a broad category, which includes a great variety of strands of thought: original institutional, post-Keynesian, Sraffian, feminist, the French regulation school and social structures of accumulation theory, along with neo-Schumpeterian, evolutionary, and Marxist economics and, according to some views (Dow, 2000; Lawson, 2006), also Austrian economics. The term 'heterodox' is controversial on two accounts. First, the variety of research programmes it includes may suggest that there is no common core and that the term boils down to 'not orthodox' (Dequech, 2007–08). Second, various research programmes in economics do not fit properly in either the mainstream or HE (Backhouse, 2004; Davis, 2008). This suggests that viewing HE as a 'fuzzy set' rather than as a strictly defined concept may be appropriate and conducive to a better understanding of the issues under inquiry (Mearman, 2012).

It is, however, the case that most heterodox economists share a common discourse over:

1. Theory: since mainstream policies miss their targets and cause economic and social costs, a more realistic theory of the economy is called for. HE, therefore, considers issues such as money, distribution, power, institutions, social classes, gender and race discrimination. Contrary to the

DAVID M. FIELDS / PAOLO RAMAZZOTTI

mainstream, these are not viewed as mere theoretical qualifications or as constraints on the proper functioning of markets. They are included as integral features of the real-world economy.
2. Methodology: this theoretical endeavour clashes with the mainstream's scientific criteria. Contrary to the latter's naturalist view of markets, HE understands the economy as a historically embedded, open system (Chick and Dow, 2005).
3. Goals: typical economic issues, such as growth and employment, are obviously important. Contrary to mainstream economics, however, HE also considers issues such as human development and the quality of life. Insofar as it conceives of the present as history (Sweezy, 1953), it entertains the possibility of a different society.

HE does not have the homogeneity that the axiomatic-deductive approach provides to the mainstream. This is less a drawback than the proof of the vitality of the heterodox research programme, as opposed to the autistic self-referentiality of the mainstream. Open issues, therefore, abound for all of the themes outlined.

From a theoretical perspective, while the importance of historical time, uncertainty and non-ergodicity is generally beyond dispute, other issues remain controversial. For instance, heterodox contributions range from the pragmatic acknowledgment that the conventional price mechanism just needs to be improved (Jo, 2016) to attempts at an altogether alternative perspective based on the claim that the mainstream is internally inconsistent or is based on irrelevant assumptions. Similar considerations apply to the economy's complexity and to power.

Differences emerge at the methodological level as well. According to some authors, the above features of real-world economies only require a change in the axioms of a deductive model (Davidson, 2011) and the inclusion of the mainstream as a special case of a broader outlook (Fontana and Gerrard, 2006). Other authors stress that underlying differences in modes of thought (Dow, 2012) and in worldviews (Lee, 2011) constrain, or even preclude, the establishment of common theoretical grounds between mainstream and HE. Underlying most discussions over these issues is the (sometimes tacit) search for rigorous ontological premises, a point particularly stressed by critical realism.

As far as the goals of the economy are concerned, a major focus is on Keynes's and Kalecki's concern for unemployment, income and wealth distribution. Another area of concern is centred on the social costs of economic activity. These include: the private costs that firms shift onto society or sections of it (for instance, pollution or shop floor accidents) (see Kapp. 1971); a composition of output that favours ceremonialism and profitability at the expense of instrumentalism and serviceability; an organization of production that reproduces a gendered division of labour; a capitalist mode of production that does not ensure either growth or the satisfaction of collective needs. These issues are often dealt with independently of one another. This suggests that there should be greater dialogue among the different strands of HE. It nonetheless points to two major issues. First, the need for a social accounting that transcends prices (Ramazzotti, 2022) and that includes qualitative elements such as capabilities (Sen, 1993). Second, the need to dispense with a scientific view of the economy and to overcome the mainstream's positive–normative dichotomy (see Putnam and Walsh, 2011).

Summing up, what heterodox economists ultimately share, although they may not stress this point, is the idea that changes in the economy feed back on society and vice versa. Consequently, neither the coordination nor the assessment of the economy can rely on relative prices alone.

PAOLO RAMAZZOTTI

See also

Complex systems; Critical realism; Feminist economics; Institutional economics; Methodology

References

Backhouse, R.E. (2004), 'A suggestion for clarifying the study of dissent in economics', *Journal of the History of Economic Thought*, **26** (2), 261–71.
Chick, V. and S. Dow (2005), 'The meaning of open systems', *Journal of Economic Methodology*, **12** (3), 363–81.
Davidson, P. (2011), 'A response to John Kay's essay on the state of economics', Institute for New Economic Thinking blog, available online at https://www.ineteconomics.org/perspectives/blog/a-response-to-john-kays-essay-on-the-state-of-economics-1 (last accessed 17 May 2019).

Davis, J.B. (2008), 'The turn in recent economics and return of orthodoxy', *Cambridge Journal of Economics*, **32** (3), 349–66.
Dequech, D. (2007–08), 'Neoclassical, mainstream, orthodox, and heterodox economics', *Journal of Post Keynesian Economics*, **30** (2), 279–302.
Dow, S.C. (2000), 'Prospects for the progress of heterodox economics', *Journal of the History of Economic Thought*, **22** (2), 157–70.
Dow, S.C. (2012), 'Babylonian mode of thought', in J. King (ed.), *The Elgar Companion to Post Keynesian Economics*, Cheltenham, UK, and Northampton, MA, USA: Edward Elgar, pp. 15–19.
Fontana, G. and B. Gerrard (2006), 'The future of post Keynesian economics', *Banca Nazionale del Lavoro Quarterly Review*, **59** (236), 49–80.
Jo, T.-H. (2016), 'Presidential address: what if there are no conventional price mechanisms?', *Journal of Economic Issues*, **50** (2), 327–44.
Kapp, K.W. (1971), *The Social Costs of Private Enterprise*, New York: Schocken Books.
Lawson, T. (2006), 'The nature of heterodox economics', *Cambridge Journal of Economics*, **30** (4), 483–505.
Lee, F.S. (2011), 'The pluralism debate in heterodox economics', *Review of Radical Political Economics*, **43** (4), 540–51.
Lee, F. (2012), 'Heterodox economics and its critics', *Review of Political Economy*, **24** (2), 337–51.
Mearman, A. (2012), ''Heterodox economics' and the problem of classification', *Journal of Economic Methodology*, **19** (4), 407–24.
Putnam, H. and V. Walsh (eds) (2011), *The End of Value-Free Economics*, London and New York: Routledge.
Ramazzotti, P. (2022), 'Heterodoxy, the mainstream and policy', *Journal of Economic Issues*, **56** (1), 59–78.
Sen, A. (1993), 'Capability and well-being', in M.C. Nussbaum and A. Sen (eds), *The Quality of Life*, Oxford: Clarendon Press, pp. 30–53.
Sweezy, P.M. (1953), *The Present as History: Essays and Reviews on Capitalism and Socialism*, New York: Monthly Review Press.

Historical time

In post-Keynesian economics the concept of historical time is independent of the use of the term in the philosophy of history. In this framework it insists that 'today is a break in time between an unknown future and an irrevocable past' (Robinson, 1962, p. 26). It is indeed contrasted with how time is treated in neoclassical economics, which views time as either 'logical time' in which the past, present and future are indistinguishable (so that movement in time is akin to movement in space) or 'mechanical time' in which all movement is along a predetermined path. In both logical and mechanical time, historical and social contexts have no meaning and thus can be assumed away.

In post-Keynesian economics the concept of historical time developed from the interpretation of Keynes's (1936) *General Theory of Employment, Interest and Money* that highlighted – rather than relegated as 'a digression' (Keynes, 1936, p. 194) – its Chapter 12 (and its own extension Chapter 17), as well as from Joan Robinson's linking of Keynes's analysis of uncertainty to the classical economists' preoccupation with the 'historical process of accumulation in a capitalist economy' (Robinson, 1980, p. 48). Indeed, '[a]s soon as the uncertainty of the expectations that guide economic behaviour is admitted, equilibrium drops out of the argument and history takes its place' (ibid.). Robinson argued that post-Keynesian insights on uncertainty apply beyond the macroeconomic topics of investment, interest rates and the price level, extending to the microeconomic issues of price determination, markets and economic decision making (p. 50).

Historical time recognizes that humans take actions informed by the past, shaped by existing social institutions, and directed towards an uncertain future about which 'there is no scientific basis on which to form any calculable probability whatever. We simply do not know' (Keynes, 1937, p. 214). This amounts to saying, as Davidson (1991) noted, that we live in a non-ergodic world. For post-Keynesians this is an ontological issue. In commenting on Davidson's assertion, Davis (1998, p. 4) observed that 'saying that the world is non-ergodic is equivalent to saying that it is transmutable, where this means the economic world may be transformed in fundamental ways as a consequence of human agency. That is, human beings are free to change not just the course of events (as orthodox thinkers allow), but are also free to change the very principles governing the economic process.'

The broader implications of historical time were recognized by Joan Robinson when she linked the post-Keynesian critique of the neoclassical theory of capital to Veblen's (1908a, 1908b) essays, 'On the nature of capital' (see Cohen, 2014, for an analysis of this link). Robinson increasingly saw that the main problem with capital theory was not how capital is measured, or any of the other technical issues that consumed the famous 'capital debates'. Capital is an aspect of the social construction of reality and has no meaning or productivity outside of its historical and social contexts (the factors that historical time brings to the forefront of economic analysis). Adoption of historical time as the basis for understanding economic change and development is a break from the natural law preconceptions that have dominated economic theory from the beginning (Clark, 1987–88; 1992, Ch. 7). It is a move towards economics as a social science, where social and historical contexts are emphasized rather than ignored, and where economists study a reality that humans make, and not, as in the natural sciences, one that they find.

CHARLES M.A. CLARK

See also

Behavioural economics; Capital theory controversies; Expectations; Neoclassical economics; Post-Keynesian economics – a big tent?

References

Clark, C.M.A. (1987–88), 'Equilibrium, market process, and historical time', *Journal of Post Keynesian Economics*, **10** (2), 270–81.
Clark, C.M.A. (1992), *Economic Theory and Natural Philosophy*, Cheltenham, UK, and Northampton, MA, USA: Edward Elgar.
Cohen, A.J. (2014), 'Veblen contra Clark and Fisher: Veblen–Robinson–Harcourt lineages in capital controversies and beyond', *Cambridge Journal of Economics*, **38** (6), 1493–515.
Davidson, P. (1991), 'Is probability theory relevant for uncertainty? A Post Keynesian perspective', *Journal of Economic Perspectives*, **5** (1), 129–43.
Davis, J.B. (1998), 'Davidson, non-ergodicity and individuals', in P. Davidson and P. Arestis (eds), *Method, Theory and Policy in Keynes: Essays in Honour of Paul Davidson, Vol. 3*, Cheltenham, UK, and Northampton, MA, USA: Edward Elgar, pp. 1–16.
Keynes, J.M. (1936), *The General Theory of Employment, Interest, and Money*, London: Macmillan.
Keynes, J.M. (1937), 'The general theory of employment', *Quarterly Journal of Economics*, **51** (2), 209–23.
Robinson, J. (1962), *Essays in the Theory of Economic Growth*, London: Macmillan.
Robinson, J. (1975/1980), 'History versus equilibrium', in *Collected Economic Papers, Volume Five*, Oxford: Basil Blackwell, pp. 48–58.
Setterfield, M. (1998), 'History versus equilibrium: Nicholas Kaldor on historical time and economic theory', *Cambridge Journal of Economics*, **22** (5), 521–37.
Veblen, T. (1908a), 'On the nature of capital I: the productivity of capital goods', *Quarterly Journal of Economics*, **22** (4), 517–42.
Veblen, T. (1908b), 'On the nature of capital II: investment, intangible assets and the pecuniary magnate', *Quarterly Journal of Economics*, **23** (1), 104–36.

Horizontalism

According to the post-Keynesian endogenous money theory, money supply is demand-determined and credit-driven. Money supply depends on the volume of loans demanded by borrowers to banks, which are able to create money *ex nihilo*, that is, without the need for a predetermined volume of savings, deposits or reserves at the central bank.

Within the post-Keynesian school of thought, two different perspectives can be identified. The first one is the horizontalist view (also improperly called the 'accommodationist' view), whereas the second one is the structuralist approach, also defined as 'structural endogeneity' (see Pollin, 1991). For an in-depth review of this debate see Rochon (1999; 2001). The supporters of the horizontalist view (see, among others, Kaldor, 1970, 1982; Eichner, 1987; Moore, 1988; Lavoie, 1996; Rochon, 1999, 2001) argue for a supply of credit and reserves infinitely elastic with respect to the interest rate, which implies that the demand for credit/reserves does not affect the level of interest rates. The horizontalist perspective is mainly grounded on a twofold argument: (i) the interest rates' exogeneity; and (ii) the accommodating behaviour of both central and commercial banks.

Concerning the determination of interest rates, horizontalists argue that the central bank exogenously sets the nominal short-run interest rate on banks' reserves (i_0).

> The nominal rate of interest administered by a central bank depends both on its policy goals and on the state of economy [that is, full employment, price stability, exchange rate, income distribution, and the liquidity of the financial system]. Endogenous market forces combined with the authorities' reaction function determine the limits within which central banks will exogenously vary nominal interest rates. ... Exogeneity simply implies that the central bank chooses its nominal

bank lending rate, and has some considerable range of discretion. (Moore, 1988, pp. 265–6)

Commercial banks determine their interest rates on loans (i_{L0}) by applying a mark-up (θ_0) over the short-run interest rate set by the central bank (i_0). Such a relationship is represented in equation (1) as follows:

$$i_{L0} = i_0 + \theta_0\,(\varepsilon, c, t) \qquad (1)$$

where i_{L0} is the sum of the mark-up (θ_0) and the short-run interest rate set by the central bank (i_0). The mark-up (θ_0) is positively influenced by the loan duration (t), the risk perceived by banks (ε) and negatively by competition among banks (c) (Eichner, 1987, p. 858). Consequently, both the interest rate set by the central bank (i_0) and the mark-up (θ_0) set by banks are exogenous variables, independently of the volume of reserves and loans granted to borrowers. Changes in the rate of interest (i_0) affect the interest rates on loans (i_{L0}), which in turn may affect the demand for credit and therefore economic activity (Rochon, 1999).

Concerning the accommodating behaviour, banks fully accommodate the creditworthy demand for loans (Robinson, 1952; Kaldor, 1982; Eichner, 1987; Moore, 1988; Rochon, 1999, 2001), namely the demand that is able to meet the collateral requirements requested by banks or in other terms 'their criteria for loans' (Rochon, 1999, p. 159). In doing so, banks are not passive institutions but are able to select good borrowers and ration credit by means of quantitative constraint (for instance changing the collateral requirements), while the interest rate 'is an inadequate exclusion mechanism' (Lavoie, 1996, p. 284).

Once loans are granted, these create an equivalent level of deposits that define the volume of reserves demanded by banks to the central bank. According to horizontalists, the central bank is fully accommodating in providing reserves to the banking sector, as the monetary authority is extremely careful about safeguarding the stability of the financial and payments system, as well as the solvency of the banking sector in order to avoid mass bankruptcies (Kaldor, 1982). The lack of accommodation, together with the quantitative control over monetary aggregates, could lead to unwanted consequences, such as the loss of control over the rate of interest and the birth of new means of payment alternative to the legal tender (Kaldor, 1970). These effects are supposed to undermine and reduce the strategic power held by the central bank in regulating the monetary and financial system (Kaldor, 1970).

MATTEO DELEIDI

See also

Central banking; Endogenous money; Monetary circuit; Money creation – nature of

References

Eichner, A.S. (1987), *The Macrodynamics of Advanced Market Economies*, Armonk, NY: M.E. Sharpe.
Kaldor, N. (1970), 'The new monetarism', *Lloyds Bank Review*, **97** (1), 18.
Kaldor, N. (1982), *The Scourge of Monetarism*, Oxford: Oxford University Press.
Lavoie, M. (1996), 'Horizontalism, structuralism, liquidity preference and the principle of increasing risk', *Scottish Journal of Political Economy*, **43** (3), 275–300.
Moore, B.J. (1988), *Horizontalists and Verticalists: The Macroeconomics of Credit Money*, Cambridge, UK: Cambridge University Press.
Pollin, R. (1991), 'Two theories of money supply endogeneity: some empirical evidence', *Journal of Post Keynesian Economics*, **13** (3), 366–96.
Robinson, J. (1952), *The Rate of Interest and Other Essays*, London: Macmillan.
Rochon, L.-P. (1999), *Credit, Money, and Production: An Alternative Post-Keynesian Approach*, Cheltenham, UK, and Northampton, MA, USA: Edward Elgar.
Rochon, L.-P. (2001), 'Horizontalism: setting the record straight', in L.-P. Rochon and M. Vernengo (eds), *Credit, Interest Rates and the Open Economy: Essays on Horizontalism*, Cheltenham, UK, and Northampton, MA, USA: Edward Elgar, pp. 31–68.

Hysteresis

Hysteresis is a form of path dependence, a process whereby the past has a lasting influence on the present and future. It provides an 'organizing concept' (similar, for example, to equilibrium) for building dynamical models that are sympathetic to the post-Keynesian notion that 'history matters' in the determination of economic outcomes.

The concept of hysteresis originated in the natural sciences, in studies of the magnetic properties of ferric metals (Cross and

Allen, 1988). Appeal to hysteresis in economics is more recent, having been popularized by critiques of the natural rate hypothesis during the 1980s (for the earliest example, see Hargreaves Heap. 1980). Several competing conceptualizations of hysteresis exist, although their properties are not mutually exclusive: the unit/zero root approach, 'true' hysteresis and hysteresis conceived as a product of historical time.

True to its name, the unit/zero root approach assumes the existence of a unit (zero) root in systems of linear difference (differential) equations. For example, if the variable x can be described by the first-order linear difference equation as follows:

$$x_t = \alpha x_{t-1} + \beta + \varepsilon_t \qquad [1]$$

where β is a constant and ε is a stochastic term, then if $\alpha = 1$ – that is, if equation [1] has a unit root – then:

$$x_t = x_0 + t\beta + \sum_{i=1}^{t} \varepsilon_i \qquad [2]$$

The current value of x thus depends on the past – specifically, initial conditions and the entire history of shocks to the system.

The unit/zero root approach has been criticized for neglecting the importance for hysteresis of non-linearities and structural change (Cross, 1994; Amable et al., 1995; Setterfield, 1998). However, models with unit/zero roots are easy to formulate, easy to contrast with traditional (ahistorical) equilibrium systems, and capture one key property of hysteresis: the propensity for transitory causes to have permanent effects. They have thus proved popular in post-Keynesian models of macrodynamic phenomena such as stabilization policy and growth (Dutt, 1997; Lavoie, 2006).

'True' hysteresis is derived from theoretical physics and, in particular, the discontinuous adjustment characteristic of a non-ideal relay. It shows how hysteresis results in macro systems as a consequence of discrete switching between outcomes, in response to behavioural stimuli (shocks), among heterogeneous decision-makers at the micro level (Cross, 1994; Setterfield, 2009). 'True' hysteresis therefore provides a micro foundation for hysteresis in aggregate outcomes. Another important feature of 'true' hysteresis is that, unlike unit/zero root systems, not all shocks affect outcomes: only non-dominated extrema have lasting effects. 'True' hysteretic systems thus have selective memory (in contrast to the complete memories of unit/zero root systems).

'True' hysteresis provides a well-specified formal model of the hysteresis process. As yet, however, this model has found relatively few applications in economics beyond a literature (exemplified by Cross, 1995) that focuses on the Phillips curve.

Inspired by the tradition's emphasis on historical time, some post-Keynesian economists have attempted to ground hysteresis in the dynamical properties of specifically social systems (Setterfield, 1998; Katzner, 1999). Setterfield (1998) considers a sequence of 'cumulatively neutral' changes in some dependent variable – in other words, an adjustment path that, starting from some initial (for instance, equilibrium) value, forces the variable back to its initial value through a sequence of changes that sums to zero. Hysteresis exists if: (a) the 'data' (the alleged exogenous parameters) that determine the variable of interest are, in fact, sensitive to changes in this variable; and (b) induced changes in the 'data' are not, themselves, cumulatively neutral (that is, do not sum to zero) – indicating that the system has undergone induced structural change. These processes can be summarized using Katzner's (1999) reduced-form equation:

$$x_t = f_t(x_{t-1}, \varepsilon_t) \qquad [3]$$

Assuming that $\varepsilon_t = 0$ for all t for simplicity, if both $f'_t \neq 0$ and $f'_t \neq f'_{t-1}$ for some t, then a hypothetical sequence of cumulatively neutral changes in x between periods $t-1$ and $t+n$ (so that $x_{t+n} = x_{t-1}$) may nevertheless imply that $x_{t+n+1} \neq x_{t+n}$. Outcomes of the system permanently reflect the legacy of the cumulatively neutral adjustment path or, in other words, display hysteresis. Note that if there are no 'deep parameters' in the social realm defining a (deterministic or stochastic) 'true' model governing the evolution of the function f_t in equation [3], then hysteresis will go hand-in-hand with fundamental uncertainty.

One of the main advantages of this approach to conceptualizing hysteresis is its sensitivity to perceived characteristics of the specifically social material that is the economist's object of analysis. One of the main drawbacks is that its formal model of hysteresis is underdeveloped.

MARK SETTERFIELD

See also

Historical time; Interest rate – natural; Microfoundations; Phillips curve; Uncertainty

References

Amable, B., J. Henry, F. Lordon and R. Topol (1995), 'Hysteresis revisited: a methodological approach', in R. Cross (ed.), *The Natural Rate of Unemployment: Reflections on 25 Years of the Hypothesis*, Cambridge: Cambridge University Press, pp. 153–80.
Cross, R. (1994), 'The macroeconomic consequences of discontinuous adjustment: selective memory of non-dominated extrema', *Scottish Journal of Political Economy*, **41** (2), 212–21.
Cross, R. (1995), 'Is the natural rate hypothesis consistent with hysteresis?', in R. Cross (ed.), *The Natural Rate of Unemployment: Reflections on 25 Years of the Hypothesis*, Cambridge, UK: Cambridge University Press, pp. 181–200.
Cross, R. and A. Allan (1988), 'On the history of hysteresis', in R. Cross (ed.), *Unemployment, Hysteresis and the Natural Rate Hypothesis*, Oxford and New York: Basil Blackwell, pp. 26–38.
Dutt, A.K. (1997), 'Equilibrium, path dependence and hysteresis in Post-Keynesian models', in P. Arestis, G. Palma and M. Sawyer (eds), *Essays in Honour of Geoff Harcourt. Volume 2: Markets, Unemployment and Economic Policy*, London and New York: Routledge, pp. 238–53.
Hargreaves Heap, S.P. (1980), 'Choosing the wrong "natural rate": accelerating inflation or decelerating employment and growth', *Economic Journal*, **90** (359), 611–20.
Katzner, D. (1999), 'Hysteresis and the modeling of economic phenomena', *Review of Political Economy*, **11** (2), 171–81.
Lavoie, M. (2006), 'A Post-Keynesian amendment to the New Consensus on monetary policy', *Metroeconomica*, **57** (2), 165–92.
Setterfield, M. (1998), 'Adjustment asymmetries and hysteresis in simple dynamic models', *The Manchester School*, **66** (3), 283–301.
Setterfield, M. (2009), 'Path dependency, hysteresis and macrodynamics', in P. Arestis and M. Sawyer (eds), *Path Dependency and Macroeconomics*, London: Palgrave Macmillan, pp. 37–79.

Imperfect competition

The theory of imperfect competition originated in Cambridge, United Kingdom, in response to the attack on the Marshallian cost and demand curves launched by Sraffa in his 1925 and 1926 articles. While challenging the consistency and lack of realism of that particular framework of analysis, Sraffa suggested to 'abandon the path of perfect competition and turn to the opposite direction, namely, towards monopoly' (Sraffa, 1926, p. 542). Lack of realism was also the reason given by Kahn (1989) for discarding perfect competition in his analysis of the cotton and coal industries in his dissertation, *The Economics of the Short Period*.

During the Great Depression of the 1920s, Kahn observed that firms earned a positive profit while working below capacity: they used 'to close down the whole plant on some days and to work the whole plant a full shift on other days' (Kahn, 1989, p. 57). The explanation was found in the shape of the cost curves; in particular, marginal costs could be thought of as having a reverse L shape; to wit, they remain constant until full capacity is reached. This was a serious challenge to the theory of perfect competition, whereby whenever the price exceeds the average cost curve, firms are supposed to be producing at full capacity. Now, if this were so, the only inefficient firms would be those that worked below capacity. Moreover, when faced by a perfectly elastic demand curve, a constant marginal cost curve loses its significance as determinant of output. However, if it is assumed that firms operate in an imperfect market, namely they are facing a downwards sloping demand curve, equilibrium (output and price) can be determined as in monopoly (Marcuzzo, 1994).

In her *Economics of Imperfect Competition*, Robinson (1933) followed a different route. She applied the technique based on average and marginal curves, incorporating various cost and demand conditions of commodities and factors of production, to all market forms. Perfect competition became a special case in a general theory of competition, allowing for various degrees of substitution and preferences on the part of consumers as captured by the value of the elasticity of demand. Perfect competition was then defined as a market condition characterized by a perfectly horizontal demand curve, that is, with infinite elasticity. On the supply side, various assumptions are allowed for in the behaviour of costs, corresponding to increasing, decreasing and constant cost cases. In fact, in an imperfect market, namely with a downwards sloping demand curve facing each firm, any assumption about the shape of the marginal cost curve provides for the determinacy of equilibrium.

MARK SETTERFIELD / MARIA CRISTINA MARCUZZO

In the hands of Joan Robinson, imperfect competition became the means by which the Marshallian–Pigouvian apparatus could again be given generality and validity against Sraffa's attack. No wonder Sraffa soon distanced himself from this line of research and pursued his research agenda against marginalist analysis in almost total isolation in Cambridge, United Kingdom (Marcuzzo, 2000).

In the mid-1930s Kalecki, too, developed an approach based on imperfect competition within a macroeconomic analysis of the economic system. In two articles published after his Cambridge period (see Kalecki, 1938, 1940), market imperfection was defined as a function that relates the elasticity of demand for the product of each industry to the ratio between the price charged by the individual firm and the average price of the industry. The degree of market imperfection is constant if, for each individual firm, the elasticity of demand is correlated solely with its price; otherwise, the degree of market imperfection varies with the average elasticity of market demand. In his 1940 paper, Kalecki dropped the assumption that firms fix prices according to the equality of marginal cost and marginal revenue – as in the Robinson–Kahn general framework of competition – and he made the case of firms setting the price at a point where marginal revenue is greater than marginal cost (Marcuzzo, 2003).

Kalecki was highly original, although at the cost of simplification, in producing a methodology to study the aggregate effects of price policy by firms in a macroeconomic representation of the economic system (Marcuzzo, 1996, pp. 11–12). Quite rightly Joan Robinson commented in the preface to the second edition of *The Economics of Imperfect Competition* that 'it was Kalecki', rather than herself, who 'brought imperfect competition in touch with the theory of employment' (Robinson, 1969, p. viii).

MARIA CRISTINA MARCUZZO

See also

Capital theory controversies; Consumer behaviour; Monopoly power; Neoclassical economics; *The Accumulation of Capital*

References

Kahn, R.F. (1989), *The Economics of the Short Period*, London: Macmillan.

Kalecki, M. (1938), 'The determinants of distribution of the national income', *Econometrica*, **6** (2), 97–112.

Kalecki, M. (1940), 'The supply curve of an industry under imperfect competition', *Review of Economic Studies*, **7** (1), 91–122.

Marcuzzo, M.C. (1994), 'R.F. Kahn and imperfect competition', *Cambridge Journal of Economics*, **18** (1), 25–39.

Marcuzzo, M.C. (2000), 'Sraffa and Cambridge economics, 1928–1931', in T. Cozzi and R. Marchionatti (eds), *Piero Sraffa's Political Economy: A Centenary Estimate*, London and New York: Routledge, pp. 81–100.

Marcuzzo, M.C. (2003), 'The first imperfect competition revolution', in J. Biddle, J. Davis and W. Samuels (eds), *The Blackwell Companion to the History of Economic Thought*, Oxford: Blackwell, pp. 294–307.

Robinson, J. (1933), *The Economics of Imperfect Competition*, London: Macmillan.

Robinson, J. (1969), 'Preface', in *The Economics of Imperfect Competition*, second edition, London: Macmillan, pp. v–xii.

Sraffa, P. (1926), 'The laws of returns under competitive conditions', *Economic Journal*, **36** (144), 535–50.

Income distribution

Post-Keynesian distribution theories are based on two traditions, each rejecting neoclassical marginal productivity theories of factor remuneration and income shares (Hein, 2014, Ch. 3–5). The first is Kaldor's (1955–56) Keynesian theory of distribution, which is inspired by Keynes's (1930, Ch. 10) *Treatise on Money*, and explains income shares mainly by capitalists' expenditures. Robinson (1956, 1962) has proposed a similar approach. For the long run, full or normal utilization of the capital stock – Kaldor (1955–56) even assumed full employment – flexible prices and rigid money wages are assumed. Applying the Keynesian notion that investment determines saving, the adjustment of saving to investment can then only take place through the variation of income shares, supposing that that the propensity to save out of profits (s_Π) is higher than the propensity to save out of wages (s_W). The latter is assumed to be given, for two reasons. First, a major part of saving is retained by corporations, and, second, private household saving propensities rise with the level of income.

For a given investment share in income (I/Y) and given propensities to save out of profits and out of wages, the share of profits in income ($h = \Pi/Y$) in a long-run goods market equilibrium ($I = S$) is thus determined by:

$$h = \frac{\Pi}{Y} = \frac{1}{s_\Pi - s_W}\frac{I}{Y} - \frac{s_W}{s_\Pi - s_W},$$
$$0 \leq s_W < s_\Pi \leq 1. \quad (1)$$

Dividing by the capital–output ratio ($v = K/Y$), which is given technologically and which, according to the results of the capital controversy (Harcourt, 1969), does not show any systematic relationship with the rate of profit (r) in a more than one-good-economy, we obtain that the long-run equilibrium rate of profit is determined by the rate of accumulation ($g = I/K$), the functional propensities to save and the capital–output ratio:

$$r = \frac{\Pi}{K} = \frac{g - \frac{s_W}{v}}{s_\Pi - s_W},$$
$$0 \leq s_W < s_\Pi \leq 1, v = \bar{v}. \quad (2)$$

Finally, assuming that workers do not save ($s_W = 0$), we arrive at the Cambridge equation, according to which, in long-run equilibrium growth, the rate of accumulation and the propensity to save out of profits determine the rate of profit, which itself can be decomposed into the profit share, the rate of capacity utilization ($u = Y/Y^p$), and the capital–output ratio:

$$r = \frac{\Pi}{K} = \frac{\Pi}{Y}\frac{Y}{Y^p}\frac{Y^p}{K} = hu\frac{1}{v} = \frac{g}{s_\Pi},$$
$$0 < s_\Pi \leq 1. \quad (3)$$

Assuming full utilization of productive capacities given by the capital stock ($u = 1$) and a given capital–output ratio, a long-run change in the rate of accumulation triggers a change in the profit share and thus in the profit rate. As shown by Pasinetti (1962), even if workers save, accumulate capital and obtain the equilibrium rate of profit on their capital, in long-run equilibrium, when workers' and capitalists' shares in the stock of capital are constant, it is only the capitalists' propensity to save (s_C) that affects the rate of profit determined by the long-run equilibrium rate of accumulation and growth:

$$r = \frac{\Pi}{K} = \frac{g}{s_C}, \quad 0 < s_C \leq 1. \quad (4)$$

Of course, the major drawback of this Kaldor–Pasinetti–Robinson approach lies in the assumptions of normal or full utilization of the capital stock, rigid money wages relative to prices, and passive adjustments of real wages and wage shares to the requirements of capital accumulation.

In the second version of post-Keynesian distribution theories, based on the works of Kalecki (1954) and Steindl (1952), these assumptions are abandoned. Here, the profit share is rather determined by active price setting of firms in oligopolistic markets, marking up constant unit variable costs up to full-capacity output, and the rate of capacity utilization is treated as an adjusting variable within bounds. According to Kalecki (1954), mark-up pricing and quantity adjustments are true in particular for industry and services where output can be varied in the short run, but not for the primary sector where changes in demand will rather trigger changes in prices. The mark-up is determined by market concentration, the relevance of price competition, overhead costs and bargaining power of trade unions. If variable costs consist of wage costs (W) and costs for (imported) raw materials and semi-finished products (M), the profit share is determined by the mark-up (m) and the ratio of material costs to wage costs ($z = M/W$):

$$h = \frac{\Pi}{Y} = \frac{\Pi}{(\Pi + W)} = \frac{(1+z)m}{(1+z)m + 1}$$
$$= \frac{1}{1 + \frac{1}{(1+z)m}}. \quad (5)$$

Any rise in the mark-up or in the ratio of material costs to wage costs, or any change in the structural composition of the economy towards high mark-up industries, will thus raise the profit share for the economy as a whole. It should be noticed that profits in this approach also include overhead costs and thus management salaries, as well as costs of fixed capital.

In a Kaleckian–Steindlian perspective, any change in capital accumulation or in the propensity to save out of profits, assuming workers do not save, will not affect the profit share but the profit rate, as can be seen in equation (3). With a profit share given by mark-up pricing and a technologically fixed capital–output ratio, the adjustment of saving to investment will now take place via the endogenous rate of capacity utilization.

Further developments of the Kaleckian approach to distribution have focused on the determination of the mark-up. Eichner (1976), Harcourt and Kenyon (1976), and Wood (1975) have argued that the mark-up is determined by firms' required internal means of finance for investment purposes. More recent developments have rather suggested that the mark-up is affected by interest and dividend payments, as well as top management salaries, and has thus focused on the distributional conflict between managers, rentiers, that is, creditors and shareholders, and workers (see Hein, 2008, Ch. 13, and Hein, 2015, for reviews).

ECKHARD HEIN

See also

Capacity utilization; Capital theory controversies; Growth – wage-led vs profit-led; Pricing; Profit

References

Eichner, A. (1976), *The Megacorp and Oligopoly*, Cambridge, UK: Cambridge University Press.
Harcourt, G.C. (1969), 'Some Cambridge controversies in the theory of capital', *Journal of Economic Literature*, **7** (2), 369–405.
Harcourt, G.C. and P. Kenyon (1976), 'Prices and investment decision', *Kyklos*, **29** (3), 449–77.
Hein, E. (2008), *Money, Distribution Conflict and Capital Accumulation: Contributions to 'Monetary Analysis'*, Basingstoke and New York: Palgrave Macmillan.
Hein, E. (2014), *Distribution and Growth after Keynes: A Post-Keynesian Guide*, Cheltenham, UK, and Northampton, MA, USA: Edward Elgar.
Hein, E. (2015), 'Finance-dominated capitalism and re-distribution of income – a Kaleckian perspective', *Cambridge Journal of Economics*, **39** (3), 907–34.
Kaldor, N. (1955–56), 'Alternative theories of distribution', *Review of Economic Studies*, **23** (2), 83–100.
Kalecki, M. (1954), *Theory of Economic Dynamics*, London: George Allen and Unwin.
Keynes, J.M. (1930), *A Treatise on Money, Volume I: The Pure Theory of Money*, London: Macmillan. Reprinted in *The Collected Writings of John Maynard Keynes, Volume V*, London: Macmillan, 1971.
Pasinetti, L.L. (1962), 'Rate of profit and income distribution in relation to the rate of economic growth', *Review of Economic Studies*, **29** (4), 267–79.
Robinson, J. (1956), *The Accumulation of Capital*, London: Macmillan.
Robinson, J. (1962), *Essays in the Theory of Economic Growth*, London: Macmillan.
Steindl, J. (1952), *Maturity and Stagnation in American Capitalism*, Oxford: Blackwell.
Wood, A. (1975), *A Theory of Profits*, Cambridge, UK: Cambridge University Press.

Income multiplier

In an economic system with spare capacity (unemployed labour in particular), 'autonomous' increases in expenditure (such as an increase in government spending) will lead to higher output, employment and thus income, as activity expands to accommodate the additional demand. The income multiplier refers to the relationship between a change in autonomous expenditure and the resulting change in total income. New spending generates new incomes, some fraction of which will also be spent, generating further new incomes. An increase in autonomous spending may therefore cause total income to expand by an amount greater than the initiating autonomous increase. In other words, the income multiplier – the ratio of the overall change in income to the initial 'autonomous' change in expenditure – is usually greater than one.

While discussion of the income multiplier is commonly focused on the 'fiscal multiplier' – the relationship between changes in government spending and changes in output – the concept refers, more broadly, to the overall change in income resulting from any change in autonomous expenditure, for example consumption, investment or demand for exports. In post-Keynesian economics, particular emphasis is placed on analysing the effects of changes in investment.

The principles involved can be illustrated in a simple way by assuming a closed economy without government expenditure. Expenditure and income, Y, will then be equal, by definition, to consumption expenditure C plus investment expenditure I. Since saving, S, is defined as income less consumption, saving and investment are identically equal by definition: $S \equiv I$. Given a positive exogenous change in investment expenditure, ΔI, either Y must increase or C must decrease, or a combination of the two must occur.

If the increase in investment is accommodated purely by an increase in output, such that $\Delta Y = \Delta I$, with no change in consumption expenditure, then the income multiplier is equal to unity. In general, however, Keynesians argue that the additional income generated as a result of the increase in investment expenditure – increased total wage payments, for example – will lead to higher consumption expenditure. In particular, if consumption expenditure is a fixed proportion, c, of total income ($C = cY$, then an increase in investment will cause consumption to increase sufficiently to maintain the ratio of income to consumption (and thus saving), so that $S = (1 - c)Y = I$ at the new level of investment.

It can readily be shown that the magnitude of the income multiplier is determined by the propensity to consume, such that $\Delta Y = \Delta I = 1/(1 - c)$, with the implication that an increase in investment expenditure requires a greater than equivalent increase in output in order to maintain equality between S and I. In contrast with 'classical' analysis, in which higher investment either leads to a higher rate of interest or to higher inflation – thus reducing consumption and/or 'crowding out' investment elsewhere – Keynesian analysis emphasizes output as the variable that adjusts to bring desired saving into equality with investment.

In the post-Keynesian literature, the multiplier has generated substantial historical debate. One strand concerns the issue of the time taken for the multiplier to work. In the simple formulation given above, it is assumed that the increase in income required to maintain the ratio of income to saving is instantaneous. In reality, it will be sequential: an increase in investment spending will generate additional income, some of which will be spent and some saved. This additional spending will generate further income, and so on, in an asymptotic process. At the end of this process, income will have increased by exactly the amount required to maintain the ratio Y/C. An implication is that the income multiplier can be regarded as a pure identity that will hold at any point in time, if I and S are measured *ex post*, during such a dynamic process. But the income multiplier can also be treated, as above, as an equilibrium condition that stipulates the required change in output for a given change in investment (see Chick, 1983, Ch. 14).

This leads to questions about finance. It was argued by Keynes – and subsequently by many post-Keynesian economists – that lack of saving can never constrain investment so long as finance is forthcoming in the form of new bank loans. This position was contested by Asimakopulos (1983) on the basis that firms and banks could face liquidity shortages during the period in which the multiplier process was not yet complete, because saving out of new income will not immediately increase to match new investment spending. This claim sparked substantial debate – see, for example, Graziani (1986), Kregel (1986) and Skott (1988), and replies by Asimakopulos (1985, 1986).

A related issue concerns whether the horizontalist approach to endogenous money invalidates the income multiplier entirely, a position argued by Moore (1988, 1994). In the case of an increase in investment, ΔI, financed by new bank lending and thus newly issued credit money (bank deposits) M, the increase in investment spending will be accompanied by growth of the money stock, $\Delta M = \Delta I$. Assuming the functioning of the multiplier, then $\Delta Y = \Delta I/(1 - c)$. If we further assume that desired money balances are a fixed proportion, h, of income Y (as a result of liquidity preference, or a constant income velocity of money), then, additionally, $\Delta M/h = \Delta Y$. The implication is that $h = (1 - c)$. In other words, desired money balances as a proportion of income must equal the proportion of total income that is saved. Given that this is unlikely to be the case in reality, Moore concludes that the income multiplier must be abandoned. A number of authors have proposed ways to reconcile this apparent conflict, by selectively loosening assumptions such as a continuously fixed propensity to consume and constant velocity of money (see for example Cottrell, 1994, and Dalziel, 1996). For a recent reappraisal of these historical debates, see Gnos and Rochon (2008).

JO MICHELL

See also

Crowding in and crowding out; Fiscal multiplier; Horizontalism; Investment theory – Keynesian; Liquidity preference

References

Asimakopulos, A. (1983), 'Kalecki and Keynes on finance, investment and saving', *Cambridge Journal of Economics*, 7 (3–4), 221–33.

Asimakopulos, A. (1985), 'The role of finance in Keynes' *General Theory*', *Economic Notes*, 14 (1), 5–16.

Asimakopulos, A. (1986), 'Finance, liquidity, saving, and investment', *Journal of Post Keynesian Economics*, 9 (1), 79–90.

Chick, V. (1983), *Macroeconomics after Keynes*, Oxford: Phillip Allen.

Cottrell, A. (1994), 'Endogenous money and the multiplier', *Journal of Post Keynesian Economics*, 17 (1), 111–20.

Dalziel, P. (1996), 'The Keynesian multiplier, liquidity preference, and endogenous money', *Journal of Post Keynesian Economics*, **18** (3), 311–31.
Gnos, C. and L.-P. Rochon (eds) (2008), *The Keynesian Multiplier*, London and New York: Routledge.
Graziani, A. (1986), 'Keynes' finance motive: a reply', *Economic Notes*, 1, 5–9.
Kregel, J. (1986), 'A note on finance, liquidity, saving, and investment', *Journal of Post Keynesian Economics*, **9** (1), 91–100.
Moore, B.J. (1988), *Horizontalists and Verticalists: The Macroeconomics of Credit Money*, Cambridge, UK: Cambridge University Press.
Moore, B.J. (1994), 'The demise of the Keynesian multiplier: a reply to Cottrell', *Journal of Post Keynesian Economics*, **17** (1), 121–33.
Skott, P. (1988), 'Finance, saving and accumulation', *Cambridge Journal of Economics*, **12** (3), 339–54.

Induction and deduction

Induction and deduction are two approaches when it comes to reasoning; two paths for the search of some 'truth'. Induction (inductive reasoning, inductive logic, inductive inference) begins with the specific and ends with the general, in contrast to deduction (deductive reasoning, deductive logic, deductive inference), which begins with the general before moving to the specific.

For induction, the process begins with observations and attempts are made to find generalizations from these parts from which one could produce a reasonable argument. The basic block of inductive reasoning is the enthymeme, which is a statement based on probabilities, thus opening the door to uncertainty. For Keynes (1921, p. 222), two parts played in the creation of inductive reasoning, namely, analogy and 'pure induction'. Analogy allowed for the creation and strengthening of one's consideration of the 'prior probability' of the situation as 'some degree of resemblance must always exist between the various instances upon which a generalisation is based', while 'pure induction' requires an increase in the number of instances being considered (ibid.). Ramsey (1964) would disagree with this 'objective probability' put forward by Keynes (1921), substituting instead a 'logic of partial belief'. According to Ramsey (1964, p. 90), '[t]hus given a single opinion, we can only praise or blame it on the ground of truth or falsity: given a habit of certain form, we can praise or blame it accordingly as the degree of belief it produces is near or far from the actual proportion in which the habit leads to truth.'

Many critiques of induction exist, the most famous of which was put forward by Hume (1739/2000, p. 64), who criticized the use of induction based on prior observations. Gordon (1991, pp. 603–4) provides a comedic rejoinder to this, when he states that 'if a philosopher were to tell a scientist that he had no warrant for asserting that the melting point of gold was 1,064.43°C because he had not melted all the gold in the universe, the scientist would be well justified in curtly bidding him to be gone'.

For deduction, the process begins with the creation of a generalized theory for which observations are collected to be able to test the validity of the preferred hypothesis. Simply put, if the premise is true, the conclusion must also be true logically. The basic blocks of deductive reasoning are syllogisms, as enthymemes are to induction, which are statements made in certitude. Deduction is the process most familiar to economists, as it is arguably the preferred method of neoclassical economics as a result of their infatuation with positivism and modernism. Indeed, it can be shown that '[m]uch of orthodox economics is based on just this kind of deductive syllogism: all consumers are assumed to be utility maximizers; Sarah purchases bundle A; therefore bundle A maximizes utility for Sarah' (Johnson, 1996, p. 292).

Critics of this deductive methodology decry the growing number of abstractions and axioms as further distancing theory from reality, fearing the misbelief that 'only the observable implications (or predictions) of a theory matter to its truth' (McCloskey, 1998, p. 143).

While Keynes (1921) considered deductive and inductive reasoning to be fundamentally alike, Ramsey (1964) disagreed. Yet, this would not be the only induction–deduction debate that Keynes would find himself embroiled in. More famously, Keynes engaged in a debate with the econometrician Jan Tinbergen in the 1930s within the pages of the *Economic Journal*. The debate, with its focus on statistical inference, involved Keynes decrying the lack of induction (or more specifically Keynes's conception of induction) within Tinbergen's econometrics, claiming that 'if the method cannot prove or disprove a qualitative theory, and if it cannot give a quantitative guide to the future, is it worthwhile?' (Keynes, 1939,

JO MICHELL / EDWARD TEATHER-POSADAS

p. 566). To this question Keynes answered with a resounding no. While proclaimed to be a 'dead issue' by Lionel Robbins in 1938, induction–deduction clearly remains an area of methodological issue.

EDWARD TEATHER-POSADAS

See also

Critical realism; Methodology; Neoclassical economics; Post-Keynesian economics – a big tent?; Uncertainty

References

Gordon, S. (1991), *The History and Philosophy of Social Science*, New York: Routledge.
Hume, D. (1739/2000), *A Treatise of Human Nature*, edited by David Fate Norton and Mary J. Norton, New York: Oxford University Press.
Johnson, C.F. (1996), 'Deductive versus inductive reasoning: a closer look at economics', *Social Science Journal*, **33** (3), 287–300.
Keynes, J.M. (1921), *A Treatise on Probability*, London: Macmillan.
Keynes, J.M. (1939), 'Professor Tinbergen's methods', *Economic Journal*, **49** (195), 558–77.
McCloskey, D.N. (1998), *The Rhetoric of Economics*, Madison: University of Wisconsin Press.
Ramsey, F.P. (1964), 'Truth and probability', in H.E. Kyburg and H.E. Smokler (eds), *Studies in Subjective Probability*, New York: John Wiley & Sons, pp. 61–92.
Robbins, L. (1938), 'Live and dead issues in the methodology of economics', *Economica*, **5** (19), 342–52.

Inequality

Inequality is a mathematical, economic, political, social and statistical fact. Its emergence within post-Keynesian economics is, however, recent, as Keynesians since Keynes have largely preoccupied themselves with macroeconomic issues: employment, inflation, output, interest and money. Inequality entered the analysis, for the most part, only in relation to the split between wages and profits, and the differing savings and consumption propensities of rich and poor (Galbraith, 2016). Also, during the High Keynesian period from 1945 until the early 1970s, income distribution appeared stable, and when rising inequality became evident in the United States in the 1980s, it was labour economists who stepped forward to discuss it (see Bound and Johnson, 1992). Inequality thus re-entered the literature as a microeconomic topic. So far, indeed, no classification code of the *Journal of Economic Literature* for 'macroeconomics of inequality' exists.

A post-Keynesian macroeconomics of inequality emerges from empirical investigation backed by elementary insight (Galbraith, 1998, 2012, 2016; Galbraith and Berner, 2001). The evidence shows a trend break in 1980–81 in inequality measures around the world, in line with the global debt crisis, followed by the collapse of the socialist regimes in the late 1980s and the Asian crisis in 1997, and continuing until conditions eased, for most countries in the developing world, around 2000. This common trend across countries is alone sufficient to demonstrate that Keynesian macrodynamics are involved.

The insight relates to the simple fact that creditors are richer than debtors, as a rule. Hence monetary policies and financial crises should be expected to have distributive impact. Interest rates and creditor/debtor relations are transmitted through foreign exchange markets, and it can be shown that for countries with open capital markets and periphery–centre trading patterns, a close relationship exists between the exchange rate and industrial pay inequality (Galbraith and Rossi, 2016), the latter in turn closely linked to household income inequality (Galbraith and Kum, 2005). This result supports the post-Keynesian New Developmentalism of Luiz Carlos Bresser-Pereira (2010). Countries suffering the 'Dutch disease' are prone to devaluation crises, which re-establish inequalities that years, even decades, of patient social-welfare programmes may have sought to reduce.

The power of the link between inequality and macrodynamics goes far beyond merely adding an extra dimension to the post-Keynesian research agenda. Indeed, if economic inequalities are driven largely by Keynesian forces, the role assigned to itself by neoclassical microeconomics is reduced *pro tanto*. The entire point of neoclassical production theory, for instance, is to establish a technological basis for the distribution of income, both between wages and profits and between workers of differing grades of skill (see Goldin and Katz, 2008). If macroeconomic forces determine these gaps – a fact that emerges plainly from the existence of a common global pattern – then they cannot also be driven by technology and skill, peculiar to bounded 'labour markets'. The artificial distinction between macroeconomics and microeconomics is erased. It becomes necessary to choose one perspective or the other, and it turns out that post-Keynesian macroeconomics provides the better guide to the data.

The proposition that global financial forces drive inequalities has a dual, to wit, that regulatory control over inequalities, including capital controls, has macroeconomic effects. Broadly and as is obvious, an egalitarian, healthy, long-lived population is happier and experiences higher social welfare. More narrowly and less well known is that compressed wage structures drive productivity growth, favouring advanced firms and integrated production methods, while discouraging the predatory use of cheap labour. This was the Meidner–Rehn model as practised in Sweden during its para-Keynesian heyday, helping to deliver egalitarian high employment in an economy with an open trading regime (Martin, 1981).

Further, countries with lower inequality, other things equal, experience systematically lower unemployment. This proposition is easily shown across Europe, where unemployment rises on a gradient from the egalitarian north to the unequal south. But it is also valid for Europe as an integrated continental economy compared to the United States. Including the large between-country differences across Europe reverses the usual notion that wages in the United States are more unequal. The result refutes the neoliberal preference for 'flexible labour markets' and argues instead that an egalitarian wages policy reduces the structural element of unemployment caused by frustrated job search (Galbraith and Garcilazo, 2007).

Finally, economies with less inequality experience less internal migration (see Harris and Todaro, 1970). This is simply because the incentive to migrate is a function of the pay differentials between origin and destination. Whether this incentive works most strongly over short or long distances depends on the geographical dispersion of rich and poor. In Europe and China, as well as between the United States and Central America, or between Europe and Africa, the distances are large and migration takes its most dramatic forms.

As a broad post-Keynesian policy condition, inequality is governed by global finance. Institutions build equality. Debt and financial crises tear it down. The precondition for sustained reduction of inequalities at global scale is control over the financial regime.

JAMES K. GALBRAITH

See also

Capital controls; Financial crises; Growth – wage-led vs profit-led; Income distribution; Monetary policy

References

Bound, J. and G. Johnson (1992), 'Changes in the structure of wages in the 1980s: an evaluation of alternative explanations', *American Economic Review*, **82** (3), 371–92.

Bresser-Pereira, L.C. (2010), *Globalization and Competition: Why Some Emergent Countries Succeed While Others Fall Behind*, Cambridge, UK: Cambridge University Press.

Galbraith, J.K. (1998), *Created Unequal: The Crisis in American Pay*, New York: Free Press.

Galbraith, J.K. (2012), *Inequality and Instability: A Study of the World Economy Just Before the Great Crisis*, New York: Oxford University Press.

Galbraith, J.K. (2016), *Inequality: What Everyone Needs to Know*, New York: Oxford University Press.

Galbraith, J.K. and M. Berner (eds) (2001), *Inequality and Industrial Change: A Global View*, New York: Cambridge University Press.

Galbraith, J.K. and E. Garcilazo (2007), 'Unemployment, inequality and the policy of Europe, 1984–2000,' in R.P.F. Holt and S. Pressman (eds), *Empirical Post Keynesian Economics: Looking at the Real World*, Armonk, NY: M.E. Sharpe, pp. 44–69.

Galbraith, J.K. and H. Kum (2005), 'Estimating the inequality of household incomes: toward a dense and consistent global data set', *Review of Income and Wealth*, **51** (1), 115–43.

Galbraith, J.K. and D. Rossi (2016), 'Exchange rates and industrial wage inequality in open economies', *University of Texas Inequality Project Working Paper*, No. 71.

Goldin, C. and L.F. Katz (2008), *The Race Between Technology and Education*, Cambridge, MA, USA: Harvard University Press.

Harris, J.R. and M.P. Todaro (1970), 'Migration, unemployment and development: a two-sector analysis', *American Economic Review*, **60** (1), 126–42.

Martin, A. (1981), 'Economic stagnation and social stalemate in Sweden', in Joint Economic Committee (ed.), *Monetary Policy, Selective Credit Policy and Industrial Policy in France, Britain, West Germany and Sweden*, Washington, DC: Joint Economic Committee, pp. 136–215.

Inflation

Inflation is a loss of money's purchasing power. As a result, there is an upward pressure on the general price level. This does not mean, however, that all prices will increase eventually because of inflation. In fact, inflation and price stability can co-exist: if technical progress reduces production costs, allowing firms to reduce their prices without reducing the mark-up and profits, then inflation may just compensate this price reduction, thereby keeping the relevant price level unchanged (see Rossi, 2001; Cencini and Rossi, 2021). There may even be a reduction in the price level despite inflation: this occurs indeed when technical progress reduces production costs – hence prices – more than inflation exerts an upward pressure on the price level.

Economists and policy makers are in general not yet aware of the essential and conceptual difference between inflation and price increases. They assimilate inflation with an increase in the (general) price level, which moreover they pretend to measure on the goods markets only, ignoring thereby real and financial assets – whose prices can also inflate obviously.

The origin of inflation is not to be found in agents' forms of behaviour, as economists try to explain referring to demand-side or supply-side phenomena (such as expansionary fiscal or monetary policies and an increase in wages beyond the increase in labour's productivity, pushing firms to transfer this excessive increase to their customers). In fact, inflation is the result of a monetary–structural disorder. It stems from a lack of distinction between money, income, and capital in banks' ledgers. As money is issued by banks every time a payment has to be made (independently of pre-existing income, in the form of savings), banks can and do provide credit lines that go beyond the real 'needs of trade' (Davidson, 1988, p. 167), or what Werner (2012, p. 29) calls 'GDP-based transactions'. Banks aim indeed at maximizing their profits, through a never-ending expansion of credit. There is therefore a mushroom growth of bank deposits (as captured by the relevant 'monetary aggregate' like M1, M2, or M3), which dilutes money's purchasing power (that is, income) into a volume of bank deposits bigger than it should be to avoid inflation.

Monetary authorities generally increase the policy rates of interest to reduce the measured rate of inflation. However, this monetary policy strategy is usually inappropriate, because it does not address the origin of inflation but merely its most evident consequence, that is, an increase in the price level. Further, increasing interest rates can even accelerate the rate of measured inflation, since firms having to pay higher rates of interest on their borrowing are induced to increase their prices on the market for produced goods and services (which may bring further increases in the policy rates of interest). A similar argument applies when the central bank aims at increasing the rate of measured inflation by reducing interest rates – in some cases below zero, as occurred after the bursting of the global financial crisis in 2008 when some central banks (notably the Swiss National Bank) adopted a negative interest rate policy (see Rossi, 2019).

To address the origin of inflation, rather than simply its most evident effect, one needs to consider the essential distinction existing between money, income, and capital. Money is a means of final payment whilst income is money's purchasing power produced on the factor market when firms pay out the wage bill. In other words, money carries out payment orders whilst income finances them, allowing the payee to have no further claims on the payer (see Goodhart, 1989, p. 26). Financial capital is by contrast the result of saving: saved income is transformed into capital, which exists in this form until it is spent on any kinds of markets – at that point of time, capital is transformed back into income, thereby financing the relevant expenditure in the marketplace.

This ontological distinction between money, income, and capital must be recognized in the banks' ledgers. Otherwise, banks can originate inflationary pressures when they open credit lines that do not rely on pre-existent deposits and are not linked to production on the factor market. To avoid this pathology, banking regulations that affect banks' behaviour are not a relevant macroprudential policy, as they are not in a position to impede banks originating inflation by granting credit lines for 'non-GDP-based transactions' (Werner, 2012, p. 29). Both liquidity and capital requirements, such as those enshrined in the Basel III agreement, concern the banks' balance sheets after the latter agents have opened a new credit line. This may affect bankers' decisions to open credit lines, but does not impede them doing so, once they consider that the underlying transactions

SERGIO ROSSI

generate enough profit to respect the relevant regulations. In fact, rather than impacting on bankers' forms of behaviour, which leaves the problem of inflation as it is to date, there must be a monetary–structural reform separating explicitly money, income, and capital in banks' bookkeeping. If so, then any 'non-GDP-based transactions' can occur only if there is enough income in the banking system, rather than being the result of a money emission starting from *tabula rasa* (see Carrera and Rossi, 2015). Further, all income that is invested to accumulate fixed capital must be transferred to a fixed-capital department in banks' accounting, to avoid this income – which is fixed forever into productive capital – being lent by the banking sector, thereby inducing further inflationary pressures when this income is spent on the products market (see Cencini, 2012, for analytical elaboration).

SERGIO ROSSI

See also

Bubbles – credit; Endogenous money; Inflation targeting; Monetary policy; Moncy as a means of payment

References

Carrera, A. and S. Rossi (2015), 'Money, income, and profit: lessons from the monetary theory of production', *Iberian Journal of the History of Economic Thought*, **2** (1), 48–60.
Cencini, A. (2012), 'Is there a common cause to economic and financial crises?', in C. Gnos and S. Rossi (eds), *Modern Monetary Macroeconomics: A New Paradigm for Economic Policy*, Cheltenham, UK, and Northampton, MA, USA: Edward Elgar, pp. 193–217.
Cencini, A. and S. Rossi (2021), 'Inflation and unemployment', in L.-P. Rochon and S. Rossi (eds), *An Introduction to Macroeconomics: A Heterodox Approach to Economic Analysis*, second edition, Cheltenham, UK, and Northampton, MA, USA: Edward Elgar, pp. 331–54.
Davidson, P. (1988), 'Endogenous money, the production process, and inflation analysis', *Économie appliquée*, **41** (1), 151–69.
Goodhart, C.A.E. (1989), *Money, Information and Uncertainty*, second edition, London and Basingstoke: Macmillan (first published 1975).
Rossi, S. (2001), *Money and Inflation: A New Macroeconomic Analysis*, Cheltenham, UK, and Northampton, MA, USA: Edward Elgar.
Rossi, S. (2019), 'The dangerous ineffectiveness of negative interest rates: the case of Switzerland', *Review of Keynesian Economics*, **7** (2), 220–32.

Werner, R. (2012), 'Economics as if banks mattered: a contribution based on the inductive methodology', *The Manchester School*, **79** (2), 25–35.

Inflation – conflict theory of

Conflict theory perspectives on inflation came to the fore in the 1970s, responding to the failures of the Phillips curve approach, as well as the industrial conflicts of the late 1960s and early 1970s over wages and profits. The essential conflict involved is that between labour and returns to capital, though other conflicts, such as those between countries, are also relevant. When pricing is viewed in terms of mark-up over costs, and notably wages, there are implications for the profit share and for the price/wage ratio. When wages are viewed in terms of striving for a form of targeted real wage (or similar), then there are implications for the wage/price ratio. There is then an inherent conflict between the claims of capitalists and the claims of workers, which can express itself in terms of rising prices and wages.

In one of the first formulations of a conflict theory of inflation, Rowthorn (1977) focused on what he termed the 'aspiration gap' of capitalists, that is, the difference between the claims of capitalists and those of workers along with claims of government (taxation) and the foreign sector. He saw this aspiration gap as 'determined by the market power of workers and capitalists and by their willingness to use this power' (Rowthorn, 1977, p. 219). The level of demand is 'a regulator of conflict, imposing a *discipline* on the price sector, and making it easier or more difficult for workers to raise wages and capitalists to raise prices' (p. 219, italics in the original). Higher taxes and higher costs of imported goods would reduce income of workers and capitalists, and both groups may resist the effects through pressing to raise their wages and their prices.

Within a conflict theory of inflation, there is a role for the level of demand (relative to capacity) and for the pace of change of demand. At high levels of demand, there would be pressures for prices to rise faster than wages from a high demand for goods and services, and for wages to rise faster than prices from a high demand for labour. The two effects together would threaten a wage–price spiral.

Prices are set in a range of ways and with different degrees of frequency, and most of them with the intention of being unchanged for a significant period of time. Wages are also set in many different ways but again typically last for a significant period of time. As such, prices and wages will reflect perceptions on recent trends in prices and wages and expectations on near future trends.

The discussion of conflict theories of inflation makes little mention of money and the money supply. It is fully compatible with the endogenous (often post-Keynesian) money analysis in which the creation of bank credit-money through the loan process is a response to rising prices and wages rather than an initiator of price rises. One part of the mechanism is that in the face of rising costs, firms have to find additional finance to enable production to occur, and this comes from provision of bank loans and thereby creation of money.

Some of the formulations of the non-accelerating inflation rate of unemployment (NAIRU), as proposed by Layard et al. (1991), have some similarities with the conflict theory of inflation, though the language and terminology may differ. Central to the Layard et al. (1991) model and similar ones is the interaction between a pricing equation and a wage determination equation, from which a level of unemployment (the NAIRU) can be derived at which price and wage inflation are consistent with no tendency to rise or fall.

Arestis and Sawyer (2005) suggest the idea of an 'inflation barrier' and indicate that there are no automatic forces leading to a level of aggregate demand consistent with constant rates of inflation. Inflationary pressures arise from, inter alia, a conflict over income shares, and from cost elements with the price of raw materials (especially oil) being the most important. There are supply-side factors impinging on the inflationary process, which arise from the level of productive capacity (relative to aggregate demand). The supply-side constraints are viewed as arising from capacity constraints, rather than from the operation of the labour market. The capacity constraints evolve over time as investment occurs and adds to the capital stock.

MALCOLM SAWYER

See also

Aggregate demand; Endogenous money; Inflation; NAIRU; Phillips curve

References

Arestis, P. and M. Sawyer (2005), 'Aggregate demand, conflict and capacity in the inflationary process', *Cambridge Journal of Economics*, 29 (6), 959–74.

Layard, R., S. Nickell and R. Jackman (1991), *Unemployment: Macroeconomic Performance and the Labour Market*, Oxford: Oxford University Press.

Rowthorn, R.E. (1977), 'Conflict, inflation and money', *Cambridge Journal of Economics*, 1 (3), 215–39.

Inflation – cost-push

Economics textbooks usually present cost-push inflation as a short-run disturbance connected with supply shocks, the oil shocks of the 1970s being the typical example in this regard. As a result, rather than a theory of inflation, cost-push is downplayed to an ad hoc explanation within a more general theory in which inflation is purely a monetary phenomenon that originates on the demand side and that monetary policy can control by maneuvering an exogenous supply of money. In post-Keynesian macroeconomics, by contrast, while money is usually explained to be endogenous, cost-push inflation is a structural phenomenon connected with market power on the supply side (see Rochon, 2006). Developing Keynes's (1936, pp. 301–2) distinction between 'semi-inflation' and 'absolute inflation', along with the basic intuitions on the labour market in Keynes's *General Theory* and Robinson (1937), post-Keynesian theory also replicates some of the original elements of the cost-push school as the latter emerged before the advent of monetarism.

Cost-push theories of inflation mushroomed during the 1950s as an alternative (or complementary) to the demand-pull explanation (Bronfenbrenner and Holzman, 1963). Within a broadly accepted, if loosely defined or unspecified, Keynesian framework, both theories reflected 'unanimity ... on the key role of the rate of increase in money wages in the inflationary process' (Kaldor, 1959, p. 292). More specifically, nominal wages increasing faster than productivity was the commonly accepted source of inflation, which the cost-push school saw as the result of distributional conflicts among wage earners and/or between wages and

MALCOLM SAWYER / CARLO CRISTIANO

profits. Market power on the side of costs – they contended – could move up prices, even in conditions in which demand was not excessive. Moreover, while the alternative approach, which would soon be related to the Phillips curve, argued that aggregate demand had to be reduced and unemployment increased in order to curb inflation, the typical cost-push policy prescription was incomes policy, aimed at price stability with full employment.

This is the milieu in which the post-Keynesian theory of inflation emerged. Kaldor (1959), for instance, presented the conflict between wages and profit as the key factor, *en passant* rejecting the Phillips curve hypothesis, while Kahn's (1960) support to incomes policy was based on a view of inflation in which the emphasis was on trade-unions rivalry. Then, the standard post-Keynesian analytical approach emerged in the United States with Weintraub (1961) and the introduction of the identity $P = k(w/A)$, where P is the price level, k is the profit markup, A is the average physical productivity of labour, w stands for nominal wages, and w/A is the unit labour cost of production (see Davidson, 1994).

Based on this identity, or variations of it, post-Keynesian models usually explain inflation either as a result of a distributional conflict among groups of workers reflected in upwards movements of w given k, or as a conflict between wage earners and profit earners as reflected in the relative rates of change of k and w. The former mechanism is usually connected to the idea of a wage-wage spiral. The latter, resulting in a wage-price spiral, is sometimes also developed within models of Kaleckian or Marxist derivation (see, for example, Rowthorn, 1977, and Myatt, 1986). These distinctions, however, should not be taken as too rigid. Combinations of the two basic mechanisms are possible, and the characteristic of this approach, as compared with mainstream theory, is eclecticism. While rejecting the neoclassical assumptions about the labour market, these theories favour more empirically and historically based analyses in which wages and/or profits are exogenous and therefore determined by a wide array of factors including moral values (such as fairness), power relations, information and institutions (see Palley, 1996, and Lavoie, 2014).

CARLO CRISTIANO

See also

Endogenous money; Income distribution; Inflation – conflict theory of; Monetary policy; Power

References

Bronfenbrenner, M. and F.D. Holzman (1963), 'Survey of inflation theory', *American Economic Review*, **53** (4), 593–661.

Davidson, P. (1994), *Post Keynesian Macroeconomic Theory: A Foundation for Successful Economic Policies for the Twenty-First Century*, Aldershot, UK, and Brookfield, USA: Edward Elgar.

Kahn, R.F. (1960), 'Memorandum of evidence submitted to the Radcliffe Committee', in *Selected Essays on Employment and Growth*, Cambridge, UK: Cambridge University Press, 1972, pp. 124–52.

Kaldor, N. (1959), 'Economic growth and the problem of inflation', *Economica*, **26** (104), 287–98.

Keynes, J.M. (1936), *The General Theory of Employment, Interest and Money*, London: Macmillan.

Lavoie, M. (2014), *Post-Keynesian Economics: New Foundations*, Cheltenham, UK, and Northampton, MA, USA: Edward Elgar.

Myatt, A. (1986), 'On the non-existence of the natural rate of unemployment and Kaleckian micro underpinnings to the Phillips curve', *Journal of Post Keynesian Economics*, **8** (3), 447–62.

Palley, T.I. (1996), *Post Keynesian Economics: Debt, Distribution and the Macro Economy*, London: Macmillan.

Robinson, J. (1937), *Essays on the Theory of Employment*, London: Macmillan.

Rochon, L.-P. (2006), 'The more things change ... inflation targeting and central bank policy', *Journal of Post Keynesian Economics*, **28** (4), 551–8.

Rowthorn, R.E. (1977), 'Conflict, inflation and money', *Cambridge Journal of Economics*, **1** (3), 215–39.

Weintraub, S. (1961), *Classical Keynesianism, Monetary Theory, and the Price Level*, Philadelphia: Chilton.

Inflation targeting

Inflation targeting is a monetary policy strategy that pursues price stability as the primary objective of central banking. It describes a set of institutional principles, practices and decision-making procedures for central banks, which are supposed to ensure low and stable inflation rates.

Inflation targeting provides a monetary outlook that consists of a predictable target and response scheme, which is optimized with a systematic policy commitment framework that 'facilitates public understanding of policy' (Woodford, 2003, p. 15). Its main tool is the announcement of an inflation target, which not only stipulates price stability for a particular economy, but also serves as an affirming letter of intent for a sound monetary policy. Its credibility is supported by the implementation of transparency to monetary policy. By this, the central bank provides a wide range of data and information (stylized facts) to report how, why and under which circumstances it is making monetary policy. Hence, inflation targeting is associated with the increased communication, (forward) guidance, transparency and accountability of central banks (see Bernanke and Woodford, 2005, p. 1).

Since the early 1990s, many countries have adopted different formal and informal variants of inflation targeting as a policy framework for central banking. It is regarded as a successful strategy because it offers a flexible and pragmatic alternative to previous monetary policy regimes like exchange-rate or monetary targeting (see Mishkin, 2002, p. 362). Its proponents argue that a projected future inflation rate and a forecast of interest rates ('forward guidance') offer an effective benchmark for a monetary economy, in which *ex ante* expectations and the *ex post* realization of prices are of major importance for decision making. From this perspective, credible targets, reliable indicators and predictable responses by a central bank contribute to stabilize prices in a sort of self-fulfilling prophecy.

The operational objectives of inflation targeting, namely a fixed point or range of targeted inflation, serve as a comprehensible feedback rule for the central bank, while the short-term interest rate is the main policy variable (Taylor, 2000, p. 92). There are two basic scenarios. If the inflation rate exceeds the targeted rate of inflation, the central bank raises its policy rate of interest and tightens the money supply. The intention is to reduce the credit providing capacity of the banking sector by increasing borrowing costs to suppress demand. In the opposite case, when the inflation rate is under the targeted rate of inflation, credit conditions are eased by lowering interest rates and improving the liquidity conditions for banks to boost demand. The economic reasoning behind this reaction pattern rests on holding consumption and investment fluctuations responsible for the deviation of the rate of inflation from its long-term path.

The way the interrelation between interest rates, inflation and GDP is operationalized makes inflation targeting a central part of the New Consensus in Macroeconomics (Taylor, 2000, p. 91; Goodfriend, 2007). In this regard, inflation targeting carries various theoretical elements from mainstream economics and can be located at the intersection of neoclassical, monetarist, new-classical and new-Keynesian theory. The way interest rates are conceptualized can be traced back to Wicksell's natural rate of interest (see Woodford, 2003). The definition of inflation rests mainly on the quantity theory of money and thus is monetarist. Nevertheless, its treatment can also be described as inspired by new-classical theory, because it adheres to the hypothesis of rational expectations as well as the time-inconsistency and inflationary bias propositions and seeks to keep governments out of monetary decisions by promoting independent central banks. And lastly, it is also new-Keynesian in its pragmatic approach for allowing limited monetary policy interventions and its acceptance of the short-run non-neutrality of money. Therefore, inflation targeting has been prominently described as 'constrained discretion' (Snowdon and Vane, 2005, p. 415).

Inflation targeting is a controversial issue in economics. While most mainstream economists praise it as an optimal policy against inflation, some point at empirical and application problems or question its real impact on inflation at all (see contributions in Bernanke and Woodford, 2005). In contrast, heterodox economists reject the limited policy approach of inflation targeting. Post-Keynesian and Marxist economists criticize it because of its narrow focus on price stability, which conveys an anti-growth bias and further depoliticizes monetary policy to a technical, exogenous task of setting interest rates (Arestis and Sawyer, 2005, p. 236; Fine and Dimakou, 2016, p. 131). This led to a systematic neglect of growing financial and economic instability that induced the global financial crisis of 2008 (Rochon and Rossi, 2021, p. 211). When policy making is measured in its impact on inflation only, other socioeconomic goals like output stabilization, employment and distribution become secondary.

Moreover, heterodox economists were pivotal in criticizing inflation targeting for treating inflation and deflation as the opposite ends of the same problem, emphasizing the peculiar dangers of deflation and the limited scope of conventional policy tools. This critique gained wider acceptance in recent years, especially since many central banks were confronted with the 'zero lower bound' problem that led to the adoption of unconventional monetary policies. Nevertheless, inflation targeting remains an established policy framework in spite of the fact that it fails to adequately address urgent issues like climate change and environmental destruction, not to mention global pandemics, which all impede social welfare.

Recent developments indicate a gradual shift of attitude towards questions of inflation target compliance and the inclusion of further socioeconomic objectives into monetary policy. New Zealand, the country that pioneered inflation targeting in 1989, moved to a double mandate in 2019 by adding 'a maximum level of sustainable employment' to its monetary objectives. In 2020, the US Federal Reserve announced a switch from fixed to average inflation targeting in order to gain more room for maintaining financial stability. In mid-2021, the European Central Bank (ECB) accordingly caught up and revised its inflation targeting strategy. In order to legitimize future unconventional monetary policy action, the ECB conceded to medium term transitory periods in which inflation could raise above its 2 percent target. It remains to be seen whether other countries will follow and whether the strategy of inflation targeting, as such, will maintain its relevance in view of future crises.

ULAŞ ŞENER

See also

Central bank independence; Central banking; Inflation; Interest rate targeting; Monetary policy

References

Arestis, P. and M. Sawyer (2005), 'New Consensus, New Keynesianism and the economics of the third way', in E. Hein, A. Heise and A. Truger (eds), *Neu-Keynesianismus: Der neue wirtschaftspolitische Mainstream?*, Marburg: Metropolis, pp. 229–46.
Bernanke, B. and M. Woodford (2005), *The Inflation-Targeting Debate*, Chicago: University of Chicago Press.
Fine, B. and O. Dimakou (2016), *Macroeconomics: A Critical Companion*, London: Pluto Press.
Goodfriend, M. (2007), 'How the world achieved consensus on monetary policy', *Journal of Economic Perspectives*, **21** (4), 47–68.
Mishkin, F.S. (2002), 'Inflation targeting', in B. Snowdon and H.R. Vane (eds), *An Encyclopedia of Macroeconomics*, Cheltenham, UK, and Northampton, MA, USA: Edward Elgar, pp. 361–5.
Rochon, L.-P. and S. Rossi (2021), 'The central bank and monetary policy', in L.-P. Rochon and S. Rossi (eds), *An Introduction to Macroeconomics: A Heterodox Approach to Economic Analysis*, second edition, Cheltenham, UK, and Northampton, MA, USA: Edward Elgar, pp. 200–29.
Snowdon, B. and H.R. Vane (2005), *Modern Macroeconomics: Its Origins, Development and Current State*, Cheltenham, UK, and Northampton, MA, USA: Edward Elgar.
Taylor, J.B. (2000), 'Teaching modern macroeconomics at the principles level', *American Economic Review*, **90** (2), 90–4.
Woodford, M. (2003), *Interest and Prices: Foundations of a Theory of Monetary Policy*, Princeton and Oxford: Princeton University Press.

Innovation

Innovation inherently implies the idea of change, and consists of 'something new' that is introduced in the economic system. The dimensions most commonly considered, which appeal to intuition, are those of product and process innovation. Product innovation has at least two sides: first, the realization of a better or new version of an existing product such as improved mechanical clocks or the creation of digital ones; second, the creation of a completely new product that did not exist, like the refrigerator or the computer. Process innovation has also at least two sides, that is, the improvement of an existing one or the creation of a completely new one – here one can think of different processes through which steel has been produced in different ages.

Let us emphasize that almost invariably the language that we use and the examples referred to suffer from an industrial bias, in the sense that we have in mind tangible products and processes. However, innovation in services is also very important: as an example, just think of the evolution of banking services – from the early establishment of automated teller machines in the late 1960s to home banking.

Another dimension that we also have in mind is some sort of classification criteria according

ULAŞ ŞENER / NICOLA DE LISO

to which we classify innovations along a scale ranging from incremental to radical. In electronics we can think of incremental improvements of valves (or vacuum tubes) in the 1940s and early 1950s before the radical innovation of transistors displaced valves completely by the late 1950s.

The latter example gives us the opportunity to clarify the fact that when we deal with innovation we deal with a process of creative destruction. This expression is due to Joseph Schumpeter (1883–1950), the scholar whose ideas have influenced most the economics of innovation research line (for a synthesis of Schumpeter's economics see De Liso, 2022). The creative side concerns both process and product innovation, and these new products and methods of production create a 'new economic space'. However, for some of the existing firms the emergence of competing innovators means economic death; for still others contraction and drifting into the background. Further, there are firms and industries that are forced to undergo a difficult and painful process of modernization, rationalization and reconstruction.

A key question thus concerns the sources of innovation. Through time economists have elaborated many tools of analysis and methodologies, from the 'technology push' and 'demand pull' perspectives, to the production function approach, to systemic views. We cannot consider all these aspects here (for exhaustive reviews see Fagerberg et al., 2005, and Swann, 2009). Let us focus here on what follows.

An innovation does not necessarily have to be based on an invention, nor need it be technological. Innovation can be an original assemblage or novel application of already existing technologies, devices and components, while there exist immaterial forms of innovation – such as organizational innovation – which do not necessarily make use of different or newer technologies. Thus, despite the fact we often observe the fusion and co-evolution of the trinomial science–technology–innovation, (just think of fields such as nanotechnology), there exist successful innovations that spread around the economy without being based on hard science and big technology, an example being the furniture industry as innovated by firms like Ikea.

An important feature of innovation is its diffusion. The initial innovation by a business unit often spreads across the economic system through a process of imitation and adoption. While the initial innovation, imitation and adoption concern individual units, the overall process leads to the diffusion phenomenon. Through diffusion, though, innovation is further developed, as imitation often leads to improvements of the original innovation, since new methods cannot simply be adopted but have to be adapted to specific needs.

There exists a special relationship between market economies and innovation. Indeed, despite the fact that creativity and innovation are intrinsic human features, within market economies there exists an endogenous driving force, that is, the search for profit, which is particularly effective in generating innovations through the work of entrepreneurs. The economic debate has thoroughly investigated the relationship that exists between firms' size (only giant firms have the resources to carry out systematic research-and-development activities), market structure (like oligopolistic markets versus competitive markets) and innovativeness.

If within market economies we have strong spontaneous incentives that stimulate innovation, we should never forget the role played by the State and public agencies in shaping an innovation-friendly environment as well as, in some cases, in directing innovation itself in certain directions, as in the case of military technologies. The concept of 'national system of innovation' and, within it, the notion of a 'science, technology and innovation policy' are particularly helpful in the understanding of the restless evolution of our economies.

NICOLA DE LISO

See also

Development; Fiscal policy; Monopoly power; Profit; Technological change

References

De Liso, N. (2022), 'Joseph Alois Schumpeter', in H. Bougrine and L.-P. Rochon (eds), *A Brief History of Economic Thought*, Cheltenham, UK, and Northampton, MA, USA: Edward Elgar, pp. 125–47.

Fagerberg, J., D.C. Mowery and R.R. Nelson (eds) (2005), *The Oxford Handbook of Innovation*, Oxford: Oxford University Press.

Metcalfe, J.S. (1998), *Evolutionary Economics and Creative Destruction*, London and New York: Routledge.

NICOLA DE LISO

Schumpeter, J.A. (1934), *The Theory of Economic Development*, Oxford: Oxford University Press.

Swann, G.M.P. (2009), *The Economics of Innovation: An Introduction*, Cheltenham, UK, and Northampton, MA, USA: Edward Elgar.

Institutional economics – core ideas

Institutional economics (or 'institutionalist economics') is a stream of thought rejecting neoclassical theory while emphasizing its difference from Marxism. It reaches its heyday between the end of the nineteenth century and the end of the 1920s.

This scientific research programme (Lakatos, 1986) includes essentially the prestigious names of Thorstein B. Veblen (1857–1929), Wesley C. Mitchell (1874–1948), John R. Commons (1862–1945) and John M. Clark (1884–1963). Some of its features allow the inclusion of such a major thinker as Karl Polanyi (1886–1964).

The expression 'institutional economics' appears for the first time in an article of Walton Hamilton published in 1919 following a convention of the American Economic Association (see Hamilton, 1919).

Contemporary with John M. Keynes, to whom some of its members were close, especially J.R. Commons (see Thabet, 2012), institutionalist economics in spite of some disagreements between its authors shares many principles (hardcore of the scientific research programme):

- What matters is not the individual (*homo œconomicus*) but the institutions (holism) as the starting point of any analysis, in an abductive perspective. Institutions (habits, customs, money, school, State) are dealt as the collective framework, formal and informal, through which individuals socialize themselves while they influence their actions.
- History is emphasized as an important explaining factor, the German historical school being one of the roots of institutionalist economics. It means that historical time streams from an irreversible past (path dependency) to a fundamentally uncertain future.
- A realist and evolutionary approach is used reflecting a Darwinian influence.
- In the field of public action, deep reforms of capitalism are advocated to avoid strongly undermining the market order (on this point, Veblen is more radical than Commons).

Institutional economics was marginalized by the 1930s crisis, by the growing mathematization of economics (econometrics) and by the hegemony of 'hydraulic Keynesianism' (Coddington, 1976). Notwithstanding this marginalization, it survived in the shadows, thanks to major authors like Allan G. Gruchy (1906–90), Warren J. Samuels (1933–2011) and still Geoffrey M. Hodgson (1946–) and William M. Dugger (1947–): the second generation of institutionalists has been rallying the *Journal of Economic Issues*. Since the 1970s, there is also a growing impact of a powerful group of authors who gave rise to 'New institutional economics'. It aims at a transformation of the ruling Walrasian paradigm rooting it in institutions and based on the works of Ronald Coase (1910–2013), Douglass North (1920–2015) and Oliver Williamson (1932–).

Since the 2008 global financial crisis, this heterodox school of thought is winning new interest because of the institutional foundations of the world financial cataclysm engineered by the collapse of the US subprime market. Rooted in the writings of Hyman Minsky on financial instability, institutional reforms and the State as an employer of last resort, institutionalist economists became closer to post-Keynesian economists: the outcome of this alliance was ultimately 'post-Keynesian institutionalism', the first contributions of which, mixing the two streams of thought, allow hope for a bright future (see Whalen, 2011).

SLIM THABET

See also

Capitalism; Employer of last resort; Neoclassical economics; Traverse, path dependency, and economic dynamics; Uncertainty

References

Coddington, A. (1976), 'Keynesian economics: the search for first principles', *Journal of Economic Literature*, **14** (4), 1258–73.

Gruchy, A.G. (1987), *The Reconstruction of Economics: An Analysis of the Fundamentals of Institutional Economics*, New York: Greenwood Press.

NICOLA DE LISO / SLIM THABET

Hamilton, W. (1919), 'The institutional approach to economic theory', *American Economic Review*, 9 (1), 309–18.

Hodgson, G.M. (1988), *Economics and Institutions: A Manifesto for a Modern Institutional Economics*, Philadelphia: University of Pennsylvania Press.

Lakatos, I. (1986), *The Methodology of Scientific Research Programmes*, Cambridge, UK: Cambridge University Press.

Thabet, S. (2012), 'Keynes et l'institutionnalisme historique américain: une perspective généalogique', *Economies et Sociétés*, **46** (7), 1297–324.

Whalen, C.J. (ed.) (2021), *Financial Instability and Economic Security after the Great Recession*, Cheltenham, UK, and Northampton, MA, USA: Edward Elgar.

Institutional economics – origins

Two institutionalist intellectual traditions, Original Institutional Economics (OIE) and New Institutional Economics (NIE), operate within the discipline. While the two movements are not without parallels, the focus below is given to OIE and its relationship to post-Keynesian economics. The inception of OIE is generally traced to the work of Thorstein Veblen, John Commons and Wesley Mitchell that first appeared in the closing decade of the nineteenth century in the United States, with the term itself later coined by Walton Hamilton (1919).

The trio of OIE authors identified above were not close collaborators, and pursued divergent research agendas, rendering any precise definition of their shared analytical framework contentious. One contributor to OIE, Clark (1936, p. 7), noted that the term 'means so many different things to so many different people that doubt has arisen whether it has any definable meaning at all'. These reservations notwithstanding, more recent surveys have seen in OIE a common attempt to integrate an evolutionary understanding of human culture and institutions into economic analysis (Mayhew, 1987). Rutherford (2011) highlights a consistent demand for empirical realism among OIE authors, coupled with a desire to move beyond the observation of social institutions, and towards active participation in their reform.

An exclusive focus on Veblen's criticisms of neoclassical economics tends to cast OIE as a heterodox movement from its inception. Institutionalist figures were, however, instrumental in founding the American Economic Association, and exercised considerable influence within the growing regulatory State of the early twentieth century. More accurately, OIE became a heterodox movement as the eclecticism of Progressive Era American economics gradually gave way to mathematical formalism.

Veblen's work, often satirical in tone, voiced strident criticisms of what he first termed 'neoclassical economics'. In attempting to abstractly analyse the isolated decisions of individuals, neoclassical economists were guilty of divorcing human behaviour and consumption choices from their social context, where they might instead play performative and symbolic functions (Veblen, 1898). Veblen (1899) understood that consumption choices often served as a means to display one's relative social position within hierarchical societies. Individual preferences were not independently constituted, and the pattern of 'pecuniary emulation' suggested that continually amplified consumption would be necessary merely to maintain one's social position. Building on Veblen, Lavoie (1994) has suggested that this 'principle of nonindependence' is part of the common ground of post-Keynesian theories of consumer choice. Moreover, an overriding focus on positions of stable equilibrium rendered neoclassical theory incapable of understanding historical dynamics and the process of change in economic systems (Schütz and Rainer, 2016). Veblen was similarly critical of the emerging neoclassical theory of distribution articulated by J.B. Clark and Irving Fisher, and maintained that the productivity of capital was necessarily a reflection of the accumulated knowledge and experience of societies as a whole (Cohen, 2014). In rejecting the measurable productivity of capital as a basis for a theory of interest, Joan Robinson (1980) herself acknowledged that Veblen had anticipated important themes that re-emerged in the 'Cambridge capital controversies'.

Commons's work evidenced far less antagonism towards the emergent neoclassical theory, seeing institutional economics as enriching rather supplanting neoclassical theories of value and distribution (Biddle and Samuels, 1998). His *Legal Foundations of Capitalism* (Commons, 1924), based in part on a close study of the Supreme Court of the United States' antitrust decisions, explored how varying structures of property rights and the relative bargaining power of agents conditioned economic value. Together with a number of his students, Commons was also a pioneering labour historian, completing extensive field research into working conditions, and producing the first scholarly treatment of the history of organized labour in the United States (Commons et al., 1918). Alongside Richard Ely, Commons was instrumental in the success of the graduate programme at the University of Wisconsin. Many graduates at this university took up positions within the growing State and federal regulatory apparatus, leading Boulding (1957, p. 7) to claim that 'through his students Commons was the intellectual origin of the New Deal, of labor legislation, of social security, of the whole movement in [the US] towards a welfare state'. On several occasions Keynes expressed an appreciation for Commons's approach, incorporating his idea that advanced economies had entered the 'era of stabilization' into several public lectures. More generally, Whalen (2008, p. 48) has suggested that Commons's and Keynes's shared precept ('[l]ook at the world, then theorize') has served as a guiding principle for a post-Keynesian institutionalism.

Completing his graduate training at the University of Chicago, where he studied under Veblen, much of Mitchell's lasting influence was exercised through his dedication to empiricism, and his criticism of purely deductive economic theorizing. Mitchell's studies of the business cycle were notably influential, his citations among macroeconomists being second only to Irving Fisher in the 1920s (Deutscher, 1990, p. 189). Mitchell helped to found the National Bureau of Economic Research, where his work on the estimation of national income, its growth and its functional distribution anticipated the systematization of national income accounting. In investigating the dynamics of business cycles, Mitchell contended that they were endogenous phenomena unique to monetary economies wherein production was organized around the profit motive (Sherman, 2001).

With the rise of the neoclassical synthesis of Keynesian economics in the United States, OIE authors' practical influence receded. OIE nevertheless remains an active tradition and, as stressed above, many of its core themes continue to find expression in post-Keynesian economics.

WILLIAM E. MCCOLLOCH

See also

Capital theory controversies; Heterodox economics; Methodology; Neoclassical economics; Post-Keynesian economics – a big tent?

References

Biddle, J.E. and W.J. Samuels (1998), 'John R. Commons and the compatibility of neoclassical and institutional economics', in R. Holt and S. Pressman (eds), *Economics and its Discontents*, Cheltenham, UK, and Northampton, MA, USA: Edward Elgar, pp. 40–55.
Boulding, K.E. (1957), 'A new look at institutional economics', *American Economic Review*, **47** (2), 1–12.
Clark, J.M. (1936), 'Past accomplishments and present prospects of American economics', *American Economic Review*, **26** (1), 1–11.
Cohen, A.J. (2014), 'Veblen *contra* Clark and Fisher: Veblen–Robinson–Harcourt lineages in capital controversies and beyond', *Cambridge Journal of Economics*, **38** (6), 1493–515.
Commons, J.R. (1924), *Legal Foundations of Capitalism*, New York: Macmillan.
Commons, J.R., D.J. Saposs, H.L. Sumner, E.B. Mittelman, H.E. Hoagland, J.B. Andrews, and S. Perlman (1918), *History of Labour in the United States*, New York: Macmillan.
Deutscher, P. (1990), *R.G. Hawtrey and the Development of Macroeconomics*, London: Macmillan.
Hamilton, W.H. (1919), 'The institutional approach to economic theory', *American Economic Review*, **9** (1), 309–18.
Lavoie, M. (1994), 'A Post Keynesian approach to consumer choice', *Journal of Post Keynesian Economics*, **16** (4), 539–62.
Mayhew, A. (1987), 'The beginning of institutionalism', *Journal of Economic Issues*, **21** (3), 971–98.
Mitchell, W.C., W.I. King, F.R. Macaulay and O.W. Knauth (1921), *Income in the United States: Its Amount and Distribution, 1909–1919*, New York: National Bureau of Economic Research.
Robinson, J.V. (1980), 'Thinking about thinking', in *Collected Economic Papers, Vol. V*, Cambridge, MA: MIT Press, pp. 110–19.
Rutherford, M. (2011), *The Institutionalist Movement in American Economics, 1918–1947*, Cambridge, UK: Cambridge University Press.
Schütz, M. and A. Rainer (2016), 'J.A. Schumpeter and T.B. Veblen on economic evolution: the dichotomy between statics and dynamics', *European Journal of the History of Economic Thought*, **23** (5), 718–42.
Sherman, H. (2001), 'The business cycle theory of Wesley Mitchell', *Journal of Economic Issues*, **35** (1), 85–97.

Veblen, T. (1898), 'Why is economics not an evolutionary science?', *Quarterly Journal of Economics*, **12** (4), 373–97.

Veblen, T. (1899), *The Theory of the Leisure Class*, New York: Macmillan.

Whalen, C.J. (2008), 'Toward "wisely managed" capitalism: Post-Keynesian institutionalism and the creative State', *Forum for Social Economics*, **37** (1), 43–60.

Interest rate – long term

The long-term interest rate is subject to great economic debate, even within post-Keynesian theory. Its importance is due to the role neoclassical economists attribute to it as a variable that balances the money market, but also as a determinant of investments and as an indicator that signals the onset of a liquidity trap.

If both classical and neoclassical economists have always maintained the existence of a natural rate of interest that is independent of economic policy decisions, post-Keynesian economists not only reject the concept altogether, but question the forces that determine its level, and the interpretation of the role it can play in economic policy decisions.

For post-Keynesian economists, the role of the central bank is crucial. It sets the interest rate at the short-end of the spectrum, which represents the base of an inverted pyramid. In turn, this determines the prevailing interest rates in the market. But at what level does the interest rate stand in the long run in an economic system?

To answer this question, post-Keynesian economists introduce several factors that help to understand the nature of the long-run rate of interest. The first is the distributive conflict. In every economic system, capital tries to extract the maximum possible value of profit from production (and the rentiers from rent), and this conflicts with the needs of workers who see their wages compressed when the economy does not grow enough. This step necessarily introduces another, namely the dependence of the interest rate on the path of economic development of a country.

The inherent nature of the interest rate is twofold. A high interest rate can represent a high level of investment profitability, or simply a high level of systemic risk of that economic system. On the other hand, a low rate of interest can be interpreted both as a sufficient level of economic stability of this system and as an absence of investment potential. For these reasons, the magnitude of the interest rate at a given historical moment and its impact on economic growth in a given country depends on the stage of economic development.

If in any case the central bank sets the first level of the interest rate, what strategies should it use? In this case, for neoclassical economist, the interest rate should be used to contain inflation. For post-Keynesian economists, it must be used to counter the rent. There are different strategies to do this: you can change its magnitude depending on the trend of the business cycle, or you can leave it stable at a very low level (or at the zero lower bound). In the second case, monetary policy would have the sole objective of contrasting the rent, while economic growth would be exclusively attributable to fiscal policy, which should be managed both to promote economic development and to mediate the distribution conflict in favour of workers.

Recent empirical evidence regarding the role of monetary policy has shown that in mature economies there is no relationship between the quantity of money in circulation and the price level (for instance, consider the changes in the quantity of money and the price level in the United States and Europe following the 2008 crisis). Central banks are losing control of the amount of money in circulation, both owing to the use of digital payment tools and above all for the endogenous part of the money supply. It is now established that commercial banks can create money independently of the policy rates of interest. Further, the compulsory reserve ratio tends to zero and is no longer used as a monetary policy tool.

Considering that mature countries represent the kind of economic system that developing countries try to reach, we can draw from these experiences some general considerations on the dynamics that the interest rate tends to show over the long run. If central banks set an interest rate low or close to zero, commercial banks may have the desired amount of resources available to make loans. The final magnitude of the interest rate will be determined by the profit prospects prevailing in that economic system or by the riskiness of the system itself. If there is no prospect of profit in the real economy, investors will move to the financial economy (financialization), or they will move capital into the global market. If banks cannot find profitable forms

WILLIAM E. MCCOLLOCH / SALVATORE PERRI

of investment, they can consider public debt as a good substitute.

Although there is no univocal theory in the post-Keynesian framework, we can conclude that the magnitude of the long-term interest rate will be influenced by the profit prospects prevailing in the economic system by the distributive conflict – which also moves in a supranational dimension (not only capital versus labour, but also real versus financial sector), and by the macroeconomic riskiness of the country considered.

SALVATORE PERRI

See also

Endogenous money; Fiscal policy; Inflation; Interest rate – natural; Monetary policy

References

Hein, E. (2017), 'Post-Keynesian macroeconomics since the mid 1990s: main developments', *European Journal of Economics and Economic Policies: Intervention*, 14 (2), 131–72.
Hein, E. and E. Stockhammer (2010), 'Macroeconomic policy mix, employment and inflation in a Post-Keynesian alternative to the New Consensus model', *Review of Political Economy*, 22 (3), 317–54.
Lavoie, M. (2006), 'A post-Keynesian amendment to the new consensus on monetary policy', *Metroeconomica*, 57 (2), 165–92.
Palley, T. (2006), 'A Post-Keynesian framework for monetary policy: why interest rate operating procedures are not enough', in C. Gnos and L.-P. Rochon (eds), *Post-Keynesian Principles of Economic Policy*, Cheltenham, UK, and Northampton, MA, USA: Edward Elgar, pp. 78–98.
Perri, S. (2013), 'The role of macroeconomic stability in the finance-growth nexus. Threshold regression approach', *Studi economici*, 110 (2), 57–81.
Rochon, L.-P. (2007), 'The state of Post Keynesian interest rate policy: where are we and where are we going?', *Journal of Post Keynesian Economics*, 30 (1), 3–11.
Rochon, L.-P. and M. Setterfield (2007), 'Post Keynesian interest rate rules and macroeconomic performance: a comparative evaluation', *Journal of Post Keynesian Economics*, 30 (1), 13–41.

Interest rate, natural

The concept of the natural rate of interest, originally developed by Knut Wicksell (1898/1965), applies in the setting of a general equilibrium model where economic outcomes are determined in real terms, hence depending on productivity and thrift. A part of output is saved and invested in a profit- and utility-maximizing way, thereby adding to the economy's capital stock. The higher the interest rate, the more agents are willing to save. Investment, on the other hand, decreases with regard to the interest rate. The natural interest rate is realized at the crossing point of the upward-sloping saving curve and the downward-sloping investment curve. Its role is to equilibrate savings and investment. Being part of the general equilibrium, the natural rate is the rate where full employment and maximum output prevail.

Since the natural interest rate is determined in a model without money, it cannot be observed in the real world, where interest rates are expressed in monetary terms much like all other economic variables. Nonetheless, the natural rate has important policy implications, because it is argued to point out the optimal conduct of monetary policy (Woodford, 2001). In this view, as expressed by the 'Taylor rule' (see Taylor, 1993), monetary policy should set its target interest rate in a way that matches the natural rate of interest. If the monetary rate is higher than the natural rate, investment is too low such that unemployment occurs. In the opposite case, investment is higher than what the availability of real savings would allow, thus giving rise to inflation.

The natural rate of interest has received renewed attention in economic theory in the era of low economic growth since the financial crisis of 2008. A major explanation of the hypothesis of 'secular stagnation' argues that owing to declining investment demand and an abundance of savings, the equilibrium interest rate may have reached negative territory (Summers, 2015). Since the monetary policy rate is constrained by the zero lower bound, it cannot shadow the natural rate anymore. The policy rate of interest is thus higher than suggested by the equilibrium, the result of which is stagnating output and unemployment.

The natural interest rate concept is rejected by post-Keynesian economists for a couple of reasons that mostly concern the foundations of neoclassical theory, where money plays no role (Rochon, 2016, p. 88). General equilibrium suggests that the availability of savings is a precondition for investment. However, in a world of endogenous money, loans create deposits, implying that savings are the simultaneous result of investment rather than the loanable funds that constrain it (see Lavoie, 2014, pp. 189–91). Since savings and investment represent an identity, the perception of the interest rate as an equilibrating variable is mistaken. The short-term interest rate, which also influences longer-term market rates, is set by the central bank and, as such, exogenous.

Whereas the Wicksellian analysis differs between the natural rate and the monetary rate of interest, post-Keynesian theory denies relevance of the former as its existence is hypothetical. Moreover, any macroeconomic framework, which takes into account the principle of effective demand and considers unemployment rather than the general equilibrium as the normal case, rejects the view that setting the interest rate at a certain equilibrium level is sufficient to ensure full employment (Serrano et al., 2020, pp. 373–6).

Finally, the natural interest rate is criticized for the policy implications that can be derived from it. Namely, the 'Taylor rule' constrains the role of monetary policy to targeting a certain hypothetical rate of interest and denies more activist interventions. In a larger sense, it also restricts fiscal policy by suggesting that the right level of the interest rate is both necessary and sufficient to meet the economy's potential output, hence its optimum. However, heterodox approaches argue that in order to overcome phenomena such as unemployment and secular stagnation, economic policies need to do more than set the interest rate right, which includes fiscal policy and long-term public investment (Di Bucchianico, 2021).

BASIL OBERHOLZER

See also

Effective demand; Endogenous money; Interest rate targeting; Monetary policy; Secular stagnation

References

Di Bucchianico, S. (2021), 'Negative interest rate policy to fight secular stagnation: unfeasible, ineffective, irrelevant, or inadequate?', *Review of Political Economy*, **33** (4), 687–710.
Lavoie, M. (2014), *Post-Keynesian Economics: New Foundations*, Cheltenham, UK, and Northampton, MA, USA: Edward Elgar.
Rochon, L.-P. (2016), 'In pursuit of the holy grail: monetary policy, the natural rate of interest, and quantitative easing', *Studies in Political Economy*, **97** (1), 87–94.
Serrano, F., R. Summa and V.G. Moreira (2020), 'Stagnation and unnaturally low interest rates: a simple critique of the amended New Consensus and the Sraffian supermultiplier alternative', *Review of Keynesian Economics*, **8** (3), 365–84.
Summers, L.H. (2015), 'Demand side secular stagnation', *American Economic Review*, **105** (5), 60–65.
Taylor, J.B. (1993), 'Discretion versus policy rules in practice', *Carnegie-Rochester Conference Series on Public Policy*, **39**, 195–214.
Wicksell, K. (1898/1965), *Interest and Prices: A Study of the Causes Regulating the Value of Money*, New York: Augustus M. Kelley.
Woodford, M. (2001), 'The Taylor rule and optimal monetary policy', *American Economic Review*, **91** (2), 232–7.

Interest rate and income distribution

The interest rate is the payment for the use of funds over time, in particular of money lent for a stated period. Since Adam Smith, the dominant view has been that monetary factors can affect the daily variations of the 'money' or market rate of interest but that, in equilibrium, this rate adjusts to its average or natural value which is determined by the same forces that determine the general rate of profits on the capital invested in the production process. In the surplus approach, this rate is determined by the methods of production and the real wage. It is divided into two components – the interest rate, which is the opportunity cost of capital, and the normal profit of enterprise that remunerates the 'risk and trouble' to employ capital productively. In neoclassical theory, in the case of perfect competition, entrepreneurial profits disappear in the long run and the rate of profit coincides with the natural rate of interest as set by 'productivity and thrift'.

In the marginalist theory, the market rate of interest can vary independently of the rate of profit, but only in the short run. More precisely, the level of interest on money is not in the last instance influenced by the relative shortage or surplus of money, but by the shortage or surplus of real capital. The idea is that an increase in the rate of return of physical capital will stimulate an increase in the demand for loans in order to acquire the 'capital' to gain the physical reward of capital. If the supply of money is fixed, the interest rate on money will rise by the same amount, whereas if there is an increase in money supply, this leads to an increase in prices and hence to a further increase in the nominal demand for loans. In both cases, the real interest rate will eventually be at a level that is consistent with equilibrium in the capital market when all resources are fully employed. Therefore, investment and savings in money are linked to investment and savings in kinds, and money and financial flows simply reflect the underlying real forces of productivity and thrift. In other words, loanable funds (money and financial flows) reflect the real forces that are behind the demand and supply of capital. Even when, as in Wicksell (1906), the influence of money on the rate of interest is recognized, market interest rates that are lower or higher than the (unobservable) natural rate will lead, respectively, to inflation or deflation, with market rates eventually adjusting to the natural rate of interest.

The monetary nature of the interest rate – notably, the fact that it can be permanently influenced by causes that are independent of what happens to the rate of profits – was stressed, however, by Tooke (1838), Stuart Mill (1852) and Marx (1894). In their view, the interest rate is affected by historical and conventional elements as well as by the policies to finance public debt and the action of the financial sector. Marx (1894), for instance, viewed the rate of profit as determined by real forces but maintained that its division between interests and profits arises from the power relation between financial and industrial capital. He also stressed that the financial sector must earn the general rate of profit on the wages and capital anticipated to carry on its activity, setting in this way some constraints linking the movements of the rates of interest and profits. Like Tooke and Stuart Mill, Marx failed, however, to advance a coherent competitive framework concerning the relation between the interest rate and the rate of profit.

An emphasis on the rate of interest as a monetary phenomenon and on money playing its own part in influencing output and distribution was later advanced also by Keynes (1936). According to him, the rate of interest is determined in the money market rather than in the investment–savings market, as a result of the relative demand for a given quantity of money and the existing stock of alternative financial assets. Moreover, Keynes (1936, p. 203) stressed the conventional character of the interest rate and the fact that monetary authorities, when acting in a coherent way, are able to influence the structure of interest rates. He also stated that it is the rate of profit (namely, in his analysis, the marginal efficiency of capital) that adapts to the money rate of interest. However, Keynes's attempt to break with the natural rate theory through his notion of liquidity preference had its own internal flaws. His assumption in *The General Theory* that an elastic decreasing investment function existed made it possible to argue that there is a rate of interest that is able to equal investment and the amount of savings corresponding to full employment. Moreover, his assumption of an exogenous nominal money supply fuelled the argument that on average a fall in prices would be able to restore full employment by lowering the rate of interest. Therefore, since Hicks (1937) and Modigliani (1944), Keynes's monetary theory of production has been mainly confined to the short run or periods of crisis.

However, Keynes's idea of the conventional nature of the interest rate can provide the basis for an alternative theory of distribution when recognizing that money supply is endogenous in a credit economy and that investments are driven by expected changes in demand rather than by the interest rate – thus depriving the loanable funds theory of its foundations. In an alternative approach, monetary policy consists of the 'terms on which' the monetary authorities are willing to accommodate demands for base money. Moreover, the adjustment of the rate of profit to the interest rate set by the central bank can pass through the action of competition in product markets. Given the money wages, the normal profit of enterprises and the methods of production, a permanent change in the interest rate affects the costs of production and prices in the same way, thus leading to a change in the rate of profit (Pivetti, 1991). This still holds when workers react to a fall in real wages by asking for higher money wages if monetary authorities change the nominal interest rate in order to maintain a certain real rate of interest whenever expected inflation changes.

Of course, monetary policy is not carried out in a vacuum and the interest rate targeted by the central bank takes into account the course of prices and its effects on the objects and constraints of monetary policy – for instance, on the external constraint, the fixed incomes and the value of accumulated financial capital. However, the fact that the rate of interest is a socially constructed variable that is targeted by monetary authorities raises the question as to what that policy should be. Several proposals have been advanced in this respect. One has been to set the 'optimum' real interest rate equal to zero and cancel out the income for rentiers. Another proposal has suggested a low but positive real interest rate, possibly lower than the growth rate of real income, in order to minimize the cost of the service of public debt while assuring a minimum income to the financial groups that are part of capitalism as a social order. Finally, it has been proposed that the real rate of interest should be equal to the increase in labour productivity. This means that a share in the rewards from current increases in productivity goes to existing financial capital, even if the essential contribution to ongoing production stems from entrepreneurs as well as workers.

ENRICO SERGIO LEVRERO

See also

Interest rate – natural; Liquidity preference; Monetary policy transmission mechanism; Monetary theory of production; Power

References

Hicks, J.R. (1937), 'Mr. Keynes and the "Classics": a suggested interpretation', *Econometrica*, **5** (2), 147–59.
Keynes, J.M. (1936), *The General Theory of Employment, Interest and Money*, London: Macmillan.
Marx, K. (1894/1967), *Capital: A Critique of Political Economy, Volume III*, New York: International Publishers.
Mill, J.S. (1852), *Principles of Political Economy, with Some of Their Application to Social Philosophy*, third edition, London: John W. Parker.
Modigliani, F. (1944), 'Liquidity preference and the theory of interest and money', *Econometrica*, **12** (1), 45–88.
Pivetti, M. (1991), *An Essay on Money and Distribution*, New York: St. Martin's Press.
Tooke, T. (1838), *A History of Prices, and the State of the Circulation, from 1793 to 1837*, vols I and II, reprint 1928, London: P.S. King and Son.
Wicksell, K. (1906), *Lectures on Political Economy*, vol. II, English translation by E. Classen and edited with an introduction by L. Robbins, 1935, reprint 1978, New Jersey: Augustus M. Kelley.

Interest rate rules

Interest rate rules stem from New Consensus Macroeconomics and are variants of the Taylor rule (see Taylor, 1993), where the central bank adjusts the policy rate of interest by responding linearly to developments in inflation and economic activity. A general formulation of the Taylor rule can be represented as follows:

$$i = a_1 (\pi - \pi_T) + a_2 (y - y_N^e) + \beta i_{-1} + r_N^e \quad (1)$$

where i is the nominal policy rate of interest, $(\pi - \pi_T)$ is the deviation of the actual from the targeted inflation rate, $(y - y_N^e)$ is the expected output gap, and r_N^e is the estimated Wicksellian natural rate of interest. Alternative specifications replace the output gap with the growth rate gap, the unemployment gap, or the wage gap that is consistent with an estimated NAIRU. The lagged term βi_{-1} is introduced in equation (1) in order to impose policy inertia and to robustify the rule from the misspecifications of exogenous shocks, or errors in the estimations of r_N^e and y_N^e. The choice of contemporaneous or lagged variables in equation (1) depends on what variables the central bank considers when setting the interest rate. Backward-looking interest rate rules utilize lagged indices, whereas forward-looking interest rate rules utilize expectations in the right-hand side of equation (1). An alternative rule that arises often is the Wicksellian rule (see Woodford, 2003, Ch. 2), where the policy rate of interest responds to the deviations of the price level from a targeted price path, making the interest rate rule price-history dependent.

Open-economy Taylor rule variants utilize linear combinations of short-term interest rates and exchange rates, in order to set a target exchange rate that satisfies purchasing power parity and to account for its effect on aggregate demand (Clarida et al., 1998). Adding to equation (1) the difference between the real exchange rate and the targeted exchange rate $(e - e_T)$ gives:

$$i = a_1 (\pi - \pi_T) + a_2 (y - y_N^e) + a_3 (e - e_T) + r_N^e \quad (2)$$

Other variants incorporate interest rate spreads, asset prices or the credit gap, by utilizing various Monetary Condition Indexes (MCI). These MCIs capture the information that financial and international developments provide to central banks when they form their expectations regarding future inflation and economic performance. The calibration of the parameters a_i depends on the relative importance that the central bank attaches to price stability, short-run income fluctuations and financial developments. Depending on whether the parameter a_1 is above or below unity, the policy rule is termed 'active' or 'passive' respectively.

Post-Keynesian economics has two approaches on interest rate rules (see Rochon and Setterfield, 2007). The first approach, called the activist approach, proposes a short-term interest rate management similar to Taylor rule formulations (Fontana and Palacio-Vera, 2006; Palley, 2006). However, the Wicksellian natural rate of interest is rejected, the ability of the central bank to target inflation by fine-tuning the policy rate of interest is discarded, and emphasis is put on accommodative policy rates of interest. These interest rate rules operate via proportional controls formally similar to equations (1) and (2) aiming to stabilize employment and private indebtedness, accounting for the effects of the interest rate on profit margins, investment, income distribution, and international flows. Focusing on stabilizing the macro-financial conditions, Brancaccio and Fontana (2013) developed a benchmark solvency rule, which guarantees the financial solvency of the private sector on average, and is formally similar to equation (1):

$$i = \psi_0 + \psi_1 \pi + \psi_2 g_Y \quad (3)$$

where ψ_i depends on the propensities to save out of profits and wages, the general rate of profit, investment decisions, income distribution, and other financial and institutional factors. The effectiveness of such Taylor-like rules in the case of small open economies with free capital flows has been questioned, owing to the impact of the global financial cycle on asset markets and credit growth (see Yilmaz and Godin, 2020).

The second approach, called the parking-it approach, suggests that short-term interest rate management distorts income distribution, via the effect of the policy rate on interest payments, macroeconomic activity, portfolio rebalancing, and indebtedness. Therefore, a reaction-function approach should be abandoned. Instead, this approach focuses on the long-term interest rate and pins it down so that it achieves a long-run, income distribution target. The focus therefore shifts from output stabilization to the stabilization of income distribution. There are three versions of this approach. The Smithin rule (Smithin, 1994) proposes a real interest rate that is zero or close to zero, aiming at the 'euthanasia of the rentier' and the reduction of interest margins. In this rule, the nominal interest rate essentially follows inflation:

$$i = \pi_T \quad (4)$$

The Kansas City rule (Mosler and Forstarter, 2004; Wray, 2007) proposes a nominal rate of interest that is zero (equation 5), hence making the real rate of interest negative in normal times. The intuition is similar to the Smithin rule, as the policy target is to redistribute income away from bankers and rentiers.

$$i = 0 \quad (5)$$

The fair rate rule, or Pasinetti rule (Lavoie and Seccareccia, 1999; Gnos and Rochon, 2007), sets the real interest rate equal to the long-run trend of labour productivity λ (equation 6). The goal of this rule is to leave income distribution between interest-earning and non-interest-earning social classes constant.

$$i = \pi_T + \lambda \quad (6)$$

In both the activist and the parking-it approaches, the main macroeconomic stabilization mechanism is fiscal policy, owing to its higher relative effectiveness.

ACHILLEAS MANTES

See also

Inflation; Interest rate – natural; Monetary policy; NAIRU; New Consensus in macroeconomics

References

Brancaccio, E. and G. Fontana (2013), '"Solvency rule" versus "Taylor rule": an alternative interpretation of the relation between monetary policy and the economic crisis', *Cambridge Journal of Economics*, 37 (1), 17–33.

Clarida, R., J. Gali and M. Gertler (1998), 'Monetary policy rules in practice: some international evidence', *European Economic Review*, 42 (6), 1033–67.

Fontana, G. and A. Palacio-Vera (2006), 'Is there an active role for monetary policy in the endogenous money approach?', in C. Gnos and L.-P. Rochon (eds), *Post Keynesian Principles of Economic Policy*, Cheltenham, UK, and Northampton, MA, USA: Edward Elgar, pp. 49–56.

Gnos, C. and L.-P. Rochon (2007), 'The New Consensus and Post-Keynesian interest rate policy', *Review of Political Economy*, **17** (3), 369–86.

Lavoie, M. and M. Seccareccia (1999), 'Interest rate: fair', in P.A. O'Hara (ed.), *Encyclopedia of Political Economy: Volume 1*, London and New York: Routledge, pp. 543–5.

Mosler, W. and M. Forsterer (2004), 'The natural rate of interest is zero', *University of Missouri Working Paper*, No. 37.

Palley, T.I. (2006), 'A Post-Keynesian framework for monetary policy: why interest rate operating procedures are not enough', in C. Gnos and L.-P. Rochon (eds), *Post-Keynesian Principles of Economic Policy*, Cheltenham, UK, and Northampton, MA, USA: Edward Elgar, pp. 78–98.

Rochon, L.-P. and M. Setterfield (2007), 'Interest rates, income distribution, and monetary policy dominance: Post Keynesians and the "fair rate" of interest', *Journal of Post Keynesian Economics*, **30** (1), 13–42.

Smithin, J. (1994), *Controversies in Monetary Economics: Ideas, Issues, and Policy*, Aldershot, UK, and Brookfield, USA: Edward Elgar.

Taylor, J.B. (1993), 'Discretion versus policy rules in practice', *Carnegie-Rochester Conference Series on Public Policy*, **39**, 195–214.

Woodford, M. (2003), *Interest and Prices: Foundations of a Theory of Monetary Policy*, Princeton: Princeton University Press.

Wray, L.R. (2004), 'The Fed and the new monetary consensus: the case for rate hikes, part two', *Levy Economics Institute of Bard College Public Policy Brief*, No. 80.

Yilmaz, S.D. and A. Godin (2020), 'Modelling small open economies in a financialized world: a stock-flow consistent prototype', *Agence Française de Développement Research Paper*, No. 125.

Interest rate targeting

Monetarists have been claiming for a long time that monetary policy is about the central bank's control of the 'quantity of money', that is, the supply of money – which would allow it to control inflation. This claim is rejected by post-Keynesian economists and by central bankers who argue that monetary policy is rather about setting interest rate targets and using policy tools to achieve those targets over the relevant time horizon. The target rate of interest is often referred to as the policy interest rate (for instance, the overnight rate in Canada, the federal funds rate in the United States, the two-week repo rate in the United Kingdom, and so on). This is the rate of interest at which financial institutions lend to, and borrow from, each other's funds, for short periods, in what is known as the 'money market' (that is, the interbank market for reserves). This rate is important, because it usually affects other interest rates, such as those charged on mortgage loans and on consumer loans.

In this regard, post-Keynesian economists agree (see Lavoie, 2019) that the available quantity of reserves has a direct impact on the level of the target rate of interest. Since this rate of interest is a short-term variable, it tends to fluctuate according to changes in the amount of available reserves. Reserves are a form of central bank money, that is to say, settlement balances used to settle interbank debts. If the central bank wants to stimulate economic activity, it sets a low target rate of interest and works to achieve it by increasing the net injections of reserves. Similarly, the central bank can create a recession by setting the target rate of interest at a high level and proceeding to withdraw more liquidity than what goes into the system.

There are several means by which the net amount of reserves can be increased or decreased. In most cases, injections and withdrawals of reserves can be carried out when the central bank buys and sells bonds, on behalf of the government, to the private sector through what are known as 'open-market operations'. However, in Canada (for instance) the main tool to control the amount of reserves in the banking system is the addition to or the removal of deposits held by the federal government in its accounts at chartered (commercial) banks (see Lavoie, 2019). Increasing the amount of reserves in the banking system puts a downward pressure on the target rate of interest, thereby lowering the cost of borrowing funds, particularly among banks. The interbank lending rate of interest is a key variable in the execution of monetary policy, but it is also directly influenced by fiscal policy through increases (decreases) in liquidity that result from net government spending. This is why it is important here to emphasize the role of fiscal policy – that is, taxing and spending by the government.

Indeed, government spending and taxing, which result in injections and withdrawals of liquidity, are important policy tools that help the government and the central bank achieve the desired target rate of interest. The 'balancing' between spending and taxing is done with this objective in mind – not for the concerns of avoiding a deficit or attempting to achieve a surplus in the public budget, as claimed by neoclassical economists.

The links between fiscal and monetary policies, which are assumed away in the orthodox view, become evident when we understand that deposits of government cheques by private agents increase the balance sheets of commercial banks both on the liabilities side (banks owe the amounts to depositors) and on the assets side (since banks now have claims of equal amounts on the government). These claims are what we refer to as 'reserves'. Banks claim these reserves at the central bank, which executes the operation simply by crediting commercial banks' accounts (that is, by adding to their reserves) and debiting the government's account by an equal amount. Government spending results in an injection of reserves (central bank money) into the private sector.

Similarly, when private agents pay their taxes or purchase government bonds, they order their banks (such as by writing cheques) to transfer a deposit from their accounts to the government's account. The operation is executed by the central bank by reducing commercial banks' reserves (debiting their accounts) and crediting the government's account. The accumulated deposits in the government's account at the central bank can now be tallied against its debts, which will be reduced or eliminated, but this has nothing to do with financing government expenditures, because the latter have already been paid. The resulting public deficit or surplus matters only insofar as it has an effect on the target rate of interest (see Bougrine, 2020). Attempts to balance the budget of the public sector are in fact attempts to stabilize the target rate of interest: adjustments in the target rate of interest can be achieved by manipulating the government's budget. Fiscal and monetary policies are intricately linked and, therefore, it is utterly wrong to claim that they can be analysed and carried out separately.

HASSAN BOUGRINE

See also

Inflation; Interest rate – natural; Monetary policy transmission mechanism; Reserves – role of; Settlement balances

References

Bougrine, H. (2020), 'The theory of money, interest and unemployment', in L.-P. Rochon and H. Bougrine (eds), *Credit, Money and Crises in Post-Keynesian Economics*, Cheltenham, UK, and Northampton, MA, USA: Edward Elgar, pp. 97–116.

Lavoie, M. (2019), 'A system with zero reserves and with clearing outside of the central bank: the Canadian case', *Review of Political Economy*, **31** (2), 145–58.

Interest rates and investment

The idea that investment is negatively affected by the rate of interest is a marginalist tenet grounded on (i) the notion of capital as a single homogeneous factor of production, (ii) the concept of a decreasing marginal productivity of capital and (iii) the idea of a substitution mechanism between capital and labour. Such a negative relationship is extremely relevant for the marginalist theory, because it would guarantee a stable full-employment equilibrium. For a given endowment of production factors, preferences and technical conditions of production, prices and quantities are simultaneously determined by the intersection between demand and supply in all markets. In the market of investment, the equilibrium condition is determined by the interaction of a downward-sloping demand curve for investment and an upward sloping supply curve of savings. In such a representation, the flexibility of the interest rate combined with a downward-sloping investment demand curve allows an economy to reach a full-employment equilibrium in which investment adapts to full-employment savings and the rate of interest gravitates towards its 'natural' level.

Starting from the assumption of a decreasing marginal productivity of production factors and a decreasing marginal utility, the marginalist theory determines the demand for production factors elastic with respect to their rates of return by means of the direct and indirect substitution mechanisms. The inverse relationship between investment and the interest rate appears as a consequence of a demand for capital highly elastic with respect to interest rates, where investment is conceived as the flow that generates the capital stock (Garegnani, 1990). According to the direct mechanism, a decrease in the rate of interest leads firms to increase investment and therefore the capital–labour ratio. Firms will save more by increasing the amount of investment and therefore of capital, namely the factor that is relatively cheaper. According to the indirect mechanism, a decrease in the rate of interest leads to a reduction in the price of capital-intensive goods. This in turn increases the demand for those goods that are produced with capital-intensive techniques, thereby raising the demand for capital. Firms cease to invest when the marginal productivity of capital is equal to the rate of interest, a condition which maximizes profits and minimizes costs.

The idea of a downward-sloping demand curve for capital was also shared by Keynes in *The General Theory* through the concept of the marginal efficiency of capital (Keynes, 1936). Indeed, according to Keynes, no relevant differences exist between the marginal efficiency of capital and the demand curve for capital envisaged by classical economists, where the classical economists Keynes referred to are Marshall and Walras (see Petri, 2015). Following Keynes (1936, p. 136), 'the inducement to invest depends partly on the investment demand-schedule and partly on the rate of interest'.

The existence of a negative relationship between the rate of interest and the demand for capital and investment has been questioned by those economists who participated in the so-called 'Cambridge capital controversy'. Specifically, according to Sraffa (1960) and Garegnani (1970), when one assumes several production techniques and heterogeneous capital goods, the possibility of reswitching of techniques and reverse capital deepening invalidates the negative relationship between investment and interest rates. Different levels of the rate of interest can allow producers to use the same method of production and thus the same factor intensity (Garegnani, 1970). Consequently, we cannot draw a downward-sloping investment demand curve, because no automatic mechanism ensures that firms adopt more capital-intensive techniques when the interest rate decreases. For more recent critiques, see Petri (2015).

The alleged negative relationship between the rate of interest and the level of investment would ensure the return to the traditional theory (Garegnani, 1979). The possibility of the investment demand being negatively affected by the rate of interest would limit in the short-run the principle of effective demand, leaving in the long run the level of investment determined by full-employment savings: 'a spontaneous tendency for investment to adjust to the saving capacity of the economy ... is the outcome of a theory of interest derived from the idea that the overall demand for "capital" is highly elastic with respect to the rate of interest' (Garegnani, 2015, p. 131).

MATTEO DELEIDI

See also

Capital theory controversies; Effective demand; Interest rate – natural; Monetary policy; Neoclassical economics

References

Garegnani, P. (1970), 'Heterogeneous capital, the production function and the theory of distribution', *Review of Economic Studies*, **37** (3), 407–36.
Garegnani, P. (1979), 'Notes on consumption, investment and effective demand: II', *Cambridge Journal of Economics*, **3** (1), 63–82.
Garegnani, P. (1990), 'Quantity of capital', in *Capital Theory*, London: Macmillan, pp. 1–78.
Garegnani, P. (2015), 'The problem of effective demand in Italian economic development: on the factors that determine the volume of investment', *Review of Political Economy*, **27** (2), 111–33.
Keynes, J.M. (1936), *The General Theory of Employment, Interest and Money*, London: Macmillan.
Petri, F. (2015), 'Neglected implications of neoclassical capital–labour substitution for investment theory: another criticism of Say's Law', *Review of Political Economy*, **27** (3), 308–40.
Sraffa, P. (1960), *Production of Commodities by Means of Commodities: Prelude to a Critique of Economic Theory*, Cambridge, UK: Cambridge University Press.

International clearing union

The idea of an international clearing union (ICU) is quite simple but has far-reaching consequences for the world economy. It is based on the role of a commercial bank in a closed system: it is well known that commercial banks today create money out of thin air simply by accepting to extend credit to creditworthy borrowers who then use these credits to pay for goods and services and to extinguish their debts (see Bougrine, 2017). If both the payer

MATTEO DELEIDI / HASSAN BOUGRINE

and the payee are clients of the same bank, then the settlement of debts consists of simply moving credits from one account to the other, and the bank would never face any difficulty honouring cheques drawn upon it. The ICU would function in essentially the same way and 'international money' would be moved from the account of the importing country to the account of the exporting country.

In the 1940s, Keynes (1941/1980, p. 29) noted that the world economy had been in 'a state of extreme disequilibrium' even prior to the Second World War and attributed that to a single reason: a transfer of value from debtor countries to creditor countries in a system that 'throws the main burden of adjustment on the country which is in the debtor position on the international balance of payments' and which therefore sought 'to force adjustments in the direction most disruptive of social order, and to throw the burden on the countries least able to support it, making the poor poorer'. Having identified this compulsory flow of capital funds out of debtor countries as the major source of instability, his solution was then to come up with a system that would force both debtor and creditor countries to share the burden of adjustment. That system was what Keynes called the International Clearing Union.

The 'international money', which Keynes called bancor, resembles commercial bank money in that it can be created to accommodate the needs of commerce. For this purpose, every member country would have an account with the ICU, with all accounts initially set to zero bancor balances. Countries will agree among themselves on 'the initial values of their own currencies in terms of bancor and also the value of bancor in terms of gold' (Keynes, 1942/1980, p. 172), and these values, that is, exchange rates, will remain fixed and cannot be altered without the permission of the governing board of the ICU. Just like private citizens have access to a line of credit and can borrow funds in their national money from a local bank, all member countries have access to an overdraft with the ICU, with a maximum amount designated as their quotas – the quota of each country being relative to its weight in international trade.

Unlike the current system, which requires importing countries to have a prior deposit of reserves, the ICU allows the importing country to use its overdraft facility. The payment is made simply by recording a 'minus' in the account of the importing country and a 'plus' in the account of the exporting country – thus making the bancor a purely scriptural money, which is created each time an importing country uses its overdraft facility to pay for its imports. This is of paramount importance for poor and developing countries, because it effectively removes their external constraint by allowing them direct access to financing imports of foreign technology. Countries with a negative (positive) balance would be in a deficit (surplus) position vis-à-vis the ICU as a whole and not vis-à-vis other countries, which 'means that overdraft facilities, whilst a relief to some, are not a real burden to others' (Keynes, 1942/1980, p. 176). However, the use of overdraft facilities is not unlimited, nor is it free. A deficit country is allowed a defined amount and an 'interval of time within which to effect a balance in its economic relations with the rest of the world' (ibid.).

The benefits of such a system for developing countries are obvious. In addition to easy access to international finance, they can also easily earn credits in 'international money', since they would sell their exports for a stable currency (the bancor) and therefore avoid the losses caused by the vagaries of exchange rates' depreciation. The deterioration in the terms of trade has been a central argument by the dependency school since the 1950s and was recently re-confirmed for the whole twentieth century in an updated study by a group of economists from the United Nations (see United Nations Conference on Trade and Development, 2005).

Since the main purpose of the ICU is to avoid the systematic build-up of long-lasting imbalances, both deficit and surplus countries are subject to certain conditions by which they are required to take appropriate measures to restore equilibrium of their international balances. For this purpose, the ICU would charge interests on both negative and positive balances when these reach a certain percentage of the country's quota. The idea of charging surplus countries a negative interest or a 'carrying cost' on their accumulated credit balances did not sit well with the orthodoxy, since these balances will be gradually depleted over time. However, from the Keynesian perspective the point is not to penalize surplus countries for having conducted successful transactions in international trade. Rather, the point is to induce them to spend these balances instead of withholding them from circulation and thus forcing a 'deflationary and contractionist pressure on the whole world, including in the end the creditor country itself' (Keynes, 1942/1980, p. 177). This measure is consistent with the general Keynesian paradigm of putting demand on the goods market at the centre of economic expansion. That is why creditor countries cannot be permitted to hoard their surpluses indefinitely. Therefore, surplus countries will have three options:

(1) spend their positive balances on buying goods and services, including from deficit countries, thereby contributing to the expansion of world trade and to a return towards equilibrium;
(2) invest these balances on a long-term basis in the form of direct investment and, therefore, contribute to the capital development of other (particularly poor and developing) countries;
(3) continue to hold their balances at the ICU but pay the carrying costs, which, as noted above, act as a tax that gradually reduces the outstanding amount of positive balances.

This last option should be the least favoured, which means that the creditor country will not remain passive and that is the idea behind the ICU plan.

HASSAN BOUGRINE

See also

Bretton Woods; Endogenous money; Keynes Plan; International financial architecture; International monetary system

References

Bougrine, H. (2017), *The Creation of Wealth and Poverty: Means and Ways*, London and New York: Routledge.
Keynes, J.M. (1941/1980), 'Proposals for an international currency union', in *The Collected Writings of John Maynard Keynes, vol. XXV, Activities 1940–1944, Shaping the Post-War World: The Clearing Union*, London and Basingstoke: Macmillan, pp. 33–40.
Keynes, J.M. (1942/1980), 'Proposals for an international clearing union', in *The Collected Writings of John Maynard Keynes, vol. XXV, Activities 1940–1944, Shaping the Post-War World: The Clearing Union*, London and Basingstoke: Macmillan, pp. 168–95.
United Nations Conference on Trade and Development (2005), 'Evolution in the terms of trade and its impact on developing countries', in *Trade and Development Report, 2005*, New York and Geneva: United Nations, pp. 85–167, available online at www.unctad.org/en/docs/tdr2005ch3_en.pdf (last accessed 8 August 2019).

International financial architecture

The international financial architecture refers to the institutions, treaties and agreements by which movements of international financial capital are affected and governed. As such and given that it includes both the developed and the developing world, the concept covers an extremely wide range of phenomena. An essential backdrop to the discussion is the contention that while the financial sector provides the liquidity absolutely necessary in a world where production takes time, it is systemically unstable. This instability manifests itself both cyclically and over the long run and is in part a function of the tendency of market participants to overestimate the likelihood that obligations (theirs and their debtors') will be fulfilled. This becomes particularly pronounced during calm periods so that financial fragility increases over the course of economic expansions and asset market booms (Minsky, 1992). The environment of fundamental uncertainty in which agents operate and their desire for quick returns combine with other psychological factors to create a world where capital flows are volatile and drawn toward short-term financial returns rather than long-term real returns.

Within that context, post-Keynesian economists are concerned with determining which aspects of the international financial architecture contribute to this instability, which moderate it and what the manifestations have been. Beginning with the institutions, at the supranational level these include most prominently the International Monetary Fund (IMF) and the World Bank. Both emerging from the Bretton Woods conference in 1944, they have been the subject of much criticism for the neoliberal policy biases that encouraged financial market liberalization not just in the developed world, but also in developing and emerging markets. The latter measures have exacerbated volatility and 'hot money' flows in the countries least able

HASSAN BOUGRINE / JOHN T. HARVEY

to cope with them (Chang and Grabel, 2014). Further, conditionality placed on borrowing nations has included not only contractionary fiscal policy, but also tight monetary policies leading to high interest rates and therefore high costs of borrowing.

While there may be some evidence that the IMF and World Bank have slightly tempered their enthusiasm for austerity and liberalization, after the Asian financial crisis many countries simply acted to reduce their dependence on them (Grabel, 2015). One strategy pursued by developing countries has been to build up large volumes of reserves so as to have funds readily available at home. There have also been regional responses involving organizations providing, among other things, loan facilities. Ilene Grabel has argued that this is a hopeful sign of pragmatic and tailor-made responses.

Another unique feature of at least some of these regional organizations is a much more democratic structure than is true at the IMF or World Bank. This raises another issue relevant to international financial architecture: power. That policy measures have been consistently stacked in favour of the interests of the wealthiest nations need not be argued here. This has manifested itself at the non-governmental organization level, in terms of national government pressure, and as financial institutions have influenced public policy and forced their preferences onto host countries. Those in the last group have also made every effort to make their activities opaque so that even extant regulations can be difficult to enforce (Outa, 2014).

Another factor working to the detriment of developing countries and their citizens is rooted in the foreign exchange market. The reasons to prefer one currency over another include the rate of return one can earn in assets denominated in that currency, the ease with which one can withdraw assets from the issuing country, and the willingness of other agents to hold that currency (Andrade and Prates, 2013; Kaltenbrunner, 2015). The international hierarchy of currencies, with the US dollar at the top, means that developing countries cannot compete in terms of the last factor. Therefore, if they are to attract capital flows of hard currencies, they have only two choices: either promise high rates of return or allow easy entrance and exit for invested funds. They are thus forced into a situation where they need to maintain rates of interest higher than might be conducive to development and to resist implementation of the very sort of capital controls necessary to combat destructive hot money flows.

An often-overlooked consequence of the current international financial architecture is its impact on women. Muchhala (2012, p. 288) has argued that there are

> three central gender biases in a liberalized and financialized international financial architecture, which work against the goals of gender equity and women's rights. These three biases, which constitute a significant discourse in feminist economics, are the 'deflationary bias', the 'male breadwinner bias' and the 'commodification or privatization bias'.

In short, not only are policy measures oriented toward changing conditions in male-dominated activities, but any attendant negative consequences tend to be concentrated among women (see also Aslanbeigui and Summerfield, 2000).

While this barely scratches the surface of the international financial architecture, the fact that it is structured so as to serve the needs of the richest nations and the financial industry (and men) is clear. One can only hope that Grabel's belief in the various regional and national efforts to create solutions superior to those offered by the IMF and World Bank is well-founded.

JOHN T. HARVEY

See also

Bretton Woods; Currency hierarchy; Financial fragility; Financial liberalization; International monetary system

References

Andrade, R.P. and D.M. Prates (2013), 'Exchange rate dynamics in a peripheral monetary economy', *Journal of Post Keynesian Economics*, **35** (3), 399–416.
Aslanbeigui, N. and G. Summerfield (2000), 'The Asian crisis, gender, and the international financial architecture', *Feminist Economics*, **6** (3), 81–103.
Chang, H.J. and I. Grabel (2014), *Reclaiming Development: An Alternative Economic Policy Manual*, London: Zed Books.
Grabel, I. (2015), 'Post-crisis experiments in development finance architectures: a Hirschmanian perspective on "productive incoherence"', *Review of Social Economy*, **73** (4), 388–414.
Kaltenbrunner, A. (2015), 'A post Keynesian framework of exchange rate determination: a Minskyan

approach', *Journal of Post Keynesian Economics*, **38** (3), 426–48.

Minsky, H. (1992), 'The financial instability hypothesis', *Jerome Levy Economics Institute of Bard College Working Paper*, No. 74, available at www.levyinstitute.org/pubs/wp74.pdf (last accessed 12 November 2020).

Muchhala, B. (2012), 'Barricades to gender equity in the international financial architecture', *Development*, **55** (3), 283–90.

Outa, E.R. (2014), 'The new international financial architecture: lessons and experiences from Africa', *AD-Minister*, **25**, 49–78.

International monetary system

The international monetary system is a set of norms and relations that ensures the settlement of transactions between different currencies. Lacking a globally accepted supranational currency, different elements and national currencies have played the predominant roles of international units of account and means of settlement (see for example Eichengreen, 2008).

Since the end of the Second World War, the US dollar has played these two roles, participating in 88 per cent of foreign-exchange transactions; the euro comes at a distant second place with 31 per cent of transactions in 2016 (Bank for International Settlements, 2016). In turn, around 40 per cent of global trade is invoiced in US dollars, four times the US weight in global trade (Gopinath, 2015).

These figures highlight the fact that the roles of an international unit of account and means of payment go beyond the mere link between transactions in goods and real assets. Just like the study of a national economy, the interlinked global economy calls for a monetary theory of production, in which (international) 'money plays a part of its own and affects motives and decisions' (Keynes, 1973a, p. 408). In this sense, the role of the US dollar is paramount to trade and investment decisions, because of its effects on exchange rates, asset prices, and credit (Harvey, 2009).

The monetary character of the international monetary system is also reflected in the role played by liquidity, in different dimensions. First of all, because of the predominant role of the US dollar as funding currency (even for non-US institutions), other currencies have to pay a liquidity premium over the US dollar, particularly at times of high liquidity preference in global financial markets (Kaltenbrunner and Lysandrou, 2017; Tooze, 2018).

Second, unlike in a barter system, it is a shortage of the means of settlement (and not necessarily of tradable goods) that harms the capabilities of a nation to make good on its commitments. As Keynes (1973b, p. 12) put it, '[a] country could be bankrupted, not because it lacked exportable goods, but merely because it lacked gold.' Gold may no longer be required to settle external contractual obligations, but a shortage of US dollars is all too frequent in the case of balance-of-payment crises triggered by excessive external borrowing, as in numerous episodes (like the Latin American debt crisis in the 1980s, the Mexican, Russian and East Asian crises in the 1990s, the Argentine crisis of 2001, and so on).

Third, since the demise of the Bretton Woods regime in the early 1970s, the creation of internationally accepted means of settlement (US dollars) has been primarily conducted by private institutions, including non-US banks (Aldasoro and Ehlers, 2018). The influence of conventional factors such as risk perceptions and asset price expectations, as stressed by Minsky (1986), holds its weight in the international financial arena. Therefore, the provision of liquidity is substantially affected by the credit conditions in global financial centres, where that liquidity is generated. 'Fundamentals' or economic conditions in countries that have a lower status in the international currency hierarchy are of smaller importance. These countries may receive or fail to receive international liquidity irrespectively of their own domestic circumstances.

Fourth, an eventual lack of access to US dollars creates an asymmetric burden of adjustments of balance-of-payments imbalances, because those in the debtor position are forced to reduce their economic activity in an effort to generate a surplus enough to face their external commitments.

This is precisely the reason that Keynes was animated in his advocacy for a global currency with an adjustment mechanism for imbalances that penalize the creditor country as well (Davidson, 1982). Imbalances denominated in this global currency (called 'bancor') would be settled through an international clearing union, with norms discouraging the accumulation of idle balances (Keynes, 1973b, pp. 33–40). Under this proposal, private creation of global liquidity in the form of capital flows would be severely restricted.

JOHN T. HARVEY / PABLO BORTZ

The international monetary system that emerged after the Second World War did not include the rebalancing mechanisms that Keynes called for during the Bretton Woods conference in 1944 and left up for the creditors the willingness to recycle their external surplus in the form of foreign investment, or to call in their claims on gold. After the abandonment of the Bretton Woods regime, there has been no agreement on a globally coordinated initiative to ensure a liquidity-provision mechanism in times of external stress, particularly aimed for developing economies. It is unlikely that any of the numerous existing proposals in this perspective (see United Nations Conference on Trade and Development, 2015) will be implemented in the near future.

PABLO BORTZ

See also

Bretton Woods; Currency hierarchy; Financial fragility; International financial architecture; Liquidity preference

References

Aldasoro, I. and T. Ehlers (2018), 'The geography of US-dollar funding of non-US banks', *Bank for International Settlements Quarterly Review*, December, pp. 15–26.
Bank for International Settlements (2016), *Triennial Central Bank Survey: Foreign Exchange Turnover in April 2016*, Basel: Bank for International Settlements.
Davidson, P. (1982), *International Money and the Real World*, London: Macmillan.
Eichengreen, B. (2008), *Globalizing Capital: A History of the International Monetary System*, Princeton, NJ: Princeton University Press.
Gopinath, G. (2015), 'The international price system', *National Bureau of Economic Research Working Paper*, No. 21646.
Harvey, J. (2009), *Currencies, Capital Flows and Crises*, London and New York: Routledge.
Kaltenbrunner, A. and P. Lysandrou (2017), 'The US dollar's continuing hegemony as an international currency: a double-matrix analysis', *Development and Change*, **48** (4), 663–91.
Keynes, J.M. (1973a), 'A monetary theory of production', in D. Moggridge (ed.), *The Collected Writings of John Maynard Keynes, Volume XIII: The General Theory and After: Part I. Preparation*, London: Royal Economic Society, pp. 408–11.
Keynes, J.M. (1973b), *The Collected Writings of John Maynard Keynes, Volume XXV: Activities 1940–1944: Shaping the Post-War World: The Clearing Union*, London: Royal Economic Society.

Minsky, H. (1986), *Stabilizing an Unstable Economy*, New York: McGraw Hill.
Tooze, A. (2018), *Crashed: How a Decade of Financial Crises Changed the World*, London: Allen Lane.
United Nations Conference on Trade and Development (2015), *Trade and Development Report*, Geneva: United Nations Conference on Trade and Development.

Investment – theories of

A cornerstone of all post-Keynesian theories of investment is the abandonment of Say's Law, and with it any stable macroeconomic relationship between *ex ante* savings and the subsequent investment decisions of firms. Keynes's (1936) own approach in *The General Theory* was not entirely a departure of extant neoclassical theory, with investment demand presented as a function of its expected profitability. Within the short period to which Keynes's analysis was confined, increases in investment would raise the supply price of capital goods, and reduce their prospective rate of return.

Keynes's perspective also emphasized the fragmentary basis of knowledge upon which profit expectations and investment decisions would inevitably be based, with the implication that 'it is our innate urge to activity that makes the wheels go round ... calculating where we can, but often falling back for our motive on whim or sentiment or chance' (Keynes, 1936, p. 163). The proper place of this fundamental uncertainty in theories of investment remains an open question. One manifestation of this tension is present in Joan Robinson's work. At times Robinson (1962a, p. 107) could insist that '[t]o understand the motives for investment, we have to understand human nature and the manner in which it reacts to the various kinds of social and economic systems in which it has to operate. We have not got far enough yet to put it into algebra.'

Efforts to extend the principle of effective demand to the long period necessarily confronted the codetermination of investment and realized profitability. As Kalecki (1936, p. 231) noted, 'Keynes takes as given the state of the expectations of returns, and from this he derives a certain definite level of investment, overlooking the effects that investment will in turn have on expectations.' The exploration of this dynamic interrelationship between past accumulation, realized profits, and the profit

PABLO BORTZ / WILLIAM E. McCOLLOCH

expectations on which subsequent investment decisions were based remained a central theme of Kalecki's work throughout his career. In her forays into explicit models of accumulation and growth, Robinson (1962b, p. 49) concisely captured this relationship in the so-called banana diagram.

While accepting that investment is not, in the aggregate, constrained by savings, the literature has also sought to better integrate finance constraints into the firm's investment function. Kalecki's (1937) 'principle of increasing risk' suggested that the size of a particular fixed investment project undertaken by an individual firm would be limited by growing prospects of financial distress or illiquidity should that investment prove unsuccessful. In this view, such a constraint would prove binding whether the firm relied upon internal or external finance, as the risk premia demanded by the banking system would be governed by the same logic. Similarly, Steindl (1952) emphasized that firms' desired leverage ratios, along with those deemed prudent by creditors, might act as constraints on investment. Explicitly incorporating the banking system's endogenous creation of credit money, Minsky's (1982) financial instability hypothesis posited a recurrent relationship between firms' finance structures and macroeconomic (in)stability. Minsky maintained that, in tranquil periods, credit conditions would tend to relax, and risk premia would tend to decline, spurring expansions of investment. The growing reliance on debt finance would, nevertheless, introduce greater fragility as debt-burdened firms would be more susceptible to variations in their short-term cash flow or borrowing costs.

Post-Keynesian departures from the neoclassical theory of the firm are also relevant in this framework. Larger firms, operating in imperfectly competitive conditions, may pursue objectives irreducible to profit maximization, including those of growth and the extension of extra-economic power. Wood's (1975, pp. 63–4) investment opportunity frontier considered the prospective growth of sales revenue as an independent determinant of investment alongside the profit margin. Eichner (1976, p. 88) emphasized that under conditions of oligopoly, where intra-industry price competition would be mutually ruinous, 'competition through investment will replace competition through price'. Eichner's framework drew distinctions between capacity-generating investment determined by firms' forecasts of future sales growth, and other forms that might enhance firms' ability to differentiate their products, and to erect barriers to entry. It was the latter forms of investment alone that gave rise to a downward-sloping investment demand schedule (Eichner, 1976, p. 192).

The literature on financialization of non-financial corporations has also brought renewed attention to the investment function, and firms' duelling objectives of growth and profitability. Stockhammer (2004) emphasized that the growing threat of hostile takeovers and the transformation of managerial compensation increasingly led firms to pursue strategies of short-run profit maximization at the expense of investment activity oriented towards long-run growth. Utilizing firm-level data for the United States, Davis (2018) drew similar conclusions, though highlighting that the negative effects of financialization on real investment were restricted to larger firms.

WILLIAM E. MCCOLLOCH

See also

Effective demand; Endogenous money; Financial instability hypothesis; Principle of increasing risk; Uncertainty

References

Davis, L.E. (2018), 'Financialization and the non-financial corporation: an investigation of firm-level investment behavior in the United States', *Metroeconomica*, **69** (1), 270–307.

Eichner, A.S. (1976), *The Megacorp and Oligopoly*, Cambridge, UK: Cambridge University Press.

Kalecki, M. (1936), 'Some remarks on Keynes's theory', in J. Osiatynski (ed.) (1990), *Collected Works of Michał Kalecki, Vol. I*, Oxford: Clarendon Press, pp. 223–32.

Kalecki, M. (1937), 'The principle of increasing risk', *Economica*, **4** (16), 440–7.

Keynes, J.M. (1936), *The General Theory of Employment, Interest and Money*, London: Macmillan.

Minsky, H.P. (1982), 'The financial-instability hypothesis: capitalist processes and the behavior of the economy', in C.P. Kindleberger and J.-P. Laffargue (eds), *Financial Crises: Theory, History, and Policy*, Cambridge, UK: Cambridge University Press, pp. 13–39.

Robinson, J. (1962a), *Economic Philosophy*, London: C.A. Watts.

Robinson, J. (1962b), *Essays in the Theory of Economic Growth*, London: Macmillan.

WILLIAM E. MCCOLLOCH

Steindl, J. (1952), *Maturity and Stagnation in American Capitalism*, Oxford: Basil Blackwell.

Stockhammer, E. (2004), 'Financialization and the slowdown of accumulation', *Cambridge Journal of Economics*, **28** (5), 719–41.

Wood, A. (1975), *A Theory of Profits*, Cambridge, UK: Cambridge University Press.

Investment theory – ecological

Even though post-Keynesian economics considers economic activity as demand driven, increasing resource consumption and environmental damages reveal a supply-side constraint given by the boundaries of the planet. Respecting those ecological constraints at a systemic level requires an appropriate analysis as provided by ecological macroeconomics. This perspective detects the important role of investment at the macroeconomic level in order to ensure the sustainable transformation of the economy.

In propositions of neoclassical ecological economics, the economy is modelled to be at a steady state in line with a sustainable use of natural resources where within this constraint factor allocation is driven by the market (Daly, 1996, p. 31). Since nature is considered as a capital stock whose deterioration makes its marginal returns increase, market regulation is basically appropriate to sustain natural resources. Investment therefore keeps the market-driven role it is assigned in conventional neoclassical theory. By contrast, in post-Keynesian economics, dynamic economic activity takes place in real time such that there is no self-adjustment of any general equilibrium to environmental requirements. Therefore, ecological investment theory obtains specific importance. Ecological transition is a process that requires appropriate investment that market forces cannot guarantee owing to uncertainty, path dependency, and instability (Courvisanos, 2009, p. 287). For this reason, the government is needed to finance investment in environmentally friendly sectors, which may require the establishment of publicly sponsored banks (Fontana and Sawyer, 2013, p. 264).

There are different views on whether or not economic growth is consistent with ecological constraints. This also involves different views on the role of investment. On the one hand, it is argued that not all sectors of the economy are energy intensive. Moreover, economic growth is required to guarantee employment and thus fulfil social needs. Hence, the economy must grow and it is able to achieve this without causing environmental damage. However, for this to happen, investment needs to be directed towards sectors without a negative environmental impact. In order to even have a positive impact, investment should be made in renewable energy, energy efficiency and circular economy approaches. Such an investment strategy, often labelled as a 'Green New Deal', supports both sustainable development and employment (Pollin, 2019). Owing to sufficient efficiency gains, the declining energy intensity of output allows for continuous economic growth while the environmental impact also decreases.

On the other hand, historical record shows that rising consumption of goods goes along with growing energy consumption. Thus, any growth-inducing investment, even if it is green investment, creates a rebound effect at the macroeconomic level since additionally created income is spent on goods and services with the respective environmental impact (Rezai et al., 2013, pp. 73–4). It may be argued that sustainability can only be achieved in a non-growing economy. Yet, such a conclusion in a post-Keynesian framework is far from a steady-state economy, because a dynamic demand-driven economy runs the risk of unemployment and instability once demand is restricted (Taylor et al., 2016, pp. 196–7). Investment as the driver of economic activity thus has a twofold task: it not only has to bring economic growth to a rate consistent with full employment but also has to align this rate with the growth rate consistent with the ecological constraint (Fontana and Sawyer, 2013, p. 261). Investment not only has to be made more sustainable with regard to its composition; its volume also should be reduced in order to respect the lower, or zero, growth rate required by the environment. This can be achieved by the regulation of lending by banks and financial institutions as well as the access to credit. To maintain employment at high levels, appropriate economic policy needs to keep up demand, which is probably ensured best by government budget deficits (ibid., p. 260). Additionally, shrinking demand for labour can be complemented on the supply side by reducing working hours, which supports employment at a given output level.

Ecological investment theory in post-Keynesian economics thus entails the regulation of investment at a macroeconomic level to direct it to environmentally friendly sectors. If sustainability is assumed to require a limitation of economic growth, a reduction of total investment volume and accompanying macroeconomic governance are needed.

BASIL OBERHOLZER

See also

Ecological macroeconomics; Fiscal policy; Growth; Neoclassical economics; Post-Keynesian economics – a big tent?

References

Courvisanos, J. (2009), 'Optimize versus satisfice: two approaches to an investment policy in sustainable development', in R.P.F. Holt, S. Pressman and C.L. Spash (eds), *Post Keynesian and Ecological Economics: Confronting Environmental Issues*, Cheltenham, UK, and Northampton, MA, USA: Edward Elgar, pp. 279–300.

Daly, H.E. (1996), *Beyond Growth: The Economics of Sustainable Development*, Boston: Beacon Press.

Fontana, G. and M. Sawyer (2013), 'Post-Keynesian and Kaleckian thoughts on ecological macroeconomics', *European Journal of Economics and Economic Policies: Intervention*, **10** (2), 256–67.

Pollin, R. (2019), 'Advancing a viable global climate stabilization project: degrowth versus the Green New Deal', *Review of Radical Political Economics*, **51** (2), 311–19.

Rezai, A., L. Taylor and R. Mechler (2013), 'Ecological macroeconomics: an application to climate change', *Ecological Economics*, **85**, 69–76.

Taylor, L., A. Rezai and D.K. Foley (2016), 'An integrated approach to climate change, income distribution, employment, and economic growth', *Ecological Economics*, **121**, 196–205.

Investment theory – Kaleckian

The simple representation of Kaleckian investment theories places emphasis on capacity utilization and profit rate or margin as the key influences on investment. The investment theories of Kalecki are more complex though featuring the effects of profits (actual or expected) and the level of economic activity on investment decisions. His investment theories went through a number of stages and come in some of his earlier papers (Kalecki, 1933) and amongst his last (Kalecki, 1968). However, Kalecki viewed 'the determination of investment decisions by, broadly speaking, the level and the rate of change of economic activity' as the *pièce de résistance* of economics (Kalecki, 1968, p. 263).

Kalecki's theories of investment were closely related with his theories of the business cycle. Steindl (1981) identified three distinct versions of Kalecki's writings on the trade cycle, each of them presenting different views of the determinants of investment, albeit with many common influences (see Sawyer, 1996).

Kalecki drew the distinction between investment decisions and implementation of those decisions, and then decisions are fully implemented in view of the time lag with production of investment goods meeting the demand for them. It is taken that credit expansion permits the investment decisions to be financed (see Kalecki, 1990, p. 489). In his first version, Kalecki focused on the rate of investment as related with both the rate of profit and the interest rate, which itself is treated as an increasing function of profitability. He argued that investment decisions will be an increasing function 'of the difference between the marginal [prospective] rate of profit and the rate of interest' (Kalecki, 1990, p. 306), with the long-term rate of interest as the relevant one but assumed constant. The marginal rate of profit is determined by the level of national income and the stock of capital equipment.

The second version (Kalecki, 1943) made the influence of the availability of finance clearer – 'the inflow of new gross savings ... push[es] forward the barriers set to investment plans by the limited accessibility of the capital market and "increasing risk"' (Kalecki, 1991, p. 164) – and also expresses the idea that previous additions to the capital stock have an adverse impact on current investment decisions. In this version, decisions on future net investment were modelled as based on net investment minus rentiers' savings, change in profits and negatively on current net addition to fixed capital equipment.

Kalecki's (1968) final discussion of investment decisions draws on the idea of looking at the parts of (existing) profits that are 'captured' by new investment. At the aggregate level, there is a rearrangement of profits between firms as well as some change in the level of profits. Kalecki related the level of investment in a particular year to the rate of profit generated on that investment, and noted that the higher the level of investment the lower is the rate of profit it yields. The direction of causation in this function runs from the level of investment to the rate

BASIL OBERHOLZER / MALCOLM SAWYER

of profit, and the negative relationship reflects competition between firms. Any new investment captures only a small proportion of the total increase in profits in a year, with the old equipment capturing the remainder. Technical progress, which leads to new machines that are more productive than old ones, and the real costs of operating old machines rise through the introduction of new machines and the consequent increases in productivity and real wages. The profit on the old machines falls and is in effect transferred to the new machines. Kalecki portrayed investment decisions as dependent on both entrepreneurial savings (the difference $I(\pi) - I$) and the stimulus from innovations.

MALCOLM SAWYER

See also

Innovation; Investment theory – Keynesian; Profit; *Selected Essays on the Dynamics of Capitalist Economy*; Technological change

References

Kalecki, M. (1933), *Essays on the Business Cycle Theory*, originally published in Polish, English translation reprinted in Kalecki (1990), pp. 66–108.
Kalecki, M. (1943), *Studies in Economic Dynamics*, London: Allen & Unwin.
Kalecki, M. (1968), 'Trend and the business cycle', *Economic Journal*, **78** (2), 263–76.
Kalecki, M. (1990), *Collected Works of Michal Kalecki, Vol. 1*, Oxford: Clarendon Press.
Kalecki, M. (1991), *Collected Works of Michal Kalecki, Vol. 2*, Oxford: Clarendon Press.
Sawyer, M. (1996), 'Kalecki on the trade cycle and economic growth', in J. King (ed.), *An Alternative Macroeconomic Theory: The Kaleckian Model and Post Keynesian Economics*, New York: Kluwer, pp. 93–114.
Steindl, J. (1981), 'Some comments on the three versions of Kalecki's theory of the trade cycle', in N. Assorodobraj-Kula, C. Bobrowski, H. Hagemejer, W. Kula and J. Loś (eds), *Studies in Economic Theory and Practice: Essays in Honour of Edward Lipinski*, Amsterdam: North-Holland, pp. 125–33. Reprinted in J. Steindl, *Economic Papers 1941–88*, London: Palgrave Macmillan, 1990, pp. 139–48.

Investment theory – Keynesian

John Maynard Keynes was not only a brilliant economist; he was a savvy investor. He actively and successfully traded money for himself, friends, family and several institutions throughout his life. He lost fortunes and built them back up – always learning and adapting to new information (one of his trademark characteristics). His investment success is even more remarkable given the times during which he was investing (two world wars, economic depressions in the United Kingdom and the United States). Keynes the economist often eclipses Keynes the investor, which is unfortunate. He has great wisdom to share with the world. Fortunately, he communicated enough of his philosophy on personal investing, speculation and financial markets that some of the most successful traders in the twentieth century (for instance John 'Jack' Bogle, Vanguard and Warren Buffett, Berkshire Hathaway) credit him with influencing their thinking about financial markets. Many investors cite Chapter 12 ('The state of long-term expectation') of Keynes's (1936/1964) *General Theory* as his greatest contribution. In many ways, Keynes's fascination with markets shaped his economic ideas and, perhaps, served as a testing ground for his thinking.

Keynes was the son of a Cambridge don and did not come from wealth. His exposure to investing was organic and self-guided. After a stint in civil service, Keynes returned to Cambridge, United Kingdom, and in 1910 started lecturing in money, credit, prices and the stock market. Wasik's (2014) *Keynes's Way to Wealth* is an excellent presentation of Keynes's investment philosophies and historical narrative during this time. After Keynes (1921/2007) wrote *A Treatise on Probability*, it is not difficult to think that he equated the stock market with a great statistical laboratory. Because Keynes understood probability and its limitations, he recognized markets (and the world) to be non-ergodic – that is to say, the past is not a good predictor of the future. Using past information to predict the future is folly. Keynes well understood the differences between calculable risk and uncertainty. True uncertainty would never yield to probabilistic rules and assurances. Nassim Nicholas Taleb, himself an investor and academic, concurs with Keynes and is helping advance this thinking.

In one of Keynes's 1910 lectures at Cambridge on the stock market he wrote that '[investing is] essentially a practical subject, which cannot properly be taught by book or lecture' (Wasik, 2014, p. 2). In these lectures, Keynes makes

MALCOLM SAWYER / ROBERT H. SCOTT

important distinctions between speculation, (long-term) investing and gambling. Keynes was soon after this time applying his investment knowledge and breaking many of his rules while learning to trade. In 1911 Keynes was appointed to the Estates Committee and was able to see how King's College handled its endowment. He found that King's held large reserves of cash, which he persuaded them to invest. But Keynes was not a dilettante investor. He often plunged heavily into and out of positions taking advantage of market movements. When currencies started floating after 1914, Keynes actively traded them. He also traded commodities. Keynes used his analytical skills to study the data generated from the markets to develop trading strategies. By the 1920s, however, Keynes had nearly lost two fortunes and was learning that speculation was a difficult way to trade profitably on a regular basis. Currencies and commodities are particularly volatile and difficult to generate consistent profits with. In 1924, Keynes became bursar and manager of King's endowment, which he managed until his death in 1946.

Keynes's experience as an investor helped refine his understanding of behaviour. Stock markets are large social networks that (prior to algorithm trading) ebb and flow according to the psychology of traders and the market overall. Keynes shared much wisdom and insight in *The General Theory*, but in Chapter 12 we learn some of his investment wisdom.

First, professional investors are not focused on buying investments 'for keeps', but rather for short-term profit. Thus, they are sensitive to the mass psychology of the market. 'This battle of wits to anticipate the basis of conventional valuation a few months hence, rather than the prospective yield of an investment over a long term of years, does not even require gulls amongst the public to feed the maws of the professional; it can be played by professionals amongst themselves' (Keynes, 1936/1964, p. 155). Keynes does hedge his viewpoint by stating that a buy-and-hold strategy is perhaps more intellectually challenging than trying to read mass market psychology because 'time and ignorance' are difficult forces to overcome.

Second, Keynes remained cautious of speculation. He states that '[s]peculators may do no harm as bubbles on a steady stream of enterprise. But the position is serious when enterprise becomes the bubble on a whirlpool of speculation. When the capital development of a country becomes a by-product of the activities of a casino, the job is likely to be ill-done' (p. 159).

Third, he introduces the idea of 'animal spirits' that serve as the initiative to engage in investment – 'a spontaneous urge to action rather than inaction, and not as the outcome of a weighted average of quantitative benefits multiplied by quantitative probabilities' (p. 161). It is these animal spirits that drive risk taking and innovation. Alternatively, 'if the animal spirits are dimmed and the spontaneous optimism falters, leaving us to depend on nothing but a mathematical expectation, enterprise will fade and die' (p. 162). The compound interest on Keynes's wisdom continues to grow.

ROBERT H. SCOTT

See also

Animal spirits; Bubbles – credit; Investment theory – Kaleckian; *The General Theory of Employment, Interest and Money*; Uncertainty

References

Keynes, J.M. (1921/2007), *A Treatise on Probability*, London: Macmillan.
Keynes, J.M. (1936/1964), *The General Theory of Employment, Interest and Money*, London: Harcourt Brace.
Wasik, J. (2014), *Keynes's Way to Wealth: Timeless Investment Lessons from the Great Economist*, New York: McGraw Hill.

Involuntary unemployment – explanations of

Involuntary unemployment occurs whenever individuals are both searching for a job and willing to accept the prevailing wage but cannot find work. It can include discouraged workers, those out of the labour force because they disbelieve in finding a job after longer-term frustrations, and employed workers who work fewer hours than desired. It is the opposite of voluntary unemployment, which comprises people of legal working age currently not seeking to work. The economy is said to be in full employment whenever involuntary unemployment is absent or quantitatively irrelevant.

ROBERT H. SCOTT / ÍTALO PEDROSA

In capitalist economies – where the great majority of people do not own the means of production – involuntary unemployment poses vital problems to society. From an individual's perspective, being unemployed often means also being unable to provide for subsistence. For society, unemployment implies a waste of resources with various detrimental social, political, and economic ramifications, such as poverty, homelessness, and educational and psychological issues.

A key contention in macroeconomic theory relates to the genesis and persistence of involuntary unemployment.

Neoclassical economics suggests that market forces would eliminate involuntary unemployment without market failures or frictions impeding the labour market clearing. It builds on well-behaved labour supply and demand schedules to determine an economy's overall level of employment. The labour supply increases with the real wage, reflecting the presupposition that an increase in labour hours requires higher pay to compensate for the higher effort or the loss of leisure time. The demand for labour schedule reflects profit maximization conditions, which in competitive goods markets require equalizing the (decreasing) marginal productivity of labour to the real wage. Under such conditions, wage flexibility ensures full employment equilibrium in the labour market because excess demand (supply) of labour bids up (down) nominal wages, changing the real wage rate.

For a given capital stock and technology, the equilibrium quantity of labour defines the economy's production independently of aggregate demand. Accordingly, the neoclassical framework employs Say's law to guarantee that aggregate demand adjusts to the level of aggregate production in the income-generating process. Typically, such adjustment gets justified by a loanable funds theory of interest rate determination or either Keynes (income) or Pigou (wealth) effects, both of which require wage and price flexibility.

In turn, post-Keynesian economists advocate that involuntary unemployment results from the normal functioning of capitalist economies because the goods market outcomes determine labour demand. Specifically, the level of employment is a by-product of spending decisions. Indeed, post-Keynesians sustain that the economy-wide spending needed to ensure full employment is typically not attained.

Accordingly, full employment is as much rare as short-lived (Keynes, 1936/1997, p. 250).

This view is fundamentally grounded in Keynes's and Kalecki's elaborations of the principle of effective demand (PED). While multiple versions of the PED exist (see Lavoie, 2014, Ch. 5), all formulations emphasize the central role of the differentiation of induced and autonomous demand. Induced demand refers to current spending decisions that depend on income-generating processes, such as workers' consumption out of wages. Autonomous expenditures, by contrast, are independent of current income.

Considering these definitions, Say's law would tacitly require all aggregate demand to be somehow induced. Post-Keynesians contend that because autonomous expenditures exist and induced expenditures depend on the marginal propensity to spend, there is no endogenous reason for overall demand to match the production needed to ensure full employment. In this sense, involuntary unemployment is the most likely outcome, meaning that labour tends to be underutilized.

Finally, contrary to mainstream interpretations of Keynes's (1936/1997) *General Theory*, post-Keynesians object that wage and price flexibility can eliminate involuntary unemployment.

First, as Harvey (2016) puts it, the supply of labour curve provides only the maximum labour supply for different real wages. It does not portray equilibrium points, as the neoclassical theory suggests. Involuntary unemployment does not self-eliminate in the labour market because lowering the asked nominal wage will not make the set of firms more willing to hire. Such a claim relies on the simple fact that wages paid by firms are a cost, on the one hand, but on the other hand, influence the ability of the set of firms to sell their products.

Second, neither Keynes's nor Pigou's effects are likely to occur, so typical neoclassical mechanisms to restore full employment are implausible. The so-called Keynes effect builds on exogenous money, implying that lower prices would increase the real money supply, reducing interest rates and increasing investment. Since post-Keynesians argue that money supply is endogenous, the Keynes effect is practically irrelevant. The Pigou effect relies on the idea that falling prices increase real wealth, then increasing autonomous consumption. However, it ignores that one agent's financial assets are another's liabilities, so the most likely outcome of falling prices is a debt-deflation process. Even if that was not the case, Stiglitz (1991) argues that the Pigou effect would be quantitatively irrelevant.

ÍTALO PEDROSA

See also

Capitalism; Effective demand; Endogenous money; Full employment; Neoclassical economics

References

Harvey, J.T. (2016), "An introduction to Post Keynesian economics: involuntary unemployment with perfectly flexible wages and prices", *American Economist*, **61** (2), pp. 140–56.
Keynes, J.M. (1936/1997), *The General Theory of Employment, Interest, and Money*, Amherst, NY: Prometheus Books.
Lavoie, M. (2014), *Post-Keynesian Economics: New Foundations*, Cheltenham, UK, and Northampton, MA, USA: Edward Elgar.
Stiglitz, J.E. (1991), "Methodological issues and the New Keynesian economics", *National Bureau of Economic Research Working Paper*, No. 3580.

Involuntary unemployment – origins of

The concept of involuntary unemployment was coined in the midst of the Great Depression of the 1930s by John Maynard Keynes, who defined it as follows: 'Men are involuntarily unemployed if, in the event of a small rise in the price of wage-goods relatively to the money-wage, both the aggregate supply of labour willing to work for the current money-wage and the aggregate demand for it at that wage would be greater than the existing volume of employment' (Keynes, 1936/2013, p. 15).

Later, Keynes (1939/2013, p. 400) made it clear that it was a mistake to see his notion of involuntary unemployment 'as a problem of supply and demand in the short period and not as a result derived from monetary factors'. Whereas Classical economists restricted involuntary unemployment to a temporary alteration caused by changes in the aggregate composition, the contemporary neoclassical authors of Keynes and those who came after (those that can be categorized as Neo-Keynesians or New Keynesians) linked it to the existence of rigidities that prevented the adjustment of prices, including wages; that is, a mismatch between supply and demand caused by the existence of factors that prevent its full flexibility. In another order, post-Keynesian authors have emphasized the monetary nature of the capitalist system, taking involuntary unemployment as a normal situation inherent to the radical uncertainty characteristic of a monetary economy. Therefore, it would not be a failure of coordination in the market, in such a way that individuals cannot be held responsible for the existence of unemployment (Chick, 1983; Davidson, 1994). In line with the latter, it is not merely a temporary mismatch between buying and selling that causes the possibility of involuntary unemployment in a money-barter economy. The radical uncertainty of a monetary economy tended to make the system operate with excess capacity and unemployment, which gave rise to a systemic deficiency in aggregate demand.

However, seriously considering the ontological difference of the post-Keynesian approach with respect to the Classical view of the world, starting from a conception of the economy where workers are paid with money, and where employees and employers do not know the value of the real wage agreed *ex ante*, necessarily precludes contemplating an economy where labour is demanded and offered for a real wage that is known to both parties, thus discarding the Classical notion of a barter economy, with which the capitalist system is dissociated in some moment of its development. In this sense, exposing a theory on the emergence of the need and acceptance of money by private agents that is not based on an extension of exchanges helps to take perspective of what is really at stake in the notion of involuntary unemployment.

Mitchell and Mosler (2006, p. 165) indicate that taxation creates unemployment in the non-governmental sector. The starting point of this perspective is that taxation works to promote the production of goods and services to the authority in exchange for the funds necessary to extinguish tax obligations. Contextualizing this fact in a capitalist system of private producers who own the means of production and where the accumulation of monetary benefits is the engine that determines the hiring of salaried labour, unemployment would only occur when net public spending is too low to adapt to the need of paying taxes and to the desire of savings (Mitchell and Muysken, 2008, p. 18). The involuntary unemployment caused by insufficient total monetary expenditure is defined by Lerner (1951, p. 15) as unemployment due to deflation. Following this approach, Tcherneva (2014, p. 50) has characterized involuntary unemployment as a monetary phenomenon. Therefore, the deficient demand of the economic system that results in the existence of involuntary unemployment is the reflection of an insufficient budget deficit (Mitchell, 1998; Mitchell and Mosler, 2002).

Esteban Cruz Hidalgo, Francisco M. Parejo Moruno and José Francisco Rangel Preciado

See also

Aggregate demand; Capitalism; Endogenous money; Fiscal deficits; *The General Theory of Employment, Interest and Money*

References

Chick, V. (1983), *Macroeconomics After Keynes: A Reconsideration of The General Theory*, London: Philip Allan.
Davidson, P. (1994), *Post Keynesian Macroeconomic Theory*, Cheltenham, UK, and Northampton, MA, USA: Edward Elgar.
Keynes, J.M. (1936/2013), *The General Theory of Employment, Interest and Money*, in *The Collected Writings of John Maynard Keynes, Vol. VII*, Cambridge, UK: Cambridge University Press.
Keynes, J.M. (1939/2013), 'Relative movements of real wages and output', in *The Collected Writings of John Maynard Keynes, Vol. VII*, Cambridge, UK: Cambridge University Press, pp. 394–412.
Lerner, A.P. (1951), *Economics of Employment*, New York: McGraw-Hill.
Mitchell, W. (1998), 'The buffer stock employment model and the NAIRU: the path to full employment', *Journal of Economic Issues*, **32** (2), 547–55.
Mitchell, W. and W. Mosler (2002), 'Fiscal policy and the job guarantee', *Australian Journal of Labour Economics*, **5** (2), 243–59.
Mitchell, W. and J. Muysken (2008), *Full Employment Abandoned: Shifting Sands and Policy Failures*, Cheltenham, UK, and Northampton, MA, USA: Edward Elgar.
Tcherneva, P.R. (2014), 'Reorienting fiscal policy: a bottom-up approach', *Journal of Post Keynesian Economics*, **37** (1), 43–66.
Wray, L.R. (1998), *Understanding Modern Money: The Key to Full Employment and Price Stability*, Cheltenham, UK, and Northampton, MA, USA: Edward Elgar.

IS–LM model

It is hard to find in the economists' toolbox a macroeconomic theoretical structure so resilient and controversial as the Hicks–Hansen IS–LM model. Since the late 1930s, this model has been extensively used for academic, political, and business purposes to study how money and product markets interact to obtain different macroeconomic short-term equilibria.

The original version – the SI–LL model (Hicks, 1937) – was initially designed to formalize the main ideas from Keynes's (1936) *General Theory* about the paramount importance of aggregate demand in a high unemployment situation and is used lately – allowing for several modifications – to provide a basis for examining different theoretical and political approaches (Keynesians, Neoclassical Synthesis, New Keynesians, New Classicals) into a unique comprehensive analytical framework.

The standard IS–LM model includes a product market with equations that equal savings (S) and investment (I) and a money market with equations that do the same for demand (L) and supply of money (M). Interactions across markets determine the macroeconomic equilibrium defined in terms of its two endogenous variables, namely, gross domestic product (GDP) and the interest rate. Using a deterministic version of the equilibrium concept, this model assumes a closed economy with labour unemployment, a short-run infinitely elastic aggregate supply curve, a traditional Keynesian saving/consumption function, a negative relationship between investment and interest rates, exogenous taxes, government spending, and money supply, and a money demand increasing with the output level and negatively related with the interest rate.

Showing high flexibility, the IS–LM model evolved incorporating open economy considerations (the Mundell–Fleming IS–LM–BP version), microfoundations and rational expectations, wealth effects and Tobin' q features, inside and outside money, and intertemporal government budget constraints. Despite many specific issues that have been addressed with these modifications, the main model contribution still relies on its simplicity to explain why fiscal, monetary, and exchange rate policies could have different results depending on the macroeconomic situation – without underestimating other analytical strengths emphasized by some New Keynesian economists like Paul Krugman, Gregory Mankiw, Bradford DeLong, or Larry Summers.

These notwithstanding, the model validity has been widely questioned: from Keynes, who pointed out that the IS–LM model should not be seen as a simplified version of his *General Theory*, because it cannot properly deal with fundamental uncertainty, structural instability, and the importance of subjective expectations; to Hicks himself, who finally recognized his model's limits to describe major Keynesian concepts and relationships (see Hicks, 1980); to a myriad of post-Keynesian contributors, focusing on IS–LM weaknesses like the absence of stock–flow consistency or the lack of theoretical foundations for the investment–interest rate negative relationship (see Robinson, 1973; Godley and Lavoie, 2012); and New Classical authors, identifying the IS–LM model as a part of a theoretical overreaction to the Great Depression, without solid microfoundations (see King, 1993, 2000).

Moreover, structuralist contributions also criticize the IS–LM model for its inability to explain key features of Latin American economies: the balance-of-payment constraint to economic growth and the cyclical relationship between income distribution, GDP, and the current account (Bielchowsky, 2009).

Despite these critiques and controversies, since the end of the Second World War the IS–LM model has shown astounding resilience, longevity, and flexibility inside academic and political circles.

FERNANDO TOLEDO AND
DEMIAN T. PANIGO

See also

Balance-of-payments constrained growth; Exogenous money; Fiscal policy; Microfoundations; Wealth effect

References

Bielchowsky, R. (2009), 'Sesenta años de la CEPAL: estructuralismo y neoestructuralismo', *Revista CEPAL*, 97, pp. 173–94.
Godley, W. and M. Lavoie (2012), *Monetary Economics: An Integrated Approach to Credit, Money, Income, Production and Wealth*, Basingstoke, UK, and New York: Palgrave Macmillan.
Hicks, J. (1937), 'Mr. Keynes and the 'Classics': a suggested interpretation', *Econometrica*, **5** (2), 147–59.
Hicks, J. (1980), 'IS–LM: an explanation', *Journal of Post Keynesian Economics*, **3** (2), 139–54.
Keynes, J.M. (1936), *The General Theory of Employment, Interest, and Money*, London: Macmillan.
King, R. (1993), 'Will the New Keynesian macroeconomics resurrect the IS–LM model?', *Journal of Economic Perspectives*, **7** (1), 67–82.
King, R. (2000), 'The new IS–LM model: language, logic, and limits', *Federal Reserve Bank of Richmond Economic Quarterly*, **86** (3), 45–103.
Robinson, J. (1973), 'What has become of the Keynesian revolution?', in J. Robinson (ed.), *After Keynes*, Oxford: Basil Blackwell, pp. 1–11.

Job guarantee

Also known as employer of last resort, the job guarantee (JG) is a central pillar of the Modern Money Theory approach. The defence of this macroeconomic stabilization mechanism is compatible with the defence of the right to work, raised in a similar way to the right to property, understood as a characteristic institution of the capitalist mode of production. In line with Keynes (1936/2013, p. 378), it is not the ownership of the means of production that is important for the State to assume, although the socialization of investment, established as one way for ensuring a de facto full employment approach eliminating involuntary unemployment, certainly claims a greater weight for it. That is the way to balance the imbalance between private affluence and public misery (as referred to by Galbraith (1958)), while the euthanasia of the rentier becomes effective.

Mosler (1997–98, p. 177) points out that the JG is a logical extension of the chartalist paradigm to the tax system. It can also be seen as the executing arm under Lerner's (1944) functional finance framework, a nondiscretionary mechanism to drive demand to the right point to achieve full employment with price stability. JG as the backbone of full functional employment is also exposed by Forstater (1998), Mitchell (1998) and Wray (1998).

The first component of JG is that the government acts as an employer of last resort, hiring all the workforce that cannot find a job in the private sector. As Minsky (1986/2008, p. 308) already pointed out, the government is the only agent that can create 'an infinitely elastic demand for labor at a floor or minimum wage that does not depend upon long-run and short-run profit expectations of business'.

However, the aforementioned authors have developed the JG as an automatic stabilization mechanism, achieving price stability through full employment, thanks to its operation as a reserve stock of employees, replacing the reserve army of unemployed justified by the notion of the non-accelerating inflation rate of unemployment (NAIRU). Mitchell (1998, p. 548) has called this reserve army of last resort employees, whose size fluctuates with the economic cycle, NAIBER (acronym for non-accelerating-inflation-buffer employment ratio). The working of this reserve stock of employees is as follows: when the economy enters a recession and companies shed a good part of their workforce, laid-off workers will be able to access one of the JG programmes available in a timely manner to absorb fluctuations in private spending and investment, thereby preventing deflation. At the height of the business cycle, the private sector would attract the workers employed in this functional reserve by offering them better working conditions. As Mitchell and Mosler (2002) explain, a policy of driving demand based on 'spending over a quantity rule' is replaced by a policy of 'spending over a price rule'. Thus, instead of the State discretionally determining how much it is going to spend and the market dictating the price, with the JG the State offers a fixed salary to anyone willing and able to work, and individuals and market forces determine the total amount of public spending with their wishes for savings and incomes. Ultimately, the JG operates as an endogenous automatic stabilizer to private activity, but, in addition, market forces would align all other wages and prices based on the salary offered in these programmes, functioning as a value standard and, therefore, as an anchor for all other prices (Mitchell and Muysken, 2008, p. 232).

Finally, it should be noted that this one-time adjustment is not inflation, as it does not imply a continuous increase in the price level. In addition, the JG promotes a sectoral restructuring by eliminating the vile effects associated with involuntary unemployment. This promotes productivity, efficiency and flexibility in the economy as a whole (see Tcherneva, 2019).

ESTEBAN CRUZ HIDALGO, FRANCISCO M. PAREJO MORUNO AND JOSÉ FRANCISCO RANGEL PRECIADO

See also

Employer of last resort; Endogenous money; Fiscal policy; Full employment; Unemployment – involuntary

References

Forstater, M. (1998), 'Flexible full employment: structural implications of discretionary public sector employment', *Journal of Economic Issues*, **32** (2), 557–63.
Galbraith, J.K. (1958), *The Affluent Society*, Boston: Houghton Mifflin.
Keynes, J.M. (1936/2013), *The General Theory of Employment, Interest and Money*, in *The Collected Writings of John Maynard Keynes, vol. VII*, third edition, Cambridge, UK: Cambridge University Press.
Lerner, A.P. (1944), *Economics of Control: Principles of Welfare Economics*, New York: Macmillan.
Minsky, H. (1986/2008), *Stabilizing an Unstable Economy*, New York: McGraw-Hill.
Mitchell, W. (1998), 'The buffer stock employment model and the NAIRU: the path to full employment', *Journal of Economic Issues*, **32** (2), 547–55.
Mitchell, W. and W. Mosler (2002), 'Fiscal policy and the job guarantee', *Australian Journal of Labour Economics*, **5** (2), 243–59.
Mitchell, W. and J. Muysken (2008), *Full Employment Abandoned: Shifting Sands and Policy Failures*, Cheltenham, UK, and Northampton, MA, USA: Edward Elgar.
Mosler, W. (1997–98), 'Full employment and price stability', *Journal of Post Keynesian Economics*, **20** (2), 167–82.
Tcherneva, P. (2019), 'The Federal Job Guarantee: prevention, not just a cure', *Challenge*, **62** (4), 253–72.
Wray, L.R. (1998), *Understanding Modern Money: The Key to Full Employment and Price Stability*, Cheltenham, UK, and Northampton, MA, USA: Edward Elgar.

Kaleckian economics

Michał Kalecki (1899–1970) developed many of the innovative ideas of Keynes's *General Theory* at the same time as Keynes but quite independently of him and in some respects arriving at a superior theoretical system. Thus, Kaleckian economics is one of the most important and influential sub-schools of post-Keynesian economics (see King, 2002, Ch. 2).

Born in Lodz, Poland, in 1899, Kalecki studied engineering and was employed as a commercial journalist before joining the Institute for

Business Cycle and Price Research in Warsaw, where he worked for seven years. He spent the period 1936–45 in the United Kingdom, mainly at the Oxford University Institute of Statistics. For the next ten years he worked (briefly) in Canada for the International Labour Organization and then for the United Nations in New York. In 1955 he returned to Poland to escape McCarthyism in the United States, serving as a government adviser and also as a professor in Warsaw, where the final years of his life were marred by official anti-Semitism and the persecution of his younger colleagues. There is an excellent two-volume biography by Jan Toporowski (2013, 2018) and a seven-volume set of his collected works (Kalecki, 1990–97).

Kalecki was self-taught in economics. He learned much from Marx and some of his less orthodox interpreters, including Rosa Luxemburg and Mikhail Tugan-Baranovksy, but he never showed any interest in the labour theory of value or in Marx's volume III analysis of the falling rate of profit. Kalecki was never afraid to use mathematical methods, and his early formal models of the business cycle place him in the top 5 per cent of the mathematical economists of the mid-1930s. But he also insisted on the need for realism in economic theory, and therefore always placed great emphasis on the class nature of the capitalist system and the power that this gave to the owners of the means of production. For Kalecki, economics and politics were inseparable. He followed Marx in emphasizing the problems associated with the realization of the surplus and the inherently cyclical nature of capitalist production, denying that a 'long run' could be defined independently of the set of short periods that constitute it, and hence rejecting neoclassical macroeconomics as a matter of methodological principle.

His approach to economic theory was original and distinctive. For Kalecki, industrial product markets are overwhelmingly oligopolistic, with free competition largely confined to agriculture, and prices are set by the application of a mark-up over the variable costs of production, which he understood to be roughly constant with respect to output. The size of the mark-up in individual industries, and hence in aggregate terms the capitalist share in total output, depends on the degree of monopoly. In his later work, Kalecki also allowed a role for trade union wage bargaining as an influence on the relative shares of wages and profits. The level of profits, however, depends upon aggregate expenditure, and in particular (since workers save little or nothing from their wage income) on capitalist investment spending. In essence, in all of Kalecki's macroeconomic models the workers spend what they get and the capitalists get what they spend.

Kalecki argued that full employment was both achievable and sustainable in capitalist economies, at least in principle, through increased government spending and the egalitarian redistribution of income. In practice, however, he believed that it would be resisted by capitalists, who feared the implications for discipline in the factories. At first, he explained the maintenance of full employment after 1945 in terms of the continuing high levels of military expenditure required during the Cold War, which provoked much less capitalist hostility than welfare spending would have done. At the end of his life, in a paper co-authored with his young Polish colleague Tadeusz Kowalik, he conceded that there had indeed been a 'crucial reform' in capitalist economies, with governments committed to full employment and strong trade unions able to ensure that real wages rose in line with labour productivity. Ironically, the 'golden age' that had resulted was already coming to an end (see King, 2013).

In his lifetime, Kalecki had a significant impact on the intellectual development of a number of influential 'left Keynesians', including Joan Robinson, Josef Steindl (who famously described him as 'my guru') and Geoff Harcourt. He also influenced the later thinking of the independent Marxist Paul Sweezy, who had befriended him in New York. The full story of the spread of Kalecki's ideas in the half century since his death has yet to be told, but the two book-length studies by Sawyer (1985) and Kriesler (1987) were important milestones in the rise of Kaleckian economics. More recently, his influence can be seen in the burgeoning post-Keynesian literature on 'wage-led growth'.

JOHN E. KING

See also

Growth – wage-led vs profit-led; Monopoly power; Neoclassical economics; Post-Keynesian economics – a big tent?; Principle of increasing risk

JOHN E. KING

References

Kalecki, M. (1990–97), *Collected Works of Michał Kalecki*, seven volumes, edited by Jerzy Osiatyński, Oxford: Clarendon Press.
King, J.E. (2002), *A History of Post Keynesian Economics since 1936*, Cheltenham, UK, and Northampton, MA, USA: Edward Elgar.
King, J.E. (2013), 'Whatever happened to the crucial reform?', in R. Bellofiore, E. Karwowski and J. Toporowski (eds), *Economic Crisis and Political Economy: Volume 2 of Essays in Honour of Tadeusz Kowalik*, Basingstoke: Palgrave Macmillan, pp. 29–41.
Kriesler, P. (1987), *Kalecki's Microanalysis: The Development of Kalecki's Analysis of Pricing and Distribution*, Cambridge, UK: Cambridge University Press.
Sawyer, M. (1985), *The Economics of Michał Kalecki*, Basingstoke: Macmillan.
Toporowski, J. (2013), *Michał Kalecki: An Intellectual Biography. Volume I: Rendez-vous in Cambridge 1899–1939*, Basingstoke: Palgrave Macmillan.
Toporowski, J. (2018), *Michał Kalecki: An Intellectual Biography. Volume II: By Intellect Alone 1939–1970*, Basingstoke: Palgrave Macmillan.

Keynes effect

The Keynes effect is a type of real-balance effect that has the potential to push an economic system from a position of unemployment towards full employment. The operation of such an effect undermines the objective of Keynes's (1936) *General Theory* to explain persistent unemployment, and so represents a problem for Keynesian theory.

Keynes's explanation of unemployment was characterized by three key features: a theory of consumption that depended on income rather than interest rates; a theory of interest based upon liquidity preference and the money supply rather than saving and investment; and the determination of output and employment by the principle of effective demand (Pasinetti, 1974, pp. 29–48). Within this system, equilibrium output could be too low to fully employ the workforce, because excess supply in the goods market even if labour was fully employed would not imply excess demand in financial markets. If it did (as in neoclassical theory), the prices of financial assets would rise and interest rates would fall, aggregate demand would rise, and this would push the system towards full employment. Since financial markets could be in equilibrium under Keynes's theory of liquidity preference even in the presence of unemployment, no adjustment to the rate of interest was necessitated by excess supply in either the goods or labour markets, and unemployment could be explained by inadequate aggregate demand.

The Keynes effect undermines this perspective. If commodity prices fall in response to excess goods market supply at full employment, the value of transactions falls, transactions demand for money falls, and downward pressure is exerted on interest rates according to Keynes's theory of interest. Lower interest rates stimulate aggregate demand, and the economy moves towards full employment (Cottrell, 1994, p. 591).

Keynes appears to have been aware of this possibility and outlines a set of forces in Chapters 17 and 19 of *The General Theory* designed to prevent it (Keynes, 1936, p. 222). These forces are linked to what he regarded as two essential features of money – zero elasticities of production and substitution – that prevent the return on money (interest) from falling when there is unemployment. These features must be understood within the context of what Keynes calls 'own rates of asset return' (Keynes, 1936, p. 234).

For assets in general, a high rate of return generates multiple responses. First, where asset supply is elastic, a high return induces increased production of that asset, which reduces the asset's expected future price and capital appreciation, and its overall return falls. However, the supply of money is fixed (that is, its elasticity of production is zero) and cannot be augmented when its rate of return is high. Second, when an asset's return is high, its price rises as demand for it increases. This stabilizes its return, and agents substitute away from it. However, according to Keynes, the elasticity of substitution for money is low because of two offsetting effects on money's liquidity premium as commodity prices fall: money's usefulness in exchange is reduced because prices are lower and less money is needed to facilitate the same transactions; and money's exchangeability is enhanced because its command over goods is increased when prices fall. These offsetting effects leave money's liquidity premium unchanged. For these reasons, the rate of interest does not thus fall even though it is too high for full employment.

Two views prevail about the success of this defence against the Keynes effect. Chick (1983)

JOHN E. KING / PETER DOCHERTY

and Maclachlan (1993) evaluate it positively. Docherty (2005, pp. 98–104), on the other hand, argues that the concept of liquidity in Keynes's own rates framework should be differentiated from price movements better handled within the capital appreciation term of an asset's return. This suggests that the overall return on money does fall if prices deflate, and that money's elasticity of substitution is not actually zero. The Keynes effect is not thus obviated by Keynes's (1936) Chapter 17 analysis, nor by additional arguments advanced in Chapter 19, which amount to either crisis-related or short-period phenomena. On this reading, Keynes's explanation for unemployment does appear vulnerable to the Keynes effect.

Two features of subsequent post-Keynesian analysis, however, address this vulnerability. The first is the assumption of endogenous money (Kaldor, 1970; Moore, 1988). If the money supply falls with demand for it as prices deflate, interest rates will not be driven down. The second is a recognition that investment spending is insensitive to interest rates, as implied by the 1960s capital debates (Harcourt, 1972). Since the structure of prices, used to aggregate heterogeneous capital goods, depends on the rate of interest, there is no guarantee that the value of aggregate capital rises monotonically with falls in interest rates. Investment spending does not therefore rise even if interest rates were to fall, and the economy is not pushed towards full employment. The Keynes effect is not, therefore, regarded by post-Keynesian economists as a phenomenon capable of undermining Keynes's explanation for persistent unemployment.

PETER DOCHERTY

See also

Capital theory controversies; Effective demand; Endogenous money; Interest rates and investment; Liquidity preference

References

Chick, V. (1983), *Macroeconomics After Keynes*, London: Philip Allan.
Cottrell, A. (1994), 'Post-Keynesian monetary economics', *Cambridge Journal of Economics*, **18** (6), 587–605.
Docherty, P. (2005), *Money and Employment: A Study of the Theoretical Implications of Endogenous Money*, Cheltenham, UK, and Northampton, MA, USA: Edward Elgar.
Harcourt, G.C. (1972), *Some Cambridge Controversies in the Theory of Capital*, Cambridge, UK: Cambridge University Press.
Kaldor, N. (1970), 'The new monetarism', *Lloyds Bank Review*, **97**, 1–17.
Keynes, J.M. (1936), *The General Theory of Employment, Interest and Money*, London: Macmillan.
Maclachlan, F.C. (1993), *Keynes' General Theory of Interest: A Reconsideration*, London and New York: Routledge.
Milgate, M. (1982), *Capital and Employment: A Study of Keynes's Economics*, London: Academic Press.
Moore, B.J. (1988), *Horizontalists and Verticalists: The Macroeconomics of Credit Money*, Cambridge, UK: Cambridge University Press.
Pasinetti, L.L. (1974), *Income Distribution and Growth*, Cambridge, UK: Cambridge University Press.

Keynes Plan

The Keynes Plan is the proposal that John Maynard Keynes put forward at the Bretton Woods conference in July 1944 regarding the international monetary system, which at that time was based on the gold standard (a 'barbarous relic' according to Keynes's own characterization of money backed up by gold).

Keynes's starting point was 'the essential principle of banking', namely, 'the necessary equality of credits and debits, of assets and liabilities' (Keynes, 1980, p. 44). Banks indeed can never be in difficulties, as credits cannot be removed from the banking system but only transferred within it (ibid.). The essential principle of double-entry bookkeeping was therefore to be applied also at international level, that is to say, between countries having different national currencies. To this end, Keynes proposed to create an international clearing union for 'the clearing and settlement of the ultimate outstanding balances between central banks' (ibid., p. 125). In order for the international payment to occur finally, Keynes imagined that an international clearing bank issued a supranational currency, which he named bancor. This means of final payment would be used for the settlement between central banks, 'private individuals, businesses and banks other than central banks, each continuing to use their own national currency as heretofore' (ibid., p. 168).

PETER DOCHERTY / SERGIO ROSSI

In this regard, Keynes aimed at making sure that trade deficit countries did not have to support alone the adjustment process to rebalance trade with their partner countries. The idea was that those countries accumulating positive bancor balances would spend them in the payment of imported goods from deficit countries, whose central banks would thereby be in a position to reimburse the credit lines they obtained earlier on from the international clearing bank. Beyond a given threshold, indeed, bancor balances were imposed a penalty if the relevant country did not spend them for the settlement of foreign trade (see Keynes, 1980, pp. 173–6).

The Keynes Plan was criticized because of its inflationary character: deficit countries were in a position to obtain a credit line (up to a certain amount) from the international clearing bank through a mere issuance of bancor, thereby confusing money and credit in the Bank's ledger. In fact, Keynes's analogy between domestic and international banking does not fully apply to his plan (see Rossi, 2007). As argued by Schumacher (1943, p. 15, emphasis in the original), '[t]he analogy with a national banking system, greatly emphasized in the Memorandum [Keynes's Plan], is justified only as far as the *creation* of bancor quotas is concerned. They indeed, like bank credit, are created out of nothing. But once bancor quotas have been allotted and fixed, the analogy becomes confusing.'

As a matter of fact, money is issued by banks as a means of final payment between non-bank agents in any payments system. It does not constitute an asset for any agent, who must earn an income to dispose of a purchasing power. By way of contrast, Keynes's bancor was meant to be issued as a reserve asset, and national central banks were allowed to use it for the final payment of international transactions. In other words, the bancor created by the international clearing bank would be a financial capital for the country that would dispose of it in order to pay for its net commercial imports. To be sure, as Keynes (1980, p. 176) explained, his plan allows each country 'a certain margin of resources and a certain interval of time within which to effect a balance in its economic relations with the rest of the world'. Keynes considered this margin as an initial reserve granted by the international clearing bank. In his own words, '[t]he margin of resources provided by the Clearing Union must be substantial .... This margin, though substantial, must be regarded solely as a reserve with which to meet temporary emergencies and to allow a breathing space' (ibid., p. 272).

In this regard, Keynes was obliged to imagine different measures, particularly a system of fines, to prevent the piling up of credit and debit balances without limit in the accounts that countries hold at the international clearing bank (ibid., pp. 173–5). These measures in fact depend on the good will of participating countries, whose behaviour may or may not abide by the system of regulations devised by Keynes. It is thus legitimate to ask whether these fines, and the other conditions stipulated by Keynes, are enough to exert pressure towards equilibrium in foreign trade. Be that as it may, there remains the logical conceptual issue of avoiding mixing up money and credit in order for an international payments system to work in an orderly way, thereby avoiding global imbalances (see Rossi, 2014).

SERGIO ROSSI

See also

Bretton Woods; International clearing union; International financial architecture; International monetary system; Money as a means of payment

References

Keynes, J.M. (1980), *The Collected Writings of John Maynard Keynes, vol. XXV, Activities 1940–1944. Shaping the Post-War World: The Clearing Union*, London and Basingstoke: Macmillan.

Rossi, S. (2007), 'The monetary-policy relevance of an international settlement institution: the Keynes plan 60 years later', in A. Giacomin and M.C. Marcuzzo (eds), *Money and Markets: A Doctrinal Approach*, London and New York: Routledge, pp. 96–114.

Rossi, S. (2014), 'A structural monetary reform to reduce global imbalances: Keynes's plan revisited to avert international payment deficits', in R. Bellofiore and G. Vertova (eds), *The Great Recession and the Contradictions of Contemporary Capitalism*, Cheltenham, UK, and Northampton, MA, USA: Edward Elgar, pp. 134–50.

Schumacher, E.F. (1943), 'The new currency plans', *Bulletin of the Oxford University Institute of Statistics*, **5** (supplement), 8–28.

Keynesian cross diagram

The Keynesian cross diagram (originally proposed by Samuelson, 1948) is a model relating national income (Y) and aggregate expenditures (AE). Its goal is to determine whether the economy is in equilibrium. It has become the starting point for economic analysis in introductory economics classes around the world and appears in virtually all undergraduate textbooks. It is meant as a simplification of the views of John Maynard Keynes (1936) in the opening chapters of *The General Theory of Employment, Interest and Money*.

The diagram contains two lines: (i) a 45-degree line that represents the equality in the goods market and the economy as a whole, and depicts any point ensuring the equilibrium condition $Y = AE$ (Mankiw, 2010, p. 27); and (ii) an AE curve, which is the sum of four main categories of expenditures, namely, private consumption (C), private investment (I), public expenditure (G), and – in an open economy – net exports (NX), which is the difference between exports (X) and imports (M). Owing to a marginal propensity to consume less than one, the slope of the AE curve is by definition and assumption less than one, and therefore less than the slope of the 45-degree line, thereby forcing it to intersect with the 45-degree line. As a result, point E in Figure 1 represents the equilibrium in the goods market for a given national economy.

This equilibrium, however, may not represent the general equilibrium of the economy at full employment. In fact, Keynes (1936, pp. 249–50) argues for the relatively rare occurrence of full employment (point E_{FE} in Figure 2).

The Keynesian cross diagram allows us to show non-optimal equilibria, namely, underemployment (point E_{UE} in Figure 2) and over-production (point E_{OP} in Figure 2) ones. According to Keynes (1936), the goal of the government should be to adjust its own expenditures (G) in order to push the economy closer to full-employment equilibrium. For instance, when the national economy is in an underemployment situation, the public expenditures' multiplier is higher than one, so a public investment of x money units shifts the AE curve upward, generating an increase of Y larger than x (Samuelson, 1948, pp. 265–7 and 276–7; see also Keynes, 1936, pp. 122–4), and moving the production activity to the full-employment level eventually.

Nevertheless, from a post-Keynesian point of view, the cross diagram as explained so far needs some revision, according to two fundamental insights of Keynes's theory. First, an identity exists between Y and the goods and services produced within a given period (Cencini, 2005, p. 68; see also Keynes, 1930/2011, p. 135; Lavoie, 2014, p. 188). Second, money has an endogenous nature (Rochon and Rossi, 2013; Lavoie, 2014, p. 186), and its issuance follows a double-entry bookkeeping principle (Davidson, 1989, pp. 550–1): money is 'credit driven and demand determined' (Moore, 1988, p. 373). Following this perspective, Y takes the form of deposits recorded in the liability side of banks' balance sheets and represents the total real output in a numerical (monetary) form (Schmitt, 1984/2021, p. 303).

Hence, AE cannot exceed Y, unless the banking system issues money for non-productive activities, namely, for an agent's expenditure (consumption or investment) exceeding the same agent's income. However, such a situation will turn, sooner or later, into a real-based income financing this (apparent) over-expenditure. In other words, the agent's over-expenditure is financed by someone else's under-expenditure (saving) within a given period (Schmitt, 1984/2021, pp. 85 and 89; Cencini, 2005, p. 84). Therefore, from a macroeconomic perspective, the AE level cannot be depicted by any point on the left of the 45-degree line.

In the same way, hoarding is meaningless in a monetary economy of production (Keynes, 1973/2013, p. 408), where the banking and financial systems work properly. Indeed, all agents' savings will be lent to someone else wishing to spend more than their own income allows (Cencini, 2005, p. 84). Therefore, any income formed within the economic system will be spent by their initial holders or by someone else, no matter if for consumption (households) or investment (firms) purposes. This is true even when we consider the general government sector: as a matter of fact, the income obtained through taxation or public indebtedness is either consumed or invested by the public sector. As a result, any point on the right of the 45-degree line should not be considered.

Therefore, in post-Keynesian analysis, the AE line is superimposed on the 45-degree line, which amounts to saying that the equilibrium condition $Y = AE$ is actually an identity ($Y \equiv AE$), despite Keynes being quite

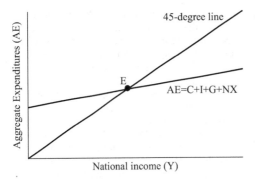

Source: Author's elaboration based on Samuelson (1948, p. 275).

Figure 1   The Keynesian cross diagram

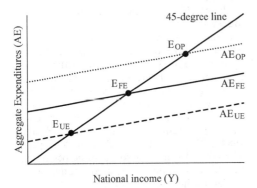

Source: Author's elaboration based on Samuelson (1948, p. 275).

Figure 2   The Keynesian cross diagram and the three equilibria

incongruous on this by explaining his own analysis in terms of 'equilibrium conditions' (see Keynes, 1930, Book III, Ch. 11, pp. 151–70). Now, an identity means an always-valid equality (that is, equilibrium). Does this statement make economic analyses and policies useless? The answer is no, because the necessary equality between AE and Y does not mean that the economy sets automatically at the full-employment level or that production has an overall positive impact on society, people, and/ or the planet. Therefore, the Keynesian cross diagram does not tell much about the goodness of economic activity: for instance, it does not show if the business cycle is upward or downward, or whether production is socially and/or ecologically sustainable or not.

A restatement of the Keynesian cross diagram is fundamental, especially considering its essential role in the IS–LM model (see Hicks, 1937; Mankiw, 2010), which is still the mainstream framework in macroeconomics. Far from the dominant equilibrium-perspective represented by any Walrasian general-equilibrium-based model, Keynes endeavoured to change macroeconomic analysis deeply, redefining it as the study of a monetary economy of production (Keynes, 1973/2013, p. 408). This is because money is endogenously issued by the banking system following a double-entry bookkeeping principle implying a necessary identity between income (formed and spent) and real output.

MAURIZIO SOLARI

See also

Aggregate demand; Endogenous money; Fiscal multiplier; Fiscal policy; Unemployment

References

Cencini, A. (2005), *Macroeconomic Foundations of Macroeconomics*, London and New York: Routledge.
Davidson, P. (1989), 'Patinkin's interpretation of Keynes and Keynesian cross', *History of Political Economy*, 21 (3), 549–53.
Hicks, J.R. (1937), 'Mr. Keynes and the "Classics": a suggested interpretation', *Econometrica*, 5 (2), 147–59.
Keynes, J.M. (1930/2011), *A Treatise on Money*, New York: Martino Publishing.
Keynes, J.M. (1936), *The General Theory of Employment, Interest and Money*, London: Macmillan.
Keynes, J.M. (1973/2013), *The Collected Writings of John Maynard Keynes, Vol. XIII. The General Theory and After: Part I, Preparation*, Cambridge, UK: Cambridge University Press.
Lavoie, M. (2014), *Post-Keynesian Economics: New Foundations*, Cheltenham, UK, and Northampton, MA, USA: Edward Elgar.
Mankiw, N.G. (2010), *Macroeconomics*, seventh edition, New York: Worth Publishers.
Moore, B.J. (1988), 'The endogenous money supply', *Journal of Post Keynesian Economics*, 10 (3), 372–85.
Rochon, L.-P. and S. Rossi (2013), 'Endogenous money: the evolutionary versus revolutionary views', *Review of Keynesian Economics*, 1 (2), 210–29.
Samuelson, P.A. (1948), *Economics: An Introductory Analysis*, New York: McGraw-Hill.
Schmitt, B. (1984/2021), *Inflation, Unemployment and Capital Malformations*, X. Bradley and A. Cencini (trans.), London and New York: Routledge.

Kuznets curve

Stemming from Simon Kuznets' (1955) exploration of the historical patterns of income inequality and growth of per capita gross domestic product in Germany, the United Kingdom and the north of the United States, the Kuznets curve, or the inverted-U hypothesis, describes an increase in income inequality both between the traditional rural sector and the modern industrial urban sector and within the latter, until this inequality reached a maximum, after which it declined.

The relationship between income inequality and economic growth has been one of the most contested issues in economics, revealing a pendulum between the prospects of equitable economic growth and acceptance of income inequality and growth trade-off (Kanbur, 1998). Kuznets himself warned first of the conflicting factors that shaped this relationship; second of the availability of adequate data; third of his country- and time-specific findings; and fourth of the necessity to investigate political aspects of social life that affected the relationship under investigation (Kuznets, 1955).

The literature on this subject matter has evolved on various paths. First, it has moved towards studying various directions of causality between the two variables. Second, it has progressed away from analysing the structural change of an economy during development and how this impacts on, or is caused by, income inequality, towards including additional explanatory factors. The mainstream political economy of both Harvard (see, for example, Alesina and Perotti, 1996) and MIT (see, for example, Acemoglou and Robinson, 2002) on international trade (see Frankel and Romer, 1999) has been particularly prolific. Yet, the effect monetary policy has on income inequality has been of interest for post-Keynesian economists (see Moore, 1989). Third, it has moved in waves after the publication of a new international data set of income inequality (Deininger and Squire, 1996) and after periods of sharp rises in inequality and poverty in both developed and developing countries. Fourth, the focus has been to look for regularities of the original inverted-U curve, which has stimulated at least two kinds of debate: one followed Kuznets' original warning about the quality of data (see Moll, 1992; Székely and Hilgert, 1999), and within this, there has been a proliferation of indexes and critiques of the widely used Gini coefficient (see Palma, 2011); the other has followed Amartya Sen's (1992) capability approach and reconceptualization of inequality, through the pivotal question of 'inequality of what?'

More recently, and within an economic and ethical debate, it is worth mentioning the much-debated work of Piketty (2013). Among its critics, Stiglitz (2013) explains how the accumulation of wealth has been due to the increase in the value of land and other rents.

Finally, this contentious relationship has also raised the question of the interpretation of Kuznets' seminal paper: Galbraith (2016) highlights that the general insight to be drawn from Kuznets' seminal paper is to expect the relationship between income inequality and economic growth to reflect the changing distribution of the population across both geographic areas and regions and countries.

The post-Keynesian tradition has tended to escape empirical findings contrary to or in acceptance of the inverted-U shape, and to be more preoccupied with the distribution of income across social classes (Kalecki, 1971) or with the distribution between wages and profits, depending on the saving propensity of capitalists and the rate of growth of the economy (Roncaglia, 2019), and, generally, with policies that could convey equity with efficiency.

DANIELA TAVASCI

See also

Growth; Income distribution; Inequality; Interest rates and income distribution; Monetary policy

References

Acemoglou, D. and J.A. Robinson (2002), 'The political economy of the Kuznets curve', *Review of Development Economics*, **6** (2), 183–203.
Alesina, A. and R. Perotti (1996), 'Income distribution, political instability, and investment', *European Economic Review*, **40** (6), 1203–28.
Deininger, K. and L. Squire (1996), 'A new data set for measuring income inequality', *World Bank Economic Review*, **10** (3), 565–91.
Frankel, J.A. and D.H. Romer (1999), 'Does trade cause growth?', *American Economic Review*, **89** (3), 379–99.
Galbraith, J.K. (2016), *What Everyone Needs to Know*, Oxford: Oxford University Press.

DANIELA TAVASCI

Kalecki, M. (1971), *Selected Essays on the Dynamics of the Capitalist Economy*, Cambridge, UK: Cambridge University Press.

Kanbur, R. (1998), 'Income distribution and development', *World Bank Working Paper*, No. 98–13.

Kuznets, S. (1955), 'Economic growth and income inequality', *American Economic Review*, **45** (1), 1–25.

Moll, T. (1992), 'Mickey Mouse numbers and inequality research in developing countries', *Journal of Development Studies*, **28** (4), 689–704.

Moore, B.J. (1989), 'The effects of monetary policy on income distribution', in P. Davidson and J. Kregel (eds), *Macroeconomic Problems and Policies of Income Distribution: Functional, Personal, International*, Aldershot, UK, and Brookfield, USA: Edward Elgar, pp. 18–41.

Palma, J.G. (2011), 'Homogeneous middles vs. heterogeneous tails, and the end of the "inverted-U": it's all about the share of the rich', *Development and Change*, **42** (1), 87–153.

Piketty, T. (2013), *Capital in the Twenty-First Century*, Cambridge, MA: Harvard University Press.

Roncaglia A. (2019), *L'età della disgregazione: storia del pensiero economico contemporaneo*, Bari: Editori Laterza.

Sen, A. (1992), *Inequality Re-Examined*, Cambridge, MA: Harvard University Press.

Stiglitz, J. (2013), *The Price of Inequality: How Today's Divided Society Endangers Our Future*, London: Penguin.

Székely, M. and M. Hilgert (1999), 'What's behind the inequality we measure: an investigation using Latin American data', *Inter-American Development Bank Working Paper*, No. 409.

Land rents

Land, which includes space and natural resources, literally provides the basis for all economic activity. Being a classical factor of production, neoclassical economists merged it with capital. Although the so-called 'capital controversies' raised awareness about these aggregation problems, post-Keynesian economists also tend to ignore the difference between land and capital (Martins, 2016).

Land differs from 'human-made' capital: land is basically fixed in supply; it can be neither accumulated nor depreciated. Land markets have effects on ecological, economic and social objectives. A substantial reduction of land sealing and fragmentation of landscape is necessary to preserve biodiversity, soil fertility and essential ecosystem services (European Union, 2013). However, this may increase social tensions especially on housing markets, as land is the bottleneck for a higher supply of affordable housing. Community interests in efficient use of the scarce resource of land and land-owner interests may conflict with each other.

Land ownership creates external effects that contribute substantially to inequality. Piketty (2014) blamed capital accumulation for leading to a concentration of wealth, causing social and economic instability. Rognlie (2015), however, finds that net capital share increases 'come entirely from the housing sector', and Knoll et al. (2017) attribute 80 per cent of rising housing costs to increases in land prices. Land values are determined primarily by 'location'. Location investments, however, depend much on both public and private investment in the surrounding area. These gains are privatized by the owner as a prime example of 'unearned income'. These 'land rents' are at odds with merit, equality and need as three major principles of justice (Richters and Siemoneit, 2021).

Attempts to improve justice and economic efficiency are based on the principle of fiscal equivalence, requiring that beneficiaries of increased land values should also bear the costs as taxpayers (Löhr, 2020). Land rents can finance the fixed costs of public expenditure (the so-called 'golden rule of local public finance', see Arnott and Stiglitz, 1979), creating fiscal space for local authorities to improve public goods.

An example is Singapore, holding more than 80 per cent of the land in public ownership. Income from long-term leasehold and public housing flats is a major source of income to finance their public infrastructure and social services (Purves, 2019).

An alternative is the introduction of land value taxes (LVT), popularized by Henry George (1881/2009). Local authorities can raise yearly taxes by multiplying a levy with a location-dependent price per square metre and the site area. This tax is paid on the value of the unimproved land, independent of buildings to avoid disincentives for investments, different to property taxes in most OECD countries (Blöchliger, 2015). LVT are difficult to pass on to tenants, because the supply and demand of rented land is unchanged by the tax. Diverting a part of the land income to the public sector reduces private investors' willingness to pay. Therefore, land prices fall until they offset the discounted tax costs, partly decapitalizing land.

DANIELA TAVASCI / DIRK LÖHR AND OLIVER RICHTERS

For land, there can be no supply response, which minimizes non-intended side effects and inefficiencies attributed to taxation.

LVT are primarily fiscal taxes generating public revenue, but with 'collateral benefits' for justice and sustainability: they ease housing markets, reduce land prices, and create pressure to use the scarce resource land more efficiently, which supports spatial and urban planning. If a land valuation register exists, LVT are easily implemented and administered.

Taxing land rents imposes costs on landowners, while the benefit is spread over today's population and future generations: it reduces inequality and enhances economic growth by putting the fiscal burden on the use of land and nature, and not on labour, investment or consumption (Harrison, 2016; Mattauch et al., 2018).

Dirk Löhr and Oliver Richters

See also

Capital theory controversies; Development; Ecological microeconomics; Fiscal policy; Inequality

References

Arnott, R.J. and J.E. Stiglitz (1979), 'Aggregate land rents, expenditure on public goods, and optimal city size', *Quarterly Journal of Economics*, **93** (4), 471–500.
Blöchliger, H. (2015), 'Reforming the tax on immovable property', *Organization for Economic Cooperation and Development Economics Department Working Paper*, No. 1205.
European Union (2013), 'The 7th Environment Action Programme to 2020', *Official Journal of the European Union*, L354/171.
George, H. (1881/2009), *Progress and Poverty*, Cambridge, UK: Cambridge University Press.
Harrison, F. (ed.) (2016), *Rent Unmasked: How to Save the Global Economy and Build a Sustainable Future*, London: Shepheard Walwyn.
Knoll, K., M. Schularick and T. Steger (2017), 'No price like home: global house prices, 1870–2012', *American Economic Review*, **107** (2), 331–53.
Löhr, D. (2020), 'Henry George: the public value of land', in F. Hertweck (ed.), *Architecture on Common Ground*, Zürich, CH: Lars Müller Publishers, pp. 50–60.
Martins, N.O. (2016), 'Political aspects of the capital controversies and capitalist crises', *Journal of Post Keynesian Economics*, **39** (4), 473–94.
Mattauch, L., J. Siegmeier, O. Edenhofer and F. Creutzig (2018), 'Financing public capital when rents are back: a macroeconomic Henry George theorem', *FinanzArchiv: Public Finance Analysis*, **74** (3), 340–60.
Piketty, T. (2014), *Capital in the Twenty-First Century*, Cambridge, MA: Harvard University Press.
Purves, A. (2019), 'Die Modelle Hongkong und Singapur – Staatliche Landverpachtung statt Verkauf', in B. Gerber and U. Kriese (eds), *Boden behalten, Stadt gestalten*, Zürich, CH: rüffer & rub, pp. 92–104.
Richters, O. and A. Siemoneit (2021), 'Making markets just: reciprocity violations as key intervention points', *Institut für zukunftsfähige Ökonomien Discussion Paper*, No. 7, available at https://hdl.handle.net/10419/235556 (last accessed 8 March 2021).
Rognlie, M. (2015), 'Deciphering the fall and rise in the net capital share: accumulation or scarcity?', *Brookings Papers on Economic Activity*, 1, 1–54.

Lender of last resort

According to Kindleberger (1978, p. 161), '[t]he lender of last resort stands ready to halt a run out of real and illiquid financial assets into money, by making more money available.' The emergence of a lender of last resort (LOLR) dates back to the eighteenth century, and one of the first written contributions on the subject was Thornton's *An Enquiry into the Nature and Effects of the Paper Credit of Great Britain* published in 1802, in which he suggested, in order to allay a panic, the Bank of England should lend freely to the money market on the basis of sound collateral (see Bordo, 2014).

Even if a central bank existed, it was often the fiscal authority that typically took on the LOLR role, with the Treasury providing liquidity through discounting of its own bills. In the United Kingdom, 'the Bank [of England] assumed the role of lender of last resort only gradually during the first half of the nineteenth century' (Kindleberger, 1978, p. 162). In the United States, prior to the creation of the Federal Reserve, '[b]anks became accustomed to looking to the Secretary of Treasury for help in an emergency' (p. 168). With the publication of Bagehot's *Lombard Street* in 1873, central banks begrudgingly accepted their role of LOLR.

Building on Thornton, Bagehot's rules for central bank action can be summarized as follows: making loans freely to all comers, on the basis of sound collateral, but at a penalty rate of interest. In practice, there are inherent ambiguities of who, when, and how much to intervene. Despite central banks periodically being accused of political motivations, they have, for the most part, adopted a strategy of bailing out large, systemically important financial institutions, leading to the concept of 'Too Big to Fail' (TBTF). Opponents of the TBTF doctrine raise the issue of moral hazard, which was one of the primary issues raised in the early nineteenth century debates over the LOLR. For example, most adherents to the Currency School believed that maintaining a constant money supply made the LOLR unnecessary, while others realized its use 'in cases of unforeseen necessity' (Kindleberger, 1978, p. 163). Most recently, when secretary of the US Treasury Henry Paulson decided not to bail out Lehman Brothers in order to 'teach the market a lesson', proponents of the moral hazard doctrine were rudely awakened to the 'unforeseen necessity' of LOLR actions.

Historically, implementation of the LOLR was performed through the discount window, with the only debate concerning the type of assets accepted as collateral. However, in 1929 the Federal Reserve Bank of New York expanded the use of open-market operations (OMOs) in excess of what was allowed by the board of governors in order to inject liquidity into a panicked market. While OMOs added another implement to the LOLR toolbox, its use by central bankers is also subject to the vagaries of when and to what extent it should be used. As Kindleberger (1978, p. 179) suggested, 'more is safer than less. The excess can be mopped up later. As for timing, it is an art. That says nothing – and everything.' Based on its response to the 2008 crisis, the US Federal Reserve certainly opted for the 'more is safer than less doctrine'.

Given the interconnectedness of global economies, there is also a need for an international LOLR. Despite the lack of a formal international LOLR, this role tends to reside with the central bank of the global hegemon and/or the country whose legal tender acts as the international reserve currency. For example, the Bank of England rescued Dutch banks in 1763, because 'British prosperity was intimately associated with Dutch' (Kindleberger, 1978, p. 183). More recently, the US Federal Reserve intervened by providing US dollar swap lines to Mexico during the so-called Tequila Crisis in 1994, and again to a number of central banks during the 2008 global financial crisis.

TED P. SCHMIDT

See also

Central banking; Currency School; Endogenous money; Monetary policy; Too-big-to-fail financial institutions

References

Bagehot, W. (1873), *Lombard Street: A Description of the Money Market*, New York: Scribner, Armstrong & Co.
Bordo, M.D. (2014), 'Rules for a lender of last resort: an historical perspective', *Journal of Economic Dynamics and Control*, **49** (C), 126–34.
Kindleberger, C.P. (1978), *Manias, Panics, and Crashes*, New York: Basic Books.

Lexicographic preferences

Given the set of alternatives $X = R_+^2$, $x \geq y$ is defined to be the lexicographic preference relation if either $x_1 > y_1$ or $x_1 = y_1$ and $x_2 \geq y_2$. The expression imitates the organization of dictionaries. In vector x, the goods are ordered according to their absolute importance. The very first of the goods in the list carries the utmost priority in consumption. Hence any bundle x with $x_1 > y_1$ will be strictly preferred over bundle y, regardless of the quantities of other goods. In other words, a consumption bundle, say, including some food and no shirts will be preferred to another bundle with no food and thousands of shirts.

Although lexicographic preferences are complete, transitive, strictly convex, strictly monotonic (hence, locally non-satiated), and homothetic, since they are not continuous the indifference sets are singletons. This means that there are no two distinct bundles for which the individual is indifferent (Mas-Colell et al., 1995). This immediately implies that lexicographic preferences cannot be represented by a continuous utility function. This is the main reason why mainstream economists rule out lexicographic preferences in their research programme. Yet, in practice, for instance in market studies, the concepts of indifference and continuity are of no relevance at all.

In post-Keynesian theory of consumer choice, lexicographic preferences are considered

TED P. SCHMIDT / ANIL ABA

to be superior to Cobb–Douglas preferences. Georgescu-Roegen (1954) argues that individuals have a hierarchy of needs and wants, and that this hierarchical ordering cannot be reduced to continuous substitution between any two goods. Roy (2005, p. 50), in similar fashion, argues that it is 'possible to classify all goods and services in groups and to state that all consumers do not access a group of a given level until they have fully satisfied the needs that the groups at lower levels are meant to fulfil'. In this regard, for a minimum-wage worker the marginal rate of substitution between foodstuff and pearl necklace would be meaningless. This is because many goods, services, needs, wants, and attributes of products are considered to be incommensurable and/or incomparable. Further, as Ariely (2008) shows, we do try to compare the goods that are somewhat easily comparable, such as jobs to jobs, cereals to cereals, or butter to margarine, but we are usually stumped when it comes to comparing two very different products, such as butter and earphones.

ANIL ABA

See also

Behavioural economics; Consumer behaviour; Consumer choice; Microfoundations; Neoclassical economics

References

Ariely, D. (2008), *Predictably Irrational*, New York: Harper Collins.
Georgescu-Roegen, N. (1954), 'Choice, expectations and measurability', *Quarterly Journal of Economics*, **68** (4), 503–34.
Mas-Colell, A., M.D. Whinston and J.R. Green (1995), *Microeconomic Theory, Vol. 1*, Oxford and New York: Oxford University Press.
Roy, R. (2005), 'The hierarchy of needs and the concept of groups in consumer choice theory [1943]', *History of Economics Review*, **42** (1), 50–56.

Limits to substitution revisited: energy

Environmental economists have criticized approaches such as post-Keynesian stock–flow consistent (SFC) models, but also new-Keynesian dynamic stochastic general equilibrium models on the grounds that they focus on the circular flow of exchange value (that is, money), rather than on the physical throughput of natural resources from which all goods and services are ultimately derived. This disregards the association between the growth of wealth and the expansion of energy services over the last several centuries (see Kronenberg, 2010, and Berg et al., 2015, and references therein). Most economists interpret energy and material services as enhanced labour or capital productivity (Kümmel, 2011) associated with technological progress, which is considered as an amorphous force that increases productive power without limit (Holt et al., 2009, p. 206).

If energy is integrated into neoclassical growth models, the responsiveness of output to a marginal change of one production factor in the neoclassical approach is given by its output elasticity, that is, the point elasticity of output with respect to a production factor. The neoclassical theory of distribution assumes that, in equilibrium, this should be identical to the cost share of the production factor (factor cost theorem), which amounts to roughly 5 per cent. This derivation has been criticized by Keynesian authors in the Cambridge 'capital controversies', and this criticism of substitutional production functions is further strengthened on the ground that they assume that production can be sustained with hardly any material input. Cost share and output elasticity are not equal once a third factor is added that is not independent of the other two (Ayres and Warr, 2005, p. 16). This is the case here, since 'capital in the absence of energy is functionally inert' (Kümmel, 2011, p. 195), and technical engineering constraints limit substitution. Empirical analyses show that the output elasticity of energy is higher than its cost share, and energy accounts for most of the economic growth usually attributed to technological progress (Kümmel, 2011, pp. 195–221).

Similar to post-Keynesian authors, ecological economists have tended to use Leontief production functions, or substitutional production functions with further technological restrictions (Kümmel, 2011). Referring to consumption theory, both fields have emphasized similar models of consumer behaviour that include procedural rationality, satiable needs or the separability of needs. These similarities and their joint emphasis on cumulative causation (path dependency), irreversibility of historical time and fundamental 'Knightian' uncertainty lead to the conclusion that post-Keynesian economics and ecological economics share substantial common ground, and are ripe for a synthesis (see Mearman, 2005; Lavoie, 2006; Holt et al., 2009; Kronenberg, 2010).

With this aim, a substantive body in 'ecological macroeconomics' has evolved (Hardt and O'Neill, 2017; Saes and Romeiro, 2019). This includes SFC input–output models based on ideas by Klein (2003) that can be extended with environmental indicators (Berg et al., 2015), demand-driven models with ecological instabilities (Barth and Richters, 2019) or the flow-fund model by Dafermos et al. (2017). They include not only the monetary balance sheets and transaction matrices to guarantee monetary stock–flow consistency as 'fundamental law of macroeconomics analogous to the principle of conservation of energy in physics' (Godley and Cripps, 1983, p. 18), but also exactly those natural 'first laws', yielding additional constraints for energy and mass conservation. Post-Keynesian environmental growth models (see Fontana and Sawyer, 2016) allow pressing problems to be studied, such as climate change and the interconnections and interdependence of the economic, biophysical and social worlds.

OLIVER RICHTERS

See also

Capital theory controversies; Ecological macroeconomics; Investment theory – ecological; Land rents; Technological change

References

Ayres, R.U. and B. Warr (2005), 'Accounting for growth: the role of physical work', *Structural Change and Economic Dynamics*, **16** (2), 181–209.

Barth, J. and O. Richters (2019), 'Demand driven ecological collapse: a stock-flow fund-service model of money, energy and ecological scale', in S. Decker, W. Elsner and S. Flechtner (eds), *Principles and Pluralist Approaches in Teaching Economics: Towards a Transformative Science*, London and New York: Routledge, pp. 169–90.

Berg, M., B. Hartley and O. Richters (2015), 'A stock–flow consistent input–output model with applications to energy price shocks, interest rates, and heat emissions', *New Journal of Physics*, **17** (1), available online at https://iopscience.iop.org/article/10.1088/1367-2630/17/1/015011/meta (last accessed 16 March 2021).

Dafermos, Y., M. Nikolaidi and G. Galanis (2017), 'A stock-flow-fund ecological macroeconomic model', *Ecological Economics*, **131**, 191–207.

Fontana, G. and M. Sawyer (2016), 'Towards post-Keynesian ecological macroeconomics', *Ecological Economics*, **121**, 186–95.

Godley, W. and F. Cripps (1983), *Macroeconomics*, Oxford: Oxford University Press.

Hardt, L. and D.W. O'Neill (2017), 'Ecological macroeconomic models: assessing current developments', *Ecological Economics*, **134**, 198–211.

Holt, R., S. Pressman and C. Spash (2009), *Post Keynesian and Ecological Economics*, Cheltenham, UK, and Northampton, MA, USA: Edward Elgar.

Klein, L. (2003), 'Some potential linkages for input-output analysis with flow-of-funds', *Economic Systems Research*, **15** (3), 269–77.

Kronenberg, T. (2010), 'Finding common ground between ecological economics and post-Keynesian economics', *Ecological Economics*, **69** (7), 1488–94.

Kümmel, R. (2011), *The Second Law of Economics: Energy, Entropy, and the Origins of Wealth*, New York: Springer.

Lavoie, M. (2006), 'Do heterodox theories have anything in common? A Post-Keynesian point of view', *European Journal of Economics and Economic Policies: Intervention*, **3** (1), 87–112.

Mearman, A. (2005), 'Why have post-Keynesians had (relatively) little to say on the economics of the environment?', *International Journal of Environment, Workplace and Employment*, **1** (2), 131–53.

Saes, B.M. and A.R. Romeiro (2019), 'Ecological macroeconomics: a methodological review', *Economia e Sociedade*, **28** (2), 365–92.

Liquidity preference

Keynes (1936) referred to the amount of savings an individual wanted to hold in money as his or her liquidity preference. The limitation of the classical interest rate theory, which viewed interest as the reward on savings, was that it did not explicitly consider the form in which savings were held. Since savings held in cash do not earn interest, interest is not the reward for savings per se. For Keynes, the interest rate was the reward for parting with liquidity: 'what can be obtained for parting with control over the money in exchange for a debt for a stated period of time' (Keynes, 1936, p. 150).

Keynes identified three motives for liquidity preference: the transactions motive, the precautionary motive, and the speculative motive. The transactions motive is the holding of money to finance daily purchases of goods and services. However, it did not explain why people hold money as a store of wealth, since money earns little or no interest. The necessary condition that made people hold some wealth as money was the uncertainty about future interest rates. This gave rise to the precautionary motive, under which people hold some wealth as cash to safeguard against income losses due to adverse movements in future interest rates, meet expenditures arising from unexpected emergencies, and honour liabilities that are fixed in money value.

The uncertainty about future interest rates also gave rise to the speculative motive, under which individuals hold some cash to profit from knowing better than the market what the future interest rate will be. An individual who expects future interest rates to be higher than the general market opinion would want to hold more wealth as cash in the present, while someone who expects future interest rates to be lower than the general opinion would hold less cash in the present.

Keynes asserted that the transactions and precautionary motives mainly depend on money income, while the speculative motive mainly depends on the divergence of the actual market interest rate from what is perceived to be a 'safe' level in the general public opinion. The perceived safe level depends on the state of expectations. Given expectations, each decrease in the interest rate reduces the actual rate relative to the perceived safe rate and lowers earnings from illiquid financial assets. This increases the speculative demand for money.

The liquidity preference concept is central to Keynes's theory of the interest rate. Interest was 'the "price" which equilibrates the desire to hold wealth in the form of cash with the available quantity of cash' (Keynes, 1936, p. 150). The liquidity preference theory implies that by increasing money supply and lowering the interest rate, monetary authorities can potentially stimulate investment and employment. However, there may be scenarios where increases in money supply may not have a significant impact on the interest rate and economic activity. If the liquidity preference of individuals is increasing faster than money supply, expanding the latter would not lower the interest rate. Additionally, if the interest rate is already at a low level, most individuals would prefer to hold all of their wealth in cash and further changes in money supply will have a negligible effect on the interest rate.

Keynes emphasized that maintaining a particular interest rate to achieve full employment would be aided by an approach under which central banks were willing to buy and sell government bonds of different maturities, and governments financed spending through short-term and long-term debt. This could help to keep interest rates lower by allowing the public to hold a more balanced wealth portfolio that catered to the desire to hold more liquid assets for precautionary purposes (Tily, 2006).

Keynes also used liquidity preference to show that when an economy is below full employment, the interest rate may not fall sufficiently to generate a level of effective demand consistent with full employment (Garegnani, 1983). Increased uncertainty may mean that an increase in money supply is accompanied by an increase in liquidity preference, resulting in either a smaller fall, or even an increase, in the interest rate. Combined with uncertainty about future profitability, investment spending would not increase adequately.

Liquidity preference has contemporary relevance to understanding the limitations of relying on global financial markets to access liquidity for pursuing domestic objectives of full employment. In a world of currency hegemony, the interest rate set by the central bank of the country with currency hegemony serves as the anchor (or safe) rate. While other countries can potentially set their interest rates at levels that deviate from this rate, there is no guarantee that they would have adequate access to liquidity at these rates. This would depend on the whims of international financial players in terms of the interest rates that they are willing to accept on assets denominated in the currencies of these countries (Bibow, 2019).

SURANJANA NABAR-BHADURI

See also

Currency hierarchy; Effective demand; Interest rates and investment; Monetary policy; Uncertainty

References

Bibow, J. (2019), 'Evolving international monetary and financial architecture and the development challenge: a liquidity preference theoretical perspective', *Levy Economics Institute Working Paper*, No. 935.

Garegnani, P. (1983), 'Two routes to effective demand: comment on Kregel', in J.A. Kregel (ed.), *Distribution, Effective Demand and International Economic Relations*, Basingstoke, UK, and New York: Macmillan, pp. 69–80.

Keynes, J.M. (1936), *The General Theory of Employment, Interest and Money*, London: Macmillan.

Tily, G. (2006), 'Keynes's theory of liquidity preference and his debt management and monetary policies', *Cambridge Journal of Economics*, **30** (5), 657–70.

Mark-up pricing

In post-Keynesian economics, mark-up pricing has two different meanings. First, it is a general concept related to price setting based on costs. Prices are not determined by a market-clearing mechanism destined to equilibrate supply and demand of commodities, but are instead set by price-making firms by adding a profit margin to a given measure of costs, such as unit labour costs. As such, mark-up pricing is sometimes employed as synonymous with cost-plus/cost-based pricing (this is, however, not the sense of mark-up pricing that will be examined below).

Second, mark-up pricing is a specific formula of cost-plus pricing, according to which the price of products is set by adding a gross profit margin to direct/prime/variable unit costs. This profit margin is then intended to cover overhead costs and generate a net profit. Mark-up pricing is considered the simplest way for businesses to set prices. Other procedures include full-cost/normal-cost pricing, consisting of adding a net profit margin to a measure of unit costs that incorporates direct/variable as well as overheads/fixed costs and which is computed for a 'normal' level of output and target-return pricing, in which the net profit margin added to unit cost is calculated so as to yield a targeted level of profit upon the value of capital assets of the firm, when actual output corresponds to its normal level.

The concept of mark-up pricing was originally developed in the writings of Michal Kalecki, where he described capitalist economies as composed of firms acting in imperfectly competitive markets, that is, having some degree of monopoly, and thus the ability to set prices higher than marginal cost. Lee (1998) asserted that mark-up pricing is very widespread in post-Keynesian models, although this might not be the most common practice among businesses in the real world. Firms may indeed prefer more sophisticated procedures like full-cost pricing or target-return pricing.

With mark-up pricing, the price of commodities is composed of two items: unit costs and a profit margin. Regarding the first component, there are three options to define unit costs – unit variable cost, unit prime cost, or unit direct cost – whose differences are explored by Lavoie (2014, Ch. 3). Although different, these measures of cost can be used in mark-up pricing, since they all have in common to exclude overhead costs. Second, what is the precise size of the gross profit margin? In post-Keynesian economics, several explanations of the size of the mark-up coexist. The first explanation, which is also put forward by Kalecki (at least in the first part of his career), links the mark-up to the degree of imperfect competition, or what Kalecki (1940, p. 91) calls 'the state of market imperfection', according to which increased competition forces firms to reduce prices and hence profit margins. This theory also refers to the work on imperfect competition by Joan Robinson (1933), who examined market structures that depart from perfect competition and their implications for prices and profit margins.

A second explanation emerged later, especially thanks to the writings of Eichner (1973), Wood (1975), and Harcourt and Kenyon (1976). In that view, mark-ups are the result of two opposite forces: a competitive force that drives mark-ups downward in order to reduce prices and gain customers, and an 'internal financing' force that drives mark-ups upwards in order to generate enough internal funds to finance the investment expenses needed to ensure the growth of the firm. The mark-up is thus the result of a process of sales growth maximizing under the constraint of internal financing of investment. A third explanation related to post-Keynesian economics is the Sraffian explanation: mark-ups are determined by the rate of interest of the central bank. Put simply, higher policy rates of interest represent higher costs for businesses, and these costs have to be incorporated into the profit margin (see Lavoie, 2014).

A very important implication of mark-up pricing in post-Keynesian economics is that it accounts for a stylized fact like price rigidity (prices that do not respond or respond slowly to short-term demand variations). With mark-up pricing, since prices depend on unit costs and profit margins, they tend to be stable (instead of sticky) as long as costs remain stable, independently of short-term variations in demand (see Melmiès, 2012).

JORDAN MELMIÈS AND
FLORIAN BOTTE

See also

Monopoly power; Post-Keynesian economics – a big tent?; Pricing; *Selected Essays on the Dynamics of Capitalist Economy*; Target-return pricing

References

Eichner, A.S. (1973), 'A theory of the determination of the mark-up under oligopoly', *Economic Journal*, **83** (332), 1184–200.
Harcourt, G.C. and P. Kenyon (1976), 'Pricing and the investment decision', *Kyklos*, **29** (3), 449–77.
Kalecki, M. (1940), 'The supply curve of an industry under imperfect competition', *Review of Economic Studies*, **7** (2), 91–112.
Lavoie, M. (2014), *Post-Keynesian Economics: New Foundations*, Cheltenham, UK, and Northampton, MA, USA: Edward Elgar.
Lee, F.S. (1998), *Post Keynesian Price Theory*, Cambridge, UK: Cambridge University Press.
Melmiès, J. (2012), 'Price rigidity', in J. King (ed.), *The Elgar Companion to Post Keynesian Economics*, second edition, Cheltenham, UK, and Northampton, MA, USA: Edward Elgar, pp. 452–6.
Robinson, J. (1933), *The Economics of Imperfect Competition*, London: Macmillan.
Wood, A. (1975), *A Theory of Profits*, Cambridge, UK: Cambridge University Press.

Maturity and Stagnation in American Capitalism

First published in 1952, Josef Steindl's *Maturity and Stagnation in American Capitalism* is an impressive intellectual effort. It not only bears the influence of Kalecki on its author, but also reminds one of Kalecki's books in its combination of detailed examination of data with conceptual (and algebraic) analysis. In comparison with the latter's work, however, Steindl's is more detailed in the discussion of data, in the comments on previous literature and in the attempt to draw the implications of his analysis for the historical tendencies of American capitalism. He claimed that the theoretical basis on which he built his analysis was 'Kalecki's economic dynamics', with one main modification: for Steindl the degree of capacity utilization is one of the main determinants of firms' actions, whereas for Kalecki 'utilization is a purely passive variable' (Steindl, 1952/1976, pp. xiii–xiv).

From a theoretical standpoint, the main contribution of the eight chapters that comprise the first part of the book is the differentiation between the pattern of competition in industries with plenty of small producers and in those where entry is difficult, that is, in competitive and in oligopolistic industries. In the first case, an eventual decline in utilization brought about by, for instance, a cyclical contraction unleashes a competitive struggle in which the high-cost firms are eliminated and the utilization is brought back to its desired level. Such adjustment of utilization is accompanied by a parallel adjustment of capital accumulation, given that the latter is influenced by the former. Steindl (1952/1976, p. 53) argues that this adjustment process is 'considerably impaired' in oligopolistic industries as, in these cases, the significant size of the high-cost firms makes their elimination in the competitive struggle more difficult. As a consequence, low utilization and high profit margins interact with accumulation in a cumulative manner, leading to stagnation. The connection suggested by Steindl between changes in the pattern of competition and their impact on accumulation of capital required a sophisticated effort to relate macroeconomic dynamics to microeconomic decisions, with which he opened the second part of the book. Then, he used this conceptual framework to offer an interpretation of the long-run decline of capital accumulation in the United States based on the tendency towards the concentration of industry.

There is no better indication of the relevance of *Maturity and Stagnation in American Capitalism* than the fact that it was the starting point of two independent intellectual enterprises. The first of them was the Marxian theory of monopoly capital, inaugurated by the book published by Baran and Sweezy in 1966. Their argument was that the monopoly stage of capitalism entailed a thorough revision of

Marxian economic theory and they based the economic theory they claimed relevant to the case of monopoly capital on Steindl's examination of the relations between concentration of industry, profit margins and investment decisions. In their book, they write that 'anyone familiar with the work of Kalecki and Steindl will readily recognize that the authors of the present work owe a great deal to them' (Baran and Sweezy, 1966, p. 56).

The second intellectual enterprise that stemmed from Steindl's book was the Kaleckian growth and distribution models (Lavoie, 2014, Chs 5–7). In the early 1980s, several authors attempted to formulate simple mathematical models connecting functional distribution of income and aggregate demand (Rowthorn, 1982; Dutt, 1984; Taylor, 1985). While much of the framework came from Kalecki, a crucial element of such models was an investment function that included the degree of capacity utilization and that was explicitly inspired by the empirical and conceptual analysis presented in *Maturity and Stagnation in American Capitalism*. These early models derived, following Steindl, a negative relation between the profit share of income and aggregate demand. However, this result was challenged a few years later by works that showed that demand could be either wage-led or profit-led (Blecker, 1989; Bhaduri and Marglin, 1990; Marglin and Bhaduri, 1990). A significant part of current post-Keynesian macroeconomics still refers to these concepts and formulations, making Steindl's contribution unavoidable after more than six decades.

FERNANDO RUGITSKY

See also

Capacity utilization; Capitalism; Growth – wage-led vs profit-led; Income distribution; Monopoly Capital

References

Baran, P. and P. Sweezy (1966), *Monopoly Capital: An Essay on the American Economic and Social Order*, New York: Monthly Review Press.

Bhaduri, A. and S. Marglin (1990), 'Unemployment and the real wage: the economic basis of contesting political ideologies', *Cambridge Journal of Economics*, **14** (4), 375–93.

Blecker, R. (1989), 'International competition, income distribution and economic growth', *Cambridge Journal of Economics*, **13** (3), 395–412.

Dutt, A. (1984), 'Stagnation, income distribution and monopoly power', *Cambridge Journal of Economics*, **8** (1), 25–40.

Lavoie, M. (2014), *Post-Keynesian Economics: New Foundations*, Cheltenham, UK, and Northampton, MA, USA: Edward Elgar.

Marglin, S. and A. Bhaduri (1990), 'Profit squeeze and Keynesian theory,' in S. Marglin and J. Schor (eds), *The Golden Age of Capitalism: Reinterpreting the Postwar Experience*, Oxford: Oxford University Press, pp. 153–86.

Rowthorn, R. (1982), 'Demand, real wages and economic growth', *Studi Economici*, **18** (1), 3–54.

Steindl, J. (1952/1976), *Maturity and Stagnation in American Capitalism*, New York: Monthly Review Press.

Taylor, L. (1985), 'A stagnationist model of economic growth', *Cambridge Journal of Economics*, **9** (4), 383–403.

Methodology

Following Eichner and Kregel's (1975) mapping-out of post-Keynesian economics as a new paradigm, it became the norm to consider defining post-Keynesian economics in terms of its methodological approach. This was evident in Dow's (1985) comparison of post-Keynesian methodology with that of other schools of thought, Hamouda and Harcourt's (1988) account of the multiple influences on and strands in post-Keynesian thought, Lavoie's (1992) exposition of the methodological foundations of his synthetic account of post-Keynesian economics, Arestis et al.'s (1999) exposition of the coherence of post-Keynesian methodology, and Dow's (1990, 2001, 2013) further accounts of that methodology.

The post-Keynesian methodological approach derives from a realist concern that methodology be designed to address the nature of the socio-economic system rather than internal disciplinary considerations. It is grounded in a particular understanding of reality (ontology) as a (partially structured) open system where components and structures evolve. From this follows an epistemology, based on Keynes (1921), which seeks knowledge in spite of the fundamental uncertainty inevitably associated with an open system. This uncertainty applies to economic actors, fostering behavioural conventions and institutional evolution designed to mitigate uncertainty. But it also applies to economists. Since no one method (or indeed any combination of methods) can demonstrate truth with respect to an open system, a pluralist methodology is required. Multiple strands of incommensurate reasoning are combined by means of context-informed judgement.

Other approaches outside of the mainstream also have an open-system ontology, which has led to attempts to downplay differences between non-mainstream schools of thought. But this attitude risks creating a duality that fits with the dualism of the mainstream approach and also risks encouraging a mainstream-like epistemology whereby one approach is seen as absolutely better than the other without need for debate. Openness/closure is not a duality since there are multiple possibilities for openness by which different non-mainstream schools of thought may be identified methodologically (Chick and Dow, 2005).

Post-Keynesianism differs from other non-mainstream approaches by an ontology that is a particular blend of agency and structure, both conditioned by fundamental uncertainty, and focusing on problems of unemployment, growth and income distribution, now extending to encompass climate change and gender, for example. The range of methods used to address these problems includes mathematical models. But it is crucial to the approach that these models feed into a broader analysis in combination with other methods, all conditioned by the evolving nature of the particular context being addressed (Kregel, 1976; Harcourt, 1995).

Since this open-system epistemology means that the validity of post-Keynesian analysis cannot be proved absolutely, it is up to post-Keynesian economists to persuade. This requires successful communication. Yet it is in the nature of different methodological approaches to be incommensurate, not least in the meaning of concepts and the use of language, but also in what is regarded as a good argument. Thus, for example, post-Keynesian economists mean something very different from mainstream economists by 'equilibrium', 'rationality' and 'uncertainty', while what is regarded as coherent depends on the type of logic employed – classical or human. The common subject matter of the economy, even if understood differently, does provide a common basis for communication. But beyond that there needs to be some mutual understanding of methodological differences if there is to be much scope for persuasion. Further, given the long-standing tradition of (post-)Keynesian ideas being transformed into something different when absorbed into the mainstream framework, an effective articulation of the methodological basis for, and thus meaning and significance of, post-Keynesian ideas is all the more crucial.

SHEILA DOW

See also

Critical realism; Income distribution; Post-Keynesian economics – a big tent?; *The General Theory of Employment, Interest and Money*; Uncertainty

References

Arestis, P., S. Dunn and M. Sawyer (1999), 'On the coherence of Post-Keynesian economics: a comment on Walters and Young', *Scottish Journal of Political Economy*, **46** (3), 339–45.

Chick, V. and S.C. Dow (2005), 'The meaning of open systems', *Journal of Economic Methodology*, **12** (3), 363–81. Reprinted in S.C. Dow, *Foundations for New Economic Thinking*, London: Palgrave Macmillan, 2012, pp. 178–96.

Dow, S.C. (1985), *Macroeconomic Thought: A Methodological Approach*, Oxford: Blackwell.

Dow, S. (1990), 'Post Keynesianism as political economy: a methodological discussion', *Review of Political Economy*, **2** (3), 345–58.

Dow, S. (2001), 'Post Keynesian methodology', in R. Holt and S. Pressman (eds), *A New Guide to Post Keynesian Economics*, London and New York: Routledge, pp. 11–20.

Dow, S. (2013), 'Methodology and Post-Keynesian economics', in G.C. Harcourt and P. Kriesler (eds), *Handbook of Post-Keynesian Economics. Volume 2: Critiques and Methodology*, Oxford: Oxford University Press, pp. 80–99.

Eichner, A.S. and J.A. Kregel (1975), 'An essay on Post-Keynesian theory: a new paradigm in economics', *Journal of Economic Literature*, **13** (4), 1293–314.

Hamouda, O. and G.C. Harcourt (1988), 'Post-Keynesianism: from criticism to coherence?', *Bulletin of Economic Research*, **40** (1), 1–33. Reprinted in J. Pheby (ed.), *New Directions in Post Keynesian Economics*, Aldershot, UK, and Brookfield, WI, USA: Edward Elgar, 1989, pp. 1–34.

Harcourt, G.C. (1995), 'On mathematics and economics', in *Capitalism, Socialism and Post-Keynesianism: Selected Essays of G.C. Harcourt*, Cheltenham, UK, and Northampton, MA, USA: Edward Elgar, pp. 201–17.

Keynes, J.M. (1921), *A Treatise on Probability*, London: Macmillan.

Kregel, J.A. (1976), 'Economic methodology in the face of uncertainty: the modelling methods of Keynes and the Post-Keynesians', *Economic Journal*, **86** (342), 209–25.

Lavoie, M. (1992), *Foundations of Post-Keynesian Economic Analysis*, Cheltenham, UK, and Northampton, MA, USA: Edward Elgar.

Microfoundations

The mainstream dogma that we must provide microfoundations for macroeconomics involves reducing macroeconomics to microeconomics and doing away with what Keynes described as the theory of output and employment as a whole (see King, 2012). If the microfoundations dogma is accepted, macroeconomics becomes nothing more than an application of microeconomic theory. The dogma also carries some very dangerous implications for macroeconomic policy, since it has often been used to justify fiscal austerity and wage cuts. Post-Keynesian economists maintain that these policy conclusions are quite wrong. A government is not a household, and the rules that quite rightly apply to the finances of individuals cannot be applied to public finance without causing serious macroeconomic damage. Further, the level of employment as a whole is determined in the product market, not in the labour market: it depends notably on the level of effective demand, which is a macroeconomic variable.

Not surprisingly, there is a strong political element in all these arguments. 'Sound finance' as well as price and wage 'flexibility' (downwards) are defended by neoliberal macroeconomists, who reject the principle of effective demand in the course of their critique of the 'traditional ad hoc Keynesian theorizing'. The upshot is an insistence on the use of models with RARE microfoundations: that is to say, models that begin by assuming the existence of representative agents with rational expectations (Ljungkvist and Sargent, 2004). Post-Keynesian economists reject both: the representative agent, which denies difference between individuals and is therefore not really microeconomics at all, and rational expectations, which rules out any serious consideration of uncertainty.

Four arguments have been used to justify the microfoundations metaphor. First, microeconomics is more basic than macroeconomics, so that in order to be persuasive, sound, reliable and robust, macroeconomics must make explicit reference to microeconomics. Second, the economy is made up of individuals, who must therefore be the starting point for any analysis of the ways in which they interact. Third, microeconomic models have been used successfully to deal with all manner of social and political questions, like voting behaviour, crime, discrimination and the family, so they should be applied also to macroeconomics. Fourth, micro-reduction has succeeded in the natural sciences, most obviously in biology with the triumph of modern genetics, and the principle should therefore be extended to economics. Richard Dawkins is sometimes cited in support of this analogy (see Dawkins, 1996).

None of these arguments is very convincing. Nothing interesting seems to follow from the statement that microeconomics is 'more basic' than macroeconomics. As for the second argument, this involves a rather elementary confusion between ontological reduction and explanatory reduction. To say that A (the economy) is made up of Bs (individual human beings) is to say something about ontology – what exists. It is rather obviously true. But it does not follow from this that A can and must be explained in terms of statements about Bs, and only in terms of statements about Bs.

The third argument relies on the extent to which mainstream microeconomic models and econometric techniques have been applied to problems that were previously the preserve of political scientists, sociologists and anthropologists. In fact, there is not much evidence to show that the 'economics imperialism' project has really succeeded, so that it does not provide a strong argument for the application of micro-reduction to macroeconomics.

Finally, there is the argument from biology. Many philosophers of science agree with Dawkins, but many do not, instead emphasizing the complexity of the relationship between an organism and its environment. Just as there is no organism without an environment, so there is no environment without an organism. Neither organism nor environment is a closed system; each is open to the other (Rose, 2005).

This indicates two insuperable difficulties with micro-reduction: downward causation and the fallacy of composition. In both economics and biology, causation runs downwards from the larger to the smaller units, and not just upwards from the smaller to the larger. The fallacy of composition arises when a statement that is true of any individual considered separately is false when applied to them all taken together. In post-Keynesian macroeconomics there are several well-known cases in which a fallacy of composition can be identified, including the paradox of thrift, the paradox of liquidity and the (Kaleckian) paradox of costs. In each case something that benefits each individual capitalist, considered separately (higher saving, more liquidity, lower wages) may well disadvantage the capitalist class as a whole.

All this raises a more general question concerning the use of metaphors in economics. The potential significance of downward causation has led some post-Keynesian economists to argue that we need macrofoundations for microeconomics. However, there is something perverse about the idea of 'foundations' that exist at a higher level than the edifice that they are supposed to be the foundations of, whether the edifice is physical or intellectual in nature. Other post-Keynesian economists claim that they are indeed providing microfoundations for macroeconomics; it is just that theirs are very different from, and much better than, those supplied by the mainstream. By adopting the mainstream's misleading metaphor, however, these post-Keynesian economists are muddying these already murky waters. Once again, this does not deny the relevance of microeconomics to macroeconomics (or for that matter vice versa), simply that the two bodies of knowledge exist side by side, neither being the foundation of the other. Both micro- and macro-foundational metaphors are best avoided.

JOHN E. KING

See also

Complex systems; Fallacy of composition; Functional finance; Paradox of costs; Paradox of thrift

References

Dawkins, R. (1996), *The Blind Watchmaker*, Harmondsworth: Penguin.
King, J.E. (2012), *The Microfoundations Delusion: Metaphor and Dogma in the History of Macroeconomics*, Cheltenham, UK, and Northampton, MA, USA: Edward Elgar.
Ljungkvist, L. and T.J. Sargent (2004), *Recursive Macroeconomic Theory*, second edition, Cambridge, MA: MIT Press.
Rose, S. (2005), *Lifelines: Life beyond the Gene*, second edition, London: Vintage.

Military Keynesianism

The expression 'military Keynesianism' seems to have originated with the American sociologist David Riesman in 1958, but the best-known statement of the underlying principles was made fifteen years earlier by the Polish economist Michał Kalecki, then in exile in Britain. Considering the prospects for full employment after the end of the Second World War, Kalecki noted that there were good reasons for capitalists to worry about the use of Keynesian fiscal policy measures to create and maintain full employment in peacetime. 'Indeed, under a regime of permanent full employment, 'the sack' would cease to play its role as a disciplinary measure', putting 'discipline in the factories' in question. Fascism, however, had removed these capitalist objections to full employment by concentrating government expenditure on armaments instead of civilian investment and consumption (Kalecki, 1943, pp. 326–7).

Kalecki did not spell out the implications for non-fascist countries but appears to have believed that militarization would stimulate patriotic sentiments among capitalists and workers, making the former less concerned about worker indiscipline and the latter less likely to indulge in it. Militarization would also be accompanied by some degree of increased repression, rendering acts of indiscipline more difficult to carry out.

These arguments were by no means new. Marxists had long claimed that there were deep economic motives behind the increasing militarism and imperialist expansion that characterized the new stage of capitalism that Rudolf Hilferding described as 'finance capital'. As early as 1888 the German socialist Max Schippel maintained that his nation's increased military expenditure was increasing aggregate output and employment, and thereby benefitting not just the armaments producers but also capital – and, more controversially, labour – as a whole. Kalecki himself later acknowledged that the benefits of military spending, which had been emphasized before 1914 by Mikhail Tugan-Baranovsky and Rosa Luxemburg, do 'find in a sense their confirmation in contemporary, in particular American, capitalism'. Indeed, 'armaments orders and ancillary expenditure ... play today a leading role in the functioning of modern capitalism' (Kalecki, 1967/1971, pp. 154–5).

JOHN E. KING

A similar case was made by Paul Baran and Paul Sweezy, who argued in their highly influential book *Monopoly Capital* that military spending benefitted not only the armaments producers but also the class interests of the oligarchy as a whole. Baran and Sweezy (1968, p. 207) noted in particular that '[w]hereas massive government spending for education and welfare tends to undermine its privileged position, the opposite is true of military spending'. 'The reason is that militarization fosters all the reactionary and irrational forces in society, and inhibits or kills everything progressive and humane' (ibid.). Cold warriors like the highly influential American Leon Kayserling found this argument convincing (see Cypher, 2015), along with many left-wing post-Keynesian economists, including Joan Robinson and Josef Steindl.

Two very large questions are posed by the doctrine of military Keynesianism. First, can it be shown that economic motives, conscious or unconscious, have dominated the decisions of capitalist powers to generate and maintain very high levels of military spending over the past century? Or, more precisely, is it the case that broad macroeconomic motives have dominated strategic decision-making (rather than the narrow sectional interests of what Dwight D. Eisenhower famously described as the 'military-industrial complex')? Second, has increased military spending actually generated the higher levels of aggregate output, employment and profits predicted by military Keynesianism, or has it come at the expense of output and employment (and profits) in non-military sectors of the economy?

The first question seems quite impossible to answer, but considerable attention has been paid to the second. Unfortunately, the substantial body of econometric research on the issue has failed to produce a conclusive answer (Dunne and Smith, 2010). As we live in a world in which tension between the major powers is again increasing, along with their already very high levels of military expenditure, this is not a comfortable conclusion. But it does appear to be inescapable.

JOHN E. KING

See also

Capitalism – stages of; Fiscal policy; Kaleckian economics; *Maturity and Stagnation in American Capitalism*; *Selected Essays on the Dynamics of Capitalist Economy*

References

Baran, P.A. and P.M. Sweezy (1968), *Monopoly Capital: An Essay on the American Economic and Social Order*, Harmondsworth: Penguin.

Cypher, J.M. (2015), 'The origins and evolution of military Keynesianism in the United States', *Journal of Post Keynesian Economics*, **38** (3), 449–76.

Dunne, J.P. and R.P. Smith (2010), 'Military expenditure and Granger causality: a critical review', *Defence and Peace Economics*, **21** (5–6), 427–41.

Kalecki, M. (1943), 'Political aspects of full employment', *Political Quarterly*, **14** (4), 322–31.

Kalecki, M. (1967/1971), 'The problem of effective demand with Tugan-Baranovsky and Luxemburg', in *Selected Essays on the Dynamics of the Capitalist Economy, 1933–1970*, Cambridge, UK: Cambridge University Press, pp. 146–55.

Modern money theory

Modern money theory (MMT) is an approach to macroeconomics that explains how a sovereign currency works and provides an analytical framework to understand the operational mechanisms of fiscal and monetary policies of a sovereign government. The national currency issued by such a government is referred to as 'sovereign currency'.

A sovereign currency is defined as existing when the federal government chooses a unit of account to denominate its currency, issues a currency denominated in that unit of account, imposes obligations (taxes, fees, fines, tribute, tithes) in its chosen unit of account and accepts the currency in payments of the imposed obligations and other settlements of debt. Examples of units of account are the US dollar, British pound, Canadian dollar, Australian dollar, Japanese yen and the euro.

This sovereign currency is called 'fiat currency', because it is not backed by reserves of precious metals and is not convertible into gold or some other commodity. The sovereign government is the monopoly issuer of the currency and needs to spend before it can tax or borrow. The acceptability of such a currency is derived from the tax obligations imposed by the government and its promises to accept the currency in discharge of tax liabilities and settlements of debt. 'Taxes drive money' is thus at the core of MMT.

A currency-issuing government does not face 'financial' affordability constraints in the same

JOHN E. KING / SHAKUNTALA DAS

manner as an individual household does. As such, the frequently used analogy between a household's budget and a government's budget is completely misleading for sound macroeconomic analysis. The government, however, may face resource constraints.

Now, since under normal circumstances anything that is available for sale domestically is in domestic currency, a currency-issuing government can always 'afford' to buy whatever is for sale in its own currency. A sovereign government also cannot become insolvent in its own currency. A sovereign government spends by crediting the bank account of the recipient and simultaneously creating reserves to the recipient's bank. Similarly, it taxes by debiting the taxpayers' account at the bank. Fiscal deficits, then, increase both the banks' reserves at the central bank and the bank deposits of government spending recipients. The initial impact of a fiscal deficit lowers the interest rate until the central bank intervenes to remove excess reserves with open-market operations.

The MMT approach explains why the conventional goal of setting an arbitrary target for public debt and deficit as percentages of GDP without considering the rate of both growth and unemployment in the economy is meaningless. Public debt and deficit largely serve a useful public purpose, and fiscal policy should be used to achieve a high level of productive employment.

MMT follows a stock–flow consistent methodological framework for macroeconomic analysis and adopts a three-sector balance approach developed by Godley (1996). Focusing on the linkages between the real and financial sectors of an economy, it ensures that there is consistency between flows (deficits) and stocks (debts). The sectoral balance method implies that, for any nation, the following macroeconomic balance equation holds true:

$$\text{domestic private balance} + \text{domestic government balance} + \text{foreign balance} = 0$$

This means that the deficit of one sector must equal the surpluses of (at least) one of the other sectors. In other words, if the government runs a deficit and if the foreigners spend less than their income, thus making the foreign balance positive, then, by macro-accounting identity, the domestic private sector must run a surplus.

All of the above principles apply to any currency-issuing nation, irrespective of their exchange-rate regime. However, a sovereign nation such as the United States with a floating exchange rate has more domestic policy space to pursue its fiscal and monetary policies than nations with fixed or managed exchange-rate regimes.

The policy implications of MMT for any currency-issuing nation with a floating-exchange-rate regime are to provide the sovereign nation with enhanced capacity to achieve the goal of full employment with price stability. Lerner's (1947) principle of functional finance is consistent with the MMT framework and specifies the operational mechanisms for fiscal and monetary policies to achieve full employment by setting the government's budget at the right level, spending more and taxing less when there is unemployment, and setting the interest rate at the right level. Tax rates should be set so that the government's budgetary outcome (whether in deficit, balanced or in surplus) is consistent with full employment.

The job guarantee programme (JG)/employer of last resort (ELR) is a policy proposal of MMT to achieve full employment, where government offers a job to anyone who is willing, able and ready to work at the programme's wage, thus providing a wage floor and effective minimum wage. This acts as a buffer and hence prevents private sector wages from falling below the minimum wage. JG/ELR provides an anchor for the internal and external value of the national currency, to actually increase macroeconomic stability. Real-world examples of ELR include Jefes de Hogar in Argentina, the National Rural Employment Guarantee Act in India, and the South African Expanded programme.

SHAKUNTALA DAS

See also

Currency hierarchy; Fiscal deficits; Fiscal policy; Monetary policy; Money creation – nature of

References

Bell, S. (2000), 'Do taxes and bonds finance government spending?', *Journal of Economic Issues*, 34 (3), 603–20.

Godley, W. (1996), 'Money, finance and national income determination: an integrated approach', *Levy Economics Institute of Bard College Working Paper*, No. 167.

Lerner, A.P. (1947), 'Money as a creature of the State', *American Economic Review*, **37** (2), 312–17.

Wray, L.R. (2015), *Modern Money Theory: A Primer on Macroeconomics for Sovereign Monetary Systems*, Basingstoke, UK, and New York: Palgrave Macmillan.

Monetary circuit

The mechanism of money creation and destruction constitutes the core of monetary circuit theory. This theory relies on the well-known fact that money is created when banks grant credits and is destroyed when these credits are reimbursed and debts are cancelled. This approach is linked to the concept of endogenous money, according to which money is created *ex nihilo* in response to the requirements of the production process. Monetary circuit theory is grounded in Keynes's finance motive and has been elaborated by Graziani (2003), Parguez (2003), Poulon (1982), Rochon (1999) and Lavoie (2022), among others.

The theory of the monetary circuit rests on four main postulates. First, money – or bank credit – constitutes an essential precondition for the production process to take place. It is therefore squarely within what Schumpeter (1954, p. 278) has called 'monetary analysis', in which money is introduced 'on the very ground floor of our analytic structure'. This stands in contradiction to neoclassical or 'real analysis', where money is not necessary to explain production, that is, where 'money enters the picture only in the modest role of a technical device' (Schumpeter, 1954, p. 278).

Second, money is endogenous; its quantity depends primarily on firms' demand for bank credits to finance the production of both consumption goods and investment goods. Hence, there is a hierarchy between monetary flows: 'firms cannot produce without having access to monetary advances from banks. Households cannot spend money as long as firms have not produced and generated revenues' (Lavoie, 1987, p. 68; our translation). This hierarchy is important. It explains the necessity of bank credit to initiate production, but also highlights the idea that the production process takes time.

Third, firms want to realize monetary profits. Indeed, the purpose of production is for firms to turn a sum obtained by bank credit into a monetary profit, that is, to somehow transform M into M' (where $M' > M$).

Finally, the monetary circuit is usually studied within periods containing two main components: the 'influx' and 'reflux' phases of production. A monetary circuit or a period of production begins with money flowing into the production sphere, as wages are paid, following an initial demand for bank credit. This observation makes it clear that money is not just a stock; it is also a flow that responds to the needs of the economic system. Provided firms are creditworthy, banks are willing to grant credit to them, so they can use these funds to remunerate their workers and purchase non-labour inputs. As firms sell their output, they recoup part of the money they initially spent or injected at the beginning of the production period. The reflux, at the end of the monetary circuit, is the moment during which credits issued at the beginning of the circuit are reimbursed. Money is then destroyed as debts are extinguished.

Two fundamental questions arise from monetary circuit theory. First, how can a crisis occur in this framework? There are several answers to this question. A first one, called 'non-opening of the circuit', corresponds to insufficient financing by the banks, which prevents the economy from functioning at its maximum capacity and from ensuring full employment. A second one, called the 'non-closure of the circuit', is the existence of excessive savings, which prevents companies from repaying the loans they have taken out from banks and can lead to bankruptcy. Savings are a drain that prevent firms from recouping their initial outlays. In both cases, the role of demand as well as expected demand is fundamental. Low expected demand will limit credit requests and make banks more wary of granting credit. Low effective demand will prevent firms from recovering the funds they borrowed to start production.

The second fundamental question, which has given rise to an abundant literature, is: how can firms make profits and repay bank credits with interest, based on the credits they have taken out to initiate their production process? This question takes the form of a paradox, since the reflux of money from households to firms and banks cannot, by construction, be greater than the influx that gave rise to it. Two main solutions have been envisaged to resolve this paradox. The first one assumes the existence of numerous phases of influx and reflux within the period (Renaud, 2000; Zezza, 2012). Thus, firms and banks will immediately spend and inject back into circulation the profits and interests they started to collect. The second solution assumes that credits can be granted over several periods and therefore do not have to be fully repaid within the period considered (Rochon, 2009; Cottin-Euziol and Rochon, 2013).

The main contributions of monetary circuit theory have been incorporated into stock–flow consistent models, which are nowadays gaining more and more influence in the economists' community.

EDOUARD COTTIN-EUZIOL AND
LOUIS-PHILIPPE ROCHON

See also

Endogenous money; Monetary theory of production; Money and banking; Money creation – nature of; Stock–flow consistent models

References

Cottin-Euziol, E. and L.-P. Rochon (2013), 'Circuit with multi-period credit', *Review of Political Economy*, **25** (3), 461–75.
Graziani, A. (2003), *The Monetary Theory of Production*, Cambridge, UK: Cambridge University Press.
Lavoie, M. (1987), 'Monnaie et production: une synthèse de la théorie du circuit', *Economies et Sociétés*, **21** (9), 65–101.
Lavoie, M. (2022), *Post-Keynesian Economics: New Foundations*, second edition, Cheltenham, UK and Northampton, MA, USA: Edward Elgar.
Parguez, A. (2003), 'Monnaie et capitalisme: la théorie générale du circuit', in P. Piégay and L.-P. Rochon (eds), *Théories monétaires post Keynésiennes*, Paris: Economica, pp. 129–42.
Poulon, F. (1982), *Macroéconomie approfondie*, Paris: Editions Cujas.
Renaud, J.-F. (2000), 'The problem of the monetary realization of profits in a Post Keynesian sequential financing model: two solutions of the Kaleckian option', *Review of Political Economy*, **12** (3), 258–303.
Rochon, L.-P. (1999), 'The creation and circulation of endogenous money: a circuit dynamique approach', *Journal of Economics Issues*, **33** (1), 1–21.
Rochon, L.-P. (2009), 'The existence of profits within the monetary circuit: the unanswered questions revisited', in J.-F. Ponsot and S. Rossi (eds), *The Political Economy of Monetary Circuits: Tradition and Change in Post-Keynesian Economics*, Basingstoke and New York: Palgrave Macmillan, pp. 56–76.

Schumpeter, J.A. (1954), *History of Economic Analysis*, London: Allen & Unwin.
Zezza, G. (2012), 'Godley and Graziani: stock-flow consistent monetary circuits', in D.B. Papadimitriou and G. Zezza (eds), *Contributions in Stock-Flow Modeling: Essays in Honor of Wynne Godley*, London: Palgrave Macmillan, pp. 154–72.

Monetary circuit – French School

In retrospect, the general theory of the monetary circuit is the most absolute negation of the neoclassical theory of money and its progeny, that is, the neo-liberal economic and social policy. Why could it be deemed the 'French school' and who are those 'French circuitists'?

The foundations of the French school of monetary circuit theory have been drafted in a book published in French (Parguez, 1975). It was the outcome of a previous and detailed proof of the total contradiction of the orthodox (neoclassical) theory of money because of its roots in Walrasian general equilibrium theory.

The monetary circuit is the fundamental process of a capitalist economy in its widest sense, explaining the creation of net wealth out of decision-makers in a non-command society. The circuit Parguez developed over time was a synthesis of Marx, Keynes and Polanyi. It perfectly integrates both money and time.

Parguez (1996) emphasized the perfect essentiality of money, as the *sine qua non* of an economic system. Real wealth is generated over time by expenditures of all economic agents in order to meet their long-run expectations. Expenditures are the outcome of initial money creation by monetary (or banking) systems. Thereby their counterpart in banks are balance-sheet bets to be repaid later when expectations are met (or should be met). This is tantamount to the definition of money as debt appearing in bank liabilities, which instantaneously generate purchasing power for spending agents. When loans are paid back, they cancel an equal amount of money. The monetary circuit is therefore enshrined in real or historical time with a past and a future to be created by expectations.

Who are the spending agents in such a monetary circuit? First, one must think of the private sector, namely, firms and household. Let us start by the role of firms directly producing real wealth to attain their long-run target profit. Private production is split between commodities for consumption and commodities to be integrated into real equipment or capital. According to the essentiality principle, the effective value of commodities is generated by their acquisition financed by money creation.

The core of the monetary circuit process can thus be shown as follows:

(1) Expectations → (2) Expenditures → (3) Production → (4) Acquisition of production → (5) Generation of value

This means that in steps (2) and (3) production appears but is yet deprived of value, as long as it is not bought out of money creation. In a given production period t, consumption goods are bought by the payment of wages in period $t-1$. Production goods are henceforth to be bought by investment decided in the past. Herein appears the explanation of the specificity of the general theory that became the 'French school' relative to other versions of the monetary circuit, notably the Schmitt school and the Italian school of Augusto Graziani. Both rely on a paramount postulate: wages are the unique source of money creation and they never truly integrated the State.

The essentiality principle relies on the existence of the State as a perfectly autonomous decision maker. First, the homogeneity of bank money is rooted into its perfect convertibility into State money essentially out of the payment of taxes. Contrary to the private sector, the State is free to create any amount of money it wants to attain its own expectations of welfare. Thereby the corollary of the essentiality principle is that the State is free to plan the required amount of public deficit or net State money creation. Taxes are part of the reflux. They destroy an equal amount of money while State initial expenditures reflect an equal amount of money creation. Being the ultimate monetary authority, the State creates directly the amount of money it needs without any borrowing from banks. At this stage, the central bank (the banking department of the State) enters the monetary system. State expenditures are reflected as pure fictitious or conventional debts in the central bank's balance sheet, while tax payments are reflected by the cancellation of this fictitious debt.

From this brief analysis, one must derive a theory of economic and social policy fully rejecting any effort to save the quantity theory of money as an explanation of inflation. It brings about the proof that full employment is the existence condition of sensible price theory. Markets do not exist as a supreme guide through price fixation. Firms fix their prices in order to attain their long-run expected profit. Herein lies the major originality of the so-called French school of the monetary circuit relative to both the Schmitt school and the Graziani-led Italian school. None can lead to a general theory of profit in a fully monetarized economy and ever explain the existence of profits.

ALAIN PARGUEZ

See also

Endogenous money; Monetary circuit – Italian school; Monetary theory of production; Money and banking; Money creation – nature of

References

Parguez, A. (1975), *Monnaie et macroéconomie*, Paris: Economica.
Parguez, A. (1996), 'Beyond scarcity: a reappraisal of the theory of the monetary circuit', in G. Deleplace and E.J. Nell (eds), *Money in Motion: The Post-Keynesian and Circulation Approaches*, London: Macmillan, pp. 155–99.

Monetary circuit – Italian School

The Italian School of the Monetary Circuit (ISMC) is a specific rendition (or branch) of monetary circuit theory. It has been developed since the mid-1970s by Augusto Graziani and his pupils (see, for instance, Graziani, 1996, 2003; but also Bellofiore and Veronese Passarella, 2016). The ISMC arose from a deep dissatisfaction with the monetary analyses provided by both the then-dominant schools in economics (new classical macroeconomics and synthesis Keynesianism) and main dissenting approaches (neo-Ricardianism, Marxism and Cambridge Keynesianism). However, while the *circuitisti* have always opposed strongly the former, they have established a mutual cross-breeding relationship with the latter. The ISMC aims at analysing the channels through which money is created, circulated and destroyed in a capitalist economy.

ALAIN PARGUEZ / MARCO VERONESE PASSARELLA

Unlike neoclassical-like economists, ISMC authors assert that money is not a commodity. It is a pure sign created *ex nihilo* by banks. While money is in the nature of credit, it is not a direct credit between two parties or agents. Rather, it is a triangular credit relationship where a third party, namely, a bank, enables a buyer (for instance, a firm purchasing labour-power from a worker) and a seller (say a worker selling her labour-power to a firm) to conclude the transaction with no debt pending between them. In this transaction, the bank does not act as a simple intermediary, lending out already-collected deposits. Rather, the bank creates means of payment by simply crediting the bank account of the buyer. When the buyer–borrower pays the seller, bank deposits are transferred from the bank account of the former to the bank account of the latter. Money is destroyed when the borrower pays back its bank credit. Therefore, it is loans that create deposits, not vice versa. A bank is an institution whose liabilities (deposits) are accepted as means of payment and are readily transferable between economic agents.

While this narrative resembles the post-Keynesian theory of endogenous money, ISMC authors focus on the process of money creation during 'normal times', rather than on uncertainty and its impact on liquidity preference (Graziani, 2003). In other words, they focus on the role of money as a means of payment (particularly, on money acting as 'capital'), rather than on its function as a store of value. Therefore, it is no surprise that ISMC authors prefer Keynes's *Treatise on Money* (1930) over *The General Theory* (Keynes, 1936). Notice that the reversed emphasis on Keynes's main works is one of the main differences between ISMC authors and other heterodox monetary approaches, including the Cambridge School of economics and the Bordeaux Circuit School led by Frédéric Poulon.

Four key classes of agents – the central bank, commercial banks, firms and workers – are considered by ISMC authors. Unlike other (French) circuitists, like the late Alain Parguez, ISMC authors do not include the State in the basic circuit abstraction. Therefore, the main steps of the monetary circuit are five. Let us expand on this.

Step one. Firms demand a bank loan to buy the labour-power necessary to start the process of production. Although the residual amount of loans at the end of the period equals firms' investment (net of retained profits and new issues of securities), firms' 'initial finance' must cover the total cost of production. If we consider firms as a consolidated and integrated sector, the only purchase they have to make is to hire workers. As a result, the initial finance must match the wage bill, while the purchase of capital goods (gross investment) is always funded *ex post* by households' saving. This assumption is another major theoretical difference between the ISMC and the approach advocated by Alain Parguez.

Step two. Firms decide both the level and the composition of output and therefore the employment level. Workers can only decide how to distribute their disposable income between consumption and saving. Workers' savings, in turn, can be held in the form of liquid balances (deposits and/or cash) and/or securities.

Step three. Firms purchase investment goods, whereas workers purchase consumer goods and securities. The former is just an internal exchange for the firm sector, that is, a zero-sum game.

Step four. As long as workers spend their income to buy consumer goods and/or securities issued by firms, money flows back to the firm sector. In fact, this 'final finance' allows firms to pay back their bank debt, thereby destroying a corresponding amount of bank deposits.

Step five. To the extent bank debt is repaid, banks can use these funds to buy consumer and/or investment goods (up to their profit). This is an additional source of final finance that allows firms to pay interests due on their loans. If there is no hoarding ('normal times' hypothesis), the monetary circuit comes to an end when the debt is fully repaid (including interests) and there is no money left in the system. If, by contrast, a positive liquidity preference exists, a residual amount of (new) loans remains at the end of the period. Firms' net bank debt equals idle balances held by workers, which, in turn, equal the 'uncovered' portion of investment.

Two major implications follow from the analysis summarized above. First, since the purchase of capital goods is an internal affair for the firm sector, while the purchase of labour-power is the only external exchange, the latter (not the former) is necessarily the source of profit for firms as a whole. Second, since the level and composition of output are decided by firms, fiscal policies can only redistribute income within classes, but not between classes.

MARCO VERONESE PASSARELLA

A direct intervention of the State is necessary for cross-class redistribution purposes.
MARCO VERONESE PASSARELLA

See also

Capitalism; Endogenous money; Monetary theory of production; Money as a means of payment; Money creation – nature of

References

Bellofiore, R. and M. Veronese Passarella (2016), 'Introduction: the theoretical legacy of Augusto Graziani', *Review of Keynesian Economics*, **4** (3), 243–9.
Graziani, A. (1996), *La teoria del circuito monetario*, Milan: Jaca Book.
Graziani, A. (2003), *The Monetary Theory of Production*, Cambridge, UK: Cambridge University Press.
Keynes, J.M. (1930), *A Treatise on Money*, London: Macmillan.
Keynes, J.M. (1936), *The General Theory of Employment, Interest and Money*, London: Macmillan.

Monetary integration

Monetary integration refers to the situation of different countries strengthening their degree of monetary connection. Consequently, monetary integration means forming a common or single currency area whose features suit the needs of each part of it.

The aim of monetary integration could be to promote trade or financial flows, but also social and political bonds. In the history of Western countries, for instance, monetary integration started with the establishment of kingships, which went hand-in-hand with centralization of political power and accelerated at the end of the nineteenth century, when these countries became nation states. The case of France comes to mind in this regard.

Likewise, the need to set up a larger domestic market with powerful economic actors can also be a motive to foster monetary integration. Switzerland's monetary history illustrates this, since the country moved gradually from a local currencies competition framework to the 'nationalization' of money at the end of the nineteenth century (see Laurent and Vallet, 2014). By the same token, the more recent example of the creation of the euro area is evidence of such a process: the euro area came into existence to enhance the functioning of the European internal market, through the 'one market, one money' logic (Emerson et al., 1992).

In the latter two cases, monetary integration rests on the view of the optimum currency area (OCA) theory (Mundell, 1961): when different countries are highly economically integrated because of trade, they are likely to abandon their own currency for a common or even a single currency. With OCA theory, the means-of-payment function of money should be a guide to contemplating monetary integration.

However, currency unification could also be 'undergone', in the sense that it is a 'second best' to other forms of monetary integration. Therefore, monetary integration can take several forms. We refer here to monetary regimes such as currency boards, dollarization, or pegged systems (see Levy-Yeyati and Sturzenegger, 2000). Through these regimes, monetary integration is intended to improve macroeconomic stability (price stability and economic growth, in particular) or other types of stability (exchange rate, assets markets). We find several examples of these forms of monetary integration: Argentina (with its currency board based on the US dollar in the 1990s), Ecuador (with dollarization today), or the Franc CFA zone since 1945.

On the whole, monetary integration cannot be viewed as a 'technical' system alone, with the means-of-payment function of money as the unique keystone of the process. What is at stake with monetary integration is economic homogeneity within the single or common currency area but, above all, political will in relation to economic prosperity at large. Consequently, two key points should be highlighted as follows.

First, monetary integration requires the design of a currency area with regard to the economic specializations of its components and their capacity for collective monetary integration. This framework implies designing both economic and political projects associated with money, defining the relationships between monetary and fiscal policy. What is at stake is competitiveness, but also solidarity and cohesion.

Second, monetary integration raises the issue of sovereignty. Economic and political choices related to monetary integration often imply a trade-off between the advantages and constraints of monetary integration. As a result, monetary integration must preserve the sovereignty of money, namely, the capacity of money to serve people's will. This explains why we should distinguish between sovereignty of money, sovereign money (legal tender), and monetary sovereignty (monetary independence through the ability to implement monetary policies and to secure the payments system). Sometimes, monetary integration is likely to entail a loss of monetary sovereignty (like when the Banque de France pegged its monetary policy to that of the Bundesbank in the early 1990s). By contrast, constrained monetary sovereignty is likely to enhance the sovereignty of money (in Ecuador, with dollarization, or during the Swiss franc/euro peg period (2011–15) for Switzerland (Ponsot et al., 2014)).

GUILLAUME VALLET AND
HAMED KARAMOKO

See also

Euro; European Monetary Union; Keynes Plan; Monetary policy; Money as a means of payment

References

Emerson, M., D. Gros, A. Italianer, J. Pisani-Ferry and H. Reichenbach (1992), *One Market, One Money: An Evaluation of the Potential Benefits and Costs of Forming an Economic and Monetary Union*, Oxford: Oxford University Press.

Laurent, A. and G. Vallet (2014), 'La construction progressive de l'avantage compétitif financier suisse (1914–1939)', *Revue d'économie financière*, **113**, 259–73.

Levy-Yeyati, E. and F. Sturzenegger (2000), 'Exchange rate regimes and economic performance', paper presented at the First Annual IMF Research Conference, 9–10 November.

Mundell, R. (1961), 'A theory of optimum currency areas', *American Economic Review*, **51** (4), 657–65.

Ponsot, J.-F., F. Ülgen and G. Vallet (2014), 'The sovereignty of money without monetary sovereignty', paper presented at the Workshop on the Future of the Euro, Grenoble, 15 May.

Monetary policy

The interest of post-Keynesian economists in monetary policy can be divided into two phases: a negative phase, which focused on criticizing orthodox approaches, and a positive phase that attempted to develop concrete alternatives. A significant contribution to the first phase was Nicholas Kaldor's attack on monetarism. Kaldor (1985, pp. 185–90) objected to Friedman's (1968) assertion that inflation was always the result of excessive money supply growth on the grounds that it assumed an exogenous money supply when in fact the money supply is endogenous. Kaldor argued that when central banks attempt to control the money supply in the face of strong increases in demand, interest rates and the velocity of circulation increase. Since extreme increases in interest rates can cause financial instability, central banks prefer to accommodate demand but at an interest rate of their choosing. However, whether the velocity of circulation of money increases or the central bank accommodates money demand, the money supply is effectively endogenous, according to Kaldor, and Friedman's theory of money-driven inflation was mistaken.

On the positive side, Kaldor identified two possibilities for monetary policy. The interest rate at which the central bank endogenously accommodates money demand could either be varied counter-cyclically (Kaldor, 1939, pp. 57–8) or it could be fixed at a low level to promote a greater volume of employment (Kaldor, 1939, p. 55). His preference was for the latter, because counter-cyclical monetary policy required higher interest rates on average, he argued, with negative implications for employment (Kaldor, 1964, p. 137). This, in fact, complemented Keynes's own scepticism about the effectiveness of counter-cyclical monetary policy (Keynes, 1936, pp. 316–17).

More recent post-Keynesian approaches to monetary policy to a large extent reflect the issues identified by Kaldor. Two questions have tended to shape the development of these approaches: the first is whether the policy rate of interest should be varied counter-cyclically or fixed according to some longer-run goal; the second is whether the nominal or the real interest rate should be targeted (Rochon and Setterfield, 2007, p. 15).

A number of post-Keynesian economists advocate varying interest rates counter-cyclically. Palley (2007) uses a backward-bending Phillips curve, reflecting real wage resistance, to define a minimum unemployment rate of inflation and argues that this should constitute the policy target. Fontana and Palacio-Vera (2006) advocate an inflation target but argue that when the Phillips curve has a large flat section, interest rates can be cut in order to reduce unemployment.

Other post-Keynesian economists follow Kaldor in advocating fixed interest rates. Smithin (2007) suggests a zero rate to promote full employment. Aspromourgos (2011) emphasises an ethical justification for this policy linking it to Keynes's 'euthanasia of the rentier' (Keynes, 1936, p. 376), which denies the ethical legitimacy of rewards from the mere ownership of capital. Wray (2007) advocates a zero rate of interest to promote this 'euthanasia' and to avoid disrupting financial markets with frequent interest rate changes. Lavoie and Seccareccia (1999) recommend setting the interest rate equal to labour productivity growth, which would (they argue) preserve real asset values in terms of labour commanded.

On the second issue of whether real or nominal rates of interest should be the policy focus, Wray (2007, pp. 129–31) argues for a nominal target, on the grounds that interest rates in Keynes's analysis function as the basis for allocating wealth between asset classes. Wray argues that only nominal rates of interest are relevant for asset comparisons, and central banks set nominal rather than real rates of interest. Aspromourgos (2011, p. 641), on the other hand, asserts that only a zero real rate of interest is consistent with Keynes's ethical justification for the 'euthanasia of the rentier' and the fair preservation of nominal asset values through time. Smithin (2007, pp. 104–5) similarly argues for a real rate of interest on the basis that this is the rate that affects entrepreneurial profits and growth, and Lavoie and Seccareccia's (1999) policy also requires setting the real rate of interest equal to labour productivity growth.

These perspectives highlight the importance of understanding monetary policy in terms of a well-specified model, since the diversity of policy recommendations to some extent reflects model variation (see Wray, 2007, p. 124).

One generally agreed post-Keynesian principle is that the transmission of monetary policy operates through changes in income distribution rather than through cost of capital effects (Rochon and Setterfield, 2007, pp. 23, 28–9, 37). More work is, however, needed to develop an agreed set of modelling frameworks within which this mechanism and other aspects of monetary policy transmission can be understood from a post-Keynesian perspective.

PETER DOCHERTY

See also

Central banking; Endogenous money; Inflation; Monetary policy transmission mechanism; Phillips curve

References

Aspromourgos, A. (2011), 'Can (and should) monetary policy pursue a zero real interest rate, permanently?', *Metroeconomica*, **62** (4), 635–55.
Fontana, G. and A. Palacio-Vera (2006), 'Is there an active role for monetary policy in the endogenous money approach?', in C. Gnos and L.-P. Rochon (eds), *Post Keynesian Principles of Economic Policy*, Cheltenham, UK, and Northampton, MA, USA: Edward Elgar, pp. 49–56.
Friedman, M. (1968), 'The role of monetary policy', *American Economic Review*, **58** (1), 1–17.
Kaldor, N. (1939), 'Speculation and economic stability', *Review of Economic Studies*, **7** (1), 1–27.
Kaldor, N. (1964/1980), 'Monetary policy, economic stability and growth', in *Collected Economic Essays: Essays on Economic Growth I*, London: Duckworth, pp. 128–53.
Kaldor, N. (1985/1989), 'How monetarism failed', in *Collected Economic Essays: Further Essays on Economic Growth*, London: Duckworth, pp. 178–97.
Keynes, J.M. (1936), *The General Theory of Employment, Interest and Money*, London: Macmillan.
Lavoie, M. and M. Seccareccia (1999), 'Interest rate: fair', in P.A. O'Hara (ed.), *Encyclopedia of Political Economy, Volume 1*, London and New York: Routledge, pp. 543–5.
Palley, T.I. (2007), 'Macroeconomics and monetary policy: competing theoretical frameworks', *Journal of Post Keynesian Economics*, **30** (1), 61–78.
Rochon, L.-P. and M. Setterfield (2007), 'Interest rates, income distribution, and monetary policy dominance: Post Keynesians and the "fair rate" of interest', *Journal of Post Keynesian Economics*, **30** (1), 13–42.
Smithin, J. (2007), 'A real interest rate rule for monetary policy?', *Journal of Post Keynesian Economics*, **30** (1), 101–18.
Wray, L.R. (2007), 'The political economy of interest rate setting, inflation and income distribution', *Journal of Post Keynesian Economics*, **30** (1), 119–41.

Monetary policy dominance

The role of money is fundamental to economic analysis. For heterodox economists, money is not neutral as it affects economic activity, in both the short run and long run. But for orthodox economists, money is neutral in the long run. Within this orthodoxy, economists of New Classical economics, such as Robert Lucas, Neil Wallace, and Thomas Sargent, believe that money is super-neutral: it can never cause any effect on economic activity whatsoever, neither in the short run nor in the long run.

For New Classical economists, central banks need to supply enough money to make sure price stability prevails on the market for goods and services. Any monetary policy that increases money supply in an attempt to accelerate economic growth will only result in inflation. Thus, according to this perspective, monetary policy is considered dominant, in the sense that it is the most important economic policy, and is considered 'better' than fiscal, exchange rate, and industrial policies. The underlying idea of monetary policy dominance is that markets are fully self-regulating and only need free floating prices in pure competitive markets to balance supply and demand in a Pareto-efficient full-employment equilibrium.

There are three perspectives with respect to monetary policy dominance. The original perspective was developed by Sargent and Wallace (1981). By the late 1980s and during the 1990s, the fiscal theory of the price level emerged, associated with Sims (1994) and Woodford (1994, 2001). By the early 2000s, Blanchard (2004) offered his view on the topic. Despite having three perspectives, they all share the same logic: without the dominance of monetary policy, inflation is inevitable. But how does inflation appear?

In its current form, inflation targeting is at the heart of the monetary policy dominance, where central banks set an inflation rate as the target that monetary policy will pursue, in a certain period of time. Fiscal policy is subsequent to monetary policy and its role is to generate the primary surpluses required to stabilize public debt, whose service varies as central banks manage the policy interest rate to attain the inflation target. However, if fiscal policy is actively undertaken and results in fiscal policy dominance – which is the case when fiscal policy is not subsequent to monetary policy – agents start losing confidence in the central bank's commitment to inflation targeting and, in turn, they begin to question the sustainability of public debt. Agents believe that if fiscal policy is not pursuing debt stabilization, inflation will arise.

The relation between fiscal dominance and inflation is twofold. First, domestic agents stop buying government bonds and begin a fast and massive demand for real sector assets, causing asset price inflation. Second, foreign investors also cease buying government bonds and leave the country, causing exchange rate depreciation and, consequently, inflation through a pass-through effect. To avoid inflation and keep markets efficiently working, the economic authorities need to commit themselves to monetary policy dominance.

A short note to conclude: post-Keynesian economists consider fiscal policy the most important policy to boost economic activity. It should be actively managed to obtain full employment and a more equitable income distribution (Arestis et al., 2018). In terms of monetary policy, Rochon and Setterfield (2007) explain that there are two approaches, which they label the 'activist' and 'parking it'. The former sees the policy interest rate as a fine-tuning instrument aimed at generating aggregate demand. The latter is concerned with both the impacts of the short-term interest rate on income distribution and its usual management based on slowing down economic activity. Therefore, the 'parking it' view proposes that monetary policy should be concerned with long-term interest rates. Moreover, the operational rule of the monetary policy should aim at 'parking' the real level of the short-term interest rate as close as possible to zero, or at a nominal zero level, or at the 'fair rate of interest', which is equal to the growth rate of labour productivity.

FÁBIO TERRA

See also

Central bank independence; Central bank–treasury relation; Debt – public; Fiscal policy; Inflation

References

Arestis, P., F. Ferrari Filho and F.B. Terra (2018), 'Keynesian macroeconomic policy: theoretical analysis and empirical evidence', *Panoeconomicus*, **65** (1), 1–20.

Blanchard, O. (2004), 'Fiscal dominance and inflation targeting: lesson from Brazil', *National Bureau of Economic Research Working Paper*, No. 10389.

Rochon, L.-P. and M. Setterfield (2007), 'Interest rates, income distribution, and monetary policy dominance: Post Keynesians and the "fair rate" of interest', *Journal of Post Keynesian Economics*, **30** (1), 12–42.

Sargent, T. and N. Wallace (1981), 'Some unpleasant monetarist arithmetic', *Federal Reserve Bank of Minneapolis Quarterly Review*, **5** (3), 1–17.

Sims, C.A. (1994), 'A simple model for study of the price level and the interaction of monetary and fiscal policy', *Economic Theory*, **4** (3), 381–99.

Woodford, M. (1994), 'Monetary policy and price level determinacy in a cash-in-advance economy', *Economic Theory*, **4** (3), 345–80.

Woodford, M. (2001), 'Fiscal requirements for price stability', *Journal of Money, Credit and Banking*, **33** (3), 669–728.

Monetary policy transmission mechanism

The monetary policy transmission mechanism refers to the channels through which monetary policy can affect aggregate demand, output, and inflation. Following the monetarist approach, these channels were initially identified considering the effects of an increase/decrease in the quantity of base money (Cecchetti, 1995; Mishkin, 1995). However, in the last couple of decades, monetary policy has shifted from managing the quantity of base money to inflation targeting via interest rate management and, correspondingly, the analysis of the transmission mechanism has also focussed on the impact of rising/falling policy rates of interest on economic activity and inflation.

Five transmission channels of monetary policy have been traditionally identified in the literature. Let us present them briefly.

Interest rate channel: An increase in the policy rate of interest leads to an increase in short-term nominal market interest rates. This increase in short-term interest rates also feeds (at least partially) into long-term interest rates. Due to sluggish price adjustment, long-term real interest rates also rise, which reduces investment and credit-financed durable and housing consumption, leading to a slowdown of both economic activity and inflation.

Credit channel: This channel operates through its impact on credit supply and credit demand. When policy rates of interest increase and economic activity declines with increasing unemployment, banks may face liquidity problems as household savings fall and external financing costs increase. As a result, banks may reduce credit supply. This mechanism is termed the bank lending channel (Ciccarelli et al., 2015). On the other hand, an increase in the policy rate of interest and a subsequent worsening of banks' balance sheets (due to non-performing loans, for instance, or falling asset prices) may also induce banks to reduce the credit supply through a decline in bank capital adequacy (Markovic, 2006). An increase in the policy rate of interest can also adversely affect credit demand through its negative impact on the balance sheets of firms and households (the balance-sheet channel). These adverse effects on credit supply and credit demand may lead to a contraction in output and a fall in inflation.

Asset price channel: This channel operates through both financial asset prices and real-estate prices (Mishkin, 2007). On the financial assets side, an increase in policy rates of interest has a dual effect on economic activity. On one hand, as short-term interest rates rise following an increase in policy rates, equity prices fall, which leads to a decrease in Tobin's q and reduces investment. On the other hand, lower asset prices reduce consumption through a negative wealth effect on households. Similarly, a higher policy rate of interest increases the cost of housing credit, pushing housing demand and growth of housing supply down, and slowing down economic activity through standard wealth effects.

Exchange rate channel: This channel has a dual effect on inflation and economic activity. On one hand, an increase in policy rates of interest makes domestic currency denominated assets more attractive relative to foreign currency denominated assets, and causes an appreciation of the domestic currency, thus increasing imports and hampering exports, which reduces domestic demand (Harrison et al., 2005). As a result, there is a decline in output and economic growth, and a downward pressure on inflation. On the other hand, the appreciation reduces the domestic currency value of imported goods and leads to a further decline in the rate of inflation.

Expectations channel: An important aspect of monetary policy is to manage expectations regarding the future path of the economy, as these expectations directly feed into price and wage formation, production/consumption decisions, and currency choice. Thus, a vital channel of monetary policy transmission operates through its impact on expectation dynamics, particularly if the credibility of the central bank is high.

Beyond these standard channels of monetary policy transmission, several recent studies have identified the importance of debt service/household indebtedness as another possible channel through which monetary policy affects output and prices (Hofmann and Peersman, 2017; Cloyne et al., 2020). Specifically, the debt-repayments-to-private-sector-income ratio may have significant macroeconomic effects, owing to higher marginal propensities to invest/consume of debtors than those of creditors. In this framework, an increase in policy rates of interest could have an additional contractionary effect on the economy by transferring income from debtors to creditors and increasing the debt service ratio (Hofmann and Peersman, 2017).

In the aftermath of the global financial crisis of 2008, central banks across the world have engaged in unconventional monetary policy in the form of large asset purchase programmes. These purchases reduce the yields on assets bought by the central banks, inducing households and investors to re-balance their portfolios in search of higher yields in other assets such as equities. This additional channel has been termed the 'portfolio balance channel' (Neri and Siviero, 2019).

DEVRIM YILMAZ

See also

Aggregate demand; Endogenous money; Inflation targeting; Interest rates and investment; Monetary policy

References

Cecchetti, S.G. (1995), 'Distinguishing theories of the monetary transmission mechanism', *Federal Reserve Bank of Saint Louis Review*, 77, 83–97.
Ciccarelli, M., A. Maddaloni and J.-L. Peydró (2015), 'Trusting the bankers: a new look at the credit channel of monetary policy', *Review of Economic Dynamics*, **18** (4), 979–1002.
Cloyne, J., C. Ferreira and P. Surico (2020), 'Monetary policy when households have debt: new evidence on the transmission mechanism', *Review of Economic Studies*, **87** (1), 102–29.
Harrison, R., K. Nikolov, M. Quinn, G. Ramsay, A. Scott and R. Thomas (2005), *The Bank of England Quarterly Model*, London: Bank of England.
Hofmann, B. and G. Peersman (2017), 'Is there a debt service channel of monetary transmission?', *Bank for International Settlements Quarterly Review*, December, 23–37.
Markovic, B. (2006), 'Bank capital channels in the monetary transmission mechanism', *Bank of England Working Paper*, No. 313.
Mishkin, F.S. (1995), 'Symposium on the monetary transmission mechanism', *Journal of Economic Perspectives*, **9** (4), 3–10.
Mishkin, F.S. (2007), 'Housing and the monetary transmission mechanism', *National Bureau of Economic Research Working Paper*, No. 13518.
Neri, S. and S. Siviero (2019), 'The non-standard monetary policy measures of the ECB: motivations, effectiveness and risks', *Bank of Italy Occasional Paper*, No. 486.

Monetary theory of production

The expression 'monetary theory of production' was first used by John Maynard Keynes in 1932 during his lectures at Cambridge (United Kingdom), as reported by one of his students, Lorie Tarshis (see Skidelsky, 1992). It was also the title of an important short piece first published in 1933 (see Keynes, 1933/1973, pp. 408–11).

In modern terms, the monetary theory of production is the logical corollary of the essentiality of money as the most fundamental existence of a non-command fully stationary society, which means a pure capitalist economy in the widest sense.

Such a society is burdened by its past, and its present is only to be defined as an effort to overcome anguish over the future out of expenditures by the set of decision-makers, namely, the private sector and the State.

Money as such is fully independent of its form. It is a mere debt to the future deprived of any intrinsic value. Money has a pure extrinsic value bestowed on it by the creation of real net wealth or income.

Herein is a crucial theorem to understand what money is: being deprived of any intrinsic value, money is created only to be spent by agents taking wagers on the far future, which is fully unknown.

From this theorem, one may derive the core characteristics of money, which are the following:

(1) Money being only a debt to the future thanks to daring expenditures, it cannot

DEVRIM YILMAZ / ALAIN PARGUEZ AND SLIM THABET

be a reserve of wealth, a 'capital' hoarded at the expense of other sources of wealth. Herein is the major weakness of Keynes's *General Theory*, especially in chapter 17 (Keynes, 1936). As shown by Parguez and Seccareccia (2000), this chapter relies on an exogenous 'preference for liquidity', which is nothing but a restatement of the marginal utility of money in neoclassical economics.

(2) Real money is thereby fully endogenous, that is, the true infrastructure of the capitalist economy open to the future.
(3) All the decision-makers striving to build the future are constrained by their targeted expenditures. Finally, money is but debts that are instantaneously transformed into expenditures. Issuers of money are indeed the private sector and mainly the State. Private issuers are constrained by their targeted profit norms, while the State is free from any constraints.
(4) Usually, debts imply interest payments. Herein appears the fundamental distinction in a genuine monetary economy of production:

- Banks charge interest fitting their own profit norms to be paid by private spenders.
- The State being the ultimate monetary authority has not to pay interest on its own money: State expenditures reflect a pure accounting system, including the spending agent, the Treasury and the money-creating agent, the central bank.

Ultimately, the pure logic of a monetary production economy bestowing as an existence condition absolute sovereignty of the State does not leave room for monetary policy as a leading force of the economy. The sole efficient economic and social policy is fiscal policy, simultaneously fixing the amount of initial producing expenditures by the State and the *ex post* tax debts imposed on society, warranting the State sovereignty on the currency.

ALAIN PARGUEZ AND SLIM THABET

See also

Endogenous money; Monetary circuit; Money and banking; Money as a means of payment; Money creation – nature of

References

Keynes, J.M. (1933/1973), 'A monetary theory of production', in *The Collected Writings of John Maynard Keynes, Vol. XIII: The General Theory and After: Preparation*, London and Basingstoke: Macmillan, pp. 408–11.

Keynes, J.M. (1936), *The General Theory of Employment, Interest and Money*, London: Macmillan.

Parguez, A. and M. Seccareccia (2000), 'A credit theory of money', in J. Smithin (ed.), *What Is Money?*, London and New York: Routledge, pp. 101–23.

Skidelsky, R. (1992), *The Economist as Saviour, 1920–1937*, London: Macmillan.

Money and banking

An original analysis of money and banking is an important element of post-Keynesian economics. Post-Keynesian economists contend that money is created 'endogenously' in the form of newly issued bank deposits whenever the banking system makes new loans. This leads to important conclusions concerning the (in)capacity of the central bank to control the money supply and concerning the mechanisms that determine interest rates. Conventional propositions such as the loanable funds theory of the rate of interest and the base money multiplier are refuted. Although many post-Keynesian claims were rejected (or ignored) at the time they were made, mainstream macroeconomists and central bankers have gradually accepted and incorporated many post-Keynesian insights and assertions (see Bindseil and König, 2013; McLeay et al., 2014).

An understanding of the way that the banking system creates new money when loans are made precedes post-Keynesian economics: it can be found in the ideas of the mid-1800s Banking School and in the work of Hayek (1933/2012), Wicksell (1936) and Schumpeter (1938/2008), among others. This understanding, however, receded from view in post-war mainstream economics discussion, before being obscured entirely with the ascent of monetarism during the 1960s and 1970s. These ideas were largely kept alive and eventually resurrected by post-Keynesian authors.

Keynes (1933/1973, p. 408) argued that 'the main reason why the problem of crises is unsolved, or at any rate why this theory is so unsatisfactory, is to be found in the lack of what might be termed a monetary theory of production'. Although Keynes's (1936) *General Theory* leaves much analysis of money and banking implicit, it is clear that the book describes a monetary economic system: one in which the binding constraint on investment spending is access to finance, not lack of saving. Important early contributions on endogenous money were made by Hyman Minsky (1957a, 1957b) and Nicholas Kaldor (1958). In this regard, Rochon (2001) argues that Joan Robinson and Richard Kahn are underappreciated as important early contributors. Kaldor (1970, p. 10) wrote notably of 'a purely Keynesian model where expenditure decisions govern incomes, and ... a purely passive monetary system ... with reserves being supplied freely at constant interest rates'.

An important step was taken with the publication in 1988 of Basil Moore's *Horizontalists and Verticalists*. Moore (1988) rejected the 'verticalist' view – then widely accepted – that the central bank could directly (or 'exogenously') determine the money supply. Instead, Moore (1988) argued, the commercial banking system supplies loans to creditworthy customers on demand, at rates of interest marked up over the cost of funding. A shortage of reserves could never constrain such lending because, at the limit, the central bank would supply reserves on demand, at its chosen rate of interest, to meet the settlement needs of the commercial banking system. While Moore (1988) argued that the central bank does this to avoid the risk of a crisis caused by liquidity shortages, this function was formalized as part of standard central bank monetary policy procedures with the advent of inflation targeting in the 1990s.

Since new lending by the commercial banking system simultaneously creates new deposits, the money supply curve is 'horizontal' at the interest rates charged by commercial banks. The central bank cannot therefore directly determine the quantity of money; it can only determine the conditions – interest rates in particular – under which eligible institutions can obtain reserves. The pace at which new money is created is determined, instead, by the interplay between demand for loans at current interest rates, and the willingness of banks to expand their balance sheets. A shortage of reserves cannot constrain lending for those institutions that have access to central bank lending facilities (and hold the collateral required to access those facilities). Banks may, however, face regulatory constraints – such as capital requirements – that limit the size of their balance sheets.

Moore's (1988) arguments triggered sustained debates between 'horizontalists', who, following Moore, argue that the supply of central bank reserves is perfectly elastic at the central bank's lending rate, and 'structuralists', who suggested reasons why interest rates might rise in line with economic activity – as a result of central bank reaction, liquidity preference on the part of banks or borrowers, or changes in balance sheet structures. While differences in opinion remain, one way to reconcile these is to view money market (very short-term) rates of interest as fixed by the central bank, while other rates of interest – and thus the shape of yield curves – are determined by factors such as liquidity preference, expectations and institutional structure (see Lavoie, 1996; Dow, 2007; Bindseil and König, 2013).

Post-Keynesian monetary analysis has important implications for banking theory. The process by which banks create new purchasing power (deposits) when loans are made means that banks are not simply financial intermediaries; they do not accept deposits (of money) on one side of their balance sheet, and lend these out on the other. Banks create new money when they lend. The fundamental role of the banking system is therefore not the efficient reallocation of currently existing savings, but substitution of its guarantee of creditworthiness for that of a borrower. By issuing a monetary liability, backed by the assets on its own balance sheet (and usually guaranteed, up to a limit, by the State), bank lending expands the quantity of money, credit and purchasing power. Bank loans thus provide a 'pre-emptive strike' on access to the resources of society.

The period preceding the 2008 financial crisis was characterized by the widespread use of securitization to convert illiquid bank assets, such as mortgage loans, into marketable securities, giving rise to what has been called the 'originate to distribute' model of banking. Securitized mortgages were sold by banks to be held in non-bank financial institutions (such as structured investment vehicles or conduits), funded with shorter maturity non-deposit liabilities such as asset-backed commercial papers or repurchase agreements (repos). The existence of large bank-like institutions funded by non-deposit liabilities does not invalidate the claim that money is endogenous: this development can be understood – without tension with post-Keynesian analysis – as the result of traditional banks reaching the limits of their capacity to issue new loans by expanding their balance sheets (as a result of capital requirements, for example). Securitization temporarily reduces the size of balance sheets while converting deposit money into near-monies, thus allowing banks to continue the process of loan issuance (Michell, 2017).

Jo Michell

See also

Credit money; Endogenous money; Monetary circuit; Money as a means of payment; Money creation – nature of

References

Bindseil, U. and P.J. König (2013), 'Basil J. Moore's *Horizontalists and Verticalists*: an appraisal 25 years later', *Review of Keynesian Economics*, **1** (4), 383–90.
Dow, S.C. (2007), 'Endogenous money: structuralist', in P. Arestis and M. Sawyer (eds), *A Handbook of Alternative Monetary Economics*, Cheltenham, UK, and Northampton, MA, USA: Edward Elgar, pp. 35–51.
Hayek, F.A. (1933/2012), 'Monetary theory and the trade cycle', in H. Klausinger (ed.), *The Collected Works of F.A. Hayek, Vol. VII: Business Cycles Part I*, Chicago: University of Chicago Press, pp. 168–283.
Kaldor, N. (1958), 'Monetary policy, economic stability and growth: a memorandum submitted to the committee of the working of the monetary system (Radcliffe Committee)', 23 June. Reprinted in *Collected Economic Papers, Volume 3: Essays on Economic Policy 1*, London: Duckworth, 1964, pp. 128–53.
Kaldor, N. (1970), 'The new monetarism', *Lloyds Bank Review*, July, pp. 1–17.
Keynes, J.M. (1933/1973), 'A monetary theory of production', in *The Collected Writings of John Maynard Keynes, vol. XIII: The General Theory and After, Part I: Presentation*, London: Macmillan, pp. 408–11.
Keynes, J.M. (1936), *The General Theory of Employment, Interest and Money*, London: Macmillan.
Lavoie, M. (1996), 'Horizontalism, structuralism, liquidity preference and the principle of increasing risk', *Scottish Journal of Political Economy*, **43** (3), 275–300.
McLeay, M., A. Radia, and R. Thomas (2014), 'Money creation in the modern economy', *Bank of England Quarterly Bulletin*, **54** (1), 14–27.
Michell, J. (2017), 'Do shadow banks create money? "Financialisation" and the monetary circuit', *Metroeconomica*, **68** (2), 354–77.

Minsky, H.P. (1957a), 'Central banking and money market changes', *Quarterly Journal of Economics*, **71** (2), 171–87.
Minsky, H.P. (1957b), 'Monetary systems and accelerator models', *American Economic Review*, **47** (6), 859–83.
Moore, B.J. (1988), Horizontalists and Verticalists: The Macroeconomics of Credit Money, Cambridge, UK: Cambridge University Press.
Rochon, L.-P. (2001), 'Cambridge's contribution to endogenous money: Robinson and Kahn on credit and money', *Review of Political Economy*, **13** (3), 287–307.
Schumpeter, J.A. (1938/2008), *The Theory of Economic Development*, New Jersey: Transaction.
Wicksell, K. (1936), *Interest and Prices: A Study of the Causes Regulating the Value of Money*, London: Macmillan.

Money as a means of payment

The nature of money has always been an issue for the economics profession, both when money was reified in a precious metal and since its gradual dematerialization. Considering that 'money is what money does' (Hicks, 1967, p. 1), the functional definition of money suggests that money plays three distinct roles: it is a unit of account, a means of payment and a store of value. In fact, the essential characteristic of money is to be a means of final payment, because there may be other units of account (such as tokens) and better stores of value (that are not subject to inflation, like gold).

A means of final payment is such when 'a seller of a good, or service, or another asset, receives something of equal value from the purchaser, which leaves the seller with no further claim on the buyer' (Goodhart, 1989, p. 26). This is what occurs when the payer disposes of a number of money units that are issued by any banks through a credit line opened to the buyer of any goods, services, or assets. As Hicks (1967, p. 11) observed, '[e]very transaction involves three parties, buyer, seller, and banker.' Bankers are go-betweens, notably because they issue the number of money units that measure both the debt and the credit of the two agents involved thereby (the payer and the payee of the relevant transaction). Money and credit are therefore two separate items, as Table 1 illustrates.

Table 1 records the result of a payment, that is, a stock magnitude in the form of a bank deposit measured by x money units.

Jo Michell / Sergio Rossi

Table 1 Money and credit are two separate items

Bank			
Assets		Liabilities	
Loan to the payer	x m.u.	Deposit of the payee	x m.u.

Note: m.u. = money units.

This number measures also the amount of the loan granted to the payer. This is why money can be defined as an 'asset–liability' (Schmitt, 1975, p. 19, our translation). As a matter of fact, banks cannot create a purchasing power starting from scratch (*tabula rasa*), because the purchasing power of money depends on production. What banks can do, and do indeed, is to split the number zero into a positive and a negative magnitude, that is, $+x$ and $-x$ money units, which they credit and debit both to the payer and the payee simultaneously (Figure 1).

The circuit of money is indeed instantaneous, that is, a circular flow whose result is a stock magnitude in the form of a bank deposit (as shown in Table 1 and explained above). Such a bank deposit has a purchasing power only as far as there is something to purchase, which is tantamount to saying that money's purchasing power strictly depends on production. In this regard, production gives a purchasing power to money, whilst the latter allows the result of production to be measured on economic grounds. This is why money must be integrated in economic analysis since the beginning of it, and not just as an ancillary issue that is meant to reduce transaction costs and avoid the 'double coincidence of wants' problem (Jevons, 1875, p. 3).

Without money, no economic transaction could be paid finally, which amounts to saying that no economic system would exist – or at least would work in an orderly way – because such a system needs an orderly working payment system to settle any debts eventually. As Servet (1994) dubbed it, 'the fable of barter' is a figment of the (neoclassical) imagination: no barter trade system could ever exist, because 'goods do not buy goods' (Clower, 1967, p. 5). Further, in such a system there would be no measurement unit, hence no objective way of measuring the value of those items that agents do (want to) exchange within the economic system.

Now, beside the need to distinguish money from credit (which is difficult apparently, as money is issued through credit), one should also understand that nobody can pay issuing one's own acknowledgment of debt. This is why banks need central bank money in order for them to pay their transactions across the interbank market. The central bank is indeed instrumental for the banking system to work properly, avoiding blurring the key distinction between the payer and the issuer of the means of final payment. As Graziani (2003, p. 60) noted, '[i]f a simple promise of payment could perform the role of final payment, buyers would be endowed with a seigniorage privilege, namely with a right of withdrawing goods from the market without giving anything in exchange'. To be sure, nobody can finally pay by surrendering a promise to pay, that is, an acknowledgment of debt (IOU); a means of final payment is required to this effect. This is the essential reason why banks are special (see Rossi, 2007, for analytical elaboration).

Sergio Rossi

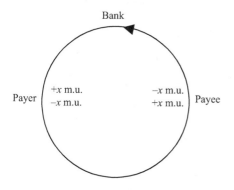

Figure 1 The instantaneous circuit of money

See also

Endogenous money; Monetary circuit – Italian school; Money and banking; Money creation – nature of; Settlement balances

References

Clower, R.W. (1967), 'A reconsideration of the microfoundations of monetary theory', *Western Economic Journal*, **6** (1), 1–8.

Goodhart, C.A.E. (1989), *Money, Information and Uncertainty*, second edition (first published 1975), London and Basingstoke: Macmillan.

Graziani, A. (2003), *The Monetary Theory of Production*, Cambridge, UK: Cambridge University Press.
Hicks, J.R. (1967), *Critical Essays in Monetary Theory*, Oxford: Clarendon Press.
Jevons, W.S. (1875), *Money and the Mechanism of Exchange*, London: Appleton.
Rossi, S. (2007), *Money and Payments in Theory and Practice*, London and New York: Routledge.
Schmitt, B. (1975), *Théorie unitaire de la monnaie, nationale et internationale*, Albeuve, CH: Castella.
Servet, J.-M. (1994), 'La fable du troc', *Dix-huitième siècle*, **26** (1), 103–15.

Money creation – history of

In terms of both monetary theory and social history, money creation has been shrouded in mystery. Throughout the ages, money has been as important to societies as it has been varied in its forms of creation. The intellectual appreciation of money has therefore been faced with two powerful distorting forces. On the one hand, when money has been controlled by the priestly castes of societies and has been an important element of social control, such castes have once and again attempted to present money creation as an element of social control determined not by humans, but rather by the gods: a divine or natural order. On the other hand, money has also been once and again created outside of the relatively rigid structures of the market and formal governance, and under many manifestations, from seeds and shells to tobacco, coloured paper and more recently bytes.

Such diversity has long perplexed economics as a social science, and to date there is still no definition of money that is accepted across the profession. Therefore, economics as a branch of ideology has long been called on to obfuscate, whereas economics as a legitimate social science has often searched fitfully, fruitlessly, for a single truth regarding money. For example, the most influential economists in Western societies, Adam Smith (1776/1976) and Karl Marx (1894), both begin their most famous works with the question of money. Scores of economists, rivers of ink and forests of paper have all been sacrificed to this task and have produced the counterintuitive conclusion that the amount written on the subject reflects how little we know.

From the beginnings of Western society, money has been present both as a tool of social control of the ruling classes and as a tool of society for economic interaction, sometimes even in the absence of money itself. For example, in Mesopotamia, social accountancy and trade was realized through tally sticks representing credit, and not money as is the typical case (Wray, 1998). In the Roman Empire, money was coined in the Temple of Juno Moneta, where the word 'money' finds its origin. After the fall of the Roman Empire, the coining of precious metals continued for centuries to be dominated by royalty. Money creation therefore obeyed a pseudo 'natural' order. Just as nobility enjoyed a mandate from God to rule, so did metallic coin money.

Such a natural order regarding money creation in the West was first challenged at a systemic level with the first manifestations of modern banking in twelfth-century Italy. Yet, while a new source of credit-money was emerging, it was still well embedded in the social order dominated by the church and nobility. By the time of the beginning of the Industrial Revolution, Adam Smith (1776/1976, p. 297) described how Scottish banks were essentially acting outside of the dictates of natural law, and how these were successful ventures that aided the growth of the overall economy as well. This era also saw the creation of the first central banks, which were often private in both ownership and operations in their original conceptions.

As the actors in the capitalist market displaced the nobles of the feudal economy in controlling European States, the ideological branch of economics slowly and partially replaced the private market and not nobility as the repository of the natural order. From Smith's time until well into the twentieth century, private banks in many countries issued the legal currency of the economy. However, such systems proved too instable for the architects of the market order. Just as central banks were made public so that private banks could seek protection by the State from the markets that they controlled and invariably ruined (Polanyi, 1944), the issue of money also became a State monopoly.

When banks could issue their own banknotes, they were typically backed by State assets and/or precious metals. For most of the nineteenth century, bonds and bills issued by States were backed by the international gold standard. During the Bretton Woods regime, gold became the backstop of the US dollar as the core international asset. With the demise of this regime, the US dollar came to fulfil the role of gold, and the international financial system became based on fiat money.

With the appearance of the first globally accepted digital currency, namely bitcoin, launched in 2009, a new form of money has appeared. The social acceptance of bitcoins did not include academia, and still largely has not, although it did provoke much debate on the nature of money. Groups that have accepted digital currencies in recent years include the world's largest banks, non-financial corporations and many central banks.

Given the fact that the internationally dominant currency has shifted from gold to the US dollar within the last half century, and now with the entrance of digital money, few still argue that money creation is a natural rather than social phenomenon. Perhaps the most interesting current debates revolve around whether money is a social convention, a view embraced by the Polanyian perspective, or an institution, as embraced from an institutionalist viewpoint.

WESLEY C. MARSHALL

See also

Bretton Woods; Credit money; International financial architecture; Money as a means of payment; Money creation – nature of

References

Marx, K. (1894), *Das Kapital: Kritik der Politischen Ökonomie. Dritter Band: Der Gesamtprozeß der Kapitalistischen Produktion*, reprinted as *Marx–Engels–Werke, Volume 25*, Berlin: Dietz Verlag, 1964. English translation: *Capital: A Critique of Political Economy*, New York: International Publisher, 1967.
Polanyi, K. (1944), *The Great Transformation*, Boston: Beacon Press.
Smith, A. (1776/1976), *An Inquiry into the Nature and Causes of the Wealth of Nations*, Oxford: Clarendon Press.
Wray, L.R. (1998), *Understanding Modern Money: The Key to Full Employment and Price Stability*, Cheltenham, UK, and Northampton, MA, USA: Edward Elgar.

Money creation – nature of

Most economic theories – including the mainstream view or any other theory based on Walrasian general equilibrium – assume the existence of money, rather than explaining it. As such, money is unnecessary (although it is useful), and is created exogenously by an institution (nowadays the central bank) with the purpose of overcoming the problem of the 'double coincidence of wants'. In this light, the role of money is to facilitate ('lubricate') exchanges, largely based on a barter system. Yet, anthropologists disprove the fundamental basis of such a framework, as barter has ever concerned a fringe ratio of all those exchanges that take place within any society (see, for instance, Graeber, 2011, pp. 29 and 40). From this perspective, money is not exogenously created and injected into an already functioning barter-trade system. On the contrary, money creation concerns the very essence of the economic system, as Keynes (1973/2013a, p. 408) recognized by arguing for the necessity of a 'monetary theory of production'.

Coming to the present, and logically speaking, no goods or services can be exchanged before they are produced. Hence, the very first creation of money cannot but concern production (Lavoie, 1996, p. 533), and more precisely the remuneration of production factors, namely labour from a post-Keynesian point of view (Keynes, 1936, p. 213; Graziani, 2003, p. 27). Schematically, a firm (F) demands and obtains a credit line, namely both a credit and a deposit recorded on its behalf on the bank's bookkeeping (Table 1), which amounts to saying that money is 'credit-driven and demand determined' (Moore, 1988, p. 373). In other

Table 1 The bank's credit line

Bank			
Assets		Liabilities	
Loan to firm F	x	Deposit of firm F	x

Source: Author's elaboration based on Rossi (2007, p. 23).

Table 2 The payment of workers and the formation of income

Bank			
Assets		Liabilities	
Loan to firm F	x	Deposit of income-holders (IH)	x

Source: Author's elaboration based on Rossi (2007, p. 23).

WESLEY C. MARSHALL / MAURIZIO SOLARI

words, money is endogenously created within the economic system and for the purposes of this system (see Rochon, 2012; Rochon and Rossi, 2013, for analytical elaboration).

Since any credit carries an interest burden, it would be nonsense not to immediately spend the obtained deposit (Graziani, 1996, pp. 21–2), for instance to pay workers and in so doing start a new cycle of production (Table 2). Therefore, workers (or, generally speaking, income holders, IH) do not obtain immediately the products resulting from their labour effort; rather, they obtain an income (initially in the form of wages), namely bank deposits charged with a positive purchasing power, which are indeed the monetary (that is, numerical) form of the aforementioned products (Schmitt, 1984/2021, p. 42).

IH have two possibilities to spend their income: (1) to purchase goods or services (that is, consumption) on the product market, giving up the product's monetary form (bank deposit) and obtaining the product in its real form; or (2) to purchase financial assets on the financial market, which consists in a transfer of income from one IH to another economic agent willing to spend it on the product market eventually. As a matter of fact, the firm will be in a position to obtain the relevant income and therefore reimburse the credit initially granted by the bank, destroying both the loan and the deposit recorded on the bank's ledger, thereby closing the production cycle. As a result, each new production cycle starts from *tabula rasa* (Rossi, 2007, p. 35). In other words, it requires the formation of a completely novel income through the granting of a new credit line by a bank (Parguez and Seccareccia, 2000, p. 106).

Money creation is enlarged or restricted following the needs of production (Rochon and Rossi, 2013, p. 214) or more precisely the effective demand (see Keynes, 1936, pp. 23–34) expected by firms. The role of banks, indeed, is to grant loans in order to monetize any production activity they consider profitable at the relevant interest rate (Rossi, 2007, p. 51; Rochon, 2012, pp. 301–2; see also Keynes, 1973/2013b, p. 219). However, banks settle all transactions between a payer and a payee, not only the payment of wages. In fact, without such an intermediation any economic agent would be able to issue its own means of payment, in the form of an IOU, allowing everyone to purchase anything in exchange for nothing (Graziani, 2003, p. 60), thus generating an unlimited accumulation of never settled debts. Conversely, the banking system ensures the monetary intermediation leaving both the payer and the payee without any further claim on one another (Rossi, 2007, pp. 43–5), and the central bank does exactly the same intermediation for interbank transactions (Rossi, 2007, pp. 65–6) with the aim to ensure the banking system's solvency when, for instance, the payer and the payee have their accounts at different banks (Rochon, 2006, pp. 174–5).

In conclusion, any transaction implies the creation of money, which, however, disappears instantaneously, to give rise to a bank deposit. Indeed, money has no value per se, being at the same time positive and negative (see Tables 1 and 2), namely an 'asset–liability' (Schmitt, 1975, p. 13, our translation). Nevertheless, when money is created to settle a transaction on the labour market, the resulting deposit is charged with purchasing power, transforming it into an income. Bank deposits and thereby income (but not money) can be replicated in a physical form (that is, visible and touchable), for instance bank notes (see Cencini, 2005, pp. 91–176, for a discussion on the conceptual difference between 'money' and 'income'). To be sure, income allows for purchasing goods and services on the product market (thereby destroying the related deposits as a result) or financial assets on the financial market (thus displacing the deposits to the sellers or issuers of these assets). Researchers as well as policy makers should acknowledge the double-entry bookkeeping nature of money (Rochon and Rossi, 2013, p. 225) in order to apply policies that ensure the proper working of the banking system as well as the economic system as a whole.

MAURIZIO SOLARI

See also

Credit money; Effective demand; Endogenous money; Monetary theory of production; Money as a means of payment

References

Cencini, A. (2005), *Macroeconomic Foundations of Macroeconomics*, London and New York: Routledge.
Graeber, D. (2011), *Debt: The First 5000 Years*, New York: Melville House.
Graziani, A. (1996), *La teoria del circuito monetario*, Milano: Jaca Book.

Graziani, A. (2003), *The Monetary Theory of Production*, Cambridge, UK: Cambridge University Press.

Keynes, J.M. (1936), *The General Theory of Employment, Interest and Money*, London: Macmillan.

Keynes, J.M. (1973/2013a), *The Collected Writings of John Maynard Keynes, Vol. XIII: The General Theory and After: Part I, Preparation*, Cambridge, UK: Cambridge University Press.

Keynes, J.M. (1973/2013b), *The Collected Writings of John Maynard Keynes, Vol. XIV: The General Theory and After: Part II, Preparation*, Cambridge, UK: Cambridge University Press.

Lavoie, M. (1996), 'Monetary policy in an economy with endogenous credit money', in G. Deleplace and E.J. Nell (eds), *Money in Motion: The Post-Keynesian and Circulation Approaches*, Basingstoke, UK, and New York: Macmillan and St. Martin's Press, pp. 532–45.

Moore, B.J. (1988), 'The endogenous money supply', *Journal of Post Keynesian Economics*, **10** (3), 372–85.

Parguez, A. and M. Seccareccia (2000), 'The credit theory of money: the monetary circuit approach', in J. Smithin (ed.), *What is Money?*, London and New York: Routledge, pp. 101–23.

Rochon, L.-P. (2006), 'Endogenous money, central banks and the banking system: Basil Moore and the supply of credit', in M. Setterfield (ed.), *Complexity, Endogenous Money and Macroeconomic Theory: Essays in Honour of Basil Moore*, Cheltenham, UK, and Northampton, MA, USA: Edward Elgar, pp. 170–86.

Rochon, L.-P. (2012), 'Money's endogeneity, Keynes's *General Theory* and beyond', in T. Cate (ed.), *Keynes's General Theory: Seventy-Five Years Later*, Cheltenham, UK, and Northampton, MA, USA: Edward Elgar, pp. 293–305.

Rochon, L.-P. and S. Rossi (2013), 'Endogenous money: the evolutionary versus revolutionary views', *Review of Keynesian Economics*, **1** (2), 210–29.

Rossi, S. (2007), *Money and Payments in Theory and Practice*, London and New York: Routledge.

Schmitt, B. (1975), *Théorie unitaire de la monnaie, nationale et internationale*, Albeuve, CH: Castella.

Schmitt, B. (1984/2021), *Inflation, Unemployment and Capital Malformations*, X. Bradley and A. Cencini (trans.), London and New York: Routledge.

Money illusion

Money illusion occurs when economic agents cannot distinguish changes in the absolute level of prices and money wages from changes in relative prices and real wages, so that monetary shocks distort decisions such as the trade-off between consumption and leisure. Keynes (1936) was often accused, groundlessly, of attributing irrational money illusion to workers, with Friedman (1968) arguing that aggregate demand stimulus would reduce unemployment below its 'natural rate' only by tricking workers into supplying more labour than they would have done if they correctly perceived the real wage.

Although absent from Keynes's *General Theory* (1936), the concept of money illusion did figure prominently in the work of his contemporary, the American economist Irving Fisher, author of *The Money Illusion* (1928). For Fisher, money illusion was not an arbitrary assumption to make about the irrationality of workers so that aggregate demand management would have real effects in a macroeconomic model. Rather, Fisher viewed widespread confusion between real and nominal values as a serious problem, the driving force behind economic fluctuations, as he argued in a serious of empirical studies, one of which (Fisher, 1926) was reprinted a quarter-century after his death as 'I discovered the Phillips curve'. Fisher devoted most of his long career to attempts to eradicate money illusion by educating the public: explaining the distinction between real and nominal interest rates in a 1896 monograph, developing the Fisher ideal index (the geometric mean of the Paasche and Laspeyres indexes) to best represent the changing purchasing power of money, establishing an index number in the basement of his home to calculate that price index each week (Fisher, 1997, Vols. 1, 4 and 7). When the public stubbornly refused to learn the difference between real and nominal variables (even during hyperinflation in Germany in 1923) and governments declined to adopt Fisher's 'compensated dollar' plan to stabilize the price level (Fisher, 1997, Vols. 4 and 6), he advocated indexation to neutralize the consequences of money illusion and pioneered the issue of bonds indexed to the price level (Fisher, 1997, Vol. 8). To Fisher, money illusion was a deplorable phenomenon, not an assumption.

As Trevithick (1975) emphasized, Keynes (1936, Ch. 2) explained how money wages could be sticky downwards without any irrational money illusion, so that a negative shock to aggregate demand and the price level would reduce employment and output. Without any failure to observe the price level or any

MAURIZIO SOLARI / ROBERT W. DIMAND

confusion between real and nominal magnitudes, workers care about their relative wages compared to others in similar jobs. Keynes (1936, p. 14, italics in the original) stressed that

> any individual or group of individuals, who consent to a reduction of money-wages relative to others, will suffer a *relative* reduction in real wages, which is a sufficient justification for them to resist it. On the other hand it would be impracticable to resist every reduction of real wages, due to a change in the purchasing-power of money which affects all workers alike ... and leave relative money-wages unchanged. ... it is unfortunate that the workers, though unconsciously, are instinctively more reasonable economists than the classical school.

Keynes (1936, Ch. 19) explained how rapid downward adjustment of money wages, such as those that occurred in the United States in 1932, could make things worse as rapid deflation lowered the marginal efficiency of capital in money terms, created expectations of future deflation, and increased the risk of bankruptcy and default (see Tobin, 1975).[1] For Keynes, downward stickiness of money wages was a recommendation, not an arbitrary assumption and not the consequence of irrational money illusion, and rapidly adjusting prices and money wages would be destabilising. Keynes's relative wages and staggered contracts explanation of downward stickiness of money wages was independently reinvented by Taylor (1980) and was acclaimed as a great advance over Keynes's supposed assumption of rigid wages due to money illusion.

While there was no money illusion in Keynes's *General Theory*, some non-Keynesian approaches to macroeconomics do depend on money illusion to explain fluctuations in employment and real output. Both Friedman's (1968) combination of adaptive expectations and the natural rate hypothesis, and Lucas's New Classical combination of the natural rate hypothesis with rational expectations and monetary misperceptions (in articles collected in Lucas, 1981) based their explanations of real fluctuations on agents failing or being unable to distinguish nominal shocks from changes in relative prices. According to Sargent (1979, p. 325), 'Lucas, in effect, constructed a simple model of 'money illusion', one compatible with rational, optimizing behavior.'

ROBERT W. DIMAND

See also

Aggregate demand; Inflation; NAIRU; Phillips curve; Wages

Note

1. Ironically, Tobin's first article (Tobin, 1941), written as an undergraduate, criticized Keynes (1936) for supposedly assuming money illusion.

References

Fisher, I. (1926), 'A statistical relation between unemployment and price changes', *International Labour Review*, **13** (6), 785–92. Reprinted as I. Fisher (1973), 'Lost and found: I discovered the Phillips curve', *Journal of Political Economy*, **81** (2), 496–502.
Fisher, I. (1928), *The Money Illusion*, New York: Adelphi.
Fisher, I. (1997), *The Works of Irving Fisher*, 14 volumes, edited by W.J. Barber assisted by R.W. Dimand and K. Foster, consulting editor J. Tobin, London: Pickering & Chatto.
Friedman, M. (1968), 'The role of monetary policy', *American Economic Review*, **58** (1), 1–17.
Keynes, J.M. (1936), *The General Theory of Employment, Interest and Money*, London: Macmillan.
Lucas, R.E., Jr. (1981), *Studies in Business Cycle Theory*, Cambridge, MA: MIT Press, and Oxford: Basil Blackwell.
Sargent, T.J. (1979), *Macroeconomic Theory*, New York: Academic Press.
Taylor, J.B. (1980), 'Aggregate dynamics and staggered contracts', *Journal of Political Economy*, **88** (1), 1–23.
Tobin, J. (1941), 'A note on the money wage problem', *Quarterly Journal of Economics*, **55** (3), 508–16.
Tobin, J. (1975), 'Keynesian models of recession and depression', *American Economic Review: Papers and Proceedings*, **65** (2), 195–202.
Trevithick, J.A. (1975), 'Keynes, inflation and money illusion', *Economic Journal*, **85** (337), 101–13.

Money in Motion

Money in Motion is the title of a book (Deleplace and Nell, 1996) collecting articles by a wide array of Circulation Approach and post-Keynesian authors. More importantly, given these authors' contributions, *Money in Motion* should be considered a research programme combining these two theoretical frameworks (and other heterodox perspectives).

ROBERT W. DIMAND / ENRIQUE DELAMÓNICA

In contrast with mainstream (Neoclassical Synthesis/New Classical/New Keynesian) ideas, the Circulation Approach emphasizes the idiosyncratic and institutional role of banks in generating money endogenously. Although this role changes across time and place, certain features/principles remain unaltered. For instance, money circulates following a specific circuit. Thus, economic activity and its aggregate components depend on how payments are organized and money created (indeed, banks finance firms, which organize production and hire workers; after output is sold, firms pay back the loans). In this framework, endogenous creation of money (not financial intermediation) is the specific characteristic/role of banks, fundamentally separating them from firms in the private sector.

Credit relations (who and when creates money, borrows and pays back) affect investment. The banks–firms relationship allows banks to endogenously create money (financing firms based on short-term interest rates). Firms selling their output (the basic relationship between customers/households and firms) or borrowing against financial instruments obtain liquidity (depending on long-term interest rates). Consequently, only the solvency and indebtedness of firms are impacted by financial market conditions, not investment decisions.

Investment decisions determine activity (employment) levels. The credit firms can obtain from banks (not savings) constrains investment. Thus, investment and savings are equal as an identity, not the result of output adjustment. Therefore, the focus is not the level of output, but analysing the conditions allowing firms to repay banks: the monetary circuit 'closure'.

This closure should not be interpreted as an equilibrium or 'steady-state loop' (identically recurring cycles). It means economic activity occurs following definite arrangements along irreversible time. This type of period analysis hearkens to Quesnay's *Tableau économique*. It involves sequentiality (a series of specifically ordered steps: firms paying wages and then workers purchasing from firms), which either demarcates intra- and inter-period activities or describes overlapping circuits of different duration (and the possibility of hoarding). Regardless, commodity production and monetary circulation are integrated through time, approaching the point when firms must repay loans to banks. Then, a symmetrical effect to money creation happens: its cancellation.

Symmetry, however, does not entail a perfect match. If, when the period ends, loans cannot be repaid, they could be converted into financial assets (long-term loans). Unspent balances in households' bank accounts would become financial claims. Thus, finance and only finance links periods. Households hoarding money (not spending all their monetary income) need not be problematic either. If firms cannot repay their loans, banks can grant them new ones. Consequently, both finance and money connect different periods. Whether finance alone or conjointly with money concatenates periods, the monetary circuit closure establishes the conditions influencing decisions for the following period.

As production and consumption decisions are decentralized (resulting in uncertainty), some expectations by firms may not be realized, leading (possibly) to bankruptcy. This effect and hoarding make the system naturally crisis-prone (requiring central banks with lender of last resort and other institutional powers to confront crises).

This brief description shows commonalities between post-Keynesian and Circulation Approach models and methodology: utilizing realistic descriptions of behaviour and institutional contexts, not suppressing uncertainty and coordination failures, endogenous money (not necessarily sufficient to sustain full employment nor avoiding excessive credit), and possibility of crises. Their differences should be considered opportunities to complement each other and to build a strong alternative to the mainstream.

For instance, in post-Keynesian analysis, mark-up pricing (in nominal terms vis-à-vis wages) ensures sufficient earnings flows to finance long-term investment plans (even if unexpected conditions require deviations from them). This analysis can offer the Circulation Approach a theory of pricing and a strengthened account of links between periods.

The Circulation Approach can provide a full description of how, and how much, money is endogenously created. Post-Keynesian economists could then eschew mainstream concepts/assumptions embedded in upward-sloping money supply curves and additive motives for money demand. Post-Keynesian economists can gain a truly non-market-clearing monetary analysis.

ENRIQUE DELAMÓNICA

Sequentiality could replace mainstream views of the macroeconomy as the aggregation of microeconomic (optimizing) agents. Integrating monetary and production circuits provides a different picture. Firms (micro-level) borrow money, produce and sell commodities, and repay loans constrained by monetary system rules and procedures (macro-level).

The pattern of circulation could assist clarifying how investments determine profits and how the wage bill in the means-of-production sector determines profits in the consumption goods sectors. Replacing comparative statics with path-dependent dynamics could facilitate these endeavours.

This shift can also help elucidate the relationship between investment and savings when there is endogenous credit-money (circumstances in which the simplistic Neoclassical Synthesis multiplier does not hold). Variations in investment lead to changes in the output of capital goods (and, concomitantly, means of production) and in employment (affecting wage earners' consumption). This sequence of changes is compatible with a Neo-Ricardian matrix multiplier. A sequential monetary-credit model is needed to fully understand this process. This understanding (generalizable to any autonomous spending) would be crucial to design economic policies to maintain full employment. Combining the Circulation Approach and post-Keynesianism can provide these answers.

ENRIQUE DELAMÓNICA

See also

Endogenous money; Interest rates and investment; Mark-up pricing; Monetary circuit; Uncertainty

Reference

Deleplace, G. and E.J. Nell (eds) (1996), *Money in Motion: The Post Keynesian and Circulation Approaches*, London and New York: Macmillan and St. Martin's Press.

Monopoly Capital

Monopoly Capital (Baran and Sweezy, 1966) represents the culmination of both authors' extensive research in the area. Sweezy had already established himself as America's foremost Marxist scholar with the publication of his definitive interpretation of Marxian political economy (*The Theory of Capitalist Development*), while Baran's *The Political Economy of Growth* was a preliminary investigation of the issues which *Monopoly Capital* was to subsequently analyse.

Underlying *Monopoly Capital* is the thesis that capitalism has evolved from its initial competitive phase to one characterized by 'large-scale enterprise[s] producing a significant share of the output of an industry, or even several industries, and able to control its prices, the volume of its production, and the type and amount of its investment' (Baran and Sweezy, 1966, p. 19). The emergence of these oligopolistic structures has transformed capitalism into its monopoly phase, which has different laws of dynamics that the book analyses, influenced by the pioneering work of Marx, Kalecki, and Steindl. The key to the transformation lies in the emergence of stagnationist tendencies associated with the tendency for the surplus to rise, with the surplus defined as 'the difference between what a society produces and the costs of producing it' (p. 23). The statistical appendix (by Joseph Phillips) estimates that the surplus was 56.1 per cent of US gross domestic product in 1963.

Baran and Sweezy start their analysis by documenting the rise of the giant corporation, which has become the major actor in capitalist society: 'The real capitalist today is not the individual businessman but the corporation' (p. 54). As a result, corporations are no longer the 'price-takers' of neoclassical competitive theory, but rather are price-makers, within a framework of implicit industry collusion, so as to avoid price wars, which has been replaced by non-price competition in the form of 'sales effort'. The rigidity of prices, coupled with strong pressures for the costs of production to fall lead to a 'strong and systematic tendency for the surplus to rise, both absolutely and as a share of total output' (p. 87).

Baran and Sweezy (1966) identify four sources for the absorption of this surplus: capitalists' consumption and investment, the sales effort, civilian government expenditure, and militarism and imperialism.

Since capitalists' consumption comes from their income, which is in the form of distributed dividends, Baran and Sweezy (1966) argue that it declines as a proportion of surplus. Absorption via increased investment meets the problem of the Kalecki paradox, that the increased investment will expand the economy's capacity – leading to the rise and growth of excess capacity. This, in turn, will put a damper on investment, leading to an economic downturn. The three main forms of exogenous investment, to meet the needs of an expanding population, new methods of production and new products, and foreign investment do not alter the picture.

Without the other ways of stimulating demand, capitalism would have a much stronger propensity to stagnate. The sales effort is important not only for its role in absorbing the surplus, but also because it replaces price competition as the main form of competition in monopoly capitalism. Advertising acts to both increase demand and to reduce demand elasticity. This is reinforced by product differentiation via the development of new products and features.

With respect to the role of civilian government, Keynes's contributions form the basis of the argument that, owing to the emergence of excess capacity and lack of effective demand under monopoly capitalism, the government can stimulate the economy through both the size of its deficit and the level of its spending. The importance of substantial growth in government spending in the post-war period as a major source of the absorption of the surplus is highlighted. Of course, this was largely reversed in the neoliberal period associated with crises and stagnation, which is foreshadowed in the book's argument that an increasing proportion of government expenditure went to defence spending, as a result of the political limits of civilian spending: 'In the case of almost every major item in the civilian budget, powerful vested interests are soon aroused to opposition as expansion proceeds beyond the necessary minimum' (p. 166).

Militarism and imperialism are not only important for their role in the absorption of the surplus, but also owing to their link to the exploitative hierarchy underlying America's 'expansionist and empire-minded' ambitions. This highlights the underlying irrationality of the system, which, instead of relying on civilian government expenditure to improve the well-being of its citizens, increasingly funds military expenditure.

The basic model is utilized to explain the history of monopoly capitalism and its role in contemporary race relations, as well as to the falling quality of society.

The main problem with *Monopoly Capital* is its relative neglect of the financial sector, which, with insurance and real estate, is discussed extremely briefly (pp. 143–4). This was rectified in subsequent analysis by Sweezy and Magdoff. These views, which are the pillar of what has become known as the Monthly Review approach, are synthesized in John Bellamy Foster's *The Theory of Monopoly Capitalism* (2014).

The importance of the Baran and Sweezy's (1966) book lies in its historical role in revitalizing the left in the 1960s, and also in its ability to explain the stagnationist tendencies of modern capitalism, which have become more apparent in the twenty-first century. The implications of the rising surplus are reinforced by the failure of the methods analysed in the book – with the addition of the role of the financial sector – to adequately stimulate demand in the market for produced goods and services.

PETER KRIESLER

See also

Capitalism; Effective demand; Kaleckian economics; Monopoly power; Paradox – Kalecki's

References

Baran, P. (1957), *The Political Economy of Growth*, New York: Monthly Review Press.
Baran, P. and P. Sweezy (1966), *Monopoly Capital: An Essay on the American Economic and Social Order*, Middlesex: Pelican Books.
Foster, J.B. (2014), *The Theory of Monopoly Capitalism: An Elaboration of Marxian Political Economy*, New York: Monthly Review Press.
Sweezy, P. (1942), *The Theory of Capitalist Development*, New York: Monthly Review Press.

Monopoly power

Imperfect competitive markets are considered by the neoclassical approach as 'market failures', because market prices do not correspond to equilibrium prices that clear markets. Hence monopoly and oligopoly cases are considered as exceptions, that is, deviations from the 'normal case'.

It is convenient to argue that in such an understanding, the concept of 'power' is 'irrelevant in a world in which freedom of entry renders monopoly positions ephemeral' (Humphrey,

PETER KRIESLER / ILHAN DÖGÜS

2013, p. 95) and 'foreign to the essential core of the neoclassical theory' (Minsky, 1986, p. 119).

The ignorance of 'power' heavily relies on the assumption of 'self-coordinating markets' in which firms' sole ontology is the reduction of transaction costs (Coase, 1937) and thereby allocating the resources in an efficient manner. This is also related to having conceived the capitalist market economy as a 'barter economy', where money possesses a 'medium of exchange' function. Hence, in industrial economics textbooks (see, for example, Belleflamme and Peitz, 2010), it is not possible to read about the concepts of money, finance, and banks.

The emphasis on the 'store of value' function of money, monetary production, capitalist investment, and fundamental uncertainty (see Keynes, 1936), however, enables the post-Keynesian approach to introduce the concept of power into economic analysis, because in that manner prices have a function to secure the firm's survival and validate its own investment and financing decisions (Minsky and Ferri, 1984, p. 490). Hence, 'market power ... may be a prerequisite for the use of expensive and highly specialized capital assets and large-scale debt financing' (Minsky, 1986, p. 181).

In Kaleckian theory (see Kalecki, 1954), it is assumed that firms are able to charge a higher mark-up rate per unit of production over their average labour and raw material costs in line with their market power. Steindl (1990, pp. 305–7) suggests that the break-even point, where revenues and total costs equalize, will be lower if the mark-up is higher. Hence the latter becomes a measure of the 'degree of monopoly'. Gordon (1988) proposes to measure it with the ratio of value added to the wage bill. In post-Keynesian studies regarding the recent increase in market concentration and monopoly power at the aggregate level, Brennan (2016) measures it by way of the 'asset share of top 100 firms', while Dögüs (2019) considers the 'the reverse of break-even point'.

Monopoly power and market concentration have been considered by mainstream economics merely as microeconomic issues. However, as pointed out by Dögüs (2023), consumption inequality consolidates and spreads the concentration across sectors by way of consumption of expensive goods produced by other dominant firms in other sectors. As a result, market concentration deserves to be examined at the macroeconomic level as well.

However, it is interesting that, despite mainstream economics having relied on assuming full-competitive markets as the normal case, while post-Keynesian economists have considered imperfect competitive markets as the normal case, there have been more New-Keynesian works in recent years on the increase in monopoly power than post-Keynesian works. Recent New-Keynesian literature has focused on the increase in monopoly power at the macroeconomic level and its implications, without referring, however, to the post-Keynesian literature (see Syverson, 2019; Dögüs, 2019). The post-Keynesian literature on functional income distribution (Stockhammer, 2017) and wage-led growth (Onaran and Galanis, 2012) has not paid attention to the increased market concentration despite considering the role of mark-up pricing in terms of income distribution. Stockhammer (2017) considers the decrease in the bargaining power of labour, but without taking into account its relationship with monopoly power.

ILHAN DÖGÜS

See also

Growth – wage-led vs profit-led; Mark-up pricing; Money and banking; Neoclassical economics; Post-Keynesian economics – a big tent?

References

Belleflamme, P. and M. Peitz (2010), *Industrial Organization: Markets and Strategies*, New York: Cambridge University Press.
Brennan, J. (2016), 'Rising corporate concentration, declining trade union power, and the growing income gap: American prosperity in historical perspective', *Levy Economics Institute of Bard College e-pamphlet*, available online at www.levyinstitute.org/pubs/e_pamphlet_1.pdf (last accessed 8 August 2019).
Coase, R.H. (1937), 'The nature of the firm', *Economica*, **4** (16), 386–405.
Dögüs, I. (2019), 'Rising wage differential between white-collar and blue-collar workers and market concentration: the case of the USA, 1964–2007', *PSL Quarterly Review*, **72** (290), 223–51.
Dögüs, I. (2023), 'Consumption differential between white-collar and blue-collar workers and rising market concentration in the USA: 1984–2017', *PSL Quarterly Review*, forthcoming.
Gordon, M.J. (1998), 'Monopoly power in the United States manufacturing sector, 1899 to 1994', *Journal of Post Keynesian Economics*, **20** (3), 323–35.

Humphrey, T.M. (2013), 'Chicago School of economics', in T. Cate (ed.), *An Encyclopedia of Keynesian Economics*, second edition, Cheltenham, UK, and Northampton, MA, USA: Edward Elgar, pp. 94–8.
Kalecki, M. (1954), *Theory of Economic Dynamics*, London: Allen & Unwin.
Keynes, J.M. (1936), *The General Theory of Employment, Interest and Money*, London: Macmillan.
Minsky, H.P. (1986), *Stabilizing an Unstable Economy*, New Haven, CT: Yale University Press.
Minsky, H.P. and P. Ferri (1984), 'Prices, employment, and profits', *Journal of Post Keynesian Economics*, **6** (4), 489–99.
Onaran, Ö. and G. Galanis (2013), 'Is aggregate demand wage-led or profit-led? A global model', in M. Lavoie and E. Stockhammer (eds), *Wage-led Growth: An Equitable Strategy for Economic Recovery*, Basingstoke, UK: Palgrave Macmillan, pp. 71–99.
Steindl, J. (1990), *Economic Papers 1941–88*, New York: St. Martin's Press.
Stockhammer, E. (2017), 'Wage-led versus profit-led demand: what have we learned? A Kaleckian–Minskyan view', *Review of Keynesian Economics*, **5** (1), 25–42.
Syverson, C. (2019), 'Macroeconomics and market power: facts, potential explanations and open questions', *The Brookings Economic Studies*, January, available online at https://www.brookings.edu/wp-content/uploads/2019/01/ES_20190116_Syverson-Macro-Micro-Market-Power.pdf (last accessed 8 August 2019).

NAIRU

The non-accelerating inflation rate of unemployment (NAIRU) is the rate of unemployment for which the inflation rate is stable. Lower (higher) rates of unemployment would increase (decrease) the rate of inflation. In New-Keynesian models the NAIRU is used as a benchmark for the estimation of the unemployment gap.

While the expressions 'NAIRU' and 'natural rate of unemployment' are often used as synonyms, they coincide only in the long period. The natural rate of unemployment is the steady state equilibrium in the labour market and changes only as a result of permanent modifications in the institutional setting or technological shocks. The NAIRU can also be modified by other types of shocks to an extent determined by the frictions existing in the labour and goods markets. In the long run, the effects of these shocks either vanish or determine changes in the natural rate of unemployment.

The acronym NAIRU was first used by Tobin (1980) in an attempt to reconcile Friedman's (1968) accelerationist hypothesis with the traditional demand management of Keynesian inspiration. According to Friedman (1968), the inflation–unemployment trade-off put to the fore by the traditional Phillips curve could exist only in the short run, defined as the period of time in which workers do not realize that their real wage has been modified by a change in the inflation rate. In the long run, workers adjust their inflation expectations and accordingly shift the supply of labour, bringing back the unemployment rate at its natural level. As a consequence, in the long run the Phillips curve is vertical at the natural rate of unemployment and policy makers can affect the real economy only through a sustained increase (acceleration) in the rate of inflation in order to defy people's expectations. Modigliani and Papademos (1975) introduced the expression 'non-inflationary rate of unemployment' as the rate of unemployment at which the conventional Phillips curve intersects Friedman's vertical curve.

Tobin and later the new-Neoclassical consensus built on this idea, conceiving the NAIRU as a tool that can be used by monetary authorities to forecast future movements of inflation rates. However, such a view of the NAIRU is in sharp contrast with the monetarist approach, which interprets it as a purely theoretical benchmark that does not need to be estimated, given that the central bank should refrain from any intervention.

The use and estimations of the NAIRU have been increasingly plagued by empirical and theoretical issues. Two of the main problems with the empirical estimation are the general lack of agreement about measurements and estimates, and the hysteresis of the unemployment rate. Empirical studies since Blanchard and Summers (1986) have established that a negative shock can permanently increase the nonaccelerating-inflation level of unemployment. In fact, the unemployment rate usually displays a strong path dependency and does not appear to revert to its pre-shock levels. The presence of hysteresis in the NAIRU is strictly related to two theoretical issues. The first is that shifts in the NAIRU are observable not in the absence of significant institutional or technological shocks but rather as a consequence of demand factors, contradicting the theory. The second issue concerns the fact that the problems in the estimation and the volatility over time imply that, even in the absence of changes in expected inflation, the expectations-augmented Phillips curve can shift over time. The consequence is that the same rate of expected inflation is compatible with different rates of unemployment, re-proposing the same theoretical conundrum that led to the dismissal of the traditional Phillips curve.

Corrado Di Guilmi

See also

Hysteresis; Inflation; Money illusion; Phillips curve; Traverse, path dependency, and economic dynamics

References

Blanchard, O. and L. Summers (1986), 'Hysteresis and the European unemployment problem', *NBER Macroeconomics Annual 1986*, 1, 15–90.
Friedman, M. (1968), 'The role of monetary policy', *American Economic Review*, **58** (1), 1–17.
Modigliani, F. and L. Papademos (1975), 'Targets for monetary policy in the coming year', *Brookings Papers on Economic Activity*, **6** (1), 141–66.
Tobin, J. (1980), 'Stabilization policy ten years after', *Brookings Papers on Economic Activity*, **11** (1), 19–90.

Negative interest rate policy

Negative interest rate policies (NIRPs) refer to central banks' decision to set their target (benchmark) short-term interest rate at less than zero percent, the latter being often called the 'zero lower bound'. These policies mostly refer to monetary policies implemented by central banks in the aftermath of the global financial crisis of 2007–08. In addition to quantitative easing (QE) policies and to zero interest rates policies (ZIRPs), both perceived as not effective enough to restore price stability and to stimulate the economy, central banks turned to NIRPs. In addition with QE and ZIRPs, NIRPs are classified as 'unconventional' monetary policies.

Although the central banks of Sweden (in 2009–10) and Denmark (in 2012) were pioneers in applying negative interest rates on some deposits, the Swiss National Bank (SNB) is doubtless the central bank that legitimized the use of NIRPs on a larger scale. In 2015, the SNB decided to set up a NIRP for a part of banks' deposits with it, paving the way for larger use of such a policy by other central banks (Rochon and Vallet, 2019).

The Swiss case is insightful and helps us to understand the underpinning motives of NIRPs. In the Swiss case, a NIRP was set up to weaken exchange rate appreciation: negative rates of interest are meant to reduce the international attractiveness of some financial investments and thus to dampen strain on exchange rates. Such an objective is particularly targeted for central banks managing 'safe-haven' currencies, such as in the Swiss case.

However, the rationale of NIRPs goes beyond this. In a sluggish growth and deflationary framework – associated with the perception of a so-called 'liquidity trap' – NIRPs are supposed to increase the efficiency of both interest rates and credit banking channels. Negative interest rates are expected to trigger a 'trickle-down effect': they act as a tax on reserves held by commercial banks in their deposit accounts with the central bank. Hence, banks are encouraged to lend, since it is preferable for them to lend reserves out instead of being taxed.

The underlying model is that there exists a negative relationship between the level of interest rate and that of investment. Moreover, there is also the belief of the existence of a positive elasticity of savings and investment to interest rate variations. For instance, since the interest rate is seen as the price of capital in its liquid form, a drop in its level will inevitably have a negative impact on the savings rate and then a positive impact on the investment rate.

From a theoretical perspective, NIRPs first rest on the 'money multiplier theory', in which banks are seen merely as financial intermediaries. According to Friedman and Schwartz (1963), the 'money multiplier' would trigger a rise in investment thanks to banking credit, enabling an increase in the 'monetary base' and in the price level. This would be the appropriate policy to get out of a deflationist spiral.

Second, NIRPs are based on the assumption that there is a natural rate of interest in the economy, at a level equilibrating *ex ante* savings and investment. In addition, this natural rate of interest involves an equilibrium with full employment and no inflation. Economists such as Wicksell (1898) and von Hayek (1941), for instance, believed in the existence of such a natural interest rate. According to them, the task of central banks is to set up their targeted interest rate close to this level.

Third, NIRPs could be related to the theory of 'melting money' – proposed in particular by Gesell (1958) – to some extent: negative interest rates would discourage savings and symmetrically increase consumption, with positive impacts on trade and economic growth.

However, NIRPs have limits and shortcomings. Negative interest rates involve discounted returns, tending to overvalue future rather than actual investments. This could trigger a deflationist spiral. Likewise, NIRPs could ease the access to monetary liquidity and reduce risk aversion: these two effects are likely to increase speculation. Last but not least, NIRPs address the following issue: how low central banks' interest rates could and should go in the negative territory.

Post-Keynesian economists reject many of the arguments of NIRPs as well as the money multiplier model in an endogenous money framework. In the end, this issue exemplifies that monetary policy cannot be the 'only game in town' – and must be associated to fiscal policy to be effective – and that economic decisions depend on a plurality of factors rather than mere reaction to 'interest rates stimulus': at stake is customers' creditworthiness and economic uncertainty in particular.

GUILLAUME VALLET AND
LOUIS-PHILIPPE ROCHON

See also

Interest rate rules; Interest rates and income distribution; Interest rates and investment; Monetary policy transmission mechanism; Reserves – role of

References

Friedman, M. and A. Schwartz (1963), *A Monetary History of the United States, 1867–1960*, Princeton, NJ: Princeton University Press.
Gesell, S. (1958), *The Natural Economic Order*, London: Peter Owen Limited.
Rochon, L.-P. and G. Vallet (2019), 'Economía del Ave María: el modelo teórico detrás de las políticas monetarias no convencionales', *Ola Financiera*, **12** (34), 1–24.
von Hayek, F. (1941), *The Pure Theory of Capital*, London: Routledge & Kegan Paul.
Wicksell, K. (1898), *Interest and Prices*, London: Macmillan.

Neoclassical economics

The birth of neoclassical economics came as an immediate reaction to the growing tensions between workers and the capitalist class and also against the critical writings that exposed the contradictions of capitalism. In this framework, the most urgent task for the early neoclassical writers was to deflect the workers' attention away from militantism and prevent a deepening of the awareness and consciousness of the masses. These writers attacked class-consciousness by praising individualism and the pursuit of self-interest. They justified private property of land and capital as a sacred gift of nature. They denied conflict between social classes and argued that workers, landlords and capitalists had mutual interests – and would be living in a 'social harmony' if only they understood the importance of their self-interest (see Bougrine and Rochon, 2021).

In the neoclassical paradigm, there is no difference between workers, capitalists and landowners. Each provides a service and, through exchange with the others, can increase their own satisfaction. Exchange becomes the crucial means by which people can increase their utility. There is less concern with the creation of value and focus is moved away from the 'sphere of production' to the 'sphere of circulation' or exchange. This groundwork has been done by early utilitarians such as Jeremy Bentham (1748–1832), Frédéric Bastiat (1801–50) and Nassau Senior (1790–1864), who were staunch defenders of the selfish, individualistic, utilitarian approach and strong believers in competition and the superiority of free markets. Later neoclassical economists, who led the so-called Marginalist Revolution, had mainly refined these arguments using mathematical rigour. The main contributors to the Marginalist Revolution were William Stanley Jevons (1835–82), Léon Walras (1834–1910) and Carl Menger (1840–1921). Let us explore their ideas and theories on important issues in economics such as value, income distribution and equilibrium.

Jevons began the first chapter of his book by assuring readers that '[r]epeated reflection and inquiry have led me to the somewhat novel opinion, that *value depends entirely upon utility*' (Jevons, 1871/2013, p. 1; italics in the original). All commodities that can produce pleasure or prevent pain possess 'utility' and therefore have 'value'. This utility, however, is not an intrinsic quality that 'useful' commodities would acquire forever. Utility, and therefore value, of the same commodity for the same person can be high under certain circumstances and may decrease to near zero under other circumstances. In this sense, it is not possible to say absolutely that some commodities are always useful while others are not. Utility, and value, is not an objective characteristic of a commodity but a subjective appreciation by the consumer. Moreover, utility depends on the 'circumstantial' feelings of the consumer, in the sense that it varies with the quantities consumed. If you are hungry, a loaf of bread gives you a great satisfaction and is, therefore, highly 'valued'. The utility you would get from a second loaf is not as high and that same loaf will have less value for you. A third and a fourth loaf will have even less utility. The addition to a person's happiness, the additional utility decreases as the quantity consumed increases. But as long as that additional, marginal utility is positive, we would continue to consume, because that increases our total utility. The latter is maximized when the additional utility becomes nil. Here, we have two dimensions of utility: one is the quantity of the commodity consumed and the other is the degree of satisfaction, the intensity of the effect it has on the consumer. This is the notion of decreasing marginal utility, which is the main innovation of the marginalist school. In mathematical terms, if $U(x)$ is the total utility gained from consuming x units of commodity X, then marginal utility is the first derivative of the total utility function: $MU_x = dU/dx$, and it is positive but decreasing: $MU_x = dU/dx > 0$; $d^2U/d^2x < 0$. Note that total utility is maximized when the marginal utility is zero and X^* units are consumed.

Neoclassical economists never accepted the class division of society, which was the framework used by the classical economists as well as Karl Marx. The philosophical foundation of neoclassical economics was (and still is) the egoistic, utilitarian and competitive individualism. The utility theory was freely applied to labour effort and earnings of factors of production in order to justify the existing type of income distribution. Therefore, labour is reduced to that 'painful exertion which we undergo to ward off pains of greater amount, or to procure pleasures which leave a balance in our favour' (Jevons, 1871/2013, p. 167). Individuals then, regardless of their social status, are somehow condemned to eternally undergo the painful exertion, which they must minimize, in order to consume and satisfy their wants. The underlying logic, of course, is that workers, capitalists and landlords – as individuals – have mutual interests and must collaborate with each other by exchanging services for their own benefit. Workers can supply their labour services in exchange for a wage that allows them to acquire the commodities they need to satisfy their wants and maximize their utility. But since labour is a pain and a disutility, workers will need to find a balance between the utility they get from consuming and the disutility they suffer by working. That balance is reached when 'the pleasure gained is exactly equal to the labour endured' (Jevons, 1871/2013, p. 173).

The notion of market equilibrium has been discussed by economists at least since Adam Smith's idea of the 'invisible hand', which implied that competition would equalize rates of profits, wages and all other prices. Several neoclassical economists such as Jevons and Menger, among others, devoted a great deal of their work to the study of equilibrium, but their analysis remained focused on separate markets and thus dealt with what became known as 'partial equilibrium'. It was Léon Walras (1874/2014) who argued that all markets are interdependent and form a general system – that is, the total economy – whose equilibrium requires that each market be in equilibrium. This is the idea of a general equilibrium. However, Walras's analysis did not differ fundamentally from that of Jevons and Menger since he also relied on the argument of competitive equilibrium in each market via supply and demand. His main point, though, was that if we had n markets and if $n-1$ markets were in equilibrium, then necessarily the nth market had to be also in equilibrium.

HASSAN BOUGRINE

See also

Capitalism; Consumer behaviour; Income distribution; Profit; Social classes

References

Bougrine, H. and L.-P. Rochon (2021), 'The neoclassical school of economics', in H. Bougrine and L.-P. Rochon (eds), *A Short History of Economic Thought*, Cheltenham, UK, and Northampton, MA, USA: Edward Elgar, forthcoming.

Jevons, W.S. (1871/2013), *The Theory of Political Economy*, fourth edition, New York: Palgrave Macmillan.

Walras, L. (1874/ 2014), *Elements of Theoretical Economics or The Theory of Social Wealth*, Cambridge, UK: Cambridge University Press.

Neo-liberalism

Neo-liberalism, broadly speaking, refers to the economic doctrine that strongly supports free-market policies for economic development. Although there is no universal agreement on its exact definition and content, markets, individualism, property rights, flexible labour markets, trickle-down economics, privatizations, abandonment of full employment goals, and international capital mobility stand out as distinguishing characteristics of neo-liberalism (Palley, 2005). Milton Friedman, Friedrich von Hayek, James M. Buchanan, George Stigler, and Gary Becker are among the pioneers of neo-liberal thought.

With the Great Depression, during the early 1930s, American capitalism came to a long-lasting halt. All macroeconomic indicators were showing signs of complete collapse. Owing to established faith in markets, the US government was reluctant to intervene in the economy. Free markets, however, have not been correcting themselves. To turn things around a major organic shift was necessary. Hence, the Roosevelt government made a deal, the so-called 'New Deal', with the American bourgeoisie.

According to this deal, the US government was going to intervene in the markets to create jobs to reduce unemployment and increase effective demand. In order to restore both the purchasing power and income stability of the citizens, the system was going to tolerate a higher rate of unionization. A banking reform was also in order. To avoid bank runs, the government established deposit insurance. To alleviate the credit crunch, the US Federal Reserve started to increase the money supply, which raised industrial production considerably.

The economic reference point of all these interventionist policies was Keynesianism. Such expansionary policies helped the United States get out of the depression and constituted the basis of the welfare state. High rates of unionization, low rates of unemployment, high tax rates, high rates of economic growth, unemployment insurance, extensive welfare benefits, and improving living standards were the characteristics of the first two decades of the post-World-War-Two era, which was, later, to be called the 'Golden Age' of American capitalism.

The welfare state brought about a relatively more equal distribution of income. The competition over the surplus had been getting tighter for capitalists. Thanks to high union density, the wage share had been on the rise. This implied, as an accounting identity, a reduction in the capital share. All these were conducive to a profit squeeze for capitalists.

The political elites of the Western world, hand in hand with Washington-based international organizations of the post-World-War-Two era, such as the International Monetary Fund (IMF) and World Bank (WB), agreed upon a political agenda. A new set of rules and policies was designed, targeting, first, Latin American countries, and then other developing countries (Williamson, 2000). The official argument was that these neo-liberal policies, dictated by the IMF and the WB, aimed to help struggling economies to catch up with the advanced world.

However, as Duménil and Levy (2005, p. 14) argue, the actual objective of this new design was 'the restoration of the income and wealth of the upper fractions of the owners of the capital'. In order to achieve this objective, many elements of the Keynesian compromise needed to be stamped out and replaced by market-oriented policies. This period, since the late 1970s, of extreme economic liberalization has been called the neo-liberal era. According to Harvey (2007), neo-liberalism should not be regarded as a brand-new ideology or even a new epoch in history; rather, it is more like an intensification of capital's dominance over the people.

Neo-liberalism promised economic development for all. However, as Crotty (2002, p. 28) states, 'the promised benefits of neoliberalism have yet to be materialized'. Real wages have been stagnant for almost five decades. GDP growth rates have been slower than they were during the Golden Age. The frequency of recessions caused by financial collapse has increased. With few exceptions, poor countries have not managed to catch up with rich ones.

On the other hand, unionization rates have been reduced dramatically, the average rate of unemployment has increased, average duration of unemployment has also increased, the tax burden has been shifted to middle- and lower-income groups, most of the national capital has been privatized into the hands of the few, a safer environment for international capital flows has been established, and tax havens and offshore financial centres have emerged. In other words, it has been a very successful era for capital. Piketty (2014) shows that, especially in the last five decades, income and wealth inequalities have reached unprecedented levels.

All in all, neo-liberalism was a conscious design. So far, its consequences have been dismal for the working people and very pleasing for capitalists. This trajectory, though, is undermining the legitimacy of the system, making the construction of consent more difficult towards further neo-liberal policies, which leads to mass protests and demonstrations.

ANIL ABA

See also

Capitalism – stages of; Development; Effective demand; Growth – wage-led vs profit-led; Income distribution

References

Crotty, J. (2002), 'Trading State-led prosperity for market-led stagnation: from the Golden Age to global neoliberalism', in G. Dymski and D. Isenberg (eds), *Seeking Shelter on the Pacific Rim: Financial Globalization, Social Change, and the Housing Market*, Armonk, NY: M.E. Sharpe, pp. 21–41.
Duménil, G. and D. Levy (2005), 'The neoliberal (counter-)revolution', in A. Saad-Filho and D. Johnston (eds), *Neoliberalism: A Critical Reader*, London and Ann Arbor, MI: Pluto Press, pp. 9–19.
Harvey, D. (2007), *A Brief History of Neoliberalism*, Oxford: Oxford University Press.
Palley, T.I. (2005), 'From Keynesianism to neoliberalism: shifting paradigms in economics', in A. Saad-Filho and D. Johnston (eds), *Neoliberalism: A Critical Reader*, London and Ann Arbor, MI: Pluto Press, pp. 20–29.
Piketty, T. (2014), *Capital in the 21st Century*, Boston: Harvard University Press.
Williamson, J. (2000), 'What should the World Bank think about the Washington Consensus?', *The World Bank Research Observer*, **15** (2), 251–64.

New Consensus in Macroeconomics

The New Consensus in Macroeconomics (NCM) is the paradigmatic answer to a series of low-intensity intellectual battles between two complementary sides of the mainstream. These are the New Classicals, who developed real business cycle (RBC) models, and the New Keynesians, who provided microeconomic foundations of market frictions and imperfections. Adherents to RBC models maintain that technology-preferences real forces and fiscal policy are at the origin of business cycles, while the New Keynesians consider that the existence of nominal or real market rigidities makes necessary the inclusion in the analysis of demand shocks and monetary policy. The consequences are clear: for RBC models the business cycle is an optimal answer of the agents to both productivity and public expenditure shocks, hence stabilization policy is innocuous. For the New Keynesians the cycles reflect the frictions and malfunctioning of the markets, thus leaving room for the macroeconomic policy of reduction of product volatility.

Methodologically, the two groups identified plentifully with the theoretical interpretation of the 'Lucas critique' to the macrostructural models in the 1960s and 1970s. This refers to the impossibility of carrying out the analysis of policy changes in the absence of the stability of the parameters of the structural equations system (Lucas, 1976). As a result, they followed rigorously the Lucas heuristic mandate: to construct micro-founded intertemporal optimization models, to incorporate the rational expectations assumption and forward-looking agents into the dynamic stochastic general equilibrium models (Goodfriend and King, 1997). Insofar as the decision rules of agents follow the 'profound parameters' of the system, the evaluation of economic policy is scientifically valid, since its microfoundation is synonymous with structural stability (Sergi, 2018).

The New Neoclassical Synthesis emerged from the recombination and integration of the two competing nuclear models. The RBC solution transformed itself in the 'neutral' norm of comparison, in which the product is supply-determined; price rigidity was introduced by means of two devices: monopolistic competition and Calvo's (1983) rule of prices, according to which the firm gets a signal with a probability (Φ) to change its price and a probability (1 − Φ) to leave it fixed. This probability is independent of the time elapsed since the last time the firm adjusted its price. Thus, in the short run, demand determines the level of production. However, 'the recommendation is that monetary policy should stabilize the path of the price level in order to keep output at its potential. This policy is activist in that the authority must manage aggregate demand to accommodate any supply-side disturbances to output' (Goodfriend and King, 1997, p. 256). The central bank resolves a problem of infinite horizon intertemporal optimization, of which the loss function is quadratic in terms of both the deviation of the output from its potential level and the deviation of the inflation rate from its target value. The optimal reaction function is an interest rate rule that depends on both the output gap and inflation gap, of which the weighting factors are determined by the inflation and unemployment preferences of monetary authorities.

The equations system that synthetizes the duality of RBC-NK is known as the Neo-Keynesian dynamic stochastic general equilibrium model (Clarida et al., 1999, p. 1662). The new macroeconomic consensus model can be summarized in three equations: the IS curve, the Phillips curve and Taylor's rule of the rate of interest. The IS equations and the Phillips curve can be obtained from the intertemporal optimization conditions of households and firms. In the case of the IS curve the Euler equations are put in the log-linear form and the macroeconomic equilibrium condition is imposed, so that consumption is equal to output minus public expenditure. The Phillips curve is obtained from the aggregation of the profit maximization conditions of firms, which fix their prices under consideration of future price adjustments (Woodford, 2003). The IS curve can be written as follows (Clarida et al., 1999):

$$y_t = E_t y_{t+1} - \beta[i_t - E_t \pi_{t+1}] + g_t \qquad (1)$$

where y_t measures the product gap, E_t is the expectations operator on the set of information available in period t, i_t is the nominal rate of interest, $E_t \pi_{t+1}$ is the inflation expectation for period $t + 1$ based on the information in period t, and g_t is a stochastic public expenditure shock. The function says that the product gap depends negatively on the real interest rate and positively on expectations about the product gap and the random public expenditure shock. The Neo-Keynesian Phillips curve is thus:

$$\pi_t = \lambda y_t + \varphi E_t \pi_{t+1} + u_t \qquad (2)$$

where π_t is the inflation rate in period t, and u_t is a supply-side cost shock. The Phillips curve establishes that inflation depends positively on both the product gap and expected inflation. Finally, the interest rate rule is:

$$i_t = \bar{r} + \bar{\pi} + \delta_\pi(\pi_t - \bar{\pi}) + \delta_y y_t \qquad (3)$$

where i_t is the interest rate of the central bank, $\bar{r} + \bar{\pi}$ is the equilibrium nominal rate of interest, and δ_π and δ_y are the weighting factors for the deviations of the inflation rate from its targeted level and the product gap. The stability of the system requires that a 1 per cent increase in the inflation rate above the target must be countered with an increase larger than 1 per cent of the nominal interest rate (Christiano et al., 2011). If the policy rate of interest is equal to the equilibrium rate of interest, then the social loss is equal to zero. This result is known as the 'divine coincidence'. Generally, for the NCM, inflation is a demand phenomenon and disinflation is a free lunch. Thus, monetary policy is neutral in the long run.

In the last years, two critiques have captured the attention. The first critique points out that the dynamic stochastic general equilibrium models do not escape the Lucas critique, and calls for a better microfoundation of the price-fixing rule (Sergi, 2018). The second critique points at the failures of the conditional expectations model and the iterated expectations in the case of unexpected changes of the distribution functions of economic variables (Hendry and Mizon, 2010).

ALVARO MARTÍN
MORENO RIVAS

See also

Aggregate demand; Fiscal policy; Microfoundations; Monetary policy; Phillips curve

References

Calvo, G. (1983), 'Staggered prices in a utility maximizing framework', *Journal of Monetary Economics*, **12** (3), 383–98.

Christiano, L., M. Trabandt and K. Walentin (2011), 'DSGE models for monetary policy analysis', in B.M. Friedman and M. Woodford (eds), *Handbook of Monetary Economic*, volume 3, Amsterdam: Elsevier, pp. 285–367.

Clarida, R., J. Galí and M. Gertler (1999), 'The science of monetary policy: a New Keynesian perspective', *Journal of Economic Literature*, **37** (4), 1661–707.

Goodfriend, M. and R.G. King (1997), 'The New Neoclassical synthesis and the role of monetary policy', in B.S. Bernanke and J.J. Rotemberg (eds), *NBER Macroeconomics Annual*, Cambridge, MA: MIT Press, pp. 231–83.

Hendry, D. and G. Mizon (2010), 'On the mathematical basis of inter-temporal optimization', *University of Oxford Department of Economics Working Paper*, No. 497.

Lucas, R. (1976), 'Econometric policy evaluation: a critique', *Carnegie Rochester Conference Series on Public Policy*, 1, 19–46.

Sergi, F. (2018), 'DSGE models and the Lucas critique: a historical appraisal', *University of West of England Working Paper*, No. 1806.

Woodford, M. (2003), *Interest and Prices: Foundations of a Theory of Monetary Policy*, Princeton and Oxford: Princeton University Press.

New fiscalism

The term 'new fiscalism' was coined by Martin Bronfenbrenner in 1979 (see Lavoie and Seccareccia, 2017), but more firmly entered into academic debate with Mario Seccareccia's (2012) article 'Understanding fiscal policy and the new fiscalism: a Canadian perspective on why budget surpluses are a public vice'. It is therefore a relatively new term, and has only been directly addressed by one other article: 'The IMF and the new fiscalism: was there a U-turn?' (Fiebiger and Lavoie, 2017). While the term has yet to enter into the mainstream debate, it encompasses several important dynamics that have not been grouped under a single term elsewhere.

Seccareccia (2012, p. 68) presents the new fiscalism as the relationship between monetary and fiscal policy in moments of normality and in moments of crisis: 'fiscal policy ought to be sidelined in favor of monetary policy ... except for the temporary budgetary stimulus through deficit spending in times of extreme crisis.' Seen from the wake of the Great Financial Crisis (GFC) of 2007–09, Seccareccia (2012) provides both a view of the history of the public policy mix and the pedigree of the idea. Seccareccia (2012, p. 66) states that 'the distinct fiscal policy approach that emerged (the new "fiscalism" of 2008–10) was not unlike the Rooseveltian "fiscalism" that emerged in the mid-1930s .... [I]n both the 1930s and after 2010, there was a dramatic policy reversal as soon as signs of recovery (the "green shoots") appeared.' Seccareccia (2012, p. 67) identifies the support for the idea in academic literature prior to the GFC: when 'monetary policy is no longer effective, one can temporarily rely on discretionary fiscal policy actions (see Allsopp and Vines 2005)'.

Giving a similar description of the phenomenon, Krugman (1999, Internet) states that 'if the liquidity trap is short-lived in any case, fiscal policy can serve as a bridge. That is, if there are good reasons to believe that after a few years of large deficits monetary policy will again be able to shoulder the load, fiscal stimulus can do its job without posing problems for solvency.'

Seccareccia (2012, p. 66) dates the first public policy use of the new fiscalism 'quite precisely to the G-20 summit in Washington, on November 14–15, 2008', with Canada's President Harper offering a concise summary: 'we did agree at the G-20 last week that additional fiscal stimulus should be used to sustain global demand if monetary policy continues to prove to be inadequate' (quoted by Seccareccia, 2012, p. 66). Seccareccia (2012, p. 68) also points to the precise moment where fiscal policy turned contractive, the G-20 Toronto summit in 2010: 'once it was observed that the Canadian economy was growing again, the return to budget balance and fiscal surpluses became once more the overwhelming concern of the fiscal authorities.'

While it is true that the mix of monetary and fiscal policies is similar after the GFC and in the previous liquidity trap of the 1930s, there is also an important difference. The overall response to the Great Depression was one engendered by a battle of ideas and for control of institutions, and manifested in academic and institutional error and incoherency. While disagreeing on the causes of the Great Depression, the inconsistent crisis response of fiscal and monetary policy makers in the United States is a point of agreement that unites the ideological gap between the twentieth century financial histories of Friedman and Schwartz (1963) and Galbraith (1954; 1975).

Whereas the mix of policies in the 1930s can be attributed to institutional incoherency reflecting an underlying ideological debate, the new fiscalism of the post-GFC years is a result of institutional and academic coherency, with the shifting of positions clearly communicated through G-20 meetings. So, while the public policy result is fairly similar in both post-crisis scenarios, their underlying dynamics are distinct.

The Fiebiger and Lavoie (2017) article updates the new fiscalism and gives it a wider geographic focus, and also problematizes its applications. The authors identify phases and regionalities of the new fiscalism, highlighting one case in which it was not applied: the European debt crisis beginning in Greece in 2010. Fiebiger and Lavoie (2017) also offer a figure to visualize the degrees of the see-saw between fiscal and monetary policy expansion and contraction.

The new fiscalism has also been present in the developing world, and the chronological trend in the mix of monetary and fiscal expansion and contraction has been generally followed, but often with much less fiscal spending and higher interest rates, both of which follow historical trends. All taken together, the new fiscalism is a global post-GFC macroeconomic response that appears similar to Depression era fiscalism, but with significant enough differences to merit the new term.

WESLEY C. MARSHALL

See also

Financial crises; Fiscal deficits; Fiscal policy; Monetary policy; Public finance

References

Allsopp, C. and D. Vines (2005), 'The macroeconomic role of fiscal policy', *Oxford Review of Economic Policy*, **21** (4), 485–508.
Fiebiger, B. and M. Lavoie (2017), 'The IMF and the new fiscalism: was there a U-turn?', *European Journal of Economics and Economic Policies: Intervention*, **14** (3), 314–32.
Friedman, M. and A. Schwartz (1963), *A Monetary History of the United States, 1867–1960*, Princeton: Princeton University Press.
Galbraith, J.K. (1954), *The Great Crash 1929*, New York: Mariner Books.
Galbraith, J.K. (1975), *Money: Whence It Came, Where It Went*, Boston: Houghton Mifflin.
Krugman, P. (1999), 'Thinking about the liquidity trap', available online at http://web.mit.edu/krugman/www/trioshrt.html (last accessed 25 May 2021).

Lavoie, M. and M. Seccareccia (2017), 'Editorial to the special issue: the political economy of the new fiscalism', *European Journal of Economics and Economic Policies: Intervention*, **14** (3), 291–5.
Seccareccia, M. (2012), 'Understanding fiscal policy and the new fiscalism: a Canadian perspective on why budget surpluses are a public vice', *International Journal of Political Economy*, **41** (2), 61–81.

New Keynesianism

Keynes (1936) showed that free-market economies, including under conditions of full price flexibility, tend to gravitate towards positions of under full-employment equilibrium. This negated the idea of the functioning of markets postulated by neoclassical economists, that is, equilibrium could only coexist with voluntary unemployment resulting from economic agents' decisions regarding their perceived trade-off between work (disutility) and leisure (utility).

Initially, neoclassical economics provided a rationale for Keynes's results, on the basis of money illusion (the confusion between a change in monetary prices and a change in relative prices). However, if economic agents acted rationally, in the sense that their subjective expectations would conform to an objective probability distribution (rational expectations), these would avoid making systematic mistakes and unemployment could not be explained on the basis of monetary/relative price misperception. Other avenues to justify Keynes's results have relied on three interrelated market imperfections: price stickiness, coordination failures, and information asymmetries. These market imperfections form, *grosso modo*, the foundation of New Keynesian economics (or Keynesianism).

Two notions of price rigidity are present in New Keynesian economics. The first centres on the notion of real price rigidity. Firms may wish to pay workers real wages that are above the labour market-clearing level to elicit effort and improve productivity. Also, firms may want to absorb an external shock, by changing their profit margins and varying their levels of production (lowering their profit margins and expanding output in the case of a positive shock). Nominal price rigidity results from the assumption that all prices and wages cannot be changed simultaneously. Price and wage negotiations are staggered, and both can be fixed

WESLEY C. MARSHALL / ESTEBAN PÉREZ CALDENTEY

for some periods (for example, a fixed fraction of firms is assumed to change their prices in a given period).

Coordination failures arise when individual decisions and actions do not lead to the best possible allocation of existing resources. The common feature underpinning coordination-failure models is an economic externality: the decision made by an economic agent can affect the utility of all other agents. Coordination failures consider two types of externalities. The first is an aggregate demand externality that occurs when the demand constraint faced by one economic agent depends on the choices of all other agents. A firm may expect a decline in economic activity and, as a result, cut production and demand from other firms, which will follow suit. The second type of externalities refers to technological externalities: economic agents' decisions affect utility or production functions (a decision of one household to reduce its working hours or effort limits the production possibilities of all households). Coordination failures fall under the umbrella of Keynesian economics, because they are compatible with under full-employment equilibrium and also because individual decisions depend on the level of aggregate market activity.

Information asymmetries provide a rationale for the existence of imperfections in financial markets. The creditworthiness of borrowers is hard to acquire and costly (when available), which increases the difficulty of estimating the probability of repayment or default. This situation can lead to phenomena such as credit rationing. Banks may lend at rates of interest below market clearing (where demand for bank loans exceeds supply), which by lowering its lending risk maximizes their expected returns. Another important contribution in this field is the financial accelerator. It is based on the idea that external finance, being costlier than internal finance, carries a premium. The external finance premium is a function of the present value of the borrower's net worth used as collateral.

Both information asymmetries and the financial accelerator provide a linkage between real and monetary variables. Information asymmetries demonstrate that interest rates do not clear the loanable funds market, and below equilibrium interest rates can provide a constraint to the financing of investment. The financial accelerator shows that changes in the value of the collateral have concomitant changes in investment swings and production.

New Keynesianism is founded upon market imperfections (which hold only in the short run). It is thus not surprising that New Keynesian economics is also referred to as 'new monetarist economics' (Mankiw and Romer, 1991, p. 3). In this sense, the characterization of the workings of free-market economies in New Keynesian economics has little to do with that of an entrepreneur or monetary economy found in Keynes's *General Theory*: 'an economy in which money plays a part of its own affects motives and decisions, so that the course of events cannot be predicted either in the long period or in the short without a knowledge of the behaviour of money' (Keynes, 1933/1973, pp. 408–9).

ESTEBAN PÉREZ CALDENTEY

See also

Aggregate demand; Effective demand; Money illusion; Neoclassical economics; Neo-liberalism

References

Keynes, J.M. (1933/1973), 'A monetary theory of production', in *The Collected Writings of John Maynard Keynes, Vol. XIII. The General Theory and After: Part I Preparation*, London: Macmillan, pp. 408–11.
Keynes, J.M. (1936), *The General Theory of Employment, Interest and Money*, London: Macmillan.
Mankiw, N.G. and D. Romer (1991), *New Keynesian Economics: Vols. I and II*, Cambridge, USA: MIT Press.

Non-ergodicity

Ergodic theory is a prohibitively technical branch of mathematics with origins in statistical mechanics (Ehrenfest and Ehrenfest, 2014). Primarily because of the work of Paul Davidson, the notion of non-ergodicity has gained prominence in discussions of methodology in post-Keynesian economics, in particular the role of econometrics, uncertainty and historical time.

To define non-ergodicity, one starts with the space Ω under consideration. For the example of a gas inside a box, this is a subset of a six-dimensional space – three coordinates for position, three coordinates for velocity – for each molecule of the gas. This space is then equipped with a measure P, which assigns a volume to subsets $A \subset \Omega$, with the total space assumed to have a finite volume. Finally, one introduces a map T representing time evolution, in the sense that a point x in Ω moves to the point $T^n(x)$ after n time steps. Because of the type of dynamics that arise in statistical mechanics, the theory was developed for measure-preserving transformations only; that is, the map T is assumed to change only the shape of a set, not its volume. With these ingredients, one says that T is ergodic if its invariant sets either have zero volume or are the complements of sets of zero volume. The importance of this definition rests on Birkhoff's ergodic theorem (see Varadhan, 2001), which states that if T is ergodic, then the limit of the time average $[f(x) + f(Tx) + ... + f(T^n x)]/n$ as n goes to infinity equals the space average $\int_\Omega f(x) dP(x)$.

In the context of stochastic processes, Ω is a sample space (say the set of sequences of coin tosses), the measure P is a probability measure (that is, $P(\Omega) = 1$), the map T shifts the process in time (say going from one coin toss to the next) and being measure-preserving means stationarity. Birkhoff's ergodic theorem then says that the average of a function f sampled on a single realization of the process at successive times converges to the expected value of the function, a procedure that forms the basis for common parameter estimation techniques in statistics. The class of ergodic processes is quite large and includes many well-known examples, such as all sequences of independent, identically distributed random variables. Whereas all ergodic processes are stationary by definition, there exist stationary processes that are non-ergodic, a trivial example being a process consisting of a single random variable repeated through time.

With these definitions in mind, we can make several observations about the status of non-ergodicity in post-Keynesian economics. First, the assertion that '[p]rior to infinity, there can be no necessary or sufficient conditions for ergodicity/nonergodicity' (O'Donnell, 2014–15, p. 195) does not conform with the notions presented above. It is true that Birkhoff's ergodic theorem, which follows from ergodicity, establishes an asymptotic result, but the definition of ergodicity itself does not invoke infinity.

Second, the common objection that ergodicity 'presumes that the economic future is governed by an already existing unchanging ergodic stochastic process' (Davidson, 2012, p. 60) is really an objection against stationarity. Third, the statement that 'there can be no *scientific basis* for calculating actuarial knowledge regarding future economic events from existing economic facts and data if *the stochastic process generating the facts and data is nonergodic*' (Davidson, 2015, p. 9, italics in the original) is puzzling in the face of the multitude of non-ergodic processes that are routinely encountered in science. In particular, ergodicity plays no essential role in Bayesian statistics, which can be taken as a scientific basis for making forecasts. Finally, if one's approach to radical uncertainty consists in rejecting the 'assumption that decision makers use probabilities to calculate an actuarially certain knowledge of future events' (Davidson, 2015, p. 5), then non-ergodicity seems like a strange standpoint, since any discussion around it necessarily relies on probability theory to make any sense. Much simpler terms such as unpredictability and complexity would still 'ram a point home' (Davidson, 2015, p. 3), without being encumbered by the technicalities surrounding the concept of non-ergodicity, which do not appear to be the heart of the matter.

MATHEUS GRASSELLI

See also

Behavioural economics; Econometrics – role of; Neoclassical economics; Post-Keynesian economics – a big tent?; Uncertainty

References

Davidson, P. (2012), 'Is economics a science? Should economics be rigorous?', *Real World Economics Review*, 59, 58–66.
Davidson, P. (2015), 'A rejoinder to O'Donnell's critique of the ergodic/nonergodic explanation of Keynes's concept of uncertainty', *Journal of Post Keynesian Economics*, **38** (1), 1–18.
Ehrenfest, P. and T. Ehrenfest (2014), *The Conceptual Foundations of the Statistical Approach in Mechanics*, New York: Dover Publications.
O'Donnell, R. (2014–15), 'A critique of the ergodic/nonergodic approach to uncertainty', *Journal of Post Keynesian Economics*, **37** (2), 187–209.
Varadhan, S.R.S. (2001), *Probability Theory*, Rhode Island, USA: American Mathematical Society.

MATHEUS GRASSELLI

Okun's law

Okun's law identifies an empirical relationship between changes in unemployment and changes in output. Originally proposed in 1962 by Arthur M. Okun, as a central piece of his procedure for empirical calculation of potential output, it has subsequently been re-estimated for different periods and different countries, and represents, along with the Phillips curve, one of the most relevant macroeconomic relationships for its frequent use in applied macroeconomic policy. Differently from the Phillips curve, which for all its popularity in mainstream economics is in reality little confirmed by empirical evidence, Okun's law found many empirical confirmations. However, in the course of its life, it has undergone both theoretical reinterpretations and empirical disputes regarding its stability.

In Okun's (1962) original analysis, the empirical estimation of the relation served the purpose to identify the coefficient linking the 'unemployment gap' (the difference between the actual rate of unemployment and a targeted rate of unemployment conventionally set by Okun at 4 per cent) and the 'output gap' (the difference between actual output and its potential level as a percentage of the former). This allowed translating the unemployment policy target into an output measure (the unobservable potential output).

Okun (1962) extracted the relation from quarterly data on the US economy (1947–60) by means of different methods: (a) the 'first differences' method, (b) the 'trial gap' method, and (c) the method of 'fitted trend and elasticity'. In method (a) first differences in actual unemployment are regressed on the actual rates of growth of real output; while methods (b) and (c) derive the coefficient by regressing unemployment gaps on output gaps, based on different hypotheses on the trend of potential output. In subsequent literature, the two procedures have been labelled 'difference specification' and 'gap specification' respectively. In Okun's (1962) original estimates, the different methods gave similar results, which brought him to establish the famous 3:1 relationship between output gaps and unemployment gaps.

A higher level of activity induces, in Okun's view, not only a reduction in unemployment but also higher labour force participation and (short-run) positive effects on productivity through more intense utilization of given resources – which explains why a one percentage point change in unemployment is associated with a greater percentage change in output. Such changes in productivity and labour force are, however, supposedly correlated with the changes in the unemployment rate, which accounts for the empirical stability of the unemployment–output relationship.

In later literature, some authors (Prachowny, 1993) have proposed a theoretical reinterpretation of Okun's law, as part of a production function relationship whereby it is employment, together with capital and the other factors, that determines output. Accordingly, Okun's law is sometimes estimated by regressing output gaps on unemployment gaps instead of the other way round (with the addition of other terms capturing the effect of the other factors).

More importantly, the post-Okun literature has almost unanimously discarded Okun's notion of a target unemployment rate, redefining the unemployment gaps as differences between actual unemployment and the natural rate (or the non-accelerating inflation rate of unemployment). This implies that, when estimating the Okun coefficient through the gap specification, both equilibrium unemployment and potential output are unobservable magnitudes. This explains why Okun's law is often estimated in a multi-equation model along with a Phillips curve (Lee, 2000).

While early estimates on US data generally confirmed the stability of Okun's law, which thus was often referred to in textbooks as a stylized fact (see Hall and Taylor, 1988), later analyses have challenged this view, either by identifying structural breaks (Gordon, 1984) or by applying rolling regressions that show the continuous variability of the coefficient over time (Knotek, 2007). A remarkably constant 2:1 relationship for the United States is instead found over a long period (1948–2013) by Ball et al. (2017), who, however, also detect short-run variability of the coefficient.

Some authors (Lee, 2000; Ball et al., 2017) explain this variability in terms of greater reactivity of unemployment to output changes in recessions. Fontanari et al. (2020) find instead empirical evidence of different values of the Okun coefficients according to the different levels of unemployment. As regards long-run stability, they detect a structural break in US data in 2009, which points to a change in Okun's law in recent years.

Cross-country analyses usually find very different coefficients for the different countries, supposedly explained by the different rules and institutions of the different labour markets (Lee, 2000).

Using a post-Keynesian (demand-led growth) approach, Fontanari et al. (2020) propose a revival of Okun's original method for potential output estimation that also involves use of Okun's law. The latter, once freed from subsequent neoclassical interpretations, expressed in the 'difference specification' and regarded (as in its original formulation) as a Keynesian relationship whereby changes in unemployment are caused by changes in economic activity, proves a useful tool for post-Keynesian applied macroeconomic analysis.

ANTONELLA PALUMBO, CLAUDIA FONTANARI AND CHIARA SALVATORI

See also

Growth; Growth – wage-led vs profit-led; NAIRU; Phillips curve; Post-Keynesian economics – a big tent?

References

Ball, L., D. Leigh and P. Loungani (2017), 'Okun's law: fit at 50?', *Journal of Money, Credit and Banking*, 49 (7), 1413–41.
Fontanari, C., A. Palumbo and C. Salvatori (2020), 'Potential output in theory and practice: a revision and update of Okun's original method', *Structural Change and Economic Dynamics*, 54 (C), 247–66.
Gordon, R.J. (1984), 'Unemployment and potential output in the 1980s', *Brookings Papers on Economic Activity*, 15 (2), 537–68.
Hall, R.E. and J.B. Taylor (1988), *Macroeconomics*, second edition, New York: Norton & Co.
Knotek, E.S. (2007), 'How useful is Okun's law?', *Federal Reserve Bank of Kansas City Economic Review*, 92 (4), 73–103.
Lee, J. (2000), 'The robustness of Okun's law: evidence from OECD countries', *Journal of Macroeconomics*, 22 (2), 331–56.
Okun, A. (1962), 'Potential GNP: its measurement and significance', *Cowles Foundation Paper*, No. 190.
Prachowny, M.F. (1993), 'Okun's law: theoretical foundations and revised estimates', *Review of Economics and Statistics*, 75 (2), 331–6.

Oligopoly and Technical Progress

Oligopoly and Technical Progress (*OTP*) was first published in Italian in 1956, with the English translation appearing in 1962. Paolo Sylos Labini (1920–2005), the author, was professor of economics initially at the universities of Bologna and Catania, then at the University of Rome La Sapienza, where he taught until his retirement. The book represents a complete innovation regarding the relations between production conditions and market structures. It is grounded not in traditional microeconomics but rather in the political economy of the Classical economists and of Marx viewed as the theorists of competitive accumulation.

The book establishes a neat link between oligopolistic conditions in production, the ensuing prices, and the principle of effective demand. In this respect Sylos Labini's analysis interacts with those of Kalecki (1971), Steindl (1952), Rothschild (1947), and Baran and Sweezy (1966). With the latter it shares the emphasis on the internal functioning of the large corporation, which explains also why *OTP* represented a crucial reference in Eichner's (1975) important volume on the megacorp and oligopoly.

Sylos Labini's monograph has had a worldwide resonance, having been translated into many languages including Korean and Japanese. In 1993 *OTP* was reprinted in the Kelley series of economic classics. The book had been discussed in a positive light well before its translation into English by Modigliani (1958), who reviewed it in the *Journal of Political Economy* along with Bain's *Barriers to New Competition* (1956). According to the late and much missed Frederic Lee, as far as the theory of price formation goes, the work of Sylos Labini is still unsurpassed (Lee, 1998, p. 183).

In *OTP* competition corresponds to that historical phase in which there are no barriers to entry and exit in an industry, so that capital mobility tends to bring about a tendency towards a uniform rate of profits. The process of competitive accumulation generates capital concentration because of the technological discontinuities connected to the emergence of large-scale firms leading to the creation of barriers to entry and exit. This new state of affairs is what defines oligopolistic conditions where, as elsewhere summarized by Sylos Labini himself:

Each firm tends to regulate price on the basis of cost variations, provided that cost variations are common to all firms, in order not to lose its market share. As a rule, demand does not affect price simply because firms tend to regulate supply in such a way as to adapt it to demand variations – which is possible not only when output is to be reduced, but also when it is to be increased, since as a rule capacity is not fully utilized; thus demand and supply vary together and price is not affected by variations. Price, then, is modified only if cost, particularly direct cost, varies. (Sylos Labini, 1993, p. 315)

Prices are set on the basis of the maximum necessary to prevent the entry of new firms into the industry, with excess capacity also used as a form of barrier to entry. These roles as entry-preventing tools explain both why prices (and capacity) do not respond to changes in demand and why they are likely to change as a result of any perceived threat of new entry.

Therefore, profit rates no longer equalize across industries and the existence of built-in unused capacity implies that the level of effective demand by and large falls short of full employment. In an oligopolistic setting there is a reason for large firms not to invest at maximum capacity. The incentive arises from the fact that large firms dominate their markets. Hence, were they to run their plants to capacity, their prices will be negatively affected. Technological discontinuities enable these firms to retain the gains ensuing from improvements in productivity. Oligopolistic structures are common in industry, since firms are not compelled to reduce prices relative to costs, while in agriculture and mining competition prevails. Hence, the terms of trade tend to move in the long run against the primary sector, because, when industries are oligopolistic, increases in industrial productivity lead either to increases in profit margins or, more frequently, to parallel increases in real wages. Thus, industrial prices do not fall relative to those of primary commodities. In industrial oligopolistic economies, demand and employment expand chiefly by means of public expenditures or exports, because profits need not be automatically invested in real activities but frozen in financial activities instead.

JOSEPH HALEVI

See also

Effective demand; Fiscal policy; Monopoly power; Pricing; Wages

References

Bain, J.S. (1956), *Barriers to New Competition*, Cambridge, MA: Harvard University Press.
Baran, P. and P. Sweezy (1966), *Monopoly Capital*, New York: Monthly Review Press.
Eichner, A. (1976), *The Megacorp and Oligopoly: Micro Foundations of Macro Dynamics*, Cambridge, UK: Cambridge University Press.
Kalecki, M. (1971), *Selected Essays on the Dynamics of the Capitalist Economy*, Cambridge, UK: Cambridge University Press.
Lee, F. (1998), *Post Keynesian Price Theory*, Cambridge, UK: Cambridge University Press.
Modigliani, F. (1958), 'New developments on the oligopoly front', *Journal of Political Economy*, 66, 215–32.
Rothschild, K. (1947), 'Price theory and oligopoly', *Economic Journal*, 57 (227), 299–320.
Steindl, J. (1952), *Maturity and Stagnation in American Capitalism*, Oxford: Oxford University Press.
Sylos Labini, P. (1956), *Oligopolio e progresso tecnico*, Milano: Giuffré.
Sylos Labini, P. (1993), 'Long-run changes in the wage and price mechanisms and the process of growth', in M. Baranzini and G.C. Harcourt (eds), *The Dynamics of the Wealth of Nations: Growth, Distribution and Structural Change*, London: Macmillan, pp. 311–47.

Open economy macro models

Post-Keynesian work on open economy macroeconomics includes many different approaches and models, some of which are covered in other entries in this volume. Post-Keynesian thinking on short-run analysis for open economies dates back to the contribution of Robinson (1947) on 'beggar-my-neighbour' trade policies (see Blecker, 2005). Whereas neoclassical economists focused on the effects of tariffs and other trade interventions on microeconomic efficiency, Robinson focused on their macroeconomic impact on aggregate demand and employment. She recognized that various means of favouring domestic industries (currency undervaluation, import protection, export subsidies, and wage suppression) could potentially increase a given country's output and employment, but argued that they would do so only at the expense of reducing output and employment in the country's trading partners. Furthermore, if many countries were to adopt such mercantilist measures simultaneously, Robinson observed that the result would be to lower global demand,

JOSEPH HALEVI / ROBERT A. BLECKER

output, and employment – as had occurred in the 1920s and 1930s.

Another key foundation is the work of Kalecki (1933/1990) on the determination of profits in an open economy (see also Blecker, 1999). Kalecki based his analysis on the national income identity, which can be written as follows:

$$R + W + T = C_K + C_W + I + G + X - M \quad (1)$$

where R is profits, W is wages, T is taxes, C_K is capitalists' consumption, C_W is workers' consumption, I is investment, G is government purchases, X is exports, and M is imports. Assuming that workers do not save (which implies $C_W = W$), Kalecki deduced that the amount of profits realized in an economy is positively related to the net export surplus $(X - M)$ as well as to the government deficit:

$$R = C_K + I + (G - T) + (X - M) \quad (2)$$

Basically, 'capitalists get what they spend' (the sum of their own consumption and investment spending), but this is modified by the fact that the government's deficit represents a surplus for the private sector while a trade (net export) surplus represents a net inflow of foreign spending that boosts domestic profits.

If we further assume that capitalists' consumption is determined by $C_K = c_K R$, where c_K is their marginal propensity to consume ($0 < c_K < 1$), while again workers consume all of their wages, the equilibrium level of realized profits is then determined by the profit multiplier equation:

$$R = \frac{I + (G - T) + (X - M)}{1 - c_K} \quad (3)$$

which is an increasing function of both the government deficit $(G - T)$ and the trade surplus $(X - M)$. These relationships were the basis for Kalecki's recognition of the expansionary role of deficit spending by governments, based on the analogy that deficit-financed government purchases are like 'domestic exports' of goods and services (Kalecki, 1933/1990, p. 168).

Later neo-Kaleckian work on open economies emphasized how international competition could affect whether national economies have wage-led or profit-led demand. Early neo-Kaleckian models imposed assumptions that made demand always wage-led, so that a rise in the (exogenously given) profit mark-up of firms and a corresponding fall in the real wage would yield economic stagnation even in an open economy (see, for example, Dutt, 1984). However, Blecker (1989) showed that if a rise in domestic wages makes home country products more expensive compared to foreign goods, this could possibly (although not necessarily) reduce net exports by more than workers' consumption would rise (with ambiguous effects on investment), resulting in a reduction rather than an increase in realized profits and domestic output. Drawing on the 1980s literature on partial pass-through of exchange rate changes (see, for example, Dornbusch, 1987), Blecker (1989) argued that a rise in domestic unit labour costs (wages adjusted for productivity) would be likely to squeeze profit mark-ups (as firms would 'price to market'), resulting in a fall in the profit share that could coincide with either an increase or decrease in domestic output (national income). Thus, an economy could have either wage-led or profit-led demand, depending on how open it is to trade and the strength of the distributional effects on consumption and investment relative to net exports (see also Bhaduri and Marglin, 1990; Blecker, 2011; Lavoie and Stockhammer, 2013).

Some recent work has criticized neo-Kaleckian open economy models. For example, Razmi (2016b) and Ros (2016) question their assumptions that domestic and foreign goods are imperfect substitutes and export prices are set in the seller's currency. These critics argue that small countries (including many developing nations) should be regarded as price-takers in global markets, in which case their costs have no impact on their export prices. Nevertheless, the outcomes of alternative, small-country models in some respects resemble those of the earlier literature. For example, wage-led demand becomes unlikely in a small open economy, because a rise in wages in tradable-goods industries reduces profits (as exporting firms cannot pass through increases in labour costs to prices), thereby depressing investment spending and aggregate demand. Also, Razmi (2016a, 2018) shows that the medium-run impact of a distributional shock (such as a change in the wage or mark-up rate) in an open economy, taking into account the dynamic stock-flow adjustments necessary to equilibrate the balance of payments, does not depend on whether the economy exhibits wage-led or profit-led demand in the short run; in some situations, the medium-run relationships can be profit-led even if the short-run relationships are wage-led.

ROBERT A. BLECKER

See also

Aggregate demand; Balance-of-payments constrained growth; Growth – wage-led vs profit-led; Mark-up pricing; Thirlwall's law

References

Bhaduri, A. and S.A. Marglin (1990), 'Unemployment and the real wage: the economic basis for contesting political ideologies', *Cambridge Journal of Economics*, **14** (4), 375–93.
Blecker, R.A. (1989), 'International competition, income distribution and economic growth', *Cambridge Journal of Economics*, **13** (3), 395–412.
Blecker, R.A. (1999), 'Kaleckian macro models for open economies', in J. Deprez and J.T. Harvey (eds), *Foundations of International Economics: Post Keynesian Perspectives*, London and New York: Routledge, pp. 116–49.
Blecker, R.A. (2005), 'International economics after Robinson', in B. Gibson (ed.), *Joan Robinson's Economics: A Centennial Celebration*, Cheltenham, UK, and Northampton, MA, USA: Edward Elgar, pp. 309–49.
Blecker, R.A. (2011), 'Open economy models of growth and distribution', in E. Hein and E. Stockhammer (eds), *A Modern Guide to Keynesian Macroeconomics and Economic Policies*, Cheltenham, UK, and Northampton, MA, USA: Edward Elgar, pp. 215–39.
Dornbusch, R. (1987), 'Exchange rates and prices', *American Economic Review*, **77** (1), 93–106.
Dutt, A.K. (1984), 'Stagnation, income distribution and monopoly power', *Cambridge Journal of Economics*, **8** (1), 25–40.
Kalecki, M. (1933), 'On foreign trade and "domestic exports"', *Ekonomista*, **3**, 27–35. Reprinted in M. Kalecki, *Collected Works of Michał Kalecki*, vol. I, *Capitalism: Business Cycles and Full Employment*, Oxford: Oxford University Press, 1990, pp. 165–73.
Lavoie, M. and E. Stockhammer (eds) (2013), *Wage-Led Growth: An Equitable Strategy for Economic Recovery*, Basingstoke, UK, and New York: Palgrave Macmillan.
Razmi, A. (2016a), 'Demand regimes and income distribution reconsidered in an open economy portfolio balance framework', *Journal of Post Keynesian Economics*, **39** (4), 516–38.
Razmi, A. (2016b), 'Growth and distribution in low-income economies: modifying post-Keynesian analysis in light of theory and history', *Review of Keynesian Economics*, **4** (4), 429–49.
Razmi, A. (2018), 'Does the demand regime matter over the medium run? Revisiting distributional issues in a portfolio framework under different exchange rate regimes', *Metroeconomica*, **69** (4), 708–36.
Robinson, J. (1947), *Essays in the Theory of Employment*, second edition, Oxford: Basil Blackwell.
Ros, J. (2016), 'Can growth be wage-led in small open developing economies?', *Review of Keynesian Economics*, **4** (4), 450–57.

Orthodox dissenters

To understand what the expression 'orthodox dissenters' means, it is worth pointing out a division in the various schools of thought in economic analysis. Economics can actually be framed into the mainstream (or orthodox) camp and the heterodox (or alternative) camp: post-Keynesian, Marxist, or French Regulation economists are labelled 'heterodox'. On the other hand, neoclassical and New Keynesian economists are classified as 'orthodox' or conventional. However, a more specific label can be used: Backhouse (2004) suggested that economics can be framed into two big branches, namely the mainstream and the dissenters.

Now, what is a dissenter? Generally speaking, a dissenter is understood as an individual who disagrees with established parameters or rules. As Backhouse (2004) claims, the idea of 'dissent' can be associated with 'disagreement'.

Thus, the dissenter category in economics can be subdivided into two groups: the orthodox dissenters and the heterodox dissenters. Lavoie (2014) defines orthodox dissenters those at the 'cutting edge' of orthodox economics, understanding 'cutting edge' as that small part of dissent that is respected by the big names and the elite in economic sciences. Consequently, orthodox dissenters can be understood as traditional mainstream economists who have even used traditional methods, but at the same time have questioned the standard receipts of the economic mainstream as austerity, privatization, and complete deregulation. Orthodox dissenters have a broad spectrum of political-economy ideas, and many of them are labelled in the left-wing of the political landscape. Nevertheless, their level of disagreement with the founding points of the discipline is not radical.

It is important to remark that the label of orthodox/heterodox dissenter is associated with the core ideas that reign in the historical moment of analysis. For example, Lavoie

ROBERT A. BLECKER / DIEGO GUEVARA

(2014) argues that Keynes, who was educated under the Marshallian paradigm, could be perceived as an orthodox dissenter after the publication of *The General Theory*. Another example is Milton Friedman, who, in the early 1950s, was an orthodox dissenter: in the golden years of Keynesian policies, Friedman was sceptical about public expenditure stabilization policies. In the 1970s, after the Keynesian Consensus crisis, Friedman's ideas became generally accepted and, as argued by Backhouse (2004), the label 'dissent' became inapplicable for him.

Current examples of orthodox dissenters are Joseph Stiglitz, Paul Krugman, and even the renowned Thomas Piketty. Stiglitz won the Nobel Prize for his clear contribution to the orthodox economics framework with his analyses on markets with asymmetric information. However, after receiving the Nobel Prize, his critiques against both globalization and free-market fundamentalism have gained media attention. Recently, Stiglitz has been close to the heterodox tradition, as he has co-authored papers in the post-Keynesian tradition, such as the one entitled 'Agent based-stock flow consistent macroeconomics: towards a benchmark model' (Caiani et al., 2016).

Krugman is another good example of an orthodox dissenter who gained wide media attention after being awarded the Nobel Prize for his contribution to international trade and new economic geography. His position to defend further stimulus in the United States in both the global financial crisis and the Covid-19 crisis, instead of the hostile austerity policies, and, in general, his opposition to many conservative economists put him in the dissent part of the orthodox spectrum. Conversely, in his approach to critical issues such as money creation, he maintains an orthodox position defending the loanable funds theory instead of an endogenous approach to money. Finally, Piketty is another orthodox dissenter who has gained recognition after the vast impact of his book *Capital in the Twenty-First Century*. Mainstream authors respect his empirical methods and formation, and his research work has made a remarkable contribution to inequality studies, a topic that was not a protagonist in the discipline during the last four decades. His political support for many left-wing positions and politicians in France put him in the economics progressist group. However, his theoretical approach to capital is narrow, and it does not recognize the Cambridge controversies and many other important concerns such that he can be called a heterodox economist. Thus, Piketty also belongs to the category of orthodox dissenters.

In conclusion, orthodox dissenters use and share the conventional mainstream economists' tools and approaches. However, they have certain disagreements with the standard communities, usually in terms of public policy recommendations and political approaches. Nonetheless, as they still are renowned and respected enough to be heard, their names are usually in prominent newspapers and debates, and they usually are asked for their opinions and economic forecasts. Many people out of heterodox circles could be named heterodox, but, clearly, they have their own category: orthodox dissenters.

DIEGO GUEVARA

See also

Capital theory controversies; Endogenous money; Money creation – nature of; Neoclassical economics; Post-Keynesian economics – a big tent?

References

Backhouse, R.E. (2004), 'A suggestion for clarifying the study of dissent in economics', *Journal of the History of Economic Thought*, **26** (2), 261–71.

Caiani, A., A. Godin, E. Caverzasi, M. Gallegati, S. Kinsella and J. Stiglitz (2016), 'Agent based-stock flow consistent macroeconomics: towards a benchmark model', *Journal of Economic Dynamics and Control*, **69** (C), 375–408.

Lavoie, M. (2014), *Post-Keynesian Economics: New Foundations*, Cheltenham, UK, and Northampton, MA, USA: Edward Elgar.

Overdraft economies

Hicks (1974, Ch. 2) introduced a dichotomy to characterize the institutional configuration of financial systems, distinguishing between the overdraft sector and the auto-sector. In the overdraft sector, deficit agents (such as firms seeking to finance an investment project) satisfy their financing needs by going into debt vis-à-vis the banking sector. In the auto-sector, by contrast, deficit agents finance their ventures by selling liquid assets or issuing bonds or shares, meaning that financing takes place via money or capital markets.

In the real world, economies exhibit a mix of both sectors, with one typically being more important than the other. The United States are usually taken to represent the archetypical example of a heavily asset-based economy, whereas the financial systems of continental Europe correspond more closely to overdraft economies. However, with the ongoing development of market-based finance in continental Europe, this distinction may become increasingly blurred. This said, it can be useful to examine the theoretical constructs of pure overdraft economies or pure auto-economies. Renversez (1996) has referred to the latter as financial-market economies; Lavoie (2001) has called them asset-based economies – the term most commonly found in the literature today. This distinction can also be applied to the analysis of central banking. For instance, in an overdraft economy, the banking sector borrows from the central bank to satisfy its need for reserves and is hence structurally indebted towards the central bank, which implements monetary policy by varying the interest rate at which banks can borrow reserves. By contrast, monetary policy implementation in asset-based economies takes place via central bank interventions in government bond markets.

Hicks's dichotomy has played a prominent role in discussions of post-Keynesian endogenous-money theory, having featured in works on the determination of interest rates (de Boissieu, 1989), government finance and monetary policy (Godley and Lavoie, 2007, Ch. 2; Lavoie, 2014, Ch. 4), monetary circuit theory (Renversez, 1996) and reserve flows in open economies (Lavoie, 2001). The endogenous nature of money, including the monetary base, is most easily demonstrated in an overdraft framework in which banks elastically supply credit at administered interest rates to creditworthy borrowers, creating deposits and thus money in the process, while the central bank elastically supplies the banking sector with reserves in order to maintain the functioning of the payments system. In such a system, it is particularly obvious that if broad money is endogenous, so must be the monetary base. The pure overdraft economy also bears similarity to the pure credit economy that has been used as an analytical device for instance by Keynes (1930) and Wicksell (1936).

Some authors appear to suggest that central tenets of post-Keynesian theory such as the causality running from investment to saving (de Boissieu, 1989) or the endogeneity of money (Renversez, 1996) are only valid in an overdraft economy. Given the prominence afforded to depictions of overdraft economies in the endogenous-money literature, it is important to discuss these arguments.

The former claim is misleading in that it is based on a confusion between saving and financing, in particular the notion that in the absence of money creation via bank lending, the financing of projects is constrained by the current flow of saving. In a stock–flow consistent framework, it is easily shown that any existing stock of savings (in the form of some means of payment) can potentially finance an arbitrarily large flow of transactions, including capital investment, which will generate a corresponding flow of saving in the national accounts (see Lindner, 2015). This echoes similar arguments made by Keynes (1937) in discussions following the publication of *The General Theory*. Such considerations do not imply that investment may not be credit-constrained, but this may also be the case in an overdraft system if banks ration the amount of loans granted.

Regarding the latter claim, even in an asset-based economy, the means of payment that are lent on capital markets must have previously been created. Given the empirical composition of broad money stocks, this will likely have happened through money creation by commercial banks. It is unclear why the money creation mechanism should be different in an asset-based economy, particularly given the shortcomings of the alternative 'money multiplier' view (Ryan-Collins et al., 2011; Werner, 2014, 2016). As argued by Lavoie and Reissl (2019), market-based financing – which merely redistributes existing means of payment – cannot logically fully replace the creation of means of payment by banks. Regarding the endogeneity of the monetary base, the detailed discussion by Lavoie (2014, Ch. 4) shows that as long as the central bank in an asset-based economy follows an interest rate target, it will have no choice but to maintain the stock of reserves close to the level demanded at this target rate, thereby making the monetary base endogenous.

Hence, while the overdraft economy represents both a theoretically and empirically important concept for the analysis of financial

SEVERIN REISSL

systems, the validity of basic post-Keynesian theory does not depend on such an institutional setting.

SEVERIN REISSL

See also

Central banking; Credit money; Endogenous money; Monetary circuit theory; Money creation – nature of

References

de Boissieu, C. (1989), 'The "overdraft economy", the "auto-economy" and the rate of interest', in A. Barrère (ed.), *Money, Credit and Prices in Keynesian Perspective*, Basingstoke: Palgrave Macmillan, pp. 79–104.
Godley, W. and M. Lavoie (2007), *Monetary Economics: An Integrated Approach to Credit, Money, Income, Production and Wealth*, Basingstoke and New York: Palgrave Macmillan.
Hicks, J.R. (1974), *The Crisis in Keynesian Economics*, Oxford: Basil Blackwell.
Keynes, J.M. (1930), *A Treatise on Money*, volumes 1 and 2, London: Macmillan.
Keynes, J.M. (1937), 'Alternative theories of the rate of interest', *Economic Journal*, **47** (186), 241–52.
Lavoie, M. (2001), 'The reflux mechanism in the open economy', in L.-P. Rochon and M. Vernengo (eds), *Credit, Interest Rates and the Open Economy: Essays on Horizontalism*, Cheltenham, UK, and Northampton, MA, USA: Edward Elgar, pp. 215–42.
Lavoie, M. (2014), *Post-Keynesian Economics: New Foundations*, Cheltenham, UK, and Northampton, MA, USA: Edward Elgar.
Lavoie, M. and S. Reissl (2019), 'Further insights on endogenous money and the liquidity preference theory of interest', *Journal of Post Keynesian Economics*, **42** (4), 503–26.
Lindner, F. (2015), 'Does saving increase the supply of credit? A critique of loanable funds theory', *World Economic Review*, 4, 1–26.
Renversez, F. (1996), 'Monetary circulation and overdraft economy', in G. Deleplace and E.J. Nell (eds), *Money in Motion: The Post Keynesian and Circulation Approaches*, Basingstoke, UK, and New York: Macmillan, pp. 465–88.
Ryan-Collins, J., T. Greenham, R. Werner and A. Jackson (2011), *Where Does Money Come From?*, London: New Economics Foundation.
Werner, R. (2014), 'Can banks individually create money out of nothing? The theories and the empirical evidence', *International Review of Financial Analysis*, 36, 1–19.
Werner, R. (2016), 'A lost century in economics: three theories of banking and the conclusive evidence', *International Review of Financial Analysis*, 46, 361–79.

Wicksell, K. (1936), *Interest and Prices*, London: Macmillan.

Paradox – Kalecki's

Kalecki identified a number of paradoxes and contradictions, which, he argued, were inherent in capitalist economies. All of these have played an important role in post-Keynesian analysis. Of these, three will be discussed in this entry: the paradox of profit margins, the contradictory role of investment, and the paradox of government debt.

Using national income accounts, Kalecki showed that total profits are determined by the expenditure decisions of capitalists, namely, by their consumption and investment decisions. Prices are determined as a mark-up on costs – which leads to the share of profits in national income being determined by the profit margins set by firms. An individual capitalist may be able to increase their total profits by increasing their profit margins (mark-ups) but capitalists as a class are unable to increase total profits beyond the level given by their expenditure decisions. Increases in profit margins (reductions of the real wage) will, therefore, lead to a fall in output (and employment) to the level where total profits are again equal to capitalist expenditure. This is an example of a fallacy of composition, and an analogue to Keynes's paradox of thrift (Kalecki, 1943a, pp. 153–4; Robinson, 1977; Kriesler, 1996).

Joan Robinson stressed the importance of Kalecki's insight as follows:

> There are two elements in Kalecki's analysis, the share of profit in the product of industry is determined by the level of gross margins, while the total flow of profits per annum depends upon the total flow of capitalists' expenditure on investment and consumption. Combining these two theories, we find the very striking proposition that firms, considered as a whole, cannot increase their profits merely by raising prices. Raising profit margins reduces real wages and consequently employment in wage-good industries. The *share* of profits is increased but the total profits remain equal to the flow of capitalists' expenditure ... In this way, Kalecki was able to weave the analysis of imperfect competition and of effective demand together and it was this that opened up the way for what goes under the name of post-Keynesian economic theory. (Robinson, 1977, pp. 192–3, original emphasis)

SEVERIN REISSL / PETER KRIESLER

The second contradiction Kalecki identified resulted from the dual nature of investment. In the short run investment increases effective demand, which is important in reducing today's unemployment, but, the long-run impact will be to increase capacity and productivity, which increases tomorrow's unemployment problem. As current investment augments the capital stock, both the economy's capacity and the productivity of labour will increase. The build-up of capacity will lead to the emergence of excess capacity, which will put downward pressure on investment, while the increase in labour productivity will reduce employment for any given level of effective demand. As a result, investment will have to increase at an increasing rate simply to stop unemployment from increasing. It is from this dual function of investment, as both a component of demand and an addition to the stock of capital, that the underlying contradiction of capitalism is most evident:

> We see that the question, 'what causes periodic crises?' could be answered briefly: the fact that the investment is not only produced but also producing. Investment considered as capitalist spending is the source of prosperity, and every increase of it improves business and stimulates a further rise of spending for investment. But, at the same time investment is an addition to the capital equipment, and right from birth it competes with the older generation of this equipment. The tragedy of investment is that it calls forth the crisis because it is useful; I do not wonder that many people consider this theory paradoxical. But it is not the theory which is paradoxical but its subject – the capitalist economy. (Kalecki, 1936-7, p. 554)

The third paradox is particularly emphasized by Lavoie (2014a, pp. 18–19 and 309–15; 2014b). Kalecki showed that, despite the fact that budget deficits would increase capitalists' profits, capitalists would resist these deficits for political reasons as outlined in his 'Political aspects of full employment' (Kalecki, 1943b).

By manipulating the national accounts for an open economy with a government sector, Kalecki shows that:

gross profits net of taxes = gross investment + export surplus + budget deficit − workers' saving + capitalists' consumption.

As a result of which, 'a budget deficit ... permits profits to increase above the level determined by private investment and capitalist consumption' (Kalecki, 1933, p. 245).

In other words, it is in the interest of individual capitalists for the government to run higher budget deficits, as this will increase their profits. However, capitalists as a class will be antagonistic to this, both because of the political impact of full employment and owing to their dislike of government intervention in determining the level of employment, which serves to reduce capitalists' political and social influence.

These three paradoxes point to contradictions at the heart of capitalism. On the one hand, investment is necessary to generate employment and economic growth; on the other hand, it makes both harder to achieve in subsequent periods. By increasing mark-ups and, therefore, reducing real wages, capitalists increase the share of profits but at the expense of lower employment and output – with no impact on total profits, as long as their expenditures remain unchanged. Government budget deficits, usually criticized by capitalists as being against their interests and those of workers, turn out to have the opposite effect – namely to increase profits and employment. Capitalists as a class often act against their interests as individuals.

PETER KRIESLER

See also

Effective demand; Fallacy of composition; Mark-up pricing; Paradox of thrift; Profit

References

Kalecki, M. (1933), 'The determinants of profits', reprinted in J. Osiatynski (ed.), *Collected Works of Michal Kalecki, Volume II*, Oxford: Clarendon Press, 1991, pp. 239–46.

Kalecki, M. (1936–37), 'A theory of the business cycle', *Review of Economic Studies*, **4** (2), 77–97, reprinted in J. Osiatynski (ed.), *Collected Works of Michal Kalecki, Volume II*, Oxford: Clarendon Press, 1991, pp. 529–57.

Kalecki, M. (1943a), *Studies in Economic Dynamics*, London: George Allen & Unwin, reprinted in J. Osiatynski (ed.), *Collected Works of Michal Kalecki: Volume I*, Oxford: Clarendon Press, 1990, pp. 117–90.

Kalecki, M. (1943b), 'Political aspects of full employment', *Political Quarterly*, **14** (4), 322–31, reprinted in J. Osiatynski (ed.), *Collected Works of Michal Kalecki: Volume I*, Oxford: Clarendon Press, 1990, pp. 347–56.

Kriesler, P. (1996), 'Microfoundations: a Kaleckian perspective', in J. King (ed.), *An Alternative*

Macroeconomic Theory: The Kaleckian Model and Post-Keynesian Economics, Boston: Kluwer, pp. 55–72, reprinted in J. Halevi, G.C. Harcourt, P. Kriesler and J. Nevile (eds), *Post-Keynesian Essays from Down Under: Theory and Policy in an Historical Context. Volume I: Essays on Keynes, Harrod and Kalecki*, Basingstoke and New York: Palgrave Macmillan, 2016, pp. 161–76.

Lavoie, M. (2014a), *Post-Keynesian Economics: New Foundations*, Cheltenham, UK, and Northampton, MA, USA: Edward Elgar.

Lavoie, M. (2014b), 'Macroeconomic paradoxes with Kalecki and Kaleckians', in R. Bellofiore, E. Karwowski and J. Toporowski (eds), *Economic Crisis and Political Economy: Volume 2 of Essays in Honour of Tadeusz Kowalik*, Cheltenham, UK, and Northampton, MA, USA: Edward Elgar, pp. 198–211.

Robinson, J. (1977), 'Michal Kalecki on the economics of capitalism', *Oxford Bulletin of Economics and Statistics*, 39 (1), 7–17.

Paradox of costs

The paradox of costs is a macroeconomic relationship between the real wage (of workers) and the profit rate (of capitalists). First, in the static version, when real wages increase, all else being constant, consumption, capacity utilization, and hence income will also increase. The profit share decreases but the profit rate does not change as a result, even though capitalists perceive the real wage increase as a rising cost. This is paradoxical from both the classical and neoclassical perspectives as, in their framework, when the wage increases, the profit rate will decrease.

This has an important implication for the rate of capital accumulation. As the profit rate is sustained, the rate of capital accumulation will also be sustained, since profitability is the main determinant of investment behaviour. Again, this is in contrast to both the classical and neoclassical perspectives, since in their framework a decrease of profit will lead to less savings by capitalists, and hence a lower rate of capital accumulation.

Second, this result is more striking in the dynamic, long-run version. When real wages increase relative to labour productivity and aggregate consumption, investment will strongly and positively respond to an increase in consumption demand owing to accelerator effects. Therefore, the overall increase in aggregate demand will be even greater and firms will experience a profit rate higher than before. It is worth highlighting that flexible capacity utilization is an important pre-condition for the validation of the paradox of costs.

The paradox of costs is one of the most well-known and important characteristics of post-Keynesian macroeconomics. The idea was discussed by Kalecki in 1939 (see Kalecki, 1969; but also Lavoie, 2015, p. 18). A dynamic, long-run version with explicit terminology of the paradox of costs was proposed by Rowthorn (1981). His model does not, however, specifically focus on the cost of workers, but on any type of production costs.

This paradox has a very significant policy implication, as it implies that the economy can redistribute income towards workers, and this does not hurt profitability of firms; it can in fact increase the latter. Redistribution will not therefore harm economic growth; it can even promote the latter.

It is important to note that this is a macroeconomic paradox. For an individual firm, rising real wages will indeed increase its production costs and hurt its profitability. But if all firms increase workers' real wages, this will generate a greater consumption demand, and hence a higher rate of capacity utilization and higher income for firms. Firms therefore can sustain their profit rate or even experience a higher one. This is another important example of the fallacy of composition at the macroeconomic level.

YK KIM

See also

Accelerator effects; Aggregate demand; Fallacy of composition; Profit; Wages

References

Kalecki, M. (1969), *Studies in the Theory of Business Cycles, 1933–1939*, Oxford: Basil Blackwell.

Lavoie, M. (2015), *Post Keynesian Economics: New Foundations*, Cheltenham, UK, and Northampton, MA, USA: Edward Elgar.

Rowthorn, B. (1981), 'Demand, real wages and economic growth', *Thames Papers in Political Economy*, Autumn.

Paradox of debt

The paradox of debt states that efforts to decrease the indebtedness (leverage) of firms may lead to a higher indebtedness. An early discussion of the paradox of debt is found in Steindl (1952, p. 114). Some authors, such as Lavoie (1995) and Hein (2007), demonstrate the idea using a formal post-Keynesian macroeconomic model.

When firms try to reduce their indebtedness, overall investment will decrease and hence there is a reduction of aggregate demand and income. Through this channel, firms' profitability and retained earnings decline. As a result, firms become more indebted than before – the exact opposite of what individual firms intended to achieve.

This process works in reverse as well. When firms increase their investment through additional borrowing, the increase of aggregate demand and income can generate stronger cash flow for firms, so that their indebtedness, as a result, declines.

It is important to note that the paradox of debt is a macroeconomic paradox. Reducing indebtedness may be a good strategy for an individual firm, but in aggregate, if there are enough firms taking the same action, this paradox can arise. This is another important example of the fallacy of composition at the macroeconomic level.

The paradox of debt is also applicable to banks and to the whole financial system as well as governments' efforts to control their indebtedness.

For example, when a government tries to reduce its indebtedness (public debt relative to GDP) through cutting public expenditures, it can result in a large reduction of aggregate demand and income through the multiplier effect, so that public indebtedness in fact increases. It works in reverse as well. Large public expenditures can result in a very strong surge in aggregate demand and generate strong growth of GDP. Therefore, public indebtedness can decrease as a result.

The paradox of debt has been used as a critique to Hyman Minsky's financial instability hypothesis, which posits that firms' indebtedness will increase during the expansion phase and decrease during the contraction phase. Some authors, such as Lavoie and Seccareccia (2001) and Bellofiore et al. (2010), argue that the financial instability hypothesis is a microeconomic phenomenon for an individual firm, and it neglects to take account of macroeconomic consequences of such behaviour by firms. In other words, the paradox of debt predicts that, if enough firms take the same action of expanding their investment, firms' indebtedness in aggregate does not have to change or even decrease during the expansion phase; similarly, if enough firms take the same action of decreasing their investment, firms' indebtedness in aggregate does not have to change or even increase during the contraction phase.

YK KIM

See also

Aggregate demand; Fallacy of composition; Financial instability hypothesis; Fiscal multiplier; Public finance

References

Bellofiore R., J. Halevi and M. Passarella (2010), 'Minsky in the "new" capitalism: the new clothes of the financial instability hypothesis', in D. Papadimitriou and L.R. Wray (eds), *The Elgar Companion to Hyman Minsky*, Cheltenham, UK, and Northampton, MA, USA: Edward Elgar, pp. 84–99.
Hein, E. (2007), 'Interest rate, debt, distribution and capital accumulation in a Post-Kaleckian model', *Metroeconomica*, **58** (2), 310–39.
Lavoie, M. (1995), 'Interest rates in Post-Keynesian models of growth and distribution', *Metroeconomica*, **46** (2), 146–77.
Lavoie, M. and M. Seccareccia (2001), 'Minsky's financial fragility hypothesis: a missing macroeconomic link?', in R. Bellofiore and P. Ferri (eds), *Financial Fragility and Investment in the Capitalist Economy: The Economic Legacy of Hyman Minsky, Volume II*, Cheltenham, UK, and Northampton, MA, USA: Edward Elgar, pp. 76–96.
Steindl, J. (1952), *Maturity and Stagnation in American Capitalism*, New York: Monthly Review Press.

Paradox of liquidity

The paradox of liquidity builds upon the concept of liquidity.

Liquidity is an attribute of real and financial assets. It can be defined as an asset's ability to be transformed into another asset on short notice, considering the potential costs (capital losses) of this transaction. The higher the liquidity premium of an asset, the faster it can be transformed into another asset and the lower the costs involved. Liquidity is measured in relative terms, as one can establish a scale to compare the degree of liquidity of different assets and situations in specific markets. Besides, the scale of liquidity varies in time and space, as what constitutes a liquid asset or market depends on social practices and institutions (Keynes, 1936/1997, p. 240).

The liquidity of assets is not entirely separable from the liquidity of markets, as market depth and scale affect how liquid one asset can be. In turn, liquid markets allow buyers and sellers to change positions without significant capital losses and feature considerable availability of credit and low borrowing costs.

In a few words, the paradox of liquidity occurs whenever the attempts to hold more liquid assets end up reducing the liquidity of assets and markets.

There are two versions of the paradox of liquidity.

The first version of this paradox relates to a more general process that may happen following an unexpected event that increases overall uncertainty and negatively impacts the value of a set of assets. Two instances of this kind of event are the collective reassessment of the future value of real-estate assets that led to the burst of the housing bubble in the financial crisis of 2008 and the COVID-19 pandemic. In such a context, agents may attempt to change their portfolios' composition towards more liquid assets, reducing the liquidity of markets for those and several other, often riskier, assets – as agents run from assets with default and capital loss risks. The decrease in markets' liquidity may generate tighter conditions for indebted parts, shrinking credit availability and hindering the rollover of outstanding debt. Those agents under financial stress may be forced to undergo asset fire sales, as they attempt to avoid default in the short run. However, when fire sales prevail, asset prices are pushed down, discouraging buyers from trading the particular asset. Eventually, there will be no buyers turning the market into a one-way market as agents want to hold the same position. As a result, liquidity vanishes.

In sum, as agents sell their assets due to their higher liquidity preference, their capital losses increase, and thus the liquidity obtained through asset sales falls. Ultimately only cash assets would still be liquid.

The second version of the paradox of liquidity, pointed out by Minsky, is associated with the development of financial markets and new credit instruments that, although intending to provide liquidity further, contribute to reducing it.

During booms, the development of financial innovations that serve both the purpose of financing business and substituting already existing cash assets may generate a liquidity illusion. The creation of securitized assets, derivatives, and swap arrangements, primarily designed to reduce individual risks, fosters the illusion of increasing overall assets' liquidity. As these innovations drive up financial asset prices, the system becomes more exhilarationist. Agents get more prone to taking on risks anchored in the belief of high liquidity and low risks. A virtuous circle is set in motion, leading to sizeable concessions of new loans and a temporary expansion of liquidity. Yet as an event breaks the confidence in financial markets, this increases the value of liquidity embodied in default-free assets and lowers the liquidity return of many private debts; it also leads to a fall in the value of capital assets and equity shares (Minsky, 1986/2008, p. 277).

In this sense, the paradox of liquidity may also implicate a paradox of risk (Lavoie, 2014): agents' willingness to take on riskier decisions based on the illusion of liquidity at the individual level mounts up systemic risk, potentially leading to financial crises and recessions.

The likelihood of these outcomes depends fundamentally on the role of the central banks as lenders of last resort. Since the monetary authority is not bound by the same liquidity constraints of private agents, it could provide banks and firms with potentially unlimited liquidity.

The paradox of liquidity also extends to the international dimension, such as in the case of capital flows to peripheral economies. During slumps or periods of low liquidity in global credit markets, both periphery and centre agents, such as households and financial institutions, increase their demand for liquid assets. As centre assets are relatively more liquid than the periphery's ones, agents move away from periphery assets pushing their prices down and contributing to the evaporation of their liquidity.

LÍDIA BROCHIER

See also

Central banking; Credit-led boom; Financial crisis; Financial instability hypothesis; Money and banking

LÍDIA BROCHIER

References

Keynes, J.M. (1936/1997), *The General Theory of Employment, Interest, and Money*, Amherst: Prometheus Books.
Lavoie, M. (2014), *Post-Keynesian Economics: New Foundations*, Cheltenham, UK, and Northampton, MA, USA: Edward Elgar.
Minsky, H.P. (1986/2008), *Stabilizing an Unstable Economy*, New York: McGraw-Hill.

Paradox of thrift

The paradox of thrift (or paradox of saving) is an excellent example of what post-Keynesian economists call the 'fallacy of composition': what is good for an individual may not be good for the economy as a whole. Specifically, the paradox of thrift means that while increased savings may be good for an individual (microeconomic level), it does not directly translate into macroeconomic benefits (investment); rather, it has the opposite effect. The paradox is simple to explain: if someone decides to increase his/her savings by not eating out at restaurants for six months and cooking cheaper meals at home, then that person will save part of his/her income and thus be better off financially by increasing their savings. However, if everyone in the same city also decided to forego eating out for six months, the macroeconomic consequences would be obvious: many restaurants would go bankrupt causing job losses, a decline in tax revenues and eventually a decrease in the overall amount people can save. Thus, increased saving among large numbers of people leads to a lesser ability to save at an aggregate level. What is good for the individual is not always applicable to society at large, especially regarding the economy.

The paradox of thrift is often attributed (in various ways) to John Maynard Keynes and his *General Theory of Employment, Interest, and Money* (1936). Bernard Mandeville's *Fable of the Bees*, which Keynes quotes in *The General Theory*, is considered the earliest reference to the paradox of thrift. Keynes never used the expression directly; however, he does present the idea. In Chapter 14, Keynes (1936) presents convincing evidence that the neoclassical causality imbedded in the idea that savings equals investment ($S = I$) is wrong. Any increase in savings is a reduction in consumption, which in turn reduces income and investment. There is no mechanism in place to ensure excess savings are used to replace lost consumption. Instead, Keynes reverses the causality by stating that investment drives saving ($I = S$). The decisions to invest and consume are the driving forces of the economy, and saving is a by-product (or afterthought) in the process.

Moreover, post-Keynesian economists generally consider public finance as a paradox-of-thrift example. Many politicians and pundits argue that federal governments should manage their finances like a household. In short, governments need to behave in a financially responsible manner – not taking on too much debt and reducing expenses – especially during times of economic crisis. The notion of balanced budgets is an example of this logic. Sovereign federal governments, however, can run deficits for far longer than households. Post-Keynesian economists assert that governments should run deficits if the additional spending (and/or loss of revenue) is due to an economic contraction. Additionally, a government's ability to deficit spend allows it to invest in long-run projects that provide an initial economic boost as well as social and economic compounding returns far into the future.

On the other hand, if the federal government is experiencing a deficit and decides to reduce spending, then it may (temporarily) save some money but will quickly exacerbate its financial problems by causing higher unemployment, lower tax revenues and greater uncertainty, which eventually reduces the ability to save. This approach is known as austerity, promoted by many governments (such as in Britain and Greece) after the Great Recession that caused them to experience significant financial shortfalls. Governments that adhere to austerity policies still believe that savings equals investment (that is, they are making the fallacy of composition) and thus disregard the paradox of thrift. As discovered by Greece and other countries whose governments adopted austerity policies, the short-term gain in savings is quickly followed by a downward spiral of unemployment, decreased investment and increased uncertainty among businesses and consumers. The financial consequences of austerity measures are disastrous – especially when employed during desperate times when a fiscal stimulus is needed rather than austerity – and predicted by post-Keynesian economists who understand the nuances of the paradox of thrift (Lavoie, 2014).

Robert H. Scott

Lídia Brochier / Robert H. Scott

See also

Fallacy of composition; Fiscal deficits; Microfoundations; Public finance; *The General Theory of Employment, Interest and Money*

References

Keynes, J.M. (1936), *The General Theory of Employment, Interest, and Money*, London: Macmillan.

Lavoie, M. (2014), *Post-Keynesian Economics: New Foundations*, Cheltenham, UK, and Northampton, MA, USA: Edward Elgar.

Paradox of tranquillity

The paradox of tranquillity is an expression coined by Lavoie (1986, p. 7) and relates to the work of Hyman P. Minsky, specifically to his financial instability hypothesis. Unlike other paradoxes identified by post-Keynesian economists, such as the well-known paradox of thrift, the paradox of tranquillity is not based on a fallacy of composition, arising in the passage from the microeconomic to the macroeconomic level of analysis.

The concept concerns the financial side of the economy and indicates the endogenous unfolding of financial fragility, due to a change in agents' expectations becoming increasingly optimistic during a period of stable economic growth. In a nutshell, 'stability is destabilizing' (Minsky, 1982, p. 26).

The paradox of tranquillity emerges from Minsky's interpretation of Keynes's *General Theory*, seen as an 'investment theory of business cycles and a financial theory of investment for capitalist economies' (Minsky, 1994, p. 3). It can be better appreciated referring to business cycles. After a crisis or an economic downturn, economic agents have negative expectations. Credit standards are strict, and investors are hesitant in engaging in risky economic activities; there are high liquidity preferences and the financial system is stable. A period of prolonged and stable economic growth modifies agents' expectations, which become more and more optimistic. Prudent forms of behaviour are progressively abandoned. Banks loosen their credit standards, while borrowers cumulate debt and opt for riskier investments. The core of the process is a stock–flow dynamics: the accumulation of debt implies a stream of payment commitments, which, if not covered with the revenues originated by investments, becomes unsustainable. The dynamics can be described at the microeconomic level referring to Minsky's taxonomy of financial positions (see for instance Minsky, 1992). Economic stability and the enhancing optimism lead an increasing number of agents to abandon 'hedge financing' positions, to engage in 'speculative finance' – with revenues covering only interest payments but not part of the debt – and then in 'Ponzi finance', with new inflows of debt needed to pay interest commitments. This increases the financial fragility of the whole economic system and eventually paves the way for a financial crisis.

The paradox of tranquillity is intimately related to three main pillars of post-Keynesian economics: fundamental uncertainty, the non-self-regulating nature of markets, and the endogenous nature of money. The progressive change in expectations driving the economy along an unstable path would not take place in an economic system with agents characterized by rational expectations as in neoclassical economics. In fact, people have limited knowledge and do not know the 'true model' of the economy, that is to say, they are not perfectly aware of how the world operates really. Therefore, the expectations driving their investment and financing decisions may prove delusional, making their debt unsustainable. Similarly, the endogenous emergence of a destabilizing process in the financial system is at odds with the neoclassical faith in market forces to lead the economy toward equilibrium.

What the paradox of tranquillity posits – that in an unregulated market, forces will endogenously emerge, which will drive the economy from financial stability to crisis – is the polar opposite of the self-regulating ability of the market. Finally, in post-Keynesian monetary theory, the number of borrowers considered creditworthy by banks represents the key limit to credit supply. The definition of creditworthiness is neither stable nor objective. The destabilizing nature of stability takes therefore the form of a loosening in that limit, hence making speculation and bubbles more likely to be fed by the banking system.

A clear example of this paradox can be found in the events that led to the subprime financial crisis. The passage from the Great Moderation (the period starting in the mid-1980s, characterized by low inflation and low volatility in the business cycle) to the Great Recession (the economic decline stemming from the subprime crisis) perfectly epitomizes the rise of destabilizing forces theorized by Minsky.

EUGENIO CAVERZASI

See also

Fallacy of composition; Financial fragility; Financial instability hypothesis; Liquidity preference; Paradox of thrift

References

Lavoie, M. (1986), 'Minsky's law or the theorem of systemic financial fragility', *Studi Economici*, **29** (2), 3–28.
Minsky, H.P. (1982), *Can 'It' Happen Again? Essays on Instability and Finance*, Armonk, NY: M.E. Sharpe.
Minsky, H.P. (1992), 'The financial instability hypothesis', *Levy Economics Institute of Bard College Working Paper*, No. 74.
Minsky, H.P. (1994), 'Financial instability and the decline (?) of banking: public policy implications', *Jerome Levy Economics Institute Working Paper*, No. 127.

Pasinetti's index

The Pasinetti index was developed by Pasinetti (1980–81) in an effort to show that a theory of interest rate and income distribution logically precedes, in a pure labour economy, the introduction of capital accumulation and profits. The author establishes a 'natural' interest rate value that leaves income distribution between creditors and debtors unchanged in such an economy. Post-Keynesian economists later used this interest rate value – the Pasinetti index – as a measure of income flowing to (or away from) rentiers (Seccareccia and Lavoie, 2016) and also as a monetary policy rule (Rochon and Setterfield, 2007).

This 'natural' interest rate is derived in a pure labour economy, which produces only perishable consumption goods. Therefore, there is neither capital accumulation nor aggregate savings, since all unconsumed goods disappear at the end of the period. However, there is room for personal savings: producers can consume less than their current production, passing the excess to other producers. Alternatively, producers can consume more than their current production, by borrowing goods from 'saver' producers. Therefore, this pure labour economy can have financial assets that represent claims on a future stream of production. The question that Pasinetti (1980–81) poses to himself is: which interest rate should be charged on those financial assets, if one wants to keep income distribution between lenders and borrowers unchanged in terms of labour time?

Supposing that it is possible to vertically integrate each industry in the economy, the average labour productivity of each industry *i* will be:

$$a_{it} = a_0 e^{\lambda_i^t t} \quad (1)$$

where λ_i^t is the exponential growth rate of labour productivity for sector *i*. Assuming mark-up pricing, it is possible to write each sector product's prices as follows:

$$p_{it} = \gamma_i w (a_{it})^{-1} \quad (2)$$

where γ is the mark-up rate and *w* represents wages, assumed constant across all sectors. Assuming wages as a *numéraire* ($w = 1$) and analysing the above equation in growth terms, we have that prices in each sector will be falling in exact proportion to the sectoral productivity growth rates:

$$\pi_i = -\lambda_i \quad (3)$$

where π_i is the rate of change of prices of each *i* sector. This implies that each 'credit' (that is, consumption goods) advanced to each sector has an 'own' rate of interest λ_i, measured in terms of labour time. This is because a credit equivalent of *x* working hours given at time *t* will represent more consumption goods at a future time, since the productivity of the same *x* working hours will have increased. Conversely, all debts of each sector *i* have an 'own' interest rate, at that same level.

If a given monetary unity is used as *numéraire*, all credits and debts should also receive as interest the inflation measured in monetary units in order to maintain their purchasing power in terms of labour time. To explain this, let us make a final simplifying assumption, integrating the whole economy in a single sector, in which case we will have:

$$\pi = -\lambda \quad (4)$$

EUGENIO CAVERZASI / SYLVIO ANTONIO KAPPES

where π is the inflation rate and λ is average labour productivity growth. If prices and wages were varying in terms of the monetary unit, the interest rate that would keep income distribution between lenders' and borrowers' constant in terms of labour time would be:

$$i = \lambda + \pi \qquad (5)$$

If the interest rate charged on loans is higher (smaller) than that, lenders will be receiving more (less) labour time than they have lent.

A numerical example may clarify the argument. For an hourly wage of 10 US dollars, a loan of 1,000 US dollars will be able to purchase 100 hours of labour time. If productivity grows by 2 per cent and the rate of inflation measured in money prices is 3 per cent, wages will increase to 10.50 US dollars per hour. With an interest rate of 5 per cent, the borrower must pay back 1,050 US dollars, which is equivalent to 100 hours of labour time at the new wage rate.

This theoretical construct was used by post-Keynesian economists both as an empirical index and as a policy rule. Seccareccia and Lavoie (2016, p. 210) aimed to build 'a simple empirical approximation that would allow an analyst to measure in a convenient way over long historical periods the evolution of rentier income'. To do so, they used i as the long-term interest rate for ten-year government bonds, π as inflation rate, and λ as measured productivity growth. The Pasinetti index (PI), then, is as follows:

$$PI = i - \pi - \lambda \qquad (6)$$

When this index is positive (negative), income is flowing to (away from) rentiers.

In conclusion, the Pasinetti index plays an important role in post-Keynesian economics, being a theoretical construct, an empirical tool of analysis, and a monetary-policy-rule point of reference.

SYLVIO ANTONIO KAPPES

See also

Income distribution; Interest rate – natural; Mark-up pricing; Profit; Rentier income

References

Pasinetti, L.L. (1980–81), 'The rate of interest and the distribution of income in a pure labor economy', *Journal of Post Keynesian Economics*, **3** (2), 170–82.

Rochon, L.-P. and M. Setterfield (2007), 'Interest rates, income distribution, and monetary policy dominance: Post Keynesians and the "fair rate" of interest', *Journal of Post Keynesian Economics*, **30** (1), 13–42.

Seccareccia, M. and M. Lavoie (2016), 'Income distribution, rentiers, and their role in a capitalist economy: a Keynes–Pasinetti perspective', *International Journal of Political Economy*, **45** (3), 200–23.

Pasinetti's paradox

Building upon Kaldor's (1956) contribution to the Cambridge theories of income distribution, Pasinetti's (1962) theorem – or 'paradox', as it has become known – put forth a model demonstrating the determination of the rate of profit – and in turn the rate of economic growth – in an economy in which both capitalists and workers save, accumulate, and earn profit income. Pasinetti's reformulation of Kaldor's model stemmed from a 'logical slip' wherein it was implicitly assumed total profits were attributed to capitalists. This shortcoming in Kaldor's model implied that all workers' savings are transferred to capitalists when, in fact, two distinct classes of savers should lead to both capitalists and workers earning profit income. This was reconciled by modifying the savings function to include workers' savings from profit income.

The unique outcome of Pasinetti's paradox is that in the steady state where both classes save and hold capital, the rate of return is determined by capitalists' propensity to save and is independent of workers' savings behaviour. In the long run, the rate of profit is equal to the ratio of the rate of economic growth to the capitalist savings rate. In addition to showing that, in the long run, the propensity to save of workers has no effect on the determination of the overall profit rate of the economy, the results demonstrate that this savings rate also has no effect on the determination of the share of total profits in national income. At the same time, the propensity to save of workers determines the distribution of profits between workers and capitalists. Intuitively it would seem that an increase in workers' propensity to save would drive down the rate of profit and bid up wages, but Pasinetti's theorem demonstrates this dynamic would not persist in the long run. Although the rate of profit may be observed to fall temporarily, this would reduce capitalists'

SYLVIO ANTONIO KAPPES / ALEX PELHAM

income. This would allow the share of wealth owned by workers to increase and since, by assumption, workers are less thrifty, this redistribution would restore the rate of profit to its long-run equilibrium level.

Since Pasinetti's seminal breakthrough, many papers have been written building upon and criticizing the assumptions necessary for the paradoxical equilibrium result. Some key components of criticism have been based on the necessary inequality requiring the capitalist savings rate being greater than the worker savings rate. Attempts have been made to incorporate this saving structure within a neoclassical framework and have been able to give rise to the extreme outcomes wherein workers hold the entirety of the capital stock or capitalists hold it entirely. Building on this criticism, Samuelson and Modigliani (1966) came up with what is known as the 'dual' Pasinetti's equilibrium by applying Pasinetti's theorem to a neoclassical model. They showed that within Pasinetti's system there could be an outcome where workers accumulate the entire share of the capital stock. If the workers' savings rate is sufficiently high, there exists a scenario where they accumulate the entirety of the capital stock and the capitalists' income share falls to zero. In the case of a Cobb–Douglas production function this will occur if the capitalists' propensity to save times the marginal product of capital is less than or equal to the workers' savings rate. In the 'dual' instance where the rentier class ceases to exist, the system becomes qualitatively similar to the single saving propensity Solow model (Samuelson and Modigliani, 1966, p. 278).

Darity (1981) applied a modified investment equation to the problem posed by Samuelson and Modigliani (1966). He found the 'dual' outcome was no longer stable and that in the presence of the neoclassical production function the Pasinetti equilibrium is the only stable outcome. Another interesting outcome from this is that under this synthesis the paradox falls away and it can be the workers' savings propensity that determines capitalists' share of the capital stock. Darity (1981) also showed, in a strictly Keynesian growth framework, that by incorporating employment fluctuations and utilization within the investment function there is an 'anti-dual' equilibrium. Depending on the parameter values of savings rates, interest rates, and investment sensitivities to utilization and profit, it is possible for the capitalists' share of the capital stock to approach unity.

The strength of Pasinetti's contribution and reason for its enduring relevance is its great generality. His results apply to almost any macroeconomic system capable of a golden age growth path and the equation holds in most diverse circumstances. Models have been built on the foundations of this finding, incorporating monetary authorities, the public sector, unstable employment dynamics, and a pure socialism scenario posed in Pasinetti's original paper.

ALEX PELHAM

See also

Cambridge equation; Capitalism; Growth; Income distribution; Profit

References

Darity, W.A. (1981), 'The simple analytics of Neo-Ricardian growth and distribution', *American Economic Review*, **71** (5), 978–93.
Kaldor, N. (1956), 'Alternative theories of distribution', *Review of Economic Studies*, **23** (2), 83–100.
Pasinetti, L.L. (1962), 'Rate of profit and income distribution in relation to the rate of economic growth', *Review of Economic Studies*, **29** (4), 267–79.
Pasinetti, L.L. (1974), *Growth and Income Distribution*, Cambridge, UK: Cambridge University Press.
Samuelson, P. and F. Modigliani (1966), 'The Pasinetti paradox in neoclassical and more general models', *Review of Economic Studies*, **33** (4), 269–301.

Phillips curve

Phillips's (1958) seminal paper, 'The relation between unemployment and the rate of change of money wage rates in the United Kingdom, 1861–1957', introduced a primitive empirical version of the so-called Phillips curve. His findings have been interpreted as the cornerstone of the debate on the interplay of inflation and (real) economic activity. Similar mechanisms had been discussed and debated both theoretically and empirically decades before.

Fisher (1926) finds a significantly negative correlation coefficient between the rate of change in the dollar value and unemployment rate in the United States (1915–25). The rise in prices improves firms' balance sheets, because their receipts increase more quickly than their expenses, where the latter are mainly interests on bonds, rents, and wages. In the same vein, Fisher (1933) provides a theory about the link between over-indebtedness, deflation, and unemployment. The argument maintains that as debt is being paid back, bank deposits are reduced, resulting in a fall in prices. This, in turn, worsens firms' net worth and profits, resulting in a reduction in output, trade, and employment.

In his theory of prices, Keynes (1936, p. 295) argues that the general price level depends partly on the wage unit and partly on the volume of employment, hence 'the effect of changes in the quantity of money on the price level can be considered as being compounded of the effect on the wage-unit and the effect on employment'. Inflationary pressures are likely to increase as the economy approaches a state of full employment, and are reduced if unutilized capacity (including labour) is abundant.

By contrast, neoclassical economists tend to undermine the beneficial effects of (moderate) inflation. The 'real-balance effect' (Pigou, 1943; Patinkin, 1948, 1965) gives important weight to the argument whereby an increase in inflation reduces real income, so that inflation, no matter its level, has mainly negative effects on aggregate demand. The neoclassical appropriation of the so-called 'Keynesian' apparatus (to wit, the IS–LM model) (see Hicks, 1937; Hansen, 1953) embedded in the neoclassical synthesis, starts from the premise that the aggregate demand curve is downward sloping, thus endorsing from the outset the real-balance effect and refuting the potential beneficial effects of (non-excessive) inflation on employment.

Phelps (1967, 1968) and Friedman (1968) set up a theoretical framework whereby inflation would be successfully predicted by economic agents, so that they adapt their expectations accordingly. As a result, the short-run Phillips curve changes with respect to past inflation. In this framework, the long-run Phillips curve is vertical, and the empirical short-term trade-off between inflation and unemployment no longer holds. The long-run equilibrium rate of unemployment is at its 'natural rate', so that monetary policy is ineffective in the long run.

In the 1970s, several theories emerged to explain the simultaneous rise in inflation and unemployment observed in that decade. Modigliani and Papademos (1975) introduced the non-inflationary rate of unemployment (NIRU, which quickly morphed into NAIRU, the non-accelerating inflation rate of unemployment), that is, the rate of unemployment below which inflation would accelerate. Lucas (1972) developed an alternative in which a positive relationship between output and inflation could arise because of imperfect information, that is, unanticipated changes. The 'policy ineffectiveness proposition' extends the model by arguing that monetary policy does not systematically influence the economy, so that monetary policy can be ineffective also in the short run.

Gordon (1982) suggested that inflation is determined by inertia, demand, and supply. He argues that, since 2000, changes have occurred in each of the three components of his triangle model (see Gordon, 2018). Among the changes, the feedback of past inflation to current inflation through the inertia effect appears to have decreased. This was interpreted by Blanchard (2016) as anchored inflation expectations. This means that no acceleration in inflation will take place if unemployment goes below its natural level, thus disproving the vertical long-run Phillips curve hypothesis.

The post-Keynesian view of the NAIRU has been described as follows:

> if it is true that there is a unique NAIRU, that really is the end of discussion of macroeconomic policy. At present I happen not to believe it and that there is no evidence of it. And I am prepared to express the value judgment that moderately higher inflation rates are an acceptable price to pay for lower unemployment. But I do not accept that it is a foregone conclusion that inflation will be higher if unemployment is lower. (Godley, 1983, p. 170)

Kriesler and Lavoie (2007) argue that inflation does not need to increase with increased capacity utilization. The authors introduced a post-Keynesian short-run Phillips curve that is flat for a range of utilization rates, and the associated long-run Phillips curve is shown as a continuum. Another view is expressed by Stockhammer (2011), who advocates that effective demand determines unemployment in the short run and the deviation of actual unemployment from the NAIRU determines the change in inflation. Nonetheless, the NAIRU is endogenous in the medium run and follows actual unemployment via hysteresis.

FLORENT MCISAAC AND LUIS REYES

See also

Aggregate demand; Inflation; Monetary policy; Money illusion; NAIRU

References

Blanchard, O. (2016), 'The US Phillips curve: back to the 60s?', *Peterson Institute for International Economics Policy Brief*, No. 16–1.
Fisher, I. (1926), 'A statistical relation between unemployment and price changes', *International Labour Review*, **13** (6), 785–92.
Fisher, I. (1933), 'The debt-deflation theory of great depressions', *Econometrica*, **1** (4), 337–57.
Friedman, M. (1968), 'The role of monetary policy', *American Economic Review*, **58** (1), 1–17.
Godley, W. (1983), 'Keynes and the management of real national income and expenditures', in D. Worswick and J. Trevithick (eds), *Money and the Modern World*, Cambridge, UK: Cambridge University Press, pp. 135–78.
Gordon, R.J. (1982), 'Price inertia and policy ineffectiveness in the United States, 1890–1980', *Journal of Political Economy*, **90** (6), 1087–17.
Gordon, R.J. (2018), 'Friedman and Phelps on the Phillips curve viewed from a half century's perspective', *Review of Keynesian Economics*, **6** (4), 425–36.
Hansen, A.H. (1953), *A Guide to Keynes*, New York: McGraw-Hill.
Hicks, J.R. (1937), 'Mr. Keynes and the 'Classics': a suggested interpretation', *Econometrica*, **5** (2), 147–59.
Keynes, J.M. (1936), *The General Theory of Employment, Interest and Money*, London: Macmillan.
Kriesler, P. and M. Lavoie (2007), 'The New Consensus on monetary policy and its post-Keynesian critique', *Review of Political Economy*, **19** (3), 387–404.
Lucas, R.E. Jr. (1972), 'Expectations and the neutrality of money', *Journal of Economic Theory*, **4** (2), 103–24.
Modigliani, F. and L. Papademos (1975), 'Targets for monetary policy in the coming year', *Brookings Papers on Economic Activity*, 1, 141–65.
Patinkin, D. (1948), 'Price flexibility and full employment', *American Economic Review*, **38** (4), 543–64.
Patinkin, D. (1965), *Money, Interest, and Prices: An Integration of Monetary and Value Theory*, New York: Harper & Row.
Phelps, E.S. (1967), 'Phillips curves, expectations of inflation and optimal unemployment over time', *Economica*, **34** (135), 254–81.
Phelps, E.S. (1968), 'Money-wage dynamics and labour-market equilibrium', *Journal of Political Economy*, **76** (4), 678–711.
Phillips, W. (1958), 'The relation between unemployment and the rate of change of money wage rates in the United Kingdom, 1861–1957', *Economica*, **25** (100), 283–99.
Pigou, A.C. (1943), 'The classical stationary state', *Economic Journal*, **53** (212), 343–51.
Samuelson, P.A. and R.M. Solow (1960), 'Analytical aspects of anti-inflation policy', *American Economic Review*, **50** (2), 177–94.
Shiller, R.J. (1997), 'Why do people dislike inflation?', in C. Romer and D. Romer (eds), *Reducing Inflation: Motivation and Strategy*, Chicago: University of Chicago Press, pp. 13–70.
Solow, R. (2018), 'A theory is a sometime thing', *Review of Keynesian Economics*, **6** (4), 421–4.
Stockhammer, E. (2011), 'Wage norms, capital accumulation, and unemployment: a post-Keynesian view', *Oxford Review of Economic Policy*, **27** (2), 295–311.

FLORENT MCISAAC AND LUIS REYES / TED P. SCHMIDT

Ponzi finance

Ponzi financing is one of three spending unit categories outlined in Minsky's (1977) 'financial instability hypothesis' (FIH), through which he explained the endogenous nature of financial crises, and, as he stated, it represents an 'interpretation of the substance of Keynes's "General Theory"' (Minsky, 1992, p. 1). In the early 1920s, Boston financier Carlos 'Charles' Ponzi was prosecuted for mail fraud in conjunction with developing a widespread pyramid investment scheme, thus earning the eponymous moniker of a 'Ponzi scheme'.

The FIH describes how an economy moves from stability to instability as spending units (Minsky focused mainly on firms) move from robust financial structures to unstable financial structures over the course of the business cycle. The financial condition of spending units is defined in terms of cash flows relative to cash commitments, which influences their need to fund expenditures with debt. Minsky's three financing units are hedged financing (a stable financial position), speculative financing (a risky financial position), and Ponzi financing (an untenable financial position).

In his original explication of the FIH, Minsky (1977, p. 14) defined Ponzi financing as 'a situation in which cash payments commitments on debt are met by increasing the amount of debt outstanding'. It is clear that Minsky has defined a situation that is untenable over time, where one must borrow to pay off previous debt commitments. In ensuing articles, Minsky would refine the definition by more explicitly focusing on cash flow measures, though not always in the most straightforward manner (see Minsky, 1978; 1982). In what would be his final write-up of the FIH in 1992, Minsky reverts to a simpler and (for the most part) clearer definition:

> For Ponzi units, the cash flows from operations are not sufficient to fulfill either the repayment of principle or the interest due on outstanding debts by their cash flows from operations. Such units can sell assets or borrow ... A unit that Ponzi finances lowers the margin of safety that it offers the holders of its debts. (Minsky, 1992, p. 7)

According to a note in Minsky's original version of the FIH,

> Charles Ponzi was a Boston 'financial wizard' who discovered that by offering high returns on 'deposits' he could acquire a large amount of 'deposits.' As long as his total borrowing grew at a faster rate than his promised 'interest,' he could fulfill his commitments by increasing his debts. Once his deposits began to grow at a slower rate than his interest obligations, he could not meet his commitments. Inasmuch as debts are used to pay interest (or dividends), a Ponzi scheme eventually collapses. (Minsky, 1977, p. 70)

According to Zuckoff (2006), however, the deposit scheme described by Minsky was actually a pyramid scheme that Ponzi learned about in 1907 while working at Banco Zarossi, in Montreal. The scheme that sent Ponzi to jail was on a much grander scale and involved International Reply Coupons (IRC), which allowed one to purchase the stamps necessary to mail an item requested from a resident in another country. Ponzi stumbled upon the fact that the dollar value of an IRC purchased in Italy was less than the actual cost of the stamps in the United States, allowing one to generate an arbitrage profit. After initially making extraordinary gains, Ponzi successfully peddled the idea to investors. However, as the number of investors exceeded the available supply of IRCs, it was impossible to generate the profits necessary to pay investors, so Ponzi resorted to paying existing investors with the funds from new participants. Ponzi pled guilty to mail fraud and other charges, spending nearly 14 years in jail from 1920 to 1934.

TED P. SCHMIDT

See also

Business cycles; Contagion effects; Financial crises; Financial fragility; Financial instability hypothesis

References

Minsky, H.P. (1977), 'The financial instability hypothesis: an interpretation of Keynes and an alternative to "standard" theory', *Nebraska Journal of Economics and Business*, **16** (1), 5–16.
Minsky, H.P. (1978), 'The financial instability hypothesis: a restatement', *Thames Papers in Political Economy*.
Minsky, H.P. (1982), *Can 'It' Happen Again?*, Armonk, NY: M.E. Sharpe.
Minsky, H.P. (1992), 'The financial instability hypothesis', *Jerome Levy Economics Institute at Bard College Working Paper*, No. 74.
Zuckoff, M. (2006), *Ponzi's Scheme: The True Story of a Financial Legend*, New York: Random House.

Post-Keynesian economics – a big tent?

On the question of whether post-Keynesian economics should be regarded as a 'big tent' there is a broad spectrum of opinion among post-Keynesians themselves. At the left extreme of this spectrum, the late Fred Lee argued tirelessly that 'heterodox economists in the United States [had] coalesced into a professional community by 2000' (Lee, 2010, p. 25), working together to pose a single coherent alternative to mainstream economics. This had gone well beyond social interaction and the occasional cross-publication. There was clear evidence of theoretical integration, Lee claimed, demonstrating the emergence of 'a group of broadly commensurable economic theories – specifically Post Keynesian-Sraffian, Marxist-radical, institutional-evolutionary, social, feminist, Austrian, and ecological economics' (*ibid.*, p. 19). For Lee the 'big tent' – though he himself did not use this metaphor – had already been erected.

At the right-hand extreme of the spectrum, Paul Davidson has maintained for half a century that Keynes's *General Theory*, correctly interpreted, provides a complete and authoritative macroeconomic theory that must be defended against allcomers. (The political implications of the terms 'left' and 'right' are

TED P. SCHMIDT / JOHN E. KING

intentional: Lee had considerable sympathy for many aspects of Marxian and radical political economy, which was emphatically not shared by Davidson.) This 'fundamentalist Keynesian' position leads Davidson not only to be suspicious of any macroeconomic analysis from other heterodox traditions, but also to resist all other variants of post-Keynesian thinking. Neither the Kaleckian nor the Minskyan sub-schools has ever attracted his support. While he has never set out his objections to Minsky in print, he has often criticized Kalecki for being unable (unlike Keynes) to deal with perfectly competitive markets and for exaggerating the macroeconomic significance of social class relations. In the second edition of his textbook, *Post Keynesian Macroeconomic Theory*, there is a single one-sentence reference to Kalecki and (judging from the index) no mention of Minsky (Davidson, 2011, p. 168).

Most of us are somewhere in the middle, recognizing first that there are several sub-species of post-Keynesian economics, all of which are essentially on the same page and, second, that while there are indeed significant differences of opinion between post-Keynesians and other schools of thought in heterodox economics, there is still considerable scope for cooperation and fruitful debate between them (King, 2013). Thus, a large majority of post-Keynesians reject both extremes. Against Lee, they suspect that the differences between the various schools of heterodox economics are so substantial that any intellectual 'popular front' that united them would prove to be a very unstable affair. Against Davidson, they deny the fundamentalist Keynesian claim that 'it is all in *The General Theory*', for several reasons. First, capitalism has changed very substantially since 1936, making it extremely unlikely that a theoretical analysis developed almost a century ago can be applied without significant revision to the third decade of the twenty-first century. Second, they can see something of value in the work of Kalecki and Minsky, some of whose ideas need to be added to (and in some cases to replace) the arguments of *The General Theory*. Third, and possibly most important, they believe that they have a lot in common with some of the other heterodox schools, whose ideas can be used both to supplement the core post-Keynesian analysis and to extend its critique of mainstream economics to other important issues (class relations, the environment, gender, ideology and institutions, to name just a few).

But this does not entail that 'anything goes': some degree of theoretical coherence is essential, as Sheila Dow (2016) reminds us.

There is also some awkwardness in the relations between post-Keynesians and some of these other heterodox schools. Three are especially interesting. First, while some post-Keynesians are sympathetic to Sraffian economics, many are unimpressed by the latter's neglect of expectations, uncertainty, and the role of money in capitalist economies. Much the same can be said, secondly, of the relationship between post-Keynesian economics and radical–Marxian political economy, with serious disagreement arising over the crucial question whether the capitalist system can be reformed or needs to be overthrown and replaced by some form of socialism. Finally, there is continuing controversy over the degree to which post-Keynesians should be receptive to the work of the 'left fringe' of New Keynesian economics, as expressed by Paul Krugman and (perhaps especially) Joseph Stiglitz, who have broken with the policy consensus of mainstream macroeconomics but still appear reluctant to abandon its underlying theoretical apparatus.

This is all very much a debate in progress, as a comparison of recently published post-Keynesian textbooks would show. Space limitations have also prevented any discussion of the related issue of the relationship between the post-Keynesians and other disciplines in the social sciences. I suspect that access to the 'big tent' should not be restricted to economists alone.

JOHN E. KING

See also

Capitalism – stages of; Capitalism – varieties of; Endogenous money; Heterodox economics; Orthodox dissenters

References

Davidson, P. (2011), *Post Keynesian Macroeconomic Theory, Second Edition: A Foundation for Successful Economic Policies for the Twenty-First Century*, Cheltenham, UK, and Northampton, MA, USA: Edward Elgar.

Dow, S. (2016), 'Consistency in pluralism and the role of microfoundations', in J. Courvisanos, J. Doughney and A. Millmow (eds), *Reclaiming Pluralism in Economics*, London and New York: Routledge, pp. 32–46.

King, J.E. (2013), 'Post Keynesians and others', in F.S. Lee and M. Lavoie (eds), *In Defense of Post-Keynesian and Heterodox Economics: Response to Their Critics*, London and New York: Routledge, pp. 1–17.

Lee, F.S. (2010), 'Pluralism in heterodox economics', in R. Garnett, E.K. Olsen and M. Starr (eds), *Economic Pluralism*, London and New York: Routledge, pp. 19–35.

Post-Keynesian economics and Marxian economics

The intellectual origins of Marxian economics differ in a significant degree from Keynes's contributions. Moreover, a researcher has to take into account that both Karl Marx and John Maynard Keynes were not exclusively economists. Both scholars took intensive courses in philosophy during their formative years. Both men only became focused on economics during their later professional life. Discerning the difference in intellectual cultures between authoritarian and semi-developed Prussia in the 1840s and liberal-imperialist Great Britain at the turn of the twentieth century is of the utmost importance for understanding the contrasts between these two men in terms of paradigmatic outlook, conceptual thinking and terminology.

Marx was educated in a time when the political philosophy and ethics of the German philosopher Georg Wilhelm Friedrich Hegel had been reinterpreted by his pupils as a legitimization of a self-asserting Prussian autocracy, emphasizing the importance of an obedient and conservative civil society and promoting a despotic administration as the epitome of rationality. Marx arrived in an intellectual atmosphere opposing the powers-to-be and joined a circle of thinkers called the Young Hegelians, who propagated a reinterpretation of Hegel as being a revolutionary liberal. However, they began to question Hegel's conceptual cornerstone, namely German idealism. This political and scientific project also required an epistemology and an ontology: Hegel's dialectics and a crude form of materialism inherited from French thinkers such as Diderot and d'Holbach. Dialectics emphasized the merits of designing thought in terms of contradictions and perpetual change, while its crude materialistic outlook wanted to explain metaphysics and religions, for example God, as a mental projection of individuals that would simultaneously determine their worldview.

Around 1845, Marx conceptually broke out of the Hegelian shell, developing a new philosophical system, in which his own version of dialectical thought was part and parcel of a new kind of materialism, that is, 'historical materialism' (Marx never used this term). Marx continued to use Hegelian terminology but succeeded in making a paradigmatic break with German idealism. For Marx, the social world should be conceived from a holistic point of view, in which economic relations, political power relations and ideological processes together transform a society throughout real historical time. Individuals were in fact historical subjects, being part of a web of many contradicting social relations, and their social practices and thoughts about the world were inherently knitted into the social fabric of a historical society. As such, for Marx, history is always in the making and without any teleological meaning, but the temporary results are always determined by the conditions of a certain historical time. Marx was never an absolute determinist and considered the future as being open-ended. His political convictions, however, made him vehemently hope for a future outcome that would be socialist in nature.

A similar trajectory can be discerned in Keynes. The young Keynes was deeply influenced by George Edward Moore, who was one of the initiators of a new tradition that would become known as 'analytical philosophy'. Moore thoroughly criticized the established Victorian traditions of individualistic and naturalist utilitarianism or British idealism, which would lead to a new paradigm of logical positivism–empiricism. However, the older Keynes would develop his own comprehensive critique of Moore's logical and epistemological propositions relating to ethics and language. A first result was his *Treatise on Probability* (Keynes, 1921), which would become a springboard for an epistemic break within prevailing analytical trends later on, resulting in Keynes's well-known economic concept of uncertainty. Gradually being absorbed by macroeconomic issues during the First World War, Keynes would ultimately make a simultaneous epistemic break with Marshallian economics. In the 1930s, Keynes was being ethically and politically propelled by the factual observation of the final demise of the classical–liberal form of capitalism. His political views were therefore

JOHN E. KING / JELLE VERSIEREN

oriented to designing a new institutional framework in which the impact of future capitalist crises could be lessened.

Marx's contributions to economics also have to be traced back to the early 1840s. German economists were then passive receptors of the English influx of Adam Smith's and David Ricardo's works while making a final break with the obsolete tradition of German cameralism. Marx's first contributions to economics could therefore be considered as still being written within the conceptual coordinates of English classical economics. In the 1850s, the intellectual climate fundamentally shifted with the emergence of a new paradigm: the 'Historische Schule der Nationalökonomie'. Marx frequently showed his reservations towards this new school, lacking logical consistency, and decided to continue to rethink the premises of classical economics instead. This would first lead to his unfinished manuscript *Grundrisse* (Marx, 1857/1993), eventually resulting in the first volume of *Capital* (Marx, 1867/1992). Marx established with his famous book the tradition of Marxian economics primarily as a conceptual overturn of classical economics, in which new concepts such as 'labour power', 'surplus value' and 'social relations of production' still remain indispensable for any Marxian economist. Also, he designed his own labour theory of value in contrast to Smith's and Ricardo's version. In addition, he also proposed his own theory of money, in which money is considered as a necessary but not sufficient precondition for capitalism – a 'value-form' next to commodities, commodified labour and prices. In a capitalist society, money fulfils four functions: 'store of value', 'means of circulation', 'measure of value' and 'means of payment'. These functions, Marx stated, are socially contradictory. For example, the hoarding/rentier logic of amassing money as a 'store of value' will contravene the demand for liquidity by industrial capital, requiring money for the 'means of circulation'. Marx also developed a crisis theory of capitalism. The precise nature of a particular crisis entirely depends on the historical evolution of capitalism. In a more abstract sense, a few variants can be discerned: overproduction by industrial capital, underconsumption forced upon workers, disproportional and uneven distribution of profits between sectors, and a general tendency of the average profit rate to fall. Many countermeasures can be taken, such as banks being deployed for flooding industrial capital with liquidity and the State fiscally intervening for redistribution purposes. In the end, however, these countermeasures cannot eliminate the inherent instability of capitalism. Rather, the dialectic between crisis and countermeasures produces a temporal solution for the fundamental problem of contradictory and opposing class relations between capital and wage earners.

JELLE VERSIEREN

See also

Capitalism; Historical time; Power; Rationality; Uncertainty

References

Keynes, J.M. (1921), *A Treatise on Probability*, London: Macmillan.
Marx, K. (1857/1993), *Grundrisse: Foundations of the Critique of Political Economy*, London: Penguin.
Marx, K. (1867/1992), *Capital: Critique of Political Economy, Volume 1*, London: Penguin.

Post-Keynesian social policy

Social policy consists of government actions to help people and protect them from life-cycle-related problems (like childcare or pensions) as well as from the negative impact of economic activities (mainly poverty and unemployment). According to mainstream models, social policy should not be needed: markets would take care of all problems optimally (private schools, private pensions, and so on). However, two issues provide a rationale for public services within the mainstream paradigm: market failures and public goods. The latter is not useful, as social services (like education, health, housing, and pensions) do not satisfy the non-exclusion and non-rivalry conditions. The former is not useful either, as markets are neither efficient nor market-clearing in the mainstream sense. A distinctive post-Keynesian articulation to understand and design social policy is therefore needed.

Maintaining the level and predictability of employment and earnings contributes to overall well-being of the population. Then, full employment (in rewarding and well-paying jobs), unemployment insurance, and pensions should be part of a post-Keynesian social policy.

JELLE VERSIEREN / ENRIQUE DELAMÓNICA

These elements were pillars of the Keynesian Welfare State, including variants in developing countries (Mkandawire, 2004). However, they were challenged by calls to reduce the role of the State (sometimes leading to improperly labelling 'post-Keynesian' the situation downgraded from the original, universalistic Keynesian Welfare State). These efforts were countered by post-Keynesian inspired and aligned suggestions for employment of last resort, universal basic income, and the decent work agenda of the International Labour Organization (Jackson, 1999; Nell, 2003). As minimum wages and income policies before, none of these elements are considered 'disruptions' or counterproductive (that is, generating or increasing unemployment) among post-Keynesian economists. Neither wages nor employment levels are optimally set by markets.

These policies redistribute income across households. Indeed, according to post-Keynesian economists, income distribution is not optimal and does not reflect 'contributions' to output by individuals. Intra-household disparities require public support for the care economy, for instance childcare, family/parental leave for mothers and fathers, and assistance for people with disabilities (Staveren, 2010).

In the health sector, uncertainties abound (timing of illness, which malady, its severity, which treatments could be applicable, and patients' reaction to treatment). The concatenation of these unpredictable features undermines the idea of 'demand' for healthcare (Dunn, 2006; Hodgson, 2007). The idiosyncratic nature and constant evolution of medical knowledge (which, unlike in production of commodities, often reverses itself) invalidate a proper 'supply' curve. A post-Keynesian social policy should be based on non-market institutional arrangements to provide healthcare. For example, uncertainty in healthcare entails that universal health insurance is the least-cost option, because the larger the group, the lower the unit cost (the same applies to pensions). Moreover, public healthcare eliminates profits and marketing costs, thus increasing resources for treatment. Large earning differentials exist within the health sector (related to income distribution). They can be publicly regulated without worrying about detrimental effects on quality, because pecuniary gains are not the (only/main) motivation for healthcare workers. Production of medicines (including research and development activities for new ones) by profit-led oligopolies does not meet social needs. Beyond FDA-type regulation, public guidance of production and research is essential (similar to Keynes's ideas about guiding/socializing investments).

In the education sector, mainstream thought argues that wages and wage differentials measure education benefits (a narrow view) and that rates of return be used to allocate scarce education resources. Keynes highlighted challenges in calculating (and basing decisions on) rates of return. In this case, a major difficulty pertains to future wages being unknown. Also, when educational opportunities expand and more people complete higher levels of education, the premium of higher education vanishes in unpredictable ways. Additionally, wages do not coincide with workers' (marginal) contribution. Moreover, wages will vary under conditions of low or high unemployment. Consequently, linking educational attainment to individual returns is impossible.

Public financing connects each sector (the core of social policy) to the macroeconomy (Todorova, 2013). Thus, a central feature of post-Keynesian social policy should be the explicit integration of all social and macroeconomic concerns under one overarching framework.

Markets being neither efficient nor optimal, a post-Keynesian social policy would eschew the private sector, public–private partnerships, managing public social services 'like' private firms, or vouchers to imitate competitive market behaviour in social services provision. Using cost–benefit analysis or random control trials to find optimal solutions for social problems would be rejected: they do not deal with uncertainty, institutional context, historical circumstances, path dependency, and structural determinants (Murnane and Nelson, 2005; Reddy, 2012). Post-Keynesian analysis complements arguments based on merit goods, decommodification, social citizenship, and human rights.

In conclusion, much exists to construct a coherent post-Keynesian social policy framework (and expand on other heterodox thinkers' ideas). Remaining gaps may be easily filled to design and implement efficient and effective alternatives to mainstream social policy.

ENRIQUE DELAMÓNICA

See also

Employer of last resort; Fiscal policy; Income distribution; Socialization of investment; Uncertainty

ENRIQUE DELAMÓNICA

References

Dunn, S.P. (2006), 'Prolegomena to a post Keynesian health economics', *Review of Social Economy*, **64** (3), 273–99.
Hodgson, G.M. (2007), 'An institutional and evolutionary perspective on health economics', *Cambridge Journal of Economics*, **32** (2), 235–56.
Jackson, W.A. (1999), 'Basic income and the right to work: a Keynesian approach', *Journal of Post Keynesian Economics*, **21** (4), 639–62.
Mkandawire, T. (2004), 'Social policy in a development context: introduction', in T. Mkandawire (ed.), *Social Policy in a Development Context*, New York: Palgrave Macmillan, pp. 1–33.
Murnane, R. and R.R. Nelson (2005), 'Improving the performance of the education sector: the valuable, challenging, and limited role of random assignment evaluations', *National Bureau of Economic Research Working Paper*, No. 11846.
Nell, E.J. (2003), 'Short-run macroeconomic stabilization by an employer of last resort', in E.J. Nell and M. Forstater (eds), *Reinventing Functional Finance: Transformational Growth and Full Employment*, Cheltenham, UK, and Northampton, MA, USA: Edward Elgar, pp. 299–318.
Reddy, S. (2012), 'Randomize this! On poor economics', *Review of Agrarian Studies*, **2** (2), 60–73.
Staveren, I.V. (2010), 'Post-Keynesianism meets feminist economics', *Cambridge Journal of Economics*, **34** (6), 1123–44.
Todorova, Z. (2013), 'Connecting social provisioning and functional finance in a post-Keynesian–institutional analysis of the public sector', *European Journal of Economics and Economic Policies: Intervention*, **10** (1), 61–75.

Power

The concept of power is virtually absent from neoclassical economics. While other social sciences take into account different approaches, typologies and dimensions of power, the topic is deeply absent in traditional economic textbooks. Of course, there is a great debate in social sciences about the nature of power. For some, power is linked to the oppression and coercion of human beings, while for others it has a positive side, being a constructive way of communication (Han, 2016) or a facilitator of the interaction that allows cooperation. Beyond these discrepancies, our notion of what power is has an important effect on the way we understand reality.

In heterodox economics, power is key in the analysis of how economies work. A long tradition that traces back to classical economics (revitalized by American institutionalism), today it forms the core of most heterodox approaches. It denotes the importance of 'the ability of persons or institutions to bend others to their purposes' (Galbraith, 2001, p. 136). Historically, property has played a decisive role in the asymmetric nature of power among different social classes. As noted by Marx (1964), peasants (without property) needed to ask permission to work the land. In the capitalist mode of production, workers do not have the same autonomy as capitalists. Recognizing this fact, heterodox economists try to understand the distributional conflict among social classes, which is regulated by institutions.

Hence, most heterodox economists (probably) would not object to the Weberian general definition of power: 'the chance of a man or of a number of men to realize their own will in a communal action even against the resistance of others who are participating in the same action' (Weber, 1968, p. 180). Accordingly, this conception of power features in much of heterodox analysis, especially with respect to the systematic inequality of social relations, for instance: between workers and capitalists; between creditors and debtors; between firms; in discussing trade between countries with different productive capacities; between monetary systems (currency hierarchy); between taxpayers; between Caucasians and racialized minorities; between women and men.

In the history of economics, classical economists were the first to draw attention to the potential conflicts that arose from the distribution of the surplus, trying to understand how the economic system can reproduce itself. The radicalization of the objective theory of value demonstrated that the capitalist class has the power to appropriate the surplus; this was later denied by the Marginalist Revolution. Based on a naturalistic view of the world taken from physics, marginalist authors reject social class analysis by making an isomorphism between the individual's psyche (utility) and the physics of energy (potential energy) (Mirowski, 1989).

One of the main reasons for the absence of a definition of power in neoclassical economics is embedded in the assumptions and meta-beliefs of its research programme (Lavoie, 2014). These premises include methodological individualism, epistemological instrumentalism, and the conception of time (reversible and

ENRIQUE DELAMÓNICA / CAMILO ANDRÉS GUEVARA

logical time). These premises, whether intentionally or not, produce a denial of social classes and uncertainty.

Methodological individualism, for instance, is key to portraying markets as non-hierarchical entities and to avoid explaining conflictual phenomena related to power. Wages are an example of this, as they are not the product of forces that are exogenous to the market – like the bargaining power of workers – but instead are the result of market forces that ultimately reveal the individual effort (the marginal product of labour). Epistemological instrumentalism, on the other hand, has served either to create an imaginary world (perfect competition in which no one has the power to distort the market) or to postulate a cognitive framework to judge reality (like the failure-markets approach, in which one explains reality as an error of that perfect world).

Nowadays, some orthodox dissenters conceptualize power in terms of asymmetric relationships 'due to political imbalances, informational asymmetries or barriers to entry' (Naidu et al., 2019, p. 1). Under this conception, governments need to address the political imbalances or correct market failures to improve economic performance. Nevertheless, there is no real questioning of the starting point, no elucidation of the origin of power before the markets. It is important to have in mind that capitalist economies are based on unequal relationships, and those relations are not an externality that results after market processes. This is paramount, because power as a market failure changes the *raison d'être* of the role of the State. It is not an intervention towards the decommodification of social relations, but one that generates greater horizontality for a competition between equals.

By way of contrast, one of the fundamental characteristics of the post-Keynesian approach is its conception of time, which is understood as an irreversible phenomenon. Hence, there is a concatenation of past and present (historical time), and the existence of uncertainty is fully recognized. For post-Keynesian economists, because the future is not given, the question of why power exists along with how power is exercised can be addressed. 'It is the presence of uncertainty that leads agents to try and secure a greater portion of the distribution of income. Given their hierarchy in the economic order, agents will be successful to various degrees' (Monvoisin and Rochon, 2007, p. 5).

As Keynes (1936) noticed, given the nature of uncertainty, conventions are fundamental for all economic agents to act. For those who build these conventions and determine how they are controlled, there is an exercise of power that can be seen, for example, in the current development of monetary policy dictated by 'independent' central banks, and financial agents such as credit rating agencies.

In post-Keynesian analysis, uncertainty and power are also tied to key elements like money, effective demand and inflation. According to Davidson (1972), for instance, the existence of a demand for money is due to uncertainty and, according to endogenous-money theory, money is a debt relation. The level of effective demand over the short run is essentially an unknown variable that has great consequences for all economic agents. Inflation is basically seen as a conflict directly linked to power, a constant tug-of-war between wages, profits and rents, in which each social class has different degrees of influence over the others.

Post-Keynesian economists have also modelled these unequal relationships. The post-Keynesian three-equation model proposed by Rochon and Setterfield (2007) established institutional parameters that involve the bargaining power of workers and firms to a target wage share.

The conceptualization of power is also fundamental in post-Keynesian microeconomics, as the objective of the firm is not profit maximization but to increase its market power at all levels. This includes its influence on consumers, suppliers, regulators and governments. Given the uncertain nature of investment decisions, firms try to maintain their influence over pricing and financing.

Regarding the international monetary regime, some heterodox schools have pointed out that there is a great power asymmetry between countries whose currencies perform their three functions internationally (such as the US dollar) and countries whose currencies are only used as speculative assets, which can generate great instabilities for those countries. Thus, these schools of thought pointed out the importance of having an international mechanism that follows the guidelines of the bancor, limiting the power of creditor countries (countries with trade surpluses) and strengthening debtor countries (countries with trade deficits).

As has been noted, the conceptualizations of post-Keynesian economists fully allow the

CAMILO ANDRÉS GUEVARA

analysis of power recognizing its origins and its exercise, and taking its consequences without rejecting or conceptualizing it as an externality.

CAMILO ANDRÉS GUEVARA

See also

Capitalism; Currency hierarchy; Heterodox economics; Income distribution; Orthodox dissenters

References

Davidson, P. (1972), *Money and the Real World*, London: Palgrave.
Galbraith, J.K. (2001), *The Essential Galbraith*, Boston: Houghton Mifflin Harcourt.
Han, B.-C. (2016), *Sobre el poder*, Barcelona: Herder.
Keynes, J.M. (1936), *The General Theory of Employment, Interest and Money*, London: Macmillan.
Lavoie, M. (2014), *Post-Keynesian Economics*, Cheltenham, UK, and Northampton, MA, USA: Edward Elgar.
Marx, K. (1964), *Pre-Capitalist Economic Formations*, London: Lawrence and Wishart.
Mirowski, P. (1989), *More Heat Than Light*, Cambridge, UK: Cambridge University Press.
Monvoisin, V. and L.-P. Rochon (2007), 'Economic power and the real world: a post-Keynesian analysis of power', *International Journal of Political Economy*, **35** (1), 5–30.
Naidu, S., D. Rodrik and G. Zucman (2019), 'Economics after neoliberalism', *Boston Review*, 15 February, available at https://bostonreview.net/forum/suresh-naidu-dani-rodrik-gabriel-zucman-economics-after-neoliberalism (last accessed 14 November 2020).
Rochon, L.-P. and M. Setterfield (2007), 'Interest rates, income distribution, and monetary policy dominance: post Keynesians and the "fair rate" of interest', *Journal of Post Keynesian Economics*, **30** (1), 13–42.
Weber, M. (1968), *Economy and Society: An Outline of Interpretive Sociology*, New York: Bedminster Press.

Pricing

In post-Keynesian economics, pricing refers to the way prices of commodities are determined in the economy. As Lee (1998, p. 10) explains, 'pricing refers to the procedures the business enterprise uses to set the price of a good before it is produced and placed on the market.' In this view, prices are determined by firms themselves and not by the market. Firms set their prices to engage in sequential transactions with their customers. The reason for this is twofold. First, firms are price setters, because markets are not perfectly competitive in the real world: there is some degree of monopoly or imperfect competition. The other reason lies in the decentralization of markets: firms need to set prices, because there are no organized markets with an auction mechanism. This explanation lies in the research work of Gardiner Means (1935, 1936) on administered prices.

The way firms set their prices is by using 'cost-plus pricing'. They add a profit margin to a measure of costs in order to generate a profit. This cost-plus practice may sometimes be called 'mark-up pricing'. Mark-up pricing, however, refers to only one of several possible formulae of cost-plus pricing. Post-Keynesian economics identify three formulas: mark-up pricing, full-cost pricing, and target-return pricing.

The specificity of mark-up pricing as a cost-plus formula is to add a gross profit margin to unit direct cost (that is, labour and raw materials variable costs), in order to cover overhead costs and generate a net profit. This practice is often linked to Kalecki's 'degree of monopoly' theory (see Kalecki, 1940). As Lee (1998) pointed out, mark-up pricing is largely widespread among post-Keynesian macroeconomic models, although not strongly supported by empirical evidence. Mark-up pricing indeed offers a realism/simplicity compromise that makes it relevant and easy to use in models.

In contrast, full-cost pricing follows a distinct logic, because it consists of calculating a unit cost incorporating all costs (variable costs and fixed/overhead costs) and adding a net profit margin. Since unit overhead costs vary with the level of output (they decline as the output goes up), this practice needs to define a 'normal' level of output at which costs are computed (full-cost pricing is quite similar to what is called 'normal cost pricing'). The first historical reference to this practice can be found in the work of Hall and Hitch (1939).

Target-return pricing is a variety of normal/full-cost pricing, in which the net profit margin added to unit costs is calculated so as to yield a targeted level of profit upon the value of capital assets of the firm, when actual output corresponds to its normal level.

Post-Keynesian pricing theory has several implications. The first one is that prices may not respond to demand changes in the same way as imagined by mainstream economics. Since prices are based on costs, they may not change when demand changes (or they may even change in the opposite direction, because unit costs can fall when output rises in the case of full-cost pricing). In that sense, costs (and not demand) may be the first reason for prices to change (see Melmiès, 2010) and this may explain the phenomenon of price rigidity. Second, post-Keynesian pricing theory leads to a different view about competition than mainstream economics. In this view, prices are not the adjustment mechanism to supply and demand disequilibria. Instead, quantity adjustments play this role in the short run. Third, the question of the determination of the profit margin is essential in post-Keynesian economics. If an explanation by the degree of monopoly or imperfect competition prevailed in the originators of post-Keynesian economics (see Robinson, 1933; Kalecki, 1940), further developments underlined the importance of internal financing of the growth of the firm as a key determinant of profit margins (see Eichner, 1973). Finally, mark-ups play a decisive role in income distribution and consequently can affect macroeconomic dynamics, depending on the demand regime.

JORDAN MELMIÈS AND
FLORIAN BOTTE

See also

Cost-plus pricing; Income distribution; Mark-up pricing; Monopoly power; Target-return pricing

References

Eichner, A.S. (1976), *The Megacorp and Oligopoly: Micro Foundations of Macro Dynamics*, New York: Cambridge University Press.
Hall, R. and C. Hitch (1939), 'Price theory and business behaviour', *Oxford Economic Papers*, 2 (1), 12–45.
Kalecki, M. (1940), 'The supply curve of an industry under imperfect competition', *Review of Economic Studies*, 7 (2), 91–112.
Lee, F.S. (1998), *Post Keynesian Price Theory*, Cambridge, UK: Cambridge University Press.
Means, G.C. (1935), *Industrial Prices and Their Relative Inflexibility*, Senate Document No. 13, 74th Congress, 1st session, Washington, DC: Government Printing Office.
Means, G.C. (1936), 'Notes on inflexible prices', *American Economic Review*, 26 (1), 23–35.
Melmiès, J. (2010), 'New Keynesians versus Post Keynesians on the theory of prices', *Journal of Post Keynesian Economics*, 32 (3), 445–66.
Robinson, J.V. (1933), *The Economics of Imperfect Competition*, London: Macmillan.

Principle of increasing risk

The principle of increasing risk (PIR) is a macroeconomic concept developed by the Polish economist Michal Kalecki in reference to a capitalist firm's ability to raise new capital and generate adequate rate of return to continue financing its operations. The PIR relates directly to the potential destabilizing threats of overleveraging that resurfaced in the 2008 Global Financial Crisis (GFC) (see Kalecki, 1937, 1970; Mott, 2009). The PIR also connects with Minsky's (1975) 'borrower's risk' (and his three financing schemes: hedge finance, speculative finance, Ponzi finance) as the borrower faces risks of rising costs of debt servicing or bankruptcy, at each subsequent loop of tapping in to capital markets. Therefore, there are strong implications for the debate on the interlink between decisions on firm financing, economic activity, and broader cyclical and structural macroeconomic effects.

According to Kalecki (1971, p. 109), '[t]he most important prerequisite for becoming an entrepreneur is the *ownership* of capital.' Similarly, the amount of capital owned by a firm defines the entrepreneurial capital. In turn, the size of the firm is limited by the availability of entrepreneurial capital. The amount of this capital conditions firms' borrowing activity in the capital markets. To comprehensively explain impediments in firms' growth, Kalecki suggests to 'drop' the assumption that 'the rate of risk is independent of the amount invested' (Kalecki, 1937, p. 442). In fact, Kalecki states that 'a firm considering expansion must face the fact that, given the amount of the entrepreneurial capital, the risk increases with the amount invested. The greater the investment in relation to the entrepreneurial capital, the greater is the reduction of the entrepreneur's income in the event of an unsuccessful business venture' (Kalecki, 2003, p. 92).

Mott (2009) clarifies the above argument by stating that the willingness to tie up liquidity into a long-term project (that is, fixed capital) is inversely related to the firm's ownership of its own invested funds. This in turn then also determines the rate of investment and a required return on investment to account for costs of capital and generate profit. There is an implicit connection with Keynes's effective demand here. A capitalist firm runs the increasing risk of loss or of going out of business, if it continuously borrows over its internal capital capacity and suffers a downturn (loss of demand for its output for whatever reason) in its operations.

It is current profits (or the rate at which they are earned, if we put them in relative terms) that determine the accumulation of capital, which in turn predetermines firms' growth. As the firm grows (with increasing internal capital), it can avoid the imperfections of capital markets and most importantly the increasing risk. In this situation, savings out of profits raise the internal capital level and allow borrowing larger amounts in the capital market. It follows that the differences in the size of entrepreneurial capital (and in the size of a firm) help explain a variety of large and small companies in the same industry at any given time. Those firms with larger capital usually claim a greater market share and can afford to borrow more to finance expansionary activity.

Kalecki argues that this dependence of the firm size on its internal capital 'goes to the very heart of the capitalist system' (Kalecki, 1970, p. 109). Even though this situation is unlikely to arise in the case of perfect foresight under perfectly competitive markets, it is realistic to suggest that imperfections exist in the real world for one reason or another.

Linking PIR with asymmetric information, Fazzari and Variato (1994) address the costs associated with bankruptcy, suggesting that the same assets might have different values depending on how informed about them are entities operating those assets. A firm trying to procure additional (financial or not) investment externally would be better off and, in fact, may reduce the risk if it possesses superior or insider information on the investment project under consideration. Thus, the limitation on investment 'is not technological' as would have been suggested under the perfect competition model, 'but inherently financial' (Fazzari and Variato, 1994, p. 6).

As an initial twist in a business cycle, the concept of the PIR may be intuitive. Yet, with every new bust following a boom period, the question remains: why would not the firms learn? There is certainly some degree of prudence in borrowing; however, in boom times investment demand is also affected by competition forces. If corporations do not seek extra funds to grow, they run a risk to be outdone by competitors. Individual firms' financing structure matters in defining the scope of its operation and productive capacity investment. Such condition then requires firms' management to balance decisions on the use of firms' own versus borrowed funds, ultimately affecting planning and production in the medium term, which transforms the structure of the individual firm, industry, and the economy (see Nell, 1992).

Hence, a firm puts itself at a correspondingly higher level of increasing risk of default with every additional loan. As such behaviour prevails across a multitude of firms, the whole economic system becomes overleveraged as the required rate of return (and the cost of borrowing) exceeds the actual generated return (return on profits). Subsequent financial collapse, a systemic breakdown, is costly, spilling outside of the group of initial investors, as they attempt to recover by relying on ever more increased borrowing with damaging claims on the real economy. This was the scenario that played itself out in 2008. After a period of adjustment, the cycle repeats, albeit possibly under a modified institutional framework and on a different monetary scale. All this makes Kalecki's contributions on a capitalist economy timelessly critical for analytical understanding of the cyclical patterns in firms' finance and adequate policy interpretation in the post-GFC global economy context.

ALEKSANDR V. GEVORKYAN

See also

Asymmetric information; Effective demand; Financial fragility; Financial instability hypothesis; *Stabilizing an Unstable Economy*

References

Fazzari, S. and A. Variato (1994), 'Asymmetric information and Keynesian theories of investment', *Journal of Post Keynesian Economics*, **16** (3), 351–69.
Kalecki, M. (1937), 'The principle of increasing risk', *Economica*, **4** (16), 440–47.
Kalecki, M. (1971), *Selected Essays on the Dynamics of the Capitalist Economy, 1933–1970*, Cambridge, UK: Cambridge University Press.
Kalecki, M. (2003), *Theory of Economic Dynamics*, London and New York: Routledge.

Minsky, H.P. (1975), *John Maynard Keynes*, New York: Columbia University Press.

Mott, T. (2009), *Kalecki's Principle of Increasing Risk and Keynesian Economics*, London and New York: Routledge.

Nell, E. (1992), *Transformational Growth and Effective Demand: Economics after the Capital Critique*, New York: New York University Press.

Production of Commodities by Means of Commodities

Some knowledge of the standpoint of 'the old classical economists from Adam Smith to Ricardo' (Sraffa, 1960, p. v) is needed to understand Sraffa's *Production of Commodities by Means of Commodities* (*PCMC*). Taking the size and composition of output, the methods of production and the subsistence wage as given, Sraffa shows that: (1) in a viable subsistence economy, relative prices are determined by the conditions of production; (2) in an economy that is capable of producing a physical surplus, the rate of profits is determined by the methods of production of the basic commodities that enter directly or indirectly into the production of all the others. In both cases, the prices of reproducible goods are not an index of scarcity.

While the data determining relative prices for Sraffa (1960) are the same as for Classical economists and Marx, the method of solution is different. Although Ricardo (1821) and Marx (1867) sought to determine r (the rate of profit) as a ratio of aggregates measured independently of distribution, Sraffa (1960) determines r and prices simultaneously. In fact, the surplus product cannot be allotted to the various industries before prices are determined, because it must be distributed in proportion to the means of production advanced in each industry and such a proportion between two aggregates of heterogeneous goods cannot be determined before commodity prices are known. On the other hand, the allotment of the surplus cannot be deferred until prices are known, because the latter cannot be determined before knowing the rate of profit.

Except for particular cases of joint production, Sraffa also shows that the properties of the price system are such that an inverse relationship between wages and profits exists and, therefore, a conflict over net product partition occurs. If the wage rate w is paid *post factum* and each industry produces only a single commodity, Sraffa's price system $\bm{Bp} = (1 + r)\bm{Ap} + \bm{l}w$ consists of k equations with $k + 2$ variables (the k prices, w and the rate of profit r), where $\bm{B}$ is the diagonal matrix of gross products, $\bm{A}$ is the matrix of techniques, and $\bm{p}$ and $\bm{l}$ are the price and labour vectors respectively. Taking the net product as the chosen standard, the price system has one degree of freedom that provides a decreasing wage–profit curve, which shows the rates of profit r associated with any particular values of the wage w. From its maximum value R when $w = 0$, the rate of profit will fall monotonically to zero when the wage rate reaches its maximum value W.

This inverse relationship between wages and profits is also shown by Sraffa (1960) by a single 'surplus equation' as in Ricardo and Marx. Without changing the methods of production, in any real system a standard system is embedded in which the composition of the means of production and the net product are the same, so that these two aggregates represent different amounts of the same composed commodity. If the wage rate is expressed as a proportion of the net product of the standard system and the labour employed is equal to 1, the proportion of the net product accruing to profits is $(1 - w)$. If the ratio of the total net product to capital is R, the linear relation $r = R(1 - w)$ holds and the rate of profit emerges as a ratio between physical quantities. This linear relationship is valid also in the real system when the standard net product is taken as its price *numéraire*, because the real system will have the same *numéraire* and the same methods of production as the standard system.

Following the Classical approach to value and distribution, price determination needs to 'close' the price system by taking one of the distributive variables as given. This variable can be the real wage, as for Classical economists and Marx, where w is determined by social and historical circumstances. However, for a wage rate above the subsistence level, Sraffa (1960, par. 44) suggests that the independent distributive variable may be the rate of profit r as determined by the level of the money rate of interest to which the former rate must conform in a competitive economy. This is reminiscent of Keynes's (1936, p. 203) remark that the rate of interest is a highly conventional phenomenon that is determined by the operations of monetary institutions.

ALEKSANDR V. GEVORKYAN / ENRICO SERGIO LEVRERO

Almost as a by-product of his examination of the properties of the price system, Sraffa also advances a critique of the marginalist theory of distribution. The reversal in the direction of the movement of relative prices when r changes 'cannot be reconciled with any notion of capital as a measurable quantity independent of distribution and prices' (Sraffa, 1960, p. 38). Moreover, in Part 3 of *PCMC*, Sraffa demonstrates that a technique that has been superseded by another technique at a higher r may prove again to be the cheapest at an even higher rate of profit. This implies that no particular ordering of techniques can be advanced and that the capital intensity of production is not an inverse function of the rate of profit.

ENRICO SERGIO LEVRERO

See also

Income distribution; Inflation – conflict theory of; Profit; Social classes; Wages

References

Keynes, J.M. (1936), *The General Theory of Employment, Interest and Money*, London: Macmillan.

Marx, K. (1867/1954), *Capital: A Critique of Political Economy, Volume I*, Moscow: Progress Publisher.

Ricardo, D. (1821/1951), 'On the principles of political economy and taxation', in *The Works and Correspondence of David Ricardo, Volume I*, Cambridge, UK: Cambridge University Press.

Sraffa, P. (1960), *Production of Commodities by Means of Commodities: Prelude to a Critique of Economic Theory*, Cambridge, UK: Cambridge University Press.

Profit

By definition, private sector profits are the difference between its incoming revenues and its costs of production. While most economists do not dispute this definition, divergences do appear when asking how profits arise. More specifically, what is the source of these profits?

Regarding the first question, the answer might seem rather obvious: profits arise when firms succeed in fixing the price of their products above unit production costs. Yet, this operation is not obvious. In neoclassical theory, when firms operate in a framework of pure and perfect competition (that is to say, when there is free entry and free exit on the market), long-run equilibrium prices and quantities in the industry tend to settle at the minimum point of the U-shaped average cost curve, where firms do not make any profit. This seemingly paradoxical result (there would be no profit in a competitive capitalist economy) is due to the fact that the remuneration of production factors is recorded in the production costs of firms, because it is supposed to remunerate the contribution of capital goods to production. If profits (distributed to the owners of the machines) are considered as a cost, then it is no surprise that there are no profits.

In the post-Keynesian tradition, by contrast, profit is duly recorded as a gain realized by the firm, part of which is used to finance investment and the other part is distributed to shareholders. In this more realistic institutional framework, companies own their equipment and do not rent it from those households that own capital goods. Dividends do not pay for productive services delivered by machines: these are property incomes claimed by the shareholders of the corporation, established precisely with a view to sharing these profits.

Concretely, since most of the time centralized markets do not exist (with an auctioneer-like mechanism), firms set their own prices, applying a predetermined margin to their production costs. Firms' pricing policies are not intended to adjust supply and demand on the market for produced goods and services in the short run, but to ensure the medium- or long-term viability of the business development project.

The theoretical question concerns how companies manage to defend the profit margins they aim for, in order to generate their proper income (profit) beyond the wages they pay as production costs (essentially). To this question, post-Keynesian economists gave three types of answers: (1) the power to extract margins may come from the need to maintain a level of self-financing sufficient to ensure medium- or long-term accumulation (Wood, 1975; Eichner, 1976); (2) it may also come from the degree of concentration of firms (Steindl, 1952) or, more broadly, from the degree of monopoly or semi-monopoly they have acquired (Kalecki, 1971); (3) finally, it can come from the evolution of wages and prices obtained respectively by wage earners and managers to achieve their conflicting income-sharing goals (Dutt, 1987).

The ultimate question to ask is how profit itself is possible. What is its source? How can

ENRICO SERGIO LEVRERO / LAURENT CORDONNIER

it be, on average (at the macroeconomic level), that businesses receive more incomes than they spend on production costs? Although this is one of the most difficult things to understand in economics, the answer seems almost contained in the question: because firms benefit from incoming revenues that exceed their expenditures in wages (which cover, as a first approximation, when spent on consumption, their own cost). These incoming revenues in excess of the costs of production, at the macroeconomic level, come from firms' investment expenditures and dividends spent on consumption (assuming the public sector budget and the current account are balanced). Indeed, these incoming revenues for businesses, which have gone well for expenses made by other companies, do not actually constitute production costs for these last ones (these are balance-sheet transactions). This result, established by Kalecki (1935), made Joan Robinson (1966, p. 341) argue that 'workers spend what they get, and capitalists get what they spend'. The particular role played by profits spent on consumption (thereby fuelling profits) had been clearly glimpsed by Keynes (1930) through his parable of the widow's cruse and the Danaid jar. It is the fact that profit is both an incentive and a condition required to finance investment as well as the result of investment itself (via current expenditure) that confers on the accumulation of capital such capricious dynamics.

LAURENT CORDONNIER

See also

Cost-plus pricing; Income distribution; Inflation – conflict theory of; Monopoly power; Pricing

References

Dutt, A.K. (1987), 'Alternative closures again: a comment on "Growth, distribution and inflation"', *Cambridge Journal of Economics*, **11** (1), 75–82.
Eichner, A.S. (1976), *The Megacorp and Oligopoly: Micro Foundations of Macro Dynamics*, Cambridge, UK: Cambridge University Press.
Kalecki, M. (1935), 'A macro-dynamic theory of business cycles', *Econometrica*, **3** (3), 327–44. Reprinted in *Collected Works of Michal Kalecki, Vol. I*, Oxford: Clarendon Press, 1990, pp. 120–38.
Kalecki, M. (1971), 'Class struggle and the distribution of national income', *Kyklos*, **24** (1), 1–9.
Keynes, J.M. (1930), *A Treatise on Money, Volume 1: The Pure Theory of Money*, London: Macmillan.
Robinson, J. (1966), 'Kalecki and Keynes', in *Economic Dynamics and Planning: Essays in Honour of Michal Kalecki*, Oxford: Pergamon, pp. 335–41.
Steindl, J. (1952), *Maturity and Stagnation in American Capitalism*, Oxford: Basil Blackwell.
Wood, A. (1975), *A Theory of Profits*, Cambridge, UK: Cambridge University Press.

Property premium

The property premium (also referred to as ownership premium) is a key element of the property theory of money and the foundation of ownership economics (see Heinsohn and Steiger, 1996, 2013). Any property asset that is unburdened (that is to say, free from claims) creates an advantage and added security to its owner, because it can be deployed to create or borrow money. All unburdened property assets therefore carry a premium: the property premium.

The property theory of money states that money creation presupposes property rights, and property assets are burdened in the process of money creation. A money-issuing creditor (such as a note-issuing bank) burdens property (bank capital) to underwrite the money notes, while the counterparty-debtor burdens property by furnishing collateral or setting aside unburdened property to enter into the money-creating loan. Both parties forgo a property premium. The creditor is compensated for this loss by an interest payment, while the debtor gains the liquidity premium associated with the created money notes. The property premium therefore leads to an interest demand and explains the existence of interest (Heinsohn and Steiger, 1996, 2008, 2013).

The concept of the property premium builds on Keynes's liquidity premium, or monetary theory of interest, formulated in his *General Theory* (Keynes, 1936). Heinsohn and Steiger (1996, 2008, 2013), however, argue that Keynes's idea that interest is the reward for parting with liquidity is incomplete. Keynes (1936) presupposes already existing money and omits an analysis of money creation. As money is not yet in existence at the beginning of the money-creation process, the money-creating creditor cannot suffer from a loss of liquidity that requires compensation. Heinsohn and Steiger, therefore, conclude that interest must

LAURENT CORDONNIER / FRANK DECKER

be explained by the creditor's loss of property premium. The creditor parts with the free disposition over her property assets (such as disposal, loan security, and other encumbrances) and must be rewarded for this loss by interest. By contrast, the liquidity premium compensates the advantage or security arising from the command over already existing money balances, which can settle obligations at any time.

This property-based explanation of interest also highlights the shortcomings of the neoclassical theory of interest, which states that interest is the reward for the deferment of consumption: (i) creditor goods and other assets are merely burdened and not actually transferred in the money-creation process; and (ii) the money-creating creditor can continue with the possession and use of the (now burdened) goods and assets.

Heinsohn and Steiger argue that the property premium is of great economic significance as it reflects the willingness to burden property in new money-creating loan contracts, which can strongly influence economic activity. In a downturn, the property premium can rise above the level of offered interest rates, which decreases the amount of new loans and the rate at which new money is created. In this situation, central bank action is hampered because its influence over the property premium is limited. Even a reduction of policy rates of interest to zero may not induce new lending, for instance when a high property premium reflects the fact that commercial banks lack capital and borrowers have insufficient collateral to enter into new loans. By contrast, central banks can increase the property premium by raising interest rates, for instance to combat inflation (Heinsohn and Steiger, 2013).

The concept of a premium on property also provides a new explanation as to why objects must be evaluated in monetary terms (that is, assigned an absolute money price), a practice that is all-pervasive in property-based systems. As the property premium implies an interest demand, the indebted producer must realize sales proceeds (a quantity of produced output times money price), the sum of which must at least equal the loan principal plus interest. Loan principal and interest, together with the associated production assets and estimated earnings from sales of products and services, are therefore assigned a price in the same, abstract money of account when the interest rate is set. As a consequence, property-based economic systems are characterized by networks of nominal obligations expressed in absolute money prices. Heinsohn and Steiger conclude that the existence of a premium on unburdened property and the associated interest demand imply that any production in this system must realize a profit.

FRANK DECKER

See also

Inflation; Liquidity preference; Money creation – nature of; Property theory of money; Settlement balances

References

Heinsohn, G. and O. Steiger (1996), *Eigentum, Zins und Geld*, Marburg: Metropolis.

Heinsohn, G. and O. Steiger (2008), 'Collateral and own capital: the missing links in the theory of the rate of interest and money', in O. Steiger (ed.), *Property Economics: Property Rights, Creditor's Money and the Foundations of the Economy*, Marburg: Metropolis, pp. 181–222.

Heinsohn, G. and O. Steiger (2013), *Ownership Economics*, London and New York: Routledge.

Keynes, J.M. (1936), *The General Theory of Employment, Interest and Money*, London: Macmillan.

Property theory of money

The property theory of money (also known as ownership theory of money; see Heinsohn and Steiger, 1996, 2013) is an important alternative to commodity and State theories of money. It defines money as a documented claim over the property of a creditor that is created in a loan contract with a debtor and is denominated in an abstract money of account (an ideal unit). For instance, money is created when a (commercial or central) bank issues promissory notes or deposits to a debtor as a result of granting a secured loan. The money notes are underpinned by property assets, which comprise the capital of the bank's creditor and the loan collateral posted by the debtor.

Bank notes issued in this way are not simply a debt and have special attributes because they are issued by a net creditor, that is, a party that has the capacity to absorb losses, maintain a positive equity position (the difference between assets and liabilities) and exchange notes at par value in interbank clearing and settlements at all times. Debtor obligations are assessed and priced by the creditor before they become the basis of a note issue. Creditor-issued notes are therefore more secure and command a higher level of trust than debtor-issued notes.

Capital (shareholders' equity) and collateral are core elements of the property-based money concept. Capital is critical as a buffer for unidentified future losses, while collateral equalizes the credit risk between creditor and debtor. Property assets are also involved when money is created in unsecured loans (Decker, 2015). The latter typically require more capital, higher credit ratings, and unencumbered debtor assets.

The property theory of money makes the important distinction between creditors' and debtors' money (Heinsohn and Steiger, 2013). Central banks create creditors' money ('sound' or 'genuine' money), when they issue notes according to banking principles with sufficient capital, sound collateral, and at market interest rates. The underlying assets, including government securities, are subject to market valuations. Bagehot's (1873) central banking rule to lend freely against good security reflects this nexus between property and money. In the 1980s, the German Bundesbank and the Swiss National Bank became the model for this type of central banking. By contrast, central banks create debtors' money (State money) when they monetize State liabilities directly, for instance through the primary issue of public debt, large-scale State debt purchases, or by granting overdrafts to governments ('money printing'). In this case, central banks act as monetary authorities, and capital or solvency risk is no longer a consideration. Debtors' money is a characteristic of command economies, where central banks allocate funds to war efforts or serve totalitarian regimes, and major fiscal policy interventions including full employment policies. Debtors' money is also historically associated with periods of high inflation.

What monetary role do commodities and State payment instruments play in a property-based monetary system? Heinsohn and Steiger (2013) interpret certain coins as bank notes printed on metal, for instance a gold coin in a nineteenth-century monetary system where note-issuing banks set the price of gold. As a broader principle, Decker (2015) argues that historically commodities, coins, and public debt attained a special monetary role, since they became the preferred or legally mandated asset to finally settle interbank debts and performed the role of 'settlement assets'. The latter are technically to be distinguished from money. In modern central bank regimes with irredeemable notes, settlement assets and money merged.

Fundamental to the property theory of money is the insight that the origins of money and the origins of private property are connected. In Heinsohn and Steiger's view (see Heinsohn, 1984, Heinsohn and Steiger, 1996, 2013), money emerged spontaneously and as a consequence of the establishment of societies based on private property (such as the Greek *polis* and Roman *civitas*). The latter were created in revolutionary acts overturning command-based regimes and distributing the former feudal land holdings to their members. Rather than engaging in barter-exchange transactions, property owners meet payment obligations by monetizing their property assets via note issue, while staying in possession and continuing with the use of their assets. The monetization of assets is enabled by the development of a legal framework that allows the separation of ownership and possession. The State comes in as the guarantor and enforcer of the rule of law. In this view, money is foremost the result of private ordering, and the paradigm that money originated from commodity barter exchanges must be rejected.

FRANK DECKER

See also

Central banking; Inflation; Money creation – nature of; Property premium; Settlement balances

References

Bagehot, W. (1873), *Lombard Street: A Description of the Money Market*, New York: Scribner, Armstrong & Co.

Decker, F. (2015), 'Property ownership and money: a new synthesis', *Journal of Economic Issues*, **49** (4), 922–46.

Heinsohn, G. (1984), *Privateigentum, Patriarchat, Geldwirtschaft*, Frankfurt am Main: Suhrkamp.

Heinsohn, G. and O. Steiger (1996), *Eigentum, Zins und Geld*, Marburg: Metropolis.

Heinsohn, G. and O. Steiger (2013), *Ownership Economics*, London and New York: Routledge.

FRANK DECKER

Public finance

One of the most controversial topics in the history of economics is related to the role of the State in the economy. What should the government do? How does the State allocate and spend its resources? Is a balanced budget necessary? In what sort of things should the government invest? What are the consequences of public debt? What is the function of taxes? These questions are at the core of the debate around public finance.

In public finance terminology, government revenues are usually divided in tax and non-tax revenues. Government expenditures are usually divided in current expenditures (goods and services, social transfers, interest payments) and capital expenditures (public investment). Based on this classification, the current budget position is defined as current expenditures minus total revenues, and the primary budget position as total expenses excluding interest payments minus total revenues. In traditional public finance these concepts are key to determine how much the government must borrow to make public investment or interest payments.

Public finance issues have a lot to do with how we see the functioning of markets. Mainstream economists for instance, believing in the market's self-adjustment mechanism, have a lot of confidence in its stability. Thus, public finance should not distort the allocation of the market but should instead behave like sound finance. This doctrine is based on the idea that (i) an increasing fiscal surplus is a necessary condition for sustainable economic growth and (ii) this fiscal surplus obtained with 'sound money' allows society to better spend public funds and it is the only way to ensure a prosperous society in the long run. In this way, fiscal deficits are a bad thing. Hence, countries with fiscal deficits need to adopt rules to achieve low budget deficits and sustainable levels of public debt. Mainstream economists believe politics should be removed from public finance decision-making and be treated only as a technocratic issue. Thus, they suggest independent fiscal institutions assuming that their conception of public finance could be neutral, as if it were a matter of clear accounting focusing on liabilities.

In theoretical terms, it is important to note that in the representative three-equation New Keynesian model (see Carlin and Soskice, 2005) there is no need for fiscal policy, because the interest rate seems sufficient to tune the economy. However, in recent years and after the widespread impacts of the 2008 Global Financial Crisis, mainstream economists have argued that if the GDP growth rate is higher than the public debt interest rate there is room for fiscal policy (Blanchard, 2019). Interestingly enough, this recognition has not come hand in hand with a change in their theoretical framework. Just as mainstream economists assumed the endogeneity of money without a theory of endogenous money (Lavoie, 2014), they assume the existence of fiscal policy without a coherent framework for it.

By contrast, for post-Keynesian economists, markets are endogenously unstable, because they are monetary economies of production (not barter economies), and investment decisions are essentially driven by uncertainty. In this sense, they develop a monetary theory of public finance in which public finance should not be judged based on an overall level of debt but rather on the net balance-sheet position (see Arestis and Sawyer, 2010). Post-Keynesian economists consider the consequences of government expenditures on production and employment (functional finance, in the language of Abba Lerner) and pursuing the goal of stabilizing the economy. Since a market economy (without nominal or real rigidities) does not lead to full employment, when the government spends there is no such thing as 'distorting the market' or 'correcting market failures'.

Another essential element of the monetary theory of public finance is the rejection of the loanable funds theory. As Parguez (2002, p. 82) notes, 'the postulate of state budget constraint is enshrined in the myth of a moneyless or real command economy. It is thus the ultimate generalization of the real loanable funds principle.' This implies that public finance does not work as household finance. Savings are not channelled to investment; they are not the key and commanding element of the economy but a residual variable. In this way, there is no upward pressure on interest rates, because the public deficit can finance itself.

For post-Keynesian economists, in order to address the important economic policy goals of our time (such as promoting sustainable structural change, achieving full employment, and reducing global inequality) the government should not commit to fiscal rules, but should lead a great fiscal activism (discretionary fiscal policy) to stabilize an unstable economy. Of course, one should keep in mind the balance-of-payments constraint and the real resources among other restrictions, but not primarily financial and capital shortage as in the mainstream outlook.

At the same time, post-Keynesian economists have depicted how financialization shapes public finance by analysing how States are forced to pay the profitability of the financial sector losing their autonomy and making States behave as households. They have also showed how countries are pressured to embrace new accounting standards to promote shareholder value in the name of adopting 'good practices'.

Some post-Keynesian economists, grouped under the label of modern monetary theory (MMT), have emphasized that taxes do not finance public spending, thus reversing the traditional logic of public finance. For them, the meaning of taxes is embedded in that they encourage the use of a sovereign currency (Wray, 1998). Taxes reduce aggregate demand and destroy private wealth when there are inflationary pressures. Some other post-Keynesian economists have criticized the way MMT have articulated some relevant proposals like job guarantee, functional finance, and endogenous money theory. Among these criticisms there is the nexus between government expenditures and the payments system (Lavoie, 2013), which leads to a separate nexus between monetary and fiscal policy. For some, in the MMT framework, it seems that interest rate decisions taken by the central bank can be set at any level without affecting the total level of expenditure (Michell, 2019). Other critiques are related to its applicability in countries with peripheral monies, showing that there are other constraints than those self-imposed politically (Vergnhanini and De Conti, 2018).

However, these discussions have enriched post-Keynesian analysis and the public finance perspectives. Post-Keynesian approaches to public finance should be part of the general conversation, which has begun with the emergence of MMT in public opinion, in a world that has shown the disastrous consequences of austerity and sound finance.

CAMILO ANDRÉS GUEVARA

See also

Balance of payments constrained growth; Debt – public; Endogenous money; Fiscal policy; Monetary theory of production

References

Arestis, P. and M. Sawyer (2010), 'The return of fiscal policy', *Journal of Post Keynesian Economics*, **32** (3), 327–46.

Blanchard, O. (2019), 'Public debt and low interest rates', *American Economic Review*, **109** (4), 1197–229.

Carlin, W. and D. Soskice (2005), 'The 3-equation New Keynesian model: a graphical exposition', *Contributions to Macroeconomics*, **5** (1), 1–36.

Lavoie, M. (2013), 'The monetary and fiscal nexus of neo-chartalism: a friendly critical look', *Journal of Economic Issues*, **47** (1), 1–31.

Lavoie, M. (2014), *Post-Keynesian Economics*, Cheltenham, UK, and Northampton, MA, USA: Edward Elgar.

Michell, J. (2019), 'Kelton and Krugman on IS-LM and MMT', *Critical Macro Finance*, available at https://criticalfinance.org/2019/03/06/kelton-and-krugman-on-is-lm-and-mmt/ (last accessed 20 November 2020).

Parguez, A. (2002), 'A monetary theory of public finance', *International Journal of Political Economy*, **32** (3), 80–97.

Vergnhanini, R. and B. De Conti (2018), 'Modern Monetary Theory: a criticism from the periphery', *Brazilian Keynesian Review*, **3** (2), 16–31.

Wray, L.R. (1998), *El papel del dinero hoy: la clave del pleno empleo y la estabilidad de precios*, Mexico: UNAM.

Quantitative easing

During the Global Financial Crisis that erupted in 2008, central banks ran many unconventional monetary policies in an attempt to rescue their economies. Quantitative easing (QE), or 'large scale asset purchases', is one such programme, which involves the central bank purchasing financial assets such as government bonds, mortgage-backed securities, and debts of government-sponsored enterprises (as well as corporate bonds in some cases) on a large scale (Lavoie, 2010).

Although many economists claimed that the mechanism through which this works is the money multiplier model, Ben Bernanke, under whom the programme was announced in November 2008 in the United States, was clear that the mechanism relied on the wealth effect (Bernanke, 2012). Bernanke's explanation is surprisingly consistent with the theory of endogenous money.

How QE works in raising output can be explained using Tobin's theory of asset allocation (see Godley and Lavoie, 2007). Because the central bank is purchasing financial assets, there is a rise in demand for them. Long-term interest rates depend on expectations of future rates as well as market segmentation or preferred habitat. Hence, we would expect long-term interest rates to fall owing to the increased demand for these securities. Since the holding of bank deposits is demand-determined, using the asset allocation theory we can conclude that QE leads to a higher demand for riskier assets. This implies higher prices of riskier assets and hence higher household wealth and, since consumption is also wealth-dependent, this increases output. Another effect is refinancing of mortgages leading to lower payments on loans and higher consumption.

How effective this is in raising economic activity is not easy to know: a full stock–flow consistent model with empirical testing is needed and this is a difficult task indeed. However, a qualitative explanation can be given as follows. First, it can be argued that expectations of future rates of interest overwhelm the preferred habitat hypothesis and, hence, that QE hardly reduces long-term interest rates. Even if long-term interest rates are reduced, how much this leads to rising prices of riskier assets would depend on the parameters of the model. Lastly, even if QE has a strong effect on prices of riskier assets, it is an open question on how much the holding gains lead to a wealth effect. Fiscal policy is the tool post-Keynesian economists would endorse to raise output – instead of QE.

Similar arguments can be made on exchange rates and rises in asset prices in emerging markets and developing economies. In stock–flow consistent models, exchange rates are determined by supply and demand for assets. QE reduces the attractiveness of financial assets in developed economies for private investors, and since in asset allocation theory asset demands are related to each other, QE can cause a rise in prices of financial assets in less advanced economies. QE does not seem to have caused a fall in the exchange rate of the US dollar but had an effect on some other currencies. This effect can be seen in the experience of India in 2013. At that time, the US Federal Reserve indicated that it was 'tapering' the purchase of assets and this is believed to have been a significant cause of the fall of the exchange rate of the Indian rupee. The effect of QE on exchange rates can also be seen in the depreciation of the Japanese yen. The USD/JPY exchange rate depreciated significantly from around 76.23 at the beginning of 2012 to 125.14 in May 2015. The QE programme of the Bank of Japan can be said to have caused a large depreciation, raising question about the 'beggar-thy-neighbour' nature of QE.

There are of course many programmes that resemble QE but should be distinguished from it. In May 2010, the national central banks of the Eurosystem (headed by the European Central Bank) started purchasing euro-area government bonds on secondary markets. The intent of this programme was far different from QE: it was to ease tensions in government bond markets and to prevent default by governments on their debt. This programme, which was called the secondary market programme, was not successful as it was limited in size, so in August 2012 the European Central Bank (ECB) announced the programme called Outright Monetary Transactions, which was not limited in size. This announcement had a huge effect in reducing bond yields and no transaction has ever been made in the programme. These programmes cannot be called QE, but nonetheless the Eurosystem had a programme similar to QE later, and has been purchasing private securities such as corporate bonds, asset-backed securities and covered bonds, and more recently government bonds (since March 2015) just like the US Federal Reserve.

Recently, in the wake of the coronavirus crisis, the US Federal Reserve once again started the asset purchase programme and included commercial asset-backed securities in its list of purchases, while the ECB announced its Pandemic Emergency Purchase Programme, deciding to increase the amount of bonds to be purchased. The latter implicitly targets spreads, that is, relative yields of bonds of various governments, so its aims go beyond standard QE.

VIJAYARAGHAVAN RAMANAN

See also

Endogenous money; Financial crises; Fiscal policy; Stock–flow consistent model; Wealth effect

References

Bernanke, B. (2012), 'Monetary policy since the onset of the crisis', Speech at the Federal Reserve Bank of Kansas City Economic Symposium, Jackson Hole, Wyoming, available online at https://www.

federalreserve.gov/newsevents/speech/bernanke20120831a.pdf (last accessed 30 November 2020).

Godley, W. and M. Lavoie (2007), *Monetary Economics*, Basingstoke and New York: Palgrave Macmillan.

Lavoie, M. (2010), 'Changes in central bank procedures during the subprime crisis and their repercussions on monetary theory', *International Journal of Political Economy*, **39** (3), 3–23.

Quantum macroeconomics

Quantum macroeconomics is a macroeconomic theory developed by the French economist Bernard Schmitt (1929–2014), who has been a professor of economics at the University of Burgundy in Dijon (France) and at the University of Fribourg (Switzerland). This is why it is also known as the 'Dijon–Fribourg School' in economic analysis (see Bailly et al., 2017, for a comprehensive survey).

The idea that produced output is a quantum of time monetized by banks when firms pay the wage bill lies at the core of quantum macroeconomics as a monetary theory of production. At the instant of time when wage earners are paid, an economic product is formed, which corresponds to the wave-like emission of a finite and indivisible period of time (a quantum of time). In this sense, production quantizes time. This implies that wages are the measurement unit in economics, and that production is an instantaneous event in the realm of economics.

Quantum macroeconomics shows that money and banking are instrumental for production, because firms need to obtain credit lines from banks in order to pay out the wage bill, thus giving rise to income and output as the two sides of the same (macroeconomic) object. The deposits that banks record on behalf of wage earners are indeed the financial representation of an income whose object is the produced output, that is, the very object of firms' debt to the banks that granted a credit to them. In this sense, as Schumpeter (1954, pp. 1110–17) already noticed, loans create deposits in the banking system.

The fact that money is issued by banks in the form of an 'asset–liability' (Schmitt, 1975, p. 19, our translation) is due to the numerical expression of the payer's debt and payee's credit recorded in the relevant bank ledger (see Rossi, 2007, for analytical elaboration). This is so much so that money measures the object of both the payer's debt and the payee's credit. To be sure, money is a purely numerical counter, whose purchasing power cannot but depend on production. In this regard, as Lavoie (1984, p. 774) observed, '[m]oney is introduced into the economy through the productive activities of the firms, as these activities generate income. There can be no money without production.'

Quantum macroeconomics is thus in a position to understand the monetary–structural origin of inflation, which is a loss in money's purchasing power that exerts an upward pressure on the general price level (see Cencini, 1995, and Rossi, 2001). Inflation originates from what Schmitt (1984, p. 507, our translation) called 'empty money', which banks issue whenever they finance final purchases through money creation. Income is thereby diluted into a higher number of money units, each of which loses therefore part of its original purchasing power. Hence, to really avoid inflation a monetary–structural reform must be put into practice, making sure that banks cannot provide new credit lines *ex nihilo* when the latter are not related to newly produced output. If so, then money and credit are explicitly separated in banks' ledgers, thereby avoiding the issuance of 'empty money' and the resulting inflationary pressures within the economic system as a whole.

The nature of money put to the fore by quantum macroeconomics also allows the understanding that the current international monetary regime, based on some national currencies (mainly the US dollar), is flawed on structural grounds. It is indeed a 'non-system' for international payments (Williamson, 1977, p. 73), since it uses these national currencies as if they were a reserve asset whilst they are both an asset and a liability as explained above. Hence, for example, when an importer in country A pays the relevant transaction by disposing of a bank deposit in country A's banking system, the latter country does not really pay the imported goods, as the relevant deposit remains in this country's banking system and the exporting country just receives the image (a 'duplicata') of it (Rueff, 1963, p. 322). This then gives rise to global imbalances, which epitomize the existence of such an international monetary disorder that only a monetary–structural reform can eradicate. As quantum macroeconomics explains, such a reform must consider the nature of money as

VIJAYARAGHAVAN RAMANAN / SERGIO ROSSI

an asset–liability and elaborate – in the spirit of Keynes (1942/1980) – an international monetary architecture based on the issuance of a supranational money to be used by central banks only, 'private individuals, businesses and banks other than central banks, each continuing to use their own national currency as heretofore' (p. 168).

Quantum macroeconomics offers much to understand and dispose of some macroeconomic issues that affect contemporary economic systems negatively. It deserves consideration by students, scholars, and policy makers.

SERGIO ROSSI

See also

Inflation; Monetary circuit – French school; Monetary theory of production; Money as a means of payment; Money creation – nature of

References

Bailly, J.-L., A. Cencini and S. Rossi (eds) (2017), *Quantum Macroeconomics: The Legacy of Bernard Schmitt*, London and New York: Routledge.
Cencini, A. (1995), *Monetary Theory, National and International*, London and New York: Routledge.
Keynes, J.M. (1942/1980), 'Proposals for an International Clearing Union', in *The Collected Writings of John Maynard Keynes, vol. XXV, Activities 1940–1944. Shaping the Post-War World: The Clearing Union*, London and Basingstoke: Macmillan, pp. 168–95.
Lavoie, M. (1984), 'The endogenous flow of credit and the Post Keynesian theory of money', *Journal of Economic Issues*, **18** (3), 771–97.
Rossi, S. (2001), *Money and Inflation: A New Macroeconomic Analysis*, Cheltenham, UK, and Northampton, MA, USA: Edward Elgar.
Rossi, S. (2007), *Money and Payments in Theory and Practice*, London and New York: Routledge.
Rueff, J. (1963), 'Gold exchange standard a danger to the West', in H.G. Grubel (ed.), *World Monetary Reform: Plans and Issues*, Stanford and London: Stanford University Press and Oxford University Press, pp. 320–28.
Schmitt, B. (1975), *Théorie unitaire de la monnaie, nationale et internationale*, Albeuve, CH: Castella.
Schmitt, B. (1984), *Inflation, chômage et malformations du capital: macroéconomie quantique*, Paris and Albeuve, CH: Economica and Castella.
Schumpeter, J.A. (1954), *History of Economic Analysis*, London: George Allen & Unwin.
Williamson, J. (1977), *The Failure of World Monetary Reform, 1971–1974*, New York: New York University Press.

Rationality

As a foundational concept in economics, rationality has received considerable attention owing to its centrality and complexity. Several aspects are relevant. First, discussion occurs at both advanced and introductory levels.[1] Second, theory/reality distinctions are involved, because economic theorizing necessarily uses theoretical constructs in its representations of the forms of behaviour of actual people engaged in economic activity in real economies. Third, rationality receives contrasting treatments in economics, a key contrast being between highly idealized conceptions of rationality and more realistic conceptions. In the space available, this entry focuses on some fundamental elements in the different treatments that rationality receives in neoclassical economics and Keynes's economics; these including agent objectives, knowledge, abilities, and environments.

In pure neoclassical theory, rationality is conceptualized in a highly idealized manner as the successful maximization of utilities by agents. To guarantee this outcome, strict assumptions are required, the following being those used in the Arrow–Debreu general equilibrium theory:

(i) All agents have sufficient initial endowments of vendible resources (human and/or natural) that generate incomes for purchasing other items.
(ii) Trading in all markets occurs only at equilibrium prices. This prevents non-maximization of agent utilities due to resources remaining unsold (or unemployed).
(iii) Market-clearing prices exist in all markets. A fictitious auctioneer discovers these by trial and error before trading starts, communicates them to all agents, and declares that exchange may now begin.
(iv) All agents have the skills to maximize mathematical functions across large numbers of commodities.
(v) All agents have perfect knowledge of their personal utility functions, available production functions, and equilibrium prices, before exchange occurs.
(vi) Firms are merely intermediaries that generate income, whether as profits to owners or sale proceeds to pay input suppliers (say workers).

SERGIO ROSSI / RODERICK O'DONNELL

(vii) All decisions concerning supplies and demands are implemented using agreed contracts at time zero. Thereafter, goods and services are simply delivered and received at specified times and places (and possibly conditions) until the end of the economy. No decision-making occurs after time zero, so that none of the dramas characteristic of real economies ever occur.

(viii) Money is irrelevant. All that is needed is a *numéraire* commodity to express relative prices in real terms.

(ix) All agents exist at the beginning of time, with no future generations produced. This is because the unknown future supplies and demands of future agents cannot be communicated to the auctioneer at time zero.

(x) Contingency (but not genuine uncertainty) is included by adding further fictions, such as a complete set of contingent markets covering all possible events at all times and places. Whatever happens, agents still successfully maximize utilities and market-clearing still occurs, because every possible future eventuality is covered at time zero. Agents just require higher computational abilities.

(xi) Full employment and/or low inflation occur automatically with no further action required.

These propositions provide the conceptual explanation of the mathematics underpinning the Arrow–Debreu general equilibrium theory. Subsequently, mathematical extensions have been developed to inter-temporal general equilibrium theory, dynamic stochastic general equilibrium theory, and 'New Keynesian' theory, but these still retain a connection to utility maximization in one form or another.

General equilibrium theory and its variants, however, are reserved for the higher levels of the economics curriculum. Undergraduate textbooks present simpler, 'partial equilibrium' scenarios based on maximization in individual markets with perfectly flexible prices and quantities, *ceteris paribus*. But while providing apparently plausible supply and demand stories about equilibration in these individual markets, the analysis remains grounded in idealized assumptions of perfect knowledge, abilities, and environments, as well as the assumption that the summation of all the interacting individual markets results in the economy as a whole also exhibiting market-clearing equilibria.[2]

By contrast, Keynes's economic theory and policy treat rationality and its aspects very differently:

(i) Theory is concerned with real agents, actual decision-making and actual capitalist economies, for which purpose realistic abstractions are deployed.

(ii) There is no auctioneer, just groups of real agents such as firms, households, wealth-holders, and governments interacting with each other without external coordination.

(iii) Agents have limited knowledge, primarily due to uncertainty about the future (for a variety of reasons).

(iv) Decision-making is dependent on expectations. Firms pursue expected rates of profit, wealth-holders pursue expected rates of return, and consumers and workers make decisions with both expected and actual prices in mind.

(v) The most important expectations arise in contexts of fundamental uncertainty, that is, uncertainty not reducible to probabilities, numerical or non-numerical.

(vi) Two broad forms of rationality then emerge, the strongly rational or probabilized form and the more important weakly rational or non-probabilized form.[3]

(vii) Money has intrinsic value, so money–real interactions occur.

(viii) Market power varies between agents and groups, with no assumption of perfect competition.

(ix) The economy is an adaptive system travelling through time from a known present to an unknown future.

(x) Long-period general equilibria occur only when the expectations of major groups are realized and the economy stabilizes at the outcomes satisfying these expectations.

(xi) Equilibrium aggregate output, employment, and inflation levels are variable over time. Only by accident will full employment and/or low inflation occur.

(xii) Theoretical individualism is rejected; the behaviour of wholes is allowed to differ from the behaviour of parts.

RODERICK O'DONNELL

Within post-Keynesianism, debates arise, however, concerning the theorization of the above issues. These often involve different assumptions about the nature of economic environments and the abilities of agents to gain whatever knowledge is relevant.

In summary, neoclassical methodology and theory began with ideas concerning the best possible outcomes and investigated what kind of ideal economy would achieve them. Keynes's methodology and theory began with reality – actual agents endowed with actual abilities and situated in actual economies – so as to investigate the actual outcomes that occur.

RODERICK O'DONNELL

See also

Behavioural economics; Money illusion; Neoclassical economics; Post-Keynesian economics – a big tent?; Uncertainty

Notes

[1] For an advanced discussion of various (largely mainstream) approaches, see Blume and Easley (2017); for a discussion of its treatment in textbooks, see Jones (2021).
[2] For an account of the origins of utility maximization and some of the problems it has encountered, see McCormick (1997).
[3] For further discussion, see O'Donnell (1991).

References

Blume, L. and D. Easley (2017), 'Rationality', in M. Vernengo, E. Perez Caldentey and B.J. Rosser Jr (eds), *The New Palgrave Dictionary of Economics*, Basingstoke, UK, and New York, pp. 5396–405.
Jones, M. (2021), 'The concept of rationality in introductory economics textbooks', *Citizenship, Social and Economics Education*, **20** (1), 37–47.
McCormick, K. (1997), 'An essay on the origin of the rational utility maximization hypothesis and a suggested modification', *Eastern Economic Journal*, **23** (1), 17–30.
O'Donnell, R. (1991), 'Keynes on probability expectations and uncertainty', in R. O'Donnell (ed.), *Keynes as Philosopher–Economist*, London: Macmillan, pp. 3–60.

Reflux mechanism

Since Moore (1988), post-Keynesian economists have actively debated various aspects of money endogeneity. One question that has attracted attention is: if loans make deposits, what happens if economic agents do not wish to hold more money balances? What brings the supply of money equal to its demand?

Moore (1988) relied on convenience lending – that is, non-volitional holding of deposits. Kaldor proposed many answers. One mechanism is the Kaldor–Trevithick (1981) reflux mechanism, according to which agents repay bank advances leading to a reduction of the money stock and another is buying of income-yielding financial assets from banks. Even Joan Robinson (1956) endorsed the reflux mechanism.

It can be said that Kaldor (1985) himself may not have thought his answer complete, and his mechanism was to highlight errors in the monetarist hot-potato process. Lavoie (1999) argues that the reflux principle not only is not inconsistent with asset allocation decisions, but also is crucial for understanding money endogeneity.

This can also be seen in stock–flow consistent models (Godley and Lavoie, 2007) based on the flow of funds. The importance of the reflux mechanism can be clearly seen in these models. Households receive income from various sources such as wages, interest payments and dividends, and make consumption and asset allocation decisions. The first stage is how much they decide to save and the second is how much they decide to allocate their saving in various assets – or between what Rochon (1999) has called hoarded savings and financial savings. They may also reduce their indebtedness towards the banking system. Firms take advances from banks to finance working capital and when they earn receipts they reduce their indebtedness to banks – highlighting the importance of the reflux mechanism.

As shown by Lavoie (2003), even in a simple model of a private economy – with firms issuing equities to households in addition to bank borrowing – there is a way in which loans are brought into equivalence with deposits. If households increase their preference to hold more deposits, firms are driven to take more loans from banks, and if households decrease their preference for deposits, this does not lead to more consumption, because that is a separate decision, but could lead to either a higher clearing price for equities or a larger issuance of equities by firms, whose proceeds will help them reduce their loans from banks. The reflux mechanism thus operates even in the framework of asset allocation.

The reflux mechanism also holds in an open economy (Lavoie, 2001). In post-Keynesian theory, the money supply is credit-led and demand-determined with both fixed and floating exchange rates. Here, the compensation thesis is important, according to which changes in the central bank's foreign reserves will be compensated endogenously. The central bank may purchase foreign exchange in fixed exchange rate regimes to defend against exchange rate appreciation in case there is a positive current account balance. Banks will see an increase in their settlement balances at the central bank as a result and will either use it to reduce their indebtedness toward the central bank (that is, a reflux) or purchase Treasury bills from the central bank. The compensation happens endogenously, because the central bank is defending an exchange rate. Short-term interest rates will fall to the floor of the monetary policy 'corridor'.

There is also a reflux mechanism concerning exporters. When exporters receive payments and exchange them for domestic currency, they may reduce their advances taken from the banking system.

Vijayaraghavan Ramanan and
Louis-Philippe Rochon

See also

Endogenous money; Money creation – nature of; Monetary circuit; Monetary theory of production; Stock–flow consistent models

References

Godley, W. and M. Lavoie (2007), *Monetary Economics*, Basingstoke, UK, and New York: Palgrave Macmillan.
Kaldor, N. (1983), 'Keynesian economics after fifty years', in D. Worswick and J. Trevithick (eds), *Keynes and the Modern World*, Cambridge, UK: Cambridge University Press, pp. 1–48.
Kaldor, N. (1985), 'How monetarism failed', *Challenge*, **28** (2), 4–13.
Kaldor, N. and J. Trevithick (1981), 'A Keynesian perspective on money', *Lloyds Bank Review*, 139, 1–19.
Lavoie, M. (1999), 'The credit-led supply of deposits and the demand for money: Kaldor's reflux mechanism as previously endorsed by Joan Robinson', *Cambridge Journal of Economics*, **23** (1), 103–13.
Lavoie, M. (2001), 'The reflux mechanism in the open economy', in L.-P. Rochon and M. Vernengo (eds), *Credit, Interest Rates and the Open Economy*, Cheltenham, UK, and Northampton, MA, USA: Edward Elgar, pp. 215–42.
Lavoie, M. (2003), 'Circuit and coherent stock–flow accounting', in R. Arena and N. Salvadori (eds), *Money, Credit and the Role of the State: Essays in Honour of Augusto Graziani*, Farnham, UK, and Burlington, VT, USA: Ashgate Publishing, pp. 136–51.
Moore, B.J. (1988), *Horizontalists and Verticalists: The Macroeconomics of Credit Money*, Cambridge, UK: Cambridge University Press.
Robinson (1956), *The Accumulation of Capital*, London: Macmillan.
Rochon, L.-P. (1999), *Credit, Money and Production: An Alternative Post-Keynesian Approach*, Cheltenham, UK, and Northampton, MA, USA: Edward Elgar.

Regional economic integration and free trade agreements

Regionalism is defined as the 'the promotion by governments of international economic linkages with countries that are geographically proximate' (Hine, 1992, p. 115). Regional economic integration, or regional trade agreements (RTAs), is a process whereby various economies in a region undergo a progressive removal of the barriers to the free movement of goods, services, capital, and labour.

RTAs consist of various levels of integration (El-Agraa, 1997). The most basic form of RTA is a preferential trade agreement, which imposes lower tariffs on imports from member countries than from non-member countries. The second level is a free trade area (FTA), which is an agreement among countries whereby tariffs and non-tariff barriers, such as quotas, licensing, and product safety regulations, are abolished among members. The third level is a customs union in which all tariffs and quantitative restrictions on trade among member countries are abolished, and a common set of tariffs is imposed for trade with non-member countries. The fourth level is a common market, which involves a customs union as well as the free movement of factors of production, such as capital and labour. The fifth level is an economic union, in which, in addition to a common market, the harmonization of fiscal, monetary, industrial, and other economic policies is included. The highest degree of economic integration is a supranational union in which member countries' governments hand over their sovereignty for economic and social policies to a supranational government.

In early 2019, 471 of a total of 685 RTAs were enforced, compared to 48 of 87 that were enforced in 1990 (World Trade Organization, 2019, p. 2). The sharp increase in the number of RTAs can be explained by the failure of multilateral trade agreements (MTAs) in liberalizing international trade. RTAs have thereby emerged as a substitute for MTAs. Most of the RTAs negotiated or signed not only cover the mobility of goods, services, and investments, but include reducing regulations and increasing the power of multinational corporations. The establishment of RTAs is part of a power game. As Mittelman (1999, p. 25) claims, 'regionalism today is emerging as a potent force in the global restructuring of power and production.'

Whether an RTA is beneficial or not depends on the magnitude of trade creation or trade diversion (Stoeckel et al., 1990, p. 23). Theoretically, an FTA is more likely to raise rather than reduce welfare: the larger the size of the market, the greater the level of intra-regional trade. The closer the members are geographically, and without trade barriers, the better the transportation of goods to member countries. Also, there would be a greater substitutability of products among member countries. With the formation of an FTA, firms and industries in the local economy would be exposed to competition from members of the FTA, and they may become more efficient. However, these gains in efficiency will not be realized overnight. To gain efficiency there should be greater competition and greater specialization that are able to reduce the intra-regional transactions costs. By opening doors for other countries to compete fairly, without the burden of trade policies, this creates the opportunity for countries to focus on what they do best, while being able to acquire goods and services at potentially the lowest price possible and increase the effective market size, decrease oligopolistic mark-ups, and reduce market segmentation (World Bank, 2000, pp. 30–34). The larger market size encourages longer production runs, and, hence, a reduction in costs.

In the process of economic integration, some higher-cost firms may be eliminated, and the demand met by imports. The increased market size that accompanies trade expansion may enable more goods to be produced profitably, thereby generating welfare gains from increased product diversity. Integration may permit firms to engage in more plant specialization, thus reducing the number of goods produced in a given plant, with attendant cost reductions. As stated by Dunning (1993, p. 486), 'economic integration offers a wider locational choice to both domestic and foreign companies to produce within the integrated region ... [I]t promotes both centripetal and centrifugal effect.' However, creating a trading bloc causes the exploitation of developing countries by industrialized countries, as in the case of the North American Free Trade Agreement for Mexico, and labour concerns over fair wages and the loss of jobs from industrialized countries to developing countries, as well as political concerns that may influence the negotiations between trading partners.

FTAs do not guarantee a 'win–win' situation. Some members of the bloc will experience trade creation while others will receive trade diversion even though intra-trade expands. Integrating countries with different levels of income and economic development could lead to an unequal distribution of gains, such as integration between developed and developing countries. It is a bad idea combining a low-skilled-job country with a high-skilled-job nation, that is, combining a high-wage country with a low-wage country (Belous and Lemco, 1995). Countries have not the same production capabilities, levels of technology, quality of human capital, or product brand. Those countries whose level of economic development is not as high as the level of developed countries will lose.

MOHAMED ASLAM

See also

Balance of payments; Capital flows; Common currency area; European Monetary Union; Trade and development

References

Belous, R.S. and J. Lemco (1995), 'The NAFTA development model of combining high- and low-wage areas: an introduction', in R.S. Belous and J. Lemco (eds), *NAFTA as a Model of Development: The Benefits and Costs of Merging High- and Low-Wage Areas*, Albany, NY: State University of New York Press, pp. 1–20.

Dunning, J.H. (1993), *Multinational Enterprises and the Global Economy*, Suffolk, UK: Addison-Wesley Publishing.
El-Agraa, A.M. (1997), 'General introduction', in A.M. El-Agraa (ed.), *Economic Integration Worldwide*, London: Macmillan, pp. 1–11.
Hine, R.C. (1992), 'Regionalism and the integration of the world economy', *Journal of Common Market Studies*, **30** (2), 115–23.
Mittleman, J.H. (1999), 'Rethinking the "New Regionalism" in the context of globalization', in B. Hettne, A. Inotai and O. Sunkel (eds), *Globalism and the New Regionalism*, London: Palgrave, pp. 25–53.
Stoeckel, A., D. Pearce and G. Banks (1990), *Western Trade Blocs*, Canberra, AU: Center for International Economics.
World Bank (2000), *Trade Blocs*, Oxford and New York: Oxford University Press.
World Trade Organization (2019), *Evolution of RTAs, 1948–2019*, available online at https://www.wto.org/english/tratop_e/region_e/region_e.htm#facts (last accessed 23 December 2020).

Regulation School

The Regulation School (RS) is a French economic theory that traces its roots to the early 1970s. Following Marxism, it focuses on the analysis of endogenous crises within capitalism and the resulting institutional transformations, understood as historical regulations to overcome those crises. It shares some roots with the social structures of accumulation (Gordon, 1978).

Coming from biology and complex system analysis, the term 'regulation', describing the different mechanisms required to maintain a system in a homeostatic equilibrium, was first introduced by the Marxist economists Paul Boccara (1973) to understand the counter-tendencies to capitalist crises. Michel Aglietta (1976), who studied the regulation of Fordism in the United States, followed then by a collection of works coordinated by Jean-Pascal Bénassy et al. (1977), developed the Parisian (now hegemonic) version of the RS. In contrast to the strict Marxist framework, the Parisian school is a critical synthesis between Althusserian and Gramscian Marxism, post-Keynesianism, the historical school of the *Annales*, and the old institutionalism. For the RS, the regulation includes all forms of rules and behaviour that contribute to the reproduction of capitalism and limit crises. It has therefore a broader meaning than 'public regulation'.

The analysis of the transformation and crises of capitalism is based on the concepts of accumulation regime (AR), mode of regulation (MR), and institutional form (IF), seen as 'intermediate concepts' between abstract structures of capitalism and empirical phenomena. The RS method is to analyse the historical succession of MR and AR in order to explain their structural crisis endogenously.

The AR describes how productivity and value are produced and distributed, and how they fuel effective demand, and reciprocally how the social demand and the norms of consumption shape the extraction of productivity. Now, since accumulation is unstable, the AR needs to be sustained by an MR, which is the set of social relations that reproduces the fundamental capitalist social relations, 'drives' the AR, and coordinates the decentralized forms of agents' behaviour (Boyer, 1986). Unfortunately, the MR can become dysfunctional to the AR. Indeed, the dynamic and innovative nature of accumulation tends in the long run to overflow the MR and to slowly transform agents behaviour, disadjusting MR with AR. When these small changes exceed some thresholds, a structural crisis occurs (Lordon, 1993), generating a political crisis and a process of socio-political transformations by trial and error.

The end of the crisis is always uncertain, depending on the institutional and political transformations. Indeed, the fundamental social relations of capitalism (money, market, and the wage–labour nexus) take historically and geographically defined institutional forms (IFs), depending on the socio-political compromises and the power relations between social groups. IFs are not transformed because of their efficiency but owing to their ability to stabilize social conflicts and political coalitions (Amable and Palombarini, 2005); to wit, they are the product of temporary institutionalized compromises. An MR is stable when a stable hierarchy between the IFs is found and when IFs are complementary, which means that the presence of several IFs together increases economic performance, and gives a systemic coherence to the MR, sustaining the AR and the dominant political compromises.

At the beginning, the RS was focused on the study of crises within Fordism, the latter being characterized by the combination of an intensive AR based on mass production, mass consumption fuelled by the growth of wages, and economy of scales, with a monopolist–inflationist and Keynesian MR. Its stagflationist crisis was explained by the slowdown of productivity gains, although the Fordist regulation based on collective wage indexation and monopolist competition was maintained.

Quickly, it appeared that Fordism was not universal and had very different national forms, owing to different forms the State may have, international integration regimes, and the idea of diachronic but also synchronic forms of capitalisms (Amable, 2003; Boyer, 2015).

In the early 2000s, Aglietta (1998), Lordon (1999), and Boyer (2000) were among the first to analyse the nature and fragility of a financialized AR, fuelled by asset bubbles and shareholder value maximization. In parallel, the RS enlarged its original macroeconomic focus to the meso-economic objects like sectors, regions (Chester, 2013; Chanteau et al., 2016), or firms (Boyer and Freyssenet, 2002) to understand the different levels of regulations and their articulation. The RS has built a general theory of institutions and institutional change and an institutionalist microeconomic theory with 'macro-foundations' following multiple sources like Bourdieu (Boyer, 2004; Klebaner and Montalban, 2020), Commons (1931; see Théret, 2001), Spinoza (Lordon, 2006; 2008; 2013) or the 'economy of conventions' (Orléan, 1994). For the RS, rationality and behaviour are embedded in social structures. Indeed, institutions are analysed at the same time as constraints and resources for individual actions, shaping representations, *habitus*, affects, and interests. Like in the sociology of Bourdieu (1992), the behaviour of agents depends on their social position, classes, and trajectory, and changes because of conflicts and learning.

MATTHIEU MONTALBAN

See also

Bubbles – credit; Capitalism; Effective demand; Institutional economics; Power

References

Aglietta, M. (1976), *Régulation et crises du capitalisme: l'expérience des Etats-Unis*, Paris: Calmann-Lévy.
Aglietta, M. (1998), *Le capitalisme de demain*, Paris: Fondation Saint-Simon.
Amable, B. (2003), *The Diversity of Modern Capitalism*, Oxford: Oxford University Press.
Amable, B. and S. Palombarini (2005), *L'économie politique n'est pas une science morale*, Paris: Raisons d'agir.
Bénassy, J.P., R. Boyer, R.M. Gelpi and A. Lipietz (1977), *Approches de l'inflation: l'exemple français*, Paris: CEPREMAP.
Boccara, P. (1973), *Etudes sur le capitalisme monopoliste d'Etat, sa crise et son issue*, Paris: Editions sociales.
Bourdieu, P. (1992), *Raisons pratiques: sur la théorie de l'action*, Paris: Editions du Seuil.
Boyer, R. (1986), *Théorie de la régulation: une analyse critique*, Paris: La Découverte.
Boyer, R. (2000), 'Is a finance-led growth regime a viable alternative to Fordism? A preliminary analysis', *Economy and Society*, **29** (1), 111–45.
Boyer, R. (2004), *Une théorie du capitalisme est-elle possible?*, Paris: Odile Jacob.
Boyer, R. (2015), *Economie politique des capitalismes*, Paris: La Découverte.
Boyer, R. and M. Freyssenet (2002), *The Productive Models: The Conditions of Profitability*, London and New York: Palgrave.
Chanteau, J.P., P. Grouiez, A. Labrousse, T. Lamarche, S. Michel, M. Nieddu and J. Vercueil (2016), 'Trois questions à la théorie de la régulation par ceux qui ne l'ont pas fondée', *Revue de la régulation: capitalisme, institutions, pouvoirs*, **19**, available online at https://journals.openedition.org/regulation/11918 (last accessed 2 December 2020).
Chester, L. (2013), 'The failure of market fundamentalism: how electricity sector restructuring is threatening the economic and social fabric', *Review of Radical Political Economy*, **45** (3), 315–22.
Commons, J.R. (1931), 'Institutional economics', *American Economic Review*, **21** (4), 648–57.
Gordon, D.M. (1978), 'Up and down the long roller coaster', in Union for Radical Political Economics (ed.), *U.S. Capitalism in Crisis*, New York: Union for Radical Political Economics, pp. 22–34.
Klebaner, S. and M. Montalban (2020), 'Cross-fertilizations between institutional economics and economic sociology: the case of régulation theory and the sociology of fields', *Review of Political Economy*, **32** (2), 180–98.
Lordon, F. (1993), 'Irrégularités des trajectoires de croissance: évolutions et dynamique non-linéaire. Vers une schématisation de l'endométabolisme', PhD dissertation, Paris: EHESS.
Lordon, F. (1999), 'Le nouvel agenda de la politique économique en régime d'accumulation financiarisé', in G. Duménil and D. Lévy (eds), *Le triangle infernal: crise, mondialisation, financiarisation*, Paris: Presses Universitaires de France, pp. 141–59.
Lordon, F. (2006), *L'intérêt souverain: essai d'anthropologie économique spinoziste*, Paris, La Découverte.
Lordon, F. (ed.) (2008), *Conflits et pouvoirs dans les institutions du capitalisme*, Paris: Presses de Sciences Po.

Lordon, F. (2013), *La société des affects: pour un structuralisme des passions*, Paris: Editions du Seuil.

Orléan, A. (ed.) (1994), *Analyse économique des conventions*, Paris: Presses Universitaires de France.

Théret, B. (2001), 'Saisir les faits économiques: la méthode Commons', *Cahiers d'économie politique*, **40–41** (2–3), 79–137.

Remittances

Remittances are the money sent by migrant workers to individuals in their home countries for personal, small business, and philanthropic uses. The role of these funds is to finance consumption and investment (Kapur, 2005). Unlike foreign aid, where good intentions do not necessarily translate into good results, remittances cut the administrative intermediary and are given directly to targeted people for the intended purposes. While it is difficult for the foreign aid giver to detect the immediate needs of the recipient (Easterly, 2008), such as the need for boreholes in a specific area, remittance givers, who come directly from the poor regions and have families there, are more privy to the specific needs of the people. As a result, remittances are more effective than foreign aid in these developing regions.

Remittance inflows make up a sizeable part of funds in developing countries. These private transfers are made through personal deliveries, wire transfers – such as Western Union and MoneyGram – and financial institutions. They serve as sources of loans from either individuals or financial institutions. Therefore, they also help to service the financial system of these countries.

Remittance transfers mostly go into developing countries, which are characterized by high levels of poverty, inequality, income volatility, and capital market imperfections (Rapoport and Docquier, 2006). They offer various benefits, especially since they meet direct needs and are channelled into the most productive uses that contribute to poverty alleviation.

The advantages of remittances can be summarized as follows.

1. Remittances are an alternative source of finance for small enterprise investment and are used to overcome liquidity constraints (Giuliano and Ruiz-Arranz, 2009).
2. At the microeconomic level, remittances aid consumption smoothing, risk diversification, and the intergenerational financing of investments (Rapoport and Docquier, 2006). These funds are used to purchase consumption goods, houses, education, healthcare, and financial instruments.
3. Remittances lower transaction costs and reduce the leakages to rent-seeking bureaucracies and consultants (Kapur, 2005).
4. By bypassing the bureaucratic red tapes of foreign aid, remittances go directly into consumption and investment, thereby boosting aggregate demand in the home country.
5. In the face of a natural disaster, recipients of remittances begin the recovery process more quickly than others in the economy (Suleri and Savage, 2006). This recovery has a multiplier effect on local expenditure, as it is used to pay local labourers. Also, remittance recipients are prone to quicker aid than those who rely on other types of foreign or governmental aid, as the latter requires bureaucratic deliberations and other forms of red tape.

Remittances are not all sunshine and rainbows. As much as they provide benefits for people in developing regions, this comes at a cost to some others. The drawbacks of remittances are notably the following:

1. According to the *Migration and Development Brief 13* of the World Bank, migrants cut costs, especially housing costs, in order to send remittances to their home countries (Mohapatra et al., 2010). This means that migrants are forced to live beneath their means in order to send money to their home countries. These migrants are therefore the sacrificial lambs/cash cows that fund the other members of their families or friends in their home countries.
2. Remittances can lead to a dependence on the inflow of capital instead of these developing countries creating sustainable development from within. Rather than using the resources they have to get what is needed, these countries have a tendency to wait for external help, just like with foreign aid. This means that these countries would be susceptible to the condition of the global economy. If there were a crisis in the issuing countries, the receiving countries would be affected.

Overall, remittances have increasingly played a large role in financing consumption, investment, and the financial sector of developing countries. They have become a recognized channel of financing development especially at the microeconomic level. These remittances meet the needs of the recipients but also have a multiplier effect on their friends, families, and workers in the home country. As a result, they contribute to poverty alleviation in developing countries.

SALEWA OLAWOYE-MANN

See also

Credit constraints; Development; Development banking; Inequality; Money and banking

References

Easterly, W. (2008), *Reinventing Foreign Aid*, volume 1, Boston: MIT Press.
Giuliano, P. and M. Ruiz-Arranz (2009), 'Remittances, financial development, and growth', *Journal of Development Economics*, **90** (1), 144–52.
Kapur, D. (2005), 'Remittances: the new development mantra?', in S.M. Maimbo and D. Ratha (eds), *Remittances: Development Impact and Future Prospects*, Washington, DC: World Bank, pp. 331–60.
Mohapatra, S., D. Ratha and A. Silwal (2010), 'Outlook for remittance flows 2011–12: recovery after the crisis, but risks lie ahead', *Migration and Development Brief 13*, Washington, DC: World Bank.
Rapoport, H. and F. Docquier (2006), 'The economics of migrants' remittances', in S.-C. Kolm and J.M. Ythier (eds), *Handbook of the Economics of Giving, Altruism and Reciprocity*, volume 2, Amsterdam: North-Holland, pp. 1135–98.
Suleri, A.Q. and K. Savage (2006), *Remittances in Crises: A Case Study from Pakistan*, London: Sustainable Development Policy Institute.

Rentier income

In post-Keynesian literature, capitalists and rentiers are defined as those who derive the majority of their income from earning profits and owning wealth. Their existence is linked to income inequality between capital and labour, as capitalists and rentiers are in conflict over the share of national income with workers (those whose livelihoods depend on paid labour).

The concept of rentier income in post-Keynesian economics can be traced back to the work of Michał Kalecki (1954) on the theory of income distribution and economic growth. Assuming an economy dominated by imperfect competition, excess capacity, constant marginal and average costs, and uncertainty, prices are set as a mark-up over wages and other variable costs (Kalecki, 1971). The mark-up is determined by firms' demand constraints and the ratio of prices to marginal costs (called the degree of monopoly). Kalecki shows that the share of wages in national income depends negatively on the degree of monopoly, and so the extent to which capitalists can increase prices without causing a fall in demand is a key determinant of the distribution of income between capital and labour.

While the terms 'capitalists' and 'rentiers' are often used interchangeably, they are fundamentally different. Capitalists have been traditionally understood as entrepreneurs, who earn variable income from profits depending on the difference between expected and actual investment. The nature of rentiers is more passive, since they receive fixed income in the form of unproductive rents from their ownership of wealth (Toporowski, 2001).

However, in the framework of an increased dominance of the financial sector over the real economy (also called financialization) and the existence of derivative trading, both capitalists and rentiers can be identified as part of one capitalist class, which pursues capital returns by investing in financial markets and owning wealth (*ibid.*). In addition to firm equity, recent post-Keynesian studies define rentier wealth (from which rentier income is derived) to include bank deposits, housing, securitized assets, and other more complex forms of wealth (see Zezza, 2008; Nikolaidi, 2015; Sawyer and Passarella Veronese, 2017).

This conception of rentiers as owners of diversified asset portfolios links the key processes of financialized capitalism to a distribution of national income that is increasingly favourable to rentiers. Shareholder value maximization has led to a higher rentier income share as firms' operations have become increasingly oriented towards short-term financial gain rather than real investment, which has skewed the price- and wage-setting power towards rentiers, or shareholders (Hein, 2015). Moreover, the rise of securitization has boosted the rentier income share through high returns on financial instruments derived from household loans

(Sawyer and Passarella Veronese, 2017). The resulting increase in household debt has contributed to a higher rentier income share by transferring income from debtor worker households to creditor rentier households through loan repayments (Palley, 2002).

Some post-Keynesian economists argue that greater complexity of household wealth under securitization has blurred the distinction between workers and rentiers. The dramatic rise in wage inequality at the turn of the twentieth century reveals that the richest individuals in the economy, who would be typically identified with rentiers, have captured an increasing share of wages, owing partly to extremely high salaries paid to financial sector executives (Kaplan and Rauh, 2010). To account for growing wage inequality, some post-Keynesian studies define a new income class earning both wages and rentier income (see Dafermos and Papatheodorou, 2015; Palley, 2015).

Lastly, some authors have introduced borrowing by the capitalist class in the definition of rentier income (Sawyer and Passarella Veronese, 2017). Because of their high income and wealth, rentiers benefit from access to larger amounts of credit at more favourable conditions and lower costs. The motives for debt accumulation among rentiers are not only to engage in consumption and investment in excess of earnings but also to take advantage of tax reliefs, such as mortgage deductions (Stiglitz, 2012).

HANNA SZYMBORSKA

See also

Capitalism; Income distribution; Mark-up pricing; Monopoly power; Profit

References

Dafermos, Y. and C. Papatheodorou (2015), 'Linking functional with personal income distribution: a stock–flow consistent approach', *International Review of Applied Economics*, **29** (6), 1–29.
Hein, E. (2015), 'Finance-dominated capitalism and re-distribution of income: a Kaleckian perspective', *Cambridge Journal of Economics*, **39** (3), 907–34.
Kalecki, M. (1954), *Theory of Economic Dynamics: An Essay on Cyclical and Long-Run Changes in Capitalist Economy*, London: George Allen and Unwin.
Kalecki, M. (1971), *Selected Essays on the Dynamics of the Capitalist Economy*, Cambridge, UK: Cambridge University Press.
Kaplan, S.N. and J. Rauh (2010), 'Wall Street and Main Street: what contributes to the rise in the highest incomes?', *Review of Financial Studies*, **23** (3), 1004–50.
Nikolaidi, M. (2015), 'Securitisation, wage stagnation and financial fragility: a stock–flow consistent perspective', *Greenwich Papers in Political Economy*, No. 14078.
Palley, T.I. (2002), 'Endogenous money: what it is and why it matters', *Metroeconomica*, **53** (2), 152–80.
Palley, T.I. (2015), 'The middle class in macroeconomics and growth theory: a three-class neo-Kaleckian–Goodwin model', *Cambridge Journal of Economics*, **39** (1), 221–43.
Sawyer, M. and M. Passarella Veronese (2017), 'The monetary circuit in the age of financialisation: a stock–flow consistent model with a twofold banking sector', *Metroeconomica*, **68** (2), 321–53.
Stiglitz, J.E. (2012), *The Price of Inequality*, London: Penguin Books.
Toporowski, J. (2001), 'Financial derivatives, liquidity preference, competition and financial inflation', in P. Arestis and M. Sawyer (eds), *Money, Finance and Capitalist Development*, Cheltenham, UK, and Northampton, MA, USA: Edward Elgar.
Zezza, G. (2008), 'U.S. growth, the housing market, and the distribution of income', *Journal of Post Keynesian Economics*, **30** (3), 375–401.

Reserves – role of

The main role of reserves (also called settlement balances) is the settlement of bilateral debt between banks through a third-party liability issued by the central bank (see Rochon and Rossi, 2007). As a matter of fact, the central bank is not only a clearing house but actually creates the means of payment needed to settle interbank debt. It ensures convertibility at par between the deposits of all banks in the system that have an account at the central bank.

The central bank has both a money creation and a credit creation role. In fact, each bank when settling replaces its debt/credit relation to another bank with a credit/debt relation to the central bank. Hence, the central bank is responsible for the smooth payment pattern of commercial banks. The bank money circuit is supplemented by a financial market circuit that ensures that debts to the central bank are repaid by using private interbank credit or by selling securities in the market.

The central bank intervenes in the financial market to foster the good functioning of it.

HANNA SZYMBORSKA / DOMENICA TROPEANO

For example, it engages in a repo transaction with a debtor bank and a reverse repo with a creditor bank using the same asset or different assets that have been approved for monetary policy operations with the central bank (Rochon and Rossi, 2007, pp. 549–50). Hence, both the money circuit and the financial circuit are involved in the normal functioning of the payments system.

The second role of reserves is related to the carrying out of monetary policy interventions by the central bank. By injecting and drawing out reserves, the central bank implements its targeted overnight rate of interest. So it accommodates the system's demand for reserves, but also injects and withdraws reserves reacting to autonomous changes in the supply of reserves, which potentially could make interbank interest rates deviate from the target. In this sense, it has both an accommodating and a defensive role (see Eichner, 1987).

Some changes to this pattern are emerging in the institutional setting of the major central banks in the world since the Global Financial Crisis that burst in 2008. The targeted overnight interest rate is being put under discussion, as it concerns only one part of the financial system, namely regular banks, neglecting non-bank financial institutions whose liabilities have started being used as money substitutes. During and after the crisis several central banks started offering facilities to non-bank financial institutions, thereby implicitly validating the near-money nature of their liabilities (Murau, 2017).

The US Federal Reserve since the 2008 crisis has carried out reverse repos with non-bank financial institutions, which means that it is not financing them but it is offering them an investment opportunity for their liquid assets. This intervention in light of the previous distinction between the accommodative and defensive roles of the central bank would fall into the latter category, drawing liquidity out of the system. Some have started to question the usefulness of targeting an interbank rate of interest and have proposed to replace it with a repo rate, which would reflect financing conditions not only among banks but also between banks and non-banks. According to some scholars, the reverse repo facility could be similar to a central bank account for non-bank financial institutions (Poszar, 2014).

The European Central Bank (ECB) is innovating the use of reserves, too. Given the distress in the interbank market, it is replacing the financial circuit and lending reserves in the long run to banks through various rounds of long-term refinancing operations. As a consequence its IOUs do not come back to the central bank any more. The circuit does not close. There is a chronic excess liquidity in the system, though asymmetrically distributed among the banks of the various countries that the ECB serves.

Here again the usefulness of targeting the interbank rate of interest for the conduct of monetary policy is discussed not because of the role of non-bank financial institutions, but because the volume of interbank unsecured loans has greatly contracted (Tropeano, 2019). It would be more convenient to opt for a repo rate given that most interbank loans are now secured and part of repo agreements. The problem would be which repo rate to target, as in the euro area there are many government bonds that are used for repos. They all command different haircuts. This points to the inexistence of a European risk-free asset.

Palley (2001) warned that changes in the financial system may eliminate the demand for liabilities of the central bank, so that the central bank would be unable to control the supply price of liquidity through open-market operations.

Another reason why reserves have seen their importance diminish is that globalization and financial integration have increased the weight of cross-border payments for which reserves are not useful. Cross-border banks and non-bank financial institutions settle their reciprocal debts using cash and cash-equivalent collateral. Financial collateral in order to be used should be liquid, marked to the market, and part of a cross-border netting agreement (Singh and Alam, 2018, p. 9).

To conclude, the role of reserves as means of payment across the interbank market has been challenged by the enlargement of the financial landscape, with the inclusion of many non-bank financial institutions whose liabilities are considered near-money and that do not have an account at the central bank. In order to preserve the ordinary workings of the payments system in the whole financial system, some central banks have started to offer facilities to non-bank financial institutions. Another blow to the reserves role has been the increase in the size of cross-border payments for which new and old settlement means are being used.

The role of reserves to achieve the overnight interest rate target has changed because of the unconventional monetary policy that has prevailed since the crisis. So the description of the role of reserves that has been made in the first part of this entry now applies only partially.

DOMENICA TROPEANO

See also

Central banking; Endogenous money; Monetary circuit; Money as a means of payment; Settlement balances

References

Eichner, A. (1987), *The Macrodynamics of Advanced Market Economies*, Armonk, NY: M.E. Sharpe.
Murau, S. (2017), 'Shadow money and the public money supply: the impact of the 2007–2009 financial crisis on the monetary system', *Review of International Political Economy*, **24** (5), 802–38.
Palley, T.I. (2001), 'The e-money revolution: challenges and implications for monetary policy', *Journal of Post Keynesian Economics*, **24** (2), 217–33.
Poszar, Z. (2014), 'Shadow banking: the money view', Office of Financial Research, London: UK Treasury.
Rochon, L.-P. and S. Rossi (2007), 'Central banking and post-Keynesian economics', *Review of Political Economy*, **19** (4), 539–54.
Singh, M. and Z. Alam (2018), 'Leverage: a broader view', *International Monetary Fund Working Paper*, No. 18/62.
Tropeano, D. (2019), 'Negative interest rates in the Eurozone', *Review of Keynesian Economics*, **7** (2), 233–46.

Satisficing

Herbert A. Simon (1955) established behavioural economics based on bounded rationality. People are unable to fully optimize due to costs of information being too high for most people and their inability to compute such behaviour for mathematical and logical limits, arguing that most people follow heuristic rules of thumb to achieve an aspirational level they hold. Most firms seek a level of profit acceptable to owners rather than a possible maximum profit level. He labelled this approach 'satisficing' (Simon, 1956), noting this word is in the *Oxford English Dictionary* from a Northumbrian dialect, basically meaning 'satisfy'. But he redefined it to describe how people behave using bounded rationality.

Some defenders of the view that economic agents fully optimize argue that all Simon did was to highlight information costs (Stigler, 1961). When it looks like people are satisficing they are actually optimizing, because they are using the optimal amount of costly information. But determining how much time one should spend gathering information raises the additional problem of determining how much time one should spend on how much time one should use in determining how much information one should gather, with this then raising an infinite regress of such problems that is fundamentally unsolvable (Conlisk, 1996), with Simon noting such issues as connected to the incompleteness theorem of Gödel. This search for information must be arbitrarily cut off, thus implying one must satisfice on this effort to determine how to optimize.

A variation on this argues that satisficing may actually be optimal often. Baumol (2003) advocates this position, noting from his observations as a witness in legal cases regarding predatory pricing how high the costs are to real-world firms of knowing their own marginal costs and the elasticities of demand they face needed for achieving theoretical profit maximization. He notes remarks he often heard from chief financial officers of corporations in such cases along the lines of 'I assume you have never worked with a company whose data are as bad as ours' (Baumol, 2003, p. 64). He argues that the value of satisficing is that it avoids costs that might be induced by trying to determine an optimum among possible alternative forms of behaviour. One such cost is undermining the morale of existing workers and suppliers of a firm, who may lose their jobs or contracts, with this undermining their productivity. A satisficing approach avoids such costs.

While Simon posed it as involving trial-and-error approaches following rules of thumb, some have argued that satisficing may imply optimization when formally posed as a system of maximizing, subject to achieving the aspiration levels of the agents as a constraint (Radner, 1975). This then focuses on what those aspiration levels are and where they come from. Simon always posed satisficing as tied to these aspiration levels. But some observers have highlighted how these are essentially arbitrary and endogenously evolve over time as a firm or

DOMENICA TROPEANO / J. BARKLEY ROSSER, JR.

individual engages in satisficing conduct over time (Bianchi, 1990).

Keynes died in 1946, a decade before Simon introduced this term into economics. However, some students of his thought have argued that Keynes was fundamentally a behavioural economist (O'Donnell, 2014–15), although Simon himself did not discuss macroeconomics or Keynes. O'Donnell's formulation of this is that Keynes emphasized human abilities and characteristics as epistemologically limiting their ability to have certainty about how to behave. Recognizing that agents cannot definitely optimize in the face of unavoidable uncertainty, Keynes (1936) argued that people rely on conventions in their conduct in the face of uncertainty. It is reasonable to see this following of conventions as consistent with satisficing conduct, if perhaps not having specific aspiration levels involved.

J. BARKLEY ROSSER, JR.

See also

Behavioural economics; Microfoundations; Neoclassical economics; Rationality; *The General Theory of Employment, Interest and Money*

References

Baumol, W.J. (2003), 'On rational satisficing', in M. Augier and J.G. March (eds), *Models of a Man: Essays in Memory of Herbert A. Simon*, Cambridge, MA: MIT Press, pp. 57–66.
Bianchi, M. (1990), 'The unsatisfactoriness of satisficing: from bounded rationality to innovative rationality', *Review of Political Economy*, **2** (2), 149–67.
Conlisk, J. (1996), 'Why bounded rationality?', *Journal of Economic Literature*, **34** (2), 669–700.
Keynes, J.M. (1936), *The General Theory of Employment, Interest and Money*, London: Macmillan.
O'Donnell, R. (2014–15), 'A critique of the ergodic/nonergodic approach to uncertainty', *Journal of Post Keynesian Economics*, **37** (2), 187–210.
Radner, R. (1975), 'Satisficing', *Journal of Mathematical Economics*, **2** (2), 253–62.
Simon, H.A. (1955), 'A behavioral model of rational choice', *Quarterly Journal of Economics*, **69** (1), 99–118.
Simon, H.A. (1956), 'Rational choice and the structure of the environment', *Psychological Review*, **63** (2), 129–38.
Stigler, G.J. (1961), 'The economics of information', *Journal of Political Economy*, **69** (3), 213–25.

Savings

A core principle that permeates any post-Keynesian approach is the idea that investment creates saving, and not the reverse. The two foundational contributions in this regard are Keynes's criticism of Say's Law in *The General Theory* (Keynes, 1936, Chs 2–3), and the works of Michał Kalecki, notably his essay on the determinants of profits (Kalecki, 1971, pp. 78–92).

If agents do not behave in accordance with Say's Law, investments determine savings regardless of how these investments were originally funded. Post-Keynesian economists place this investment/saving relationship within an endogenous money approach, which separates the determination of these two real variables from that of the interest rate, which is a monetary variable. Saving decisions and interest rates can influence each other, depending on agents' portfolio choice and the influence of the central bank in interest rate setting. But in a post-Keynesian approach, portfolio decisions do not necessarily limit the size of investments and the ensuing savings.

If we consider foreign trade and the government sector, then net exports and net public spending are additional sources of savings for the economy. Conversely, net imports reduce domestic savings. In fact, if investments in a closed economy or on a global scale 'finance' themselves, the relation does not hold for a regional open economy with a current account deficit. Imports and exports cancel out on a world scale. Government budget deficits, instead, positively affect savings globally and post-Keynesian economists have opposed unanimously austerity policies imposed by the Washington Consensus, and implemented by many governments historically, reaffirming that a fiscal deficit may well derive from government spending too little rather than too much.

As we have seen, in this approach, aggregate savings are a 'passive' variable. However, the propensity to save is an important factor determining effective demand, including the amount of investment necessary to achieve a desired level or growth rate of income. Exploring these relations dynamically, post-Keynesian scholars have produced several growth models, confirming the validity of the paradox of thrift for the short run and, more controversially, also for the long run. In the latter case, some scholars argue that this paradox may not hold, if we assume that an economy's capacity utilization is full or 'normal'.

The determination of the marginal and average propensities to save in post-Keynesian literature depends on psychological and distributional issues. Since affluent individuals tend to save more out of their incomes, an unequal distribution of income should increase the average propensity to save. A large literature has focused on the definition of different growth regimes, in the simplest form defined as wage-led and profit-led. In a profit-led regime, the positive effect of an increase in the profit share (or rate) on capital accumulation exceeds the negative effect of the parallel decrease in consumption expenditures. Hence, there can be a positive relation between the higher propensity to save, associated with an increase in the profit share, and economic growth, via investment. In a wage-led regime, the effect of lower consumption expenditures prevails, affecting negatively entrepreneurial expectations of future sales and investment decisions. Household access to credit complicates the picture. In fact, their borrowing reduces the impact of inequality on aggregate household spending. On the other hand, the unequal distribution of savings within the sector may increase financial fragility, if the lower income groups get chronically into debt.

A literature on the portfolio decision of agents, including firms, and their liquidity preference, has been generated from a mixture of macro and micro insights, partly associated with the institutionalist tradition of Thorstein Veblen, James Duesenberry, and Hyman Minsky and with the work of Alfred Chandler and Alfred Eichner on the theory of the firm (see Eichner, 1976; Chandler, 1977).

Some authors have argued that, since the 1970s, financial speculative opportunities have tended to depress the incentives to engage in productive investments and innovation, reducing the corporate sector to a net lender rather than a net borrower in some periods of time and regions.

While all post-Keynesian economists would agree that the deregulation of finance has contributed to an increase in the corporate marginal propensity to save, some refuse to see it as its main or necessary cause. Being no trade-off between investment in financial assets and in real production projects, the low real investment rate, if confirmed, would have to derive from on independent causes. For instance, observing the recent decade-long process of wage repression and dual labour market formation, scholars often suggest that inequality, and not finance, would be at the origin of stagnation in many developed countries. Despite these two views often seeming to differ on theoretical grounds, they are better described as conflicting historical reconstructions of the interaction between specific deregulation policies in financial and labour markets, macroeconomic dynamics, and firms' decisions.

Many contributions have focused also on the unprecedented levels of household indebtedness, found especially in Anglo-Saxon countries. The arguments here concern, on the demand side, the mimetic and emulative behaviour of consumers, the stickiness of consumption habits, and the role of positional goods. All of them much reduced the marginal propensity to save across income groups of households as well as the effect of inequality on the average propensity to save. On the supply side, speculative credit, predatory lending, and insufficient pension schemes have also been identified as causes of a reduction of saving out of income.

ORSOLA COSTANTINI

See also

Effective demand; Fiscal deficits; Growth – wage-led vs profit-led; Paradox of thrift; Washington Consensus

References

Chandler, A.D. Jr. (1977), *The Visible Hand: The Managerial Revolution in American Business*, Cambridge, MA: The Belknap Press of Harvard University Press.
Eichner, A.S. (1976), *The Megacorp and Oligopoly: Micro Foundations of Macro Dynamics*, Cambridge, UK: Cambridge University Press.
Kalecki, M. (1971), *Selected Essays on the Dynamics of the Capitalist Economy 1933–1970*, Cambridge, UK: Cambridge University Press.
Keynes, J.M. (1936), *The General Theory of Employment, Interest and Money*, London: Macmillan.

Secular stagnation

The genesis and revival of the concept of secular stagnation is a testament to Joseph

Schumpeter's (1954, p. 4) suggestion that economic analysis 'is an incessant struggle with creations of our own and our predecessors' minds'. Concerns over capitalism's continued dynamism pervade much of classical political economy, and subsequent Marxian analysis, making any simplistic genealogy of the theory of stagnation dubious. Nevertheless, the theory of secular stagnation was first explicitly proposed by Alvin Hansen (1887–1975), an American economist who spent the majority of his academic career at Harvard University. Though principally remembered for his popular textbook presentations that introduced a generation of American students to the core of Keynesian theory, Hansen's engagement with business cycle theory was long-standing, beginning with his doctoral dissertation (1927). In much of his early work Hansen treated the business cycle downturns, and their accompanying unemployment, as the necessary mechanism through which factor prices adjusted to account for technological shocks that raised the relative productivity of capital (Hansen, 1932, p. 27). Several proximate causes for the subsequent shift in Hansen's thinking have been suggested. The term itself first appears in Hansen (1934), but William Barber (1987) has argued that the US economy's return to recession in 1937 undermined Hansen's understanding of the Great Depression as a severe episode of factor price adjustment, and thereby prompted a substantial elaboration of the concept. Backhouse and Boianovsky (2016) emphasize the stimulus of Keynes's (1937) article for the *Eugenics Review*. There Keynes proposed that declining population growth in Britain would, in the absence of redistributive policies and a reduction in the long-term rate of interest, result in inadequate consumption growth.

Hansen's subsequent reinterpretation of the downturn, detailed in *Full Recovery or Stagnation?* (Hansen, 1938), argued that in a departure from the preceding 150 years, persistent population growth in the United States could no longer be expected. Likewise, the closing of the frontier precluded continued extensive expansion. These factors alone were, however, insufficient to generate secular stagnation. While new epochal industries such as the railroads, or later automobiles and the construction of public roads, had previously fuelled massive waves of investment, the continued emergence of comparable industries was by no means assured. For Hansen (1941, p. 336) it was 'definitely clear that the mere fact that there are seemingly unlimited consumer wants cannot of itself ensure full-employment even with the most perfectly functioning price system'. In such a 'non-expansionist economy' (ibid.) secular stagnation was to be expected in the absence of supplementary demand in the form of public expenditures.

Hansen's thesis attracted considerable contemporary attention. Paul Sweezy adopted much of Hansen's argument in his own *Theory of Capitalist Development* (Sweezy, 1942), and secular stagnation featured prominently in early editions of Paul Samuelson's (1948, pp. 418–23) undergraduate textbook. Still, robust post-war economic growth served to allay the fears of many, and stagnationist models became once more the domain of those outside of the economics profession's mainstream.

First championed by Summers (2013), in the wake of the Great Recession a variety of reworked conceptions of secular stagnation rose to prominence. In Summer's (2014) account, a confluence of forces from reduced population growth, to a slower pace of technological change, income inequality, and increased risk-aversion served to drive a greater wedge between actual rates and the natural rate of interest at which actual and potential output would coincide. By contrast, others like Robert Gordon have suggested that post-war rates of economic growth should be understood as the exception rather than the rule (Gordon, 2015). In this view, productivity stimulus from the increase in mass education that followed the Second World War had run its course by the late 1970s, and secular stagnation constitutes a return to typical rates of potential output growth. As suggested by Hein (2016), the possibility that demand growth might influence the economy's potential rate of growth has been absent from this reanimated discussion of secular stagnation. Whereas Hanson's argument drew explicitly and liberally from classical political economy and the array of contemporary under-consumptionist theories with which he had engaged, much of the twenty-first century discourse of secular stagnation omits any substantive engagement with Marxist and post-Keynesian models of stagnation.

WILLIAM E. McCOLLOCH

See also

Business cycles; Capitalism; Financial crises; Fiscal policy; Inequality

References

Backhouse, R.E. and M. Boianovsky (2016), 'Secular stagnation: the history of a macroeconomic heresy', *European Journal of the History of Economic Thought*, **23** (6), 946–70.
Barber, W.J. (1987), 'The career of Alvin Hansen: a study in intellectual transformation', *History of Political Economy*, **19** (2), 191–205.
Gordon, R.J. (2015), 'Secular stagnation: a supply-side view', *American Economic Review: Papers & Proceedings*, **105** (5), 54–9.
Hansen, A.H. (1927), *Business Cycle Theory: Its Development and Present Status*, New York: Ginn and Co.
Hansen, A.H. (1932), 'The theory of technological progress and the dislocation of employment', *American Economic Review*, **22** (1), 25–31.
Hansen, A.H. (1934), 'Capital goods and the restoration of purchasing power', *Proceedings of the Academy of Political Science*, **16** (1), 11–19.
Hansen, A.H. (1938), *Full Recovery or Stagnation?*, New York: W.W. Norton.
Hansen, A.H. (1941), *Fiscal Policy and Business Cycles*, New York: W.W. Norton.
Hein, E. (2016), 'Secular stagnation or stagnation policy: Steindl after Summers', *PSL Quarterly Review*, **69** (267), 3–47.
Keynes, J.M. (1937), 'Some economic consequences of declining population', *Eugenics Review*, **29** (1), 13–17.
Samuelson, P.A. (1948), *Economics: An Introductory Analysis*, New York: McGraw-Hill.
Schumpeter, J.A. (1954), *History of Economic Analysis*, New York: Oxford University Press.
Summers, L.H. (2013), 'Have we entered an age of secular stagnation?', International Monetary Fund Fourteenth Annual Research Conference in Honor of Stanley Fischer, 8 November, Washington, DC, USA.
Summers, L.H. (2014), 'Reflections on the new secular stagnation hypothesis', in C. Teulings and R. Baldwin (eds), *Secular Stagnation: Facts, Causes, and Cures*, London: CEPR Press, pp. 27–38.
Sweezy, P.M. (1942), *The Theory of Capitalist Development: Principles of Marxian Political Economy*, Oxford: Oxford University Press.

Securitization

Securitization refers to the process of transforming a pool of loans into securities that will be rated and sold in the capital markets, and whose principal and interest payments derive from the income flows generated by the pool of loans held by an independent entity called a 'special purpose vehicle' (SPV). As such, these securities – known as asset-backed securities (ABS), collateralized debt obligations (CDOs), or mortgage-backed securities in the case of a pool of mortgage loans – are claims on the cash flows from the pool of loans (Gorton and Metrick, 2013, p. 2).

Securitization has become significant in the context of the emergence of the new 'originate and distribute' model of banking, which is itself subsumed into the contemporaneous phenomenon of financialization (see Epstein, 2005, p. 3). SPVs, whose role is to issue ABS and manage the pools of loans, are part of the so-called shadow banking, namely those financial institutions that are much less regulated than traditional banking activities and which play a substantial and growing role in the working of our modern economies.

In the traditional 'originate and hold' model of banking, which prevailed in the pre-financialization era, banks would grant credit for production activities and would then hold the loan until maturity. In this framework, identifying the borrower's ability to make timely payments in reimbursing the loan was a central task of banks. Yet, in the 1980s, this formula slowly started to change, as banking was shifting toward the new 'originate and distribute' model, where 'banks can originate loans [mostly to the household sector], earn their fees, and then sell these assets off to investors who would be prepared to accept different layers of exposure to risk' (Seccareccia, 2012, pp. 288–9). Therefore, in the 'originate and distribute' model, banks can remove the loans – and the risks associated to them – from their balance sheet.

In the new model of banking, the role of credit risk assessment has been significantly downplayed, given that the banks originating the loans have supposedly become disconnected from the capital losses associated with non-performing loans (Monvoisin, 2017, p. 187). Because banks are transferring the risks to other market participants, it may appear that securitization is equivalent to eliminating the risks altogether. However, the 2007–2009 Global Financial Crisis and the dire situation of banks at that time strongly contradict this view. Indeed, Gutmann (2008, p. 15)

WILLIAM E. MCCOLLOCH / CARRYL OBERSON

observes that '[i]f anything, securitization just transforms a credit risk into a combination of market and counterparty risks'. To be sure, in light of the complex nature of these instruments, banks themselves were lured into massively investing in these securities, given their apparently appealing risk–return characteristics.

According to orthodox finance theory, securitization might bring about social benefits because, on the one hand, it allows risks to be spread more efficiently among investors with different needs (through the different risk levels associated to each of the tranches of ABS and CDOs) and shall therefore lower the costs of credit. On the other hand, securitized assets can be used as collateral in repurchasing agreements (repos). These factors are believed to both bolster economic growth through increased lending and increase the resilience of the banking system. This view relies on the acceptance of the efficient market hypothesis and, as pointed out by Arcand et al. (2012, p. 23), it is based on the naive 'assumption that larger financial sectors are always good for economic growth'. In fact, the validity of the social benefit hypothesis is seriously questioned even among mainstream economists.

On the contrary, numerous economists emphasize that securitization is associated with high social costs, as it reduces credit quality and increases financial fragility. Lavoie (2012, p. 231) suggests that because of securitization, credit defaults spilled over to the payments system, which was supposedly safer as banks can get rid of the loans. Unprecedented central bank interventions were required to prevent a complete meltdown of the clearing and settlement system, as ABS – which were used to a large extent as collateral in repo transactions – incurred significant impairments when a large number of mortgage holders in the United States were unable to service their debt. Minsky (2008, p. 3) observed already in 1987 that '[s]ecuritization implies that there is no limit to bank initiative in creating credits for there is no recourse to bank capital', which indicates that securitization allows banks to circumvent Basel-type regulation on capital requirements. Lavoie (2012, p. 229) claims that this is certainly the main objective pursued by securitization. Overall, securitization induces banks to originate an ever-greater volume of credits in order to earn fees, and they are encouraged to do so by a myriad of other stakeholders – such as investment banks, rating agencies, insurance companies (as they sell credit default swaps), real estate firms, and so on – that also benefit from it.

The 2007–2009 Global Financial Crisis has left no doubt about the deleterious nature of securitization. However, while the volume of securitized assets has decreased significantly since the 2007 peak, little has been done as regards regulation. The heterodox view seems to converge towards forbidding securitization rather than regulating it, given that developments in financial innovation might (again) allow the regulatory framework to be circumvented (Lavoie, 2012, p. 232; Seccareccia, 2012, p. 297). Finally, we may ask if securitization and financialization at large are the cause of the financial crisis, or if they are a major symptom of a more profound issue affecting the working of our monetary economies. Rossi (2011) argues in favour of the latter, as he identifies the structural origin of the 2007–2009 Global Financial Crisis and proposes to reform the payments system at both domestic and international levels.

CARRYL OBERSON

See also

Bubbles – financial; Financial crises; Financial fragility; Financialization; Shadow banking

References

Arcand, J.-L., E. Berkes and U. Panizza (2012), 'Too much finance?', *International Monetary Fund Working Paper*, No. 161.

Epstein, G. (2005), 'Introduction', in G. Epstein (ed.), *Financialization and the World Economy*, Cheltenham, UK, and Northampton, MA, USA: Edward Elgar, pp. 3–16.

Gorton, G. and A. Metrick (2013), 'Securitization', in G.M. Constantinides, M. Harris and R.M. Stulz (eds), *Handbook of the Economics of Finance – Volume 2A: Corporate Finance*, Amsterdam: Elsevier, North Holland, pp. 1–70.

Gutmann, R. (2008), 'A primer on finance-led capitalism and its crisis', *Revue de la régulation*, 3–4, available at https://journals.openedition.org/regulation/5843 (last accessed 28 December 2020).

Lavoie, M. (2012), 'Financialization, neo-liberalism, and securitization', *Journal of Post Keynesian Economics*, 35 (2), 215–33.

Minsky, H.P. (2008), 'Securitization', *Levy Institute of Bard College Policy Note*, No. 2.

Monvoisin, V. (2017), 'Rethinking the role of banks', in L.-P. Rochon and S. Rossi (eds), *A Modern*

Guide to Rethinking Economics, Cheltenham, UK, and Northampton, MA, USA: Edward Elgar, pp. 182–98.

Rossi, S. (2011), 'Can it happen again? Structural policies to avert further systemic crises', *International Journal of Political Economy*, **40** (2), 61–78.

Seccareccia, M. (2012), 'Financialization and the transformation of commercial banking: understanding the recent Canadian experience before and during the international financial crisis', *Journal of Post Keynesian Economics*, **35** (2), 277–300.

Stockhammer, E. (2010), 'Financialization and the global economy', *Political Economy Research Institute Working Paper*, No. 240.

Selected Essays on the Dynamics of Capitalist Economy 1933–1970

Selected Essays on the Economic Growth of the Socialist and the Mixed Economy (Kalecki, 1972) was published in 1971, a year after the death of Kalecki, and contains 15 chapters based on papers written over 35 years (1933 to 1968) divided into three parts and often in revised form from the initial publication. It includes most, though not all, of Kalecki's important ideas on capitalist economies. It is complemented by similar volumes on planning and socialist economies and on developing economies (see Kalecki, 1972, 1976). A full collection of Kalecki's works is available in the seven volumes of his *Collected Works* edited by Jerzy Osiatynski (see Kalecki 1990–97).

Part I opens with an 'Outline of a theory of business cycle' (Chapter 1) based on the dual relationships between investment and profits: the drive to invest dependent on the rate of profit, and aggregate profits related to accumulation and autonomous consumption. Chapter 3 ('The mechanism of the business upswing') exposes the futility of wage reductions as a means of generating employment. The emphasis is placed on the role of investment stimulating any upswing, while an increase in investment unaccompanied by a wage reduction causes a rise in output.

Chapter 2 ('On foreign trade') is an early expression of the significance of a net export position and the fiscal deficit (here termed 'domestic exports') for the level of economic activity. This provides an early statement, in the framework of workers' savings treated as zero, of the equality between aggregate profits and capitalists' consumption plus investment plus foreign trade balance plus budget deficit.

Chapter 4 ('A theory of commodity, income and capital taxation' written in 1937) was an early analysis of tax incidence outside of a neoclassical framework with allowance for the effects of the tax structure on investment. It concludes that 'capital taxation is perhaps the best way to stimulate business and reduce unemployment' (Kalecki, 1972, p. 42) but that capital taxation would not be applied as it would undermine the 'principle of private property'.

In Part II, Chapter 5 ('Costs and prices') distinguishes between cost-determined prices (mainly identified with manufactured products) and demand-determined prices (mainly identified with commodities), with the focus on cost-determined prices. These prices are set by mark-ups over costs dependent on the 'degree of monopoly', and the chapter continues by discussing the causes of changes in the degree of monopoly. This leads into Chapter 6 ('Distribution of national income'), which develops the significant relationship between the wage share and the degree of monopoly, and the ratio of material bill to wages bill.

Chapter 7 ('The determinants of profits') sets out the profits determination equation as mentioned in Chapter 2 though here including workers' savings. Capitalists' consumption and investment are then modelled to arrive at the equation for the evolution of profits, which is then reviewed empirically.

Chapter 8 ('Determination of national income and consumption') arrives at an equation relating (changes in) income to (changes in) investment in a multiplier-like relationship dependent on the propensity to save out of profits and the (incremental) profit share.

Chapter 9 ('Entrepreneurial capital and investment') is a revised version of the paper on the 'principle of increasing risk', which forms a good basis for understanding credit rationing and limitations on the size of business.

Chapter 10 returns to the theme of 'Determinants of investment' and the generation of business cycles. Investment is viewed here in terms of prior savings out of profits and change in profits (bringing in a form of accelerator). This leads into Chapter 11 ('The business cycle') further developing the analysis of a business cycle.

CARRYL OBERSON / MALCOLM SAWYER

Part III opens with Chapter 12 ('Political aspects of full employment') with Kalecki's warnings on the political constraints on the achievement of full employment through the reactions of bosses, following from arguments elsewhere on the need for fiscal policy and budget deficits to secure full employment.

Chapter 13 ('The problem of effective demand') discusses works of Tugan-Baranovski and Rosa Luxembourg. Chapter 14 covers 'Class struggle and distribution of national income', Kalecki's last published paper in which the concept of the degree of monopoly is broadened out to bring in workers' power and has overtones of the conflict theory of inflation.

Chapter 15 ('Trend and the business cycle') published in 1968 returns to a further formulation of and addresses the relationships between short run and long run summed up in the phrase 'the long-run trend is but a slowly changing component of a chain of short-term situations: it has not independent entity' (p. 165).

MALCOLM SAWYER

See also

Accelerator effects; Business cycles; Inflation – conflict theory of; Mark-up pricing; Profit

References

Kalecki, M. (1972), *Selected Essays on the Economic Growth of the Socialist and the Mixed Economy*, Cambridge, UK: Cambridge University Press.
Kalecki, M. (1976), *Essays on Developing Economies*, Hassocks: Harvester Press.
Kalecki, M. (1990–97), *Collected Works of Michał Kalecki*, volumes 1 to 7, Oxford: Clarendon Press.

Settlement balances

The Bank for International Settlements (BIS) defines 'settlement' as 'an act that discharges obligations in respect of funds or securities transfers between two or more parties', specifying that it is 'the completion of a transaction, wherein the seller transfers securities or financial instruments to the buyer and the buyer transfers money to the seller. A settlement may be final or provisional' (Committee on Payments and Settlement Systems, 2003a, p. 45). Digging into economic literature, in the mid-nineteenth century, some economists found it worth mentioning that the notions of 'settlement' and 'balance' taken separately imply two different mechanisms – 'hence, balance implies not settlement merely, but settlement and pay' (Adams, 1849, p. 29).

In the current framework, a 'settlement balance' can be defined as the positive or negative position with an economic agent like a bank, which results from the completion of a set of transactions in a given space of time like a business day. Moreover, as pointed out by Rogers and Rymes (2000, p. 80), it is by far not unlikely for central banks like the Bank of Canada and the Reserve Bank of Australia to charge higher rates of interest on banks' negative settlement balances while paying lower interest rates on banks' positive settlement balances such that banks might await to have a zero settlement balance.

Indeed, 'the emission of money is the result of a demand for settlement balances from the banking system (in the form of central bank money) or from non-bank agents (in the form of commercial bank money)' (Rossi, 2006, p. 9). The Committee on Payments and Settlement Systems (2003b, p. 2) confirms this in writing that '[d]eposits at the settlement institution and the credit of the settlement institution (when available) are both accepted as money by all the participants in the system'.

The role of central banks as settlement institutions is also 'crucial for the payment system safety. Settlement represents the final execution of payment transaction through money transfer between counterparties. For the settlement to be made, the counterparties, i.e. participants in the transaction, must have open accounts with the settlement institution. Participants' confidence in the settlement procedure depends primarily on the security of the payment instrument in which the settlement is performed (money) and the safety of the institution that performs it' (National Bank of Serbia, 2019, Internet). In general, large-value payment systems as well as securities settlement systems are mostly characterized by the 'use [of] settlement balances at a central bank account to discharge the payment obligations of participants' (Tennekoon, 2015, p. 456).

EDOARDO BERETTA

See also

Central banking; Monetary policy; Money and banking; Money as a means of payment; Settlement system

MALCOLM SAWYER / EDOARDO BERETTA

References

Adams, D. (1849), *Book-Keeping, Containing a Lucid Explanation of the Common Method of Book-Keeping by Single Entry; a New, Concise, and Common-Sense Method of Book-Keeping, for Farmers, Mechanics, Retailers, and Professional Men; Methods of Keeping Books by Figures; Short Methods of Keeping Accounts in a Limited Business; Exercises for the Pupil; and Various Forms Necessary for the Transaction of Business. Accompanied with Blank Books for the Use of Learners. Designed for Schools and Academies*, Keene, NH: J.W. Prentiss & Co.

Committee on Payments and Settlement Systems (2003a), *A Glossary of Terms Used in Payments and Settlement Systems*, Basel: Bank for International Settlements.

Committee on Payments and Settlement Systems (2003b), *The Role of Central Bank Money in Payment Systems*, Basel: Bank for International Settlements.

National Bank of Serbia (2019), *Central Bank Oversight of Payment Systems*, Belgrade: National Bank of Serbia, available online at https://www.nbs.rs/internet/english/35/nadgledanje/funkcija_nadgledanja.html (last accessed on 23 May 2019).

Rogers, C. and T.K. Rymes (2000), 'On "money" in ISLM and AD/AS models', in W. Young and B.Z. Zilberfarb (eds), *IS-LM and Modern Macroeconomics*, Dordrecht: Springer, pp. 77–90.

Rossi, S. (2006), 'Inflation targeting: a conceptual appraisal', paper presented at the international conference on 'Developments in Economic Theory and Policy', University of the Basque Country, Bilbao, Spain, 6–7 July, available online at http://sugarhoover.co.uk/articulosrecibidos/Rossi.pdf (last accessed on 23 May 2019).

Tennekoon, V.S. (2015), 'Settlement balances', in L.-P. Rochon and S. Rossi (eds), *The Encyclopedia of Central Banking*, Cheltenham, UK, and Northampton, MA, USA: Edward Elgar, pp. 455–6.

Settlement system

A settlement system is usually defined as 'a system used to facilitate the settlement of transfers of funds or financial instruments' (Committee on Payments and Settlement Systems, 2003, p. 46). If it is a gross settlement system, then the settlement of funds, as well as securities transfer instructions, takes place on an individual (namely instruction by instruction) basis. At the same time, a real-time gross settlement (RTGS) system represents a specific typology of it, 'in which processing and settlement take place on an order-by-order basis (without netting) in real time (continuously)' (European Central Bank, 2007, p. 452). Time as well as individual basis approach are, therefore, the main characteristics of this typology of settlement systems. A net settlement system involves instead settlement operations being completed on a bilateral or multilateral net basis at one or various 'discrete, prespecified times during the processing day' (Committee on Payments and Settlement Systems, 2003, p. 34). Sometimes, a distinction between types of transfer orders might occur while payment orders might for instance be settled on a net basis and securities transfer orders on an individual basis.

According to Marquardt (1994, p. 52), '[m]ultilateral net settlement systems tend to economize on the use of central bank money relative to gross settlement systems, essentially by substituting explicit or implicit interbank intraday credit, extended through netting for central bank money.' In fact, as also pointed out by Geva (2012, p. 519), gross settlement systems are particularly likely to create liquidity shortfalls because of their high intensity of central bank money. 'Further, the relevant opportunity cost for settling payments using a real-time gross settlement system that operates during the banking day is the opportunity cost of obtaining central bank money during the day to settle payments' (Marquardt, 1994, p. 45).

Since settlement systems aim at facilitating the settlement of transfers of funds, assets or other kinds of financial instruments – in fact, 'most if not all economic transactions involve some form of payment' (Rossi, 2007, p. 64) – it is also possible to distinguish between securities settlement systems and funds transfer systems, where the first ones enable 'transfer[s] of securities, either free of payment (FOP) or against payment (delivery versus payment)' (European Central Bank, 2009, Internet). The second ones (namely funds transfer systems) represent instead an arrangement between several members to set common rules and standardize procedures to handle the transfer, clearing, netting and/or settlement of any kind of monetary obligations concerning their members. As recognized by the Committee on Payments and Settlement Systems (1992, p. 15) in early days, the highest level of credit risk in securities settlement occurs on the settlement date itself. On the contrary, if the securities settlement system is conceived on the basis of delivery-versus-payment mechanisms making

EDOARDO BERETTA

sure that delivery occurs only if the corresponding payment has taken place, too, liquidity risks shrink. In general, '[t]he debate over what constitutes an optimal settlement arrangement, however, has only recently been started' (Vital, 1997, p. 319). In derivatives clearing and settlement, as pointed out by Karacadag et al. (2003, p. 28), a central counterparty is also required, since the central system would absorb the risk of failure of the members involved. As the Bank for International Settlements (2018, Internet) highlights, countries may also differ widely in terms of:

- *system types:* while large-value payments systems (LPVS), which are also known as whole payments systems, are intended to deal with 'large value money transfers' (Kumar Khandelwal, 2007, Internet), retail payments systems are intended to deal with large volumes of relatively small-value payments made by cheques, credit transfers, direct debits and card payments, as reminded by the Bank for International Settlements (2012, Internet). In turn, fast payments systems rather presume the ability to 'complete a payment almost immediately and at any time' (Bech et al., 2017, p. 59);
- *settlement types:* some payments systems are characterized by RTGS mechanisms, which handle transactions on a continuous order-by-order basis, while others have adopted a multilateral netting approach, which means that they offset 'obligations between or among multiple participants to result in a single net position per participant' (Bank for International Settlements, 2016c, Internet). By contrast, a payments system based on bilateral netting implies the 'offsetting of obligations between two parties thereby reducing the number and value of payments or deliveries needed to settle a set of transactions' (Bank for International Settlements, 2016b, Internet), which in turn aims at limiting the operational effort involved by every transaction undertaken/ received by each affiliated member. As the term 'batch settlement' implies, such payments systems involve the settlement of payments, transfer instructions or other obligations on a grouped basis at one or several times during each processing day (Bank for International Settlements, 2016a, Internet);
- *ownership and degree of centralization:* the central bank and commercial banks as well as payments associations can be the legal owners of the payments system, which might be accordingly more (or less) centralized.

As Rossi (2004, p. 16) points out, '[w]hat cross-border settlement systems are still lacking is a settlement institution for national central banks themselves that would homogenize the various national currencies by the emission of a supranational central bank money.' More precisely, 'Rossi suggests the introduction of a real-time gross-settlement system between countries, to be run by an international settlement institution issuing supranational currency every time a final payment has to be carried out between any two monetary spaces' (Bellofiore, 2014, p. 4). This would allow for payment finality, which corresponds to 'a transfer of funds [or] a transfer of securities that have become irrevocable and unconditional' (Auer, 2019, p. 11; see also Committee on Payments and Settlement Systems, 2003, p. 496). '[O]nce a payment has made its way through the national payment system and into the books of the central bank, it is final by law and cannot be revoked' (Auer, 2019, p. 11). At the international level this would represent a necessary step towards a payments system guaranteeing for the final settlement of every cross-border transaction. In other words, the above-mentioned institutional setting would transpose at the global level the principle that 'neither can pay through its own acknowledgement of debt – which is a mere promise of payment and does not constitute a final debt' (Rossi, 2017, p. 118).

EDOARDO BERETTA

See also

Central banking; International clearing union; Money and banking; Money as a means of payment; Settlement balances

References

Auer, R. (2019), 'Beyond the doomsday economics of "proof-of-work" in cryptocurrencies', *Bank for International Settlements Working Paper*, No. 765.
Bank for International Settlements (2012), *Retail Payment System*, Basel: Bank for International Settlements, available online at https://www.bis.org/cpmi/publ/d00b.htm?&selection=61&scop

e=CPMI&c=a&base=term (last accessed on 28 February 2019).
Bank for International Settlements (2016a), *Batch Settlement*, Basel: Bank for International Settlements, available online at https://www.bis.org/cpmi/publ/d00b.htm?&selection=4&scope=CPMI&c=a&base=term (last accessed on 28 February 2019).
Bank for International Settlements (2016b), *Bilateral Netting*, Basel: Bank for International Settlements, available online at https://www.bis.org/cpmi/publ/d00b.htm?&selection=178&scope=CPMI&c=a&base=term (last accessed on 28 February 2019).
Bank for International Settlements (2016c), *Multilateral Netting*, Basel: Bank for International Settlements, available online at https://www.bis.org/cpmi/publ/d00b.htm?&selection=178&scope=CPMI&c=a&base=term (last accessed on 28 February 2019).
Bank for International Settlements (2018), *Table PS1: Features of Selected Payment Systems*, Basel: Bank for International Settlements, available online at https://www.bis.org/statistics/payment_stats/rb_qual_inf_table_ps1.pdf (last accessed on 27 February 2019).
Bech, M., Y. Shimizu and P. Wong (2017), 'The quest for speed in payments', *Bank for International Settlements Quarterly Review*, March, 57–68.
Bellofiore, R. (2014), 'The Great Recession and the contradictions of contemporary capitalism', in R. Bellofiore and G. Vertova (eds), *The Great Recession and the Contradictions of Contemporary Capitalism*, Cheltenham, UK, and Northampton, MA, USA: Edward Elgar, pp. 7–25.
Caprio, G. (ed.), *Handbook of Key Global Financial Markets, Institutions, and Infrastructure*, Boston: Elsevier.
Committee on Payments and Settlement Systems (1992), *Delivery Versus Payment in Securities Settlement Systems – Report prepared by the Committee on Payments and Settlement Systems of the Central Banks of the Group of Ten Countries*, Basel: Bank for International Settlements.
Committee on Payments and Settlement Systems (2003), *A Glossary of Terms Used in Payments and Settlement Systems*, Basel: Bank for International Settlements.
European Central Bank (2007), *Blue Book: Payment and Securities Settlement Systems in the European Union (Volume I) – Euro Area Countries (August 2007)*, Frankfurt am Main: European Central Bank.
European Central Bank (2009), *Glossary of Terms Related to Payment, Clearing and Settlement Systems*, Frankfurt am Main: European Central Bank, available online at https://www.ecb.europa.eu/pub/pdf/other/glossaryrelatedtopaymentclearingandsettlementsystemsen.pdf (last accessed on 25 February 2019).
Geva, B. (2012), 'Global payment and settlement systems', in G. Caprio, D.W. Arner, T. Beck, C.W. Calomiris, L. Neal, C. Veron Karacadag, V. Sundararajan and J. Elliott (2003), 'Managing risks in financial market development: the role of sequencing', *International Monetary Fund Working Paper*, No. WP/03/116.
Karacadag, C., V. Sundararajan and J. Elliott (2003), 'Managing risks in financial market development: the role of sequencing', *International Monetary Fund Working Paper*, No. 03/116.
Kumar Khandelwal, S. (2007), 'Risks in large value payment systems', *Journal of Internet Banking and Commerce*, **12** (1), available online at https://papers.ssrn.com/sol3/papers.cfm?abstract_id=1330893 (last accessed on 27 February 2019).
Marquardt, J.C. (1994), 'Monetary issues and payment system design', in B.J. Summers (ed.), *The Payment System: Design, Management, and Supervision*, Washington, DC: International Monetary Fund, pp. 41–52.
Rossi, S. (2004), 'Central bank money and payment finality', *Research Laboratory of Monetary Economics Working Paper*, No. 11.
Rossi, S. (2007), *Money and Payments in Theory and Practice*, London and New York: Routledge.
Rossi, S. (2017), 'Money and interest-rate determination in a system with no reserve requirements', in L.-P. Rochon and S. Rossi (eds), *Advances in Endogenous Money Analysis*, Cheltenham, UK, and Northampton, MA, USA: Edward Elgar, pp. 111–28.
Vital, C. (1997), 'The architecture of real time gross settlement system', *Swiss National Bank Quarterly Bulletin*, 4, 319–37.

Shadow banking – extent of

The term 'shadow banking' was coined by McCulley (2007) in a speech that he gave at the Jackson Hole symposium. McCulley used this metaphor to compare the activity of some entities that were part of the securitization chain with that of 'real banks'. This comparison relied on a specific conception of banking, according to which banks are mere intermediaries of loanable funds. Indeed, for McCulley (2009) banks are in the business of 'maturity and credit quality transformation': they borrow depositors' savings on a short-term basis and 'redeploy that money' into longer-term and riskier loans. Banks can do so because of their public backstop (their access to the US Federal Reserve and deposit insurance). Seen from this perspective, his comparison with banks seems relevant. If one believes that a bank is a regulated and publicly backstopped intermediary that borrows depositors' savings at short notice to make long-term loans, it makes sense to consider that unregulated financial intermediaries (conduits, investment vehicles, and so on) that rely on short-term borrowing (commercial paper, repos, and so forth) to buy long-term assets (mortgage-backed securities, collateralized debt obligations, and you name it) are 'shadow banks'.

After McCulley's speech, the concept of shadow banking gained in popularity and a thriving literature emerged. The authors of this literature analysed shadow banking as a new form of credit intermediation (Bouguelli, 2019). In the traditional banking system, banks directly intermediate savers' deposits to borrowers. In contrast, the intermediation chain is longer in the shadow banking system, where several intermediaries stand in between savers and borrowers. In their intermediation process, banks are supposed to transform risk-free, liquid and short-term deposits into riskier, illiquid and long-term loans. The shadow banking system is said to perform similar functions following a functional division of labour: some intermediaries transform credit risk, others transform maturity or liquidity risks. But the outcome of the intermediation process is the same: borrowers obtain credit and savers get a deposit-like claim. Since the shadow banking system is supposed to perform these useful functions (credit intermediation and production of safe assets), it follows that regulation should be aimed at preserving its main benefits while managing the risks that it poses.

Two views on shadow banking can be found in post-Keynesian economics (Lavoie, 2019). The first strand is associated with the horizontalist approach and with monetary circuit theory. According to this view, the shadow banking metaphor is irrelevant. This is because the shadow banking system does something that is fundamentally different from what traditional banks do (Bouguelli, 2019). While banks grant loans by issuing money *ex nihilo*, the shadow banking system only kicks in afterwards, to provide an alternative way to fund these loans. Indeed, the bulk of the shadow banking system is not a source of credit for the non-financial private sector: it simply turns the claims originated by banks (loans) into securities. Put simply, banks grant loans and move a part of these loans off their balance sheets, in the shadow banking system that will use them to produce securities. And since the shadow banking system is composed of mere intermediaries, it has to borrow the funds to carry out its operations. When banks grant loans, they create the 'raw materials' used by the shadow banking system to produce securities (loans) and the deposits that it will need to borrow to acquire these claims (or securities backed by them). It follows that the shadow banking system cannot grow if the traditional banking system does not expand in the first place.

The second strand is related to the structuralist approach. These authors abandon the traditional post-Keynesian distinction between banks and non-bank financial institutions (NBFIs). Instead of differentiating money creation from intermediation, they focus on liquidity creation (Nersisyan and Dantas, 2017). Seen from this perspective, banks and NBFIs play a similar role: they both create liquidity. This view, which is based on the famous hierarchy of money, leads to the conclusion that NBFIs face little constraints in their expansion.

Apart from their differences, both views share common grounds. Most importantly, all post-Keynesian economists agree on the fact that the development of the shadow banking system increases financial fragility. Hence, they believe that it should be eliminated or substantially constrained.

RUDY BOUGUELLI

See also

Banking and finance; Financial fragility; Horizontalism; Monetary circuit; Structuralism

References

Bouguelli, R. (2019), 'Is shadow banking really akin to banking? A critical analysis in light of monetary theory', *Journal of Post Keynesian Economics*, 43 (1), 1–27.

Lavoie, M. (2019), 'Advances in the Post-Keynesian analysis of money and finance', in P. Arestis and M. Sawyer (eds), *Frontiers of Heterodox Macroeconomics*, Cham: Springer International Publishing, pp. 89–129.

McCulley, P. (2007), 'Teton reflections', *PIMCO Global Central Bank Focus*, Newport Beach, CA, available at https://www.pimco.com/en-us/insights/economic-and-market-commentary/global-central-bank-focus/teton-reflections/ (last accessed on 17 May 2021).

McCulley, P. (2009), 'Saving capitalistic banking from itself', *PIMCO Global Central Bank Focus*, Newport Beach, CA, available at https://www.

pimco.com/en-us/insights/economic-and-market-commentary/global-central-bank-focus/saving-capitalistic-banking-from-itself (last accessed on 17 May 2021).

Nersisyan, Y. and F. Dantas (2017), 'Rethinking liquidity creation: banks, shadow banks and the elasticity of finance', *Journal of Post Keynesian Economics*, **40** (3), 279–99.

Shadow banking – origins

The origin of the shadow banking system, previously known as the parallel banking system, is located in the blurring of the operations carried out by banks in the North American payments system. This was a concerning issue for Minsky, D'Arista, and Schlesinger at The Declining Role of Banking conference in 1994, and consists in the presence of financial intermediation operations carried out by 'multifunctional financial conglomerates and the emergence of an unregulated parallel banking system. Along with other powerful trends like securitization, these events have broken down the carefully compartmentalized credit and capital marketplace established in New Deal legislation 60 years ago. Mortgage companies, less regulated than their thrift competitors, constitute a parallel housing finance system. Similarly, finance companies anchor the lending side of a parallel banking system. The finance companies obtain their funds from banks as well as from the money market mutual funds (MMMFs) that buy their notes, bonds, and commercial paper' (D'Arista and Schlesinger, 1994, p. 289).

For Minsky (1994, p. 55), this disintermediation and the 'declining' role of banks relate to the 'efficacy of monetary policy operations. The channels by which Federal Reserve operations impact upon the economy may no longer be through the availability or cost of financing but rather by affecting uncertainty, by affecting the evaluation by portfolio managers of the viability of enterprises and the stability of markets. When Central Bank operations affect the evaluation of uncertainty by financial market agents, market reactions will often be out of line with the size of the operation.'

Concerns about the increase in parallel banking operations were even manifested years later in Greenspan's question about "'irrational exuberance" [that] has unduly escalated asset values, which then become subject to unexpected and prolonged contractions as they have in Japan over the past decade' (Greenspan, 1996, Internet). The exponential growth of the parallel banking system's operations made it necessary to repeal large parts of the Glass–Steagall Act, which had separated commercial and investment banking since 1933 in order to approve the Financial Services Modernization Act known as the Gramm–Leach–Bliley Act in 1999. This favoured the inclusion of investment operations and commercial banks in investment funds. An example, before the proclamation of that Act, is the merger of Citicorp and Travelers Group to form Citigroup (1998).

Within the framework of gradual financial deregulation, set in motion during the 1970s, off-balance-sheet operations' bases for commercial banks were provided. Subsequently, operations of the parallel banking system deepened because of legal changes. The 'over the counter' operations, along with technological innovation were moulding the shadow banking system and also creating international liquidity, which would cause the Global Financial Crisis along with the fall of Lehman Brothers in 2008. When pointing at the Federal Reserve as responsible for uncertainty, Minsky anticipated how the shadow banking system's 'approach had opened up gaps in oversight of critical areas with trillions of dollars at risk, such as the SBS [shadow banking system] and over-the-counter derivatives markets' (National Commission on the Causes of the Financial and Economic Crisis in the United States, 2011, p. xviii). While the shadow banking system contributed to the Global Financial Crisis, it also contributed to reducing the risk of financial instability by following it up, using the Monitoring Universe of Non-bank Financial Intermediation through the Financial Stability Board (FSB) created after the eruption of that crisis.

The parallel or shadow banking system cannot be comprehended without understanding financialization and securitization (Girón, 2013, p. 513). Villeroy de Galhau (2018, p. 8) mentions how 'this welcome diversification of financing can be achieved through the development of sound securitization in order to free up banks' balance sheets and thus encourage the issuance of new loans, while providing safe assets to investors and offering bond market exposure to borrowers who generally do not have access to this form of financing, such as small and medium-sized enterprises. At the same time, the development of new forms of debt such as microcredit, solidarity-based finance and marketplace lending are filling some gaps, especially for micro-enterprises.'

The FSB created a classification for non-bank financial institutions by taking into account the economic functions they perform: (1) money mutual funds, fixed-income funds, mixed funds, credit hedge funds, real estate funds; (2) finance companies, leasing/factoring companies, consumer credit companies; (3) brokers-dealers, securities finance companies; (4) credit insurance companies, financial guarantors, monolines; (5) securitization vehicles, structured finance vehicles, asset-backed branches (Financial Stability Board, 2018, p. 45).

ALICIA GIRÓN

See also

Banking and finance; Banking regulations; Financial crises; Financial liberalization; Money and banking

References

D'Arista, J. and T. Schlesinger (1994), 'The parallel banking system', *Annual Conference on Bank Structure and Competition*, Chicago: Federal Reserve of Chicago.
Financial Stability Board (2018), *Global Shadow Banking Monitoring Report 2017*, available at https://www.fsb.org/2018/03/global-shadow-banking-monitoring-report-2017/ (last accessed on 17 May 2021).
Girón, A. (2013), 'Crisis, dollar and shadow financial system', *Journal of Economic Issues*, **46** (2), 511–17.
Greenspan, A. (1996), 'The challenge of central banking in a democratic society', *Lecture for the American Enterprise*, Institute for Public Policy Research, Washington, DC, available at https://www.aei.org/research-products/speech/the-challenge-of-central-banking-in-a-democratic-society/ (last accessed 17 May 2021).
Minsky, H. (1994), 'Financial instability and the decline (?) of banking: public policy implications', *Annual Conference on Bank Structure and Competition*, Federal Reserve Bank of Chicago.
National Commission on the Causes of the Financial and Economic Crisis in the United States (2011), *The Financial Crisis Inquiry Report*, Washington, DC: U.S. Government Printing Office.
Villeroy de Galhau, F. (2018), 'Between "shadow" banking and an angelic vision of the market: towards a balanced development of non-bank finance', *Financial Stability Review*, Paris: Banque de France, pp. 7–12.

ALICIA GIRÓN / JOHN E. KING

Social classes

Two hundred years ago no-one would have doubted the importance of social classes in the formulation of economic theory. David Ricardo in particular based his entire theoretical system on distinguishing the three classes in early nineteenth-century Britain, namely land owners, capitalists and workers. They owned three distinct productive inputs (land, capital, and labour) and received three different types of income (rent, profits, and wages). In Ricardo's model, only capitalists save; workers are too poor, and land owners too profligate, so that the relative income shares of the three classes have very significant implications for economic growth in addition to the distribution of income. Half a century later, Karl Marx also emphasized the class nature of contemporary British capitalism, making particular reference to the deep-rooted conflict between capitalists and workers.

Only with the onset of neoclassical economic theory in the final quarter of the nineteenth century was the attention paid to social classes replaced by a focus on individual behaviour. This survived the revival of macroeconomics in the Keynesian Revolution, with the so-called Grand Neoclassical Synthesis treating individuals as somehow outside society and ignoring issues of power, role conflict, and class struggle. Critics noted that mainstream theorists also treated production as 'asocial', seeing it as a natural process rather than a social one. Post-Keynesian economics, in contrast, 'is based on the premise that capitalism is a class-divided society' (Arestis, 1992, p. 101).

Keynes himself did of course understand that he was living in a capitalist society. He wrote a lot about it in his political essays, including discussion of the different social classes and the political parties that represented them. But these comments are found only in his political writings, and there is not a trace of them in his economic texts, least of all in *The General Theory*, where the celebrated reference to the 'euthanasia of the rentier' concerns the distributive consequences of a policy of very low interest rates and has no theoretical significance. And the 373-page index to his *Collected Writings* contains just four references to 'class war'. Two of these appear in letters addressed to Keynes and one is an editorial note, so the only mention that can be found in the

29 volumes (admittedly a famous one) comes in his address to a Liberal Party summer school, where he announced that 'the *class* war will find me on the side of the educated *bourgeoisie*' (Keynes, 1925/2010, p. 297; italics in the original). He did not say whether he expected this to place him at odds with the uneducated bourgeoisie.

Michał Kalecki's position was very different, as Sawyer (1985, pp. 149–53) noted in his intellectual biography of the Polish theorist, in which a four-page section on the 'similarities between Kalecki and Marx' is devoted to the class nature of capitalist society and the related class antagonisms. For Kalecki, capitalism is not a harmonious regime but is instead characterized by continual conflict between capital and labour over the distribution of income. His last paper, published a year after his death, was entitled 'Class struggle and the distribution of income' (Kalecki, 1971). In Kaleckian models the profit share is determined by the outcome of social conflict, including wage bargaining in the labour market and the average profit mark-up in the product market. It has important macroeconomic consequences. Since workers save little or nothing, '[s]avings are largely made by capitalists, for reasons connected with production and profits, and not as part of utility calculations over the optimal split between consumption and saving' (Sawyer, 1985, p. 151). And they are 'ploughed back, usually (but not always) by the firm making the saving (i.e. internal finance) into investment' (ibid.).

These insights have been formalized by the Kaleckian current in post-Keynesian thought, in elaborate class-based macroeconomic models (see Arestis, 1992, for an early example). More recently, a substantial literature has emerged on wage-led growth, a macroeconomic regime in which capitalists benefit as a class from the consumption spending of workers, even though individual capitalists always have an incentive to resist wage increases for their own employees (King, 2019). However, nothing at all like any of this can be found in the work of the 'fundamentalist Keynesian' current, represented by Paul Davidson, which regards *The General Theory* as the source of its fundamental theoretical insights. The third current, represented by Hyman Minsky, does focus on the decisions (and the errors) of a section of the capitalist class. Minsky's representative agent is a financial capitalist, not a classless consumer, as in neoclassical theory, nor an industrial capitalist, as in Marx and Kalecki, and class conflict does not play an essential role in his analysis.

A rather similar distinction between entrepreneurs and rentiers can be found in the work of some other post-Keynesian theorists, such as Lavoie (1992, pp. 370–71); the rentiers of today's capitalist economy are comparable in some respects with the land owners of Ricardo's day. Arestis (1992, p. 103) points to the emergence of 'a new class of professionally trained managers and executives, who are at the centre of decision-making', even though they are not, strictly speaking, themselves capitalists. And Kalecki himself identified what he termed 'intermediate regimes' in developing countries, characterized by 'a powerful lower-middle class and rich or medium-rich peasants amalgamated with state capitalism (the managers' class)' (Sawyer, 1985, p. 153). Thus, post-Keynesian economists do recognize that class structure is more complicated than a simple division between capitalists and workers.

JOHN E. KING

See also

Capitalism; Euthanasia of the rentier; Growth – wage-led vs profit-led; Income distribution; Power

References

Arestis, P. (1992), *The Post-Keynesian Approach to Economics*, Aldershot, UK, and Brookfield, VT, USA: Edward Elgar.

Kalecki, M. (1971), 'Class struggle and the distribution of national income', *Kyklos*, **24** (1), 1–9.

Keynes, J.M. (1925/2010), 'Am I a liberal?', in *The Collected Writings of John Maynard Keynes. Vol. IX: Essays in Persuasion*, Cambridge, UK: Cambridge University Press, pp. 295–306.

Keynes, J.M. (1936), *The General Theory of Employment, Interest and Money*, London: Macmillan.

King, J.E. (2019), 'Some obstacles to wage-led growth', *Review of Keynesian Economics*, **7** (3), 308–20.

Lavoie, M. (1992), *Foundations of Post-Keynesian Economic Analysis*, Aldershot, UK, and Brookfield, VT, USA: Edward Elgar.

Sawyer, M. (1985), *The Economics of Michał Kalecki*, Basingstoke: Macmillan.

JOHN E. KING

Socialization of investment

The concept of 'socialization of investment' embodies key aspects of Keynes's theorizing and policy-making. This expression occurs in *The General Theory*'s concluding discussion of economic policies, this apparently being its only explicit occurrence in his published writings: 'I conceive, therefore, that a somewhat comprehensive socialisation of investment will prove the only means of securing an approximation to full employment' (Keynes, 1936, p. 378).

However, the concept of socialization has a much longer history in Keynes's policy writings from at least 1920 onwards, as he pursued desirable economic and social outcomes in democratic capitalist economies.

Being a politically loaded term signifying different things to different people in the political spectrum, one needs to distinguish between what Keynes does, and does not, mean. In general terms, his writings indicate that the socialization of X means policies to bring X under State influence, management or control, where X is some desirable social objective that *laissez-faire* fails to deliver adequately. Both X and its socialization can take various forms:

(i) control of the level of a critical variable, such as aggregate investment, using State-sponsored additions to private sector levels (say directly by public works or indirectly by contracting out);
(ii) changes to policy instruments (such as tax, subsidy or interest rates) to influence key variables (such as investment, consumption, inflation or exchange rates);
(iii) the establishment of public or semi-public institutions with socio-economic functions;
(iv) nationalization (State ownership) to some degree in rare instances.

In this framework, socialization refers to significant State activities of well-judged kinds aimed at desirable social objectives within a system allowing market forces to play major (but not exclusive) roles.

Reflecting his ethical philosophy and liberal–socialist politics, Keynes saw full employment and lower inequality as highly desirable objectives. Movement towards them not only directly increased the ethical goodness of society, but also reduced the appeal of revolution as the only process for righting social ills, a process capable of sliding into authoritarianism and the suppression of valuable goodness-promoting freedoms. His stance opposed extreme versions of socialization that replaced the market system with State ownership, central planning and a command economy, that is, a 'State socialism' covering 'most of the economic life of the community', (Keynes, 1936, p. 378). Markets and their advantages were retained, but their major shortcomings corrected using social means to serve social ends. The result was modified forms of capitalism, with the State (not markets alone) in the saddle and aimed at well-managed market societies.

Of Keynes's many explicit or implicit references to policies of socialization, only a summary is given here. In 1920, in interest rate policy, he favoured dear money over a discriminatory policy that assumed 'a *very high degree* of socialisation' of the supply of capital that neither the government nor the market were at present capable of implementing wisely (Keynes, 1977, pp. 182–3, emphasis added). In 1924–6, the State's most important agenda concerned those 'decisions made by *no one*' if the State did not make them (Keynes, 1972, p. 291, emphasis added). In 1927, State policy focused on 'deliberate regulation from the centre' in spheres of action where individuals were powerless on their own (Keynes, 1981a, p. 647). In 1929, an economics general staff was proposed to assist the 'organisation of industry and commerce, national finance and the distribution of wealth' and hence the 'purposive guidance of the evolution of economic life' (Keynes, 1981b, pp. 22, 27).

In 1930, he suggested the level of investment become a State affair based on 'collective wisdom and long views', and less on 'individual caprice' (Keynes, 1971, p. 145). In 1932, he welcomed a Labour Party proposal to establish a national investment board and argued that its scope should be widened (Keynes, 1982, pp. 133–7). In 1936, the 'two outstanding faults' of economic society were suboptimal levels of employment in production, and high income/wealth inequalities in distribution (Keynes, 1936, pp. 372–4), both requiring State activity for their reduction.

In 1940 his deferred wages plan aimed to control war-time inflation and assist post-war recovery. In 1942, he offered strong, but qualified, support for Beveridge's proposals concerning social insurance, but went further in generalizing them.

RODERICK O'DONNELL

We need to extend, rather than curtail, the theory and practice of extra-budgetary funds for state operated or supported functions. Whether it is the transport system, the Electricity Board ... or Social Security. The more socialised we become, the more important it is to associate as closely as possible, the cost of particular services with the sources out of which they are provided .... This is the only way to preserve sound accounting, to measure efficiency, to maintain economy, and to keep the public properly aware of what things cost. (Keynes, 1980, pp. 224–5 and p. 252)

In 1944, he favoured the fuller nationalization of electricity production and distribution, while objecting to the unfairness of the proposed financial technique – existing shareholders should be completely bought out, not be left bearing the risk without influence over management (Keynes, 1978, pp. 454–8).

In summary, socialization (in the above sense) was a longstanding theme in Keynes's thought. Of its many forms, the socialization of aggregate investment was typically the most important for achieving full employment and lower inequality in a democratic society.

RODERICK O'DONNELL

See also

Fiscal policy; Full employment; Inequality; Investment – theories of; *The General Theory of Employment, Interest and Money*

References

Keynes, J.M. (1936), *The General Theory of Employment, Interest and Money*, London: Macmillan.
Keynes, J.M. (1971), *A Treatise on Money: The Applied Theory of Money*, in *The Collected Writings of John Maynard Keynes, Volume VI*, London: Macmillan.
Keynes, J.M. (1972), *Essays in Persuasion*, in *The Collected Writings of John Maynard Keynes, Volume IX*, London: Macmillan.
Keynes, J.M. (1977), *Activities 1920–1922. Treaty Revision and Reconstruction*, in *The Collected Writings of John Maynard Keynes, Volume XVII*, London: Macmillan.
Keynes, J.M. (1978), *Activities 1939–1945. Internal War Finance*, in *The Collected Writings of John Maynard Keynes, Volume XXII*, London: Macmillan.
Keynes, J.M. (1980), *Activities 1940–1946. Shaping the Post-War World: Employment and Commodities*, in *The Collected Writings of John Maynard Keynes, Volume XXVII*, London: Macmillan.
Keynes, J.M. (1981a), *Activities 1922–1929. The Return to Gold and Industrial Policy Part II*, in *The Collected Writings of John Maynard Keynes, Volume XIX*, London: Macmillan.
Keynes, J.M. (1981b), *Activities 1929–1931. Rethinking Employment and Unemployment Policies*, in *The Collected Writings of John Maynard Keynes, Volume XX*, London: Macmillan.
Keynes, J.M. (1982), *Activities 1931–1939. World Crises and Policies in Britain and America*, in *The Collected Writings of John Maynard Keynes, Volume XXI*, London: Macmillan.

Sraffian economics

By Sraffian economics one generally means the set of lines of analysis that originated from Piero Sraffa's contributions.

In his two major publications, the 'Introduction' (Sraffa, 1951) to his edition of *The Works and Correspondence of David Ricardo* and *Production of Commodities by Means of Commodities* (Sraffa, 1960), Sraffa rediscovered the logical structure of the classical approach to the theory of value and distribution. He also proposed a solution of analytical problems left open by the classical authors and laid the foundations for a criticism of marginalist theories. Sraffian economics deepens as well as extends these contributions (see Aspromourgos, 2004).

Since the end of the 1920s (see Garegnani, 2005), Sraffa discovered the diversity of the structure of classical theory compared to that of contemporary marginalist theories, with the notion of 'surplus' and thereby the conditions of reproduction being crucial for the former and unimportant for the latter. The thesis of the continuity between the two approaches, which had even determined the attribute of 'neoclassical' for marginalist authors, was thus overturned.

Sraffa, however, also reformulates classical theories, by overcoming the problem of the treatment of value in terms of incorporated labour with his price equations, which simultaneously determine relative prices and the uniform profit rate. However, the structure of the classical theory is maintained: the main determinants of the value of commodities are the real wage (separately determined by historical, social and institutional circumstances), the quantities produced, and the technical conditions of production (see Roncaglia, 1978;

RODERICK O'DONNELL / ATTILIO TREZZINI

Garegnani, 1984; Kurz and Salvadori, 1995). Sraffa also shows the possibility of taking the profit rate, instead of the real wage rate, as the distributive variable separately determined.

The rediscovery and reformulation of classical political economy is such a crucial contribution that most authors working in developing it would reject the expression 'Sraffian economics' and indicate their theoretical position as the 'modern reappraisal of the surplus approach'.

In his book, Sraffa (1960) shows that the change in the value of heterogeneous capital goods following any change in distribution is as complex and unpredictable that when the means of production are treated as a single productive factor, capital, conceived as a homogeneous quantity and measured in value, it is impossible to order the techniques according to their *capital intensity*. It is therefore impossible to consistently construct demand functions for factors with the formal properties necessary for the marginalist explanation of distribution and prices.

These insights develop into an articulated critique of the marginalist notion of capital becoming one of the lines of research of Sraffian economics. In the 1960s and 1970s, a first phase of the debate was centred on the notion of capital proper to the traditional long-period versions of marginalist theories. Marginalist authors, mainly Samuelson (1966), reacted to Sraffa's criticism by trying to redefine capital so as to represent the essence of marginalist theories but avoid the phenomena of reverse capital deepening and re-switching of techniques. Direct pupils of Sraffa, but also authors less close to his theses, demonstrated that the principles and theorems developed to contrast those criticisms were inconsistent, as Samuelson (1966) himself had to admit.

The debate on capital then went through a second phase. Marginalist authors reacted by abandoning long-run equilibria and adopting neo-Walrasian temporary or intertemporal equilibria. According to Sraffian economists, however, these reformulations only apparently overcame the inconsistencies: on the one hand, the positions determined by the new versions of the theory cannot act as centers of gravity for actual magnitudes, thereby losing relevance for the study of reality; on the other hand, the new formulations can only apparently do without a notion of capital in value that, actually, reappears in the equality between saving and investments, which the theory requires to be studied in terms of value. (For guidance on this complex debate, see Lazzarini (2011) on the first phase, and Fratini (2019) on the second.)

Demonstrating the impossibility of constructing decreasing demand functions for factors is an alternative route to the principle of effective demand (Garegnani, 1983), which moving on the ground of the long-run tendencies of economies appears more solid than the short-period Keynesian route.

The reappraisal of classical theories – neutral with respect to output determination – constitutes a sounder basis for extending the principle of effective demand and, in particular, the Keynesian hypothesis on saving and investment to the analysis of economic growth. Thus, since the 1990s, a classical–Keynesian approach to economic growth has developed, which takes into account the crucial role of demand expansion in determining the level of output but also the development over time of productive capacity (see Trezzini and Palumbo, 2016).

The classical–Keynesian approach to the theory of output has been the basis for a strand of works on economic policy issues. Deprived of the constraint of the tendency to full employment and, with it, of the notion of Pareto optimum, the analysis of policy issues can be reversed in almost all its main aspects and on almost all the themes. The issue of public debt, the notion of potential output, the effects of expansionary policies and different monetary phenomena have been the objects of analyses by Sraffian economists since the 2000s.

Although the analyses based on it are not quantitatively dominant, the breadth of issues treated and their diffusion among younger generations of scholars make Sraffian economics one of the most promising among non-mainstream economic approaches.

ATTILIO TREZZINI

See also

Capital theory controversies; Effective demand; Neoclassical economics; *Production of Commodities by Means of Commodities*; Profit

References

Aspromourgos, T. (2004), 'Sraffian research programmes and unorthodox economics', *Review of Political Economy*, **16** (2), 179–206.

Fratini, S.M. (2019), 'On the second stage of the Cambridge capital controversy', *Journal of Economic Surveys*, **33** (4), 1073–93.

Garegnani, P. (1983), 'Two routes to effective demand: comment on Kregel', in J. Kregel (ed.), *Distribution, Effective Demand and International Economic Relations*, London: Macmillan, pp. 69–80.

Garegnani, P. (1984), 'Value and distribution in the classical economists and Marx', *Oxford Economic Papers*, **36** (2), 291–325.

Garegnani, P. (2005), 'On a turning point in Sraffa's theoretical and interpretative position in the late 1920s', *European Journal of the History of Economic Thought*, **12** (3), 453–92.

Kurz, H.D. and N. Salvadori (1995), *Theory of Production: A Long-Period Analysis*, Cambridge, UK: Cambridge University Press.

Lazzarini, A. (2011), *Revisiting the Cambridge Capital Theory Controversies: A Historical and Analytical Study*, Pavia, IT: Pavia University Press.

Roncaglia, A. (1978), *Sraffa and the Theory of Prices*, New York: Wiley.

Samuelson, P.A. (1966), 'A summing up', *Quarterly Journal of Economics*, **80** (4), 568–83.

Sraffa, P. (1951), 'Introduction', in P. Sraffa (ed.), *The Works and Correspondence of David Ricardo*, Cambridge, UK: Cambridge University Press, vol. 1, pp. xiii–xiv.

Sraffa, P. (1960), *Production of Commodities by Means of Commodities: Prelude to a Critique of Economic Theory*, Cambridge, UK: Cambridge University Press.

Trezzini, A. and A. Palumbo (2016), 'The theory of output in the modern classical approach: main principles and controversial issues', *Review of Keynesian Economics*, **4** (4), 503–22.

Stabilizing an Unstable Economy

Stabilizing an Unstable Economy (*SUE*) is a book written in 1986 by the American economist Hyman P. Minsky (1919–96) and is considered to be his seminal work. In the words of Tobin (1989, p. 106), *SUE* is 'a full and mature statement of a thesis he has been advancing for three decades: capitalist economies are unstable because of capitalist financial markets and institutions'. The book develops Minsky's financial instability hypothesis, addressing the problems of the origins of the boom–bust cycles as well as the role of regulatory agencies in stabilizing a capitalist economy.

Advancing a general framework (including in a dedicated algebraic appendix), *SUE* identifies three interconnected phases of modern financing: 'hedge', 'speculative', and 'Ponzi', all appearing to be relevant to the contemporary understanding of boom–bust cycles. Under hedge financing, borrowers repay the interest and the principal on incurred debt. At the speculative stage, borrowers' revenues are sufficient to cover interest expenses but are limited, and the principal periodically needs to be refinanced; and the third type is when borrowers' income stream is insufficient to cover either the interest or the principal, forcing them to rely on capital gains or appreciation in value of the underlying asset. Bernard et al. (2014) argue that the logic of the financial instability hypothesis explains a business cycle from a perspective of the inherent interlock of the real economy with financial markets' gyrations. This in turn leads to more profound long-term transformation of the economic system, as short-term-based policy decisions fundamentally reshape the economy's structure.

One might imagine the process as a rising spiral with every new twist leading to a greater degree of financial deepening and proliferation of new instruments, increasingly being detached from the real asset, led by the most conservative vis-à-vis risk, yet most adaptable in its profit-seeking behaviour modern financial system. Much of this is a natural behaviour by economic agents who tend to curtail their business activity on the downside and expand on the expansionary side of the cycle. At this latter stage, spotted by a new twist of financial innovation, financial commitments rise, often disproportionally high, and diluted risk perceptions shake the institutional foundations of the system, pushing the economy out of the comfortable equilibrium towards a new twist of unsustainable risk-taking activity ending with a financial crisis.

Therefore, the instability is endogenous and comes from within the operations of what initially may have been characterized as an efficient market. This is contrary to the established views of self-calibrating equilibrium models of the economy, where the main instability shock is exogenous (Gevorkyan, 2015). In Minsky's own words, 'stability is destabilizing' and instability becomes 'a fundamental characteristic of an economy' (Minsky, 1986, p. 58) with advanced and flexible financial institutions (Minsky in *SUE* relies on the example of the US economy since the 1960s, but today's reader quickly recognizes parallels across many open economies globally). Perhaps it is not surprising that Minsky's work jumped in popularity during the 2008 financial and economic tsunamis (Pressman, 2013). Ever since then investors have been on a look out for a 'Minsky moment' (McCulley, 2009).

SUE concludes with policy proposals hoped to avert future crises (almost warning about a 2008 Global Financial Crisis (GFC)-like meltdown), yet remaining somewhat difficult to accept by economists and the general public even today. Minsky advocates for an active fiscal and monetary policy regulatory intervention in the economy. Opposing the deregulatory push of the 1980s, Minsky advocates adopting proactive measures and warns against adopting policies *post factum*.

Minsky supports the idea of a 'big government' as a pragmatic proactive policy mechanism that stabilizes the economy by contracyclically adjusting taxation and expenditure, while acting as an employer of last resort. The latter is the New Deal inspired idea, with employment guarantees helping workers to transition into higher-paying private sector jobs and offering opportunities to boost professional skills (a recurring theme since the GFC and more recently in the background of rising automation across all sectors of the global economy). However, Minsky warns, relying too much on a State-led economic growth might lead to spiralling inflation.

In this framework, the US Federal Reserve System, on top of its strict monetary policy targets, also acts as a lender of last resort (as it technically did in the aftermath of the GFC) and acting as a watchdog that 'needs to continuously "lean against" the use of speculative and Ponzi finance' (Minsky, 1986, p. 364). Yet, Minsky continues, Ponzi is the common debt-finance of investment in a capitalist society and severely constraining deeper financial systems in overzealous efforts to ensure stability 'might very well take part of the spark of creativity out of the capitalist system' (ibid.).

Mixed with somewhat repetitively raised points and out-dated technical examples, the above outlined duality of the conceptually meaningful but practically doubtful proposals leads Minsky to call for an analytically superior, more qualitative and nuanced approach in steering towards a macroeconomic balance. And though today's demanding reader might require a more rigorous justification, the crisis-prone financial tendencies identified and conceptual overview of stability ensuring policies developed within *SUE* undoubtedly serve as solid guiding posts for contemporary policy makers.

ALEKSANDR V. GEVORKYAN

See also

Bubbles – credit; Business cycles; Financial crises; Financial instability hypothesis; Financial regulations

References

Bernard, L., A.V. Gevorkyan, T. Palley and W. Semmler (2014), 'Time scales and mechanisms of economic cycles: a review of theories of long waves', *Review of Keynesian Economics*, 2 (1), 87–107.
Gevorkyan, A.V. (2015), 'Economic crisis', in C. Cooper, M. Vodosek and D. den Hartog (eds), *Wiley Encyclopedia of Management*, Vol. 6, New York: Wiley-Blackwell, pp. 1–5.
McCulley, P. (2009), 'The shadow banking system and Hyman Minsky's economic journey', *PIMCO: Global Central Bank Focus*, May, available online at https://www.iosco.org/library/annual_conferences/pdf/ac34-5.pdf (last accessed on 27 August 2019).
Minsky, H. (1986), *Stabilizing an Unstable Economy*, New Haven and London: Yale University Press.
Pressman, S. (2013), *Fifty Major Economists*, London and New York: Routledge.
Tobin, J. (1989), 'Review of *Stabilizing an Unstable Economy* by Hyman P. Minsky', *Journal of Economic Literature*, 27 (1), 105–8.

Stagflation

Stagflation is a *portmanteau* of the words stagnation and inflation. The coincidence of inflation (which generates a persistent and general rise in prices) with an economic *malaise* is significant both as a policy problem and for its role in the conventional history of economic thought. It is most usually understood as a specific reference to the high unemployment and double-digit inflation among many high-income countries in the 1970s. The academic literature, both post-Keynesian and mainstream, thus centres around the North American, European and Japanese experience in this period. Of course, stagflation is not at all unfamiliar to many low- and middle-income countries prior to (and after) the 1970s. The pattern of 'creeping' inflation throughout the 1960s, the spike in 1973, and the double peaks in the mid 1970s and early 1980s are common to virtually all of the G-7 countries. Throughout this period, rates of unemployment were much higher than the averages of the 1950s and 1960s.

The era of stagflation coincided with a number of shocks that are relevant to understanding the period. In 1971, Nixon closed the gold window, ending convertibility and marking the end of the Bretton Woods era. The US dollar depreciated and exchange rates remained volatile for some time. Nixon also imposed temporary wage and price controls in 1971, only to lift them in 1973 (after his re-election). Despite their half-hearted and inconsistent application, the controls worked initially, but prices spiked dramatically when lifted. Additionally, in 1972 the Soviet Union purchased an enormous amount of grain from the United States and other countries after a massive crop failure, leading to soaring global food prices by 1973. Finally, between 1973 and 1974 the Organization of Petroleum Exporting Countries engaged in an oil embargo of the United States and other supporters of Israel during the Yom Kippur War. Oil prices jumped globally.

Though the conventional history of economic thought recognizes these cost shocks, it frames stagflation as an empirical challenge to dominant beliefs of economic theorists and policymakers of the 1960s and 1970s (see Snowdon and Vane, 2005; Mankiw, 1990; Sargent, 1999; but also Forder, 2014). In particular it presents stagflation as a challenge to the dominant version of Keynesianism.

By the 1950s, the profession coalesced around a 'neoclassical synthesis' macroeconomics. This was a two-part model with the Hicks (1937) IS–LM version of Keynesianism governing the short run (with the possibility of underemployment equilibrium), and the classical position of full employment governing the long run. To this core, it is claimed a Phillips curve relation is tacked on, which posits a long-run trade-off between unemployment and inflation.

The story goes that economists and policymakers of the 1960s understood the Phillips curve relation as a consistent and exploitable one. This amounts to saying that policymakers can choose greater inflation and lower unemployment or vice versa depending on their (or the electorate's) preferences. The experience of both high unemployment and inflation is then supposed to have been an empirical failing, which laid the groundwork for a paradigm shift in macroeconomics towards a more classically inspired macroeconomics, including the rise of monetarism.

The monetarists and New Classicals questioned the ability of policymakers to influence the long-run state of the macroeconomy. Phelps (1967) and Friedman (1968) are said to have anticipated stagflation in their contributions that emphasized real incomes and the independent role of expectations in the inflationary process. When workers and firms correctly anticipate the actual rate of inflation, the Phillips curve trade-off disappears, and prices are only stable at a long-run 'natural rate' of unemployment. If the unemployment rate is below this rate, inflation (even accelerating inflation) is the consequence.

The problem with this story is that it vastly overstates the importance of the Phillips curve in influencing policymakers (there is little evidence that anyone 'chooses' inflation as a price to pay for employment) and even among academics. Forder (2014) reviews the relevant literature and finds that the understanding of inflation at the time was far more nuanced, and that the 'myth' of the Phillips curve as central was constructed after the fact to justify the abandonment of Keynesianism.

Mainstream economists still debate whether inflation was due to cost shocks, or whether it was due to misguided monetary and fiscal policy premised on the Phillips curve (see, for instance, Blinder and Rudd, 2013). Post-Keynesian analysis of inflation in general, and of stagflation in particular, rejects single causal explanations, instead favouring historically and institutionally specific explanations. Post-Keynesian economists are also distinct in their preference for incomes policy, competition policy, and commodity market stabilization as policy measures to control inflation.

Perhaps the best-known intervention by a post-Keynesian is Kaldor's (1976) argument that inflation originated in commodity markets that were unstable and prone to speculation. He maintained the common post-Keynesian assumption that industrial prices are administered and generally unresponsive to demand, while commodity prices are quite volatile. The creeping wage inflation of the 1960s was then a very different animal than the commodity price inflation of later years. The solution, he argued, was to maintain global buffer stocks of commodities (possibly even creating a currency backed by them).

To these factors, Means (1975) adds the possibility that a good portion of the inflation can be attributed to concentrated industries whose prices are administered as they attempt to widen profit margins. In a somewhat similar vein, Marxian political economists like Bowles et al. (1990) and Devine (2000) emphasize a distributional conflict originating from a profit squeeze.

In addition to supply shocks, post-Keynesians have emphasized the wage–wage and wage–price spirals that occur when workers experience declines in living standards contrary to their aspirations (Cornwall and Cornwall, 2001). These aspirations may be set in such a way that they are not wholly determined by unemployment (Atesoglu, 1981).

The end of stagflation was brought about by a combination of the exceptionally tight monetary policy of Paul Volker, the consequent significant depression of the early 1980s, and the rise of a new right-wing politics that shrunk the welfare state and attacked labour unions. The distributional battle was thus resolved. The decades that followed were marked by a 'revenge of the rentier', as interest rates remained high relative to wage growth (see Pasinetti, 1997).

NATHANIEL CLINE

See also

Bretton Woods; Inflation; Money illusion; NAIRU; Phillips curve

References

Atesoglu, H.S. (1981), 'Wages and stagflation', *Journal of Post Keynesian Economics*, **4** (2), 271–6.
Blinder, A.S. and J.B. Rudd (2013), 'The supply-shock explanation of the Great Stagflation revisited', in M.D. Bordo and A. Orphanides (eds), *The Great Inflation: The Rebirth of Modern Central Banking*, Chicago: University of Chicago Press, pp. 119–75.
Bowles, S., D.M. Gordon and T.E. Weisskopf (1990), *After the Waste Land: A Democratic Economics for the Year 2000*, New York: M.E. Sharpe.
Cornwall, J. and W. Cornwall (2001), *Capitalist Development in the Twentieth Century: An Evolutionary Keynesian Analysis*, Cambridge, UK: Cambridge University Press.
Devine, J. (2000), 'The rise and fall of stagflation: preliminary results', *Review of Radical Political Economics*, **32** (3), 398–407.
Forder, J. (2014), *Macroeconomics and the Phillips Curve Myth*, Oxford: Oxford University Press.
Friedman, M. (1968), 'The role of monetary policy', *American Economic Review*, **58** (1), 1–17.
Hicks, J.R. (1937), 'Mr. Keynes and the "Classics": a suggested interpretation', *Econometrica*, **5** (2), 147–59.
Kaldor, N. (1976), 'Inflation and recession in the world economy', *Economic Journal*, **86** (344), 703–14.
Mankiw, N.G. (1990), 'A quick refresher course in macroeconomics', *Journal of Economic Literature*, **28** (4), 1645–60.
Means, G.C. (1975), 'Simultaneous inflation and unemployment: a challenge to theory and policy', *Challenge*, **18** (4), 6–20.
Pasinetti, L.L. (2005), 'The social "burden" of high interest rates', in P. Arestis, G. Palma and M. Sawyer (eds), *Capital Controversy, Post Keynesian Economics and the History of Economic Thought*, London and New York: Routledge, pp. 173–80.
Phelps, E.S. (1967), 'Phillips curves, expectations of inflation and optimal unemployment over time', *Economica*, **34** (135), 254–81.
Sargent, T.J. (1999), *The Conquest of American Inflation*, Princeton, NJ: Princeton University Press.
Snowdon, B. and H.R. Vane (2005), *Modern Macroeconomics: Its Origins, Development and Current State*, Cheltenham, UK, and Northampton, MA, USA: Edward Elgar.

Stagnation policy

According to Steindl (1952), mature capitalism faces the fundamental problem of stagnation because of tendencies towards oligopolies causing rising profit shares and higher income inequality. These then trigger problems of effective demand, under-utilization of productive capacities and hence stagnant investment, capital accumulation and economic growth. In the post-World War II period, however, these tendencies were more than balanced by several counter-tendencies, according to Steindl (1976, 1979): increasing public expenditures financed to a large extent by taxes on profits, high investment in research and development activities driven by the competition between capitalist and socialist systems, close cooperation of the capitalist economies under the leadership of the United States and the introduction of stabilizing and growth-enhancing institutions (Bretton Woods, Marshall Plan), as well as the catching-up of Western Europe and Japan towards the more advanced US technological level. Since the 1970s, however, these tendencies have been reversed and the problems associated with oligopoly have been reinforced through several channels (Steindl, 1979): the reduction of tensions between the superpowers, an increase in internal rivalries among the capitalist economies, the decay of US leadership and the collapse of the Bretton Woods international financial system, the fading out of the catching-up potential of Europe and Japan towards the United States, increasing environmental and energy problems, rising capital productivity, and rising propensities to save, partly caused by redistribution of income towards capital and high-income households.

However, the most important factor that explains the re-emergence of stagnation tendencies was, according to Steindl (1976, 1979), 'stagnation policy' in the major capitalist economies: 'thus we witness stagnation not as an incomprehensible fate, as in the 1930s, but stagnation as policy' (Steindl, 1976, p. xvii). This refers to Kalecki's (1971, Ch. 12) *Political Aspects of Full Employment*, in which Kalecki argued that, although governments might know how to maintain full employment in a capitalist economy, they will not do so, because of capitalists' opposition.

Whereas in Kalecki (1971, p. 144) the opposition of the capitalist class towards full-employment policies gave rise to a 'political business cycle', Steindl (1979, p. 9) argues that business opposition towards full-employment policies generates a 'political trend' causing or contributing to stagnation. Facing full employment and increasing rates of inflation in the 1970s, governments moved away from targeting full employment by means of active demand management and turned towards targeting price stability by means of restrictive monetary policies, reducing public deficits and debt, as well as supply-side policies. In particular governments refrained from required deficit spending and investment in research and development activities in the face of high private saving rates – partly due to redistribution in favour of profits – and low private investment rates.

In his latest contributions, Steindl even relates stagnation tendencies and stagnation policy to an increasing dominance of the financial sector in modern capitalist economies. According to Bhaduri and Steindl (1985), stagnation policies are associated with 'the rise of monetarism as a social doctrine', because monetarism is inherently linked with restrictive fiscal and monetary policies, which are supported by banks and the financial sector (or the rentiers). The application of monetarist policies thus indicates a shift of power from industry to banks, or from the non-financial to the financial sector, which occurred in the course of national and international financial liberalization and rapidly increasing financial activity in the 1970s and early 1980s.

Steindl's notion of stagnation policy has recently been applied in order to provide an alternative explanation for stagnation tendencies after the crisis of finance-dominated capitalism, the Great Recession (Hein, 2016). Stagnation is thus seen as a result of the increasing dominance of finance before the crisis, contributing to redistribution of income at the expense of labour and low-income households, as well as weak private investment in the capital stock, and then fiscal austerity policies in several countries after the crisis. Furthermore, Steindl's approach has been used to relate the long-run stagnation tendencies in the European Union and the euro area before and after the Great Recession to the institutional setup and assignment of restrictive macroeconomic policies, that is, monetary policies geared towards price stability, fiscal policies towards balanced budgets, and wage and labour market policies towards reducing the non-accelerating inflation rate of unemployment (NAIRU) by means of 'structural reforms' (Guger et al., 2006; Hein, 2018).

ECKHARD HEIN

See also

Capitalism; Effective demand; Inequality; *Maturity and Stagnation in American Capitalism*; Phillips curve

References

Bhaduri, A. and J. Steindl (1985), 'The rise of monetarism as a social doctrine', in P. Arestis and T. Skouras (eds), *Post-Keynesian Economic Theory: A Challenge to Neo-Classical Economics*, Sussex: Wheatsheaf, pp. 56–78.

Guger, A., M. Marterbauer and E. Walterskirchen (2006), 'Growth policy in the spirit of Steindl and Kalecki', *Metroeconomica*, **57** (3), 428–42.

ECKHARD HEIN

Hein, E. (2016), 'Secular stagnation or stagnation policy? Steindl after Summers', *PSL Quarterly Review*, **69** (276), 3–47.
Hein, E. (2018), 'Stagnation policy in the Eurozone and economic policy alternatives: A Steindlian/ neo-Kaleckian perspective', *Wirtschaft und Gesellschaft*, **44** (3), 315–48.
Kalecki, M. (1971), *Selected Essays on the Dynamics of the Capitalist Economy, 1933–1970*, Cambridge: Cambridge University Press.
Steindl, J. (1952), *Maturity and Stagnation in American Capitalism*, Oxford: Blackwell.
Steindl, J. (1976), 'Introduction', in *Maturity and Stagnation in American Capitalism*, second edition, New York and London: Monthly Review Press, pp. ix–xvii.
Steindl, J. (1979), 'Stagnation theory and stagnation policy', *Cambridge Journal of Economics*, **3** (1), 1–14.

State – entrepreneurial

In an interview for *Bloomberg Businessweek* (Lisy, 2014) on 14 December 2001, Steve Wozniak, co-founder of Apple, destroyed a myth enshrined in the well-known brand: the first computers were never conceived in Steve Jobs' family house in Los Altos (California). Despite the hard fact that this place played no role at all, a legend was born bestowing a special aura in the brand history. According to *The Guardian* (Gibbs, 2014), in 2013 the famous garage became a historical site.

Wozniak, however, could have gone further in his revelation: he should have strongly emphasized that what explains the success of his firm is the determining role of the American government. The State acted through subsidies granted to his firm in the early phase. There is more: some of the crucial technologies enshrined in the symbolic product of Apple, namely the iPhone, are the outcome of the enormous intervention of the State. What were the channels of this intervention? First, the State was a genuine source of finance for fundamental research; second, it played the role of a crucial agent for radical innovations; third, it created new markets for the final outcome of these innovations. For decades, it invested vast sums of money into research and development activities of public laboratories from which appeared key technologies benefiting private firms. In this role, the State accepted the risk that could not have been taken by the private sector, since costs relative to future incomes – at this stage still too uncertain – were too high.

The story above is explained in great detail by Mariana Mazzucato in *The Entrepreneurial State: Debunking Public vs. Private Sector Myths*. In this book, published in 2013, she fully proves that the neo-liberal vision of a minimal State only capable of acting as a regulator of markets, of which it also finances failures, is wrong. Mazzucato goes much further than many post-Keynesians' vision of the State, which is too often reduced to short-term stabilization of the economy by fiscal deficits (Parguez and Thabet, 2017). She shows that the State can also be the 'architect of the future', widening economic agents' long-term horizon of uncertainties.

There are no breakthrough innovations that are not the outcome of the engine role of the State: internet, bio-technologies, and nano-technologies are not the outcome of the 'genius entrepreneurs' of Silicon Valley. The case of the pharmaceutical industry is decisive proof: from 1993 to 2004, 75 per cent of the new molecules approved in the United States came from public research (Mazzucato, 2013). Private firms in this sector concentrated their financial resources in copying radical public discoveries or to buy their own stocks for the benefit of their shareholders and managers.

Private firms were never the victims of some crowding-out effect. They could never have developed their activity had the State not initially created the field by its investment, essentially in fundamental research. Private firms could also never have undertaken these investments, because of the lack of available financial resources and long-run strategies. The so-called venture capital (the assumed essential factor of any system of innovations) appears only 15 or 20 years (Mazzucato, 2013) after the fundamental investments of the State, when technological risks have been greatly eliminated, which gives assurance of rising profit opportunities.

Therefore, Mariana Mazzucato warns against the disaster effects of austerity: tax cuts for the ruling class and squeezing of public expenditures (especially in research and development) instead of providing opportunities for capitalism are lethal dangers to its own development.

SLIM THABET

See also

Crowding in and crowding out; Debt – public; Fiscal deficits; Fiscal policy; Public finance

References

Gibbs, S. (2014), 'Steve Wozniak: Apple starting in a garage is a myth', *The Guardian*, 5 December, available online at https://www.theguardian.com/technology/2014/dec/05/steve-wozniak-apple-starting-in-a-garage-is-a-myth (last accessed on 29 March 2021).

Lisy, B. (2014), 'Steve Wozniak on Apple, the computer revolution, and working with Steve Jobs', *Bloomberg Businessweek*, 14 December, available online at https://www.bloomberg.com/news/articles/2014-12-04/apple-steve-wozniak-on-the-early-years-with-steve-jobs (last accessed on 29 March 2021).

Mazzucato, M. (2013), *The Entrepreneurial State: Debunking Public Vs. Private Sector Myths*, London: Anthem Press.

Parguez, A. and S. Thabet (2017), '¿Economía capitalista monetaria sin deflación? Enfoque circuitista-institucionalista', *Ola Financiera*, **10** (26), 1–31.

State – role of

Capitalism does not embody a social system that harmonizes individual interests in the process of promoting collective social welfare, as mainstream economics contends. Rather, the kernel of truth lies in an inherently unstable historical evolution of antithetical social relations. The role of the State manifests the socio-political problem whereby the contradictions of class conflict are continually fought out. The question is how? By way of fiscal policy, the role of the State defines the nature of economic organization (Campbell, 1993). The means by which the State has the magnitude to perform this duty is regulated by the power of central bank policy (Vernengo, 2018). The State installs a macroeconomic configuration to make capitalist investment outcomes less uncertain and more predictable (Pressman, 2006), that is, a system of stabilization (Kaldor, 1938).

As a premise, let us abstractly demonstrate Karl Marx's process of capital accumulation, whereby $M - C\,(LP, MP) - P - C' - M'$. This chain captures the capitalist procedure of producing an economic surplus, realized by capitalists who possess a monopoly over the means of production (MP). Workers are forced to sell their capacity to produce, namely labour power (LP), and obtain wages for sustenance. Capitalists invest money (M) to buy productive inputs (C), in the form of LP and additional MP. The actual process of economic production (P), in which commodities (C') are produced, constitutes the combination of LP and MP in order to ensure a net profit (M') for the capitalists in the market sphere of commodity circulation, which depends on the level of effective demand.

Since capitalism presupposes its 'own legal relations, form of government, etc.' (Marx, 1973, p. 242), the fundamental concern is under what conditions a particular historically specific institutional structure (McDonough, 2011) fosters the capacity for the capitalist process, as described above, to be reproduced. To ensure a suitable social surrounding, what is requisite is steady macroeconomic coordination.

James O'Connor's (2002) *The Fiscal Crisis of the State* exhibits a crucial integrative fiscal sociological framework. The model denotes that a State's fiscal dimension is subdivided into three categories, which correspond to Marx's reproductive schema:

1. Social capital expenditure (constant capital) consists of expenditures on capitalist means of production that include physical economic infrastructure, research and development, and outlays on various forms of investment that enhance the productivity of labour power.
2. Social consumption expenditures (variable capital, that is, living labour), which consists of allocations devoted to training services, housing, education, health, and various forms of social insurance.
3. Social legitimization expenditures, which are outlays to legitimate the capitalist social structure and serve as a source of aggregate demand management, that is, surplus capital absorption (Baran and Sweezy, 1966).

The specific elements of public spending, which condition the level of economic stability for capitalists to make reasonable calculations about expected rates of return on investment, are acutely made apparent.

The State assumes the responsibilities for maintaining capitalist economic growth and social stability. In the long run, however, the assumption is that fiscal policy becomes 'more and more out of proportion to the requirements

SLIM THABET / DAVID M. FIELDS

of capital accumulation. ... [T]here is a tendency for the level of State "waste" to expand more rapidly than the capacity of the system' (Wright, 1993, p. 159). The increasing pertinence of fiscal policy outweighs the State's capacity to finance it through tax receipts, especially if social consumption and legitimization expenditures take more of the State's fiscal outlays. The impression is that balanced budgets should be enshrined, to allow for 'sound finance' to prevent potential fiscal crises as a result of excessive government deficits ensuing hyperinflation (Block, 1981).

What is missing is the extent to which the central bank provides a guarantee for State debt (Knapp. 1924, pp. 299–303), which delivers a secure financial asset to allow for credit conditions to propel capitalist investment (Fields and Vernengo, 2013). By providing a guarantee for State debt, the central bank allows the State to use budget deficits to stimulate economic activity. This process of 'monetization' could lead to inflation, but only under very specific conditions, whereby expansionary measures lead to overheating as a result of an already established position of durable full employment.

The appearance of public deficits is not necessarily a sign of fiscal precariousness, but the workings of an institutionalized accounting process that ensures the State's fiscal solvency to ensure capitalist stability. Concerns over public deficits should be a matter of what degree to reach a sustainable position of capital accumulation, which ultimately rests on the nature of monetary policy (see Lerner, 1943; Domar, 1944).

DAVID M. FIELDS

See also

Capitalism; Effective demand; Fiscal policy; Monetary policy; Social classes

References

Baran, P. and P. Sweezy (1966), *Monopoly Capital: An Essay on the American Economic and Social Order*, New York: Monthly Review Press.
Block, F. (1981), 'The fiscal crisis of the capitalist State', *Annual Review of Sociology*, 7, 1–27.
Campbell, J.L. (1993), 'The State and fiscal sociology', *Annual Review of Sociology*, 19, 163–85.
Domar, E. (1944), 'The "burden of the debt" and the national income', *American Economic Review*, 34 (4), 798–827.
Fields, D. and M. Vernengo (2013), 'Hegemonic currencies during the crisis: the dollar versus the euro in a cartalist perspective', *Review of International Political Economy*, 20 (4), 740–59.
Kaldor, N. (1938), 'Stability and full employment', *Economic Journal*, 48 (182), 642–57.
Knapp, G.F. (1924), *The State Theory of Money*, London: Macmillan.
Lerner, A.P. (1943), 'Functional finance and the federal debt', *Social Research*, 10 (1), 38–51.
Marx, K. (1973), *Grundrisse*, London: Penguin.
McDonough, T. (2011), 'Social structures of accumulation: a "punctuated" view of embeddedness', *American Journal of Economics and Sociology*, 70 (5), 1234–47.
O'Connor, J. (2002), *The Fiscal Crisis of the State*, New Brunswick, NJ: Transaction Publishers.
Pressman, S. (2006), 'Economic power, the State, and post-Keynesian economics', *International Journal of Political Economy*, 35 (4), 67–86.
Vernengo, M. (2018), 'Classical political economy and the evolution of central banks: endogenous money and the fiscal–military State', *Review of Radical Political Economics*, 50 (4), 660–7.
Wright, E.O. (1993), *Class, Crisis and the State*, London and New York: Verso.

Stock–flow consistent models

Stock–flow consistent (SFC) models are macroeconomic models constructed around a rigorous accounting framework and a strong theoretical background, usually post-Keynesian even if some additions have been made around Schumpeterian (Caiani et al., 2014) or ecological (see Bovari et al., 2018, and Dafermos et al., 2017, among others) approaches (see Godley and Lavoie, 2007, for the most extensive description of the approach, and Caverzasi and Godin, 2015, and Nikiforos and Zezza, 2017, for recent literature surveys).

The accounting framework is typically built on different matrices. The balance sheet contains the distribution of assets across sectors, emphasizing who is the liability emitter and who is the asset holder. The transaction-flow matrix contains all the non-financial transactions, that is, the monetary flows in the economy such as the various components of total demand (consumption, investment), primary distribution flows (wages, taxes) or secondary income distribution (rents, interests or dividends). The flow-of-funds matrix contains financial transactions, that is, the emission of liabilities and the corresponding financial investment leading to

DAVID M. FIELDS / ANTOINE GODIN

accumulation of assets. Finally, when needed, the revaluation matrix contains the changes in value of the different assets and liabilities modelled, owing to price movements or default by the liability emitter. These matrices are strongly connected to the sectorial accounts data and hence bear an important empirical content.

The main interest of the approach (aside from the theoretical content and topic of study, which are typically related to heterodox schools of thought) is that it highlights the important feedbacks due to the accounting structure. These real–financial feedbacks can be categorized into two broad categories: explicit ones and implicit ones. Explicit feedbacks are those embedded into forms of behaviour, and hence are more theoretical in nature, such as wealth effects on investment or consumption, redistribution impacts through interest or rent payments or even capital gains dynamics. Implicit feedbacks are those relating to the financial structure and thus captured by the accounting framework.

For example, the clearing mechanism related to any bank transfer between two private agents implies a transfer of reserves between the two banks where the paying and receiving accounts are lodged. This transfer of reserves creates a movement in the balance sheets of agents (the two banks and the central bank) that are completely passive in the transaction. This implicit feedback is at the core of the emergence of agent-based stock–flow-consistent (AB-SFC) models where the SFC-ness of the model adds a third layer of complexity onto the other two layers: heterogeneity and interactions (see Caiani et al., 2016, and Caverzasi and Russo, 2018, for more details).

This fundamental insight of SFC models can be summarized in a nutshell: economies can be represented by dynamic and evolving multi-layered networks of financial relationships. These networks can then be populated by sectors, as is traditionally the case in SFC models, or agents, as for AB-SFC models.

At the origin of the SFC approach another insight was highlighted by Wynne Godley, particularly in his seminal paper entitled 'Seven unsustainable processes' (Godley, 1999) in which he rightly warns against the emergence of a financial crisis in the United States. This insight is that imbalances between sectors are the norm and can lead to unsustainable dynamics, depending on the structure of those imbalances. Sectorial imbalances are indeed normal. In order to finance investment, it is often the case that firms have to take a loan or emit liabilities such as bonds or equity. Similarly, it is often the case that households save part of their income, leading to asset accumulation for the household sector. The fundamental question, however, is not whether there are sectorial imbalances, but which sector is running an imbalanced budget. Indeed, as shown by Godley (1999), the situation is problematic when households are running prolonged deficits and firms running surpluses. Contrary to most mainstream economic theory, the SFC approach thus shows that while it is theoretically possible to reach a balanced growth path, the economy might not reach that state of affairs and hence includes the possibility of financial crises.

Owing to the combination of these two insights (namely, real–financial feedbacks and the importance of financial imbalances), SFC models are a very effective tool to understand the dynamics of financialized economies and the interactions between monetary/financial dynamics (for instance, macroprudential policies, interbank market or portfolio allocations) and real dynamics (like the emergence of new sectors, products, technologies, decisions to invest in physical capital or consumption behaviour). Further, the strong empirical connection via the national accounts combined with the intrinsic dynamic nature of the approach make SFC models an interesting tool to analyse medium- to long-run dynamics of specific countries, with econometric estimates as proposed by Zezza and Zezza (2019) or calibrated methods (Burgess et al., 2016), and even to compare countries (Gimet et al., 2019).

ANTOINE GODIN

See also

Financial crises; Income distribution; Modern money theory; Monetary circuit; Wealth effect

References

Bovari, E., G. Giraud and F. McIsaac (2018), 'Coping with collapse: a stock–flow consistent monetary macrodynamics of global warming', *Ecological Economics*, **147**, 383–98.

Burgess, S., O. Burrows, A. Godin, S. Kinsella and S. Millard (2016), 'A dynamic model of financial balances for the United Kingdom', *Bank of England Staff Working Paper*, No. 614.

ANTOINE GODIN

Caiani, A., A. Godin and S. Lucarelli (2014), 'Innovation and finance: a stock flow consistent analysis of great surges of development', *Journal of Evolutionary Economics*, **24** (2), 421–48.

Caiani, A., A. Godin, E. Caverzasi, M. Gallegati, S. Kinsella and J.E. Stiglitz (2016), 'Agent based-stock flow consistent macroeconomics: towards a benchmark model', *Journal of Economic Dynamics and Control*, **69**, 375–408.

Caverzasi, E. and A. Godin (2015), 'Post-Keynesian stock–flow-consistent modelling: a survey', *Cambridge Journal of Economics*, **39** (1), 157–87.

Caverzasi, E. and A. Russo (2018), 'Toward a new microfounded macroeconomics in the wake of the crisis', *Industrial and Corporate Change*, **27** (6), 999–1014.

Dafermos, Y., M. Nikolaidi and G. Galanis (2017), 'A stock–flow-fund ecological macroeconomic model', *Ecological Economics*, **131**, 191–207.

Gimet, C., T. Lagoarde-Segot and L. Reyes-Ortiz (2019), 'Financialization and the macroeconomy: theory and empirical evidence', *Economic Modelling*, **81**, 89–110.

Godley, W. (1999), 'Seven unsustainable processes', *Jerome Levy Economics Institute of Bard College Special Report*.

Godley, W. and M. Lavoie (2007), *Monetary Economics: An Integrated Approach to Credit, Money, Income, Production and Wealth*, Basingstoke and New York: Palgrave Macmillan.

Nikiforos, M. and G. Zezza (2017), 'Stock-flow consistent macroeconomic models: a survey', *Journal of Economic Surveys*, **31** (5), 1204–39.

Zezza, G. and F. Zezza (2019), 'On the design of empirical stock–flow consistent models', *European Journal of Economics and Economic Policies: Intervention*, **16** (1), 134–58.

Structural economic dynamics

Structural economic dynamics is a theoretical approach to the study of economic growth. It investigates the long-run evolution of the structure of industrial systems, characterized by technical progress, a high degree of dynamism and uneven development from sector to sector – and from region to region.

The dynamic structure of modern economic systems is continuously changing owing to the effect of variations in the sectoral composition of productivity – because of technical change – and of aggregate demand – because of changes in the level and distribution of income. This makes industrial systems intrinsically unstable.

As a consequence of such uneven evolution of labour productivity and demand on the market for produced goods and services, the whole sectoral structure of production, employment, and so on is continuously changing through time.

On the contrary, traditional aggregate growth models imply a conception of dynamics basically given by stationary expansion with uniform technical progress and aggregate demand expansion.

It is not always easy, in the short run, to distinguish between genuine structural change (that is, change in the composition of the economic variables that are permanent and irreversible) and change that is purely transitory and reversible. However, as time goes on, the transitory variables in either direction cancel out, while structural changes not only remain, but tend to become more accentuated. In the study of these dynamic movements, economic theory has too often confused these two types of variations. It has also generally considered the study of structural change as being subordinate to the study of macroeconomic movements. A more accurate analysis has revealed that dynamic macroeconomic movements are not at all to be considered as a simplified expression of structural dynamics and cannot be ignored. It has become clear that the study of structural economic dynamics is not merely complementary to macroeconomic dynamics: it is something more profound. In many cases, the analytical results of the former can even be incompatible with the latter. Essentially, the two approaches incorporate two different visions of the industrial world.

Any multisector model is characterized, at a certain point in time, by a particular structure; and the aggregate dimension of production of the entire economic system will result from a weighted mean of the output of the various sectors. The weights are determined by the sectoral proportion of aggregate output. The proportions for the entire economic system follow on the one side from the technology applied in the various productive branches, and on the other from the composition of sectoral demand. It thus follows that both technology and demand, in their various combinations, will shape the structure of the entire economic system.

This framework is unique to each single period of time. When introducing time, the entire framework will progressively change. It is precisely this characteristic that creates the complementarity between the two approaches.

Traditional literature on economic growth (including the famous von Neumann model of an expanding economy) has focused attention on economic systems growing in absolute terms, but maintaining relative quantities constant. However, it can be shown (see for example Pasinetti, 1981) that uniform growth is a particular case – so particular that it almost never occurs in real-world economic systems.

In all realistic cases, structural dynamics – of productivity on the one side, and of demand for consumption on the other – make all sectors grow at different rates. This is what happens in all industrial systems.

It is precisely structural dynamics that rule out the existence of any automatism whatsoever leading to a stable equilibrium. Equilibrium (in the sense of full utilization of productive capacity and full employment of the labour force) can only be approached by actively adjusting sectoral magnitudes, and accordingly redistributing investment and employment.

This is the object of all our investigations and research in structural economic dynamics (see Pasinetti, 1993, 2012a, 2012b), which, unfortunately, theoretical economists have tended to ignore. Yet, it is these types of investigations that should be most encouraged in order to enable us to understand the characteristics and shapes of the globalized post-industrial society of the third millennium.

Luigi L. Pasinetti and Nadia Garbellini

See also

Aggregate demand; Growth; Income distribution; Traverse, path dependency, and economic dynamics

References

Pasinetti, L.L. (1981), *Structural Change and Economic Growth: A Theoretical Essay on the Dynamics of the Wealth of Nations*, Cambridge, UK: Cambridge University Press.
Pasinetti, L.L. (1993), *Structural Economic Dynamics: A Theory of the Economic Consequences of Human Learning*, Cambridge, UK: Cambridge University Press.
Pasinetti, L.L. (2012a), 'Growth and structural change: perspectives for the future', in R. Arena and P.-L. Porta (eds), *Structural Dynamics and Economic Growth*, Cambridge, UK: Cambridge University Press, pp. 276–82.
Pasinetti, L.L. (2012b), 'Second afterword: the significance of structural economic dynamics', in R. Arena and P.-L. Porta (eds), *Structural Dynamics and Economic Growth*, Cambridge, UK: Cambridge University Press, pp. 283–7.

Structuralism

In general, structuralism refers to a form of social analysis that starts with the study of how a social system as a whole is constituted, that is, what structure it has (how different parts of the system are related to each other), and how this structure possibly changes over time. This approach can be contrasted with an analysis that starts with individual units taken in isolation, from which the relations between these units can be examined, to analyse the system as a whole (an approach followed by neoclassical economics).

Structuralism has existed in many disciplines, including linguistics, social anthropology, and psychology, among others. In economics, it is associated with approaches to development economics that emerged after the Second World War: in Europe and the United States, where it was often based on the idea that less-developed countries exhibit several kinds of distortions and rigidities that prevent them from experiencing development based on market mechanisms; and in Latin America, where it was argued that the structure of the global economy, resulting from the history of colonialism, placed impediments on the development of peripheral or lower-income countries, which also had internal structures that were very different from those of central or higher-income countries. These structures emphasized specialization of production in primary products and simple manufactures, underemployment, heterogeneous production systems in the periphery, and institutional constraints on agriculture in the periphery. These earlier approaches have given rise to various newer approaches to structuralism in development economics (see Dutt, 2019).

In his paper published just after *The General Theory*, Keynes (1937) emphasized that one of the two central messages of his 1936 book is that it is necessary to examine the supply and demand of output as a whole (the other concerning the role of uncertainty). In light of this, Keynes's systemic approach reveals close connections between his analysis, structuralism, and post-Keynesian economics.

However, while early structuralist development economists emphasized the role of the State in overcoming structural barriers, and even in pursuing counter-cyclical macroeconomic policies, they generally did not use Keynesian ideas, because they believed that aggregate demand issues were relevant for the analysis of mature capitalist countries in the short run, whereas development problems were caused by supply-side issues such as saving, agricultural problems, and foreign-exchange constraints, where long-run considerations mattered most.

Raul Prebisch, the leader of Latin American structuralism, was critical of Keynes's *General Theory* for its focus on short-run equilibrium, and saw saving, rather than aggregate demand, as a major constraint on development (see Pérez Caldentey and Vernengo, 2015). However, Celso Furtado (1964), a major Brazilian structuralist, seems to refer to aggregate demand issues when he argues that high income inequality reduces the size of the domestic market and results in low rates of capital accumulation (see Dutt, 2019).

It is only later, for instance in the writings of Taylor (1983, 1991) and others who call themselves structuralist macroeconomists, that aggregate demand began to have a major role in development economics. Drawing on the Kaleckian, post-Keynesian, and Marxian traditions, this approach examines how output and capacity utilization are determined by aggregate demand with excess capacity, and introduces different classes with different saving propensities to examine the interaction between output, economic growth, and distribution. This approach is extended to take into account conflict inflation, financial markets, technological change, agriculture–industry interactions, fiscal constraints, and open-economy issues. These extensions allow for the incorporation of many of the early structuralist ideas related to conflict inflation, supply bottlenecks in agriculture, and foreign-exchange constraints. Indeed, supply constraints need not be independent of aggregate demand: an increase in the latter can increase economic growth and raise productivity owing to learning by doing and increased exports, thereby easing foreign-exchange constraints. Bresser-Pereira (2012), a follower of Furtado, also emphasizes the role of aggregate demand, although stressing the importance of the real exchange rate in promoting manufacturing exports.

AMITAVA DUTT

See also

Aggregate demand; Development; Inequality; Structuralism – Latin American; Structuralism and post-Keynesianism

References

Bresser-Pereira, L.C. (2012), 'Structuralist macroeconomics and the new developmentalism', *Brazilian Journal of Political Economy*, 32 (3), 347–66.
Dutt, A.K. (2019), 'Structuralists, structures and economic development', in M. Nissanke and J.A. Ocampo (eds), *The Palgrave Handbook of Development Economics: Critical Reflections on Globalization and Development*, Basingstoke, UK, and New York: Palgrave Macmillan, pp. 109–41.
Furtado, C. (1964), *Development and Underdevelopment*, Berkeley, CA: University of California Press.
Keynes, J.M. (1937), 'General theory of employment', *Quarterly Journal of Economics*, 51 (2), 209–23.
Pérez Caldentey, E. and M. Vernengo (2015), 'Reading Keynes in Buenos Aires: Prebisch and the dynamics of capitalism', *Cambridge Journal of Economics*, 40 (6), 1725–41.
Taylor, L. (1983), *Structuralist Macroeconomics: Applicable Models for the Third World*, New York: Basic Books.
Taylor, L. (1991), *Income Distribution, Inflation and Growth: Lectures on Structuralist Macroeconomic Theory*, Cambridge, MA: MIT Press.

Structuralism and post-Keynesianism

Structuralism is associated with a group of economists working out of the Economic Commission for Latin America and the Caribbean (ECLAC) and the Higher Institute of Brazilian Studies (ISEB), which between 1940 and 1965 provided a body of independent economic theorizing based on the development experience of Latin America and the Caribbean. For structuralists, underdevelopment was not due to exogenous forces or shocks or to bad economic policy. It was rather an intrinsic feature of Latin America and the Caribbean ingrained in its own social and economic structure. As a way to conceptualize Latin American and Caribbean reality, structuralism became a practice, before being a policy and a policy prior to becoming a theory. The most renowned economists within the group include Celso Furtado (1920–2004), Arthur C. Lewis (1915–91), Raúl Prebisch (1901–86), Juan Noyola (1922–62), Aníbal Pinto Santa Cruz (1919–96), Osvaldo Sunkel (1929–), and Ignacio Rangel (1914–94).

AMITAVA DUTT / ESTEBAN PÉREZ CALDENTEY

Structuralist thinking is articulated around the following themes: power relations between centre and periphery, the criticism of comparative advantage and the prominence of the external constraint, the dual character of economic development, a vision of development as structural change, the need for an adequate regional and international insertion, and the necessity of a development policy guided by the government especially in infrastructure and productive development.

Structuralist ideas were influenced by the thinking of economists belonging to the Keynesian, post-Keynesian, and Schumpeterian traditions. Particular mention should be made of the influence on the Latin American structuralist school of John Maynard Keynes (1883–1946), Roy Harrod (1900–78), Nicholas Kaldor (1908–86), and Michal Kalecki (1899–1970).

As part of the Argentine delegation to the World Economic Conference (London, 1933), Prebisch became exposed to Keynes's ideas to stimulate worldwide demand to overcome the effects of the Great Depression (Keynes, 1933/1972). Keynes's influence was partly reflected in the formulation of the National Plan for Economic Action launched in Argentina at the end of 1933, which combined expansionary economic policies with exchange-rate controls to isolate the economy from external fluctuations. These elements also provided the foundations for an autonomous national monetary policy that Prebisch (1944a/1991, 1944b/1991) developed during his tenure as first president of the Central Bank of Argentina (1935–43). Prebisch analysed the validity of Keynes's clearing union plan in terms of its compatibility with his autonomous national monetary policy plan.

Kalecki was also a major influencer in the development of structuralist inflation theory, whose originality was underscored by Kaldor. Kaldor was closest to Latin America and the Caribbean, structuralism, and ECLAC, and covered a wide spectrum of subjects, including issues affecting developing countries and Latin America. At the urging of Prebisch, in 1956 Kaldor worked as an ECLAC consultant and wrote 'Economic problems of Chile' (Kaldor, 1956), which analysed the problem of income inequality and advocated a structuralist interpretation of inflation. During his visits to Latin America, Kaldor developed a number of concepts that would dominate his thinking (such as cumulative causation, technical progress, industrial concentration, and the limits to industrial growth) and that are fundamental to the conceptualization of structural change. Latin America also provided the inspiration for Kaldor's exchange-rate strategy for promoting economic development.

Both post-Keynesian and structuralist thoughts identify three basic failings in the workings of market economies: (1) their inability to ensure full employment and create decent jobs as standard, (2) their tendency to generate an arbitrary and unequal distribution of income and wealth, and (3) their propensity to financial fragility and instability. Also within the sphere of methodology, economic research and policies, structuralism, and post-Keynesian theories share the following similarities: the emphasis on reality-based theorizing, the conception of the individual as a social and institutional animal, the autonomy of institutions, the perception that individuals are under major restraints when it comes to obtaining and processing information, the centrality of production (rather than exchange) and of the economic structure, and the importance of the State (government) in regulating the functioning of markets.

Esteban Pérez
Caldentey

See also

Cumulative causation; Inequality; International clearing union; Financial fragility; Structuralism – Latin American

References

Kaldor, N. (1956), 'Economic problems of Chile', in *Essays on Economic Policy*, New York: Holmes & Meier Publishers, pp. 233–87.
Keynes, J.M. (1933/1972), 'The means to prosperity', in *The Collected Writings of John Maynard Keynes. Vol. IX: Essays in Persuasion*, London: Macmillan, pp. 335–66.
Prebisch, R. (1944a/1991), 'Lineamientos de una política monetaria nacional', in *Obras 1919–1949, vol. III*, Buenos Aires: Fundación Raúl Prebisch, pp. 123–88.
Prebisch, R. (1944b/1991), 'La política monetaria nacional y los planes monetarios internacionales', in *Obras 1919–1949, vol. III*, Buenos Aires: Fundación Raúl Prebisch, pp. 189–206.

Esteban Pérez Caldentey

Structuralism – Latin American

In the decade following the end of the Second World War, one of the most active fields of research in economics was development (Hirschman, 1981; Arndt, 1987; Krugman, 1993). Several researchers dedicated their work to understanding the reasons why so many countries remained underdeveloped, at the periphery of the world economy, and how this situation could be overcome. They would later be called the 'pioneers in development' (Meier and Seers, 1984). An important part of this collective research effort was undertaken by Latin American economists working at the United Nations' Economic Commission for Latin American and the Caribbean (ECLAC), led by Raúl Prebisch. This particular strand of early development thinking is referred to as Latin American structuralism.

According to Furtado (1975, p. 83), Latin American structuralism 'had as its main goal to put in evidence the importance of "non-economic parameters" for macroeconomic models. As the behavior of the economic variables depends to a great extent on these parameters and their nature can change significantly in phases of rapid social change ... they must be studied meticulously. This observation is particularly pertinent with respect to social and technologically heterogeneous economic systems, like the underdeveloped economies.' Such emphasis led these economists to argue that Latin American countries needed an economic theory of their own. In the words of Prebisch (1950, p. 7, fn. 1), '[o]ne of the most conspicuous deficiencies of general economic theory, from the point of view of the periphery, is its false sense of universality' (on the methodology of Latin American structuralism, see Boianovsky, 2015).

Latin American structuralism dealt with many issues and shifted its focus along with the changing challenges faced by Latin American economies (a short summary can be found in Palma, 2008, and a longer one in Bielschowsky, 2016). But two issues are prominent among the formulations of this school of thought: the tendency of the terms of trade to deteriorate (also called the Prebisch–Singer hypothesis) and the interaction between the structure of demand and the structure of supply. The Prebisch–Singer hypothesis claimed that the terms of trade of underdeveloped countries specializing in the production and exports of primary commodities tended to deteriorate, pushing down their real income and dividing the world economy into two regions, a core and a periphery. This was one of the main arguments for the industrialization of Latin American economies.

The second issue, namely the interaction between the structure of demand and the structure of supply, is best understood as a critical extension of Lewis's (1954) model of economic development with unlimited supplies of labour. Lewis argued that economic development was characterized by a shift of the labour force from the subsistence sector to the capitalist sector, which would increase labour productivity, enlarge the surplus available to be accumulated as capital and, in the end, allow the capitalist sector to absorb the entire labour force. Furtado (1965) and Pinto (1976) extended such a model to incorporate a crucial structural dynamics: the income distribution that resulted from the dual nature of the economy would determine the consumption patterns and the latter, in their turn, would determine the sectoral composition of output and employment. The main implication of this analysis was that, contra Lewis, a process of development did not necessarily lead to the absorption of the entire labour force in high-productivity capitalist sectors, but could reproduce continuously massive underemployment and high inequality. If, in Lewis's model, increasing inequality would be a temporary phenomenon, being attenuated once the unlimited labour supply was extinguished, for Furtado and Pinto inequality could become a permanent feature of underdeveloped countries, being a result of what Pinto (1970) called 'structural heterogeneity'.

This formulation is particularly relevant for post-Keynesian economics, because such structural dynamics can be fruitfully incorporated as a mediation between income distribution and aggregate demand in post-Keynesian growth and distribution models (Rugitsky, 2016). In this way, shifts in income distribution impact aggregate demand not only through different propensities to consume between social classes and through its impact on aggregate investment. It can also impact aggregate demand through changes in consumption patterns that, in their turn, impact the sectoral composition of output and employment. Such interaction can lead to cumulative processes in which economic growth is accompanied by

FERNANDO RUGITSKY

either rising or falling inequality. This extension of post-Keynesian growth and distribution models, which was suggested by Taylor (1983, 1989), may be particularly important in order for them to be relevant to interpret the trajectories of underdeveloped countries, which are still characterized by a high degree of sectoral heterogeneity.

FERNANDO RUGITSKY

See also

Development; Income distribution; Inequality; Structuralism and post-Keynesianism; Terms of trade

References

Arndt, H.W. (1987), *Economic Development: The History of an Idea*, Chicago: University of Chicago Press.
Bielschowsky, R. (2016), 'Fifty years of ECLAC thought: a review', in R. Bielschowsky (ed.), *ECLAC Thinking: Selected Texts (1948–1998)*, Santiago: United Nations/ECLAC, pp. 7–43.
Boianovsky, M. (2015), 'Between Lévi-Strauss and Braudel: Furtado and the historical–structural method in Latin American political economy', *Journal of Economic Methodology*, **22** (4), 413–38.
Furtado, C. (1965), 'Development and stagnation in Latin America: a structuralist approach', *Studies in Comparative International Development*, **1** (11), 159–75.
Furtado, C. (1975), *Teoria e Política do Desenvolvimento Econômico*, fifth edition, São Paulo: Editora Nacional.
Hirschman, A.O. (1981), 'The rise and decline of development economics', in *Essays in Trespassing: Economics to Politics and Beyond*, Cambridge, UK: Cambridge University Press, pp. 1–24.
Krugman, P. (1993), 'Toward a counter-counterrevolution in development theory', *Proceedings of the World Bank Annual Conference on Development Economics 1992*, Washington, DC: World Bank, pp. 15–38.
Lewis, W.A. (1954), 'Economic development with unlimited supplies of labour', *Manchester School of Economic and Social Studies*, **22** (2), 139–91.
Meier, G.M. and D. Seers (eds) (1984), *Pioneers in Development*, Oxford: Oxford University Press.
Palma, J.G. (2008), 'Structuralism', in A. Dutt and J. Ros (eds), *International Handbook of Development Economics*, Cheltenham, UK and Northampton, MA, USA: Edward Elgar, vol. 1, pp. 136–43.
Pinto, A. (1970), 'Naturaleza y implicaciones de la "heterogeneidad structural" de la América Latina', *El Trimestre Económico*, **37** (145), 83–100.
Pinto, A. (1976), 'Notas sobre estilos de desarrollo en América Latina', *Revista de la Cepal*, 1, 97–128.
Prebisch, R. (1950), *The Economic Development of Latin America and Its Principal Problems*, Lake Success, NY: United Nations.
Rugitsky, F. (2016), 'Growth, distribution, and sectoral heterogeneity: reading the Kaleckians in Latin America', *EconomiA*, **17** (3), 265–78.
Taylor, L. (1983), *Structuralist Macroeconomics: Applicable Models for the Third World*, New York: Basic Books.
Taylor, L. (1989), 'Demand composition, income distribution, and growth', in G. Feiwel (ed.), *Joan Robinson and Modern Economic Theory*, London: Macmillan, pp. 623–37.

Subprime financial crisis

The subprime financial crisis is a major financial crisis that hit the US financial system in 2007 and triggered the so-called Great Recession, a general economic downturn of the world economy between 2008 and 2010.

This crisis owes its name to the subprime mortgages sector, in which it ignited. Subprime mortgages are a kind of real-estate loan to risky borrowers, namely those with a poor credit history or with high debt-to-income ratios. Until the early 2000s, subprime mortgages represented a small portion of the whole mortgages issued (8 per cent in 2003), but this share rapidly increased, accounting for one fifth of newly originated mortgages in 2005 and 2006 (Harvard Joint Center for Housing Studies, 2008). The great majority of these subprime mortgages were adjustable-rate mortgages (ARMs), with an interest rate rising after the first years of the loan. Rising house prices (between 1997 and 2006 housing prices in the United States rose by 124 per cent according to the Case–Shiller index) allowed borrowers to refinance their debt and thus circumvent the rise in interest rates. When the growth of housing prices suddenly stopped in 2006, such possibility vanished and the whole system started to crumble. Interest rates dramatically increased and mortgage delinquencies soared, peaking at more than 40 per cent of all subprime ARMs in 2009. The crisis rapidly spread to the other mortgages sectors and to the whole US financial system eventually.

In 2007, HSBC wrote down 10.5 billion US dollar subprime mortgage-related securities. In September 2008, all major US investment banks had been hit by the crisis. The most iconic event was probably the bankruptcy of

FERNANDO RUGITSKY / EUGENIO CAVERZASI

Lehman Brothers in September 2008; the same year, Merrill Lynch, on the brink of collapsing, was acquired by Bank of America; Goldman Sachs and Morgan Stanley had to become traditional commercial banks, subject to stricter regulation by the US Federal Reserve (Fed) in exchange for the possibility of accessing the Fed's lending facilities; the insurance company AIG was bailed out by the government for 100 billion US dollars; Fannie Mae and Freddie Mac, two government-sponsored enterprises, were taken over by the US federal government. Meanwhile, more than one hundred mortgage companies filed for bankruptcy.

It was not only the financial market to be severely hit, with the main indexes such as Nasdaq, S&P500 and the Dow Jones Industrial Average facing losses for 54.9 per cent, 56.9 per cent, and 54.1 per cent, respectively, between 2007 and 2009. Also the real sector was stormed by these events: the unemployment rate increased from 4.7 per cent in January 2007 to 9.7 per cent in the same month of 2010, while GDP growth fell into negative territory (−0.137 per cent in 2008 and −2.537 per cent in 2009). The crisis soon propagated from the United States to Europe, paving the way to the euro-area crisis (see Arestis and Sawyer, 2012).

The epidemic diffusion of the crisis, which from a segment of the mortgage market infected the whole financial system, finds its main explanation in the evolution of the financial sector. Owing to the securitization process, mortgages had become the input for the issuance of complex financial assets (Caverzasi et al., 2019), namely mortgage-backed securities and collateralized debt obligations, which spread widely in the 2000s.

Securitization allowed banks to move loans from their balance sheets and sidestep balance-sheet regulations. This in turn favoured a massive credit boom and the consequent housing-price bubble, as well as the detachment of the holders of the credit assets from any evaluation of the creditworthiness of borrowers (Kregel, 2008), hence incentivizing a general riskier lending behaviour. Moreover, the sophistication of these instruments made it more difficult for investors to appreciate the real riskiness of the relevant assets, which also involved the responsibility of credit-rating agencies that regularly assigned triple-A ratings to mortgage-related securities (Financial Crisis Inquiry Commission, 2011, p. xxv). The triple-A rating made these instruments highly attractive and therefore very popular, with investment institutions using them as collateral in the repo market (Gabor, 2016), which was vastly used by investment funds and which collapsed after the crisis (Gorton and Metrick, 2012). In relation to that, credit-default swaps (CDSs), a form of derivative used to hedge against the risk of default of securities, spread the risk even further.

The aspects of novelty of the financial system (see also Crotty, 2009) nested on a wider transformation of the US economy, in which finance became increasingly more important with respect to the real economy, and inequality and households' indebtedness (the households' debt to disposal income ratio reached 137 per cent in 2007) increased dramatically (see Bellofiore and Halevi, 2009; Onaran et al., 2011). In fact, the new financial structure and the overall financialization of the economy enabled wealth owners and the financial system to drain resources from the ever-growing indebtedness of poorer households (Lapavitsas, 2009; Botta et al., 2019).

EUGENIO CAVERZASI

See also

Bubbles – credit; Eurozone imbalances; Financial crises; Financial regulations; Securitization

References

Arestis, P. and M. Sawyer (eds) (2012), *The Euro Crisis*, Basingstoke, UK, and New York: Palgrave Macmillan.
Bellofiore, R. and J. Halevi (2009), 'A Minsky moment? The subprime crisis and the "new" capitalism', in C. Gnos and L.-P. Rochon (eds), *Credit, Money and Macroeconomic Policy: A Post-Keynesian Approach*, Cheltenham, UK, and Northampton, MA, USA: Edward Elgar, pp. 13–32.
Botta, A., E. Caverzasi, A. Russo, M. Gallegati and J.E. Stiglitz (2019), 'Inequality and finance in a rent economy', *Journal of Economic Behavior and Organization*, **183**, 998–1029.
Caverzasi, E., A. Botta and C. Capelli (2019), 'Shadow banking and the financial side of financialisation', *Cambridge Journal of Economics*, **43** (4), 1029–51.
Crotty, J. (2009), 'Structural causes of the global financial crisis: a critical assessment of the 'new financial architecture'', *Cambridge Journal of Economics*, **33** (4), 563–80.
Financial Crisis Inquiry Commission (2011), *The Financial Crisis Inquiry Report – Final Report of the National Commission on the Causes of*

the Financial and Economic Crisis in the United States, Washington, DC: Official Government Edition.

Gabor, D. (2016), 'The (impossible) repo trinity: the political economy of repo markets', *Review of International Political Economy*, **23** (6), 967–1000.

Gorton, G.B. and A. Metrick (2012), 'Securitized banking and the run on repo', *Journal of Financial Economics*, **104** (3), 425–51.

Harvard Joint Center for Housing Studies (2008), *The State of the Nation's Housing*, Harvard, MA: Harvard Joint Center for Housing Studies, available online at www.jchs.harvard.edu/publications/markets/son2008/son2008.pdf (last accessed on 29 March 2021).

Kregel, J. (2008), 'Using Minsky's cushions of safety to analyze the crisis in the U.S. subprime mortgage market', *International Journal of Political Economy*, **37** (1), 3–23.

Lapavitsas, C. (2009), 'Financialised capitalism: crisis and financial expropriation', *Historical Materialism*, **17** (2), 114–48.

Onaran, O., E. Stockhammer and L. Grafl (2011), 'Financialisation, income distribution and aggregate demand in the USA', *Cambridge Journal of Economics*, **35** (4), 637–61.

Supermultiplier

The expression 'supermultiplier' was first coined by John Hicks in 1950 to refer to a dynamically unstable multiplier–accelerator growth and business cycle model in which explosive short-period fluctuations of output were driven by aggregate demand but the trend was driven by the full-employment labour supply 'ceiling' growth (Hicks, 1950). The Sraffian supermultiplier developed by Franklin Serrano in 1995 combined a similar multiplier–accelerator mechanism (assumed to be dynamically stable) with non-capacity creating autonomous demand (NCCAD) to advance the research agenda proposed by Pierangelo Garegnani for the analysis of demand-led growth based on the modern Classical surplus approach (see Sraffa, 1960; Garegnani, 1962/2015; Serrano, 1995). Nowadays, besides some Sraffians, other leading heterodox economists such as Marc Lavoie, Steven Fazzari, Amitava Dutt, Thomas Palley, and Mariana Mazzucato have also adopted and developed their own versions of this fully demand-led supermultiplier (see Lavoie, 2016; Deleidi and Mazzucato, 2019; Dutt, 2019; Palley, 2019; Fazzari et al., 2020).

The demand-led supermultiplier theory is based on the principle of effective demand, according to which the level of real aggregate expenditures, measured at their supply prices, determines the (profitable) levels of real output. By extending this principle to longer periods to consider the capacity effects of business investment and the tendency of capacity to adjust to demand, the supermultiplier shows that the trend of effective demand will also determine the level of productive capacity or potential output (at an exogenous normal or planned degree of capacity utilization).

The supermultiplier theory separates expenditures into two categories, namely, induced and autonomous expenditures. Autonomous demand is defined as the part of aggregate demand that is not systematically related to the level of output. This separation is made in two different steps. First, in the circular flow of income, only part of consumption is induced, since the purchasing power introduced in the economy by current production decisions as contractual income (wages) paid to workers induces consumption expenditures. At this level of analysis, the other expenditures are considered autonomous and financed out of new credit or the monetization of accumulated wealth. In a second step, considering a longer-time horizon, business investment is seen as totally induced, since these expenditures (in aggregate) must be systematically related to the capacity requirements to produce the levels of output. Following the capital-stock adjustment principle, business investment is seen as a derived demand. Investment goods are purchased and added to the capital stock to increase productive capacity, allowing production to meet the expected trend of effective demand. Individual investment decisions are autonomous injections of purchasing power from the point of view of the circular flow of income. But competition between firms forces them to try to adjust the capital stock and capacity to the trend of demand as the underestimation of demand trends entails the risk of losing market share to rival firms and overestimation leads to very costly levels of undesired excess capacity.

Another important theoretical point is that the 'marginal propensity to spend' (the sum of the marginal propensities to consume and invest) must be lower than one for the system to be truly demand-led; that is, an increase in output must induce a less than proportional level of aggregate demand (notice that a marginal propensity to spend equal to one would mean that Say's Law holds). This requires the introduction of additional purchasing power injected in the economy by NCCAD as necessary to determine a positive level of output. Moreover, the presence of these expenditures is also necessary for the process of adjusting capacity to demand, since business investment and the capital stock can grow faster or slower than aggregate demand, ensuring the logical possibility of this adjustment. Among these expenditures we find (at least part of) residential investment, consumption financed by credit, discretionary consumption expenditures of the wealthy, government expenditures, and exports. These expenditures have multiple determinants that reflect social, political, and institutional settings of specific economies and are influenced by their particular economic policy framework.

According to the supermultiplier, the trend rate of economic growth is driven by the expansion of the NCCAD and changes in the propensity to spend, although a single shift in the latter (owing to changes in distributive shares, for example) will have only a temporary effect on economic growth and a permanent level effect on output/capacity. The induced business investment share will be positively related to the rate of economic growth and capacity utilization will tend to adjust slowly to the exogenous normal level.

The recent research agenda on the supermultiplier has advanced to better specify the theoretical determinants of the various NCCAD; the relationships between the supermultiplier and economic policy regimes; the relation between demand-led growth, accommodating supply (labour force and productivity) and conflict inflation. It has also been applied (using econometric, historical, aggregate, and input–output multisectoral/multi-country calibrated models) to analyse concrete experiences in advanced and developing countries.

RICARDO SUMMA

See also

Accelerator effects; Aggregate demand; Capacity utilization; Effective demand; Monetary circuit

References

Deleidi, M. and M. Mazzucato (2019), 'Putting austerity to bed: technical progress, aggregate demand and the supermultiplier', *Review of Political Economy*, **31** (3), 315–35.

Dutt, A.K. (2019), 'Some observations on models of growth and distribution with autonomous demand growth', *Metroeconomica*, **70** (2), 288–301.

Fazzari, S.M., P. Ferri and A.M. Variato (2020), 'Demand-led growth and accommodating supply', *Cambridge Journal of Economics*, **44** (3), 583–605.

Garegnani, P. (1962/2015), 'The problem of effective demand in Italian economic development: on the factors that determine the volume of investment', *Review of Political Economy*, **27** (2), 111–33.

Hicks, J.R. (1950), *A Contribution to the Theory of the Trade Cycle*, Oxford: Clarendon Press.

Lavoie, M. (2016), 'Convergence towards the normal rate of capacity utilization in neo-Kaleckian models: the role of non-capacity creating autonomous expenditures', *Metroeconomica*, **67** (1), 172–201.

Palley, T. (2019), 'The economics of the supermultiplier: a comprehensive treatment with labor markets', *Metroeconomica*, **70** (2), 325–40.

Serrano, F. (1995), 'Long period effective demand and the Sraffian supermultiplier', *Contributions to Political Economy*, **14** (1), 67–90.

Sraffa, P. (1960), *Production of Commodities by Means of Commodities: Prelude to a Critique of Economic Theory*, Cambridge, UK: Cambridge University Press.

Sustainable development

From a 'sustainable' economic development perspective, post-Keynesian economics has potential to effectively challenge the mainstream approach of maximizing economic growth. Mainstream economics has a 'weak' form of ecological sustainability embedded, where monetary (not ecosystem) valuation of the environment is calculated; for instance, what is the price of a 500-year-old tree (Costanza and Daly, 1992)? Sustainable development (SD) in its 'strong' form is the heterodox economics perspective to development that embraces a bottom-up approach, allowing both social equity and ecological viability to operate, with transformative innovations taking up regional and sectoral opportunities that address local constraints (Courvisanos, 2012).

Post-Keynesian economics has very limited theoretical discussion of the SD concept or policy guidance (Berr, 2009). Holt (2009) details analytical relevance of post-Keynesian economics for SD. Mearman (2009, p. 97) explains that economists in this tradition have 'inadequately dealt' with environmental issues owing to a lack of expertise and interest in the myriad of micro-environment issues involved in SD.

Berr (2009, p. 23) notes Keynes's philosophy of uncertainty has elements in common with operationalizing SD by the 'strong sustainability' rule in which natural (capital) resources are not substitutable with human-made (capital) resources, which is counter to neoclassical economists' monetary valuation of the environment. However, Keynes underestimates the role of natural resources and the power of vested interests in decision-making (Berr, 2009, pp. 33–4).

Michał Kalecki in his body of work identifies limits to economic growth; with developed countries owing to political constraints on full employment and with less-developed countries because of insufficient productive capacities. These limits inspire a SD framework in which demand-side perspective planning requires 'a set of procedures to promote the societal debate on the "project", to stimulate the social imagination ... with environmental prudence' (Sachs, 1996, p. 318). A historically based approach emerges where past decisions crucially influence future rational decisions. On the margins of post-Keynesian economics this designing rationality approach has various forms.

From the perspective of consumption, Lavoie (2009) has consumer choice allocated in a hierarchical order with essential needs purchased first, followed by higher order desires. This allows exploration of income boundaries to consuming specific classes of goods and services depending on sustainable levels in needs/desires. Based on this ordering, Jespersen (2004) argues for work permits equally to all employed persons as a first step to SD, reducing average working hours with unchanged real income and variations through trading these permits according to need. Mathieu (1993) proposes a negative income tax linked to sustainability to limit conspicuous consumption and provide 'ecobonuses' for low carbon emissions.

From a capital investment perspective, fiscal policy can stimulate SD as proposed in a Green New Deal (GND). This is centred on strong active fiscal policy prescriptions of infrastructure investment, tax credits, loan guarantees and carbon pricing aimed at shifting economies away from dominant oil-based, heavy pollution, high-carbon industrial structure (Fontana and Sawyer, 2016). GND can stimulate 'sustainably' economies out of recession as proposed by the New Economics Foundation in the United Kingdom, the United Nations Environment Programme and European Green parties. In the United States, the Political Economy Research Institute, led by Robert Pollin, has concentrated on providing a set of programmes for building a clean-energy US economy while creating employment and reducing poverty (Dafermos and Nicolaidi, 2019). Another approach, led by Mathew Forstater and the Global Institute for Sustainable Prosperity, argues for green jobs created using State counter-cyclical policy as employer of last resort. In this way jobs are designed on functional finance principles to avoid structural bottlenecks in a market economy, using 'appropriate technology' and providing skilling-up to work (Tcherneva, 2009).

None of the above Keynes/Kalecki-inspired initiatives have been incorporated into standard post-Keynesian economic theory. Courvisanos (2012) attempts this through an eco-sustainable framework to guide policy with a public–private sector cooperative process of innovation and investment underpinning appropriate satisficing paths to SD. Also of note is the critique of green post-Keynesianism from the Center for a New American Dream because of its inability to decouple economic growth from the ecosystem, leading to the alternative 'people-centric degrowth model' inspired by steady-state economics (Schor and Jorgenson, 2019).

JERRY COURVISANOS

See also

Development; Ecological macroeconomics; Employer of last resort; Fiscal policy; Growth – wage-led vs profit-led

References

Berr, E. (2009), 'Keynes and sustainable development', *International Journal of Political Economy*, **38** (3), 22–38.

Costanza, R. and H. Daly (1992), 'Natural capital and sustainable development', *Conservation Biology*, **6** (1), 37–46.

Courvisanos, J. (2012), *Cycles, Crises and Innovation: Path to Sustainable Development – A Kaleckian–Schumpeterian Synthesis*, Cheltenham, UK, and Northampton, MA, USA: Edward Elgar.

Dafermos, Y. and M. Nicolaidi (2019), 'Fiscal policy and ecological sustainability: a post-Keynesian perspective', *Post-Keynesian Economics Society Working Paper*, No. 1912.

JERRY COURVISANOS

Fontana, G. and M. Sawyer (2016), 'Towards post-Keynesian ecological macroeconomics', *Ecological Economics*, **121** (1), 186–95.
Holt, R.F. (2009), 'The relevance of Post-Keynesian economics to sustainable development', in P. Lawn (ed.), *Environment and Employment: A Reconciliation*, London and New York: Routledge, pp. 146–59.
Jespersen, J. (2004), 'Macroeconomic stability: sustainable development and full employment', in L. Reisch and I. Røpke (eds), *The Ecological Economics of Consumption*, Cheltenham, UK, and Northampton, MA, USA: Edward Elgar, pp. 233–49.
Lavoie, M. (2009), 'Post Keynesian consumer choice theory and ecological economics', in R.F. Holt, S. Pressman and C.L. Spash (eds), *Post Keynesian and Ecological Economics: Confronting Environmental Issues*, Cheltenham, UK, and Northampton, MA, USA: Edward Elgar, pp. 141–57.
Mathieu, K.-H. (1993), 'Bioeconomics and post Keynesian economics: a search for common ground', *Ecological Economics*, **8** (1), 11–16.
Mearman, A. (2009), 'Why have Post-Keynesians (perhaps) inadequately dealt with issues related to the environment?', in P. Lawn (ed.), *Environment and Employment: A Reconciliation*, London and New York: Routledge, pp. 97–125.
Sachs, I. (1996), 'What State, what markets, for what development? The social, ecological and economical dimensions of planning', *Social Indicators Research*, **39** (3), 311–20.
Schor, J.B. and A.K. Jorgenson (2019), 'Is it too late for growth?', *Review of Radical Political Economics*, **51** (2), 320–9.
Tcherneva, P. (2009), 'Evaluating the economic and environmental viability of basic income and job guarantees', in P. Lawn (ed.), *Environment and Employment: A Reconciliation*, London and New York: Routledge, pp. 184–205.

Target-return pricing

Target-return pricing is one among several pricing procedures businesses can use to set the prices of their commodities. It is a variant of normal-cost pricing. In this procedure, firms set their prices by adding a profit margin to a measure of unit (normal) cost so as to yield a precise and targeted rate of return on capital assets, when output corresponds to a normal or standard level. This procedure is one of the most sophisticated of all pricing procedures: as recalled by Lavoie (2014), it requires to define standard and full-capacity volumes of output, so as to calculate a normal rate of capacity utilization, and a normal unit cost, as well as to calculate the value of capital assets of a plant so as to apply the targeted profit rate. Although sophisticated, this procedure seems very widespread among businesses, be they large or small (see Lee, 1998).

When actual sales exceed normal or standard output, the actual rate of capacity is higher than the standard rate and the actual rate of profit is higher than the targeted rate. When sales are lower than normal output, the rate of capacity utilization is lower than the standard rate and the actual profit rate is lower than the targeted profit rate. In that sense, target-return pricing has to be conceived not as a short-term rate of profit that is always reached, but as a mean over several periods. In periods of booms, firms may reach better rates than the targeted rate, and in periods of recessions the converse may occur.

To our knowledge, the first historical identification of the principle of target return pricing can be found in an article of a management engineer, Donaldson Brown, in 1924 (also mentioned by Means (1962)). Brown describes the five steps of this procedure as follows:

- decide on a normal/standard rate of capacity utilization;
- calculate or estimate the full unit cost at the standard rate of utilization;
- decide on a targeted rate of return;
- calculate the price that follows;
- consider the price in light of market conditions.

Later, this principle was described by Lanzillotti (1958) and Kaplan et al. (1958). In their study, two interviews taken several years apart with each of 20 among the largest US corporations reported the widespread existence of target return as a pricing objective. It was even the first objective for one half of these companies, the several years between the two interviews showing an increasing tendency to adopt it (Lanzillotti, 1958).

For companies, target-return pricing has several advantages:

- It allows for different profit margins of different products, all compatible with the global targeted rate of return decided at the level of the plant/firm.
- It provides price stabilization over the business cycle, because prices are

determined under long-term considerations and not by profit maximization in the current period.

This procedure has also some limits. It does not explain the value of the targeted rate of profit. In that sense it is not a theory of the desired profit margin. Further, it explains the fluctuation of actual rates of profit, but not how firms have decided to incorporate one value or another of the profit rate in their target calculus. This refers to several post-Keynesian explanations of profit margins: degree of monopoly/imperfect competition, needs for internal finance.

JORDAN MELMIÈS AND
FLORIAN BOTTE

See Also

Capacity utilization; Mark-up pricing; Monopoly power; Pricing; Profit

References

Brown, D. (1924), 'Pricing policy in relation to financial control', *Management and Administration*, 7 (2), 283–6.
Kaplan, A.D.H., J.B. Dirlam and R.F. Lanzillotti (1958), *Pricing in Big Business: A Case Approach*, Washington, DC: Brookings Institution.
Lanzillotti, R.F. (1958), 'Pricing objectives in large companies', *American Economic Review*, 48 (5), 921–40.
Lavoie, M. (2014), *Post-Keynesian Economics: New Foundations*, Cheltenham, UK, and Northampton, MA, USA: Edward Elgar.
Lee, F.S. (1998), *Post Keynesian Price Theory*, Cambridge, UK: Cambridge University Press.
Means, G.C. (1962), *Pricing Power and the Public Interest*, New York: Harper and Brothers.

TARGET2 system

TARGET2 is the acronym for the 'Trans-European Automated Real-Time Gross Settlement Express Transfer' system. This is the payment system set up when the euro area was created as a result of the European Monetary Union in January 1999.

Cross-border payments within the euro area are carried out through TARGET2, involving the national central banks of both the payer's and the payee's countries. As the European Central Bank (2007, p. 34) explains, '[c]ross-border TARGET[2] payments are processed via the national RTGS [standing for Real-Time Gross Settlement] systems and exchanged directly on a bilateral basis between NCBs [standing for national central banks].' There is therefore a two-tier structure for processing payment orders within TARGET2. The first tier includes commercial banks across the euro area, whilst their national central banks are gathered in the second tier. 'Once the sending NCB has checked the validity of a payment message and the availability of funds or sufficient overdraft facilities, the amount of the payment is debited irrevocably and without delay from the RTGS account of the sending credit institution and credited to the Interlinking account of the receiving NCB' (European Central Bank, 2007, p. 35). To this end, each national central bank in the euro area holds an 'Interlinking account' in the Interlinking mechanism, which assembles 'the infrastructures and procedures which link domestic RTGS systems in order to enable the processing of inter-Member State payments within TARGET[2]' (European Central Bank, 2011, p. 58). After the receiving national central bank has carried out all security checks and message verifications, it 'converts, where appropriate, the message from the Interlinking standard into the domestic standard, debits the Interlinking account of the sending NCB, credits the beneficiary's RTGS account and delivers a positive acknowledgement to the sending NCB' (European Central Bank, 2007, p. 35).

This infrastructure is not yet up to the task of making sure that cross-border payments are finally settled internationally, to wit, between the national central banks involved thereby. This is so because the European Central Bank (ECB) does not intervene as an international settlement institution when a cross-border payment order is carried out through TARGET2. As a matter of fact, these payment orders are executed by national central banks instead of being settled through the ECB, whose role should be to act as the central bank for NCBs – similarly to the role the latter play with regard to commercial banks in their own countries (see Rossi, 2007).

Lacking payment finality at international level (that is, between euro-area countries each considered as a whole), TARGET2 payments have been inflating net balances that national central banks hold within this system: net exporting countries like Germany have been thus accumulating an increasing volume of positive balances within TARGET2 since the euro-area crisis burst, whilst net importing countries (such as Greece) have been accumulating an increasing volume of negative balances within it. These so-called 'TARGET2 imbalances' (see for instance Sinn and Wollmershäuser, 2012) are a result of the euro-area crisis that erupted at the end of 2009, as earlier on the net exporting countries' banks were purchasing those financial assets that net importing countries' agents wanted to sell in order to finance their commercial deficits thereby and hence reduced net balances close to zero within the TARGET2 system for both deficit and surplus countries.

To avoid the monetary disorder that the ECB originates within TARGET2, the latter central bank must issue the means of final payment that national central banks need to finally pay a cross-border transaction for the countries involved thereby. This is in line with the Keynes Plan that he proposed at the Bretton Woods conference in 1944, to set up an international clearing union with an international clearing bank issuing a means of final payment to be used by national central banks only (which Keynes called 'bancor') (see Keynes, 1980).

SERGIO ROSSI

See also

Euro; European Monetary Union; Eurozone imbalances; International clearing union; Settlement system

References

European Central Bank (2007), *Payment and Securities Settlement Systems in the European Union, Volume 1: Euro Area Countries*, Frankfurt am Main: European Central Bank.
European Central Bank (2011), *TARGET Annual Report 2010*, Frankfurt am Main: European Central Bank.
Keynes, J.M. (1980), *The Collected Writings of John Maynard Keynes*, vol. XXV, *Activities 1940–1944. Shaping the Post-War World: The Clearing Union*, London and Basingstoke: Macmillan.
Rossi, S. (2007), *Money and Payments in Theory and Practice*, London and New York: Routledge.
Sinn, H.-W. and T. Wollmershäuser (2012), 'Target loans, current account balances and capital flows: the ECB's rescue facility', *International Tax and Public Finance*, **19** (4), 468–508.

Technological change

Technology is as old as humanity, and technological change has incessantly occurred throughout human history. Technology can be looked at according to three dimensions, that is, technology as knowledge, skills, and artefacts. These three dimensions are intertwined and feed one another. Technology creation is based on 'acts of insight', which concern each dimension. What has changed radically through time are the breadth of technology creation and the speed of change, particularly since the relationship between technology and science has become close (Metcalfe, 2010; De Liso, 2013).

Let us consider only the economic analysis of technological change, which concerns market economies where profit constitutes a fundamental lever. We consider how technological change is studied within the Classical, Neoclassical, and Evolutionary schools of thought.

Technical change is a central feature of the Classical school since the publication of Adam Smith's *Wealth of Nations* in 1776. Classical economics deals with structural economic dynamics, so that different sectors emerge and evolve and their relative importance changes through time. Along the path, technological change plays an essential role. Technology affects the way in which the fundamental economic magnitudes (profit, wage, rent, prices, and employment) are set. As we cannot provide here a full summary of Classical analysis (see Kurz and Salvadori, 2003), let us focus on two central themes: the division of labour and the automation of work processes. The division of labour can be looked at on two different levels: a first level refers to the separation of employments and professions within society, and a second level refers to the detailed tasks that develop within a factory or office, or within a single industry. A more detailed division of labour implies higher productivity of the economic system as a whole. Automation of human activities is a constituent part of capitalist systems whose technological basis is revolutionary by definition: the search for profit stimulates the search for more efficient production techniques, besides the creation of new products and services that, in turn, further stimulate technology creation.

The Neoclassical school has its origins in the works of the founders of the Marginalist

SERGIO ROSSI / NICOLA DE LISO

Revolution in the 1870s. Technical change has become central to this school only from the mid-1950s. This approach was originally based on the measurement of 'total factor productivity' and the so-called 'residual'. The main point lies in the fact that a large proportion of economic growth observed in advanced economies cannot be justified by the substitution of capital for labour or by the availability of more capital per unit of labour. Rather, both capital and labour become more productive. Put another way, a certain capital-to-labour ratio in a given year is characterized by a higher productivity with respect to the same ratio referring to a previous year. The difference between productivities is called the 'residual' and is justified by the occurrence of technological change. This residual can be illustrated graphically by means of production functions. At first, economists simply measured the residual without being able to explain it, and technical change was synthesized as being a function of time. Then a process of 'endogenization' of technical progress, that is, an explanation of what explains progress itself, has taken place. Recent explanations refer to intentional actions of firms to create new knowledge and to the existence and development of human capital (see Aghion and Howitt, 1998).

The Evolutionary, or Neo-Schumpeterian, school established itself as a coherent body of research in the early 1980s, and the role played by technical change has always been central to it. Following Nelson and Winter (1982), it looks at firms as being run on the basis of three different routines: standard operating procedures, routines that determine the investment behaviour, and routines according to which the firm decides to look for better ways of doing things. Profit-oriented behaviour implies that technical change can take place within each routine, the third type being the strongest in order to promote technical progress. When something 'happens' – for instance the product's price changes – firms activate their search strategy. The outcome of the actions taken can be a better or new technology and may lead to the development of broadly useful new knowledge. Technological variety characterizes the productive panorama of evolutionary theory, and the market, through consumers' choice, will implicitly select the technology. Technological change and variety, though, are limited by two forces, namely path-dependence and the paradigmatic nature of technology: as a rule, what a firm does at time t is affected by what it did at time $t-1$; secondly, technologies tend to be organized around a basic principle or device – for example internal combustion for engines, semiconductors for computers – and they develop along a trajectory.

Scholars belonging to any of these schools always consider the importance of non-economic factors in shaping technology, the role played by governments through science and technology policy, and the impact on employment.

NICOLA DE LISO

See also

Consumer choice; Growth; Innovation; Neoclassical economics; Profit; Traverse, path dependency and economic dynamics

References

Aghion, P. and P. Howitt (1998), *Endogenous Growth Theory*, Cambridge, USA: MIT Press.

De Liso, N. (2013), 'From mechanical arts to the philosophy of technology', *Economics of Innovation and New Technology*, **22** (7–8), 726–50.

Kurz, H.D. and N. Salvadori (2003), *Classical Economics and Modern Theory: Studies in Long-Period Analysis*, London and New York: Routledge.

Metcalfe, J.S. (2010), 'Technical change', in S.N. Durlauf and L.E. Blume (eds), *Economic Growth*, London: Macmillan, pp. 237–48.

Nelson, R.R. and S.G. Winter (1982), *An Evolutionary Theory of Economic Change*, Cambridge, USA: Belknap Press.

Terms of trade

Terms of trade are defined as the ratio between the prices of the exports of a country and the price of its imports. They can thus be interpreted as the inverse of the real exchange rate, being negatively correlated with competitiveness (Carlin and Soskice, 2006, p. 302). The concept, however, is usually associated with the Prebisch–Singer hypothesis (Prebisch, 1950; Singer, 1950), which maintains that the terms of trade of underdeveloped countries tend to deteriorate. This hypothesis resulted from independent efforts by Prebisch and Singer to provide explanations for the empirical findings reported in a United Nations document

NICOLA DE LISO / FERNANDO RUGITSKY

elaborated by Singer in the late 1940s: the ratio between the prices of primary commodities and the prices of manufactured goods declined by about a third between the 1870s and the 1940s (Toye and Toye, 2003).

Given that trade between developed and underdeveloped countries, at that time, consisted predominantly in the exchange of primary commodities produced in underdeveloped countries against manufactured goods produced in developed countries, the above-mentioned ratio could be interpreted as an approximation of the terms of trade of underdeveloped economies. Singer's explanation for that decline was mainly based on the low price and income elasticities of primary goods, whereas Prebisch also focused on the role played by differences between the structures of the labour markets of the two regions. These elements explained why productivity gains in the production of manufactured goods generally resulted in higher wages, with prices remaining stable, while the (less frequent) productivity gains in the production of primary commodities tended to result in lower prices. This contrast implied that developed countries not only kept to themselves the fruits of their technical progress, but also were able to appropriate part of the fruits of the technical progress that took place in underdeveloped countries.

The Prebisch–Singer hypothesis put forward, in this way, an explanation for the continuous reproduction of two polarized regions in the world economy: developed countries at the core and underdeveloped countries at the periphery. In the early days of development thinking, this hypothesis was one of the most influential bases for the defence of State-led industrialization in the periphery. Industrialization was seen as a way to defend the economy against the negative effects of deteriorating terms of trade between primary commodities and manufactured goods.

But if the terms of trade can be interpreted as the inverse of the real exchange rate, is it not possible to claim that their deterioration is expansionary through their positive impact on exports? Thirlwall (1983, p. 252) raised this question in the following terms, when he examined Prebisch's work: '[i]t is often forgotten that when countries devalue their currency they deliberately deteriorate their terms of trade in the hope of real income gains from a greater volume of home production.' The Prebisch–Singer hypothesis assumed that these real income gains would not materialize owing to low price elasticities of exports and imports of underdeveloped countries, in a framework of specialization in the production of primary commodities and high dependence on foreign goods not produced domestically. In technical terms, the Marshall–Lerner condition does not hold for these economies and the terms of trade deterioration (or, equivalently, an exchange-rate devaluation) is contractionary, a possibility that was entertained by Hirschman (1949) and Díaz-Alejandro (1963) and further elaborated by Krugman and Taylor (1978).

After almost seven decades, one is allowed to ask how the Prebisch–Singer hypothesis stood the test of time. Abundant empirical research suggests that the deterioration of the terms of trade between primary commodities and manufactured goods remains observable in the data and that the recent commodities prices boom was but a cycle around a declining trend (see, for instance, Harvey et al., 2010; Erten and Ocampo, 2013; Baffes and Etienne, 2016). It is true that the international division of labour has changed considerably since the 1950s, especially with the shift of the production of manufacturing goods to Asia, shielding the countries of the region from the negative effects of the declining relative prices of primary commodities. However, some regions of the underdeveloped world, especially in Africa and South America, remain highly dependent on the exports of primary commodities and still face the challenges identified long ago by Prebisch and Singer.

FERNANDO RUGITSKY

See also

Balance of payments; Balance-of-payments constrained growth; Development; Exchange rates; Foreign-exchange reserves

References

Baffes, J. and X. Etienne (2016), 'Analysing food price trends in the context of Engel's Law and the Prebisch–Singer hypothesis', *Oxford Economic Papers*, **68** (3), 688–713.

Carlin, W. and D. Soskice (2006), *Macroeconomics: Imperfections, Institutions and Policies*, Oxford: Oxford University Press.

Díaz-Alejandro, C.F. (1963), 'A note on the impact of devaluation and the redistributive effect', *Journal of Political Economy*, **71** (6), 577–80.

Erten, B. and J.A. Ocampo (2013), 'Super cycles of commodity prices since the mid-nineteenth century', *World Development*, **44** (C), 14–30.

Harvey, D., N. Kellard, J. Madsen and M. Wohar (2010), 'The Prebisch–Singer hypothesis: four centuries of evidence', *Review of Economics and Statistics*, **92** (2), 367–77.

Hirschman, A.O. (1949), 'Devaluation and the trade balance: a note', *Review of Economics and Statistics*, **31** (1), 50–53.

Krugman, P. and L. Taylor (1978), 'Contractionary effects of devaluation', *Journal of International Economics*, **8** (3), 445–56.

Prebisch, R. (1950), *The Economic Development of Latin America and Its Principal Problems*, Lake Success, NY: United Nations.

Singer, H. (1950), 'The distribution of gains between investing and borrowing countries', *American Economic Review*, **40** (2), 473–85.

Thirlwall, A. (1983), 'Foreign trade elasticities in centre–periphery models of growth and development', *Banca Nazionale del Lavoro Quarterly Review*, **36** (146), 249–61.

Toye, J. and R. Toye (2003), 'The origins and interpretation of the Prebisch–Singer thesis', *History of Political Economy*, **35** (3), 437–67.

The Accumulation of Capital

Joan Robinson saw Keynes's (1936) *General Theory* and its application of the principle of effective demand to the short run as having initiated a revolutionary rupture with neoclassical theory. In her account, the book 'broke through the unnatural barrier and brought history and theory together again. But for theorists the descent into time has not been easy. After twenty years, the awakened Princess is still dazed and groggy' (Robinson, 1962a, p. 78). Keynes's work thus roused in Robinson the ambition to provide 'a generalization of the *General Theory*, that is, an extension of Keynes' short-period analysis to long-run development' (Robinson, 1956, p. vi).

This engagement with the theory of accumulation featured early and often in Robinson's work, beginning with her *Essays in the Theory of Employment* (1937). Given her penchant for autocriticism, Robinson would readily acknowledge that her *Accumulation of Capital* (*AC*) (1956) was an imperfect effort in service of her ambition, and indeed saw her subsequent *Essays in the Theory of Economic Growth* (1962b) as a necessary revision and introduction to her earlier book.

While enjoying a wide audience upon its immediate publication, reviewers regularly objected to both the opaque style and theoretical propositions of *AC*. Further, despite the considerable energies that post-Keynesian authors have devoted to models of economic growth and income distribution in the past thirty years, Robinson's *AC* features as little more than a footnote in these discussions (King, 2016). Thus, for modern readers, the book primarily offers a window into Robinson's own process of intellectual growth and development and, more broadly, into the adolescence of post-Keynesian economics. The problems of re-switching and reverse capital deepening that, years later, would become central to the Cambridge capital controversies make a hesitant first appearance. Similarly, other readers have found in Robinson's discussion of money and finance an anticipation of the theory of the monetary circuit (Rochon, 2005).

The book is at once a work of criticism and construction, highlighting as it does the logical inconsistencies of the neoclassical theory of the rate of profit as a measure of the relative scarcity of capital (Bhaduri, 1996). In Robinson's model, investment decisions are understood to be governed by profit expectations and the 'animal spirits' of the capitalist class, influences that are ultimately unobservable. The relationship is, however, double-sided in the sense that desired investment determines the *ex post* rate of profit. The practical limit to the rate of profit is given by the minimum socially acceptable level of real wages, or what Robinson terms the 'inflation barrier'. Past this point, pressure for nominal wages to rise emerges, and '[e]ither the system explodes in a hyper-inflation, or some check operates to curtail investment' (Robinson, 1956, p. 48). Importantly, the particular real-wage level that serves as the inflation barrier is not a physiological minimum required for workers' survival and productivity, and instead depends on labour's degree of organization and bargaining power.

AC also evinces Robinson's discomfort with the idea that the actual long-run development of capitalist economies could be meaningfully captured by any singular equilibrium growth path. Sensitivity to the true nature of historical change requires one to 'give up the idea of equilibrium and exhibit an economy blundering on from one situation to another (as happens in the world we live in) following no simple predictable path' (Robinson, 1961, p. 361).

AC's analytical core is found in its Book II, 'Accumulation in the long run', where Robinson sets out the distributive consequences of various patterns of capital accumulation. She describes the potential growth path wherein labour would be fully employed, with a steady rate of profit, and real wage increases mirroring the rate of productivity growth, as a 'golden age'. The practical demands of such a fortuitous developmental path amount to 'a mythical state of affairs not likely to obtain in any actual economy' (Robinson, 1956, p. 99).

Having established the book's foundational model early on, Robinson (1956, p. ix) suggests that 'the rest of the book may be regarded as complications and qualifications surrounding this central core'. Outside of golden age tranquillity, a range of alternative scenarios corresponding to varying forms and rates of technical progress are also admitted for analysis. The final half of the book contains significant digressions into the influence of finance, agriculture and balance of payments. Absent from all this exposition are explicit connections to the lived history of capitalist economies that might illustrate the patterns of accumulation she describes. The reader is instead left to find their own place amidst the muddle.

WILLIAM E. MCCOLLOCH

See also

Animal spirits; Capital theory controversies; Effective demand; Income distribution; Monetary circuit

References

Bhaduri, A. (1996), 'Economic growth and the theory of capital: an evaluation of Joan Robinson's contribution', in M.C. Marcuzzo, L.L. Pasinetti and A. Roncaglia (eds), *The Economics of Joan Robinson*, London: Routledge, pp. 200–6.
Keynes, J.M. (1936), *The General Theory of Employment, Interest and Money*, London: Macmillan.
King, J.E. (2016), 'Joan Robinson's *Accumulation of Capital* after 60 years', *Review of Keynesian Economics*, **4** (3), 316–30.
Robinson, J. (1937), *Essays in the Theory of Employment*, London: Macmillan.
Robinson, J.V. (1956), *The Accumulation of Capital*, London: Macmillan.
Robinson, J.V. (1961), 'Equilibrium growth models: a review article', *American Economic Review*, **51** (3), 360–9.
Robinson, J.V. (1962a), *Economic Philosophy*, London: C.A. Watts.
Robinson, J.V. (1962b), *Essays in the Theory of Economic Growth*, London: Macmillan.

Rochon, L.-P. (2005), 'Robinson on credit, money and finance', in B. Gibson (ed.), *Joan Robinson's Economics: A Centennial Celebration*, Cheltenham, UK, and Northampton, MA, USA: Edward Elgar, pp. 267–82.

The Great Transformation

The Great Transformation (originally titled *The Origins of Our Time*) is the work for which the Austro-Hungarian socialist and polymath Karl Polanyi is known. Its central thesis is that the events through which its author was living – two world wars, fascism and the Great Depression – formed an interconnected cataclysm whose origins lay 'in the utopian endeavor of economic liberalism to set up a self-regulating market system' (Polanyi, 1944/2001, p. 31). What was it about the market system that had brought the world to the brink? When land, labour and money are treated as commodities, society as a whole becomes subject to the laws of the market, while simultaneously, at the institutional level, the economy becomes separated from politics. This marked a novel departure from all previous social formations.

According to Polanyi, the very extremism of the self-regulating market ensures it cannot govern unchallenged. With this we arrive at his second thesis: the subsuming of vital elements of human life and the natural environment beneath the calculus of purchase and sale gives rise to such corrosive tendencies that spontaneous reactions of 'social protection' (or the 'countermovement') are inevitable. The countermovements of the nineteenth century provided support for market expansion by checking its destructive tendencies, but in the twentieth century they conflicted with market principles, giving rise to 'disruptive strains' that brought the market system to collapse. On one hand, protective measures such as trade union practices and economic nationalism (Dale, 2016) were needed to prevent society from self-destruction; on the other hand, these same measures exacerbated slumps and protectionism. (Polanyi subscribed to the pre-Keynesian tenet that interference with markets causes them to malfunction.)

We should also read *The Great Transformation* as a theorization of Europe's fascist irruption of the interwar period. For what, in its author's view, was fascism? It was the last throw of the dice by embattled capitalist elites, as they confronted working-class revolt and a series of crises culminating in the Great Depression. And what was the Great Depression? It was the outcome of the aforementioned 'disruptive strains' – notably the social fall-out from the operation of the gold standard. And what was the gold standard? It was the global institutional embodiment of free-market economics. Hence Polanyi's (2001, p. 32) famous phrase: 'In order to comprehend German fascism, we must revert to Ricardian England' – the setting of the book's central chapters. It is in these chapters, too, that a further major thesis is proposed. Contrary to those explanations that posit the Industrial Revolution as a purely private process supervised by a minimal State, Polanyi shows that behind the construction of the market system there is a programme of social engineering steered by States that were far more intrusive than their pre-modern predecessors. In this thesis, Polanyi inverts the Hayekian indictment against socialism – that it represents an artificial experiment in social engineering, anti-human in its suppression of catallactic spontaneity. In *The Great Transformation* the tables are turned: economic liberals are the utopian extremists; their opponents are the bearers of a spontaneous reaction demanding social protection.

If we turn to look at internal tensions and ambiguities, the most obvious concern the book title itself. To what does 'the great transformation' refer? The usual interpretation, amplified by the book's Wikipedia entry, is that it refers to the eighteenth and nineteenth century rise of market society. This is not wholly misleading. Polanyi does see this as one of world history's major revolutionary transformations. But during his research on the book, and in its pages too, he associated 'transformation' and 'great transformation' far more frequently with the breakdown and replacement of market society, which he believed was occurring in the first half of the twentieth century, with the 1930s as the pivotal ('revolutionary') decade. In Chapter 1 he makes this perfectly plain: 'Nineteenth-century civilization has collapsed. This book is concerned with the political and economic origins of this event, as well as with the great transformation which it ushered in' (Polanyi, 2001, p. 3).

The inner meaning and objective of *The Great Transformation* have been the subject of some debate, which Szelényi (1991) usefully summarized as the 'hard' and the 'soft' Polanyi. The former advocated a socialist mixed economy dominated by redistributive mechanisms; the latter believed the market should remain the dominant coordinating mechanism within a capitalist mixed economy. Other interpretative arguments have arisen over the meaning of the 'countermovement', his analysis of the gold standard (Knafo, 2019), questions of neoclassical economics, functionalism and determinism in Polanyi's method (Bockman, 2011; Dale, 2014; Gemici, 2015), and the ambiguity of his concept of 'protection' (is Polanyi referring to the protection of labour from the volatility of a market economy, or of the rural community – including employers' interests?).

Following its publication in 1944, *The Great Transformation* occupied a relatively marginal role for several decades. It gained a readership among anthropologists, but it made little headway in the fields of economics or political economy, or as a touchstone for socialists. But with the rise of neoliberalism in the 1980s it began to appear more relevant to contemporary debates, its audience grew, and its status as a classic became assured.

GARETH DALE

See also

Capitalism; Income distribution; Neoclassical economics; Social classes; State–entrepreneurial

References

Bockman, J. (2011), *Markets in the Name of Socialism: The Left-Wing Origins of Neoliberalism*, Stanford: Stanford University Press.
Dale, G. (2014), 'The iron law of democratic socialism: British and Austrian influences on the young Karl Polanyi', *Economy and Society*, **43** (4), 650–67.
Dale, G. (2016), 'In search of Karl Polanyi's international relations theory', *Review of International Studies*, **42** (3), 401–24.
Gemici, K. (2015), 'The neoclassical origins of Polanyi's self-regulating market', *Sociological Theory*, **33** (2), 125–47.
Knafo, S. (2019), 'The gold standard', in G. Dale, C. Holmes and M. Markantōnatou (eds), *Karl Polanyi's Political and Economic Thought: A Critical Guide*, Newcastle upon Tyne: Agenda Publishing, pp. 89–108.
Polanyi, K. (1944/2001), *The Great Transformation*, Boston: Beacon Press.
Szelényi, I. (1991), 'Karl Polanyi and the theory of a socialist mixed economy', in M. Mendell and D. Salée (eds), *The Legacy of Karl Polanyi: Market, State and Society at the End of the Twentieth Century*, Houndmills: Macmillan, pp. 231–48.

GARETH DALE

The Path of Economic Growth

The Path of Economic Growth was published in 1976 by Cambridge University Press and represents the culmination of its author's lifetime work on the structural features of an industrial economy and on the business cycle.

Adolph Lowe (1893–1995) was born in Stuttgart, Germany, as Adolf Löwe. In 1933, upon his dismissal by the Hitlerite regime from the University of Frankfurt, he was compelled to leave his country for the United Kingdom, where he was naturalized. However, as stated on the History of Economic Thought website, 'when World War II began, Lowe found his position as an "enemy alien" caused discomfort and therefore resolved on leaving England in 1940.' Adolph Lowe became Professor of Economics at the Graduate Faculty of the New School for Social Research in New York, where he served as the most senior faculty until his retirement in 1983. Afterwards he returned to Germany to live in the city of Wolfenbüttel, where he died in 1995 aged 102.

During Weimar's Germany, Lowe founded the Kiel Institute of World Economics in 1926, where he published a seminal paper on the business cycle, outlining elements of his subsequent theorizing. The first presentation of his theoretical approach appeared in the early 1950s in the New School's well-known journal *Social Research* (Lowe, 1952; see also Hagemann and Kurz, 1998).

The objective of *The Path of Economic Growth* is to analyse the structural changes entailed in the process of capital accumulation as well as in its opposite, namely that of capital liquidation. To highlight the logic in the complexity of structural change, Lowe considers what happens if the initial stationary state is disturbed, starting with the simplest possible question. What processes should a stationary system undergo in order to meet a once and for all increase in population? The initial state of the economy is therefore characterized by full capacity and full employment under conditions of simple reproduction, with no technical progress. The study of the adjustment process is conducted by means of instrumental analysis, which combines the postulated macroeconomic goal of attaining a new state of stationariness – but at a higher level of employment in the wake of the once over expansion of population – with the structural analysis of sectoral movements. After dealing with the sectoral changes required to attain the new stationary state, Lowe addresses the issues of economic growth and of the changes in the techniques of production, including the requirements for the recycling of production residuals. The transition of the economic system from one state to the next is called 'traverse', a term borrowed from John Hicks (1965). In the latter's framework, the trajectory of the traverse depends on the configuration of the technical coefficients of production, whereas in Lowe's it is conditional upon the institutional framework.

Economic theory must show and explain how a system can get into a new state. For this purpose, Lowe builds a three-sector model based on two capital goods sectors and one consumption goods sector. The first capital goods sector produces machine tools that can reproduce themselves and/or the machines for the second capital goods sector, which produces the specific machine for the consumption goods sector. The stated macroeconomic goal is to absorb the new labour force; thus, new capacity must be created in order to expand the capital stock by the required amount. It follows that the machine tools sector will have to concentrate on its own expansion, reducing the supply of machinery to the intermediate sector producing the equipment for the consumption goods sector. Given the initial stationary conditions, this means that the consumption goods industries will receive less equipment, thereby reducing the supply of consumption goods, which is tantamount to a fall in real wages. Market forces have a limited role to play. The increase in the supply of labour may reduce wages, thereby liberating capacity for the self-expansion of the machine tools sector. However, if institutions fail to achieve the macroeconomic goal of full employment, the market-induced reduction in real wages will translate into unused capacity and into industrial unemployment rather than in a greater output of machine tools. Although Lowe shows that there may be a traverse leading to a new full-employment steady state, the market is very unlikely to deliver it, as it transmits the wrong signals in terms of the optimal structure of production and the necessary intersectoral flows. A full-employment outcome, as with Keynesian analysis, is a fluke.

Lowe's book constitutes the most comprehensive treatment to date of the dynamics within capital goods sectors and it establishes

Joseph Halevi

a bridge between structural and Keynesian analyses.

JOSEPH HALEVI

See also

Business cycles; Growth; Post-Keynesian economics – a big tent?; Traverse, path dependency, and economic dynamics; Traverse, path dependency, and economic equilibrium

References

Hagemann, H. and H. Kurz (eds) (1998), *Political Economics in Retrospect*, Cheltenham, UK, and Northampton, MA, USA: Edward Elgar.
Hicks, J. (1965), *Capital and Growth*, Oxford: Clarendon Press.
Lowe, A. (1952), 'A structural model of production', *Social Research*, 19, 135–76.
Lowe, A. (1976), *The Path of Economic Growth*, Cambridge: Cambridge University Press.

The Scourge of Monetarism

Kaldor's *The Scourge of Monetarism* is a short book of just over 100 pages. It is comprised of two lectures delivered at the University of Warwick in 1981 to commemorate the life and work of Lord Radcliffe; and Kaldor's evidence to the 1980 Treasury and Civil Service Committee inquiry into monetary policy. Originally published in 1982 with a second edition in 1986, it represents an excellent summary of Kaldor's monetary thought, its policy implications, and Kaldor's strong opposition to the tenets of monetarism.

Kaldor's first lecture in this work provides a detailed background to the appointment in 1957 of the Radcliffe Committee, which examined the working of Britain's monetary and credit system. It also summarizes the Radcliffe Committee's findings. Kaldor explains that after a number of years in which aggregate demand had been managed using fiscal policy to deliver full employment with low inflation, the re-emergence of inflation in the mid-1950s re-ignited interest in monetary policy to manage the macroeconomy, particularly inflation. Initial attempts to use monetary policy, however, were not very effective. The Radcliffe Committee's (1960) *Report* famously expressed scepticism about whether this ineffectiveness could be overcome and about the possibility of a close relationship between the amount of money in circulation and the level of income. It acknowledged the potential for variations in the velocity of monetary circulation, it employed a relatively broad definition of liquidity, and it enumerated the difficulties faced by central banks attempting to limit spending by monetary policy interventions (Kaldor, 1986, pp. 3–10). Kaldor observes that none of these conclusions were friendly to monetarism.

His second lecture contains a crisp summary of his own monetary thought. Within just a few pages, Kaldor outlines the ideas of reverse causation flowing from income to the money supply, a version of the Classical doctrine of reflux by which superfluous money balances are returned to the banking system rather than used for inflationary spending, he presents the famous diagram in which the money supply curve is horizontal rather than vertical, and he explains exogenously fixed interest rates in terms of the central bank's objective of maintaining banking system stability (Kaldor, 1986, pp. 21–6; see also Lavoie, 1999).

Of particular importance to Kaldor in this discussion, is Friedman's (1956, 1969) interpretation of Keynes's (1936) liquidity preference theory of interest. Friedman saw liquidity preference theory as predicting instability in the demand for money when expressed as a function of nominal income. An increase in nominal income, for Friedman, implied a predictable and stable increase in money demand. When such a function was combined with an exogenous increase in money supply, higher prices would inevitably result. But if money demand varied with interest rates as suggested by Keynes, it would be an unstable function of nominal income. In this case, an increased money supply could reduce interest rates, the velocity of circulation of money would fall, and this would increase the demand for money at the same level of nominal income without increasing prices. Friedman thus asserted that the Keynesian theory could be evaluated by testing whether the demand for money function was unstable. He found that it was in fact stable, contra Keynes.

Kaldor (1986, pp. 22–8) argues, however, that it is only when central banks refuse to accommodate changes in money demand that interest rates change, money's velocity of circulation varies, and the money demand function appears

JOSEPH HALEVI / PETER DOCHERTY

to be unstable in the Keynesian argument. The more usual case is that central banks accommodate variations in money demand at the prevailing interest rate in order to prevent financial instability. In this case, money demand does in fact appear to be stable, but the money supply is not exogenously exerting an influence on prices, as asserted by Friedman: it is endogenously responding to the needs of trade.

Money endogeneity for Kaldor is thus a complex of central bank accommodation and velocity variability, and it flatly contradicts Friedman's theory of inflation (Kaldor, 1986, p. 29; see Docherty, 2005, p. 124). The possibility that Keynes's concept of liquidity preference could be misinterpreted in this way led Kaldor to question whether it should be regarded as a fundamental determinant of interest rates (Kaldor, 1986, p. 26; Desai, 1989, p. 175). For Kaldor, the rate of interest is determined by central bank policy, and liquidity preference provides a theory of the term structure of interest rates rather than a theory of their level (Kaldor, 1986, pp. 95–6; see Docherty, 2005, pp. 160–4).

Kaldor's evidence to the Treasury and Civil Service Committee in the second part of *The Scourge of Monetarism* engages with the British version of monetarism. This embodiment of Friedman's ideas argued in the 1970s and 1980s for reductions in public sector deficits because they were inflationary. British monetarists based this argument on the claim that unfunded deficits increase the monetary base and hence the money supply (Kaldor, 1986, p. 48). Where public deficits are, however, fully funded, they simply drive up interest rates, which crowds out private sector expenditure with no effect on output or employment (Kaldor, 1986, p. 98). Kaldor's response employed both his theory of endogenous money and his argument that the structure of interest rates was determined by a combination of central bank policy and liquidity preference.

In the case of an unfunded public deficit at less than full employment (which was the only context in which Keynesians, at least, would recommend such a measure), Kaldor argued that the monetary base may well be expanded, but the associated government expenditure would generate higher output and employment rather than higher prices. The additional saving generated by this expansion of income would be held partly in bank deposits (which would be consistent with an expanded money supply) and partly in government securities. But this choice would not alter the savings decision of households, and would not, therefore, generate any additional spending effects that could further increase aggregate demand and drive up prices (Kaldor, 1986, pp. 49–50). A fully funded public deficit, on the other hand, may well have the initial effect of raising long-term interest rates, but this would tempt savers out of short-term securities rewarded at the same short-term rate of interest, and release funds to finance the larger public deficit. This would, in turn, place upward pressure on short-term rates of interest. But if the central bank wished to maintain the existing short-term rate of interest, it would need to purchase short-term securities, endogenously providing additional liquidity that would flow through to finance the higher level of government spending without a permanent increase in the long-term rate of interest (Kaldor, 1986, pp. 47–9). Monetary endogeneity thus performs the dual function of stabilizing the structure of interest rates and meeting the short-term financing needs of an expanding economy. British monetarism was, therefore, wrong in its assertions that public deficits were inflationary, according to Kaldor.

In this Treasury evidence, Kaldor also advances a number of alternative explanations to monetarism for the effectiveness of restrictive macroeconomic policies in reducing inflation. His emphasis here is on how restrictive fiscal policy weakens real-wage resistance by the labour movement (Kaldor, 1986, p. 55). Contractionary policy reduces aggregate demand, which causes a fall in output and raises unemployment. Higher unemployment undermines the bargaining power of labour, which is therefore more willing to accept lower nominal-wage increases, and the resulting lower labour costs enable firms to raise prices by a smaller proportion. A second alternative operates through the exchange rate. Higher interest rates cause a currency over-valuation by attracting additional foreign capital (Kaldor, 1986, p. 58). This over-valuation reduces net exports, aggregate demand and output, with similar effects on unemployment and real-wage resistance to those outlined above. A third alternative works in the opposite direction. In an argument similar to that advanced by Thomas Tooke and the nineteenth century Banking School (see Green, 1992, p. 172), Kaldor (1986, p. 63) identifies the possibility that higher interest rates may actually raise the rate of inflation, because interest constitutes an operating expense for firms.

The Scourge of Monetarism thus represents an important initial statement of the post-Keynesian theory of endogenous money. This theory was later developed by Moore (1988) with an expanded treatment for the role of banks and their use of wholesale markets to induce credit supply elasticity. But the significance of Kaldor's treatment of central bank policy and interest rates in *The Scourge of Monetarism* cannot be overestimated for the development of this important post-Keynesian doctrine.

PETER DOCHERTY

See also

Endogenous money; Inflation; Liquidity preference; Monetary policy; Money illusion

References

Committee on the Working of the Monetary System (Radcliffe Committee) (1960), *Report*, London: Her Majesty's Stationery Office.
Desai, M. (1989), 'The scourge of the monetarists: Kaldor on monetarism and money', *Cambridge Journal of Economics*, **13** (1), 171–82.
Docherty, P. (2005), *Money and Employment: A Study of the Theoretical Implications of Endogenous Money*, Cheltenham, UK, and Northampton, MA, USA: Edward Elgar.
Friedman, M. (1956), 'The quantity theory of money: a restatement', in M. Friedman (ed.), *Studies in the Quantity Theory of Money*, Chicago: Chicago University Press, pp. 3–21.
Friedman, M. (1969), 'The quantity theory of money: a restatement', in *The Optimum Quantity of Money and Other Essays*, London: Macmillan, pp. 51–68.
Green, R. (1992), *Classical Theories of Money, Output and Inflation: A Study in Historical Economics*, New York: St. Martin's Press.
Kaldor, N. (1986), *The Scourge of Monetarism*, second edition, Oxford: Oxford University Press.
Keynes, J.M. (1936), *The General Theory of Employment, Interest and Money*, London: Macmillan.
Lavoie, M. (1999), 'The credit-led supply of deposits and the demand for money: Kaldor's reflux mechanism as previously endorsed by Joan Robinson', *Cambridge Journal of Economics*, **23** (1), 103–13.
Moore, B.J. (1988), *Horizontalists and Verticalists: The Macroeconomics of Credit Money*, Cambridge, UK: Cambridge University Press.

The Structure of Post-Keynesian Economics

Geoffrey Colin Harcourt is one of the two most eminent world scholars of the Cambridge (UK) tradition, the other being Luigi Lodovico Pasinetti. In *The Structure of Post-Keynesian Economics*, Harcourt (2006) shows how the different strands of post-Keynesian economics can be brought together to form a coherent whole, without having to conceal their respective differences.

The book represents the most complete treatment of the ideas that came from Cambridge, UK, and from the people linked to that school, particularly the late Athanasios (Tom) Asimakopoulos in Canada and Stephen Marglin of Harvard, who feature significantly. The volume is characterized by a smooth and didactically very effective integration of analytical economics with the history of the theories concerned, with an appendix containing the biographies of the main players. Further, as he proceeds with the investigation, Harcourt brings in the relevance of contributions, such as Salter's (1960) theory of technical change, not formally associated with the Cambridge tradition, as well as of neoclassical economists such as Harry Johnson and Frank Hahn. The author's approach is a model of the method of intellectual openness and its combination with rigour.

After the introductory chapter, the book presents a new view of the macroeconomic theories of distribution. It starts with the Kaldor–Pasinetti model, which is juxtaposed by Kalecki's three sector mark-up theory. One can immediately grasp their common grounds and their marked differences. Then very elegantly through Joan Robinson and a contribution by Harry Johnson, the same Kaleckian approach is directed towards issues of economic development where the technical limits to the production of capital goods are brought to the fore. Having assigned centre stage to Kalecki's oligopolistic view of capitalism, Harcourt moves on to the discussion of theories dealing with the determination of the mark-up, reiterating Kalecki's emphasis on the importance of internal finance. Two models are analysed: Adrian Wood's golden-age theory of profit set in logical time and the Harcourt–Kenyon theory of pricing and investment decisions set in historical time. The merits and limitations of both are shown in detail. Logical time is needed for thought experiments whereas for actual analysis historical time is more appropriate. The ensuing discussion of the relation between investment decisions and the choice of techniques proves the case. The next step is to address the macroeconomic theories of accumulation, namely, the determination of investment. Lerner's, Kalecki's, and Asimakopoulos's critiques of Keynes's marginal efficiency of investment schedule are shown to be valid, from which Harcourt goes on to scrutinize both Joan Robinson's (via the banana diagram) and Kalecki's attempts to build a theory of investment decisions. This, the author observes, 'is still the Holy Grail of modern economics and of policy makers', because 'animal spirits cannot be bottled' (Harcourt, 2006, p. 65).

Harcourt claims that he is a real rather than a money man, yet the chapter on money and finance is exquisite; he deals with the issue succinctly and clearly. Building on Sheila Dow's contribution, it is argued that Keynes did not posit money as an exogenous stock but rather as a given amount in the short period, and that finance, not saving, 'is the ultimate binding macroeconomic constraint' (p. 71).

At this point the complete post-Keynesian short-run model is ready for presentation. The framework chosen is that of the inflationary episodes of the 1970s. The post-Keynesian approach emerges as particularly enlightening for the understanding of class conflicts in those years, through the Marglin–Rowthorn model.

The seventh chapter deals with growth theory and it is the longest one in the book. It spans from Adam Smith to endogenous growth theory. By reading it one realizes that it is possible to move from the Classics, to Marx, Harrod and Kaldor in a coherent manner without ever having to go through neoclassical concepts. The latter reappear only because of Swan and Solow's treatment of Harrod's problem – with Harcourt expressing preference for Swan's treatment both for teaching and for clarity of the issues analysed. The chapter has a cogent critique of the representative firm as used by Kaldor, before the latter broke with his earlier smooth approach to economic growth. The neoclassical theory of endogenous growth, arising from Chicago, is treated sympathetically, owing to its resurrecting issues of Classical concern.

The concluding chapter raises the question of the links between vision and policies setting in the framework of Kalecki's (1943) essay on the political aspects of full employment and in Salter's analysis of technical progress. This is a beautiful chapter that shows that economic theorizing always requires a moral philosophy to go with it, and 'suggests a package deal of policies' (Harcourt, 2006, p. 157).

Two appendices, one on the biographies of the post-Keynesians, and one on the capital theory debates, close the book.

The achievement of the book is to present the structure of the Cambridge post-Keynesian economists in an overall framework – where all the different units contribute to an organic whole that has both strong contemporary relevance and provides an excellent guide to policy.

JOSEPH HALEVI AND PETER KRIESLER

See also

Animal spirits; Income distribution; Mark-up pricing; Neoclassical economics; Post-Keynesian economics – a big tent?

References

Harcourt, G.C. (2006), *The Structure of Post-Keynesian Economics: The Core Contributions of the Pioneers*, Cambridge, UK: Cambridge University Press.
Kalecki, M. (1943), 'Political aspects of full employment', *Political Quarterly*, 14, 322–31. Reprinted in J. Osiatynski (ed.), *Collected Works of Michal Kalecki, Vol. I*, Oxford: Clarendon Press, 1990, pp. 347–56.
Salter, W.E.G. (1960), *Productivity and Technical Change*, Cambridge, UK: Cambridge University Press.

The Theory of the Leisure Class

The Theory of the Leisure Class, the pioneer work of Thornstein Veblen, published in 1899, constitutes a cornerstone in economic thinking. The post-Darwinian method of scientific inquiry employed by Veblen set forth a dynamic analysis of the social structures and the habits of thought that prevail in modern affluent societies. The innovative methodological framework of Veblen gave rise to the schools of institutional and evolutionary economics and the post-Darwinian economics (Hodgson, 1992, 1998).

The book is usually associated with the expression 'conspicuous consumption', doing great injustice to the complexity and the multidimensionality of Veblen's analysis. Conspicuous consumption, which is erroneously used interchangeably with the term 'keeping up with the Joneses', is a symptom of the institutions that govern the behaviour of the upper classes of industrialized economies, such as exploit and ownership, and not a causal factor per se.

Veblen traces the roots of the social structure in predatory societies in which a higher status within the members of such societies was granted upon exploit. The dichotomy between worthy and unworthy employment holds a central role in Veblen's analysis. Unworthy employment refers to everyday non-prestigious activities, with prestige being determined by the element of exploit in the activity per se. In this context, ownership is an essential indicator of exploit and thus of worthy employment. Activities that allow the accumulation of personal wealth, both in terms of goods as well as persons, that is, slavery, constitute a critical incentive for economic and social behaviour. Thereby, in Veblen's terms it is not the economic motive, as defined in mainstream economic thinking, that governs agents' actions, but the pecuniary motive that establishes the respectability of a person within the society.

The dichotomy is also evident in contemporary or, according to Veblen, semi-barbaric societies. The evolution of the modes of labour transformed unworthy employment in industrial work, while worthy employment becomes a synonym of leisure. Indeed, for Veblen, ownership and leisure are strongly interconnected. Ownership eventually does not suffice to ensure the respective status for a member of the upper class. Individuals should express their wealth through a set of pecuniary activities, such as leisure, which allow them to avoid industrial work. On the contrary, members of the lower classes are expected to rely strictly on industrial, yet non-respectable, work in order to secure a higher standard of living. Of course, the Veblenian system of analysis is much more complex, since a number of other activities, that is, nineteenth-century pastoral and military activities, are also considered as prestigious, though to a lesser extent as compared to those of the upper class.

The evolutionary nature of Veblen's analysis is evident in how the expression of pecuniary behaviour evolves across time, even though the motive is practically the same. As societies grow and become wealthier, conspicuous leisure gradually becomes conspicuous consumption. The need to distinguish oneself from the other members of the class and more importantly from the lower classes dictates the adoption of more ostentatious forms of behaviour. Therefore, in a wealthy society, conspicuous leisure is not adequate to characterize an individual as wealthy and prestigious. A flamboyant pattern of consumption becomes essential in order to ensure a higher status for the individual in the society. Thereby, conspicuous consumption is not a characteristic of the lower classes in their attempt to emulate the behaviour of the upper classes, as is often believed, but on the contrary it is a habit of thought of the upper classes, which allows its members to distinguish themselves from the lower classes.

Further, Veblen attempts a more detailed description of particular behavioural patterns of affluent societies attributed to their core pecuniary incentives, for instance the canons of taste. Veblen's analysis covers the full spectrum of the habits of thought that prevail in Western societies, with a direct applicability to the present. Of critical importance are two final remarks. Contrary to the contemporaneous trend in social sciences, expressed in the works of Spencer and the likes, Veblen did not attribute the evolutionary process, as described above, to the strict biological sphere in analytical terms, but to a more complex interaction between economics and biology in a non-teleological manner. Secondly, Veblen holds an exceptional role for women in his analysis, since on the one hand they are considered as the greatest victims of exploit, while on the other, gender equality is viewed as a factor that would substantially ameliorate the (semi)barbaric nature of modern societies (Gilman, 1999).

CHRISTOS PIERROS

See also

Consumer behaviour; Income distribution; Institutional economics; Land rents; Methodology

References

Gilman, N. (1999), 'Thorstein Veblen's neglected feminism', *Journal of Economic Issues*, **33** (3), 689–711.

Hodgson, G.M. (1992), 'Thorstein Veblen and post-Darwinian economics', *Cambridge Journal of Economics*, **16** (3), 285–301.
Hodgson, G.M. (1998), 'On the evolution of Thorstein Veblen's evolutionary economics', *Cambridge Journal of Economics*, **22** (4), 415–31.
Veblen, T.D. (1899/2007), *The Theory of the Leisure Class*, Oxford and New York: Oxford University Press.

Thirlwall's law

Thirlwall's law (TL) (see Thirlwall, 1979, 2011) is a dynamized version of Roy Harrod's foreign trade multiplier (Harrod, 1933). TL states that the long-run rate of growth of an economy compatible with balance-of-payments equilibrium (y_{bpc}) can be approximated by the product of the rate of economic growth of the rest of the world (y_{rw}) and the ratio of the income elasticity of the demand for exports (ε) to the income elasticity of the demand for imports π, or by the simple rule of the rate of growth of exports (x) divided by the income elasticity of demand for imports:

$$y_{bpc} = \frac{\varepsilon}{\pi} y_{rw} = \frac{x}{\pi}$$

where $\varepsilon, \pi > 0$ and $x = \varepsilon y_{rw}$.

TL encapsulates several key post-Keynesian principles. First, the balance-of-payments constrained rate of economic growth represents an under full-employment equilibrium, as it falls below the rate of economic growth determined by the maximum expansion of output from the supply side. As a result, balance-of-payments constrained economic growth implies the existence of excess capacity, low rates of accumulation and of technical progress, and the existence of unemployment and underemployment. The degree and binding character of the balance-of-payments constraint depends on the characteristics of a given economy as well as those of the existing external framework. The external constraint manifests itself with particular strength in those countries that do not issue a reserve currency but that are highly dependent on it for their productive development.

Second, TL shows that economic growth is driven through a multiplier process by autonomous demand. Within an open-economy framework, exports are the only true component of autonomous demand in the sense of demand emanating from outside the system, and also the only component of demand that can pay for the import requirements for economic growth (Kaldor, 1981; Thirlwall, 2002).

Third, according to TL, income effects predominate over substitution effects. Variations in income provide the mechanism that brings about the adjustment between internal and external economic conditions. For a given ratio of income elasticities, an increase in the rate of economic growth of the rest of the world translates into a rise in exports over imports and thus generates the space for the expansion of aggregate demand. The consequent increase in income and thus in imports restores the balance-of-payments equilibrium.

Relative prices play no role in the adjustment process. TL assumes the near constancy of real exchange rates, as variations in internal prices adjust to those of nominal exchange rates. Adjustment is also prevented by the existence of price setting behaviour and wage bargaining clauses (McCombie and Thirlwall, 1994).

Fourth, TL presupposes that money is not neutral in the long run. The external constraint is directly related to the workings of the international monetary architecture and is especially binding for those countries that do not issue a currency that is accepted as an international means of payment. Moreover, countries that face a binding external constraint tend to have a high import elasticity of income combined with a low export elasticity of income. This condemns them to recurrent adjustments and to grow at a rate below that compatible with full employment. Long-term capital flows can soften the external constraint, insofar as its most important determinant is the basic balance (current account and long-term capital flows).

Finally, TL underscores the importance of progressive structural change as key to shift the long-term rate of growth of an economy. The degree to which a faster rate of economic growth of the rest of the world will raise the balance-of-payments constrained equilibrium growth rate depends on the ratio of exports to income elasticities. While any given country cannot control the long-term rate of economic growth of the rest of the world, it can influence its impact on the domestic economy by increasing exports elasticity of income and/or decreasing the imports elasticity of income. The magnitude of these parameters depends on the diversification and upgrading of the productive

CHRISTOS PIERROS / ESTEBAN PÉREZ CALDENTEY

basis and structure (McCombie and Thirlwall, 1994; Thirlwall, 2019).

ESTEBAN PÉREZ CALDENTEY

See also

Aggregate demand; Balance-of-payments constrained growth; Currency hierarchy; Free trade; Growth

References

Harrod, R. (1933), *International Economics*, Cambridge, UK: Cambridge University Press.
Kaldor, N. (1981), 'The role of increasing returns, technical progress and cumulative causation in the theory of international trade and economic growth', *Economie Appliquée*, **34** (4), 593–617.
McCombie, J.S.L. and A.P. Thirlwall (1994), *Economic Growth and the Balance of Payments Constraint*, New York: Macmillan.
Thirlwall, A.P. (1979), 'The balance of payments constraint as an explanation of international growth rate differences', *Banca Nazionale del Lavoro Quarterly Review*, **32** (128), 45–53.
Thirlwall, A.P. (2002), *The Nature of Economic Growth*, Cheltenham, UK, and Northampton, MA, USA: Edward Elgar.
Thirlwall, A.P. (2011), 'Balance of payments constrained growth models: history and overview', *PSL Quarterly Review*, **64** (259), 307–51.
Thirlwall, A.P. (2019), 'Thoughts on balance-of-payments constrained growth after 40 years', *Review of Keynesian Economics*, **7** (4), 554–67.

Tobin tax

Tobin's (1979) original proposal was to improve the financial market's efficiency in allocating resources by restricting short-term capital flows that have led to increased volatility in the foreign-exchange market. In this way, the autonomy of monetary and fiscal policies would be restored, and supranational institutions, such as the International Monetary Fund and the World Bank, would increase their income. According to Tobin (1979), this purpose would be achieved through a uniform tax on all financial transactions that make conversions from one currency to another to discourage short-term capital flows.

Frankel (1996) presents a simple formalization of the Tobin tax, assuming i^* as the return on the external asset, i the return on the domestic asset, t the investment time in years, and α the Tobin tax rate. First, he analyses the case of an investment that pays the tax twice: when the asset is bought and when the asset is sold.

$$(1 + i't)(1 - \alpha) - \alpha = 1 + it \quad (1)$$

$$i' = \frac{1 + \frac{2\alpha}{t}}{1 - \alpha} \quad (2)$$

Second, he studies when the interests return to their country of origin, but the principal remains in foreign currency.

$$(i't)(1 - \alpha) - \alpha = it \quad (3)$$

$$i' = \frac{1 + \frac{\alpha}{t}}{1 - \alpha} \quad (4)$$

Following equation (4), if the tax rate is 1 per cent, the domestic interest rate is 10 per cent and the values of t are 1, 12 or 52, interpreted as annual, monthly or weekly investments, respectively, it can be observed that Tobin's tax penalizes shorter-term investments such as weekly ones, where $t = 52$. This occurs because the interest rate that the external asset needs to be profitable must reach 62 per cent. In comparison, an annual investment must guarantee a return higher than 11 per cent.

At the same time, Frankel (1996) argues that the exchange rate's harmful volatility, referred to by Tobin (1979), must be interpreted by dividing the foreign-exchange market between long-term investors and short-term speculators. For this he puts forward the following formula of the variance of the spot exchange rate:

$$var(s) = \frac{Var(m + u)}{[1 + wf_i\Phi - (1 - w)f_s\delta]} \quad (5)$$

where w is the participation of long-term investors (i), and ($1 - w$) corresponds to speculators (s); f_i and f_s represent the elasticities of demand for external assets of each group, m is the supply of local assets compared to the amount from abroad, and u is an unknown error term.

According to equation (5), greater participation of long-term investors and a higher elasticity of the demand for assets of this group would stabilize the exchange rate, which will throw the usual stabilizing mechanism of arbitrage in the markets. The opposite happens with the movements of the speculative group, which act as destabilizers.

One of the most studied effects is that of net capital flows on nominal and real exchange rates. This impact ends up triggering a change in the productive structure that accentuates problems such as the 'Dutch disease', which for financial reasons distorts relative prices and favours the regressive forces of the productive structure (Botta, 2015; Bresser-Pereira et al., 2015). This occurs in addition to increasing the economy's dependence on primary sectors and sectors of low technological complexity and prone to income concentration (Hartmann et al., 2017).

Some authors, such as Garber (1996) and Kenen (1996), however, have criticized Tobin's (1979) original tax proposal. They argue that the implementation problem is more political than technical, because there is a need to coordinate several countries and to create and finance supranational institutions, which means a significant challenge. Further, the type of transactions subject to the Tobin tax must also be carefully selected, because spot contracts would be the candidates, but there are also futures, options and derivatives. The possibility of geographical evasion and asset substitution has to be cautiously monitored as well. Another problem is to set a tax rate that discourages speculation but does not inhibit long-term investment activity.

Undoubtedly, the most substantial criticism of Tobin's tax comes from Davidson (1999): he mentions that by considering the capital flows issue as one of microeconomic imperfection, where the social cost is raised until it is equated with the social benefit, the real problem is omitted. This means that fluctuations in expectations about the valuation of assets denominated in foreign currency, in a scenario of fundamental uncertainty, may be so significant that Tobin's tax rate may not be able to correct the imbalances caused by exchange rate crises. Therefore, Davidson (1999) mentions that the solution is not to make the system work by rectifying an imperfection but seeking to reform it from the root: starting from Keynes's proposal to create the bancor, where the circulation of merely speculative capital is prohibited, and countries that are affected by balance-of-payments crises or foreign-exchange crises are easily rescued.

GONZALO COMBITA MORA

See also

Bubbles – financial; Capital flows; Dutch disease; Exchange rates; International financial architecture

References

Botta, A. (2015), 'The macroeconomics of a financial Dutch disease', *Levy Economics Institute of Bard College Working Paper*, No. 850.
Bresser-Pereira, L., J.L. Oreiro and N. Marconi (2015), *Macroeconomía desenvolvimentista*, Sao Pablo: Elsevier.
Davidson, P. (1999), 'Global employment and open economy macroeconomics', in J. Deprez and J. Harvey (eds), *Foundation of International Economics: A Post Keynesian Perspective*, London and New York: Routledge, pp. 9–35.
Frankel, J. (1996), 'How well do markets work: might a Tobin tax help?', in M. ul Haq, I. Kaul and I. Grunberg (eds), *The Tobin Tax: Coping with Financial Volatility*, Oxford: Oxford University Press, pp. 42–83.
Garber, P.M. (1996), 'Issues of enforcement and evasion in a tax on foreign exchange transactions', in M. ul Haq, I. Kaul and I. Grunberg (eds), *The Tobin Tax: Coping with Financial Volatility*, Oxford: Oxford University Press, pp. 129–42.
Hartmann, D., M. Guevara, C. Figueroa, M. Aristáran and C. Hidalgo (2017), 'Linking economic complexity, institutions and income inequality', *World Development*, 93 (C), 75–93.
Kenen, P. (1996), 'The feasibility of taxing foreign exchange transaction', in M. ul Haq, I. Kaul and I. Grunberg (eds), *The Tobin Tax: Coping with Financial Volatility*, Oxford: Oxford University Press, pp. 109–28.
Tobin, J. (1979), 'A proposal for international monetary reform', *Eastern Economic Journal*, 4 (3–4), 156–9.

Too-big-to-fail financial institutions

Financial institutions designated as too-big-to-fail (TBTF) are those megabanks that are considered sufficiently large, complex, and interconnected that their failure would cause disastrous effects on the financial system, which would eventually impose high costs on the whole economic system. Therefore, when the bankruptcy of a TBTF financial institution is imminent, it is expected that the government will bail out the failing institution (Cetorelli and Traina, 2018, p. 3). It follows that TBTF financial institutions benefit from an 'implicit government guarantee', which represents a substantial subsidy granted by taxpayers. The value of this subsidy is usually measured by the spread between the average cost of capital for smaller banks and the cost of capital for TBTF banks. For the year 2009, Baker and McArthur (2009, pp. 2–4) have estimated the value of the subsidy to TBTF banks operating in the United States to oscillate between 6.3 billion US dollars and 34.1 billion US dollars, which amounts to a significant share of their profits (between 8.8 and 47.7 per cent). In order to account for the total cost incurred by taxpayers, one should also consider – besides the ongoing transfer of income resulting from lower capital costs – the one-time contributions of the public sector that occur when the government actually provides bailouts. In the 2007–09 Global Financial Crisis (GFC), national governments in the United States and Europe committed 679 billion US dollars to their banks' recapitalization (Ioannou et al., 2019, p. 365). In addition to being enormously costly, the implicit government guarantee leads TBTF financial institutions to engage in excessive risk-taking activities (Panzera and Rossi, 2011, p. 316), as they do not bear the consequences of downside risks.

During the 2007–09 GFC, policy makers across various countries massively intervened to prevent the default of TBTF financial institutions – which are more commonly referred to as 'large and complex financial institutions' (LCFIs) in the field of regulation. Undoubtedly, these interventions have successfully avoided the adverse externalities that would have likely resulted from the failure of one or several systemically important financial institutions. However, these interventions also reinforced the market belief that governments would back up the debts of LCFIs if conditions of distress materialize again in the future, thereby increasing the value of the implicit subsidy and the associated competitive advantage of LCFIs over smaller banks in the conduct of their businesses.

Authorities in the United States have responded to these issues by introducing so-called 'living wills' as part of the Dodd–Franck Act regulation that was enacted in 2010. Each LCFI is thus required to fill a 'living will', whose goal is to create the conditions for an orderly liquidation in the event of financial distress, such that the need to bail out these institutions is reduced or even eliminated. Cetorelli and Traina (2018) find that 'living will' regulation has increased the average cost of capital incurred by LCFIs by at least 22 basis points, thereby reducing the State guarantee that these institutions enjoy. According to Cetorelli and Traina (2018, p. 21), this reduction in the cost of capital is the result of a decrease in systemic risk, which would itself result from the new regulation.

However, this type of regulation cannot prevent the occurrence of future systemic crises for at least two reasons. First, the authors (ibid.) themselves recognize that 'living wills' have only achieved a reduction of the ongoing TBTF subsidy, which means that the problem is persistent despite the new regulation. Second and more importantly, 'living will' regulation – along with other regulations such as capital requirements – relies on market mechanisms to address the systemic threat posed by TBTF financial institutions. Indeed, when the two Fed economists conclude that 'living wills' contribute to financial stability (ibid.), their argument is based on their belief in the financial market efficiency, as they investigate the response of financial markets – all the more in a period of relative financial stability – to the new regulation. But Minsky (1977) warned that financial stability sows the seeds of instability. More generally, heterodox economists argue that markets left on their own are unstable, and that 'financial markets tend to blow up on their own' (Lavoie, 2012, p. 231). Consequently, Cetorelli and Traina (2018) would come to a different conclusion had they conducted their empirical analysis during a period of financial turmoil. Besides, the design and assessment of a regulation seeking financial stability should not rely on the premise that financial markets are really efficient.

More than a decade after the 2007–09 GFC, the global megabanking sector is still very large and powerful and remains a threat to financial stability. Ioannou et al. (2019, p. 376) explain that this results notably from the fact that TBTF banking is embedded in a set of five self-reinforcing policies: consolidation, quantitative easing, favourable regulations, bank lobbying, and geo-economic and geopolitical considerations. Another reason for the failure of TBTF banks to shrink is the persisting view that 'banks' default role is one that promotes the overall-efficiency in economic transactions (ibid.). In this framework,

CARRYL OBERSON

banks are mere financial intermediaries and instability stems mostly from moral-hazard issues. Obviously, this view – which is prevailing among regulators and mainstream economists – is flawed, as it overlooks the fundamental and singular role played by banks. Current regulations will therefore fail to prevent the occurrence of future systemic crises. However, more promising avenues exist. For instance, Marshall and Rochon (2019) suggest the use of public banks to promote more-favourable financial conditions and alleviate the problems TBTF banks have caused and perpetuated, while Panzera and Rossi (2011) propose a structural reform that would prevent banks from opening credit lines to finance speculative transactions for which no available income exists yet.

CARRYL OBERSON

See also

Basel Agreements; Capital requirements; Financial instability hypothesis; Financial regulations; International financial architecture

References

Baker, D. and T. McArthur (2009), 'The value of the "too big to fail" big bank subsidy', *Center for Economic and Policy Research Issue Brief*, Washington, DC: Center for Economic and Policy Research.
Cetorelli, N. and J. Traina (2018), 'Resolving "too big to fail"', *Federal Reserve Bank of New York Staff Report*, No. 859.
Ioannou, S., D. Wójcik and G. Dymski (2019), 'Too-big-to-fail: why megabanks have not become smaller since the global financial crisis?', *Review of Political Economy*, 31 (2), 356–81.
Lavoie, M. (2012), 'Financialization, neo-liberalism, and securitization', *Journal of Post Keynesian Economics*, 35 (2), 215–33.
Marshall, W.C. and L.-P. Rochon (2019), 'Public banking and post-Keynesian economic theory', *International Journal of Political Economy*, 48 (1), 60–75.
Minsky, H.P. (1977), 'The financial instability hypothesis: an interpretation of Keynes and an alternative to "standard" theory', *Nebraska Journal of Economics and Business*, 16 (1), 5–16.
Panzera, F. and S. Rossi (2011), '"Too-big-to-fail" financial institutions: risks and remedies', *International Journal of Trade and Global Markets*, 4 (3), 311–27.

Trade and development

International trade, which refers to the purchase or sale of goods and services across national borders, has been widely considered to have a major impact on economic development, both positive and negative. While international trade has occurred for a long time, policy changes have reduced trade barriers, and technological changes have reduced transport and communication costs and have made possible the dispersal of production of components of goods and services across national borders. All this has resulted in an enormous growth in international trade.

Mainstream economists typically argue, using theoretical and empirical analysis, that international trade promotes economic development and increases economic wellbeing. In theoretical terms, it does so by increasing efficiency by improving resource allocation according to comparative advantage, by expanding markets to reap the advantages of scale economies and learning by doing, by promoting competition and by allowing the transfer of technology through learning by seeing imported products. Empirical evidence has been amassed to suggest that economic growth and income distribution are improved using econometric analysis showing how trade flows and trade liberalization have positive effects (see Edwards, 1998; Dollar and Kraay, 2004), and case studies have been interpreted to show how trade liberalization has promoted economic development in East Asia, China and India, among other countries (Bhagwati, 2004). Non-mainstream economists, including post-Keynesian and structuralist economists, however, argued that trade liberalization and the expansion of international trade can have negative effects, especially for lower-income countries (Dutt, 2023). This can happen as a result of the loss of output and employment caused by the inability to withstand foreign competition due to low productivity (and the full employment of resources is not assured due to the lack of effective demand), especially of manufactured goods, and cause balance-of-payments problems. It can also reinforce the 'colonial' pattern of trade with lower-income countries specializing in exports of primary products and low-skilled manufactures and services, thereby depriving them of the possibility of developing technological capability, and leading to deteriorating and fluctuating external terms of trade. Indeed, currently high-income countries resorted to import tariffs to develop their industries in their early stages of industrialization (Chang, 2002). Trade liberalization episodes also suggest that lower-income countries have experienced reduced economic growth, deindustrialization and increased inequality (Dutt, 2023).

International trade can foster economic development, but this is unlikely to happen due to indiscriminate trade liberalization. The effects of international trade on lower-income countries depend on what products they import and export, and who are their trading partners. This requires strategic trade policies and not blanket adherence to neoliberal policies.

AMITAVA DUTT AND NAJIB KHAN

See also

Development; Free trade; Growth; Regional economic integration and free trade agreements; Terms of trade

References

Bhagwati, J.N. (2004), *In Defense of Globalization*, Oxford: Oxford University Press.
Chang, H.-J. (2002), *Kicking Away the Ladder: Development Strategy in Historical Perspective*, London: Anthem Press.
Dollar, D. and A. Kraay (2004), 'Trade, growth, and poverty', *Economic Journal*, **114** (493), F22–F49.
Dutt, A.K. (2023), 'International trade and economic development', in F. Obeng-Odoom (ed.), *The Elgar Handbook of Alternative Global Development*, Cheltenham, UK and Northampton, MA, USA: Edward Elgar, forthcoming.
Edwards, S. (1998), 'Openness, productivity and growth: what do we really know?', *Economic Journal*, **108** (447), 383–98.

Trade cycles

Also known as business cycles, trade cycles depict the phenomena of the rise and fall of production, and therefore of employment, inherent in a monetary production economy, whose production processes begin with the granting of credit and end with its repayment after the sale of produced goods and services (see Schumpeter, 1912; Graziani, 2003). In this historical and specific system that is capitalism, production is a fragmented and private process, directed by individual producers without a joint plan, and who hire labour and invest in capital based on the expectations of obtaining monetary profits to continue their capital accumulation. In this process, banks' credit plays a crucial role, since the validation that commercial banks make of these private expectations allows for the beginning of new productive processes.

Mitchell (1913, p. 449) defines the trade cycle as a process by which 'the recurrent phases presented by economic activity, wherever it is dominated by the quest of profits, grow out of and grow into each other'. The business cycle is characterized as an endogenous process within a for-profit capitalist economy, where each phase of the cycle determines the next phase. This is an aspect shared by the business cycle approaches of John Maynard Keynes, Karl Marx and Michal Kalecki.

For Keynes (1936, Ch. 22), the fluctuation around the expected profitability of the additional capital invested in the development of an economic boom, which he calls the 'marginal efficiency of capital', causes excess capacity leading to the accumulation of goods in firms' inventory. This increase in inventories causes investment to be reduced, leading to an economic crisis, which in turn increases agents' liquidity preference, further aggravating the situation.

Marx also has an explanation focused on the role of investment. He affirms that competition between capitalists continually forces the improvement of the means of production by modifying the relationship between capital invested in means of production and that invested in labour power, which he calls the 'organic composition of capital', and that it collides with formation of the general rate of profit. In his words, '[t]he rate of profit does not fall because the worker is less exploited, but rather because less labour is generally applied in relation to the capital invested' (Marx, 1867b/1991, p. 354). However, commercial banks are only going to bet on those production processes that show expectations of obtaining profits. This point is consistent with the post-Keynesian endogenous-money approach, according to which the money supply responds endogenously to the demands of solvent firms (see Lavoie, 1984). However, there may be the temporary impulse of animal spirits, waves of optimism referred to by Keynes (1936, pp. 161–2), which can fuel this overproduction thanks to increased investment credit.

Kalecki, who can be seen as a bridge between Keynes and Marx, is very explicit about the paradox that investment creates a central contradiction of the capitalist system. He asks, 'What causes periodical crises?' His answer is 'the fact that investment is not only produced but also producing' (Kalecki, 1939, p. 148).

In the transition from the boom phase to the depression phase, the three positions appear similar, but not the other way around. Marx (1867a/1982, p. 770) argues that, because of the increase of the industrial reserve army, '[t]he price of labour falls again to a level corresponding with capital's requirements for self-valorization', creating an automatic take off. Kalecki, by contrast, emphasizes that the cycle will not be reversed unless some 'external market' supports the realization of earnings with additional purchasing power outside the capital–labour ratio (Kalecki and Kowalik, 1971), even if it is 'only pretext for digging holes', as Keynes (1936, p. 130) points out, in the absence of a better use. This external market is public sector spending.

Esteban Cruz Hidalgo, Francisco
M. Parejo Moruno and José
Francisco Rangel Preciado

See also

Animal spirits; Business cycles; Endogenous money; Liquidity preference; Monetary circuit

References

Graziani, A. (2003), *The Monetary Theory of Production*, Cambridge, UK: Cambridge University Press.
Kalecki, M. (1939), *Essays in the Theory of Economic Fluctuations*, London: Allen & Unwin.
Kalecki, M. and T. Kowalik (1971/1991), 'Observations on the crucial reform', in J. Osiatynski (ed.), *Collected Works of Michal Kalecki, Vol. II: Capitalism*, Oxford and New York: Clarendon Press, pp. 466–76.
Keynes, J.M. (1936), *The General Theory of Employment, Interest and Money*, London, Macmillan.
Lavoie, M. (1984), 'The endogenous flow of credit and the post Keynesian theory of money', *Journal of Economic Issues*, **18** (3), 771–97.
Marx, K. (1867a/1982), *Capital, Volume I*, London: Penguin Classics.
Marx, K. (1867b/1991), *Capital, Volume III*, London: Penguin Classics.
Minsky, H. (1986/2008), *Stabilizing an Unstable Economy*, New York: McGraw-Hill.
Mitchell, W.C. (1913), *Business Cycles*, Berkeley: University of California Press.
Schumpeter, J.A. (1912/1949), *The Theory of Economic Development*, Cambridge, MA, USA: Harvard University Press.

Transformational growth

Transformational growth is a framework that analyses the central features of macroeconomic fluctuations and economic growth in advanced capitalism as part of an (endogenous) process of structural change (see Nell, 1992; 1998a). It has also been applied to developing countries and thinking about 'greening' the economy.

Transformational growth is founded on the ontological premise that the economy is constantly evolving. It does not settle in, nor is it converging to, an equilibrium or steady state. This proposition does not entail the economy moving randomly or chaotically. Transformational growth helps to decipher how definite patterns and cycles (including stagnation) emerge, persist, and evolve as total output increases (and its components change). Transformational growth offers a comprehensive perspective to understand all of these changes endogenously. The basic premise is that firms are involved in investment and innovation processes that are not coordinated. Consequently, economic growth is irregular. This irregular and differential pace of economic growth among industries and sectors introduces market disruptions to which firms need to adjust. These adjustments lead to (endogenous) business cycles. In addition, as the pace of expansion of various sectors and industries is different, economic growth does not follow a steady-state path, but an uneven one along which the economic structure itself changes. Thus, the stylized facts of economic cycles differ in various historical periods (which also means different economic models are needed to explain them).

A simple way to visualize these elements is to think of two central pillars of transformational growth: 'old' and 'new' business cycles (see Nell, 1992; 1998b). In rich countries, during the nineteenth century, business cycles presented large price fluctuations (often drastic declines, including for manufacturing output and wages) and (relative to prices) smaller fluctuations in employment. The reasons for these patterns can be found in the conditions influencing firms' behaviour. Markets (rather competitive), technologies (craft-based), and institutions (un-unionized labour force) led firms to maintain their level of production and adjust prices (and wages) in the face of a supply and demand mismatch. This could be considered a 'Marshallian' world. Starting in the 1900s, and even more pronouncedly after the Second World War, business cycles have been almost a mirror image of this process. Unemployment fluctuates more than in the past and more than wages and manufacturing prices (which rarely decline in a significant way). In this 'Keynesian' world, price (and wage) adjustments are less common than fluctuations in output (and employment) owing to mass production technologies (which lead to oligopolistic markets), the expansion of unions and labour rights, and the need to secure steady and predictable financial flows to invest in (and replace) large manufacturing plants.

It is important to highlight four points to fully understand the transformational growth perspective. First, these characteristics are not independent of each other. Mass production and Fordism require sizeable investments. In order to pay loans (or cover opportunity cost of own funds) it is important to guarantee steady revenue streams. Non-decreasing nominal prices (based on mark-ups, not mainstream competitive market adjustment) allow that.

Secondly, these changes do not arise all of a sudden, but gradually and endogenously as part of the transformational growth process. Oligopolies were introduced and expanded at the end of the nineteenth century, partly due to opportunities provided by new technologies as well as by the need to prevent price declines (and they were facilitated by the high entry cost of setting up large factories). The efforts of workers to unionize and obtain legislation to protect them (such as the eight-hour workday, vacations, working conditions, pensions, and unemployment insurance) were easier to accommodate in an oligopolistic market structure. Higher and steady wages combined with unemployment insurance promoted a reliable level of demand for these firms.

Moreover, innovations (and their concomitant new market behaviour and structures) also emerge slowly. As firms attempt to increase profits (not maximize them), they innovate their business practices, impacting output structures and prices. Thus, input–output equations (and their price duals) do not represent an equilibrium but the crystallization of the most recent production period. This is the starting point to calculate a new array of prices, quantities, and profits that are only limited by the uncertain prospect of future demand. Paraphrasing Adam Smith, one can argue that the size of aggregate demand influences economically viable technologies and market structures. Economic growth expands aggregate income, which in turn makes new technologies, products, and firms profitable. Thus, the timing and pace of innovations are endogenous. Their diffusion contributes to further economic growth and expansion of aggregate demand.

Thirdly, economic changes and social changes are intertwined. As economic structures change and expand, so do consumption patterns and income distribution (relative bargaining power of workers and capitalists change through cycles and as transformational growth unfolds) as well as demographics, politics, and institutions – like urbanization, family structures, and size and regulatory role of government. All these changes impact economic agents' behaviour.

Fourthly, transformational growth offers alternative views for practical policy making, ranging from monetary policy based on endogenous money/credit through the employer of last resort programme to applications of functional finance. As there is no market clearing based on optimizing behaviour, the notion that taxes or import duties introduce distortions loses its theoretical grounding, opening doors to progressive taxation and trade/industrial policies.

In summary, transformational growth combines theory, methodology, history, and philosophy to describe how markets are constantly changing. These changes prompt households, firms, and governments to alter their behaviour. Given these changes, the process starts again (following, however, different paths and adjustment patterns). Thus, there is no equilibrium or steady state. Patterns of market adjustment and macroeconomic cycles vary as the economy evolves and undergoes structural change. Understanding different historical periods requires different economic principles.

ENRIQUE DELAMÓNICA

See also

Aggregate demand; Business cycles; Endogenous money; Growth; Profit

References

Nell, E.J. (1992), *Transformational Growth and Effective Demand: Economics After the Capital Critique*, London and New York: Palgrave Macmillan.

Nell, E.J. (1998a), *The General Theory of Transformational Growth: Keynes after Sraffa*, Cambridge: Cambridge University Press.

Nell, E.J. (ed.) (1998b), *Transformational Growth and the Business Cycle*, London and New York: Routledge.

Transmission mechanism of monetary policy – income distribution

The distributional impact of monetary policy is a topic that is receiving greater attention by mainstream economists and policymakers. Beyond a profusion of empirical studies, there are official publications by institutions such as the International Monetary Fund, the Bank for International Settlements, the US Federal Reserve, the World Bank and the European Central Bank (Kappes, 2021). However, attention to this theme is not new: heterodox economists, especially post-Keynesian authors, have been exploring this issue since at least the 1980s (Rochon and Seccareccia, 2022).

There are many ways by which monetary policy can affect income distribution. In order to better organize this discussion and present a systematic account of them, we will start with a definition of net financial income:

Net Financial Income
 = Wages + Interest + Business profits
 + Transfers + Capital Gains − Debt payments

The above equation shows that the net financial income of a given household can be split between labour income (wages); interest receipts from various sources such as deposits and government bonds; business profits, which can be either the direct profit of a firm or the dividends of stocks; government transfers; and capital gains arising from various asset types, such as housing, bonds and equities. Debt payments are reduced from those various income sources.

Monetary policy can affect almost all components of net financial income. The most obvious one, which is called the 'direct' channel by Rochon and Seccareccia (2022), is the impact on interest receipts and debt payments after a change in interest rates. A lower rate of interest will reduce both income and payments, and its overall impact on net financial income will depend on the individual's net wealth. A lower-class household with a mortgage-financed house will probably benefit from a reduction in the rates of interest, since its payments will be lower and the household most likely has no financial wealth upon which interest is received. On the other hand, a rich individual is probably worse off from such a reduction, since she/he is likely to hold bonds and has little debt. Therefore, the expected overall impact on income distribution of an expansionary monetary policy is to reduce income inequality through this channel. The effect can be lower or higher according to the flexible or fixed-rate character of a household's debt and on the easiness (or difficulty) of renegotiating the mortgage loan agreement. Countries in which fixed-rate mortgages are more common and in which renegotiation is more difficult will likely face a reduced impact of monetary policy on income distribution through this channel.

There are, however, more 'indirect' ways in which an interest rate change can impact the income distribution. An expansionary monetary policy should increase output and reduce unemployment, and this manifests itself at the individual level as a higher wage rate and as the achievement of a job for those previously unemployed. Some authors name these effects the 'earnings heterogeneity channel' for the change in the wage rate, and the 'job creation channel' for the change in the employment status. The impact of these changes on income distribution can vary from country to country, according to the responses of low-skilled and high-skilled workers to the changes in unemployment rate. Countries in which high-skilled workers' earnings grow more relative to low-skilled workers' earnings will probably face an increase in inequality after an expansionary monetary policy. In the job creation channel, countries in which low-skilled workers are the first to be unemployed in a slump and the first to be hired on the recovery will likely experience a reduction in inequality following an expansionary monetary policy and an increase after a contractionary policy.

Monetary policy also affects asset prices, leading to capital gains/losses, whose final impact on inequality measures depends on the distribution of assets among income (or wealth) percentiles and on the degree by which each asset class responds to changes in interest rates. If, for instance, equity prices rise more than housing prices after a given interest rate cut and if equities are more unevenly distributed amongst households, then an expansionary monetary policy will lead to increased inequality through this channel. An opposite case occurs if housing prices increase more than equity prices after the interest rate cut, with housing being more evenly distributed: then, the impact on inequality will be more egalitarian.

Given all the possibilities explained above, it is clear that the overall impact of monetary policy on income distribution cannot be determined *a priori*, as it depends on several empirical facts. For instance, it depends on the job creation and the wage rate elasticities of different skill levels for a given change in the aggregate unemployment rate; the proportions of labour and capital income in each percentile; the distribution of assets and of net wealth; the proportion of household debt with fixed rate or flexible rate; and the easiness (or difficulty) in renegotiating debt. All these factors interact with monetary policy in delivering the final distributional impacts.

The evidence, however, points to, in most cases, an expansionary monetary policy tending to improve income distribution. The most important channel for this effect is the 'indirect' or 'job creation channel': the output expansion that follows a lower interest rate lowers the unemployment rate, and these newly employed individuals are usually in the bottom percentiles of the income distribution.

The empirical evidence that is recently being presented by mainstream authors points to the relevance of post-Keynesian thinking that has been exploring the connection between interest rates and income distribution since at least the works of Pasinetti. Unfortunately, heterodox economists are rarely cited in these recent works, pointing to the urgent need for heterodox authors to reclaim this topic.

SYLVIO ANTONIO KAPPES

See also

Income distribution; Inequality; Interest rates and income distribution; Monetary policy; Post-Keynesian economics – a big tent?

References

Kappes, S.A. (2021), 'Monetary policy and personal income distribution: a survey of the empirical literature', *Review of Political Economy*, forthcoming.

Rochon, L.-P. and M. Seccareccia (2022), 'A primer on monetary policy and its effect on income distribution: a heterodox perspective', in S.A. Kappes, L.-P. Rochon and G. Vallet (eds), *Central Banking, Monetary Policy and Income Distribution*, Cheltenham, UK, and Northampton, MA, USA: Edward Elgar, forthcoming.

Traverse, path dependency, and economic dynamics

The traverse describes the movement from one steady-state position to another in a dynamical system. The term was coined in *Capital and Growth* by Sir John Hicks (1965), who was the first to develop traverse models (see also Hicks, 1973). The issue of the traverse is of key importance in growth models, as it involves the description of out-of-equilibrium dynamics in economic systems. Traverse analysis acquires a peculiar role in post-Keynesian growth theory, as it pairs with the idea that economic equilibria ought to be path dependent. More specifically, path dependency describes the particular property exhibited by a dynamical system in which earlier states influence later ones. In other words, an economic system is characterized by path dependency if the path taken during the traverse 'has a long-persisting effect upon the position that it reaches' (Robinson, 1956, p. 58). Broadly speaking, the importance of the traverse and path dependency for post-Keynesian economists can be summarized by two simple principles: first, disequilibrium is the rule rather than the exception, and, second, history matters.

Fundamentally, dynamical systems can be of two types: path independent and path dependent.

In path-independent systems the movement between equilibrium positions – the traverse – does not influence the final outcome of the system. Following the taxonomy proposed by Kaldor (1934), we may call path-independent systems determined, given that the resulting outcome of a change in the parameter space or in exogenous variables is known *a priori*, that is, not affected by the path taken towards the new

SYLVIO ANTONIO KAPPES / ETTORE GALLO

equilibrium. Accordingly, path-independent systems are strongly stable, often displaying asymptotic stability. This means that the system will always go back to equilibrium when hit by an arbitrary shock. Examples of path-independent systems are the Solow model and neoclassical endogenous growth models. Path-independent systems tend to be strongly tied with the organizing concept of traditional equilibrium in macroeconomic modelling.

In path-dependent systems, by contrast, the movement between equilibrium positions is influenced by what happens during the traverse. In other words, there is no independence between the outcome and the adjustment path towards it. According to Kaldor (1934, p. 132), path-dependent systems may also be called indeterminate, 'as the successive moves undertaken in order to reach equilibrium will influence the nature of the final position'. There are various specific concepts of path dependency; among them, it is worth mentioning cumulative causation, lock-in and hysteresis. Of course, these different types of path dependency may coexist in macroeconomic modelling. In this sense, an example is provided by the Kaldorian growth model developed by Setterfield (2002).

At this stage, it should be clear that path dependency is in stark contrast with the notion of traditional equilibrium. As such, on the basis of the simple idea that history matters, path dependency constitutes the organizing principle upon which post-Keynesian growth theory ought to be constructed. Accordingly, if what happens during the traverse affects the resulting outcome of the dynamical system, we must focus our attention on disequilibrium dynamics, thus entering the realm of traverse analysis. Moreover, as real-world economic processes take place in historical rather than logical time, they cannot be reversed. Therefore, the traverse becomes the fundamental bridge between the past and the future. In the words of Robinson (1962, p. 25), 'observed history cannot be interpreted in terms of a movement along an equilibrium path ... A model applicable to actual history has to be capable of getting out of equilibrium.' This presupposition becomes particularly central for evaluating a model's policy implications. As pointed out by Hicks (1980, p. 153), '[i]t may be hoped that, after the change in policy, the economy will ... settle into ... a new equilibrium; but there must necessarily be a stage before that equilibrium is reached. There must always be a problem of traverse.'

However, there is major trouble with traverse analysis, namely, its mathematical intractability. If, for instance, we turn to the analysis of a non-linear path-dependent growth model, we soon realize that a general solution to the differential equation (or system of differential equations) governing its out-of-equilibrium dynamics cannot be found. In other terms, the description of 'the contortions that any economic system must undergo during such an adjustment process ... requires mathematics of such complexity that any formal advantages would have to be purchased at the sacrifice of analytical transparency' (Lowe, 1976, p. 114). This aspect leads Solow (1984, p. 21) to ironically note that the traverse 'is the easiest part of skiing, but the hardest part of economics'. Still, this should not be seen as an excuse to abandon traverse analysis. Even though an analytical solution cannot be found explicitly, numerical methods for differential equations may be adopted to evaluate the direction and the time dimension of the adjustment path. This methodology, precluded to Hicks, Lowe, Robinson and others, can now be carried out thanks to the wide availability of personal computers and programming languages that allow easy calibration and simulation of economic models.

ETTORE GALLO

See also

Cumulative causation; Growth; Hysteresis; Neoclassical economics; Traverse, path dependency, and economic equilibrium

References

Hicks, J.R. (1965), *Capital and Growth*, Oxford: Oxford University Press.
Hicks, J.R. (1973), *Capital and Time: A Neo-Austrian Theory*, Oxford: Clarendon Press.
Hicks, J.R. (1980), 'IS-LM: an explanation', *Journal of Post Keynesian Economics*, 3 (2), 139–54.
Kaldor, N. (1934), 'A classificatory note on the determinateness of equilibrium', *Review of Economic Studies*, 1 (2), 122–36.
Lowe, A. (1976), *The Path of Economic Growth*, Cambridge: Cambridge University Press.
Robinson, J. (1956), *The Accumulation of Capital*, London: Macmillan.
Robinson, J. (1962), *Essays in the Theory of Economic Growth*, London: Macmillan.
Setterfield, M. (2002), 'A model of Kaldorian traverse: cumulative causation, structural change and evolutionary hysteresis', in M. Setterfield (ed.),

The Economics of Demand-Led Growth: Challenging the Supply Side Vision of the Long Run, Cheltenham, UK, and Northampton, MA, USA: Edward Elgar, pp. 215–33.

Solow, R.M. (1984), 'Mr Hicks and the Classics', *Oxford Economic Papers*, 36, 13–25.

Traverse, path dependency, and economic equilibrium

Economics has traditionally relied on some notion of equilibrium as a central organizing concept. A major methodological difference between different schools of thought has been the operational significance that each ascribed to that concept. For some economists, equilibrium is important for organizing ideas, and as an idealized point of reference. Others see it as being descriptive, with either actual economies showing strong tendencies towards equilibrium, which would be achievable except for constant shocks, or, in the case of new classical macroeconomists (and dynamic stochastic general equilibrium models), economies are always in equilibrium. However, despite the importance of the concept of equilibrium, little is said about the process whereby the economy achieves it. For equilibrium to serve the function that economists have assigned to it, there must be forces pushing the economy towards equilibrium, and the path the economy takes (its adjustment path) must not influence the equilibrium to which it is tending. In the absence of these conditions, the analysis of equilibria, independent of the 'traverse', becomes pointless.

Hicks (1973, p. 81) first introduced the term 'traverse' into economics, characterizing it as 'the path which will be followed when the steady state is subjected to some kind of disturbance'. In other words, the traverse describes the economy's dynamic out-of-equilibrium adjustment path in historical time. The importance of historical time is its direction: time can only move forward, with the link between time periods given by the stock of capital inherited from the past, and the expectations embodied in it (see Robinson, 1974; Setterfield, 1995).

Although initially the traverse was used to describe the path between equilibria, later the traverse itself was seen to be the end of the story. Post-Keynesian economists, amongst other heterodox economists (especially evolutionary and institutional economists), deny the usefulness of equilibrium analysis independently of the study of the path that the economy takes to 'get into' equilibrium. In other words, they believe either that the economy is never in equilibrium with no tendency towards it, or that the equilibrium it approaches is determined by the path taken to get there. More pointedly, Joan Robinson often criticized the separation of equilibrium analysis from the analysis of the traverse, as she believed that the actual equilibrium an economy achieves (if it is capable of achieving one) will be vitally dependent on the path it takes, so that equilibrium would always be path dependent (Robinson, 1974).

The importance of path dependency is related to the role of historical time and uncertainty in post-Keynesian thought. Decisions taken today are influenced both by the past and by our expectations of the future. These decisions will, in turn, influence current events and so will lead to different forms of behaviour of individuals, firms and institutions. With historical time, the past is unchangeable, though its influence is felt in the present and therefore in the future. All aspects of the economy are in a state of flux, changing and evolving as a result of decisions taken currently as well as those taken in the past. Today's events and decisions are profoundly influenced by what has gone on before, by history, so that the sequence of events leading up to the present is extremely important. Everything that happens today is a product of its past. As history matters, the future cannot be predicted with perfect foresight, so future outcomes cannot be predestined, as they also crucially depend on current events, and the history of events leading to those outcomes. This explains why post-Keynesian economists believe that the movement of the economy, and its destination (if it has one) are path determined.

Post-Keynesian economists rarely use equilibrium concepts in their analysis of capitalist economies, as they are concerned with cumulative change and dynamic paths. Inherent in their analysis is the concept of cumulative causation, which is extremely destructive of the concept of equilibrium, since it implies that any movement away from an initial position will be amplified and generate further movements away from that position for a long period of time. 'Cumulative causation is the idea of reinforcing processes by which the patterns of uneven development between regions, between countries and between economic and social phenomena may be perpetuated and even accentuated' (Thirlwall, 1994, p. 62, commenting on Myrdal, 1957). In other words, 'change becomes progressive and propagates itself in a cumulative way' (Young, 1928, p. 533).

The traverse, which defines the movement of the economy outside equilibrium, plays a particularly important role in post-Keynesian theory. Hicks (1965, 1973) and Lowe (1976) undertook detailed analysis of the adjustment paths economies take outside equilibrium. They considered the question of whether the market would send the correct signals to allow the structure of production to adjust in response to a shock. 'The necessary *adjustment path* requires both *time* and *costs*, and faces difficulties which arise from disproportions between sectors and misleading market signals' (Hagemann, 1992, p. 235, italics in the original). Most work on the traverse has concluded that markets transmit 'the "wrong" signals in terms of the optimal structure of production and intersectoral flows' (Kriesler, 1999, p. 410), thereby making the achievement of equilibrium extremely unlikely.

PETER KRIESLER

See also

Animal spirits; Cumulative causation; Institutional economics; Traverse, path dependency, and economic dynamics; Uncertainty

References

Hagemann, H. (1992), 'Traverse analysis in a post-Classical model', in J. Halevi, D. Laibman and E. Nell (eds), *Beyond the Steady State: A Revival of Growth Theory*, London: Macmillan, pp. 235–63.
Halevi, J., G.C. Harcourt, P. Kriesler and J. Nevile (2016), *Post-Keynesian Essays from Down Under: Essays on Theory. Volume IV: Theory and Policy in an Historical Context*, Basingstoke and New York: Palgrave Macmillan.
Halevi, J., N. Hart and P. Kriesler (2013), 'The traverse and equilibrium analysis', in G.C. Harcourt and P. Kriesler (eds), *Oxford Handbook of Post-Keynesian Economics: Volume 2, Critiques and Methodology*, Oxford: Oxford University Press, pp. 175–97.
Harcourt, G.C. (2007), 'Markets, madness and a middle way revisited', *Economic and Labour Relations Review*, **18** (1), 1–10.
Hicks, J. (1965), *Capital and Growth*, Oxford: Clarendon Press.
Hicks, J. (1973), *Capital and Time: A Neo-Austrian Theory*, Oxford: Clarendon Press.
Kriesler, P. (1999), 'Harcourt, Hicks and Lowe: incompatible bedfellows?', in C. Sardoni and P. Kriesler (eds), *Keynes, Post-Keynesianism and Political Economy: Essays in Honour of Geoff Harcourt, Volume 3*, London and New York: Routledge, pp. 400–17.
Lowe, A. (1976), *The Path of Economic Growth*, Cambridge, UK: Cambridge University Press.
Myrdal, G. (1957), *Economic Theory and Underdeveloped Regions*, London: University Paperbacks.
Robinson, J. (1974), 'History vs. equilibrium', *Thames Papers in Political Economy*. Reprinted in J. Robinson, *Contributions to Modern Economics*, Oxford: Basil Blackwell, 1978, pp. 126–36.
Setterfield, M. (1995), 'Historical time and economic theory', *Review of Political Economy*, **7** (1), 1–27.
Thirlwall, A.P. (1994), 'Cumulative causation', in P. Arestis and M. Sawyer (eds), *The Elgar Companion to Radical Political Economics*, Aldershot, UK, and Brookfield, USA, Edward Elgar, pp. 62–5.
Young, A.A. (1928), 'Increasing returns and economic progress', *Economic Journal*, **38** (152), 527–40.

Twin deficits

A twin-deficit situation can arise when a country is simultaneously in a situation of public deficit and external deficit (current-account deficit). As is often the case in macroeconomics, the direction of causality between the two deficits can go both ways.

In order to explain the macroeconomic mechanisms behind a twin deficit, let us start from a theoretical situation where the public sector's balance and the external balance are balanced at the accounting level. An asymmetric policy carried out in a country that increases public spending (or tax cuts) financed by debt can in theory generate a public deficit and an external deficit through increased imports. If public expenditure concerns imported goods and services, the country's trade balance will deteriorate by the amount of imports. In addition, under the Keynesian multiplier effect of public expenditure, the increase in national income will lead to an increase in the consumption of goods and services and, with it, to an increase in imports. All other things being equal, in periods of under-utilization of production capacity, the increase in income leads to an increase in the utilization rate and an increase in investment, which in turn leads to an increase in imports.

The extent of the link between the public deficit and the external deficit depends on the asymmetry of fiscal policy (a fiscal stimulus will further worsen the current-account balance if the demand of the country's trading partners is lower) and the degree of openness of the country (the higher the import contents of expenditure on goods and services, the more an expansionary fiscal policy will cause a twin deficit).

On the other hand, the explanation for a twin deficit may come from an increase in the external deficit, caused by an appreciation of the currency and/or higher private demand in a country with regard to its trading partners (Nikiforos et al., 2015). An overvalued currency will favour imports and penalize exports, resulting in an external deficit (Duwicquet et al., 2018). The deterioration in the trade balance will lead to a slowdown in economic activity and an increase in unemployment. The economic and social deterioration will reduce the State's tax revenues and increase public spending through social benefits. The country will therefore have a twin deficit, but the cause is monetary, with no link to fiscal policy.

This twin deficit may persist for many years but may appear unsustainable. Here again, a distinction must be made between macroeconomic adjustments according to the nature of the twin deficit. If the twin deficit is caused by an overvaluation of the currency, the adjustment may be made by a depreciation of the currency. Consider the situation in the United States in the mid-1980s, where following a sharp appreciation of the US dollar between 1980 and 1985 the US external deficit increased and was partly offset by the depreciation of the US dollar allowed by the so-called 'Plaza agreements', thus showing the importance of international cooperation in adjusting external imbalances.

The twin deficit observed in the United States since the early 2000s is a sign of public and private sectors' debt. From 2001 to 2008, the dynamism of consumption driven by credit, real estate and financial bubbles stimulated imports and widened the external deficit. Using Godley's (1999) financial sector's approach, the 2008 crisis showed the very strong link between the private sector balance, the public sector balance and the external balance.

In the United States, the 2009 recession reduced the country's external deficit but significantly increased its public deficit, showing the small impact of a sharp increase in the public deficit on the external balance in a context where the private sector is spending less.

In Greece, the twin deficit was significantly reduced between 2009 and 2019 through fiscal and wage austerity policies. The fall in imports following the contraction of domestic demand has virtually eliminated the external and public deficits. The adjustment of a twin deficit can therefore be abrupt and socially very costly, if it is carried out through a reduction in public spending or an increase in taxes.

The exchange-rate regime appears important, because in a currency union the nominal exchange rate can no longer be used as an adjustment variable for a twin deficit. The US twin deficit, by contrast, appears more sustainable, as far as the US dollar remains today the most liquid currency at the international level. Nevertheless, excessive private debt combined with public debt can lead to a twin deficit that will be offset by a contraction in aggregate demand, following a financial and/or real-estate crisis (Wray, 2006).

The mechanisms at work during the subprime crisis and the euro-area crisis should encourage us to study the link between the public deficit and the external deficit in a macroeconomic approach that includes the private sector.

VINCENT DUWICQUET

See also

Balance of trade; Debt – public; Exchange rates; Fiscal deficit; Fiscal multiplier

References

Duwicquet, V., J. Mazier and J. Saadaoui (2018), 'Dealing with the consequences of exchange rate misalignments for macroeconomic adjustments in the EMU', *Metroeconomica*, **69** (4), 737–67.

Godley, W. (1999), 'Seven unsustainable processes: medium-term prospects and policies for the United States and the world', *Levy Economics Institute Special Report*.

Nikiforos, M., L. Carvalho and C. Schoder (2015), '"Twin deficits" in Greece: in search of causality', *Journal of Post Keynesian Economics*, **38** (2), 302–30.

Wray, L.R. (2006), 'Twin deficits and sustainability', *Levy Economics Institute Policy Note*, No. 2006/3.

VINCENT DUWICQUET

Uncertainty

Most post-Keynesian economists follow Keynes (1936) in emphasizing uncertainty, some explicitly, by making the concept central to their analysis of the behaviour of decision makers and the systemic consequences of such behaviour (see, for instance, Shackle, 1974; Minsky, 1975; Davidson, 1991), while others more implicitly, by incorporating the role of uncertainty in the behavioural and institutional relations used in their analysis (for instance, Kalecki's followers who use his approach to mark-up pricing and investment behaviour; see, for instance, Lavoie, 2014).

In a much-quoted passage, Keynes (1937, pp. 213–14) states that

> [b]y 'uncertain' knowledge ... I do not mean merely to distinguish what is known for certain from what is only probable. The game of roulette is not subject, in this sense, to uncertainty .... The sense in which I am using the term is that in which the prospect of a European war is uncertain, or the price of copper and the rate of interest twenty years hence, or the obsolescence of a new invention .... About these matters there is no scientific basis on which to form any calculable probability whatsoever. We simply do not know.

Thus, risk exists when the expected outcome of a future event is known in terms of an objective probability distribution, either through repeated occurrences of the event under the same (or at least similar) conditions, or through logical reasoning, while uncertainty exists when no such objective probability distribution exists (see Davidson, 1991).

For Keynes (1936), although uncertainty affects most decisions involving future consequences, it is particularly relevant for those that have more long-term implications, such as the investment decisions of firms, which depend on long-term expectations, the state of which depend not just on the most probable forecast of the future, but also on the confidence with which such a forecast is made.

Keynes (1936, p. 149) recognizes that not much *a priori* can be said about the state of confidence, and what we can say about it 'must mainly depend on the actual observation of markets and business psychology'. From such observation, Keynes (1936, 1937) argues that people have devised a variety of techniques to deal with uncertainty, or rules of thumb, relying on:

(1) facts – such as present conditions – about which they are more confident even though they may not be as relevant to the issue as facts about which people's knowledge is vague and scanty;
(2) opinions embodied in actual prices of goods and financial instruments, for instance, stock-market valuations;
(3) the judgment of the majority or average, that is, a conventional judgment, under the assumption that others are better informed than themselves; and
(4) the opinion of 'experts' who, however, are merely trying to ascertain how to obtain returns by buying assets, the prices of which are affected by mass psychology, as in the so-called 'beauty contest' (Keynes, 1936, p. 156).

According to Keynes and post-Keynesians, people and firms also try to avoid uncertainty by postponing decisions, by maintaining liquidity (for instance, by holding liquid assets such as money), or by maintaining excess capacity, allowing them to alter their production levels. Finally, people try to reduce uncertainty by entering into long-term arrangements, for instance, about the money wage, which reduces uncertainty about the future both for workers who receive wages and for firms whose costs and hence profits depend on them.

Such coping mechanisms may sometimes lead to fairly stable behaviour patterns but, in others, expectations and hence behaviour can change suddenly and violently – as in Shackle's (1974) kaleidic image.

Several systemic implications follow. First, animal spirits – the spontaneous urge for action – may be depressed for long periods of time, resulting in low levels of investment and aggregate demand, making unemployment persist. Second, small changes in the economy can, sometimes, lead to large changes in expectations, since they are based on rather flimsy foundations. Third, periods in which optimism leads to further optimism – making lending, investment and output increase – and in which pessimism reinforces itself – reducing aggregate demand and output – may alternate. Fourth, a reduction in the interest rate may not restore investment spending and output, when animal spirits are weak and investors believe the future is bleak, and a reduction in the wage in the presence of unemployment may not increase employment when aggregate demand is low, and wage flexibility is likely to increase uncertainty and reduce aggregate demand.

AMITAVA DUTT

See also

Aggregate demand; Animal spirits; Liquidity preference; Mark-up pricing; Uncertainty – ontological and epistemological accounts

References

Davidson, P. (1991), 'Is probability theory relevant for uncertainty? A post Keynesian perspective', *Journal of Economic Perspectives*, **5** (1), 129–43.
Keynes, J.M. (1936), *The General Theory of Employment, Interest and Money*, London: Macmillan.
Keynes, J.M. (1937), 'The general theory of employment', *Quarterly Journal of Economics*, **51** (2), 209–23.
Lavoie, M. (2014), *Post-Keynesian Economics: New Foundations*, Cheltenham, UK, and Northampton, MA, USA: Edward Elgar.
Minsky, H.P. (1975), *John Maynard Keynes*, New York: Columbia University Press.
Shackle, G.L.S. (1974), *Keynesian Kaleidics*, Edinburgh: University of Edinburgh Press.

Uncertainty – ontological and epistemological accounts

A key feature of Keynes's break with orthodox economics was his emphasis on uncertainty, especially irreducible uncertainty. In his theory, this factor critically influenced all decision-making and was a central cause of variable aggregate output and employment in all runs. This conflicts with the core theory of orthodox economics, where genuine uncertainty is absent because all agents have (or quickly acquire) perfect knowledge of all relevant variables for decision-making, whether as certainties or numerical probabilities. Such assumptions then guarantee the maximization of agents' objective functions (utility or profit in actual or probabilistic terms) and the full employment of resources. These outcomes favour policies of zero (or at most temporary) government economic activity in the economy.

The General Theory (Keynes, 1936) takes a more realistic stance. It views uncertainties, especially those not reducible to probabilities, as central factors in agent decision-making, particularly (but not exclusively) in relation to investment. Incorporating irreducible uncertainty into economic theory has the consequence that agents do not always achieve their goals and that unsatisfactory outcomes occur with significant resources left unemployed. If full employment is socially desirable, government needs to assist private sector economic activity in suitable ways.

Although post-Keynesian economics emphasizes uncertainty, it divides into two camps concerning its foundations. Each framework contains ontological and epistemological components but differ as to which is the primary cause of uncertainty, and hence its consequences.

The ontological account

(i) Probabilities are relative frequencies: probabilities are always numerical and contain objective information about reality.
(ii) Uncertainty means a complete lack of knowledge, including of probabilities.
(iii) Risk and uncertainty describe two opposing epistemological situations. Risk occurs when probabilities are known so that uncertainty is absent. Uncertainty occurs when there is no knowledge, including that of probabilities.
(iv) Two ontological worlds are distinguished:
   a. Ergodic worlds, where reality is governed by a fixed, immutable set of probabilities (relative frequencies). Humans gain knowledge of these by observation or purchase and are then able to predict the future statistically. Such worlds are characterized as having risk but not uncertainty.
   b. Nonergodic worlds, where reality is unconstrained and hence ungoverned by frequencies. Instead of being pre-determined and immutable, reality is undetermined and mutable. Decision-makers (especially those engaged in investment) can now create their own futures. Such worlds are characterized as having uncertainty but not risk.
(v) The difference between *The General Theory* and orthodox economics lies in their assumed ontologies. The former assumes the world is nonergodic, the latter assumes it is ergodic.
(vi) The ontological account views both uncertainty and risk as originating in

AMITAVA DUTT / RODERICK O'DONNELL

the nature of reality independently of humans. Humans must then discover by observation which reality they inhabit – the ergodic world of risk, or the nonergodic world of uncertainty – and act appropriately.

(vii) The approach relies heavily on Frank Knight's risk-uncertainty distinction, and ideas borrowed from physics.

The epistemological account

(i) Uncertainty means lack of certainty. It takes two primary forms: probabilistic uncertainty (reducible uncertainty, or risk), and non-probabilistic uncertainty (irreducible or fundamental uncertainty). Both are types of uncertainty.
(ii) The difference depends on whether humans can or cannot determine probabilities in given situations.
(iii) Probabilities deal with relationships between propositions – those that are known (say past prices) and those that are unknown (say future prices). The relationships express the degree of support that the former give to that latter. If the degree of support can be perceived, then a known probability results and probabilistic uncertainty occurs. If it cannot, then the probability is unknown and non-probabilistic uncertainty arises.
(iv) This interpretation of probability is the logical interpretation developed by Keynes, this finally being published in 1921 as *A Treatise on Probability* (Keynes, 1973).
(v) Whether probabilities are known or unknown depends on human abilities in perceiving logical relations between propositions.
(vi) Probabilities can be cardinal (or numerical) or ordinal (or non-numerical, as in greater or less than).
(vii) Orthodox economics is grounded on forms of certainty either directly or indirectly using subjective numerical probabilities. *The General Theory* allows for various kinds of uncertainty but focuses primarily on irreducible uncertainty.

In short, the epistemological account views both kinds of uncertainty (reducible or irreducible) as originating with humans independently of the ontology they inhabit, while the ontological account views uncertainty only as irreducible uncertainty, which is caused by the nonergodic nature of economic reality. Critics of the latter argue that the definitions used for ergodicity and nonergodicity make it impossible for humans to determine which state they inhabit, because that knowledge relies on outcomes only available after the passage of infinite time and the traverse of infinite space. Human limitations make both impossible, so that the necessary knowledge of the ruling ontology lies out of reach.

RODERICK O'DONNELL

See also

Aggregate demand; Animal spirits; Post-Keynesian economics – a big tent?; *The General Theory of Employment, Interest and Money*; Uncertainty

References

Keynes, J.M. (1936), *The General Theory of Employment, Interest and Money*, London: Macmillan.
Keynes, J.M. (1973), *A Treatise on Probability*, in *The Collected Writings of John Maynard Keynes, Volume VIII*, London: Macmillan.
O'Donnell, R.M. (2013), 'Two Post-Keynesian approaches to uncertainty and irreducible uncertainty', in G.C. Harcourt and P. Kriesler (eds), *Oxford Handbook of Post-Keynesian Economics*, Oxford: Oxford University Press, vol. 2, 124–42.
See also the debates in 2014–2016 in the *Journal of Post Keynesian Economics*.

Unemployment

Unemployment is a regular, persisting outcome of the normal functioning of capitalist economies, even in times of economic growth. Of course, supply-side disturbances such as a major global pandemic or permanent structural technological changes are inevitable, often unpredictable, and do lead to fluctuations in the level of employment at any given point in time, but unemployment is generally a matter of insufficient effective demand and, ultimately, a failure of economic policy. Particularly, post-Keynesian economists focus on the persistence of involuntary unemployment in monetary production economies, where employment decisions are taken with the sole purpose of producing monetary returns in the future.

Post-Keynesian economists build upon Keynes's theories of effective demand and liquidity preference to explain the determination of income and the level of employment in monetary production economies (Keynes, 1936; 1937). In a system where the means of production are privately owned and production takes place through time for the purpose of monetary accumulation, the private sector determines the level of employment based on the expected proceeds from that amount of employment relative to the costs of production incurred today and into the future, or, more simply, based on the relationship between money today (spot price) and money tomorrow (forward price) (see Kregel, 1998). There is no reason to assume that the aggregate of these private decisions will coincide with full employment.

Fundamental uncertainty and complex financial relations (see Davidson, 1972; Minsky, 1986) imply that private investment is generally insufficient or too volatile to close the gap between income and consumption at full employment. The return on money and other liquid assets (liquidity preference) often sets a standard that is too high relative to the expected returns from other employment-creating investments. Monetary relations are not temporary disturbances, but a 'real factor' that fundamentally affects the determination of output and employment (see Davidson, 1972; Kregel, 1998) and that subjects monetary economies to frequent periods of boom and bust (see Minsky, 1975; 1986). Distributional conflicts, market power, and economic inequality aggravate the chronic insufficient effective demand problem.

In contrast to the self-correcting classical system, Keynes's theory applied to the general case that multiple levels of employment and output are consistent with equilibrium – defined as a position of rest – before full employment. There are no short or long run automatic self-correcting adjustments to full employment, even in the absence of wage and price rigidities, imperfect competition, asymmetric information, or other market imperfections. In fact, falling wages exacerbate the demand problem, and reduce profit expectations and employment.

To some degree, the mainstream today – be it 'Keynesian' or not – accepts that economic policy has some role to play during recessions to address unemployment and falling output, or to counter secular stagnation. However, mainstream economists generally see a role for fiscal stimulus only after all monetary policy tools have been exhausted. Further, in their view expansionary fiscal policy is to be limited and short-lived not to cause accelerating inflation, crowd-out private investment, disrupt the private sector efficient allocation of resources, or bring public indebtedness to unsustainable levels. This view is consistent with the New Monetary Consensus, where supply-side forces still determine equilibrium in the long run with the implication that employment policy focus on the structural attenuation of price stickiness and wage rigidities. Low, stable inflation is seen as a necessary (sometimes sufficient) condition to stable economic growth and maximum employment.

In contrast, post-Keynesian economists reject the 'Keynesian' trade-off between inflation and employment as much as they reject, theoretically and empirically, the monetarist concept of the 'natural rate of unemployment' or its New Keynesian sister NAIRU (non-accelerating inflation rate of unemployment). In terms of policy, these models establish the primacy of inflation over employment – 'full employment' is whatever unemployment rate is consistent with stable prices – and the fear of (wage-led) inflation becomes a major political barrier to full employment.

They also eliminate the centrality of effective demand and 'involuntary' unemployment from theory and policy (see Kregel, 1987), reduce the determination of employment in the long run to supply-side factors (though some NAIRU models do allow for hysteresis), and offer no compelling empirical evidence (see Galbraith, 1997).

While most heterodox economists have long argued that it is time to 'ditch' the NAIRU (Galbraith, 1997), others have proposed a reformulation consistent with post-Keynesian theory (see Stockhammer, 2011). Regardless, nearly all post-Keynesian authors agree that policymakers must abandon the narrow focus on the NAIRU in favour of broader alternate measures of labour underutilization such as the employment-to-population ratio or labour force participation. Policy should target unemployment measures that account for the duration of unemployment, the number of discouraged workers, and the underemployed. Further, the formulation of any meaningful employment policy must start with the

FLAVIA DANTAS

recognition that unemployment is more pervasive for certain demographic groups, and that significant disparities exist when race, ethnicity, age, gender, and education are considered. Full employment policy – in the post-Keynesian sense – is first and foremost a matter of equity and social justice.

To the fear that 'too low' unemployment will cause inflation, post-Keynesian authors remind us that inflation is usually cost-push and a result of mark-up power and distributional conflicts (see Rowthorn, 1977; Arestis and Sawyer, 2005). Inflation is never a monetary phenomenon (in the too-much-money-chasing-too-few-goods sense) and is rarely demand-push when the economy is far below full employment. There are many historical examples of low unemployment coinciding with (very) low inflation, including the recent case of the US economy pre-COVID-19. Post-Keynesian economists do admit that as the economy approaches full employment, demand-led inflationary pressures may start to build up. However, that is due to the obvious fact that not all segments of the economy (or demographics) experience economic growth; the tide does not lift all boats – in fact, when the wave comes, some boats capsize while others barely move. To reflect this point, Keynes astutely distinguished between 'semi-inflation' and 'true inflation' – which only happens at full employment – and made the argument that 'rightly distributed demand' was key to deal with the 'semi-inflation' problem before full employment (see Kregel, 2008).

Other post-Keynesian authors developed this point further: Minsky (2013) insisted that generic aggregate demand policies produce a myriad of intended and unintended final demand impacts. For example, public spending in the postwar period had been biased towards high-earning industries, capital formation, and research and development, favouring the demand for highly skilled, and specialized labour. For that reason, most post-Keynesian economists do not subscribe to fine-tuning or the general 'pump priming' aggregate demand policies associated with the IS–LM orthodox Keynesianism of the 1960s, or the New Keynesianism of today. Demand policy needs to be targeted towards effective demand, economic stability, and maximum employment (see Kregel, 2008; Tcherneva, 2008; Wray, 2009; Minsky, 2013). Generic aggregate demand policy may or may not induce entrepreneurs to undertake job-creating investments, and investment-oriented policies may increase financial fragility and inequality. Further, periods of generalized prosperity tend to fuel speculative behaviour from households and firms, who assume riskier balance sheet positions that make the economy even more fragile and prone to instability (see Minsky, 1986).

Joblessness is a persistent, normal feature of capitalist economies, even during periods of growth and relatively low official rates of unemployment. The closer the economy is to full employment, the more challenging it becomes to 'get there'. Government policy needs to target socially purposeful job creation particularly for the underemployed, long-term unemployed, discouraged workers, and for demographic groups that are disproportionally impacted by persistent joblessness. Some post-Keynesian economists argue that a job guarantee or employer of last resort programme (see Wray et al., 2018) is fundamental for true full employment with both price and economic stability.

FLAVIA DANTAS

See also

Effective demand; Employer of last resort; Involuntary unemployment – origins of; NAIRU; Phillips curve

References

Arestis, P. and M. Sawyer (2005), 'Aggregate demand, conflict and capacity in the inflationary process', *Cambridge Journal of Economics*, **29** (6), 959–74.
Davidson, P. (1972), *Money and the Real World*, London: Macmillan.
Galbraith, J.K. (1997), 'Time to ditch the NAIRU', *Journal of Economic Perspectives*, **11** (1), 93–108.
Keynes, J.M. (1936), *The General Theory of Employment, Interest and Money*, London: Macmillan.
Keynes, J.M. (1937), 'The general theory of employment', *Quarterly Journal of Economics*, **41** (2), 209–23.
Kregel, J.A. (1987), 'The effective demand approach to employment and inflation', *Journal of Post Keynesian Economics*, **10** (1), 133–45.
Kregel, J.A. (1998), 'Aspects of a Post Keynesian theory of finance', *Journal of Post Keynesian Economics*, **21** (1), 111–33.
Kregel, J.A. (2008), 'The continuing policy relevance of Keynes's *General Theory*', in M. Forstater and L.R. Wray (eds), *Keynes for the Twenty-First Century: The Continuing Relevance of the General Theory*, London: Palgrave Macmillan, pp. 127–44.

Minsky, H.P. (1975), 'Financial resources in a fragile financial environment', *Challenge*, **18** (3), 6–13.
Minsky, H.P. (1986), *Stabilizing an Unstable Economy*, New Haven, USA: Yale University Press.
Minsky, H.P. (2013), *Ending Poverty: Jobs not Welfare*, Annandale-on-Hudson, NY: Levy Economics Institute of Bard College.
Rowthorn, R.E. (1977), 'Conflict, inflation, and money', *Cambridge Journal of Economics*, **1** (3), 215–39.
Stockhammer, E. (2011), 'Wage norms, capital accumulation, and unemployment: a Post-Keynesian view', *Oxford Review of Economic Policy*, **27** (2), 295–311.
Tcherneva, P. (2008), 'Keynes's approach to full employment: aggregate or targeted demand', *Levy Economics Institute of Bard College Working Paper*, No. 542.
Wray, L.R. (2009), 'The social and economic importance of full employment', *Levy Economics Institute of Bard College Working Paper*, No. 560.
Wray, L.R. (2016), *Why Minsky Matters: An Introduction to the Work of a Maverick Economist*, Princeton: NJ: Princeton University Press.
Wray, L.R., F. Dantas, S. Fullwiler, P. Tcherneva and S. Kelton (2018), 'Public service employment: a path to full employment', *Levy Economics Institute of Bard College Research Project Report*.

Universal basic income

Universal basic income ('guaranteed income', 'unconditional cash transfers') refers to a public policy of recurrent cash payments to individuals or households unconnected with market labour supply or with other notions of individual entitlement, as is the case with social insurance.

The macroeconomic significance of universal basic income (UBI) is in its effect on household consumption, and thus its utility as an intervention both to measure the marginal propensity to consume quasi-experimentally and to stimulate the economy through the household consumption channel (Nifikoros et al., 2017).

UBI contrasts in two respects with dominant welfare paradigms in the post-Great-Society era: benefits should be 'phased in', that is, unavailable to those without market labour income, to incentivize the supply of market labour and inhibit subsistence on transfers, and they should be 'phased out' to avoid a benefit cliff, that is, a very high effective marginal tax on income above a benefit threshold or from supplying market labour at all, if that income replaces means-tested benefits. Both elements of that post-Great-Society paradigm are premised on the assumption that welfare programmes engender dependence and substitute for market labour income.

The combination of these two concerns gives rise to the so-called trapezoid structure (expressing benefit levels as a function of pre-policy income) describing policies such as earnings subsidies and child tax credits (Bruenig, 2018; 2019). Moreover, underlying both the phase-in and phase-out components of such programmes is concern over excessive government spending, and thus confining the beneficiary population through such a 'targeted' approach serves to curtail 'wasteful' expenditure. More recently, this concern has been partly replaced by a distributional one: that absent a programme-specific phase-out, benefits risk accruing to the well-off, worsening inequality.

As the name suggests, UBI has neither a phase-in nor a phase-out. In that respect it can be compared to a negative income tax (NIT), that is, a tax bracket with a negative statutory rate at the low end of the income distribution within an overall progressive income tax system. This idea has been proposed as a less distortionary alternative to cash welfare, because it lacks a benefit cliff, and thus the earliest experiments with UBI/NIT are in the tradition of post-Great-Society welfare skepticism about penalizing labour supply. If UBI is fully income-taxable and implemented within a progressive tax system, there is no qualitative difference between the two policies, and the progressivity of the overall income tax can counter-act either of the concerns about excessive spending or distributional inequity.

Another impetus for UBI is as permanent unemployment insurance or strike fund, that is, a payment to workers other than from their employer that reduces dependence on any one employer and thus increases worker bargaining power vis-à-vis individual employers through the creation of a viable outside option. Unlike with unemployment insurance or payouts from a strike fund, UBI is independent of labour market status, which would make it even more effective as a tool for increasing worker bargaining power than either of those means. Moreover, unemployment insurance typically eliminates eligibility for those who refuse a bona fide offer of work, and recipience of a strike fund is conditional on prior union membership and the strike's official status.

FLAVIA DANTAS / MARSHALL STEINBAUM

Finally, UBI has been conceived as a solution for technological unemployment short of redistributing the ownership of productive capital. In that schematization, UBI in a progressive tax system substitutes for market labour by redistributing income from the owners of capital, whose share of income increases in response to the replacement of workers with machines, to the owners (or former owners) of labour rendered economically superfluous by that trend.

Actual UBI has not ever been implemented in any real-world context, but several programmes display some of its features:

- *Bolsa familia*: unconditional cash grants to poor families in Brazil. This programme grew out of a conditional cash grant for school attendance. It differs from UBI in that it is means-tested.
- Alaska Permanent Fund: cash grants to all residents of the State of Alaska. They are not means-tested, but they are conditional on the general revenues of the State agency that holds claims on crude oil extracted from Alaska. Hence, the payments vary with the value of the fund and its assets, similar to pay-outs from a non-profit endowment. Research shows recipience of this benefit has a minimal effect on labour supply at either the intensive or extensive margins (Marinescu and Jones, 2022).
- NIT experiments: between 1968 and 1982, and in response to concerns about labour supply disincentives in traditional welfare programs, the US government undertook four experiments with an NIT. At the time, most researchers concluded that experimental treatment reduced labour supply (although some doubted this finding, given the incentive for inaccurate reporting and other features of the experimental design), and subsequent research found lasting reductions in market income due to early retirement and increased disability claims (Burtless and Greenberg, 1983; Burtless, 1986; Marinescu, 2018; Price and Song, 2018).
- Native American casino dividends: tribal affiliation entitles enrolled members to income from tribal assets that is otherwise unconditional. Research has found salutary effects of that income on indices of social wellbeing and no reduction in labour supply by recipients (Akee et al., 2010).

MARSHALL STEINBAUM

See also

Aggregate demand; Demand-led growth; Fiscal policy; Inequality; Involuntary unemployment – origins of

References

Akee, R.K.Q., W.E. Copeland, G. Keeler, A. Angold and E.J. Costello, (2010), 'Parents' incomes and children's outcomes: a quasi-experiment using transfer payments from casino profits', *American Economic Journal: Applied Economics*, **2** (1), 86–115.

Bruenig, M. (2018), 'Do we really need a second earned income tax credit?', *People's Policy Project*, available online at https://www.peoplespolicyproject.org/2018/10/19/do-we-really-need-a-second-earned-income-tax-credit/ (last accessed 21 May 2021).

Bruenig, M. (2019), 'Are benefit phase-ins completely pointless?'. *People's Policy Project*, available online at https://www.peoplespolicyproject.org/2019/05/09/are-benefit-phase-ins-completely-pointless/ (last accessed 21 May 2021).

Burtless, G. (1986), 'The work response to a guaranteed income: a survey of experimental evidence', in A.H. Munnell (ed.), *Lessons from the Income Maintenance Experiments*, Boston: Federal Reserve Bank of Boston, pp. 22–53.

Burtless, G. and D. Greenberg (1983), 'Measuring the impact of NIT experiments on work effort', *International Labor Review*, **36** (4), 592–605.

Marinescu, I. (2018), 'No strings attached: the behavioral effects of U.S. unconditional cash transfer programs', *National Bureau of Economic Research Working Paper*, No. 24337.

Marinescu, I. and D. Jones (2022), 'The labor market impacts of universal and permanent cash transfers: evidence from the Alaska Permanent Fund', *American Economic Journal: Economic Policy*, **14** (2), 315–40.

Nikiforos, M., M. Steinbaum and G. Zezza (2017), 'Modeling the macroeconomic effects of a universal basic income', *Roosevelt Institute Working Paper*, available at https://rooseveltinstitute.org/wp-content/uploads/2020/07/RI-Macroeconomic-Effects-of-UBI-201708.pdf (last accessed 21 May 2021).

Price, D. and J. Song (2018), 'The long-term effects of cash assistance', *Princeton University Industrial Relations Section Working Paper*, available online at https://www.davidjonathanprice.com/docs/djprice_jsong_simedime_WP621.pdf (last accessed 21 May 2021).

Veblen effect

In *The Theory of the Leisure Class*, Veblen (1899/1975) argues that the primary motive for consumption, apart from the consumption devoted to satisfying basic needs, is ostentation. This particularly affects the leisure class – whose main aim is to preserve its reputation, as well as to keep the gap between its own living standard and that of the lower class almost constant – and, as regards the class of goods, to preserve 'the more desirable things', such as 'rare articles of adornment' (Veblen, 1899/1975, p. 69).

These goods (the so-called 'Veblen goods') are not desired (only) for their intrinsic utility, insofar as they serve no other purpose apart from ostentation. They are desired because they are scarce, and because they fit the prevailing norms of taste. Further, a 'Veblen good' is a good for which the quantity demanded rises when its price rises: 'The consumption of expensive goods is meritorious, and the goods which contain an appreciable element of cost in excess of what goes to give them serviceability for their ostensible mechanical purpose are honorific' (Veblen, 1899/1975, pp. 154–5).

Veblen refers to the 'invidious comparison' effect: according to him, envy is a strong motive for striving to succeed. 'An invidious comparison is a process of valuation of persons in respect of worth' (Veblen, 1899/1975, p. 34). Accordingly, the accumulation of wealth, and its consequent ostentation, is not the result of the purpose of satisfying needs, via consumption: it is an intermediate goal in order to gain reputation, esteem, and respect within a given social group. In other words, consumption is not an end in itself, as in the standard neoclassical view: it is, above all, a means to excel (see Varian, 1974; Edgell, 1999, 2001).

Two considerations are worth noting in this regard. First, as opposed to the dominant view, competition is not a 'struggle for survival', but – at least within the leisure class – it is solely a struggle to excel: 'the struggle is substantially a race of reputability on the basis of invidious comparison' (Veblen, 1899/1975, p. 32). Second, by developing Veblen's argument, competitive consumption generates waste. Waste can be seen in at least two different ways. First, a wasteful activity is such that it does not contribute to the production of goods or services. Second, a wasteful activity is such that with or without the effort it requires, agents achieve exactly the same results (O'Hara, 2000).

Veblen's argument is that while individuals of the lower classes can increase consumption (also for ostentatious purposes) only by means of 'efficiency and thrift', for members of the upper class the 'taboo on labour' holds: therefore, they do not contribute to economic growth, mainly because they consume without working.

Ostentation involves waste (in Veblen's terms, this is 'the law of conspicuous waste'). In *The Theory of the Leisure Class*, waste is defined as 'usefulness as seen from the point of view of the generically human' (Veblen, 1899/1975, p. 51). Waste can be seen in at least two different ways. First, a wasteful activity is such that it does not contribute to the production of goods or services and, more generally, it does not contribute to economic growth (O'Hara, 2000). Second, a wasteful activity is such that with or without the effort it requires, agents achieve exactly the same results. This second meaning particularly pertains to the process of competitive consumption (see Forges Davanzati, 2006).

In modern macroeconomics, the Veblen effect is also used to study the dynamics of international trade (see Tilman, 2003; Forges Davanzati and Giangrande, 2020). In particular, it is argued that the export of luxury goods is driven by non-price competitiveness, which is particularly relevant for countries that are specialized in the production of such goods, and that mainly export these luxury goods (think, for instance, of Italian wines). It is relevant because, in such a condition, economic policies devoted to stimulating exports via deflationary measures – which, in turn, presuppose wage moderation – are unable to reach the desired outcome (since exports are driven by high prices) and are counterproductive for economic growth (insofar as they reduce domestic demand) (see Forges Davanzati et al., 2017).

GUGLIELMO FORGES DAVANZATI

See also

Consumer behaviour; Consumption theory; Income distribution; *The Theory of the Leisure Class*; Wealth effect

References

Edgell, S. (1999), 'Veblen's theory of conspicuous consumption after 100 years', *History of Economic Ideas*, **7** (3), 99–125.

Edgell, S. (2001), *Veblen in Perspective: His Life and Thought*, New York: M.E. Sharpe.
Forges Davanzati, G. (2006), *Ethical Codes and Income Distribution: A Study of John Bates Clark and Thorstein Veblen*, London and New York: Routledge.
Forges Davanzati, G. and N. Giangrande (2020), 'Labour market deregulation and labour productivity in a Marxian–Kaldorian theoretical framework: the case of Italy', *Cambridge Journal of Economics*, **44** (2), 371–90.
Forges Davanzati, G., R. Patalano and G. Traficante (2017), 'The Italian economic stagnation in a Kaldorian theoretical perspective', *Economia Politica: Journal of Analytical and Institutional Economics*, **36** (3), 841–61.
O'Hara, P.A. (2000), *Marx, Veblen, and Contemporary Institutional Political Economy*, Cheltenham, UK, and Northampton, MA, USA: Edward Elgar.
Tilman, R. (2003), *The Legacy of Thorstein Veblen*, Cheltenham, UK, and Northampton, MA, USA: Edward Elgar, 3 volumes.
Varian, H. (1974), 'Equity, envy and efficiency', *Journal of Economic Theory*, **9** (1), 63–91.
Veblen, T.B. (1899/1975), *The Theory of the Leisure Class*, New York: A.M. Kelley.

Verdoorn's law

Verdoorn's law states that there is a long-run stable relation between the growth rate of labour productivity in manufacture and the growth rate of product in industry. This empirical regularity was discovered by Dutch economist Petrus J. Verdoorn in 1949, when working for the Research and Planning Division of the Economic Commission for Europe in Genoa (see Soro, 2002; Thirlwall, 2018). The purpose of the original investigation was to estimate the future behaviour of labour productivity in order to establish the consistency of the economic reconstruction plans of the European countries.

After collecting the statistical information available for 18 countries for the periods 1870–1914 and 1914–30, he concluded that '[f]rom analyzing the historical series for industry as a whole and for individual industrial sectors, for the two time periods, it is found that the average value of the elasticity of productivity with respect to output is approximately 0.45 (with limits of 0.41 and 0.57). This means that over the long period a change in the volume of production, say of about 10 per cent, tends to be associated with an average increase in labour productivity of 4.5 per cent' (Verdoorn, 1949, p. 28).

Formally, Verdoorn's law can be represented as follows:

$$p = c + v * q \qquad (1)$$

where p is the growth rate of industrial labour productivity, c reflects the autonomous technical change, v is the elasticity between p and q (measured as the ratio between the growth rate of labour productivity and the growth rate of the industrial GDP), and q is the growth rate of the manufactured product. In the appendix of his original paper, Verdoorn uses both a Cobb–Douglas production function and Tinbergen's growth model in order to establish formally the stability conditions of parameter v.

Verdoorn considered that the existence of the regularity expressed in equation (1) was due to the existence of static and dynamic increasing returns to scale, both internal and external to the firm. 'In fact, one could have expected a priori to find a correlation between labour productivity and output, given that the division of labour only comes about through increases in the volume of production; therefore the expansion of production creates the possibility of further rationalization which has the same effects as mechanization' (Verdoorn, 1949, p. 28). This is a widely shared idea and is stated precisely in a later work in which Verdoorn introduces the learning curve. There he assumes that the productivity of labour depends positively on the accumulated product and not on the scale of production at a particular moment in time (Verdoorn, 1956). This reference was one of Arrow's (1962) starting points for the construction of his 'learning by doing' growth model.

However, in his last writing on the issue, Verdoorn (1980) emphasizes the interpretation of his 'rule' set in the 1949 appendix, where he assumed perfect substitutability between capital and labour (Soro, 2002). The consequence of this was to recognize that the stability of the elasticity (v) between p and q can only be attained asymptotically in Solow's steady state equilibrium. Thus, 'the "law" that has been given my name appears therefore to be much less generally valid than I was led to believe in 1949' (Verdoorn, 1980, p. 385).

It was the Cambridge economist Nicholas Kaldor (1966) who first named equation (1) 'Verdoorn's law'. Kaldor met Verdoorn in

Genoa when he took office as the Director of the Research and Planning Division of the Economic Commission for Europe. No doubt he then got first-hand acquainted with Verdoorn's 1949 results. In his inaugural speech at Cambridge University in 1966, Kaldor used Verdoorn's law to explain the weak economic performance of the United Kingdom between 1953–4 and 1963–4. On this occasion Kaldor estimated equation (1) for 12 developed countries confirming the results obtained by Verdoorn (1949). In order to avoid the problems of spurious correlation, Kaldor transformed equation (1) using the identity $p = q - e$, where p is the productivity growth rate, q the growth rate of the industrial GDP product, and e the growth rate of employment. Mathematically, the equation can be written as follows:

$$e = -c + (1 - v) * q \qquad (2)$$

where $0 < v < 1$. Kaldor's econometric estimation of equation (2) yielded a value of the industrial employment elasticity equal to 0.56. Thus, if the industrial product increases by 1 per cent, then employment will increase by 0.5 per cent and labour productivity will increase by 0.5 per cent.

For Kaldor, Verdoorn's law was foremost a dynamic relation, hence the variables should be expressed in terms of growth rates and not in terms of their level (see McCombie, 2002). In this regard, increasing returns are not limited to the reduction of the average costs owing to a larger scale of production, as they arise essentially as a result of the division of labour due to sectoral specialization as well as industrial and regional diversification.

Kaldor's open rejection of neoclassical theory of production and distribution allowed him to explain Verdoorn's law using the Smith–Young–Myrdal circular cumulative causation models linked to the idea of increasing macroeconomic returns, that is, irreversible learning processes of specialization and labour division at firm level of both sectors and regions (see McCombie and Thirlwall, 1994; McCombie, 2002, Moreno, 2008).

To this end, the industrial sector became the motor for growth in capitalist economies. Kaldor (1975) defended equations (1) and (2) against criticism pointing at the endogeneity of q (see Rowthorn, 1975a, 1975b), and showed that the model consistent with Verdoorn's law is demand constraint and not supply constraint. So, the supply of productive factors is endogenous to output growth, while exports are the source of economic growth – through Harrod's supermultiplier – in an open economy (Kaldor, 1981). Magacho and McCombie (2017) estimate Verdoorn's law using panel data for a 70-country sample between 1963 and 2009. When they introduce the demand constraint, their results confirm the existence of increasing returns and the determination of the growth rate of productivity by the growth rate of output.

Feynman (1992, p. 33) wrote in *The Character of Physical Law* that 'the most impressive fact is that gravity is simple. It is simple to state the principles completely and not have left any vagueness for anybody to change the ideas of the law. It is simple, and therefore it is beautiful.' The same can be said of Verdoorn's law.

ALVARO MARTÍN MORENO RIVAS

See also

Aggregate demand; Cumulative causation; Growth; Income distribution; Supermultiplier

References

Arrow, K.J. (1962), 'The economic implications of learning by doing', *Review of Economic Studies*, **29** (3), 155–73.

Feynman, R. (1992), *The Character of Physical Law*, Cambridge, USA, and London: MIT Press.

Kaldor, N. (1966), 'Causes of the slow rate of economic growth in the United Kingdom', in F. Targetti and A.P. Thirlwall (1989), *The Essential Kaldor*, London: Duckworth, pp. 229–81.

Kaldor, N. (1975), 'Economic growth and the Verdoorn Law: a comment on Mr Rowthorn's article', *Economic Journal*, **85** (340), 891–6.

Kaldor, N. (1981), 'The role increasing returns, technical progress and cumulative causation in the theory of international trade and economic growth', *Economie Appliquée*, **34** (4), 593–617.

Magacho, G.R. and J.S.L. McCombie (2017), 'Verdoorn's law and productivity dynamics: an empirical investigation into the demand and supply approaches', *Journal of Post Keynesian Economics*, **40** (4), 600–21.

McCombie, J.S.L. (2002), 'Increasing returns and the Verdoorn law from a Kaldorian perspective', in J.S.L. McCombie and B. Soro (eds), *Productivity Growth and Economic Performance: Essays on Verdoorn's Law*, Basingstoke and New York: Palgrave Macmillan, pp. 64–114.

McCombie, J.S.L. and A.P. Thirlwall (1994), *Economic Growth and the Balance of Payments Constraint*, New York: St. Martin's Press.

Moreno Rivas, A.M. (2008), 'Las leyes del desarrollo económico endógeno de Kaldor: el caso colombiano', *Revista de Economía Institucional*, **10** (18), 129–47.

Rowthorn, R.E. (1975a), 'What remains of Kaldor's law?', *Economic Journal*, **85** (337), 10–19.

Rowthorn, R.E. (1975b), 'A reply to Lord Kaldor's comment', *Economic Journal*, **85** (340), 897–901.

Soro, B. (2002), "Fattori che regolano lo sviluppo della produttività del lavoro' fifty years on', in J.S.L. McCombie and B. Soro (eds), *Productivity Growth and Economic Performance: Essays on Verdoorn's Law*, Basingstoke and New York: Palgrave Macmillan, pp. 37–63.

Thirlwall, A.P. (2018), 'John McCombie's contribution to the applied economics of growth in a closed and open economy', in P. Arestis (ed.), *Alternative Approaches in Macroeconomics: Essays in Honour of John McCombie*, Basingstoke and New York: Palgrave Macmillan, pp. 23–56.

Verdoorn, P.J. (1949), 'Factors that determine the growth of labour productivity'. Reprinted in J.S.L. McCombie and B. Soro (eds), *Productivity Growth and Economic Performance: Essays on Verdoorn's Law*, Basingstoke and New York: Palgrave Macmillan, 2002, pp. 28–36.

Verdoorn, P.J. (1956), 'Complementarity and long-range projections', *Econometrica*, **24** (4), 429–50.

Verdoorn, P.J. (1980), 'Verdoorn's law in retrospect: a comment', *Economic Journal*, **90** (358), 382–5.

Wages

The wage rate is the price of labour services for a specific time period. It is paid by adopting piece or time rates, or a mix of these methods of payment. With the formation and strengthening of trade unions, its determination has been progressively driven by collective bargaining (see Dobb, 1959). In real terms, it is calculated by referring to a bundle of wage goods. Therefore, for the same money wages, the real wage rate w_r will change for changes in the kinds and prices of wage commodities.

Prior to the eighteenth century, a low fraction of the labour force passed through a free labour market and long periods of constant money wages were observed, because they were fixed by custom and laws. Since the cost of foodstuffs fluctuated widely, this relative constancy of money wages was associated with wide fluctuations in real wages. In the nineteenth century, money wages became more sensitive to the state of the labour market as shaped by the industrial trade cycle, and real wages began to rise more steadily owing to a continuous increase in labour productivity (see Phelps Brown and Browne, 1968), although they were not strictly determined by it: even in the major industrialized countries, changes in the wage share $q_w = \frac{w_r p_w}{\pi\, p_y}$ occurred on average according to the trend of real wages relative to the product per worker π, and according to changes in the price of the bundle of wage commodities p_w relative to the product price p_y.

Different explanations of the determinants of real wages have been advanced in economic theory. In the surplus approach of Smith, Ricardo and Marx, the wage rate is determined by the relative strength of the parties involved (see Levrero, 2013; 2018). Since workers start from a disadvantage in wage bargaining due to their immediate need to work in order to survive, Classical economists thought that wages were normally set at a minimum level compatible with 'common humanity' (Smith, 1776/1976, pp. 75–80). This subsistence wage was viewed as an essential material necessity of production unlike profits and rents, which are paid out of the surplus product. However, the subsistence wage was not conceived of as physiologically determined. It includes goods and services that the habits of a country, which operate as a 'second nature', make necessary for the maintenance and reproduction of labourers (Ricardo, 1821/1951, pp. 96–7). Moreover, improvements in workers' living standard were admitted when a lower level of unemployment or the rise and action of trade unions strengthened the workers' position in wage bargaining. In these circumstances, the wage rate may remain over the subsistence level for a long period of time, thus modifying it.

The reference to a historically determined subsistence wage implies that no iron law of wages is traceable in Smith, Ricardo and Marx, although they considered mechanisms – as in Marx's theory of the 'industrial reserve army' (Marx, 1867/1961) – limiting the increase in real wages if it impairs capital accumulation. A mechanical determination of the wage rate was first put forward by the wage-fund doctrine, according to which the wage rate is set by the ratio between a given wage fund independent of income distribution available at the beginning of the production process and the working age population. This led to the argument that an inverse relationship between wages and employment exists and that trade unions cannot ameliorate the conditions of the working class.

These ideas have been refined by the marginalist theory, according to which income distribution is set by the relative scarcity of factors of production and any action raising wages above the level that equals the net labour marginal product with labour disutility implies a lower level of employment and, therefore, a consequent fall in real wages under the pressure of competition. In this framework, a definite inverse relationship between wages and the level of employment is advanced and each factor of production receives at equilibrium a remuneration that is equal to its contribution to production at the margin. Moreover, social and institutional factors acting in the labour market are treated as disturbances or 'obstacles' to free competition that determine a misallocation of resources and will be bypassed in the long run by the 'forces of demand and supply' (Marshall, 1920/1959, pp. 465 and 577). This is not the case in the Classical–Keynesian and other heterodox approaches, where different levels of employment are admitted for a given wage rate and state of technique, higher wages fuelling aggregate demand may lead to a higher (and not lower) level of employment, and social and institutional factors combine to determine the normal wage rate in a condition of free competition.

These heterodox approaches differentiate from each other, however, when explaining the forces that set wages when they are higher than the subsistence level. Alongside a determination of the 'surplus wage' by forces acting in the labour market as for Classical economists and Marx, other approaches consider it as a residuum after the rate of profit is determined. In a strand of the Classical–Keynesian approach, the rate of profit is seen to be influenced by the interest rate on riskless long-term loans as determined by monetary policy (Pivetti, 1991). In post-Keynesian theory, capitalists earn what they spend and the higher the rate of accumulation is, the lower the real wages. On the assumptions of long-run output inelasticity and a propensity of workers to save that is lower than that of capitalists, a higher amount of investment per unit of capital would require a shift of income distribution towards profits to generate a corresponding higher amount of savings per unit of capital (see Robinson, 1956).

ENRICO SERGIO LEVRERO

See also

Aggregate demand; Growth – wage-led vs profit-led; Income distribution; Profit; Trade cycles

References

Dobb, M. (1959), *Wages*, fifth edition, Cambridge, UK: Cambridge University Press.
Levrero, E.S. (2013), 'Marx on absolute and relative wages and the modern theory of distribution', *Review of Political Economy*, **25** (1), 91–116.
Levrero, E.S. (2018), 'The classical theory of wages and its interpretations: a critique to the canonical classical model', *Bulletin of Political Economy*, **12** (1–2), 55–76.
Marshall, A. (1920/1959), *Principles of Economics*, eighth edition, London: Macmillan.
Marx, K. (1867/1967), *Capital: A Critique of Political Economy*, Volume I, New York: International Publishers.
Phelps Brown, E.H. and M.H. Browne (1968), *A Century of Pay*, New York: St. Martin Press.
Pivetti, M. (1991), *An Essay on Money and Distribution*, London: Macmillan.
Ricardo, D. (1821/1951), *On the Principles of Political Economy and Taxation*, in *The Works and Correspondence of David Ricardo*, Volume I, Cambridge, UK: Cambridge University Press.
Robinson, J. (1956), *The Accumulation of Capital*, London: Macmillan.
Smith, A. (1776/1976), *An Inquiry into the Nature and Causes of the Wealth of Nations*, Chicago: University of Chicago Press.

Washington Consensus

The Washington Consensus is a set of ten macroeconomic policies and reforms of neoliberal flavour, namely: fiscal discipline, reordering public expenditures priorities, tax reform, liberalizing interest rates, competitive exchange rates, trade liberalization, liberalization of inward foreign direct investment, privatization, deregulation, and property rights. According to Williamson (1990), 'Washington', that is, the International Monetary Fund (IMF), the World Bank (WB), and the US Treasury, considered as desirable for Latin American countries, at the end of the 1980s, to recover from the debt crisis that had hit the continent at the beginning of the decade (Cedrini, 2008).

Employed also as needed ideological support for the triumph of capitalism over socialism in the post-cold-war world, the Washington Consensus – better, a more radical version including capital market liberalization as a fundamental pillar – rapidly became the economic policy paradigm used by the IMF and the WB in elaborating the 'conditionalities' for the concession of financial assistance to developing countries during the 1990s. Aiming at restoring the confidence of international financial markets by a reversal of traditional 'development economics' prescriptions (State-led industrialization and import-substitution strategies), the paradigm exalted trade as a precondition for economic growth, and competitiveness as a policy target, substituting openness to competition and capital flows for autonomy in monetary policy and discretion in trade policies (Gore, 2000).

Anti-inflationist adjustment policies in Latin America gave rise to high levels of capital inflows, tendencies to currency appreciation, and current account deficits, while favouring financial assets and rentiers over the domestic restructuring required to set these economies on a growth path (Kregel, 2008). Neoliberal economists could, however, identify the key factor behind the East Asian miracle in the Washington Consensus, at least until the 1997 crisis cast doubts on this vision. Instead of recognizing the contribution of 'heterodox' elements to the miracle, the IMF blamed crisis-hit countries for inconsistencies and insufficient ambition in implementing the Washington Consensus reform package, thus pushing the agenda even further (Stiglitz, 2002). Attempts to reform the agenda after disappointing results produced not the restoration of the policy space required to remedy the too-narrow concept of macroeconomic stability embedded in the paradigm, but rather an undue enlargement of the agenda itself to a series of institutional prescriptions.

Argentina, the main laboratory for the aggressively neoliberal vision lying behind IMF programmes, financially collapsed in 2001 (in this regard, Williamson (2004) has strongly denied any continuity with the original Washington Consensus). The crisis showed the impracticality of this 'golden straitjacket' model, which requires the full subordination of political and economic policy choices to the ultimate aims of growing by free-market policies (Rodrik, 2011). Argentina's default represented the failure of hyperglobalization, or the attempt to govern the global economy by means of one-size-fits-all neoliberal prescriptions. These latter favoured an abuse of export-led growth strategies and the diffusion of mercantilism at the global level, thereby promoting a deflationary international environment (Davidson, 2004).

The lesson emerging countries learned was that it is better to self-protect through increased liquidity rather than put development at the mercy of liberalized and volatile international capital markets. The so-called regime of Bretton Woods II and developing countries' accumulation of exchange reserves are a legacy of the Washington Consensus epoch. The Bretton Woods institutions partly revised their attitude: structural adjustment programmes show now a remarkable degree of inconsistency, as well as a timid emphasis on the need for policy diversity. The multipolar and fragmented form of governance that shapes the post-Washington Consensus era (Grabel, 2011) may finally widen the policy space available to developing countries and the possibilities for policy and institutional experimentation.

Mario Cedrini

See also

Bretton Woods; Current accounts; Financial crises; Fiscal policy; Trade and development

References

Cedrini, M. (2008), 'Consensus versus freedom or consensus upon freedom? From Washington disorder to the rediscovery of Keynes', *Journal of Post Keynesian Economics*, **30** (4), 499–522.

Davidson, P. (2004), 'A Post Keynesian view of the Washington Consensus and how to improve it', *Journal of Post Keynesian Economics*, **27** (2), 208–30.

Gore, C. (2000), 'The rise and fall of the Washington Consensus as a paradigm for developing countries', *World Development*, **28** (5), 789–804.

Grabel, I. (2011), 'Not your grandfather's IMF: global crisis, "productive incoherence" and developmental policy space', *Cambridge Journal of Economics*, **35** (5), 805–30.

Kregel, J. (2008), 'The discrete charm of the Washington Consensus', *Journal of Post Keynesian Economics*, **30** (4), 541–60.

Rodrik, D. (2011), *The Globalization Paradox: Democracy and the Future of the World Economy*, New York: Norton.

Stiglitz, J.E. (2002), *Globalization and Its Discontents*, New York: Norton.
Williamson, J. (ed.) (1990), *Latin American Adjustment: How Much Has Happened?*, Washington, DC: Institute for International Economics.
Williamson, J. (2004), 'The strange history of the Washington Consensus', *Journal of Post Keynesian Economics*, **27** (2), 195–206.

Wealth distribution

In the preface to his *Principles of Political Economy and Taxation*, Ricardo (1821, p. 5) famously claimed that the 'principal problem of Political Economy' was determining the laws by which income is distributed between three classes: landowners, capitalists, and workers. The focus on the distribution of income overcasts an implicit assumption regarding the distribution of wealth. The existence of these three classes depends on the distribution of income not altering substantially the distribution of wealth, allowing the land to remain owned by landowners and the capital by capitalists, whereas workers do not accumulate wealth in a significant amount. What is implicit in Ricardo becomes explicit in Marx. In the latter's view, capitalist production is not only the production of goods and services but also the continuous reproduction of 'the working man as a working man, and the capitalist as a capitalist', by incessantly separating the workers from the means of production (Marx, 1865, p. 42), that is, by reproducing continuously a certain distribution of wealth.

In spite of this relationship between the functional distribution of income and the distribution of wealth, the debate on the former often disregards the latter, probably in part owing to the predominant focus of economic theorizing on flows rather than stocks. The issue of wealth distribution, however, re-surfaced again in the mid-1960s, in the debates around the so-called Pasinetti theorem, one of the last chapters of the Cambridge capital controversies (see Harcourt, 1972). In their reaction to Pasinetti's (1962) formulation, Samuelson and Modigliani (1966a) argued that an 'anti-Pasinetti regime' could be derived, in which the accumulation of wealth by workers ended up eliminating capitalists.

This opened an empirical debate on whether wealth distribution underlying the class structure supposed by Classical political economists was stable or not (besides Samuelson and Modigliani, 1966a, see Kaldor, 1966, Pasinetti, 1966, Samuelson and Modigliani, 1966b). The controversy focused on the empirical meaning of the conditions for the Pasinetti and anti-Pasinetti regimes, especially the heterogeneous saving propensities from different kinds of income, and the connection between income and wealth distributions would soon be pushed aside to the margins of post-Keynesian debates, surviving only in a few attempts to re-examine the issues raised by Pasinetti in a Kaleckian growth and distribution setting (Dutt, 1990; Lavoie, 1998; Palley, 2012).

Recently, however, the studies on inequality based on tax data allowed the issue to be empirically reassessed. The Classical political economists' indication that wages were determined by subsistence – a plausible interpretation of the situation in Western Europe in the first half of the nineteenth century (Allen, 2009) – ruled out the possibility that workers would accumulate any significant amount of wealth. However, the trajectory of wages in the following two centuries raised the question of whether there was a reduction of wealth inequality. In fact, Piketty (2014, pp. 336–76) has shown that wealth inequality, after increasing mildly in the nineteenth century, fell markedly in the first half of the twentieth century in the United Kingdom, France, Sweden, and the United States, as a result of capital destruction during the wars and the Great Depression as well as a result of economic policies adopted in the period. Concretely, the top 10 per cent of wealth holders owned 80 to 90 per cent of all wealth in the eve of the First World War. By the 1970s, these shares were reduced to 60 to 70 percent, recovering slightly ever since.

Such a reduction of wealth inequality, however significant, did not alter substantially the polarized class structure assumed by Classical political economists. The reduction of the wealth share of the top decile resulted in the emergence of what Piketty (2014, pp. 346–7) calls a 'patrimonial middle class', but this did not entail that such a class became capitalist: it was able generally to buy a home, but it could not live out of capital income. US data from 2001 shows that the bottom 98 per cent of the population received around 90 per cent of its income as wages, a share that drops significantly once one moves up the social pyramid (Duménil and Lévy, 2004, p. 107). The top 2 per cent earns almost half of its income from sources other than wages (including capital income, capital gains, and sole proprietor income) and the share of wages in the income of the top thousandth goes down, depending on the country, to around 20 to 30 per cent (Piketty, 2014, pp. 277 and 302). Despite its changes in the twentieth century, wealth distribution remains polarized and income from capital remains concentrated at the top.

FERNANDO RUGITSKY

See also

Capital theory controversies; Capitalism – varieties of; Growth; Income distribution; Pasinetti's paradox

References

Allen, R. (2009), 'Engels' pause: technical change, capital accumulation, and inequality in the British industrial revolution', *Explorations in Economic History*, 46 (4), 418–35.
Duménil, G. and D. Lévy (2004), 'Neoliberal income trends: wealth, class and ownership in the USA', *New Left Review*, 30, 105–33.
Dutt, A.K. (1990), 'Growth, distribution and capital ownership: Kalecki and Pasinetti revisited', in B. Dutta, S. Gangopadhayay, D. Mookherjee and D. Ray (eds), *Economic Theory and Policy: Essays in Honor of Dipak Banerjee*, Bombay: Oxford University Press, pp. 130–45.
Harcourt, G.C. (1972), *Some Cambridge Controversies in the Theory of Capital*, Cambridge, UK: Cambridge University Press.
Kaldor, N. (1966), 'Marginal productivity and the macro-economic theories of distribution: comment on Samuelson and Modigliani', *Review of Economic Studies*, 33 (4), 309–19.
Lavoie, M. (1998), 'The neo-Pasinetti theorem in Cambridge and Kaleckian models of growth and distribution', *Eastern Economic Journal*, 24 (4), 417–34.
Marx, K. (1865), 'Value, price and profit'. Reprinted in K. Marx, *Wage-Labor and Capital & Value, Price and Profit*, New York: International Publishers, 1976, pp. 5–62.
Palley, T.I. (2012), 'Wealth and wealth distribution in the neo-Kaleckian growth model', *Journal of Post Keynesian Economics*, 34 (3), 453–74.
Pasinetti, L.L. (1962), 'Rate of profit and income distribution in relation to the rate of economic growth', *Review of Economic Studies*, 29 (4), 267–79.
Pasinetti, L.L. (1966), 'New results in an old framework', *Review of Economic Studies*, 33 (4), 303–6.
Piketty, T. (2014), *Capital in the Twenty-First Century*, Cambridge, MA: Harvard University Press.

Ricardo, D. (1821), *Principles of Political Economy and Taxation*. Reprinted in *The Works and Correspondence of David Ricardo, Vol. I*, Indianapolis: Liberty Fund, 2004.
Samuelson, P. and F. Modigliani (1966a), 'The Pasinetti paradox in neoclassical and more general models', *Review of Economic Studies*, 33 (4), 269–301.
Samuelson, P. and F. Modigliani (1966b), 'Marginal productivity and the macro-economic theories of distribution: reply to Pasinetti and Robinson', *Review of Economic Studies*, 33 (4), 321–30.

Wealth effect

The traditional preoccupation with the wealth effect focuses on the quantification of changes in household propensity to consume relative to actual or perceived changes in real and financial wealth (a positive or a negative shock to wealth). The subject is thus of particular importance in the sphere of policy deliberation, and, more specifically, to monetary policy decision-making, which is concerned with the effects of changes to the policy rate of interest on various sectors of the economy, and not least with the impact on consumer spending of changing values of real and financial assets. Longitudinal empirical studies aiming to explain changes in the magnitude of the wealth effect over time examine the effects of long-term changes in productivity, demographics, financial developments and long-term interest-rate dynamics, amongst other potentially critical variables. This consideration highlights the existence of complex networks of interlinkages and interdependencies determining economic outcomes as well as the dynamic nature of economic growth, concepts central to macroeconomic analysis in a post-Keynesian theoretical framework (Dianova, 2018, pp. 86–8).

Theoretical and empirical analyses of the wealth effect distinguish between the impact on consumption of changes in financial wealth, or the value of the aggregate household financial portfolio comprised of stocks, bonds and other financial instruments, from the effect of changes in housing wealth, derived from variations in the value of the aggregate household real-estate portfolio. With some notable exceptions (Juster et al., 2006; Calomiris et al., 2009), there appears to be a general agreement in the empirical literature that the housing wealth effect is greater in magnitude (Mishkin, 2007; Carroll

FERNANDO RUGITSKY / VERA DIANOVA

et al., 2011) than the financial wealth effect, the traditional interpretation of which has focused on the impact of fluctuations in equity prices on the aggregate value of the household financial portfolio, neglecting the possible income effects of corresponding changes of income flows from the fixed-income portion of the aggregate financial portfolio.

The post-2008 crisis period, which has been characterized by an unprecedented period of low interest rates, has provided rich empirical ground for the re-evaluation of theoretical wealth effects on household consumption from heterodox perspectives. For instance, while empirical research shows that balance-sheet shocks experienced by high-leverage (lower income) households in light of the collapse of residential housing prices are responsible for a sharp decrease in consumption in the post-crisis period (Mian and Sufi, 2012), it is unlikely that such effects are symmetrical. This implies that a recovery of residential housing prices is unlikely to be followed by a proportional increase in household spending, especially given households' recent experience of crisis-related economic hardship. This theoretical supposition is supported by empirical consumption trends one decade after the financial crisis (Dianova, 2018, p. 123).

It is likewise crucial to consider the effects of the extended period of low interest rates on disposable income and hence households' perception of current wealth and resulting propensity to spend. Specifically, the 'negative income effect' (also known as the 'negative wealth effect') considers the effects of prolonged low-interest-rate policy on the income and wealth of households dependent on financial income either exclusively or as supplement to labour income. The existence and importance of the negative wealth effect has been supported by recent empirical research, which has suggested that the household sector (a net creditor) has lost significantly more interest income than it has gained as a result of a lower interest expense (Dobbs et al., 2013, p. 20).

More generally, in mainstream theoretical literature supply-side changes are believed to be a dominant force in determining economic growth and developments relative to demand-side dynamics, including the potential impact of an increase or a decrease in household consumption as a result of changing real or perceived wealth. Post-Keynesian economic theory, by contrast, assigns greater importance to potential household wealth effects as well as to household consumption more generally in determining economic outcomes, suggesting the need for further investigation of the link between policy, households' real and financial wealth, and resulting consumption dynamics.

VERA DIANOVA

See also

Consumption theory; Growth; Interest rates and income distribution; Monetary policy transmission mechanism; Wealth distribution

References

Calomiris, C., S. Longhofer and W. Miles (2009), 'The (mythical?) housing wealth effect', *National Bureau of Economic Research Working Paper*, No. 15075.

Carroll, C., M. Otsuka and J. Slacalek (2011), 'How large are housing and financial wealth effects? A new approach', *European Central Bank Working Paper*, No. 1283.

Dianova, V.G. (2018), *The Effectiveness of Monetary Policy after the Financial Crisis: Redefining the Role of the Central Bank*, PhD dissertation, University of Fribourg, Switzerland.

Dobbs, R., S. Lund, T. Koller and A. Shwayder (2013), 'QE and ultra-low interest rates: distributional effects and risks', *McKinsey Global Institute Discussion Paper*, November.

Juster, F., J. Lupton, J. Smith and F. Stafford (2006), 'The decline in household savings and the wealth effect', *Review of Economics and Statistics*, **88** (1), 20–7.

Mian, A.R. and A. Sufi (2012), 'What explains high unemployment? The aggregate demand channel', *National Bureau of Economic Research Working Paper*, No. 17830.

Mishkin, F. (2007), 'Housing and the monetary transmission mechanism', *National Bureau of Economic Research Working Paper*, No. 13518.

Zero interest rate policy

The policy in which the central bank lowers its key interest rate to zero and holds it there for an extended period of time has acquired great prominence in the wake of the Global Financial Crisis of 2007–09, since the Central Bank of Japan inaugurated it in 1999. Zero interest rate policy (ZIRP) stands at the boundary between conventional and unconventional monetary policy and, as such, is best discussed in connection with those measures that aim to influence the entire yield curve (see Turner, 2014).

The idea of adopting 'extraordinary' monetary policy measures against deflation and crisis can be traced back to Keynes's *Treatise on Money*, and the indication to 'maintain a very low level of the short-term rate of interest, and buy long-dated securities against an expansion of central bank money or against the sale of short-dated securities' (Keynes, 1930/1971, pp. 346–7). With time, as Kregel (2013, p. 146) observes, Keynes's confidence in these measures gave way to a recognition of the 'need to provide an external source of demand through government expenditure' (ibid.), if monetary expansion alone proved insufficient (see also Lavoie, 2016).

Traces of Keynes's ideas re-emerged in the works of the UK Radcliffe Committee, which recommended to adopt open-market operations *à outrance* in short as well as long-dated securities to restrain inflation without compromising full employment and economic growth (Committee on the Working of the Monetary System (Radcliffe Committee), 1960). On this point, the Radcliffe Committee claimed to follow Kahn's advice to consider 'the structure of interest rates rather than some notion of the "supply of money" as the centre-piece of monetary action' (Radcliffe Committee, 1960, par. 395).

Albeit the link between Kahn's (and Keynes's) ideas and those of the Radcliffe Committee is problematic (see Cristiano and Paesani, 2018), there is little doubt about the fact that the publication of the Radcliffe Report, and of analogous reports in the United States, Canada and Italy (see Paesani, 2018), gave the occasion, in the 1960s, to debate innovative ideas in the field of monetary policy.

These ideas resound today in the debates on ZIRP, financial stability and the liquidity trap (see, for instance, Kregel, 2014; Pilkington, 2015; Fischer, 2016). In the mainstream field, apart from Friedman's early advocacy of a zero nominal interest rate rule (Friedman, 1969), different ways exist to reconcile ZIRP with the New Consensus approach to monetary policy modelling by means of Taylor rules (see, for example, Hurn et al., 2018). This approach, however, presents significant shortcomings, which Gnos and Rochon (2007) discuss together with post-Keynesian alternatives to Taylor rules.

Rochon and Setterfield (2007) identify two strands in this respect: one advocates the use of interest rates to fine-tune aggregate demand, whereas the other proposes to 'park' the (nominal or real) interest rate at a given level. Within this second strand, the Kansas City rule recommends setting the nominal rate of interest to zero. According to the Smithin (2007) rule, an 'optimal' interest rate policy is achieved when nominal interest rates move in step with inflation, leaving real interest rates at (or very close to) zero. Finally, a 'fair' interest rate rule, also known as the Pasinetti rule (see Pasinetti, 1981, p. 170), leaves the distribution of income between interest and non-interest income groups unchanged (see Lavoie and Seccareccia, 1999). Combining these rules with active fiscal policy, while taking the endogeneity of money and financial structure into account, provides a valuable alternative to the New Consensus approach to monetary policy.

PAOLO PAESANI

See also

Endogenous money; Financial instability hypothesis; Interest rate rules; Monetary policy transmission mechanism; Wealth effect

References

Committee on the Working of the Monetary System (Radcliffe Committee) (1960), *Report*, London: HMSO.

Cristiano, C. and P. Paesani (2018), 'Unconventional monetary policy *ante litteram*: Richard Kahn and the monetary policy debate during the works of the Radcliffe Committee', *Cambridge Journal of Economics*, **42** (4), 1145–64.

Fischer, S. (2016), 'Monetary policy, financial stability, and the zero lower bound', *American Economic Review*, **106** (5), 39–42.

Friedman, M. (1969), 'The optimum quantity of money', in *The Optimum Quantity of Money*, London: Macmillan, pp. 1–50.

Gnos, C. and L.-P. Rochon (2007), 'The New Consensus and post-Keynesian interest rate policy', *Review of Political Economy*, **19** (3), 369–86.

Hurn, S., N. Johnson, A. Silvennoinen and T. Teräsvirta (2018), 'Transition from the Taylor rule to the zero lower bound', *CREATES Research Paper*, No. 2018-31.

Keynes, J.M. (1930/1971), *A Treatise on Money, Vol. II: The Applied Theory of Money*, reprinted in *The Collected Writings of John Maynard Keynes, Vol. VI*, London: Macmillan.

Kregel, J. (2013), 'Was Keynes's monetary policy, à outrance in the *Treatise*, the model for ZIRP and QE?', in H. Toshiaki, M.C. Marcuzzo and P. Mehrling (eds), *Keynesian Reflections: Effective Demand, Money, Finance, and Policies in the Crisis*, Oxford: Oxford University Press, pp. 135–48.

Kregel, J. (2014), 'Liquidity preference and the entry and exit to ZIRP and QE', *Levy Economics Institute Policy Note*, No. 2014/5.

Lavoie, M. (2016), 'Rethinking monetary theory in light of Keynes and the crisis', *Brazilian Keynesian Review*, **2** (2), 174–88.

Lavoie, M. and M. Seccareccia (1999), 'Interest rate: fair', in P.A. O'Hara (ed.), *Encyclopedia of Political Economy*, London and New York: Routledge, pp. 543–5.

Paesani, P. (2018), 'Reception and scientific dissemination of the Radcliffe Report in Italy', *Pensiero Economico Italiano*, **26** (1), 105–24.

Pasinetti, L.L. (1981), *Structural Change and Economic Growth*, Cambridge, UK: Cambridge University Press.

Pilkington, P. (2015), 'Zero interest-rate policy', in L.-P. Rochon and S. Rossi (eds), *The Encyclopedia of Central Banking*, Cheltenham, UK, and Northampton, MA, USA: Edward Elgar, pp. 508–10.

Rochon, L.-P. and M. Setterfield (2007), 'Interest rates, income distribution and monetary policy dominance: post Keynesians and the "fair rate" of interest', *Journal of Post Keynesian Economics*, **30** (1), 13–42.

Smithin, J. (2007), 'A real interest rate rule for monetary policy?', *Journal of Post Keynesian Economics*, **30** (1), 101–18.

Turner, P. (2014), 'Is the long-term interest rate a policy victim, a policy variable or a policy lodestar?', in J.S. Chadha, A.C.J. Durré, M.A.S. Joyce and L. Sarno (eds), *Developments in Macro-Finance Yield Curve Modelling*, Cambridge, UK: Cambridge University Press, pp. 19–55.

PAOLO PAESANI